A Mechanical Translation of the Book of Exodus

A Mechanical Translation
of the Book of Exodus

The Hebrew text literally
translated word for word

~~~~~~

Jeff A. Benner

Cover design by Jeff A. Benner.

"A Mechanical Translation of the Book of Exodus," by Jeff A. Benner. ISBN 978-1-60264-391-8.

Manufactured in the United States of America.

This book is dedicated to our many readers who have encouraged and supported us in our work.

To all of you, my wife Denise and I, thank you from the bottom of our heart.

Table of Contents

Acknowledgments

I would first like to thank my wife Denise and our three boys, Josiah, Jeremiah and Jedidiah, for their support and encouragement while working on this project.

I also want to thank my publisher Bobby Bernshausen of Virtual Bookworm Publishing. He has always been there when I needed him and has been very helpful and encouraging with the pubishing of my materials.

Many other people deserve my special thanks and recognition for their dedication to this project. Each of the following individuals volunteered their time and energies to read and reread the manuscript and provide valuable comments and suggestions that contributed immensely to the quality of this translation. However, any mistakes, omissions or oversights that may be found within this book are mine and mine alone.

Holly Begley	Gordon Hayes	Edward MacIsaac
Richard Conaway	Myhrrhleine Hunter	Terry Smith
LuAna Craig	Jeanne M Irons	Frances Stolz
Ken Finn	Tim Jones	Randy Talbot
Steve Foisy	Kathy Kindall	Yvonne Todd
Devora Forsman	Jerry R Lambert	Lisa Anne Vallee
Kathy Hamlett	Paul Lurk	

Philosophy and Methodology

The *Mechanical Translation of the Hebrew Bible* project* began in 2005 with the publication of the *Ancient Hebrew Lexicon of the Bible*. This lexicon laid the foundation for a mechanical translation of the Hebrew Bible, where each Hebrew word would be translated faithfully and consistently according to its original linguistic and cultural perspective. The Mechanical Translation uses a new and unique methodology and philosophy that revolutionizes how we read the Bible.

1. The Mechanical Translation eliminates personal and religious bias on the part of the translator.
2. The Mechanical Translation translates each Hebrew word, prefix and suffix, exactly the same way, in every occurrence within the Hebrew text.
3. The Mechanical Translation can be read and understood by the average person who has no prior knowledge of the Hebrew language.
4. The Mechanical Translation includes a dictionary and concordance of each word used in the translation.
5. The Mechanical Translation reflects the original concrete meaning of Hebrew words and phrases.
6. The Mechanical Translation can be used as a tool by those who are learning to read Biblical Hebrew.

Personal and Religious Bias

It has been argued that it is impossible to eliminate bias into any translation, especially one of a religious nature. However, the Mechanical Translation incorporates a method that almost completely removes the possibility of any personal or religious bias within the translation through a two-fold process.

The first part of the process is through the Lexicon. Each translation and definition of each Hebrew word in the lexicon is chosen based primarily on its etymology (what the meaning of a word is based on its relationship to other words and roots), context (how the word is used throughout the Bible) and culture (what the word meant to those who lived within that culture).

---

* http://www.mechanical-translation.org

The second part of the process simply involves replacing the Hebrew word, prefix or suffix with its corresponding English word from the Lexicon. This method of translation also has the unique quality that a reader, who disagrees with the translation of a given word, may simply replace that word with one of his own choosing. As the translation is accompanied with a concordance, finding the location of each occurrence of that word in the book of Exodus is fairly simple.

A word for word translation

Every translation to date, including interlinears and literal translations, translates the Hebrew text according to context. The problem with this is that the context can be interpreted differently based upon the translator's personal opinions of what that context is. In contrast, a word for word, prefix for prefix and suffix for suffix translation is very mechanical and prevents the translator from inserting his own opinion into the text.

One advantage to this method of translation is that the reader is able to see the text in its pure and original Hebrew format. However, there is one major drawback to this method of translation. Hebrew syntax (sentence structure and style) is very different from English syntax and a reader that has no background in Hebrew syntax would be completely lost in the translation. To alleviate this problem, the "Mechanical Translation" is accompanied with a "Revised Mechanical Translation."

Easily read and understood

The Revised Mechanical Translation re-arranges the words of the Mechanical Translation into a more readable and understandable format for the English reader. This method of translation is common among other translations, but those changes are invisible to the reader. With the Mechanical and Revised Mechanical Translations side by side, the reader is able to see all the changes that are made within the Revised Mechanical Translation.

There are times when the Revised Mechanical Translation is difficult to read and may not make perfect sense, but this is due to the fact that the Hebrew structure of a given sentence is sometimes difficult to read itself. While most other translations "fix" the text so that it will always be read easily, this translation preserves the difficulties. It is the opinion of the author of this translation, that those who will be interested in this translation will be willing to put in the extra effort to examine these difficulties with more detail.

A dictionary and concordance

No one English word can fully convey the meaning of one Hebrew word. For this reason, the translation will include a dictionary that will more finely define each word within its linguistic, contextual and cultural setting. In addition, for an in-depth study of the words in the Book of Exodus, a concordance will be included that will identify the location of each word within the text.

Concrete meaning of Hebrew words

The Hebrew language of the Bible is a concrete language, where each word is related to an image of action. In contrast, our own English language, as well as most all other modern languages, relies heavily on abstract ideas. The English translations of the Hebrew words in this translation will reflect the concrete nature of the original Hebrew.

A tool for learning Hebrew

Learning Hebrew is much more than memorizing the meaning of Hebrew words. It involves learning to recognize prefixes and suffixes attached to a word (very common in Hebrew, much more so than English), verb conjugations (which include subject, tense, gender, number, mood, voice and sometimes the object of the verb) and syntax. When reading the Hebrew text of the Bible, the reader will come across words which will be difficult to decipher. The reader can check the Mechanical Translation to help assist with deciphering the word. The reader is also able to check the "revised mechanical" translation if he is unable to determine the meaning of the sentence itself.

Contents

The Book of Exodus

Hebrew

Each verse includes the Hebrew text as well as a transliteration of the Hebrew. Appendix F is a pronunciation guide for pronouncing the transliterations of the Hebrew text.

Mechanical Translation

The Mechanical Translation translates each Hebrew word, prefix and suffix exactly the same way each time it occurs and in the same order as they appear in the Hebrew text. This translation demonstrates the Hebrew syntax of the verse and is very useful for anyone learning to read and understand Hebrew. This translation includes special codes for identifying specific parts of speech.

Words

Hebrew words, including nouns, adjectives, prepositions, etc., are written in all upper case letters. If two English words are used to translate a single Hebrew word, a dash (-) will be placed between the two words. Each Hebrew word translation is listed in the dictionary which follows the book of Exodus. Hebrew words will frequently include one or two prefixes. Prefixes are written in all lower case letters and are followed by the tilde (~). Some words will include a suffix, which is also written in all lower case letters, and is preceded by the tilde (~). The dictionary also includes a list of all the prefixes and suffixes found in the Mechanical Translation. Below are examples of words with prefixes and suffixes, which appear in the Mechanical Translation.

Hebrew	Prefix	Word	Suffix	Mech. Trans.
היבשה	the~	DRY-GROUND		the~DRY-GROUND
כאשר	like~	WHICH		like~WHICH
ידך		HAND	~you(ms)	HAND~you(ms)
ובנים	and~	SON	~s	and~SON~s

Verbs

Hebrew Verbs are written in all upper case letters and are underlined for easy identification. Each Hebrew verb translation is listed in the dictionary, which follows the book of Exodus, and is also underlined. Verbs may also include a prefix as well as a suffix. Hebrew verb conjugations identify such aspects as the gender and number of the subject (he, she, they, etc), gender and number of the object (him, her, you, etc.), the tense (did, will), and verb form (make, be, etc.). The translations of these aspects are written in all lower case and in italics. The dictionary also includes a list of all the conjugations and their meanings. Below are examples of verbs with prefixes, suffixes and conjugations, which appear in the Mechanical Translation.

Hebrew	Prefix	Conj.	Verb	Suffix	Mech. Trans.
יאמר		he~will~	SAY		he~will~SAY
ושמרת	and~	you(ms)~did~	SAFE-GUARD		and~you(ms)~did~SAFE-GUARD
דברך		>~much~	SPEAK	~you(ms)	>~much~SPEAK~you(ms)

Names

Each name in the Mechanical Translation is a transliteration of the Hebrew and begins with an upper case letter. The Mechanical Translation of the name appears in brackets and written in superscript. Each Hebrew name is listed in the dictionary following the book of Exodus. Names may also include prefixes and suffixes such as can be seen in the examples below.

Hebrew	Prefix	Name	Meaning	Suffix	Mech. Trans.
במצרים	in~	Mits'rayim	STRAIT~s2		in~"Mits'rayim STRAIT~ s2„
סכתה		Sukhot	BOOTH~s	~unto	Sukhot BOOTH~ s„~ unto

Revised Mechanical Translation

The Revised Mechanical Translation re-arranges the words of the Mechanical Translation to more closely reflect English syntax, making the translation understood by all. At times, it is necessary to make some changes between the Mechanical

Translation and the Revised Mechanical Translation. For this reason, different styles of brackets are added to show these various changes.

Alternate Translations - (...)

Where the Mechanical Translation of a given Hebrew word will make no sense in English, it will be necessary to change the translation of that Hebrew word. As an example, the Hebrew word בית (bayit) is always translated as "house" in the Mechanical Translation, but in the phrase מבית ומחוץ (from the house and from the outside) the translation "house" does not make any sense in English. Therefore, the word "house" is changed to "inside" (another meaning of the Hebrew word בית), but written as "(inside)" in the Revised Mechanical Translation. Appendix A is a complete list of these alternate translations followed by how they are translated in the Mechanical Translation.

Compound Phrases - <...>

Certain combinations of Hebrew words have a specific meaning. For example, the Hebrew phrase על כן (al keyn) would literally be translated as "upon so" but means "therefore." This phrase is then translated in the Revised Mechanical Translation as "<therefore>." Another example is the word כאשר (k'asher), which literally means "like which," but is translated as "<just as>" in the Revised Mechanical Translation. Appendix B is a complete list of these compound phrases followed by how they are translated in the Mechanical Translation.

Verb Forms - [...]

Different verb forms can change the meaning of a verb. For instance, the Hebrew verb אמן (aman) means "secure, "but when this verb is written in the hiphil form (identified as *make*~SECURE in the Mechanical Translation), it literally means "to cause to be secure" meaning "support." Therefore, this verb will be written as "[support]" in the Revised Mechanical Translation. Appendix C is a complete list of these verb forms followed by how they are translated in the Mechanical Translation.

Plural Forms - \.../

The Hebrew word אף (aph) means "nose," but when it is written in the plural form, אפים (aphiym), it means "nostrils." Therefore, this plural form will appear in the Revised Mechanical Translation as "\nostrils/." Appendix D is a complete list of these plural forms followed by how they are translated in the Mechanical Translation.

Intensifying Infinitive Absolute - :...:

The Hebrew language uses the unique style of doubling the use of a verb to show intensity. As an example, the phrase ראה ראיתי (ra'oh ra'iy'tiy) includes the Hebrew verb ראה (R.A.H), meaning "see," twice and is translated in the Revised Mechanical Translation as "I :surely: saw."

Past Perfect Verbs - |...|

In Hebrew Syntax, the subject of the verb follows the verb. For instance, we would say in English, "Mosheh walked," but in Hebrew it would be, "walked Mosheh." However, there are times when the subject of the verb precedes the verb. In this case, the structure is identifying the verb as a past perfect. As an example, the Hebrew phrase היה משה (hayah mosheh) would be translated in the Revised Mechanical Translation as "Mosheh existed," but when this phrase is written as משה היה (mosheh hayah), it is translated as "Mosheh |had| existed."

Added Words - {...}

It is frequently required to add words in the Revised Mechanical Translation that do not exist within the Hebrew text in order to have the translation make sense in English. A common example in the Hebrew text is the phrase בני ישראל (b'ney yisra'el), which is translated in the Mechanical Translation as "SON~s Yisra'el," but appears in the Revised Mechanical Translation as "{the} sons {of} Yisra'el," where the words "the" and "of" have been added to the text.

Changes not identified by codes

Pronouns are changed without any identifying codes. For instance, the Mechanical Translation may have the pronoun "you" but may be translated as "your" in the Revised Mechanical Translation.

Most plural forms of nouns are simply the singular form with the letter "s" suffixed to the noun. Examples from the Mechanical Translation are the plural HAND~s and HOUSE~s, which simply appear as "hands" and "houses" in the Revised Mechanical Translation. However, the plural words MAN~s and FOOT~s will be translated in the Revised Mechanical Translation as "men" and "feet," but are not identified by any codes.

The Hebrew verb אמר (amar) is translated as "*he~did~*SAY" in the Mechanical Translation, where the word "he" identifies the gender (masculine) and number (singular) of the subject of the verb and the word "did" identifies the tense (perfect, similar to the English past tense) of the verb. This word is translated as "he said" in the

Revised Mechanical Translation. The dropping of the word "did" and the change from "say" to "said" are not identified by any code. When the prefix "and~" is attached to a verb, the tense of the verb is reversed. So, the verb ואמר (wa'omar) would be translated in the Mechanical Translation as "and~*he~did*~SAY," but as "and he will say" in the Revised Mechanical Translation. The word "did" is changed to "will" because of the prefixed letter meaning "and," but is not identified by any code. Below are a few examples of how a verb and its subject would be translated in the Mechanical Translation and the Revised Mechanical Translation.

Mech. Trans.	Revised Mech. Trans.
he~did~HELP Elohiym	Elohiym helped
and~*he~did*~HELP Elohiym	and Elohiym will help
Elohiym *he~did*~HELP	Elohiym |had| helped
he~will~HELP Elohiym	Elohiym will help
and~*he~will*~HELP Elohiym	and Elohiym helped

Punctuation

The original Hebrew text does not include any punctuation. However, it is necessary to add comas in the Revised Mechanical Translation in order to show breaks in the sentences which are implied through the grammar of the Hebrew. In addition, the question mark (?) is added for sentences that are constructed in the interrogative form.

Names

As previously discussed, Hebrew names are written in the Mechanical Translation as "Yisra'el *he~will*~TURN-ASIDE~+~MIGHTY-ONE„". The only change between the Mechanical Translation and the Revised Mechanical is the Revised Mechanical Translation of the meaning of the name, which will appear as "Yisra'el He turns El aside„ .

Dictionary

Words and Verbs

Translation

Each word and verb translation found in the Mechanical Translation is listed alphabetically. As an example, the phrase "in~HAND~you(ms)" appears in the Mechanical Translation and only the word "HAND" is included in this list. For the words "in~" and "~you(mp) see "Prefixes and Suffixes" below. Note, only the words of the Mechanical Translation appear in the dictionary and not those found in the Revised Mechanical Translation.

Hebrew

Each entry includes Hebrew spelling of the word (in Ancient and Modern Hebrew) along with a transliteration of the Hebrew word. All Hebrew nouns are gender specific and the words gender will also be identified. Some Hebrew words have alternate spellings, which are also included.

Definition

Because each Hebrew word has a specific meaning within its etymological and cultural background, one or two English words cannot completely convey its meaning. Therefore, a more detailed definition of each word is provided.

References

Each Hebrew word is cross-referenced, by number, with the *Ancient Hebrew Lexicon of the Bible* and *Strong's Dictionary*.

Concordance

Each verse in the book of Exodus, in which a word appears, is identified. If the word appears more than once in a given verse, the number of times it appears in that verse is written in brackets - { }.

Names

Each Hebrew name is listed alphabetically, followed by the Hebrew spelling (in Ancient and Modern Hebrew), transliteration, gender, meaning, Strong's number and the verses of each occurrence in the book of Exodus.

Prefixes and Suffixes

Each prefix and suffix found within the Mechanical Translation is listed alphabetically followed by its Hebrew spelling (in Ancient and Modern Hebrew) and its meaning.

Verb Conjugations

Each word used in the Mechanical Translation representing the verb conjugations is listed alphabetically followed by its meaning.

Appendices

Appendix A - Alternate Translations

This is an alphabetical list of all the alternate translations used in the Revised Mechanical Translation for words found in the Mechanical Translation.

Appendix B - Compound Phrases

This is an alphabetical list of all the words used in the Revised Mechanical Translation for translating compound phrases found in the Mechanical Translation.

Appendix C - Verb Forms

This is an alphabetical list of all the words used in the Revised Mechanical Translation for translating complex verb forms found in the Mechanical Translation.

Appendix D - Plural Forms

This is an alphabetical list of all the words used in the Revised Mechanical Translation for translating specific plural forms found in the Mechanical Translation.

Appendix E - Pronunciation Guide

The chart included in this appendix provides the pronunciation for the transliterations of the Hebrew used in the book of Exodus and in the dictionary.

Appendix F – Changes since the Mechanical Translation of Genesis

As the Mechanical Translation is a work in progress, some changes have occurred since the publishing of *A Mechanical Translation of the Book of Genesis*, specifically, the translation of some Hebrew words. This is an alphabetical list of translations used in the book of Genesis and their revised translation used in the book of Exodus.

Bibliography

This is a list of resources that have been helpful with translating and defining Hebrew words found in the book of Exodus, as well as a list of Bible translations consulted for the translational process.

The Mechanical Translation of the Book of Exodus

Chapter 1

1:1   וְאֵלֶּה שְׁמוֹת בְּנֵי יִשְׂרָאֵל הַבָּאִים מִצְרָיְמָה אֵת יַעֲקֹב אִישׁ וּבֵיתוֹ בָּאוּ

we'ey'leh she'mot be'ney yis'ra'eyl ha'ba'im mits'rai'mah eyt ya'a'qov ish u'vey'to ba'u

and~THESE TITLE~s SON~s "Yisra'el ^{he~will~} ^{TURN-ASIDE~+~MIGHTY-ONE}" the~COME~ing/er(mp) "Mits'rayim ^{STRAIT~s2}"~unto AT "Ya'aqov ^{he~will~} ^{RESTRAIN}" MAN and~HOUSE~him *they~did~* COME□

and* these {are the} titles {of the} sons {of} "Yisra'el ^{He turns El aside}", the {one}s coming unto "Mits'rayim ^{Two straits}" (with) "Ya'aqov ^{He restrains}", (each) and his house |had| come,□

1:2   רְאוּבֵן שִׁמְעוֹן לֵוִי וִיהוּדָה

re'u'veyn shim'on ley'wi wi'hu'dah

"Re'uven ^{SEE~+~l(ms)~+~SON}" "Shimon ^{HEARER}" "Lewi ^{JOINING~me}" and~"Yehudah ^{THANKSGIVING}"□

"Re'uven ^{See a son}", "Shimon ^{Hearer}", "Lewi ^{My joining}", and "Yehudah ^{Thanksgiving}",□

1:3   יִשָּׂשכָר זְבוּלֻן וּבִנְיָמִן

yis'sas'khar ze'vu'lun u'vin'ya'min

"Yis'sas'khar ^{THERE-IS~+~WAGE}" "Zevulun ^{RESIDENT}" and~"Binyamin ^{SON~+~RIGHT-HAND}"□

"Yis'sas'kar ^{He hires}", "Zevulun ^{Resident}", and "Binyamin ^{Son of the right hand}",□

1:4   דָּן וְנַפְתָּלִי גָּד וְאָשֵׁר

dan we'naph'ta'li gad we'asheyr

"Dan ^{MODERATOR}" and~"Naphtali ^{WRESTLING~me}" "Gad ^{FORTUNE}" and~"Asher ^{HAPPY}"□

"Dan ^{Moderator}", and "Naphtali ^{My wrestling}", "Gad ^{Fortune}" and "Asher ^{Happy}",□

1:5   וַיְהִי כָּל נֶפֶשׁ יֹצְאֵי יֶרֶךְ יַעֲקֹב שִׁבְעִים נָפֶשׁ וְיוֹסֵף הָיָה בְמִצְרָיִם

wai'hi kol ne'phesh yots'ey ye'rekh ya'a'qov shiv'im na'phesh we'yo'seyph hai'yah ve'mits'ra'yim

and~he~will~EXIST ALL BEING GO-OUT~ ing/er(mp) MIDSECTION "Ya'aqov ^{he~will~} ^{RESTRAIN}" SEVEN~s BEING and~"Yoseph ^{ADD~}

and (it) (came to pass), all {the} being{s} going out {of the} midsection {of} "Ya'aqov ^{He restrains}" {were} \seventy/ being{s} and "Yoseph ^{Adding}"

---

* The first verse of the book of Exodus begins with "and," indicating that this is a continuation of the final verse of Genesis.

Revised Mechanical Translation Codes

(..) Alt Trans/App A	<..> Comp Phrase/App B	[..] Verb Form/App C	\../ Plural Form/App D
:...: Int Inf Abs	|..| Past Perf Verb	{...} Added Word	

ing/er(ms)" *he~did~*<u>EXIST</u> in~"Mits'rayim STRAIT~s2" □

|had| existed in "Mits'rayim ^{Two straits}", □

1:6

וַיָּמָת יוֹסֵף וְכָל אֶחָיו וְכֹל הַדּוֹר הַהוּא

wai'ya'mat yo'seyph we'khol e'hhaw we'khol ha'dor ha'hu

and~*he~will~*<u>DIE</u> "Yoseph ^{ADD~ing/er(ms)"} and~ALL BROTHER~s~him and~ALL the~GENERATION the~HE□

and "Yoseph ^{Adding}" died and all his brothers and all (that) generation, □

1:7

וּבְנֵי יִשְׂרָאֵל פָּרוּ וַיִּשְׁרְצוּ וַיִּרְבּוּ וַיַּעַצְמוּ בִּמְאֹד מְאֹד וַתִּמָּלֵא הָאָרֶץ אֹתָם

uv'ney yis'ra'eyl pa'ru wai'yish're'tsu wai'yir'bu wai'ya'ats'mu bim'od me'od wa'ti'ma'ley ha'a'rets o'tam

and~SON~s "Yisra'el ^{he~will~TURN-ASIDE~+~MIGHTY-ONE"} *they~did~*<u>REPRODUCE</u> and~*they(m)~will~*<u>SWARM</u> and~*they(m)~will~*<u>INCREASE</u> and~*they(m)~will~*<u>BE-ABUNDANT</u> in~MANY MANY and~ she~*will~be~*<u>FILL</u> the~LAND AT~them(m)□

and {the} sons {of} "Yisra'el ^{He turns El aside}" |had| reproduced and they swarmed and they increased and they were abundant (with) {a} (great) many, and the land was filled (with) them, □

1:8

וַיָּקָם מֶלֶךְ חָדָשׁ עַל מִצְרָיִם אֲשֶׁר לֹא יָדַע אֶת יוֹסֵף

wai'ya'qam me'lekh hha'dash al mits'ra'yim a'sher lo ya'da et yo'seyph

and~*he~will~*<u>RISE</u> KING NEW UPON "Mits'rayim ^{STRAIT~s2"} WHICH NOT *he~did~*<u>KNOW</u> AT "Yoseph ^{ADD~ing/er(ms)"} □

and {a} new king rose upon "Mits'rayim ^{Two straits}" (who) did not know "Yoseph ^{Adding}", □

1:9

וַיֹּאמֶר אֶל עַמּוֹ הִנֵּה עַם בְּנֵי יִשְׂרָאֵל רַב וְעָצוּם מִמֶּנּוּ

wai'yo'mer el a'mo hin'neyh am be'ney yis'ra'eyl rav we'a'tsum mi'me'nu

and~*he~will~*<u>SAY</u> TO PEOPLE~him LOOK PEOPLE SON~s "Yisra'el ^{he~will~TURN-ASIDE~+~MIGHTY-ONE"} ABUNDANT and~NUMEROUS FROM~us□

and he said to his people, look, {the} people {of the} sons {of} "Yisra'el ^{He turns El aside}" {are} abundant and numerous, (more than) us, □

1:10

הָבָה נִתְחַכְּמָה לוֹ פֶּן יִרְבֶּה וְהָיָה כִּי תִקְרֶאנָה מִלְחָמָה וְנוֹסַף גַּם הוּא עַל שֹׂנְאֵינוּ וְנִלְחַם בָּנוּ וְעָלָה מִן הָאָרֶץ

ha'vah nit'hhak'mah lo pen yir'beh we'hai'yah ki tiq're'nah mil'hha'mah we'no'seyph gam hu al shon'ey'nu we'nil'hham ba'nu we'a'lah min ha'a'rets

!(ms)~<u>PROVIDE</u>~^ *we~will~* self~<u>BE-SKILLED</u>~^ to~him OTHERWISE *he~will~*

(come), we will (act) skill{fully} to{ward} him*, otherwise he will increase, and (it) will (come

---

* Referring to the "people" (of verse 9) a masculine singular word in Hebrew.

Mechanical Translation Codes

<u>WORD</u> – Verb	WORD – Noun	Word – Name	word – Pre/Suff	*word* – Conj.

INCREASE and~he~did~EXIST GIVEN-THAT
they(f)~will~MEET BATTLE and~he~did~ADD
ALSO HE UPON HATE~ing/er(mp)~us and~
he~did~be~FIGHT in~us and~he~did~GO-UP
FROM the~LAND□

to pass) that {a} battle will meet us*, also {in}
add{ition}, our haters will [wage war] (with)
us, and he will go up from the land,□

1:11 וַיָּשִׂימוּ עָלָיו שָׂרֵי מִסִּים לְמַעַן עַנֹּתוֹ בְּסִבְלֹתָם וַיִּבֶן עָרֵי מִסְכְּנוֹת לְפַרְעֹה אֶת פִּתֹם וְאֶת רַעַמְסֵס

wai'ya'si'mu a'law sa'rey mi'sim le'ma'an an'no'to be'siv'lo'tam wai'yi'ven a'rey mis'ke'not
le'phar'oh et pi'tom we'et ra'am'seys

and~they(m)~will~PLACE UPON~him
NOBLE~s TASK-WORK~s to~THAT >~much~
AFFLICT~him in~BURDEN~s~them(m) and~
he~will~BUILD CITY~s STOREHOUSE~s to~
"Paroh GREAT-HOUSE" AT "Pitom CITY-OF-JUSTICE"
and~AT "Ra'meses CHILD-OF-THE-SUN"□

and they placed nobles {of the} task works
upon him† (so) that he {was} afflicted in their
burdens, and he built storehouse cities (for)
"Paroh Great house" at "Pitom City of justice" and at
"Ra'meses Child of the sun",□

1:12 וְכַאֲשֶׁר יְעַנּוּ אֹתוֹ כֵּן יִרְבֶּה וְכֵן יִפְרֹץ וַיָּקֻצוּ מִפְּנֵי בְּנֵי יִשְׂרָאֵל

we'kha'a'sher ye'a'nu o'to keyn yir'beh we'kheyn yiph'rots wai'ya'qu'tsu mip'ney be'ney
yis'ra'eyl

and~like~WHICH they(m)~will~AFFLICT AT~
him SO he~will~INCREASE and~SO he~will~
BREAK-OUT and~they(m)~will~LOATHE
from~FACE~s SON~s "Yisra'el he~will~TURN-ASIDE~
+~MIGHTY-ONE"□

and <just as> they will afflict him‡, so he will
increase, and so, he will break out, and they
loathed {the} face {of the} sons {of} "Yisra'el He
turns El aside",□

1:13 וַיַּעֲבִדוּ מִצְרַיִם אֶת בְּנֵי יִשְׂרָאֵל בְּפָרֶךְ

wai'ya'a'vi'du mits'ra'yim et be'ney yis'ra'eyl be'pha'rek

and~they(m)~will~make~SERVE "Mits'rayim
STRAIT~s2" AT SON~s "Yisra'el he~will~TURN-ASIDE~+~
MIGHTY-ONE" in~WHIP□

and "Mits'rayim Two straits" made {the} sons {of}
"Yisra'el He turns El aside" serve (by) {the} whip,□

1:14 וַיְמָרְרוּ אֶת חַיֵּיהֶם בַּעֲבֹדָה קָשָׁה בְּחֹמֶר וּבִלְבֵנִים וּבְכָל עֲבֹדָה בַּשָּׂדֶה אֵת כָּל עֲבֹדָתָם אֲשֶׁר עָבְדוּ בָהֶם בְּפָרֶךְ

wai'mar'ru et hhai'yey'him ba'a'vo'dah qa'shah be'hho'mer u'vil'vey'nim uv'khol a'vo'dah

---

* The phrase תִקְרֶאנָה מִלְחָמָה is grammatically incorrect. The subject of the verb is the word מִלְחָמָה (Battle), which is a feminine singular noun. However, the verb identifies the subject of the verb as a feminine plural. If the final letters of the verb were originally נוּ(meaning "us," the object of the verb) instead of נָה (meaning "she," the subject of the verb), then this would read "a battle will meet us," which makes more contextual and grammatical sense.
† Referring to the "people" (of verse 9) a masculine singular word in Hebrew.
‡ Referring to the "people" (of verse 9) a masculine singular word in Hebrew.

Revised Mechanical Translation Codes
(..) Alt Trans/App A   <..> Comp Phrase/App B   [..] Verb Form/App C   \../ Plural Form/App D
:..: Int Inf Abs |..| Past Perf Verb   {...} Added Word

ba'sa'deh eyt kol a'vo'da'tam a'sher av'du va'hem be'pha'rek

and~*they(m)~will~much~*<u>BE-BITTER</u> AT LIVING~s~them(m) in~the~SERVICE HARD in~MORTAR and~in~BRICK~s and~in~ALL SERVICE in~the~FIELD AT ALL SERVICE~ them(m) WHICH *they~did~*<u>SERVE</u> in~ them(m) in~WHIP□	and their \life/ was (very) bitter (with) the hard service, (with) mortar and (with) bricks and (with) all {the} service in the field, all their service which they served in them (with) {the} whip,□

1:15 וַיֹּאמֶר מֶלֶךְ מִצְרַיִם לַמְיַלְּדֹת הָעִבְרִיֹּת אֲשֶׁר שֵׁם הָאַחַת שִׁפְרָה וְשֵׁם הַשֵּׁנִית פּוּעָה

wai'yo'mer me'lekh mits'ra'yim lam'yal'dot ha'iv'ri'yot a'sher sheym ha'a'hhat shiph'rah we'sheym ha'shey'nit pu'ah

and~*he~will~*<u>SAY</u> KING "Mits'rayim ^{STRAIT~s2}„ to~the~*much~*<u>BRING-FORTH</u>~*ing/er(fp)* the~ "Ever ^{OTHER-SIDE}„~s WHICH TITLE the~UNIT "Shiphrah ^{BRIGHTNESS}„ and~TITLE the~SECOND "Pu'ah ^{SPLENDID}„□	and {the} king {of} "Mits'rayim ^{Two straits}„ said to the [midwives] {of} "Ever ^{Other side}„, {of} (whom) {the} title {of} the (one) {is} "Shiphrah ^{Brightness}„ and {the} title {of} the second {is} "Pu'ah ^{Splendid}„,□

1:16 וַיֹּאמֶר בְּיַלֶּדְכֶן אֶת הָעִבְרִיּוֹת וּרְאִיתֶן עַל הָאָבְנָיִם אִם בֵּן הוּא וַהֲמִתֶּן אֹתוֹ וְאִם בַּת הִיא וָחָיָה

wai'yo'mer be'ya'led'khen et ha'iv'ri'yot ur'i'ten al ha'av'na'yim im beyn hu wa'ha'mi'ten o'to we'im bat hi wa'hhai'yah

and~*he~will~*<u>SAY</u> in~>~*much~*<u>BRING-FORTH</u>~them(f) AT the~"Ever ^{OTHER-SIDE}„~s and~*you(fp)~did~*<u>SEE</u> UPON the~STONE-STOOL IF SON HE and~*you(fp)~make~* <u>DIE</u> AT~him and~IF DAUGHTER SHE and~ *she~did~*<u>LIVE</u>□	and he said (with) the {one}s {of} "Ever ^{Other side}„ {acting as a} [midwife], if you see upon the stone stool {that} he {is a} son, (then) you will [kill] him, and if she {is a} daughter, (then) she will live,□

1:17 וַתִּירֶאןָ הַמְיַלְּדֹת אֶת הָאֱלֹהִים וְלֹא עָשׂוּ כַּאֲשֶׁר דִּבֶּר אֲלֵיהֶן מֶלֶךְ מִצְרָיִם וַתְּחַיֶּיןָ אֶת הַיְלָדִים

wa'ti're'na ham'yal'dot et ha'e'lo'him we'lo a'su ka'a'sheyr di'ber a'ley'hen me'lekh mits'ra'yim wat'hha'yey'na et ha'ye'la'dim

and~*they(f)~will~*<u>FEAR</u> the~*much~*<u>BRING-FORTH</u>~*ing/er(fp)* AT the~"Elohiym ^{POWER~s}„ and~NOT *they~did~*<u>DO</u> like~WHICH *he~did~ much~*<u>SPEAK</u> TO~them(f) KING "Mits'rayim ^{STRAIT~s2}„ and~*they(f)~will~much~*<u>LIVE</u> AT the~BOY~s□	and the [midwives] feared the "Elohiym ^{Powers}„ and they did not do <just as> {the} king {of} "Mits'rayim ^{Two straits}„ spoke to them, and they [kept alive] the boys,□

1:18 וַיִּקְרָא מֶלֶךְ מִצְרַיִם לַמְיַלְּדֹת וַיֹּאמֶר לָהֶן מַדּוּעַ עֲשִׂיתֶן הַדָּבָר הַזֶּה וַתְּחַיֶּיןָ אֶת הַיְלָדִים

wai'yiq'ra me'lekh mits'ra'yim lam'yal'dot wai'yo'mer la'hen ma'du'a a'si'ten ha'da'var ha'zeh wat'hha'yey'na et ha'ye'la'dim

Mechanical Translation Codes

<u>WORD</u> – Verb	WORD – Noun	Word – Name	word – Pre/Suff	*word* – Conj.

and~*he*~*will*~<u>CALL-OUT</u> KING "Mits'rayim ^{STRAIT~s2}„ to~the~*much*~<u>BRING-FORTH</u>~*ing/er(fp)* and~*he*~*will*~<u>SAY</u> to~them(f) WHY you(fp)~*did*~<u>DO</u> the~WORD the~THIS and~you(fp)~*will*~*much*~<u>LIVE</u> AT the~BOY~s□

and {the} king {of} "Mits'rayim ^{Two straits}„ called out to the [midwives] and he said to them, why did you do this (matter) and [kept alive] the boys?□

1:19 וַתֹּאמַרְןָ הַמְיַלְּדֹת אֶל פַּרְעֹה כִּי לֹא כַנָּשִׁים הַמִּצְרִיֹּת הָעִבְרִיֹּת כִּי חָיוֹת הֵנָּה בְּטֶרֶם תָּבוֹא אֲלֵהֶן הַמְיַלֶּדֶת וְיָלָדוּ

wa'to'ma'na ham'yal'dot el par'oh ki lo ka'na'shim ha'mits'ri'yot ha'iv'ri'yot ki hhai'ot heyn'nah be'te'rem ta'vo a'ley'hen ham'ya'le'det we'ya'la'du

and~*they(f)*~*will*~<u>SAY</u> the~*much*~<u>BRING-FORTH</u>~*ing/er(fp)* TO "Paroh ^{GREAT-HOUSE}„ GIVEN-THAT NOT like~the~WOMAN~s the~"Mits'rayim ^{STRAIT~s2}„~s the~"Ever ^{OTHER-SIDE}„~s GIVEN-THAT LIVELY~s THEY(f) in~BEFORE she~*will*~<u>COME</u> TO~them(f) the~*much*~<u>BRING-FORTH</u>~*ing/er(fs)* and~*they*~*did*~<u>BRING-FORTH</u>□

and the [midwives] said to "Paroh ^{Great house}„, (because) the women {of} "Mits'rayim ^{Two straits}„ {are} not like the {one}s {of} "Ever ^{Other side}„, (because) they {are} lively before the [midwife] comes to them, and they bring forth,□

1:20 וַיֵּיטֶב אֱלֹהִים לַמְיַלְּדֹת וַיִּרֶב הָעָם וַיַּעַצְמוּ מְאֹד

wai'yey'tev e'lo'him lam'yal'dot wai'yi'rev ha'am wai'ya'ats'mu me'od

and~*he*~*will*~*make*~<u>DO-WELL</u> "Elohiym ^{POWER~s}„ to~the~*much*~<u>BRING-FORTH</u>~*ing/er(fp)* and~*he*~*will*~<u>INCREASE</u> the~PEOPLE and~*they(m)*~*will*~<u>BE-ABUNDANT</u> MANY□

and "Elohiym ^{Powers}„ made {it} [go well] (for) the [midwives] and the people increased and they be{came} (greatly) abundant,□

1:21 וַיְהִי כִּי יָרְאוּ הַמְיַלְּדֹת אֶת הָאֱלֹהִים וַיַּעַשׂ לָהֶם בָּתִּים

wai'hi ki yar'u ham'yal'dot et ha'e'lo'him wai'ya'as la'hem ba'tim

and~*he*~*will*~<u>EXIST</u> GIVEN-THAT *they*~*did*~<u>FEAR</u> the~*much*~<u>BRING-FORTH</u>~*ing/er(fp)* AT the~"Elohiym ^{POWER~s}„ and~*he*~*will*~<u>DO</u> to~them(m) HOUSE~s□

and (it) (came to pass) that the [midwives] feared the "Elohiym ^{Powers}„ and he made houses (for) them,□

1:22 וַיְצַו פַּרְעֹה לְכָל עַמּוֹ לֵאמֹר כָּל הַבֵּן הַיִּלּוֹד הַיְאֹרָה תַּשְׁלִיכֻהוּ וְכָל הַבַּת תְּחַיּוּן

wai'tsaw par'oh le'khol a'mo ley'mor kol ha'beyn hai'yi'lod hai'o'rah tash'li'khu'hu we'khol ha'bat te'hhai'yun

and~*he*~*will*~*much*~<u>DIRECT</u> "Paroh ^{GREAT-HOUSE}„ to~ALL PEOPLE~him to~>~<u>SAY</u> ALL the~SON the~BIRTHED the~STREAM~unto you(mp)~*will*~*make*~<u>THROW-OUT</u>~him and~ALL the~DAUGHTER you(mp)~*will*~*much*~

and "Paroh ^{Great house}„ directed all his people say{ing}, you will throw all the birthed son{s} out unto the stream and you must [keep alive] all the daughter{s},□

Revised Mechanical Translation Codes

(..) Alt Trans/App A   <..> Comp Phrase/App B   [..] Verb Form/App C   \../ Plural Form/App D

:...: Int Inf Abs |..| Past Perf Verb   {...} Added Word

LIVE~must□

Chapter 2

2:1　　　　　　　וַיֵּלֶךְ אִישׁ מִבֵּית לֵוִי וַיִּקַּח אֶת בַּת לֵוִי

wai'yey'lekh ish mi'beyt ley'wi wai'yi'qahh et bat ley'wi

and~*he~will*~<u>WALK</u> MAN from~HOUSE "Lewi ^{JOINING~me}" and~*he~will*~<u>TAKE</u> AT DAUGHTER "Lewi ^{JOINING~me}"□

and {a} man from {the} house {of} "Lewi ^{My joining}" walked* and he took {a} daughter {of} "Lewi ^{My joining}",□

2:2　　　　וַתַּהַר הָאִשָּׁה וַתֵּלֶד בֵּן וַתֵּרֶא אֹתוֹ כִּי טוֹב הוּא וַתִּצְפְּנֵהוּ שְׁלֹשָׁה יְרָחִים

wa'ta'har ha'i'shah wa'tey'led beyn wa'tey're o'to ki tov hu wa'tits'pe'ney'hu she'lo'shah ye'ra'hhim

and~ she~*will*~<u>CONCEIVE</u> the~WOMAN and~ she~*will*~<u>BRING-FORTH</u> SON and~ she~*will*~<u>SEE</u> AT~him GIVEN-THAT FUNCTIONAL HE and~ she~*will*~<u>CONCEAL</u>~him THREE MOON~s□

and the woman conceived and she brought forth {a} son and she saw that he {was} functional and she concealed him {for} three moons,□

2:3　　　וְלֹא יָכְלָה עוֹד הַצְּפִינוֹ וַתִּקַּח לוֹ תֵּבַת גֹּמֶא וַתַּחְמְרָה בַחֵמָר וּבַזָּפֶת וַתָּשֶׂם בָּהּ אֶת הַיֶּלֶד וַתָּשֶׂם בַּסּוּף עַל שְׂפַת הַיְאֹר

we'lo yakh'lah od hats'phi'no wa'ti'qahh lo tey'vat go'me wa'tahh'me'rah ba'hhey'mar u'va'za'phet wa'ta'sem bah et ha'ye'led wa'ta'sem ba'suph al she'phat hai'or

and~NOT she~*did*~<u>BE-ABLE</u> YET-AGAIN >~*make*~<u>CONCEAL</u>~him and~ she~*will*~<u>TAKE</u> to~him VESSEL BULRUSH and~ she~*will*~<u>PASTE</u> in~the~TAR and~in~the~PITCH and~ she~*will*~<u>PLACE</u> in~her AT the~BOY and~ she~*will*~<u>PLACE</u> in~the~REEDS UPON LIP the~STREAM□

and she was not able to (continue) {to} make him concealed and she took (for) him {a} vessel {of} bulrush and she pasted {it} (with) the tar and (with) the pitch and she placed the boy in her† and she placed {it} in the reeds upon {the} lip {of} the stream,□

2:4　　　　　　　וַתֵּתַצַּב אֲחֹתוֹ מֵרָחֹק לְדֵעָה מַה יֵּעָשֶׂה לוֹ

wa'tey'ta'tsav a'hho'to mey'ra'hhoq le'dey'ah mah yey'a'seh lo

and~ she~*will*~ self~<u>STATION</u> SISTER~him from~DISTANCE to~>~<u>KNOW</u> WHAT *he~will*~be~<u>DO</u> to~him□

and his sister stationed {her}self (at) {a} distance to know what will be done to him,□

---

* Or "went."

† Referring to the vessel, a feminine word in Hebrew.

Mechanical Translation Codes

<u>WORD</u> – Verb	WORD – Noun	Word – Name	word – Pre/Suff	*word* – Conj.

2:5

וַתֵּרֶד בַּת פַּרְעֹה לִרְחֹץ עַל הַיְאֹר וְנַעֲרֹתֶיהָ הֹלְכֹת עַל יַד הַיְאֹר וַתֵּרֶא אֶת הַתֵּבָה בְּתוֹךְ הַסּוּף וַתִּשְׁלַח אֶת אֲמָתָהּ וַתִּקָּחֶהָ

wa'tey'red bat par'oh lir'hhots al hai'or we'na'a'ro'tey'ah hol'khot al yad hai'or wa'tey're et ha'tey'vah be'tokh ha'suph wa'tish'lahh et a'ma'tah wa'ti'qa'hhe'ha

and~ she~*will*~GO-DOWN DAUGHTER "Paroh GREAT-HOUSE" to~>~BATHE UPON the~STREAM and~YOUNG-WOMAN~s~her WALK~*ing/er(fp)* UPON HAND the~STREAM and~ she~*will*~SEE AT the~VESSEL in~MIDST the~REEDS and~ she~*will*~SEND AT BONDWOMAN~her and~ she~*will*~TAKE~her□

and {the} daughter {of} "Paroh Great house" went down to bathe upon the stream, and her young women {were} walking upon {the} hand* {of} the stream, and she saw the vessel in {the} midst {of} the reeds and she sent her bondwoman, and she took her†,□

2:6

וַתִּפְתַּח וַתִּרְאֵהוּ אֶת הַיֶּלֶד וְהִנֵּה נַעַר בֹּכֶה וַתַּחְמֹל עָלָיו וַתֹּאמֶר מִיַּלְדֵי הָעִבְרִים זֶה

wa'tiph'tahh wa'tir'ey'hu et ha'ye'led we'hin'neyh na'ar bo'kheh wa'tahh'mol a'law wa'to'mer mi'yal'dey ha'iv'rim zeh

and~ she~*will*~OPEN and~ she~*will*~SEE~him AT the~BOY and~LOOK YOUNG-MAN WEEP~*ing/er(ms)* and~ she~*will*~SHOW-PITY UPON~him and~ she~*will*~SAY from~BOY~s the~"Ever OTHER-SIDE"~s THIS□

and she opened {it} and she saw the boy, and look, {a} young man {was} weeping and she showed pity upon him, and she said, this {is} from {the} boys {of} the {one}s {of} "Ever Other side",□

2:7

וַתֹּאמֶר אֲחֹתוֹ אֶל בַּת פַּרְעֹה הַאֵלֵךְ וְקָרָאתִי לָךְ אִשָּׁה מֵינֶקֶת מִן הָעִבְרִיֹּת וְתֵינִק לָךְ אֶת הַיָּלֶד

wa'to'mer a'hho'to el bat par'oh ha'ey'leykh we'qa'ra'ti lakh i'shah mey'ne'qet min ha'iv'ri'yot we'tey'niq lakh et hai'ya'led

and~ she~*will*~SAY SISTER~him TO DAUGHTER "Paroh GREAT-HOUSE" ?~*I*~*will*~WALK and~*I*~*did*~CALL-OUT to~you(fs) WOMAN *make*~SUCKLE~*ing/er(fs)* FROM the~"Ever OTHER-SIDE"~s and~ she~*will*~*make*~SUCKLE to~you(fs) AT the~BOY□

and his sister said to {the} daughter {of} "Paroh Great house", {should} I walk and {should} I call out (for) you {a} woman, {a} [nurse] from the {one}s {of} "Ever Other side", and {should} she [nurse] the boy (for) you?□

2:8

וַתֹּאמֶר לָהּ בַּת פַּרְעֹה לֵכִי וַתֵּלֶךְ הָעַלְמָה וַתִּקְרָא אֶת אֵם הַיָּלֶד

wa'to'mer lah bat par'oh ley'khi wa'tey'lekh ha'al'mah wa'tiq'ra et eym hai'ya'led

and~ she~*will*~SAY to~her DAUGHTER "Paroh GREAT-HOUSE" *I(fs)*~WALK and~ she~*will*~WALK the~YOUNG-MAIDEN and~ she~*will*~CALL-OUT AT MOTHER the~BOY□

and {the} daughter {of} "Paroh Great house" said to her, walk, and the young maiden walked and she called out (to) {the} mother {of} the boy,□

---

* The word "Hand" may be in error and may have originally been "Lip," meaning "edge."
† Referring to the vessel, a feminine word in Hebrew.

Revised Mechanical Translation Codes

(..) Alt Trans/App A	<..> Comp Phrase/App B	[..] Verb Form/App C	\../ Plural Form/App D
:..: Int Inf Abs	|..| Past Perf Verb	{...} Added Word	

2:9 וַתֹּאמֶר לָהּ בַּת פַּרְעֹה הֵילִיכִי אֶת הַיֶּלֶד הַזֶּה וְהֵינִקִהוּ לִי וַאֲנִי אֶתֵּן אֶת שְׂכָרֵךְ וַתִּקַּח הָאִשָּׁה הַיֶּלֶד וַתְּנִיקֵהוּ

wa'to'mer lah bat par'oh hey'li'khi et ha'ye'led ha'zeh we'hey'ni'qi'hu li wa'ani e'teyn et se'kha'reykh wa'ti'qahh ha'i'shah ha'ye'led wa'te'ni'qey'hu

and~ she~*will*~SAY to~her DAUGHTER "Paroh ᴳᴿᴱᴬᵀ⁻ᴴᴼᵁˢᴱ" *make~!(fs)*~WALK AT the~ BOY the~THIS and~*make~!(fs)*~SUCKLE~him to~me and~*I I*~*will*~GIVE AT WAGE~you(fs) and~ she~*will*~TAKE the~WOMAN the~BOY and~ she~*will*~*make*~SUCKLE~him□

and {the} daughter {of} "Paroh ᴳʳᵉᵃᵗ ʰᵒᵘˢᵉ" said to her, [take] this boy and [nurse] him (for) me and I will give your wage, and the woman took the boy and she [nursed] him,□

2:10 וַיִּגְדַּל הַיֶּלֶד וַתְּבִאֵהוּ לְבַת פַּרְעֹה וַיְהִי לָהּ לְבֵן וַתִּקְרָא שְׁמוֹ מֹשֶׁה וַתֹּאמֶר כִּי מִן הַמַּיִם מְשִׁיתִהוּ

wai'yig'dal ha'ye'led wat'vi'ey'hu le'vat par'oh wai'hi lah le'veyn wa'tiq'ra she'mo mo'sheh wa'to'mer ki min ha'ma'yim me'shi'ti'hu

and~*he*~*will*~MAGNIFY the~BOY and~ she~ *will*~*make*~COME~him to~DAUGHTER "Paroh ᴳᴿᴱᴬᵀ⁻ᴴᴼᵁˢᴱ" and~*he*~*will*~EXIST to~her to~SON and~ she~*will*~CALL-OUT TITLE~him "Mosheh ᴾᴸᵁᶜᴷᴱᴰ⁻ᴼᵁᵀ" and~ she~*will*~SAY GIVEN-THAT FROM the~WATER~s2 *I*~*did*~ PLUCK-OUT~him□

and the boy magnified, and she [brought] him to {the} daughter {of} "Paroh ᴳʳᵉᵃᵗ ʰᵒᵘˢᵉ", and he existed to her (for) {a} son, and she called out his title "Mosheh ᴾˡᵘᶜᵏᵉᵈ ᵒᵘᵗ", and she said, given that from the waters I plucked him out,□

2:11 וַיְהִי בַּיָּמִים הָהֵם וַיִּגְדַּל מֹשֶׁה וַיֵּצֵא אֶל אֶחָיו וַיַּרְא בְּסִבְלֹתָם וַיַּרְא אִישׁ מִצְרִי מַכֶּה אִישׁ עִבְרִי מֵאֶחָיו

wai'hi bai'ya'mim ha'heym wai'yig'dal mo'sheh wai'yey'tsey el e'hhaw wai'yar be'siv'lo'tam wai'yar ish mits'ri ma'keh ish iv'ri mey'e'hhaw

and~*he*~*will*~EXIST in~the~DAY~s the~ THEY(m) and~*he*~*will*~MAGNIFY "Mosheh ᴾᴸᵁᶜᴷᴱᴰ⁻ᴼᵁᵀ" and~*he*~*will*~GO-OUT TO BROTHER~s~him and~*he*~*will*~SEE in~ BURDEN~s~them(m) and~*he*~*will*~SEE MAN "Mits'rayim ˢᵀᴿᴬᴵᵀ~ˢ²"~of *make*~HIT~ ing/er(ms) MAN "Ever ᴼᵀᴴᴱᴿ⁻ˢᴵᴰᴱ"~of from~ BROTHER~s~him□

and (it) (came to pass) in (those) days (that) "Mosheh ᴾˡᵘᶜᵏᵉᵈ ᵒᵘᵗ" magnified, and he went out to his brothers and he saw {them} (with) their burdens, and he saw {a} man of "Mits'rayim ᵀʷᵒ ˢᵗʳᵃⁱᵗˢ" hitting {a} man of "Ever ᴼᵗʰᵉʳ ˢⁱᵈᵉ", {one} from his brothers,□

2:12 וַיִּפֶן כֹּה וָכֹה וַיַּרְא כִּי אֵין אִישׁ וַיַּךְ אֶת הַמִּצְרִי וַיִּטְמְנֵהוּ בַּחוֹל

wai'yi'phen koh wa'khoh wai'yar ki eyn ish wai'yakh et ha'mits'ri wai'yit'me'ney'hu ba'hhul

and~*he*~*will*~TURN IN-THIS-WAY and~IN-THIS-WAY and~*he*~*will*~SEE GIVEN-THAT WITHOUT MAN and~*he*~*will*~*make*~HIT AT the~"Mits'rayim ˢᵀᴿᴬᴵᵀ~ˢ²"~of and~*he*~*will*~

and he turned this way and (that way), and he saw that {there was} (no) man, and he hit the {one} of "Mits'rayim ᵀʷᵒ ˢᵗʳᵃⁱᵗˢ" and he submerged him in the sand,□

Mechanical Translation Codes

WORD – Verb	WORD – Noun	Word – Name	word – Pre/Suff	*word* – Conj.

SUBMERGE~him in~the~SAND□

2:13

וַיֵּצֵא בַּיוֹם הַשֵּׁנִי וְהִנֵּה שְׁנֵי אֲנָשִׁים עִבְרִים נִצִּים וַיֹּאמֶר לָרָשָׁע לָמָּה תַכֶּה רֵעֶךָ

wai'yey'tsey ba'yom ha'shey'ni we'hin'neyh she'ney a'na'shim iv'rim ni'tsim wai'yo'mer la'ra'sha la'mah ta'keh rey'e'kha

and~he~will~<u>GO-OUT</u> in~the~DAY the~SECOND and~LOOK TWO MAN~s "Ever ^{OTHER-SIDE}"~s be~<u>STRUGGLE</u>~ing/er(mp) and~he~will~<u>SAY</u> to~the~LOST to~WHAT you(ms)~will~make~<u>HIT</u> COMPANION~you(ms)□

and he went out in the second day, and look, two men {of} "Ever ^{Other side}" were struggling, and he said to the lost {one}*, why would you hit your companion?□

2:14

וַיֹּאמֶר מִי שָׂמְךָ לְאִישׁ שַׂר וְשֹׁפֵט עָלֵינוּ הַלְהָרְגֵנִי אַתָּה אֹמֵר כַּאֲשֶׁר הָרַגְתָּ אֶת הַמִּצְרִי וַיִּירָא מֹשֶׁה וַיֹּאמַר אָכֵן נוֹדַע הַדָּבָר

wai'yo'mer mi sam'kha le'ish sar we'sho'pheyt a'ley'nu hal'har'gey'ni a'tah o'meyr ka'a'sheyr ha'rag'ta et ha'mits'ri wai'yi'ra mo'sheh wai'yo'mar a'kheyn no'da ha'da'var

and~he~will~<u>SAY</u> WHO he~did~<u>PLACE</u>~you(ms) to~MAN NOBLE and~<u>DECIDE</u>~ing/er(ms) UPON~us ?~to~>~<u>KILL</u>~me YOU(ms) <u>SAY</u>~ing/er(ms) like~WHICH you(ms)~did~<u>KILL</u> AT the~"Mits'rayim ^{STRAIT~s2}"~of and~he~will~<u>FEAR</u> "Mosheh ^{PLUCKED-OUT}" and~he~will~<u>SAY</u> SURELY he~did~be~<u>KNOW</u> the~WORD□

and he said, who placed you (as) {a} noble man and decider† (over) us? {are you} say{ing} you {will} kill me <just as> you killed the {one} of "Mits'rayim ^{Two straits}"? and "Mosheh ^{Plucked out}" feared, and he said, surely the (matter) is known,□

2:15

וַיִּשְׁמַע פַּרְעֹה אֶת הַדָּבָר הַזֶּה וַיְבַקֵּשׁ לַהֲרֹג אֶת מֹשֶׁה וַיִּבְרַח מֹשֶׁה מִפְּנֵי פַרְעֹה וַיֵּשֶׁב בְּאֶרֶץ מִדְיָן וַיֵּשֶׁב עַל הַבְּאֵר

wai'yish'ma par'oh et ha'da'var ha'zeh wai'va'qeysh la'ha'rog et mo'sheh wai'yiv'rahh mo'sheh mip'ney phar'oh wai'yey'shev be'e'rets mid'yan wai'yey'shev al ha'be'eyr

and~he~will~<u>HEAR</u> "Paroh ^{GREAT-HOUSE}" AT the~WORD the~THIS and~he~will~much~<u>SEARCH-OUT</u> to~>~<u>KILL</u> AT "Mosheh ^{PLUCKED-OUT}" and~he~will~<u>FLEE-AWAY</u> "Mosheh ^{PLUCKED-OUT}" from~FACE~s "Paroh ^{GREAT-HOUSE}" and~he~will~<u>SETTLE</u> in~LAND "Mid'yan ^{QUARREL}" and~he~will~<u>SETTLE</u> UPON the~WELL□

and "Paroh ^{Great house}" heard {of} this (matter), and he searched out to kill "Mosheh ^{Plucked out}", and "Mosheh ^{Plucked out}" fled away from {the} face {of} "Paroh ^{Great house}", and he settled in {the} land {of} "Mid'yan ^{Quarrel}" and he settled upon the well,□

2:16

וּלְכֹהֵן מִדְיָן שֶׁבַע בָּנוֹת וַתָּבֹאנָה וַתִּדְלֶנָה וַתְּמַלֶּאנָה אֶת הָרְהָטִים לְהַשְׁקוֹת צֹאן אֲבִיהֶן

ul'kho'heyn mid'yan she'va ba'not wa'ta'vo'nah wa'tid'le'nah wat'ma'le'nah et har'ha'tim

---

* The "lost one" is the one who is in the wrong.

† That is, a judge.

le'hash'qot tson a'vi'hen

and~to~ADMINISTRATOR "Mid'yan ^{QUARREL}" SEVEN DAUGHTER~s and~they(f)~will~COME and~they(f)~will~DRAW-UP and~they(f)~ will~FILL AT the~TROUGH~s to~>~*make*~ DRINK FLOCKS FATHER~them(f)□	and to {the} administrator {of} "Mid'yan ^{Quarrel}" {were} seven daughters, and they came and they drew up and they filled the troughs to make {the} flocks {of} their father drink,□

2:17   וַיָּבֹאוּ הָרֹעִים וַיְגָרְשׁוּם וַיָּקָם מֹשֶׁה וַיּוֹשִׁעָן וַיַּשְׁקְ אֶת צֹאנָם

wai'ya'vo'u ha'ro'im wai'gar'shum wai'ya'qam mo'sheh wai'yo'shi'an wai'ya'sheq et tso'nam

and~*they(m)*~*will*~COME the~FEED~ *ing/er(mp)* and~*they(m)*~*will*~CAST-OUT~ them(m) and~*he*~*will*~RISE "Mosheh ^{PLUCKED-OUT}" and~*he*~*will*~*make*~RESCUE~them(f) and~*he*~*will*~*make*~DRINK AT FLOCKS~ them(m)□	and the feeders* came and they cast them out, and "Mosheh ^{Plucked out}" rose and he rescued them and he made their flocks drink,□

2:18   וַתָּבֹאנָה אֶל רְעוּאֵל אֲבִיהֶן וַיֹּאמֶר מַדּוּעַ מִהַרְתֶּן בֹּא הַיּוֹם

wa'ta'vo'nah el re'u'eyl a'vi'hen wai'yo'mer ma'du'a mi'har'ten bo hai'yom

and~*they(f)*~*will*~COME TO "Re'u'el ^{COMPANION~+~MIGHTY-ONE}" FATHER~them(f) and~ *he*~*will*~SAY WHY *you(fp)*~*did*~*much*~HURRY >~COME the~DAY□	and they came to "Re'u'el ^{Companion of El}" their father, and he said, why did you hurry {to}† come <today>? □

2:19   וַתֹּאמַרְןָ אִישׁ מִצְרִי הִצִּילָנוּ מִיַּד הָרֹעִים וְגַם דָּלֹה דָּלָה לָנוּ וַיַּשְׁקְ אֶת הַצֹּאן

wa'to'ma'na ish mits'ri hi'tsi'la'nu mi'yad ha'ro'im we'gam da'loh da'lah la'nu wai'ya'sheq et ha'tson

and~*they(f)*~*will*~SAY MAN "Mits'rayim ^{STRAIT~s2}"~*of* *he*~*did*~*make*~DELIVER~us from~ HAND the~FEED~*ing/er(mp)* and~ALSO >~DRAW-UP *he*~*did*~DRAW-UP to~us and~ *he*~*will*~*make*~DRINK AT the~FLOCKS□	and they said, {a} man of "Mits'rayim ^{Two straits}" |had| delivered us from {the} hand {of} the feeders‡, and also, he :surely: drew {it} up (for) us and he made the flocks drink,□

2:20   וַיֹּאמֶר אֶל בְּנֹתָיו וְאַיּוֹ לָמָּה זֶּה עֲזַבְתֶּן אֶת הָאִישׁ קִרְאֶן לוֹ וְיֹאכַל לָחֶם

wai'yo'mer el be'no'taw we'ai'o la'mah zeh a'zav'ten et ha'ish qir'en lo we'yo'khal la'hhem

and~*he*~*will*~SAY TO DAUGHTER~s~him	and he said to his daughters, and where {is}

---

* That is "shepherds."

† The word בֹ֗א appears to be missing the prefix "to."

‡ That is "shepherds."

Mechanical Translation Codes

<u>WORD</u> – Verb	WORD – Noun	Word – Name	word – Pre/Suff	*word* – Conj.

and~WHERE~him to~WHAT THIS *you(fp)*~
did~LEAVE AT the~MAN *!(fp)*~CALL-OUT to~
him and~*he~will*~EAT BREAD□

he? <for what reason> did you leave the man?
call out to him and he will eat bread,□

2:21 וַיּוֹאֶל מֹשֶׁה לָשֶׁבֶת אֶת הָאִישׁ וַיִּתֵּן אֶת צִפֹּרָה בִתּוֹ לְמֹשֶׁה

wai'yo'el mo'sheh la'she'vet et ha'ish wai'yi'teyn et tsi'po'rah vi'to le'mo'sheh

and~*he~will~make*~TAKE-UPON "Mosheh
PLUCKED-OUT" to~>~SETTLE AT the~MAN and~
he~will~GIVE AT "Tsiporah BIRD" DAUGHTER~
him to~"Mosheh PLUCKED-OUT"□

and "Mosheh Plucked out" [agreed] to settle
(with) the man, and he gave "Tsiporah Bird", his
daughter, to "Mosheh Plucked out",□

2:22 וַתֵּלֶד בֵּן וַיִּקְרָא אֶת שְׁמוֹ גֵּרְשֹׁם כִּי אָמַר גֵּר הָיִיתִי בְּאֶרֶץ נָכְרִיָּה

wa'tey'led beyn wai'yiq'ra et she'mo ger'shom ki a'mar geyr hai'yi'ti be'e'rets nakh'ri'yah

and~ *she~will*~BRING-FORTH SON and~*he*~
will~CALL-OUT AT TITLE~him "Gershom
EVICTED" GIVEN-THAT *he~will*~SAY STRANGER
l~did~EXIST in~LAND FOREIGN□

and she brought forth {a} son, and he called
out his title "Gershom Evicted" given that he
said, I existed {as a} stranger in {a} foreign
land,□

2:23 וַיְהִי בַיָּמִים הָרַבִּים הָהֵם וַיָּמָת מֶלֶךְ מִצְרַיִם וַיֵּאָנְחוּ בְנֵי יִשְׂרָאֵל מִן
הָעֲבֹדָה וַיִּזְעָקוּ וַתַּעַל שַׁוְעָתָם אֶל הָאֱלֹהִים מִן הָעֲבֹדָה

wai'hi vai'ya'mim ha'ra'bim ha'heym wai'ya'mat me'lekh mits'ra'yim wai'yey'an'hu ve'ney
yis'ra'eyl min ha'a'vo'dah wai'yiz'a'qu wa'ta'al sha'a'tam el ha'e'lo'him min ha'a'vo'dah

and~*he~will*~EXIST in~the~DAY~s the~
ABUNDANT~s the~THEY(m) and~*he~will*~DIE
KING "Mits'rayim STRAIT~s2" and~*they(m)~will*~
SIGH SON~s "Yisra'el *he~will*~TURN-ASIDE~+~MIGHTY-
ONE" FROM the~SERVICE and~*they(m)~will*~
YELL-OUT and~ *she~will*~GO-UP OUTCRY~
them(m) TO the~"Elohiym POWER~s" FROM
the~SERVICE□

and (it) (came to pass) in (those) abundance
{of} days, and {the} king {of} "Mits'rayim Two
straits" died, and {the} sons {of} "Yisra'el He turns El
aside" sighed from the service and they yelled
out, and their outcry went up to the "Elohiym
Powers" from the service,□

2:24 וַיִּשְׁמַע אֱלֹהִים אֶת נַאֲקָתָם וַיִּזְכֹּר אֱלֹהִים אֶת בְּרִיתוֹ אֶת אַבְרָהָם
אֶת יִצְחָק וְאֶת יַעֲקֹב

wai'yish'ma e'lo'him et na'a'qa'tam wai'yiz'kor e'lo'him et be'ri'to et av'ra'ham et
yits'hhaq we'et ya'a'qov

and~*he~will*~HEAR "Elohiym POWER~s" AT
GROANING~them(m) and~*he~will*~
REMEMBER "Elohiym POWER~s" AT
COVENANT~him AT "Avraham FATHER~+~LIFTED"
AT "Yits'hhaq *he~will*~LAUGH" and~AT "Ya'aqov
he~will~RESTRAIN"□

and "Elohiym Powers" heard their groaning, and
"Elohiym Powers" remembered his covenant
(with) "Avraham Father lifted", (with) "Yits'hhaq He
laughs" and (with) "Ya'aqov He restrains",□

Revised Mechanical Translation Codes

| (..) Alt Trans/App A | <..> Comp Phrase/App B | [..] Verb Form/App C | \../ Plural Form/App D |
| :..: Int Inf Abs | |..| Past Perf Verb | {...} Added Word | |

~ 23 ~

2:25 וַיַּרְא אֱלֹהִים אֶת בְּנֵי יִשְׂרָאֵל וַיֵּדַע אֱלֹהִים

wai'yar e'lo'him et be'ney yis'ra'eyl wai'yey'da e'lo'him

and~*he~will*~<u>SEE</u> "Elohiym ^{POWER~s}" AT SON~s and~*he~ will*~<u>KNOW</u> "Elohiym ^{POWER~s}"□

"Yisra'el ^{he~will~}<u>TURN-ASIDE</u>~+~MIGHTY-ONE"

and "Elohiym ^{Powers}" saw {the} sons {of} "Yisra'el ^{He turns El aside}" and "Elohiym ^{Powers}" knew,□

Chapter 3

3:1 וּמֹשֶׁה הָיָה רֹעֶה אֶת צֹאן יִתְרוֹ חֹתְנוֹ כֹּהֵן מִדְיָן וַיִּנְהַג אֶת הַצֹּאן אַחַר הַמִּדְבָּר וַיָּבֹא אֶל הַר הָאֱלֹהִים חֹרֵבָה

u'mo'sheh hai'yah ro'eh et tson yit'ro hhot'no ko'heyn mid'yan wai'yon'hag et ha'tson a'hhar ha'mid'bar wai'ya'vo el har ha'e'lo'him hhor'vah

and~"Mosheh ^{PLUCKED-OUT}" *he~did*~<u>EXIST</u> <u>FEED</u>~*ing/er(ms)* AT FLOCKS "Yitro ^{REMAINDER~him}" <u>BE-AN-IN-LAW</u>~*ing/er(ms)*~him ADMINISTRATOR "Mid'yan ^{QUARREL}" and~*he~ will*~<u>DRIVE</u> AT the~FLOCKS AFTER the~ WILDERNESS and~*he~will*~<u>COME</u> TO HILL the~"Elohiym ^{POWER~s}" "Hhorev ^{PARCHING-HEAT}"~ unto□

and "Mosheh ^{Plucked out}" |had| {been} feeding {the} flocks {of} "Yitro ^{His remainder}", his in-law, {the} administrator {of} "Mid'yan ^{Quarrel}", and he drove the flocks (behind) the wilderness and he came to {the} hill {of} the "Elohiym ^{Powers}", unto "Hhorev ^{Parching heat}",□

3:2 וַיֵּרָא מַלְאַךְ יְהֹוָה אֵלָיו בְּלַבַּת אֵשׁ מִתּוֹךְ הַסְּנֶה וַיַּרְא וְהִנֵּה הַסְּנֶה בֹּעֵר בָּאֵשׁ וְהַסְּנֶה אֵינֶנּוּ אֻכָּל

wai'yey'ra mal'akh YHWH ey'law be'la'bat eysh mi'tokh has'neh wai'yar we'hin'neyh has'neh bo'eyr ba'eysh we'has'neh ey'ne'nu u'kal

and~*he~will~be*~<u>SEE</u> MESSENGER "Yhwh ^{he~ will~}<u>BE</u>" TO~him in~GLIMMERING FIRE from~ MIDST the~THORN-BUSH and~*he~will*~<u>SEE</u> and~LOOK the~THORN-BUSH <u>BURN</u>~ *ing/er(ms)* in~the~FIRE and~the~THORN-BUSH WITHOUT~him <u>EAT</u>~*ed(ms)*□

and {the} messenger {of} "Yhwh ^{He is}" [appeared] to him in {a} glimmering {of} fire from {the} midst {of} the thorn bush, and he saw, and look, the thorn bush {was} burning (with) the fire and the thorn bush {was} (not) eaten,□

3:3 וַיֹּאמֶר מֹשֶׁה אָסֻרָה נָּא וְאֶרְאֶה אֶת הַמַּרְאֶה הַגָּדֹל הַזֶּה מַדּוּעַ לֹא יִבְעַר הַסְּנֶה

wai'yo'mer mo'sheh a'su'rah na we'er'eh et ha'mar'eh ha'ga'dol ha'zeh ma'du'a lo yiv'ar has'neh

and~*he~will*~<u>SAY</u> "Mosheh ^{PLUCKED-OUT}" *I~will*~ <u>TURN-ASIDE</u> PLEASE and~*I~will*~<u>SEE</u> AT the~ APPEARANCE the~GREAT the~THIS WHY NOT *he~will*~<u>BURN</u> the~THORN-BUSH□

and "Mosheh ^{Plucked out}" said, please, I will turn aside and I will see this great appearance, why the thorn bush will not burn,□

Mechanical Translation Codes

| <u>WORD</u> – Verb | WORD – Noun | Word – Name | word – Pre/Suff | *word* – Conj. |

3:4

וַיַּרְא יְהוָה כִּי סָר לִרְאוֹת וַיִּקְרָא אֵלָיו אֱלֹהִים מִתּוֹךְ הַסְּנֶה וַיֹּאמֶר מֹשֶׁה מֹשֶׁה וַיֹּאמֶר הִנֵּנִי

wai'yar YHWH ki sar lir'ot wai'yiq'ra ey'law e'lo'him mi'tokh has'neh wai'yo'mer mo'sheh mo'sheh wai'yo'mer hin'ney'ni

and~he~will~<u>SEE</u> "Yhwh ^{he~will~<u>BE</u>}" GIVEN-THAT he~did~<u>TURN-ASIDE</u> to~>~<u>SEE</u> and~ he~will~<u>CALL-OUT</u> TO~him "Elohiym ^{POWER~s}" from~MIDST the~THORN-BUSH and~he~ will~<u>SAY</u> "Mosheh ^{PLUCKED-OUT}" "Mosheh ^{PLUCKED-OUT}" and~he~will~<u>SAY</u> LOOK~me☐

and "Yhwh ^{He is}" saw that he turned aside to see, and "Elohiym ^{Powers}" called out to him from {the} midst {of} the thorn bush, and he said, "Mosheh ^{Plucked out}" "Mosheh ^{Plucked out}", and he said, (here) I {am},☐

3:5

וַיֹּאמֶר אַל תִּקְרַב הֲלֹם שַׁל נְעָלֶיךָ מֵעַל רַגְלֶיךָ כִּי הַמָּקוֹם אֲשֶׁר אַתָּה עוֹמֵד עָלָיו אַדְמַת קֹדֶשׁ הוּא

wai'yo'mer al tiq'rav ha'lom shal ne'a'ley'kha mey'al rag'ley'kha ki ha'ma'qom a'sher a'tah o'meyd a'law ad'mat qo'desh hu

and~he~will~<u>SAY</u> DO-NOT you(ms)~will~ <u>COME-NEAR</u> AT-THIS-POINT !(ms)~<u>CAST-OFF</u> SANDAL~s~you(ms) from~UPON FOOT~s2~ you(ms) GIVEN-THAT the~AREA WHICH YOU(ms) <u>STAND</u>~ing/er(ms) UPON~him GROUND SPECIAL HE☐

and he said, do not come near to this point, cast off your sandals from upon your feet, given that the area which you {are} standing upon {is the} ground {of a} special* {place}, ☐

3:6

וַיֹּאמֶר אָנֹכִי אֱלֹהֵי אָבִיךָ אֱלֹהֵי אַבְרָהָם אֱלֹהֵי יִצְחָק וֵאלֹהֵי יַעֲקֹב וַיַּסְתֵּר מֹשֶׁה פָּנָיו כִּי יָרֵא מֵהַבִּיט אֶל הָאֱלֹהִים

wai'yo'mer a'no'khi e'lo'hey a'vi'kha e'lo'hey av'ra'ham e'lo'hey yits'hhaq wey'lo'hey ya'a'qov wai'yas'teyr mo'sheh pa'naw ki ya'rey mey'ha'bit el ha'e'lo'him

and~he~will~<u>SAY</u> I "Elohiym ^{POWER~s}" FATHER~you(ms) "Elohiym ^{POWER~s}" "Avraham ^{FATHER~+~LIFTED}" "Elohiym ^{POWER~s}" "Yits'hhaq ^{he~will~<u>LAUGH</u>}" and~"Elohiym ^{POWER~s}" "Ya'aqov ^{he~will~<u>RESTRAIN</u>}" and~he~will~make~ <u>HIDE</u> "Mosheh ^{PLUCKED-OUT}" FACE~s~him GIVEN-THAT he~did~<u>FEAR</u> from~>~make~ <u>STARE</u> TO the~"Elohiym ^{POWER~s}"☐

and he said, I {am} "Elohiym ^{Powers}" {of} your father, "Elohiym ^{Powers}" {of} "Avraham ^{Father lifted}", "Elohiym ^{Powers}" {of} "Yits'hhaq ^{He laughs}" and "Elohiym ^{Powers}" {of} "Ya'aqov ^{He restrains}", and "Mosheh ^{Plucked out}" hid his face, given that he feared from staring to{ward} the "Elohiym ^{Powers}",☐

3:7

וַיֹּאמֶר יְהוָה רָאֹה רָאִיתִי אֶת עֳנִי עַמִּי אֲשֶׁר בְּמִצְרָיִם וְאֶת צַעֲקָתָם שָׁמַעְתִּי מִפְּנֵי נֹגְשָׂיו כִּי יָדַעְתִּי אֶת מַכְאֹבָיו

---

* The Hebrew word קֹדֶשׁ (qodesh) is translated as "holy," an adjective, in all other translations. While this word can be used as an adjective, it cannot here and in many other occurrences of this word. The reason being, the word קֹדֶשׁ is a masculine word while the word for ground, אֲדָמָה (adamah), is a feminine word and in Hebrew, the adjective and the noun it modifies must match in gender. In addition, the word אֲדָמָה is written as אַדְמַת, indicating the phrase אַדְמַת קֹדֶשׁ is in the construct state and should be translated as "ground of a special place."

Revised Mechanical Translation Codes

(..) Alt Trans/App A	<..> Comp Phrase/App B	[..] Verb Form/App C	\..\ Plural Form/App D
:..: Int Inf Abs	|..| Past Perf Verb	{...} Added Word	

wai'yo'mer YHWH ra'oh ra'i'ti et a'ni a'mi a'sher be'mits'ra'yim we'et tsa'a'qa'tam sha'ma'ti mip'ney nog'saw ki ya'da'ti et makh'o'vaw

and~*he~will~*<u>SAY</u> "Yhwh *he~will~*<u>BE</u>" >~<u>SEE</u> *I~did~*<u>SEE</u> AT AFFLICTION PEOPLE~me WHICH in~"Mits'rayim ^{STRAIT~s2}" and~AT CRY~them(m) *I~did~*<u>HEAR</u> from~FACE~s <u>PUSH</u>~*ing/er(mp)*~him GIVEN-THAT *I~did~*<u>KNOW</u> AT MISERY~s~him□

and "Yhwh ^{He is}" said, I :surely: saw {the} affliction {of} my people (who) {are} in "Mits'rayim ^{Two straits}", and I heard their* cry from {the} faces {of} his pushers† given that I know his miseries,□

3:8

וָאֵרֵד לְהַצִּילוֹ מִיַּד מִצְרַיִם וּלְהַעֲלֹתוֹ מִן הָאָרֶץ הַהִוא אֶל אֶרֶץ טוֹבָה וּרְחָבָה אֶל אֶרֶץ זָבַת חָלָב וּדְבָשׁ אֶל מְקוֹם הַכְּנַעֲנִי וְהַחִתִּי וְהָאֱמֹרִי וְהַפְּרִזִּי וְהַחִוִּי וְהַיְבוּסִי

wa'ey'reyd le'ha'tsi'lo mi'yad mits'ra'yim ul'ha'a'lo'to min ha'a'rets ha'hi el e'rets to'vah ur'hha'vah el e'rets za'vat hha'lav ud'vash el me'qom ha'ke'na'a'ni we'ha'hhi'ti we'ha'e'mo'ri we'ha'pe'ri'zi we'ha'hhi'wi we'hai'vu'si

and~*I~will~*<u>GO-DOWN</u> to~>~*make~*<u>DELIVER</u>~him from~HAND "Mits'rayim ^{STRAIT~s2}" and~to~>~*make~*<u>GO-UP</u>~him FROM the~LAND the~ she TO LAND FUNCTIONAL and~WIDE TO LAND <u>ISSUE</u>~*ing/er(fs)* FAT and~HONEY TO AREA the~"Kena'an ^{LOWERED}"~of and~the~"Hhet ^{TREMBLING-IN-FEAR}"~of and~the~"Emor ^{SAYER}"~of and~the~"Perez ^{PEASANT}"~of and~the~"Hhiw ^{TOWN}"~of and~the~"Yevus ^{he~will~}<u>TRAMPLE-DOWN</u>"~of□

and I will go down to deliver him from {the} hand {of} "Mits'rayim ^{Two straits}", and to make him go up from (that) land to {a} functional and wide land, to {a} land issuing fat‡ and honey§, to {the} area {of} the {one} of "Kena'an ^{Lowered}" and the {one} of "Hhet ^{Trembling in fear}" and the {one} of "Emor ^{Sayer}" and the {one} of "Perez ^{Peasant}" and the {one} of "Hhiw ^{Town}" and the {one} of "Yevus ^{He will trample down}",□

3:9

וְעַתָּה הִנֵּה צַעֲקַת בְּנֵי יִשְׂרָאֵל בָּאָה אֵלָי וְגַם רָאִיתִי אֶת הַלַּחַץ אֲשֶׁר מִצְרַיִם לֹחֲצִים אֹתָם

we'a'tah hin'neyh tsa'a'qat be'ney yis'ra'eyl ba'ah ey'lai we'gam ra'i'ti et ha'la'hhats a'sher mits'ra'yim lo'hha'thsim o'tam

and~NOW LOOK CRY SON~s "Yisra'el ^{he~will~}<u>TURN-ASIDE</u>~+~MIGHTY-ONE" she~*djd~*<u>COME</u> TO~me and~ALSO *I~did~*<u>SEE</u> AT the~SQUEEZING WHICH "Mits'rayim ^{STRAIT~s2}" <u>SQUEEZE</u>~*ing/er(mp)* AT~them(m)□

and now look, {the} cry {of the} sons {of} "Yisra'el ^{He turns El aside}" |had| come to me, and also, I saw the squeezing (because) "Mits'rayim ^{Two straits}" {is} squeezing them,□

3:10

וְעַתָּה לְכָה וְאֶשְׁלָחֲךָ אֶל פַּרְעֹה וְהוֹצֵא אֶת עַמִּי בְנֵי יִשְׂרָאֵל מִמִּצְרָיִם

---

* The Hebrew word צַעֲקָתָם (their cry) should be written as צַעֲקָתוֹ (his cry) as the pronoun is referring to עַם (people), a masculine singular noun. This is also evident in the fact that the pronoun "his" is used with the following words.

† Or "oppressors."

‡ Or "milk."

§ The Hebrew word דבש means a "sticky mass" and can also mean "dates" from the palm tree.

Mechanical Translation Codes

<u>WORD</u> – Verb	WORD – Noun	Word – Name	word – Pre/Suff	*word* – Conj.

we'a'tah le'khah we'esh'la'hha'kha el par'oh we'ho'tsey et a'mi ve'ney yis'ra'eyl mi'mits'ra'yim

and~NOW !(ms)~<u>WALK</u>~^ and~*I~will*~<u>SEND</u>~ you(ms) TO "Paroh ^{GREAT-HOUSE}" and~>~*make*~ <u>GO-OUT</u> AT PEOPLE~me SON~s "Yisra'el ^{he~} ^{*will*~TURN-ASIDE~+~MIGHTY-ONE}" from~"Mits'rayim ^{STRAIT~s2}"□

and now walk, and I will send you to "Paroh ^{Great house}", and make my people, {the} sons {of} "Yisra'el ^{He turns El aside}", go out from "Mits'rayim ^{Two straits}",□

3:11   וַיֹּאמֶר מֹשֶׁה אֶל הָאֱלֹהִים מִי אָנֹכִי כִּי אֵלֵךְ וְכִי אוֹצִיא אֶת בְּנֵי יִשְׂרָאֵל מִמִּצְרָיִם

wai'yo'mer mo'sheh el ha'elo'him mi a'no'khi ki ey'leykh el par'oh we'khi o'tsi et be'ney yis'ra'eyl mi'mits'ra'yim

and~*he~will*~<u>SAY</u> "Mosheh ^{PLUCKED-OUT}" TO the~"Elohiym ^{POWER~s}" WHO I <u>GIVEN-THAT</u> *I~ will*~<u>WALK</u> TO "Paroh ^{GREAT-HOUSE}" and~ GIVEN-THAT *I~will*~*make*~<u>GO-OUT</u> AT SON~s "Yisra'el ^{he~will~<u>TURN-ASIDE</u>~+~MIGHTY-ONE}" from~ "Mits'rayim ^{STRAIT~s2}"□

and "Mosheh ^{Plucked out}" said to the "Elohiym ^{Powers}", who {am} I that I should walk to "Paroh ^{Great house}" and that I will make {the} sons {of} "Yisra'el ^{He turns El aside}", go out from "Mits'rayim ^{Two straits}"?□

3:12   וַיֹּאמֶר כִּי אֶהְיֶה עִמָּךְ וְזֶה לְּךָ הָאוֹת כִּי אָנֹכִי שְׁלַחְתִּיךָ בְּהוֹצִיאֲךָ אֶת הָעָם מִמִּצְרַיִם תַּעַבְדוּן אֶת הָאֱלֹהִים עַל הָהָר הַזֶּה

wai'yo'mer ki eh'yeh i'makh we'zeh le'kha ha'ot ki a'no'khi she'lahh'ti'kha be'ho'tsi'a'kha et ha'am mi'mits'ra'yim ta'av'dun et ha'elo'him al ha'har ha'zeh

and~*he~will*~<u>SAY</u> GIVEN-THAT *I~will*~<u>EXIST</u> WITH~you(fs) and~THIS to~you(ms) the~ SIGN GIVEN-THAT I *I~did*~<u>SEND</u>~you(ms) in~ >~*make*~<u>GO-OUT</u>~you(ms) AT the~PEOPLE from~"Mits'rayim ^{STRAIT~s2}" *you(mp)~will*~ <u>SERVE</u>~must AT the~"Elohiym ^{POWER~s}" UPON the~HILL the~THIS□

and he said, given that I will exist with you, and this {is} the sign (for) you that I |had| sent you, in your making the people go out from "Mits'rayim ^{Two straits}", you must serve the "Elohiym ^{Powers}" upon this hill,□

3:13   וַיֹּאמֶר מֹשֶׁה אֶל הָאֱלֹהִים הִנֵּה אָנֹכִי בָא אֶל בְּנֵי יִשְׂרָאֵל וְאָמַרְתִּי לָהֶם אֱלֹהֵי אֲבוֹתֵיכֶם שְׁלָחַנִי אֲלֵיכֶם וְאָמְרוּ לִי מַה שְּׁמוֹ מָה אֹמַר אֲלֵהֶם

wai'yo'mer mo'sheh el ha'elo'him hin'neyh a'no'khi va el be'ney yis'ra'eyl we'a'mar'ti la'hem e'lo'hey a'vo'tey'khem she'la'hha'ni a'ley'khem we'am'ru li mah she'mo mah o'mar a'ley'hem

and~*he~will*~<u>SAY</u> "Mosheh ^{PLUCKED-OUT}" TO the~"Elohiym ^{POWER~s}" LOOK I <u>COME</u>~ *ing/er(ms)* TO SON~s "Yisra'el ^{he~will~<u>TURN-ASIDE</u>~} ^{+~MIGHTY-ONE}" and~*I~did*~<u>SAY</u> to~them(m) "Elohiym ^{POWER~s}" FATHER~s~you(mp) *he~* *did*~<u>SEND</u>~me TO~you(mp) and~*they~did*~ <u>SAY</u> to~me WHAT TITLE~him WHAT *I~will*~

and "Mosheh ^{Plucked out}" said to the "Elohiym ^{Powers}", Look, I {am} coming to {the} sons {of} "Yisra'el ^{He turns El aside}" and I will say to them, "Elohiym ^{Powers}" {of} your fathers |had| sent me to you, and they will say to me, what {is} his title? what will I say to them?□

Revised Mechanical Translation Codes
(..) Alt Trans/App A   <..> Comp Phrase/App B   [..] Verb Form/App C   \../ Plural Form/App D
:..: Int Inf Abs |..| Past Perf Verb   {...} Added Word

SAY TO~them(m)□

3:14

וַיֹּאמֶר אֱלֹהִים אֶל מֹשֶׁה אֶהְיֶה אֲשֶׁר אֶהְיֶה וַיֹּאמֶר כֹּה תֹאמַר לִבְנֵי
יִשְׂרָאֵל אֶהְיֶה שְׁלָחַנִי אֲלֵיכֶם

wai'yo'mer e'lo'him el mo'sheh eh'yeh a'sher eh'yeh wai'yo'mer koh to'mar liv'ney
yis'ra'eyl eh'yeh she'la'hha'ni a'ley'khem

and~*he~will*~<u>SAY</u> "Elohiym ^{POWER~s}" TO "Mosheh ^{PLUCKED-OUT}" *I~will*~<u>EXIST</u> WHICH *I~ will*~<u>EXIST</u> and~*he~will*~<u>SAY</u> IN-THIS-WAY *you(ms)~will*~<u>SAY</u> to~SON~s "Yisra'el ^{he~will~ TURN-ASIDE~+~MIGHTY-ONE}" "Ehyeh ^{I~will~EXIST}" *he~ did*~<u>SEND</u>~me TO~you(mp)□

and "Elohiym ^{Powers}" said to "Mosheh ^{Plucked out}", I will exist which I will exist, and he said, in this way you will say to {the} sons {of} "Yisra'el ^{He turns El aside}", "Ehyeh ^{I exist}" |had| sent me to you,□

3:15

וַיֹּאמֶר עוֹד אֱלֹהִים אֶל מֹשֶׁה כֹּה תֹאמַר אֶל בְּנֵי יִשְׂרָאֵל יְהוָה אֱלֹהֵי
אֲבֹתֵיכֶם אֱלֹהֵי אַבְרָהָם אֱלֹהֵי יִצְחָק וֵאלֹהֵי יַעֲקֹב שְׁלָחַנִי אֲלֵיכֶם זֶה
שְׁמִי לְעֹלָם וְזֶה זִכְרִי לְדֹר דֹּר

wai'yo'mer od e'lo'him el mo'sheh koh to'mar el be'ney yis'ra'eyl YHWH e'lo'hey
a'vo'tey'khem e'lo'hey av'ra'ham e'lo'hey yits'hhaq wey'lo'hey ya'a'qov she'la'hha'ni
a'ley'khem zeh she'mi le'o'lam we'zeh zikh'ri le'dor dor

and~*he~will*~<u>SAY</u> YET-AGAIN "Elohiym ^{POWER~s}" TO "Mosheh ^{PLUCKED-OUT}" IN-THIS-WAY *you(ms)~will*~<u>SAY</u> TO SON~s "Yisra'el ^{he~will~ TURN-ASIDE~+~MIGHTY-ONE}" "Yhwh ^{he~will~BE}" "Elohiym ^{POWER~s}" FATHER~s~you(mp) "Elohiym ^{POWER~s}" "Avraham ^{FATHER~+~LIFTED}" "Elohiym ^{POWER~s}" "Yits'hhaq ^{he~will~LAUGH}" and~ "Elohiym ^{POWER~s}" "Ya'aqov ^{he~will~RESTRAIN}" *he~ did*~<u>SEND</u>~me TO~you(mp) THIS TITLE~me to~<u>DISTANT</u> and~THIS MEMORIAL~me to~ GENERATION GENERATION□

and "Elohiym ^{Powers}" said yet again to "Mosheh ^{Plucked out}", in this way you will say to {the} sons {of} "Yisra'el ^{He turns El aside}", "Yhwh ^{He is}" {the} "Elohiym ^{Powers}" {of} your fathers, "Elohiym ^{Powers}" {of} "Avraham ^{Father lifted}", "Elohiym ^{Powers}" {of} "Yits'hhaq ^{He laughs}" and "Elohiym ^{Powers}" {of} "Ya'aqov ^{He restrains}" |had| sent me to you, this {is} my title (for) {a} distant {time} and this {is} my memorial (for) {a} generation {and a} generation*, □

3:16

לֵךְ וְאָסַפְתָּ אֶת זִקְנֵי יִשְׂרָאֵל וְאָמַרְתָּ אֲלֵהֶם יְהוָה אֱלֹהֵי אֲבֹתֵיכֶם
נִרְאָה אֵלַי אֱלֹהֵי אַבְרָהָם יִצְחָק וְיַעֲקֹב לֵאמֹר פָּקֹד פָּקַדְתִּי אֶתְכֶם
וְאֶת הֶעָשׂוּי לָכֶם בְּמִצְרָיִם

leykh we'a'saph'ta et ziq'ney yis'ra'eyl we'a'mar'ta a'ley'hem YHWH e'lo'hey
a'vo'tey'khem nir'ah ey'lai e'lo'hey av'ra'ham yits'hhaq le'ya'a'qov ley'mor pa'qod
pa'qad'ti et'khem we'et he'a'su'i la'khem be'mits'ra'yim

!(ms)~<u>WALK</u> and~*you(ms)~did*~<u>GATHER</u> AT BEARD~s "Yisra'el ^{he~will~TURN-ASIDE~+~MIGHTY-ONE}" and~*you(ms)~did*~<u>SAY</u> TO~them(m) "Yhwh ^{he~will~BE}" "Elohiym ^{POWER~s}" FATHER~s~

walk and you will gather {the} beard{ed one}s† {of} "Yisra'el ^{He turns El aside}", and you will say to them, "Yhwh ^{He is}" {the} "Elohiym ^{Powers}" {of} your fathers |had| [appeared] to me,

---

* "For a generation and a generation" is an idiom meaning "throughout the generations," or "for all time."

† "Bearded ones" is a euphemism for "elders."

Mechanical Translation Codes

<u>WORD</u> – Verb	WORD – Noun	Word – Name	word – Pre/Suff	*word* – Conj.

you(mp) he~did~be~<u>SEE</u> TO~me "Elohiym
POWER~s„ "Avraham FATHER~+~LIFTED„ "Yits'hhaq
he~will~<u>LAUGH</u>„ and~"Ya'aqov he~will~<u>RESTRAIN</u>„ to~
>~<u>SAY</u> >~<u>REGISTER</u> I~did~REGISTER AT~
you(mp) and~AT the~<u>DO</u>~ed(ms) to~
you(mp) in~"Mits'rayim STRAIT~s2„□

"Elohiym Powers„ {of} "Avraham Father lifted„,
"Yits'hhaq He laughs„ and "Ya'aqov He restrains„,
say{ing}, I :surely: registered you and {what}
was done to you in "Mits'rayim Two straits„,□

3:17 וָאֹמַר אַעֲלֶה אֶתְכֶם מֵעֳנִי מִצְרַיִם אֶל אֶרֶץ הַכְּנַעֲנִי וְהַחִתִּי וְהָאֱמֹרִי וְהַפְּרִזִּי וְהַחִוִּי וְהַיְבוּסִי אֶל אֶרֶץ זָבַת חָלָב וּדְבָשׁ

wa'o'mar a'a'leh et'khem mey'a'ni mits'ra'yim el e'rets ha'ke'na'a'ni we'ha'hhi'ti
we'ha'e'mo'ri we'ha'pe'ri'zi we'ha'hhi'wi we'hai'vu'si el e'rets za'vat hha'lav ud'vash

and~I~will~<u>SAY</u> I~will~make~<u>GO-UP</u> AT~
you(mp) from~AFFLICTION "Mits'rayim
STRAIT~s2„ TO LAND the~"Kena'an LOWERED„~of
and~the~"Hhet TREMBLING-IN-FEAR„~of and~the~
"Emor SAYER„~of and~the~"Perez PEASANT„~of
and~the~"Hhiw TOWN„~of and~the~"Yevus he~
will~<u>TRAMPLE-DOWN</u>„~of TO LAND <u>ISSUE</u>~ing/er(fs)
FAT and~HONEY□

and I said, I will make you go up from {the}
affliction {of} "Mits'rayim Two straits„ to {the}
land {of} the {one} of "Kena'an Lowered„ and the
{one} of "Hhet Trembling in fear„ and the {one} of
"Emor Sayer„ and the {one} of "Perez Peasant„ and
the {one} of "Hhiw Town„ and the {one} of
"Yevus He will trample down„, to {a} land issuing fat*
and honey†,□

3:18 וְשָׁמְעוּ לְקֹלֶךָ וּבָאתָ אַתָּה וְזִקְנֵי יִשְׂרָאֵל אֶל מֶלֶךְ מִצְרַיִם וַאֲמַרְתֶּם אֵלָיו יְהוָה אֱלֹהֵי הָעִבְרִיִּים נִקְרָה עָלֵינוּ וְעַתָּה נֵלְכָה נָּא דֶּרֶךְ שְׁלֹשֶׁת יָמִים בַּמִּדְבָּר וְנִזְבְּחָה לַיהוָה אֱלֹהֵינוּ

we'sham'u le'qo'le'kha u'va'ta a'tah we'ziq'ney yis'ra'eyl el me'lekh mits'ra'yim
wa'a'mar'tem ey'law YHWH e'lo'hey ha'iv'ri'yim niq'rah a'ley'nu we'a'tah neyl'khah na
de'rekh she'lo'shet ya'mim ba'mid'bar we'niz'be'hhah la'YHWH e'lo'hey'nu

and~they~did~<u>HEAR</u> to~VOICE~you(ms)
and~you(ms)~did~<u>COME</u> YOU(ms) and~
BEARD~s "Yisra'el he~will~<u>TURN-ASIDE</u>+~MIGHTY-ONE„
TO KING "Mits'rayim STRAIT~s2„ and~you(mp)~
did~<u>SAY</u> TO~him "Yhwh he~will~<u>BE</u>„ "Elohiym
POWER~s„ the~"Ever OTHER-SIDE„~s he~did~be~
<u>MEET</u> UPON~us and~NOW we~will~<u>WALK</u>~^
PLEASE ROAD THREE DAY~s in~the~
WILDERNESS and~we~will~<u>SACRIFICE</u>~^ to~
"Yhwh he~will~<u>BE</u>„ "Elohiym POWER~s„~us□

and they heard your voice, and you will come,
you and the beard{ed one}s‡ {of} "Yisra'el He
turns El aside„, to {the} king {of} "Mits'rayim Two
straits„ and you will say to him, "Yhwh He is„ {the}
"Elohiym Powers„ {of} the {one}s {of} "Ever Other
side„ |had| met (with) us, and now, please, we
will walk {the} road {for} three days in the
wilderness and we will sacrifice to "Yhwh He is„
our "Flohiym Powers„,□

3:19 וַאֲנִי יָדַעְתִּי כִּי לֹא יִתֵּן אֶתְכֶם מֶלֶךְ מִצְרַיִם לַהֲלֹךְ וְלֹא בְּיָד חֲזָקָה

wa'ani ya'da'ti ki lo yi'teyn et'khem me'lekh mits'ra'yim la'ha'lokh we'lo be'yad
hha'za'qah

---

* Or "milk."

† The Hebrew word דבש means a "sticky mass" and can also mean "dates" from the palm tree.

‡ "Bearded ones" is a euphemism for "elders."

Revised Mechanical Translation Codes

(..) Alt Trans/App A	<..> Comp Phrase/App B	[..] Verb Form/App C	\../ Plural Form/App D
:..: Int Inf Abs	|..| Past Perf Verb	{...} Added Word	

and~I *I~did~*<u>KNOW</u> GIVEN-THAT NOT *he~* *will~*<u>GIVE</u> AT~you(mp) KING "Mits'rayim ^{STRAIT~s2}" *to~>~*<u>WALK</u> and~NOT in~HAND FORCEFUL□

and I |had| known that {the} king {of} "Mits'rayim ^{Two straits}" will not (allow) you to walk <without> {a} forceful hand,□

3:20   וְשָׁלַחְתִּי אֶת יָדִי וְהִכֵּיתִי אֶת מִצְרַיִם בְּכֹל נִפְלְאֹתַי אֲשֶׁר אֶעֱשֶׂה בְּקִרְבּוֹ וְאַחֲרֵי כֵן יְשַׁלַּח אֶתְכֶם

we'sha'lahh'ti et ya'di we'hi'key'ti et mits'ra'yim be'khol niph'le'o'tai a'sher e'e'seh be'qir'bo we'a'hha'rey kheyn ye'sha'lahh et'khem

and~*I~did~*<u>SEND</u> AT HAND~me and~*I~did~* *make~*<u>HIT</u> AT "Mits'rayim ^{STRAIT~s2}" in~ALL *be~*<u>PERFORM</u>~*ing/er(fp)~*me WHICH *I~will~* <u>DO</u> in~WITHIN~him and~AFTER SO *he~will~* *much~*<u>SEND</u> AT~you(mp)□

and I will send my hand and I will hit "Mits'rayim ^{Two straits}" (with) all my [performances] which I will do within him, and <afterward> he will send you,□

3:21   וְנָתַתִּי אֶת חֵן הָעָם הַזֶּה בְּעֵינֵי מִצְרָיִם וְהָיָה כִּי תֵלֵכוּן לֹא תֵלְכוּ רֵיקָם

we'na'ta'ti et hheyn ha'am ha'zeh be'ey'ney mits'ra'yim we'hai'yah ki tey'ley'khun lo teyl'khu rey'qam

and~*I~did~*<u>GIVE</u> AT BEAUTY the~PEOPLE the~THIS in~EYE~s2 "Mits'rayim ^{STRAIT~s2}" and~*he~did~*<u>EXIST</u> GIVEN-THAT *you(mp)~* *will~*<u>WALK</u>~must NOT *you(mp)~will~*<u>WALK</u> EMPTINESS□

and I will (place) {the} beauty* {of} this people in {the} eyes {of}† "Mits'rayim ^{Two straits}", and (it) will (come to pass), (when) you must walk, you will not walk empty,□

3:22   וְשָׁאֲלָה אִשָּׁה מִשְּׁכֶנְתָּהּ וּמִגָּרַת בֵּיתָהּ כְּלֵי כֶסֶף וּכְלֵי זָהָב וּשְׂמָלֹת וְשַׂמְתֶּם עַל בְּנֵיכֶם וְעַל בְּנֹתֵיכֶם וְנִצַּלְתֶּם אֶת מִצְרָיִם

we'sha'a'lah i'shah mish'khe'ne'tah u'mi'ga'rat bey'tah ke'ley ke'seph ukh'ley za'hav us'ma'lot we'sam'tem al be'ney'khem we'al be'no'tey'khem we'ni'tsal'tem et mits'ra'yim

and~ *she~did~*<u>ENQUIRE</u> WOMAN from~ DWELLER~her and~*from~*<u>SOJOURN</u>~ *ing/er(fs)* HOUSE~her ITEM~s SILVER and~ ITEM~s GOLD and~APPAREL~s and~ *you(mp)~did~*<u>PLACE</u> UPON SON~s~you(mp) and~UPON DAUGHTER~s~you(mp) and~ *you(mp)~did~much~*<u>DELIVER</u> AT "Mits'rayim ^{STRAIT~s2}"□

and {a} woman will enquire from her dweller, and from {the} sojourner {of} her house, items {of} silver, and items {of} gold, and apparels, and you will place {them} upon your sons and upon your daughters, and you will deliver "Mits'rayim ^{Two straits}",□

---

* "Place the beauty" means to "make accepted."
† "To the eyes of" is an idiom meaning "in the sight of."

Mechanical Translation Codes

<u>WORD</u> – Verb	WORD – Noun	Word – Name	word – Pre/Suff	*word* – Conj.

Chapter 4

4:1 וַיַּעַן מֹשֶׁה וַיֹּאמֶר וְהֵן לֹא יַאֲמִינוּ לִי וְלֹא יִשְׁמְעוּ בְּקֹלִי כִּי יֹאמְרוּ לֹא נִרְאָה אֵלֶיךָ יְהוָה

wai'ya'an mo'sheh wai'yo'mer we'heyn lo ya'a'mi'nu li we'lo yish'me'u be'qo'li ki yom'ru lo nir'ah ey'ley'kha YHWH

and~*he~will*~<u>ANSWER</u> "Mosheh ^{PLUCKED-OUT}" and~*he~will*~<u>SAY</u> and~THOUGH NOT *they(m)~will*~make~<u>SECURE</u> to~me and~ NOT *they(m)~will*~<u>HEAR</u> in~VOICE~me GIVEN-THAT *they(m)~will*~<u>SAY</u> NOT *he~did*~ be~<u>SEE</u> TO~you(ms) "Yhwh ^{*he~will*~<u>BE</u>}"□

and "Mosheh ^{Plucked out}" answered and he said, <but> they will not [support] me, and they will not hear my voice given that they will say, "Yhwh ^{He is}" did not [appear] to you,□

4:2 וַיֹּאמֶר אֵלָיו יְהוָה מַזֶּה בְּיָדֶךָ וַיֹּאמֶר מַטֶּה

wai'yo'mer ey'law YHWH ma-zeh be'ya'de'kha wai'yo'mer ma'teh

and~*he~will*~<u>SAY</u> TO~him "Yhwh ^{*he~will*~<u>BE</u>}" WHAT THIS in~HAND~you(ms) and~*he~will*~ <u>SAY</u> BRANCH□

and "Yhwh ^{He is}" said to him, what {is} this* in your hand? and he said, {a} branch,□

4:3 וַיֹּאמֶר הַשְׁלִיכֵהוּ אַרְצָה וַיַּשְׁלִכֵהוּ אַרְצָה וַיְהִי לְנָחָשׁ וַיָּנָס מֹשֶׁה מִפָּנָיו

wai'yo'mer hash'li'key'hu ar'tsah wai'yash'li'khey'hu ar'tsah wai'hi le'na'hhash wai'ya'nas mo'sheh mi'pa'naw

and~*he~will*~<u>SAY</u> !*(ms)~make*~<u>THROW-OUT</u>~him LAND~unto and~*he~will*~make~ <u>THROW-OUT</u>~him LAND~unto and~*he~will*~ <u>EXIST</u> to~SERPENT and~*he~will*~<u>FLEE</u> "Mosheh ^{PLUCKED-OUT}" from~FACE~s~him□

and he said, throw him out unto {the} land, and he threw him out unto {the} land, and he existed (as) {a} serpent, and "Mosheh ^{Plucked out}" fled from his face,□

4:4 וַיֹּאמֶר יְהוָה אֶל מֹשֶׁה שְׁלַח יָדְךָ וֶאֱחֹז בִּזְנָבוֹ וַיִּשְׁלַח יָדוֹ וַיַּחֲזֶק בּוֹ וַיְהִי לְמַטֶּה בְּכַפּוֹ

wai'yo'mer YHWH el mo'sheh she'lahh yad'kha we'e'hhoz biz'na'vo wai'yish'lahh ya'do wai'ya'hha'zeq bo wai'hi le'ma'teh be'kha'po

and~*he~will*~<u>SAY</u> "Yhwh ^{*he~will*~<u>BE</u>}" TO "Mosheh ^{PLUCKED-OUT}" !*(ms)~*<u>SEND</u> HAND~ you(ms) and~!*(ms)~*<u>TAKE-HOLD</u> in~TAIL~him and~*he~will*~<u>SEND</u> HAND~him and~*he~will*~ make~<u>SEIZE</u> in~him and~*he~will*~<u>EXIST</u> to~ BRANCH in~PALM~him□

and "Yhwh ^{He is}" said to "Mosheh ^{Plucked out}", send your hand and take hold (by) his tail, and he sent his hand and he seized him, and he existed (as) {a} branch in his palm,□

---

* The Hebrew word מַזֶּה is written defectively and should be written as מָה זֶה, meaning "what is this."

Revised Mechanical Translation Codes

(..) Alt Trans/App A   <..> Comp Phrase/App B   [..] Verb Form/App C   \..\ Plural Form/App D
:..: Int Inf Abs |..| Past Perf Verb   {...} Added Word

~ 31 ~

4:5 לְמַעַן יַאֲמִינוּ כִּי נִרְאָה אֵלֶיךָ יְהוָה אֱלֹהֵי אֲבֹתָם אֱלֹהֵי אַבְרָהָם אֱלֹהֵי יִצְחָק וֵאלֹהֵי יַעֲקֹב

le'ma'an ya'a'mi'nu ki nir'ah ey'ley'kha YHWH e'lo'hey a'vo'tam e'lo'hey av'ra'ham e'lo'hey yits'hhaq wey'lo'hey ya'a'qov

to~THAT *they(m)~will~make~*<u>SECURE</u> GIVEN-THAT *he~did~be~*<u>SEE</u> TO~you(ms) "Yhwh *he~will~*<u>BE</u>" "Elohiym POWER~s" FATHER~s~ them(m) "Elohiym POWER~s" "Avraham FATHER~+~ LIFTED" "Elohiym POWER~s" "Yits'hhaq *he~will~* <u>LAUGH</u>" and~"Elohiym POWER~s" "Ya'aqov *he~will~* <u>RESTRAIN</u>,"□

(so) that they will [support], given that "Yhwh ^He is^ {the} "Elohiym ^Powers^ {of} their fathers, "Elohiym ^Powers^ {of} "Avraham ^Father lifted^, "Elohiym ^Powers^ {of} "Yits'hhaq ^He laughs^ and "Elohiym ^Powers^ {of} "Ya'aqov ^He restrains^,□

4:6 וַיֹּאמֶר יְהוָה לוֹ עוֹד הָבֵא נָא יָדְךָ בְּחֵיקֶךָ וַיָּבֵא יָדוֹ בְּחֵיקוֹ וַיּוֹצִאָהּ וְהִנֵּה יָדוֹ מְצֹרַעַת כַּשָּׁלֶג

wai'yo'mer YHWH lo od ha'veyh na yad'kha be'hhey'qe'kha wai'ya'vey ya'do be'hhey'qo wai'yo'tsi'ah we'hin'neyh ya'do me'tso'ra'at ka'sha'leg

and~*he~will~*<u>SAY</u> "Yhwh ^he~will~^<u>BE</u>" to~him YET-AGAIN !(ms)~make~<u>COME</u> PLEASE HAND~you(ms) in~BOSOM~you(ms) and~ *he~will~make~*<u>COME</u> HAND~him in~ BOSOM~him and~*he~will~make~*<u>GO-OUT</u>~ her and~LOOK HAND~him *be~much~* <u>INFECT</u>~*ing/er(fs)* like~the~<u>SNOW</u>□

and "Yhwh ^He is^" said to him yet again, please [bring] your hand in your bosom, and he [brought] his hand in his bosom, and he made her* go out, and look, his hand {was} being infected like the snow,□

4:7 וַיֹּאמֶר הָשֵׁב יָדְךָ אֶל חֵיקֶךָ וַיָּשֶׁב יָדוֹ אֶל חֵיקוֹ וַיּוֹצִאָהּ מֵחֵיקוֹ וְהִנֵּה שָׁבָה כִּבְשָׂרוֹ

wai'yo'mer ha'sheyv yad'kha el hhey'qe'kha wai'ya'shev ya'do el hhey'qo wai'yo'tsi'ah ma'hhey'qo we'hin'neyh sha'vah kiv'sa'ro

and~*he~will~*<u>SAY</u> !(ms)~make~<u>TURN-BACK</u> HAND~you(ms) TO BOSOM~you(ms) and~ *he~will~make~*<u>TURN-BACK</u> HAND~him TO BOSOM~him and~*he~will~make~*<u>GO-OUT</u>~ her from~BOSOM~him and~LOOK *she~did~* <u>TURN-BACK</u> like~FLESH~him□

and he said, make your hand turn back to your bosom, and he made his hand turn back to his bosom, and he made her† go out from his bosom, and look, she turned back like his flesh,□

4:8 וְהָיָה אִם לֹא יַאֲמִינוּ לָךְ וְלֹא יִשְׁמְעוּ לְקֹל הָאֹת הָרִאשׁוֹן וְהֶאֱמִינוּ לְקֹל הָאֹת הָאַחֲרוֹן

we'hai'yah im lo ya'a'mi'nu lakh we'lo yish'me'u le'qol ha'ot ha'ri'shon we'he'e'mi'nu le'qol ha'ot ha'a'hha'ron

---

* referring to the "hand," a feminine word in Hebrew.
† referring to the "hand," a feminine word in Hebrew.

Mechanical Translation Codes

<u>WORD</u> – Verb	WORD – Noun	Word – Name	word – Pre/Suff	*word* – Conj.

and~he~did~EXIST IF NOT *they(m)~will~* make~SECURE to~you(fs) and~NOT *they(m)~ will~*HEAR to~VOICE the~SIGN the~FIRST and~*they~did~*make~SECURE to~VOICE the~ SIGN the~LAST□

and (it) will (come to pass)*, if they will not [support] you, and they will not hear {the} voice† {of} the first sign and they will not [support] {the} voice {of} the last sign,□

4:9 וְהָיָה אִם לֹא יַאֲמִינוּ גַּם לִשְׁנֵי הָאֹתוֹת הָאֵלֶּה וְלֹא יִשְׁמְעוּן לְקֹלֶךָ וְלָקַחְתָּ מִמֵּימֵי הַיְאֹר וְשָׁפַכְתָּ הַיַּבָּשָׁה וְהָיוּ הַמַּיִם אֲשֶׁר תִּקַּח מִן הַיְאֹר וְהָיוּ לְדָם בַּיַּבָּשֶׁת

we'hai'yah im lo ya'a'mi'nu gam lish'ney ha'ot'ot ha'ey'leh we'lo yish'me'un le'qo'le'kha we'la'qahh'ta mi'mey'mey hai'or we'sha'phakh'ta hai'ya'ba'shah we'hai'u ha'ma'yim a'sher ti'qahh min hai'or we'hai'u le'dam bai'ya'ba'shet

and~he~did~EXIST IF NOT *they(m)~will~* make~SECURE ALSO to~TWO the~SIGN~s the~THESE and~NOT *they(m)~will~*HEAR~ must to~VOICE~*you(ms)* and~*you(ms)~did~* TAKE from~WATER~s2 the~STREAM and~ *you(ms)~did~*POUR-OUT the~DRY-GROUND and~*they~did~*EXIST the~WATER~s2 WHICH *you(ms)~will~*TAKE FROM the~STREAM and~ *they~did~*EXIST to~BLOOD in~the~DRY-LAND□

and (it) will (come to pass), if they will not [support] (both) {of} these two signs, and they will not hear your voice, (then) you will take from {the} waters {of} the stream and you will pour {it} out {to}‡ the dry ground, and the waters, which you took from the stream, will exist, and they will exist (as) blood in the dry land,□

4:10 וַיֹּאמֶר מֹשֶׁה אֶל יְהוָה בִּי אֲדֹנָי לֹא אִישׁ דְּבָרִים אָנֹכִי גַּם מִתְּמוֹל גַּם מִשִּׁלְשֹׁם גַּם מֵאָז דַּבֶּרְךָ אֶל עַבְדֶּךָ כִּי כְבַד פֶּה וּכְבַד לָשׁוֹן אָנֹכִי

wai'yo'mer mo'sheh el YHWH bi a'do'nai lo ish de'va'rim a'no'khi gam mit'mol gam mi'shil'shom gam mey'az da'ver'kha el av'de'kha ki khe'vad peh u'khe'vad la'shon a'no'khi

and~he~will~SAY "Mosheh ᴾᴸᵁᶜᴷᴱᴰ⁻ᴼᵁᵀ" TO "Yhwh ʰᵉ~ʷⁱˡˡ~ᴮᴱ" EXCUSE-ME "Adonai ᴸᴼᴿᴰ~ˢ~ ᵐᵉ" NOT MAN WORD~s I ALSO from~ YESTERDAY ALSO from~THREE-DAYS-AGO ALSO from~AT-THAT-TIME >~*much~*SPEAK~ you(ms) TO SERVANT~you(ms) GIVEN-THAT HEAVY MOUTH and~HEAVY TONGUE I□

and "Mosheh ᴾˡᵘᶜᵏᵉᵈ ᵒᵘᵗ" said to "Yhwh ᴴᵉ ⁱˢ", excuse me "Adonai ᴹʸ ˡᵒʳᵈˢ", I {am} not {a} man {of} words, <since> <previously> , <since> that time you spoke to your servant, given that I {have a} heavy mouth and heavy tongue,□

---

* The first word may be in error and might have originally been the word וַיֹּאמֶר (and he said) as the following words are the words of Yhwh to Mosheh. Because the first four words of this verse are the same as the next verse, the scribe may have mistakenly used the word וְהָיָה from the next verse.

† In context, the phrase "hear the voice" means "heed the message."

‡ The word הַיַּבָּשָׁה (the dry ground) is grammatically incorrect and should be written as לַיַּבָּשָׁה (to the dry ground).

Revised Mechanical Translation Codes

(..) Alt Trans/App A   <..> Comp Phrase/App B   [..] Verb Form/App C   \../ Plural Form/App D
:..: Int Inf Abs |..| Past Perf Verb   {...} Added Word

4:11

וַיֹּאמֶר יְהוָה אֵלָיו מִי שָׂם פֶּה לָאָדָם אוֹ מִי־יָשׂוּם אִלֵּם אוֹ חֵרֵשׁ אוֹ פִקֵּחַ אוֹ עִוֵּר הֲלֹא אָנֹכִי יְהוָה

wai'yo'mer YHWH ey'law mi sham peh la'a'dam o mi ya'sum i'leym o hhey'reysh o phi'qey'ahh o i'weyr ha'lo a'no'khi YHWH

and~he~will~SAY "Yhwh _he~will~BE_" TO~him WHO he~did~PLACE MOUTH to~the~ HUMAN OR WHO he~will~PLACE MUTE OR SILENT OR SEEING OR BLIND ?~NOT I "Yhwh _he~will~BE_"□

and "Yhwh _He is_" said to him, who placed the mouth (of) the human? or who placed {the} mute or {the} silent or {the} seeing or {the} blind? {is it} not I, "Yhwh _He is_"?□

4:12

וְעַתָּה לֵךְ וְאָנֹכִי אֶהְיֶה עִם־פִּיךָ וְהוֹרֵיתִיךָ אֲשֶׁר תְּדַבֵּר

we'a'tah leykh we'a'no'khi eh'yeh im pi'kha we'ho'rey'ti'kha a'sher te'da'beyr

and~NOW !(ms)~WALK and~I I~will~EXIST WITH MOUTH~you(ms) and~I~did~make~ THROW~you(ms) WHICH you(ms)~will~ much~SPEAK□

and now walk, and I will exist with your mouth, and I will [teach] you (what) you will speak,□

4:13

וַיֹּאמֶר בִּי אֲדֹנָי שְׁלַח־נָא בְּיַד־תִּשְׁלָח

wai'yo'mer bi a'do'nai she'lahh na be'yad tish'lahh

and~he~will~SAY EXCUSE-ME "Adonai _LORD~s~ me_" !(ms)~SEND PLEASE in~HAND you(ms)~ will~SEND□

and he said, excuse me "Adonai _My lords_", please send (by) {the} hand, can send,*□

4:14

וַיִּחַר אַף יְהוָה בְּמֹשֶׁה וַיֹּאמֶר הֲלֹא אַהֲרֹן אָחִיךָ הַלֵּוִי יָדַעְתִּי כִּי־דַבֵּר יְדַבֵּר הוּא וְגַם הִנֵּה־הוּא יֹצֵא לִקְרָאתֶךָ וְרָאֲךָ וְשָׂמַח בְּלִבּוֹ

wai'yi'hhar aph YHWH be'mo'sheh wai'yo'mer ha'lo a'ha'ron a'hhi'kha ha'ley'wi ya'da'ti ki da'beyr ye'da'beyr hu we'gam hin'neyh hu yo'tsey liq'ra'te'kha we'ra'a'kha we'sa'mahh be'li'bo

and~he~will~FLARE-UP NOSE "Yhwh _he~will~ BE_" in~"Mosheh _PLUCKED-OUT_" and~he~will~SAY ?~NOT "Aharon _LIGHT-BRINGER_" BROTHER~ you(ms) the~"Lewi _JOINING~me_" I~did~KNOW GIVEN-THAT >~much~SPEAK he~will~much~ SPEAK HE and~ALSO LOOK HE GO-OUT~ ing/er(ms) to~>~MEET~you(ms) and~he~ did~SEE~you(ms) and~he~did~REJOICE in~ HEART~him□

and "Yhwh _He is_" flared up {the} nose† (with) "Mosheh _Plucked out_" and he said, {is} not "Aharon _Light bringer_" your brother, the {one} of "Lewi _My joining_"? I know that he will :surely: speak well, also look, he {is} going out to meet you and he will see you and he will rejoice in his heart,□

4:15

וְדִבַּרְתָּ אֵלָיו וְשַׂמְתָּ אֶת־הַדְּבָרִים בְּפִיו וְאָנֹכִי אֶהְיֶה עִם־פִּיךָ וְעִם־פִּיהוּ

---

* The Hebrew text appears to be missing text. The Septuagint, which may preserve the original wording, reads, "please send another by the hand that you can send."

† The "flaring of the nose" is an idiom for a fierce anger.

Mechanical Translation Codes

<u>WORD</u> – Verb	WORD – Noun	Word – Name	word – Pre/Suff	_word_ – Conj.

וְהוֹרֵיתִי אֶתְכֶם אֵת אֲשֶׁר תַּעֲשׂוּן

we'di'bar'ta ey'law we'sam'ta et had'va'rim be'phiw we'a'no'khi eh'yeh im pi'kha we'im pi'hu we'ho'rey'ti et'khem eyt a'sher ta'a'sun

and~you(ms)~did~much~SPEAK TO~him and~you(ms)~did~PLACE AT the~WORD~s in~MOUTH~him and~I ~will~EXIST WITH MOUTH~you(ms) and~WITH MOUTH~him and~I~did~make~THROW AT~you(mp) AT WHICH you(ms)~will~DO~must□

and you will speak to him, and you will place the words in his mouth, and I will exist with your mouth and with his mouth, and I will [teach] you (what) you must do,□

4:16

וְדִבֶּר הוּא לְךָ אֶל הָעָם וְהָיָה הוּא יִהְיֶה לְּךָ לְפֶה וְאַתָּה תִּהְיֶה לּוֹ לֵאלֹהִים

we'di'ber hu le'kha el ha'am we'hai'yah hu yih'yeh le'kha le'pheh we'a'tah tih'yeh lo ley'lo'him

and~he~did~much~SPEAK HE to~you(ms) TO the~PEOPLE and~he~did~EXIST HE he~will~EXIST to~you(ms) to~MOUTH and~YOU(ms) you(ms)~will~EXIST to~him to~"Elohiym POWER~s"□

and he will speak (for) you to the people, and (it) will (come to pass), he will exist (for) you (as) {a} mouth and you, you will exist (for) him (as) "Elohiym Powers",□

4:17

וְאֶת הַמַּטֶּה הַזֶּה תִּקַּח בְּיָדֶךָ אֲשֶׁר תַּעֲשֶׂה בּוֹ אֶת הָאֹתֹת

we'et ha'ma'teh ha'zeh ti'qahh be'ya'de'kha a'sher ta'a'seh bo et ha'ot'ot

and~AT the~BRANCH the~THIS you(ms)~ will~TAKE in~HAND~you(ms) WHICH you(ms)~will~DO in~him AT the~SIGN~s□

and this branch, you will take in your hand, which {is what} you will do the signs (with),□

4:18

וַיֵּלֶךְ מֹשֶׁה וַיָּשָׁב אֶל יֶתֶר חֹתְנוֹ וַיֹּאמֶר לוֹ אֵלְכָה נָּא וְאָשׁוּבָה אֶל אַחַי אֲשֶׁר בְּמִצְרַיִם וְאֶרְאֶה הַעוֹדָם חַיִּים וַיֹּאמֶר יִתְרוֹ לְמֹשֶׁה לֵךְ לְשָׁלוֹם

wai'yey'lekh mo'sheh wai'ya'shav el ye'ter hhot'no wai'yo'mer lo eyl'khah na we'a'shu'vah el a'hhai a'sher be'mits'ra'yim we'er'eh ha'o'dam hai'yim wai'yo'mer yit'ro le'mo'sheh leykh le'sha'lom

and~he~will~WALK "Mosheh PLUCKED-OUT" and~he~will~TURN-BACK TO "Yeter REMAINDER" BE-AN-IN-LAW~ing/er(ms)~him and~he~will~SAY to~him I~will~WALK~^ PLEASE and~I~will~TURN-BACK~^ TO BROTHER~s~me WHICH in~"Mits'rayim STRAIT~s2" and~I~will~SEE ?~YET-AGAIN~ them(m) LIVING~s and~he~will~SAY "Yitro REMAINDER~him" to~"Mosheh PLUCKED-OUT" !(ms)~

and "Mosheh Plucked out" walked and he turned back to "Yeter Remainder"*, his in-law, and he said to him, please, I will walk and I will turn back to my brothers (who) {are} in "Mits'rayim Two straits", and I will see, {are} they (still) living? and "Yitro His remainder" said to "Mosheh Plucked out", walk to completeness,□

---

* Mosheh's father-in-law is identified by two different names in this text, יתר (yeter) and יתרו (yitro).

Revised Mechanical Translation Codes

(..) Alt Trans/App A   <..> Comp Phrase/App B   [..] Verb Form/App C   \../ Plural Form/App D
:..: Int Inf Abs |..| Past Perf Verb   {...} Added Word

~ 35 ~

WALK to~COMPLETENESS□

4:19

וַיֹּאמֶר יְהוָה אֶל מֹשֶׁה בְּמִדְיָן לֵךְ שֻׁב מִצְרָיִם כִּי מֵתוּ כָּל הָאֲנָשִׁים
הַמְבַקְשִׁים אֶת נַפְשֶׁךָ

wai'yo'mer YHWH el mo'sheh be'mid'yan leykh shuv mits'ra'yim ki mey'tu kol
ha'a'na'shim ham'vaq'shim et naph'she'kha

and~he~will~SAY "Yhwh ^(he~will~BE)" TO "Mosheh ^(PLUCKED-OUT)" in~"Mid'yan ^(QUARREL)" !(ms)~WALK !(ms)~TURN-BACK "Mits'rayim ^(STRAIT~s2)" GIVEN-THAT they~did~DIE ALL the~ MAN~s the~much~SEARCH-OUT~ing/er(mp) AT BEING~you(ms)□

and "Yhwh ^(He is)" said to "Mosheh ^(Plucked out)" in "Mid'yan ^(Quarrel)", walk, turn back {unto}* "Mits'rayim ^(Two straits)", given that all the men died, the {one}s searching out your being,□

4:20

וַיִּקַּח מֹשֶׁה אֶת אִשְׁתּוֹ וְאֶת בָּנָיו וַיַּרְכִּבֵם עַל הַחֲמֹר וַיָּשָׁב אַרְצָה
מִצְרָיִם וַיִּקַּח מֹשֶׁה אֶת מַטֵּה הָאֱלֹהִים בְּיָדוֹ

wai'yi'qahh mo'sheh et ish'to we'et ba'naw wai'yar'ki'veym al ha'hha'mor wai'ya'shav
ar'tsah mits'ra'yim wai'yi'qahh mo'sheh et ma'tey ha'e'lo'him be'ya'do

and~he~will~TAKE "Mosheh ^(PLUCKED-OUT)" AT WOMAN~him and~AT SON~s~him and~he~ will~make~RIDE~them(m) UPON the~ DONKEY and~he~will~TURN-BACK LAND~ unto "Mits'rayim ^(STRAIT~s2)" and~he~will~TAKE "Mosheh ^(PLUCKED-OUT)" AT BRANCH the~ "Elohiym ^(POWER~s)" in~HAND~him□

and "Mosheh ^(Plucked out)" took his woman and his sons, and he made them ride upon the donkey, and he turned back unto {the} land {of} "Mits'rayim ^(Two straits)", and "Mosheh ^(Plucked out)" took {the} branch {of} the "Elohiym ^(Powers)" in his hand,□

4:21

וַיֹּאמֶר יְהוָה אֶל מֹשֶׁה בְּלֶכְתְּךָ לָשׁוּב מִצְרַיְמָה רְאֵה כָּל הַמֹּפְתִים
אֲשֶׁר שַׂמְתִּי בְיָדֶךָ וַעֲשִׂיתָם לִפְנֵי פַרְעֹה וַאֲנִי אֲחַזֵּק אֶת לִבּוֹ וְלֹא
יְשַׁלַּח אֶת הָעָם

wai'yo'mer YHWH el mo'sheh be'lekh'te'kha la'shuv mits'rai'mah re'eyh kol ha'moph'tim
a'sher sam'ti be'ya'de'kha we'a'si'tam liph'ney phar'oh wa'ani a'hha'zeyq et li'bo we'lo
ye'sha'lahh et ha'am

and~he~will~SAY "Yhwh ^(he~will~BE)" TO "Mosheh ^(PLUCKED-OUT)" in~>~WALK~you(ms) to~>~TURN-BACK "Mits'rayim ^(STRAIT~s2)"~unto !(ms)~SEE ALL the~WONDER~s WHICH I~ did~PLACE in~HAND~you(ms) and~you(ms)~ will~DO~them(m) to~FACE~s "Paroh ^(GREAT-HOUSE)" and~I I~will~SEIZE AT HEART~him and~NOT he~will~much~SEND AT the~ PEOPLE□

and "Yhwh ^(He is)" said to "Mosheh ^(Plucked out)", in your walking to turn back unto "Mits'rayim ^(Two straits)", see all the wonders which I placed in your hand, and you will do them <in front of> "Paroh ^(Great house)", and I will seize his heart and he will not send the people,□

4:22

וְאָמַרְתָּ אֶל פַּרְעֹה כֹּה אָמַר יְהוָה בְּנִי בְכֹרִי יִשְׂרָאֵל

---

* The word Mits'rayim appears to be missing the suffix "unto," the prefix "to" or the word "To."

Mechanical Translation Codes

WORD – Verb	WORD – Noun	Word – Name	word – Pre/Suff	word – Conj.

we'a'mar'ta el par'oh koh a'mar YHWH be'ni be'khi'ri yis'ra'eyl

and~you(ms)~did~<u>SAY</u> TO "Paroh ^{GREAT-HOUSE}" IN-THIS-WAY he~did~<u>SAY</u> "Yhwh ^{he~will~}<u>BE</u>" SON~me FIRSTBORN~me "Yisra'el ^{he~will~}<u>TURN-ASIDE</u>~+~MIGHTY-ONE" □

and you will say to "Paroh ^{Great house}" in this way, "Yhwh ^{He is}" said, my firstborn son {is} "Yisra'el ^{He turns El aside}", □

4:23 וָאֹמַר אֵלֶיךָ שַׁלַּח אֶת בְּנִי וְיַעַבְדֵנִי וַתְּמָאֵן לְשַׁלְּחוֹ הִנֵּה אָנֹכִי הֹרֵג אֶת בִּנְךָ בְּכֹרֶךָ

wa'o'mar ey'ley'kha sha'lahh et be'ni we'ya'av'dey'ni wat'ma'eyn le'shal'hho hin'neyh a'no'khi ho'reyg et bin'kha be'kho're'kha

and~I~will~<u>SAY</u> TO~you(ms) !(ms)~much~<u>SEND</u> AT SON~me and~he~will~<u>SERVE</u>~me and~you(ms)~will~much~<u>REFUSE</u> to~>~much~<u>SEND</u>~him LOOK I <u>KILL</u>~ing/er(ms) AT SON~you(ms) FIRSTBORN~you(ms)□

and I say to you, send my son and he will serve me, and you refused to send him, look, I {am} killing your firstborn son,□

4:24 וַיְהִי בַדֶּרֶךְ בַּמָּלוֹן וַיִּפְגְּשֵׁהוּ יְהֹוָה וַיְבַקֵּשׁ הֲמִיתוֹ

wai'hi va'de'rekh ba'ma'lon wai'yiph'ge'shey'hu YHWH wai'va'qeysh ha'mi'to

and~he~will~<u>EXIST</u> in~the~<u>ROAD</u> in~the~PLACE-OF-LODGING and~he~will~<u>ENCOUNTER</u>~him "Yhwh ^{he~will~}<u>BE</u>" and~he~will~much~<u>SEARCH-OUT</u> >~make~<u>DIE</u>~him□

and (it) (came to pass), in the road, in the place of lodging, and "Yhwh ^{He is}" encountered him* and he searched out {to}† [kill] him,□

4:25 וַתִּקַּח צִפֹּרָה צֹר וַתִּכְרֹת אֶת עָרְלַת בְּנָהּ וַתַּגַּע לְרַגְלָיו וַתֹּאמֶר כִּי חֲתַן דָּמִים אַתָּה לִי

wa'ti'qahh tsi'po'rah tsor wa'tikh'rot et ar'lat be'nah wa'ta'ga le'rag'law wa'to'mer ki hha'tan da'mim a'tah li

and~ she~will~<u>TAKE</u> "Tsiporah ^{BIRD}" SHARP-STONE and~ she~will~<u>CUT</u> AT FORESKIN SON~her and~ she~will~make~<u>TOUCH</u> to~FOOT~s2~him and~ she~will~<u>SAY</u> GIVEN-THAT IN-LAW BLOOD~s YOU(ms) to~me□

and "Tsiporah ^{Bird}" took {a} sharp stone and she cut {the} foreskin {of} her son, and she touched {it} to his feet, and she said, given that you {are an} in-law {of} \bloodshed/ to me,□

4:26 וַיִּרֶף מִמֶּנּוּ אָז אָמְרָה חֲתַן דָּמִים לַמּוּלֹת

wai'yi'reph mi'me'nu az am'rah hha'tan da'mim la'mu'lot

and~he~will~<u>SINK-DOWN</u> FROM~him AT-THAT-TIME she~did~<u>SAY</u> IN-LAW BLOOD~s to~the~CIRCUMCISION~s□

and he sunk down from him, at that time she said, {an} in-law {of} \bloodshed/ (for) the circumcisions,□

---

* The "him" may be Mosheh, but may also be his son (see 4:25).
† The prefix ל appears to be missing from the word הֲמִיתוֹ.

Revised Mechanical Translation Codes

(..) Alt Trans/App A	<..> Comp Phrase/App B	[..] Verb Form/App C	\../ Plural Form/App D
:..: Int Inf Abs	|..| Past Perf Verb	{...} Added Word	

4:27   וַיֹּאמֶר יְהוָה אֶל אַהֲרֹן לֵךְ לִקְרַאת מֹשֶׁה הַמִּדְבָּרָה וַיֵּלֶךְ וַיִּפְגְּשֵׁהוּ בְּהַר הָאֱלֹהִים וַיִּשַּׁק לוֹ

wai'yo'mer YHWH el a'ha'ron leykh liq'rat mo'sheh ha'mid'ba'rah wai'yey'lekh wai'yiph'ge'shey'hu be'har ha'elo'him wai'yi'shaq lo

and~he~will~SAY "Yhwh ^{he~will~BE}" TO "Aharon ^{LIGHT-BRINGER}" !(ms)~WALK to~ >~MEET "Mosheh ^{PLUCKED-OUT}" the~ WILDERNESS~unto and~he~will~WALK and~ he~will~ENCOUNTER~him in~HILL the~ "Elohiym ^{POWER~s}" and~he~will~KISS to~him□

and "Yhwh ^{He is}" said to "Aharon ^{Light bringer}", walk unto the wilderness to meet "Mosheh ^{Plucked out}", and he walked and he encountered him in {the} hill {of} the "Elohiym ^{Powers}", and he kissed him,□

4:28   וַיַּגֵּד מֹשֶׁה לְאַהֲרֹן אֵת כָּל דִּבְרֵי יְהוָה אֲשֶׁר שְׁלָחוֹ וְאֵת כָּל הָאֹתֹת אֲשֶׁר צִוָּהוּ

wai'ya'geyd mo'sheh le'a'ha'ron eyt kol div'rey YHWH a'sher she'la'hho we'eyt kol ha'ot'ot a'sher tsi'wa'hu

and~he~will~make~BE-FACE-TO-FACE "Mosheh ^{PLUCKED-OUT}" to~"Aharon ^{LIGHT-BRINGER}" AT ALL WORD~s "Yhwh ^{he~will~BE}" WHICH he~ did~SEND~him and~AT ALL the~SIGN~s WHICH he~did~much~DIRECT~him□

and "Mosheh ^{Plucked out}" [told] "Aharon ^{Light bringer}" all {the} words {of} "Yhwh ^{He is}" which he sent him and all the signs which he directed him,□

4:29   וַיֵּלֶךְ מֹשֶׁה וְאַהֲרֹן וַיַּאַסְפוּ אֶת כָּל זִקְנֵי בְּנֵי יִשְׂרָאֵל

wai'yey'lekh mo'sheh we'a'ha'ron wai'ya'as'phu et kol ziq'ney be'ney yis'ra'eyl

and~he~will~WALK "Mosheh ^{PLUCKED-OUT}" and~"Aharon ^{LIGHT-BRINGER}" and~they(m)~will~ GATHER AT ALL BEARD~s SON~s "Yisra'el ^{he~will~TURN-ASIDE~+~MIGHTY-ONE}"□

and "Mosheh ^{Plucked out}" walked, and "Aharon ^{Light bringer}", and they gathered all {the} beard{ed one}s* {of the} sons {of} "Yisra'el ^{He turns El aside}",□

4:30   וַיְדַבֵּר אַהֲרֹן אֵת כָּל הַדְּבָרִים אֲשֶׁר דִּבֶּר יְהוָה אֶל מֹשֶׁה וַיַּעַשׂ הָאֹתֹת לְעֵינֵי הָעָם

wai'da'beyr a'ha'ron eyt kol had'va'rim a'sher di'ber YHWH el mo'sheh wai'ya'as ha'ot'ot le'ey'ney ha'am

and~he~will~much~SPEAK "Aharon ^{LIGHT-BRINGER}" AT ALL the~WORD~s WHICH he~did~ much~SPEAK "Yhwh ^{he~will~BE}" TO "Mosheh ^{PLUCKED-OUT}" and~he~will~DO the~SIGN~s to~ EYE~s2 the~PEOPLE□

and "Aharon ^{Light bringer}" spoke all the words which "Yhwh ^{He is}" spoke to "Mosheh ^{Plucked out}", and he did the signs to {the} eyes {of} the people,□

4:31   וַיַּאֲמֵן הָעָם וַיִּשְׁמְעוּ כִּי פָקַד יְהוָה אֶת בְּנֵי יִשְׂרָאֵל וְכִי רָאָה אֶת עָנְיָם וַיִּקְּדוּ וַיִּשְׁתַּחֲווּ

wai'ya'a'meyn ha'am wai'yish'me'u ki pha'qad YHWH et be'ney yis'ra'eyl we'khi ra'ah et

---

* "Bearded ones" is a euphemism for "elders."

Mechanical Translation Codes

WORD – Verb	WORD – Noun	Word – Name	word – Pre/Suff	word – Conj.

an'yam wai'yiq'du wai'yish'ta'hhaw'u

and~*he~will~make~*<u>SECURE</u> the~PEOPLE and~*they(m)~will~*<u>HEAR</u> GIVEN-THAT *he~did~*<u>REGISTER</u> "Yhwh ^{*he~will~*<u>BE</u>"} AT SON~s "Yisra'el ^{*he~will~*<u>TURN-ASIDE</u>~+~MIGHTY-ONE"} and~GIVEN-THAT *he~did~*<u>SEE</u> AT AFFLICTION~them(m) and~*they(m)~will~*<u>BOW-THE-HEAD</u> and~*they(m)~will~* self~<u>BEND-DOWN</u>▢	and the people [supported], and they heard that "Yhwh ^{He is}" registered {the} sons {of} "Yisra'el ^{He turns El aside}", and that he saw their affliction, and they bowed the head and they bent {them}selves down,▢

Chapter 5

5:1 וְאַחַר בָּאוּ מֹשֶׁה וְאַהֲרֹן וַיֹּאמְרוּ אֶל פַּרְעֹה כֹּה אָמַר יְהֹוָה אֱלֹהֵי יִשְׂרָאֵל שַׁלַּח אֶת עַמִּי וְיָחֹגּוּ לִי בַּמִּדְבָּר

we'a'hhar ba'u mo'sheh we'a'ha'ron wai'yom'ru el par'oh koh a'mar YHWH e'lo'hey yis'ra'eyl sha'lahh et a'mi we'ya'hho'gu li ba'mid'bar

and~AFTER *they~did~*<u>COME</u> "Mosheh ^{PLUCKED-OUT}" and~"Aharon ^{LIGHT-BRINGER}" and~*they(m)~will~*<u>SAY</u> TO "Paroh ^{GREAT-HOUSE}" IN-THIS-WAY *he~did~*<u>SAY</u> "Yhwh ^{*he~will~*<u>BE</u>"} "Elohiym POWER~s" "Yisra'el ^{*he~will~*<u>TURN-ASIDE</u>~+~MIGHTY-ONE"} !*(ms)~much~*<u>SEND</u> AT PEOPLE~me and~*they(m)~will~*<u>HOLD-A-FEAST</u> to~me in~the~WILDERNESS▢	and after{ward}, "Mosheh ^{Plucked out}" and "Aharon ^{Light bringer}" came, and they said to "Paroh ^{Great house}", in this way "Yhwh ^{He is}" {the} "Elohiym ^{Powers}" {of} "Yisra'el ^{He turns El aside}" said, send my people and they will hold a feast to me in the wilderness,▢

5:2 וַיֹּאמֶר פַּרְעֹה מִי יְהֹוָה אֲשֶׁר אֶשְׁמַע בְּקֹלוֹ לְשַׁלַּח אֶת יִשְׂרָאֵל לֹא יָדַעְתִּי אֶת יְהֹוָה וְגַם אֶת יִשְׂרָאֵל לֹא אֲשַׁלֵּחַ

wai'yo'mer par'oh mi YHWH a'sher esh'ma be'qo'lo le'sha'lahh et yis'ra'eyl lo ya'da'ti et YHWH we'gam et yis'ra'eyl lo a'sha'ley'ahh

and~*he~will~*<u>SAY</u> "Paroh ^{GREAT-HOUSE}" WHO "Yhwh ^{*he~will~*<u>BE</u>"} WHICH *I~will~*<u>HEAR</u> in~VOICE~him to~>~*much~*<u>SEND</u> AT "Yisra'el ^{*he~will~*<u>TURN-ASIDE</u>~+~MIGHTY-ONE"} NOT *I~did~*<u>KNOW</u> AT "Yhwh ^{*he~will~*<u>BE</u>"} and~ALSO AT "Yisra'el ^{*he~will~*<u>TURN-ASIDE</u>~+~MIGHTY-ONE"} NOT *I~will~much~*<u>SEND</u>▢	and "Paroh ^{Great house}" said, who {is} "Yhwh ^{He is}" (that) I should listen (to) his voice to send "Yisra'el ^{He turns El aside}"? I do not know "Yhwh ^{He is}", and also, I will not send "Yisra'el ^{He turns El aside}",▢

5:3 וַיֹּאמְרוּ אֱלֹהֵי הָעִבְרִים נִקְרָא עָלֵינוּ נֵלְכָה נָּא דֶּרֶךְ שְׁלֹשֶׁת יָמִים בַּמִּדְבָּר וְנִזְבְּחָה לַיהֹוָה אֱלֹהֵינוּ פֶּן יִפְגָּעֵנוּ בַּדֶּבֶר אוֹ בֶחָרֶב

wai'yom'ru e'lo'hey ha'iv'rim niq'ra a'ley'nu neyl'khah na de'rekh she'lo'shet ya'mim ba'mid'bar we'niz'be'hhah la'YHWH e'lo'hey'nu pen yiph'ga'ey'nu ba'de'ver o be'hha'rev

and~*they(m)~will~*<u>SAY</u> "Elohiym ^{POWER~s}" the~"Ever ^{OTHER-SIDE}~s *he~did~be~*<u>MEET</u>	and they said, "Elohiym ^{Powers}" {of} the {one}s {of} "Ever ^{Other side}" has met (with) us, please,

Revised Mechanical Translation Codes

(..) Alt Trans/App A	<..> Comp Phrase/App B	[..] Verb Form/App C	\../ Plural Form/App D
:..: Int Inf Abs	|..| Past Perf Verb	{...} Added Word	

UPON~us *we~will*~UNDERLINE WALK~^ PLEASE ROAD THREE DAY~s in~the~WILDERNESS and~*we~will*~SACRIFICE~^ to~"Yhwh *he~will~BE*" "Elohiym *POWER~s*"~us OTHERWISE *he~will~*REACH~us in~the~EPIDEMIC OR in~the~SWORD□

we will walk {the} road {for} three days in the wilderness, and we will sacrifice to "Yhwh *He is*" our "Elohiym *Powers*", otherwise, he will reach us (with) the epidemic or (with) the sword,□

5:4

וַיֹּאמֶר אֲלֵהֶם מֶלֶךְ מִצְרַיִם לָמָּה מֹשֶׁה וְאַהֲרֹן תַּפְרִיעוּ אֶת הָעָם מִמַּעֲשָׂיו לְכוּ לְסִבְלֹתֵיכֶם

wai'yo'mer a'ley'hem me'lekh mits'ra'yim la'mah mo'sheh we'a'ha'ron taph'ri'u et ha'am mi'ma'a'saw le'khu le'siv'lo'tey'khem

and~*he~will*~SAY TO~them(m) KING "Mits'rayim *STRAIT~s2*" to~WHAT "Mosheh *PLUCKED-OUT*" and~"Aharon *LIGHT-BRINGER*" *you(mp)~will*~make~LOOSE AT the~PEOPLE from~WORK~him *!(mp)*~WALK to~BURDEN~s~you(mp)□

and {the} king {of} "Mits'rayim *Two straits*" said to them, <why> will you, "Mosheh *Plucked out*" and "Aharon *Light bringer*", loose the people from his work? Walk to your burdens,□

5:5

וַיֹּאמֶר פַּרְעֹה הֵן רַבִּים עַתָּה עַם הָאָרֶץ וְהִשְׁבַּתֶּם אֹתָם מִסִּבְלֹתָם

wai'yo'mer par'oh heyn ra'bim a'tah am ha'a'rets we'hish'ba'tem o'tam mi'siv'lo'tam

and~*he~will*~SAY "Paroh *GREAT-HOUSE*" THOUGH ABUNDANT~s NOW PEOPLE the~LAND and~*you(mp)~did*~make~CEASE AT~them(m) from~BURDEN~s~them(m)□

and "Paroh *Great house*" said, though {the} people {of} the land {are} now abundant, will you make them cease from their burdens?□

5:6

וַיְצַו פַּרְעֹה בַּיּוֹם הַהוּא אֶת הַנֹּגְשִׂים בָּעָם וְאֶת שֹׁטְרָיו לֵאמֹר

wai'tsaw par'oh ba'yom ha'hu et ha'nog'sim ba'am we'et shot'raw ley'mor

and~*he~will*~much~DIRECT "Paroh *GREAT-HOUSE*" in~the~DAY the~HE AT the~PUSH~ing/er(mp) in~the~PEOPLE and~AT DOMINATE~ing/er(mp)~him to~>~SAY□

and in (that) day, "Paroh *Great house*" directed the pushers (over) the people and his dominators, say{ing},□

5:7

לֹא תֹאסִפוּן לָתֵת תֶּבֶן לָעָם לִלְבֹּן הַלְּבֵנִים כִּתְמוֹל שִׁלְשֹׁם הֵם יֵלְכוּ וְקֹשְׁשׁוּ לָהֶם תֶּבֶן

lo to'si'phun la'teyt te'ven la'am lil'bon hal'bey'nim kit'mol shil'shom heym yeyl'khu we'qosh'shu la'hem te'ven

NOT *you(mp)~will*~make~ADD~must to~>~GIVE STRAW to~the~PEOPLE to~>~MAKE-BRICKS the~BRICK~s like~YESTERDAY THREE-DAYS-AGO THEY(m) *they(m)~will*~WALK and~*they~did*~much~COLLECT to~them(m) STRAW□

you must not [again] give straw to the people to make bricks like the bricks <previously> , they will walk and they, they will collect straw (for) them{selves},□

Mechanical Translation Codes

<u>WORD</u> – Verb	WORD – Noun	Word – Name	word – Pre/Suff	*word* – Conj.

5:8 וְאֶת מַתְכֹּנֶת הַלְּבֵנִים אֲשֶׁר הֵם עֹשִׂים תְּמוֹל שִׁלְשֹׁם תָּשִׂימוּ עֲלֵיהֶם לֹא תִגְרְעוּ מִמֶּנּוּ כִּי נִרְפִּים הֵם עַל כֵּן הֵם צֹעֲקִים לֵאמֹר נֵלְכָה נִזְבְּחָה לֵאלֹהֵינוּ

we'et mat'ko'net hal'bey'nim a'sher heym o'sim te'mol shil'shom ta'si'mu a'ley'hem lo tig're'u mi'me'nu ki nir'pim heym al keyn heym tso'a'qim ley'mor neyl'khah niz'be'hhah ley'lo'hey'nu

and~AT SUM the~BRICK~s WHICH THEY(m) DO~ing/er(mp) YESTERDAY THREE-DAYS-AGO you(mp)~will~PLACE UPON~them(m) NOT you(mp)~will~TAKE-AWAY FROM~him GIVEN-THAT be~SINK-DOWN~ing/er(mp) THEY(m) UPON SO THEY(m) CRY-OUT~ing/er(mp) to~>~SAY we~will~WALK~^ we~will~SACRIFICE~^ to~"Elohiym POWER~s"~us□

and {the} sum {of} the bricks which they {were} doing <previously> , you will place upon them, you will not take away from him given that they {are} [lazy], <therefore> , they {are} crying out say{ing}, we will walk, we will sacrifice to our "Elohiym Powers",□

5:9 תִּכְבַּד הָעֲבֹדָה עַל הָאֲנָשִׁים וְיַעֲשׂוּ בָהּ וְאַל יִשְׁעוּ בְּדִבְרֵי שָׁקֶר

tikh'bad ha'a'vo'dah al ha'a'na'shim we'ya'a'su vah we'al yish'u be'div'rey sha'qer

she~will~BE-HEAVY the~SERVICE UPON the~MAN~s and~they(m)~will~DO in~her and~DO-NOT they(m)~will~DO in~WORD~s FALSE□

the service will be heavy upon the men and they will do her*, and do not do words {of} false{ness},□

5:10 וַיֵּצְאוּ נֹגְשֵׂי הָעָם וְשֹׁטְרָיו וַיֹּאמְרוּ אֶל הָעָם לֵאמֹר כֹּה אָמַר פַּרְעֹה אֵינֶנִּי נֹתֵן לָכֶם תֶּבֶן

wai'yeyts'u nog'sey ha'am we'shot'raw wai'yom'ru el ha'am ley'mor koh a'mar par'oh ey'ne'ni no'teyn la'khem te'ven

and~they(m)~will~GO-OUT PUSH~ing/er(mp) the~PEOPLE and~DOMINATE~s~him and~they(m)~will~SAY TO the~PEOPLE to~>~SAY IN-THIS-WAY he~did~SAY "Paroh GREAT-HOUSE" WITHOUT~me GIVE~ing/er(ms) to~you(mp) STRAW□

and {the} pushers {of} the people, and his dominators, went out and they said to the people say{ing}, in this way "Paroh Great house" said, I {am} (not) giving straw to you,□

5:11 אַתֶּם לְכוּ קְחוּ לָכֶם תֶּבֶן מֵאֲשֶׁר תִּמְצָאוּ כִּי אֵין נִגְרָע מֵעֲבֹדַתְכֶם דָּבָר

a'tem le'khu qe'hhu la'khem te'ven mey'a'sher tim'tsa'u ki eyn nig'ra mey'a'vo'dat'khem da'var

YOU(mp) !(mp)~WALK !(mp)~TAKE to~you(mp) STRAW from~WHICH you(mp)~will~FIND GIVEN-THAT WITHOUT be~TAKE-AWAY~ing/er(ms) from~SERVICE~you(mp) WORD□

you, walk, take straw (for) your{self} from which you will find, given that (not) {a} (thing) {will} be taken away from your service,□

---

* Referring to the "service," a feminine word in Hebrew.

Revised Mechanical Translation Codes
(..) Alt Trans/App A   <..> Comp Phrase/App B   [..] Verb Form/App C   \../ Plural Form/App D
:..: Int Inf Abs |..| Past Perf Verb   {...} Added Word

5:12

וַיָּפֶץ הָעָם בְּכָל אֶרֶץ מִצְרָיִם לְקֹשֵׁשׁ קַשׁ לַתֶּבֶן

wai'ya'phets ha'am be'khol e'rets mits'ra'yim le'qo'sheysh qash la'te'ven

and~*he*~*will*~make~<u>SCATTER-ABROAD</u> the~ PEOPLE in~ALL LAND "Mits'rayim STRAIT~s2„ to~*much*~<u>COLLECT</u> STUBBLE to~STRAW□	and the people scattered abroad in all {the} land {of} "Mits'rayim Two straits„ to collect stubble (for) straw,□

5:13

וְהַנֹּגְשִׂים אָצִים לֵאמֹר כַּלּוּ מַעֲשֵׂיכֶם דְּבַר יוֹם בְּיוֹמוֹ כַּאֲשֶׁר בִּהְיוֹת הַתֶּבֶן

we'ha'nog'sim a'tsim ley'mor ka'lu ma'a'sey'khem de'var yom be'yo'mo ka'a'sheyr bih'yot ha'te'ven

and~the~<u>PUSH</u>~*ing/er(mp)* <u>COMPEL</u>~ *ing/er(mp)* to~>~<u>SAY</u> !(mp)~*much*~<u>FINISH</u> WORK~s~*you(mp)* WORD DAY in~DAY~him like~WHICH in~>~<u>EXIST</u> the~STRAW□	and the pushers {were} compelling, say{ing}, finish your work, {it is a} (matter) {of the} day in his day*, <just as> (with) {the} exist{ence of} the straw,□

5:14

וַיֻּכּוּ שֹׁטְרֵי בְּנֵי יִשְׂרָאֵל אֲשֶׁר שָׂמוּ עֲלֵהֶם נֹגְשֵׂי פַרְעֹה לֵאמֹר מַדּוּעַ לֹא כִלִּיתֶם חָקְכֶם לִלְבֹּן כִּתְמוֹל שִׁלְשֹׁם גַּם תְּמוֹל גַּם הַיּוֹם

wai'yu'ku shot'rey be'ney yis'ra'eyl a'sher sha'mu a'ley'hem nog'sey phar'oh ley'mor ma'du'a lo ki'li'tem hhaq'khem lil'bon kit'mol shil'shom gam te'mol gam hai'yom

and~*they(m)*~*will*~be~make~<u>HIT</u> <u>DOMINATE</u>~*ing/er(mp)* SON~s "Yisra'el *he*~*will*~ <u>TURN-ASIDE</u>~+~MIGHTY-ONE„ WHICH *they*~*did*~<u>PLACE</u> UPON~them(m) <u>PUSH</u>~*ing/er(mp)* "Paroh GREAT-HOUSE„ to~>~<u>SAY</u> WHY NOT *you(mp)*~ *did*~*much*~<u>FINISH</u> CUSTOM~*you(mp)* to~ >~<u>MAKE-BRICKS</u> like~YESTERDAY THREE-DAYS-AGO ALSO YESTERDAY ALSO the~ DAY□	and {the} dominators {of the} sons {of} "Yisra'el He turns El aside„, which {the} pushers {of} "Paroh Great house„ placed upon them, were hit, say{ing}, why did you not finish your custom to make bricks, (both) yesterday (and) <today> like <previously>?□

5:15

וַיָּבֹאוּ שֹׁטְרֵי בְּנֵי יִשְׂרָאֵל וַיִּצְעֲקוּ אֶל פַּרְעֹה לֵאמֹר לָמָּה תַעֲשֶׂה כֹה לַעֲבָדֶיךָ

wai'ya'vo'u shot'rey be'ney yis'ra'eyl wai'yits'a'qu el par'oh ley'mor la'mah ta'a'seh koh la'a'va'dey'kha

and~*they(m)*~*will*~<u>COME</u> <u>DOMINATE</u>~ *ing/er(mp)* SON~s "Yisra'el *he*~*will*~<u>TURN-ASIDE</u>~+~ MIGHTY-ONE„ and~*they(m)*~*will*~<u>CRY-OUT</u> TO "Paroh GREAT-HOUSE„ to~>~<u>SAY</u> to~WHAT *you(ms)*~*will*~<u>DO</u> IN-THIS-WAY to~ SERVANT~s~*you(ms)*□	and {the} dominators {of the} sons {of} "Yisra'el He turns El aside„ came and they cried out to "Paroh Great house„ say{ing}, <why> will you do {this} to your servants in this way?□

---

* "Matter of the day in his day" is an idiom meaning a "daily matter."

Mechanical Translation Codes

<u>WORD</u> – Verb	WORD – Noun	Word – Name	word – Pre/Suff	*word* – Conj.

5:16   תֶּבֶן אֵין נִתָּן לַעֲבָדֶיךָ וּלְבֵנִים אֹמְרִים לָנוּ עֲשׂוּ וְהִנֵּה עֲבָדֶיךָ מֻכִּים וְחָטָאת עַמֶּךָ

te'ven eyn ni'tan la'a'va'dey'kha ul'vey'nim om'rim la'nu a'su we'hin'neyh a'va'dey'kha mu'kim we'hha'tat a'me'kha

STRAW WITHOUT be~GIVE~ing/er(ms) to~ SERVANT~s~you(ms) and~BRICK~s SAY~ ing/er(mp) to~us !(mp)~DO and~LOOK SERVANT~s~you(ms) be~make~HIT~ ing/er(mp) and~ERROR PEOPLE~you(ms)☐

(no) straw {is} being given to your servants, and {they are} say{ing} to us, (make) bricks, and look, your servants {are} being hit, and {it is an} error {of} your people,☐

5:17   וַיֹּאמֶר נִרְפִּים אַתֶּם נִרְפִּים עַל כֵּן אַתֶּם אֹמְרִים נֵלְכָה נִזְבְּחָה לַיהוָה

wai'yo'mer nir'pim a'tem nir'pim al keyn a'tem om'rim neyl'khah niz'be'hhah la'YHWH

and~he~will~SAY be~SINK-DOWN~ ing/er(mp) YOU(mp) be~SINK-DOWN~ ing/er(mp) UPON SO YOU(mp) SAY~ ing/er(mp) we~will~WALK~^ we~will~ SACRIFICE~^ to~"Yhwh ^{he~will~BE}"☐

and he said, you {are} :very: [lazy], <therefore> , you {are} say{ing}, we will walk, we will sacrifice to "Yhwh ^{He is}",☐

5:18   וְעַתָּה לְכוּ עִבְדוּ וְתֶבֶן לֹא יִנָּתֵן לָכֶם וְתֹכֶן לְבֵנִים תִּתֵּנוּ

we'a'tah le'khu iv'du we'te'ven lo yi'na'teyn la'khem we'to'khen le'vey'nim ti'tey'nu

and~NOW !(mp)~WALK !(mp)~SERVE and~ STRAW NOT he~will~be~GIVE to~you(mp) and~MEASURED-AMOUNT BRICK~s you(mp)~will~GIVE☐

and now, walk, serve, and straw will not be given to you, and you will give {the} measured amount {of} bricks,☐

5:19   וַיִּרְאוּ שֹׁטְרֵי בְנֵי יִשְׂרָאֵל אֹתָם בְּרָע לֵאמֹר לֹא תִגְרְעוּ מִלִּבְנֵיכֶם דְּבַר יוֹם בְּיוֹמוֹ

wai'yir'u shot'rey ve'ney yis'ra'eyl o'tam be'ra ley'mor lo tig're'u mi'liv'ney'khem de'var yom be'yo'mo

and~they(m)~will~SEE DOMINATE~ ing/er(mp) SON~s "Yisra'el ^{he~will~TURN-ASIDE~+~ MIGHTY-ONE}" AT~them(m) in~DYSFUNCTIONAL to~>~SAY NOT you(mp)~will~TAKE-AWAY from~BRICK~s~you(mp) WORD DAY in~DAY~ him☐

and {the} dominators {of the} sons {of} "Yisra'el ^{He turns El aside}" saw them in dysfunction, say{ing}, you will not take away from your bricks, {it is a} (matter) {of the} day in his day*,☐

5:20   וַיִּפְגְּעוּ אֶת מֹשֶׁה וְאֶת אַהֲרֹן נִצָּבִים לִקְרָאתָם בְּצֵאתָם מֵאֵת פַּרְעֹה

wai'yiph'ge'u et mo'sheh we'et a'ha'ron ni'tsa'vim liq'ra'tam be'tsey'tam mey'eyl par'oh

and~they(m)~will~REACH AT "Mosheh ^{PLUCKED-OUT}" and~AT "Aharon ^{LIGHT-BRINGER}" be~

and they reached "Mosheh ^{Plucked out}" and "Aharon ^{Light bringer}" standing to meet them in

---

* "Matter of the day in his day" is an idiom meaning a "daily matter."

Revised Mechanical Translation Codes

(..) Alt Trans/App A   <..> Comp Phrase/App B   [..] Verb Form/App C   \..\ Plural Form/App D
:..: Int Inf Abs |..| Past Perf Verb   {...} Added Word

STAND-UP~*ing/er*(mp) to~>~<u>MEET</u>~them(m)   their go{ing} out from "Paroh ^{Great house}",☐
in~>~<u>GO-OUT</u>~them(m) from~AT "Paroh
^{GREAT-HOUSE}"☐

5:21 וַיֹּאמְרוּ אֲלֵהֶם יֵרֶא יְהֹוָה עֲלֵיכֶם וְיִשְׁפֹּט אֲשֶׁר הִבְאַשְׁתֶּם אֶת רֵיחֵנוּ
בְּעֵינֵי פַרְעֹה וּבְעֵינֵי עֲבָדָיו לָתֶת חֶרֶב בְּיָדָם לְהָרְגֵנוּ

wai'yom'ru a'ley'hem yey're YHWH a'ley'khem we'yish'pot a'sher hiv'ash'tem et
rey'hey'nu be'ey'ney phar'oh uv'ey'ney a'va'daw la'tet hhe'rev be'ya'dam le'har'gey'nu

and~*they*(m)~*will*~<u>SAY</u> TO~them(m) he~will~
<u>SEE</u> "Yhwh ^{he~will~BE}" UPON~you(mp) and~*he*~
will~<u>DECIDE</u> WHICH *you*(mp)~*did*~*make*~
<u>STINK</u> AT AROMA~us in~EYE~s2 "Paroh ^{GREAT-HOUSE}" and~in~EYE~s2 SERVANT~s~him to~
>~<u>GIVE</u> SWORD in~HAND~them(m) to~
>~<u>KILL</u>~us☐

and they said to them, "Yhwh ^{He is}" will (look) upon you, and he will decide, (because) you made our aroma stink in {the} eyes {of} "Paroh ^{Great house}" and in {the} eyes {of} his servants, to give {a} sword in their hand to kill us,☐

5:22 וַיָּשָׁב מֹשֶׁה אֶל יְהֹוָה וַיֹּאמַר אֲדֹנָי לָמָה הֲרֵעֹתָה לָעָם הַזֶּה לָמָּה זֶּה
שְׁלַחְתָּנִי

wai'ya'shav mo'sheh el YHWH wai'yo'mar a'do'nai la'mah ha'rey'o'tah la'am ha'zeh
la'mah zeh she'lahh'ta'ni

and~*he*~*will*~<u>TURN-BACK</u> "Mosheh ^{PLUCKED-OUT}" TO "Yhwh ^{he~will~BE}" and~*he*~*will*~<u>SAY</u>
"Adonai ^{LORD~s~me}" to~WHAT *you*(ms)~*did*~
make~<u>BE-DYSFUNCTIONAL</u>~^ to~the~
PEOPLE the~THIS to~WHAT THIS *you*(ms)~
did~<u>SEND</u>~me☐

and "Mosheh ^{Plucked out}" turned back to "Yhwh ^{He is}" and he said, "Adonai ^{My lords}", <why> did you make {it} dysfunctional (for) this people? <what is the reason> you sent me?☐

5:23 וּמֵאָז בָּאתִי אֶל פַּרְעֹה לְדַבֵּר בִּשְׁמֶךָ הֵרַע לָעָם הַזֶּה וְהַצֵּל לֹא הִצַּלְתָּ
אֶת עַמֶּךָ

u'mey'az ba'ti el par'oh le'da'beyr bish'me'kha hey'ra la'am ha'zeh we'ha'tseyl lo
hi'tsal'ta et a'me'kha

and~from~AT-THAT-TIME *I*~*did*~<u>COME</u> TO "Paroh ^{GREAT-HOUSE}" to~>~*much*~<u>SPEAK</u> in~
TITLE~you(ms) he~*did*~*make*~<u>BE-DYSFUNCTIONAL</u> to~the~PEOPLE the~THIS
and~>~*make*~<u>DELIVER</u> NOT *you*(ms)~*did*~
make~<u>DELIVER</u> AT PEOPLE~you(ms)☐

and from that time, I came to "Paroh ^{Great house}" to speak in your title, he made {it} dysfunctional to this people and you :never: delivered your people,☐

Chapter 6

6:1 וַיֹּאמֶר יְהֹוָה אֶל מֹשֶׁה עַתָּה תִרְאֶה אֲשֶׁר אֶעֱשֶׂה לְפַרְעֹה כִּי בְיָד חֲזָקָה
יְשַׁלְּחֵם וּבְיָד חֲזָקָה יְגָרְשֵׁם מֵאַרְצוֹ

Mechanical Translation Codes

<u>WORD</u> – Verb   WORD – Noun   Word – Name   word – Pre/Suff   *word* – Conj.

~ 44 ~

wai'yo'mer YHWH el mo'sheh a'tah tir'eh a'sher e'e'seh le'phar'oh ki be'yad hha'za'qah
ye'shal'hheym uv'yad hha'za'qah ye'gar'sheym mey'ar'tso

and~*he~will~*<u>SAY</u> "Yhwh ^{he~will~<u>BE</u>} TO
"Mosheh ^{PLUCKED-OUT}" NOW *you(ms)~will~*<u>SEE</u>
WHICH *I~will~*<u>DO</u> to~"Paroh ^{GREAT-HOUSE}"
GIVEN-THAT in~HAND FORCEFUL *he~will~*
much~<u>SEND</u>~them(m) and~in~HAND
FORCEFUL *he~will~much~*<u>CAST-OUT</u>~
them(m) from~LAND~him□

and "Yhwh ^{He is}" said to "Mosheh ^{Plucked out}",
now you will see (what) I will do to "Paroh ^{Great house}", given that (with) {a} forceful hand he
will send them, and (with) {a} forceful hand he
will cast them out from his land,□

6:2 וַיְדַבֵּר אֱלֹהִים אֶל מֹשֶׁה וַיֹּאמֶר אֵלָיו אֲנִי יְהֹוָה

wai'da'beyr e'lo'him el mo'sheh wai'yo'mer ey'law a'ni YHWH

and~*he~will~much~*<u>SPEAK</u> "Elohiym ^{POWER~s}"
TO "Mosheh ^{PLUCKED-OUT}" and~*he~will~*<u>SAY</u>
TO~him I "Yhwh ^{he~will~<u>BE</u>}"□

and "Elohiym ^{Powers}" spoke to "Mosheh ^{Plucked out}" and he said to him, I {am} "Yhwh ^{He is}",□

6:3 וָאֵרָא אֶל אַבְרָהָם אֶל יִצְחָק וְאֶל יַעֲקֹב בְּאֵל שַׁדָּי וּשְׁמִי יְהֹוָה לֹא
נוֹדַעְתִּי לָהֶם

wa'ey'ra el av'ra'ham el yits'hhaq we'el ya'a'qov be'eyl sha'dai ush'mi YHWH lo no'da'ti
la'hem

and~*I~will~be~*<u>SEE</u> TO "Avraham ^{FATHER~+~}
^{LIFTED}" TO "Yits'hhaq ^{he~will~<u>LAUGH</u>}" and~TO
"Ya'aqov ^{he~will~<u>RESTRAIN</u>}" in~MIGHTY-ONE
"Shaddai ^{BREAST~s~me}" and~TITLE~me "Yhwh
^{he~will~<u>BE</u>}" NOT *I~did~be~*<u>KNOW</u> to~them(m)□

and I [appeared] to "Avraham ^{Father lifted}", to
"Yits'hhaq ^{He laughs}", and to "Ya'aqov ^{He restrains}"
(with) {the} mighty one {of} "Shaddai ^{My breasts}",
and my title {is} "Yhwh ^{He is}", I was not known
to them*, □

6:4 וְגַם הֲקִמֹתִי אֶת בְּרִיתִי אִתָּם לָתֵת לָהֶם אֶת אֶרֶץ כְּנַעַן אֵת אֶרֶץ
מְגֻרֵיהֶם אֲשֶׁר גָּרוּ בָהּ

we'gam ha'qi'mo'ti et be'ri'ti i'tam la'teyt la'hem et e'rets ke'na'an eyt e'rets
me'gu'rey'hem a'sher ga'ru vah

and~ALSO *I~did~make~*<u>RISE</u> AT COVENANT~
me AT~them(m) to~>~<u>GIVE</u> to~them(m) AT
LAND "Kena'an ^{LOWERED}" AT LAND
PILGRIMAGE~them(m) WHICH *they~did~*
<u>SOJOURN</u> in~her□

and also, I made my covenant rise (with)
them, to give to them {the} land {of} "Kena'an ^{Lowered}", {the} land {of} their pilgrimage which
they sojourned in,□

6:5 וְגַם אֲנִי שָׁמַעְתִּי אֶת נַאֲקַת בְּנֵי יִשְׂרָאֵל אֲשֶׁר מִצְרַיִם מַעֲבִדִים אֹתָם
וָאֶזְכֹּר אֶת בְּרִיתִי

we'gam a'ni sha'ma'ti et na'a'qat be'ney yis'ra'eyl a'sher mits'ra'yim ma'a'vi'dim o'tam
wa'ez'kor et be'ri'ti

and~ALSO I *I~did~*<u>HEAR</u> AT GROANING

and also, I |had| heard the groaning {of the}

---

* Compare with Genesis 17:1, but also see Genesis 15:7 and 28:13.

Revised Mechanical Translation Codes

(..) Alt Trans/App A	<..> Comp Phrase/App B	[..] Verb Form/App C	\..\ Plural Form/App D
:..: Int Inf Abs	|..| Past Perf Verb	{...} Added Word	

SON~s "Yisra'el ^{he~will~}<u>TURN-ASIDE</u>~+~<u>MIGHTY-ONE</u>" WHICH "Mits'rayim ^{STRAIT~s2}" *make*~<u>SERVE</u>~ *ing/er(mp)* AT~them(m) and~*I~will~* <u>REMEMBER</u> AT COVENANT~me□

sons {of} "Yisra'el ^{He turns El aside}", (because) "Mits'rayim ^{Two straits}" {was} making them serve, and I remembered my covenant,□

6:6 לָכֵן אֱמֹר לִבְנֵי יִשְׂרָאֵל אֲנִי יְהֹוָה וְהוֹצֵאתִי אֶתְכֶם מִתַּחַת סִבְלֹת מִצְרַיִם וְהִצַּלְתִּי אֶתְכֶם מֵעֲבֹדָתָם וְגָאַלְתִּי אֶתְכֶם בִּזְרוֹעַ נְטוּיָה וּבִשְׁפָטִים גְּדֹלִים

la'kheyn e'mor liv'ney yis'ra'eyl a'ni YHWH we'ho'tsey'ti et'khem mi'ta'hhat siv'lot mits'ra'yim we'hi'tsal'ti et'khem mey'a'vo'da'tam we'ga'al'ti et'khem biz'ro'a ne'tu'yah u'vish'pha'tim ge'do'lim

to~SO !(*ms*)~<u>SAY</u> to~SON~s "Yisra'el ^{he~will~}<u>TURN-ASIDE</u>~+~<u>MIGHTY-ONE</u>" I "Yhwh ^{he~will~}<u>BE</u>" and~*I~ did~make*~<u>GO-OUT</u> AT~you(mp) from~ UNDER BURDEN~s "Mits'rayim ^{STRAIT~s2}" and~ *I~did~make*~<u>DELIVER</u> AT~you(mp) from~ SERVICE~them(m) and~*I~did*~<u>REDEEM</u> AT~ you(mp) in~ARM <u>EXTEND</u>~*ed(fs)* and~in~ JUDGMENT~s GREAT~s□

<because of this> , say to {the} sons {of} "Yisra'el ^{He turns El aside}", I {am} "Yhwh ^{He is}", and I will make you go out from under {the} burdens {of} "Mits'rayim ^{Two straits}", and I will deliver you from their service, and I will redeem you (with) {an} extended arm, and (with) great judgments,□

6:7 וְלָקַחְתִּי אֶתְכֶם לִי לְעָם וְהָיִיתִי לָכֶם לֵאלֹהִים וִידַעְתֶּם כִּי אֲנִי יְהֹוָה אֱלֹהֵיכֶם הַמּוֹצִיא אֶתְכֶם מִתַּחַת סִבְלוֹת מִצְרָיִם

we'la'qahh'ti et'khem li le'am we'hai'yi'ti la'khem ley'lo'him wi'da'tem ki a'ni YHWH e'lo'hey'khem ha'mo'tsi et'khem mi'ta'hhat siv'lot mits'ra'yim

and~*I~did*~<u>TAKE</u> AT~you(mp) to~me to~ PEOPLE and~*I~did*~<u>EXIST</u> to~you(mp) to~ "Elohiym ^{POWER~s}" and~*you(mp)~did*~<u>KNOW</u> GIVEN-THAT I "Yhwh ^{he~will~}<u>BE</u>" "Elohiym ^{POWER~s}"~you(mp) the~*make*~<u>GO-OUT</u>~ *ing/er(ms)* AT~you(mp) from~UNDER BURDEN~s "Mits'rayim ^{STRAIT~s2}"□

and I will take you (for) me (for) {a} people, and I will exist (for) you (for) "Elohiym ^{Powers}", and you will know that I {am} "Yhwh ^{He is}" your "Elohiym ^{Powers}", the {one} making you go out from under {the} burdens {of} "Mits'rayim ^{Two straits}",□

6:8 וְהֵבֵאתִי אֶתְכֶם אֶל הָאָרֶץ אֲשֶׁר נָשָׂאתִי אֶת יָדִי לָתֵת אֹתָהּ לְאַבְרָהָם לְיִצְחָק וּלְיַעֲקֹב וְנָתַתִּי אֹתָהּ לָכֶם מוֹרָשָׁה אֲנִי יְהֹוָה

we'hey'vey'ti et'khem el ha'a'rets a'sher na'sa'ti et ya'di la'teyt o'tah le'av'ra'ham le'yits'hhaq ul'ya'a'qov we'na'ta'ti o'tah la'khem mo'ra'shah a'ni YHWH

and~*I~will~make*~<u>COME</u> AT~you(mp) TO the~LAND WHICH *I~did*~<u>LIFT-UP</u> AT HAND~ me to~>~<u>GIVE</u> AT~her to~"Avraham ^{FATHER~+~} ^{LIFTED}" to~"Yits'hhaq ^{he~will~}<u>LAUGH</u>" and~to~ "Ya'aqov ^{he~will~}<u>RESTRAIN</u>" and~*I~did*~<u>GIVE</u> AT~

and I will [bring] you to the land which I lifted up (with) my hand to give to "Avraham ^{Father lifted}", to "Yits'hhaq ^{He laughs}", and to "Ya'aqov ^{He restrains}", and I gave her* to you {for}† {a} possession, I {am} "Yhwh ^{He is}",□

---

* Referring to the "land," a feminine word in Hebrew.

† The word "Possession" appears to be missing the prefix "to," which would then be translated as "for a possession,"

Mechanical Translation Codes

<u>WORD</u> – Verb	WORD – Noun	Word – Name	word – Pre/Suff	*word* – Conj.

her to~you(mp) POSSESSION I "Yhwh ^{he~will~}
^{BE}"□

6:9 וַיְדַבֵּר מֹשֶׁה כֵּן אֶל בְּנֵי יִשְׂרָאֵל וְלֹא שָׁמְעוּ אֶל מֹשֶׁה מִקֹּצֶר רוּחַ
וּמֵעֲבֹדָה קָשָׁה

wai'da'beyr mo'sheh keyn el be'ney yis'ra'eyl we'lo sham'u el mo'sheh mi'qo'tser ru'ahh
u'me'a'vo'dah qa'shah

and~he~will~much~SPEAK "Mosheh ^{PLUCKED-}
^{OUT}" SO TO SON~s "Yisra'el ^{he~will~TURN-ASIDE~+~}
^{MIGHTY-ONE}" and~NOT *they~did*~HEAR TO
"Mosheh ^{PLUCKED-OUT}" from~SHORTNESS
WIND and~from~SERVICE HARD□

and "Mosheh ^{Plucked out}" spoke to {the} sons {of}
"Yisra'el ^{He turns El aside}", and they did not hear
Mosheh from {the} shortness {of} wind* and
from {the} hard service,□

6:10 וַיְדַבֵּר יְהוָה אֶל מֹשֶׁה לֵּאמֹר

wai'da'beyr YHWH el mo'sheh ley'mor

and~he~will~much~SPEAK "Yhwh ^{he~will~BE}"
TO "Mosheh ^{PLUCKED-OUT}" to~>~SAY□

and "Yhwh ^{He is}" spoke to "Mosheh ^{Plucked out}"
say{ing},□

6:11 בֹּא דַבֵּר אֶל פַּרְעֹה מֶלֶךְ מִצְרָיִם וִישַׁלַּח אֶת בְּנֵי יִשְׂרָאֵל מֵאַרְצוֹ

bo da'beyr el par'oh me'lekh mits'ra'yim wi'sha'lahh et be'ney yis'ra'eyl mey'ar'tso

!(ms)~COME !(ms)~much~SPEAK TO "Paroh
^{GREAT-HOUSE}" KING "Mits'rayim ^{STRAIT~s2}" and~
he~will~SEND AT SON~s "Yisra'el ^{he~will~TURN-}
^{ASIDE~+~MIGHTY-ONE}" from~LAND~him□

come, speak to "Paroh ^{Great house}", king {of}
"Mits'rayim ^{Two straits}", and he will send {the}
sons {of} "Yisra'el ^{He turns El aside}" from his land,□

6:12 וַיְדַבֵּר מֹשֶׁה לִפְנֵי יְהוָה לֵאמֹר הֵן בְּנֵי יִשְׂרָאֵל לֹא שָׁמְעוּ אֵלַי וְאֵיךְ
יִשְׁמָעֵנִי פַרְעֹה וַאֲנִי עֲרַל שְׂפָתָיִם

wai'da'beyr mo'sheh liph'ney YHWH ley'mor heyn be'ney yis'ra'eyl lo sham'u ey'lai
we'eykh yish'ma'ey'ni phar'oh wa'ani a'ral se'pha'ta'yim

and~he~will~much~SPEAK "Mosheh ^{PLUCKED-}
^{OUT}" to~FACE~s "Yhwh ^{he~will~BE}" to~>~SAY
THOUGH SON~s "Yisra'el ^{he~will~TURN-ASIDE~+~}
^{MIGHTY-ONE}" NOT *they~did*~HEAR TO~me and~
HOW *he~will*~HEAR~me "Paroh ^{GREAT-HOUSE}"
and~I UNCIRCUMCISED LIP~s2□

and "Mosheh ^{Plucked out}" spoke <in front of>
"Yhwh ^{He is}" say{ing}, (since) {the} sons {of}
"Yisra'el ^{He turns El aside}" |had| not heard me,
(then) how will "Paroh ^{Great house}" hear me and I
{am of} uncircumcised lips?□

6:13 וַיְדַבֵּר יְהוָה אֶל מֹשֶׁה וְאֶל אַהֲרֹן וַיְצַוֵּם אֶל בְּנֵי יִשְׂרָאֵל וְאֶל פַּרְעֹה
מֶלֶךְ מִצְרָיִם לְהוֹצִיא אֶת בְּנֵי יִשְׂרָאֵל מֵאֶרֶץ מִצְרָיִם

wai'da'beyr YHWH el mo'sheh we'el a'ha'ron wai'tsa'weym el be'ney yis'ra'eyl we'el

---

* The phrase "shortness of wind," being paralleled with "hard service," means "shortness of
breath."

Revised Mechanical Translation Codes

(..) Alt Trans/App A	<..> Comp Phrase/App B	[..] Verb Form/App C	\../ Plural Form/App D
:..: Int Inf Abs	|..| Past Perf Verb	{...} Added Word	

par'oh me'lekh mits'ra'yim le'ho'tsi et be'ney yis'ra'eyl mey'e'rets mits'ra'yim

and~*he~will~much~*<u>SPEAK</u> "Yhwh *he~will~*<u>BE</u>„ TO "Mosheh PLUCKED-OUT„ and~TO "Aharon LIGHT-BRINGER„ and~*he~will~much~*<u>DIRECT</u>~ them(m) TO SON~s "Yisra'el *he~will~*<u>TURN-ASIDE</u>~+~ MIGHTY-ONE„ and~TO "Paroh GREAT-HOUSE„ KING "Mits'rayim STRAIT~s2„ to~>~*make~*<u>GO-OUT</u> AT SON~s "Yisra'el *he~will~*<u>TURN-ASIDE</u>~+~MIGHTY-ONE„ from~LAND "Mits'rayim STRAIT~s2„ □	and "Yhwh He is„ spoke to "Mosheh Plucked out„ and to "Aharon Light bringer„, and he directed them to {the} sons {of} "Yisra'el He turns El aside„ and to "Paroh Great house„, king {of} "Mits'rayim Two straits„, to make {the} sons {of} "Yisra'el He turns El aside„ go out from {the} land {of} "Mits'rayim Two straits„, □

6:14 אֵלֶּה רָאשֵׁי בֵית אֲבֹתָם בְּנֵי רְאוּבֵן בְּכֹר יִשְׂרָאֵל חֲנוֹךְ וּפַלּוּא חֶצְרֹן וְכַרְמִי אֵלֶּה מִשְׁפְּחֹת רְאוּבֵן

ey'leh ra'shey veyt a'vo'tam be'ney re'u'veyn e'khor yis'ra'eyl hha'nokh u'pha'lu hhets'ron we'khar'mi ey'leh mish'pe'hhot re'u'veyn

THESE HEAD~s HOUSE FATHER~s~them(m) SON~s "Re'uven <u>SEE</u>~+~!(ms)~+~SON„ FIRSTBORN "Yisra'el *he~will~*<u>TURN-ASIDE</u>~+~MIGHTY-ONE„ "Hhanokh DEVOTED„ and~"Palu PERFORMING„ "Hhetsron SURROUNDED-BY-A-WALL„ and~"Karmi VINEYARD~me„ THESE FAMILY~s "Re'uven <u>SEE</u>~+~!(ms)~+~SON„ □	these {are the} heads {of the} house {of} their fathers, {the} sons {of} "Re'uven See a son„, firstborn {of} "Yisra'el He turns El aside„, "Hhanokh Devoted„ and "Palu Performing„, "Hhetsron Surrounded by a wall„ and "Karmi My vineyard„, these {are the} families {of} "Re'uven See a son„, □

6:15 וּבְנֵי שִׁמְעוֹן יְמוּאֵל וְיָמִין וְאֹהַד וְיָכִין וְצֹחַר וְשָׁאוּל בֶּן הַכְּנַעֲנִית אֵלֶּה מִשְׁפְּחֹת שִׁמְעוֹן

uv'ney shim'on ye'mu'eyl we'ya'min we'o'had we'ya'khin we'tso'hhar we'sha'ul ben ha'ke'na'a'nit ey'leh mish'pe'hhot shim'on

and~SON~s "Shimon HEARER„ "Yemu'el DAY~+~MIGHTY-ONE„ and~"Yamin RIGHT-HAND„ and~"Ohad SHOUTING„ and~"Yakhin *he~will~*<u>PREPARE</u>„ and~ "Tsohhar REDDISH-GRAY„ and~"Sha'ul <u>ENQUIRE</u>~ ed(ms)„ SON the~"Kena'an LOWERED~s THESE FAMILY~s "Shimon HEARER„ □	and {the} sons {of} "Shimon Hearer„, "Yemu'el Day of El„ and "Yamin Right hand„ and "Ohad Shouting„ and "Yakhin He will prepare„ and "Tsohhar Reddish gray„ and "Sha'ul Enquired„, {a} son {of} the {one}s {of} "Kena'an Lowered„, these {are the} families {of} "Shimon Hearer„, □

6:16 וְאֵלֶּה שְׁמוֹת בְּנֵי לֵוִי לְתֹלְדֹתָם גֵּרְשׁוֹן וּקְהָת וּמְרָרִי וּשְׁנֵי חַיֵּי לֵוִי שֶׁבַע וּשְׁלֹשִׁים וּמְאַת שָׁנָה

we'ey'leh she'mot be'ney ley'wi le'tol'do'tam geyr'shon uq'hat um'ra'ri ush'ney hhai'yey ley'wi she'va ush'lo'shim um'at sha'nah

and~THESE TITLE~s SON~s "Lewi JOINING~me„ to~BIRTHING~s~them(m) "Gershon EVICTED„ and~"Qehat ALLIED„ and~"Merari BITTERNESS~me„ and~YEAR~s LIVING~s "Lewi JOINING~me„ SEVEN and~THREE~s and~HUNDRED YEAR□	and these {are the} titles {of the} sons {of} "Lewi My joining„, to their birthings, "Gershon Evicted„ and "Qehat Allied„ and "Merari My bitterness„, and {the} years {of the} \life/ {of} "Lewi My joining„ {is} seven and \thirty/ and {a} hundred year{s}, □

6:17 בְּנֵי גֵרְשׁוֹן לִבְנִי וְשִׁמְעִי לְמִשְׁפְּחֹתָם

be'ney ger'shon liv'ni we'shim'i le'mish'pe'hho'tam

SON~s "Gershon ^{EVICTED}" "Liyvniy ^{WHITE~me}" and~"Shiymiy ^{REPORT~me}" to~FAMILY~s~ them(m)□

{the} sons {of} "Gershon ^{Evicted}", "Liyvniy ^{My white}" and "Shiymiy ^{My report}", to their families,□

6:18 וּבְנֵי קְהָת עַמְרָם וְיִצְהָר וְחֶבְרוֹן וְעֻזִּיאֵל וּשְׁנֵי חַיֵּי קְהָת שָׁלֹשׁ וּשְׁלֹשִׁים וּמְאַת שָׁנָה

uv'ney qe'hat am'ram we'yits'har we'hhev'ron we'u'zi'eyl ush'ney hhai'yey qe'hat sha'losh ush'lo'shim um'at sha'nah

and~SON~s "Qehat ^{ALLIED}" "Amram ^{PEOPLE~+~RAISED}" and~"Yits'har ^{he~will~PRESS-OUT-OIL}" and~ "Hhevron ^{ASSOCIATION}" and~"Uziy'eyl ^{BOLDNESS~ me~+~MIGHTY-ONE}" and~YEAR~s LIVING~s "Qehat ^{ALLIED}" THREE and~THREE~s and~HUNDRED YEAR□

and {the} sons {of} "Qehat ^{Allied}", "Amram ^{People raised}" and "Yits'har ^{He presses out oil}" and "Hhevron ^{Association}" and "Uziy'eyl ^{My boldness is El}", and {the} years {of the} \life/ {of} "Qehat ^{Allied}" {is} three and \thirty/ and {a} hundred year{s},□

6:19 וּבְנֵי מְרָרִי מַחְלִי וּמוּשִׁי אֵלֶּה מִשְׁפְּחֹת הַלֵּוִי לְתֹלְדֹתָם

uv'ney me'ra'ri mahh'li u'mush'i ey'leh mish'pe'hhot ha'ley'wi le'tol'do'tam

and~SON~s "Merari ^{BITTERNESS~me}" "Mahh'liy ^{SICKNESS~me}" and~"Mushiy ^{MOVING~me}" THESE FAMILY~s the~"Lewi ^{JOINING~me}" to~ BIRTHING~s~them(m)□

and {the} sons {of} "Merari ^{My bitterness}", "Mahh'liy ^{My sickness}" and "Mushiy ^{My moving}", these {are the} families {of} the "Lewi ^{My joining}" to their birthings,□

6:20 וַיִּקַּח עַמְרָם אֶת יוֹכֶבֶד דֹּדָתוֹ לוֹ לְאִשָּׁה וַתֵּלֶד לוֹ אֶת אַהֲרֹן וְאֶת מֹשֶׁה וּשְׁנֵי חַיֵּי עַמְרָם שֶׁבַע וּשְׁלֹשִׁים וּמְאַת שָׁנָה

wai'yi'qahh am'ram et yo'khe'ved do'da'to lo le'i'shah wa'tey'led lo et a'ha'ron we'et mo'sheh ush'ney hhai'yey am'ram she'va ush'lo'shim um'at sha'nah

and~he~will~<u>TAKE</u> "Amram ^{PEOPLE~+~RAISED}" AT "Yokheved ^{EXISTING~+~HEAVY}" AUNT~him to~him to~WOMAN and~ she~<u>will~BRING-FORTH</u> to~him AT "Aharon ^{LIGHT-BRINGER}" and~AT "Mosheh ^{PLUCKED-OUT}" and~YEAR~s LIVING~s "Amram ^{PEOPLE~+~RAISED}" SEVEN and~THREE~s and~HUNDRED YEAR□

and "Amram ^{People raised}" took "Yokheved ^{Yah is heavy}", his aunt, (for) him (for) {a} woman, and she brought forth (for) him, "Aharon ^{Light bringer}" and "Mosheh ^{Plucked out}", and {the} years {of the} \life/ {of} "Amram ^{People raised}" {is} seven and \thirty/ and {a} hundred year{s},□

6:21 וּבְנֵי יִצְהָר קֹרַח וָנֶפֶג וְזִכְרִי

uv'ney yits'har qo'rahh wa'ne'pheg we'zikh'ri

and~SON~s "Yits'har ^{he~will~PRESS-OUT-OIL}" "Qorahh ^{BALDING}" and~"Nepheg ^{SPROUT-UP}" and~"Zikh'riy ^{MEMORIAL~me}"□

and {the} sons {of} "Yits'har ^{He presses out oil}", "Qorahh ^{Balding}" and "Nepheg ^{Sprout up}" and "Zikh'riy ^{My memorial}",□

6:22 וּבְנֵי עֻזִּיאֵל מִישָׁאֵל וְאֶלְצָפָן וְסִתְרִי

uv'ney u'zi'eyl mi'sha'eyl we'el'tsa'phon we'sit'ri

and~SON~s "Uziy'eyl BOLDNESS~me~+~MIGHTY-ONE" "Miysha'eyl WHO~+~he~did~ENQUIRE" and~ "Eliytsaphan MIGHTY-ONE~me~+~he~did~CONCEAL" and~"Sitriy PROTECTION~me" □

and {the} sons {of} "Uziy'eyl My boldness is El", "Miysha'eyl Who enquired" and "Eliytsaphan My El conceals" and "Sitriy My hiding", □

6:23 וַיִּקַּח אַהֲרֹן אֶת אֱלִישֶׁבַע בַּת עַמִּינָדָב אֲחוֹת נַחְשׁוֹן לוֹ לְאִשָּׁה וַתֵּלֶד לוֹ אֶת נָדָב וְאֶת אֲבִיהוּא אֶת אֶלְעָזָר וְאֶת אִיתָמָר

wai'yi'qahh a'ha'ron et e'li'she'va bat a'mi'na'dav a'hhot nahh'shon lo le'i'shah wa'tey'led lo et na'dav we'et a'vi'hu et el'a'zar we'et i'ta'mar

and~he~will~TAKE "Aharon LIGHT-BRINGER" AT "Eliysheva MIGHTY-ONE~me~+~he~did~SWEAR" DAUGHTER "Amiynadav PEOPLE~me~+~OFFERED-WILLINGLY" SISTER "Nahhshon DIVINER" to~him to~WOMAN and~ she~will~BRING-FORTH to~him AT "Nadav he~did~OFFER-WILLINGLY" and~ AT "Aviyhu FATHER~me~+~HE" AT "Elazar MIGHTY-ONE~+~he~did~HELP" and~AT "Iytamar ISLAND~+~DATE-PALM" □

and "Aharon Light bringer" took "Eliysheva My El swears", daughter {of} "Amiynadav My people offered willingly", sister {of} "Nahhshon Diviner", (for) him (for) {a} woman, and she brought forth (for) him "Nadav He offered willingly" and "Aviyhu He is my father", "Elazar El helps" and "Iytamar Island of the date palm", □

6:24 וּבְנֵי קֹרַח אַסִּיר וְאֶלְקָנָה וַאֲבִיאָסָף אֵלֶּה מִשְׁפְּחֹת הַקָּרְחִי

uv'ney qo'rahh a'sir we'el'qa'nah wa'a'vi'a'saph ey'leh mish'pe'hhot ha'qar'hhi

and~SON~s "Qorahh BALDING" "Asiyr PRISONER" and~"Elqanah MIGHTY-ONE~+~he~did~PURCHASE" and~ "Aviyasaph FATHER~me~+~he~did~GATHER" THESE FAMILY~s the~"Qorahh BALDING"~of □

and {the} sons {of} "Qorahh Balding", "Asiyr Prisoner" and "Elqanah El purchased" and "Aviyasaph My father gathers", these {are the} families {of} the {one} of "Qorahh Balding", □

6:25 וְאֶלְעָזָר בֶּן אַהֲרֹן לָקַח לוֹ מִבְּנוֹת פּוּטִיאֵל לוֹ לְאִשָּׁה וַתֵּלֶד לוֹ אֶת פִּינְחָס אֵלֶּה רָאשֵׁי אֲבוֹת הַלְוִיִּם לְמִשְׁפְּחֹתָם

we'el'a'zar ben a'ha'ron la'qahh lo mi'be'not pu'ti'eyl lo le'i'shah wa'tey'led lo et pin'hhas ey'leh ra'shey a'vot hal'wi'yim le'mish'pe'hho'tam

and~"Elazar MIGHTY-ONE~+~he~did~HELP" SON "Aharon LIGHT-BRINGER" he~did~TAKE to~him from~DAUGHTER~s "Puthiy'eyl BELONGING~of~+~MIGHTY-ONE" to~him to~WOMAN and~ she~will~BRING-FORTH to~him AT "Piynhhas MOUTH~+~SERPENT" THESE HEAD~s FATHER~s the~"Lewi JOINING~me"~s to~FAMILY~s~ them(m) □

and "Elazar El helps", son {of} "Aharon Light bringer", |had| taken (for) him from {the} daughters {of} "Puthiy'eyl Belonging of El", (for) him (for) {a} woman, and she brought forth (for) him "Piynhhas Mouth of the serpent", these {are the} heads {of the} fathers {of} the {one}s {of} "Lewi My joining" to their families, □

6:26 הוּא אַהֲרֹן וּמֹשֶׁה אֲשֶׁר אָמַר יְהוָה לָהֶם הוֹצִיאוּ אֶת בְּנֵי יִשְׂרָאֵל מֵאֶרֶץ מִצְרַיִם עַל צִבְאֹתָם

hu a'ha'ron u'mo'sheh a'sher a'mar YHWH la'hem ho'tsi'u et be'ney yis'ra'eyl mey'e'rets

Mechanical Translation Codes

| <u>WORD</u> – Verb | WORD – Noun | Word – Name | word – Pre/Suff | *word* – Conj. |

mits'ra'yim al tsiv'o'tam

HE "Aharon ^{LIGHT-BRINGER}" and~"Mosheh ^{PLUCKED-OUT}" WHICH *he~did~*SAY "Yhwh ^{he~will~BE}" to~them(m) !(mp)~make~GO-OUT AT SON~s "Yisra'el ^{he~will~TURN-ASIDE~+~MIGHTY-ONE}" from~LAND "Mits'rayim ^{STRAIT~s2}" UPON ARMY~s~them(m)□

(this) {is} (what) "Yhwh ^{He is}" said to "Aharon ^{Light bringer}" and "Mosheh ^{Plucked out}", make {the} sons {of} "Yisra'el ^{He turns El aside}" go out from {the} land {of} "Mits'rayim ^{Two straits}" upon their armies,□

6:27 הֵם הַמְדַבְּרִים אֶל פַּרְעֹה מֶלֶךְ מִצְרַיִם לְהוֹצִיא אֶת בְּנֵי יִשְׂרָאֵל מִמִּצְרָיִם הוּא מֹשֶׁה וְאַהֲרֹן

heym ham'da'be'rim el par'oh me'lekh mits'ra'yim le'ho'tsi et be'ney yis'ra'eyl mi'mits'ra'yim hu mo'sheh we'a'ha'ron

THEY(m) the~*much~*SPEAK~ing/er(mp) TO "Paroh ^{GREAT-HOUSE}" KING "Mits'rayim ^{STRAIT~s2}" to~>~*make~*GO-OUT AT SON~s "Yisra'el ^{he~will~TURN-ASIDE~+~MIGHTY-ONE}" from~"Mits'rayim ^{STRAIT~s2}" HE "Mosheh ^{PLUCKED-OUT}" and~ "Aharon ^{LIGHT-BRINGER}"□

they, the {one}s speaking to "Paroh ^{Great house}", king {of} "Mits'rayim ^{Two straits}", {are} to make {the} sons {of} "Yisra'el ^{He turns El aside}" go out from "Mits'rayim ^{Two straits}", (this) {is} "Mosheh ^{Plucked out}" and "Aharon ^{Light bringer}",□

6:28 וַיְהִי בְּיוֹם דִּבֶּר יְהוָה אֶל מֹשֶׁה בְּאֶרֶץ מִצְרָיִם

wai'hi be'yom di'ber YHWH el mo'sheh be'e'rets mits'ra'yim

and~*he~will~*EXIST in~DAY *he~did~much~*SPEAK "Yhwh ^{he~will~BE}" TO "Mosheh ^{PLUCKED-OUT}" in~LAND "Mits'rayim ^{STRAIT~s2}"□

and (it) (came to pass), in {the} day "Yhwh ^{He is}" spoke to "Mosheh ^{Plucked out}" in {the} land {of} "Mits'rayim ^{Two straits}",□

6:29 וַיְדַבֵּר יְהוָה אֶל מֹשֶׁה לֵּאמֹר אֲנִי יְהוָה דַּבֵּר אֶל פַּרְעֹה מֶלֶךְ מִצְרָיִם אֵת כָּל אֲשֶׁר אֲנִי דֹבֵר אֵלֶיךָ

wai'da'beyr YHWH el mo'sheh ley'mor a'ni YHWH da'beyr el par'oh me'lekh mits'ra'yim eyt kol a'sher a'ni do'veyr ey'ley'kha

and~*he~will~much~*SPEAK "Yhwh ^{he~will~BE}" TO "Mosheh ^{PLUCKED-OUT}" to~>~SAY I "Yhwh ^{he~will~BE}" !(ms)~*much~*SPEAK TO "Paroh ^{GREAT-HOUSE}" KING "Mits'rayim ^{STRAIT~s2}" AT ALL WHICH I SPEAK~ing/er(ms) TO~you(ms)□

and "Yhwh ^{He is}" spoke to "Mosheh ^{Plucked out}" say{ing}, I {am} "Yhwh ^{He is}", speak to "Paroh ^{Great house}", king {of} "Mits'rayim ^{Two straits}", all which I {am} speaking to you,□

6:30 וַיֹּאמֶר מֹשֶׁה לִפְנֵי יְהוָה הֵן אֲנִי עֲרַל שְׂפָתַיִם וְאֵיךְ יִשְׁמַע אֵלַי פַּרְעֹה

wai'yo'mer mo'sheh liph'ney YHWH heyn a'ni a'ral she'pha'ta'yim we'eykh yish'ma ey'lai par'oh

and~*he~will~*SAY "Mosheh ^{PLUCKED-OUT}" to~FACE~s "Yhwh ^{he~will~BE}" THOUGH I UNCIRCUMCISED LIP~s2 and~HOW *he~will~*HEAR TO~me "Paroh ^{GREAT-HOUSE}"□

and "Mosheh ^{Plucked out}" said <in front of> "Yhwh ^{He is}", (since) I {am of} uncircumcised lips, (then) how will "Paroh ^{Great house}" hear me?□

Chapter 7

7:1 וַיֹּאמֶר יְהֹוָה אֶל מֹשֶׁה רְאֵה נְתַתִּיךָ אֱלֹהִים לְפַרְעֹה וְאַהֲרֹן אָחִיךָ יִהְיֶה נְבִיאֶךָ

wai'yo'mer YHWH el mo'sheh re'eyh ne'ta'ti'kha e'lo'hiym le'phar'oh we'a'ha'ron a'hhi'kha yih'yeh ne'vi'e'kha

and~*he~will~*<u>SAY</u> "Yhwh ^{*he~will~*<u>BE</u>}" TO "Mosheh ^{PLUCKED-OUT}" !(*ms*)~<u>SEE</u> *I~did~*<u>GIVE</u>~ you(ms) "Elohiym ^{POWER~s}" to~"Paroh ^{GREAT-HOUSE}" and~"Aharon ^{LIGHT-BRINGER}" BROTHER~ you(ms) *he~will~*<u>EXIST</u> PROPHET~you(ms)□

and "Yhwh ^{He is}" said to "Mosheh ^{Plucked out}", See, I gave you "Elohiym ^{Powers}" (for) "Paroh ^{Great house}", and "Aharon ^{Light bringer}", your brother, he exists {as} your prophet,□

7:2 אַתָּה תְדַבֵּר אֵת כָּל אֲשֶׁר אֲצַוֶּךָּ וְאַהֲרֹן אָחִיךָ יְדַבֵּר אֶל פַּרְעֹה וְשִׁלַּח אֶת בְּנֵי יִשְׂרָאֵל מֵאַרְצוֹ

a'tah te'da'beyr eyt kol a'sher a'tsa'we'kha we'a'ha'ron a'hhi'kha ye'da'beyr el par'oh we'shi'lahh et be'ney yis'ra'eyl mey'ar'tso

YOU(ms) *you(ms)~will~much~*<u>SPEAK</u> AT ALL WHICH *I~will~much~*<u>DIRECT</u>~you(ms) and~ "Aharon ^{LIGHT-BRINGER}" BROTHER~you(ms) *he~ will~much~*<u>SPEAK</u> TO "Paroh ^{GREAT-HOUSE}" and~*he~did~much~*<u>SEND</u> AT SON~s "Yisra'el ^{*he~will~*<u>TURN-ASIDE</u>~+~<u>MIGHTY-ONE</u>}" from~LAND~him□

you, you will speak all which I will direct you, and "Aharon ^{Light bringer}", your brother, will speak to "Paroh ^{Great house}" and he will send {the} sons {of} "Yisra'el ^{He turns El aside}" from his land,□

7:3 וַאֲנִי אַקְשֶׁה אֶת לֵב פַּרְעֹה וְהִרְבֵּיתִי אֶת אֹתֹתַי וְאֶת מוֹפְתַי בְּאֶרֶץ מִצְרָיִם

wa'ani aq'sheh et leyv par'oh we'hir'bey'ti et o'to'tai we'et moph'tai be'e'rets mits'ra'yim

and~I *I~will~make~*<u>BE-HARD</u> AT HEART "Paroh ^{GREAT-HOUSE}" and~*I~did~make~* <u>INCREASE</u> AT SIGN~s~me and~AT WONDER~s~me in~LAND "Mits'rayim ^{STRAIT~s2}"□

and I will make {the} heart {of} "Paroh ^{Great house}" be hard, and I will make my signs and my wonders increase in {the} land {of} "Mits'rayim ^{Two straits}",□

7:4 וְלֹא יִשְׁמַע אֲלֵכֶם פַּרְעֹה וְנָתַתִּי אֶת יָדִי בְּמִצְרָיִם וְהוֹצֵאתִי אֶת צִבְאֹתַי אֶת עַמִּי בְנֵי יִשְׂרָאֵל מֵאֶרֶץ מִצְרַיִם בִּשְׁפָטִים גְּדֹלִים

we'lo yish'ma a'ley'khem par'oh we'na'ta'ti et ya'di be'mits'ra'yim we'ho'tsey'ti et tsiv'o'tai et a'mi ve'ney yis'ra'eyl mey'e'rets mits'ra'yim bish'pha'tim ge'do'lim

and~NOT *he~will~*<u>HEAR</u> TO~you(mp) "Paroh ^{GREAT-HOUSE}" and~*I~did~*<u>GIVE</u> AT HAND~me in~ "Mits'rayim ^{STRAIT~s2}" and~*I~did~make~*<u>GO-OUT</u> AT ARMY~s~me AT PEOPLE~me SON~s

and "Paroh ^{Great house}" will not hear you, and I will give my hand in "Mits'rayim ^{Two straits}", and I will make my armies, my people, {the} sons {of} "Yisra'el ^{He turns El aside}", go out from {the}

Mechanical Translation Codes

<u>WORD</u> – Verb	WORD – Noun	Word – Name	word – Pre/Suff	*word* – Conj.

"Yisra'el ^{he~will~TURN-ASIDE~+~MIGHTY-ONE}" from~ LAND "Mits'rayim ^{STRAIT~s2}" in~JUDGMENT~s GREAT~s□

land {of} "Mits'rayim ^{Two straits}" (with) great judgments,□

7:5

וְיָדְעוּ מִצְרַיִם כִּי אֲנִי יְהוָה בִּנְטֹתִי אֶת יָדִי עַל מִצְרָיִם וְהוֹצֵאתִי אֶת בְּנֵי יִשְׂרָאֵל מִתּוֹכָם

we'yad'u mits'ra'yim ki a'ni YHWH bin'to'ti et ya'di al mits'ra'yim we'ho'tsey'ti et be'ney yis'ra'eyl mit'o'kham

and~*they~did~*KNOW "Mits'rayim ^{STRAIT~s2}" GIVEN-THAT I "Yhwh ^{he~will~BE}" in~>~EXTEND~ me AT HAND~me UPON "Mits'rayim ^{STRAIT~s2}" and~*I~did~make~*GO-OUT AT SON~s "Yisra'el ^{he~will~TURN-ASIDE~+~MIGHTY-ONE}" from~ MIDST~them(m)□

and "Mits'rayim ^{Two straits}" will know that I {am} "Yhwh ^{He is}" (with) my extending {of} my hand upon "Mits'rayim ^{Two straits}", and I will make {the} sons {of} "Yisra'el ^{He turns El aside}" go out from {the} midst {of} them,□

7:6

וַיַּעַשׂ מֹשֶׁה וְאַהֲרֹן כַּאֲשֶׁר צִוָּה יְהוָה אֹתָם כֵּן עָשׂוּ

wai'ya'as mo'sheh we'a'ha'ron ka'a'sheyr tsi'wah YHWH o'tam keyn a'su

and~*he~will~*DO "Mosheh ^{PLUCKED-OUT}" and~ "Aharon ^{LIGHT-BRINGER}" like~WHICH *he~did~* much~DIRECT "Yhwh ^{he~will~BE}" AT~them(m) SO *they~did~*DO□

and "Mosheh ^{Plucked out}" did, and "Aharon ^{Light bringer}", <just as> "Yhwh ^{He is}" directed them, so they did,□

7:7

וּמֹשֶׁה בֶּן שְׁמֹנִים שָׁנָה וְאַהֲרֹן בֶּן שָׁלֹשׁ וּשְׁמֹנִים שָׁנָה בְּדַבְּרָם אֶל פַּרְעֹה

u'mo'sheh ben she'mo'nim sha'nah we'a'ha'ron ben sha'losh u'she'mo'nim sha'nah be'da'be'ram el par'oh

and~"Mosheh ^{PLUCKED-OUT}" SON EIGHT~s YEAR and~"Aharon ^{LIGHT-BRINGER}" SON THREE and~ EIGHT~s YEAR in~>~*much~*SPEAK~them(m) TO "Paroh ^{GREAT-HOUSE}"□

and "Mosheh ^{Plucked out}" {was a} son {of} \eighty/ year{s}* and "Aharon ^{Light bringer}" {was a} son {of} three and \eighty/ year{s} in their speaking to "Paroh ^{Great house}",□

7:8

וַיֹּאמֶר יְהוָה אֶל מֹשֶׁה וְאֶל אַהֲרֹן לֵאמֹר

wai'yo'mer YHWH el mo'sheh we'el a'ha'ron ley'mor

and~*he~will~*SAY "Yhwh ^{he~will~BE}" TO "Mosheh ^{PLUCKED-OUT}" and~TO "Aharon ^{LIGHT-BRINGER}" to~>~SAY□

and "Yhwh ^{He is}" said to "Mosheh ^{Plucked out}" and to "Aharon ^{Light bringer}" say{ing},□

7:9

כִּי יְדַבֵּר אֲלֵכֶם פַּרְעֹה לֵאמֹר תְּנוּ לָכֶם מוֹפֵת וְאָמַרְתָּ אֶל אַהֲרֹן קַח אֶת מַטְּךָ וְהַשְׁלֵךְ לִפְנֵי פַרְעֹה יְהִי לְתַנִּין

ki ye'da'beyr a'ley'khem par'oh ley'mor te'nu la'khem mo'pheyt we'a'mar'ta el a'ha'ron

---

* "A son of..." is an idiom for the age of a person.

Revised Mechanical Translation Codes

| (..) Alt Trans/App A | <..> Comp Phrase/App B | [..] Verb Form/App C | \../ Plural Form/App D |
| :..: Int Inf Abs | \|..\| Past Perf Verb | {...} Added Word | |

qahh et mat'kha we'hash'leykh liph'ney phar'oh ye'hi le'ta'nin

GIVEN-THAT *he~will~much~*<u>SPEAK</u> TO~ you(mp) "Paroh ^{GREAT-HOUSE},, to~>~<u>SAY</u> !(mp)~ <u>GIVE</u> to~you(mp) WONDER and~*you(ms)~ did~*<u>SAY</u> TO "Aharon ^{LIGHT-BRINGER},, !(ms)~<u>TAKE</u> AT BRANCH~you(ms) and~*!(ms)~make~* <u>THROW-OUT</u> to~FACE~s "Paroh ^{GREAT-HOUSE},, *he~will~*<u>EXIST</u> to~TANIYN□

given that "Paroh ^{Great house},, will speak to you say{ing}, give (for) you {a} wonder, and you will say to "Aharon ^{Light bringer},, take your branch and throw {it} out <in front of> "Paroh ^{Great house},, he will exist (as) {a} taniyn*, □

7:10 וַיָּבֹא מֹשֶׁה וְאַהֲרֹן אֶל פַּרְעֹה וַיַּעֲשׂוּ כֵן כַּאֲשֶׁר צִוָּה יְהוָה וַיַּשְׁלֵךְ אַהֲרֹן אֶת מַטֵּהוּ לִפְנֵי פַרְעֹה וְלִפְנֵי עֲבָדָיו וַיְהִי לְתַנִּין

wai'ya'vo mo'sheh we'a'ha'ron el par'oh wai'ya'a'su kheyn ka'a'sheyr tsi'wah YHWH wai'yash'leykh a'ha'ron et ma'tey'hu liph'ney phar'oh we'liph'ney a'va'daw wai'hi le'ta'nin

and~*he~will~*<u>COME</u> "Mosheh ^{PLUCKED-OUT},, and~"Aharon ^{LIGHT-BRINGER},, TO "Paroh ^{GREAT-HOUSE},, and~*they(m)~will~*<u>DO</u> SO like~WHICH *he~did~much~*<u>DIRECT</u> "Yhwh ^{he~will~}<u>BE</u>,, and~ *he~will~make~*<u>THROW-OUT</u> "Aharon ^{LIGHT-BRINGER},, AT BRANCH~him to~FACE~s "Paroh ^{GREAT-HOUSE},, and~to~FACE~s SERVANT~s~him and~*he~will~*<u>EXIST</u> to~TANIYN□

and "Mosheh ^{Plucked out},, came, and "Aharon ^{Light bringer},, to "Paroh ^{Great house},, and they did so, <just as> "Yhwh ^{He is},, directed, and "Aharon ^{Light bringer},, threw out his branch <in front of> "Paroh ^{Great house},, and <in front of> his servants, and he existed (as) {a} taniyn†, □

7:11 וַיִּקְרָא גַם פַּרְעֹה לַחֲכָמִים וְלַמְכַשְּׁפִים וַיַּעֲשׂוּ גַם הֵם חַרְטֻמֵי מִצְרַיִם בְּלַהֲטֵיהֶם כֵּן

wai'yiq'ra gam par'oh la'hha'kha'mim we'lam'khash'phim wai'ya'a'su gam heym hhar'tu'mey mits'ra'yim be'la'ha'tey'hem keyn

and~*he~will~*<u>CALL-OUT</u> ALSO "Paroh ^{GREAT-HOUSE},, to~SKILLED-ONE~s and~to~*much~* <u>SORCERY</u>~*ing/er*(mp) and~*they(m)~will~*<u>DO</u> ALSO THEY(m) MAGICIAN~s "Mits'rayim ^{STRAIT~s2},, in~BLAZING~s~them(m) SO□

and "Paroh ^{Great house},, also called out to {the} skilled ones and to {the} sorcerers, and they, {the} magicians {of} "Mits'rayim ^{Two straits},, also did so (with) their blazings‡,□

7:12 וַיַּשְׁלִיכוּ אִישׁ מַטֵּהוּ וַיִּהְיוּ לְתַנִּינִם וַיִּבְלַע מַטֵּה אַהֲרֹן אֶת מַטֹּתָם

wai'yash'li'khu ish ma'tey'hu wai'yih'yu le'ta'ni'nim wai'yiv'la ma'tey a'ha'ron et ma'to'tam

---

* This Hebrew word is translated in various ways including; whale, sea-monster, dragon, serpent, asp and jackal (see Genesis 1:21, Deuteronomy 32:33, Nehemiah 2:13, Job 7:12), but its original meaning is unknown.

† The original meaning of this word is unknown (see Footnote in 7:9).

‡ The word "blazing" is the same word used (for) the sword of the Keruv (cherub in most other translations) in Genesis 3:24, but the meaning of its use in this verse is obscure.

Mechanical Translation Codes

<u>WORD</u> – Verb	WORD – Noun	Word – Name	word – Pre/Suff	*word* – Conj.

and~they(m)~will~make~<u>THROW-OUT</u> MAN BRANCH~him and~they(m)~will~<u>EXIST</u> to~ TANIYN~s and~he~will~<u>SWALLOW</u> BRANCH "Aharon ^{LIGHT-BRINGER}" AT BRANCH~s~ them(m)□

and (each) threw* out his branch and they existed (as) taniyns†, and {the} branch {of} "Aharon ^{Light bringer}" swallowed their branches,□

7:13   וַיֶּחֱזַק לֵב פַּרְעֹה וְלֹא שָׁמַע אֲלֵהֶם כַּאֲשֶׁר דִּבֶּר יְהוָה

wa'ye'hhe'zaq leyv par'oh we'lo sha'ma a'ley'hem ka'a'sheyr di'ber YHWH

and~he~will~<u>SEIZE</u> HEART "Paroh ^{GREAT-HOUSE}" and~NOT he~did~<u>HEAR</u> TO~them(m) like~ WHICH he~did~much~<u>SPEAK</u> "Yhwh ^{he~will~BE}"□

and he seized {the} heart‡ {of} "Paroh ^{Great house}" and he did not hear them, <just as> "Yhwh ^{He is}" spoke,□

7:14   וַיֹּאמֶר יְהוָה אֶל מֹשֶׁה כָּבֵד לֵב פַּרְעֹה מֵאֵן לְשַׁלַּח הָעָם

wai'yo'mer YHWH el mo'sheh ka'veyd leyv par'oh mey'eyn le'sha'lahh ha'am

and~he~will~<u>SAY</u> "Yhwh ^{he~will~BE}" TO "Mosheh ^{PLUCKED-OUT}" HEAVY HEART "Paroh ^{GREAT-HOUSE}" he~did~much~<u>REFUSE</u> to~ >~much~<u>SEND</u> the~PEOPLE□

and "Yhwh ^{He is}" said to "Mosheh ^{Plucked out}", heavy {is the} heart {of} "Paroh ^{Great house}", he refuses to send the people,□

7:15   לֵךְ אֶל פַּרְעֹה בַּבֹּקֶר הִנֵּה יֹצֵא הַמַּיְמָה וְנִצַּבְתָּ לִקְרָאתוֹ עַל שְׂפַת הַיְאֹר וְהַמַּטֶּה אֲשֶׁר נֶהְפַּךְ לְנָחָשׁ תִּקַּח בְּיָדֶךָ

leykh el par'oh ba'bo'qer hin'neyh yo'tsey ha'mai'mah we'ni'tsav'ta liq'ra'to al she'phat hai'or we'ha'ma'teh a'sher neh'pakh le'na'hhash ti'qahh be'ya'de'kha

!(ms)~<u>WALK</u> TO "Paroh ^{GREAT-HOUSE}" in~the~ MORNING LOOK <u>GO-OUT</u>~ing/er(ms) the~ WATER~s2~unto and~you(ms)~did~be~ <u>STAND-UP</u> to~>~<u>MEET</u>~him UPON LIP the~ STREAM and~the~BRANCH WHICH he~did~ be~<u>OVERTURN</u> to~SERPENT you(ms)~will~ <u>TAKE</u> in~HAND~you(ms)□

walk to "Paroh ^{Great house}" in the morning, look, {he}§ {is} going out unto the waters, and you will be standing up to meet him upon {the} lip {of} the stream, and the branch, (which) was overturned to {a} serpent, you will take in your hand,□

7:16   וְאָמַרְתָּ אֵלָיו יְהוָה אֱלֹהֵי הָעִבְרִים שְׁלָחַנִי אֵלֶיךָ לֵאמֹר שַׁלַּח אֶת עַמִּי וְיַעַבְדֻנִי בַּמִּדְבָּר וְהִנֵּה לֹא שָׁמַעְתָּ עַד כֹּה

---

* The verb וַיַּשְׁלִיכוּ (and they threw out) identifies the subject of the verb (they) as masculine plural. However, the word אִישׁ (man or each, the subject of the verb) is a masculine singular word. Therefore, the verb should be written as וַיַּשְׁלִיךְ (and he threw out).

† The original meaning of this word is unknown (see Footnote in 7:9).

‡ The phrase וַיֶּחֱזַק לֵב פַּרְעֹה can also be translated as "and the heart seized Paroh" but compare with Exodus 4:21 and 9:12.

§ The Hebrew literally reads, "look, going out," and appears to be missing the word "he."

we'a'mar'ta ey'law YHWH e'lo'hey ha'iv'rim she'la'hha'ni ey'ley'kha ley'mor sha'lahh et a'mi we'ya'av'du'ni ba'mid'bar we'hin'neyh lo sha'ma'ta ad koh

and~*you(ms)~did*~<u>SAY</u> TO~him "Yhwh ^{he~will~}<u>BE</u>" "Elohiym ^{POWER~s} the~"Ever ^{OTHER-SIDE}"~s *he~did~*<u>SEND</u>~me TO~you(ms) to~>~<u>SAY</u> *!(ms)~much~*<u>SEND</u> AT PEOPLE~me and~ *they(m)~will~*<u>SERVE</u>~me in~the~ WILDERNESS and~LOOK NOT *you(ms)~did~* <u>HEAR</u> UNTIL IN-THIS-WAY□	and you will say to him, "Yhwh ^{He is} {the} "Elohiym ^{Powers}" {of} the {one}s {of} "Ever ^{Other side}" sent me to you say{ing}, send my people and they will serve me in the wilderness, and look, you <still> did not hear,□

7:17 כֹּה אָמַר יְהֹוָה בְּזֹאת תֵּדַע כִּי אֲנִי יְהֹוָה הִנֵּה אָנֹכִי מַכֶּה בַּמַּטֶּה אֲשֶׁר בְּיָדִי עַל הַמַּיִם אֲשֶׁר בַּיְאֹר וְנֶהֶפְכוּ לְדָם

koh a'mar YHWH be'zot tey'da ki a'ni YHWH hin'neyh a'no'khi ma'keh ba'ma'teh a'sher be'ya'di al ha'ma'yim a'sher bai'or we'ne'heph'khu le'dam

IN-THIS-WAY *he~did~*<u>SAY</u> "Yhwh ^{he~will~}<u>BE</u>" in~ THIS *you(ms)~will~*<u>KNOW</u> GIVEN-THAT I "Yhwh ^{he~will~}<u>BE</u>" LOOK I *make~*<u>HIT</u>*~ing/er(ms)* in~the~BRANCH WHICH in~HAND~me UPON the~WATER~s2 WHICH in~the~STREAM and~*they~did~be~*<u>OVERTURN</u> to~BLOOD□	in this way, "Yhwh ^{He is}" said, in this you will know that I {am} "Yhwh ^{He is}", look, I {am} hitting, (with) the branch which {is} in my hand, upon the waters which {are} in the stream, and they will be overturned to blood,□

7:18 וְהַדָּגָה אֲשֶׁר בַּיְאֹר תָּמוּת וּבָאַשׁ הַיְאֹר וְנִלְאוּ מִצְרַיִם לִשְׁתּוֹת מַיִם מִן הַיְאֹר

we'ha'da'gah a'sher bai'or ta'mut u'va'ash hai'or we'nil'u mits'ra'yim lish'tot ma'yim min hai'or

and~the~FISH WHICH in~the~STREAM *she~will~*<u>DIE</u> and~*he~did~*<u>STINK</u> the~STREAM and~*they~did~be~*<u>WEARY</u> "Mits'rayim ^{STRAIT~s2}" to~>~<u>GULP</u> WATER~s2 FROM the~ STREAM□	and the fish, which {are} in the stream, will die and the stream will stink, and "Mits'rayim ^{Two straits}" will be {to} weary to gulp waters from the stream,□

7:19 וַיֹּאמֶר יְהֹוָה אֶל מֹשֶׁה אֱמֹר אֶל אַהֲרֹן קַח מַטְּךָ וּנְטֵה יָדְךָ עַל מֵימֵי מִצְרַיִם עַל נַהֲרֹתָם עַל יְאֹרֵיהֶם וְעַל אַגְמֵיהֶם וְעַל כָּל מִקְוֵה מֵימֵיהֶם וְיִהְיוּ דָם וְהָיָה דָם בְּכָל אֶרֶץ מִצְרַיִם וּבָעֵצִים וּבָאֲבָנִים

wai'yo'mer YHWH el mo'sheh e'mor el a'ha'ron qahh mat'kha un'teyh yad'kha al mey'mey mits'ra'yim al na'ha'ro'tam al ye'o'rey'hem we'al ag'mey'hem we'al kol miq'weh mey'mey'hem we'yih'yu dam we'hai'yah dam be'khol e'rets mits'ra'yim u'va'ey'tsim u'va'a'va'nim

and~*he~will~*<u>SAY</u> "Yhwh ^{he~will~}<u>BE</u>" TO "Mosheh ^{PLUCKED-OUT}" *!(ms)~*<u>SAY</u> TO "Aharon ^{LIGHT-BRINGER}" *!(ms)~*<u>TAKE</u> BRANCH~you(ms) and~*!(ms)~*<u>EXTEND</u> HAND~you(ms) UPON WATER~s2 "Mits'rayim ^{STRAIT~s2}" UPON RIVER~s~them(m) UPON STREAM~s~	and "Yhwh ^{He is}" said to "Mosheh ^{Plucked out}", say to "Aharon ^{Light bringer}", take your branch and extend your hand upon {the} waters {of} "Mits'rayim ^{Two straits}", upon their rivers, upon their streams, and upon their pools and upon all {the} collection{s of} their waters, and they

Mechanical Translation Codes

<u>WORD</u> – Verb	WORD – Noun	Word – Name	word – Pre/Suff	*word* – Conj.

them(m) and~UPON POOL~s~them(m) and~
UPON ALL COLLECTION WATER~s2~them(m)
and~*they(m)~will*~EXIST BLOOD and~*he~
did*~EXIST BLOOD in~ALL LAND "Mits'rayim
STRAIT~s2" and~in~the~TREE~s and~in~the~
STONE~s□

will exist {as} blood, and blood will exist in all
{the} land {of} "Mits'rayim Two straits" and in the
\wood/ and in the stones*,□

7:20 וַיַּעֲשׂוּ כֵן מֹשֶׁה וְאַהֲרֹן כַּאֲשֶׁר צִוָּה יְהוָה וַיָּרֶם בַּמַּטֶּה וַיַּךְ אֶת הַמַּיִם
אֲשֶׁר בַּיְאֹר לְעֵינֵי פַרְעֹה וּלְעֵינֵי עֲבָדָיו וַיֵּהָפְכוּ כָּל הַמַּיִם אֲשֶׁר בַּיְאֹר
לְדָם

wai'ya'a'su kheyn mo'sheh we'a'ha'ron ka'a'sheyr tsi'wah YHWH wai'ya'rem ba'ma'teh
wai'yakh et ha'ma'yim a'sher bai'or le'ey'ney phar'oh ul'ey'ney a'va'daw wai'ye'haph'khu
kol ha'ma'yim a'sher bai'or le'dam

and~*they(m)~will*~DO SO "Mosheh PLUCKED-
OUT" and~"Aharon LIGHT-BRINGER" like~WHICH
he~did~much~DIRECT "Yhwh *he~will*~BE" and~
he~will~make~RAISE in~the~BRANCH and~
he~will~make~HIT AT the~WATER~s2
WHICH in~the~STREAM to~EYE~s2 "Paroh
GREAT-HOUSE" and~to~EYE~s SERVANT~s~him
and~*they(m)~will*~*be*~OVERTURN ALL the~
WATER~s2 WHICH in~the~STREAM to~
BLOOD□

and "Mosheh Plucked out" and "Aharon Light bringer"
did <just as> "Yhwh He is" directed, and he rose
(with) the branch, and he hit the waters,
which {were} in the stream, to {the} eyes {of}
"Paroh Great house" and to {the} eyes {of} his
servants, and all the waters which {were} in
the stream were overturned to blood,□

7:21 וְהַדָּגָה אֲשֶׁר בַּיְאֹר מֵתָה וַיִּבְאַשׁ הַיְאֹר וְלֹא יָכְלוּ מִצְרַיִם לִשְׁתּוֹת מַיִם
מִן הַיְאֹר וַיְהִי הַדָּם בְּכָל אֶרֶץ מִצְרָיִם

we'ha'da'gah a'sher bai'or mey'tah wai'yiv'ash hai'or we'lo yakh'lu mits'ra'yim lish'tot
ma'yim min hai'or wai'hi ha'dam be'khol e'rets mits'ra'yim

and~the~FISH WHICH in~the~STREAM she~
did~DIE and~*he~will*~STINK the~STREAM
and~NOT *they~did*~BE-ABLE "Mits'rayim
STRAIT~s2" to~>~GULP WATER~s2 FROM the~
STREAM and~*he~will*~EXIST the~BLOOD in~
ALL LAND "Mits'rayim STRAIT~s2"□

and the fish which {were} in the stream died
and the stream stank, and "Mits'rayim Two
straits" was not able to gulp waters from the
stream, and the blood existed in all {the} land
{of} "Mits'rayim Two straits",□

7:22 וַיַּעֲשׂוּ כֵן חַרְטֻמֵּי מִצְרַיִם בְּלָטֵיהֶם וַיֶּחֱזַק לֵב פַּרְעֹה וְלֹא שָׁמַע אֲלֵהֶם
כַּאֲשֶׁר דִּבֶּר יְהוָה

wai'ya'a'su kheyn hhar'tu'mey mits'ra'yim be'la'tey'hem wa'ye'hhe'zaq leyv par'oh we'lo
sha'ma a'ley'hem ka'a'sheyr di'ber YHWH

and~*they(m)~will*~DO SO MAGICIAN~s
"Mits'rayim STRAIT~s2" in~SECRET~s~them(m)

and {the} magicians {of} "Mits'rayim Two straits"
did so (with) their secrets, and he seized {the}

---

* Probably referring to containers made of wood and stone.
Revised Mechanical Translation Codes
(..) Alt Trans/App A   <..> Comp Phrase/App B   [..] Verb Form/App C   \../ Plural Form/App D
:..: Int Inf Abs |..| Past Perf Verb   {...} Added Word

and~he~will~<u>SEIZE</u> HEART "Paroh ^{GREAT-HOUSE}„ and~NOT he~did~<u>HEAR</u> TO~them(m) like~WHICH he~did~much~<u>SPEAK</u> "Yhwh ^{he~will~<u>BE</u>}„□

heart* {of} "Paroh ^{Great house}„ and he did not hear them <just as> "Yhwh ^{He is}„ spoke,□

7:23

וַיִּ֤פֶן פַּרְעֹה֙ וַיָּבֹ֣א אֶל־בֵּית֔וֹ וְלֹא־שָׁ֥ת לִבּ֖וֹ גַּם־לָזֹֽאת

wai'yi'phen par'oh wai'ya'vo el bey'to we'lo shat li'bo gam la'zot

and~he~will~<u>TURN</u> "Paroh ^{GREAT-HOUSE}„ and~he~will~<u>COME</u> TO HOUSE~him and~NOT he~did~<u>SET-DOWN</u> HEART~him ALSO to~THIS□

and "Paroh ^{Great house}„ turned and he came to his house and he also did not set his heart down (by) this,□

7:24

וַיַּחְפְּר֧וּ כָל־מִצְרַ֛יִם סְבִיבֹ֥ת הַיְאֹ֖ר מַ֣יִם לִשְׁתּ֑וֹת כִּ֣י לֹ֤א יָֽכְלוּ֙ לִשְׁתֹּ֔ת מִמֵּימֵ֖י הַיְאֹֽר

wai'yahh'pe'ru khol mits'ra'yim se'vi'vot hai'or ma'yim lish'tot ki lo yakh'lu lish'tot mi'mey'mey hai'or

and~they(m)~will~<u>DIG-OUT</u> ALL "Mits'rayim ^{STRAIT~s2}„ ALL-AROUND~s the~STREAM WATER~s2 to~>~<u>GULP</u> GIVEN-THAT NOT they~did~<u>BE-ABLE</u> to~>~<u>GULP</u> from~WATER~s2 the~STREAM□

and all {of} "Mits'rayim ^{Two straits}„ dug out all around the stream {of} waters to gulp given that they were not able to gulp from {the} waters {of} the stream,□

7:25

וַיִּמָּלֵ֖א שִׁבְעַ֣ת יָמִ֑ים אַחֲרֵ֥י הַכּוֹת־יְהוָ֖ה אֶת־הַיְאֹֽר

wai'yi'ma'ley shiv'at ya'mim a'hha'rey ha'kot YHWH et hai'or

and~he~will~be~<u>FILL</u> SEVEN DAY~s AFTER >~make~<u>HIT</u> "Yhwh ^{he~will~<u>BE</u>}„ AT the~STREAM□

and seven days were filled after "Yhwh ^{He is}„ hit the stream,□

7:26(1)

וַיֹּ֤אמֶר יְהוָה֙ אֶל־מֹשֶׁ֔ה בֹּ֖א אֶל־פַּרְעֹ֑ה וְאָמַרְתָּ֣ אֵלָ֗יו כֹּ֚ה אָמַ֣ר יְהוָ֔ה שַׁלַּ֥ח אֶת־עַמִּ֖י וְיַֽעַבְדֻֽנִי

wai'yo'mer YHWH el mo'sheh bo el par'oh we'a'mar'ta ey'law koh a'mar YHWH sha'lahh et a'mi we'ya'av'du'ni

and~he~will~<u>SAY</u> "Yhwh ^{he~will~<u>BE</u>}„ TO "Mosheh ^{PLUCKED-OUT}„ !(ms)~<u>COME</u> TO "Paroh ^{GREAT-HOUSE}„ and~you(ms)~did~<u>SAY</u> TO~him IN-THIS-WAY he~did~<u>SAY</u> "Yhwh ^{he~will~<u>BE</u>}„ !(ms)~much~<u>SEND</u> AT PEOPLE~me and~they(m)~will~<u>SERVE</u>~me□

and "Yhwh ^{He is}„ said to "Mosheh ^{Plucked out}„, come to "Paroh ^{Great house}„ and you will say to him in this way, "Yhwh ^{He is}„ said, send my people and they will serve me,†□

---

* The phrase וַיֶּחֱזַק לֵב פַּרְעֹה can also be translated as "and the heart seized Paroh" but compare with Exodus 4:21 and 9:12.

† This verse is the first verse of chapter 8 in Christian Bibles. For the remainder of chapter 7 and all of chapter 8, the verse numbers in Christian Bibles will be four numbers higher.

Mechanical Translation Codes

<u>WORD</u> – Verb	WORD – Noun	Word – Name	word – Pre/Suff	*word* – Conj.

7:27(2) וְאִם מָאֵן אַתָּה לְשַׁלֵּחַ הִנֵּה אָנֹכִי נֹגֵף אֶת כָּל גְּבוּלְךָ בַּצְפַרְדְּעִים

we'im ma'eyn a'tah le'sha'ley'ahh hin'neyh a'no'khi no'geyph et kol ge'vul'kha bats'phar'de'im

and~IF REFUSING YOU(ms) to~>~*much*~ SEND LOOK I SMITE~*ing/er(ms)* AT ALL BORDER~you(ms) in~the~FROG~s□

and if you {are} refusing to send {them}, look, I {am} smiting all your border{s} (with) the frogs,□

7:28(3) וְשָׁרַץ הַיְאֹר צְפַרְדְּעִים וְעָלוּ וּבָאוּ בְּבֵיתֶךָ וּבַחֲדַר מִשְׁכָּבְךָ וְעַל מִטָּתֶךָ וּבְבֵית עֲבָדֶיךָ וּבְעַמֶּךָ וּבְתַנּוּרֶיךָ וּבְמִשְׁאֲרוֹתֶיךָ

we'sha'rats hai'or tse'phar'de'im we'a'lu u'va'u be'vey'te'kha u'va'hha'dar mish'kav'kha we'al mi'ta'te'kha uv'beyt a'va'dey'kha uv'a'me'kha uv'ta'nu'rey'kha uv'mish'a'ro'tey'kha

and~*he~did*~SWARM the~STREAM FROG~s and~*they~did*~GO-UP and~*they~did*~COME in~HOUSE~you(ms) and~in~CHAMBER LAYING-PLACE~you(ms) and~UPON BED~ you(ms) and~in~HOUSE SERVANT~s~ you(ms) and~in~PEOPLE~you(ms) and~in~ OVEN~s~you(ms) and~in~KNEADING-BOWL~s~you(ms)□

and the stream will swarm {with} frogs, and they will go up, and they will come in your house, and in {the} chamber {of} your laying place, and upon your bed, and in {the} house {of} your servants, and in your people, and in your ovens, and in your kneading bowls,□

7:29(4) וּבְכָה וּבְעַמְּךָ וּבְכָל עֲבָדֶיךָ יַעֲלוּ הַצְפַרְדְּעִים

uv'khah uv'am'kha uv'khol a'va'dey'kha ya'a'lu ha'tse'phar'de'im

and~in~you(ms) and~in~PEOPLE~you(ms) and~in~ALL SERVANT~s~you(ms) *they(m)~ will*~GO-UP the~FROG~s□

and in you, and in your people, and in all your servants the frogs will go up,□

Chapter 8

8:1(5) וַיֹּאמֶר יְהוָה אֶל מֹשֶׁה אֱמֹר אֶל אַהֲרֹן נְטֵה אֶת יָדְךָ בְּמַטֶּךָ עַל הַנְּהָרֹת עַל הַיְאֹרִים וְעַל הָאֲגַמִּים וְהַעַל אֶת הַצְפַרְדְּעִים עַל אֶרֶץ מִצְרָיִם

wai'yo'mer YHWH el mo'sheh e'mor el a'ha'ron ne'teyh et yad'kha be'ma'te'kha al han'ha'rot al hai'o'rim we'al ha'a'ga'mim we'ha'al et ha'tse'phar'de'im al e'rets mits'ra'yim

and~*he~will*~SAY "Yhwh *he~will~BE*" TO "Mosheh PLUCKED-OUT" !(ms)~SAY TO "Aharon LIGHT-BRINGER" !(ms)~EXTEND AT HAND~ you(ms) in~BRANCH~you(ms) UPON the~ RIVER~s UPON the~STREAM~s and~UPON the~POOL~s and~!(ms)~make~GO-UP AT the~FROG~s UPON LAND "Mits'rayim

and "Yhwh He is" said to "Mosheh Plucked out", say to "Aharon Light bringer", extend your hand, (with) your branch, upon the rivers, upon the streams and upon the pools, and make the frogs upon {the} land {of} "Mits'rayim Two straits" go up,□

Revised Mechanical Translation Codes

(..) Alt Trans/App A   <..> Comp Phrase/App B   [..] Verb Form/App C   \../ Plural Form/App D
:..: Int Inf Abs |..| Past Perf Verb   {...} Added Word

STRAIT~s2„ □

8:2(6) וַיֵּט אַהֲרֹן אֶת יָדוֹ עַל מֵימֵי מִצְרַיִם וַתַּעַל הַצְּפַרְדֵּעַ וַתְּכַס אֶת אֶרֶץ מִצְרָיִם

wai'yeyt a'ha'ron et ya'do al mey'mey mits'ra'yim wa'ta'al hats'phar'dey'a wat'khas et e'rets mits'ra'yim

and~*he*~*will*~<u>EXTEND</u> "Aharon ^{LIGHT-BRINGER}„ AT HAND~him UPON WATER~s2 "Mits'rayim ^{STRAIT~s2}„ and~ *she*~*will*~<u>GO-UP</u> the~FROG and~ *she*~*will*~much~<u>COVER-OVER</u> AT LAND "Mits'rayim ^{STRAIT~s2}„ □

and "Aharon ^{Light bringer}„ extended his hand upon {the} waters {of} "Mits'rayim ^{Two straits}„, and the frog{s} went up and she* covered over {the} land {of} "Mits'rayim ^{Two straits}„, □

8:3(7) וַיַּעֲשׂוּ כֵן הַחַרְטֻמִּים בְּלָטֵיהֶם וַיַּעֲלוּ אֶת הַצְפַרְדְּעִים עַל אֶרֶץ מִצְרָיִם

wai'ya'a'su kheyn ha'hhar'tu'mim be'la'tey'hem wai'ya'a'lu et ha'tse'phar'de'im al e'rets mits'ra'yim

and~*they(m)*~*will*~<u>DO</u> SO the~MAGICIAN~s in~SECRET~s~them(m) and~*they(m)*~*will*~ make~<u>GO-UP</u> AT the~FROG~s UPON LAND "Mits'rayim ^{STRAIT~s2}„ □

and the magicians did so (with) their secrets, and they made the frogs go up upon {the} land {of} "Mits'rayim ^{Two straits}„, □

8:4(8) וַיִּקְרָא פַרְעֹה לְמֹשֶׁה וּלְאַהֲרֹן וַיֹּאמֶר הַעְתִּירוּ אֶל יְהוָה וְיָסֵר הַצְפַרְדְּעִים מִמֶּנִּי וּמֵעַמִּי וַאֲשַׁלְּחָה אֶת הָעָם וְיִזְבְּחוּ לַיהוָה

wai'yiq'ra phar'oh le'mo'sheh ul'a'ha'ron wai'yo'mer ha'ti'ru el YHWH we'ya'seyr ha'tse'phar'de'im mi'me'ni u'mey'a'mi wa'a'shal'hhah et ha'am we'yiz'be'hhu la'YHWH

and~*he*~*will*~<u>CALL-OUT</u> "Paroh ^{GREAT-HOUSE}„ to~"Mosheh ^{PLUCKED-OUT}„ and~to~"Aharon ^{LIGHT-BRINGER}„ and~*he*~*will*~<u>SAY</u> !(mp)~make~ <u>INTERCEDE</u> TO "Yhwh ^{*he*~*will*~<u>BE</u>}„ and~*he*~*will*~ make~<u>TURN-ASIDE</u> the~FROG~s FROM~me and~from~PEOPLE~me and~*I*~*will*~much~ <u>SEND</u>~^ AT the~PEOPLE and~*they(m)*~*will*~ <u>SACRIFICE</u> to~"Yhwh ^{*he*~*will*~<u>BE</u>}„ □

and "Paroh ^{Great house}„ called out to "Mosheh ^{Plucked out}„ and to "Aharon ^{Light bringer}„ and he said, intercede to "Yhwh ^{He is}„ and he will make the frogs turn aside from me and from my people, and I will send the people and they will sacrifice to "Yhwh ^{He is}„, □

8:5(9) וַיֹּאמֶר מֹשֶׁה לְפַרְעֹה הִתְפָּאֵר עָלַי לְמָתַי אַעְתִּיר לְךָ וְלַעֲבָדֶיךָ וּלְעַמְּךָ לְהַכְרִית הַצֲפַרְדְּעִים מִמְּךָ וּמִבָּתֶּיךָ רַק בַּיְאֹר תִּשָּׁאַרְנָה

wai'yo'mer mo'sheh le'phar'oh hit'pa'eyr a'lai le'ma'tai a'tir le'kha we'la'a'va'dey'kha ul'am'kha le'hakh'rit ha'tse'phar'de'im mim'kha u'mi'ba'tey'kha raq bai'or ti'sha'ar'nah

and~*he*~*will*~<u>SAY</u> "Mosheh ^{PLUCKED-OUT}„ to~ "Paroh ^{GREAT-HOUSE}„ !(ms)~ self~<u>DECORATE</u> UPON~me to~HOW-LONG *I*~*will*~make~ <u>INTERCEDE</u> to~you(ms) and~to~SERVANT~s~

and "Mosheh ^{Plucked out}„ said to "Paroh ^{Great house}„, decorate yourself upon me† (for) how long I will intercede (for) you and (for) your servants and (for) your people, to make the

---

* Referring to the "frogs," a feminine word in Hebrew.

† The meaning of the phrase "decorate yourself upon me" is uncertain.

Mechanical Translation Codes

<u>WORD</u> – Verb	WORD – Noun	Word – Name	word – Pre/Suff	*word* – Conj.

you(ms) and~to~PEOPLE~you(ms) to~
>~*make*~CUT the~FROG~s FROM~you(ms)
and~from~HOUSE~s~you(ms) ONLY in~the~
STREAM *they(f)~will~be*~REMAIN□

frogs cut from you and from your houses, only
in the streams will they remain,□

8:6(10)   וַיֹּאמֶר לְמָחָר וַיֹּאמֶר כִּדְבָרְךָ לְמַעַן תֵּדַע כִּי אֵין כַּיהוָה אֱלֹהֵינוּ

wai'yo'mer le'ma'hhar wai'yo'mer kid'var'kha le'ma'an tey'da ki eyn ka'YHWH e'lo'hey'nu

and~*he~will~*SAY to~TOMORROW and~*he~
will~*SAY like~WORD~you(ms) to~THAT
*you(ms)~will~*KNOW GIVEN-THAT WITHOUT
like~"Yhwh *he~will~*BE" "Elohiym POWER~s"~~us□

and he said, tomorrow, and he said, {it will be}
like your word (so) that you will know that
{there is} (none) like "Yhwh He is" our "Elohiym
Powers",□

8:7(11)   וְסָרוּ הַצְפַרְדְּעִים מִמְּךָ וּמִבָּתֶּיךָ וּמֵעֲבָדֶיךָ וּמֵעַמֶּךָ רַק בַּיְאֹר תִּשָּׁאַרְנָה

we'sa'ru ha'tse'phar'de'im mim'kha u'mi'ba'tey'kha u'mey'a'va'dey'kha u'mey'a'me'kha raq
bai'or ti'sha'ar'nah

and~*they~did~*TURN-ASIDE the~FROG~s
FROM~you(ms) and~from~HOUSE~s
you(ms) and~from~SERVANT~s~you(ms)
and~from~PEOPLE~you(ms) ONLY in~the~
STREAM *they(f)~will~be*~REMAIN□

and the frogs will turn aside from you and
from your houses and from your servants and
from your people, only in the stream will they
remain,□

8:8(12)   וַיֵּצֵא מֹשֶׁה וְאַהֲרֹן מֵעִם פַּרְעֹה וַיִּצְעַק מֹשֶׁה אֶל יְהוָה עַל דְּבַר
הַצְפַרְדְּעִים אֲשֶׁר שָׂם לְפַרְעֹה

wai'yey'tsey mo'sheh we'a'ha'ron mey'im par'oh wai'yits'aq mo'sheh el YHWH al de'var
ha'tse'phar'de'im a'sher sham le'phar'oh

and~*he~will~*GO-OUT "Mosheh PLUCKED-OUT"
and~"Aharon LIGHT-BRINGER" from~WITH "Paroh
GREAT-HOUSE" and~*he~will~*CRY-OUT "Mosheh
PLUCKED-OUT" TO "Yhwh *he~will~*BE" UPON WORD
the~FROG~s WHICH *he~did~*PLACE to~
"Paroh GREAT-HOUSE"□

and "Mosheh Plucked out" went out, and "Aharon
Light bringer", <away from> "Paroh Great house", and
"Mosheh Plucked out" cried out to "Yhwh He is"
(with) {the} (matter) {of} the frogs which he
placed (for) "Paroh Great house",□

8:9(13)   וַיַּעַשׂ יְהוָה כִּדְבַר מֹשֶׁה וַיָּמֻתוּ הַצְפַרְדְּעִים מִן הַבָּתִּים מִן הַחֲצֵרֹת וּמִן
הַשָּׂדֹת

wai'ya'as YHWH kid'var mo'sheh wai'ya'mu'tu ha'tse'phar'de'im min ha'ba'tim min
ha'hha'tsey'rot u'min ha'sa'dot

and~*he~will~*DO "Yhwh *he~will~*BE" like~WORD
"Mosheh PLUCKED-OUT" and~*they(m)~will~*DIE
the~FROG~s FROM the~HOUSE~s FROM
the~YARD~s and~FROM the~FIELD~s□

and "Yhwh He is" did {just} like {the} word {of}
"Mosheh Plucked out", and the frogs died, from
the houses, from the yards, and from the
fields,□

8:10(14)   וַיִּצְבְּרוּ אֹתָם חֳמָרִם חֳמָרִם וַתִּבְאַשׁ הָאָרֶץ

---

wai'yits'be'ru o'tam hha'ma'rim hha'ma'rim wa'tiv'ash ha'a'rets

and~*they(m)~will*~UNDERLINE PILE-UP AT~them(m) TAR~s TAR~s and~ *she~will*~STINK the~ LAND□

and they piled them up {like} tar*, and the land stank,□

8:11(15) וַיַּרְא פַּרְעֹה כִּי הָיְתָה הָרְוָחָה וְהַכְבֵּד אֶת לִבּוֹ וְלֹא שָׁמַע אֲלֵהֶם כַּאֲשֶׁר דִּבֶּר יְהוָה

wai'yar par'oh ki hai'tah har'wa'hhah we'hakh'beyd et li'bo we'lo sha'ma a'ley'hem ka'a'sheyr di'ber YHWH

and~*he~will*~SEE "Paroh GREAT-HOUSE" GIVEN-THAT *she~did*~EXIST the~RESPITE and~ >~*make*~BE-HEAVY AT HEART~him and~NOT *he~did*~HEAR TO~them(m) like~WHICH *he~did~much*~SPEAK "Yhwh *he~will*~BE"□

and "Paroh Great house" saw that the respite existed, and his heart {was} made heavy, and he did not hear them <just as> "Yhwh He is" spoke,□

8:12(16) וַיֹּאמֶר יְהוָה אֶל מֹשֶׁה אֱמֹר אֶל אַהֲרֹן נְטֵה אֶת מַטְּךָ וְהַךְ אֶת עֲפַר הָאָרֶץ וְהָיָה לְכִנִּם בְּכָל אֶרֶץ מִצְרָיִם

wai'yo'mer YHWH el mo'sheh e'mor el a'ha'ron ne'teyh et mat'kha we'hakh et a'phar ha'a'rets we'hai'yah le'khi'nim be'khol e'rets mits'ra'yim

and~*he~will*~SAY "Yhwh *he~will*~BE" TO "Mosheh PLUCKED-OUT" *!(ms)~SAY* TO "Aharon LIGHT-BRINGER" *!(ms)~EXTEND* AT BRANCH~ you(ms) and~*!(ms)~make*~HIT AT POWDER the~LAND and~*he~did*~EXIST to~GNAT~s in~ ALL LAND "Mits'rayim STRAIT~s2"□

and "Yhwh He is" said to "Mosheh Plucked out", say to "Aharon Light bringer", extend your branch and hit {the} powder {of} the land and he† will exist (as) gnats in all {the} land {of} "Mits'rayim Two straits",□

8:13(17) וַיַּעֲשׂוּ כֵן וַיֵּט אַהֲרֹן אֶת יָדוֹ בְמַטֵּהוּ וַיַּךְ אֶת עֲפַר הָאָרֶץ וַתְּהִי הַכִּנָּם בָּאָדָם וּבַבְּהֵמָה כָּל עֲפַר הָאָרֶץ הָיָה כִנִּים בְּכָל אֶרֶץ מִצְרָיִם

wai'ya'a'su kheyn wai'yeyt a'ha'ron et ya'do ve'ma'tey'hu wai'yakh et a'phar ha'a'rets wat'hi ha'ki'nam ba'a'dam u'va'be'hey'mah kol a'phar ha'a'rets hai'yah khi'nim be'khol e'rets mits'ra'yim

and~*they(m)~will*~DO SO and~*he~will*~ EXTEND "Aharon LIGHT-BRINGER" AT HAND~him in~BRANCH~him and~*he~will*~make~HIT AT POWDER the~LAND and~ *she~will*~EXIST the~GNAT~s in~the~HUMAN and~in~the~ BEAST ALL POWDER the~LAND *he~did*~EXIST

and they did so, and "Aharon Light bringer" extended his hand, (with) his branch, and he hit {the} powder {of} the land and the gnats‡ existed in the human and in the beast, all {the} powder {of} the land |had| existed {as} gnats in all {the} land {of} "Mits'rayim Two straits",□

---

* The grammar of the first part of this verse would literally be translated as, "and tars of tars piled them up" and appears to be written defectively. A possible correction is that the second occurrence of the word "Tars" is a duplication by scribal error and the first occurrence is missing the prefix "like."

† Referring to the "powder," a masculine word in Hebrew.

‡ The word הַכִּנָּם is probably written defectively and should be הַכִּנִּים.

Mechanical Translation Codes

WORD – Verb	WORD – Noun	Word – Name	word – Pre/Suff	*word* – Conj.

GNAT~s in~ALL LAND "Mits'rayim STRAIT~s2„□

8:14(18)

וַיַּעֲשׂוּ כֵן הַחַרְטֻמִּים בְּלָטֵיהֶם לְהוֹצִיא אֶת הַכִּנִּים וְלֹא יָכֹלוּ וַתְּהִי הַכִּנָּם בָּאָדָם וּבַבְּהֵמָה

wai'ya'a'su kheyn ha'hhar'tu'mim be'la'tey'hem le'ho'tsi et ha'ki'nim we'lo ya'kho'lu wat'hi ha'ki'nam ba'a'dam u'va'be'hey'mah

and~they(m)~will~<u>DO</u> SO the~MAGICIAN~s in~SECRET~s~them(m) to~>~make~<u>GO-OUT</u> AT the~GNAT~s and~NOT they~did~<u>BE-ABLE</u> and~ she~will~<u>EXIST</u> the~GNAT~s in~the~ HUMAN and~in~the~BEAST□

and the magicians did so (with) their secrets, to make the gnats go out, and they were not able, and the gnats* existed in the human and in the beast,□

8:15(19)

וַיֹּאמְרוּ הַחַרְטֻמִּם אֶל פַּרְעֹה אֶצְבַּע אֱלֹהִים הִוא וַיֶּחֱזַק לֵב פַּרְעֹה וְלֹא שָׁמַע אֲלֵהֶם כַּאֲשֶׁר דִּבֶּר יְהוָה

wai'yom'ru ha'hhar'tu'mim el par'oh ets'ba e'lo'him hi wa'ye'hhe'zaq leyv par'oh we'lo sha'ma a'ley'hem ka'a'sheyr di'ber YHWH

and~they(m)~will~<u>SAY</u> the~MAGICIAN~s TO "Paroh GREAT-HOUSE„ FINGER "Elohiym POWER~s„ she and~he~will~<u>SEIZE</u> HEART "Paroh GREAT-HOUSE„ and~NOT he~did~<u>HEAR</u> TO~them(m) like~WHICH he~did~much~<u>SPEAK</u> "Yhwh he~will~<u>BE</u>„ □

and the magicians said to "Paroh Great house„, (this) {is the} finger {of} "Elohiym Powers„, and he seized {the} heart† {of} "Paroh Great house„ and he did not hear them, <just as> "Yhwh He is„ spoke,□

8:16(20)

וַיֹּאמֶר יְהוָה אֶל מֹשֶׁה הַשְׁכֵּם בַּבֹּקֶר וְהִתְיַצֵּב לִפְנֵי פַרְעֹה הִנֵּה יֹצֵא הַמָּיְמָה וְאָמַרְתָּ אֵלָיו כֹּה אָמַר יְהוָה שַׁלַּח עַמִּי וְיַעַבְדֻנִי

wai'yo'mer YHWH el mo'sheh hash'keym ba'bo'qer we'hit'ya'tseyv liph'ney phar'oh hin'neyh yo'tsey ha'mai'mah we'a'mar'ta ey'law koh a'mar YHWH sha'lahh a'mi we'ya'av'du'ni

and~he~will~<u>SAY</u> "Yhwh he~will~<u>BE</u>„ TO "Mosheh PLUCKED-OUT„ !(mp)~make~<u>DEPART-EARLY</u> in~the~MORNING and~!(ms)~ self~<u>STAND-UP</u> to~FACE~s "Paroh GREAT-HOUSE„ LOOK <u>GO-OUT</u>~ing/er(ms) the~WATER~s2~ unto and~you(ms)~did~<u>SAY</u> TO~him IN-THIS-WAY he~did~<u>SAY</u> "Yhwh he~will~<u>BE</u>„ !(ms)~ much~<u>SEND</u> PEOPLE~me and~they(m)~will~ <u>SERVE</u>~me□

and "Yhwh He is„ said to "Mosheh Plucked out„, depart early in the morning and stand {your}self up <in front of> "Paroh Great house„, look, {he is} going out unto the waters, and you will say to him in this way, "Yhwh He is„ said, send my people and they will serve me,□

8:17(21)

כִּי אִם אֵינְךָ מְשַׁלֵּחַ אֶת עַמִּי הִנְנִי מַשְׁלִיחַ בְּךָ וּבַעֲבָדֶיךָ וּבְעַמְּךָ וּבְבָתֶּיךָ אֶת הֶעָרֹב וּמָלְאוּ בָּתֵּי מִצְרַיִם אֶת הֶעָרֹב וְגַם הָאֲדָמָה אֲשֶׁר הֵם עָלֶיהָ

---

* The word הַכִּנָּם is probably written defectively and should be הַכִּנִּים.

† The phrase וַיֶּחֱזַק לֵב פַּרְעֹה can also be translated as "and the heart seized Paroh" but compare with Exodus 4:21 and 9:12.

Revised Mechanical Translation Codes

(..) Alt Trans/App A	<..> Comp Phrase/App B	[..] Verb Form/App C	\../ Plural Form/App D
:..: Int Inf Abs	|..| Past Perf Verb	{...} Added Word	

ki im eyn'kha me'sha'ley'ahh et a'mi hin'ni mash'li'ahh be'kha u'va'a'va'dey'kha uv'am'kha uv'va'tey'kha et he'a'rov u'mal'u ba'tey mits'ra'yim et he'a'rov we'gam ha'a'da'mah a'sher heym a'ley'ah

GIVEN-THAT IF WITHOUT~you(ms) *much*~ SEND~*ing/er(ms)* AT PEOPLE~me LOOK~me *make*~SEND~*ing/er(ms)* in~you(ms) and~*in*~ SERVANT~*s*~you(ms) and~*in*~PEOPLE~ you(ms) and~*in*~HOUSE~*s*~you(ms) AT the~ HORDE and~*they~did*~FILL HOUSE~s "Mits'rayim STRAIT~s2" AT the~HORDE and~ ALSO the~GROUND WHICH THEY(m) UPON~ her□

<instead> you {are} (not) sending my people, look {at} me, {I am} sending the horde in you and in your servants and in your people and in your houses, and {the} houses {of} "Mits'rayim Two straits" will be filled (with) the horde, and also the ground which they {are} upon,□

8:18(22) וְהִפְלֵיתִי בַיּוֹם הַהוּא אֶת אֶרֶץ גֹּשֶׁן אֲשֶׁר עַמִּי עֹמֵד עָלֶיהָ לְבִלְתִּי הֱיוֹת שָׁם עָרֹב לְמַעַן תֵּדַע כִּי אֲנִי יְהוָה בְּקֶרֶב הָאָרֶץ

we'hiph'ley'ti vai'yom ha'hu et e'rets go'shen a'sher a'mi o'meyd a'ley'ah le'vil'ti he'yot sham a'rov le'ma'an tey'da ki a'ni YHWH be'qe'rev ha'a'rets

and~*I~did~make*~BE-DISTINCT in~the~DAY the~HE AT LAND "Goshen DRAWING-NEAR" WHICH PEOPLE~me STAND~*ing/er(ms)* UPON~her to~EXCEPT >~EXIST THERE HORDE to~THAT *you(ms)~will*~KNOW GIVEN-THAT I "Yhwh *he~will~BE*" in~WITHIN the~LAND□

and I will make {the} land {of} "Goshen Drawing near", which my people {are} standing upon, be distinct in (this) day, <by not> {letting the} horde exist there, so that you will know that I {am} "Yhwh He is" within the land,□

8:19(23) וְשַׂמְתִּי פְדֻת בֵּין עַמִּי וּבֵין עַמֶּךָ לְמָחָר יִהְיֶה הָאֹת הַזֶּה

we'sam'ti phe'dut beyn a'mi u'veyn a'me'kha le'ma'hhar yih'yeh ha'ot ha'zeh

and~*I~did*~PLACE RANSOM BETWEEN PEOPLE~me and~BETWEEN PEOPLE~ you(ms) to~TOMORROW *he~will*~EXIST the~ SIGN the~THIS□

and I will place {a} ransom between my people and your people, tomorrow this sign will exist,□

8:20(24) וַיַּעַשׂ יְהוָה כֵּן וַיָּבֹא עָרֹב כָּבֵד בֵּיתָה פַרְעֹה וּבֵית עֲבָדָיו וּבְכָל אֶרֶץ מִצְרַיִם תִּשָּׁחֵת הָאָרֶץ מִפְּנֵי הֶעָרֹב

wai'ya'as YHWH keyn wai'ya'vo a'rov ka'veyd bey'tah phar'oh u'veyt a'va'daw uv'khol e'rets mits'ra'yim ti'sha'hheyt ha'a'rets mip'ney he'a'rov

and~*he~will*~DO "Yhwh *he~will~BE*" SO and~*he~ will*~COME HORDE HEAVY HOUSE~unto "Paroh GREAT-HOUSE" and~HOUSE SERVANT~*s*~ him and~*in*~ALL LAND "Mits'rayim STRAIT~s2" *she~will~be*~DAMAGE the~LAND from~ FACE~s the~HORDE□

and "Yhwh He is" did so, and {the} horde came heavy unto {the} house {of} "Paroh Great house" and {the} house {of} his servants and in all {the} land {of} "Mits'rayim Two straits", the land was damaged from {the} face {of} the horde,□

8:21(25) וַיִּקְרָא פַרְעֹה אֶל מֹשֶׁה וּלְאַהֲרֹן וַיֹּאמֶר לְכוּ זִבְחוּ לֵאלֹהֵיכֶם בָּאָרֶץ

Mechanical Translation Codes

<u>WORD</u> – Verb	WORD – Noun	Word – Name	word – Pre/Suff	*word* – Conj.

wai'yiq'ra phar'oh el mo'sheh ul'a'ha'ron wai'yo'mer le'khu ziv'hhu ley'lo'hey'khem ba'a'rets

and~*he~will~*<u>CALL-OUT</u> "Paroh ^{GREAT-HOUSE}„ TO "Mosheh ^{PLUCKED-OUT}„ and~to~"Aharon ^{LIGHT-BRINGER}„ and~*he~will~*<u>SAY</u> !(*mp*)~<u>WALK</u> !(*mp*)~<u>SACRIFICE</u> to~"Elohiym ^{POWER~s}„~ you(mp) in~the~LAND□	and "Paroh ^{Great house}„ called out to "Mosheh ^{Plucked out}„ and to "Aharon ^{Light bringer}„, and he said, walk, sacrifice to your "Elohiym ^{Powers}„ in the land,□

8:22(26) וַיֹּאמֶר מֹשֶׁה לֹא נָכוֹן לַעֲשׂוֹת כֵּן כִּי תּוֹעֲבַת מִצְרַיִם נִזְבַּח לַיהוָה אֱלֹהֵינוּ הֵן נִזְבַּח אֶת תּוֹעֲבַת מִצְרַיִם לְעֵינֵיהֶם וְלֹא יִסְקְלֻנוּ

wai'yo'mer mo'sheh lo na'khon la'a'shot keyn ki to'a'vat mits'ra'yim niz'bahh la'YHWH e'lo'hey'nu heyn niz'bahh et to'a'vat mits'ra'yim le'ey'ney'hem we'lo yis'qe'lu'nu

and~*he~will~*<u>SAY</u> "Mosheh ^{PLUCKED-OUT}„ NOT *be~*<u>PREPARE</u>~*ing/er(ms)* to~>~<u>DO</u> SO GIVEN-THAT DISGUSTING "Mits'rayim ^{STRAIT~s2}„ *we~will~*<u>SACRIFICE</u> to~"Yhwh ^{he~will~BE}„ "Elohiym ^{POWER~s}„~us THOUGH *we~will~*<u>SACRIFICE</u> AT DISGUSTING "Mits'rayim ^{STRAIT~s2}„ to~ EYE~s2~them(m) and~NOT *they(m)~will~*<u>STONE</u>~us□	and "Mosheh ^{Plucked out}„ said, {it is} not being prepared to do so, given that we will sacrifice to "Yhwh ^{He is}„ our "Elohiym ^{Powers}„ {it is a} disgusting {thing to} "Mits'rayim ^{Two straits}„, (since) we sacrifice {a} disgusting {thing to} "Mits'rayim ^{Two straits}„ to their eyes, (then) will they not stone us?□

8:23(27) דֶּרֶךְ שְׁלֹשֶׁת יָמִים נֵלֵךְ בַּמִּדְבָּר וְזָבַחְנוּ לַיהוָה אֱלֹהֵינוּ כַּאֲשֶׁר יֹאמַר אֵלֵינוּ

de'rekh she'lo'shet ya'mim ney'leykh ba'mid'bar we'za'vahh'nu la'YHWH e'lo'hey'nu ka'a'sheyr yo'mar ey'ley'nu

ROAD THREE DAY~s *we~will~*<u>WALK</u> in~the~ WILDERNESS and~*we~did~*<u>SACRIFICE</u> to~ "Yhwh ^{he~will~BE}„ "Elohiym ^{POWER~s}„~us like~ WHICH *he~will~*<u>SAY</u> TO~us□	we will walk {the} road {for} three days in the wilderness, and we will sacrifice to "Yhwh ^{He is}„ our "Elohiym ^{Powers}„, <just as> he said to us,□

8:24(28) וַיֹּאמֶר פַּרְעֹה אָנֹכִי אֲשַׁלַּח אֶתְכֶם וּזְבַחְתֶּם לַיהוָה אֱלֹהֵיכֶם בַּמִּדְבָּר רַק הַרְחֵק לֹא תַרְחִיקוּ לָלֶכֶת הַעְתִּירוּ בַּעֲדִי

wai'yo'mer par'oh a'no'khi a'sha'lahh et'khem uz'vahh'tem la'YHWH e'lo'hey'khem ba'mid'bar raq har'hheyq lo tar'hhi'qu la'le'khet ha'ti'ru ba'a'di

and~*he~will~*<u>SAY</u> "Paroh ^{GREAT-HOUSE}„ I *I~will~* much~<u>SEND</u> AT~you(mp) and~*you(mp)~did~*<u>SACRIFICE</u> to~"Yhwh ^{he~will~BE}„ "Elohiym ^{POWER~s}„~you(mp) in~the~WILDERNESS ONLY >~*make~*<u>BE-FAR</u> NOT *you(mp)~will~make~*<u>BE-FAR</u> to~>~<u>WALK</u> !(*mp*)~*make~*<u>INTERCEDE</u> ROUND-ABOUT~me□	and "Paroh ^{Great house}„ said, I will send you and you will sacrifice to "Yhwh ^{He is}„ your "Elohiym ^{Powers}„ in the wilderness, only you will not walk :very: far, intercede (concerning) me,□

8:25(29) וַיֹּאמֶר מֹשֶׁה הִנֵּה אָנֹכִי יוֹצֵא מֵעִמָּךְ וְהַעְתַּרְתִּי אֶל יְהוָה וְסָר הֶעָרֹב

מִפַּרְעֹה מֵעֲבָדָיו וּמֵעַמּוֹ מָחָר רַק אַל יֹסֵף פַּרְעֹה הָתֵל לְבִלְתִּי שַׁלַּח אֶת הָעָם לִזְבֹּחַ לַיהוָה

wai'yo'mer mo'sheh hin'neyh a'no'khi yo'tsey mey'i'makh we'ha'tar'ti el YHWH we'sar he'a'rov mi'par'oh mey'a'va'daw u'mey'a'mo ma'hhar raq al yo'seyph par'oh ha'teyl le'vil'ti sha'lahh et ha'am liz'bo'ahh la'YHWH

and~*he~will~*<u>SAY</u> "Mosheh ^{PLUCKED-OUT}" LOOK I <u>GO-OUT</u>~*ing/er*(ms) from~WITH~you(ms) and~*I~did~make~*<u>INTERCEDE</u> TO "Yhwh ^{he~will~<u>BE</u>}" and~*he~did~*<u>TURN-ASIDE</u> the~HORDE from~"Paroh ^{GREAT-HOUSE}" from~SERVANT~s~him and~from~PEOPLE~him TOMORROW ONLY DO-NOT *he~will~*<u>ADD</u> "Paroh ^{GREAT-HOUSE}" >~*make~*<u>DEAL-DECEITFULLY</u> to~ EXCEPT !(ms)~*much~*<u>SEND</u> AT the~PEOPLE to~>~<u>SACRIFICE</u> to~"Yhwh ^{he~will~<u>BE</u>}"□

and "Mosheh ^{Plucked out}" said, look, I {am} going out <away from> you, and I will intercede to "Yhwh ^{He is}", and he will turn aside the horde from "Paroh ^{Great house}", from his servants, and from his people tomorrow, only do not {let} "Paroh ^{Great house}" [again] deal deceitfully, <by not> sending the people to sacrifice to "Yhwh ^{He is}",□

8:26(30)

וַיֵּצֵא מֹשֶׁה מֵעִם פַּרְעֹה וַיֶּעְתַּר אֶל יְהוָה

wai'yey'tsey mo'sheh mey'im par'oh wai'ye'tar el YHWH

and~*he~will~*<u>GO-OUT</u> "Mosheh ^{PLUCKED-OUT}" from~WITH "Paroh ^{GREAT-HOUSE}" and~*he~will~* <u>INTERCEDE</u> TO "Yhwh ^{he~will~<u>BE</u>}"□

and "Mosheh ^{Plucked out}" went out <away from> "Paroh ^{Great house}" and he interceded to "Yhwh ^{He is}",□

8:27(31)

וַיַּעַשׂ יְהוָה כִּדְבַר מֹשֶׁה וַיָּסַר הֶעָרֹב מִפַּרְעֹה מֵעֲבָדָיו וּמֵעַמּוֹ לֹא נִשְׁאַר אֶחָד

wai'ya'as YHWH kid'var mo'sheh wai'ya'sar he'a'rov mi'par'oh mey'a'va'daw u'mey'a'mo lo nish'ar e'hhad

and~*he~will~*<u>DO</u> "Yhwh ^{he~will~<u>BE</u>}" like~WORD "Mosheh ^{PLUCKED-OUT}" and~*he~will~make~* <u>TURN-ASIDE</u> the~HORDE from~"Paroh ^{GREAT-HOUSE}" from~SERVANT~s~him and~from~ PEOPLE~him NOT *he~did~be~*<u>REMAIN</u> UNIT□

and "Yhwh ^{He is}" did {just} like {the} word {of} "Mosheh ^{Plucked out}", and he made the horde turn aside from "Paroh ^{Great house}", from his servants, and from his people, not (one) was remaining,□

8:28(32)

וַיַּכְבֵּד פַּרְעֹה אֶת לִבּוֹ גַּם בַּפַּעַם הַזֹּאת וְלֹא שִׁלַּח אֶת הָעָם

wai'yakh'beyd par'oh et li'bo gam ba'pa'am ha'zot we'lo shi'lahh et ha'am

and~*he~will~make~*<u>BE-HEAVY</u> "Paroh ^{GREAT-HOUSE}" AT HEART~him ALSO in~the~ FOOTSTEP the~THIS and~NOT *he~did~* *much~*<u>SEND</u> AT the~PEOPLE□

and "Paroh ^{Great house}" made his heart heavy, also in this footstep*, and he did not send the people,□

---

* The phrase "also in this footstep" means "also at this time."

Mechanical Translation Codes

<u>WORD</u> – Verb	WORD – Noun	Word – Name	word – Pre/Suff	*word* – Conj.

Chapter 9

9:1 וַיֹּאמֶר יְהוָה אֶל מֹשֶׁה בֹּא אֶל פַּרְעֹה וְדִבַּרְתָּ אֵלָיו כֹּה אָמַר יְהוָה אֱלֹהֵי הָעִבְרִים שַׁלַּח אֶת עַמִּי וְיַעַבְדֻנִי

wai'yo'mer YHWH el mo'sheh bo el par'oh we'di'bar'ta ey'law koh a'mar YHWH e'lo'hey ha'iv'rim sha'lahh et a'mi we'ya'av'du'ni

and~he~will~<u>SAY</u> "Yhwh ^{he~will~<u>BE</u>}" TO "Mosheh ^{PLUCKED-OUT}" !(ms)~<u>COME</u> TO "Paroh ^{GREAT-HOUSE}" and~you(ms)~did~much~<u>SPEAK</u> TO~him IN-THIS-WAY he~did~<u>SAY</u> "Yhwh ^{he~will~<u>BE</u>}" "Elohiym ^{POWER~s}" the~"Ever ^{OTHER-SIDE}"~s !(ms)~much~<u>SEND</u> AT PEOPLE~me and~they(m)~will~<u>SERVE</u>~me☐

and "Yhwh ^{He is}" said to "Mosheh ^{Plucked out}", come to "Paroh ^{Great house}" and you will speak to him in this way, "Yhwh ^{He is}" {the} "Elohiym ^{Powers}" {of} the {one}s {of} "Ever ^{Other side}" said, send my people and they will serve me,☐

9:2 כִּי אִם מָאֵן אַתָּה לְשַׁלֵּחַ וְעוֹדְךָ מַחֲזִיק בָּם

ki im ma'eyn a'tah le'sha'ley'ahh we'od'kha ma'hha'ziq bam

GIVEN-THAT IF REFUSING YOU(ms) to~ >~much~<u>SEND</u> and~YET-AGAIN~you(ms) make~<u>SEIZE</u>~ing/er(ms) in~them(m)☐

<instead> you {are} refusing to send {them}, and you (continue) seizing them,☐

9:3 הִנֵּה יַד יְהוָה הוֹיָה בְּמִקְנְךָ אֲשֶׁר בַּשָּׂדֶה בַּסּוּסִים בַּחֲמֹרִים בַּגְּמַלִים בַּבָּקָר וּבַצֹּאן דֶּבֶר כָּבֵד מְאֹד

hin'neyh yad YHWH ho'yah be'miq'ne'kha a'sher ba'sa'deh ba'su'sim ba'hha'mo'rim bag'ma'lim ba'ba'qar u'va'tson de'ver ka'veyd me'od

LOOK HAND "Yhwh ^{he~will~<u>BE</u>}" <u>EXIST</u>~ing/er(fs) in~LIVESTOCK~you(ms) WHICH in~the~FIELD in~the~HORSE~s in~the~DONKEY~s in~the~CAMEL~s in~the~CATTLE and~in~the~FLOCKS EPIDEMIC HEAVY MANY☐

look, {the} hand {of} "Yhwh ^{He is}" {is} existing in your livestock, which {are} in the field, in the horses, in the donkeys, in the camels, in the cattle, and in the flocks, {it is a} (very) heavy epidemic,☐

9:4 וְהִפְלָה יְהוָה בֵּין מִקְנֵה יִשְׂרָאֵל וּבֵין מִקְנֵה מִצְרָיִם וְלֹא יָמוּת מִכָּל לִבְנֵי יִשְׂרָאֵל דָּבָר

we'hiph'lah YHWH beyn miq'neyh yis'ra'eyl u'veyn miq'neyh mits'ra'yim we'lo ya'mut mi'kol liv'ney yis'ra'eyl da'var

and~he~did~make~<u>BE-DISTINCT</u> "Yhwh ^{he~will~<u>BE</u>}" BETWEEN LIVESTOCK "Yisra'el ^{he~will~<u>TURN-ASIDE</u>~+~MIGHTY-ONE}" and~BETWEEN LIVESTOCK "Mits'rayim ^{STRAIT~s2}" and~NOT he~will~<u>DIE</u> from~ALL to~SON~s "Yisra'el ^{he~will~<u>TURN-ASIDE</u>~+~MIGHTY-ONE}" WORD☐

and "Yhwh ^{He is}" will make {a} distinct{ion} between {the} livestock {of} "Yisra'el ^{He turns El aside}" and {the} livestock {of} "Mits'rayim ^{Two straits}", and not {a} (thing) will die from <among> {the} sons {of} "Yisra'el ^{He turns El aside}",☐

9:5 וַיָּשֶׂם יְהוָה מוֹעֵד לֵאמֹר מָחָר יַעֲשֶׂה יְהוָה הַדָּבָר הַזֶּה בָּאָרֶץ

wai'ya'sem YHWH mo'eyd ley'mor ma'hhar ya'a'seh YHWH ha'da'var ha'zeh ba'a'rets

and~he~will~UNDERLINE{PLACE} "Yhwh ^(he~will~BE)" APPOINTED to~>~UNDERLINE{SAY} TOMORROW he~will~ UNDERLINE{DO} "Yhwh ^(he~will~BE)" the~WORD the~THIS in~ the~LAND□

and "Yhwh ^(He is)" placed {an} appointed {time} say{ing}, tomorrow "Yhwh ^(He is)" will do this (matter) in the land,□

9:6 וַיַּעַשׂ יְהוָה אֶת הַדָּבָר הַזֶּה מִמָּחֳרָת וַיָּמָת כֹּל מִקְנֵה מִצְרַיִם וּמִמִּקְנֵה בְּנֵי יִשְׂרָאֵל לֹא מֵת אֶחָד

wai'ya'as YHWH et ha'da'var ha'zeh mi'ma'hhu'rat wai'ya'mat kol miq'neyh mits'ra'yim u'mi'miq'neyh ve'ney yis'ra'eyl lo meyt e'hhad

and~he~will~UNDERLINE{DO} "Yhwh ^(he~will~BE)" AT the~ WORD the~THIS from~MORROW and~he~ will~UNDERLINE{DIE} ALL LIVESTOCK "Mits'rayim ^(STRAIT~s2)" and~from~LIVESTOCK SON~s "Yisra'eyl ^(he~will~ UNDERLINE{TURN-ASIDE}+~MIGHTY-ONE)" NOT he~did~UNDERLINE{DIE} UNIT□

and "Yhwh ^(He is)" did this (matter) <the next day> , and all {the} livestock {of} "Mits'rayim ^(Two straits)" died, and from {the} livestock {of the} sons {of} "Yisra'el ^(He turns El aside)" not (one) died,□

9:7 וַיִּשְׁלַח פַּרְעֹה וְהִנֵּה לֹא מֵת מִמִּקְנֵה יִשְׂרָאֵל עַד אֶחָד וַיִּכְבַּד לֵב פַּרְעֹה וְלֹא שִׁלַּח אֶת הָעָם

wai'yish'lahh par'oh we'hin'neyh lo meyt mi'miq'neyh yis'ra'eyl ad e'hhad wai'yikh'bad leyv par'oh we'lo shi'lahh et ha'am

and~he~will~UNDERLINE{SEND} "Paroh ^(GREAT-HOUSE)" and~ LOOK NOT he~did~UNDERLINE{DIE} from~LIVESTOCK "Yisra'el ^(he~will~UNDERLINE{TURN-ASIDE}+~MIGHTY-ONE)" UNTIL UNIT and~he~will~UNDERLINE{BE-HEAVY} HEART "Paroh ^(GREAT-HOUSE)" and~NOT he~did~much~UNDERLINE{SEND} AT the~PEOPLE□

and "Paroh ^(Great house)" sent, and look, not {a} <single one> died from {the} livestock {of} "Yisra'el ^(He turns El aside)", and {the} heart {of} "Paroh ^(Great house)" was heavy, and he did not send the people,□

9:8 וַיֹּאמֶר יְהוָה אֶל מֹשֶׁה וְאֶל אַהֲרֹן קְחוּ לָכֶם מְלֹא חָפְנֵיכֶם פִּיחַ כִּבְשָׁן וּזְרָקוֹ מֹשֶׁה הַשָּׁמַיְמָה לְעֵינֵי פַרְעֹה

wai'yo'mer YHWH el mo'sheh we'el a'ha'ron qe'hhu la'khem me'lo hhaph'ney'khem pi'ahh kiv'shan uz'ra'qo mo'sheh ha'sha'mai'mah le'ey'ney phar'oh

and~he~will~UNDERLINE{SAY} "Yhwh ^(he~will~BE)" TO "Mosheh ^(PLUCKED-OUT)" and~TO "Aharon ^(LIGHT-BRINGER)" !(mp)~UNDERLINE{TAKE} to~you(mp) FILLING CUPPED-HAND~s2~you(mp) SOOT FURNACE and~he~did~UNDERLINE{SPRINKLE}~him "Mosheh ^(PLUCKED-OUT)" the~SKY~s2~unto to~EYE~s2 "Paroh ^(GREAT-HOUSE)"□

and "Yhwh ^(He is)" said to "Mosheh ^(Plucked out)" and to "Aharon ^(Light bringer)", take (for) you {the} soot {of the} furnace, filling your cupped hands, and "Mosheh ^(Plucked out)" will sprinkle him unto the skies to {the} eyes {of}* "Paroh ^(Great house)",□

9:9 וְהָיָה לְאָבָק עַל כָּל אֶרֶץ מִצְרָיִם וְהָיָה עַל הָאָדָם וְעַל הַבְּהֵמָה לִשְׁחִין

---

* "To the eyes of" is an idiom meaning "in the sight of."

Mechanical Translation Codes

UNDERLINE{WORD} – Verb	WORD – Noun	Word – Name	word – Pre/Suff	*word* – Conj.

פֹּרֵחַ אֲבַעְבֻּעֹת בְּכָל אֶרֶץ מִצְרָיִם

we'hai'yah le'a'vaq al kol e'rets mits'ra'yim we'hai'yah al ha'a'dam we'al ha'be'hey'mah lish'hhin po'rey'ahh a'va'bu'ot be'khol e'rets mits'ra'yim

and~*he~did*~<u>EXIST</u> to~DUST UPON ALL LAND "Mits'rayim ^{STRAIT~s2}" and~*he~did*~<u>EXIST</u> UPON the~HUMAN and~UPON the~BEAST to~BOILS <u>BURST-OUT</u>~*ing/er(ms)* BLISTER~s in~ALL LAND "Mits'rayim ^{STRAIT~s2}"□	and he will exist (as) dust upon all {the} land {of} "Mits'rayim ^{Two straits}", and he will exist upon the human and upon the beast (as) boils, bursting out blisters in all {the} land {of} "Mits'rayim ^{Two straits}",□

9:10

וַיִּקְחוּ אֶת פִּיחַ הַכִּבְשָׁן וַיַּעַמְדוּ לִפְנֵי פַרְעֹה וַיִּזְרֹק אֹתוֹ מֹשֶׁה הַשָּׁמָיְמָה וַיְהִי שְׁחִין אֲבַעְבֻּעֹת פֹּרֵחַ בָּאָדָם וּבַבְּהֵמָה

wai'yiq'hhu et pi'ahh ha'kiv'shan wai'ya'am'du liph'ney phar'oh wai'yiz'roq o'to mo'sheh ha'sha'mai'mah wai'hi she'hhin a'va'bu'ot po'rey'ahh ba'a'dam u'va'be'hey'mah

and~*they(m)~will*~<u>TAKE</u> AT SOOT the~ FURNACE and~*they(m)~will*~<u>STAND</u> to~ FACE~s "Paroh ^{GREAT-HOUSE}" and~*he~will*~ <u>SPRINKLE</u> AT~him "Mosheh ^{PLUCKED-OUT}" the~ SKY~s2~unto and~*he~will*~<u>EXIST</u> BOILS BLISTER~s <u>BURST-OUT</u>~*ing/er(ms)* in~the~ HUMAN and~in~the~BEAST□	and they took {the} soot {of} the furnace and they stood <in front of> "Paroh ^{Great house}", and "Mosheh ^{Plucked out}" sprinkled him* unto the skies and boils existed, blisters bursting out in the human and in the beast,□

9:11

וְלֹא יָכְלוּ הַחַרְטֻמִּים לַעֲמֹד לִפְנֵי מֹשֶׁה מִפְּנֵי הַשְּׁחִין כִּי הָיָה הַשְּׁחִין בַּחַרְטֻמִּם וּבְכָל מִצְרָיִם

we'lo yakh'lu ha'hhar'tu'mim la'a'mod liph'ney mo'sheh mip'ney hash'hhin ki hai'yah hash'hhin ba'hhar'tu'mim uv'khol mits'ra'yim

and~NOT *they~did*~<u>BE-ABLE</u> the~ MAGICIAN~s to~><u>STAND</u> to~FACE~s "Mosheh ^{PLUCKED-OUT}" from~FACE~s the~BOILS GIVEN-THAT *he~did*~<u>EXIST</u> the~BOILS in~ the~MAGICIAN and~in~ALL "Mits'rayim ^{STRAIT~s2}"□	and the magicians were not able to stand <in front of> "Mosheh ^{Plucked out}" (at) {the} face {of} the boils given that the boils existed in the magicians and in all "Mits'rayim ^{Two straits}",□

9:12

וַיְחַזֵּק יְהוָה אֶת לֵב פַּרְעֹה וְלֹא שָׁמַע אֲלֵהֶם כַּאֲשֶׁר דִּבֶּר יְהוָה אֶל מֹשֶׁה

wai'hha'zeyq YHWH et leyv par'oh we'lo sha'ma a'ley'hem ka'a'sheyr di'ber YHWH el mo'sheh

and~*he~will*~*much*~<u>SEIZE</u> "Yhwh ^{he~will~BE}" AT HEART "Paroh ^{GREAT-HOUSE}" and~NOT *he~did*~ <u>HEAR</u> TO~them(m) like~WHICH and~*he~did*~ *much*~<u>SPEAK</u> "Yhwh ^{he~will~BE}" TO "Mosheh ^{PLUCKED-OUT}"□	and "Yhwh ^{He is}" seized {the} heart {of} "Paroh ^{Great house}" and he did not hear them, <just as> "Yhwh ^{He is}" spoke to "Mosheh ^{Plucked out}",□

---

* Referring to the "soot" a masculine word in Hebrew.

Revised Mechanical Translation Codes

(..) Alt Trans/App A	<..> Comp Phrase/App B	[..] Verb Form/App C	\../ Plural Form/App D
:..: Int Inf Abs	|..| Past Perf Verb	{...} Added Word	

9:13

וַיֹּאמֶר יְהוָה אֶל מֹשֶׁה הַשְׁכֵּם בַּבֹּקֶר וְהִתְיַצֵּב לִפְנֵי פַרְעֹה וְאָמַרְתָּ
אֵלָיו כֹּה אָמַר יְהוָה אֱלֹהֵי הָעִבְרִים שַׁלַּח אֶת עַמִּי וְיַעַבְדֻנִי

wai'yo'mer YHWH el mo'sheh hash'keym ba'bo'qer we'hit'ya'tseyv liph'ney phar'oh
we'a'mar'ta ey'law koh a'mar YHWH e'lo'hey ha'iv'rim sha'lahh et a'mi we'ya'av'du'ni

and~he~will~<u>SAY</u> "Yhwh ^{he~will~<u>BE</u>} TO "Mosheh ^{PLUCKED-OUT,,} !(mp)~make~<u>DEPART-EARLY</u> in~the~MORNING and~!(ms)~ self~<u>STAND-UP</u> to~FACE~s "Paroh ^{GREAT-HOUSE,,} and~you(ms)~did~<u>SAY</u> TO~him IN-THIS-WAY he~did~<u>SAY</u> "Yhwh ^{he~will~<u>BE</u>} "Elohiym ^{POWER~s,,} the~"Ever ^{OTHER-SIDE~s} !(ms)~much~<u>SEND</u> AT PEOPLE~me and~they(m)~will~<u>SERVE</u>~me□

and "Yhwh ^{He is,,} said to "Mosheh ^{Plucked out,,}, depart early in the morning and stand {your}self up <in front of> "Paroh ^{Great house,,} and you will say to him in this way, "Yhwh ^{He is,,} {the} "Elohiym ^{Powers,,} {of} the {one}s {of} "Ever ^{Other side,,} said, send my people and they will serve me,□

9:14

כִּי בַּפַּעַם הַזֹּאת אֲנִי שֹׁלֵחַ אֶת כָּל מַגֵּפֹתַי אֶל לִבְּךָ וּבַעֲבָדֶיךָ וּבְעַמֶּךָ
בַּעֲבוּר תֵּדַע כִּי אֵין כָּמֹנִי בְּכָל הָאָרֶץ

ki ba'pa'am ha'zot a'ni sho'ley'ahh et kol ma'gey'pho'tai el li'be'kha u'va'a'va'dey'kha
uv'a'me'kha ba'a'vur tey'da ki eyn ka'mo'ni be'khol ha'a'rets

GIVEN-THAT in~the~FOOTSTEP the~THIS I <u>SEND</u>~ing/er(ms) AT ALL PESTILENCE~s~me TO HEART~you(ms) and~in~SERVANT~s~ you(ms) and~in~PEOPLE~you(ms) in~ INTENTION you(ms)~will~<u>KNOW</u> GIVEN-THAT WITHOUT like~THAT-ONE~me in~ALL the~LAND□

given that in this footstep*, I {am} sending all my pestilences to your heart and in your servants and in your people, (with) {the} intention, you will know that {there is} (not) one like me in all the land,□

9:15

כִּי עַתָּה שָׁלַחְתִּי אֶת יָדִי וָאַךְ אוֹתְךָ וְאֶת עַמְּךָ בַּדָּבֶר וַתִּכָּחֵד מִן הָאָרֶץ

ki a'tah sha'lahh'ti et ya'di wa'akh ot'kha we'et am'kha ba'da'ver wa'ti'ka'hheyd min
ha'a'rets

GIVEN-THAT NOW I~did~<u>SEND</u> AT HAND~me and~I~will~make~<u>HIT</u> AT~you(ms) and~AT PEOPLE~you(ms) in~the~EPIDEMIC and~ you(ms)~will~be~<u>KEEP-SECRET</u> FROM the~ LAND□

given that now I sent my hand, and I hit you and your people (with) the epidemic, and you will be kept secret from the land,□

9:16

וְאוּלָם בַּעֲבוּר זֹאת הֶעֱמַדְתִּיךָ בַּעֲבוּר הַרְאֹתְךָ אֶת כֹּחִי וּלְמַעַן סַפֵּר
שְׁמִי בְּכָל הָאָרֶץ

we'u'lam ba'a'vur zot he'e'mad'ti'kha ba'a'vur har'ot'kha et ko'hhi ul'ma'an sa'peyr
she'mi be'khol ha'a'rets

and~BUT in~INTENTION THIS I~did~make~ <u>STAND</u>~you(ms) in~INTENTION >~make~

but, (with) this intention, I made you stand, (with) the intention {to} [show] you my

---

* The phrase "in this footstep" means "at this time."

Mechanical Translation Codes

<u>WORD</u> – Verb	WORD – Noun	Word – Name	word – Pre/Suff	*word* – Conj.

SEE~you(ms) AT STRENGTH~me and~to~ THAT >~*much*~COUNT TITLE~me in~ALL the~ LAND□

strength, and (so) that {there will be a} [recount]{ing of} my title in all the land,□

9:17 עוֹדְךָ מִסְתּוֹלֵל בְּעַמִּי לְבִלְתִּי שַׁלְּחָם

od'kha mis'to'leyl be'a'mi le'vil'ti shal'hham

YET-AGAIN~you(ms) self~BUILD-UP~ *ing/er(ms)* in~PEOPLE~me to~EXCEPT >~*much*~SEND~them(m)□

yet again, you {are} building {your}self up (with) my people, <by not> sending them,□

9:18 הִנְנִי מַמְטִיר כָּעֵת מָחָר בָּרָד כָּבֵד מְאֹד אֲשֶׁר לֹא הָיָה כָמֹהוּ בְּמִצְרַיִם לְמִן הַיּוֹם הִוָּסְדָה וְעַד עָתָּה

hin'ni mam'tir ka'eyt ma'hhar ba'rad ka'veyd me'od a'sher lo hai'yah kha'mo'hu be'mits'ra'yim le'min hai'yom hi'was'dah we'ad a'tah

LOOK~me *make*~PRECIPITATE~*ing/er(ms)* like~the~APPOINTED-TIME TOMORROW HAILSTONES HEAVY MANY WHICH NOT *he*~*did*~EXIST like~THAT-ONE~him in~ "Mits'rayim [STRAIT~s2]" to~FROM the~DAY >~*be*~FOUND~her and~UNTIL NOW□

look {at} me, (about) {this} time tomorrow, {will be a} precipitating {of} (very) heavy hailstones, which |had| not existed like <this> in "Mits'rayim [Two straits]", <before> the day she {was} found{ed} and until now,□

9:19 וְעַתָּה שְׁלַח הָעֵז אֶת מִקְנְךָ וְאֵת כָּל אֲשֶׁר לְךָ בַּשָּׂדֶה כָּל הָאָדָם וְהַבְּהֵמָה אֲשֶׁר יִמָּצֵא בַשָּׂדֶה וְלֹא יֵאָסֵף הַבַּיְתָה וְיָרַד עֲלֵהֶם הַבָּרָד וָמֵתוּ

we'a'tah she'lahh ha'eyz et miq'ne'kha we'eyt kol a'sher le'kha ba'sa'deh kol ha'a'dam we'ha'be'hey'mah a'sher yi'ma'tsey va'sa'deh we'lo ye'a'seyph ha'bai'tah we'ya'rad a'ley'hem ha'ba'rad wa'mey'tu

and~NOW *!(ms)*~SEND *!(ms)*~*make*~BE-BOLD AT LIVESTOCK~you(ms) and~AT ALL WHICH to~you(ms) in~the~FIELD ALL the~ HUMAN and~the~BEAST WHICH *he*~*will*~ *be*~FIND in~the~FIELD and~NOT *he*~*will*~*be*~ GATHER the~HOUSE~unto and~*he*~*did*~GO-DOWN UPON~them(m) the~HAILSTONES and~*they*~*did*~DIE□

and now, send, [seek refuge] (with) your livestock and (with) all which {belongs} to you in the field, all the human{s} and the beast{s} which will be found in the field, and {those} not gathered unto the house, (then) the hailstones will go down upon them and they will die,□

9:20 הַיָּרֵא אֶת דְּבַר יְהוָה מֵעַבְדֵי פַּרְעֹה הֵנִיס אֶת עֲבָדָיו וְאֶת מִקְנֵהוּ אֶל הַבָּתִּים

hai'ya'rey et de'var YHWH mey'av'dey par'oh hey'nis et a'va'daw we'et miq'ney'hu el ha'ba'tim

the~FEAR~*ing/er(ms)* AT WORD "Yhwh [*he*~*will*~BE]" from~SERVANT~s "Paroh [GREAT-HOUSE]" *he*~*did*~*make*~FLEE AT SERVANT~s~him and~AT

the {one} fearing {the} word {of} "Yhwh [He is]" from {the} servants {of} "Paroh [Great house]", he will make his servants and his livestock flee to

LIVESTOCK~him TO the~HOUSE~s□   the houses,□

9:21 וַאֲשֶׁר לֹא שָׂם לִבּוֹ אֶל דְּבַר יְהוָה וַיַּעֲזֹב אֶת עֲבָדָיו וְאֶת מִקְנֵהוּ בַּשָּׂדֶה

wa'a'sher lo sham li'bo el de'var YHWH wai'ya'a'zov et a'va'daw we'et miq'ney'hu ba'sa'deh

and~WHICH NOT *he~did~*PLACE HEART~him TO WORD "Yhwh ^{he~will~BE}" and~*he~will~*LEAVE AT SERVANT~s~him and~AT LIVESTOCK~him in~the~FIELD□

and (who) does not place his heart to{ward the} word {of} "Yhwh ^{He is}", (then) he will leave his servants and his livestock in the field,□

9:22 וַיֹּאמֶר יְהוָה אֶל מֹשֶׁה נְטֵה אֶת יָדְךָ עַל הַשָּׁמַיִם וִיהִי בָרָד בְּכָל אֶרֶץ מִצְרָיִם עַל הָאָדָם וְעַל הַבְּהֵמָה וְעַל כָּל עֵשֶׂב הַשָּׂדֶה בְּאֶרֶץ מִצְרָיִם

wai'yo'mer YHWH el mo'sheh ne'teyh et yad'kha al ha'sha'ma'yim wi'hi va'rad be'khol e'rets mits'ra'yim al ha'a'dam we'al ha'be'hey'mah we'al kol ey'sev ha'sa'deh be'e'rets mits'ra'yim

and~*he~will~*SAY "Yhwh ^{he~will~BE}" TO "Mosheh ^{PLUCKED-OUT}" !(ms)~EXTEND AT HAND~you(ms) UPON the~SKY~s2 and~*he~will~*EXIST HAILSTONES in~ALL LAND "Mits'rayim ^{STRAIT~s2}" UPON the~HUMAN and~UPON the~BEAST and~UPON ALL HERB the~FIELD in~LAND "Mits'rayim ^{STRAIT~s2}"□

and "Yhwh ^{He is}" said to "Mosheh ^{Plucked out}", extend your hand upon the skies and hailstones will exist in all {the} land {of} "Mits'rayim ^{Two straits}", upon the human and upon the beast and upon all {the} herb{s of} the field in {the} land {of} "Mits'rayim ^{Two straits}",□

9:23 וַיֵּט מֹשֶׁה אֶת מַטֵּהוּ עַל הַשָּׁמַיִם וַיהוָה נָתַן קֹלֹת וּבָרָד וַתִּהֲלַךְ אֵשׁ אַרְצָה וַיַּמְטֵר יְהוָה בָּרָד עַל אֶרֶץ מִצְרָיִם

wai'yeyt mo'sheh et ma'tey'hu al ha'sha'ma'yim wa'YHWH na'tan qo'lot u'va'rad wa'ti'ha'lakh eysh ar'tsah wai'yam'teyr YHWH ba'rad al e'rets mits'ra'yim

and~*he~will~*EXTEND "Mosheh ^{PLUCKED-OUT}" AT BRANCH~him UPON the~SKY~s2 and~ "Yhwh ^{he~will~BE}" *he~did~*GIVE VOICE~s and~ HAILSTONES and~ she~*will~*WALK FIRE LAND~unto and~*he~will~make~*PRECIPITATE "Yhwh ^{he~will~BE}" HAILSTONES UPON LAND "Mits'rayim ^{STRAIT~s2}"□

and "Mosheh ^{Plucked out}" extended his branch upon the skies, and "Yhwh ^{He is}" |had| given \thunder/ and hailstones, and fire walked unto {the} land, and "Yhwh ^{He is}" made {it} precipitate hailstones upon {the} land {of} "Mits'rayim ^{Two straits}",□

9:24 וַיְהִי בָרָד וְאֵשׁ מִתְלַקַּחַת בְּתוֹךְ הַבָּרָד כָּבֵד מְאֹד אֲשֶׁר לֹא הָיָה כָמֹהוּ בְּכָל אֶרֶץ מִצְרַיִם מֵאָז הָיְתָה לְגוֹי

wai'hi va'rad we'eysh mit'la'qa'hhat be'tokh ha'ba'rad ka'veyd me'od a'sher lo hai'yah kha'mo'hu be'khol e'rets mits'ra'yim mey'az hai'tah le'goi

and~*he~will~*EXIST HAILSTONES and~FIRE self~*TAKE~*ing/er(ms) in~MIDST the~ HAILSTONES HEAVY MANY WHICH NOT *he~did~*EXIST like~THAT-ONE~him in~ALL LAND

and hailstones existed, and fire {was} taking {it}self in {the} midst {of} the (very) heavy hailstones, which |had| not existed like <this> in all {the} land {of} "Mits'rayim ^{Two straits}", from

---

Mechanical Translation Codes

<u>WORD</u> – Verb	WORD – Noun	Word – Name	word – Pre/Suff	*word* – Conj.

"Mits'rayim ^{STRAIT~s2}" from~AT-THAT-TIME   the time she* existed (as) {a} nation,▢
she~*did*~EXIST to~NATION▢

9:25   וַיַּךְ הַבָּרָד בְּכָל אֶרֶץ מִצְרַיִם אֵת כָּל אֲשֶׁר בַּשָּׂדֶה מֵאָדָם וְעַד בְּהֵמָה וְאֵת כָּל עֵשֶׂב הַשָּׂדֶה הִכָּה הַבָּרָד וְאֶת כָּל עֵץ הַשָּׂדֶה שִׁבֵּר

wai'yakh ha'ba'rad be'khol e'rets mits'ra'yim eyt kol a'sher ba'sa'deh mey'a'dam we'ad be'hey'mah we'eyt kol ey'sev ha'sa'deh hi'kah ha'ba'rad we'et kol eyts ha'sa'deh shi'beyr

and~he~will~make~<u>HIT</u> the~HAILSTONES in~ ALL LAND "Mits'rayim ^{STRAIT~s2}" AT ALL WHICH in~the~FIELD from~HUMAN and~ UNTIL BEAST and~AT ALL HERB the~FIELD *he~did*~make~<u>HIT</u> the~HAILSTONES and~AT ALL TREE the~FIELD *he~did*~much~<u>CRACK</u>▢	and the hailstones hit in all {the} land {of} "Mits'rayim ^{Two straits}", all which {were} in the field, from {the} human and (even) {the} beast, and all {the} herb{s of} the field, the hailstones hit, and all {the} tree{s of} the field he✝ [shattered],▢

9:26   רַק בְּאֶרֶץ גֹּשֶׁן אֲשֶׁר שָׁם בְּנֵי יִשְׂרָאֵל לֹא הָיָה בָּרָד

raq be'e'rets go'shen a'sher sham be'ney yis'ra'eyl lo hai'yah ba'rad

ONLY in~LAND "Goshen ^{DRAWING-NEAR}" WHICH THERE SON~s "Yisra'el ^{he~will~<u>TURN-ASIDE</u>~+~MIGHTY-ONE}" NOT *he~did*~<u>EXIST</u> HAILSTONES▢	only in {the} land {of} "Goshen ^{Drawing near}", which there {is the} sons {of} "Yisra'el ^{He turns El aside}", {the} hailstones did not exist,▢

9:27   וַיִּשְׁלַח פַּרְעֹה וַיִּקְרָא לְמֹשֶׁה וּלְאַהֲרֹן וַיֹּאמֶר אֲלֵהֶם חָטָאתִי הַפָּעַם יְהוָה הַצַּדִּיק וַאֲנִי וְעַמִּי הָרְשָׁעִים

wai'yish'lahh par'oh wai'yiq'ra le'mo'sheh ul'a'ha'ron wai'yo'mer a'ley'hem hha'ta'ti ha'pa'am YHWH ha'tsa'diq wa'ani we'a'mi har'sha'im

and~he~will~<u>SEND</u> "Paroh ^{GREAT-HOUSE}" and~ he~will~<u>CALL-OUT</u> to~"Mosheh ^{PLUCKED-OUT}" and~to~"Aharon ^{LIGHT-BRINGER}" and~he~will~ <u>SAY</u> TO~them(m) *I~did*~<u>ERR</u> the~FOOTSTEP "Yhwh ^{he~will~<u>BE</u>}" the~CORRECT and~I and~ PEOPLE~me the~LOST~s▢	and "Paroh ^{Great house}" sent and he called out to "Mosheh ^{Plucked out}" and "Aharon ^{Light bringer}", and he said to them, I erred <this time> , "Yhwh ^{He is}" {is} the correct {one} and I and my people{are} the lost {one}s,▢

9:28   הַעְתִּירוּ אֶל יְהוָה וְרַב מִהְיֹת קֹלֹת אֱלֹהִים וּבָרָד וַאֲשַׁלְּחָה אֶתְכֶם וְלֹא תֹסִפוּן לַעֲמֹד

ha'ti'ru el YHWH we'rav mih'yot qo'lot e'lo'him u'va'rad wa'a'shal'hhah et'khem we'lo to'si'phun la'a'mod

!(mp)~make~<u>INTERCEDE</u> TO "Yhwh ^{he~will~<u>BE</u>}" and~ABUNDANT from~>~<u>EXIST</u> VOICE~s "Elohiym ^{POWER~s}" and~HAILSTONES and~I~ will~much~<u>SEND</u>~^ AT~you(mp) and~NOT	intercede to "Yhwh ^{He is}", <there is enough> \thunder/ {of} "Elohiym ^{Powers}" and hailstones, and I will send you, and you must not [again] stand {here},▢

---

* Referring to the "land," a feminine word in Hebrew.
✝ Referring to the "hailstones" a masculine word in Hebrew.

Revised Mechanical Translation Codes

(..) Alt Trans/App A   <..> Comp Phrase/App B   [..] Verb Form/App C   \../ Plural Form/App D
:..: Int Inf Abs |..| Past Perf Verb   {...} Added Word

you(mp)~will~make~<u>ADD</u>~must to~
>~<u>STAND</u>◻

9:29 וַיֹּאמֶר אֵלָיו מֹשֶׁה כְּצֵאתִי אֶת הָעִיר אֶפְרֹשׂ אֶת כַּפַּי אֶל יְהוָה הַקֹּלוֹת
יֶחְדָּלוּן וְהַבָּרָד לֹא יִהְיֶה עוֹד לְמַעַן תֵּדַע כִּי לַיהוָה הָאָרֶץ

wai'yo'mer ey'law mo'sheh ke'tsey'ti et ha'ir eph'rosh et ka'pai el YHWH ha'qo'lot
yehh'da'lun we'ha'ba'rad lo yih'yeh od le'ma'an tey'da ki la'YHWH ha'a'rets

and~he~will~<u>SAY</u> TO~him "Mosheh ^{PLUCKED-OUT}" like~>~<u>GO-OUT</u>~me AT the~CITY I~will~<u>SPREAD-OUT</u> AT PALM~s2~me TO "Yhwh ^{he~will~<u>BE</u>}" the~VOICE~s *they(m)~will~*<u>TERMINATE</u>~must and~the~HAILSTONES NOT *he~will~*<u>EXIST</u> YET-AGAIN to~THAT *you(ms)~will~*<u>KNOW</u> GIVEN-THAT to~"Yhwh ^{he~will~<u>BE</u>}" the~LAND◻	and "Mosheh ^{Plucked out}" said to him, {in} my go{ing} out* {of} the city, I will spread out my palms to "Yhwh ^{He is}", the \thunder/ must terminate, and the hailstones will not exist again, (so) that you will know that the land {belongs} to "Yhwh ^{He is}",◻

9:30 וְאַתָּה וַעֲבָדֶיךָ יָדַעְתִּי כִּי טֶרֶם תִּירְאוּן מִפְּנֵי יְהוָה אֱלֹהִים

we'a'tah wa'a'va'dey'kha ya'da'ti ki te'rem tir'un mip'ney YHWH e'lo'him

and~YOU(ms) and~SERVANT~s~you(ms) *I~did~*<u>KNOW</u> GIVEN-THAT BEFORE *you(mp)~will~*<u>FEAR</u>~must from~FACE~s "Yhwh ^{he~will~<u>BE</u>}" "Elohiym ^{POWER~s}"◻	and you, and your servants, I know that {you do} (not yet) fear {the} face {of} "Yhwh ^{He is}" {the} "Elohiym ^{Powers}",◻

9:31 וְהַפִּשְׁתָּה וְהַשְּׂעֹרָה נֻכָּתָה כִּי הַשְּׂעֹרָה אָבִיב וְהַפִּשְׁתָּה גִּבְעֹל

we'ha'pish'tah we'has'o'rah nu'ka'tah ki has'o'rah a'viv we'ha'pish'tah giv'ol

and~the~FLAX and~the~BARLEY she~*did~*be~much~<u>HIT</u> GIVEN-THAT the~BARLEY GREEN-GRAIN and~the~FLAX BUDDING◻	and the flax and the barley was hit, given that the barley {was} green and the flax {was} budding,◻

9:32 וְהַחִטָּה וְהַכֻּסֶּמֶת לֹא נֻכּוּ כִּי אֲפִילֹת הֵנָּה

we'ha'hhi'tah we'ha'ku'se'met lo nu'ku ki a'phi'lot heyn'nah

and~the~WHEAT and~the~SPELT NOT *they~did~*<u>HIT</u> GIVEN-THAT LATE~s THEY(f)◻	and the wheat and the spelt were not hit given that they {were} late,◻

9:33 וַיֵּצֵא מֹשֶׁה מֵעִם פַּרְעֹה אֶת הָעִיר וַיִּפְרֹשׂ כַּפָּיו אֶל יְהוָה וַיַּחְדְּלוּ
הַקֹּלוֹת וְהַבָּרָד וּמָטָר לֹא נִתַּךְ אָרְצָה

wai'yey'tsey mo'sheh mey'im par'oh et ha'ir wai'yiph'ros ka'paw el YHWH wai'yahh'de'lu
ha'qo'lot we'ha'ba'rad u'ma'tar lo ni'takh ar'tsah

and~*he~will~*<u>GO-OUT</u> "Mosheh ^{PLUCKED-OUT}"	and "Mosheh ^{Plucked out}" went out {of} the city,

---

* The word כְּצֵאתִי (like my going out) appears to be written defectively and may have originally been written as בְּצֵאתִי (with my going out).

Mechanical Translation Codes

<u>WORD</u> – Verb	WORD – Noun	Word – Name	word – Pre/Suff	*word* – Conj.

from~WITH "Paroh ^{GREAT-HOUSE}" AT the~CITY and~he~will~SPREAD-OUT PALM~s2~him TO "Yhwh ^{he~will~BE}" and~they(m)~will~ TERMINATE the~VOICE~s and~the~ HAILSTONES and~PRECIPITATION NOT he~ did~be~DROP-DOWN LAND~unto□

<away from> "Paroh ^{Great house}", and he spread out his palms to "Yhwh ^{He is}" and the \thunder/ terminated, and the hailstones and precipitation did not drop down unto {the} land,□

9:34   וַיַּרְא פַּרְעֹה כִּי חָדַל הַמָּטָר וְהַבָּרָד וְהַקֹּלֹת וַיֹּסֶף לַחֲטֹא וַיַּכְבֵּד לִבּוֹ הוּא וַעֲבָדָיו

wai'yar par'oh ki hha'dal ha'ma'tar we'ha'ba'rad we'ha'qo'lot wai'yo'seph la'hha'to wai'yakh'beyd li'bo hu wa'a'va'daw

and~he~will~SEE "Paroh ^{GREAT-HOUSE}" GIVEN-THAT he~did~TERMINATE the~ PRECIPITATION and~the~HAILSTONES and~ the~VOICE~s and~he~will~make~ADD to~ >~ERR and~he~will~make~BE-HEAVY HEART~him HE and~SERVANT~s~him□

and "Paroh ^{Great house}" saw that the precipitation and the hailstones and the \thunder/ terminated, and he [again] erred and his heart was made heavy, he and his servants,□

9:35   וַיֶּחֱזַק לֵב פַּרְעֹה וְלֹא שִׁלַּח אֶת בְּנֵי יִשְׂרָאֵל כַּאֲשֶׁר דִּבֶּר יְהֹוָה בְּיַד מֹשֶׁה

wa'ye'hhe'zaq leyv par'oh we'lo shi'lahh et be'ney yis'ra'eyl ka'a'sheyr di'ber YHWH be'yad mo'sheh

and~he~will~SEIZE HEART "Paroh ^{GREAT-HOUSE}" and~NOT he~did~much~SEND AT SON~s "Yisra'el ^{he~will~TURN-ASIDE~+~MIGHTY-ONE}" like~ WHICH he~did~much~SPEAK "Yhwh ^{he~will~BE}" in~HAND "Mosheh ^{PLUCKED-OUT}"□

and he seized {the} heart {of} "Paroh ^{Great house}"*, and he did not send {the} sons {of} "Yisra'el ^{He turns El aside}" <just as> "Yhwh ^{He is}" spoke (by) {the} hand {of} "Mosheh ^{Plucked out}",□

Chapter 10

10:1   וַיֹּאמֶר יְהֹוָה אֶל מֹשֶׁה בֹּא אֶל פַּרְעֹה כִּי אֲנִי הִכְבַּדְתִּי אֶת לִבּוֹ וְאֶת לֵב עֲבָדָיו לְמַעַן שִׁתִי אֹתֹתַי אֵלֶּה בְּקִרְבּוֹ

wal'yo'mer YHWH el mo'sheh bo el par'oh ki a'ni hikh'bad'ti et li'bo we'et leyv a'va'daw le'ma'an shi'ti o'to'tai ey'leh be'qir'bo

and~he~will~SAY "Yhwh ^{he~will~BE}" TO "Mosheh ^{PLUCKED-OUT}" !(ms)~COME TO "Paroh ^{GREAT-HOUSE}" GIVEN-THAT I l~did~make~BE-HEAVY AT HEART~him and~AT HEART SERVANT~s~him to~THAT >~SET-DOWN~me

and "Yhwh ^{He is}" said to "Mosheh ^{Plucked out}", come to "Paroh ^{Great house}" given that I made his heart heavy, and {the} heart {of} his servants, (so) that I {can} set down these, my signs, within him,□

---

* The phrase וַיֶּחֱזַק לֵב פַּרְעֹה can also be translated as "and the heart seized Paroh" but compare with Exodus 4:21 and 9:12.

Revised Mechanical Translation Codes

(..) Alt Trans/App A	<..> Comp Phrase/App B	[..] Verb Form/App C	\../ Plural Form/App D
:..: Int Inf Abs	|..| Past Perf Verb	{...} Added Word	

SIGN~s~me THESE in~WITHIN~him□

10:2 וּלְמַעַן תְּסַפֵּר בְּאָזְנֵי בִנְךָ וּבֶן בִּנְךָ אֵת אֲשֶׁר הִתְעַלַּלְתִּי בְּמִצְרַיִם וְאֶת
אֹתֹתַי אֲשֶׁר שַׂמְתִּי בָם וִידַעְתֶּם כִּי אֲנִי יְהֹוָה

ul'ma'an te'sa'peyr be'az'ney vin'kha u'ven bin'kha eyt a'sher hit'a'lal'ti be'mits'ra'yim
we'et o'to'tai a'sher sam'ti vam wi'da'tem ki a'ni YHWH

and~to~THAT *you(ms)~did~much~*<u>COUNT</u>
in~EAR~s2 SON~you(ms) and~SON SON~
you(ms) AT WHICH *I~did~* self~<u>WORK-OVER</u>
in~"Mits'rayim ᔆᵀᴿᴬᴵᵀ~ˢ²" and~AT SIGN~s~me
WHICH *I~did~*<u>PLACE</u> in~them(m) and~
you(mp)~did~<u>KNOW</u> GIVEN-THAT I "Yhwh ʰᵉ~
ʷⁱˡˡ~<u>BE</u>"□

and (so) that you will [recount] in {the} ears
{of} your son and {the} son {of} your son,
(that) I [abused] "Mits'rayim ᵀʷᵒ ˢᵗʳᵃⁱᵗˢ" (with)
my signs which I placed in them, (then) you
will know that I {am} "Yhwh ᴴᵉ ⁱˢ",□

10:3 וַיָּבֹא מֹשֶׁה וְאַהֲרֹן אֶל פַּרְעֹה וַיֹּאמְרוּ אֵלָיו כֹּה אָמַר יְהֹוָה אֱלֹהֵי
הָעִבְרִים עַד מָתַי מֵאַנְתָּ לֵעָנֹת מִפָּנָי שַׁלַּח עַמִּי וְיַעַבְדֻנִי

wai'ya'vo mo'sheh we'a'ha'ron el par'oh wai'yom'ru ey'law koh a'mar YHWH e'lo'hey
ha'iv'rim ad ma'tai mey'an'ta ley'a'not mi'pa'nai sha'lahh a'mi we'ya'av'du'ni

and~*he~will~*<u>COME</u> "Mosheh ᴾᴸᵁᶜᴷᴱᴰ-ᴼᵁᵀ"
and~"Aharon ᴸᴵᴳᴴᵀ-ᴮᴿᴵᴺᴳᴱᴿ" TO "Paroh ᴳᴿᴱᴬᵀ-
ᴴᴼᵁˢᴱ" and~*they(m)~will~*<u>SAY</u> TO~him IN-
THIS-WAY *he~did~*<u>SAY</u> "Yhwh ʰᵉ~ʷⁱˡˡ~<u>BE</u>"
"Elohiym ᴾᴼᵂᴱᴿ~ˢ" the~"Ever ᴼᵀᴴᴱᴿ-ˢᴵᴰᴱ"~s
UNTIL HOW-LONG *you(ms)~did~much~*
<u>REFUSE</u> to~>~much~<u>AFFLICT</u> from~FACE~s~
me !*(ms)~much~*<u>SEND</u> PEOPLE~me and~
they(m)~will~<u>SERVE</u>~me□

and "Mosheh ᴾˡᵘᶜᵏᵉᵈ ᵒᵘᵗ", and "Aharon ᴸⁱᵍʰᵗ
ᵇʳⁱⁿᵍᵉʳ", came to "Paroh ᴳʳᵉᵃᵗ ʰᵒᵘˢᵉ" and they said
to him, in this way "Yhwh ᴴᵉ ⁱˢ" {the} "Elohiym
ᴾᵒʷᵉʳˢ" {of} the {one}s {of} "Ever ᴼᵗʰᵉʳ ˢⁱᵈᵉ" said,
(for) how long will you refuse to afflict
{yourself} (at) my face? send my people and
they will serve me,□

10:4 כִּי אִם מָאֵן אַתָּה לְשַׁלֵּחַ אֶת עַמִּי הִנְנִי מֵבִיא מָחָר אַרְבֶּה בִּגְבֻלֶךָ

ki im ma'eyn a'tah le'sha'ley'ahh et a'mi hin'ni me'vi ma'hhar ar'beh big'vu'le'kha

GIVEN-THAT IF REFUSING YOU(ms) to~
>~much~<u>SEND</u> AT PEOPLE~me LOOK~me
make~<u>COME</u>~*ing/er(ms)* TOMORROW
LOCUST in~BORDER~you(ms)□

<instead> you {are} refusing to send my
people, look {at} me, tomorrow {I am}
[bring]ing locust in your borders,□

10:5 וְכִסָּה אֶת עֵין הָאָרֶץ וְלֹא יוּכַל לִרְאֹת אֶת הָאָרֶץ וְאָכַל אֶת יֶתֶר
הַפְּלֵטָה הַנִּשְׁאֶרֶת לָכֶם מִן הַבָּרָד וְאָכַל אֶת כָּל הָעֵץ הַצֹּמֵחַ לָכֶם מִן
הַשָּׂדֶה

we'khi'sah et eyn ha'a'rets we'lo yu'khal lir'ot et ha'a'rets we'a'khal et ye'ter hap'ley'tah
ha'nish'e'ret la'khem min ha'ba'rad we'a'khal et kol ha'eyts ha'tso'mey'ahh la'khem min
ha'sa'deh

Mechanical Translation Codes

<u>WORD</u> – Verb   WORD – Noun   Word – Name   word – Pre/Suff   *word* – Conj.

~ 76 ~

and~he~did~much~UNDERLINE{COVER-OVER} AT EYE the~LAND and~NOT he~will~UNDERLINE{BE-ABLE} to~ >~UNDERLINE{SEE} AT the~LAND and~he~did~UNDERLINE{EAT} AT REMAINDER the~ESCAPE the~be~UNDERLINE{REMAIN}~ ing/er(fs) to~you(mp) FROM the~ HAILSTONES and~he~did~UNDERLINE{EAT} AT ALL the~ TREE the~UNDERLINE{SPRING-UP}~ing/er(ms) to~ you(mp) FROM the~FIELD□

and he* will cover over {the} eye {of} the land, and he† will not be able to see the land, and he will eat {the} remainder {of} the {ones} escap{ing}, the {ones} remaining to you from the hailstones, and he will eat all the springing up tree{s that belong} to you from the field,□

10:6 וּמָלְאוּ בָתֶּיךָ וּבָתֵּי כָל עֲבָדֶיךָ וּבָתֵּי כָל מִצְרַיִם אֲשֶׁר לֹא רָאוּ אֲבֹתֶיךָ וַאֲבוֹת אֲבֹתֶיךָ מִיּוֹם הֱיוֹתָם עַל הָאֲדָמָה עַד הַיּוֹם הַזֶּה וַיִּפֶן וַיֵּצֵא מֵעִם פַּרְעֹה

u'mal'u va'tey'kha u'va'tey khol a'va'dey'kha u'va'tey khol mits'ra'yim a'sher lo ra'u a'vo'tey'kha wa'a'vot a'vo'tey'kha mi'yom he'yo'tam al ha'a'da'mah ad hai'yom ha'zeh wai'yi'phen wai'yey'tsey mey'im par'oh

and~they~did~UNDERLINE{FILL} HOUSE~s~you(ms) and~ HOUSE~s ALL SERVANT~s~you(ms) and~ HOUSE~s ALL "Mits'rayim $^{STRAIT~s2}$" WHICH NOT they~did~UNDERLINE{SEE} FATHER~s~you(ms) and~ FATHER~s FATHER~s~you(ms) from~DAY >~UNDERLINE{EXIST}~you(mp) UPON the~GROUND UNTIL the~DAY the~THIS and~he~will~UNDERLINE{TURN} and~he~will~UNDERLINE{GO-OUT} from~WITH "Paroh GREAT-HOUSE"□

and they will fill your houses and {the} houses {of} all your servants and {the} houses {of} all "Mits'rayim $^{Two straits}$", which your fathers, and {the} fathers {of} your fathers, did not see, from {the} day you existed upon the ground until this day, and he turned and he went out <away from> "Paroh $^{Great house}$",□

10:7 וַיֹּאמְרוּ עַבְדֵי פַרְעֹה אֵלָיו עַד מָתַי יִהְיֶה זֶה לָנוּ לְמוֹקֵשׁ שַׁלַּח אֶת הָאֲנָשִׁים וְיַעַבְדוּ אֶת יְהֹוָה אֱלֹהֵיהֶם הֲטֶרֶם תֵּדַע כִּי אָבְדָה מִצְרָיִם

wai'yom'ru av'dey phar'oh ey'law ad ma'tai yih'yeh zeh la'nu le'mo'qeysh sha'lahh et ha'a'na'shim we'ya'av'du et YHWH e'lo'hey'hem ha'te'rem tey'da ki av'dah mits'ra'yim

and~they(m)~will~UNDERLINE{SAY} SERVANT~s "Paroh GREAT-HOUSE" TO~him UNTIL HOW-LONG he~ will~UNDERLINE{EXIST} THIS to~us to~UNDERLINE{SNARE} !(ms)~ much~UNDERLINE{SEND} AT the~MAN~s and~they(m)~ will~UNDERLINE{SERVE} AT "Yhwh $^{he~will~BE}$" "Elohiym $^{POWER~s}$"~them(m) ?~BEFORE you(ms)~will~ UNDERLINE{KNOW} GIVEN-THAT she~did~UNDERLINE{PERISH} "Mits'rayim $^{STRAIT~s2}$"□

and {the} servants {of} "Paroh $^{Great house}$" said to him, (for) how long will this exist to us (as) {a} snare? send the men and they will serve "Yhwh $^{He is}$" their "Elohiym ^{Powers}", {do} you (not yet) know that "Mits'rayim $^{Two straits}$" {is} perished?□

10:8 וַיּוּשַׁב אֶת מֹשֶׁה וְאֶת אַהֲרֹן אֶל פַּרְעֹה וַיֹּאמֶר אֲלֵהֶם לְכוּ עִבְדוּ אֶת יְהֹוָה אֱלֹהֵיכֶם מִי וָמִי הַהֹלְכִים

wai'yu'shav et mo'sheh we'et a'ha'ron el par'oh wai'yo'mer a'ley'hem le'khu iv'du et

---

* Referring to the "locust," a masculine singular word in Hebrew.
† Grammatically, this is referring to the locust, but contextually it is referring to the people.

Revised Mechanical Translation Codes

(..) Alt Trans/App A	<..> Comp Phrase/App B	[..] Verb Form/App C	\..\ Plural Form/App D
:...: Int Inf Abs	|..| Past Perf Verb	{...} Added Word	

YHWH e'lo'hey'khem mi wa'mi ha'hol'khim

and~*he*~will~*be*~make~<u>TURN-BACK</u> AT "Mosheh ^{PLUCKED-OUT}" and~AT "Aharon ^{LIGHT-BRINGER}" TO "Paroh ^{GREAT-HOUSE}" and~*he*~will~<u>SAY</u> TO~them(m) !(mp)~<u>WALK</u> !(mp)~<u>SERVE</u> AT "Yhwh ^{*he*~will~<u>BE</u>}" "Elohiym ^{POWER~s}~ you(mp) WHO and~WHO the~<u>WALK</u>~ing/er(mp)□	and "Mosheh ^{Plucked out}" was turned back, and "Aharon ^{Light bringer}", to "Paroh ^{Great house}", and he said to them, walk, serve "Yhwh ^{He is}" your "Elohiym ^{Powers}", who and who* {are} the {one}s walking?□

10:9   וַיֹּאמֶר מֹשֶׁה בִּנְעָרֵינוּ וּבִזְקֵנֵינוּ נֵלֵךְ בְּבָנֵינוּ וּבִבְנוֹתֵנוּ בְּצֹאנֵנוּ וּבִבְקָרֵנוּ נֵלֵךְ כִּי חַג יְהוָה לָנוּ

wai'yo'mer mo'sheh bin'a'rey'nu u'viz'qey'ney'nu ney'leykh be'va'ney'nu u'viv'no'tey'nu be'tso'ney'nu u'viv'qa'rey'nu ney'leykh ki hhag YHWH la'nu

and~*he*~will~<u>SAY</u> "Mosheh ^{PLUCKED-OUT}" in~YOUNG-MAN~s~us and~in~BEARD~us *we*~will~<u>WALK</u> in~SON~s~us and~in~DAUGHTER~s~us in~FLOCKS~us and~in~CATTLE~us *we*~will~<u>WALK</u> GIVEN-THAT FEAST "Yhwh ^{*he*~will~<u>BE</u>}" to~us□	and "Mosheh ^{Plucked out}" said, (with) our young men and (with) our beard{ed ones}† we will walk, (with) our sons and (with) our daughters, (with) our flocks and (with) our cattle we will walk, given that {a} feast {of} "Yhwh ^{He is}" {is} (for) us,□

10:10   וַיֹּאמֶר אֲלֵהֶם יְהִי כֵן יְהוָה עִמָּכֶם כַּאֲשֶׁר אֲשַׁלַּח אֶתְכֶם וְאֶת טַפְּכֶם רְאוּ כִּי רָעָה נֶגֶד פְּנֵיכֶם

wai'yo'mer a'ley'hem ye'hi kheyn YHWH i'ma'khem ka'a'sheyr a'sha'lahh et'khem we'et tap'khem re'u ki ra'ah ne'ged pe'ney'khem

and~*he*~will~<u>SAY</u> TO~them(m) *he*~will~<u>EXIST</u> SO "Yhwh ^{*he*~will~<u>BE</u>}" WITH~you(mp) like~WHICH *I*~will much~<u>SEND</u> AT~you(mp) and~AT CHILDREN~you(mp) !(mp)~<u>SEE</u> GIVEN-THAT DYSFUNCTIONAL OPPOSITE FACE~s~you(mp)□	and he said to them, "Yhwh ^{He is}" will exist so with you, <just as> I will send you and your children, see that dysfunction {is} (before) your face,□

10:11   לֹא כֵן לְכוּ נָא הַגְּבָרִים וְעִבְדוּ אֶת יְהוָה כִּי אֹתָהּ אַתֶּם מְבַקְשִׁים וַיְגָרֶשׁ אֹתָם מֵאֵת פְּנֵי פַרְעֹה

lo kheyn le'khu na hag'va'rim we'iv'du et YHWH ki o'tah a'tem me'vaq'shim wai'ga'resh o'tam mey'eyt pe'ney phar'oh

NOT SO !(mp)~<u>WALK</u> PLEASE the~WARRIOR~s and~!(mp)~<u>SERVE</u> AT "Yhwh ^{*he*~will~<u>BE</u>}" GIVEN-THAT AT~her YOU(mp) *much*~<u>SEARCH-OUT</u>~ing/er(mp) and~*he*~will~*much*~<u>CAST-OUT</u> AT~them(m) from~AT	not so, please walk the warriors and serve "Yhwh ^{He is}", given that you {are} searching (this) out, and he cast them out from {the} face {of} "Paroh ^{Great house}",□

---

* "Who and who are the ones walking" means "who all are going."
† "Bearded ones" is a euphemism for "elders."

Mechanical Translation Codes

<u>WORD</u> – Verb	WORD – Noun	Word – Name	word – Pre/Suff	*word* – Conj.

FACE~s "Paroh ^GREAT-HOUSE„□

10:12

וַיֹּאמֶר יְהוָה אֶל מֹשֶׁה נְטֵה יָדְךָ עַל אֶרֶץ מִצְרַיִם בָּאַרְבֶּה וְיַעַל עַל אֶרֶץ מִצְרַיִם וְיֹאכַל אֶת כָּל עֵשֶׂב הָאָרֶץ אֵת כָּל אֲשֶׁר הִשְׁאִיר הַבָּרָד

wai'yo'mer YHWH el mo'sheh ne'teyh yad'kha al e'rets mits'ra'yim ba'ar'beh we'ya'al al e'rets mits'ra'yim we'yo'khal et kol ey'sev ha'a'rets eyt kol a'sher hish'ir ha'ba'rad

and~he~will~<u>SAY</u> "Yhwh ^he~will~<u>BE</u>„ TO "Mosheh ^PLUCKED-OUT„ !(ms)~<u>EXTEND</u> HAND~ you(ms) UPON LAND "Mits'rayim ^STRAIT~s2„ in~ the~LOCUST and~he~will~<u>GO-UP</u> UPON LAND "Mits'rayim ^STRAIT~s2„ and~he~will~<u>EAT</u> AT ALL HERB the~LAND AT ALL WHICH he~ did~make~<u>REMAIN</u> the~HAILSTONES□

and "Yhwh ^He is„ said to "Mosheh ^Plucked out„, extend your hand upon {the} land {of} "Mits'rayim ^Two straits„ (with) the locust, and he will go up upon {the} land {of} "Mits'rayim ^Two straits„, and he will eat all {the} herb{s of} the land, all which the hailstones [left],□

10:13

וַיֵּט מֹשֶׁה אֶת מַטֵּהוּ עַל אֶרֶץ מִצְרַיִם וַיהוָה נִהַג רוּחַ קָדִים בָּאָרֶץ כָּל הַיּוֹם הַהוּא וְכָל הַלַּיְלָה הַבֹּקֶר הָיָה וְרוּחַ הַקָּדִים נָשָׂא אֶת הָאַרְבֶּה

wai'yeyt mo'sheh et ma'tey'hu al e'rets mits'ra'yim wa'YHWH ni'hag ru'ahh qa'dim ba'a'rets kol hai'yom ha'hu we'khol ha'lai'lah ha'bo'qer hai'yah we'ru'ahh ha'qa'dim na'sa et ha'ar'beh

and~he~will~<u>EXTEND</u> "Mosheh ^PLUCKED-OUT„ AT BRANCH~him UPON LAND "Mits'rayim ^STRAIT~s2„ and~"Yhwh ^he~will~<u>BE</u>„ he~did~much~ <u>DRIVE</u> WIND EAST-WIND in~the~LAND ALL the~DAY the~HE and~ALL the~NIGHT the~ MORNING he~did~<u>EXIST</u> and~WIND the~ EAST-WIND he~did~<u>LIFT-UP</u> AT the~ LOCUST□

and "Mosheh ^Plucked out„ extended his branch upon {the} land {of} "Mits'rayim ^Two straits„, and "Yhwh ^He is„ |had| driven {a} wind {of the} east wind in the land all (that) day and all the night, the morning |had| existed and {the} wind {of} the east wind |had| lifted up the locust,□

10:14

וַיַּעַל הָאַרְבֶּה עַל כָּל אֶרֶץ מִצְרַיִם וַיָּנַח בְּכֹל גְּבוּל מִצְרָיִם כָּבֵד מְאֹד לְפָנָיו לֹא הָיָה כֵן אַרְבֶּה כָּמֹהוּ וְאַחֲרָיו לֹא יִהְיֶה כֵּן

wai'ya'al ha'ar'beh al kol e'rets mits'ra'yim wai'ya'nahh be'khol ge'vul mits'ra'yim ka'veyd me'od le'pha'naw lo hai'yah kheyn ar'beh ka'mo'hu we'a'hha'raw lo yih'yeh keyn

and~he~will~<u>GO-UP</u> the~LOCUST UPON ALL LAND "Mits'rayim ^STRAIT~s2„ and~he~will~<u>REST</u> in~ALL BORDER "Mits'rayim ^STRAIT~s2„ HEAVY MANY to~FACE~s~him NOT he~did~<u>EXIST</u> SO LOCUST like~THAT-ONE~him and~AFTER~ him NOT he~will~<u>EXIST</u> SO□

and the locust went up upon all {the} land {of} "Mits'rayim ^Two straits„, and he* rested in all {the} border{s of} "Mits'rayim ^Two straits„, (very) heavy <in front of> him, locust like <this> did not exist so, and after he will not exist so,□

10:15

וַיְכַס אֶת עֵין כָּל הָאָרֶץ וַתֶּחְשַׁךְ הָאָרֶץ וַיֹּאכַל אֶת כָּל עֵשֶׂב הָאָרֶץ וְאֵת כָּל פְּרִי הָעֵץ אֲשֶׁר הוֹתִיר הַבָּרָד וְלֹא נוֹתַר כָּל יֶרֶק בָּעֵץ וּבְעֵשֶׂב הַשָּׂדֶה בְּכָל אֶרֶץ מִצְרָיִם

---

* Referring to the "locust," a masculine singular word in Hebrew.

Revised Mechanical Translation Codes

| (..) Alt Trans/App A | <..> Comp Phrase/App B | [..] Verb Form/App C | \../ Plural Form/App D |
| :..: Int Inf Abs | \|..\| Past Perf Verb | {...} Added Word | |

wai'khas et eyn kol ha'a'rets wa'tehh'shakh ha'a'rets wai'yo'khal et kol ey'sev ha'a'rets
we'eyt kol pe'ri ha'eyts a'sher ho'tir ha'ba'rad we'lo no'tar kol ye'req ba'eyts uv'ey'sev
ha'sa'deh be'khol e'rets mits'ra'yim

and~*he~will~much~*<u>COVER-OVER</u> AT EYE ALL the~LAND and~ she~*will~*<u>DARKEN</u> the~LAND and~*he~will~*<u>EAT</u> AT ALL HERB the~LAND and~AT ALL PRODUCE the~TREE WHICH *he~ did~make~*<u>LEAVE-BEHIND</u> the~HAILSTONES and~NOT *he~did~be~*<u>LEAVE-BEHIND</u> ALL GREEN in~the~TREE and~in~HERB the~FIELD in~ALL LAND "Mits'rayim ^{STRAIT~s2}"□	and he* covered over {the} eye {of} all the land, and the land was darkened, and he ate all {the} herb{s of} the land and all {the} produce {of} the tree{s} which the hailstones left behind, and not (any) {of the} green in the tree{s} was left behind (or) in {the} herb{s of} the field, in all {the} land {of} "Mits'rayim ^{Two straits}",□

10:16 וַיְמַהֵר פַּרְעֹה לִקְרֹא לְמֹשֶׁה וּלְאַהֲרֹן וַיֹּאמֶר חָטָאתִי לַיהוָה אֱלֹהֵיכֶם וְלָכֶם

wai'ma'heyr par'oh liq'ro le'mo'sheh ul'a'ha'ron wai'yo'mer hha'ta'ti la'YHWH
e'lo'hey'khem we'la'khem

and~*he~will~much~*<u>HURRY</u> "Paroh ^{GREAT-HOUSE}" to~>~<u>CALL-OUT</u> to~"Mosheh ^{PLUCKED-OUT}" and~to~"Aharon ^{LIGHT-BRINGER}" and~*he~ will~*<u>SAY</u> *I~did~*<u>ERR</u> to~"Yhwh ^{*he~will~*<u>BE</u>}" "Elohiym ^{POWER~s}"~you(mp) and~to~you(mp)□	and "Paroh ^{Great house}" hurried to call out to "Mosheh ^{Plucked out}" and to "Aharon ^{Light bringer}" and he said, I erred to "Yhwh ^{He is}" your "Elohiym ^{Powers}" and to you,□

10:17 וְעַתָּה שָׂא נָא חַטָּאתִי אַךְ הַפַּעַם וְהַעְתִּירוּ לַיהוָה אֱלֹהֵיכֶם וְיָסֵר מֵעָלַי רַק אֶת הַמָּוֶת הַזֶּה

we'a'tah sa na hha'ta'ti akh ha'pa'am we'ha'ti'ru la'YHWH e'lo'hey'khem we'ya'seyr
mey'a'lai raq et ha'ma'wet ha'zeh

and~NOW *!(ms)~*<u>LIFT-UP</u> PLEASE ERROR~me SURELY the~FOOTSTEP and~*!(mp)~*<u>INTERCEDE</u> to~"Yhwh ^{*he~will~*<u>BE</u>}" "Elohiym ^{POWER~s}"~you(mp) and~*he~will~make~*<u>TURN-ASIDE</u> from~UPON~me ONLY AT the~DEATH the~THIS□	and now, please lift up my error, (only) <this time>, and intercede to "Yhwh ^{He is}" your "Elohiym ^{Powers}", and he will turn aside this death from upon me only,□

10:18 וַיֵּצֵא מֵעִם פַּרְעֹה וַיֶּעְתַּר אֶל יְהוָה

wai'yey'tsey mey'im par'oh wai'ye'tar el YHWH

and~*he~will~*<u>GO-OUT</u> from~WITH "Paroh ^{GREAT-HOUSE}" and~*he~will~*<u>INTERCEDE</u> TO "Yhwh ^{*he~will~*<u>BE</u>}"□	and he went out <away from> "Paroh ^{Great house}" and he interceded to "Yhwh ^{He is}",□

10:19 וַיַּהֲפֹךְ יְהוָה רוּחַ יָם חָזָק מְאֹד וַיִּשָּׂא אֶת הָאַרְבֶּה וַיִּתְקָעֵהוּ יָמָּה סּוּף לֹא נִשְׁאַר אַרְבֶּה אֶחָד בְּכֹל גְּבוּל מִצְרָיִם

---

* Referring to the "locust," a masculine singular word in Hebrew.

Mechanical Translation Codes

<u>WORD</u> – Verb	WORD – Noun	Word – Name	word – Pre/Suff	*word* – Conj.

wai'ya'ha'phokh YHWH ru'ahh yam hha'zaq me'od wai'yi'sa et ha'ar'beh wai'yit'qa'ey'hu ya'mah suph lo nish'ar ar'beh e'hhad be'khol ge'vul mits'ra'yim

and~*he~will*~UNDERLINE OVERTURN "Yhwh ^{he~will~BE}"
WIND SEA FORCEFUL MANY and~*he~will*~
LIFT-UP AT the~LOCUST and~*he~will*~
THRUST~him SEA~unto REEDS NOT *he~did*~
be~REMAIN LOCUST UNIT in~ALL BORDER
"Mits'rayim ^{STRAIT~s2}",□

and "Yhwh ^{He is}" overturned {a} (very) forceful
wind {of the} sea*, and he lifted up the locust,
and he thrust him† unto the sea {of} reeds‡,
not (one) locust was remaining in all {the}
border{s of} "Mits'rayim ^{Two straits}",□

10:20 וַיְחַזֵּק יְהוָה אֶת לֵב פַּרְעֹה וְלֹא שִׁלַּח אֶת בְּנֵי יִשְׂרָאֵל

wai'hha'zeyq YHWH et leyv par'oh we'lo shi'lahh et be'ney yis'ra'eyl

and~*he~will*~*much*~SEIZE "Yhwh ^{he~will~BE}" AT
HEART "Paroh ^{GREAT-HOUSE}" and~NOT *he~did*~
much~SEND AT SON~s "Yisra'el ^{he~will~TURN-ASIDE~+~MIGHTY-ONE}"□

and "Yhwh ^{He is}" seized {the} heart {of} "Paroh
^{Great house}", and he did not send {the} sons {of}
"Yisra'el ^{He turns El aside}",□

10:21 וַיֹּאמֶר יְהוָה אֶל מֹשֶׁה נְטֵה יָדְךָ עַל הַשָּׁמַיִם וִיהִי חֹשֶׁךְ עַל אֶרֶץ מִצְרָיִם וְיָמֵשׁ חֹשֶׁךְ

wai'yo'mer YHWH el mo'sheh ne'teyh yad'kha al ha'sha'ma'yim wi'hi hho'shekh al e'rets mits'ra'yim we'ya'meysh hho'shekh

and~*he~will*~SAY "Yhwh ^{he~will~BE}" TO
"Mosheh ^{PLUCKED-OUT}" !(ms)~EXTEND HAND~
you(ms) UPON the~SKY~s2 and~*he~will*~
EXIST DARKNESS UPON LAND "Mits'rayim
^{STRAIT~s2}" and~*he~will*~*make*~GROPE
DARKNESS□

and "Yhwh ^{He is}" said to "Mosheh ^{Plucked out}",
extend your hand upon the skies and darkness
will exist upon {the} land {of} "Mits'rayim <sup>Two
straits</sup>", and {the} darkness will make {one}
grope,□

10:22 וַיֵּט מֹשֶׁה אֶת יָדוֹ עַל הַשָּׁמָיִם וַיְהִי חֹשֶׁךְ אֲפֵלָה בְּכָל אֶרֶץ מִצְרַיִם שְׁלֹשֶׁת יָמִים

wai'yeyt mo'sheh et ya'do al ha'sha'ma'yim wai'hi hho'shekh a'phey'lah be'khol e'rets mits'ra'yim she'lo'shet ya'mim

and~*he~will*~EXTEND "Mosheh ^{PLUCKED-OUT}"
AT HAND~him UPON the~SKY~s2 and~*he~*
will~EXIST DARKNESS THICK-GLOOMINESS
in~ALL LAND "Mits'rayim ^{STRAIT~s2}" THREE
DAY~s□

and "Mosheh ^{Plucked out}" extended his hand
upon the skies, and {a} darkness {of} thick
gloominess existed in all {the} land {of}
"Mits'rayim ^{Two straits}" {for} three days,□

10:23 לֹא רָאוּ אִישׁ אֶת אָחִיו וְלֹא קָמוּ אִישׁ מִתַּחְתָּיו שְׁלֹשֶׁת יָמִים וּלְכָל בְּנֵי יִשְׂרָאֵל הָיָה אוֹר בְּמוֹשְׁבֹתָם

---

* Meaning the "west."
† Referring to the "locust," a masculine singular word in Hebrew.
‡ "Sea of reeds," or "Yam Suph," is usually mistranslated as "red sea."

Revised Mechanical Translation Codes

(..) Alt Trans/App A	<..> Comp Phrase/App B	[..] Verb Form/App C	\..\ Plural Form/App D
:..: Int Inf Abs	|..| Past Perf Verb	{...} Added Word	

lo ra'u ish et a'hhiw we'lo qa'mu ish mi'tahh'taw she'lo'shet ya'mim ul'khol be'ney yis'ra'eyl hai'yah or be'mosh'vo'tam

NOT *they~did*~<u>SEE</u> MAN AT BROTHER~him and~NOT *they~did*~<u>RISE</u> MAN from~ UNDER~s~him THREE DAY~s and~to~ALL SON~s "Yisra'el *he~will*~<u>TURN-ASIDE</u>~+~MIGHTY-ONE„ *he~did*~<u>EXIST</u> LIGHT in~<u>SETTLING</u>~them(m)▢

(each) could not see his brother, and (each) could not rise from \underneath/ him* {for} three days, and to all {the} sons {of} "Yisra'el ^{He} turns El aside" light existed in their settling {place},▢

10:24

וַיִּקְרָא פַרְעֹה אֶל מֹשֶׁה וַיֹּאמֶר לְכוּ עִבְדוּ אֶת יְהוָה רַק צֹאנְכֶם וּבְקַרְכֶם יֻצָּג גַּם טַפְּכֶם יֵלֵךְ עִמָּכֶם

wai'yiq'ra phar'oh el mo'sheh wai'yo'mer le'khu iv'du et YHWH raq tson'khem uv'qar'khem yu'tsag gam tap'khem yey'leykh i'ma'khem

and~*he~will*~<u>CALL-OUT</u> "Paroh ^{GREAT-HOUSE}„ TO "Mosheh ^{PLUCKED-OUT}„ and~*he~will*~<u>SAY</u> !(mp)~<u>WALK</u> !(mp)~<u>SERVE</u> AT "Yhwh ^{he~will~}<u>BE</u>„ ONLY FLOCKS~you(mp) and~CATTLE~ you(mp) *he~will~be~make*~<u>LEAVE-IN-PLACE</u> ALSO CHILDREN~you(mp) *he~will*~<u>WALK</u> WITH~you(mp)▢

and "Paroh ^{Great house}„ called out to "Mosheh ^{Plucked out}„ and he said, walk, serve "Yhwh ^{He is}„, only your flocks and your cattle will be left in place, also your children will walk with you,▢

10:25

וַיֹּאמֶר מֹשֶׁה גַּם אַתָּה תִּתֵּן בְּיָדֵנוּ זְבָחִים וְעֹלֹת וְעָשִׂינוּ לַיהוָה אֱלֹהֵינוּ

wai'yo'mer mo'sheh gam a'tah ti'teyn be'ya'dey'nu ze'va'hhim we'o'lot we'a'si'nu la'YHWH e'lo'hey'nu

and~*he~will*~<u>SAY</u> "Mosheh ^{PLUCKED-OUT}„ ALSO YOU(ms) *you(ms)~will*~<u>GIVE</u> in~HAND~us SACRIFICE~s and~RISING~s and~*we~did*~<u>DO</u> to~"Yhwh ^{he~will~}<u>BE</u>„ "Elohiym ^{POWER~s}„~us▢

and "Mosheh ^{Plucked out}„ said, also you, you will (place) in our hand {the} sacrifices and rising {sacrifice}s, and we will do {them} (for) "Yhwh ^{He is}„ our "Elohiym ^{Powers}„,▢

10:26

וְגַם מִקְנֵנוּ יֵלֵךְ עִמָּנוּ לֹא תִשָּׁאֵר פַּרְסָה כִּי מִמֶּנּוּ נִקַּח לַעֲבֹד אֶת יְהוָה אֱלֹהֵינוּ וַאֲנַחְנוּ לֹא נֵדַע מַה נַּעֲבֹד אֶת יְהוָה עַד בֹּאֵנוּ שָׁמָּה

we'gam miq'ney'nu yey'leykh i'ma'nu lo ti'sha'eyr par'sah ki mi'me'nu ni'qahh la'a'vod et YHWH e'lo'hey'nu wa'a'nahh'nu lo ney'da mah na'a'vod et YHWH ad bo'ey'nu sham'mah

and~ALSO LIVESTOCK~us *he~will*~<u>WALK</u> WITH~us NOT *she~will~be*~<u>REMAIN</u> SPLIT-HOOF GIVEN-THAT FROM~him *we~will*~<u>TAKE</u> to~>~<u>SERVE</u> AT "Yhwh ^{he~will~BE}„ "Elohiym ^{POWER~s}„~us and~WE NOT *we~will*~<u>KNOW</u> WHAT *we~will*~<u>SERVE</u> AT "Yhwh ^{he~will~BE}„ UNTIL >~<u>COME</u>~us THERE~unto▢

and also our livestock will walk with us, {a} split hoof will not remain, given that from him we will take to serve "Yhwh ^{He is}„ our "Elohiym ^{Powers}„, and we will not know what we will serve "Yhwh ^{He is}„ until we come unto there,▢

10:27

וַיְחַזֵּק יְהוָה אֶת לֵב פַּרְעֹה וְלֹא אָבָה לְשַׁלְּחָם

---

* Referring to the "darkness" in verse 22, a masculine word in Hebrew.

Mechanical Translation Codes

<u>WORD</u> – Verb	WORD – Noun	Word – Name	word – Pre/Suff	*word* – Conj.

wai'hha'zeyq YHWH et leyv par'oh we'lo a'vah le'shal'hham

and~he~will~much~<u>SEIZE</u> "Yhwh ^{he~will~<u>BE</u>}" AT HEART "Paroh ^{GREAT-HOUSE}" and~NOT he~did~ <u>CONSENT</u> to~>~much~<u>SEND</u>~them(m)□	and "Yhwh ^{He is}" seized {the} heart {of} "Paroh ^{Great house}" and he did not consent to send them,□

10:28 וַיֹּאמֶר לוֹ פַרְעֹה לֵךְ מֵעָלָי הִשָּׁמֶר לְךָ אַל תֹּסֶף רְאוֹת פָּנַי כִּי בְּיוֹם רְאֹתְךָ פָנַי תָּמוּת

wai'yo'mer lo phar'oh leykh mey'a'lai hi'sha'mer le'kha al to'seph re'ot pa'nai ki be'yom re'ot'kha pha'nai ta'mut

and~he~will~<u>SAY</u> to~him "Paroh ^{GREAT-HOUSE}" !(ms)~<u>WALK</u> from~UPON~me !(ms)~be~ <u>SAFEGUARD</u> to~you(ms) DO-NOT you(ms)~ will~make~<u>ADD</u> >~<u>SEE</u> FACE~s~me GIVEN-THAT in~DAY >~<u>SEE</u>~you(ms) FACE~s~me you(ms)~will~<u>DIE</u>□	and "Paroh ^{Great house}" said to him, walk from upon me, safeguard your{selves}, do not [again] see my face, given that in {the} day you see my face, you will die,□

10:29 וַיֹּאמֶר מֹשֶׁה כֵּן דִּבַּרְתָּ לֹא אֹסִף עוֹד רְאוֹת פָּנֶיךָ

wai'yo'mer mo'sheh keyn di'bar'ta lo o'siph od re'ot pa'ney'kha

and~he~will~<u>SAY</u> "Mosheh ^{PLUCKED-OUT}" SO you(ms)~did~much~<u>SPEAK</u> NOT I~will~ make~<u>ADD</u> YET-AGAIN >~<u>SEE</u> FACE~s~ you(ms)□	and "Mosheh ^{Plucked out}" said, so you spoke, I will not (ever) [again] see your face,□

Chapter 11

11:1 וַיֹּאמֶר יְהוָה אֶל מֹשֶׁה עוֹד נֶגַע אֶחָד אָבִיא עַל פַּרְעֹה וְעַל מִצְרַיִם אַחֲרֵי כֵן יְשַׁלַּח אֶתְכֶם מִזֶּה כְּשַׁלְּחוֹ כָּלָה גָּרֵשׁ יְגָרֵשׁ אֶתְכֶם מִזֶּה

wai'yo'mer YHWH el mo'sheh od ne'ga e'hhad a'vi al par'oh we'al mits'ra'yim a'hha'rey kheyn ye'sha'lahh et'khem mi'zeh ke'shal'hho ka'lah ga'reysh ye'ga'reysh et'khem mi'zeh

and~he~will~<u>SAY</u> "Yhwh ^{he~will~<u>BE</u>}" TO "Mosheh ^{PLUCKED-OUT}" YET-AGAIN PLAGUE UNIT I~will~make~<u>COME</u> UPON "Paroh ^{GREAT-HOUSE}" and~UPON "Mits'rayim ^{STRAIT~s2}" AFTER SO he~will~much~<u>SEND</u> AT~you(mp) from~ THIS like~>~much~<u>SEND</u>~him COMPLETION >~much~<u>CAST-OUT</u> he will much~<u>CAST OUT</u> AT~you(mp) from~THIS□	and "Yhwh ^{He is}" said to "Mosheh ^{Plucked out}", I will [bring] (one) (more) plague upon "Paroh ^{Great house}" and upon "Mits'rayim ^{Two straits}", <afterward> he will send you from this {place}, (as) he {is} complete{ly} sending {you}, he will :surely: cast you out from this {place},□

11:2 דַּבֶּר נָא בְּאָזְנֵי הָעָם וְיִשְׁאֲלוּ אִישׁ מֵאֵת רֵעֵהוּ וְאִשָּׁה מֵאֵת רְעוּתָהּ כְּלֵי כֶסֶף וּכְלֵי זָהָב

da'ber na be'az'ney ha'am we'yish'a'lu ish mey'eyt rey'ey'hu we'i'shah mey'eyt re'u'tah

Revised Mechanical Translation Codes

(..) Alt Trans/App A	<..> Comp Phrase/App B	[..] Verb Form/App C	\../ Plural Form/App D
:...: Int Inf Abs	|..| Past Perf Verb	{...} Added Word	

ke'ley ke'seph ukh'ley za'hav

>~*much*~<u>SPEAK</u> PLEASE in~EAR~s2 the~ PEOPLE and~*they(m)*~will~<u>ENQUIRE</u> MAN from~AT COMPANION~him and~WOMAN from~AT FRIEND~her ITEM~s SILVER and~ ITEM~s GOLD□	please speak in {the} ears {of} the people and (each) will enquire, from his companion and (each) from her friend, items {of} silver and items {of} gold,□

11:3 וַיִּתֵּן יְהוָה אֶת חֵן הָעָם בְּעֵינֵי מִצְרַיִם גַּם הָאִישׁ מֹשֶׁה גָּדוֹל מְאֹד בְּאֶרֶץ מִצְרַיִם בְּעֵינֵי עַבְדֵי פַרְעֹה וּבְעֵינֵי הָעָם

wai'yi'teyn YHWH et hheyn ha'am be'ey'ney mits'ra'yim gam ha'ish mo'sheh ga'dol me'od be'e'rets mits'ra'yim be'ey'ney av'dey phar'oh uv'ey'ney ha'am

and~he~will~<u>GIVE</u> "Yhwh *he~will~<u>BE</u>*" AT BEAUTY the~PEOPLE in~EYE~s2 "Mits'rayim STRAIT~s2" ALSO the~MAN "Mosheh PLUCKED-OUT" GREAT MANY in~LAND "Mits'rayim STRAIT~s2" in~EYE~s2 SERVANT~s "Paroh GREAT-HOUSE" and~in~EYE~s2 the~PEOPLE□	and "Yhwh He is" (placed) {the} beauty* {of} the people in {the} eyes {of} "Mits'rayim Two straits", also the man "Mosheh Plucked out" {was} (very) great in {the} land {of} "Mits'rayim Two straits" in {the} eyes {of the} servants {of} "Paroh Great house" and in {the} eyes {of} the people,□

11:4 וַיֹּאמֶר מֹשֶׁה כֹּה אָמַר יְהוָה כַּחֲצֹת הַלַּיְלָה אֲנִי יוֹצֵא בְּתוֹךְ מִצְרָיִם

wai'yo'mer mo'sheh koh a'mar YHWH ka'hha'tsot ha'lai'lah a'ni yo'tsey be'tokh mits'ra'yim

and~he~will~<u>SAY</u> "Mosheh PLUCKED-OUT" IN-THIS-WAY he~did~<u>SAY</u> "Yhwh *he~will~<u>BE</u>*" like~ CENTER the~NIGHT I <u>GO-OUT</u>~*ing/er(ms)* in~ MIDST "Mits'rayim STRAIT~s2"□	and "Mosheh Plucked out" said, in this way "Yhwh He is" said, (about) {the} center {of} the night†, I {am} going out in {the} midst {of} "Mits'rayim Two straits",□

11:5 וּמֵת כָּל בְּכוֹר בְּאֶרֶץ מִצְרַיִם מִבְּכוֹר פַּרְעֹה הַיֹּשֵׁב עַל כִּסְאוֹ עַד בְּכוֹר הַשִּׁפְחָה אֲשֶׁר אַחַר הָרֵחָיִם וְכֹל בְּכוֹר בְּהֵמָה

u'meyt kol be'khor be'e'rets mits'ra'yim mi'be'khor par'oh hai'yo'sheyv al kis'o ad be'khor ha'shiph'hhah a'sher a'hhar ha'rey'hha'yim we'khol be'khor be'hey'mah

and~he~did~<u>DIE</u> ALL FIRSTBORN in~LAND "Mits'rayim STRAIT~s2" from~FIRSTBORN "Paroh GREAT-HOUSE" the~<u>SETTLE</u>~*ing/er(ms)* UPON SEAT~him UNTIL FIRSTBORN the~ MAID WHICH AFTER the~MILLSTONE~s and~ ALL FIRSTBORN BEAST□	and all {the} firstborn in {the} land {of} "Mits'rayim Two straits" will die, from {the} firstborn {of} "Paroh Great house", the {one} settling upon his seat, (unto) {the} firstborn {of} the maid which {is} (behind) the millstones, and all {the} firstborn beast{s},□

11:6 וְהָיְתָה צְעָקָה גְדֹלָה בְּכָל אֶרֶץ מִצְרַיִם אֲשֶׁר כָּמֹהוּ לֹא נִהְיָתָה וְכָמֹהוּ לֹא תֹסִף

we'hai'tah tse'a'qah ge'do'lah be'khol e'rets mits'ra'yim a'sher ka'mo'hu lo nih'ya'tah

---

* "Place the beauty" means to "make accepted."

† "Center of the night" is midnight.

Mechanical Translation Codes

<u>WORD</u> – Verb	WORD – Noun	Word – Name	word – Pre/Suff	*word* – Conj.

we'kha'mo'hu lo to'siph

and~ she~*did*~EXIST CRY GREAT in~ALL LAND "Mits'rayim ^{STRAIT~s2}" WHICH like~THAT-ONE~ him NOT she~*did*~be~EXIST and~like~THAT-ONE~him NOT she~*will*~make~ADD☐	and {a} great cry will exist in all {the} land {of} "Mits'rayim ^{Two straits}", which |had| not existed like <this> and will not [again] exist like <this>,☐

11:7 וּלְכֹל בְּנֵי יִשְׂרָאֵל לֹא יֶחֱרַץ כֶּלֶב לְשֹׁנוֹ לְמֵאִישׁ וְעַד בְּהֵמָה לְמַעַן תֵּדְעוּן אֲשֶׁר יַפְלֶה יְהוָה בֵּין מִצְרַיִם וּבֵין יִשְׂרָאֵל

ul'khol be'ney yis'ra'eyl lo ye'hhe'rats ke'lev le'sho'no le'mey'ish we'ad be'hey'mah le'ma'an teyd'un a'sher yaph'leh YHWH beyn mits'ra'yim u'veyn yis'ra'eyl

and~to~ALL SON~s "Yisra'el ^{he~will~TURN-ASIDE~+~MIGHTY-ONE}" NOT he~*will*~CUT-SHARPLY DOG TONGUE~him to~from~MAN and~UNTIL BEAST to~THAT you(mp)~*will*~KNOW~must WHICH he~*will*~make~BE-DISTINCT "Yhwh ^{he~will~BE}" BETWEEN "Mits'rayim ^{STRAIT~s2}" and~ BETWEEN "Yisra'el ^{he~will~TURN-ASIDE~+~MIGHTY-ONE}"☐	and to all {of the} sons {of} "Yisra'el ^{He turns El aside}", {the} dog will not cut his tongue sharply*, from {the} man and (even) {the} beast, so that you must know that "Yhwh ^{He is}" will make {a} distinct{ion} between "Mits'rayim ^{Two straits}" and "Yisra'el ^{He turns El aside}",☐

11:8 וְיָרְדוּ כָל עֲבָדֶיךָ אֵלֶּה אֵלַי וְהִשְׁתַּחֲווּ לִי לֵאמֹר צֵא אַתָּה וְכָל הָעָם אֲשֶׁר בְּרַגְלֶיךָ וְאַחֲרֵי כֵן אֵצֵא וַיֵּצֵא מֵעִם פַּרְעֹה בָּחֳרִי אָף

we'yar'du khol a'va'dey'kha ey'leh ey'lai we'hish'ta'hha'wu li ley'mor tsey a'tah we'khol ha'am a'sher be'rag'ley'kha we'a'hha'rey kheyn ey'tsey wai'yey'tsey mey'im par'oh ba'hha'ri aph

and~*they*~*will*~GO-DOWN ALL SERVANT~s~ you(ms) THESE TO~me and~*they*~*did*~ self~ BEND-DOWN to~me to~>~SAY !(ms)~GO-OUT YOU(ms) and~ALL the~PEOPLE WHICH in~FOOT~s~you(ms) and~AFTER SO I~*will*~ GO-OUT and~he~*will*~GO-OUT from~WITH "Paroh ^{GREAT-HOUSE}" in~the~FLAMING NOSE☐	and all these, your servants, will go down to me and they will bend {them}selves down to me say{ing}, go out, you and all the people which {are} (with) your feet†, and <afterward> I will go out, and he went out <away from> "Paroh ^{Great house}" (with) the flaming nose‡,☐

11:9 וַיֹּאמֶר יְהוָה אֶל מֹשֶׁה לֹא יִשְׁמַע אֲלֵיכֶם פַּרְעֹה לְמַעַן רְבוֹת מוֹפְתַי בְּאֶרֶץ מִצְרָיִם

wai'yo'mer YHWH el mo'sheh lo yish'ma a'ley'khem par'oh le'ma'an re'vot moph'tai be'e'rets mits'ra'yim

and~he~*will*~SAY "Yhwh ^{he~will~BE}" TO "Mosheh ^{PLUCKED-OUT}" NOT he~*will*~HEAR TO~	and "Yhwh ^{He is}" said to "Mosheh ^{Plucked out}", "Paroh ^{Great house}" will not hear you so that my

---

* "The dog will not cut his tongue sharply" is probably an idiom, but of unknown meaning.

† "With your feet" is an idiom meaning "following after you."

‡ "Flaming nose" is an idiom for "fierce anger."

Revised Mechanical Translation Codes

(..) Alt Trans/App A	<..> Comp Phrase/App B	[..] Verb Form/App C	\..\ Plural Form/App D
	:...: Int Inf Abs	|..| Past Perf Verb	{...} Added Word

you(mp) "Paroh ^{GREAT-HOUSE}" to~THAT >~<u>INCREASE</u> WONDER~s~me in~LAND "Mits'rayim ^{STRAIT~s2}"□

wonders {will} increase in {the} land {of} "Mits'rayim ^{Two straits}",□

11:10 וּמֹשֶׁה וְאַהֲרֹן עָשׂוּ אֶת כָּל הַמֹּפְתִים הָאֵלֶּה לִפְנֵי פַרְעֹה וַיְחַזֵּק יְהוָה אֶת לֵב פַּרְעֹה וְלֹא שִׁלַּח אֶת בְּנֵי יִשְׂרָאֵל מֵאַרְצוֹ

u'mo'sheh we'a'ha'ron a'su et kol ha'moph'tim ha'ey'leh liph'ney phar'oh wai'hha'zeyq YHWH et leyv par'oh we'lo shi'lahh et be'ney yis'ra'eyl mey'ar'tso

and~"Mosheh ^{PLUCKED-OUT}" and~"Aharon ^{LIGHT-BRINGER}" *they~did*~<u>DO</u> AT ALL the~WONDER~s the~THESE to~FACE~s "Paroh ^{GREAT-HOUSE}" and~*he~will*~much~<u>SEIZE</u> "Yhwh ^{he~will~BE}" AT HEART "Paroh ^{GREAT-HOUSE}" and~NOT *he~did*~ much~<u>SEND</u> AT SON~s "Yisra'el ^{he~will~TURN-ASIDE~+~MIGHTY-ONE}" from~LAND~him□

and "Mosheh ^{Plucked out}" and "Aharon ^{Light bringer}" did all these wonders <in front of> "Paroh ^{Great house}", and "Yhwh ^{He is}" seized {the} heart {of} "Paroh ^{Great house}" and he did not send {the} sons {of} "Yisra'el ^{He turns El aside}" from his land,□

Chapter 12

12:1 וַיֹּאמֶר יְהוָה אֶל מֹשֶׁה וְאֶל אַהֲרֹן בְּאֶרֶץ מִצְרַיִם לֵאמֹר

wai'yo'mer YHWH el mo'sheh we'el a'ha'ron be'e'rets mits'ra'yim ley'mor

and~*he~will*~<u>SAY</u> "Yhwh ^{he~will~BE}" TO "Mosheh ^{PLUCKED-OUT}" and~TO "Aharon ^{LIGHT-BRINGER}" in~LAND "Mits'rayim ^{STRAIT~s2}" to~ >~<u>SAY</u>□

and "Yhwh ^{He is}" said to "Mosheh ^{Plucked out}" and to "Aharon ^{Light bringer}" in {the} land {of} "Mits'rayim ^{Two straits}",□

12:2 הַחֹדֶשׁ הַזֶּה לָכֶם רֹאשׁ חֳדָשִׁים רִאשׁוֹן הוּא לָכֶם לְחָדְשֵׁי הַשָּׁנָה

ha'hho'desh ha'zeh la'khem rosh hha'da'shim ri'shon hu la'khem le'hhad'shey ha'sha'nah

the~NEW-MOON the~THIS to~you(mp) HEAD NEW-MOON~s FIRST HE to~you(mp) to~NEW-MOON~s the~YEAR□

this new moon {is} (for) you {the} head {of the} new moons, he {is the} first (for) you (for) {the} new moons {of} the year,□

12:3 דַּבְּרוּ אֶל כָּל עֲדַת יִשְׂרָאֵל לֵאמֹר בֶּעָשֹׂר לַחֹדֶשׁ הַזֶּה וְיִקְחוּ לָהֶם אִישׁ שֶׂה לְבֵית אָבֹת שֶׂה לַבָּיִת

da'be'ru el kol a'dat yis'ra'eyl ley'mor be'a'sor la'hho'desh ha'zeh we'yiq'hhu la'hem ish seh le'veyt a'vot seh la'ba'yit

!(mp)~much~<u>SPEAK</u> TO ALL COMPANY "Yisra'el ^{he~will~TURN-ASIDE~+~MIGHTY-ONE}" to~>~<u>SAY</u> in~the~TENTH-ONE to~the~NEW-MOON the~THIS and~*they(m)~will*~<u>TAKE</u> to~

speak to all {the} company {of} "Yisra'el ^{He turns El aside}" say{ing}, in the tenth one* to this new moon, (each) will take (for) them{selves a}

---

* Meaning "the tenth day."

Mechanical Translation Codes

<u>WORD</u> – Verb	WORD – Noun	Word – Name	word – Pre/Suff	*word* – Conj.

them(m) MAN RAM to~HOUSE FATHER~s RAM to~the~HOUSE□

ram to {the} house {of the} fathers, {a} ram to the house,□

12:4 וְאִם יִמְעַט הַבַּיִת מִהְיֹת מִשֶּׂה וְלָקַח הוּא וּשְׁכֵנוֹ הַקָּרֹב אֶל בֵּיתוֹ בְּמִכְסַת נְפָשֹׁת אִישׁ לְפִי אָכְלוֹ תָּכֹסּוּ עַל הַשֶּׂה

we'im yim'at ha'ba'yit mih'yot mi'seh we'la'qahh hu ush'khey'no ha'qa'rov el bey'to be'mikh'sat ne'pha'shot ish le'phi akh'lo ta'kho'su al ha'seh

and~IF he~will~BE-LESS the~HOUSE from~ >~EXIST from~RAM and~he~did~TAKE HE and~DWELLER~him the~NEAR TO HOUSE~ him in~VALUE BEING~s MAN to~MOUTH >~EAT~him you(mp)~will~ESTIMATE UPON the~RAM□

and if the house will be less <than what is needed> from {a} ram, (then) he and his dweller, the {one} near to his house, will take {one that is} (with) {the} value {of the} beings {of} (each)*, {according} to {the} mouth {of} his eating, you will estimate upon the ram,□

12:5 שֶׂה תָמִים זָכָר בֶּן שָׁנָה יִהְיֶה לָכֶם מִן הַכְּבָשִׂים וּמִן הָעִזִּים תִּקָּחוּ

seh ta'mim za'khar ben sha'nah yih'yeh la'khem min hak'va'sim u'min ha'i'zim ti'qa'hhu

RAM WHOLE MALE SON YEAR he~will~EXIST to~you(mp) FROM the~SHEEP~s and~FROM the~SHE-GOAT~s you(mp)~will~TAKE□

{a} ram will exist (for) you, {it will be} whole, {a} male, {a} son {of a} year†, you will take {it} from the sheep and from the she-goats,□

12:6 וְהָיָה לָכֶם לְמִשְׁמֶרֶת עַד אַרְבָּעָה עָשָׂר יוֹם לַחֹדֶשׁ הַזֶּה וְשָׁחֲטוּ אֹתוֹ כֹּל קְהַל עֲדַת יִשְׂרָאֵל בֵּין הָעַרְבָּיִם

we'hai'yah la'khem le'mish'me'ret ad ar'ba'ah a'sar yom la'hho'desh ha'zeh we'sha'hha'tu o'to kol qe'hal a'dat yis'ra'eyl beyn ha'ar'ba'yim

and~he~did~EXIST to~you(mp) to~CHARGE UNTIL FOUR TEN DAY to~the~NEW-MOON the~THIS and~they~did~SLAY AT~him ALL ASSEMBLY COMPANY "Yisra'el he~will~TURN-ASIDE~+~MIGHTY-ONE„ BETWEEN the~EVENING~s□

and he will exist (for) you (for) {a} charge until the <fourteen>{th} day to this new moon, and all the assembly {of the} company {of} "Yisra'el He turns El aside„ will slay him between the evenings‡,□

12:7 וְלָקְחוּ מִן הַדָּם וְנָתְנוּ עַל שְׁתֵּי הַמְּזוּזֹת וְעַל הַמַּשְׁקוֹף עַל הַבָּתִּים אֲשֶׁר יֹאכְלוּ אֹתוֹ בָּהֶם

we'laq'hhu min ha'dam we'nat'nu al she'tey ham'zu'zot we'al ha'mash'qoph al ha'ba'tim a'sher yokh'lu o'to ba'hcm

and~they~did~TAKE FROM the~BLOOD and~ they~did~GIVE UPON TWO the~ DOORPOST~s and~UPON the~LINTEL UPON

and they will take from the blood, and they will (place) {it} upon the two doorposts and upon the lintel upon the houses which they

---

* "one that is with the value of the beings of each" means "one that is sufficient for all those eating it."
† The phrase "son of a year" is an idiom meaning "a year old."
‡ The phrase "between the evenings" is of uncertain meaning, but may be the time between sunset and dark.

Revised Mechanical Translation Codes

(..) Alt Trans/App A   <..> Comp Phrase/App B   [..] Verb Form/App C   \../ Plural Form/App D
:..: Int Inf Abs |..| Past Perf Verb   {...} Added Word

~ 87 ~

the~HOUSE~s WHICH *they(m)~will*~EAT AT~ him in~them(m)□

will eat him in,□

12:8 וְאָכְלוּ אֶת הַבָּשָׂר בַּלַּיְלָה הַזֶּה צְלִי אֵשׁ וּמַצּוֹת עַל מְרֹרִים יֹאכְלֻהוּ

we'akh'lu et ha'ba'sar ba'lai'lah ha'zeh tse'li eysh u'ma'tsot al me'ro'rim yokh'lu'hu

and~*they~did*~EAT AT the~FLESH in~the~ NIGHT the~THIS ROAST FIRE and~ UNLEAVENED-BREAD~s UPON BITTER-HERBS~s *they(m)~will*~EAT~him□

and they will eat the flesh in this night, {a} roast {of} fire, and unleavened bread, upon bitter herbs they will eat him,□

12:9 אַל תֹּאכְלוּ מִמֶּנּוּ נָא וּבָשֵׁל מְבֻשָּׁל בַּמָּיִם כִּי אִם צְלִי אֵשׁ רֹאשׁוֹ עַל כְּרָעָיו וְעַל קִרְבּוֹ

al tokh'lu mi'me'nu na u'va'sheyl me'vu'shal ba'ma'yim ki im tse'li eysh ro'sho al ke'ra'aw we'al qir'bo

DO-NOT *you(mp)~will*~EAT FROM~him RAW and~BOILED from~*be~much*~BOIL~ *ing/er(ms)* in~the~WATER~s2 GIVEN-THAT IF ROAST FIRE HEAD~him UPON LEG~s~him and~UPON WITHIN~him□

you will not eat from him raw (or) boiled (by) being boiled in the waters, <instead>, {a} roast {of} fire, his head, (also) his legs and (also) his within{s}*,□

12:10 וְלֹא תוֹתִירוּ מִמֶּנּוּ עַד בֹּקֶר וְהַנֹּתָר מִמֶּנּוּ עַד בֹּקֶר בָּאֵשׁ תִּשְׂרֹפוּ

we'lo to'ti'ru mi'me'nu ad bo'qer we'ha'no'tar mi'me'nu ad bo'qer ba'eysh tis'ro'phu

and~NOT *you(mp)~will~make*~LEAVE-BEHIND FROM~him UNTIL MORNING and~ *be*~LEAVE-BEHIND~*ing/er(ms)* FROM~him UNTIL MORNING in~the~FIRE *you(mp)~will*~ CREMATE□

and you will not leave him behind until morning, and {what is} being left behind {of} him until morning, you will cremate in the fire,□

12:11 וְכָכָה תֹּאכְלוּ אֹתוֹ מָתְנֵיכֶם חֲגֻרִים נַעֲלֵיכֶם בְּרַגְלֵיכֶם וּמַקֶּלְכֶם בְּיֶדְכֶם וַאֲכַלְתֶּם אֹתוֹ בְּחִפָּזוֹן פֶּסַח הוּא לַיהוָה

we'kha'khah tokh'lu o'to mat'ney'khem hha'gu'rim na'a'ley'khem be'rag'ley'khem u'ma'qel'khem be'yed'khem wa'a'khal'tem o'to be'hhi'paz'on pe'sahh hu la'YHWH

and~like~IN-THIS-WAY *you(mp)~will*~EAT AT~him WAIST~s~you(mp) GIRD-UP~*ed(mp)* SANDAL~s~you(mp) in~FOOT~s~you(mp) and~ROD~you(mp) in~HAND~you(mp) and~ *you(mp)~did*~EAT AT~him in~HASTE “Pesahh HOPPING” HE to~“Yhwh *he~will*~BE”□

and <just like this> you will eat him, your waists girded up, your sandals in your feet, and your rod in your hand, and you will eat him in haste, he {is the} “Pesahh hopping” (for) “Yhwh He is”,□

12:12 וְעָבַרְתִּי בְאֶרֶץ מִצְרַיִם בַּלַּיְלָה הַזֶּה וְהִכֵּיתִי כָל בְּכוֹר בְּאֶרֶץ מִצְרַיִם מֵאָדָם וְעַד בְּהֵמָה וּבְכָל אֱלֹהֵי מִצְרַיִם אֶעֱשֶׂה שְׁפָטִים אֲנִי יְהוָה

* The word “withins” mean the “insides.”

Mechanical Translation Codes

WORD – Verb WORD – Noun Word – Name word – Pre/Suff *word* – Conj.

we'a'var'ti be'e'rets mits'ra'yim ba'lai'lah ha'zeh we'hi'key'ti khol be'khor be'e'rets mits'ra'yim mey'a'dam we'ad be'hey'mah uv'khol e'lo'hey mits'ra'yim e'e'seh she'pha'tim a'ni YHWH

and~I~did~<u>CROSS-OVER</u> in~LAND "Mits'rayim ^{STRAIT~s2}" in~the~NIGHT the~THIS and~I~did~make~<u>HIT</u> ALL FIRSTBORN in~ LAND "Mits'rayim ^{STRAIT~s2}" from~HUMAN and~UNTIL BEAST and~in~ALL "Elohiym ^{POWER~s}~s "Mits'rayim ^{STRAIT~s2}" I~will~<u>DO</u> JUDGMENT~s I "Yhwh ^{he~will~<u>BE</u>}" □

and I will cross over in {the} land {of} "Mits'rayim ^{Two straits}" in this night, and I will hit all {the} firstborn in {the} land {of} "Mits'rayim ^{Two straits}", from {the} human and (even) {the} beast, and in all {the} "Elohiym ^{Powers}" {of} "Mits'rayim ^{Two straits}" I will do judgments, I {am} "Yhwh ^{He is}",□

12:13 וְהָיָה הַדָּם לָכֶם לְאֹת עַל הַבָּתִּים אֲשֶׁר אַתֶּם שָׁם וְרָאִיתִי אֶת הַדָּם וּפָסַחְתִּי עֲלֵכֶם וְלֹא יִהְיֶה בָכֶם נֶגֶף לְמַשְׁחִית בְּהַכֹּתִי בְּאֶרֶץ מִצְרָיִם

we'hai'yah ha'dam la'khem le'ot al ha'ba'tim a'sher a'tem sham we'ra'i'ti et ha'dam u'pha'sahh'ti a'ley'khem we'lo yih'yeh va'khem ne'geph le'mash'hhit be'ha'ko'ti be'e'rets mits'ra'yim

and~he~did~<u>EXIST</u> the~BLOOD to~you(mp) to~SIGN UPON the~HOUSE~s WHICH YOU(mp) THERE and~I~did~<u>SEE</u> AT the~ BLOOD and~I~did~<u>HOP</u> UPON~you(mp) and~NOT he~will~<u>EXIST</u> in~you(mp) STRIKING to~DESTRUCTION in~>~make~HIT~ me in~LAND "Mits'rayim ^{STRAIT~s2}" □

and the blood will exist (for) you (for) {a} sign upon the houses which you {are} (in), and I will see the blood and I will hop upon you* and {the} striking to destruction will not exist in you in my hitting in {the} land {of} "Mits'rayim ^{Two straits}",□

12:14 וְהָיָה הַיּוֹם הַזֶּה לָכֶם לְזִכָּרוֹן וְחַגֹּתֶם אֹתוֹ חַג לַיהוָה לְדֹרֹתֵיכֶם חֻקַּת עוֹלָם תְּחָגֻּהוּ

we'hai'yah hai'yom ha'zeh la'khem le'zi'ka'ron we'hha'go'tem o'to hhag la'YHWH le'do'ro'tey'khem hhu'qat o'lam te'hha'gu'hu

and~he~did~<u>EXIST</u> the~DAY the~THIS to~ you(mp) to~REMEMBRANCE and~you(mp)~ did~<u>HOLD-A-FEAST</u> AT~him FEAST to~"Yhwh ^{he~will~<u>BE</u>}" to~GENERATION~s~you(mp) RITUAL DISTANT you(mp)~will~<u>HOLD-A-FEAST</u>□

and this day will exist to you (for) {a} remembrance, and you will hold a feast (with) him†, {a} feast to "Yhwh ^{He is}" (for) your generations, you will hold a feast, {it is a} ritual {of a} distant {time},□

12:15 שִׁבְעַת יָמִים מַצּוֹת תֹּאכֵלוּ אַךְ בַּיּוֹם הָרִאשׁוֹן תַּשְׁבִּיתוּ שְּׂאֹר מִבָּתֵּיכֶם כִּי כָּל אֹכֵל חָמֵץ וְנִכְרְתָה הַנֶּפֶשׁ הַהִוא מִיִּשְׂרָאֵל מִיּוֹם הָרִאשֹׁן עַד יוֹם הַשְּׁבִעִי

shiv'at ya'mim ma'tsot to'khey'lu akh ha'yom ha'ri'shon tash'bi'tu she'or mi'ba'tey'khem ki kol o'kheyl hha'meyts we'nikh're'tah ha'ne'phesh ha'hi mi'yis'ra'eyl mi'yom ha'ri'shon ad yom hash'vi'i

---

* "Upon you" may also be translated as "over you."
† Referring to "this day."

Revised Mechanical Translation Codes

(..) Alt Trans/App A   <..> Comp Phrase/App B   [..] Verb Form/App C   \../ Plural Form/App D
:..: Int Inf Abs |..| Past Perf Verb   {...} Added Word

SEVEN DAY~s UNLEAVENED-BREAD~s
you(mp)~will~EAT SURELY in~the~DAY the~
FIRST you(mp)~will~make~CEASE LEAVEN
from~HOUSE~s~you(mp) GIVEN-THAT ALL
EAT~ing/er(ms) LEAVENED-BREAD and~ she~
did~be~CUT the~BEING the~ she from~
"Yisra'el ^he~will~TURN-ASIDE~+~MIGHTY-ONE" from~
DAY the~FIRST UNTIL DAY the~SEVENTH□

you will eat unleavened bread {for} seven
days, in the first day you will surely make
leaven cease from your houses, given that
(any) {one} eating leavened bread from the
first {day} until the seventh day, (that) being
will be cut from "Yisra'el ^He turns El aside",□

12:16 וּבַיּוֹם הָרִאשׁוֹן מִקְרָא קֹדֶשׁ וּבַיּוֹם הַשְּׁבִיעִי מִקְרָא קֹדֶשׁ יִהְיֶה לָכֶם
כָּל מְלָאכָה לֹא יֵעָשֶׂה בָהֶם אַךְ אֲשֶׁר יֵאָכֵל לְכָל נֶפֶשׁ הוּא לְבַדּוֹ יֵעָשֶׂה
לָכֶם

u'va'yom ha'ri'shon miq'ra qo'desh u'va'yom hash'vi'i miq'ra qo'desh yih'yeh la'khem kol
me'la'khah lo yey'a'seh va'hem akh a'sher yey'a'kheyl le'khol ne'phesh hu le'va'do
yey'a'seh la'khem

and~in~the~DAY the~FIRST MEETING
SPECIAL and~in~the~DAY the~SEVENTH
MEETING SPECIAL he~will~EXIST to~you(mp)
ALL BUSINESS NOT he~will~be~DO in~
them(m) SURELY WHICH he~will~be~EAT to~
ALL BEING HE to~STICK~him he~will~be~DO
to~you(mp)□

and in the first day {a} meeting {of a} special
{time}*, and in the seventh day {a} meeting {of
a} special {time} will exist (for) you, no
business will be done in them, (only) (what)
<everyone> will be eat{ing}, <that alone> will
be done (for) you,□

12:17 וּשְׁמַרְתֶּם אֶת הַמַּצּוֹת כִּי בְּעֶצֶם הַיּוֹם הַזֶּה הוֹצֵאתִי אֶת צִבְאוֹתֵיכֶם
מֵאֶרֶץ מִצְרָיִם וּשְׁמַרְתֶּם אֶת הַיּוֹם הַזֶּה לְדֹרֹתֵיכֶם חֻקַּת עוֹלָם

ush'mar'tem et ha'ma'tsot ki be'e'tsem hai'yom ha'zeh ho'tsey'ti et tsiv'o'tey'khem
mey'e'rets mits'ra'yim ush'mar'tem et hai'yom ha'zeh le'do'ro'tey'khem hhu'qat o'lam

and~you(mp)~did~SAFEGUARD AT the~
UNLEAVENED-BREAD~s GIVEN-THAT in~
BONE the~DAY the~THIS I~did~make~GO-
OUT AT ARMY~s~you(mp) from~LAND
"Mits'rayim ^STRAIT~s2" and~you(mp)~did~
SAFEGUARD AT the~DAY the~THIS to~
GENERATION~s~you(mp) RITUAL DISTANT□

and you will safeguard the unleavened bread,
given that in {the} bone {of} this day† I will
make your armies go out from {the} land {of}
"Mits'rayim ^Two straits", and you will safeguard
this day (for) your generations, {it is a} ritual
{of a} distant {time}‡,□

12:18 בָּרִאשֹׁן בְּאַרְבָּעָה עָשָׂר יוֹם לַחֹדֶשׁ בָּעֶרֶב תֹּאכְלוּ מַצֹּת עַד יוֹם הָאֶחָד
וְעֶשְׂרִים לַחֹדֶשׁ בָּעָרֶב

ba'ri'shon be'ar'ba'ah a'sar yom la'hho'desh ba'e'rev tokh'lu ma'tsot ad yom ha'e'hhad
we'es'rim la'hho'desh ba'a'rev

---

* the words לָכֶם יִהְיֶה (will exist for you) appears to be missing here (compare with the next
phrase).
† The "bone of the day" is an idiom, probably meaning "noon."
‡ See Footnote at Exodus 12:14.

Mechanical Translation Codes

| <u>WORD</u> – Verb | WORD – Noun | Word – Name | word – Pre/Suff | *word* – Conj. |

in~the~FIRST in~FOUR TEN DAY to~the~
NEW-MOON in~the~EVENING *you(mp)~will~*
EAT UNLEAVENED-BREAD~s UNTIL DAY the~
UNIT and~TEN~s to~the~NEW-MOON in~
the~EVENING□

in the first {month}, in the <fourteen>{th} day
to* the new moon in the evening, you will eat
unleavened bread until {the} day {of} the (one)
and \twenty/ to† the new moon in the
evening,□

12:19 שִׁבְעַת יָמִים שְׂאֹר לֹא יִמָּצֵא בְּבָתֵּיכֶם כִּי כָּל אֹכֵל מַחְמֶצֶת וְנִכְרְתָה הַנֶּפֶשׁ הַהִוא מֵעֲדַת יִשְׂרָאֵל בַּגֵּר וּבְאֶזְרַח הָאָרֶץ

shiv'at ya'mim se'or lo yi'ma'tsey be'va'tey'khem ki kol o'kheyl mahh'me'tset
we'nikh're'tah ha'ne'phesh ha'hi mey'a'dat yis'ra'eyl ba'geyr uv'ez'rahh ha'a'rets

SEVEN DAY~s LEAVEN NOT *he~will~be~*FIND
in~HOUSE~s~you(mp) GIVEN-THAT ALL EAT~
ing/er(ms) make~BE-SOUR~*ing/er(fs)* and~
she~*did~be~*CUT the~BEING the~ she from~
COMPANY "Yisra'el *he~will~*TURN-ASIDE~+~MIGHTY-
ONE" in~the~STRANGER and~in~NATIVE the~
LAND□

{for} seven days leaven will not be found in
your houses, given that (any) {one} eating
[leaven], (that) being will be cut from {the}
company {of} "Yisra'el ^(He turns El aside)", (with) the
stranger and (with) {the} native {of} the land,□

12:20 כָּל מַחְמֶצֶת לֹא תֹאכֵלוּ בְּכֹל מוֹשְׁבֹתֵיכֶם תֹּאכְלוּ מַצּוֹת

kol mahh'me'tset lo to'khey'lu be'khol mosh'vo'tey'khem tokh'lu ma'tsot

ALL make~BE-SOUR~*ing/er(fs)* NOT
*you(mp)~will~*EAT in~ALL SETTLING~s~
you(mp) *you(mp)~will~*EAT UNLEAVENED-
BREAD~s□

you will not eat (any) [leaven] in (any) {of}
your settlings, you will eat unleavened
bread,□

12:21 וַיִּקְרָא מֹשֶׁה לְכָל זִקְנֵי יִשְׂרָאֵל וַיֹּאמֶר אֲלֵהֶם מִשְׁכוּ וּקְחוּ לָכֶם צֹאן לְמִשְׁפְּחֹתֵיכֶם וְשַׁחֲטוּ הַפָּסַח

wai'yiq'ra mo'sheh le'khol ziq'ney yis'ra'eyl wai'yo'mer a'ley'hem mish'khu uq'hhu
la'khem tson le'mish'pe'hho'tey'khem we'sha'hha'tu ha'pa'sahh

and~he~will~CALL-OUT "Mosheh ^(PLUCKED-OUT)"
to~ALL BEARD~s "Yisra'el *he~will~*TURN-ASIDE~+~
MIGHTY-ONE" and~he~will~SAY TO~them(m)
*!(mp)~*DRAW and~*!(mp)~*TAKE to~you(mp)
FLOCKS to~FAMILY~s~you(mp) and~*!(mp)~*
SLAY the~"Pesahh ^(HOPPING)"□

and "Mosheh ^(Plucked out)" called out to all {the}
beard{ed one}s‡ {of} "Yisra'el ^(He turns El aside)" and
he said to them, draw and take (for) your{self
one from the}§ flocks (for) your families and

---

* Or "after."
† Or "after."
‡ "Bearded ones" is a euphemism for "elders."
§ The Hebrew phrase וּקְחוּ לָכֶם צֹאן should grammatically be translated as "and take for yourself the flock." However, as the Pesahh is "one" from the flock, the prefix "from" may be missing from the word "flocks."

Revised Mechanical Translation Codes

(..) Alt Trans/App A	<..> Comp Phrase/App B	[..] Verb Form/App C	\../ Plural Form/App D
:..: Int Inf Abs	|..| Past Perf Verb	{...} Added Word	

hopping„,◻

12:22 וּלְקַחְתֶּם אֲגֻדַּת אֵזוֹב וּטְבַלְתֶּם בַּדָּם אֲשֶׁר בַּסַּף וְהִגַּעְתֶּם אֶל הַמַּשְׁקוֹף וְאֶל שְׁתֵּי הַמְּזוּזֹת מִן הַדָּם אֲשֶׁר בַּסָּף וְאַתֶּם לֹא תֵצְאוּ אִישׁ מִפֶּתַח בֵּיתוֹ עַד בֹּקֶר

ul'qahh'tem a'gu'dat ey'zov ut'val'tem ba'dam a'sher ba'saph we'hi'ga'tem el ha'mash'qoph we'el she'tey ham'zu'zot min ha'dam a'sher ba'saph we'a'tem lo teyts'u ish mi'pe'tahh bey'to ad bo'qer

and~*you(mp)*~did~<u>TAKE</u> BUNCH HYSSOP and~*you(mp)*~did~<u>DIP</u> in~the~BLOOD WHICH in~the~TUB and~*you(mp)*~did~ *make*~<u>SMITE</u> TO the~LINTEL and~TO TWO the~DOORPOST~s FROM the~BLOOD WHICH in~the~TUB and~YOU(mp) NOT *you(mp)*~ *will*~<u>GO-OUT</u> MAN from~OPENING HOUSE~ him UNTIL MORNING◻

and you will take {a} bunch {of} hyssop, and you will dip {it} in the blood which {is} in the tub, and you will smite {it} (on) the lintel and (on) the two doorposts, from the blood which {is} in the tub, you will not go out, (each) from {the} opening {of} his house until morning,◻

12:23 וְעָבַר יְהוָה לִנְגֹּף אֶת מִצְרַיִם וְרָאָה אֶת הַדָּם עַל הַמַּשְׁקוֹף וְעַל שְׁתֵּי הַמְּזוּזֹת וּפָסַח יְהוָה עַל הַפֶּתַח וְלֹא יִתֵּן הַמַּשְׁחִית לָבֹא אֶל בָּתֵּיכֶם לִנְגֹּף

we'a'var YHWH lin'goph et mits'ra'yim we'ra'ah et ha'dam al ha'mash'qoph we'al she'tey ham'zu'zot u'pha'sahh YHWH al ha'pe'tahh we'lo yi'teyn ha'mash'hhit la'vo el ba'tey'khem lin'goph

and~he~did~<u>CROSS-OVER</u> "Yhwh ^*he~will~*<u>BE</u>" to~>~<u>SMITE</u> AT "Mits'rayim ^STRAIT~s2" and~he~ did~<u>SEE</u> AT the~BLOOD UPON the~LINTEL and~UPON TWO the~DOORPOST~s and~he~ did~<u>HOP</u> "Yhwh ^*he~will~*<u>BE</u>" UPON the~ OPENING and~NOT *he~will~*<u>GIVE</u> the~ *make*~<u>DAMAGE</u>~*ing/er(ms)* to~>~<u>COME</u> TO HOUSE~s~*you(mp)* to~>~<u>SMITE</u>◻

and "Yhwh ^He is" will cross over to smite "Mits'rayim ^Two straits", and he will see the blood upon the lintel and upon the two doorposts, and "Yhwh ^He is" will hop upon* the opening, and he will not (allow) the damager to come to your houses to smite,◻

12:24 וּשְׁמַרְתֶּם אֶת הַדָּבָר הַזֶּה לְחָק לְךָ וּלְבָנֶיךָ עַד עוֹלָם

ush'mar'tem et ha'da'var ha'zeh le'hhaq le'kha ul'va'ney'kha ad o'lam

and~*you(mp)*~did~<u>SAFEGUARD</u> AT the~ WORD the~THIS to~CUSTOM to~*you(ms)* and~to~GENERATION~s~*you(ms)* UNTIL DISTANT◻

and you will safeguard this word (for) {a} custom (for) you, and (for) your generations until† {a} distant {time},◻

12:25 וְהָיָה כִּי תָבֹאוּ אֶל הָאָרֶץ אֲשֶׁר יִתֵּן יְהוָה לָכֶם כַּאֲשֶׁר דִּבֵּר וּשְׁמַרְתֶּם אֶת הָעֲבֹדָה הַזֹּאת

---

* The word "upon" may also be translated as "over."

† Or "unto."

Mechanical Translation Codes

<u>WORD</u> – Verb	WORD – Noun	Word – Name	word – Pre/Suff	*word* – Conj.

we'hai'yah ki ta'vo'u el ha'a'rets a'sher yi'teyn YHWH la'khem ka'a'sheyr di'beyr ush'mar'tem et ha'a'vo'dah ha'zot

and~he~did~EXIST GIVEN-THAT *you(mp)*~ *will*~COME TO the~LAND WHICH *he*~*will*~ GIVE "Yhwh *he~will~*BE" to~*you(mp)* like~ WHICH *he~did~much*~SPEAK and~*you(mp)*~ *did*~SAFEGUARD AT the~SERVICE the~THIS□

and (it) will (come to pass), you will come to the land, which "Yhwh He is" will give to you <just as> he spoke, and you will safeguard this service,□

12:26 וְהָיָה כִּי יֹאמְרוּ אֲלֵיכֶם בְּנֵיכֶם מָה הָעֲבֹדָה הַזֹּאת לָכֶם

we'hai'yah ki yom'ru a'ley'khem be'ney'khem mah ha'a'vo'dah ha'zot la'khem

and~he~did~EXIST GIVEN-THAT *they(m)*~ *will*~SAY TO~*you(mp)* SON~s~*you(mp)* WHAT the~SERVICE the~THIS to~*you(mp)*□

and (it) will (come to pass) that your sons will say to you, what {is} this service to you?□

12:27 וַאֲמַרְתֶּם זֶבַח פֶּסַח הוּא לַיהוָה אֲשֶׁר פָּסַח עַל בָּתֵּי בְנֵי יִשְׂרָאֵל בְּמִצְרַיִם בְּנָגְפּוֹ אֶת מִצְרַיִם וְאֶת בָּתֵּינוּ הִצִּיל וַיִּקֹּד הָעָם וַיִּשְׁתַּחֲווּ

wa'a'mar'tem ze'vahh pe'sahh hu la'YHWH a'sher pa'sahh al ba'tey ve'ney yis'ra'eyl be'mits'ra'yim be'nag'po et mits'ra'yim we'et ba'tey'nu hi'tsil wai'yi'qod ha'am wai'yish'ta'hhaw'u

and~*you(mp)*~*did*~SAY SACRIFICE "Pesahh HOPPING" HE to~"Yhwh *he~will~*BE" WHICH *he*~ *did*~HOP UPON HOUSE~s SON~s "Yisra'el *he~will~*TURN-ASIDE~+~MIGHTY-ONE" in~"Mits'rayim STRAIT~s2" in~>~SMITE~him AT "Mits'rayim STRAIT~s2" and~AT HOUSE~s~us *he~did~make*~ DELIVER and~*he~will*~BOW-THE-HEAD the~ PEOPLE and~*they(m)*~*will*~ self~BEND-DOWN□

and you will say, he {is a} sacrifice {of} "Pesahh hopping" (for) "Yhwh He is", who hopped upon* {the} houses {of the} sons {of} "Yisra'el He turns El aside" in "Mits'rayim Two straits", in his smiting {of} "Mits'rayim Two straits", and he delivered our houses, and the people bowed the head and they bent {them}selves down†, □

12:28 וַיֵּלְכוּ וַיַּעֲשׂוּ בְּנֵי יִשְׂרָאֵל כַּאֲשֶׁר צִוָּה יְהוָה אֶת מֹשֶׁה וְאַהֲרֹן כֵּן עָשׂוּ

wai'yeyl'khu wai'ya'a'su be'ney yis'ra'eyl ka'a'sheyr tsi'wah YHWH et mo'sheh we'a'ha'ron keyn a'su

and~*they(m)*~*will*~WALK and~*they(m)*~*will*~ DO SON~s "Yisra'el *he~will~*TURN-ASIDE~+~MIGHTY-ONE" like~WHICH *he~did~much*~DIRECT "Yhwh *he~will~*BE" AT "Mosheh PLUCKED-OUT" and~ "Aharon LIGHT-BRINGER" SO *they*~*did*~DO□

and {the} sons {of} "Yisra'el He turns El aside" will walk and they did <just as> "Yhwh He is" directed "Mosheh Plucked out" and "Aharon Light bringer", so they did,□

12:29 וַיְהִי בַּחֲצִי הַלַּיְלָה וַיהוָה הִכָּה כָל בְּכוֹר בְּאֶרֶץ מִצְרַיִם מִבְּכֹר פַּרְעֹה

---

* The word "upon" may also be translated as "over."

† "Bending oneself down" means to prostrate oneself down to the ground in respect to another.

Revised Mechanical Translation Codes

(..) Alt Trans/App A	<..> Comp Phrase/App B	[..] Verb Form/App C	\../ Plural Form/App D
:..: Int Inf Abs	|..| Past Perf Verb	{...} Added Word	

הַיּשֵׁב עַל כִּסְאוֹ עַד בְּכוֹר הַשְּׁבִי אֲשֶׁר בְּבֵית הַבּוֹר וְכֹל בְּכוֹר בְּהֵמָה

wai'hi ba'hha'tsi ha'lai'lah wa'YHWH hi'kah khol be'khor be'e'rets mits'ra'yim mi'be'khor par'oh hai'yo'sheyv al kis'o ad be'khor hash'vi a'sher be'veyt ha'bor we'khol be'khor be'hey'mah

and~*he~will*~UNDERLINE:EXIST in~HALF the~NIGHT and~ "Yhwh *he~will*~BE" he~did~make~HIT ALL FIRSTBORN in~LAND "Mits'rayim STRAIT~s2" from~FIRSTBORN "Paroh GREAT-HOUSE" the~ SETTLE~*ing/er(ms)* UPON SEAT~him UNTIL FIRSTBORN the~CAPTIVE WHICH in~HOUSE the~CISTERN and~ALL FIRSTBORN BEAST□	and (it) (came to pass) in {the} (middle) {of} the night, and "Yhwh He is" |had| hit all {the} firstborn in {the} land {of} "Mits'rayim Two straits", from {the} firstborn {of} "Paroh Great house", the {one} settling upon his seat, (unto) {the} firstborn {of} the captive{s}, which {are} in {the} house {of} the cistern*, and all {the} firstborn {of the} beast{s},□

12:30   וַיָּקָם פַּרְעֹה לַיְלָה הוּא וְכָל עֲבָדָיו וְכָל מִצְרַיִם וַתְּהִי צְעָקָה גְדֹלָה בְּמִצְרָיִם כִּי אֵין בַּיִת אֲשֶׁר אֵין שָׁם מֵת

wai'ya'qam par'oh lai'lah hu we'khol a'va'daw we'khol mits'ra'yim wat'hi tse'a'qah ge'do'lah be'mits'ra'yim ki eyn ba'yit a'sher eyn sham meyt

and~*he~will*~RISE "Paroh GREAT-HOUSE" NIGHT HE and~ALL SERVANT~s~him and~ALL "Mits'rayim STRAIT~s2" and~ she~*will*~EXIST CRY GREAT in~"Mits'rayim STRAIT~s2" GIVEN-THAT WITHOUT HOUSE WHICH WITHOUT THERE DIE~*ing/er(ms)*□	and "Paroh Great house" rose (that) night and all his servants and all "Mits'rayim Two straits", and {a} great cry existed in "Mits'rayim Two straits", given that there {was} (not) {a} house which {was} without {a} dying {one},□

12:31   וַיִּקְרָא לְמֹשֶׁה וּלְאַהֲרֹן לַיְלָה וַיֹּאמֶר קוּמוּ צְּאוּ מִתּוֹךְ עַמִּי גַּם אַתֶּם גַּם בְּנֵי יִשְׂרָאֵל וּלְכוּ עִבְדוּ אֶת יְהוָה כְּדַבֶּרְכֶם

wai'yiq'ra le'mo'sheh ul'a'ha'ron lai'lah wai'yo'mer qu'mu tse'u mi'tokh a'mi gam a'tem gam be'ney yis'ra'eyl ul'khu iv'du et YHWH ke'da'ber'khem

and~*he~will*~CALL-OUT to~"Mosheh PLUCKED-OUT" and~to~"Aharon LIGHT-BRINGER" NIGHT and~*he~will*~SAY !(*mp*)~RISE !(*mp*)~GO-OUT from~MIDST PEOPLE~me ALSO YOU(*mp*) ALSO SON~s "Yisra'el *he~will*~TURN-ASIDE~+~MIGHTY-ONE" and~!(*mp*)~WALK !(*mp*)~SERVE AT "Yhwh *he~will*~BE" like~>~*much*~SPEAK~ you(*mp*)□	and he called out to "Mosheh Plucked out" and to "Aharon Light bringer" {in the}† Night and he said, rise, go out from {the} midst {of} my people, (both) you, (and) {the} sons {of} "Yisra'el He turns El aside" and walk, serve "Yhwh He is" (as) you spoke,□

12:32   גַּם צֹאנְכֶם גַּם בְּקַרְכֶם קְחוּ כַּאֲשֶׁר דִּבַּרְתֶּם וָלֵכוּ וּבֵרַכְתֶּם גַּם אֹתִי

gam tson'khem gam be'qar'khem qe'hhu ka'a'sheyr de'bar'tem wa'ley'khu u'vey'rakh'tem gam o'ti

---

* The "house of the cistern" is probably a prison.
† The word "night" is missing the prefix "in."

Mechanical Translation Codes

<u>WORD</u> – Verb	WORD – Noun	Word – Name	word – Pre/Suff	*word* – Conj.

ALSO FLOCKS~you(mp) ALSO CATTLE~ you(mp) !(mp)~TAKE like~WHICH you(mp)~ did~much~SPEAK and~!(mp)~WALK and~ you(mp)~did~much~KNEEL ALSO AT~me□

also your flocks (and) your cattle, take {them} <just as> you spoke, and walk, and you will [respect] me also,□

12:33

וַתֶּחֱזַק מִצְרַיִם עַל הָעָם לְמַהֵר לְשַׁלְּחָם מִן הָאָרֶץ כִּי אָמְרוּ כֻּלָּנוּ מֵתִים

wa'te'hhe'zaq mits'ra'yim al ha'am le'ma'heyr le'shal'hham min ha'a'rets ki am'ru ku'la'nu mey'tim

and~ she~will~SEIZE "Mits'rayim STRAIT~s2″ UPON the~PEOPLE to~>~much~HURRY to~ >~much~SEND~them(m) FROM the~LAND GIVEN-THAT they~did~SAY ALL~us DIE~ ing/er(mp)□

and "Mits'rayim Two straits″ seized upon the people to hurry to send them from the land, given that they said, all {of} us {are} dying,□

12:34

וַיִּשָּׂא הָעָם אֶת בְּצֵקוֹ טֶרֶם יֶחְמָץ מִשְׁאֲרֹתָם צְרֻרֹת בְּשִׂמְלֹתָם עַל שִׁכְמָם

wai'yi'sa ha'am et be'tsey'qo te'rem yehh'mats mish'a'ro'tam tse'ru'rot be'sim'lo'tam al shikh'mam

and~he~will~LIFT-UP the~PEOPLE AT DOUGH~him BEFORE he~will~BE-SOUR KNEADING-BOWL~s~them(m) PRESS-IN~ ed(fp) in~APPAREL~s~them(m) UPON SHOULDER~them(m)□

and the people lifted up his* dough before he was soured, their kneading bowls {were} pressed in (with) their apparel upon their shoulder,□

12:35

וּבְנֵי יִשְׂרָאֵל עָשׂוּ כִּדְבַר מֹשֶׁה וַיִּשְׁאֲלוּ מִמִּצְרַיִם כְּלֵי כֶסֶף וּכְלֵי זָהָב וּשְׂמָלֹת

uv'ney yis'ra'eyl a'su kid'var mo'sheh wai'yish'a'lu mi'mits'ra'yim ke'ley ke'seph ukh'ley za'hav us'ma'lot

and~SON~s "Yisra'el he~will~TURN-ASIDE+~MIGHTY-ONE″ they~did~DO like~WORD "Mosheh PLUCKED-OUT″ and~they(m)~will~ENQUIRE from~"Mits'rayim STRAIT~s2″ ITEM~s SILVER and~ITEM~s GOLD and~APPAREL~s□

and {the} sons {of} "Yisra'el He turns El aside″ |had| done like {the} word {of} "Mosheh Plucked out″, and they enquired from "Mits'rayim Two straits″ items {of} silver and items {of} gold and apparel,□

12:36

וַיהוָה נָתַן אֶת חֵן הָעָם בְּעֵינֵי מִצְרַיִם וַיַּשְׁאִלוּם וַיְנַצְּלוּ אֶת מִצְרָיִם

wa'YHWH na'tan et hheyn ha'am be'ey'ney mits'ra'yim wai'yash'i'lum wai'nats'lu et mits'ra'yim

and~"Yhwh he~will~BE″ he~did~GIVE AT BEAUTY the~PEOPLE in~EYE~s2 "Mits'rayim

and "Yhwh He is″ |had| (placed) {the} beauty† {of} the people in {the} eyes {of} "Mits'rayim

_____

* The Hebrew word for "people" is a masculine singular word.

† "Place the beauty" means to "make accepted."

Revised Mechanical Translation Codes

(..) Alt Trans/App A	<..> Comp Phrase/App B	[..] Verb Form/App C	\../ Plural Form/App D
:..: Int Inf Abs	|..| Past Perf Verb	{..} Added Word	

STRAIT~s2″ and~*they(m)~will~make~*ENQUIRE~ them(m) and~*they(m)~will~much~*DELIVER AT "Mits'rayim STRAIT~s2″□

the people in {the} eyes {of} "Mits'rayim Two straits″, and they [granted] {it to} them and they delivered "Mits'rayim Two straits″,□

12:37 וַיִּסְעוּ בְנֵי יִשְׂרָאֵל מֵרַעְמְסֵס סֻכֹּתָה כְּשֵׁשׁ מֵאוֹת אֶלֶף רַגְלִי הַגְּבָרִים לְבַד מִטָּף

wai'yis'u ve'ney yis'ra'eyl mey'ra'me'seys su'ko'tah ke'sheysh mey'ot e'leph rag'li hag'va'rim le'vad mi'taph

and~*they(m)~will~*JOURNEY SON~s "Yisra'el *he~will~*TURN-ASIDE~+~MIGHTY-ONE″ from~"Ra'meses CHILD-OF-THE-SUN″ "Sukhot BOOTH~s″~unto like~SIX HUNDRED~s THOUSAND ON-FOOT the~WARRIOR~s to~STICK from~CHILDREN□

and {the} sons {of} "Yisra'el He turns El aside″ journeyed from "Ra'meses Child of the sun″ unto "Sukhot Booths″, (about) six hundred thousand warriors on foot, <aside> from {the} children,□

12:38 וְגַם עֵרֶב רַב עָלָה אִתָּם וְצֹאן וּבָקָר מִקְנֶה כָּבֵד מְאֹד

we'gam ey'rev rav a'lah i'tam we'tson u'va'qar miq'neh ka'veyd me'od

and~ALSO MIXTURE ABUNDANT *he~did~*GO-UP AT~them(m) and~FLOCKS and~CATTLE LIVESTOCK HEAVY MANY□

and also {an} abundant mixture |had| gone up (with) them, and flocks and cattle, {the} livestock {was} (very) heavy*,□

12:39 וַיֹּאפוּ אֶת הַבָּצֵק אֲשֶׁר הוֹצִיאוּ מִמִּצְרַיִם עֻגֹת מַצּוֹת כִּי לֹא חָמֵץ כִּי גֹרְשׁוּ מִמִּצְרַיִם וְלֹא יָכְלוּ לְהִתְמַהְמֵהַּ וְגַם צֵדָה לֹא עָשׂוּ לָהֶם

wai'yo'phu et ha'ba'tseyq a'sher ho'tsi'u mi'mits'ra'yim u'got ma'tsot ki lo hha'meyts ki gor'shu mi'mits'ra'yim we'lo yakh'lu le'hit'mah'mey'ah we'gam tsey'dah lo a'su la'hem

and~*they(m)~will~*BAKE AT the~DOUGH WHICH *they~did~make~*GO-OUT from~"Mits'rayim STRAIT~s2″ BREAD-CAKE~s UNLEAVENED-BREAD~s GIVEN-THAT NOT *he~did~*BE-SOUR GIVEN-THAT *they~did~be~ much~*CAST-OUT from~"Mits'rayim STRAIT~s2″ and~NOT *they~did~*BE-ABLE to~>~ self~LINGER and~ALSO PROVISIONS NOT *they~did~*DO to~them(m)□

and they will bake the dough which they made go out from "Mits'rayim Two straits″, {these are} bread cakes {of} unleavened bread, given that he† was not soured, given that they were cast out from "Mits'rayim Two straits″, and they were not able to linger, and also, they did not do provisions (for) them{selves},□

12:40 וּמוֹשַׁב בְּנֵי יִשְׂרָאֵל אֲשֶׁר יָשְׁבוּ בְּמִצְרָיִם שְׁלֹשִׁים שָׁנָה וְאַרְבַּע מֵאוֹת שָׁנָה

u'mo'shav be'ney yis'ra'eyl a'sher yash'vu be'mits'ra'yim she'lo'shim sha'nah we'ar'ba mey'ot sha'nah

and~SETTLING SON~s "Yisra'el *he~will~*TURN-ASIDE~+~MIGHTY-ONE″ WHICH *they~did~*SETTLE in~"Mits'rayim STRAIT~s2″ THREE~s YEAR and~

and {the} settling {of the} sons {of} "Yisra'el He turns El aside″, who settled in "Mits'rayim Two straits″, {was} \thirty/ and four hundred year{s},□

---

* "Very heavy" means a great abundance.

† Referring to the "dough," a masculine word.

Mechanical Translation Codes

<u>WORD</u> – Verb	WORD – Noun	Word – Name	word – Pre/Suff	*word* – Conj.

FOUR HUNDRED~s YEAR□

12:41

וַיְהִי מִקֵּץ שְׁלֹשִׁים שָׁנָה וְאַרְבַּע מֵאוֹת שָׁנָה וַיְהִי בְּעֶצֶם הַיּוֹם הַזֶּה
יָצְאוּ כָּל צִבְאוֹת יְהוָה מֵאֶרֶץ מִצְרָיִם

wai'hi mi'qeyts she'lo'shim sha'nah we'ar'ba mey'ot sha'nah wai'hi be'e'tsem hai'yom ha'zeh yats'u kol tsiv'ot YHWH mey'e'rets mits'ra'yim

and~he~will~EXIST from~CONCLUSION THREE~s YEAR and~FOUR HUNDRED~s YEAR and~he~will~EXIST in~BONE the~DAY the~THIS they~did~GO-OUT ALL ARMY~s "Yhwh ^(he~will~BE)" from~LAND "Mits'rayim ^(STRAIT~s2)"□

and (it) (came to pass), (at) {the} conclusion {of the} \thirty/ and four hundred year{s}, and (it) (came to pass) in the bone {of} this day*, all the armies {of} "Yhwh ^(He is)" went out from {the} land {of} "Mits'rayim ^(Two straits)",□

12:42

לֵיל שִׁמֻּרִים הוּא לַיהוָה לְהוֹצִיאָם מֵאֶרֶץ מִצְרָיִם הוּא הַלַּיְלָה הַזֶּה
לַיהוָה שִׁמֻּרִים לְכָל בְּנֵי יִשְׂרָאֵל לְדֹרֹתָם

leyl shi'mu'rim hu la'YHWH le'ho'tsi'am mey'e'rets mits'ra'yim hu ha'lai'lah ha'zeh la'YHWH shi'mu'rim le'khol be'ney yis'ra'eyl le'do'ro'tam

NIGHT SAFEGUARDING~s HE to~"Yhwh ^(he~will~BE)" to~>~make~GO-OUT~them(m) from~LAND "Mits'rayim ^(STRAIT~s2)" HE the~NIGHT the~THIS to~"Yhwh ^(he~will~BE)" SAFEGUARDING~s to~ALL SON~s "Yisra'el ^(he~will~TURN-ASIDE~+~MIGHTY-ONE)" to~GENERATION~s~them(m)□

(this) {is a} night {of} safeguardings to "Yhwh ^(He is)", to make them go out from {the} land {of} "Mits'rayim ^(Two straits)", (that) this night {is} to "Yhwh ^(He is)", safeguardings to all {the} sons {of} "Yisra'el ^(He turns El aside)", to their generations,□

12:43

וַיֹּאמֶר יְהוָה אֶל מֹשֶׁה וְאַהֲרֹן זֹאת חֻקַּת הַפָּסַח כָּל בֶּן נֵכָר לֹא יֹאכַל בּוֹ

wai'yo'mer YHWH el mo'sheh we'a'ha'ron zot hhu'qat ha'pa'sahh kol ben ney'khar lo yo'khal bo

and~he~will~SAY "Yhwh ^(he~will~BE)" TO "Mosheh ^(PLUCKED-OUT)" and~"Aharon ^(LIGHT-BRINGER)" THIS RITUAL the~"Pesahh ^(HOPPING)" ALL SON FOREIGNER NOT he~will~EAT in~him□

and "Yhwh ^(He is)" said to "Mosheh ^(Plucked out)" and "Aharon ^(Light bringer)", this {is the} ritual {of} the "Pesahh ^(hopping)", not {one} son {of a} foreigner will eat him,□

12:44

וְכָל עֶבֶד אִישׁ מִקְנַת כָּסֶף וּמַלְתָּה אֹתוֹ אָז יֹאכַל בּוֹ

we'khol e'ved ish miq'nat ka'seph u'mal'tah o'to az yo'khal bo

and~ALL SERVANT MAN ACQUIRED SILVER and~you(ms)~did~CIRCUMCISE AT~him AT-THAT-TIME he~will~EAT in~him□

and you will circumcise (every) man servant acquired {by} silver, at that time he will eat him,□

---

* The "bone of the day" is an idiom, probably meaning "noon."

Revised Mechanical Translation Codes

| (..) Alt Trans/App A | <...> Comp Phrase/App B | [..] Verb Form/App C | \../ Plural Form/App D |
| :..: Int Inf Abs | |..| Past Perf Verb | {...} Added Word | |

12:45

תּוֹשָׁב וְשָׂכִיר לֹא יֹאכַל בּוֹ

to'shav we'sa'khir lo yo'khal bo

SOJOURNER and~HIRELING NOT *he~will*~<u>EAT</u> in~him◻

{a} sojourner (or) {a} hireling will not eat him,◻

12:46

בְּבַיִת אֶחָד יֵאָכֵל לֹא תוֹצִיא מִן הַבַּיִת מִן הַבָּשָׂר חוּצָה וְעֶצֶם לֹא תִשְׁבְּרוּ בוֹ

be'va'yit e'hhad yey'a'kheyl lo to'tsi min ha'ba'yit min ha'ba'sar hhu'tsah we'e'tsem lo tish'be'ru bo

in~HOUSE UNIT *he~will~be*~<u>EAT</u> NOT *you(ms)~will~make*~<u>GO-OUT</u> FROM the~HOUSE FROM the~FLESH OUTSIDE~unto and~BONE NOT *you(mp)~will*~<u>CRACK</u> in~him◻

he will be eaten in (one) house, you will not make {anything} from the flesh go out from the house unto {the} outside, and you will not crack {a} bone {of} him,◻

12:47

כָּל עֲדַת יִשְׂרָאֵל יַעֲשׂוּ אֹתוֹ

kol a'dat yis'ra'eyl ya'a'su o'to

ALL COMPANY "Yisra'el *he~will~*<u>TURN-ASIDE</u>~+~ MIGHTY-ONE„ *they(m)~will*~<u>DO</u> AT~him◻

all {the} company {of} "Yisra'el He turns El aside„ will do him,◻

12:48

וְכִי יָגוּר אִתְּךָ גֵּר וְעָשָׂה פֶסַח לַיהוָה הִמּוֹל לוֹ כָל זָכָר וְאָז יִקְרַב לַעֲשֹׂתוֹ וְהָיָה כְּאֶזְרַח הָאָרֶץ וְכָל עָרֵל לֹא יֹאכַל בּוֹ

we'khi ya'gur it'kha geyr we'a'sah phe'sahh la'YHWH hi'mol lo khol za'khar we'az yiq'rav la'a'so'to we'hai'yah ke'ez'rahh ha'a'rets we'khol a'reyl lo yo'khal bo

and~GIVEN-THAT *he~will*~<u>SOJOURN</u> AT~ you(ms) STRANGER and~*he~did*~<u>DO</u> "Pesahh HOPPING„ to~"Yhwh *he~will*~<u>BE</u>„ >~be~ <u>CIRCUMCISE</u> to~him ALL MALE and~AT-THAT-TIME *he~will~*<u>COME-NEAR</u> to~>~<u>DO</u>~ him and~*he~did*~<u>EXIST</u> like~NATIVE the~ LAND and~ALL UNCIRCUMCISED NOT *he~ will*~<u>EAT</u> in~him◻

and (if) {a} stranger will sojourn (with) you, and he will do {the} "Pesahh hopping„ to "Yhwh He is„, all {the} male{s will} be circumcis{ed} to him, and at that time, he will come near to do him, and he will exist like {a} native {of} the land, and all {the} uncircumcised will not eat him,◻

12:49

תּוֹרָה אַחַת יִהְיֶה לָאֶזְרָח וְלַגֵּר הַגָּר בְּתוֹכְכֶם

to'rah a'hhat yih'yeh la'ez'rahh we'la'geyr ha'gar be'tokh'khem

TEACHING UNIT *he~will*~<u>EXIST</u> to~NATIVE and~to~STRANGER the~<u>SOJOURN</u>~ *ing/er(ms)* in~MIDST~you(mp)◻

(one) teaching will exist to {the} native and to {the} stranger, the sojourner in {the} midst {of} you,◻

12:50

וַיַּעֲשׂוּ כָּל בְּנֵי יִשְׂרָאֵל כַּאֲשֶׁר צִוָּה יְהוָה אֶת מֹשֶׁה וְאֶת אַהֲרֹן כֵּן עָשׂוּ

wai'ya'a'su kol be'ney yis'ra'eyl ka'a'sheyr tsi'wah YHWH et mo'sheh we'et a'ha'ron keyn a'su

Mechanical Translation Codes

| <u>WORD</u> – Verb | WORD – Noun | Word – Name | word – Pre/Suff | *word* – Conj. |

and~they(m)~will~<u>DO</u> ALL SON~s "Yisra'el ^{he~} ^{will~}<u>TURN-ASIDE</u>~+~MIGHTY-ONE„ like~WHICH he~did~ much~<u>DIRECT</u> "Yhwh ^{he~will~}<u>BE</u>„ AT "Mosheh ^{PLUCKED-OUT}„ and~AT "Aharon ^{LIGHT-BRINGER}„ SO they~did~<u>DO</u>□

and all {the} sons {of} "Yisra'el ^{He turns El aside}„ did <just as> "Yhwh ^{He is}„ directed "Mosheh ^{Plucked out}„ and "Aharon ^{Light bringer}„, so they did,□

12:51 וַיְהִי בְּעֶצֶם הַיּוֹם הַזֶּה הוֹצִיא יְהוָה אֶת בְּנֵי יִשְׂרָאֵל מֵאֶרֶץ מִצְרַיִם עַל צִבְאֹתָם

wai'hi be'e'tsem hai'yom ha'zeh ho'tsi YHWH et be'ney yis'ra'eyl mey'e'rets mits'ra'yim al tsiv'o'tam

and~he~will~<u>EXIST</u> in~BONE the~DAY the~ THIS he~did~make~<u>GO-OUT</u> "Yhwh ^{he~will~}<u>BE</u>„ AT SON~s "Yisra'el ^{he~will~}<u>TURN-ASIDE</u>~+~MIGHTY-ONE„ from~LAND "Mits'rayim ^{STRAIT~s2}„ UPON ARMY~s~them(m)□

and (it) (came to pass), in {the} bone {of} this day*, "Yhwh ^{He is}„ made {the} sons {of} "Yisra'el ^{He turns El aside}„ go out from {the} land {of} "Mits'rayim ^{Two straits}„, (with) their armies,□

Chapter 13

13:1 וַיְדַבֵּר יְהוָה אֶל מֹשֶׁה לֵּאמֹר

wai'da'beyr YHWH el mo'sheh ley'mor

and~he~will~much~<u>SPEAK</u> "Yhwh ^{he~will~}<u>BE</u>„ TO "Mosheh ^{PLUCKED-OUT}„ to~>~<u>SAY</u>□

and "Yhwh ^{He is}„ spoke to "Mosheh ^{Plucked out}„ say{ing},□

13:2 קַדֶּשׁ לִי כָל בְּכוֹר פֶּטֶר כָּל רֶחֶם בִּבְנֵי יִשְׂרָאֵל בָּאָדָם וּבַבְּהֵמָה לִי הוּא

qa'desh li khol be'khor pe'ter kol re'hhem biv'ney yis'ra'eyl ba'a'dam u'va'be'hey'mah li hu

!(ms)~much~<u>SET-APART</u> to~me ALL FIRSTBORN BURSTING ALL BOWELS in~ SON~s "Yisra'el ^{he~will~}<u>TURN-ASIDE</u>~+~MIGHTY-ONE„ in~the~HUMAN and~in~the~BEAST to~me HE□

set apart (for) me all {the} firstborn bursting {of} all {the} bowels† in {the} sons {of} "Yisra'el ^{He turns El aside}„, in the human and in the beast, he {belongs} to me,□

13:3 וַיֹּאמֶר מֹשֶׁה אֶל הָעָם זָכוֹר אֶת הַיּוֹם הַזֶּה אֲשֶׁר יְצָאתֶם מִמִּצְרַיִם מִבֵּית עֲבָדִים כִּי בְּחֹזֶק יָד הוֹצִיא יְהוָה אֶתְכֶם מִזֶּה וְלֹא יֵאָכֵל חָמֵץ

wai'yo'mer mo'sheh el ha'am za'khor et hai'yom ha'zeh a'sher ye'tsa'tem mi'mits'ra'yim mi'beyt a'va'dim ki be'hho'zeq yad ho'tsi YHWH et'khem mi'zeh we'lo yey'a'kheyl hha'meyts

---

* The "bone of the day" is an idiom, probably meaning "noon."

† "Bursting of all the bowels" is an idiom for "births."

Revised Mechanical Translation Codes

(..) Alt Trans/App A	<..> Comp Phrase/App B	[..] Verb Form/App C	\../ Plural Form/App D
:..: Int Inf Abs	|..| Past Perf Verb	{...} Added Word	

and~he~will~SAY "Mosheh PLUCKED-OUT" TO the~PEOPLE >~REMEMBER AT the~DAY the~THIS WHICH you(mp)~did~GO-OUT from~"Mits'rayim STRAIT~s2" from~HOUSE SERVANT~s GIVEN-THAT in~GRASP HAND he~did~make~GO-OUT "Yhwh he~will~BE" AT~you(mp) from~THIS and~NOT he~will~be~EAT LEAVENED-BREAD□

and "Mosheh Plucked out" said to the people, remember this day, (which is when) you went out from "Mits'rayim Two straits", from {the} house {of} servants, given that (with) {a} grasp {of the} hand "Yhwh He is" made you go out from this, and leavened bread will not be eaten,□

13:4

הַיּוֹם אַתֶּם יֹצְאִים בְּחֹדֶשׁ הָאָבִיב

hai'yom a'tem yots'im be'hho'desh ha'a'viv

the~DAY YOU(mp) GO-OUT~ing/er(mp) in~NEW-MOON the~GREEN-GRAIN□

<today> you {are} going out in {the} new moon {of} the green grain,□

13:5 וְהָיָה כִי יְבִיאֲךָ יְהוָה אֶל אֶרֶץ הַכְּנַעֲנִי וְהַחִתִּי וְהָאֱמֹרִי וְהַחִוִּי וְהַיְבוּסִי אֲשֶׁר נִשְׁבַּע לַאֲבֹתֶיךָ לָתֶת לָךְ אֶרֶץ זָבַת חָלָב וּדְבָשׁ וְעָבַדְתָּ אֶת הָעֲבֹדָה הַזֹּאת בַּחֹדֶשׁ הַזֶּה

we'hai'yah khi ye'vi'a'kha YHWH el e'rets ha'ke'na'a'ni we'ha'hhi'ti we'ha'e'mo'ri we'ha'hhi'wi we'hai'vu'si a'sher nish'ba la'a'vo'tey'kha la'tet lakh e'rets za'vat hha'lav ud'vash we'a'vad'ta et ha'a'vo'dah ha'zot ba'hho'desh ha'zeh

and~he~did~EXIST GIVEN-THAT he~will~make~COME~you(ms) "Yhwh he~will~BE" TO LAND the~"Kena'an LOWERED"~of and~the~"Hhet TREMBLING-IN-FEAR"~of and~the~"Emor SAYER"~of and~the~"Hhiw TOWN"~of and~the~"Yevus he~will~TRAMPLE-DOWN"~of WHICH he~did~be~SWEAR to~FATHER~s~you(ms) to~>~GIVE to~you(fs) LAND ISSUE~ing/er(fs) FAT and~HONEY and~you(ms)~did~SERVE AT the~SERVICE the~THIS in~the~NEW-MOON the~THIS□

and (it) will (come to pass) that "Yhwh He is" will [bring] you to {the} land {of} the {one} of "Kena'an Lowered" and the {one} of "Hhet Trembling in fear" and the {one} of "Emor Sayer" and the {one} of "Hhiw Town" and the {one} of "Yevus He will trample down", which was sworn to your fathers to give to you, {a} land issuing fat* and honey†, and you will serve this service in this new moon,□

13:6 שִׁבְעַת יָמִים תֹּאכַל מַצֹּת וּבַיּוֹם הַשְּׁבִיעִי חַג לַיהוָה

shiv'at ya'mim to'khal ma'tsot u'va'yom hash'vi'i hhag la'YHWH

SEVEN DAY~s you(ms)~will~EAT UNLEAVENED-BREAD~s and~in~the~DAY the~SEVENTH FEAST to~"Yhwh he~will~BE"□

seven {of the} days you will eat unleavened bread, and in the seventh day {is the} feast to "Yhwh He is",□

13:7 מַצּוֹת יֵאָכֵל אֵת שִׁבְעַת הַיָּמִים וְלֹא יֵרָאֶה לְךָ חָמֵץ וְלֹא יֵרָאֶה לְךָ שְׂאֹר בְּכָל גְּבֻלֶךָ

---

* Or "milk."

† The Hebrew word דבש means a "sticky mass" and can also mean "dates" from the palm tree.

Mechanical Translation Codes

WORD – Verb	WORD – Noun	Word – Name	word – Pre/Suff	word – Conj.

ma'tsot yey'a'kheyl eyt shiv'at hai'ya'mim we'lo yey'ra'eh le'kha hha'meyts we'lo yey'ra'eh le'kha se'or be'khol ge'vu'le'kha

UNLEAVENED-BREAD~s *he~will~be~*<u>EAT</u> AT SEVEN the~DAY~s and~NOT *he~will~be~*<u>SEE</u> to~you(ms) LEAVENED-BREAD and~NOT *he~ will~be~*<u>SEE</u> to~you(ms) LEAVEN in~ALL BORDER~you(ms)□	unleavened bread will be eaten seven {of} the days, and leavened bread will not [appear] to you, and leaven will not [appear] to you in all your border{s},□

13:8 וְהִגַּדְתָּ לְבִנְךָ בַּיּוֹם הַהוּא לֵאמֹר בַּעֲבוּר זֶה עָשָׂה יְהוָה לִי בְּצֵאתִי מִמִּצְרָיִם

we'hi'gad'ta le'vin'kha ba'yom ha'hu ley'mor ba'a'vur zeh a'sah YHWH li be'tsey'ti mi'mits'ra'yim

and~*you(ms)~did~make~*<u>BE-FACE-TO-FACE</u> to~SON~you(ms) in~the~DAY the~HE to~ >~<u>SAY</u> in~INTENTION THIS *he~did~*<u>DO</u> "Yhwh *he~will~*<u>BE</u>" to~me in~>~<u>GO-OUT</u>me from~ "Mits'rayim ^{STRAIT~s2}"□	and you will [tell] to your son in (that) day say{ing}, (with) this intention, "Yhwh ^{He is}" did to me in my go{ing} out from "Mits'rayim ^{Two straits}",□

13:9 וְהָיָה לְךָ לְאוֹת עַל יָדְךָ וּלְזִכָּרוֹן בֵּין עֵינֶיךָ לְמַעַן תִּהְיֶה תּוֹרַת יְהוָה בְּפִיךָ כִּי בְּיָד חֲזָקָה הוֹצִאֲךָ יְהוָה מִמִּצְרָיִם

we'hai'yah le'kha le'ot al yad'kha ul'zi'ka'ron beyn ey'ney'kha le'ma'an tih'yeh to'rat YHWH be'phi'kha ki be'yad hha'za'qah ho'tsi'a'kha YHWH mi'mits'ra'yim

and~*he~did~*<u>EXIST</u> to~you(ms) to~SIGN UPON HAND~you(ms) and~to~ REMEMBRANCE BETWEEN EYE~s2~you(ms) to~THAT *she~will~*<u>EXIST</u> TEACHING "Yhwh *he~will~*<u>BE</u>" in~MOUTH~you(ms) GIVEN-THAT in~HAND FORCEFUL *he~did~make~*<u>GO-OUT</u>~ you(ms) "Yhwh *he~will~*<u>BE</u>" from~"Mits'rayim ^{STRAIT~s2}"□	and he will exist (for) you (for) {a} sign upon your hand, and (for) {a} remembrance between your eyes, (so) that {the} teaching {of} "Yhwh ^{He is}" will exist in your mouth, given that (with) {a} forceful hand "Yhwh ^{He is}" made you go out from "Mits'rayim ^{Two straits}",□

13:10 וְשָׁמַרְתָּ אֶת הַחֻקָּה הַזֹּאת לְמוֹעֲדָהּ מִיָּמִים יָמִימָה

we'sha'mar'ta et ha'hhu'qah ha'zot le'mo'a'dah mi'ya'mim ya'mi'mah

and~*you(ms)~did~*<u>SAFEGUARD</u> AT the~ RITUAL the~THIS to~APPOINTED~her from~ DAY~s DAY~s~unto□	and you will safeguard this ritual {according} to her* appointed {time}, from days unto days†,□

13:11 וְהָיָה כִּי יְבִאֲךָ יְהוָה אֶל אֶרֶץ הַכְּנַעֲנִי כַּאֲשֶׁר נִשְׁבַּע לְךָ וְלַאֲבֹתֶיךָ

---

* Referring to "ritual," a feminine word in Hebrew.
† "From days unto days" is a Hebrew idiom meaning "continually."

Revised Mechanical Translation Codes

(..) Alt Trans/App A	<..> Comp Phrase/App B	[..] Verb Form/App C	\../ Plural Form/App D
:..: Int Inf Abs	|..| Past Perf Verb	{...} Added Word	

וּנְתָנָהּ לָךְ

we'hai'yah ki ye'vi'a'kha YHWH el e'rets ha'ke'na'a'ni ka'a'sheyr nish'ba le'kha
we'la'a'vo'tey'kha un'ta'nah lakh

and~*he*~*did*~<u>EXIST</u> GIVEN-THAT *he*~*will*~ *make*~<u>COME</u>~you(ms) "Yhwh *he*~*will*~<u>BE</u>" TO LAND the~"Kena'an ^{LOWERED}"~of like~WHICH *he*~*did*~*be*~<u>SWEAR</u> to~you(ms) and~to~ FATHER~s~you(ms) and~*he*~*did*~<u>GIVE</u>~her to~you(fs)□	and (it) will (come to pass), that "Yhwh ^{He is}" will [bring] you to {the} land {of} the {one} of "Kena'an ^{Lowered}", <just as> he swore to you and to your fathers, and he will give her* to you,□

13:12 וְהַעֲבַרְתָּ כָל פֶּטֶר רֶחֶם לַיהוָה וְכָל פֶּטֶר שֶׁגֶר בְּהֵמָה אֲשֶׁר יִהְיֶה לְךָ הַזְּכָרִים לַיהוָה

we'ha'a'var'ta khol pe'ter re'hhem la'YHWH we'khol pe'ter she'ger be'hey'mah a'sher
yih'yeh le'kha haz'kha'rim la'YHWH

and~*you(ms)*~*did*~*make*~<u>CROSS-OVER</u> ALL BURSTING BOWELS to~"Yhwh ^{he~will~}<u>BE</u>" and~ ALL BURSTING BIRTH BEAST WHICH *he*~*will*~ <u>EXIST</u> to~you(ms) the~MALE~s to~"Yhwh ^{he}~^{will~}<u>BE</u>"□	and you will make all {the} bursting{s of the} bowels† cross over to "Yhwh ^{He is}", and all {the} bursting{s of the} birth{s of the} beast{s} will exist (for) you, the males {belong} to "Yhwh ^{He is}",□

13:13 וְכָל פֶּטֶר חֲמֹר תִּפְדֶּה בְשֶׂה וְאִם לֹא תִפְדֶּה וַעֲרַפְתּוֹ וְכֹל בְּכוֹר אָדָם בְּבָנֶיךָ תִּפְדֶּה

we'khol pe'ter hha'mor tiph'deh ve'sheh we'im lo tiph'deh wa'a'raph'to we'khol be'khor
a'dam be'va'ney'kha tiph'deh

and~ALL BURSTING DONKEY *you(ms)*~*will*~ <u>RANSOM</u> in~RAM and~IF NOT *you(ms)*~*will*~ <u>RANSOM</u> and~*you(ms)*~*did*~<u>BEHEAD</u>~him and~ALL FIRSTBORN HUMAN in~SON~s~ you(ms) *you(ms)*~*will*~<u>RANSOM</u>□	and you will ransom all {the} bursting {of the} donkey{s} (with) {a} ram, and if you will not ransom {it}, then you will behead‡ him, and all {the} firstborn {of the} human{s} (among) your sons, you will ransom,□

13:14 וְהָיָה כִּי יִשְׁאָלְךָ בִנְךָ מָחָר לֵאמֹר מַה זֹּאת וְאָמַרְתָּ אֵלָיו בְּחֹזֶק יָד הוֹצִיאָנוּ יְהוָה מִמִּצְרַיִם מִבֵּית עֲבָדִים

we'hai'yah ki yish'a'le'kha vin'kha ma'hhar ley'mor mah zot we'a'mar'ta ey'law
be'hho'zeq yad ho'tsi'a'nu YHWH mi'mits'ra'yim mi'beyt a'va'dim

and~*he*~*did*~<u>EXIST</u> GIVEN-THAT *he*~*will*~ <u>ENQUIRE</u>~you(ms) SON~you(ms) TOMORROW to~>~<u>SAY</u> WHAT THIS and~ *you(ms)*~*did*~<u>SAY</u> TO~him in~GRASP HAND *he*~*did*~*make*~<u>GO-OUT</u>~us "Yhwh ^{he~will~}<u>BE</u>"	and (it) will (come to pass) tomorrow§, that your son will enquire {of} you say{ing}, what {is} this, and you will say to him, (with) {the} grasp {of the} hand, "Yhwh ^{He is}" made us go out from "Mits'rayim ^{Two straits}", from {the}

---

* Referring to "land," a feminine word in Hebrew.
† "Bursting of the bowels" is an idiom meaning "births."
‡ This Hebrew verb can mean to "behead" or "break the neck."
§ "Tomorrow" can mean "later," a time in the future.

Mechanical Translation Codes

<u>WORD</u> – Verb	WORD – Noun	Word – Name	word – Pre/Suff	*word* – Conj.

from~"Mits'rayim ^{STRAIT~s2}" from~HOUSE SERVANT~s□

house {of} servants,□

13:15

וַיְהִי כִּי הִקְשָׁה פַרְעֹה לְשַׁלְּחֵנוּ וַיַּהֲרֹג יְהֹוָה כָּל בְּכוֹר בְּאֶרֶץ מִצְרַיִם מִבְּכֹר אָדָם וְעַד בְּכוֹר בְּהֵמָה עַל כֵּן אֲנִי זֹבֵחַ לַיהֹוָה כָּל פֶּטֶר רֶחֶם הַזְּכָרִים וְכָל בְּכוֹר בָּנַי אֶפְדֶּה

wai'hi ki hiq'shah phar'oh le'shal'hhey'nu wai'ya'ha'rog YHWH kol be'khor be'e'rets mits'ra'yim mi'be'khor a'dam we'ad be'khor be'hey'mah al keyn a'ni zo'vey'ahh la'YHWH kol pe'ter re'hhem haz'kha'rim we'khol be'khor ba'nai eph'deh

and~he~will~<u>EXIST</u> GIVEN-THAT he~did~ make~BE-HARD "Paroh ^{GREAT-HOUSE}" to~ >~much~<u>SEND</u>~us and~he~will~<u>KILL</u> "Yhwh ^{he~will~<u>BE</u>}" ALL FIRSTBORN in~LAND "Mits'rayim ^{STRAIT~s2}" from~FIRSTBORN HUMAN and~UNTIL FIRSTBORN BEAST UPON SO I <u>SACRIFICE</u>~ing/er(ms) to~"Yhwh ^{he~will~<u>BE</u>}" ALL BURSTING BOWELS the~ MALE~s and~ALL FIRSTBORN SON~s~me I~ will~<u>RANSOM</u>□

and (it) (came to pass), that "Paroh ^{Great house}" made {it} hard to send us, and "Yhwh ^{He is}" killed all {the} firstborn in {the} land {of} "Mits'rayim ^{Two straits}", from the firstborn human and (even) the firstborn beast, <therefore> I am sacrificing to "Yhwh ^{He is}" all {the} bursting {of the} bowels*, the males, and all {the} firstborn {of} my sons I will ransom,□

13:16

וְהָיָה לְאוֹת עַל יָדְכָה וּלְטוֹטָפֹת בֵּין עֵינֶיךָ כִּי בְּחֹזֶק יָד הוֹצִיאָנוּ יְהֹוָה מִמִּצְרָיִם

we'hai'yah le'ot al yad'khah ul'to'ta'phot beyn ey'ney'kha ki be'hho'zeq yad ho'tsi'a'nu YHWH mi'mits'ra'yim

and~he~did~<u>EXIST</u> to~SIGN UPON HAND~ you(ms) and~to~MARKER~s BETWEEN EYE~s2~you(ms) GIVEN-THAT in~GRASP HAND he~did~make~<u>GO-OUT</u>~us "Yhwh ^{he~ will~<u>BE</u>}" from~"Mits'rayim ^{STRAIT~s2}"□

and he will exist (for) {a} sign upon your hand, and (for) markers between your eyes, given that (with) {the} grasp {of the} hand, "Yhwh ^{He is}" made us go out from "Mits'rayim ^{Two straits}",□

13:17

וַיְהִי בְּשַׁלַּח פַּרְעֹה אֶת הָעָם וְלֹא נָחָם אֱלֹהִים דֶּרֶךְ אֶרֶץ פְּלִשְׁתִּים כִּי קָרוֹב הוּא כִּי אָמַר אֱלֹהִים פֶּן יִנָּחֵם הָעָם בִּרְאֹתָם מִלְחָמָה וְשָׁבוּ מִצְרָיְמָה

wai'hi be'sha'lahh par'oh et ha'am we'lo na'hham e'lo'him de'rekh e'rets pe'lish'tim ki qa'rov hu ki a'mar e'lo'him pen yi'na'hheym ha'am bir'o'tam mil'hha'mah we'sha'vu mits'rai'mah

and~he~will~<u>EXIST</u> in~>~much~<u>SEND</u> "Paroh ^{GREAT-HOUSE}" AT the~PEOPLE and~NOT he~did~ <u>GUIDE</u>~them(m) "Elohiym ^{POWFR~s}" ROAD LAND "Peleshet ^{IMMIGRANT}~s GIVEN-THAT NEAR HE GIVEN-THAT he~did~<u>SAY</u> "Elohiym

and (it) (came to pass), (with) "Paroh ^{Great house}" sending the people, and "Elohiym ^{Powers}" did not guide them {on the} road {to the} land {of the one}s {of} "Peleshet ^{Immigrant}" (when) he† {was} near, given that "Elohiym ^{Powers}" said,

---

* "Bursting of the bowels" is an idiom meaning "births."
† That is, "the people," a masculine singular word in Hebrew.

Revised Mechanical Translation Codes

| (..) Alt Trans/App A | <..> Comp Phrase/App B | [..] Verb Form/App C | \../ Plural Form/App D |
| :..: Int Inf Abs | |..| Past Perf Verb | {...} Added Word | |

POWER~s„ OTHERWISE he~will~be~COMFORT the~PEOPLE in~>~SEE~them(m) BATTLE and~they~did~TURN-BACK "Mits'rayim STRAIT~s2„~unto□

otherwise, the people will [repent] in their seeing {the} battle, and they will turn back unto "Mits'rayim Two straits„,□

13:18

וַיַּסֵּב אֱלֹהִים אֶת־הָעָם דֶּרֶךְ הַמִּדְבָּר יַם־סוּף וַחֲמֻשִׁים עָלוּ בְנֵי יִשְׂרָאֵל מֵאֶרֶץ מִצְרָיִם

wai'ya'seyv e'lo'him et ha'am de'rekh ha'mid'bar yam suph wa'hha'mu'shim a'lu ve'ney yis'ra'eyl mey'e'rets mits'ra'yim

and~he~will~make~GO-AROUND "Elohiym POWER~s„ AT the~PEOPLE ROAD the~ WILDERNESS SEA REEDS and~ARM-FOR-BATTLE~ed(mp) they~did~GO-UP SON~s "Yisra'el he~will~TURN-ASIDE~+~MIGHTY-ONE„ from~ LAND "Mits'rayim STRAIT~s2„□

and "Elohiym Powers„ made the people go around {the} road {of} the wilderness {of the} sea {of} reeds*, and armed for battle, {the} sons {of} "Yisra'el He turns El aside„ went up from {the} land {of} "Mits'rayim Two straits„,□

13:19

וַיִּקַּח מֹשֶׁה אֶת־עַצְמוֹת יוֹסֵף עִמּוֹ כִּי הַשְׁבֵּעַ הִשְׁבִּיעַ אֶת־בְּנֵי יִשְׂרָאֵל לֵאמֹר פָּקֹד יִפְקֹד אֱלֹהִים אֶתְכֶם וְהַעֲלִיתֶם אֶת־עַצְמֹתַי מִזֶּה אִתְּכֶם

wai'yi'qahh mo'sheh et ats'mot yo'seyph i'mo ki hash'bey'a hish'bi'a et be'ney yis'ra'eyl ley'mor pa'qod yiph'qod e'lo'him et'khem we'ha'a'li'tem et ats'mo'tai mi'zeh it'khem

and~he~will~TAKE "Mosheh PLUCKED-OUT„ AT BONE~s "Yoseph ADD~ing/er(ms)„ WITH~him GIVEN-THAT >~make~SWEAR he~did~make~ SWEAR AT SON~s "Yisra'el he~will~TURN-ASIDE~+~ MIGHTY-ONE„ to~>~SAY >~REGISTER he~will~ REGISTER "Elohiym POWER~s„ AT~you(mp) and~you(mp)~did~make~GO-UP AT BONE~s~me from~THIS AT~you(mp)□

and "Mosheh Plucked out„ took {the} bones {of} "Yoseph Adding„ with him, given that he :surely: made {the} sons {of} "Yisra'el He turns El aside„ swear, say{ing}, "Elohiym Powers„ will :surely: register (with) you, and you will make my bones go up from this {place} (with) you,□

13:20

וַיִּסְעוּ מִסֻּכֹּת וַיַּחֲנוּ בְאֵתָם בִּקְצֵה הַמִּדְבָּר

wai'yis'u mi'su'kot wai'ya'hha'nu ve'ey'tam biq'tseyh ha'mid'bar

and~they(m)~will~JOURNEY from~"Sukhot BOOTH~s„ and~they(m)~will~CAMP in~"Eytam PLOWSHARE~them(m)„ in~EXTREMITY the~ WILDERNESS□

and they journeyed from "Sukhot Booths„, and they camped in "Eytam Their plowshare„, in {the} extremity {of} the wilderness,□

13:21

וַיהוָה הֹלֵךְ לִפְנֵיהֶם יוֹמָם בְּעַמּוּד עָנָן לַנְחֹתָם הַדֶּרֶךְ וְלַיְלָה בְּעַמּוּד אֵשׁ לְהָאִיר לָהֶם לָלֶכֶת יוֹמָם וָלָיְלָה

wa'YHWH ho'leykh liph'ney'hem yo'mam be'a'mud a'nan lan'hho'tam ha'de'rekh we'lai'lah be'a'mud eysh le'ha'ir la'hem la'le'khet yo'mam wa'lai'lah

---

* "Sea of reeds," or "Yam Suph," is usually mistranslated as "red sea."

Mechanical Translation Codes

WORD – Verb	WORD – Noun	Word – Name	word – Pre/Suff	word – Conj.

and~"Yhwh ^{he~will~<u>BE</u>}" <u>WALK</u>~*ing/er(ms)* to~
FACE~s~them(m) DAYTIME in~PILLAR
CLOUD to~>~*make*~<u>GUIDE</u>~them(m) the~
ROAD and~NIGHT in~PILLAR FIRE to~
>~*make*~<u>LIGHT</u> to~them(m) to~>~<u>WALK</u>
DAYTIME and~NIGHT□

and "Yhwh ^{He is}" {was} walking to their face*,
{by} daytime in {a} pillar {of} cloud to guide
them {in} the road, and {by} night in {a} pillar
{of} fire to make light (for) them to walk,
daytime and night,□

13:22 לֹא יָמִישׁ עַמּוּד הֶעָנָן יוֹמָם וְעַמּוּד הָאֵשׁ לַיְלָה לִפְנֵי הָעָם

lo ya'mish a'mud he'a'nan yo'mam we'a'mud ha'eysh lai'lah liph'ney ha'am

NOT *he*~*will*~*make*~<u>MOVE-AWAY</u> PILLAR
the~CLOUD DAYTIME and~PILLAR the~FIRE
NIGHT to~FACE~s the~PEOPLE□

he will not make {the} pillar {of} the cloud {of
the} daytime and {the} pillar {of} the fire {of
the} night move away {from} <in front of> the
people,□

Chapter 14

14:1 וַיְדַבֵּר יְהֹוָה אֶל מֹשֶׁה לֵּאמֹר

wai'da'beyr YHWH el mo'sheh ley'mor

and~*he*~*will*~*much*~<u>SPEAK</u> "Yhwh ^{he~will~<u>BE</u>}"
TO "Mosheh ^{PLUCKED-OUT}" to~>~<u>SAY</u>□

and "Yhwh ^{He is}" spoke to "Mosheh ^{Plucked out}"
say{ing},□

14:2 דַּבֵּר אֶל בְּנֵי יִשְׂרָאֵל וְיָשֻׁבוּ וְיַחֲנוּ לִפְנֵי פִּי הַחִירֹת בֵּין מִגְדֹּל וּבֵין הַיָּם
לִפְנֵי בַּעַל צְפֹן נִכְחוֹ תַחֲנוּ עַל הַיָּם

da'beyr el be'ney yis'ra'eyl we'ya'shu'vu we'yahh'nu liph'ney pi ha'hhi'rot beyn mig'dol
u'veyn hai'yam liph'ney ba'al tse'phon nikh'hho ta'hha'nu al hai'yam

!*(ms)*~*much*~<u>SPEAK</u> TO SON~s "Yisra'el ^{he~will~}
^{<u>TURN-ASIDE</u>~+~<u>MIGHTY-ONE</u>}" and~*they(m)*~*will*~
<u>TURN-BACK</u> and~*they(m)*~*will*~<u>CAMP</u> to~
FACE~s "Piy-Hahhiyrot ^{MOUTH~+~the~CISTERN~s}"
BETWEEN "Migdol ^{TOWER}" and~BETWEEN
the~SEA to~FACE~s "Ba'al-Tsephon ^{MASTER~+~}
^{NORTH}" IN-FRONT~him *you(mp)*~*will*~<u>CAMP</u>
UPON the~SEA□

speak to {the} sons {of} "Yisra'el ^{He turns El aside}"
and they will turn back and they will camp <in
front of> "Piy-Hahhiyrot ^{Mouth of the cisterns}",
between "Migdol ^{Tower}" and the sea, <in front
of> "Ba'al-Tsephon ^{Master of the north}", in front {of}
him you will camp, upon the sea,□

14:3 וְאָמַר פַּרְעֹה לִבְנֵי יִשְׂרָאֵל נְבֻכִים הֵם בָּאָרֶץ סָגַר עֲלֵיהֶם הַמִּדְבָּר

we'a'mar par'oh liv'ney yis'ra'eyl ne'vu'khim heym ba'a'rets sa'gar a'ley'hem ha'mid'bar

---

* "To their face" is an idiom meaning "in front of them."

Revised Mechanical Translation Codes

(..) Alt Trans/App A	<..> Comp Phrase/App B	[..] Verb Form/App C	\..\ Plural Form/App D
:..: Int Inf Abs	|..| Past Perf Verb	{...} Added Word	

and~he~did~SAY "Paroh ^{GREAT-HOUSE}„ to~ SON~s "Yisra'el ^{he~will~TURN-ASIDE~+~MIGHTY-ONE}„ be~ENTANGLED~ing/er(mp) THEY(m) in~ the~LAND he~did~SHUT UPON~them(m) the~WILDERNESS□

and "Paroh ^{Great house}„ will say to* {the} sons {of} "Yisra'el ^{He turns El aside}„, they {are} being entangled in the land, the wilderness shut {in} upon them,□

14:4

וְחִזַּקְתִּי אֶת לֵב פַּרְעֹה וְרָדַף אַחֲרֵיהֶם וְאִכָּבְדָה בְּפַרְעֹה וּבְכָל חֵילוֹ וְיָדְעוּ מִצְרַיִם כִּי אֲנִי יְהֹוָה וַיַּעֲשׂוּ כֵן

we'hhi'zaq'ti et leyv par'oh we'ra'daph a'hha'rey'hem we'i'kav'dah be'phar'oh uv'khol hhey'lo we'yad'u mits'ra'yim ki a'ni YHWH wai'ya'a'su kheyn

and~I~did~much~SEIZE AT HEART "Paroh ^{GREAT-HOUSE}„ and~he~did~PURSUE AFTER~ them(m) and~I~will~be~BE-HEAVY~^ in~ "Paroh ^{GREAT-HOUSE}„ and~in~ALL FORCE~him and~they~did~KNOW "Mits'rayim ^{STRAIT~s2}„ GIVEN-THAT I "Yhwh ^{he~will~BE}„ and~they(m)~ will~DO SO□

and I will seize {the} heart {of} "Paroh ^{Great house}„, and he will pursue after them, and I will be heavy in "Paroh ^{Great house}„, and in all his force{s}, and "Mits'rayim ^{Two straits}„ will know that I {am} "Yhwh ^{He is}„, and they will do so,□

14:5

וַיֻּגַּד לְמֶלֶךְ מִצְרַיִם כִּי בָרַח הָעָם וַיֵּהָפֵךְ לְבַב פַּרְעֹה וַעֲבָדָיו אֶל הָעָם וַיֹּאמְרוּ מַה זֹּאת עָשִׂינוּ כִּי שִׁלַּחְנוּ אֶת יִשְׂרָאֵל מֵעָבְדֵנוּ

wai'yu'gad le'me'lekh mits'ra'yim ki va'rahh ha'am wai'yey'ha'pheykh le'vav par'oh wa'a'va'daw el ha'am wai'yom'ru mah zot a'si'nu ki shi'lahh'nu et yis'ra'eyl mey'av'dey'nu

and~he~will~be~make~BE-FACE-TO-FACE to~KING "Mits'rayim ^{STRAIT~s2}„ GIVEN-THAT he~did~FLEE-AWAY the~PEOPLE and~he~ will~be~OVERTURN MIND "Paroh ^{GREAT-HOUSE}„ and~SERVANT~s~him TO the~PEOPLE and~ they(m)~will~SAY WHAT THIS we~did~DO GIVEN-THAT we~did~much~SEND AT "Yisra'el ^{he~will~TURN-ASIDE~+~MIGHTY-ONE}„ from~ >~SERVE~us□

and (it) was [told] to {the} king {of} "Mits'rayim ^{Two straits}„ that the people fled away, and {the} mind {of} "Paroh ^{Great house}„, and his servants, were overturned to the people, and they said, what {is} this we did, given that we sent "Yisra'el ^{He turns El aside}„ from serving us?□

14:6

וַיֶּאְסֹר אֶת רִכְבּוֹ וְאֶת עַמּוֹ לָקַח עִמּוֹ

wai'ye'sor et rikh'bo we'et a'mo la'qahh i'mo

and~he~will~TIE-UP AT VEHICLE~him and~ AT PEOPLE~him he~did~TAKE WITH~him□

and he tied up† his vehicle, and he took his people with him,□

14:7

וַיִּקַּח שֵׁשׁ מֵאוֹת רֶכֶב בָּחוּר וְכֹל רֶכֶב מִצְרַיִם וְשָׁלִשִׁם עַל כֻּלּוֹ

wai'yi'qahh sheysh mey'ot re'khev ba'hhur we'khol re'khev mits'ra'yim we'sha'li'shim al ku'lo

---

* The word "to" may be interpreted as "concerning."

† Meaning "harnessed."

Mechanical Translation Codes

<u>WORD</u> – Verb	WORD – Noun	Word – Name	word – Pre/Suff	*word* – Conj.

and~he~will~TAKE SIX HUNDRED~s VEHICLE CHOOSE~ed(*ms*) and~ALL VEHICLE "Mits'rayim ^{STRAIT~s2}" and~LIEUTENANT~s UPON ALL~him□

and he took six hundred chosen vehicle{s}, and all {the} vehicle{s of} "Mits'rayim ^{Two straits}", and {the} lieutenants (over) all {of} them*,□

14:8 וַיְחַזֵּק יְהוָה אֶת לֵב פַּרְעֹה מֶלֶךְ מִצְרַיִם וַיִּרְדֹּף אַחֲרֵי בְּנֵי יִשְׂרָאֵל וּבְנֵי יִשְׂרָאֵל יֹצְאִים בְּיָד רָמָה

wai'hha'zeyq YHWH et leyv par'oh me'lekh mits'ra'yim wai'yir'doph a'hha'rey be'ney yis'ra'eyl uv'ney yis'ra'eyl yots'im be'yad ra'mah

and~he~will~much~SEIZE "Yhwh ^{he~will~BE}" AT HEART "Paroh ^{GREAT-HOUSE}" KING "Mits'rayim ^{STRAIT~s2}" and~he~will~PURSUE AFTER SON~s "Yisra'el ^{he~will~TURN-ASIDE~+~MIGHTY-ONE}" and~ SON~s "Yisra'el ^{he~will~TURN-ASIDE~+~MIGHTY-ONE}" GO-OUT~*ing/er*(*mp*) in~HAND RAISE~ *ing/er*(*fs*)□

and "Yhwh ^{He is}" seized {the} heart {of} "Paroh ^{Great house}", {the} king {of} "Mits'rayim ^{Two straits}", and he pursued after {the} sons {of} "Yisra'el ^{He turns El aside}", and {the} sons {of} "Yisra'el ^{He turns El aside}" {were} going out (with) {the} hand raising†,□

14:9 וַיִּרְדְּפוּ מִצְרַיִם אַחֲרֵיהֶם וַיַּשִּׂיגוּ אוֹתָם חֹנִים עַל הַיָּם כָּל סוּס רֶכֶב פַּרְעֹה וּפָרָשָׁיו וְחֵילוֹ עַל פִּי הַחִירֹת לִפְנֵי בַּעַל צְפֹן

wai'yir'de'phu mits'ra'yim a'hha'rey'hem wai'ya'si'gu o'tam hho'nim al hai'yam kol sus re'khev par'oh u'pha'ra'shaw we'hhey'lo al pi ha'hhi'rot liph'ney ba'al tse'phon

and~they(*m*)~will~PURSUE "Mits'rayim ^{STRAIT~s2}" AFTER~them(*m*) and~they(*m*)~will~ make~OVERTAKE AT~them(*m*) CAMP~ *ing/er*(*fp*) UPON the~SEA ALL HORSE VEHICLE "Paroh ^{GREAT-HOUSE}" and~ HORSEMAN~s~him and~FORCE~him UPON "Piy-Hahhiyrot ^{MOUTH~+~the~CISTERN~s}" to~FACE~s "Ba'al-Tsephon ^{MASTER~+~NORTH}"□

and "Mits'rayim ^{Two straits}" pursued after them, and all {the} horse{s of the} vehicle{s of} "Paroh ^{Great house}", and his horsemen, and his force{s} overtook them camping upon the sea, upon "Piy-Hahhiyrot ^{Mouth of the cisterns}", <in front of> "Ba'al-Tsephon ^{Master of the north}",□

14:10 וּפַרְעֹה הִקְרִיב וַיִּשְׂאוּ בְנֵי יִשְׂרָאֵל אֶת עֵינֵיהֶם וְהִנֵּה מִצְרַיִם נֹסֵעַ אַחֲרֵיהֶם וַיִּירְאוּ מְאֹד וַיִּצְעֲקוּ בְנֵי יִשְׂרָאֵל אֶל יְהוָה

u'phar'oh hiq'riv wai'yish'u ve'ney yis'ra'eyl et ay'ney'hem we'hin'neyh mits'ra'yim no'sey'a a'hha'rey'hem wai'yir'u me'od wai'yits'a'qu ve'ney yis'ra'eyl el YHWH

and~"Paroh ^{GREAT-HOUSE}" he~did~make~ COME-NEAR and~they(*m*)~will~LIFT-UP SON~s "Yisra'el ^{he~will~TURN-ASIDE~+~MIGHTY-ONE}" AT EYE~s2~them(*m*) and~LOOK "Mits'rayim ^{STRAIT~s2}" JOURNEY~*ing/er*(*ms*) AFTER~ them(*m*) and~they(*m*)~will~FEAR MANY and~they(*m*)~will~CRY-OUT SON~s "Yisra'el

and "Paroh ^{Great house}" |had| come near, and {the} sons {of} "Yisra'el ^{He turns El aside}" lifted up their eyes and (saw) "Mits'rayim ^{Two straits}" journeying after them, and they feared (greatly), and {the} sons {of} "Yisra'el ^{He turns El aside}" cried out to "Yhwh ^{He is}",□

---

* Literally "him," as the word "vehicle" is a singular word in Hebrew.
† "The hand raising" is an idiom meaning "boldly."

Revised Mechanical Translation Codes

(..) Alt Trans/App A	<..> Comp Phrase/App B	[..] Verb Form/App C	\../ Plural Form/App D
:...: Int Inf Abs	|..| Past Perf Verb	{...} Added Word	

he~will~<u>TURN-ASIDE</u>~+~<u>MIGHTY-ONE</u>„ TO "Yhwh *he~will~*
<u>BE</u>„□

14:11 וַיֹּאמְרוּ אֶל מֹשֶׁה הֲמִבְּלִי אֵין קְבָרִים בְּמִצְרַיִם לְקַחְתָּנוּ לָמוּת בַּמִּדְבָּר מַה זֹּאת עָשִׂיתָ לָּנוּ לְהוֹצִיאָנוּ מִמִּצְרָיִם

wai'yom'ru el mo'sheh ha'mi'be'li eyn qe'va'rim be'mits'ra'yim le'qahh'ta'nu la'mut ba'mid'bar mah zot a'si'ta la'nu le'ho'tsi'a'nu mi'mits'ra'yim

and~*they(m)~will~*<u>SAY</u> TO "Mosheh ᴾᴸᵁᶜᴷᴱᴰ⁻ᴼᵁᵀ„ ?~from~<u>UNAWARE WITHOUT GRAVE</u>~s in~"Mits'rayim ˢᵀᴿᴬᴵᵀ~ˢ²„ *you(ms)~did~*<u>TAKE</u>~us to~>~<u>DIE</u> in~the~<u>WILDERNESS</u> WHAT THIS *you(ms)~did~*<u>DO</u> to~us to~>~*make~*<u>GO-OUT</u>~us from~"Mits'rayim ˢᵀᴿᴬᴵᵀ~ˢ²„□

and they said to "Mosheh ᴾˡᵘᶜᵏᵉᵈ ᵒᵘᵗ„, {is it} from {a} <lack of> graves in "Mits'rayim ᵀʷᵒ ˢᵗʳᵃⁱᵗˢ„ {that} you took us to die in the wilderness? what {is} this you did to us, to make us go out from "Mits'rayim ᵀʷᵒ ˢᵗʳᵃⁱᵗˢ„?□

14:12 הֲלֹא זֶה הַדָּבָר אֲשֶׁר דִּבַּרְנוּ אֵלֶיךָ בְמִצְרַיִם לֵאמֹר חֲדַל מִמֶּנּוּ וְנַעַבְדָה אֶת מִצְרָיִם כִּי טוֹב לָנוּ עֲבֹד אֶת מִצְרַיִם מִמֻּתֵנוּ בַּמִּדְבָּר

ha'lo zeh ha'da'var a'sher di'bar'nu ey'ley'kha ve'mits'ra'yim ley'mor hha'dal mi'me'nu we'na'av'dah et mits'ra'yim ki tov la'nu a'vod et mits'ra'yim mi'mu'tey'nu ba'mid'bar

?~NOT THIS the~<u>WORD</u> WHICH *we~did~much~*<u>SPEAK</u> TO~*you(ms)* in~"Mits'rayim ˢᵀᴿᴬᴵᵀ~ˢ²„ to~>~<u>SAY</u> *!(ms)~*<u>TERMINATE</u> FROM~us and~*we~will~*<u>SERVE</u>~^ AT "Mits'rayim ˢᵀᴿᴬᴵᵀ~ˢ²„ GIVEN-THAT FUNCTIONAL to~us >~<u>SERVE</u> AT "Mits'rayim ˢᵀᴿᴬᴵᵀ~ˢ²„ from~ >~<u>DIE</u>~us in~the~<u>WILDERNESS</u>□

{is} not this the word which we spoke to you in "Mits'rayim ᵀʷᵒ ˢᵗʳᵃⁱᵗˢ„ say{ing}, terminate from us and we will serve "Mits'rayim ᵀʷᵒ ˢᵗʳᵃⁱᵗˢ„? given that {it is} functional (for) us {to} serve "Mits'rayim ᵀʷᵒ ˢᵗʳᵃⁱᵗˢ„ (rather than) us dying in the wilderness,□

14:13 וַיֹּאמֶר מֹשֶׁה אֶל הָעָם אַל תִּירָאוּ הִתְיַצְּבוּ וּרְאוּ אֶת יְשׁוּעַת יְהוָה אֲשֶׁר יַעֲשֶׂה לָכֶם הַיּוֹם כִּי אֲשֶׁר רְאִיתֶם אֶת מִצְרַיִם הַיּוֹם לֹא תֹסִפוּ לִרְאֹתָם עוֹד עַד עוֹלָם

wai'yo'mer mo'sheh el ha'am al ti'ra'u hit'yats'vu ur'u et ye'shu'at YHWH a'sher ya'a'seh la'khem hai'yom ki a'sher re'i'tem et mits'ra'yim hai'yom lo to'si'phu lir'o'tam od ad o'lam

and~*he~will~*<u>SAY</u> "Mosheh ᴾᴸᵁᶜᴷᴱᴰ⁻ᴼᵁᵀ„ TO the~<u>PEOPLE</u> DO-NOT *you(mp)~will~*<u>FEAR</u> *!(mp)~* self~<u>STATION</u> and~*!(mp)~*<u>SEE</u> AT RELIEF "Yhwh *he~will~*<u>BE</u>„ WHICH *he~will~*<u>DO</u> to~*you(mp)* the~<u>DAY</u> GIVEN-THAT WHICH *you(mp)~did~*<u>SEE</u> AT "Mits'rayim ˢᵀᴿᴬᴵᵀ~ˢ²„ the~<u>DAY</u> NOT *you(mp)~will~make~*<u>ADD</u> to~<u>SEE</u>~them(m) YET-AGAIN UNTIL <u>DISTANT</u>□

and "Mosheh ᴾˡᵘᶜᵏᵉᵈ ᵒᵘᵗ„ said to the people, do not fear, station {your}self and see {the} relief {of} "Yhwh ᴴᵉ ⁱˢ„, which he will do (for) you <today>, <even though> you saw "Mits'rayim ᵀʷᵒ ˢᵗʳᵃⁱᵗˢ„ <today>, you will not [again] see them, (even) (unto) {a} distant {time}, □

14:14 יְהוָה יִלָּחֵם לָכֶם וְאַתֶּם תַּחֲרִשׁוּן

YHWH yi'la'heym la'khem we'a'tem ta'hha'ri'shun

"Yhwh *he~will~*<u>BE</u>„ *will~be~*<u>FIGHT</u> to~*you(mp)*

"Yhwh ᴴᵉ ⁱˢ„ will [wage war] (for) you, and you

Mechanical Translation Codes

<u>WORD</u> – Verb	WORD – Noun	Word – Name	word – Pre/Suff	*word* – Conj.

| and~YOU(mp) you(mp)~will~make~KEEP-SILENT~must☐ | must keep silent,☐ |

14:15 וַיֹּאמֶר יְהֹוָה אֶל מֹשֶׁה מַה תִּצְעַק אֵלָי דַּבֵּר אֶל בְּנֵי יִשְׂרָאֵל וְיִסָּעוּ

wai'yo'mer YHWH el mo'sheh mah tits'aq ey'lai da'beyr el be'ney yis'ra'eyl we'yi'sa'u

| and~*he~will*~SAY "Yhwh ^{he~will~BE}" TO "Mosheh ^{PLUCKED-OUT}" WHAT *you(ms)~will*~CRY-OUT TO~me !(ms)~much~SPEAK TO SON~s "Yisra'el ^{he~will~TURN-ASIDE~+~MIGHTY-ONE}" and~*they(m)~will*~JOURNEY☐ | and "Yhwh ^{He is}" said to "Mosheh ^{Plucked out}", what will you cry out to me?* speak to {the} sons {of} "Yisra'el ^{He turns El aside}" and they will journey,☐ |

14:16 וְאַתָּה הָרֵם אֶת מַטְּךָ וּנְטֵה אֶת יָדְךָ עַל הַיָּם וּבְקָעֵהוּ וְיָבֹאוּ בְנֵי יִשְׂרָאֵל בְּתוֹךְ הַיָּם בַּיַּבָּשָׁה

we'a'tah ha'reym et mat'kha un'teyh et yad'kha al hai'yam uv'qa'ey'hu we'ya'vo'u ve'ney yis'ra'eyl be'tokh hai'yam ba'ya'ba'shah

| and~YOU(ms) !(ms)~make~RAISE AT BRANCH~you(ms) and~!(ms)~EXTEND AT HAND~you(ms) UPON the~SEA and~!(ms)~CLEAVE~him and~*they(m)~will*~COME SON~s "Yisra'el ^{he~will~TURN-ASIDE~+~MIGHTY-ONE}" in~MIDST the~SEA in~the~DRY-GROUND☐ | and you, raise your branch and extend your hand upon the sea and cleave him†, and {the} sons {of} "Yisra'el ^{He turns El aside}" will come‡ in {the} midst {of} the sea (on) the dry ground,☐ |

14:17 וַאֲנִי הִנְנִי מְחַזֵּק אֶת לֵב מִצְרַיִם וְיָבֹאוּ אַחֲרֵיהֶם וְאִכָּבְדָה בְּפַרְעֹה וּבְכָל חֵילוֹ בְּרִכְבּוֹ וּבְפָרָשָׁיו

wa'ani hin'ni me'hha'zeyq et leyv mits'ra'yim we'ya'vo'u a'hha'rey'hem we'i'kav'dah be'phar'oh uv'khol hhey'lo be'rikh'bo uv'pha'ra'shaw

| and~I LOOK~me much~SEIZE~ing/er(ms) AT HEART "Mits'rayim ^{STRAIT~s2}" and~*they(m)~will*~COME AFTER~them(m) and~*I~will*~be~BE-HEAVY~^ in~"Paroh ^{GREAT-HOUSE}" and~in~ALL FORCE~him in~VEHICLE~him and~in~HORSEMAN~s~him☐ | and I, look {at} me, seizing {the} heart {of} "Mits'rayim ^{Two straits}", and they will come after them, and I will be heavy§ (with) "Paroh ^{Great house}", and (with) all his force{s}, (with) his vehicle{s}, and (with) his horsemen,☐ |

14:18 וְיָדְעוּ מִצְרַיִם כִּי אֲנִי יְהֹוָה בְּהִכָּבְדִי בְּפַרְעֹה בְּרִכְבּוֹ וּבְפָרָשָׁיו

we'yad'u mits'ra'yim ki a'ni YHWH be'hi'kav'di be'phar'oh be'rikh'bo uv'pha'ra'shaw

---

* The phrase, "What will you cry out to me?" may also be translated as "What? Will you cry out to me?"

† Referring to the "sea," a masculine word in Hebrew.

‡ Or "go."

§ "Being heavy" means that YHWH will bring his power on Mits'rayim to show his might.

Revised Mechanical Translation Codes

| (..) Alt Trans/App A | <..> Comp Phrase/App B | [..] Verb Form/App C | \../ Plural Form/App D |
| :..: Int Inf Abs | |..| Past Perf Verb | {...} Added Word | |

and~*they~did*~<u>KNOW</u> "Mits'rayim ^{STRAIT~s2}"
GIVEN-THAT I "Yhwh ^{he~will~BE}" in~>~*be*~<u>BE-</u>
<u>HEAVY</u>~me in~"Paroh ^{GREAT-HOUSE}" in~
VEHICLE~him and~in~HORSEMAN~s~him□

and "Mits'rayim ^{Two straits}" will know that I {am}
"Yhwh ^{He is}" (with) my be{ing} heavy* (with)
"Paroh ^{Great house}", (with) his vehicle{s}, and
(with) his horsemen,□

14:19 וַיִּסַּע מַלְאַךְ הָאֱלֹהִים הַהֹלֵךְ לִפְנֵי מַחֲנֵה יִשְׂרָאֵל וַיֵּלֶךְ מֵאַחֲרֵיהֶם וַיִּסַּע עַמּוּד הֶעָנָן מִפְּנֵיהֶם וַיַּעֲמֹד מֵאַחֲרֵיהֶם

wai'yi'sa mal'akh ha'e'lo'him ha'ho'leykh liph'ney ma'hha'neyh yis'ra'eyl wai'yey'lekh
mey'a'hha'rey'hem   wai'yi'sa   a'mud   he'a'nan   mi'pe'ney'hem   wai'ya'a'mod
mey'a'hha'rey'hem

and~*he~will*~<u>JOURNEY</u> MESSENGER the~
"Elohiym ^{POWER~s}" the~<u>WALK</u>~*ing/er(ms)* to~
FACE~s CAMPSITE "Yisra'el ^{he~will~TURN-ASIDE~+~}
^{MIGHTY-ONE}" and~*he~will*~<u>WALK</u> from~AFTER~
them(m) and~*he~will*~<u>JOURNEY</u> PILLAR the~
CLOUD from~FACE~s~them(m) and~*he~will*~
<u>STAND</u> from~AFTER~them(m)□

and {the} messenger {of} the "Elohiym ^{Powers}",
the {one} walking <in front of> {the} campsite
{of} "Yisra'el ^{He turns El aside}", journeyed, and he
walked <behind> them, and {the} pillar {of}
the cloud journeyed from their face, and he†
stood <behind> them,□

14:20 וַיָּבֹא בֵּין מַחֲנֵה מִצְרַיִם וּבֵין מַחֲנֵה יִשְׂרָאֵל וַיְהִי הֶעָנָן וְהַחֹשֶׁךְ וַיָּאֶר אֶת הַלָּיְלָה וְלֹא קָרַב זֶה אֶל זֶה כָּל הַלָּיְלָה

wai'ya'vo beyn ma'hha'neyh mits'ra'yim u'veyn ma'hha'neyh yis'ra'eyl wai'hi he'a'nan
we'ha'hho'shekh wai'ya'er et ha'lai'lah we'lo qa'rav zeh el zeh kol ha'lai'lah

and~*he~will*~<u>COME</u> BETWEEN CAMPSITE
"Mits'rayim ^{STRAIT~s2}" and~BETWEEN
CAMPSITE "Yisra'el ^{he~will~TURN-ASIDE~+~MIGHTY-}
^{ONE}" and~*he~will*~<u>EXIST</u> the~CLOUD and~
the~DARKNESS and~*he~will~make*~<u>LIGHT</u>
AT the~NIGHT and~NOT *he~did*~<u>COME-</u>
<u>NEAR</u> THIS TO THIS ALL the~NIGHT□

and he‡ came between {the} campsite {of}
"Mits'rayim ^{Two straits}" and {the} campsite {of}
"Yisra'el ^{He turns El aside}", and the cloud existed,
and the darkness, and he made the night light,
and this {one} did not come near (that) {one}
all the night,□

14:21 וַיֵּט מֹשֶׁה אֶת יָדוֹ עַל הַיָּם וַיּוֹלֶךְ יְהֹוָה אֶת הַיָּם בְּרוּחַ קָדִים עַזָּה כָּל הַלָּיְלָה וַיָּשֶׂם אֶת הַיָּם לֶחָרָבָה וַיִּבָּקְעוּ הַמָּיִם

wai'yeyt mo'sheh et ya'do al hai'yam wai'yo'lekh YHWH et hai'yam be'ru'ahh qa'dim
a'zah kol ha'lai'lah wai'ya'sem et hai'yam le'hha'ra'vah wai'yi'baq'u ha'ma'yim

and~*he~will*~<u>EXTEND</u> "Mosheh ^{PLUCKED-OUT}"
AT HAND~him UPON the~SEA and~*he~will*~
make~<u>WALK</u> "Yhwh ^{he~will~BE}" AT the~SEA in~
WIND EAST-WIND STRONG ALL the~NIGHT
and~*he~will*~<u>PLACE</u> AT the~SEA to~

and "Mosheh ^{Plucked out}" extended his hand
upon the sea, and "Yhwh ^{He is}" made the sea
walk (with) {a} strong east wind all the night,
and he placed§ the sea (for) {a} wasteland,
and the waters were cleaved,□

---

* "Being heavy"means that YHWH will bring his power on Mits'rayim to show his might.
† Referring to the "pillar," a masculine word in Hebrew.
‡ Referring to the "pillar" in verse 19, a masculine word in Hebrew.
§ This verb, שים, appears to be out of context and may be an error. A possible correction may be the verb עשה meaning "to make."

Mechanical Translation Codes

<u>WORD</u> – Verb	WORD – Noun	Word – Name	word – Pre/Suff	*word* – Conj.

WASTELAND and~*they(m)*~*will*~*be*~<u>CLEAVE</u>
the~<u>WATER</u>~s2□

14:22 וַיָּבֹאוּ בְנֵי יִשְׂרָאֵל בְּתוֹךְ הַיָּם בַּיַּבָּשָׁה וְהַמַּיִם לָהֶם חוֹמָה מִימִינָם וּמִשְּׂמֹאלָם

wai'ya'vo'u ve'ney yis'ra'eyl be'tokh hai'yam ba'ya'ba'shah we'ha'ma'yim la'hem hho'mah mi'mi'nam u'mis'mo'lam

and~*they(m)*~*will*~<u>COME</u> SON~s "Yisra'el ^{he~}^{*will*~<u>TURN-ASIDE</u>+~<u>MIGHTY-ONE</u>„} in~MIDST the~SEA in~the~DRY-GROUND and~the~WATER~s2 to~them(m) RAMPART from~RIGHT-HAND~ them(m) and~from~LEFT-HAND~them(m)□

and {the} sons {of} "Yisra'el ^{He turns El aside„} came in {the} midst {of} the sea in the dry ground, and the waters {were a} rampart (for) them, (at) their right hand and (at) their left hand,□

14:23 וַיִּרְדְּפוּ מִצְרַיִם וַיָּבֹאוּ אַחֲרֵיהֶם כֹּל סוּס פַּרְעֹה רִכְבּוֹ וּפָרָשָׁיו אֶל תּוֹךְ הַיָּם

wai'yir'de'phu mits'ra'yim wai'ya'vo'u a'hha'rey'hem kol sus par'oh rikh'bo u'pha'ra'shaw el tokh hai'yam

and~*they(m)*~*will*~<u>PURSUE</u> "Mits'rayim ^{STRAIT~s2„} and~*they(m)*~*will*~<u>COME</u> AFTER~ them(m) ALL HORSE "Paroh ^{GREAT-HOUSE„} VEHICLE~him and~HORSEMAN~s~him TO MIDST the~SEA□

and "Mits'rayim ^{Two straits„} pursued, and all {the} horse{s of} "Paroh ^{Great house„}, his chariot{s} and his vehicle, came after them to {the} midst {of} the sea,□

14:24 וַיְהִי בְּאַשְׁמֹרֶת הַבֹּקֶר וַיַּשְׁקֵף יְהוָה אֶל מַחֲנֵה מִצְרַיִם בְּעַמּוּד אֵשׁ וְעָנָן וַיָּהָם אֵת מַחֲנֵה מִצְרָיִם

wai'hi be'ash'mo'ret ha'bo'qer wai'yash'qeyph YHWH el ma'hha'neyh mits'ra'yim be'a'mud eysh we'a'nan wai'ya'ham eyt ma'hha'neyh mits'ra'yim

and~*he*~*will*~<u>EXIST</u> in~NIGHT-WATCH the~ MORNING and~*he*~*will*~make~<u>LOOK-DOWN</u> "Yhwh ^{he~will~<u>BE</u>„} TO CAMPSITE "Mits'rayim ^{STRAIT~s2„} in~PILLAR FIRE and~CLOUD and~*he*~ *will*~<u>CONFUSE</u> AT CAMPSITE "Mits'rayim ^{STRAIT~s2„}□

and (it) (came to pass) in {the} night watch {of} the morning, and "Yhwh ^{He is„} looked down to {the} campsite {of} "Mits'rayim ^{Two straits„}, in {the} pillar {of} fire and {the} cloud, and he confused {the} campsite {of} "Mits'rayim ^{Two straits„},□

14:25 וַיָּסַר אֵת אֹפַן מַרְכְּבֹתָיו וַיְנַהֲגֵהוּ בִּכְבֵדֻת וַיֹּאמֶר מִצְרַיִם אָנוּסָה מִפְּנֵי יִשְׂרָאֵל כִּי יְהוָה נִלְחָם לָהֶם בְּמִצְרָיִם

wai'ya'sar eyt o'phan mar'ke'vo'taw wai'na'ha'gey'hu bikh'vey'dut wai'yo'mer mits'ra'yim a'nu'sah mip'ney yis'ra'eyl ki YHWH nil'hham la'hem be'mits'ra'yim

and~*he*~*will*~make~<u>TURN-ASIDE</u> AT WHEEL CHARIOT~s~him and~*he*~*will*~much~<u>DRIVE</u>~

and he made {the} wheel{s of} his chariots turn aside*, and he* drove him† (with)

---

* Probably meaning to "turn heavily." Some translations have "fell off," but see Footnote for the pronoun "him."

Revised Mechanical Translation Codes
(..) Alt Trans/App A   <..> Comp Phrase/App B   [..] Verb Form/App C   \../ Plural Form/App D
:..: Int Inf Abs |..| Past Perf Verb   {...} Added Word

him in~HEAVINESS and~*he~will*~SAY "Mits'rayim ^{STRAIT~s2}" *I~will*~FLEE from~ FACE~s "Yisra'el ^{*he~will*~TURN-ASIDE~+~MIGHTY-ONE}" GIVEN-THAT "Yhwh ^{*he~will*~BE}" *be*~FIGHT~ *ing/er(ms)* to~them(m) in~"Mits'rayim ^{STRAIT~s2}"□

him† (with) heaviness‡, and "Mits'rayim ^{Two straits}" said, I will flee from {the} face {of} "Yisra'el ^{He turns El aside}", given that "Yhwh ^{He is}" {will} [wage war] (for) them (among) "Mits'rayim ^{Two straits}",□

14:26 וַיֹּאמֶר יְהוָה אֶל מֹשֶׁה נְטֵה אֶת יָדְךָ עַל הַיָּם וְיָשֻׁבוּ הַמַּיִם עַל מִצְרַיִם עַל רִכְבּוֹ וְעַל פָּרָשָׁיו

wai'yo'mer YHWH el mo'sheh ne'teyh et yad'kha al hai'yam we'ya'shu'vu ha'ma'yim al mits'ra'yim al rikh'bo we'al pa'ra'shaw

and~*he~will*~SAY "Yhwh ^{*he~will*~BE}" TO "Mosheh ^{PLUCKED-OUT}" *!(ms)*~EXTEND AT HAND~you(ms) UPON the~SEA and~ *they(m)~will*~TURN-BACK the~WATER~s2 UPON "Mits'rayim ^{STRAIT~s2}" UPON VEHICLE~ him and~UPON HORSEMAN~s~him□

and "Yhwh ^{He is}" said to "Mosheh ^{Plucked out}", extend your hand upon the sea and the waters will turn back upon "Mits'rayim ^{Two straits}", upon his vehicle{s}, and upon his horsemen,□

14:27 וַיֵּט מֹשֶׁה אֶת יָדוֹ עַל הַיָּם וַיָּשָׁב הַיָּם לִפְנוֹת בֹּקֶר לְאֵיתָנוֹ וּמִצְרַיִם נָסִים לִקְרָאתוֹ וַיְנַעֵר יְהוָה אֶת מִצְרַיִם בְּתוֹךְ הַיָּם

wai'yeyt mo'sheh et ya'do al hai'yam wai'ya'shav hai'yam liph'not bo'qer le'ey'ta'no u'mits'ra'yim na'sim liq'ra'to wai'na'eyr YHWH et mits'ra'yim be'tokh hai'yam

and~*he~will*~EXTEND "Mosheh ^{PLUCKED-OUT}" AT HAND~him UPON the~SEA and~*he~will*~ TURN-BACK the~SEA to~>~TURN MORNING to~CONSISTENCY~him and~"Mits'rayim ^{STRAIT~s2}" FLEE~*ing/er(mp)* to~>~MEET~him and~*he~will*~much~SHAKE-OFF "Yhwh ^{*he~will*~ BE}" AT "Mits'rayim ^{STRAIT~s2}" in~MIDST the~ SEA□

and "Mosheh ^{Plucked out}" extended his hand upon the sea and the sea turned back to his consistency (by) the turning {of the} morning, and "Mits'rayim ^{Two straits}" {was} fleeing to meet him, and "Yhwh ^{He is}" shook off "Mits'rayim ^{Two straits}" in {the} midst {of} the sea,□

14:28 וַיָּשֻׁבוּ הַמַּיִם וַיְכַסּוּ אֶת הָרֶכֶב וְאֶת הַפָּרָשִׁים לְכֹל חֵיל פַּרְעֹה הַבָּאִים אַחֲרֵיהֶם בַּיָּם לֹא נִשְׁאַר בָּהֶם עַד אֶחָד

wai'ya'shu'vu ha'ma'yim wai'kha'su et ha're'khev we'et ha'pa'ra'shim le'khol hheyl par'oh ha'ba'im a'hha'rey'hem ba'yam lo nish'ar ba'hem ad e'hhad

and~*they(m)~will*~TURN-BACK the~ WATER~s2 and~*they(m)~will*~much~COVER-OVER AT the~VEHICLE and~AT the~

and the waters turned back and they covered over the vehicle{s}, and the horsemen, {and}§ all the force{s of} "Paroh ^{Great house}", the {ones}

---

* Probably referring to Mits'rayim.

† This pronoun cannot be referring to the chariots as the word is feminine in Hebrew. Therefore, this pronoun must be referring to the wheels.

‡ "Heaviness" in this context means "with difficulty."

§ The word לְכֹל (to all) may be written defectively and may originally have been written as וְכֹל (and all).

Mechanical Translation Codes

WORD – Verb	WORD – Noun	Word – Name	word – Pre/Suff	*word* – Conj.

HORSEMAN~s to~ALL FORCE "Paroh ^{GREAT-HOUSE}" the~COME~ing/er(mp) AFTER~ them(m) in~the~SEA NOT he~did~be~ REMAIN in~them(m) UNTIL UNIT□

house", the {ones} coming after them in the sea, not {a} <single one> was remain{ing} (with) them,□

14:29 וּבְנֵי יִשְׂרָאֵל הָלְכוּ בַיַּבָּשָׁה בְּתוֹךְ הַיָּם וְהַמַּיִם לָהֶם חֹמָה מִימִינָם וּמִשְּׂמֹאלָם

uv'ney yis'ra'eyl hal'khu vai'ya'ba'shah be'tokh hai'yam we'ha'ma'yim la'hem hho'mah mi'mi'nam u'mis'mo'lam

and~SON~s "Yisra'el ^{he~will~TURN-ASIDE~+~MIGHTY-ONE}" they~did~WALK in~the~DRY-GROUND in~MIDST the~SEA and~the~WATER~s2 to~ them(m) RAMPART from~RIGHT-HAND~ them(m) and~from~LEFT-HAND~them(m)□

and {the} sons {of} "Yisra'el ^{He turns El aside}" |had| walked (on) the dry ground in {the} midst {of} the sea, and the waters {were a} rampart (for) them, (at) their right hand and (at) their left hand,□

14:30 וַיּוֹשַׁע יְהוָה בַּיּוֹם הַהוּא אֶת יִשְׂרָאֵל מִיַּד מִצְרָיִם וַיַּרְא יִשְׂרָאֵל אֶת מִצְרַיִם מֵת עַל שְׂפַת הַיָּם

wai'yo'sha YHWH ba'yom ha'hu et yis'ra'eyl mi'yad mits'ra'yim wai'yar yis'ra'eyl et mits'ra'yim meyt al she'phat hai'yam

and~he~will~make~RESCUE "Yhwh ^{he~will~BE}" in~the~DAY the~HE AT "Yisra'el ^{he~will~TURN-ASIDE~+~MIGHTY-ONE}" from~HAND "Mits'rayim ^{STRAIT~s2}" and~he~will~SEE "Yisra'el ^{he~will~TURN-ASIDE~+~MIGHTY-ONE}" AT "Mits'rayim ^{STRAIT~s2}" DIE~ ing/er(ms) UPON LIP the~SEA□

and "Yhwh ^{He is}" rescued "Yisra'el ^{He turns El aside}" from {the} hand {of} "Mits'rayim ^{Two straits}" in (that) day, and "Yisra'el ^{He turns El aside}" saw "Mits'rayim ^{Two straits}" dying upon {the} lip* {of} the sea,□

14:31 וַיַּרְא יִשְׂרָאֵל אֶת הַיָּד הַגְּדֹלָה אֲשֶׁר עָשָׂה יְהוָה בְּמִצְרַיִם וַיִּירְאוּ הָעָם אֶת יְהוָה וַיַּאֲמִינוּ בַּיהוָה וּבְמֹשֶׁה עַבְדּוֹ

wai'yar yis'ra'eyl et hai'yad hag'do'lah a'sher a'sah YHWH be'mits'ra'yim wai'yir'u ha'am et YHWH wai'ya'a'mi'nu ba'YHWH uv'mo'sheh av'do

and~he~will~SEE "Yisra'el ^{he~will~TURN-ASIDE~+~MIGHTY-ONE}" AT the~HAND the~GREAT WHICH he~did~DO "Yhwh ^{he~will~BE}" in~"Mits'rayim ^{STRAIT~s2}" and~they(m)~will~FEAR the~PEOPLE AT "Yhwh ^{he~will~BE}" and~they(m)~will~make~ SECURE in~"Yhwh ^{he~will~BE}" and~in~"Mosheh ^{PLUCKED-OUT}" SERVANT~him□

and "Yisra'el ^{He turns El aside}" saw the great hand†, which "Yhwh ^{He is}" did in "Mits'rayim ^{Two straits}", and the people feared "Yhwh ^{He is}", and they [supported] "Yhwh ^{He is}" and "Mosheh ^{Plucked out}", his servant,□

---

* Or "edge."
† A "great hand" is a "powerful action."

Revised Mechanical Translation Codes

| (..) Alt Trans/App A | <..> Comp Phrase/App B | [..] Verb Form/App C | \..\ Plural Form/App D |
| :..: Int Inf Abs | |..| Past Perf Verb | {...} Added Word | |

Chapter 15

15:1 אָז יָשִׁיר מֹשֶׁה וּבְנֵי יִשְׂרָאֵל אֶת הַשִּׁירָה הַזֹּאת לַיהוָה וַיֹּאמְרוּ לֵאמֹר אָשִׁירָה לַיהוָה כִּי גָאֹה גָּאָה סוּס וְרֹכְבוֹ רָמָה בַיָּם

az ya'shir mo'sheh uv'ney yis'ra'eyl et ha'shi'rah ha'zot la'YHWH wai'yom'ru ley'mor a'shi'rah la'YHWH ki ga'oh ga'ah sus we'rokh'vo ra'mah vai'yam

AT-THAT-TIME *he~will~*<u>SING</u> "Mosheh ^{PLUCKED-OUT}*"* and~SON~s "Yisra'el *he~will~*<u>TURN-ASIDE</u>~+~<u>MIGHTY-ONE</u>*"* AT the~SONG the~THIS to~ "Yhwh ^{*he~will~*<u>BE</u>}*"* and~*they(m)~will~*<u>SAY</u> to~ >~<u>SAY</u> *I~will~*<u>SING</u>~^ to~"Yhwh ^{*he~will~*<u>BE</u>}*"* GIVEN-THAT >~<u>RISE-UP</u> *he~did~*<u>RISE-UP</u> HORSE and~<u>RIDE</u>~*ing/er(ms)*~him *he~did~* <u>THROW-DOWN</u> in~the~SEA□

at that time, Mosheh, ^{Plucked out}*"*, and {the} sons {of} "Yisra'el ^{He turns El aside}*"*, will sing this song to "Yhwh ^{He is}*"*, and they said say{ing}, I will sing to "Yhwh ^{He is}*"* given that he :surely: rose up, {the} horse and his rider, he threw down in the sea,□

15:2 עָזִּי וְזִמְרָת יָהּ וַיְהִי לִי לִישׁוּעָה זֶה אֵלִי וְאַנְוֵהוּ אֱלֹהֵי אָבִי וַאֲרֹמְמֶנְהוּ

a'zi we'zim'rat yah wai'hi li li'shu'ah zeh ey'li we'an'wey'hu e'lo'hey a'vi wa'a'rom'men'hu

BOLDNESS~me and~MUSIC "Yah ^{EXISTING}*"* and~*he~will~*<u>EXIST</u> to~me to~RELIEF THIS MIGHTY-ONE~me and~*I~will~make~*<u>ABIDE</u>~ him "Elohiym ^{POWER~s}*"* FATHER~me and~*I~ will~much~*<u>RAISE</u>~him□

my boldness and music {is} "Yah ^{Existing}*"*, and he will exist (to) me (for) {a} relief, this {is} my mighty one, and I will make him abide, "Elohiym ^{Powers}*"* {of} my father, and I will raise him,□

15:3 יְהוָה אִישׁ מִלְחָמָה יְהוָה שְׁמוֹ

YHWH ish mil'hha'mah YHWH she'mo

"Yhwh ^{*he~will~*<u>BE</u>}*"* MAN BATTLE "Yhwh ^{*he~will~*<u>BE</u>}*"* TITLE~him□

"Yhwh ^{He is}*"* {is a} man {of} battle, "Yhwh ^{He is}*"* {is} his title,□

15:4 מַרְכְּבֹת פַּרְעֹה וְחֵילוֹ יָרָה בַיָּם וּמִבְחַר שָׁלִשָׁיו טֻבְּעוּ בְיַם סוּף

mar'ke'vot par'oh we'hhey'lo ya'rah vai'yam u'miv'hhar sha'li'shaw tu'be'u ve'yam suph

CHARIOT~s "Paroh ^{GREAT-HOUSE}*"* and~FORCE~ him *he~did~*<u>THROW</u> in~the~SEA and~ CHOSEN LIEUTENANT~s~him *they~did~be~* *much~*<u>SINK</u> in~the~SEA REEDS□

he threw {the} chariots {of} "Paroh ^{Great house}*"* and his force{s} in the sea, and his chosen lieutenants |had| sunk in the sea {of} reeds*, □

15:5 תְּהֹמֹת יְכַסְיֻמוּ יָרְדוּ בִמְצוֹלֹת כְּמוֹ אָבֶן

te'ho'mot ye'khas'yu'mu yar'du vim'tso'lot ke'mo a'ven

DEEP-SEA~s *they(m)~will~much~*<u>COVER-</u>

{the} deep seas will cover them over, they will

---

* "Sea of reeds," or "Yam Suph," is usually mistranslated as "red sea."

Mechanical Translation Codes

<u>WORD</u> – Verb	WORD – Noun	Word – Name	word – Pre/Suff	*word* – Conj.

OVER~them(m) *they~will~*GO-DOWN in~
DEPTH~s like~THAT-ONE STONE□

go down in {the} depths like {a} stone,□

15:6

יְמִינְךָ יְהוָה נֶאְדָּרִי בַּכֹּחַ יְמִינְךָ יְהוָה תִּרְעַץ אוֹיֵב

ye'min'kha YHWH ne'da'ri ba'ko'ahh ye'min'kha YHWH tir'ats o'yeyv

RIGHT-HAND~you(ms) "Yhwh *he~will~*BE" *be~*
BE-EMINENT~*ing/er(ms)* in~the~STRENGTH
RIGHT-HAND~you(ms) "Yhwh *he~will~*BE" *she~*
*will~*DASH-TO-PIECES ATTACK~*ing/er(ms)*□

Yhwh [He is], your right hand {is} being
eminent, (with) the strength {of} your right
hand "Yhwh *He is*", she* will dash to pieces
{the} attacker,□

15:7

וּבְרֹב גְּאוֹנְךָ תַּהֲרֹס קָמֶיךָ תְּשַׁלַּח חֲרֹנְךָ יֹאכְלֵמוֹ כַּקַּשׁ

uv'rov ge'on'kha ta'ha'ros qa'mey'kha te'sha'lahh hha'ron'kha yokh'ley'mo ka'qash

and~in~ABUNDANCE MAJESTY~you(ms)
*you(ms)~will~*CAST-DOWN RISE~*ing/er(mp)~*
you(ms) *you(ms)~will~much~*SEND
BURNING-WRATH~you(ms) *he~will~*EAT~
them(m) like~the~STUBBLE□

and (with) {the} abundance {of} your majesty,
you will demolish {the} rising {one}, you will
send your burning wrath, he† will eat them
like the stubble,□

15:8

וּבְרוּחַ אַפֶּיךָ נֶעֶרְמוּ מַיִם נִצְּבוּ כְמוֹ נֵד נֹזְלִים קָפְאוּ תְהֹמֹת בְּלֶב יָם

uv'ru'ahh a'pey'kha ne'er'mu ma'yim nits'vu khe'mo neyd noz'lim qaph'u te'ho'mot
be'lev yam

and~in~WIND NOSE~s~you(ms) *they~did~*
*be~*PILE WATER~s2 *they~did~be~*STAND-UP
like~THAT-ONE HEAP FLOW~*ing/er(mp)*
*they~did~*CURDLE DEPTH~s in~HEART SEA□

and (with) {the} wind {of} your nose, {the}
waters were piled, they were stood up like {a}
flowing heap, the depths curdled in {the}
heart {of the} sea,□

15:9

אָמַר אוֹיֵב אֶרְדֹּף אַשִּׂיג אֲחַלֵּק שָׁלָל תִּמְלָאֵמוֹ נַפְשִׁי אָרִיק חַרְבִּי
תּוֹרִישֵׁמוֹ יָדִי

a'mar o'yeyv er'doph a'sig a'hha'leyq sha'lal tim'la'ey'mo naph'shi a'riq har'bi
to'ri'shey'mo ya'di

*he~did~*SAY ATTACK~*ing/er(ms)* *I~will~*
PURSUE *I~will~make~*OVERTAKE *I~will~*
*much~*APPORTION SPOIL *she~will~be~*FILL~
them(m) BEING~me *I~will~make~*DRAW-
OUT SWORD~me *she~will~make~*POSSESS~
them(m) HAND~me□

{the} attacker said, I will pursue, I will
overtake, I will apportion {the} spoil, my being
will be filled‡ {with} them, I will make my
sword drawn out, my hand will [dispossess]
them,□

15:10

נָשַׁפְתָּ בְרוּחֲךָ כִּסָּמוֹ יָם צָלֲלוּ כַּעוֹפֶרֶת בְּמַיִם אַדִּירִים

---

* Referring to the "hand," a feminine word in Hebrew.
† Referring to "wrath," a masculine word in Hebrew.
‡ "Be filled" probably means "outraged," in the sense of being filled with anger.

Revised Mechanical Translation Codes

(..) Alt Trans/App A	<..> Comp Phrase/App B	[..] Verb Form/App C	\../ Plural Form/App D
:..: Int Inf Abs	|..| Past Perf Verb	{...} Added Word	

na'shaph'ta ve'ru'hha'kha ki'sa'mo yam tsal'lu ka'o'phe'ret be'ma'yim adi'rim

you(ms)~did~<u>BLOW</u> in~WIND~*you(ms) he~did~much~*<u>COVER-OVER</u>~*them(m)* SEA *they~did~*<u>BE-OVERSHADOWED</u> *like~*LEAD in~WATER~s2 EMINENT~s□

you blew (with) your wind, {the} sea covered them over, they were overshadowed* like lead in {the} eminent waters,□

15:11   מִי כָמֹכָה בָּאֵלִם יְהוָה מִי כָּמֹכָה נֶאְדָּר בַּקֹּדֶשׁ נוֹרָא תְהִלֹּת עֹשֵׂה פֶלֶא

mi kha'mo'khah ba'ey'lim YHWH mi ka'mo'khah ne'dar ba'qo'desh no'ra te'hi'lot o'seyh phe'le

WHO *like~*THAT-ONE~*you(ms)* in~the~MIGHTY-ONE~s "Yhwh *he~will~*<u>BE</u>" WHO *like~*THAT-ONE~*you(ms) be~*<u>BE-EMINENT</u>~*ing/er(ms)* in~the~SPECIAL *be~*<u>FEAR</u>~*ing/er(ms)* ADORATION~s <u>DO</u>~*ing/er(ms)* PERFORMANCE□

who {is} like you (among) the mighty ones? "Yhwh *He is*", who {is} like you, being eminent in special{ness}, being fear{ed of} adorations, doing performance{s}?□

15:12   נָטִיתָ יְמִינְךָ תִּבְלָעֵמוֹ אָרֶץ

na'ti'ta ye'min'kha tiv'la'ey'mo a'rets

you(ms)~did~<u>EXTEND</u> RIGHT-HAND~*you(ms) she~will~*<u>SWALLOW</u>~*them(m)* LAND□

you extended your right hand and {the} land swallowed them,□

15:13   נָחִיתָ בְחַסְדְּךָ עַם זוּ גָּאָלְתָּ נֵהַלְתָּ בְעָזְּךָ אֶל נְוֵה קָדְשֶׁךָ

na'hhi'ta ve'hhas'de'kha am zu ga'al'ta ney'hal'ta ve'az'kha el ne'weyh qad'she'kha

you(ms)~did~<u>GUIDE</u> in~KINDNESS~*you(ms)* PEOPLE WHEREIN *you(ms)~did~*<u>REDEEM</u> *you(ms)~did~much~*<u>LEAD</u> in~BOLDNESS~*you(ms)* TO ABODE SPECIAL~*you(ms)*□

you guided {the} people (with) your kindness, wherein you redeemed, you lead (with) your boldness to {the} abode {of} your special {place},□

15:14   שָׁמְעוּ עַמִּים יִרְגָּזוּן חִיל אָחַז יֹשְׁבֵי פְּלָשֶׁת

sham'u a'mim yir'ga'zun hhil a'hhaz yosh'vey pe'la'shet

they~did~<u>HEAR</u> PEOPLE~s *they(m)~will~*<u>SHAKE</u>~*must* AGONY *he~did~*<u>TAKE-HOLD</u> <u>SETTLE</u>~*ing/er(mp)* "Peleshet ^{IMMIGRANT}"□

the people heard, they [trembled], agony |had| taken hold {of the} settlers {of} "Peleshet ^{Immigrant}",□

15:15   אָז נִבְהֲלוּ אַלּוּפֵי אֱדוֹם אֵילֵי מוֹאָב יֹאחֲזֵמוֹ רָעַד נָמֹגוּ כֹּל יֹשְׁבֵי כְנָעַן

az niv'ha'lu a'lu'phey e'dom ey'ley mo'av yo'hha'zey'mo ra'ad na'mo'gu kol yosh'vey khe'na'an

---

* Meaning "they dropped to the dark depths."

Mechanical Translation Codes

<u>WORD</u> – Verb	WORD – Noun	Word – Name	word – Pre/Suff	*word* – Conj.

AT-THAT-TIME they~did~be~STIR CHIEF~s "Edom RED" BUCK~s "Mo'av THAT-ONE~+~FATHER" he~will~TAKE-HOLD~them(m) SHAKING-IN-FEAR they~did~be~DISSOLVE ALL SETTLE~ing/er(mp) "Kena'an LOWERED"□

at that time, {the} chiefs {of} "Edom Red" were stirred, {the} bucks* {of} "Mo'av That one is father", {a} shaking in fear will take hold {of} them, all {the} settlers {of} "Kena'an Lowered" were dissolved,□

15:16

תִּפֹּל עֲלֵיהֶם אֵימָתָה וָפַחַד בִּגְדֹל זְרוֹעֲךָ יִדְּמוּ כָּאָבֶן עַד יַעֲבֹר עַמְּךָ יְהוָה עַד יַעֲבֹר עַם זוּ קָנִיתָ

ti'pol a'ley'hem ey'ma'tah wa'pha'hhad big'dol ze'ro'a'kha yid'mu ka'a'ven ad ya'a'vor am'kha YHWH ad ya'a'vor am zu qa'ni'ta

she~will~FALL UPON~them(m) TERROR and~AWE in~GREAT ARM~you(ms) they(m)~will~BE-SILENT like~STONE UNTIL he~will~CROSS-OVER PEOPLE~you(ms) "Yhwh he~will~BE" UNTIL he~will~CROSS-OVER PEOPLE WHEREIN you(ms)~did~PURCHASE□

terror will fall upon them, and awe, (with) your great arm they will be silent like {a} stone, until your people "Yhwh He is", will cross over, until {the} people wherein you purchased, cross over,□

15:17

תְּבִאֵמוֹ וְתִטָּעֵמוֹ בְּהַר נַחֲלָתְךָ מָכוֹן לְשִׁבְתְּךָ פָּעַלְתָּ יְהוָה מִקְּדָשׁ אֲדֹנָי כּוֹנְנוּ יָדֶיךָ

te'vi'ey'mo we'ti'ta'ey'mo be'har na'hha'lat'kha ma'khon le'shiv'te'kha pa'al'ta YHWH miq'dash a'do'nai kon'nu ya'dey'kha

you(ms)~will~make~COME~them(m) and~you(ms)~will~PLANT~them(m) in~HILL INHERITANCE~you(ms) PEDESTAL to~>~SETTLE~you(ms) you(ms)~did~MAKE "Yhwh he~will~BE" SANCTUARY "Adonai LORD~s~me" they~did~much~PREPARE HAND~s2~you(ms)□

you will bring them, and you will plant them in {the} hill {of} your inheritance, {a} pedestal (for) your settling, "Yhwh He is", you made {a} sanctuary, "Adonai My lords", your hands prepared {it},□

15:18

יְהוָה יִמְלֹךְ לְעֹלָם וָעֶד

YHWH yim'lokh le'o'lam wa'ed

"Yhwh he~will~BE" he~will~REIGN to~DISTANT and~UNTIL□

"Yhwh He is" will reign to {a} distant {time} and (beyond),□

15:19

כִּי בָא סוּס פַּרְעֹה בְּרִכְבּוֹ וּבְפָרָשָׁיו בַּיָּם וַיָּשֶׁב יְהוָה עֲלֵהֶם אֶת מֵי הַיָּם וּבְנֵי יִשְׂרָאֵל הָלְכוּ בַיַּבָּשָׁה בְּתוֹךְ הַיָּם

ki va sus par'oh be'rikh'bo uv'pha'ra'shaw ba'yam wai'ya'shev YHWH a'ley'hem et mey hai'yam uv'ney yis'ra'eyl hal'khu vai'ya'ba'shah be'tokh hai'yam

GIVEN-THAT he~did~COME HORSE "Paroh GREAT-HOUSE" in~VEHICLE~him and~in~HORSEMAN~s~him in~the~SEA and~he~

given that {the} horse {of} "Paroh Great house", (with) his vehicle and (with) his horsemen, came in the sea, and "Yhwh He is" made {the}

---

* Meaning "mighty men."

Revised Mechanical Translation Codes

| (..) Alt Trans/App A | <..> Comp Phrase/App B | [..] Verb Form/App C | \../ Plural Form/App D |
| :...: Int Inf Abs | |..| Past Perf Verb | {...} Added Word | |

will~make~TURN-BACK "Yhwh ^{he~will~BE}„ UPON~them(m) AT WATER~s2 the~SEA and~ SON~s "Yisra'el ^{he~will~TURN-ASIDE~+~MIGHTY-ONE}„ they~did~WALK in~the~DRY-GROUND in~ MIDST the~SEA□

waters {of} the sea turn back upon them, and {the} sons {of} "Yisra'el ^{He turns El aside}„ |had| walked (on) the dry ground in {the} midst {of} the sea,□

15:20 וַתִּקַּח מִרְיָם הַנְּבִיאָה אֲחוֹת אַהֲרֹן אֶת הַתֹּף בְּיָדָהּ וַתֵּצֶאןָ כָל הַנָּשִׁים אַחֲרֶיהָ בְּתֻפִּים וּבִמְחֹלֹת

wa'ti'qahh mir'yam han'vi'ah a'hhot a'ha'ron et ha'toph be'ya'dah wa'tey'tse'na khol ha'na'shim a'hha'rey'ah be'tu'pim u'vim'hho'lot

and~ she~will~TAKE "Mir'yam ^{BITTER~+~SEA}„ the~PROPHETESS SISTER "Aharon ^{LIGHT-BRINGER}„ AT the~TAMBOURINE in~HAND~her and~they(f)~will~GO-OUT ALL the~ WOMAN~s AFTER~her in~TAMBOURINE~s and~in~DANCE~s□

and "Mir'yam ^{Bitter sea}„, the prophetess, sister {of} "Aharon ^{Light bringer}„, took the tambourine in her hand, and all the women went out after her, (with) tambourines and (with) dances,□

15:21 וַתַּעַן לָהֶם מִרְיָם שִׁירוּ לַיהוָה כִּי גָאֹה גָּאָה סוּס וְרֹכְבוֹ רָמָה בַיָּם

wa'ta'an la'hem mir'yam shi'ru la'YHWH ki ga'oh ga'ah sus we'rokh'vo ra'mah vai'yam

and~ she~will~ANSWER to~them(m) "Mir'yam ^{BITTER~+~SEA}„ !(mp)~SING to~"Yhwh ^{he~will~BE}„ GIVEN-THAT >~RISE-UP he~did~ RISE-UP HORSE and~RIDE~ing/er(ms)~him he~did~THROW-DOWN in~the~SEA□

and "Mir'yam ^{Bitter sea}„ answered them, sing to "Yhwh ^{He is}„, given that he :surely: rose up, {the} horse and his rider, he threw down in the sea,□

15:22 וַיַּסַּע מֹשֶׁה אֶת יִשְׂרָאֵל מִיַּם סוּף וַיֵּצְאוּ אֶל מִדְבַּר שׁוּר וַיֵּלְכוּ שְׁלֹשֶׁת יָמִים בַּמִּדְבָּר וְלֹא מָצְאוּ מָיִם

wai'ya'sa mo'sheh et yis'ra'eyl mi'yam suph wai'yeyts'u el mid'bar shur wai'yeyl'khu she'lo'shet ya'mim ba'mid'bar we'lo mats'u ma'yim

and~he~will~JOURNEY "Mosheh ^{PLUCKED-OUT}„ AT "Yisra'el ^{he~will~TURN-ASIDE~+~MIGHTY-ONE}„ from~ SEA REEDS and~they(m)~will~GO-OUT TO WILDERNESS "Shur ^{ROCK-WALL}„ and~they(m)~ will~WALK THREE DAY~s in~the~ WILDERNESS and~NOT they~did~FIND WATER~s2□

and "Mosheh ^{Plucked out}„ journeyed "Yisra'el ^{He turns El aside}„ from {the} sea {of} reeds*, and they went out to {the} wilderness {of} "Shur ^{Rock wall}„, and they walked three days in the wilderness, and they did not find water,□

15:23 וַיָּבֹאוּ מָרָתָה וְלֹא יָכְלוּ לִשְׁתֹּת מַיִם מִמָּרָה כִּי מָרִים הֵם עַל כֵּן קָרָא שְׁמָהּ מָרָה

wai'ya'vo'u ma'ra'tah we'lo yakh'lu lish'tot ma'yim mi'ma'rah ki ma'rim heym al keyn qa'ra she'mah ma'rah

and~they(m)~will~COME "Marah ^{BITTER}„~

and they came unto "Marah ^{Bitter}„, and they

---

* "Sea of reeds," or "Yam Suph," is usually mistranslated as "red sea."

Mechanical Translation Codes

<u>WORD</u> – Verb	WORD – Noun	Word – Name	word – Pre/Suff	*word* – Conj.

unto and~NOT they~did~BE-ABLE to~
>~GULP WATER~s2 from~"Marah ^{BITTER}"
GIVEN-THAT BITTER~s THEY(m) UPON SO
he~did~CALL-OUT TITLE~her "Marah ^{BITTER}"□

were not able to gulp water from "Marah
^{Bitter}", given that they {were} bitter,
<therefore>, he called out her title "Marah
^{Bitter}",□

15:24   וַיִּלֹּנוּ הָעָם עַל מֹשֶׁה לֵּאמֹר מַה נִּשְׁתֶּה

wai'yi'lo'nu ha'am al mo'sheh ley'mor mah nish'teh

and~they(m)~will~be~MURMUR the~
PEOPLE UPON "Mosheh ^{PLUCKED-OUT}" to~>~SAY
WHAT we~will~GULP□

and the people were murmur{ing} upon
"Mosheh ^{Plucked out}" say{ing}, what will we
gulp?□

15:25   וַיִּצְעַק אֶל יְהוָה וַיּוֹרֵהוּ יְהוָה עֵץ וַיַּשְׁלֵךְ אֶל הַמַּיִם וַיִּמְתְּקוּ הַמָּיִם שָׁם
שָׁם לוֹ חֹק וּמִשְׁפָּט וְשָׁם נִסָּהוּ

wai'yits'aq el YHWH wai'yo'rey'hu YHWH eyts wai'yash'leykh el ha'ma'yim wai'yim'te'qu
ha'ma'yim sham sham lo hhoq u'mish'pat we'sham ni'sa'hu

and~he~will~CRY-OUT TO "Yhwh ^{he~will~BE}"
and~he~will~make~THROW~him "Yhwh <sup>he~
will~BE</sup>" TREE and~he~will~make~THROW-
OUT TO the~WATER~s2 and~they(m)~will~
TASTE-SWEET the~WATER~s2 THERE he~
did~PLACE to~him CUSTOM and~DECISION
and~THERE he~did~much~TEST~him□

and he cried out to "Yhwh ^{He is}", and "Yhwh <sup>He
is</sup>" [pointed] {to} him {a} tree, and he threw {it}
out to the waters and the waters tasted
sweet, there he placed* (for) him {a} custom
and {a} decision, and there he tested him,□

15:26   וַיֹּאמֶר אִם שָׁמוֹעַ תִּשְׁמַע לְקוֹל יְהוָה אֱלֹהֶיךָ וְהַיָּשָׁר בְּעֵינָיו תַּעֲשֶׂה
וְהַאֲזַנְתָּ לְמִצְוֺתָיו וְשָׁמַרְתָּ כָּל חֻקָּיו כָּל הַמַּחֲלָה אֲשֶׁר שַׂמְתִּי
בְמִצְרַיִם לֹא אָשִׂים עָלֶיךָ כִּי אֲנִי יְהוָה רֹפְאֶךָ

wai'yo'mer im sha'mo'a tish'ma le'qol YHWH e'lo'hey'kha we'ha'ya'shar be'ey'naw
ta'a'seh we'ha'a'zan'ta le'mits'o'taw we'sha'mar'ta kol hhu'qaw kol ha'ma'hha'lah a'sher
sam'ti ve'mits'ra'yim lo a'sim a'ley'kha ki a'ni YHWH roph'e'kha

and~he~will~SAY IF >~HEAR you(ms)~will~
HEAR to~VOICE "Yhwh ^{he~will~BE}" "Elohiym
^{POWER~s}"~you(ms) and~the~STRAIGHT in~
EYE~s2~him you(ms)~will~DO and~you(ms)~
did~make~GIVE-AN-EAR to~DIRECTIVE~s~
him and~you(ms)~did~SAFEGUARD ALL
CUSTOM~s~him ALL the~SICKNESS WHICH I~
did~PLACE in~"Mits'rayim ^{STRAIT~s2}" NOT I~
will~PLACE UPON~you(ms) GIVEN-THAT I
"Yhwh ^{he~will~BE}" HEAL~ing/er(ms)~you(ms)□

and he said, if you :surely: hear {the} voice {of}
"Yhwh ^{He is}" your "Elohiym ^{Powers}", and you will
do {what is} straight in his eyes, and you will
give an ear to his directives, and you will
safeguard all his customs, all the sickness
which I placed in "Mits'rayim ^{Two straits}", I will
not place upon you, given that I {am} "Yhwh <sup>He
is</sup>", your healer,□

15:27   וַיָּבֹאוּ אֵילִמָה וְשָׁם שְׁתֵּים עֶשְׂרֵה עֵינֹת מַיִם וְשִׁבְעִים תְּמָרִים וַיַּחֲנוּ

---

* Meaning "established" or "appointed."

Revised Mechanical Translation Codes
(..) Alt Trans/App A   <..> Comp Phrase/App B   [..] Verb Form/App C   \../ Plural Form/App D
:..: Int Inf Abs |..| Past Perf Verb   {...} Added Word

שֵׁם עַל הַמָּיִם

wai'ya'vo'u ey'li'mah we'sham she'teym es'reyh ey'not ma'yim we'shiv'im te'ma'rim wai'ya'hha'nu sham al ha'ma'yim

and~*they(m)~will~*<u>COME</u> "Eyliym ^{BUCK~s}"~ unto and~THERE TWO TEN EYE~s WATER~s2 and~SEVEN~s DATE-PALM~s and~*they(m)~will~*<u>CAMP</u> THERE UPON the~WATER~s2☐	and they came unto "Eyliym ^{Bucks}", and there {were} <twelve> eyes* {of} water, and \seventy/ date palms, and they camped there upon the waters,☐

Chapter 16

16:1

וַיִּסְעוּ מֵאֵילִם וַיָּבֹאוּ כָּל עֲדַת בְּנֵי יִשְׂרָאֵל אֶל מִדְבַּר סִין אֲשֶׁר בֵּין אֵילִם וּבֵין סִינַי בַּחֲמִשָּׁה עָשָׂר יוֹם לַחֹדֶשׁ הַשֵּׁנִי לְצֵאתָם מֵאֶרֶץ מִצְרָיִם

wai'yis'u mey'ey'lim wai'ya'vo'u kol a'dat be'ney yis'ra'eyl el mid'bar sin a'sher beyn ey'lim u'veyn si'nai ba'hha'mi'shah a'sar yom la'hho'desh ha'shey'ni le'tsey'tam mey'e'rets mits'ra'yim

and~*they(m)~will~*<u>JOURNEY</u> from~ "Eyliym ^{BUCK~s}" and~*they(m)~will~*<u>COME</u> ALL COMPANY SON~s "Yisra'el ^{he~will~<u>TURN-ASIDE</u>~+~ MIGHTY-ONE}" TO WILDERNESS "Sin ^{SHARP-THORN}" WHICH BETWEEN "Eyliym ^{BUCK~s}" and~ BETWEEN "Sinai ^{SHARP-THORN~s~me}" in~the~FIVE TEN DAY to~the~NEW-MOON the~SECOND to~>~<u>GO-OUT</u>~them(m) from~LAND "Mits'rayim ^{STRAIT~s2}"☐	and all {the} company {of the} sons {of} "Yisra'el ^{He turns El aside}" journeyed from "Eyliym ^{Bucks}" and they came to {the} wilderness {of} "Sin ^{Sharp thorn}", which {is} between "Eyliym ^{Bucks}" and "Sinai ^{My sharp thorns}", (on) the <fifteen>{th} day to the second new moon {of} their go{ing} out from {the} land {of} "Mits'rayim ^{Two straits}",☐

16:2

וַיִּלּוֹנוּ כָּל עֲדַת בְּנֵי יִשְׂרָאֵל עַל מֹשֶׁה וְעַל אַהֲרֹן בַּמִּדְבָּר

wai'yi'li'nu kol a'dat be'ney yis'ra'eyl al mo'sheh we'al a'ha'ron ba'mid'bar

and~*they(m)~will~*be~<u>MURMUR</u> ALL COMPANY SON~s "Yisra'el ^{he~will~<u>TURN-ASIDE</u>~+~ MIGHTY-ONE}" UPON "Mosheh ^{PLUCKED-OUT}" and~ UPON "Aharon ^{LIGHT-BRINGER}" in~the~ WILDERNESS☐	and all {the} company {of the} sons {of} "Yisra'el ^{He turns El aside}" were murmur{ing}† upon "Mosheh ^{Plucked out}" and upon "Aharon ^{Light bringer}" in the wilderness,☐

16:3

וַיֹּאמְרוּ אֲלֵהֶם בְּנֵי יִשְׂרָאֵל מִי יִתֵּן מוּתֵנוּ בְיַד יְהוָה בְּאֶרֶץ מִצְרַיִם בְּשִׁבְתֵּנוּ עַל סִיר הַבָּשָׂר בְּאָכְלֵנוּ לֶחֶם לָשֹׂבַע כִּי הוֹצֵאתֶם אֹתָנוּ אֶל הַמִּדְבָּר הַזֶּה לְהָמִית אֶת כָּל הַקָּהָל הַזֶּה בָּרָעָב

wai'yom'ru a'ley'hem be'ney yis'ra'eyl mi yi'teyn mu'tey'nu ve'yad YHWH be'e'rets

---

* That is, a spring.

† The Hebrew word וַיִּלִּינוּ, meaning "and they stayed the night," is written defectively and should be written as וַיִּלּוֹנוּ, meaning "and they were murmuring."

Mechanical Translation Codes

<u>WORD</u> – Verb	WORD – Noun	Word – Name	word – Pre/Suff	*word* – Conj.

mits'ra'yim be'shiv'tey'nu al sir ha'ba'sar be'akh'ley'nu le'hhem la'sho'va ki ho'tsey'tem o'ta'nu el ha'mid'bar ha'zeh le'ha'mit et kol ha'qa'hal ha'zeh ba'ra'av

and~*they(m)~will~*<u>SAY</u> TO~them(m) SON~s "Yisra'el *he~will~*<u>TURN-ASIDE</u>~+~<u>MIGHTY-ONE</u>" WHO *he~ will~*<u>GIVE</u> >~<u>DIE</u>~us in~HAND "Yhwh *he~will~*<u>BE</u>" in~LAND "Mits'rayim *STRAIT~s2*" in~<u>SETTLE</u>~us UPON POT the~FLESH in~>~<u>EAT</u>~us BREAD to~<u>SATISFACTION</u> GIVEN-THAT *you(mp)~ did~make~*<u>GO-OUT</u> AT~us TO the~ WILDERNESS the~THIS to~>~*make~*<u>DIE</u> AT ALL the~ASSEMBLY the~THIS in~the~ HUNGER□	and {the} sons {of} "Yisra'el *He turns El aside*" said, who will (allow) us {to} die (by) {the} hand {of} "Yhwh *He is*" in {the} land {of} "Mits'rayim *Two straits*"? (with) our settling upon {the} pot {of} flesh (with) us eating bread to satisfaction, given that you made us go out to this wilderness to [kill] this assembly (with) hunger,□

16:4 וַיֹּאמֶר יְהוָה אֶל מֹשֶׁה הִנְנִי מַמְטִיר לָכֶם לֶחֶם מִן הַשָּׁמַיִם וְיָצָא הָעָם וְלָקְטוּ דְּבַר יוֹם בְּיוֹמוֹ לְמַעַן אֲנַסֶּנּוּ הֲיֵלֵךְ בְּתוֹרָתִי אִם לֹא

wai'yo'mer YHWH el mo'sheh hin'ni mam'tir la'khem le'hhem min ha'sha'ma'yim we'ya'tsa ha'am we'laq'tu de'var yom be'yo'mo le'ma'an a'na'se'nu ha'yey'leykh be'to'ra'ti im lo

and~*he~will~*<u>SAY</u> "Yhwh *he~will~*<u>BE</u>" TO "Mosheh *PLUCKED-OUT*" <u>LOOK</u>~me *make~* <u>PRECIPITATE</u>~*ing/er(ms)* to~you(mp) BREAD FROM the~SKY~s2 and~*he~will~*<u>GO-OUT</u> the~PEOPLE and~*they~did~*<u>PICK-UP</u> WORD DAY in~DAY~him to~THAT *I~will~*<u>TEST</u>~him ?~*he~will~*<u>WALK</u> in~TEACHING~me IF NOT□	and "Yhwh *He is*" said to "Mosheh *Plucked out*", look {at} me making {it} precipitate bread (for) you from the skies, and the people will go out and they will pick {it} up, {it is a} (matter) {of the} day in his day*, (so) that I will test him, will he walk in my teaching (or) not?□

16:5 וְהָיָה בַּיּוֹם הַשִּׁשִּׁי וְהֵכִינוּ אֵת אֲשֶׁר יָבִיאוּ וְהָיָה מִשְׁנֶה עַל אֲשֶׁר יִלְקְטוּ יוֹם יוֹם

we'hai'yah ba'yom ha'shi'shi we'hey'khi'nu eyt a'sher ya'vi'u we'hai'yah mish'neh al a'sher yil'qe'tu yom yom

and~*he~did~*<u>EXIST</u> in~the~DAY the~SIXTH and~*they~did~make~*<u>PREPARE</u> AT WHICH *they(m)~will~make~*<u>COME</u> and~*he~did~* <u>EXIST</u> DOUBLE UPON WHICH *they(m)~will~* <u>PICK-UP</u> DAY DAY□	and (it) will (come to pass), in the sixth day, and they will prepare (what) they will [bring], and double will exist (in addition) {to} (what) they will pick up <daily>,□

16:6 וַיֹּאמֶר מֹשֶׁה וְאַהֲרֹן אֶל כָּל בְּנֵי יִשְׂרָאֵל עֶרֶב וִידַעְתֶּם כִּי יְהוָה הוֹצִיא אֶתְכֶם מֵאֶרֶץ מִצְרָיִם

wai'yo'mer mo'sheh we'a'ha'ron el kol be'ney yis'ra'eyl e'rev wi'da'tem ki YHWH ho'tsi et'khem mey'e'rets mits'ra'yim

and~*he~will~*<u>SAY</u> "Mosheh *PLUCKED-OUT*" and~ "Aharon *LIGHT-BRINGER*" TO ALL SON~s "Yisra'el	and "Mosheh *Plucked out*", and "Aharon *Light bringer*" said to all {the} sons {of} "Yisra'el *He turns El aside*",

---

* "It is a matter of the day in his day" is an idiom meaning a "daily matter."

Revised Mechanical Translation Codes

(..) Alt Trans/App A   <..> Comp Phrase/App B   [..] Verb Form/App C   \../ Plural Form/App D

:..: Int Inf Abs |..| Past Perf Verb   {...} Added Word

he~will~<u>TURN-ASIDE</u>~+~MIGHTY-ONE" EVENING and~
you(mp)~did~<u>KNOW</u> GIVEN-THAT "Yhwh ^{he~}
^{will~<u>BE</u>}" he~did~make~<u>GO-OUT</u> AT~you(mp)
from~LAND "Mits'rayim ^{STRAIT~s2}"□

evening*, and you will know that "Yhwh ^{He is}"
|had| made you go out from {the} land {of}
"Mits'rayim ^{Two straits}",□

16:7 וּבֹקֶר וּרְאִיתֶם אֶת כְּבוֹד יְהוָה בְּשָׁמְעוֹ אֶת תְּלֻנֹּתֵיכֶם עַל יְהוָה וְנַחְנוּ
מָה כִּי תַלּוֹנוּ עָלֵינוּ

u'vo'qer ur'i'tem et ke'vod YHWH be'sham'o et te'lu'no'tey'khem al YHWH we'nahh'nu
mah ki ta'lo'nu a'ley'nu

and~MORNING and~you(mp)~did~<u>SEE</u> AT
ARMAMENT "Yhwh ^{he~will~<u>BE</u>}" in~>~<u>HEAR</u>~him
AT MURMURING~s~you(mp) UPON "Yhwh
^{he~will~<u>BE</u>}" and~WE WHAT GIVEN-THAT
you(mp)~will~be~<u>MURMUR</u> UPON~us□

and morning†, and you will see {the}
armament {of} "Yhwh ^{He is}", in his hearing {of}
your murmurings upon "Yhwh ^{He is}", and what
{are} we that you will murmur‡ upon us?□

16:8 וַיֹּאמֶר מֹשֶׁה בְּתֵת יְהוָה לָכֶם בָּעֶרֶב בָּשָׂר לֶאֱכֹל וְלֶחֶם בַּבֹּקֶר לִשְׂבֹּעַ
בִּשְׁמֹעַ יְהוָה אֶת תְּלֻנֹּתֵיכֶם אֲשֶׁר אַתֶּם מַלִּינִם עָלָיו וְנַחְנוּ מָה לֹא
עָלֵינוּ תְלֻנֹּתֵיכֶם כִּי עַל יְהוָה

wai'yo'mer mo'sheh be'teyt YHWH la'khem ba'e'rev ba'sar le'e'khol we'le'hhem
ba'bo'qer lish'bo'a bish'mo'a YHWH et te'lu'no'tey'khem a'sher a'tem ma'li'nim a'law
we'nahh'nu mah lo a'ley'nu te'lu'no'tey'khem ki al YHWH

and~he~will~<u>SAY</u> "Mosheh ^{PLUCKED-OUT}" in~
>~<u>GIVE</u> "Yhwh ^{he~will~<u>BE</u>}" to~you(mp) in~the~
EVENING FLESH to~>~<u>EAT</u> and~BREAD in~
the~MORNING to~>~<u>BE-SATISFIED</u> in~
>~<u>HEAR</u> "Yhwh ^{he~will~<u>BE</u>}" AT MURMURING~s~
you(mp) WHICH YOU(mp) make~MURMUR~
ing/er(mp) UPON~him and~WE WHAT NOT
UPON~us MURMURING~s~you(mp) GIVEN-
THAT UPON "Yhwh ^{he~will~<u>BE</u>}"□

and "Mosheh ^{Plucked out}" said, (with) "Yhwh ^{He is}"
giving you flesh to eat in the evening, and
bread in the morning to be satisfied, (with)
"Yhwh ^{He is}" hearing your murmurings which
you {are} murmuring upon him, and what
{are} we? your murmurings {are} not upon us,
given that {they are} upon "Yhwh ^{He is}",□

16:9 וַיֹּאמֶר מֹשֶׁה אֶל אַהֲרֹן אֱמֹר אֶל כָּל עֲדַת בְּנֵי יִשְׂרָאֵל קִרְבוּ לִפְנֵי יְהוָה
כִּי שָׁמַע אֵת תְּלֻנֹּתֵיכֶם

wai'yo'mer mo'sheh el a'ha'ron e'mor el kol a'dat be'ney yis'ra'eyl qir'vu liph'ney YHWH
ki sha'ma eyt te'lu'no'tey'khem

and~he~will~<u>SAY</u> "Mosheh ^{PLUCKED-OUT}" TO
"Aharon ^{LIGHT-BRINGER}" !(ms)~<u>SAY</u> TO ALL

and "Mosheh ^{Plucked out}" said to "Aharon ^{Light}
^{bringer}", say to all {the} company {of the} sons

---

* The passage does not make sense contextually and appears to be written defectively. A
possible solution is that the passage originally read, "and in the evening you will eat flesh"
(compare with verse 8 and 12).

† The passage does not make sense contextually and appears to be written defectively. A
possible solution is that the passage originally read, "and in the morning you will eat bread"
(compare with verse 8 and 12).

‡ The Hebrew word תַלּוֹנוּ is written defectively and should be written as תָלִינוּ.

Mechanical Translation Codes

<u>WORD</u> – Verb	WORD – Noun	Word – Name	word – Pre/Suff	*word* – Conj.

COMPANY SON~s "Yisra'el ^{he~will~TURN-ASIDE~+~MIGHTY-ONE}" !(mp)~COME-NEAR to~FACE~s "Yhwh ^{he~will~BE}" GIVEN-THAT he~did~HEAR AT MURMURING~s~you(mp)□

{of} "Yisra'el ^{He turns El aside}", come near <in front of> "Yhwh ^{He is}" given that he heard your murmurings,□

16:10

וַיְהִי כְּדַבֵּר אַהֲרֹן אֶל כָּל עֲדַת בְּנֵי יִשְׂרָאֵל וַיִּפְנוּ אֶל הַמִּדְבָּר וְהִנֵּה כְּבוֹד יְהוָה נִרְאָה בֶּעָנָן

wai'hi ke'da'beyr a'ha'ron el kol a'dat be'ney yis'ra'eyl wai'yiph'nu el ha'mid'bar we'hin'neyh ke'vod YHWH nir'ah be'a'nan

and~he~will~EXIST like~>~much~SPEAK "Aharon ^{LIGHT-BRINGER}" TO ALL COMPANY SON~s "Yisra'el ^{he~will~TURN-ASIDE~+~MIGHTY-ONE}" and~they(m)~will~TURN TO the~WILDERNESS and~LOOK ARMAMENT "Yhwh ^{he~will~BE}" he~did~be~SEE in~CLOUD□

and (it) (came to pass) (as) "Aharon ^{Light bringer}" spoke to all {the} company {of the} sons {of} "Yisra'el ^{He turns El aside}", and they turned to the wilderness, and look, {the} armament {of} "Yhwh ^{He is}" [appeared] in {the} cloud,□

16:11

וַיְדַבֵּר יְהוָה אֶל מֹשֶׁה לֵּאמֹר

wai'da'beyr YHWH el mo'sheh ley'mor

and~he~will~much~SPEAK "Yhwh ^{he~will~BE}" TO "Mosheh ^{PLUCKED-OUT}" to~>~SAY□

and "Yhwh ^{He is}" spoke to "Mosheh ^{Plucked out}" say{ing},□

16:12

שָׁמַעְתִּי אֶת תְּלוּנֹת בְּנֵי יִשְׂרָאֵל דַּבֵּר אֲלֵהֶם לֵאמֹר בֵּין הָעַרְבַּיִם תֹּאכְלוּ בָשָׂר וּבַבֹּקֶר תִּשְׂבְּעוּ לָחֶם וִידַעְתֶּם כִּי אֲנִי יְהוָה אֱלֹהֵיכֶם

sha'ma'ti et te'lu'not be'ney yis'ra'eyl da'beyr a'ley'hem ley'mor beyn ha'ar'ba'yim tokh'lu va'sar u'va'bo'qer tis'be'u la'hhem wi'da'tem ki a'ni YHWH e'lo'hey'khem

I~did~HEAR AT MURMURING~s SON~s "Yisra'el ^{he~will~TURN-ASIDE~+~MIGHTY-ONE}" !(ms)~much~SPEAK TO~them(m) to~>~SAY BETWEEN the~EVENING~s you(mp)~will~EAT FLESH and~in~the~MORNING you(mp)~will~BE-SATISFIED BREAD and~you(mp)~did~KNOW GIVEN-THAT I "Yhwh ^{he~will~BE}" "Elohiym ^{POWER~s}"~you(mp)□

I heard {the} murmurings {of the} sons {of} "Yisra'el ^{He turns El aside}", speak to them say{ing}, between the evenings* you will eat flesh and in the morning you will be satisfied {with} bread, and you will know that I {am} "Yhwh ^{He is}" your "Elohiym ^{Powers}",□

16:13

וַיְהִי בָעֶרֶב וַתַּעַל הַשְּׂלָו וַתְּכַס אֶת הַמַּחֲנֶה וּבַבֹּקֶר הָיְתָה שִׁכְבַת הַטָּל סָבִיב לַמַּחֲנֶה

wai'hi va'e'rev wa'ta'al has'law wat'khas et ha'ma'hha'neh u'va'bo'qer hai'tah shikh'vat ha'tal sa'viv la'ma'hha'neh

and~he~will~EXIST in~the~EVENING and~she~will~GO-UP the~QUAIL and~ she~will~

and (it) (came to pass) in the evening, and the quail went up and she covered over the

---

* The phrase "between the evenings" is of uncertain meaning, but may be the time between sunset and dark.

Revised Mechanical Translation Codes

(..) Alt Trans/App A   <..> Comp Phrase/App B   [..] Verb Form/App C   \../ Plural Form/App D
:..: Int Inf Abs |..| Past Perf Verb   {...} Added Word

much~COVER-OVER AT the~CAMPSITE and~ in~the~MORNING she~did~EXIST LYING-DOWN the~DEW ALL-AROUND to~the~ CAMPSITE□

campsite, and in the morning the lying down {of} the dew existed all around the campsite,□

16:14 וַתַּעַל שִׁכְבַת הַטָּל וְהִנֵּה עַל פְּנֵי הַמִּדְבָּר דַּק מְחֻסְפָּס דַּק כַּכְּפֹר עַל הָאָרֶץ

wa'ta'al shikh'vat ha'tal we'hin'neyh al pe'ney ha'mid'bar daq me'hhus'pas daq ka'ke'phor al ha'a'rets

and~ she~will~GO-UP LYING-DOWN the~ DEW and~LOOK UPON FACE~s the~ WILDERNESS SCRAWNY be~much~FLAKE-OFF~ing/er(ms) SCRAWNY like~HOARFROST UPON the~LAND□

and the lying down {of} the dew went up, and look, upon {the} face {of} the wilderness {was a} scrawny flake, scrawny like {the} hoarfrost upon the land,□

16:15 וַיִּרְאוּ בְנֵי יִשְׂרָאֵל וַיֹּאמְרוּ אִישׁ אֶל אָחִיו מָן הוּא כִּי לֹא יָדְעוּ מַה הוּא וַיֹּאמֶר מֹשֶׁה אֲלֵהֶם הוּא הַלֶּחֶם אֲשֶׁר נָתַן יְהֹוָה לָכֶם לְאָכְלָה

wai'yir'u ve'ney yis'ra'eyl wai'yom'ru ish el a'hhiw man hu ki lo yad'u mah hu wai'yo'mer mo'sheh a'ley'hem hu ha'le'hhem a'sher na'tan YHWH la'khem le'akh'lah

and~they(m)~will~SEE SON~s "Yisra'el ^He~will~TURN-ASIDE~+~MIGHTY-ONE" and~they(m)~will~SAY MAN TO BROTHER~him "Mahn ^SHARE" HE GIVEN-THAT NOT they~did~KNOW WHAT HE and~he~will~SAY "Mosheh ^PLUCKED-OUT" TO~ them(m) HE the~BREAD WHICH he~did~ GIVE "Yhwh ^he~will~BE" to~you(mp) to~FOOD□

and {the} sons {of} "Yisra'el ^He turns El aside" saw, and they said (each) to his brother, he {is} "Mahn ^share"*, given that they did not know what he {was}, and "Mosheh ^Plucked out" said to them, he {is} the bread which "Yhwh ^He is" gave to you (for) food,□

16:16 זֶה הַדָּבָר אֲשֶׁר צִוָּה יְהֹוָה לִקְטוּ מִמֶּנּוּ אִישׁ לְפִי אָכְלוֹ עֹמֶר לַגֻּלְגֹּלֶת מִסְפַּר נַפְשֹׁתֵיכֶם אִישׁ לַאֲשֶׁר בְּאָהֳלוֹ תִּקָּחוּ

zeh ha'da'var a'sher tsi'wah YHWH liq'tu mi'me'nu ish le'phi akh'lo o'mer la'gul'go'let mis'par naph'sho'tey'khem ish la'a'sheyr be'a'ha'lo ti'qa'hhu

THIS the~WORD WHICH he~did~much~ DIRECT "Yhwh ^he~will~BE" !(mp)~PICK-UP FROM~him MAN to~MOUTH >~EAT~him OMER to~the~SKULL NUMBER BEING~s~ you(mp) MAN to~WHICH in~TENT~him

this {is} the word which "Yhwh ^He is" directed, pick him† up, (each) {according} to {the} mouth {of} his eating‡, {an} omer to the skull§, {a} number {of} your beings, you will take {for} (each) <that> {is} in his tent,□

---

* The phrase מָן הוּא (mahn hu) means, "Mahn is he" or "he is Mahn" (where Mahn is the bread-like substance). However, if the text originally read, מָה הוּא (mah hu), then this would be translated as "What is he," which explains the next phrase which states, "given that they did not know what he was," where "what he was" is מָה הוּא in Hebrew.

† Referring to the "mahn," a masculine word in Hebrew.

‡ "According to the mouth of his eating" means that each person was to gather only what was needed for their meals.

§ "Skull" is a euphemism for a "person."

Mechanical Translation Codes

| <u>WORD</u> – Verb | WORD – Noun | Word – Name | word – Pre/Suff | *word* – Conj. |

you(mp)~will~<u>TAKE</u>□

16:17

וַיַּעֲשׂוּ כֵן בְּנֵי יִשְׂרָאֵל וַיִּלְקְטוּ הַמַּרְבֶּה וְהַמַּמְעִיט

wai'ya'a'su kheyn be'ney yis'ra'eyl wai'yil'qe'tu ha'mar'beh we'ha'mam'it

and~they(m)~will~<u>DO SO SON</u>~s "Yisra'el *he~* ^will~<u>TURN-ASIDE</u>~+~<u>MIGHTY-ONE</u>„ *and~they(m)~will~* <u>PICK-UP</u> *the~make~*<u>INCREASE</u>~*ing/er(ms)* *and~the~make~*<u>BE-LESS</u>~*ing/er(ms)*□

and {the} sons {of} "Yisra'el ^He turns El aside„ did so, and they picked {it} up, the {one} (tak)ing {an} increase and the {other} (tak)ing less,□

16:18

וַיָּמֹדּוּ בָעֹמֶר וְלֹא הֶעְדִּיף הַמַּרְבֶּה וְהַמַּמְעִיט לֹא הֶחְסִיר אִישׁ לְפִי אָכְלוֹ לָקָטוּ

wai'ya'mo'du va'o'mer we'lo he'diph ha'mar'beh we'ha'mam'it lo hehh'sir ish le'phi akh'lo la'qa'tu

and~they(m)~will~<u>MEASURE</u> *in~the~*<u>OMER</u> *and~*NOT *he~did~make~*<u>EXCEED</u> *the~make~* <u>INCREASE</u>~*ing/er(ms)* *and~the~make~*<u>BE-LESS</u>~*ing/er(ms)* NOT *he~did~make~* <u>DIMINISH</u> MAN *to~*<u>MOUTH</u> >~<u>EAT</u>~him *they~did~*<u>PICK-UP</u>□

and they measured (with) the omer, and the {one} mak{ing an} increase was not made {to} exceed, and the {one} (tak)ing less was not diminished, (each) picked up {according} to {the} mouth {of} his eating*,□

16:19

וַיֹּאמֶר מֹשֶׁה אֲלֵהֶם אִישׁ אַל יוֹתֵר מִמֶּנּוּ עַד בֹּקֶר

wai'yo'mer mo'sheh a'ley'hem ish al yo'teyr mi'me'nu ad bo'qer

and~he~will~<u>SAY</u> "Mosheh ^<u>PLUCKED-OUT</u>„ TO~ them(m) MAN DO-NOT *he~will~make~* <u>LEAVE-BEHIND</u> FROM~him UNTIL MORNING□

and "Mosheh ^Plucked out„ said to them, {a} man will not leave him† behind until morning,□

16:20

וְלֹא שָׁמְעוּ אֶל מֹשֶׁה וַיּוֹתִרוּ אֲנָשִׁים מִמֶּנּוּ עַד בֹּקֶר וַיָּרֻם תּוֹלָעִים וַיִּבְאַשׁ וַיִּקְצֹף עֲלֵהֶם מֹשֶׁה

we'lo sham'u el mo'sheh wai'yo'ti'ru a'na'shim mi'me'nu ad bo'qer wai'ya'rum to'la'im wai'yiv'ash wai'yiq'tsoph a'ley'hem mo'sheh

*and~*NOT *they~did~*<u>HEAR</u> TO "Mosheh ^<u>PLUCKED-OUT</u>„ *and~they(m)~will~make~*<u>LEAVE-BEHIND</u> MAN~s FROM~him UNTIL MORNING *and~he~will~*<u>RAISE</u> KERMES~s *and~he~will~* <u>STINK</u> *and~he~will~*<u>SNAP</u> UPON~them(m) "Mosheh ^<u>PLUCKED-OUT</u>„□

and they did not hear "Mosheh ^Plucked out„ and the men left him‡ behind until morning, and kermes raised§ and he stank and "Mosheh ^Plucked out„ snapped upon them,□

---

* "According to the mouth of his eating" means that each person gathered what was needed for their meals.

† Referring to the "mahn," a masculine word in Hebrew.

‡ Referring to the "mahn," a masculine word in Hebrew.

§ Kermes, a species of worms, were found on the mahn (compare with verse 24).

Revised Mechanical Translation Codes

(..) Alt Trans/App A   <..> Comp Phrase/App B   [..] Verb Form/App C   \../ Plural Form/App D

:..: Int Inf Abs |..| Past Perf Verb   {...} Added Word

16:21 וַיִּלְקְטוּ אֹתוֹ בַּבֹּקֶר בַּבֹּקֶר אִישׁ כְּפִי אָכְלוֹ וְחַם הַשֶּׁמֶשׁ וְנָמָס

wai'yil'qe'tu o'to ba'bo'qer ba'bo'qer ish ke'phi akh'lo we'hham ha'she'mesh we'na'mas

and~*they(m)~will*~UNDERLINE:PICK-UP AT~him in~the~ MORNING in~the~MORNING MAN like~ MOUTH >~UNDERLINE:EAT~him and~*he~did*~be~UNDERLINE:BE-WARM the~SUN and~*he~did*~be~UNDERLINE:MELT-AWAY□

and they picked him* up morning (by) morning, (each) {according} to {the} mouth {of} his eating†, and the sun will be warm and he will be melted away,□

16:22 וַיְהִי בַּיּוֹם הַשִּׁשִּׁי לָקְטוּ לֶחֶם מִשְׁנֶה שְׁנֵי הָעֹמֶר לָאֶחָד וַיָּבֹאוּ כָּל נְשִׂיאֵי הָעֵדָה וַיַּגִּידוּ לְמֹשֶׁה

wai'hi ba'yom ha'shi'shi laq'tu le'hhem mish'neh she'ney ha'o'mer la'e'hhad wai'ya'vo'u kol ne'si'ey ha'ey'dah wai'ya'gi'du le'mo'sheh

and~*he~will*~UNDERLINE:EXIST in~the~DAY the~SIXTH *they~did*~UNDERLINE:PICK-UP BREAD DOUBLE TWO the~ OMER to~UNIT and~*they(m)~will*~UNDERLINE:COME ALL CAPTAIN~s the~COMPANY and~*they(m)~ will*~make~UNDERLINE:BE-FACE-TO-FACE to~"Mosheh PLUCKED-OUT"□

and (it) (came to pass) in the sixth day, they picked up double {the} bread, two {of} the omer{s} (for) {a} unit, and all {the} captains {of} the company came, and they [told] {this} to "Mosheh Plucked out",□

16:23 וַיֹּאמֶר אֲלֵהֶם הוּא אֲשֶׁר דִּבֶּר יְהוָה שַׁבָּתוֹן שַׁבַּת קֹדֶשׁ לַיהוָה מָחָר אֵת אֲשֶׁר תֹּאפוּ אֵפוּ וְאֵת אֲשֶׁר תְּבַשְּׁלוּ בַּשֵּׁלוּ וְאֵת כָּל הָעֹדֵף הַנִּיחוּ לָכֶם לְמִשְׁמֶרֶת עַד הַבֹּקֶר

wai'yo'mer a'ley'hem hu a'sher di'ber YHWH sha'ba'ton sha'bat qo'desh la'YHWH ma'hhar eyt a'sher to'phu ey'phu we'eyt a'sher te'vash'lu ba'shey'lu we'eyt kol ha'o'deyph ha'ni'hhu la'khem le'mish'me'ret ad ha'bo'qer

and~*he~will*~UNDERLINE:SAY TO~them(m) HE WHICH *he~did*~much~UNDERLINE:SPEAK "Yhwh *he~will*~UNDERLINE:BE" REST- DAY CEASING SPECIAL to~"Yhwh *he~will*~UNDERLINE:BE" TOMORROW AT WHICH *you(mp)~will*~UNDERLINE:BAKE !(mp)~UNDERLINE:BAKE and~AT WHICH *you(mp)~will*~ much~UNDERLINE:BOIL !(mp)~UNDERLINE:BOIL and~AT ALL the~ UNDERLINE:EXCEED~*ing/er(ms)* !(mp)~make~UNDERLINE:REST to~ you(mp) to~CHARGE UNTIL the~MORNING□

and he said to them, (that) {is} (what) "Yhwh He is" said, tomorrow {is a} rest day, {a} ceasing, {a} special {time} (for) "Yhwh He is", bake (what) you will bake, boil (what) you will boil, and [leave] (for) your{self} all the exceeding (for) a charge until the morning,□

16:24 וַיַּנִּיחוּ אֹתוֹ עַד הַבֹּקֶר כַּאֲשֶׁר צִוָּה מֹשֶׁה וְלֹא הִבְאִישׁ וְרִמָּה לֹא הָיְתָה בּוֹ

wai'ya'ni'hhu o'to ad ha'bo'qer ka'a'sheyr tsi'wah mo'sheh we'lo hiv'ish we'ri'mah lo hai'tah bo

---

* Referring to the "mahn," a masculine word in Hebrew.
† "According to the mouth of his eating" means that each person gathered what was needed for their meals.

Mechanical Translation Codes

<u>WORD</u> – Verb	WORD – Noun	Word – Name	word – Pre/Suff	*word* – Conj.

and~*they(m)*~will~make~REST AT~him UNTIL the~MORNING like~WHICH *he~did~much*~DIRECT "Mosheh ^{PLUCKED-OUT}" and~NOT *he~did~*make~STINK and~MAGGOT NOT *she~did~*EXIST in~him□

and they [left] him* until the morning, <just as> "Mosheh ^{Plucked out}" directed, and he did not stink and maggot{s} did not exist in him,□

16:25 וַיֹּאמֶר מֹשֶׁה אִכְלֻהוּ הַיּוֹם כִּי שַׁבָּת הַיּוֹם לַיהוָה הַיּוֹם לֹא תִמְצָאֻהוּ בַּשָּׂדֶה

wai'yo'mer mo'sheh ikh'lu'hu hai'yom ki sha'bat hai'yom la'YHWH hai'yom lo tim'tsa'u'hu ba'sa'deh

and~*he~will~*SAY "Mosheh ^{PLUCKED-OUT}" *!(mp)*~EAT~him the~DAY GIVEN-THAT CEASING the~DAY to~"Yhwh ^{he~will~BE}" the~DAY NOT *you(mp)~will~*FIND~him in~the~FIELD□

and "Mosheh ^{Plucked out}" said, eat him <today>, given that <today> {is a} ceasing (for) "Yhwh ^{He is}", <today> you will not find him† in the field,□

16:26 שֵׁשֶׁת יָמִים תִּלְקְטֻהוּ וּבַיּוֹם הַשְּׁבִיעִי שַׁבָּת לֹא יִהְיֶה בּוֹ

shey'shet ya'mim til'qe'tu'hu u'va'yom hash'vi'i sha'bat lo yih'yeh bo

SIX DAY~s *you(mp)~will~*PICK-UP~him and~in~the~DAY the~SEVENTH CEASING NOT *he~will~*EXIST in~him□

six days you will pick him‡ up, and in the seventh day {is a} ceasing, he will not exist in him,□

16:27 וַיְהִי בַּיּוֹם הַשְּׁבִיעִי יָצְאוּ מִן הָעָם לִלְקֹט וְלֹא מָצָאוּ

wai'hi ba'yom hash'vi'i yats'u min ha'am lil'qot we'lo ma'tsa'u

and~*he~will~*EXIST in~the~DAY the~SEVENTH *they~did~*GO-OUT FROM the~PEOPLE to~>~PICK-UP and~NOT *they~did~*FIND□

and (it) (came to pass) in the seventh day, they went out from the people to pick {it} up and they did not find {it},□

16:28 וַיֹּאמֶר יְהוָה אֶל מֹשֶׁה עַד אָנָה מֵאַנְתֶּם לִשְׁמֹר מִצְו‍ֹתַי וְתוֹרֹתָי

wai'yo'mer YHWH el mo'sheh ad a'nah mey'an'tem lish'mor mits'o'tai we'to'ro'tai

and~*he~will~*SAY "Yhwh ^{he~will~BE}" TO "Mosheh ^{PLUCKED-OUT}" UNTIL WHEREVER *you(mp)~did~*much~REFUSE to~>~SAFEGUARD DIRECTIVE~s~me and~TEACHING~s~me□

and "Yhwh ^{He is}" said to "Mosheh ^{Plucked out}", <how long> will§ you refuse to safeguard my directives and my teachings?□

---

* Referring to the "mahn," a masculine word in Hebrew.
† Referring to the "mahn," a masculine word in Hebrew.
‡ Referring to the "mahn," a masculine word in Hebrew.
§ The verb is written in the perfect tense but contextually it appears that this verb should have been written in the imperfect tense.

Revised Mechanical Translation Codes

(..) Alt Trans/App A	<..> Comp Phrase/App B	[..] Verb Form/App C	\..∕ Plural Form/App D
:..: Int Inf Abs	|..| Past Perf Verb	{...} Added Word	

16:29 רְאוּ כִּי יְהוָה נָתַן לָכֶם הַשַּׁבָּת עַל כֵּן הוּא נֹתֵן לָכֶם בַּיּוֹם הַשִּׁשִּׁי לֶחֶם
יוֹמָיִם שְׁבוּ אִישׁ תַּחְתָּיו אַל יֵצֵא אִישׁ מִמְּקֹמוֹ בַּיּוֹם הַשְּׁבִיעִי

re'u ki YHWH na'tan la'khem ha'sha'bat al keyn hu no'teyn la'khem ba'yom ha'shi'shi
le'hhem yo'ma'yim she'vu ish tahh'taw al yey'tsey ish mim'qo'mo ba'yom hash'vi'i

!(mp)~SEE GIVEN-THAT "Yhwh ^(he~will~BE)" he~ did~GIVE to~you(mp) the~CEASING UPON SO HE GIVE~ing/er(ms) to~you(mp) in~the~DAY the~SIXTH BREAD DAY~s2 !(mp)~SETTLE MAN UNDER~s~him DO-NOT he~will~GO-OUT MAN from~AREA~him in~the~DAY the~SEVENTH□

see, given that "Yhwh ^(He is)" |had| given to you the ceasing, <therefore> he {is} giving to you in the sixth day {the} bread {of} two days, (each) {will} settle \underneath/*, (each) will not go out from his area in the seventh day,□

16:30 וַיִּשְׁבְּתוּ הָעָם בַּיּוֹם הַשְּׁבִעִי

wai'yish'be'tu ha'am ba'yom hash'vi'i

and~they(m)~will~CEASE the~PEOPLE in~the~DAY the~SEVENTH□

and the people will cease in the seventh day,□

16:31 וַיִּקְרְאוּ בֵית יִשְׂרָאֵל אֶת שְׁמוֹ מָן וְהוּא כְּזֶרַע גַּד לָבָן וְטַעְמוֹ כְּצַפִּיחִת בִּדְבָשׁ

wai'yiq're'u veyt yis'ra'eyl et she'mo man we'hu ke'ze'ra gad la'van we'ta'mo ke'tsa'pi'hhit bid'vash

and~they(m)~will~CALL-OUT HOUSE "Yisra'el ^(he~will~TURN-ASIDE~+~MIGHTY-ONE)" AT TITLE~him "Mahn ^(SHARE)" and~HE like~SEED CORIANDER WHITE and~FLAVOR~him like~WAFER in~HONEY□

and {the} house {of} "Yisra'el ^(He turns El aside)" called out his title "Mahn ^(share)", and he {was} like {the} seed {of a} coriander, {it was} white, and his flavor {was} like {a} wafer in honey,□

16:32 וַיֹּאמֶר מֹשֶׁה זֶה הַדָּבָר אֲשֶׁר צִוָּה יְהוָה מְלֹא הָעֹמֶר מִמֶּנּוּ לְמִשְׁמֶרֶת
לְדֹרֹתֵיכֶם לְמַעַן יִרְאוּ אֶת הַלֶּחֶם אֲשֶׁר הֶאֱכַלְתִּי אֶתְכֶם בַּמִּדְבָּר
בְּהוֹצִיאִי אֶתְכֶם מֵאֶרֶץ מִצְרָיִם

wai'yo'mer mo'sheh zeh ha'da'var a'sher tsi'wah YHWH me'lo ha'o'mer mi'me'nu
le'mish'me'ret le'do'ro'tey'khem le'ma'an yir'u et ha'le'hhem a'sher he'e'khal'ti et'khem
ba'mid'bar be'ho'tsi'i et'khem mey'e'rets mits'ra'yim

and~he~will~SAY "Mosheh ^(PLUCKED-OUT)" THIS the~WORD WHICH he~did~much~DIRECT "Yhwh ^(he~will~BE)" FILLING the~OMER FROM~him to~CHARGE to~GENERATION~s~you(mp) to~THAT they(m)~will~SEE AT the~BREAD WHICH I~did~make~EAT AT~you(mp) in~the~WILDERNESS in~>~make~GO-OUT~me AT~you(mp) from~LAND "Mits'rayim

and "Mosheh ^(Plucked out)" said, this {is} the word which "Yhwh ^(He is)" directed, {make a} filling {of} the omer from him† {for} {a} charge (for) your generations (so) that they will see the bread which I made you eat in the wilderness (with) my making you go out from the land {of} "Mits'rayim ^(Two straits)",□

---

* Probably meaning "underneath his tent."
† Referring to the "mahn," a masculine word in Hebrew.

Mechanical Translation Codes

<u>WORD</u> – Verb	WORD – Noun	Word – Name	word – Pre/Suff	*word* – Conj.

STRAIT~s2„☐

16:33 וַיֹּאמֶר מֹשֶׁה אֶל אַהֲרֹן קַח צִנְצֶנֶת אַחַת וְתֶן שָׁמָּה מְלֹא הָעֹמֶר מָן וְהַנַּח אֹתוֹ לִפְנֵי יְהוָה לְמִשְׁמֶרֶת לְדֹרֹתֵיכֶם

wai'yo'mer mo'sheh el a'ha'ron qahh tsin'tse'net a'hhat we'ten sham'mah me'lo ha'o'mer man we'ha'nahh o'to liph'ney YHWH le'mish'me'ret le'do'ro'tey'khem

and~he~will~<u>SAY</u> "Mosheh ^{PLUCKED-OUT}„ TO "Aharon ^{LIGHT-BRINGER}„ !(ms)~<u>TAKE</u> WOVEN-BASKET UNIT and~!(ms)~<u>GIVE</u> THERE~unto FILLING the~OMER "Mahn ^{SHARE}„ and~!(ms)~make~<u>REST</u> AT~him to~FACE~s "Yhwh ^{he~will~}^{BE}„ to~CHARGE to~GENERATION~s~ you(mp)☐

and "Mosheh ^{Plucked out}„ said to "Aharon ^{Light bringer}„, take (one) woven basket and (place) unto there {the} filling {of} the Omer {of the} "Mahn ^{share}„, and make him rest <in front of> "Yhwh ^{He is}„ (for) {a} charge (for) your generations,☐

16:34 כַּאֲשֶׁר צִוָּה יְהוָה אֶל מֹשֶׁה וַיַּנִּיחֵהוּ אַהֲרֹן לִפְנֵי הָעֵדֻת לְמִשְׁמָרֶת

ka'a'sheyr tsi'wah YHWH el mo'sheh wai'ya'ni'hhey'hu a'ha'ron liph'ney ha'ey'dut le'mish'ma'ret

like~WHICH he~did~much~<u>DIRECT</u> "Yhwh ^{he~}^{will~BE}„ TO "Mosheh ^{PLUCKED-OUT}„ and~he~will~make~<u>REST</u>~him "Aharon ^{LIGHT-BRINGER}„ to~FACE~s the~EVIDENCE to~CHARGE☐

<just as> "Yhwh ^{He is}„ directed to "Mosheh ^{Plucked out}„, and "Aharon ^{Light bringer}„ [left] him* <in front of> the evidence (for) {a} charge,☐

16:35 וּבְנֵי יִשְׂרָאֵל אָכְלוּ אֶת הַמָּן אַרְבָּעִים שָׁנָה עַד בֹּאָם אֶל אֶרֶץ נוֹשָׁבֶת אֶת הַמָּן אָכְלוּ עַד בֹּאָם אֶל קְצֵה אֶרֶץ כְּנָעַן

uv'ney yis'ra'eyl akh'lu et ha'man ar'ba'im sha'nah ad bo'am el e'rets no'sha'vet et ha'man akh'lu ad bo'am el qe'tseyh e'rets ke'na'an

and~SON~s "Yisra'el ^{he~will~TURN-ASIDE~+~MIGHTY-ONE}„ they~did~<u>EAT</u> AT the~"Mahn ^{SHARE}„ FOUR~s YEAR UNTIL >~<u>COME</u>~them(m) TO LAND be~<u>SETTLE</u>~ing/er(fs) AT the~"Mahn ^{SHARE}„ they~did~<u>EAT</u> UNTIL >~<u>COME</u>~them(m) TO EXTREMITY LAND "Kena'an ^{LOWERED}„☐

and {the} sons {of} "Yisra'el ^{He turns El aside}„ |had| eaten the "Mahn ^{share}„ \forty/ year{s} until they came to {the} land being settled, they |had| eaten the "Mahn ^{share}„ until they came to {the} extremity {of the} land {of} "Kena'an ^{Lowered}„,☐

16:36 וְהָעֹמֶר עֲשִׂרִית הָאֵיפָה הוּא

we'ha'o'mer a'si'rit ha'ey'phah hu

and~the~OMER TENTH the~EYPHAH HE☐

and the omer {is a} tenth {of} the eyphah,☐

---

* Referring to the "mahn," a masculine word in Hebrew.

Revised Mechanical Translation Codes

(..) Alt Trans/App A	<..> Comp Phrase/App B	[..] Verb Form/App C	\../ Plural Form/App D
:..: Int Inf Abs	|..| Past Perf Verb	{...} Added Word	

Chapter 17

17:1 וַיִּסְעוּ כָּל עֲדַת בְּנֵי יִשְׂרָאֵל מִמִּדְבַּר סִין לְמַסְעֵיהֶם עַל פִּי יְהֹוָה וַיַּחֲנוּ בִּרְפִידִים וְאֵין מַיִם לִשְׁתֹּת הָעָם

wai'yis'u kol a'dat be'ney yis'ra'eyl mi'mid'bar sin le'mas'ey'hem al pi YHWH wai'ya'hha'nu bir'phi'dim we'eyn ma'yim lish'tot ha'am

and~*they(m)~will*~<u>JOURNEY</u> ALL COMPANY SON~s "Yisra'el *he~will*~<u>TURN-ASIDE</u>~+~MIGHTY-ONE" from~WILDERNESS "Sin ^{SHARP-THORN}" to~ BREAKING-CAMP~s~them(m) UPON MOUTH "Yhwh ^{he~will~BE}" and~*they(m)~will*~<u>CAMP</u> in~ "Rephiydiym ^{BOTTOM}" and~WITHOUT WATER~s2 to~>~<u>GULP</u> the~PEOPLE□

and all {the} company {of the} sons {of} "Yisra'el ^{He turns El aside}" journeyed from {the} wilderness {of} "Sin ^{Sharp thorn}", {according} to their breaking camps (by) {the} mouth {of} "Yhwh ^{He is}", and they camped in "Rephiydiym ^{Bottom}", and the people {were} without water to gulp,□

17:2 וַיָּרֶב הָעָם עִם מֹשֶׁה וַיֹּאמְרוּ תְּנוּ לָנוּ מַיִם וְנִשְׁתֶּה וַיֹּאמֶר לָהֶם מֹשֶׁה מַה תְּרִיבוּן עִמָּדִי מַה תְּנַסּוּן אֶת יְהֹוָה

wai'ya'rev ha'am im mo'sheh wai'yom'ru te'nu la'nu ma'yim we'nish'teh wai'yo'mer la'hem mo'sheh mah te'ri'vun i'ma'di mah te'na'sun et YHWH

and~*he~will*~<u>DISPUTE</u> the~PEOPLE WITH "Mosheh ^{PLUCKED-OUT}" and~*they(m)~will*~<u>SAY</u> !(mp)~<u>GIVE</u> to~us WATER~s2 and~*we~will*~ <u>GULP</u> and~*he~will*~<u>SAY</u> to~them(m) "Mosheh ^{PLUCKED-OUT}" WHAT *you(mp)~will*~ <u>DISPUTE</u>~must BY~me WHAT *you(mp)~will*~ <u>TEST</u>~must AT "Yhwh ^{he~will~BE}"□

and the people disputed with "Mosheh ^{Plucked out}" and they said, give us water and we will gulp, and "Mosheh ^{Plucked out}" said to them, (why) must you dispute (with) me? (why) must you test "Yhwh ^{He is}"?□

17:3 וַיִּצְמָא שָׁם הָעָם לַמַּיִם וַיָּלֶן הָעָם עַל מֹשֶׁה וַיֹּאמֶר לָמָּה זֶּה הֶעֱלִיתָנוּ מִמִּצְרַיִם לְהָמִית אֹתִי וְאֶת בָּנַי וְאֶת מִקְנַי בַּצָּמָא

wai'yits'ma sham ha'am la'ma'yim wai'ya'len ha'am al mo'sheh wai'yo'mer la'mah zeh he'e'li'ta'nu mi'mits'ra'yim le'ha'mit o'ti we'et ba'nai we'et miq'nai ba'tsa'ma

and~*he~will*~<u>THIRST</u> THERE the~PEOPLE to~ WATER~s2 and~*he~will*~*make*~<u>MURMUR</u> the~PEOPLE UPON "Mosheh ^{PLUCKED-OUT}" and~ *he~will*~<u>SAY</u> to~WHAT THIS *you(ms)~did*~ *make*~<u>GO-UP</u>~us from~"Mits'rayim ^{STRAIT~s2}" to~>~*make*~<u>DIE</u> AT~me and~AT SON~s~me and~AT ACQUIRED~s~me in~the~THIRST□

and the people thirsted there (for) water, and the people murmured upon "Mosheh ^{Plucked out}", and he* said, <for what reason> did you make us go up from "Mits'rayim ^{Two straits}"? to kill me and my sons, and my acquir{ing}s (with) the thirst?□

17:4 וַיִּצְעַק מֹשֶׁה אֶל יְהֹוָה לֵאמֹר מָה אֶעֱשֶׂה לָעָם הַזֶּה עוֹד מְעַט וּסְקָלֻנִי

wai'yits'aq mo'sheh el YHWH ley'mor mah e'e'seh la'am ha'zeh od me'at us'qa'lu'ni

and~*he~will*~<u>CRY-OUT</u> "Mosheh ^{PLUCKED-OUT}"

and "Mosheh ^{Plucked out}" cried out to "Yhwh ^{He}

---

* Referring to the "people," a masculine singular word in Hebrew.

Mechanical Translation Codes

<u>WORD</u> – Verb	WORD – Noun	Word – Name	word – Pre/Suff	*word* – Conj.

TO "Yhwh ^{he~will~}<u>BE</u>" to~>~<u>SAY</u> WHAT I~will~ <u>DO</u> to~the~PEOPLE the~THIS YET-AGAIN SMALL-AMOUNT and~*they~did~*<u>STONE</u>~ me☐

^{is}" say{ing}, what will I do (for) this people, <in a moment> they will stone me,☐

17:5 וַיֹּאמֶר יְהוָה אֶל מֹשֶׁה עֲבֹר לִפְנֵי הָעָם וְקַח אִתְּךָ מִזִּקְנֵי יִשְׂרָאֵל וּמַטְּךָ אֲשֶׁר הִכִּיתָ בּוֹ אֶת הַיְאֹר קַח בְּיָדְךָ וְהָלָכְתָּ

wai'yo'mer YHWH el mo'sheh a'vor liph'ney ha'am we'qahh it'kha mi'ziq'ney yis'ra'eyl u'mat'kha a'sher hi'ki'ta bo et hai'or qahh be'yad'kha we'ha'lakh'ta

and~he~will~<u>SAY</u> "Yhwh ^{he~will~}<u>BE</u>" TO "Mosheh ^{PLUCKED-OUT}" !(ms)~<u>CROSS-OVER</u> to~ FACE~s the~PEOPLE and~!(ms)~<u>TAKE</u> AT~ you(ms) from~BEARD~s "Yisra'el ^{he~will~TURN-ASIDE~+~MIGHTY-ONE}" and~BRANCH~you(ms) WHICH you(ms)~*did~make~*<u>HIT</u> in~him AT the~STREAM !(ms)~<u>TAKE</u> in~HAND~you(ms) and~you(ms)~*did~*<u>WALK</u>☐

and "Yhwh ^{He is}" said to "Mosheh ^{Plucked out}", cross over <in front of> the people and take (with) you from {the} beard{ed one}s* {of} "Yisra'el ^{He turns El aside}", and your branch, which you hit the stream (with), take {it} in your hand and you will walk,☐

17:6 הִנְנִי עֹמֵד לְפָנֶיךָ שָּׁם עַל הַצּוּר בְּחֹרֵב וְהִכִּיתָ בַצּוּר וְיָצְאוּ מִמֶּנּוּ מַיִם וְשָׁתָה הָעָם וַיַּעַשׂ כֵּן מֹשֶׁה לְעֵינֵי זִקְנֵי יִשְׂרָאֵל

hin'ni o'meyd le'pha'ney'kha sham al ha'tsur be'hho'reyv we'hi'ki'ta va'tsur we'yats'u mi'me'nu ma'yim we'sha'tah ha'am wai'ya'as keyn mo'sheh le'ey'ney ziq'ney yis'ra'eyl

LOOK~me <u>STAND</u>~ing/er(ms) to~FACE~s~ you(ms) THERE UPON the~BOULDER in~ "Hhorev ^{PARCHING-HEAT}" and~you(ms)~*did~ make~*<u>HIT</u> in~the~BOULDER and~*they~did~* <u>GO-OUT</u> FROM~him WATER~s2 and~*he~ did~*<u>GULP</u> the~PEOPLE and~he~will~<u>DO</u> SO "Mosheh ^{PLUCKED-OUT}" to~EYE~s2 BEARD~s "Yisra'el ^{he~will~TURN-ASIDE~+~MIGHTY-ONE}"☐

(here), I {am} standing <in front of> you, there upon the boulder in "Hhorev ^{Parching heat}", and you will hit the boulder and waters will go out from him, and the people will gulp, and "Mosheh ^{Plucked out}" did so to {the} eyes {of the} beard{ed one}s† {of} "Yisra'el ^{He turns El aside}",☐

17:7 וַיִּקְרָא שֵׁם הַמָּקוֹם מַסָּה וּמְרִיבָה עַל רִיב בְּנֵי יִשְׂרָאֵל וְעַל נַסֹּתָם אֶת יְהוָה לֵאמֹר הֲיֵשׁ יְהוָה בְּקִרְבֵּנוּ אִם אָיִן

wai'yiq'ra sheym ha'ma'qom ma'sah um'ri'vah al riv be'ney yis'ra'eyl we'al na'so'tam et YHWH ley'mor ha'yeysh YHWH be'qir'bey'nu im a'yin

and~he~will~<u>CALL-OUT</u> TITLE the~AREA "Masah ^{TRIAL}" and~"Meriyvah ^{CONTENTION}" UPON DISPUTE SON~s "Yisra'el ^{he~will~TURN-ASIDE~+~MIGHTY-ONE}" and~UPON >~*much~*<u>TEST</u>~ them(m) AT "Yhwh ^{he~will~}<u>BE</u>" to~>~<u>SAY</u> ?~THERE-IS "Yhwh ^{he~will~}<u>BE</u>" in~WITHIN~us IF

and he called out {the} title {of} the area, "Masah ^{Trial}" and "Meriyvah ^{Contention}", (because) {of the} dispute {of the} sons {of} "Yisra'el ^{He turns El aside}", and (because) {of} their testing "Yhwh ^{He is}" say{ing}, {is} "Yhwh ^{He is}" <among> us <or not>?☐

---

* "Bearded ones" is a euphemism for "elders."
† "Bearded ones" is a euphemism for "elders."

Revised Mechanical Translation Codes

(..) Alt Trans/App A	<..> Comp Phrase/App B	[..] Verb Form/App C	\../ Plural Form/App D
:..: Int Inf Abs	|..| Past Perf Verb	{...} Added Word	

WITHOUT□

17:8 וַיָּבֹא עֲמָלֵק וַיִּלָּחֶם עִם יִשְׂרָאֵל בִּרְפִידִם

wai'ya'vo a'ma'leyq wai'yi'la'hhem im yis'ra'eyl bir'phi'dim

and~*he~will*~<u>COME</u> "Amaleq ^{PEOPLE~+~GATHERED-UP}" and~*he~will~be*~<u>FIGHT</u> WITH "Yisra'el ^{*he~will*~TURN-ASIDE~+~MIGHTY-ONE}" in~"Rephiydiym BOTTOM"□

and "Amaleq ^{People gathered up}" came and he [waged war] with "Yisra'el ^{He turns El aside}" in "Rephiydiym ^{Bottom}",□

17:9 וַיֹּאמֶר מֹשֶׁה אֶל יְהוֹשֻׁעַ בְּחַר לָנוּ אֲנָשִׁים וְצֵא הִלָּחֵם בַּעֲמָלֵק מָחָר אָנֹכִי נִצָּב עַל רֹאשׁ הַגִּבְעָה וּמַטֵּה הָאֱלֹהִים בְּיָדִי

wai'yo'mer mo'sheh el ye'ho'shu'a be'hhar la'nu a'na'shim we'tsey hi'la'hheym ba'a'ma'leyq ma'hhar a'no'khi ni'tsav al rosh ha'giv'ah u'ma'tey ha'e'lo'him be'ya'di

and~*he~will*~<u>SAY</u> "Mosheh ^{PLUCKED-OUT}" TO "Yehoshu'a ^{EXISTING~+~*he~will*~RESCUE}" !*(ms)*~<u>CHOOSE</u> to~us MAN~s and~!*(ms)*~<u>GO-OUT</u> !*(ms)*~*be*~<u>FIGHT</u> in~the~"Amaleq ^{PEOPLE~+~GATHERED-UP}" TOMORROW I *be*~<u>STAND-UP</u>~ing/er*(ms)* UPON HEAD the~KNOLL and~BRANCH the~"Elohiym ^{POWER~s}" in~HAND~me□

and "Mosheh ^{Plucked out}" said to "Yehoshu'a ^{Yah will rescue}", choose (for) us men and go out, [wage war] (with) the "Amaleq ^{People gathered up}", tomorrow I will be standing up upon {the} head {of} the knoll, and {the} branch {of} the "Elohiym ^{Powers}" {will be} in my hand,□

17:10 וַיַּעַשׂ יְהוֹשֻׁעַ כַּאֲשֶׁר אָמַר לוֹ מֹשֶׁה לְהִלָּחֵם בַּעֲמָלֵק וּמֹשֶׁה אַהֲרֹן וְחוּר עָלוּ רֹאשׁ הַגִּבְעָה

wai'ya'as ye'ho'shu'a ka'a'sheyr a'mar lo mo'sheh le'hi'la'hheym ba'a'ma'leyq u'mo'sheh a'ha'ron we'hhur a'lu rosh ha'giv'ah

and~*he~will*~<u>DO</u> "Yehoshu'a ^{EXISTING~+~*he~will*~RESCUE}" like~WHICH *he~did*~<u>SAY</u> to~him "Mosheh ^{PLUCKED-OUT}" to~>~*be*~<u>FIGHT</u> in~the~"Amaleq ^{PEOPLE~+~GATHERED-UP}" and~"Mosheh ^{PLUCKED-OUT}" "Aharon ^{LIGHT-BRINGER}" and~"Hhur ^{CISTERN}" *they~did*~<u>GO-UP</u> HEAD the~KNOLL□

and "Yehoshu'a ^{Yah will rescue}" did <just as> "Mosheh ^{Plucked out}" said to him, to [wage war] (with) the "Amaleq ^{People gathered up}", and "Mosheh ^{Plucked out}", "Aharon ^{Light bringer}" and "Hhur ^{Cistern}", |had| gone up {to the} head {of} the knoll,□

17:11 וְהָיָה כַּאֲשֶׁר יָרִים מֹשֶׁה יָדוֹ וְגָבַר יִשְׂרָאֵל וְכַאֲשֶׁר יָנִיחַ יָדוֹ וְגָבַר עֲמָלֵק

we'hai'yah ka'a'sheyr ya'rim mo'sheh ya'do we'ga'var yis'ra'eyl we'kha'a'sher ya'ni'ahh ya'do we'ga'var a'ma'leyq

and~*he~did*~<u>EXIST</u> like~WHICH *he~will*~*make*~<u>RAISE</u> "Mosheh ^{PLUCKED-OUT}" HAND~him and~*he~did*~<u>OVERCOME</u> "Yisra'el ^{*he~will*~TURN-ASIDE~+~MIGHTY-ONE}" and~like~WHICH *he~will*~*make*~<u>REST</u> HAND~him and~*he~did*~<u>OVERCOME</u> "Amaleq ^{PEOPLE~+~GATHERED-UP}"□

and (it) (came to pass), <just as> "Mosheh ^{Plucked out}" made his hand rise, (then) "Yisra'el ^{He turns El aside}" will overcome, and <just as> he made his hand rest, then "Amaleq ^{People gathered up}" will overcome,□

Mechanical Translation Codes

<u>WORD</u> – Verb	WORD – Noun	Word – Name	word – Pre/Suff	*word* – Conj.

17:12

וִידֵי מֹשֶׁה כְּבֵדִים וַיִּקְחוּ אֶבֶן וַיָּשִׂימוּ תַחְתָּיו וַיֵּשֶׁב עָלֶיהָ וְאַהֲרֹן וְחוּר
תָּמְכוּ בְיָדָיו מִזֶּה אֶחָד וּמִזֶּה אֶחָד וַיְהִי יָדָיו אֱמוּנָה עַד בֹּא הַשָּׁמֶשׁ

wi'dey mo'sheh ke'vey'dim wai'yiq'hhu e'ven wai'ya'si'mu tahh'taw wai'yey'shev a'ley'ah
we'a'ha'ron we'hhur tam'khu ve'ya'daw mi'zeh e'hhad u'mi'zeh e'hhad wai'hi ya'daw
e'mu'nah ad bo ha'sha'mesh

and~HAND~s2 "Mosheh ^{PLUCKED-OUT}" HEAVY~s and~*they(m)~will*~<u>TAKE</u> STONE and~*they(m)~will*~<u>PLACE</u> UNDER~s~him and~*he~will*~<u>SETTLE</u> UPON~her and~"Aharon ^{LIGHT-BRINGER}" and~"Hhur ^{CISTERN}" *they~did*~<u>UPHOLD</u> in~HAND~s2~him from~THIS UNIT and~from~THIS UNIT and~*he~will*~<u>EXIST</u> HAND~s2~him FIRMNESS UNTIL >~<u>COME</u> the~SUN□

and {the} hands {of} "Mosheh ^{Plucked out}" {were} heavy, and they took {a} stone and they placed {it} \underneath/ him, and he settled upon her, and "Aharon ^{Light bringer}" and "Hhur ^{Cistern}" upheld his hands, from this (one) and from (that) (one)*, and his hands (were) firm until {the} coming† {of} the sun,□

17:13

וַיַּחֲלֹשׁ יְהוֹשֻׁעַ אֶת עֲמָלֵק וְאֶת עַמּוֹ לְפִי חָרֶב

wai'ya'hha'losh ye'ho'shu'a et a'ma'leyq we'et a'mo le'phi hha'rev

and~*he~will*~<u>WEAKEN</u> "Yehoshu'a ^{EXISTING~+~he~will~<u>RESCUE</u>}" AT "Amaleq ^{PEOPLE~+~GATHERED-UP}" and~AT PEOPLE~him to~MOUTH SWORD□

and "Yehoshu'a ^{Yah will rescue}" weakened "Amaleq ^{People gathered up}" and his people (by) {the} mouth {of the} sword,□

17:14

וַיֹּאמֶר יְהוָה אֶל מֹשֶׁה כְּתֹב זֹאת זִכָּרוֹן בַּסֵּפֶר וְשִׂים בְּאָזְנֵי יְהוֹשֻׁעַ כִּי
מָחֹה אֶמְחֶה אֶת זֵכֶר עֲמָלֵק מִתַּחַת הַשָּׁמָיִם

wai'yo'mer YHWH el mo'sheh ke'tov zot zi'ka'ron ba'sey'pher we'sim be'az'ney
ye'ho'shu'a ki ma'hhoh em'hheh et zey'kher a'ma'leyq mi'ta'hhat ha'sha'ma'yim

and~*he~will*~<u>SAY</u> "Yhwh ^{he~will~<u>BE</u>}" TO "Mosheh ^{PLUCKED-OUT}" *!(ms)~*<u>WRITE</u> THIS REMEMBRANCE in~the~SCROLL and~*!(ms)~*<u>PLACE</u> in~EAR~s2 "Yehoshu'a ^{EXISTING~+~he~will~<u>RESCUE</u>}" GIVEN-THAT >~<u>WIPE-AWAY</u> *I~will*~<u>WIPE-AWAY</u> AT MEMORIAL "Amaleq ^{PEOPLE~+~GATHERED-UP}" from~UNDER the~SKY~s2□

and "Yhwh ^{He is}" said to "Mosheh ^{Plucked out}", write this remembrance in the scroll and place {it} in {the} ears‡ {of} "Yehoshu'a ^{Yah will rescue}", given that I will :surely: wipe away {the} memorial {of} "Amaleq ^{People gathered up}" from under the skies,□

17:15

וַיִּבֶן מֹשֶׁה מִזְבֵּחַ וַיִּקְרָא שְׁמוֹ יְהוָה נִסִּי

wai'yi'ven mo'sheh miz'bey'ahh wai'yiq'ra she'mo YHWH ni'si

and~*he~will*~<u>BUILD</u> "Mosheh ^{PLUCKED-OUT}" ALTAR and~*he~will*~<u>CALL-OUT</u> TITLE~him

and "Mosheh ^{Plucked out}" built {an} altar and he called out his title "Yhwh-Nisiy ^{Yhwh is my}

---

* The phrase "from this one and from that one" means "one on this side and one on the other side."

† The Hebrew verb may mean "come" or "go" and probably refers to the "going down" of the sun.

‡ "Place it in the ears" is an idiom meaning to "speak."

Revised Mechanical Translation Codes

(..) Alt Trans/App A	<..> Comp Phrase/App B	[..] Verb Form/App C	\../ Plural Form/App D
:...: Int Inf Abs	|..| Past Perf Verb	{...} Added Word	

"Yhwh-Nisiy ^{he~will~BE~+~STANDARD~me}"□ standard", □

17:16 וַיֹּאמֶר כִּי יָד עַל כֵּס יָה מִלְחָמָה לַיהוָה בַּעֲמָלֵק מִדֹּר דֹּר

wai'yo'mer ki yad al keys yah mil'hha'mah la'YHWH ba'a'ma'leyq mi'dor dor

and~*he~will*~<u>SAY</u> GIVEN-THAT HAND UPON STOOL "Yah ^{EXISTING}" BATTLE to~"Yhwh ^{he~will~}<u>BE</u>" in~the~"Amaleq ^{PEOPLE~+~GATHERED-UP}" from~ GENERATION GENERATION□

and he said, given that {a} hand {is} upon {the} stool {of} "Yah ^{Existing}"*, {the} battle {is} (for) "Yhwh ^{He is}" (with) the {ones of} "Amaleq ^{People gathered up}", from {a} generation {and a} generation†, □

Chapter 18

18:1 וַיִּשְׁמַע יִתְרוֹ כֹהֵן מִדְיָן חֹתֵן מֹשֶׁה אֵת כָּל אֲשֶׁר עָשָׂה אֱלֹהִים לְמֹשֶׁה וּלְיִשְׂרָאֵל עַמּוֹ כִּי הוֹצִיא יְהוָה אֶת יִשְׂרָאֵל מִמִּצְרָיִם

wai'yish'ma yit'ro kho'heyn mid'yan hho'teyn mo'sheh eyt kol a'sher a'sah e'lo'him le'mo'sheh ul'yis'ra'eyl a'mo ki ho'tsi YHWH et yis'ra'eyl mi'mits'ra'yim

and~*he~will*~<u>HEAR</u> "Yitro ^{REMAINDER~him}" ADMINISTRATOR "Mid'yan ^{QUARREL}" <u>BE-AN-IN-LAW</u>~*ing/er(ms)* "Mosheh ^{PLUCKED-OUT}" AT ALL WHICH *he~did~*<u>DO</u> "Elohiym ^{POWER~s}" to~ "Mosheh ^{PLUCKED-OUT}" and~to~"Yisra'el ^{he~will~}<u>TURN-ASIDE~+~MIGHTY-ONE</u>" PEOPLE~him GIVEN-THAT *he~did~make~*<u>GO-OUT</u> "Yhwh ^{he~will~}<u>BE</u>" AT "Yisra'el ^{he~will~}<u>TURN-ASIDE~+~MIGHTY-ONE</u>" from~ "Mits'rayim ^{STRAIT~s2}"□

and "Yitro ^{His remainder}", administrator {of} "Mid'yan ^{Quarrel}", in-law {of} "Mosheh ^{Plucked out}", heard all which "Elohiym ^{Powers}" did (for) "Mosheh ^{Plucked out}" and (for) "Yisra'el ^{He turns El aside}" his people, given that "Yhwh ^{He is}" made "Yisra'el ^{He turns El aside}" go out from "Mits'rayim ^{Two straits}", □

18:2 וַיִּקַּח יִתְרוֹ חֹתֵן מֹשֶׁה אֶת צִפֹּרָה אֵשֶׁת מֹשֶׁה אַחַר שִׁלּוּחֶיהָ

wai'yi'qahh yit'ro hho'teyn mo'sheh et tsi'po'rah ey'shet mo'sheh a'hhar shi'lu'hhey'ah

and~*he~will*~<u>TAKE</u> "Yitro ^{REMAINDER~him}" <u>BE-AN-IN-LAW</u>~*ing/er(ms)* "Mosheh ^{PLUCKED-OUT}" AT "Tsiporah ^{BIRD}" WOMAN "Mosheh ^{PLUCKED-OUT}" AFTER SEND-OFF~s~her□

and "Yitro ^{His remainder}", in-law {of} "Mosheh ^{Plucked out}", took "Tsiporah ^{Bird}", Woman {of} "Mosheh ^{Plucked out}", after send{ing} her off,□

18:3 וְאֵת שְׁנֵי בָנֶיהָ אֲשֶׁר שֵׁם הָאֶחָד גֵּרְשֹׁם כִּי אָמַר גֵּר הָיִיתִי בְּאֶרֶץ נָכְרִיָּה

we'eyt she'ney va'ney'ah a'sher sheym ha'e'hhad ger'shom ki a'mar geyr hai'yi'ti

---

* The phrase "a hand is upon the stool (or throne) of Yah" is of uncertain meaning.

† "For a generation and a generation" is an idiom meaning "throughout the generations," or "for all time."

Mechanical Translation Codes

<u>WORD</u> – Verb	WORD – Noun	Word – Name	word – Pre/Suff	*word* – Conj.

be'e'rets nakh'ri'yah

and~AT TWO SON~s~her WHICH TITLE the~ UNIT "Gershom ^{EVICTED}" GIVEN-THAT *he~did~* SAY STRANGER *I~did~*EXIST in~LAND FOREIGN□	and (with) her two sons, which {the} title {of} the (one) {is} "Gershom ^{Evicted}", given that he said, I existed {as a} stranger in {a} foreign land,□

18:4 וְשֵׁם הָאֶחָד אֱלִיעֶזֶר כִּי אֱלֹהֵי אָבִי בְּעֶזְרִי וַיַּצִּלֵנִי מֵחֶרֶב פַּרְעֹה

we'sheym ha'e'hhad e'li'e'zer ki e'lo'hey a'vi be'ez'ri wai'ya'tsi'ley'ni mey'hhe'rev par'oh

and~TITLE the~UNIT "Eli'ezer ^{MIGHTY-ONE~me~+~} *he~did~*HELP" GIVEN-THAT "Elohiym ^{POWER~s}" FATHER~me in~HELP~me and~*he~will~* DELIVER~me from~SWORD "Paroh ^{GREAT-HOUSE}"□	and {the} title {of} the {other} one {is} "Eli'ezer ^{My El helps}", given that "Elohiym ^{Powers}" {of} my father {is} in my help, he will deliver me from {the} sword {of} "Paroh ^{Great house}",□

18:5 וַיָּבֹא יִתְרוֹ חֹתֵן מֹשֶׁה וּבָנָיו וְאִשְׁתּוֹ אֶל מֹשֶׁה אֶל הַמִּדְבָּר אֲשֶׁר הוּא חֹנֶה שָׁם הַר הָאֱלֹהִים

wai'ya'vo yit'ro hho'teyn mo'sheh u'va'naw we'ish'to el mo'sheh el ha'mid'bar a'sher hu hho'neh sham har ha'e'lo'him

and~*he~will~*COME "Yitro ^{REMAINDER~him}" BE-AN-IN-LAW~*ing/er(ms)* "Mosheh ^{PLUCKED-OUT}" and~SON~s~him and~WOMAN~him TO "Mosheh ^{PLUCKED-OUT}" TO the~WILDERNESS WHICH HE CAMP~*ing/er(ms)* THERE HILL the~"Elohiym ^{POWER~s}"□	and "Yitro ^{His remainder}", in-law {of} "Mosheh ^{Plucked out}", and his sons and his woman, came to "Mosheh ^{Plucked out}", to the wilderness, where he {was} camping, there {was the} hill {of} the "Elohiym ^{Powers}",□

18:6 וַיֹּאמֶר אֶל מֹשֶׁה אֲנִי חֹתֶנְךָ יִתְרוֹ בָּא אֵלֶיךָ וְאִשְׁתְּךָ וּשְׁנֵי בָנֶיהָ עִמָּהּ

wai'yo'mer el mo'sheh a'ni hho'ten'kha yit'ro ba ey'ley'kha we'ish'te'kha ush'ney va'ney'ah i'mah

and~*he~will~*SAY TO "Mosheh ^{PLUCKED-OUT}" I BE-AN-IN-LAW~*ing/er(ms)*~you(ms) "Yitro ^{REMAINDER~him}" COME~*ing/er(ms)* TO~you(ms) and~WOMAN~you(ms) and~TWO SON~s~ her WITH~her□	and he said to "Mosheh ^{Plucked out}", I am your in-law "Yitro ^{His remainder}", coming to you, and your woman and her two sons with her,□

18:7 וַיֵּצֵא מֹשֶׁה לִקְרַאת חֹתְנוֹ וַיִּשְׁתַּחוּ וַיִּשַּׁק לוֹ וַיִּשְׁאֲלוּ אִישׁ לְרֵעֵהוּ לְשָׁלוֹם וַיָּבֹאוּ הָאֹהֱלָה

wai'yey'tsey mo'sheh liq'rat hhot'no wai'yish'ta'hhu wai'yi'shaq lo wai'yish'a'lu ish le'rey'ey'hu le'sha'lom wai'ya'vo'u ha'o'he'lah

and~*he~will~*GO-OUT "Mosheh ^{PLUCKED-OUT}" to~>~MEET BE-AN-IN-LAW~*ing/er(ms)*~him and~*he~will~* self~BEND-DOWN and~*he~ will~*KISS to~him and~*they(m)~will~*	and "Mosheh ^{Plucked out}" went out to meet his in-law, and he bent {him}self down and he kissed him, and (each) enquired to his companion {according} to {the} completeness,

Revised Mechanical Translation Codes

(..) Alt Trans/App A	<..> Comp Phrase/App B	[..] Verb Form/App C	\..\ Plural Form/App D
∴: Int Inf Abs	|..| Past Perf Verb	{...} Added Word	

ENQUIRE MAN to~COMPANION~him to~ COMPLETENESS and~*they(m)~will~*COME the~TENT~unto□

and they came unto the tent,□

18:8 וַיְסַפֵּר מֹשֶׁה לְחֹתְנוֹ אֵת כָּל אֲשֶׁר עָשָׂה יְהוָה לְפַרְעֹה וּלְמִצְרַיִם עַל אוֹדֹת יִשְׂרָאֵל אֵת כָּל הַתְּלָאָה אֲשֶׁר מְצָאָתַם בַּדֶּרֶךְ וַיַּצִּלֵם יְהוָה

wai'sa'peyr mo'sheh le'hhot'no eyt kol a'sher a'sah YHWH le'phar'oh ul'mits'ra'yim al o'dot yis'ra'eyl eyt kol hat'la'ah a'sher me'tsa'a'tam ba'de'rekh wai'ya'tsi'leym YHWH

and~he~will~much~<u>COUNT</u> "Mosheh ^{PLUCKED-OUT}" to~<u>BE-AN-IN-LAW</u>~*ing/er(ms)~*him AT ALL WHICH *he~did~*<u>DO</u> "Yhwh ^{he~will~BE}" to~ "Paroh ^{GREAT-HOUSE}" and~to~"Mits'rayim ^{STRAIT~s2}" UPON CONCERNING~s "Yisra'el ^{he~will~TURN-ASIDE~+~MIGHTY-ONE}" AT ALL the~TROUBLE WHICH *she~did~*<u>FIND</u>~*them(m)* in~the~ ROAD and~*he~will~make~*<u>DELIVER</u>~*them(m)* "Yhwh ^{he~will~BE}"□

and "Mosheh ^{Plucked out}" [recounted] to his in-law all which "Yhwh ^{He is}" did to "Paroh ^{Great house}" and to "Mits'rayim ^{Two straits}" <on account of> "Yisra'el ^{He turns El aside}", all the trouble which found them in the road, and "Yhwh ^{He is}" delivered them,□

18:9 וַיִּחַדְּ יִתְרוֹ עַל כָּל הַטּוֹבָה אֲשֶׁר עָשָׂה יְהוָה לְיִשְׂרָאֵל אֲשֶׁר הִצִּילוֹ מִיַּד מִצְרָיִם

wai'yi'hhad yit'ro al kol ha'to'vah a'sher a'sah YHWH le'yis'ra'eyl a'sher hi'tsi'lo mi'yad mits'ra'yim

and~he~will~<u>BE-AMAZED</u> "Yitro ^{REMAINDER~him}" UPON ALL the~FUNCTIONAL WHICH *he~did~*<u>DO</u> "Yhwh ^{he~will~BE}" to~"Yisra'el ^{he~will~TURN-ASIDE~+~MIGHTY-ONE}" WHICH *he~did~make~*<u>DELIVER</u>~*them(m)* from~HAND "Mits'rayim ^{STRAIT~s2}"□

and "Yitro ^{His remainder}" was amazed (over) all the functional {things} which "Yhwh ^{He is}" did (for) "Yisra'el ^{He turns El aside}", (when) he delivered them from {the} hand {of} "Mits'rayim ^{Two straits}",□

18:10 וַיֹּאמֶר יִתְרוֹ בָּרוּךְ יְהוָה אֲשֶׁר הִצִּיל אֶתְכֶם מִיַּד מִצְרַיִם וּמִיַּד פַּרְעֹה אֲשֶׁר הִצִּיל אֶת הָעָם מִתַּחַת יַד מִצְרָיִם

wai'yo'mer yit'ro ba'rukh YHWH a'sher hi'tsil et'khem mi'yad mits'ra'yim u'mi'yad par'oh a'sher hi'tsil et ha'am mi'ta'hhat yad mits'ra'yim

and~he~will~<u>SAY</u> "Yitro ^{REMAINDER~him}" <u>KNEEL</u>~*ed(ms)* "Yhwh ^{he~will~BE}" WHICH *he~did~make~*<u>DELIVER</u> AT~you(mp) from~HAND "Mits'rayim ^{STRAIT~s2}" and~from~HAND "Paroh ^{GREAT-HOUSE}" WHICH *he~did~make~*<u>DELIVER</u> AT the~PEOPLE from~UNDER HAND "Mits'rayim ^{STRAIT~s2}"□

and "Yitro ^{His remainder}" said, [respected] {is} "Yhwh ^{He is}" (who) delivered you from {the} hand {of} "Mits'rayim ^{Two straits}", and from {the} hand {of} "Paroh ^{Great house}" (who) delivered the people from under {the} hand {of} "Mits'rayim ^{Two straits}",□

18:11 עַתָּה יָדַעְתִּי כִּי גָדוֹל יְהוָה מִכָּל הָאֱלֹהִים כִּי בַדָּבָר אֲשֶׁר זָדוּ עֲלֵיהֶם

a'tah ya'da'ti ki ga'dol YHWH mi'kol ha'e'lo'him ki va'da'var a'sher za'du a'ley'hem

NOW *I~did~*<u>KNOW</u> GIVEN-THAT GREAT

now I know that "Yhwh ^{He is}" {is} great, (more

Mechanical Translation Codes

<u>WORD</u> – Verb	WORD – Noun	Word – Name	word – Pre/Suff	*word* – Conj.

"Yhwh ^(he~will~)BE" from~ALL the~"Elohiym ^(POWER~s)" GIVEN-THAT in~the~WORD WHICH *they~did~*SIMMER UPON~them(m)□

than) all the "Elohiym ^(Powers)", (because) {of} the (matter) which they simmered* upon them,□

18:12

וַיִּקַּח יִתְרוֹ חֹתֵן מֹשֶׁה עֹלָה וּזְבָחִים לֵאלֹהִים וַיָּבֹא אַהֲרֹן וְכֹל זִקְנֵי יִשְׂרָאֵל לֶאֱכָל לֶחֶם עִם חֹתֵן מֹשֶׁה לִפְנֵי הָאֱלֹהִים

wai'yi'qahh yit'ro hho'teyn mo'sheh o'lah uz'va'hhim ley'lo'him wai'ya'vo a'ha'ron we'khol ziq'ney yis'ra'eyl le'e'khol le'hhem im hho'teyn mo'sheh liph'ney ha'e'lo'him

and~*he~will~*TAKE "Yitro ^(REMAINDER~him)" BE-AN-IN-LAW~*ing/er(ms)* "Mosheh ^(PLUCKED-OUT)" RISING and~SACRIFICE~s to~"Elohiym ^(POWER~s)" and~*he~will~*COME "Aharon ^(LIGHT-BRINGER)" and~ALL BEARD~s "Yisra'el ^(he~will~)TURN-ASIDE~+~MIGHTY-ONE" to~>~EAT BREAD WITH BE-AN-IN-LAW~*ing/er(ms)* "Mosheh ^(PLUCKED-OUT)" to~FACE~s the~"Elohiym ^(POWER~s)"□

and "Yitro ^(His remainder)", in-law {of} "Mosheh ^(Plucked out)", took a rising {sacrifice} and sacrifices (for) "Elohiym ^(Powers)", and "Aharon ^(Light bringer)" came, and all {the} beard{ed one}s† {of} "Yisra'el ^(He turns El aside)", to eat bread with {the} in-law {of} "Mosheh ^(Plucked out)" <in front of> the "Elohiym ^(Powers)",□

18:13

וַיְהִי מִמָּחֳרָת וַיֵּשֶׁב מֹשֶׁה לִשְׁפֹּט אֶת הָעָם וַיַּעֲמֹד הָעָם עַל מֹשֶׁה מִן הַבֹּקֶר עַד הָעָרֶב

wai'hi mi'ma'hha'rat wai'yey'shev mo'sheh lish'pot et ha'am wai'ya'a'mod ha'am al mo'sheh min ha'bo'qer ad ha'a'rev

and~*he~will~*EXIST from~MORROW and~*he~will~*SETTLE "Mosheh ^(PLUCKED-OUT)" to~ >~DECIDE AT the~PEOPLE and~*he~will~*STAND the~PEOPLE UPON "Mosheh ^(PLUCKED-OUT)" FROM the~MORNING UNTIL the~EVENING□

and (it) (came to pass) (on) {the} morrow, and "Mosheh ^(Plucked out)" settled to decide‡ the people, and the people stood upon "Mosheh ^(Plucked out)" from the morning until the evening,□

18:14

וַיַּרְא חֹתֵן מֹשֶׁה אֵת כָּל אֲשֶׁר הוּא עֹשֶׂה לָעָם וַיֹּאמֶר מָה הַדָּבָר הַזֶּה אֲשֶׁר אַתָּה עֹשֶׂה לָעָם מַדּוּעַ אַתָּה יוֹשֵׁב לְבַדֶּךָ וְכָל הָעָם נִצָּב עָלֶיךָ מִן בֹּקֶר עַד עָרֶב

wai'yar hho'teyn mo'sheh eyt kol a'sher hu o'seh la'am wai'yo'mer mah ha'da'var ha'zeh a'sher a'tah o'seh la'am ma'du'a a'tah yo'sheyv le'va'de'kha we'khol ha'am ni'tsav a'ley'kha min bo'qer ad a'rev

and~*he~will~*SEE BE-AN-IN-LAW~*ing/er(ms)* "Mosheh ^(PLUCKED-OUT)" AT ALL WHICH HE DO~*ing/er(ms)* to~the~PEOPLE and~*he~will~*SAY WHAT the~WORD the~THIS WHICH YOU(ms) DO~*ing/er(ms)* to~the~PEOPLE WHY YOU(ms) SETTLE~*ing/er(ms)* to~STICK~

and {the} in-law {of} "Mosheh ^(Plucked out)" saw all which he {was} doing (for) the people, and he said, what {is} this (matter) which you {are} doing (for) the people? why {are} you settling (by) your<self>, and all the people {are} standing upon you from morning until

---

* Probably referring to the hard labor forced on the people.
† "Bearded ones" is a euphemism for "elders."
‡ Or, to judge.

Revised Mechanical Translation Codes

(..) Alt Trans/App A	<..> Comp Phrase/App B	[..] Verb Form/App C	\../ Plural Form/App D
:..: Int Inf Abs	|..| Past Perf Verb	{...} Added Word	

you(ms) and~ALL the~PEOPLE be~STAND-
UP~ing/er(ms) UPON~you(ms) FROM
MORNING UNTIL EVENING□   evening?□

18:15   וַיֹּאמֶר מֹשֶׁה לְחֹתְנֹו כִּי יָבֹא אֵלַי הָעָם לִדְרֹשׁ אֱלֹהִים

wai'yo'mer mo'sheh le'hhot'no ki ya'vo ey'lai ha'am lid'rosh e'lo'him

and~he~will~SAY "Mosheh ᴾᴸᵁᶜᴷᴱᴰ⁻ᴼᵁᵀ" to~   and "Mosheh ᴾˡᵘᶜᵏᵉᵈ ᵒᵘᵗ" said to his in-law,
BE-AN-IN-LAW~ing/er(ms)~him GIVEN-THAT   (because) the people will come to me to seek
he~will~COME TO~me the~PEOPLE to~   "Elohiym ᴾᵒʷᵉʳˢ",□
>~SEEK "Elohiym ᴾᴼᵂᴱᴿ~s"□

18:16   כִּי יִהְיֶה לָהֶם דָּבָר בָּא אֵלַי וְשָׁפַטְתִּי בֵּין אִישׁ וּבֵין רֵעֵהוּ וְהֹודַעְתִּי אֶת חֻקֵּי הָאֱלֹהִים וְאֶת תֹּורֹתָיו

ki yih'yeh la'hem da'var ba ey'lai we'sha'phat'ti beyn ish u'veyn rey'ey'hu we'ho'da'ti et
hhu'qey ha'e'lo'him we'et to'ro'taw

GIVEN-THAT he~will~EXIST to~them(m)   given that {a} (matter) will exist (for) them, {it
WORD COME~ing/er(ms) TO~me and~I~did~   is} coming to me and I will decide between
DECIDE BETWEEN MAN and~BETWEEN   (each) and his companion, and I will make
COMPANION~him and~I~did~make~KNOW   known {the} customs {of} the "Elohiym ᴾᵒʷᵉʳˢ"
AT CUSTOM~s the~"Elohiym ᴾᴼᵂᴱᴿ~s" and~AT   and his teachings,□
TEACHING~s~him□

18:17   וַיֹּאמֶר חֹתֵן מֹשֶׁה אֵלָיו לֹא טֹוב הַדָּבָר אֲשֶׁר אַתָּה עֹשֶׂה

wai'yo'mer hho'teyn mo'sheh ey'law lo tov ha'da'var a'sher a'tah o'seh

and~he~will~SAY BE-AN-IN-LAW~ing/er(ms)   and {the} in-law {of} "Mosheh ᴾˡᵘᶜᵏᵉᵈ ᵒᵘᵗ" said to
"Mosheh ᴾᴸᵁᶜᴷᴱᴰ⁻ᴼᵁᵀ" TO~him NOT   him, the (matter) which you {are} doing {is}
FUNCTIONAL the~WORD WHICH YOU(ms)   not functional,□
DO~ing/er(ms)□

18:18   נָבֹל תִּבֹּל גַּם אַתָּה גַּם הָעָם הַזֶּה אֲשֶׁר עִמָּךְ כִּי כָבֵד מִמְּךָ הַדָּבָר לֹא תוּכַל עֲשֹׂהוּ לְבַדֶּךָ

na'vol ti'bol gam a'tah gam ha'am ha'zeh a'sher i'makh ki kha'veyd mim'kha ha'da'var
lo tu'khal a'so'hu le'va'de'kha

>~FADE you(ms)~will~FADE ALSO YOU(ms)   you will :surely: fade, (both) you and this
ALSO the~PEOPLE the~THIS WHICH WITH~   people which {are} with you, given that the
you(fs) GIVEN-THAT HEAVY FROM~you(ms)   (matter) {is} heavi{er} than you, you will not
the~WORD NOT you(ms)~will~BE-ABLE   be able {to} do him (by) your<self>,□
>~DO~him to~STICK~you(ms)□

18:19   עַתָּה שְׁמַע בְּקֹלִי אִיעָצְךָ וִיהִי אֱלֹהִים עִמָּךְ הֱיֵה אַתָּה לָעָם מוּל הָאֱלֹהִים וְהֵבֵאתָ אַתָּה אֶת הַדְּבָרִים אֶל הָאֱלֹהִים

a'tah she'ma be'qo'li i'ats'kha wi'hi e'lo'him i'makh he'yeh a'tah la'am mul ha'e'lo'him
we'hey'vey'ta a'tah et had'va'rim el ha'e'lo'him

Mechanical Translation Codes

<u>WORD</u> – Verb	WORD – Noun	Word – Name	word – Pre/Suff	*word* – Conj.

NOW !(ms)~<u>HEAR</u> in~VOICE~me I~will~<u>GIVE-ADVICE</u>~you(ms) and~he~will~<u>EXIST</u> "Elohiym ^{POWER~s}" WITH~you(fs) !(ms)~<u>EXIST</u> YOU(ms) to~the~PEOPLE FOREFRONT the~ "Elohiym ^{POWER~s}" and~you(ms)~did~make~ <u>COME</u> YOU(ms) AT the~WORD~s TO the~ "Elohiym ^{POWER~s}"□

now, hear my voice, I will give you advice, and "Elohiym ^{Powers}" will exist with you, you {will} exist (for) the people, (in place) {of} "Elohiym ^{Powers}", and you will [bring] the (matters) to the "Elohiym ^{Powers}"*,□

18:20 וְהִזְהַרְתָּה אֶתְהֶם אֶת הַחֻקִּים וְאֶת הַתּוֹרֹת וְהוֹדַעְתָּ לָהֶם אֶת הַדֶּרֶךְ יֵלְכוּ בָהּ וְאֶת הַמַּעֲשֶׂה אֲשֶׁר יַעֲשׂוּן

we'hiz'har'tah et'hem et ha'hhu'qim we'et ha'to'rot we'ho'da'ta la'hem et ha'de'rekh yeyl'khu vah we'et ha'ma'a'seh a'sher ya'a'sun

and~you(ms)~did~make~<u>WARN</u> AT~ them(m) AT the~CUSTOM~s and~AT the~ TEACHING~s and~you(ms)~did~make~ <u>KNOW</u> to~them(m) AT the~ROAD they(m)~ will~<u>WALK</u> in~her and~AT the~WORK WHICH they(m)~will~<u>DO</u>~must□

and you will warn them {of} the customs and the teachings, and you will make them know the road they will walk in and the work which they must do,□

18:21 וְאַתָּה תֶחֱזֶה מִכָּל הָעָם אַנְשֵׁי חַיִל יִרְאֵי אֱלֹהִים אַנְשֵׁי אֱמֶת שֹׂנְאֵי בָצַע וְשַׂמְתָּ עֲלֵהֶם שָׂרֵי אֲלָפִים שָׂרֵי מֵאוֹת שָׂרֵי חֲמִשִּׁים וְשָׂרֵי עֲשָׂרֹת

we'a'tah te'hhe'zeh mi'kol ha'am an'shey hha'yil yir'ey e'lo'him an'shey e'met son'ey va'tsa we'sam'ta a'ley'hem sa'rey a'la'phim sa'rey mey'ot sa'rey hha'mi'shim we'sa'rey a'sa'rot

and~YOU(ms) you(ms)~will~<u>PERCEIVE</u> from~ ALL the~PEOPLE MAN~s FORCE FEARFUL~s "Elohiym ^{POWER~s}" MAN~s TRUTH <u>HATE</u>~ ing/er(mp) PROFIT and~you(ms)~did~<u>PLACE</u> UPON~them(m) NOBLE~s THOUSAND~s NOBLE~s HUNDRED~s NOBLE~s FIVE~s and~ NOBLE~s TEN~s□

and you, you will perceive (out of) all the people, men {of} force, fearful {of} "Elohiym ^{Powers}", men {of} truth, hating profit, and you will place upon them nobles {of} thousands, nobles {of} hundreds, nobles {of} fifties† and nobles {of} tens,□

18:22 וְשָׁפְטוּ אֶת הָעָם בְּכָל עֵת וְהָיָה כָּל הַדָּבָר הַגָּדֹל יָבִיאוּ אֵלֶיךָ וְכָל הַדָּבָר הַקָּטֹן יִשְׁפְּטוּ הֵם וְהָקֵל מֵעָלֶיךָ וְנָשְׂאוּ אִתָּךְ

we'shaph'tu et ha'am be'khol eyt we'hai'yah kol ha'da'var ha'ga'dol ya'vi'u ey'ley'kha we'khol ha'da'var ha'qa'ton yish'pe'tu heym we'ha'qeyl mey'a'ley'kha we'nas'u i'takh

and~they~did~<u>DECIDE</u> AT the~PEOPLE in~ ALL APPOINTED-TIME and~he~did~<u>EXIST</u> ALL the~WORD the~GREAT they(m)~will~make~

and they will decide {for} the people <at all times>, and (it) will (come to pass), {of} all the great (matter){s} they will [bring] to you, and

---

* The word Elohiym may refer to the judges, but the Hebrew word for judges is usually שׁוֹפְטִים (shoftim).
† The Hebrew word חֲמִשִּׁים, the plural form of חָמֵשׁ, means fifty. However, the context of the word חֲמִשִּׁים in this verse means fifties.

Revised Mechanical Translation Codes

(..) Alt Trans/App A	<..> Comp Phrase/App B	[..] Verb Form/App C	\../ Plural Form/App D
:..: Int Inf Abs	|..| Past Perf Verb	{...} Added Word	

COME TO~you(ms) and~ALL the~WORD the~
SMALL they(m)~will~<u>DECIDE</u> THEY(m) !(ms)~
make~<u>BELITTLE</u> from~UPON~you(ms) and~
they~did~<u>LIFT-UP</u> AT~you(ms)□

{of} all the small (matter){s} they will decide
them{selves}, {it will} be made little upon you,
and they will lift you up,□

18:23

אִם אֶת הַדָּבָר הַזֶּה תַּעֲשֶׂה וְצִוְּךָ אֱלֹהִים וְיָכָלְתָּ עֲמֹד וְגַם כָּל הָעָם
הַזֶּה עַל מְקֹמוֹ יָבֹא בְשָׁלוֹם

im et ha'da'var ha'zeh ta'a'seh we'tsiw'kha e'lo'him we'ya'khal'ta a'mod we'gam kol
ha'am ha'zeh al me'qo'mo ya'vo ve'sha'lom

IF AT the~WORD the~THIS you(ms)~will~<u>DO</u>
and~he~did~much~<u>DIRECT</u>~you(ms)
"Elohiym ^{POWER~s}" and~you(ms)~did~<u>BE-ABLE</u>
>~<u>STAND</u> and~ALL the~PEOPLE the~
THIS UPON AREA~him he~will~<u>COME</u> in~
COMPLETENESS□

if you will do this (matter), and "Elohiym
^{Powers}" will direct you, (then) you will be able
{to} stand, and also, this people will come
upon his* area in completeness,□

18:24

וַיִּשְׁמַע מֹשֶׁה לְקוֹל חֹתְנוֹ וַיַּעַשׂ כֹּל אֲשֶׁר אָמָר

wai'yish'ma mo'sheh le'qol hhot'no wai'ya'as kol a'sher a'mar

and~he~will~<u>HEAR</u> "Mosheh ^{PLUCKED-OUT}" to~
VOICE <u>BE-AN-IN-LAW</u>~ing/er(ms)~him and~
he~will~<u>DO</u> ALL WHICH he~did~<u>SAY</u>□

and "Mosheh ^{Plucked out}" heard {the} voice {of}
his in-law and he did all which he said,□

18:25

וַיִּבְחַר מֹשֶׁה אַנְשֵׁי חַיִל מִכָּל יִשְׂרָאֵל וַיִּתֵּן אֹתָם רָאשִׁים עַל הָעָם שָׂרֵי
אֲלָפִים שָׂרֵי מֵאוֹת שָׂרֵי חֲמִשִּׁים וְשָׂרֵי עֲשָׂרֹת

wai'yiv'hhar mo'sheh an'shey hha'yil mi'kol yis'ra'eyl wai'yi'teyn o'tam ra'shim al ha'am
sa'rey a'la'phim sa'rey mey'ot sa'rey hha'mi'shim we'sa'rey a'sa'rot

and~he~will~<u>CHOOSE</u> "Mosheh ^{PLUCKED-OUT}"
MAN~s FORCE from~ALL "Yisra'el <sup>he~will~TURN-
ASIDE~+~MIGHTY-ONE</sup>" and~he~will~<u>GIVE</u> AT~
them(m) HEAD~s UPON the~PEOPLE
NOBLE~s THOUSAND~s NOBLE~s
HUNDRED~s NOBLE~s FIVE~s and~NOBLE~s
TEN~s□

and "Mosheh ^{Plucked out}" chose men {of} force
from all {of} "Yisra'el ^{He turns El aside}", and he gave
them heads upon the people, nobles {of}
thousands, nobles {of} hundreds, nobles {of}
fifties† and nobles {of} tens,□

18:26

וְשָׁפְטוּ אֶת הָעָם בְּכָל עֵת אֶת הַדָּבָר הַקָּשֶׁה יְבִיאוּן אֶל מֹשֶׁה וְכָל
הַדָּבָר הַקָּטֹן יִשְׁפּוּטוּ הֵם

we'shaph'tu et ha'am be'khol eyt et ha'da'var ha'qa'sheh ye'vi'un el mo'sheh we'khol
ha'da'var ha'qa'ton yish'pu'tu heym

and~they~did~<u>DECIDE</u> AT the~PEOPLE in~
ALL APPOINTED-TIME AT the~WORD the~

and they will decide {for} the people <at all
times>, they must [bring] the hard (matter){s}

---

* The "his" is "the people," a masculine singular word in Hebrew.
† The Hebrew word חֲמִשִּׁים, the plural form of חָמֵשׁ, means fifty. However, the context of the
word חֲמִשִּׁים in this verse means fifties.

Mechanical Translation Codes

| <u>WORD</u> – Verb | WORD – Noun | Word – Name | word – Pre/Suff | *word* – Conj. |

HARD *they(m)~will~make~*<u>COME</u>*~must* TO "Mosheh ^{PLUCKED-OUT}" and~ALL the~WORD the~SMALL *they(m)~did~*<u>DECIDE</u> THEY(m)□

to "Mosheh ^{Plucked out}", and they will decide all the small (matter){s} them{selves},□

18:27   וַיְשַׁלַּח מֹשֶׁה אֶת חֹתְנוֹ וַיֵּלֶךְ לוֹ אֶל אַרְצוֹ

wai'sha'lahh mo'sheh et hhot'no wai'yey'lekh lo el ar'tso

and~*he~will~much~*<u>SEND</u> "Mosheh ^{PLUCKED-OUT}" AT <u>BE-AN-IN-LAW</u>*~ing/er(ms)~*him and~ *he~will~*<u>WALK</u> to~him TO LAND~him□

and "Mosheh ^{Plucked out}" sent his in-law, and he walked him{self}, to his land,□

Chapter 19

19:1   בַּחֹדֶשׁ הַשְּׁלִישִׁי לְצֵאת בְּנֵי יִשְׂרָאֵל מֵאֶרֶץ מִצְרָיִם בַּיּוֹם הַזֶּה בָּאוּ מִדְבַּר סִינָי

ba'hho'desh hash'li'shi le'tseyt be'ney yis'ra'eyl mey'e'rets mits'ra'yim ba'yom ha'zeh ba'u mid'bar si'nai

in~the~NEW-MOON the~THIRD to~>~<u>GO-OUT</u> SON~s "Yisra'el ^{he~will~TURN-ASIDE~+~MIGHTY-ONE}" from~LAND "Mits'rayim ^{STRAIT~s2}" in~the~ DAY the~THIS *they~did~*<u>COME</u> WILDERNESS "Sinai ^{SHARP-THORN~s~me}"□

in the third new moon to {the} go{ing} out {of} the} sons {of} "Yisra'el ^{He turns El aside}" from {the} land {of} "Mits'rayim ^{Two straits}", in this day they came {to the} wilderness {of} "Sinai ^{My sharp thorns}",□

19:2   וַיִּסְעוּ מֵרְפִידִים וַיָּבֹאוּ מִדְבַּר סִינַי וַיַּחֲנוּ בַּמִּדְבָּר וַיִּחַן שָׁם יִשְׂרָאֵל נֶגֶד הָהָר

wai'yis'u meyr'phi'dim wai'ya'vo'u mid'bar si'nai wai'ya'hha'nu ba'mid'bar wai'yi'hhan sham yis'ra'eyl ne'ged ha'har

and~*they(m)~will~*<u>JOURNEY</u> from~ "Rephiydiym ^{BOTTOM}" and~*they(m)~will~* <u>COME</u> WILDERNESS "Sinai ^{SHARP-THORN~s~me}" and~*they(m)~will~*<u>CAMP</u> in~the~ WILDERNESS and~*he~will~*<u>CAMP</u> THERE "Yisra'el ^{he~will~TURN-ASIDE~+~MIGHTY-ONE}" OPPOSITE the~HILL□

and they journeyed from "Rephiydiym ^{Bottom}", and they came {to the} wilderness {of} "Sinai ^{My sharp thorns}", and they camped in the wilderness, and "Yisra'el ^{He turns El aside}" camped there, opposite the hill,□

19:3   וּמֹשֶׁה עָלָה אֶל הָאֱלֹהִים וַיִּקְרָא אֵלָיו יְהוָה מִן הָהָר לֵאמֹר כֹּה תֹאמַר לְבֵית יַעֲקֹב וְתַגֵּיד לִבְנֵי יִשְׂרָאֵל

u'mo'sheh a'lah el ha'e'lo'him wai'yiq'ra ey'law YHWH min ha'har ley'mor koh to'mar le'veyt ya'a'qov we'ta'geyd liv'ney yis'ra'eyl

and~"Mosheh ^{PLUCKED-OUT}" *he~did~*<u>GO-UP</u> TO the~"Elohiym ^{POWER~s}" and~*he~will~*<u>CALL-OUT</u> TO~him "Yhwh ^{he~will~BE}" FROM the~HILL

and "Mosheh ^{Plucked out}" |had| gone up to the "Elohiym ^{Powers}" and "Yhwh ^{He is}" called out to him from the hill say{ing}, in this way you will

to~>~<u>SAY</u> IN-THIS-WAY *you(ms)~will~*<u>SAY</u> to~HOUSE "Ya'aqov ^{he~will~<u>RESTRAIN</u>}″ and~ *you(ms)~will~make~*<u>BE-FACE-TO-FACE</u> to~ SON~s "Yisra'el ^{he~will~<u>TURN-ASIDE</u>~+~<u>MIGHTY-ONE</u>}″□

say to {the} house {of} "Ya'aqov ^{He restrains}″, and you will [tell] to {the} sons {of} "Yisra'el ^{He turns El aside}″,□

19:4

אַתֶּם רְאִיתֶם אֲשֶׁר עָשִׂיתִי לְמִצְרָיִם וָאֶשָּׂא אֶתְכֶם עַל כַּנְפֵי נְשָׁרִים וָאָבִא אֶתְכֶם אֵלָי

a'tem re'i'tem a'sher a'si'ti le'mits'ra'yim wa'e'sa et'khem al kan'phey ne'sha'rim wa'a'vi et'khem ey'lai

<u>YOU(mp)</u> *you(mp)~did~*<u>SEE</u> WHICH *I~did~*<u>DO</u> to~"Mits'rayim ^{STRAIT~s2}″ and~*I~will~*<u>LIFT-UP</u> AT~you(mp) UPON WING~s NESHER~s and~ *I~will~make~*<u>COME</u> AT~you(mp) TO~me□

you saw (what) I did to "Mits'rayim ^{Two straits}″, and I will lift you up upon {the} wings {of the} nesher*, and I will [bring] you to me,□

19:5

וְעַתָּה אִם שָׁמוֹעַ תִּשְׁמְעוּ בְּקֹלִי וּשְׁמַרְתֶּם אֶת בְּרִיתִי וִהְיִיתֶם לִי סְגֻלָּה מִכָּל הָעַמִּים כִּי לִי כָּל הָאָרֶץ

we'a'tah im sha'mo'a tish'me'u be'qo'li ush'mar'tem et be'ri'ti wih'yi'tem li se'gu'lah mi'kol ha'a'mim ki li kol ha'a'rets

and~NOW IF >~<u>HEAR</u> *you(mp)~will~*<u>HEAR</u> in~VOICE~me and~*you(mp)~did~* <u>SAFEGUARD</u> AT COVENANT~me and~ *you(mp)~did~*<u>EXIST</u> to~me JEWEL from~ALL the~PEOPLE~s GIVEN-THAT to~me ALL the~ LAND□

and now, if you will :carefully: hear my voice, and you will safeguard my covenant, (then) you will exist (for) me {as a} jewel (more than) all the peoples, given that all the land{s belong} to me,□

19:6

וְאַתֶּם תִּהְיוּ לִי מַמְלֶכֶת כֹּהֲנִים וְגוֹי קָדוֹשׁ אֵלֶּה הַדְּבָרִים אֲשֶׁר תְּדַבֵּר אֶל בְּנֵי יִשְׂרָאֵל

we'a'tem tih'yu li mam'le'khet ko'ha'nim we'goy qa'dosh ey'leh had'va'rim a'sher te'da'beyr el be'ney yis'ra'eyl

and~YOU(mp) *you(mp)~will~*<u>EXIST</u> to~me KINGDOM ADMINISTRATOR~s and~NATION UNIQUE THESE the~WORD~s WHICH *you(ms)~will~much~*<u>SPEAK</u> TO SON~s "Yisra'el ^{he~will~<u>TURN-ASIDE</u>~+~<u>MIGHTY-ONE</u>}″□

and you will exist (for) me {as a} kingdom {of} administrators and {a} unique nation, these {are} the words which you will speak to {the} sons {of} "Yisra'el ^{He turns El aside}″,□

19:7

וַיָּבֹא מֹשֶׁה וַיִּקְרָא לְזִקְנֵי הָעָם וַיָּשֶׂם לִפְנֵיהֶם אֵת כָּל הַדְּבָרִים הָאֵלֶּה אֲשֶׁר צִוָּהוּ יְהֹוָה

wai'ya'vo mo'sheh wai'yiq'ra le'ziq'ney ha'am wai'ya'sem liph'ney'hem eyt kol had'va'rim ha'ey'leh a'sher tsi'wa'hu YHWH

and~*he~will~*<u>COME</u> "Mosheh ^{PLUCKED-OUT}″ and~*he~will~*<u>CALL-OUT</u> to~BEARD~s the~

and "Mosheh ^{Plucked out}″ came and he called out to {the} beard{ed one}s† {of} the people, and

---

* An unknown bird, but probably a hawk or eagle.

† "Bearded ones" is a euphemism for "elders."

Mechanical Translation Codes

<u>WORD</u> – Verb	WORD – Noun	Word – Name	word – Pre/Suff	*word* – Conj.

PEOPLE and~he~will~<u>PLACE</u> to~FACE~s~ them(m) AT ALL the~WORD~s the~THESE WHICH he~did~much~<u>DIRECT</u>~him "Yhwh ^{he~}^{will~<u>BE</u>}"□

he placed all these words, which "Yhwh ^{He is}" directed him, <in front of> them,□

19:8   וַיַּעֲנוּ כָל הָעָם יַחְדָּו וַיֹּאמְרוּ כֹּל אֲשֶׁר דִּבֶּר יְהֹוָה נַעֲשֶׂה וַיָּשֶׁב מֹשֶׁה אֶת דִּבְרֵי הָעָם אֶל יְהֹוָה

wai'ya'a'nu khol ha'am yahh'daw wai'yom'ru kol a'sher di'ber YHWH na'a'seh wai'ya'shev mo'sheh et div'rey ha'am el YHWH

and~they(m)~will~<u>ANSWER</u> ALL the~PEOPLE TOGETHER and~they(m)~will~<u>SAY</u> ALL WHICH he~did~much~<u>SPEAK</u> "Yhwh ^{he~will~<u>BE</u>}" we~will~<u>DO</u> and~he~will~make~<u>TURN-BACK</u> "Mosheh ^{PLUCKED-OUT}" AT WORD~s the~ PEOPLE TO "Yhwh ^{he~will~<u>BE</u>}"□

and all the people answered together, and they said, all which "Yhwh ^{He is}" spoke, we will do, and "Mosheh ^{Plucked out}" [returned] {the} words {of} the people to "Yhwh ^{He is}",□

19:9   וַיֹּאמֶר יְהֹוָה אֶל מֹשֶׁה הִנֵּה אָנֹכִי בָּא אֵלֶיךָ בְּעַב הֶעָנָן בַּעֲבוּר יִשְׁמַע הָעָם בְּדַבְּרִי עִמָּךְ וְגַם בְּךָ יַאֲמִינוּ לְעוֹלָם וַיַּגֵּד מֹשֶׁה אֶת דִּבְרֵי הָעָם אֶל יְהֹוָה

wai'yo'mer YHWH el mo'sheh hin'neyh a'no'khi ba ey'ley'kha be'av he'a'nan ba'a'vur yish'ma ha'am be'da'be'ri i'makh we'gam be'kha ya'a'mi'nu le'o'lam wai'ya'geyd mo'sheh et div'rey ha'am el YHWH

and~he~will~<u>SAY</u> "Yhwh ^{he~will~<u>BE</u>}" TO "Mosheh ^{PLUCKED-OUT}" LOOK I <u>COME</u>~ ing/er(ms) TO~you(ms) in~THICK the~CLOUD in~INTENTION he~will~<u>HEAR</u> the~PEOPLE in~>~much~<u>SPEAK</u>~me WITH~you(fs) and~ ALSO in~you(ms) they(m)~will~make~ <u>SECURE</u> to~DISTANT and~he~will~make~<u>BE-</u> <u>FACE-TO-FACE</u> "Mosheh ^{PLUCKED-OUT}" AT WORD~s the~PEOPLE TO "Yhwh ^{he~will~<u>BE</u>}"□

and "Yhwh ^{He is}" said to "Mosheh ^{Plucked out}", look, I {am} coming to you in {the} thick {of} the} cloud, (with) {the} intention {that} the people will hear me speak{ing} with you, and also, they will [support] you (for) {a} distant {time}, and "Mosheh ^{Plucked out}" [told] {the} words {of} the people to "Yhwh ^{He is}",□

19:10   וַיֹּאמֶר יְהֹוָה אֶל מֹשֶׁה לֵךְ אֶל הָעָם וְקִדַּשְׁתָּם הַיּוֹם וּמָחָר וְכִבְּסוּ שִׂמְלֹתָם

wai'yo'mer YHWH el mo'sheh leykh el ha'am we'qi'dash'tam hai'yom u'ma'hhar we'khi'be'su sim'lo'tam

and~he~will~<u>SAY</u> "Yhwh ^{he~will~<u>BE</u>}" TO "Mosheh ^{PLUCKED-OUT}" !(ms)~<u>WALK</u> TO the~ PEOPLE and~you(ms)~did~much~<u>SET-</u> <u>APART</u>~them(m) the~DAY and~TOMORROW and~they~did~much~<u>WASH</u> APPAREL~s~ them(m)□

and "Yhwh ^{He is}" said to "Mosheh ^{Plucked out}", walk to the people and you will set them apart <today> and tomorrow, and they will wash their apparel,□

19:11   וְהָיוּ נְכֹנִים לַיּוֹם הַשְּׁלִישִׁי כִּי בַּיּוֹם הַשְּׁלִשִׁי יֵרֵד יְהֹוָה לְעֵינֵי כָל הָעָם

Revised Mechanical Translation Codes

(..) Alt Trans/App A	<..> Comp Phrase/App B	[..] Verb Form/App C	\../ Plural Form/App D
:..: Int Inf Abs	|..| Past Perf Verb	{...} Added Word	

עַל הַר סִינָי

we'hai'u ne'kho'nim la'yom hash'li'shi ki ba'yom hash'li'shi yey'reyd YHWH le'ey'ney khol ha'am al har si'nai

and~*they*~*did*~EXIST be~PREPARE~ *ing/er*(mp) to~the~DAY the~THIRD GIVEN-THAT in~the~DAY the~THIRD he~*will*~GO-DOWN "Yhwh ^{he~will~BE}" to~EYE~s2 ALL the~PEOPLE UPON HILL "Sinai ^{SHARP-THORN~s~me}"□	and they will <be ready> (for) the third day, given that in the third day "Yhwh ^{He is}" will go down to {the} eyes {of} all the people upon {the} hill {of} "Sinai ^{My sharp thorns}",□

19:12 וְהִגְבַּלְתָּ אֶת הָעָם סָבִיב לֵאמֹר הִשָּׁמְרוּ לָכֶם עֲלוֹת בָּהָר וּנְגֹעַ בְּקָצֵהוּ כָּל הַנֹּגֵעַ בָּהָר מוֹת יוּמָת

we'hig'bal'ta et ha'am sa'viv ley'mor hi'sham'ru la'khem a'lot ba'har un'go'a be'qa'tsey'hu kol ha'no'gey'a ba'har mot yu'mat

and~*you*(ms)~*did*~make~BOUND AT the~PEOPLE ALL-AROUND to~>~SAY !(mp)~be~SAFEGUARD to~you(mp) >~GO-UP in~the~HILL and~>~TOUCH in~EXTREMITY~him ALL the~TOUCH~*ing/er*(ms) in~the~HILL >~DIE he~*will*~be~make~DIE□	and you will make bounds all around the people say{ing}, safeguard your{selves}, go up in the hill*, and touch his extremity, all the {ones} touching the hill will :surely: be [killed],□

19:13 לֹא תִגַּע בּוֹ יָד כִּי סָקוֹל יִסָּקֵל אוֹ יָרֹה יִיָּרֶה אִם בְּהֵמָה אִם אִישׁ לֹא יִחְיֶה בִּמְשֹׁךְ הַיֹּבֵל הֵמָּה יַעֲלוּ בָהָר

lo ti'ga bo yad ki sa'qol yi'sa'qeyl o ya'roh yi'ya'reh im be'hey'mah im ish lo yihh'yeh bim'shokh hai'yo'veyl hey'mah ya'a'lu va'har

NOT she~*will*~TOUCH in~him HAND GIVEN-THAT >~STONE he~*will*~be~STONE OR >~THROW he~*will*~be~THROW IF BEAST IF MAN NOT he~*will*~LIVE in~>~DRAW the~TRUMPET THEY(m) *they*(m)~*will*~GO-UP in~the~HILL□	{the} hand will not touch him, given that he will :surely: be stoned or he will :surely: be thrown, if {it is a} beast, if {it is a} man, he will not live, (with) {the} draw{ing of} the trumpet, they, they will go up in the hill,□

19:14 וַיֵּרֶד מֹשֶׁה מִן הָהָר אֶל הָעָם וַיְקַדֵּשׁ אֶת הָעָם וַיְכַבְּסוּ שִׂמְלֹתָם

wai'yey'red mo'sheh min ha'har el ha'am wai'qa'deysh et ha'am wai'kha'be'su sim'lo'tam

and~he~*will*~GO-DOWN "Mosheh ^{PLUCKED-OUT}" FROM the~HILL TO the~PEOPLE and~he~*will*~much~SET-APART AT the~PEOPLE and~*they*(m)~*will*~much~WASH APPAREL~s~them(m)□	and "Mosheh ^{Plucked out}" went down from the hill to the people, and he set apart the people, and they washed their apparel,□

19:15 וַיֹּאמֶר אֶל הָעָם הֱיוּ נְכֹנִים לִשְׁלֹשֶׁת יָמִים אַל תִּגְּשׁוּ אֶל אִשָּׁה

---

* The passage written as is, is a contradiction. It appears the word אֹל (not) is missing and should read "do not go up in the hill..."

Mechanical Translation Codes

<u>WORD</u> – Verb	WORD – Noun	Word – Name	word – Pre/Suff	*word* – Conj.

wai'yo'mer el ha'am he'yu ne'kho'nim lish'lo'shet ya'mim al tig'shu el i'shah

and~*he~will~*<u>SAY</u> TO the~PEOPLE !(mp)~ <u>EXIST</u> be~<u>PREPARE</u>~ing/er(mp) to~THREE DAY~s <u>DO-NOT</u> you(mp)~*will~*<u>DRAW-NEAR</u> TO WOMAN□

and he said to the people, <be ready> (for) three days, do not draw near to {a} woman,□

19:16　　וַיְהִי בַיּוֹם הַשְּׁלִישִׁי בִּהְיֹת הַבֹּקֶר וַיְהִי קֹלֹת וּבְרָקִים וְעָנָן כָּבֵד עַל הָהָר וְקֹל שֹׁפָר חָזָק מְאֹד וַיֶּחֱרַד כָּל הָעָם אֲשֶׁר בַּמַּחֲנֶה

wai'hi vai'yom hash'li'shi bih'yot ha'bo'qer wai'hi qo'lot uv'ra'qim we'a'nan ka'veyd al ha'har we'qol sho'phar hha'zaq me'od wai'ye'hhe'rad kol ha'am a'sher ba'ma'hha'neh

and~*he~will~*<u>EXIST</u> in~the~DAY the~THIRD in~>~<u>EXIST</u> the~MORNING and~*he~will~* <u>EXIST</u> VOICE~s and~FLASH~ś and~CLOUD HEAVY UPON the~HILL and~VOICE RAM-HORN FORCEFUL MANY and~*he~will~* <u>TREMBLE</u> ALL the~PEOPLE WHICH in~the~ CAMPSITE□

and (it) (came to pass) in the third day, in {the} exist{ing of} the morning, and (it) (came to pass), \thunder/ and flashes and {a} heavy cloud {were} upon the hill, and {the} voice {of the} ram horn {was} (very) forceful, and all the people, which {were} in the campsite, trembled,□

19:17　　וַיּוֹצֵא מֹשֶׁה אֶת הָעָם לִקְרַאת הָאֱלֹהִים מִן הַמַּחֲנֶה וַיִּתְיַצְּבוּ בְּתַחְתִּית הָהָר

wai'yo'tsey mo'sheh et ha'am liq'rat ha'e'lo'him min ha'ma'hha'neh wai'yit'yats'vu be'tahh'tit ha'har

and~*he~will~*make~<u>GO-OUT</u> "Mosheh ᴾᴸᵁᶜᴷᴱᴰ⁻ᴼᵁᵀ„" AT the~PEOPLE to~>~<u>MEET</u> the~ "Elohiym ᴾᴼᵂᴱᴿ~ˢ„" FROM the~CAMPSITE and~ *they(m)~will~be~*make~<u>STAND-UP</u> in~ LOWER-PART the~HILL□

and "Mosheh ᴾˡᵘᶜᵏᵉᵈ ᵒᵘᵗ„" made the people go out from the campsite to meet the "Elohiym ᴾᵒʷᵉʳˢ„", and they were made {to} stand up in {the} lower part {of} the hill,□

19:18　　וְהַר סִינַי עָשַׁן כֻּלּוֹ מִפְּנֵי אֲשֶׁר יָרַד עָלָיו יְהוָה בָּאֵשׁ וַיַּעַל עֲשָׁנוֹ כְּעֶשֶׁן הַכִּבְשָׁן וַיֶּחֱרַד כָּל הָהָר מְאֹד

we'har si'nai a'shan ku'lo mip'ney a'sher ya'rad a'law YHWH ba'eysh wai'ya'al a'sha'no ke'e'shen ha'kiv'shan wai'ye'hhe'rad kol ha'har me'od

and~HILL "Sinai ˢᴴᴬᴿᴾ⁻ᵀᴴᴼᴿᴺ~ˢ~ᵐᵉ„" *he~did~* <u>SMOKE</u> ALL~him from~FACE~s WHICH *he~* *did~*<u>GO-DOWN</u> UPON~him "Yhwh ʰᵉ~ʷⁱˡˡ⁻ᴮᴱ„" in~the~FIRE and~*he~will~*<u>GO-UP</u> SMOKE~ him like~SMOKE the~FURNACE and~*he~* *will~*<u>TREMBLE</u> ALL the~HILL MANY□

and all {of the} hill {of} "Sinai ᴹʸ ˢʰᵃʳᵖ ᵗʰᵒʳⁿˢ„" |had| smoked, all his face*, (because) "Yhwh ᴴᵉ ⁱˢ„" went down upon him in the fire, and his smoke went up like {the} smoke {of} the furnace, and all the hill trembled (greatly),□

19:19　　וַיְהִי קוֹל הַשֹּׁפָר הוֹלֵךְ וְחָזֵק מְאֹד מֹשֶׁה יְדַבֵּר וְהָאֱלֹהִים יַעֲנֶנּוּ בְקוֹל

wai'hi qol ha'sho'phar ho'leykh we'hha'zeyq me'od mo'sheh ye'da'beyr we'ha'e'lo'him

---

* "All his face" means the entire surface.

Revised Mechanical Translation Codes

(..) Alt Trans/App A	<..> Comp Phrase/App B	[..] Verb Form/App C	\../ Plural Form/App D
:..: Int Inf Abs	|..| Past Perf Verb	{...} Added Word	

ya'a'ne'nu ve'qol

and~*he~will*~<u>EXIST</u> VOICE the~RAM-HORN <u>WALK</u>~*ing/er(ms)* and~FORCEFUL MANY "Mosheh ^{PLUCKED-OUT}" *he~will~much~*<u>SPEAK</u> and~the~"Elohiym ^{POWER~s}" *he~will~* <u>ANSWER</u>~him in~VOICE◻	and {the} voice {of} the ram horn (was) walking* and {was} (very) forceful, "Mosheh ^{Plucked out}" will speak and the "Elohiym ^{Powers}" will answer him (with) {the} voice,◻

19:20 נֵיֵרֶד יְהוָה עַל הַר סִינַי אֶל רֹאשׁ הָהָר וַיִּקְרָא יְהוָה לְמֹשֶׁה אֶל רֹאשׁ הָהָר וַיַּעַל מֹשֶׁה

wai'yey'red YHWH al har si'nai el rosh ha'har wai'yiq'ra YHWH le'mo'sheh el rosh ha'har wai'ya'al mo'sheh

and~*he~will*~<u>GO-DOWN</u> "Yhwh ^{he~will~BE}" UPON HILL "Sinai ^{SHARP-THORN~s~me}" TO HEAD the~HILL and~*he~will~*<u>CALL-OUT</u> "Yhwh ^{he~will~BE}" to~"Mosheh ^{PLUCKED-OUT}" TO HEAD the~ HILL and~*he~will~*<u>GO-UP</u> "Mosheh ^{PLUCKED-OUT}"◻	and "Yhwh ^{He is}" went down upon {the} hill {of} "Sinai ^{My sharp thorns}", to {the} head {of} the hill, and "Yhwh ^{He is}" called out to "Mosheh ^{Plucked out}" to {the} head {of} the hill, and "Mosheh ^{Plucked out}" went up,◻

19:21 וַיֹּאמֶר יְהוָה אֶל מֹשֶׁה רֵד הָעֵד בָּעָם פֶּן יֶהֶרְסוּ אֶל יְהוָה לִרְאוֹת וְנָפַל מִמֶּנּוּ רָב

wai'yo'mer YHWH el mo'sheh reyd ha'eyd ba'am pen ye'her'su el YHWH lir'ot we'na'phal mi'me'nu rav

and~*he~will*~<u>SAY</u> "Yhwh ^{he~will~BE}" TO "Mosheh ^{PLUCKED-OUT}" *!(ms)~*<u>GO-DOWN</u> *!(ms)~ make~*<u>WRAP-AROUND</u> in~the~PEOPLE OTHERWISE *they(m)~will~*<u>CAST-DOWN</u> TO "Yhwh ^{he~will~BE}" to~>~<u>SEE</u> and~*he~did~*<u>FALL</u> FROM~him ABUNDANT◻	and "Yhwh ^{He is}" said to "Mosheh ^{Plucked out}", go down, [warn] the people, otherwise, they will cast down† to "Yhwh ^{He is}" to see, and many will fall from him,◻

19:22 וְגַם הַכֹּהֲנִים הַנִּגָּשִׁים אֶל יְהוָה יִתְקַדָּשׁוּ פֶּן יִפְרֹץ בָּהֶם יְהוָה

we'gam ha'ko'ha'nim ha'ni'ga'shim el YHWH yit'qa'da'shu pen yiph'rots ba'hem YHWH

and~ALSO the~ADMINISTRATOR~s the~*be~* <u>DRAW-NEAR</u>~*ing/er(mp)* TO "Yhwh ^{he~will~BE}" *they(m)~be~make~*<u>SET-APART</u> OTHERWISE *he~will~*<u>BREAK-OUT</u> in~ them(m) "Yhwh ^{he~will~BE}"◻	and also the administrators, drawing near to "Yhwh ^{He is}", they will be made set apart, otherwise, "Yhwh ^{He is}" will break out in them,◻

19:23 וַיֹּאמֶר מֹשֶׁה אֶל יְהוָה לֹא יוּכַל הָעָם לַעֲלֹת אֶל הַר סִינַי כִּי אַתָּה הַעֵדֹתָה בָּנוּ לֵאמֹר הַגְבֵּל אֶת הָהָר וְקִדַּשְׁתּוֹ

wai'yo'mer mo'sheh el YHWH lo yu'khal ha'am la'a'lot el har si'nai ki a'tah ha'ey'do'tah

---

* Meaning "sounding."

† "Cast down" probably means to "throw down" the boundary that was to be made (see 19:12).

Mechanical Translation Codes

<u>WORD</u> – Verb	WORD – Noun	Word – Name	word – Pre/Suff	*word* – Conj.

ba'nu ley'mor hag'beyl et ha'har we'qi'dash'to

and~he~will~<u>SAY</u> "Mosheh ^{PLUCKED-OUT}" TO "Yhwh ^{he~will~BE}" NOT he~will~<u>BE-ABLE</u> the~ PEOPLE to~>~<u>GO-UP</u> TO HILL "Sinai ^{SHARP-THORN~s~me}" GIVEN-THAT YOU(ms) you(ms)~ did~make~<u>WRAP-AROUND</u>~^ in~us to~ >~<u>SAY</u> !(ms)~make~<u>BOUND</u> AT the~HILL and~you(ms)~did~much~<u>SET-APART</u>~him□

and "Mosheh ^{Plucked out}" said to "Yhwh ^{He is}", the people will not be able to go up to {the} hill {of} "Sinai ^{My sharp thorns}" given that you, you [warned] us say{ing}, make bound{s} at the hill, and you will set him* apart,□

19:24 וַיֹּאמֶר אֵלָיו יְהוָה לֶךְ רֵד וְעָלִיתָ אַתָּה וְאַהֲרֹן עִמָּךְ וְהַכֹּהֲנִים וְהָעָם אַל יֶהֶרְסוּ לַעֲלֹת אֶל יְהוָה פֶּן יִפְרָץ בָּם

wai'yo'mer ey'law YHWH lekh reyd we'a'li'ta a'tah we'a'ha'ron i'makh we'ha'ko'ha'nim we'ha'am al ye'her'su la'a'lot el YHWH pen yiph'rats bam

and~he~will~<u>SAY</u> TO~him "Yhwh ^{he~will~BE}" !(ms)~<u>WALK</u> !(ms)~<u>GO-DOWN</u> and~ you(ms)~did~<u>GO-UP</u> YOU(ms) and~"Aharon ^{LIGHT-BRINGER}" WITH~you(fs) and~the~ ADMINISTRATOR~s and~the~PEOPLE DO-NOT they(m)~will~<u>CAST-DOWN</u> to~>~<u>GO-UP</u> TO "Yhwh ^{he~will~BE}" OTHERWISE he~will~ <u>BREAK-OUT</u> in~them(m)□

and "Yhwh ^{He is}" said to him, walk, go down, and you will go up, you and "Aharon ^{Light bringer}" with you, and the administrators, and do not {let} the people cast down† to go up to "Yhwh ^{He is}", otherwise he will break out (with) them,□

19:25 וַיֵּרֶד מֹשֶׁה אֶל הָעָם וַיֹּאמֶר אֲלֵהֶם

wai'yey'red mo'sheh el ha'am wai'yo'mer a'ley'hem

and~he~will~<u>GO-DOWN</u> "Mosheh ^{PLUCKED-OUT}" TO the~PEOPLE and~he~will~<u>SAY</u> TO~ them(m)□

and "Mosheh ^{Plucked out}" went down to the people and he said to them‡,□

Chapter 20

20:1 וַיְדַבֵּר אֱלֹהִים אֵת כָּל הַדְּבָרִים הָאֵלֶּה לֵאמֹר

wai'da'beyr e'lo'him eyt kol had'va'rim ha'ey'leh ley'mor

and~he~will~much~<u>SPEAK</u> "Elohiym ^{POWER~s}" AT ALL the~WORD~s the~THESE to~>~<u>SAY</u>□

and "Elohiym ^{Powers}" spoke all these words say{ing},□

---

* Referring to the "hill," a masculine word in Hebrew.
† "Cast down" probably means to "throw down" the boundary that was to be made (see 19:12).
‡ The text appears to be missing what Mosheh said to the people.

Revised Mechanical Translation Codes

(..) Alt Trans/App A	<..> Comp Phrase/App B	[..] Verb Form/App C	\../ Plural Form/App D
:..: Int Inf Abs	|..| Past Perf Verb	{...} Added Word	

20:2

אָנֹכִי יְהוָה אֱלֹהֶיךָ אֲשֶׁר הוֹצֵאתִיךָ מֵאֶרֶץ מִצְרַיִם מִבֵּית עֲבָדִים

a'no'khi YHWH e'lo'hey'kha a'sher ho'tsey'ti'kha mey'e'rets mits'ra'yim mi'beyt a'va'dim

I "Yhwh *he~will~*<u>BE</u>" "Elohiym ^{POWER~s}"~you(ms) WHICH *I~did~make~*<u>GO-OUT</u>~you(ms) from~LAND "Mits'rayim ^{STRAIT~s2}" from~ HOUSE SERVANT~s□

I {am} "Yhwh ^{He is}" your "Elohiym ^{Powers}", who made you go out from {the} land {of} "Mits'rayim ^{Two straits}", from {the} house {of} servants,□

20:3

לֹא יִהְיֶה לְךָ אֱלֹהִים אֲחֵרִים עַל פָּנָי

lo yih'yeh le'kha e'lo'him a'hhey'rim al pa'nai

NOT *he~will~*<u>EXIST</u> to~you(ms) "Elohiym ^{POWER~s}" OTHER~s UPON FACE~s~me□

other "Elohiym ^{Powers}" will not exist (for) you upon my face*,□

20:4

לֹא תַעֲשֶׂה לְךָ פֶסֶל וְכָל תְּמוּנָה אֲשֶׁר בַּשָּׁמַיִם מִמַּעַל וַאֲשֶׁר בָּאָרֶץ מִתַּחַת וַאֲשֶׁר בַּמַּיִם מִתַּחַת לָאָרֶץ

lo ta'a'seh le'kha phe'sel we'khol te'mu'nah a'sher ba'sha'ma'ma'yim mi'ma'al wa'a'sher ba'a'rets mi'ta'hhat wa'a'sher ba'ma'yim mi'ta'hhat la'a'rets

NOT *you(ms)~will~*<u>DO</u> to~you(ms) SCULPTURE and~ALL RESEMBLANCE WHICH in~the~SKY~s2 from~UPWARD and~WHICH in~the~LAND from~UNDER and~WHICH in~ the~WATER~s2 from~UNDER to~the~ LAND□

you will not (make) (for) you {a} sculpture and (any) resemblance which {is} in the skies <above>, and which {is} in the land <below>, and which {is} in the waters <below> the land,□

20:5

לֹא תִשְׁתַּחֲוֶה לָהֶם וְלֹא תָעָבְדֵם כִּי אָנֹכִי יְהוָה אֱלֹהֶיךָ אֵל קַנָּא פֹּקֵד עֲוֹן אָבֹת עַל בָּנִים עַל שִׁלֵּשִׁים וְעַל רִבֵּעִים לְשֹׂנְאָי

lo tish'ta'hha'weh la'hem we'lo ta'av'deym ki a'no'khi YHWH e'lo'hey'kha eyl qa'na po'qeyd a'won a'vot al ba'nim al shi'ley'shim we'al ri'bey'im le'shon'ai

NOT *you(ms)~will~* self~<u>BEND-DOWN</u> to~ them(m) and~NOT *you(ms)~will~be~make~* <u>SERVE</u>~them(m) GIVEN-THAT I "Yhwh *he~will~* <u>BE</u>" "Elohiym ^{POWER~s}"~you(ms) MIGHTY-ONE ZEALOUS <u>REGISTER</u>~*ing/er(ms)* INIQUITY FATHER~s UPON SON~s UPON THIRD-GENERATION~s and~UPON FOURTH-GENERATION~s to~<u>HATE</u>~*ing/er(mp)*~me□

you will not bend {your}self down to them, and you will not be made {to} serve them, given that I {am} "Yhwh ^{He is}" your "Elohiym ^{Powers}", {the} mighty one {of} zealous{ness}, registering {the} iniquity {of the} fathers upon {the} sons, upon {the} third generation, and upon {the} fourth generation, to {the one}s hating me,□

20:6

וְעֹשֶׂה חֶסֶד לַאֲלָפִים לְאֹהֲבַי וּלְשֹׁמְרֵי מִצְוֹתָי

we'o'seh hhe'sed la'a'la'phim le'o'ha'vai ul'shom'rey mits'otai

and~<u>DO</u>~*ing/er(ms)* KINDNESS to~the~ THOUSAND~s to~<u>LOVE</u>~*ing/er(mp)*~me and~ to~<u>SAFEGUARD</u>~*ing/er(mp)* DIRECTIVE~s~

and doing kindness to the thousands, to {the one}s loving me, and to {the one}s safeguarding my directives,□

---

* "Upon my face" means "in my presence."

Mechanical Translation Codes

| <u>WORD</u> – Verb | WORD – Noun | Word – Name | word – Pre/Suff | *word – Conj.* |

me□

20:7

לֹא תִשָּׂא אֶת שֵׁם יְהוָה אֱלֹהֶיךָ לַשָּׁוְא כִּי לֹא יְנַקֶּה יְהוָה אֵת אֲשֶׁר יִשָּׂא אֶת שְׁמוֹ לַשָּׁוְא

lo ti'sa et sheym YHWH e'lo'hey'kha la'sha'we ki lo ye'na'qeh YHWH eyt a'sher yi'sa et she'mo la'sha'we

NOT you(ms)~will~<u>LIFT-UP</u> AT TITLE "Yhwh ^{he~will~}<u>BE</u>" "Elohiym ^{POWER~s}~you(ms) to~the~ FALSENESS GIVEN-THAT NOT he~will~much~ <u>ACQUIT</u> "Yhwh ^{he~will~}<u>BE</u>" AT WHICH he~will~ <u>LIFT-UP</u> AT TITLE~him to~the~FALSENESS□

you will not lift up {the} title {of} "Yhwh ^{He is}" your "Elohiym ^{Powers}" (for) the falseness, given that "Yhwh ^{He is}" will not acquit {one} (who) will lift up his title (for) the falseness,□

20:8

זָכוֹר אֶת יוֹם הַשַּׁבָּת לְקַדְּשׁוֹ

za'khor et yom ha'sha'bat le'qad'sho

>~<u>REMEMBER</u> AT DAY the~CEASING to~ >~much~<u>SET-APART</u>~him□

remember {the} day {of} ceasing, to set him* apart,□

20:9

שֵׁשֶׁת יָמִים תַּעֲבֹד וְעָשִׂיתָ כָּל מְלַאכְתֶּךָ

shey'shet ya'mim ta'a'vod we'a'si'ta kol me'lakh'te'kha

SIX DAY~s you(ms)~will~<u>SERVE</u> and~ you(ms)~did~<u>DO</u> ALL BUSINESS~you(ms)□

six days you will serve, and you will do all your business,□

20:10

וְיוֹם הַשְּׁבִיעִי שַׁבָּת לַיהוָה אֱלֹהֶיךָ לֹא תַעֲשֶׂה כָל מְלָאכָה אַתָּה וּבִנְךָ וּבִתֶּךָ עַבְדְּךָ וַאֲמָתְךָ וּבְהֶמְתֶּךָ וְגֵרְךָ אֲשֶׁר בִּשְׁעָרֶיךָ

we'yom hash'vi'i sha'bat la'YHWH e'lo'hey'kha lo ta'a'seh khol me'la'khah a'tah u'vin'kha u'vi'te'kha av'de'kha wa'a'mat'kha uv'hem'te'kha we'ger'kha a'sher bish'a'rey'kha

and~DAY the~SEVENTH CEASING to~"Yhwh ^{he~will~}<u>BE</u>" "Elohiym ^{POWER~s}~you(ms) NOT you(ms)~will~<u>DO</u> ALL BUSINESS YOU(ms) and~SON~you(ms) and~DAUGHTER~ you(ms) SERVANT~you(ms) and~ BONDWOMAN~you(ms) and~BEAST~ you(ms) and~STRANGER~you(ms) WHICH in~GATE~s~you(ms)□

and the seventh day {is a} ceasing to "Yhwh ^{He is}" your "Elohiym ^{Powers}", you will not do (any) business, you and your son and your daughter, your servant and your bondwoman, and your beast, and your stranger which {is} in your gates,□

20:11

כִּי שֵׁשֶׁת יָמִים עָשָׂה יְהוָה אֶת הַשָּׁמַיִם וְאֶת הָאָרֶץ אֶת הַיָּם וְאֶת כָּל אֲשֶׁר בָּם וַיָּנַח בַּיּוֹם הַשְּׁבִיעִי עַל כֵּן בֵּרַךְ יְהוָה אֶת יוֹם הַשַּׁבָּת וַיְקַדְּשֵׁהוּ

ki shey'shet ya'mim a'sah YHWH et ha'sha'ma'yim we'et ha'a'rets et hai'yam we'et kol a'sher bam wai'ya'nahh ba'yom hash'vi'i al keyn bey'rakh YHWH et yom ha'sha'bat

---

* Referring to the "day," a masculine word in Hebrew.

Revised Mechanical Translation Codes

(..) Alt Trans/App A   <..> Comp Phrase/App B   [..] Verb Form/App C   \..\ Plural Form/App D

:..: Int Inf Abs |..| Past Perf Verb   {...} Added Word

wai'qad'shey'hu

GIVEN-THAT SIX DAY~s he~did~<u>DO</u> "Yhwh ^{he~}^{will~BE}" AT the~SKY~s2 and~AT the~LAND AT the~SEA and~AT ALL WHICH in~them(m) and~he~will~<u>REST</u> in~the~DAY the~ SEVENTH UPON SO he~did~much~<u>KNEEL</u> "Yhwh ^{he~will~BE}" AT DAY the~CEASING and~ he~will~much~<u>SET-APART</u>~him□

given that six days "Yhwh ^{He is}" (made) the skies and the land, the sea and all which {is} in them, and he rested in the seventh day, <therefore>, "Yhwh ^{He is}" [respected] {the} day {of} the ceasing, and he set him* apart,□

20:12 כַּבֵּד אֶת אָבִיךָ וְאֶת אִמֶּךָ לְמַעַן יַאֲרִכוּן יָמֶיךָ עַל הָאֲדָמָה אֲשֶׁר יְהוָה אֱלֹהֶיךָ נֹתֵן לָךְ

ka'beyd et a'vi'kha we'et i'me'kha le'ma'an ya'a'ri'khun ya'mey'kha al ha'a'da'mah a'sher YHWH e'lo'hey'kha no'teyn lakh

!(ms)~much~<u>BE-HEAVY</u> AT FATHER~you(ms) and~AT MOTHER~you(ms) to~THAT they(m)~will~make~<u>PROLONG</u>~must DAY~s~ you(ms) UPON the~GROUND WHICH "Yhwh ^{he~will~BE}" "Elohiym ^{POWER~s}"~you(ms) <u>GIVE</u>~ ing/er(ms) to~you(fs)□

[honor] your father and your mother (so) that your days will {be} made long upon the ground which "Yhwh ^{He is}" your "Elohiym ^{Powers}" {is} giving to you,□

20:13 לֹא תִרְצָח

lo tir'tsahh

NOT you(ms)~will~<u>MURDER</u>□

you will not murder,□

20:14 לֹא תִנְאָף

lo tin'aph

NOT you(ms)~will~<u>COMMIT-ADULTERY</u>□

you will not commit adultery,□

20:15 לֹא תִגְנֹב

lo tig'nov

NOT you(ms)~will~<u>STEAL</u>□

you will not steal,□

20:16 לֹא תַעֲנֶה בְרֵעֲךָ עֵד שָׁקֶר

lo ta'a'neh ve'rey'a'kha eyd sha'qer

NOT you(ms)~will~<u>AFFLICT</u> in~COMPANION~ you(ms) WITNESS FALSE□

you will not afflict your companion (with) {a} witness {of} false{ness},□

20:17 לֹא תַחְמֹד בֵּית רֵעֶךָ לֹא תַחְמֹד אֵשֶׁת רֵעֶךָ וְעַבְדּוֹ וַאֲמָתוֹ וְשׁוֹרוֹ וַחֲמֹרוֹ וְכֹל אֲשֶׁר לְרֵעֶךָ

---

* Referring to the "day," a masculine word in Hebrew.

Mechanical Translation Codes

<u>WORD</u> – Verb	WORD – Noun	Word – Name	word – Pre/Suff	*word* – Conj.

lo tahh'mod beyt rey'e'kha lo tahh'mod ey'shet rey'e'kha we'av'do wa'a'ma'to we'sho'ro
wa'hha'mo'ro we'khol a'sher le'rey'e'kha

NOT *you(ms)~will~*<u>CRAVE</u> HOUSE COMPANION~*you(ms)* NOT *you(ms)~will~* <u>CRAVE</u> WOMAN COMPANION~*you(ms)* and~ SERVANT~him and~BONDWOMAN~him and~OX~him and~DONKEY~him and~ALL WHICH to~COMPANION~*you(ms)*◻	you will not crave {the} house {of} your companion, you will not crave {the} woman {of} your companion, and his servant, and his bondwoman, and his ox, and his donkey, and all which {belongs} to your companion,◻

20:18 וְכָל הָעָם רֹאִים אֶת הַקּוֹלֹת וְאֶת הַלַּפִּידִם וְאֵת קוֹל הַשֹּׁפָר וְאֶת הָהָר עָשֵׁן וַיַּרְא הָעָם וַיָּנֻעוּ וַיַּעַמְדוּ מֵרָחֹק

we'khol ha'am ro'im et ha'qo'lot we'et ha'la'pi'dim we'eyt qol ha'sho'phar we'et ha'har
a'sheyn wai'yar ha'am wai'ya'nu'u wai'ya'am'du mey'ra'hhoq

and~ALL the~PEOPLE <u>SEE</u>~*ing/er(mp)* AT the~VOICE~s and~AT the~TORCH~s and~AT VOICE the~RAM-HORN and~AT the~HILL SMOKE and~*he~will~*<u>SEE</u> the~PEOPLE and~ *they(m)~will~*<u>STAGGER</u> and~*they(m)~will~* <u>STAND</u> from~DISTANCE◻	and all the people {were} seeing the \thunder/ and the torches and {the} voice {of} the ram horn and the hill {of} smoke, and the people saw, and staggered, and they stood from {a} distance,◻

20:19 וַיֹּאמְרוּ אֶל מֹשֶׁה דַּבֵּר אַתָּה עִמָּנוּ וְנִשְׁמָעָה וְאַל יְדַבֵּר עִמָּנוּ אֱלֹהִים פֶּן נָמוּת

wai'yom'ru el mo'sheh da'beyr a'tah i'ma'nu we'nish'ma'ah we'al ye'da'beyr i'ma'nu
e'lo'him pen na'mut

and~*they(m)~will~*<u>SAY</u> TO "Mosheh ^{PLUCKED-OUT}" !*(ms)~much~*<u>SPEAK</u> YOU(ms) WITH~us and~*we~will~*<u>HEAR</u>~^ and~DO-NOT *he~will~* *much~*<u>SPEAK</u> WITH~us "Elohiym ^{POWER~s}" OTHERWISE *we~will~*<u>DIE</u>◻	and they said to "Mosheh ^{Plucked out}", you {will} speak with us and we will hear, and do not {let} "Elohiym ^{Powers}" speak with us, otherwise we will die,◻

20:20 וַיֹּאמֶר מֹשֶׁה אֶל הָעָם אַל תִּירָאוּ כִּי לְבַעֲבוּר נַסּוֹת אֶתְכֶם בָּא הָאֱלֹהִים וּבַעֲבוּר תִּהְיֶה יִרְאָתוֹ עַל פְּנֵיכֶם לְבִלְתִּי תֶחֱטָאוּ

wai'yo'mer mo'sheh el ha'am al ti'ra'u ki le'va'a'vur na'sot et'khem ba ha'e'lo'him
u'va'a'vur tih'yeh yir'a'to al pe'ney'khem le'vil'ti te'hhe'ta'u

and~*he~will~*<u>SAY</u> "Mosheh ^{PLUCKED-OUT}" TO the~PEOPLE DO-NOT *you(mp)~will~*<u>FEAR</u> GIVEN-THAT to~in~INTENTION >~*much~* <u>TEST</u> AT~*you(mp)* *he~did~*<u>COME</u> the~ "Elohiym ^{POWER~s}" and~in~INTENTION *she~ will~*<u>EXIST</u> FEARFULNESS~him UPON FACE~s~*you(mp)* to~EXCEPT *you(mp)~will~* <u>ERR</u>◻	and "Mosheh ^{Plucked out}" said to the people, do not fear, given that "Elohiym ^{Powers}" came (with) {the} intention to test you, and (with) {the} intention {that} his fearfulness will exist upon your faces (so) you will (not) err,◻

Revised Mechanical Translation Codes

(..) Alt Trans/App A	<..> Comp Phrase/App B	[..] Verb Form/App C	\../ Plural Form/App D
:..: Int Inf Abs	|..| Past Perf Verb	{...} Added Word	

20:21 וַיַּעֲמֹד הָעָם מֵרָחֹק וּמֹשֶׁה נִגַּשׁ אֶל הָעֲרָפֶל אֲשֶׁר שָׁם הָאֱלֹהִים

wai'ya'a'mod ha'am mey'ra'hhoq u'mo'sheh ni'gash el ha'a'ra'phel a'sher sham ha'e'lo'him

and~*he*~*will*~<u>STAND</u> the~PEOPLE from~ DISTANCE and~"Mosheh ^{PLUCKED-OUT}" *he*~*did*~ *be*~<u>DRAW-NEAR</u> TO the~THICK-DARKNESS WHICH THERE the~"Elohiym ^{POWER~s}"□

and the people stood from a distance, and "Mosheh ^{Plucked out}" |had| been drawn near to the thick darkness which there, {is} the "Elohiym ^{Powers}",□

20:22 וַיֹּאמֶר יְהוָה אֶל מֹשֶׁה כֹּה תֹאמַר אֶל בְּנֵי יִשְׂרָאֵל אַתֶּם רְאִיתֶם כִּי מִן הַשָּׁמַיִם דִּבַּרְתִּי עִמָּכֶם

wai'yo'mer YHWH el mo'sheh koh to'mar el be'ney yis'ra'eyl a'tem re'i'tem ki min ha'sha'ma'yim di'bar'ti i'ma'khem

and~*he*~*will*~<u>SAY</u> "Yhwh ^{*he*~*will*~<u>BE</u>}" TO "Mosheh ^{PLUCKED-OUT}" IN-THIS-WAY *you(ms)*~ *will*~<u>SAY</u> TO SON~s "Yisra'el ^{*he*~*will*~<u>TURN-ASIDE</u>~+~MIGHTY-ONE}" YOU(mp) *you(mp)*~*did*~<u>SEE</u> GIVEN-THAT FROM the~SKY~s2 *I*~*did*~*much*~ <u>SPEAK</u> WITH~*you(mp)*□

and "Yhwh ^{He is}" said to "Mosheh ^{Plucked out}", in this way you will say to {the} sons {of} "Yisra'el ^{He turns El aside}", you saw that I spoke with you from the skies,□

20:23 לֹא תַעֲשׂוּן אִתִּי אֱלֹהֵי כֶסֶף וֵאלֹהֵי זָהָב לֹא תַעֲשׂוּ לָכֶם

lo ta'a'sun i'ti e'lo'hey ke'seph wey'lo'hey za'hav lo ta'a'su la'khem

NOT *you(ms)*~*will*~<u>DO</u>~must AT~me "Elohiym ^{POWER~s}" SILVER and~"Elohiym ^{POWER~s}" GOLD NOT *you(mp)*~*will*~<u>DO</u> to~ *you(mp)*□

you must not (make) me {a} "Elohiym ^{Powers}" {of} silver and {a} "Elohiym ^{Powers}" {of} gold, you will not (make) {them} (for) your{selves},□

20:24 מִזְבַּח אֲדָמָה תַּעֲשֶׂה לִּי וְזָבַחְתָּ עָלָיו אֶת עֹלֹתֶיךָ וְאֶת שְׁלָמֶיךָ אֶת צֹאנְךָ וְאֶת בְּקָרֶךָ בְּכָל הַמָּקוֹם אֲשֶׁר אַזְכִּיר אֶת שְׁמִי אָבוֹא אֵלֶיךָ וּבֵרַכְתִּיךָ

miz'bahh a'da'mah ta'a'seh li we'za'vahh'ta a'law et o'lo'tey'kha we'et she'la'mey'kha et tson'kha we'et be'qa're'kha be'khol ha'ma'qom a'sher az'kir et she'mi a'vo ey'ley'kha u'vey'rakh'ti'kha

ALTAR GROUND *you(ms)*~*will*~<u>DO</u> to~me and~*you(ms)*~*did*~<u>SACRIFICE</u> UPON~him AT RISING~s~*you(ms)* and~AT COMPLETE~s~ *you(ms)* AT FLOCKS~*you(ms)* and~AT CATTLE~*you(ms)* in~ALL the~AREA WHICH *I*~ *will*~*make*~<u>REMEMBER</u> AT TITLE~me *I*~*will*~ <u>COME</u> TO~*you(ms)* and~*I*~*did*~*much*~ <u>KNEEL</u>~*you(ms)*□

you will (make) {an} altar {of} ground (for) me, and you will sacrifice upon him your rising {sacrifice}s and your complete {sacrifice}s, your flocks and your cattle, in all the area (where) I will make my title remembered, I will come to you and I will [respect] you,□

20:25 וְאִם מִזְבַּח אֲבָנִים תַּעֲשֶׂה לִּי לֹא תִבְנֶה אֶתְהֶן גָּזִית כִּי חַרְבְּךָ הֵנַפְתָּ עָלֶיהָ וַתְּחַלְלֶהָ

Mechanical Translation Codes

<u>WORD</u> – Verb	WORD – Noun	Word – Name	word – Pre/Suff	*word* – Conj.

we'im miz'bahh a'va'nim ta'a'seh li lo tiv'neh et'hen ga'zit ki hhar'be'kha hey'naph'ta a'ley'ah wat'hhal'le'le'ah

and~IF ALTAR STONE~s *you(ms)~will~*<u>DO</u> to~ me NOT *you(ms)~will~*<u>BUILD</u> AT~them(f) HEWN-STONE GIVEN-THAT SWORD~you(ms) *you(ms)~did~make~*<u>WAVE</u> UPON~her and~ *you(ms)~will~much~*<u>PIERCE</u>~her□	and if you will (make) {an} altar {of} stones, you will not build them {of} hewn stone, given that you waved your sword* upon her†, and you (made) her [common],□

20:26　　וְלֹא תַעֲלֶה בְמַעֲלֹת עַל מִזְבְּחִי אֲשֶׁר לֹא תִגָּלֶה עֶרְוָתְךָ עָלָיו

we'lo ta'a'leh ve'ma'a'lot al miz'be'hhi a'sher lo ti'ga'leh er'wat'kha a'law

and~NOT *you(ms)~will~*<u>GO-UP</u> in~STEP~s UPON ALTAR~me WHICH NOT *you(ms)~will~* *be~*<u>REMOVE-THE-COVER</u> NAKEDNESS~ you(ms) UPON~him□	and you will not go up (with) steps upon my altar, (because) you will not [uncover] your nakedness upon him‡,□

Chapter 21

21:1　　וְאֵלֶּה הַמִּשְׁפָּטִים אֲשֶׁר תָּשִׂים לִפְנֵיהֶם

we'ey'leh ha'mish'pa'tim a'sher ta'sim liph'ney'hem

and~THESE the~DECISION~s WHICH *you(ms)~will~*<u>PLACE</u> to~FACE~s~them(m)□	and these {are} the decisions which you will place <in front of> them,□

21:2　　כִּי תִקְנֶה עֶבֶד עִבְרִי שֵׁשׁ שָׁנִים יַעֲבֹד וּבַשְּׁבִעַת יֵצֵא לַחָפְשִׁי חִנָּם

ki tiq'neh e'ved iv'ri sheysh sha'nim ya'a'vod u'vash'bi'it yey'tsey la'hhaph'shi hhi'nam

GIVEN-THAT *you(ms)~will~*<u>PURCHASE</u> SERVANT "Ever ^{OTHER-SIDE}"~of SIX YEAR~s *he~* *will~*<u>SERVE</u> and~in~the~SEVENTH *he~will~* <u>GO-OUT</u> to~FREE FREELY□	if you will purchase {a} servant of "Ever ^{Other side}", he will serve six years, and in the seventh he will go out freely to free{dom},□

21:3　　אִם בְּגַפּוֹ יָבֹא בְּגַפּוֹ יֵצֵא אִם בַּעַל אִשָּׁה הוּא וְיָצְאָה אִשְׁתּוֹ עִמּוֹ

im be'ga'po ya'vo be'ga'po yey'tsey im ba'al i'shah hu we'yats'ah ish'to i'mo

IF in~ARCH~him *he~will~*<u>COME</u> in~ARCH~ him *he~will~*<u>GO-OUT</u> IF MASTER WOMAN HE and~ *she~did~*<u>GO-OUT</u> WOMAN~him WITH~him□	if he comes (by) <himself>, he will go out (by) <himself>, if he {is the} master {of a} woman, (then) his woman will go out with him,□

---

* Probably meaning any sharp instrument used for shaping stone.
† Referring to the "hewn stone," a feminine word in Hebrew.
‡ Referring to the "altar," a masculine word in Hebrew.

Revised Mechanical Translation Codes

(..) Alt Trans/App A	<..> Comp Phrase/App B	[..] Verb Form/App C	\../ Plural Form/App D
:..: Int Inf Abs	|..| Past Perf Verb	{...} Added Word	

21:4 אִם אֲדֹנָיו יִתֶּן לוֹ אִשָּׁה וְיָלְדָה לוֹ בָנִים אוֹ בָנוֹת הָאִשָּׁה וִילָדֶיהָ תִּהְיֶה לַאדֹנֶיהָ וְהוּא יֵצֵא בְגַפּוֹ

im a'do'naw yi'ten lo i'shah we'yal'dah lo va'nim o va'not ha'i'shah wi'la'dey'ah tih'yeh la'do'ney'ah we'hu yey'tsey ve'ga'po

IF LORD~s~him *he~will*~<u>GIVE</u> to~him WOMAN and~ *she~did*~<u>BRING-FORTH</u> to~ him SON~s OR DAUGHTER~s the~WOMAN and~BOY~s~her *she~will*~<u>EXIST</u> to~LORD~s~ her and~HE *he~will*~<u>GO-OUT</u> in~ARCH~ him□

if his lord will give him {a} woman, and she will bring forth (for) him sons or daughters, the woman and her boys* will exist (for) her lord, and he, he will go out (by) <himself>,□

21:5 וְאִם אָמֹר יֹאמַר הָעֶבֶד אָהַבְתִּי אֶת אֲדֹנִי אֶת אִשְׁתִּי וְאֶת בָּנַי לֹא אֵצֵא חָפְשִׁי

we'im a'mor yo'mar ha'e'ved a'hav'ti et a'do'ni et ish'ti we'et ba'nai lo ey'tsey hhaph'shi

and~IF >~<u>SAY</u> *he~will*~<u>SAY</u> the~SERVANT *I~ did*~<u>LOVE</u> AT LORD~me AT WOMAN~me and~AT SON~s~me NOT *I~will*~<u>GO-OUT</u> FREE□

(but) if the servant will say, I love my lord, my woman and my sons, I will not go out free,□

21:6 וְהִגִּישׁוֹ אֲדֹנָיו אֶל הָאֱלֹהִים וְהִגִּישׁוֹ אֶל הַדֶּלֶת אוֹ אֶל הַמְּזוּזָה וְרָצַע אֲדֹנָיו אֶת אָזְנוֹ בַּמַּרְצֵעַ וַעֲבָדוֹ לְעֹלָם

we'hi'gi'sho a'do'naw el ha'e'lo'him we'hi'gi'sho el ha'de'let o el ham'zu'zah we'ra'tsa a'do'naw et az'no ba'mar'tsey'a wa'a'vad'o le'o'lam

and~*he~did~make*~<u>DRAW-NEAR</u>~him LORD~s~him TO the~"Elohiym POWER~s" and~ *he~did~make*~<u>DRAW-NEAR</u>~him TO the~ DOOR OR TO the~DOORPOST and~*he~did*~ <u>BORE-THROUGH</u> LORD~s~him AT EAR~him in~the~AWL and~*he~did*~<u>SERVE</u>~him to~ DISTANT□

(then) his lord will make him draw near to the "Elohiym Powers"†, and he will make him draw near to the door, or to the doorpost, and his lord will bore through his ear (with) the awl and he will serve him to a distant {time},□

21:7 וְכִי יִמְכֹּר אִישׁ אֶת בִּתּוֹ לְאָמָה לֹא תֵצֵא כְּצֵאת הָעֲבָדִים

we'khi yim'kor ish et bi'to le'a'mah lo tey'tsey ke'tseyt ha'a'va'dim

and~GIVEN-THAT *he~will*~<u>SELL</u> MAN AT DAUGHTER~him to~BONDWOMAN NOT *she~will*~<u>GO-OUT</u> like~>~<u>GO-OUT</u> the~ SERVANT~s□

and (if) {a} man will sell his daughter (as) {a} bondwoman, she will not go out like {the} go{ing} out {of} the servants,□

---

* The masculine plural suffix (ים) may be used for a group of males or males and females. In the context of this verse, the word "boys" refers to the children, the sons and daughter.

† The word Elohiym may refer to the judges, but the Hebrew word for judges is usually שׁוֹפְטִים (shoftim).

Mechanical Translation Codes

<u>WORD</u> – Verb	WORD – Noun	Word – Name	word – Pre/Suff	*word* – Conj.

21:8

אִם רָעָה בְּעֵינֵי אֲדֹנֶיהָ אֲשֶׁר לֹא יְעָדָהּ וְהֶפְדָּהּ לְעַם נָכְרִי לֹא יִמְשֹׁל לְמָכְרָהּ בְּבִגְדוֹ בָהּ

im ra'ah be'ey'ney a'do'ney'ah a'sher lo ye'a'dah we'heph'dah le'am nakh'ri lo yim'shol le'makh'rah be'vig'do vah

IF DYSFUNCTIONAL in~EYE~s2 LORD~s~her WHICH NOT *he~did*~APPOINT~her and~*he~ did~make*~RANSOM~her to~PEOPLE FOREIGN NOT *he~will*~REGULATE to~ >~SELL~her in~>~ACT-TREACHEROUSLY~him in~her□

if {she is} dysfunctional in {the} eyes {of} her lord, which he did not appoint*, (then) he will ransom her, he will not regulate† to sell her in his treacherous act (with) her,□

21:9

וְאִם לִבְנוֹ יִיעָדֶנָּה כְּמִשְׁפַּט הַבָּנוֹת יַעֲשֶׂה לָּהּ

we'im liv'no yi'a'de'nah ke'mish'pat ha'ba'not ya'a'seh lah

and~IF to~SON~him *he~will*~APPOINT~her like~DECISION the~DAUGHTER~s *he~will*~ DO to~her□

and if he will appoint her to his son, he will do to her {just} like {the} decision‡ {of} the daughters,□

21:10

אִם אַחֶרֶת יִקַּח לוֹ שְׁאֵרָהּ כְּסוּתָהּ וְעֹנָתָהּ לֹא יִגְרָע

im a'hhe'ret yi'qahh lo she'ey'rah ke'su'tah we'o'na'tah lo yig'ra

IF OTHER *he~will*~TAKE to~him REMAINS~ her RAIMENT~her and~HABITATION~her NOT *he~will*~TAKE-AWAY□

if he will take {an}other, he will not take away her remains§, her raiment and her habitation,□

21:11

וְאִם שְׁלָשׁ אֵלֶּה לֹא יַעֲשֶׂה לָהּ וְיָצְאָה חִנָּם אֵין כָּסֶף

we'im she'lash ey'leh lo ya'a'seh lah we'yats'ah hhi'nam eyn ka'seph

and~IF THREE THESE NOT *he~will*~DO to~her and~ *she~did*~GO-OUT FREELY WITHOUT SILVER□

and if he will not do these three to her, (then) she will go out freely without silver,□

21:12

מַכֵּה אִישׁ וָמֵת מוֹת יוּמָת

ma'keyh ish wa'meyt mot yu'mat

make~HIT~*ing/er(ms)* MAN and~*he~did*~DIE >~DIE *he~will~be~make*~DIE□

{anyone} hitting {a} man, and dies, he will be [killed],□

---

* The Hebrew word לֹא (pronounced "lo" and meaning "no") in the phrase, "which he did not appoint," may be written defectively for לוֹ (also pronounced "lo," but meaning "to himself") and would then be translated as "who appointed her to himself."
† That is to "rule" or "decide."
‡ Or "manner."
§ Probably referring to her relatives.

Revised Mechanical Translation Codes
(..) Alt Trans/App A   <..> Comp Phrase/App B   [..] Verb Form/App C   \../ Plural Form/App D
:..: Int Inf Abs |..| Past Perf Verb   {...} Added Word

21:13 וַאֲשֶׁר לֹא צָדָה וְהָאֱלֹהִים אִנָּה לְיָדוֹ וְשַׂמְתִּי לְךָ מָקוֹם אֲשֶׁר יָנוּס שָׁמָּה

wa'a'sher lo tsa'dah we'ha'e'lo'him i'nah le'ya'do we'sam'ti le'kha ma'qom a'sher ya'nus sham'mah

and~WHICH NOT he~did~LAY-IN-WAIT and~ the~"Elohiym ᴾᴼᵂᴱᴿˢ" he~did~much~ APPROACH to~HAND~him and~I~did~PLACE to~you(ms) AREA WHICH he~will~FLEE THERE~unto□

and (when) he did not lay in wait, and the "Elohiym ᴾᵒʷᵉʳˢ"* [delivers] {him} to his hand, (then) I will place {an} area (for) you (where) he will flee unto,□

21:14 וְכִי יָזִד אִישׁ עַל רֵעֵהוּ לְהָרְגוֹ בְעָרְמָה מֵעִם מִזְבְּחִי תִּקָּחֶנּוּ לָמוּת

we'khi ya'zid ish al rey'ey'hu le'har'go ve'ar'mah mey'im miz'be'hhi ti'qa'hhe'nu la'mut

and~GIVEN-THAT he~will~make~SIMMER MAN UPON COMPANION~him to~>~KILL~ him in~SUBTLETY from~WITH ALTAR~me you(ms)~will~TAKE~him to~>~DIE□

and (if) {a} man simmers† upon his companion to kill him (with) subtlety, you will take him from my altar to die,□

21:15 וּמַכֵּה אָבִיו וְאִמּוֹ מוֹת יוּמָת

u'ma'keyh a'viw we'i'mo mot yu'mat

and~make~HIT~ing/er(ms) FATHER~him and~MOTHER~him >~DIE he~will~be~make~ DIE□

and {anyone} hitting his father (or) his mother, will :surely: be [killed],□

21:16 וְגֹנֵב אִישׁ וּמְכָרוֹ וְנִמְצָא בְיָדוֹ מוֹת יוּמָת

we'go'neyv ish um'kha'ro we'nim'tsa be'ya'do mot yu'mat

and~STEAL~ing/er(ms) MAN and~he~did~ SELL~him and~he~did~be~FIND in~HAND~ him >~DIE he~will~be~make~DIE□

and {anyone} stealing {a} man and sells him (or) is found in his hand‡, he will :surely: be [killed],□

21:17 וּמְקַלֵּל אָבִיו וְאִמּוֹ מוֹת יוּמָת

um'qa'leyl a'viw we'i'mo mot yu'mat

and~much~BELITTLE~ing/er(ms) FATHER~ him and~MOTHER~him >~DIE he~will~be~ make~DIE□

and {anyone} belittling his father (or) his mother, he will :surely: be [killed],□

21:18 וְכִי יְרִיבֻן אֲנָשִׁים וְהִכָּה אִישׁ אֶת רֵעֵהוּ בְּאֶבֶן אוֹ בְאֶגְרֹף וְלֹא יָמוּת וְנָפַל לְמִשְׁכָּב

---

* The word Elohiym may refer to the judges, but the Hebrew word for judges is usually שׁופטים (shoftim).
† Possibly meaning a premeditated action.
‡ Meaning "in his possession."

Mechanical Translation Codes

WORD – Verb	WORD – Noun	Word – Name	word – Pre/Suff	word – Conj.

we'khi ye'ri'vun a'na'shim we'hi'kah ish et rey'ey'hu be'e'ven o ve'eg'roph we'lo ya'mut we'na'phal le'mish'kav

and~GIVEN-THAT *they(m)~will*~DISPUTE~ must MAN~s and~*he~did~make*~HIT MAN AT COMPANION~him in~STONE OR in~FIST and~NOT *he~will*~DIE and~*he~did*~FALL to~ LAYING-PLACE□

and (if) men must dispute, and a man will hit his companion (with) {a} stone, or (with) {a} fist, and he does not die, (then) he will fall to {the} laying place,□

21:19 אִם יָקוּם וְהִתְהַלֵּךְ בַּחוּץ עַל מִשְׁעַנְתּוֹ וְנִקָּה הַמַּכֶּה רַק שִׁבְתּוֹ יִתֵּן וְרַפֹּא יְרַפֵּא

im ya'qum we'hit'ha'leykh ba'hhuts al mish'a'ne'to we'ni'qah ha'ma'keh raq shiv'to yi'teyn we'ra'po ye'ra'pey

IF *he~will*~RISE and~*he~did*~ self~WALK in~ the~OUTSIDE UPON STAVE~him and~*he~ did~be*~ACQUIT make~HIT~*ing/er(ms)* ONLY CEASING~him *he~will*~GIVE and~>~*much*~ HEAL *he~will*~much~HEAL□

if he will rise, and he walks {him}self (to) the outside upon his stave, (then) {the one} hitting {him} will be acquitted, only his ceasing he will give {him}* and he will be :completely: healed†,□

21:20 וְכִי יַכֶּה אִישׁ אֶת עַבְדּוֹ אוֹ אֶת אֲמָתוֹ בַּשֵּׁבֶט וּמֵת תַּחַת יָדוֹ נָקֹם יִנָּקֵם

we'khi ya'keh ish et av'do o et a'ma'to ba'shey'vet u'meyt ta'hhat ya'do na'qom yi'na'qeym

and~GIVEN-THAT *he~will~make*~HIT MAN AT SERVANT~him OR AT BONDWOMAN~him in~the~BRANCH and~*he~did*~DIE UNDER HAND~him >~AVENGE *he~will~be*~ AVENGE□

and (if) {a} man hits his servant or his bondwoman (with) the branch, and he dies (by) his hand, he will :surely: be avenged,□

21:21 אַךְ אִם יוֹם אוֹ יוֹמַיִם יַעֲמֹד לֹא יֻקַּם כִּי כַסְפּוֹ הוּא

akh im yom o yo'ma'yim ya'a'mod lo yu'qam ki khas'po hu

SURELY IF DAY OR DAY~s2 *he~will*~STAND NOT *he~will~be~make*~AVENGE GIVEN-THAT SILVER~him HE□

(however), if he will stand‡ {for a} day or two days, he will not be avenged, given that he {is} his silver,□

21:22 וְכִי יִנָּצוּ אֲנָשִׁים וְנָגְפוּ אִשָּׁה הָרָה וְיָצְאוּ יְלָדֶיהָ וְלֹא יִהְיֶה אָסוֹן עָנוֹשׁ יֵעָנֵשׁ כַּאֲשֶׁר יָשִׁית עָלָיו בַּעַל הָאִשָּׁה וְנָתַן בִּפְלִלִים

---

* The phrase "only his ceasing he will give" is probably an idiom for compensating the injured person for his time lost.
† The injured is physically healed as well financially compensated.
‡ Literally meaning "to be able to stand," but figuratively "to continue."

Revised Mechanical Translation Codes

(..) Alt Trans/App A   <..> Comp Phrase/App B   [..] Verb Form/App C   \..\ Plural Form/App D
:..: Int Inf Abs |..| Past Perf Verb   {...} Added Word

~ 157 ~

we'khi yi'na'tsu a'na'shim we'nag'phu i'shah ha'rah we'yats'u ye'la'dey'ah we'lo yih'yeh a'son a'nosh yey'a'neysh ka'a'sheyr ya'shit a'law ba'al ha'i'shah we'na'tan biph'li'lim

and~GIVEN-THAT *they(m)~will~be~* STRUGGLE MAN~s and~*they~did~*SMITE WOMAN PREGNANT and~*they~did~*GO-OUT BOY~s~her and~NOT *he~will~*EXIST HARM >~FINE *he~will~be~*FINE like~WHICH *he~ will~*SET-DOWN UPON~him MASTER the~ WOMAN and~*he~did~*GIVE in~JUDGE~s□

and (if) men struggle, and they smite {a} pregnant woman, and her boys* go out, (but) harm did not exist, he will :surely: be fined <just as> {the} master {of} the woman will set down upon him, and he will give {the} judg{ment}s,□

21:23

וְאִם אָסוֹן יִהְיֶה וְנָתַתָּה נֶפֶשׁ תַּחַת נָפֶשׁ

we'im a'son yih'yeh we'na'ta'tah ne'phesh ta'hhat na'phesh

and~IF HARM *he~will~*EXIST and~*you(ms)~ did~*GIVE~^ BEING UNDER BEING□

(but) if harm {does} exist, (then) you will give {a} being (in place of) {a} being,□

21:24

עַיִן תַּחַת עַיִן שֵׁן תַּחַת שֵׁן יָד תַּחַת יָד רֶגֶל תַּחַת רָגֶל

a'yin ta'hhat a'yin sheyn ta'hhat sheyn yad ta'hhat yad re'gel ta'hhat ra'gel

EYE UNDER EYE TOOTH UNDER TOOTH HAND UNDER HAND FOOT UNDER FOOT□

{an} eye (in place of) {an} eye, {a} tooth (in place of) {a} tooth, {a} hand (in place of) {a} hand, {a} foot (in place of) {a} foot,□

21:25

כְּוִיָּה תַּחַת כְּוִיָּה פֶּצַע תַּחַת פָּצַע חַבּוּרָה תַּחַת חַבּוּרָה

ke'wi'yah ta'hhat ke'wi'yah pe'tsa ta'hhat pa'tsa hha'bu'rah ta'hhat hha'bu'rah

SINGEING UNDER SINGEING BRUISE UNDER BRUISE STRIPED-BRUISE UNDER STRIPED-BRUISE□

{a} singeing (in place of) {a} singeing, {a} bruise (in place of) {a} bruise, {a} striped bruise (in place of) {a} striped bruise,□

21:26

וְכִי יַכֶּה אִישׁ אֶת עֵין עַבְדּוֹ אוֹ אֶת עֵין אֲמָתוֹ וְשִׁחֲתָהּ לַחָפְשִׁי יְשַׁלְּחֶנּוּ תַּחַת עֵינוֹ

we'khi ya'keh ish et eyn av'do o et eyn a'ma'to we'shi'hha'tah la'hhaph'shi ye'shal'hhe'nu ta'hhat ey'no

and~GIVEN-THAT *he~will~make~*HIT MAN AT EYE SERVANT~him OR AT EYE BONDWOMAN~him and~*he~did~much~* DAMAGE~her to~FREE *he~will~much~* SEND~him UNDER EYE~him□

(but) (if) {a} man will hit {the} eye {of} his servant, or {the} eye {of} his bondwoman, and he damages her, he will send him to free{dom} (in place of) his eye,□

21:27

וְאִם שֵׁן עַבְדּוֹ אוֹ שֵׁן אֲמָתוֹ יַפִּיל לַחָפְשִׁי יְשַׁלְּחֶנּוּ תַּחַת שִׁנּוֹ

---

* The masculine plural suffix (ים) may be used for a group of males or males and females. In the context of this verse, the word "boys" refers to the children, the sons and daughters.

Mechanical Translation Codes

| <u>WORD</u> – Verb | WORD – Noun | Word – Name | word – Pre/Suff | *word* – Conj. |

we'im sheyn av'do o sheyn a'ma'to ya'pil la'hhaph'shi ye'shal'hhe'nu ta'hhat shi'no

and~IF TOOTH SERVANT~him OR TOOTH BONDWOMAN~him *he~will~make~*FALL to~ FREE *he~will~much~*SEND~him UNDER TOOTH~him▢

and if {the} tooth {of} his servant, or {the} tooth {of} his bondwoman, is made to fall {out}, he will send him to free{dom} (in place of) his tooth,▢

21:28 וְכִי יִגַּח שׁוֹר אֶת אִישׁ אוֹ אֶת אִשָּׁה וָמֵת סָקוֹל יִסָּקֵל הַשּׁוֹר וְלֹא יֵאָכֵל אֶת בְּשָׂרוֹ וּבַעַל הַשּׁוֹר נָקִי

we'khi yi'gahh shor et ish o et i'shah wa'meyt sa'qol yi'sa'qeyl ha'shor we'lo yey'a'kheyl et be'sar'o u'va'al ha'shor na'qi

and~GIVEN-THAT *he~will~*GORE OX AT MAN OR AT WOMAN and~*he~did~*DIE >~STONE *he~will~be~*STONE the~OX and~NOT *he~ will~be~*EAT AT FLESH~him and~MASTER the~OX INNOCENT▢

and (if) {an} ox will gore {a} man, or {a} woman, {and} he dies, the ox will :surely: be stoned, and his flesh will not be eaten, and {the} master {of} the ox {is} innocent,▢

21:29 וְאִם שׁוֹר נַגָּח הוּא מִתְּמֹל שִׁלְשֹׁם וְהוּעַד בִּבְעָלָיו וְלֹא יִשְׁמְרֶנּוּ וְהֵמִית אִישׁ אוֹ אִשָּׁה הַשּׁוֹר יִסָּקֵל וְגַם בְּעָלָיו יוּמָת

we'im shor na'gahh hu mit'mol shil'shom we'hu'ad biv'a'law we'lo yish'me're'nu we'hey'mit ish o i'shah ha'shor yi'sa'qeyl we'gam be'a'law yu'mat

and~IF OX GORER HE from~YESTERDAY THREE-DAYS-AGO and~*he~did~be~make~* WRAP-AROUND in~MASTER~s~him and~ NOT *he~will~*SAFEGUARD~him and~*he~did~ make~*DIE MAN OR WOMAN the~OX *he~ will~be~*STONE and~ALSO MASTER~s~him *he~will~be~make~*DIE▢

(but) if (that) ox {was a} gorer <previously>, and his master was [warned], and he does not safeguard him, and he [kills] {a} man or {a} woman, the ox will be stoned, and also his master will be [killed],▢

21:30 אִם כֹּפֶר יוּשַׁת עָלָיו וְנָתַן פִּדְיֹן נַפְשׁוֹ כְּכֹל אֲשֶׁר יוּשַׁת עָלָיו

im ko'pher yu'shat a'law we'na'tan pid'yon naph'sho ke'khol a'sher yu'shat a'law

IF COVERING *he~will~*SET-DOWN~*ed(ms)* UPON~him and~*he~did~*GIVE RANSOM-PRICE BEING~him like~ALL WHICH *he~will~* SET-DOWN~*ed(ms)* UPON~him▢

if {a} covering {is} set down upon him*, and he will give {the} ransom price {of} his being, {just} like all (that) was set down upon him,▢

21:31 אוֹ בֵן יִגָּח אוֹ בַת יִגָּח כַּמִּשְׁפָּט הַזֶּה יֵעָשֶׂה לּוֹ

o veyn yi'gahh o vat yi'gahh ka'mish'pat ha'zeh yey'a'seh lo

OR SON *he~will~*GORE OR DAUGHTER *he~ will~*GORE like~the~DECISION the~THIS *he~ will~be~*DO to~him▢

or he gores {a} son, or he gores {a} daughter, like{wise}, this decision, will be done to him,▢

---

* "A covering set down upon him" means "a ransom is laid upon him.

Revised Mechanical Translation Codes

(..) Alt Trans/App A   <..> Comp Phrase/App B   [..] Verb Form/App C   \../ Plural Form/App D

:...: Int Inf Abs |..| Past Perf Verb   {...} Added Word

21:32 אִם עֶבֶד יִגַּח הַשּׁוֹר אוֹ אָמָה כֶּסֶף שְׁלֹשִׁים שְׁקָלִים יִתֵּן לַאדֹנָיו וְהַשּׁוֹר יִסָּקֵל

im e'ved yi'gahh ha'shor o a'mah ke'seph she'lo'shim she'qa'lim yi'teyn la'donaw we'ha'shor yi'sa'qeyl

IF SERVANT he~will~<u>GORE</u> the~OX OR BONDWOMAN SILVER THREE~s SHEQEL~s he~will~<u>GIVE</u> to~the~LORD~s~him and~the~ OX he~will~be~<u>STONE</u>◻

if the ox gores {a} servant, or {a} bondwoman, he will give to his lords {a} silver {of} three sheqels, and the ox will be stoned,◻

21:33 וְכִי יִפְתַּח אִישׁ בּוֹר אוֹ כִּי יִכְרֶה אִישׁ בֹּר וְלֹא יְכַסֶּנּוּ וְנָפַל שָׁמָּה שׁוֹר אוֹ חֲמוֹר

we'khi yiph'tahh ish bor o ki yikh'reh ish bor we'lo ye'kha'se'nu we'na'phal sham'mah shor o hha'mor

and~GIVEN-THAT he~will~<u>OPEN</u> MAN CISTERN OR GIVEN-THAT he~will~<u>DIG</u> MAN CISTERN and~NOT he~will~much~<u>COVER-OVER</u>~him and~he~did~<u>FALL</u> THERE~unto OX OR DONKEY◻

and (if) {a} man opens {a} cistern, or (if) {a} man digs {a} cistern, and he does not cover him over, and {an} ox or {a} donkey falls unto {it},◻

21:34 בַּעַל הַבּוֹר יְשַׁלֵּם כֶּסֶף יָשִׁיב לִבְעָלָיו וְהַמֵּת יִהְיֶה לּוֹ

ba'al ha'bor ye'sha'leym ke'seph ya'shiv liv'a'law we'ha'meyt yih'yeh lo

MASTER the~CISTERN he~will~much~<u>MAKE-RESTITUTION</u> SILVER he~will~make~<u>TURN-BACK</u> to~MASTER~s~him and~the~<u>DIE</u>~ing/er(ms) he~will~<u>EXIST</u> to~him◻

{the} master {of} the cistern will make restitution, he will [return] silver to his master, and the dead {one} will exist (for) him{self},◻

21:35 וְכִי יִגֹּף שׁוֹר אִישׁ אֶת שׁוֹר רֵעֵהוּ וָמֵת וּמָכְרוּ אֶת הַשּׁוֹר הַחַי וְחָצוּ אֶת כַּסְפּוֹ וְגַם אֶת הַמֵּת יֶחֱצוּן

we'khi yi'goph shor ish et shor rey'ey'hu wa'meyt u'makh'ru et ha'shor ha'hhai we'hha'tsu et kas'po we'gam et ha'meyt ye'hhe'tsun

and~GIVEN-THAT he~will~<u>SMITE</u> OX MAN AT OX COMPANION~him and~he~did~<u>DIE</u> and~ they~did~<u>SELL</u> AT the~OX the~LIVING and~ they~did~<u>DIVIDE</u> AT SILVER~him and~ALSO AT the~<u>DIE</u>~ing/er(ms) they(m)~will~ <u>DIVIDE</u>~must◻

and (if) {the} ox {of a} man smites {the} ox {of} his companion, and he dies, (then) they will sell the living ox, and they will divide his silver, (then) they must also divide the dead {one},◻

21:36 אוֹ נוֹדַע כִּי שׁוֹר נַגָּח הוּא מִתְּמוֹל שִׁלְשֹׁם וְלֹא יִשְׁמְרֶנּוּ בְּעָלָיו שַׁלֵּם יְשַׁלֵּם שׁוֹר תַּחַת הַשּׁוֹר וְהַמֵּת יִהְיֶה לּוֹ

o no'da ki shor na'gahh hu mit'mol shil'shom we'lo yish'me're'nu be'a'law sha'leym ye'sha'leym shor ta'hhat ha'shor we'ha'meyt yih'yeh lo

OR he~did~be~<u>KNOW</u> GIVEN-THAT OX

or {if it} was known that (that) ox {was a}

Mechanical Translation Codes

<u>WORD</u> – Verb   WORD – Noun   Word – Name   word – Pre/Suff   *word* – Conj.

~ 160 ~

GORER HE from~YESTERDAY THREE-DAYS-AGO and~NOT he~will~SAFEGUARD~him MASTER~s~him >~much~MAKE-RESTITUTION he~will~much~MAKE-RESTITUTION OX UNDER the~OX and~the~DIE~ing/er(ms) he~will~EXIST to~him□

gorer <previously>, and he does not safeguard him, his master will make :full: restitution, {an} ox (in place of) the ox, and the dead {one} will exist (for) him{self},□

21:37(1) כִּי יִגְנֹב אִישׁ שׁוֹר אוֹ שֶׂה וּטְבָחוֹ אוֹ מְכָרוֹ חֲמִשָּׁה בָקָר יְשַׁלֵּם תַּחַת הַשּׁוֹר וְאַרְבַּע צֹאן תַּחַת הַשֶּׂה

ki yig'nov ish shor o seh ut'va'hho o me'kha'ro hha'mi'shah va'qar ye'sha'leym ta'hhat ha'shor we'ar'ba tson ta'hhat ha'seh

GIVEN-THAT he~will~STEAL MAN OX OR RAM and~he~did~BUTCHER~him OR he~did~SELL~him FIVE CATTLE he~will~much~MAKE-RESTITUTION UNDER the~OX and~FOUR FLOCKS UNDER the~RAM□

(if) {a} man steals {an} ox or {a} ram, and he butchers him, or he sells him, he will make restitution {with} five cattle (in place of) the ox, and four flocks (in place of) the ram,*□

Chapter 22

22:1(2) אִם בַּמַּחְתֶּרֶת יִמָּצֵא הַגַּנָּב וְהֻכָּה וָמֵת אֵין לוֹ דָּמִים

im ba'mahh'te'ret yi'ma'tsey ha'ga'nav we'hu'kah wa'meyt eyn lo da'mim

IF in~the~SEARCHING he~will~be~FIND the~THIEF and~he~did~be~make~HIT and~he~did~DIE WITHOUT to~him BLOOD~s□

if the thief is found in the {act of} searching, and he is hit, and he dies, {the} \bloodshed/ {does} (not) {belong} to him,□

22:2(3) אִם זָרְחָה הַשֶּׁמֶשׁ עָלָיו דָּמִים לוֹ שַׁלֵּם יְשַׁלֵּם אִם אֵין לוֹ וְנִמְכַּר בִּגְנֵבָתוֹ

im zar'hhah ha'she'mesh a'law da'mim lo sha'leym ye'sha'leym im eyn lo we'nim'kar big'ney'va'to

IF she~did~COME-UP the~SUN UPON~him BLOOD~s to~him >~much~MAKE-RESTITUTION he~will~much~MAKE-RESTITUTION IF WITHOUT to~him and~he~did~be~SELL in~THEFT~him□

if the sun comes up upon him, {the} \bloodshed/ {belongs} to him, he will make :full: restitution, if (nothing) {belongs} to him, (then) he will be sold (with) his theft,□

22:3(4) אִם הִמָּצֵא תִמָּצֵא בְיָדוֹ הַגְּנֵבָה מִשּׁוֹר עַד חֲמוֹר עַד שֶׂה חַיִּים שְׁנַיִם יְשַׁלֵּם

im hi'ma'tsey ti'ma'tsey be'ya'do hag'ney'vah mi'shor ad hha'mor ad seh hai'yim

---

* This verse is the first verse of chapter 22 in Christian Bibles. In all of chapter 22, the verse numbers in Christian Bibles will be one number higher.

Revised Mechanical Translation Codes

(..) Alt Trans/App A	<..> Comp Phrase/App B	[..] Verb Form/App C	\../ Plural Form/App D
:..: Int Inf Abs	|..| Past Perf Verb	{...} Added Word	

she'na'yim ye'sha'leym

IF >~*be*~<u>FIND</u> she~*will*~*be*~<u>FIND</u> in~HAND~ him the~THEFT from~OX UNTIL DONKEY UNTIL RAM LIVING~s TWO he~*will*~*much*~ <u>MAKE-RESTITUTION</u>□	if the theft is :surely: found in his hand, from {the} ox, (even) {the} donkey, (even) {a} ram, he will make restitution {with} (double) {the} \life/,□

22:4(5)   כִּי יַבְעֶר אִישׁ שָׂדֶה אוֹ כֶרֶם וְשִׁלַּח אֶת בְּעִירֹה וּבִעֵר בִּשְׂדֵה אַחֵר מֵיטַב שָׂדֵהוּ וּמֵיטַב כַּרְמוֹ יְשַׁלֵּם

ki yav'er ish sa'deh o khe'rem we'shi'lahh et be'i'roh u'vi'eyr bis'deyh a'hheyr mey'tav
sa'dey'hu u'mey'tav kar'mo ye'sha'leym

GIVEN-THAT he~*will*~*make*~<u>BURN</u> MAN FIELD OR VINEYARD and~*he*~*did*~*much*~ <u>SEND</u> AT CATTLE~her and~*he*~*did*~*much*~ <u>BURN</u> in~FIELD OTHER BEST FIELD~him and~ BEST VINEYARD~him he~*will*~*much*~<u>MAKE-RESTITUTION</u>□	(if) {a} man (causes) {a} field or vineyard {to} burn*, and he sends his† cattle, and they‡ [ignite]§ {an}other field, he will make restitution {with} his best field and his best vineyard,□

22:5(6)   כִּי תֵצֵא אֵשׁ וּמָצְאָה קֹצִים וְנֶאֱכַל גָּדִישׁ אוֹ הַקָּמָה אוֹ הַשָּׂדֶה שַׁלֵּם יְשַׁלֵּם הַמַּבְעִר אֶת הַבְּעֵרָה

ki tey'tsey eysh u'mats'ah qo'tsim we'ne'e'khal ga'dish o ha'qa'mah o ha'sa'deh sha'leym
ye'sha'leym ha'mav'ir et ha'be'ey'rah

GIVEN-THAT she~*will*~<u>GO-OUT</u> FIRE and~ she~*did*~<u>FIND</u> BRAMBLE~s and~*he*~*did*~*be*~ <u>EAT</u> STACK OR the~GRAIN-STALK OR the~ FIELD >~*much*~<u>MAKE-RESTITUTION</u> he~*will*~ *much*~<u>MAKE-RESTITUTION</u> the~*make*~ BURN~*ing*/*er*(ms) AT the~BURNING□	(if) {a} fire will go out**, and she†† finds brambles, and stack{s}, or grain stalk{s}, or {a} field is eaten‡‡, the {one} making the burning will make :full: restitution,□

22:6(7)   כִּי יִתֵּן אִישׁ אֶל רֵעֵהוּ כֶּסֶף אוֹ כֵלִים לִשְׁמֹר וְגֻנַּב מִבֵּית הָאִישׁ אִם יִמָּצֵא הַגַּנָּב יְשַׁלֵּם שְׁנָיִם

ki yi'teyn ish el rey'ey'hu ke'seph o khey'lim lish'mor we'gu'nav mi'beyt ha'ish im
yi'ma'tsey ha'ga'nav ye'sha'leym she'na'yim

---

* The "burning" in this context implies that the field or vineyard is completely devoured.

† The word בְּעִירֹה (her cattle) is grammatically incorrect and should be written as בְּעִירוֹ (his cattle).

‡ The Hebrew reads "he," referring to the "cattle," as the Hebrew word for "cattle" is a masculine singular noun. Since the English word "cattle" is plural, the translation uses the pronoun "they" instead.

§ The "igniting" in this context implies that the field or vineyard is being eaten.

** Referring to the "fire," a feminine word in Hebrew.

†† Meaning to "spread," not in the sense of being extinguished.

‡‡ This Hebrew word means to eat, but also to devour or destroy.

Mechanical Translation Codes

<u>WORD</u> – Verb	WORD – Noun	Word – Name	word – Pre/Suff	*word* – Conj.

GIVEN-THAT *he~will*~<u>GIVE</u> MAN TO COMPANION~him SILVER OR ITEM~s to~ >~<u>SAFEGUARD</u> and~*he~did~be~much*~<u>STEAL</u> from~HOUSE the~MAN IF *he~will~be*~<u>FIND</u> the~THIEF *he~will~much*~<u>MAKE-RESTITUTION</u> TWO□

(if) {a} man gives silver or items to his companion (for) safeguard{ing}, and he* was stolen from {the} house {of} the man, if the thief is found, he will make restitution {of} two {times},□

22:7(8) אִם לֹא יִמָּצֵא הַגַּנָּב וְנִקְרַב בַּעַל הַבַּיִת אֶל הָאֱלֹהִים אִם לֹא שָׁלַח יָדוֹ בִּמְלֶאכֶת רֵעֵהוּ

im lo yi'ma'tsey ha'ga'nav we'niq'rav ba'al ha'ba'yit el ha'e'lo'him im lo sha'lahh ya'do bim'le'khet rey'ey'hu

IF NOT *he~will~be*~<u>FIND</u> the~THIEF and~*he~did~be*~<u>COME-NEAR</u> MASTER the~HOUSE TO the~"Elohiym ᴾᴼᵂᴱᴿ˜ˢ" IF NOT *he~did*~<u>SEND</u> HAND~him in~BUSINESS COMPANION~him□

if the thief is not found, (then) {the} master {of} the house will [be brought near] to the "Elohiym ᴾᵒʷᵉʳˢ"†, {to see}‡ if he did not send his hand in{to the} business {of} his companion,□

22:8(9) עַל כָּל דְּבַר פֶּשַׁע עַל שׁוֹר עַל חֲמוֹר עַל שֶׂה עַל שַׂלְמָה עַל כָּל אֲבֵדָה אֲשֶׁר יֹאמַר כִּי הוּא זֶה עַד הָאֱלֹהִים יָבֹא דְּבַר שְׁנֵיהֶם אֲשֶׁר יַרְשִׁיעֻן אֱלֹהִים יְשַׁלֵּם שְׁנַיִם לְרֵעֵהוּ

al kol de'var pe'sha al shor al hha'mor al seh al sal'mah al kol a'vey'dah a'sher yo'mar ki hu zeh ad ha'e'lo'him ya'vo de'var she'ney'hem a'sher yar'shi'un e'lo'him ye'sha'leym she'na'yim le'rey'ey'hu

UPON ALL WORD TRANSGRESSION UPON OX UPON DONKEY UPON RAM UPON OUTER-GARMENT UPON ALL LOST-THING WHICH *he~will*~<u>SAY</u> GIVEN-THAT HE THIS UNTIL the~"Elohiym ᴾᴼᵂᴱᴿ˜ˢ" *he~will*~<u>COME</u> WORD TWO~them(m) WHICH *he~will~make*~<u>DEPART</u>~must "Elohiym ᴾᴼᵂᴱᴿ˜ˢ" *he~will~much*~<u>MAKE-RESTITUTION</u> TWO to~ COMPANION~him□

(over) all (manner){s of} transgression, (over) {an} ox, (over) {a} donkey, (over) {a} ram, (over) {an} outer garment, (over) all lost thing{s}, {of} which (it) is said, that (one) {is} this, {the} (manner) {of the} two {of} them will come unto the "Elohiym ᴾᵒʷᵉʳˢ"§, {the one} which "Elohiym ᴾᵒʷᵉʳˢ" must [convict], he will make :full: restitution {of} two {times} to his companion,□

---

* Referring to the silver or items.
† The word Elohiym may refer to the judges, but the Hebrew word for judges is usually שׁופטים (shoftim).
‡ The text appears to be missing text at this point and may have originally included "to see," or "to determine."
§ The word Elohiym may refer to the judges, but the Hebrew word for judges is usually שׁופטים (shoftim). Unlike the other uses of this word in this section, the verb associated with Elohiym is singular (he).

Revised Mechanical Translation Codes

(..) Alt Trans/App A	<..> Comp Phrase/App B	[..] Verb Form/App C	\../ Plural Form/App D
:..: Int Inf Abs	|..| Past Perf Verb	{...} Added Word	

22:9(10) כִּי יִתֵּן אִישׁ אֶל רֵעֵהוּ חֲמוֹר אוֹ שׁוֹר אוֹ שֶׂה וְכָל בְּהֵמָה לִשְׁמֹר וּמֵת אוֹ נִשְׁבַּר אוֹ נִשְׁבָּה אֵין רֹאֶה

ki yi'teyn ish el rey'ey'hu hha'mor o shor o seh we'khol be'hey'mah lish'mor u'meyt o nish'bar o nish'bah eyn ro'eh

GIVEN-THAT he~will~<u>GIVE</u> MAN TO COMPANION~him DONKEY OR OX OR RAM and~ALL BEAST to~>~<u>SAFEGUARD</u> and~he~ did~<u>DIE</u> OR he~did~be~<u>CRACK</u> OR he~did~ be~<u>CAPTURE</u> WITHOUT <u>SEE</u>~ing/er(ms)□

(if) {a} man will give to his companion {a} donkey, or {an} ox, or {a} ram (or) (any) beast (for) safeguard{ing}, and he dies, or he is cracked, or he is captured, without being seen,□

22:10(11) שְׁבֻעַת יְהוָה תִּהְיֶה בֵּין שְׁנֵיהֶם אִם לֹא שָׁלַח יָדוֹ בִּמְלֶאכֶת רֵעֵהוּ וְלָקַח בְּעָלָיו וְלֹא יְשַׁלֵּם

she'vu'at YHWH tih'yeh beyn she'ney'hem im lo sha'lahh ya'do bim'le'khet rey'ey'hu we'la'qahh be'a'law we'lo ye'sha'leym

SWEARING "Yhwh ^{he~will~}<u>^{BE}</u>" she~will~<u>EXIST</u> BETWEEN TWO~them(m) IF NOT he~did~ <u>SEND</u> HAND~him in~BUSINESS COMPANION~him and~he~did~<u>TAKE</u> MASTER~s~him and~NOT he~will~much~ <u>MAKE-RESTITUTION</u>□

{a} swearing {of} "Yhwh ^{He is}" will exist between {the} two {of} them, if he did not send his hand in{to the} business {of} his companion, (then) his* master will take† {it}, and he will not make restitution,□

22:11(12) וְאִם גָּנֹב יִגָּנֵב מֵעִמּוֹ יְשַׁלֵּם לִבְעָלָיו

we'im ga'nov yi'ga'neyv mey'i'mo ye'sha'leym liv'a'law

and~IF >~<u>STEAL</u> he~will~be~<u>STEAL</u> from~ WITH~him he~will~much~<u>MAKE-</u> <u>RESTITUTION</u> to~MASTER~s~him□

(but) if he was :surely: stolen <away from> him, he will make restitution to his‡ master,□

22:12(13) אִם טָרֹף יִטָּרֵף יְבִאֵהוּ עֵד הַטְּרֵפָה לֹא יְשַׁלֵּם

im ta'roph yi'ta'reyph ye'vi'ey'hu eyd hat'rey'phah lo ye'sha'leym

IF >~<u>TEAR-INTO-PIECES</u> he~will~be~<u>TEAR-</u> <u>INTO-PIECES</u> he~will~make~<u>COME</u>~him WITNESS the~TORN NOT he~will~much~ <u>MAKE-RESTITUTION</u>□

if he was :surely: torn into pieces, he will [bring] him {as a} witness, he will not make restitution {of the} torn {thing}, □

22:13(14) וְכִי יִשְׁאַל אִישׁ מֵעִם רֵעֵהוּ וְנִשְׁבַּר אוֹ מֵת בְּעָלָיו אֵין עִמּוֹ שַׁלֵּם יְשַׁלֵּם

we'khi yish'al ish mey'im rey'ey'hu we'nish'bar o meyt be'a'law eyn i'mo sha'leym ye'sha'leym

---

* "His master" is the owner of the beast.
† Meaning "accept."
‡ "His master" is the owner of the beast.

Mechanical Translation Codes

<u>WORD</u> – Verb	WORD – Noun	Word – Name	word – Pre/Suff	*word* – Conj.

and~GIVEN-THAT *he~will~*ENQUIRE MAN from~WITH COMPANION~him and~*he~did~* be~CRACK OR *he~did~*DIE MASTER~s~him WITHOUT WITH~him >~*much~*MAKE-RESTITUTION *he~will~much~*MAKE-RESTITUTION□

and (if) {a} man will enquire <away from> * his companion, and he is cracked, or he dies, {and} his master {is} not with him, he will make :full: restitution,□

22:14(15)   אִם בְּעָלָיו עִמּוֹ לֹא יְשַׁלֵּם אִם שָׂכִיר הוּא בָּא בִּשְׂכָרוֹ

im be'a'law i'mo lo ye'sha'leym im sa'khir hu ba bis'kha'ro

IF MASTER~s~him WITH~him NOT *he~will~ much~*MAKE-RESTITUTION IF HIRELING HE *he~did~*COME in~WAGE~him□

if his master {is} with him, he will not make restitution, if he {is a} hireling, he, he came (with) his wage,□

22:15(16)   וְכִי יְפַתֶּה אִישׁ בְּתוּלָה אֲשֶׁר לֹא אֹרָשָׂה וְשָׁכַב עִמָּהּ מָהֹר יִמְהָרֶנָּה לּוֹ לְאִשָּׁה

we'khi ye'pha'teh ish be'tu'lah a'sher lo o'ra'sah we'sha'khav i'mah ma'hor yim'ha're'nah lo le'i'shah

and~GIVEN-THAT *he~will~much~*SPREAD-WIDE MAN VIRGIN WHICH NOT *she~did~be~ much~*BETROTH and~*he~did~*LAY-DOWN WITH~her >~HURRY *he~will~*HURRY~her to~ him to~WOMAN□

and (if) {a} man will [persuade] {a} virgin who has not been betrothed, and he lays down with her, he will :quickly: hurry her to {be a} woman (for) him{self}, □

22:16(17)   אִם מָאֵן יְמָאֵן אָבִיהָ לְתִתָּהּ לוֹ כֶּסֶף יִשְׁקֹל כְּמֹהַר הַבְּתוּלֹת

im ma'eyn ye'ma'eyn a'vi'ah le'ti'tah lo ke'seph yish'qol ke'mo'har ha'be'tu'lot

IF >~*much~*REFUSE *he~will~much~*REFUSE FATHER~her to~>~GIVE~her to~him SILVER *he~will~*WEIGH like~BRIDE-PRICE the~ VIRGIN□

if her father :completely: refuses to give her to him, he will weigh {out} silver {just} like {the} bride price {of} the virgin,□

22:17(18)   מְכַשֵּׁפָה לֹא תְחַיֶּה

me'kha'shey'phah lo te'hha'yeh

*much~*SORCERY~*ing/er(fs)* NOT *you(ms)~ will~much~*LIVE□

you will not [keep alive] {a} sorceress,□

22:18(19)   כָּל שֹׁכֵב עִם בְּהֵמָה מוֹת יוּמָת

kol sho'kheyv im be'hey'mah mot yu'mat

ALL LAY-DOWN~*ing/er(ms)* WITH BEAST >~DIE *he~will~be~make~*DIE□

all laying down with {a} beast will :surely: be [killed],□

---

* "Enquire away from" means to "borrow from."

Revised Mechanical Translation Codes

(..) Alt Trans/App A   <..> Comp Phrase/App B   [..] Verb Form/App C   \../ Plural Form/App D
:...: Int Inf Abs |..| Past Perf Verb   {...} Added Word

22:19(20)

זֹבֵחַ לָאֱלֹהִים יָחֳרָם בִּלְתִּי לַיהוָה לְבַדּוֹ

zo'vey'ahh la'e'lo'him ya'hha'ram bil'ti la'YHWH le'va'do

SACRIFICE~*ing/er(ms)* to~the~"Elohiym POWER~s" *he~will~be~*make~PERFORATE EXCEPT to~"Yhwh *he~will~BE*" to~STICK~him☐

{anyone} sacrificing to the "Elohiym Powers", except to "Yhwh He is" <himself>, will be [destroyed],☐

22:20(21)

וְגֵר לֹא תוֹנֶה וְלֹא תִלְחָצֶנּוּ כִּי גֵרִים הֱיִיתֶם בְּאֶרֶץ מִצְרָיִם

we'ger lo to'neh we'lo til'hha'tse'nu ki gey'rim he'yi'tem be'e'rets mits'ra'yim

and~STRANGER NOT *you(ms)~will~*make~SUPPRESS and~NOT *you(ms)~will~*SQUEEZE~him GIVEN-THAT STRANGER~s *you(mp)~did~*EXIST in~LAND "Mits'rayim STRAIT~s2"☐

and you will not suppress {a} stranger, and you will not squeeze* him, given that you existed {as} strangers in {the} land {of} "Mits'rayim Two straits",☐

22:21(22)

כָּל אַלְמָנָה וְיָתוֹם לֹא תְעַנּוּן

kol al'ma'nah we'ya'tom lo te'a'nun

ALL WIDOW and~ORPHAN NOT *you(ms)~will~*much~AFFLICT~must☐

you must not afflict (any) widow (or) orphan,☐

22:22(23)

אִם עַנֵּה תְעַנֶּה אֹתוֹ כִּי אִם צָעֹק יִצְעַק אֵלַי שָׁמֹעַ אֶשְׁמַע צַעֲקָתוֹ

im a'neyh te'a'neh o'to ki im tsa'oq yits'aq ey'lai sha'mo'a esh'ma tsa'a'qa'to

IF >~*much~*AFFLICT *you(ms)~will~*much~AFFLICT AT~him GIVEN-THAT IF >~CRY-OUT *he~will~*CRY-OUT TO~me >~HEAR *I~will~*HEAR CRY~him☐

if you :greatly: afflict him <instead>, he will :greatly: cry out to me, I will :surely: hear his cry,☐

22:23(24)

וְחָרָה אַפִּי וְהָרַגְתִּי אֶתְכֶם בֶּחָרֶב וְהָיוּ נְשֵׁיכֶם אַלְמָנוֹת וּבְנֵיכֶם יְתֹמִים

we'hha'rah a'pi we'ha'rag'ti et'khem be'hha'rev we'hai'u ne'shey'khem al'ma'not uv'ney'khem ye'to'mim

and~*he~did~*FLARE-UP NOSE~me and~*I~did~*KILL AT~you(mp) in~SWORD and~*they~did~*EXIST WOMAN~s~you(mp) WIDOW~s and~SON~s~you(mp) ORPHAN~s☐

and my nose will flare up†, and I will kill you (with) {the} sword, and your women will exist {as} widows, and your sons {as} orphans,☐

22:24(25)

אִם כֶּסֶף תַּלְוֶה אֶת עַמִּי אֶת הֶעָנִי עִמָּךְ לֹא תִהְיֶה לוֹ כְּנֹשֶׁה לֹא תְשִׂימוּן עָלָיו נֶשֶׁךְ

im ke'seph tal'weh et a'mi et he'a'ni i'makh lo tih'yeh lo ke'no'sheh lo te'si'mun a'law ne'shekh

---

* Meaning "opresss."

† "My nose will flare up" is an idiom meaning "I will be fiercely angry."

Mechanical Translation Codes

<u>WORD</u> – Verb	WORD – Noun	Word – Name	word – Pre/Suff	*word* – Conj.

IF SILVER you(ms)~will~make~JOIN AT PEOPLE~me AT the~AFFLICTION WITH~ you(fs) NOT you(ms)~will~EXIST to~him like~ DECEIVE~ing/er(ms) NOT you(ms)~will~ PLACE~must UPON~him USURY▫

if you [loan] silver {to} my people, the {ones} afflicted with{in} you, you will not exist to him (as) {a} deceiver, you must not place {a} usury upon him,▫

22:25(26)   אִם חָבֹל תַּחְבֹּל שַׂלְמַת רֵעֶךָ עַד בֹּא הַשֶּׁמֶשׁ תְּשִׁיבֶנּוּ לוֹ

im hha'vol tahh'bol sal'mat rey'e'kha ad bo ha'she'mesh te'shi've'nu lo

IF >~TAKE-AS-A-PLEDGE you(ms)~will~TAKE-AS-A-PLEDGE OUTER-GARMENT COMPANION~you(ms) UNTIL >~COME the~ SUN you(ms)~will~make~TURN-BACK~him to~him▫

if you :insist to: take {the} outer garment {of} your companion as a pledge, you will [return] him* to him (by) the com{ing of}† the sun,▫

22:26(27)   כִּי הִוא כְסוּתֹה לְבַדָּהּ הִוא שִׂמְלָתוֹ לְעֹרוֹ בַּמֶּה יִשְׁכָּב וְהָיָה כִּי יִצְעַק אֵלַי וְשָׁמַעְתִּי כִּי חַנּוּן אָנִי

ki hi khe'su'toh le'va'dah hi sim'la'to le'o'ro ba'meh yish'kav we'hai'yah ki yits'aq ey'lai we'sha'ma'ti ki hha'nun a'ni

GIVEN-THAT she RAIMENT~her to~STICK~ her she APPAREL~him to~SKIN~him in~ WHAT he~will~LAY-DOWN and~he~did~ EXIST GIVEN-THAT he~will~CRY-OUT TO~me and~I~did~HEAR GIVEN-THAT GRACIOUS I▫

given that she‡ {is} his§ <only> raiment, she {is} his apparel (for) his skin, <how> will he lay down? and (it) will (come to pass) that he will cry out to me and I will hear {him} given that I {am} gracious,▫

22:27(28)   אֱלֹהִים לֹא תְקַלֵּל וְנָשִׂיא בְעַמְּךָ לֹא תָאֹר

e'lo'him lo te'qa'leyl we'na'si ve'am'kha lo ta'or

"Elohiym POWER~s" NOT you(ms)~will~much~ BELITTLE and~CAPTAIN in~PEOPLE~you(ms) NOT you(ms)~will~SPIT-UPON▫

you will not belittle "Elohiym Powers"**, and you will not spit upon {the} captain{s} (among) your people,▫

22:28(29)   מְלֵאָתְךָ וְדִמְעֲךָ לֹא תְאַחֵר בְּכוֹר בָּנֶיךָ תִּתֶּן לִי

me'ley'at'kha we'dim'a'kha lo te'a'hheyr be'khor ba'ney'kha ti'ten li

RIPE-FRUIT~you(ms) and~JUICE~you(ms)

you will not delay your ripe fruit and your

---

* Referring to the "outer garment," which is a feminine word in Hebrew. However, the Hebrew pronoun is written defectively as masculine.
† The Hebrew verb may mean "come" or "go" and contextually must be referring to the "going down" of the sun.
‡ Referring to the "outer garment," a feminine word in Hebrew.
§ The word כְסוּתֹה (her raiment) is grammatically incorrect and should be written as כְסוּתוֹ (his raiment).
** Context suggests this may be the judges, but the Hebrew word for judges is usually שופטים (shoftim).

Revised Mechanical Translation Codes

(..) Alt Trans/App A	<..> Comp Phrase/App B	[..] Verb Form/App C	\../ Plural Form/App D
:..: Int Inf Abs	|..| Past Perf Verb	{..} Added Word	

NOT *you(ms)~will~much~*<u>DELAY</u> FIRSTBORN SON~s~*you(ms) you(ms)~will~*<u>GIVE</u> to~me□

juice, you will give to me your firstborn sons,□

22:29(30) כֵּן תַּעֲשֶׂה לְשֹׁרְךָ לְצֹאנֶךָ שִׁבְעַת יָמִים יִהְיֶה עִם אִמּוֹ בַּיּוֹם הַשְּׁמִינִי תִּתְּנוֹ לִי

keyn ta'a'seh le'shor'kha le'tso'ne'kha shiv'at ya'mim yih'yeh im i'mo ba'yom hash'mini tit'no li

SO *you(ms)~will~*<u>DO</u> to~OX~*you(ms)* to~ FLOCKS~*you(ms)* SEVEN DAY~s *he~will~* <u>EXIST</u> WITH MOTHER~him in~the~DAY the~ EIGHTH *you(ms)~will~*<u>GIVE</u>~him to~me□

(thus) you will do to your ox, to your flocks, he will exist with his mother {for} seven days, in the eighth day you will give him to me,□

22:30(31) וְאַנְשֵׁי קֹדֶשׁ תִּהְיוּן לִי וּבָשָׂר בַּשָּׂדֶה טְרֵפָה לֹא תֹאכֵלוּ לַכֶּלֶב תַּשְׁלִכוּן אֹתוֹ

we'an'shey qo'desh tih'yun li u'va'sar ba'sa'deh te'rey'pha lo to'khey'lu la'kelev tash'li'khun o'to

and~MAN~s SPECIAL *you(mp)~will~*<u>EXIST</u>~ must to~me and~FLESH in~the~FIELD TORN NOT *you(mp)~will~*<u>EAT</u> to~the~DOG *you(mp)~will~make~*<u>THROW-OUT</u>~must AT~ him□

and you must exist {as} men {of} special{ness} (for) me, and you will not eat torn flesh in the field, you must throw {it} to the dog,□

Chapter 23

23:1 לֹא תִשָּׂא שֵׁמַע שָׁוְא אַל תָּשֶׁת יָדְךָ עִם רָשָׁע לִהְיֹת עֵד חָמָס

lo ti'sa shey'ma sha'we al ta'shet yad'kha im ra'sha lih'yot eyd hha'mas

NOT *you(ms)~will~*<u>LIFT-UP</u> REPORT FALSENESS DO-NOT *you(ms)~will~*<u>SET-DOWN</u> HAND~*you(ms)* WITH LOST to~ >~<u>EXIST</u> WITNESS VIOLENCE□

you will not lift up {a} report {of} falseness, you will not set your hand down with {the} lost to (be) {a} witness {of} violence,□

23:2 לֹא תִהְיֶה אַחֲרֵי רַבִּים לְרָעֹת וְלֹא תַעֲנֶה עַל רִב לִנְטֹת אַחֲרֵי רַבִּים לְהַטֹּת

lo tih'yeh a'hha'rey ra'bim le'ra'ot we'lo ta'a'neh al riv lin'tot a'hha'rey ra'bim le'ha'tot

NOT *you(ms)~will~*<u>EXIST</u> AFTER ABUNDANT~s to~DYSFUNCTIONAL~s and~ NOT *you(ms)~will~*<u>ANSWER</u> UPON DISPUTE to~>~<u>EXTEND</u> AFTER ABUNDANT~s to~ >~*make~*<u>EXTEND</u>□

you will not [follow] {the} abundant* to dysfunction, and you will not answer upon {a} dispute, extend{ing} after {the} abundant† (by) [turn{ing} away from] {it}, □

---

* That is, a "crowd," as a great multitude, the majority.
† That is, a "crowd," as a great multitude, the majority.

Mechanical Translation Codes

<u>WORD</u> – Verb	WORD – Noun	Word – Name	word – Pre/Suff	*word* – Conj.

23:3 וְדָל לֹא תֶהְדַּר בְּרִיבוֹ

we'dal lo teh'dar be'ri'vo

and~WEAK NOT *you(ms)~will*~<u>SWELL</u> in~ DISPUTE~him□

and you will not swell {the} weak in his dispute,□

23:4 כִּי תִפְגַּע שׁוֹר אֹיִבְךָ אוֹ חֲמֹרוֹ תֹּעֶה הָשֵׁב תְּשִׁיבֶנּוּ לוֹ

ki tiph'ga shor oi'yiv'kha o hha'mo'ro to'eh ha'sheyv te'shi've'nu lo

GIVEN-THAT *you(ms)~will*~<u>REACH</u> OX <u>ATTACK</u>~*ing/er(ms)*~*you(ms)* OR DONKEY~ him <u>WANDER</u>~*ing/er(ms)* >~*make*~<u>TURN-BACK</u> *you(ms)~will*~*make*~<u>TURN-BACK</u>~him to~him□

(if) you reach {the} ox {of} your attacker, or his donkey, {and it is} wandering, you will :surely: [return] him to him,□

23:5 כִּי תִרְאֶה חֲמוֹר שֹׂנַאֲךָ רֹבֵץ תַּחַת מַשָּׂאוֹ וְחָדַלְתָּ מֵעֲזֹב לוֹ עָזֹב תַּעֲזֹב עִמּוֹ

ki tir'eh hha'mor so'na'a'kha ro'veyts ta'hhat ma'sa'o we'hha'dal'ta mey'a'zov lo a'zov ta'a'zov i'mo

GIVEN-THAT *you(ms)~will*~<u>SEE</u> DONKEY <u>HATE</u>~*ing/er(ms)*~*you(ms)* <u>STRETCH-OUT</u>~ *ing/er(ms)* UNDER LOAD~him and~*you(ms)*~ *did*~<u>TERMINATE</u> from~>~<u>LEAVE</u> to~him >~<u>LEAVE</u> *you(ms)~will*~<u>LEAVE</u> WITH~him□

(if) you see {the} donkey {of} your hater stretching out under his load*, you will terminate from leav{ing it} to† him, you will :surely: leave {it} with him,‡□

23:6 לֹא תַטֶּה מִשְׁפַּט אֶבְיֹנְךָ בְּרִיבוֹ

lo ta'teh mish'pat ev'yon'kha be'ri'vo

NOT *you(ms)~will*~*make*~<u>EXTEND</u> DECISION NEEDY~*you(ms)* in~DISPUTE~him□

you will not [turn away from] {a} decision {of} your needy in his dispute,□

23:7 מִדְּבַר שֶׁקֶר תִּרְחָק וְנָקִי וְצַדִּיק אַל תַּהֲרֹג כִּי לֹא אַצְדִּיק רָשָׁע

mid'var she'qer tir'hhaq we'na'qi we'tsa'tiq al ta'ha'rog ki lo ats'diq ra'sha

from~WORD FALSE *you(ms)~will*~<u>BE-FAR</u> and~INNOCENT and~CORRECT DO-NOT *you(ms)~will*~<u>KILL</u> GIVEN-THAT NOT *I~will*~ *make*~<u>BE-CORRECT</u> LOST□

you will be far from {a} false word, and you will not kill {the} innocent (or) {the} correct, given that I will not correct {the} lost,□

---

* "Stretching out under his load" means "laying down from the heavy load."
† Or "for."
‡ The second part of this passage is ambiguous. One possible interpretation is, "you will not leave the donkey to struggle with its load, but will help it with its load." Another interpretation is, "you will not release the load from the donkey and leave it behind, but will help it up to carry its load."

Revised Mechanical Translation Codes

(..) Alt Trans/App A   <..> Comp Phrase/App B   [..] Verb Form/App C   \../ Plural Form/App D
:...: Int Inf Abs |..| Past Perf Verb   {...} Added Word

23:8

וְשֹׁחַד לֹא תִקָּח כִּי הַשֹּׁחַד יְעַוֵּר פִּקְחִים וִיסַלֵּף דִּבְרֵי צַדִּיקִים

we'sho'hhad lo ti'qahh ki ha'sho'hhad ye'a'weyr piq'hhim wi'sa'leyph div'rey tsa'di'qim

and~BRIBE NOT *you(ms)~will~*<u>TAKE</u> GIVEN-THAT the~BRIBE *he~will~much~*<u>BLIND</u> SEEING~s and~*he~will~much~*<u>TWIST-BACKWARDS</u> WORD~s CORRECT~s☐

and you will not take {a} bribe, given that the bribe will blind {the} seeing {one}s, and he will twist correct words backwards,☐

23:9

וְגֵר לֹא תִלְחָץ וְאַתֶּם יְדַעְתֶּם אֶת נֶפֶשׁ הַגֵּר כִּי גֵרִים הֱיִיתֶם בְּאֶרֶץ מִצְרָיִם

we'ger lo til'hhats we'a'tem ye'da'tem et ne'phesh ha'geyr ki gey'rim he'yi'tem be'e'rets mits'ra'yim

and~STRANGER NOT *you(ms)~will~*<u>SQUEEZE</u> and~YOU(mp) *you(mp)~did~*<u>KNOW</u> AT BEING the~STRANGER GIVEN-THAT STRANGER~s *you(mp)~did~*<u>EXIST</u> in~LAND "Mits'rayim ^{STRAIT~s2}"☐

and you will not squeeze {a} stranger, and you know {the} being {of} the stranger, given that you existed {as} strangers in {the} land {of} "Mits'rayim ^{Two straits}",☐

23:10

וְשֵׁשׁ שָׁנִים תִּזְרַע אֶת אַרְצֶךָ וְאָסַפְתָּ אֶת תְּבוּאָתָהּ

we'sheysh sha'nim tiz'ra et ar'tse'kha we'a'saph'ta et te'vu'a'tah

and~SIX YEAR~s *you(ms)~will~*<u>SOW</u> AT LAND~you(ms) and~*you(ms)~did~*<u>GATHER</u> AT PRODUCTION~her☐

and you will sow your land six years, and you will gather her* production,☐

23:11

וְהַשְּׁבִיעִת תִּשְׁמְטֶנָּה וּנְטַשְׁתָּהּ וְאָכְלוּ אֶבְיֹנֵי עַמֶּךָ וְיִתְרָם תֹּאכַל חַיַּת הַשָּׂדֶה כֵּן תַּעֲשֶׂה לְכַרְמְךָ לְזֵיתֶךָ

we'hash'vi'it tish'me'te'nah un'tash'tah we'akh'lu ev'yo'ney a'me'kha we'yit'ram to'khal hhai'yat ha'sa'deh keyn ta'a'seh le'khar'me'kha le'zey'te'kha

and~the~SEVENTH *you(ms)~will~*<u>RELEASE</u>~her and~*you(ms)~did~*<u>LET-ALONE</u>~her and~*they~did~*<u>EAT</u> NEEDY~s PEOPLE~you(ms) and~REMAINDER~them(m) *she~will~*<u>EAT</u> LIVING the~FIELD SO *you(ms)~will~*<u>DO</u> to~VINEYARD~you(ms) to~OLIVE~you(ms)☐

and {in} the seventh you will release her†, and you will let her alone, and {the} needy {one}s {of} your people will eat, and {the} living {ones of} the field‡ will eat their remainder§, so you will do to your vineyard, {and} to your olive {grove},☐

23:12

שֵׁשֶׁת יָמִים תַּעֲשֶׂה מַעֲשֶׂיךָ וּבַיּוֹם הַשְּׁבִיעִי תִּשְׁבֹּת לְמַעַן יָנוּחַ שׁוֹרְךָ וַחֲמֹרֶךָ וְיִנָּפֵשׁ בֶּן אֲמָתְךָ וְהַגֵּר

shey'shet ya'mim ta'a'seh ma'a'sey'kha u'va'yom hash'vi'i tish'bot le'ma'an ya'nu'ahh

---

* Referring to the "land," a feminine word in Hebrew.
† Referring to the "land," a feminine word in Hebrew.
‡ "The living ones of the field" is an idiom meaning "wild animals."
§ What the needy ones leave behind.

Mechanical Translation Codes

<u>WORD</u> – Verb	WORD – Noun	Word – Name	word – Pre/Suff	*word* – Conj.

shor'kha wa'hha'mo're'kha we'yi'na'pheysh ben a'mat'kha we'ha'geyr

SIX DAY~s *you(ms)~will~*<u>DO</u> WORK~s~ *you(ms)* and~in~the~DAY the~SEVENTH *you(ms)~will~*<u>CEASE</u> to~THAT *he~will~*<u>REST</u> OX~*you(ms)* and~DONKEY~*you(ms)* and~*he~ will~*<u>BREATHE-DEEPLY</u> SON BONDWOMAN~ *you(ms)* and~the~STRANGER☐	six days you will do your work, and in the seventh day you will cease, (so) that your ox and your donkey will rest, and {the} son {of} your bondwoman and the stranger will breathe deeply*,☐

23:13 וּבְכֹל אֲשֶׁר אָמַרְתִּי אֲלֵיכֶם תִּשָּׁמֵרוּ וְשֵׁם אֱלֹהִים אֲחֵרִים לֹא תַזְכִּירוּ לֹא יִשָּׁמַע עַל פִּיךָ

uv'khol a'sher a'mar'ti a'ley'khem ti'sha'mey'ru we'sheym e'lo'him a'hhey'rim lo taz'ki'ru
lo yi'sha'ma al pi'kha

and~in~ALL WHICH *I~did~*<u>SAY</u> TO~*you(mp)* *you(mp)~will~be~*<u>SAFEGUARD</u> and~TITLE "Elohiym ^POWER~s^" AFTER~s NOT *you(mp)~ will~make~*<u>REMEMBER</u> NOT *he~will~be~* <u>HEAR</u> UPON MOUTH~*you(ms)*☐	and in all which I said to you, you will be safeguarded, and you will not remember {the} title {of} <other> "Elohiym ^Powers^", he† will not be heard upon your mouth,☐

23:14 שָׁלֹשׁ רְגָלִים תָּחֹג לִי בַּשָּׁנָה

sha'losh re'ga'lim ta'hhog li ba'sha'nah

THREE FOOT~s *you(ms)~will~*<u>HOLD-A-FEAST</u> to~me in~the~YEAR☐	you will hold a feast three (times) (for) me in the year,☐

23:15 אֶת חַג הַמַּצּוֹת תִּשְׁמֹר שִׁבְעַת יָמִים תֹּאכַל מַצּוֹת כַּאֲשֶׁר צִוִּיתִךָ לְמוֹעֵד חֹדֶשׁ הָאָבִיב כִּי בוֹ יָצָאתָ מִמִּצְרָיִם וְלֹא יֵרָאוּ פָנַי רֵיקָם

et hhag ha'ma'tsot tish'mor shiv'at ya'mim to'khal ma'tsot ka'a'sheyr tsi'wi'ti'kha
le'mo'eyd hho'desh ha'a'viv ki bo ya'tsa'ta mi'mits'ra'yim we'lo yey'ra'u pha'nai rey'qam

AT FEAST the~UNLEAVENED-BREAD~s *you(ms)~will~*<u>SAFEGUARD</u> SEVEN DAY~s *you(ms)~will~*<u>EAT</u> UNLEAVENED-BREAD~s like~WHICH *I~did~much~*<u>DIRECT</u>~*you(ms)* to~APPOINTED NEW-MOON the~GREEN-GRAIN GIVEN-THAT in~him *you(ms)~did~* <u>GO-OUT</u> from~"Mits'rayim ^STRAIT~s2^" and~NOT *they(m)~will~be~*<u>SEE</u> FACE~s~me EMPTINESS☐	you will safeguard {the} feast {of} unleavened bread, {for} seven days you will eat unleavened bread, <just as> I directed you, {it is} (for) {an} appointed {time in the} (month) {of} the green grain, given that in him‡ you went out from "Mits'rayim ^Two straits^", and they will not [appear] (in front of)§ me empty,☐

---

* "Breathe deeply" means to take a break, to refresh oneself.
† Referring to the "title," a masculine word in Hebrew.
‡ Referring to the "month," a masculine word in Hebrew.
§ The word פָנַי (my face) appears to be missing the prefix "to." As it is written, the sentence could be translated as "and my face will not appear empty."

Revised Mechanical Translation Codes

(..) Alt Trans/App A	<..> Comp Phrase/App B	[..] Verb Form/App C	\../ Plural Form/App D
:..: Int Inf Abs	|..| Past Perf Verb	{...} Added Word	

23:16 וְחַג הַקָּצִיר בִּכּוּרֵי מַעֲשֶׂיךָ אֲשֶׁר תִּזְרַע בַּשָּׂדֶה וְחַג הָאָסִף בְּצֵאת הַשָּׁנָה בְּאָסְפְּךָ אֶת מַעֲשֶׂיךָ מִן הַשָּׂדֶה

we'hhag ha'qa'tsir bi'ku'rey ma'a'sey'kha a'sher tiz'ra ba'sa'deh we'hhag ha'a'siph be'tseyt ha'sha'nah be'as'pe'kha et ma'a'sey'kha min ha'sa'deh

and~FEAST the~HARVEST FIRSTFRUIT~s WORK~s~you(ms) WHICH you(ms)~will~ SOW in~the~FIELD and~FEAST the~ GATHERING in~>~GO-OUT the~YEAR in~ >~GATHER~you(ms) AT WORK~s~you(ms) FROM the~FIELD□

and {the} feast {of} the harvest, {the} firstfruits {of} your works, which you will sow in the field, and {the} feast {of} the gathering in {the} go{ing} out {of} the year*, (with) your gather{ing of} your works from the field,□

23:17 שָׁלֹשׁ פְּעָמִים בַּשָּׁנָה יֵרָאֶה כָּל זְכוּרְךָ אֶל פְּנֵי הָאָדֹן יְהוָה

sha'losh pe'a'mim ba'sha'nah yey'ra'eh kol zekhur'kha el pe'ney ha'a'don YHWH

THREE FOOTSTEP~s in~the~YEAR he~will~ be~SEE ALL MEN~you(ms) TO FACE~s the~ LORD "Yhwh ^(he~will~BE)"□

three footsteps† in the year, your men will [appear] to {the} face {of} the lord "Yhwh ^(He is)",□

23:18 לֹא תִזְבַּח עַל חָמֵץ דַּם זִבְחִי וְלֹא יָלִין חֵלֶב חַגִּי עַד בֹּקֶר

lo tiz'bahh al hha'meyts dam ziv'hhi we'lo ya'lin hhey'lev hha'gi ad bo'qer

NOT you(ms)~will~SACRIFICE UPON LEAVENED-BREAD BLOOD SACRIFICE~me and~NOT he~will~STAY-THE-NIGHT FAT FEAST~me UNTIL MORNING□

you will not sacrifice {the} blood {of} my sacrifice upon leavened bread, and {the} fat {of} my feast will not stay the night until morning,□

23:19 רֵאשִׁית בִּכּוּרֵי אַדְמָתְךָ תָּבִיא בֵּית יְהוָה אֱלֹהֶיךָ לֹא תְבַשֵּׁל גְּדִי בַּחֲלֵב אִמּוֹ

rey'shit bi'ku'rey ad'mat'kha ta'vi beyt YHWH e'lo'hey'kha lo te'va'sheyl ge'di ba'hha'leyv i'mo

SUMMIT FIRSTFRUIT~s GROUND~you(ms) you(ms)~will~make~COME HOUSE "Yhwh ^(he~will~BE)" "Elohiym ^(POWER~s)"~you(ms) NOT you(ms)~will~much~BOIL MALE-KID in~the~ FAT MOTHER~him□

you will [bring] {the} summit‡ {of the} firstfruits {of} your ground to§ {the} house {of} "Yhwh ^(He is)" your "Elohiym ^(Powers)", you will not boil {a} male kid in the fat** {of} his mother,□

23:20 הִנֵּה אָנֹכִי שֹׁלֵחַ מַלְאָךְ לְפָנֶיךָ לִשְׁמָרְךָ בַּדָּרֶךְ וְלַהֲבִיאֲךָ אֶל הַמָּקוֹם אֲשֶׁר הֲכִנֹתִי

hin'neyh a'no'khi sho'ley'ahh mal'akh le'pha'ney'kha lish'mar'kha ba'da'rekh

---

* "In the going out of the year" meaning "at the end of the year."
† Or "times."
‡ "The summit of the firstfruits" may mean the "first" or the "best" of the firstfruits.
§ The word "house" appears to be missing the prefix "to" or the suffix "unto."
** Or "milk."

Mechanical Translation Codes

<u>WORD</u> – Verb	WORD – Noun	Word – Name	word – Pre/Suff	*word* – Conj.

we'la'ha'vi'a'kha el ha'ma'qom a'sher ha'khi'no'ti

LOOK I <u>SEND</u>~*ing/er(ms)* MESSENGER to~ FACE~s~you(ms) to~>~<u>SAFEGUARD</u>~you(ms) in~the~ROAD and~to~>~*make*~<u>COME</u>~ you(ms) TO the~AREA WHICH *I~did~make~* <u>PREPARE</u>□	look, I {am} sending {a} messenger <in front of> you to safeguard you in the road, and to [bring] you to the area which I prepared,□

23:21 הִשָּׁמֶר מִפָּנָיו וּשְׁמַע בְּקֹלוֹ אַל תַּמֵּר בּוֹ כִּי לֹא יִשָּׂא לְפִשְׁעֲכֶם כִּי שְׁמִי בְּקִרְבּוֹ

hi'sha'mer mi'pa'naw ush'ma be'qo'lo al ta'meyr bo ki lo yi'sa le'phish'a'khem ki she'mi be'qir'bo

!*(ms)*~*be*~<u>SAFEGUARD</u> from~FACE~s~him and~!*(ms)*~<u>HEAR</u> in~VOICE~him DO-NOT *you(ms)*~*will*~*make*~<u>BE-BITTER</u> in~him GIVEN-THAT NOT *he~will*~<u>LIFT-UP</u> to~ TRANSGRESSION~you(mp) GIVEN-THAT TITLE~me in~WITHIN~him□	be safeguarded from his face, and hear his voice, you will not [provoke] him, given that he will not lift up* your transgression, given that my title {is} within him,□

23:22 כִּי אִם שָׁמֹעַ תִּשְׁמַע בְּקֹלוֹ וְעָשִׂיתָ כֹּל אֲשֶׁר אֲדַבֵּר וְאָיַבְתִּי אֶת אֹיְבֶיךָ וְצַרְתִּי אֶת צֹרְרֶיךָ

ki im sha'mo'a tish'ma be'qo'lo we'a'si'ta kol a'sher a'da'beyr we'a'yav'ti et oi'vey'kha we'tsar'ti et tsor'rey'kha

GIVEN-THAT IF >~<u>HEAR</u> *you(ms)*~*will*~<u>HEAR</u> in~VOICE~him and~*you(ms)*~*did*~<u>DO</u> ALL WHICH *I~will~much*~<u>SPEAK</u> and~*I~did~* <u>ATTACK</u> AT <u>ATTACK</u>~*ing/er(mp)*~you(ms) and~*I~did*~<u>SMACK</u> AT <u>PRESS-IN</u>~*ing/er(mp)*~ you(ms)□	<instead> you will :surely: hear his voice, and you will do all which I will speak, (then) I will attack your attackers, and I will smack your {op}pressors,□

23:23 כִּי יֵלֵךְ מַלְאָכִי לְפָנֶיךָ וֶהֱבִיאֲךָ אֶל הָאֱמֹרִי וְהַחִתִּי וְהַפְּרִזִּי וְהַכְּנַעֲנִי הַחִוִּי וְהַיְבוּסִי וְהִכְחַדְתִּיו

ki yey'leykh mal'a'khi le'pha'ney'kha we'he'vi'a'kha el ha'e'mo'ri we'ha'hhi'ti we'ha'pe'ri'zi we'hak'na'a'ni ha'hhi'wi we'hai'vu'si we'hikh'hhad'tiw

GIVEN-THAT *he~will*~<u>WALK</u> MESSENGER~me to~FACE~s~you(ms) and~*he~did~make~* <u>COME</u>~you(ms) TO the~"Emor ^{SAYER}"~of and~ the~"Hhet ^{TREMBLING-IN-FEAR}"~of and~the~ "Perez ^{PEASANT}"~of and~the~"Kena'an ^{LOWERED}"~of the~"Hhiw ^{TOWN}"~of and~the~ "Yevus ^{he~will~}<u>TRAMPLE-DOWN</u>"~of and~*I~did~* *make*~<u>KEEP-SECRET</u>~him□	given that, my messenger will walk <in front of> you, and he will [bring] you to the {one} of "Emor ^{Sayer}" and the {one} of "Hhet ^{Trembling in fear}" and the {one} of "Perez ^{Peasant}" and the {one} of "Kena'an ^{Lowered}", the {one} of "Hhiw ^{Town}" and the {one} of "Yevus ^{He will trample down}", and I will [hide] him†,□

---

* Meaning to "remove" or "forgive."

† In context, probably meaning to remove these people from the land.

Revised Mechanical Translation Codes

(..) Alt Trans/App A	<..> Comp Phrase/App B	[..] Verb Form/App C	\../ Plural Form/App D
:...: Int Inf Abs	|..| Past Perf Verb	{...} Added Word	

23:24 לֹא תִשְׁתַּחֲוֶה לֵאלֹהֵיהֶם וְלֹא תָעָבְדֵם וְלֹא תַעֲשֶׂה כְּמַעֲשֵׂיהֶם כִּי הָרֵס תְּהָרְסֵם וְשַׁבֵּר תְּשַׁבֵּר מַצֵּבֹתֵיהֶם

lo tish'ta'hha'weh ley'lo'hey'hem we'lo ta'av'deym we'lo ta'a'seh ke'ma'a'sey'hem ki ha'reys te'har'seym we'sha'beyr te'sha'beyr ma'tsey'vo'tey'hem

NOT *you(ms)~will~* self~<u>BEND-DOWN</u> to~ "Elohiym ^POWER~s^~them(m) and~NOT *you(ms)~will~be~make~*<u>SERVE</u>~them(m) and~NOT *you(ms)~will~*<u>DO</u> like~WORK~s~ them(m) GIVEN-THAT >~*much*~<u>CAST-DOWN</u> *you(ms)~will~much~*<u>CAST-DOWN</u>~them(m) and~>~*much*~<u>CRACK</u> *you(ms)~will~much~* <u>CRACK</u> MONUMENT~s~them(m)□

you will not bend {your}self down to their "Elohiym ^Powers^", and you will not be made {to} serve them, and you will not do like their works, given that you will :surely: cast them down, and you will :surely: [shatter] their monuments,□

23:25 וַעֲבַדְתֶּם אֵת יְהֹוָה אֱלֹהֵיכֶם וּבֵרַךְ אֶת לַחְמְךָ וְאֶת מֵימֶיךָ וַהֲסִרֹתִי מַחֲלָה מִקִּרְבֶּךָ

wa'a'vad'tem eyt YHWH e'lo'hey'khem u'vey'rakh et lahh'me'kha we'et mey'mey'kha wa'ha'si'ro'ti ma'hha'lah mi'qir'be'kha

and~*you(mp)~will~*<u>SERVE</u> AT "Yhwh ^he~will~<u>BE</u>^ "Elohiym ^POWER~s^~you(mp) and~*he~did~ much~*<u>KNEEL</u> AT BREAD~you(ms) and~AT WATER~s2~you(ms) and~*I~did~make~* <u>TURN-ASIDE</u> SICKNESS from~WITHIN~ you(ms)□

and you will serve "Yhwh ^He is^ your "Elohiym ^Powers^", and he will [respect] your bread and your waters, and I will [remove] sickness from within you,□

23:26 לֹא תִהְיֶה מְשַׁכֵּלָה וַעֲקָרָה בְּאַרְצֶךָ אֶת מִסְפַּר יָמֶיךָ אֲמַלֵּא

lo tih'yeh me'sha'key'lah wa'a'qa'rah be'ar'tse'kha et mis'par ya'mey'kha a'ma'ley

NOT *you(ms)~will~*<u>EXIST</u> *much~*<u>BE-CHILDLESS</u>~*ing/er(fs)* and~STERILE in~LAND~ you(ms) AT NUMBER DAY~s~you(ms) *I~will~ much~*<u>FILL</u>□

you will not [miscarry] (or) {be} sterile in your land, I will [fulfill] {the} number {of} your days,□

23:27 אֵת אֵימָתִי אֲשַׁלַּח לְפָנֶיךָ וְהַמֹּתִי אֶת כָּל הָעָם אֲשֶׁר תָּבֹא בָּהֶם וְנָתַתִּי אֶת כָּל אֹיְבֶיךָ אֵלֶיךָ עֹרֶף

et ey'ma'ti a'sha'lahh le'pha'ney'kha we'ha'mo'ti et kol ha'am a'sher ta'vo ba'hem we'na'ta'ti et kol oi'vey'kha ey'ley'kha o'reph

AT TERROR~me *I~will~much~*<u>SEND</u> to~ FACE~s~you(ms) and~*I~did~*<u>CONFUSE</u> AT ALL the~PEOPLE WHICH *you(ms)~will~*<u>COME</u> in~them(m) and~*I~did~*<u>GIVE</u> AT ALL

I will send my terror <in front of> you, and I will confuse all the people which you come (to), and I will give {the} neck {of} all your attackers to you*,□

---

* "Give the neck of all your attackers to you" is an idiom meaning "all your enemies will be defeated." In the Ancient Near East, the victorious king would place his foot on the neck of his enemy as a sign of victory over the defeated.

Mechanical Translation Codes

<u>WORD</u> – Verb	WORD – Noun	Word – Name	word – Pre/Suff	*word* – Conj.

ATTACK~*ing/er(mp)*~you(ms) TO~you(ms) NECK□

23:28 וְשָׁלַחְתִּי אֶת הַצִּרְעָה לְפָנֶיךָ וְגֵרְשָׁה אֶת הַחִוִּי אֶת הַכְּנַעֲנִי וְאֶת הַחִתִּי מִלְּפָנֶיךָ

we'sha'lahh'ti et ha'tsir'ah le'pha'ney'kha we'ger'shah et ha'hhi'wi et ha'ke'na'a'ni we'et ha'hhi'ti mil'pha'ney'kha

and~*I~did*~SEND AT the~HORNET to~FACE~s~you(ms) and~ she~*did~much*~CAST-OUT AT the~"Hhiw ^TOWN^"~of AT the~ "Kena'an ^LOWERED^"~of and~AT the~"Hhet ^TREMBLING-IN-FEAR^"~of from~to~FACE~s~ you(ms)□

and I will send the hornet <in front of> you, and she will cast out the {one} of "Hhiw ^Town^", the {one} of "Kena'an ^Lowered^" and the {one} of "Hhet ^Trembling in fear^", from <in front of> you,□

23:29 לֹא אֲגָרְשֶׁנּוּ מִפָּנֶיךָ בְּשָׁנָה אֶחָת פֶּן תִּהְיֶה הָאָרֶץ שְׁמָמָה וְרַבָּה עָלֶיךָ חַיַּת הַשָּׂדֶה

lo a'gar'she'nu mi'pa'ney'kha be'sha'nah e'hhat pen tih'yeh ha'a'rets she'ma'mah we'ra'bah a'ley'kha hhai'yat ha'sa'deh

NOT *I~will~much*~CAST-OUT~him from~FACE~s~you(ms) in~YEAR UNIT OTHERWISE she~*will*~EXIST the~LAND DESOLATE and~ she~*did*~INCREASE-IN-NUMBER UPON~ you(ms) LIVING the~FIELD□

I will not cast him out from your face* in (one) year, otherwise, the land will (be) desolate and {the} living {ones of} the field† will increase in number upon you,□

23:30 מְעַט מְעַט אֲגָרְשֶׁנּוּ מִפָּנֶיךָ עַד אֲשֶׁר תִּפְרֶה וְנָחַלְתָּ אֶת הָאָרֶץ

me'at me'at a'gar'she'nu mi'pa'ney'kha ad a'sher teph'reh we'na'hhal'ta et ha'a'rets

SMALL-AMOUNT SMALL-AMOUNT *I~will~ much*~CAST-OUT~him from~FACE~s~ you(ms) UNTIL WHICH *you(ms)~will*~ REPRODUCE and~*you(ms)~did*~INHERIT AT the~LAND□

I will cast him out <little by little> from your face‡, until you reproduce and you inherit the land,□

23:31 וְשַׁתִּי אֶת גְּבֻלְךָ מִיַּם סוּף וְעַד יָם פְּלִשְׁתִּים וּמִמִּדְבָּר עַד הַנָּהָר כִּי אֶתֵּן בְּיֶדְכֶם אֵת יֹשְׁבֵי הָאָרֶץ וְגֵרַשְׁתָּמוֹ מִפָּנֶיךָ

we'sha'ti et ge'vul'kha mi'yam suph we'ad yam pe'lish'tim u'mi'mid'bar ad ha'na'har ki e'teyn be'yed'khem eyt yosh'vey ha'a'rets we'gey'rash'ta'mo mi'pa'ney'kha

and~*I~did*~SET-DOWN AT BORDER~you(ms) from~SEA REEDS and~UNTIL SEA "Peleshet

and I will set down your border from {the} sea {of} reeds§ and unto {the} sea {of the} one{s

---

* "From your face" is an idiom meaning "from your presence."
† "The living ones of the field" is an idiom meaning "wild animals."
‡ "From your face" is an idiom meaning "from your presence."
§ "Sea of reeds," or "Yam Suph," is usually mistranslated as "red sea."

Revised Mechanical Translation Codes

(..) Alt Trans/App A	<..> Comp Phrase/App B	[..] Verb Form/App C	\../ Plural Form/App D
:..: Int Inf Abs	|..| Past Perf Verb	{...} Added Word	

IMMIGRANT_"~s and~from~WILDERNESS UNTIL the~RIVER GIVEN-THAT *I*~will~<u>GIVE</u> in~ HAND~you(mp) AT <u>SETTLE</u>~*ing/er*(mp) the~ LAND and~*you*(ms)~*did*~much~<u>CAST-OUT</u>~ them(m) from~FACE~s~you(ms)□

of} "Peleshet ^{Immigrant}", and from {the} wilderness unto the river, given that I will give {the} settlers {of} the land in your hand, and you will cast them out from your face*,□

23:32

לֹא תִכְרֹת לָהֶם וְלֵאלֹהֵיהֶם בְּרִית

lo tikh'rot la'hem we'ley'lo'hey'hem be'rit

NOT *you*(ms)~*will*~<u>CUT</u> to~them(m) and~to~ "Elohiym ^{POWER~s}"~them(m) COVENANT□

you will not cut {a} covenant (with) them (or) (with) their "Elohiym ^{Powers}",□

23:33   לֹא יֵשְׁבוּ בְּאַרְצְךָ פֶּן יַחֲטִיאוּ אֹתְךָ לִי כִּי תַעֲבֹד אֶת אֱלֹהֵיהֶם כִּי יִהְיֶה לְךָ לְמוֹקֵשׁ

lo yesh'vu be'arts'kha pen ya'hha'ti'u ot'kha li ki ta'a'vod et e'lo'hey'hem ki yih'yeh le'kha le'mo'qeysh

NOT *they*(m)~*will*~<u>SETTLE</u> in~LAND~you(ms) OTHERWISE *they*(m)~*will*~make~<u>ERR</u> AT~ you(ms) to~me GIVEN-THAT *you*(ms)~*will*~ <u>SERVE</u> AT "Elohiym ^{POWER~s}"~them(m) GIVEN-THAT *he*~*will*~<u>EXIST</u> to~you(ms) to~SNARE□

they will not settle in your land, otherwise, they will make you err to me, given that you will serve their "Elohiym ^{Powers}", given that he will exist (for) you (for) {a} snare,□

Chapter 24

24:1   וְאֶל מֹשֶׁה אָמַר עֲלֵה אֶל יְהוָה אַתָּה וְאַהֲרֹן נָדָב וַאֲבִיהוּא וְשִׁבְעִים מִזִּקְנֵי יִשְׂרָאֵל וְהִשְׁתַּחֲוִיתֶם מֵרָחֹק

we'el mo'sheh a'mar a'leyh el YHWH a'tah we'a'ha'ron na'dav wa'a'vi'hu we'shiv'im mi'ziq'ney yis'ra'eyl we'hish'ta'hha'wi'tem mey'ra'hhoq

and~TO "Mosheh ^{PLUCKED-OUT}" *he*~*did*~<u>SAY</u> !(ms)~<u>GO-UP</u> TO "Yhwh ^{he~will~<u>BE</u>}" YOU(ms) and~"Aharon ^{LIGHT-BRINGER}" "Nadav ^{he~did~<u>OFFER-WILLINGLY</u>}" and~"Aviyhu ^{FATHER~me~+~HE}" and~ SEVEN~s from~BEARD~s "Yisra'el ^{he~will~<u>TURN-ASIDE</u>~+~<u>MIGHTY-ONE</u>}" and~*you*(mp)~*did*~ self~ <u>BEND-DOWN</u> from~DISTANCE□

and to "Mosheh ^{Plucked out}" he said, go up to "Yhwh ^{He is}", you and "Aharon ^{Light bringer}", "Nadav ^{He offered willingly}" and "Aviyhu ^{He is my father}", and \seventy/ from {the} beard{ed one}s† {of} "Yisra'el ^{He turns El aside}", and you will bend {your}self down (at) {a} distance,□

24:2   וְנִגַּשׁ מֹשֶׁה לְבַדּוֹ אֶל יְהוָה וְהֵם לֹא יִגָּשׁוּ וְהָעָם לֹא יַעֲלוּ עִמּוֹ

we'ni'gash mo'sheh le'va'do el YHWH we'heym lo yi'ga'shu we'ha'am lo ya'a'lu i'mo

and~*he*~*did*~be~<u>DRAW-NEAR</u> "Mosheh

and "Mosheh ^{Plucked out}" <alone> will be drawn

---

* "From your face" is an idiom meaning "from your presence."
† "Bearded ones" is a euphemism for "elders."

Mechanical Translation Codes

<u>WORD</u> – Verb	WORD – Noun	Word – Name	word – Pre/Suff	*word* – Conj.

PLUCKED-OUT„ to~STICK~him TO "Yhwh ^{he~will~BE}„ and~THEY(m) NOT *they(m)~will~*DRAW-NEAR and~the~PEOPLE NOT *they(m)~will~* GO-UP WITH~him□

near to "Yhwh ^{He is}„, and they will not draw near, and the people will not go up with him,□

24:3 וַיָּבֹא מֹשֶׁה וַיְסַפֵּר לָעָם אֵת כָּל דִּבְרֵי יְהֹוָה וְאֵת כָּל הַמִּשְׁפָּטִים וַיַּעַן כָּל הָעָם קוֹל אֶחָד וַיֹּאמְרוּ כָּל הַדְּבָרִים אֲשֶׁר דִּבֶּר יְהֹוָה נַעֲשֶׂה

wai'ya'vo mo'sheh wai'sa'peyr la'am eyt kol div'rey YHWH we'eyt kol ha'mish'pa'tim wai'ya'an kol ha'am qol e'hhad wai'yom'ru kol had'va'rim a'sher di'ber YHWH na'a'seh

and~*he~will~*COME "Mosheh ^{PLUCKED-OUT}„ and~*he~will~much~*COUNT to~the~PEOPLE AT ALL WORD~s "Yhwh ^{he~will~BE}„ and~AT ALL the~DECISION~s and~*he~will~*ANSWER ALL the~PEOPLE VOICE UNIT and~*they(m)~will~* SAY ALL the~WORD~s WHICH *he~did~much~* SPEAK "Yhwh ^{he~will~BE}„ *we~will~*DO□

and "Mosheh ^{Plucked out}„ came and he [recounted] to the people all {the} words {of} "Yhwh ^{He is}„ and all the decisions, and all the people answered {with}* (one) voice, and they said, all the words which "Yhwh ^{He is}„ spoke, we will do,□

24:4 וַיִּכְתֹּב מֹשֶׁה אֵת כָּל דִּבְרֵי יְהֹוָה וַיַּשְׁכֵּם בַּבֹּקֶר וַיִּבֶן מִזְבֵּחַ תַּחַת הָהָר וּשְׁתֵּים עֶשְׂרֵה מַצֵּבָה לִשְׁנֵים עָשָׂר שִׁבְטֵי יִשְׂרָאֵל

wai'yikh'tov mo'sheh eyt kol div'rey YHWH wai'yash'keym ba'bo'qer wai'yi'ven miz'bey'ahh ta'hhat ha'har ush'teym es'reyh ma'tsey'vah lish'neym a'sar shiv'tey yis'ra'eyl

and~*he~will~*WRITE "Mosheh ^{PLUCKED-OUT}„ AT ALL WORD~s "Yhwh ^{he~will~BE}„ and~*he~will~* *make~*DEPART-EARLY in~the~MORNING and~*he~will~*BUILD ALTAR UNDER the~HILL and~TWO TEN MONUMENT to~TWO TEN STAFF~s "Yisra'el ^{he~will~TURN-ASIDE~+~MIGHTY-ONE}„□

and "Mosheh ^{Plucked out}„ wrote all {the} words {of} "Yhwh ^{He is}„, and he departed early in the morning, and he built {an} altar under† the hill, and <twelve> monument{s} (for) {the} <twelve> staffs‡ {of} "Yisra'el ^{He turns El aside}„,□

24:5 וַיִּשְׁלַח אֶת נַעֲרֵי בְּנֵי יִשְׂרָאֵל וַיַּעֲלוּ עֹלֹת וַיִּזְבְּחוּ זְבָחִים שְׁלָמִים לַיהֹוָה פָּרִים

wai'yish'lahh et na'a'rey be'ney yis'ra'eyl wai'ya'a'lu o'lot wai'yiz'be'hhu ze'va'hhim she'la'mim la'YHWH pa'rim

and~*he~will~*SEND AT YOUNG-MAN~s SON~s "Yisra'el ^{he~will~TURN-ASIDE~+~MIGHTY-ONE}„ and~*they(m)~will~make~*GO-UP RISING and~*they(m)~will~*SACRIFICE SACRIFICE~s COMPLETE~s to~"Yhwh ^{he~will~BE}„ BULL~s□

and he sent {the} young men {of the} sons {of} "Yisra'el ^{He turns El aside}„, and they [brought up] {a} rising {sacrifice}, and they sacrificed sacrifices, complete {sacrifices of} bulls to "Yhwh ^{He is}„,□

24:6 וַיִּקַּח מֹשֶׁה חֲצִי הַדָּם וַיָּשֶׂם בָּאַגָּנֹת וַחֲצִי הַדָּם זָרַק עַל הַמִּזְבֵּחַ

wai'yi'qahh mo'sheh hha'tsi ha'dam wai'ya'sem ba'a'ga'not wa'hha'tsi ha'dam za'raq al

---

* The Hebrew text appears to be missing the word "with" or the prefix "in."
† Meaning "the base."
‡ Also meaning "tribe," as each tribe was represented by a staff or standard.

Revised Mechanical Translation Codes

(..) Alt Trans/App A	<..> Comp Phrase/App B	[..] Verb Form/App C	\../ Plural Form/App D
:..: Int Inf Abs	|..| Past Perf Verb	{...} Added Word	

ha'miz'bey'ahh

and~*he~will*~<u>TAKE</u> "Mosheh ^{PLUCKED-OUT}„ HALF the~BLOOD and~*he~will*~<u>PLACE</u> in~the~GOBLET~s and~HALF the~BLOOD *he~did*~<u>SPRINKLE</u> UPON the~ALTAR□

and "Mosheh ^{Plucked out}„ took half {of} the blood and he placed {it} in the goblets, and half {of} the blood he sprinkled upon the altar,□

24:7 וַיִּקַּח סֵפֶר הַבְּרִית וַיִּקְרָא בְּאָזְנֵי הָעָם וַיֹּאמְרוּ כֹּל אֲשֶׁר דִּבֶּר יְהוָה נַעֲשֶׂה וְנִשְׁמָע

wai'yi'qahh sey'pher ha'be'rit wai'yiq'ra be'az'ney ha'am wai'yom'ru kol a'sher di'ber YHWH na'a'seh we'nish'ma

and~*he~will*~<u>TAKE</u> SCROLL the~COVENANT and~*he~will*~<u>CALL-OUT</u> in~EAR~s2 the~PEOPLE and~*they(m)~will*~<u>SAY</u> ALL WHICH *he~did~much*~<u>SPEAK</u> "Yhwh ^{*he~will*~<u>BE</u>}„ *we~will*~<u>DO</u> and~*we~will*~<u>HEAR</u>□

and he took {the} scroll {of} the covenant and he called {it} out* in {the} ears {of} the people, and they said, all which "Yhwh ^{He is}„ spoke, we will do and we will hear,□

24:8 וַיִּקַּח מֹשֶׁה אֶת הַדָּם וַיִּזְרֹק עַל הָעָם וַיֹּאמֶר הִנֵּה דַם הַבְּרִית אֲשֶׁר כָּרַת יְהוָה עִמָּכֶם עַל כָּל הַדְּבָרִים הָאֵלֶּה

wai'yi'qahh mo'sheh et ha'dam wai'yiz'roq al ha'am wai'yo'mer hin'neyh dam ha'be'rit a'sher ka'rat YHWH i'ma'khem al kol had'va'rim ha'ey'leh

and~*he~will*~<u>TAKE</u> "Mosheh ^{PLUCKED-OUT}„ AT the~BLOOD and~*he~will*~<u>SPRINKLE</u> UPON the~PEOPLE and~*he~will*~<u>SAY</u> LOOK BLOOD the~COVENANT WHICH *he~did*~<u>CUT</u> "Yhwh ^{*he~will*~<u>BE</u>}„ WITH~*you(mp)* UPON ALL the~WORD~s the~THESE□

and "Mosheh ^{Plucked out}„ took the blood and he sprinkled {it} upon the people, and he said, look, {the} blood {of} the covenant, which "Yhwh ^{He is}„ cut with you (concerning) all these words,□

24:9 וַיַּעַל מֹשֶׁה וְאַהֲרֹן נָדָב וַאֲבִיהוּא וְשִׁבְעִים מִזִּקְנֵי יִשְׂרָאֵל

wai'ya'al mo'sheh we'a'ha'ron na'dav wa'a'vi'hu we'shiv'im mi'ziq'ney yis'ra'eyl

and~*he~will*~<u>GO-UP</u> "Mosheh ^{PLUCKED-OUT}„ and~"Aharon ^{LIGHT-BRINGER}„ "Nadav ^{*he~did*~<u>OFFER-WILLINGLY</u>}„ and~"Aviyhu ^{FATHER~me+HE}„ and~SEVEN~s from~BEARD~s "Yisra'el ^{*he~will*~<u>TURN-ASIDE~+~MIGHTY-ONE</u>}„□

and "Mosheh ^{Plucked out}„ went up, and "Aharon ^{Light bringer}„, "Nadav ^{He offered willingly}„ and "Aviyhu ^{He is my father}„, and \seventy/ from {the} beard{ed one}s† {of} "Yisra'el ^{He turns El aside}„,□

24:10 וַיִּרְאוּ אֵת אֱלֹהֵי יִשְׂרָאֵל וְתַחַת רַגְלָיו כְּמַעֲשֵׂה לִבְנַת הַסַּפִּיר וּכְעֶצֶם הַשָּׁמַיִם לָטֹהַר

wai'yir'u eyt e'lo'hey yis'ra'eyl we'ta'hhat rag'law ke'ma'a'seyh liv'nat ha'sa'pir ukh'e'tsem ha'sha'ma'yim la'to'har

and~*they(m)~will*~<u>SEE</u> AT "Elohiym ^{POWER~s}„

and they saw "Elohiym ^{Powers}„ {of} "Yisra'el ^{He}

---

* Or "read it."

† "Bearded ones" is a euphemism for "elders."

Mechanical Translation Codes

<u>WORD</u> – Verb	WORD – Noun	Word – Name	word – Pre/Suff	*word* – Conj.

"Yisra'el ^{he~will~}<u>TURN-ASIDE</u>~+~^{MIGHTY-ONE}" and~ UNDER FOOT~s2~him like~WORK BRICK the~LAPIS-LAZULI and~like~BONE the~ SKY~s2 to~CLEANLINESS□

^{turns El aside}", and under his feet {was} like {a} work {of} brick* {of} the lapis-lazuli, and like {a} bone {of} the skies (for) cleanliness†,□

24:11 וְאֶל אֲצִילֵי בְּנֵי יִשְׂרָאֵל לֹא שָׁלַח יָדוֹ וַיֶּחֱזוּ אֶת הָאֱלֹהִים וַיֹּאכְלוּ וַיִּשְׁתּוּ

we'el a'tsi'ley be'ney yis'ra'eyl lo sha'lahh ya'do wai'ye'hhe'zu et ha'e'lo'him wai'yokh'lu wai'yish'tu

and~TO LEADER~s SON~s "Yisra'el ^{he~will~}<u>TURN-ASIDE</u>~+~^{MIGHTY-ONE}" NOT he~did~<u>SEND</u> HAND~ him and~they(m)~will~<u>PERCEIVE</u> AT the~ "Elohiym ^{POWER~s}" and~they(m)~will~<u>EAT</u> and~they(m)~will~<u>GULP</u>□

and to {the} leaders {of the} sons {of} "Yisra'el ^{He turns El aside}" he did not send his hand‡, and they perceived the "Elohiym ^{Powers}", and they ate and they gulped,□

24:12 וַיֹּאמֶר יְהוָה אֶל מֹשֶׁה עֲלֵה אֵלַי הָהָרָה וֶהְיֵה שָׁם וְאֶתְּנָה לְךָ אֶת לֻחֹת הָאֶבֶן וְהַתּוֹרָה וְהַמִּצְוָה אֲשֶׁר כָּתַבְתִּי לְהוֹרֹתָם

wai'yo'mer YHWH el mo'sheh a'leyh ey'lai ha'ha'rah weh'yey sham we'et'nah le'kha et lu'hhot ha'e'ven we'ha'to'rah we'ha'mits'wah a'sher ka'tav'ti le'ho'ro'tam

and~he~will~<u>SAY</u> "Yhwh ^{he~will~}<u>BE</u>" TO "Mosheh ^{PLUCKED-OUT}" !(ms)~<u>GO-UP</u> TO~me the~HILL~unto and~!(ms)~<u>EXIST</u> THERE and~ I~will~<u>GIVE</u>~^ to~you(ms) AT SLAB~s the~ STONE and~the~TEACHING and~the~ DIRECTIVE WHICH I~did~<u>WRITE</u> to~>~make~ THROW~them(m)□

and "Yhwh ^{He is}" said to "Mosheh ^{Plucked out}", go up to me unto the hill and exist there, and I will give to you slabs {of} the stone, and the teaching and the directive which I wrote to [teach] them,□

24:13 וַיָּקָם מֹשֶׁה וִיהוֹשֻׁעַ מְשָׁרְתוֹ וַיַּעַל מֹשֶׁה אֶל הַר הָאֱלֹהִים

wai'ya'qam mo'sheh wi'ho'shu'a me'shar'to wai'ya'al mo'sheh el har ha'e'lo'him

and~he~will~<u>RISE</u> "Mosheh ^{PLUCKED-OUT}" and~ "Yehoshu'a ^{EXISTING~+~he~will~}<u>RESCUE</u>" much~ MINISTER~ing/er(ms)~him and~he~will~<u>GO-UP</u> "Mosheh ^{PLUCKED-OUT}" TO HILL the~ "Elohiym ^{POWER~s}"□

and "Mosheh ^{Plucked out}" rose, and "Yehoshu'a ^{Yah will rescue}" his minister, and "Mosheh ^{Plucked out}" went up to {the} hill {of} the "Elohiym ^{Powers}",□

24:14 וְאֶל הַזְּקֵנִים אָמַר שְׁבוּ לָנוּ בָזֶה עַד אֲשֶׁר נָשׁוּב אֲלֵיכֶם וְהִנֵּה אַהֲרֹן וְחוּר עִמָּכֶם מִי בַעַל דְּבָרִים יִגַּשׁ אֲלֵהֶם

we'el haz'qey'nim a'mar she'vu la'nu va'zeh ad a'sher na'shuv a'ley'khem we'hin'neyh a'ha'ron we'hhur i'ma'khem mi va'al de'va'rim yi'gash a'ley'hem

---

* This Hebrew word may also mean a "poplar" or the "moon."
† The meaning of the phrase "like a bone of the skies for cleanliness" is uncertain.
‡ "He did not send his hand" probably means that "he did not strike" them.

Revised Mechanical Translation Codes

(..) Alt Trans/App A   <..> Comp Phrase/App B   [..] Verb Form/App C   \../ Plural Form/App D
:..: Int Inf Abs |..| Past Perf Verb   {...} Added Word

and~TO the~BEARD~s he~did~<u>SAY</u> !(mp)~ <u>SETTLE</u> to~us in~THIS UNTIL WHICH *we~will~* <u>TURN-BACK</u> TO~you(mp) and~LOOK "Aharon ^{LIGHT-BRINGER}" and~"Hhur ^{CISTERN}" WITH~ you(mp) WHO MASTER WORD~s he~will~ <u>DRAW-NEAR</u> TO~them(m)□

and to the beard{ed one}s* he said, settle (for) us <here>, until we turn back to you, and look, "Aharon ^{Light bringer}" and "Hhur ^{Cistern}" {are} with you, who{ever is a} master {of} words† will draw near to them,□

24:15

וַיַּעַל מֹשֶׁה אֶל הָהָר וַיְכַס הֶעָנָן אֶת הָהָר

wai'ya'al mo'sheh el ha'har wai'khas he'a'nan et ha'har

and~he~will~<u>GO-UP</u> "Mosheh ^{PLUCKED-OUT}" TO the~HILL and~he~will~much~<u>COVER-OVER</u> the~CLOUD AT the~HILL□

and "Mosheh ^{Plucked out}" went up to the hill, and the cloud covered over the hill,□

24:16

וַיִּשְׁכֹּן כְּבוֹד יְהוָה עַל הַר סִינַי וַיְכַסֵּהוּ הֶעָנָן שֵׁשֶׁת יָמִים וַיִּקְרָא אֶל מֹשֶׁה בַּיּוֹם הַשְּׁבִיעִי מִתּוֹךְ הֶעָנָן

wai'yish'kon ke'vod YHWH al har si'nai wai'kha'sey'hu he'a'nan shey'shet ya'mim wai'yiq'ra el mo'sheh ba'yom hash'vi'i mi'tokh he'a'nan

and~he~will~<u>DWELL</u> ARMAMENT "Yhwh ^{he~will~<u>BE</u>}" UPON HILL "Sinai ^{SHARP-THORN~s~me}" and~ he~will~much~<u>COVER-OVER</u>~him the~ CLOUD SIX DAY~s and~he~will~<u>CALL-OUT</u> TO "Mosheh ^{PLUCKED-OUT}" in~the~DAY the~ SEVENTH from~MIDST the~CLOUD□

and {the} armament {of} "Yhwh ^{He is}" dwelled upon {the} hill {of} "Sinai ^{My sharp thorns}", and the cloud covered over him‡ {for} six days, and he called out to "Mosheh ^{Plucked out}" in the seventh day from {the} midst {of} the cloud,□

24:17

וּמַרְאֵה כְּבוֹד יְהוָה כְּאֵשׁ אֹכֶלֶת בְּרֹאשׁ הָהָר לְעֵינֵי בְּנֵי יִשְׂרָאֵל

u'mar'eyh ke'vod YHWH ke'eysh o'khe'let be'rosh ha'har le'ey'ney be'ney yis'ra'eyl

and~APPEARANCE ARMAMENT "Yhwh ^{he~will~<u>BE</u>}" like~FIRE <u>EAT</u>~ing/er(fs) in~HEAD the~ HILL to~EYE~s2 SON~s "Yisra'el ^{he~will~<u>TURN-ASIDE</u>~+~MIGHTY-ONE}"□

and {the} appearance {of the} armament {of} "Yhwh ^{He is}" {was} like {a} fire eating in {the} head {of} the hill§ to {the} eyes {of the} sons {of} "Yisra'el ^{He turns El aside}",□

24:18

וַיָּבֹא מֹשֶׁה בְּתוֹךְ הֶעָנָן וַיַּעַל אֶל הָהָר וַיְהִי מֹשֶׁה בָּהָר אַרְבָּעִים יוֹם וְאַרְבָּעִים לָיְלָה

wai'ya'vo mo'sheh be'tokh he'a'nan wai'ya'al el ha'har wai'hi mo'sheh ba'har ar'ba'im yom we'ar'ba'im lai'lah

and~he~will~<u>COME</u> "Mosheh ^{PLUCKED-OUT}" in~ MIDST the~CLOUD and~he~will~<u>GO-UP</u> TO the~HILL and~he~will~<u>EXIST</u> "Mosheh ^{PLUCKED-}

and "Mosheh ^{Plucked out}" came in {the} midst {of} the cloud, and he went up to the hill, and "Mosheh ^{Plucked out}" existed in the hill {for}

---

* "Bearded ones" is a euphemism for "elders."

† The phrase "master of words" apparently means "one with a dispute."

‡ Referring to the "hill," a masculine word in Hebrew.

§ The phrase "like a fire eating in the head of the hill" means "like a fire devouring everything on top of the hill."

Mechanical Translation Codes

<u>WORD</u> – Verb	WORD – Noun	Word – Name	word – Pre/Suff	*word* – Conj.

^{OUT}„ in~the~HILL FOUR~s DAY and~FOUR~s NIGHT☐

\forty/ day{s} and \forty/ night{s},☐

Chapter 25

25:1

וַיְדַבֵּר יְהוָה אֶל מֹשֶׁה לֵּאמֹר

wai'da'beyr YHWH el mo'sheh ley'mor

and~he~will~much~<u>SPEAK</u> "Yhwh ^{he~will~BE}„ TO "Mosheh ^{PLUCKED-OUT}„ to~>~<u>SAY</u>☐

and "Yhwh ^{He is}„ spoke to "Mosheh ^{Plucked out}„ say{ing},☐

25:2

דַּבֵּר אֶל בְּנֵי יִשְׂרָאֵל וְיִקְחוּ לִי תְּרוּמָה מֵאֵת כָּל אִישׁ אֲשֶׁר יִדְּבֶנּוּ לִבּוֹ תִּקְחוּ אֶת תְּרוּמָתִי

da'beyr el be'ney yis'ra'eyl we'yiq'hhu li te'ru'mah mey'eyt kol ish a'sher yid've'nu li'bo tiq'hhu et te'ru'ma'ti

!(ms)~much~<u>SPEAK</u> TO SON~s "Yisra'el ^{he~will~TURN-ASIDE~+~MIGHTY-ONE}„ and~they(m)~will~<u>TAKE</u> to~me OFFERING from~AT ALL MAN WHICH he~will~<u>OFFER-WILLINGLY</u>~him HEART~him you(mp)~will~<u>TAKE</u> AT OFFERING~me☐

speak to {the} sons {of} "Yisra'el ^{He turns El aside}„ and they will take (for) me {an} offering from (every) man (whose) heart will offer willingly, you will take my offering,☐

25:3

וְזֹאת הַתְּרוּמָה אֲשֶׁר תִּקְחוּ מֵאִתָּם זָהָב וָכֶסֶף וּנְחֹשֶׁת

we'zot hat'ru'mah a'sher tiq'hhu mey'i'tam za'hav wa'ke'seph un'hho'shet

and~THIS the~OFFERING WHICH you(mp)~will~<u>TAKE</u> from~AT~them(m) GOLD and~SILVER and~COPPER☐

and this {is} the offering which you will take from them, gold and silver and copper,☐

25:4

וּתְכֵלֶת וְאַרְגָּמָן וְתוֹלַעַת שָׁנִי וְשֵׁשׁ וְעִזִּים

ut'khey'let we'ar'ga'man we'to'la'at sha'ni we'sheysh we'i'zim

and~BLUE and~PURPLE and~KERMES SCARLET and~LINEN and~SHE-GOAT~s☐

and blue and purple and kermes {of} scarlet and linen and she-goats,☐

25:5

וְעֹרֹת אֵילִם מְאָדָּמִים וְעֹרֹת תְּחָשִׁים וַעֲצֵי שִׁטִּים

we'o'rot ey'lim me'a'da'mim we'o'rot te'hha'sim wa'a'tsey shi'tim

and~SKIN~s BUCK~s be~much~<u>BE-RED</u>~ing/er(mp) and~SKIN~s TAHHASH~s and~TREE~s ACACIA~s☐

and skins {of} bucks being red, and {the} skins {of the} tahhashs*, and \wood/ {of} acacia,☐

---

* The Tahhash is an unknown species of animal.

Revised Mechanical Translation Codes

(..) Alt Trans/App A   <..> Comp Phrase/App B   [..] Verb Form/App C   \../ Plural Form/App D
:..: Int Inf Abs |..| Past Perf Verb   {...} Added Word

25:6

שֶׁמֶן לַמָּאֹר בְּשָׂמִים לְשֶׁמֶן הַמִּשְׁחָה וְלִקְטֹרֶת הַסַּמִּים

she'men la'ma'or be'sa'mim le'she'men ha'mish'hhah we'liq'to'ret ha'sa'mim

OIL to~the~LUMINARY SWEET-SPICE~s to~ OIL the~OINTMENT and~to~INCENSE the~ AROMATIC-SPICE~s□

oil (for) the luminary, sweet spices (for) the oil {of} ointment and (for) the incense {of} aromatic spices,□

25:7

אַבְנֵי שֹׁהַם וְאַבְנֵי מִלֻּאִים לָאֵפֹד וְלַחֹשֶׁן

av'ney sho'ham we'av'ney mi'lu'im la'ey'phod we'lahh'shen

STONE~s ONYX and~STONE~s INSTALLATION~s to~the~EPHOD and~to~ the~BREASTPLATE□

stones {of the} onyx* and stones {of the} installations (for) the ephod and (for) the breastplate,□

25:8

וְעָשׂוּ לִי מִקְדָּשׁ וְשָׁכַנְתִּי בְּתוֹכָם

we'a'su li miq'dash we'sha'khan'ti be'to'kham

and~*they~did~*<u>DO</u> to~me SANCTUARY and~ *I~did~*<u>DWELL</u> in~MIDST~them(m)□

and they will (make) (for) me {a} sanctuary, and I will dwell in their midst,□

25:9

כְּכֹל אֲשֶׁר אֲנִי מַרְאֶה אוֹתְךָ אֵת תַּבְנִית הַמִּשְׁכָּן וְאֵת תַּבְנִית כָּל כֵּלָיו וְכֵן תַּעֲשׂוּ

ke'khol a'sher a'ni mar'eh ot'kha eyt tav'nit ha'mish'kan we'eyt tav'nit kol key'law we'kheyn ta'a'su

like~ALL WHICH I *make~*<u>SEE</u>~*ing/er(ms)* AT~ you(ms) AT PATTERN the~DWELLING and~ AT PATTERN ALL ITEM~s~him and~SO *you(mp)~will~*<u>DO</u>□

like (every) {thing} (that) I [showed] you, {the} pattern {of} the dwelling and {the} pattern {of} all his items, and so you will (make),□

25:10

וְעָשׂוּ אֲרוֹן עֲצֵי שִׁטִּים אַמָּתַיִם וָחֵצִי אָרְכּוֹ וְאַמָּה וָחֵצִי רָחְבּוֹ וְאַמָּה וָחֵצִי קֹמָתוֹ

we'a'su a'ron a'tsey shi'tim a'ma'ta'yim wa'hhey'tsi ar'ko we'a'mah wa'hhey'tsi rahh'bo we'a'mah wa'hhey'tsi qo'ma'to

and~*they~did~*<u>DO</u> BOX TREE~s ACACIA~s FOREARM~s2 and~HALF LENGTH~him and~ FOREARM and~HALF WIDTH~him and~ FOREARM and~HALF HEIGHT~him□

and they will (make) {a} box {of} \wood/ {of} acacia, two forearms and {a} half {is} his length, and {a} forearm and {a} half {is} his width, and {a} forearm and {a} half {is} his height,□

25:11

וְצִפִּיתָ אֹתוֹ זָהָב טָהוֹר מִבַּיִת וּמִחוּץ תְּצַפֶּנּוּ וְעָשִׂיתָ עָלָיו זֵר זָהָב סָבִיב

we'tsi'pi'ta o'to za'hav ta'hor mi'ba'yit u'mi'hhuts te'tsa'pe'nu we'a'si'ta a'law zeyr za'hav sa'viv

---

* The "shoham" is unknown stone.

Mechanical Translation Codes

| <u>WORD</u> – Verb | WORD – Noun | Word – Name | word – Pre/Suff | *word* – Conj. |

and~you(ms)~did~much~<u>OVERLAY</u> AT~him GOLD PURE from~HOUSE and~from~ OUTSIDE you(ms)~will~much~<u>OVERLAY</u>~him and~you(ms)~did~<u>DO</u> UPON~him MOLDING GOLD ALL-AROUND□

and you will overlay him* {with} pure gold, from {the} (inside) and {the} outside you will overlay him, and you will (make) upon him {a} molding {of} gold all around,□

25:12 וְיָצַקְתָּ לּוֹ אַרְבַּע טַבְּעֹת זָהָב וְנָתַתָּה עַל אַרְבַּע פַּעֲמֹתָיו וּשְׁתֵּי טַבָּעֹת עַל צַלְעוֹ הָאֶחָת וּשְׁתֵּי טַבָּעֹת עַל צַלְעוֹ הַשֵּׁנִית

we'ya'tsaq'ta lo ar'ba ta'be'ot za'hav we'na'ta'tah al ar'ba pa'a'mo'taw ush'tey ta'ba'ot al tsal'o ha'e'hhat ush'tey ta'ba'ot al tsal'o ha'shey'nit

and~you(ms)~did~<u>POUR-DOWN</u> to~him FOUR RING~s GOLD and~you(ms)~did~ <u>GIVE</u>~^ UPON FOUR FOOTSTEP~s~him and~ TWO RING~s UPON RIB~him the~UNIT and~ TWO RING~s UPON RIB~him the~SECOND□

and you will pour down† (for) him four rings {of} gold, and you will (place) upon {it} his four footsteps‡, and two rings upon his (one) rib, and two rings upon his second rib,□

25:13 וְעָשִׂיתָ בַדֵּי עֲצֵי שִׁטִּים וְצִפִּיתָ אֹתָם זָהָב

we'a'si'ta va'dey a'tsey shi'tim we'tsi'pi'ta o'tam za'hav

and~you(ms)~did~<u>DO</u> STICK~s TREE~s ACACIA~s and~you(ms)~did~much~<u>OVERLAY</u> AT~them(m) GOLD□

and you will (make) sticks {of} \wood/ {of} acacia, and you will overlay them {with} gold,□

25:14 וְהֵבֵאתָ אֶת הַבַּדִּים בַּטַּבָּעֹת עַל צַלְעֹת הָאָרֹן לָשֵׂאת אֶת הָאָרֹן בָּהֶם

we'hey'vey'ta et ha'ba'dim ba'ta'ba'ot al tsal'ot ha'a'ron la'seyt et ha'a'ron ba'hem

and~you(ms)~did~make~<u>COME</u> AT the~ STICK~s in~the~RING~s UPON RIB~s the~ BOX to~>~<u>LIFT-UP</u> AT the~BOX in~them(m)□

and you will [bring] the sticks in the rings upon {the} ribs {of} the box to lift up the box (with) them,□

25:15 בְּטַבְּעֹת הָאָרֹן יִהְיוּ הַבַּדִּים לֹא יָסֻרוּ מִמֶּנּוּ

be'ta'be'ot ha'a'ron yih'yu ha'ba'dim lo ya'su'ru mi'me'nu

in~RING~s the~BOX they(m)~will~<u>EXIST</u> the~ STICK~s NOT they(m)~will~<u>TURN-ASIDE</u> FROM~him□

the sticks will exist in {the} rings {of} the box, they will not turn aside from him,□

25:16 וְנָתַתָּ אֶל הָאָרֹן אֵת הָעֵדֻת אֲשֶׁר אֶתֵּן אֵלֶיךָ

we'na'ta'ta el ha'a'ron eyt ha'ey'dut a'sher e'teyn ey'ley'kha

and~you(ms)~did~<u>GIVE</u> TO the~BOX AT the~ EVIDENCE WHICH I~will~<u>GIVE</u> TO~you(ms)□

and you will (place) (by) the box, the evidence which I will give to you,□

---

* Referring to the "box," a masculine word in Hebrew.
† In this context, to "pour down" means to "cast" an object from a molten metal.
‡ Or "feet."

Revised Mechanical Translation Codes
(..) Alt Trans/App A   <..> Comp Phrase/App B   [..] Verb Form/App C   \../ Plural Form/App D
:..: Int Inf Abs |..| Past Perf Verb   {...} Added Word

25:17 וְעָשִׂיתָ כַפֹּרֶת זָהָב טָהוֹר אַמָּתַיִם וָחֵצִי אָרְכָּהּ וְאַמָּה וָחֵצִי רָחְבָּהּ

we'a'si'ta kha'po'ret za'hav ta'hor a'ma'ta'yim wa'hhey'tsi ar'kah we'a'mah wa'hhey'tsi rahh'bah

and~you(ms)~did~<u>DO</u> LID GOLD PURE FOREARM~s2 and~HALF LENGTH~her and~FOREARM and~HALF WIDTH~her□

and you will (make) {a} lid {of} pure gold, two forearms and {a} half {is} her length, and {a} forearm and {a} half {is} her width,□

25:18 וְעָשִׂיתָ שְׁנַיִם כְּרֻבִים זָהָב מִקְשָׁה תַּעֲשֶׂה אֹתָם מִשְּׁנֵי קְצוֹת הַכַּפֹּרֶת

we'a'si'ta she'na'yim ke'ru'vim za'hav miq'shah ta'a'seh o'tam mish'ney qe'tsot ha'ka'po'ret

and~you(ms)~did~<u>DO</u> TWO KERUV~s GOLD BEATEN-WORK you(ms)~will~<u>DO</u> AT~them(m) from~TWO EXTREMITY~s the~LID□

and you will (make) two keruvs {of} gold {of} beaten work, you will (make) them (at) {the} two extremities {of} the lid,*□

25:19 וַעֲשֵׂה כְּרוּב אֶחָד מִקָּצָה מִזֶּה וּכְרוּב אֶחָד מִקָּצָה מִזֶּה מִן הַכַּפֹּרֶת תַּעֲשׂוּ אֶת הַכְּרֻבִים עַל שְׁנֵי קְצוֹתָיו

wa'a'seyh ke'ruv e'hhad mi'qa'tsah mi'zeh ukh'ruv e'hhad mi'qa'tsah mi'zeh min ha'ka'po'ret ta'a'su et hak'ru'vim al she'ney qe'tso'taw

and~!(ms)~<u>DO</u> KERUV UNIT from~EXTREMITY from~THIS and~KERUV UNIT from~EXTREMITY from~THIS FROM the~LID you(mp)~will~<u>DO</u> AT the~KERUV~s UPON TWO EXTREMITY~s~him□

and (make) (one) keruv (at) this extremity, and (one) keruv (at) (that) extremity, from the lid you will (make) the keruvs upon two {of} his extremities,□

25:20 וְהָיוּ הַכְּרֻבִים פֹּרְשֵׂי כְנָפַיִם לְמַעְלָה סֹכְכִים בְּכַנְפֵיהֶם עַל הַכַּפֹּרֶת וּפְנֵיהֶם אִישׁ אֶל אָחִיו אֶל הַכַּפֹּרֶת יִהְיוּ פְּנֵי הַכְּרֻבִים

we'hai'u hak'ru'vim por'sey khe'na'pha'yim le'ma'lah sokh'khim be'khan'phey'hem al ha'ka'po'ret uph'ney'hem ish el a'hhiw el ha'ka'po'ret yih'yu pe'ney hak'ru'vim

and~they~did~<u>EXIST</u> the~KERUV~s <u>SPREAD-OUT</u>~ing/er(mp) WING~s2 to~UPWARD~ unto <u>FENCE-AROUND</u>~ing/er(mp) in~WING~s~them(m) UPON the~LID and~FACE~s~them(m) MAN TO BROTHER~him TO the~LID they(m)~will~<u>EXIST</u> FACE~s the~KERUV~s□

and the keruvs will (be) spreading out {the} wings <above>, fencing around (with) their wings upon the lid, and their faces (each) to his brother, {the} faces {of} the keruvs will exist to{ward} the lid,□

25:21 וְנָתַתָּ אֶת הַכַּפֹּרֶת עַל הָאָרֹן מִלְמָעְלָה וְאֶל הָאָרֹן תִּתֵּן אֶת הָעֵדֻת אֲשֶׁר אֶתֵּן אֵלֶיךָ

we'na'ta'ta et ha'ka'po'ret al ha'a'ron mil'ma'lah we'el ha'a'ron ti'teyn et ha'ey'dut

---

* This verse may also be translated as, "and you will make two keruvs of gold, of beaten work you will make them, at the two ends of the lid."

Mechanical Translation Codes

<u>WORD</u> – Verb	WORD – Noun	Word – Name	word – Pre/Suff	*word* – Conj.

a'sher e'teyn ey'ley'kha

and~you(ms)~did~<u>GIVE</u> AT the~LID UPON the~BOX from~to~UPWARD~unto and~TO the~BOX you(ms)~will~<u>GIVE</u> AT the~ EVIDENCE WHICH I~will~<u>GIVE</u> TO~you(ms)□	and you will (place) the lid upon {the} <top> {of} the box, and (by) the box you will (place) the evidence which I will give to you,□

25:22 וְנוֹעַדְתִּי לְךָ שָׁם וְדִבַּרְתִּי אִתְּךָ מֵעַל הַכַּפֹּרֶת מִבֵּין שְׁנֵי הַכְּרֻבִים אֲשֶׁר עַל אֲרֹן הָעֵדֻת אֵת כָּל אֲשֶׁר אֲצַוֶּה אוֹתְךָ אֶל בְּנֵי יִשְׂרָאֵל

we'no'ad'ti le'kha sham we'di'bar'ti it'kha mey'al ha'ka'po'ret mi'beyn she'ney hak'ru'vim a'sher al a'ron ha'ey'dut eyt kol a'sher a'tsa'weh ot'kha el be'ney yis'ra'eyl

and~I~did~be~<u>APPOINT</u> to~you(ms) THERE and~I~did~much~<u>SPEAK</u> AT~you(ms) from~ UPON the~LID from~BETWEEN TWO the~ KERUV~s WHICH UPON BOX the~EVIDENCE AT ALL WHICH I~will~much~<u>DIRECT</u> AT~ you(ms) TO SON~s "Yisra'el ^{he~will~}<u>TURN-ASIDE</u>~+~ MIGHTY-ONE"□	and I was appointed to you there, and from upon the lid, from between {the} two keruvs, which {are} upon the box {of the} evidence, I will speak (with) you {of} all which I will direct you (for) {the} sons {of} "Yisra'el ^{He turns El aside}",□

25:23 וְעָשִׂיתָ שֻׁלְחָן עֲצֵי שִׁטִּים אַמָּתַיִם אָרְכּוֹ וְאַמָּה רָחְבּוֹ וְאַמָּה וָחֵצִי קֹמָתוֹ

we'a'si'ta shul'hhan a'tsey shi'tim a'ma'ta'yim ar'ko we'a'mah rahh'bo we'a'mah wa'hhey'tsi qo'ma'to

and~you(ms)~did~<u>DO</u> TABLE TREE~s ACACIA~s FOREARM~s2 LENGTH~him and~ FOREARM WIDTH~him and~FOREARM and~ HALF HEIGHT~him□	and you will (make) {a} table {of} \wood/ {of} acacia, two forearms {is} his length, and {a} forearm {is} his width, and {a} forearm and {a} half {is} his height,□

25:24 וְצִפִּיתָ אֹתוֹ זָהָב טָהוֹר וְעָשִׂיתָ לּוֹ זֵר זָהָב סָבִיב

we'tsi'pi'ta o'to za'hav ta'hor we'a'si'ta lo zeyr za'hav sa'viv

and~you(ms)~did~much~<u>OVERLAY</u> AT~him GOLD PURE and~you(ms)~did~<u>DO</u> to~him MOLDING GOLD ALL-AROUND□	and you will overlay him* {with} pure gold, and you will (make) (for) him {a} molding {of} gold all around,□

25:25 וְעָשִׂיתָ לּוֹ מִסְגֶּרֶת טֹפַח סָבִיב וְעָשִׂיתָ זֵר זָהָב לְמִסְגַּרְתּוֹ סָבִיב

we'a'si'ta lo mis'ge'ret to'phahh sa'viv we'a'si'ta zeyr za'hav le'mis'gar'to sa'viv

and~you(ms)~did~<u>DO</u> to~him RIM HAND-SPAN ALL-AROUND and~you(ms)~did~<u>DO</u> MOLDING GOLD to~RIM~him ALL-AROUND□	and you will (make) (for) him {a} rim {of a} hand span all around, and you will (make) {a} molding {of} gold (for) his rim all around,□

25:26 וְעָשִׂיתָ לּוֹ אַרְבַּע טַבְּעֹת זָהָב וְנָתַתָּ אֶת הַטַּבָּעֹת עַל אַרְבַּע הַפֵּאֹת אֲשֶׁר

---

* Referring to the "table," a masculine word in Hebrew.

Revised Mechanical Translation Codes

(..) Alt Trans/App A	<..> Comp Phrase/App B	[..] Verb Form/App C	\../ Plural Form/App D
:..: Int Inf Abs	|..| Past Perf Verb	{...} Added Word	

לְאַרְבַּע רַגְלָיו

we'a'si'ta lo ar'ba ta'be'ot za'hav we'na'ta'ta et ha'ta'ba'ot al ar'ba ha'pey'ot a'sher le'ar'ba rag'law

and~*you(ms)*~*did*~<u>DO</u> to~him FOUR RING~s GOLD and~*you(ms)*~*did*~<u>GIVE</u> AT the~ RING~s UPON FOUR the~EDGE~s WHICH to~ FOUR FOOT~s2~him□	and you will (make) (for) him four rings {of} gold, and you will (place) the rings upon the four edges which {belong} to his four feet,□

25:27 לְעֻמַּת הַמִּסְגֶּרֶת תִּהְיֶיןָ הַטַּבָּעֹת לְבָתִּים לְבַדִּים לָשֵׂאת אֶת הַשֻּׁלְחָן

le'u'mat ha'mis'ge'ret tih'yey'na ha'ta'ba'ot le'va'tim le'va'dim la'seyt et ha'shul'hhan

to~ALONGSIDE the~RIM *they(f)*~*will*~<u>EXIST</u> the~RING~s to~HOUSE~s to~STICK~s to~ >~<u>LIFT-UP</u> AT the~TABLE□	the rings will exist alongside the rim (for) houses* (for) {the} sticks to lift up the table,□

25:28 וְעָשִׂיתָ אֶת הַבַּדִּים עֲצֵי שִׁטִּים וְצִפִּיתָ אֹתָם זָהָב וְנִשָּׂא בָם אֶת הַשֻּׁלְחָן

we'a'si'ta et ha'ba'dim a'tsey shi'tim we'tsi'pi'ta o'tam za'hav we'ni'sa vam et ha'shul'hhan

and~*you(ms)*~*did*~<u>DO</u> AT the~STICK~s TREE~s ACACIA~s and~*you(ms)*~*did*~*much*~ <u>OVERLAY</u> AT~them(m) GOLD and~*he*~*did*~ *be*~<u>LIFT-UP</u> in~them(m) AT the~TABLE□	and you will (make) the sticks {of} \wood/ {of} acacia, and you will overlay them {with} gold, and the table will be lifted up (with) them,□

25:29 וְעָשִׂיתָ קְּעָרֹתָיו וְכַפֹּתָיו וּקְשׂוֹתָיו וּמְנַקִּיֹּתָיו אֲשֶׁר יֻסַּךְ בָּהֵן זָהָב טָהוֹר תַּעֲשֶׂה אֹתָם

we'a'si'ta qe'a'ro'taw we'kha'po'taw uq'so'taw um'na'qi'taw a'sher yu'sakh ba'heyn za'hav ta'hor ta'a'seh o'tam

and~*you(ms)*~*did*~<u>DO</u> PLATTER~s~him and~ PALM~s~him and~JUG~s~him and~ SACRIFICIAL-BOWL~s~him WHICH *he*~*will*~ *be*~*make*~<u>POUR</u> in~them(f) GOLD PURE *you(ms)*~*will*~<u>DO</u> AT~them(m)□	and you will (make) his platters, and his palms† and his jugs and his sacrificial bowls, which will be {for} pour{ing}, {with} pure gold you will (make) them,□

25:30 וְנָתַתָּ עַל הַשֻּׁלְחָן לֶחֶם פָּנִים לְפָנַי תָּמִיד

we'na'ta'ta al ha'shul'hhan le'hhem pa'nim le'pha'nai ta'mid

and~*you(ms)*~*did*~<u>GIVE</u> UPON the~TABLE BREAD FACE~s to~FACE~s~me CONTINUALLY□	and you will (place) upon the table {the} bread {of the} face, <in front of> me continually,□

---

* Or "housings."
† The Hebrew word for the "palms" can also mean "palm" shaped and here refers to "spoons" or "shovels."

Mechanical Translation Codes

<u>WORD</u> – Verb	WORD – Noun	Word – Name	word – Pre/Suff	*word* – Conj.

25:31 וְעָשִׂיתָ מְנֹרַת זָהָב טָהוֹר מִקְשָׁה תֵּעָשֶׂה הַמְּנוֹרָה יְרֵכָהּ וְקָנָהּ גְּבִיעֶיהָ כַּפְתֹּרֶיהָ וּפְרָחֶיהָ מִמֶּנָּה יִהְיוּ

we'a'si'ta me'no'rat za'hav ta'hor miq'shah tey'a'seh ham'no'rah ye'rey'khah we'qa'nah ge'vi'ey'ah kaph'to'rey'ah uph'ra'hhey'ah mi'me'nah yih'yu

and~you(ms)~did~<u>DO</u> LAMPSTAND GOLD PURE BEATEN-WORK she~will~be~<u>DO</u> the~ LAMPSTAND MIDSECTION~her and~STALK~ her BOWL~s~her KNOB~s~her and~BUD~s~ her FROM~her they(m)~will~<u>EXIST</u>□

and you will (make) {a} lampstand {of} pure gold, the midsection {of the} lampstand will be (made) {of} beaten work, and her stalk, her bowls, her knobs and her buds will exist (out of) her*,□

25:32 וְשִׁשָּׁה קָנִים יֹצְאִים מִצִּדֶּיהָ שְׁלֹשָׁה קְנֵי מְנֹרָה מִצִּדָּהּ הָאֶחָד וּשְׁלֹשָׁה קְנֵי מְנֹרָה מִצִּדָּהּ הַשֵּׁנִי

we'shi'shah qa'nim yots'im mi'tsi'dey'ah she'lo'shah qe'ney me'no'rah mi'tsi'dah ha'e'hhad ush'lo'shah qe'ney me'no'rah mi'tsi'dah ha'shey'ni

and~SIX STALK~s GO-OUT~ing/er(mp) from~ SIDE~s~her THREE STALK~s LAMPSTAND from~SIDE~her the~UNIT and~THREE STALK~s LAMPSTAND from~SIDE~her the~ SECOND□

and six stalks {are} going out from her sides, three stalks {of the} lampstand (out of) her† (one) side, and three stalks {of the} lampstand (out of) her second side,□

25:33 שְׁלֹשָׁה גְבִעִים מְשֻׁקָּדִים בַּקָּנֶה הָאֶחָד כַּפְתֹּר וָפֶרַח וּשְׁלֹשָׁה גְבִעִים מְשֻׁקָּדִים בַּקָּנֶה הָאֶחָד כַּפְתֹּר וָפָרַח כֵּן לְשֵׁשֶׁת הַקָּנִים הַיֹּצְאִים מִן הַמְּנֹרָה

she'lo'shah ge'vi'im me'shu'qa'dim ba'qa'neh ha'e'hhad kaph'tor wa'phe'rahh ush'lo'shah ge'vi'im me'shu'qa'dim ba'qa'neh ha'e'hhad kaph'tor wa'pha'rahh keyn le'shey'shet ha'qa'nim hai'yots'im min ham'no'rah

THREE BOWL~s be~much~<u>BE-ALMOND-SHAPED</u>~ing/er(mp) in~the~STALK the~UNIT KNOB and~BUD and~THREE BOWL~s be~ much~<u>BE-ALMOND-SHAPED</u>~ing/er(mp) in~ the~STALK the~UNIT KNOB and~BUD SO to~ SIX the~STALK~s the~<u>GO-OUT</u>~ing/er(mp) FROM the~LAMPSTAND□

three bowls, being almond shaped in the stalk {of} the (one) {with a} knob and {a} bud, and three bowls, being almond shaped in the stalk {of} the (other) {with a} knob and {a} bud, so {it is} (for) the six stalks going out from the lampstand,□

25:34 וּבַמְּנֹרָה אַרְבָּעָה גְבִעִים מְשֻׁקָּדִים כַּפְתֹּרֶיהָ וּפְרָחֶיהָ

u'vam'no'rah ar'ba'ah ge'vi'im me'shu'qa'dim kaph'to'rey'ah uph'ra'hhey'ah

and~in~the~LAMPSTAND FOUR BOWL~s be~ much~<u>BE-ALMOND-SHAPED</u>~ing/er(mp)

and in the lampstand {are} four bowls being almond shaped {with} her knobs and her

---

* "out of her" means that each of these parts is beaten (molded) out of the one piece.

† "out of her" means that each of these parts is beaten (molded) out of the one piece.

KNOB~s~her and~BUD~s~her□   buds,□

25:35 וְכַפְתֹּר תַּחַת שְׁנֵי הַקָּנִים מִמֶּנָּה וְכַפְתֹּר תַּחַת שְׁנֵי הַקָּנִים מִמֶּנָּה

וְכַפְתֹּר תַּחַת שְׁנֵי הַקָּנִים מִמֶּנָּה לְשֵׁשֶׁת הַקָּנִים הַיֹּצְאִים מִן הַמְּנֹרָה

we'khaph'tor ta'hhat she'ney ha'qa'nim mi'me'nah we'khaph'tor ta'hhat she'ney
ha'qa'nim mi'me'nah we'khaph'tor ta'hhat she'ney ha'qa'nim mi'me'nah le'shey'shet
ha'qa'nim hai'yots'im min ham'no'rah

and~KNOB UNDER TWO the~STALK~s FROM~her and~KNOB UNDER TWO the~STALK~s FROM~her and~KNOB UNDER TWO the~STALK~s FROM~her to~SIX the~STALK~s the~<u>GO-OUT</u>~*ing/er(mp)* FROM the~ LAMPSTAND□	and {a} knob under two {of} the stalks (out of) her*, and {a} knob under two {of} the stalks (out of) her, and {a} knob under two {of} the stalks (out of) her, (for) the six stalks going out from the lampstand,□

25:36 כַּפְתֹּרֵיהֶם וּקְנֹתָם מִמֶּנָּה יִהְיוּ כֻּלָּהּ מִקְשָׁה אַחַת זָהָב טָהוֹר

kaph'to'rey'hem uq'no'tam mi'me'nah yih'yu ku'lah miq'shah a'hhat za'hav ta'hor

KNOB~s~them(m) and~STALK~s~them(m) FROM~her *they(m)~will~*<u>EXIST</u> ALL~her BEATEN-WORK UNIT GOLD PURE□	their knobs and their stalks (out of) her†, all {of} her will exist {as} (one) beaten work {of} pure gold,□

25:37 וְעָשִׂיתָ אֶת נֵרֹתֶיהָ שִׁבְעָה וְהֶעֱלָה אֶת נֵרֹתֶיהָ וְהֵאִיר עַל עֵבֶר פָּנֶיהָ

we'a'si'ta et ney'ro'te'yah shiv'ah we'he'e'lah et ney'ro'te'yah we'hey'ir al ey'ver
pa'ney'ah

and~you(ms)~*did~*<u>DO</u> AT LAMP~s~her SEVEN and~*he~did~make~*<u>GO-UP</u> AT LAMP~s~her and~*he~did~make~*<u>LIGHT</u> UPON OTHER-SIDE FACE~s~her□	and you will (make) her seven lamps, and he will make her lamps go up‡, and he will make light upon {the} other side {of} her face,□

25:38 וּמַלְקָחֶיהָ וּמַחְתֹּתֶיהָ זָהָב טָהוֹר

u'mal'qa'hhey'ah u'mahh'to'tey'ah za'hav ta'hor

and~TONG~s~her and~FIRE-PAN~s~her GOLD PURE□	and her tongs and her fire pans {with} pure gold,□

25:39 כִּכָּר זָהָב טָהוֹר יַעֲשֶׂה אֹתָהּ אֵת כָּל הַכֵּלִים הָאֵלֶּה

ki'kar za'hav ta'hor ya'a'seh o'tah eyt kol ha'key'lim ha'ey'leh

KIKAR GOLD PURE *he~will~*<u>DO</u> AT~her AT	{a} kikar {of} pure gold he will (make) her

---

* "out of her" means that each of these parts is beaten (molded) out of the one piece.

† "out of her" means that each of these parts is beaten (molded) out of the one piece.

‡ "Make her lamps go up" means to light the wicks.

Mechanical Translation Codes

<u>WORD</u> – Verb	WORD – Noun	Word – Name	word – Pre/Suff	*word* – Conj.

ALL the~ITEM~s the~THESE□   (with) all these items,□

25:40   וּרְאֵה וַעֲשֵׂה בְּתַבְנִיתָם אֲשֶׁר אַתָּה מָרְאֶה בָּהָר

ur'eyh wa'a'seyh be'tav'ni'tam a'sher a'tah mar'eh ba'har

and~!(ms)~SEE and~!(ms)~DO in~PATTERN~ them(m) WHICH YOU(ms) be~make~SEE~ ing/er(ms) in~the~HILL□

and see and do {them} (with) their pattern which you {were} being [shown] in the hill,□

Chapter 26

26:1   וְאֶת הַמִּשְׁכָּן תַּעֲשֶׂה עֶשֶׂר יְרִיעֹת שֵׁשׁ מָשְׁזָר וּתְכֵלֶת וְאַרְגָּמָן וְתֹלַעַת שָׁנִי כְּרֻבִים מַעֲשֵׂה חֹשֵׁב תַּעֲשֶׂה אֹתָם

we'et ha'mish'kan ta'a'seh e'ser ye'ri'ot sheysh mash'zar ut'khey'let we'ar'ga'man we'to'la'at sha'ni ke'ru'vim ma'a'seyh hho'sheyv ta'a'seh o'tam

and~AT the~DWELLING you(ms)~will~DO TEN TENT-WALL~s LINEN be~make~TWIST-TOGETHER~ing/er(ms) and~BLUE and~ PURPLE and~KERMES SCARLET KERUV~s WORK THINK~ing/er(ms) you(ms)~will~DO AT~them(m)□

and you will (make) the dwelling, ten tent walls {of} [twisted] linen and blue and purple and kermes {of} scarlet, you will (make) them {with} keruvs {of a} work {of} thinking*,□

26:2   אֹרֶךְ הַיְרִיעָה הָאַחַת שְׁמֹנֶה וְעֶשְׂרִים בָּאַמָּה וְרֹחַב אַרְבַּע בָּאַמָּה הַיְרִיעָה הָאֶחָת מִדָּה אַחַת לְכָל הַיְרִיעֹת

o'rekh hai'ri'ah ha'a'hhat she'mo'neh we'es'rim ba'a'mah we'ro'hhav ar'ba ba'a'mah hai'ri'ah ha'e'hhat mi'dah a'hhat le'khol hai'ri'ot

LENGTH the~TENT-WALL the~UNIT EIGHT and~TEN~s in~the~FOREARM and~WIDTH FOUR in~the~FOREARM the~TENT-WALL the~UNIT MEASUREMENT UNIT to~ALL the~ TENT-WALL~s□

{the} length {of} the (one) tent wall {is} eight and \twenty/ (by) the forearm, and the width {is} four (by) the forearm, the (one) tent wall measurement {is} (one) (for) all the tent walls,□

26:3   חֲמֵשׁ הַיְרִיעֹת תִּהְיֶיןָ חֹבְרֹת אִשָּׁה אֶל אֲחֹתָהּ וְחָמֵשׁ יְרִיעֹת חֹבְרֹת אִשָּׁה אֶל אֲחֹתָהּ

hha'meysh hai'ri'ot tih'yey'na hhov'rot i'shah el a'hho'tah we'hha'meysh ye'ri'ot hhov'rot i'shah el a'hho'tah

FIVE the~TENT-WALL~s they(f)~will~EXIST COUPLE~ing/er(fp) WOMAN TO SISTER~her and~FIVE TENT-WALL~s COUPLE~ing/er(fp)

five {of} the tent walls will exist, coupling (each) to her sister, and five tent walls coupling (each) to her sister,□

---

* This may be a work of an intricate design or made by "a thinker" in the sense of a designer.

Revised Mechanical Translation Codes
(..) Alt Trans/App A   <..> Comp Phrase/App B   [..] Verb Form/App C   \../ Plural Form/App D
:..: Int Inf Abs |..| Past Perf Verb   {...} Added Word
~ 189 ~

WOMAN TO SISTER~her☐

26:4

וְעָשִׂיתָ לֻלְאֹת תְּכֵלֶת עַל שְׂפַת הַיְרִיעָה הָאֶחָת מִקָּצָה בַּחֹבָרֶת וְכֵן תַּעֲשֶׂה בִּשְׂפַת הַיְרִיעָה הַקִּיצוֹנָה בַּמַּחְבֶּרֶת הַשֵּׁנִית

we'a'si'ta lul'ot te'khey'let al she'phat hai'ri'ah ha'e'hhat mi'qa'tsah ba'hho'va'ret we'kheyn ta'a'seh bis'phat hai'ri'ah ha'qi'tso'nah ba'mahh'be'ret ha'shey'nit

and~*you(ms)~did*~<u>DO</u> LOOP~s BLUE UPON LIP the~TENT-WALL the~UNIT from~ EXTREMITY in~the~COUPLING and~SO *you(ms)~will*~<u>DO</u> in~LIP the~TENT-WALL the~OUTER in~the~JOINT the~SECOND☐	and you will (make) loops {of} blue upon {the} lip {of} the (one) tent wall from {the} extremity in the coupling, and so you will (make) in {the} lip {of} the outer tent wall in the joint {of} the second,☐

26:5

חֲמִשִּׁים לֻלָאֹת תַּעֲשֶׂה בַּיְרִיעָה הָאֶחָת וַחֲמִשִּׁים לֻלָאֹת תַּעֲשֶׂה בִּקְצֵה הַיְרִיעָה אֲשֶׁר בַּמַּחְבֶּרֶת הַשֵּׁנִית מַקְבִּילֹת הַלֻּלָאֹת אִשָּׁה אֶל אֲחֹתָהּ

hha'mi'shim lu'la'ot ta'a'seh bai'ri'ah ha'e'hhat wa'hha'mi'shim lu'la'ot ta'a'seh biq'tseyh hai'ri'ah a'sher ba'mahh'be'ret ha'shey'nit maq'bi'lot ha'lu'la'ot i'shah el a'hho'tah

FIVE~s LOOP~s *you(ms)~will*~<u>DO</u> in~the~ TENT-WALL the~UNIT and~FIVE~s LOOP~s *you(ms)~will*~<u>DO</u> in~EXTREMITY the~TENT-WALL WHICH in~the~JOINT the~SECOND *make*~<u>RECEIVE</u>~*ing/er(fp)* the~LOOP~s WOMAN TO SISTER~her☐	you will (make) \fifty/ loops in the (one) tent wall, and you will (make) \fifty/ loops in {the} extremity {of} the tent wall which {is} in the joint {of} the second receiving the loops {of} (each) to her sister,☐

26:6

וְעָשִׂיתָ חֲמִשִּׁים קַרְסֵי זָהָב וְחִבַּרְתָּ אֶת הַיְרִיעֹת אִשָּׁה אֶל אֲחֹתָהּ בַּקְּרָסִים וְהָיָה הַמִּשְׁכָּן אֶחָד

we'a'si'ta hha'mi'shim qar'sey za'hav we'hhi'bar'ta et hai'ri'ot i'shah el a'hho'tah baq'ra'sim we'hai'yah ha'mish'kan e'hhad

and~*you(ms)~did*~<u>DO</u> FIVE~s HOOK~s GOLD and~*you(ms)~did*~*much*~<u>COUPLE</u> AT the~ TENT-WALL~s WOMAN TO SISTER~her in~ the~HOOK~s and~*he~did*~<u>EXIST</u> the~ DWELLING UNIT☐	and you will (make) \fifty/ hooks {of} gold, and you will couple the tent walls (each) to her sister in the hooks, and the dwelling will exist {as a} unit,☐

26:7

וְעָשִׂיתָ יְרִיעֹת עִזִּים לְאֹהֶל עַל הַמִּשְׁכָּן עַשְׁתֵּי עֶשְׂרֵה יְרִיעֹת תַּעֲשֶׂה אֹתָם

we'a'si'ta ye'ri'ot i'zim le'o'hel al ha'mish'kan ash'tey es'reyh ye'ri'ot ta'a'seh o'tam

and~*you(ms)~did*~<u>DO</u> TENT-WALL~s SHE-GOAT~s to~TENT UPON the~DWELLING ONE TEN TENT-WALL~s *you(ms)~will*~<u>DO</u> AT~ them(m)☐	and you will (make) {the} tent walls {of} she-goats* (for) {the} tent upon the dwelling, <eleven> tent walls you will (make),☐

---

* Specifically, the hair of the she-goats.

Mechanical Translation Codes

<u>WORD</u> – Verb	WORD – Noun	Word – Name	word – Pre/Suff	*word* – Conj.

26:8 אֹרֶךְ הַיְרִיעָה הָאַחַת שְׁלֹשִׁים בָּאַמָּה וְרֹחַב אַרְבַּע בָּאַמָּה הַיְרִיעָה הָאֶחָת מִדָּה אַחַת לְעַשְׁתֵּי עֶשְׂרֵה יְרִיעֹת

o'rekh hai'ri'ah ha'a'hhat she'lo'shim ba'a'mah we'ro'hhav ar'ba ba'a'mah hai'ri'ah ha'e'hhat mi'dah a'hhat le'ash'tey es'reyh ye'ri'ot

LENGTH the~TENT-WALL the~UNIT THREE~s in~the~FOREARM and~WIDTH FOUR in~the~FOREARM the~TENT-WALL the~UNIT MEASUREMENT UNIT to~ONE TEN TENT-WALL~s□	{the} length {of} the (one) tent wall {is} \thirty/ (by) the forearm, and {the} width {is} four (by) the forearm, the (one) tent wall measurement {is} (one) (for) {the} <eleven> tent walls,□

26:9 וְחִבַּרְתָּ אֶת חֲמֵשׁ הַיְרִיעֹת לְבָד וְאֶת שֵׁשׁ הַיְרִיעֹת לְבָד וְכָפַלְתָּ אֶת הַיְרִיעָה הַשִּׁשִּׁית אֶל מוּל פְּנֵי הָאֹהֶל

we'hhi'bar'ta et hha'meysh hai'ri'ot le'vad we'et sheysh hai'ri'ot le'vad we'kha'phal'ta et hai'ri'ah ha'shi'shit el mul pe'ney ha'o'hel

and~*you(ms)*~did~much~<u>COUPLE</u> AT FIVE the~TENT-WALL~s to~STICK and~AT SIX the~TENT-WALL~s to~STICK and~*you(ms)*~did~<u>DOUBLE-OVER</u> AT the~TENT-WALL the~SIXTH TO FOREFRONT FACE~s the~TENT□	and you will couple five {of} the tent walls <alone> and six {of} the tent walls <alone>, and you will double over the sixth tent wall to {the} forefront face {of} the tent,□

26:10 וְעָשִׂיתָ חֲמִשִּׁים לֻלָאֹת עַל שְׂפַת הַיְרִיעָה הָאֶחָת הַקִּיצֹנָה בַּחֹבָרֶת וַחֲמִשִּׁים לֻלָאֹת עַל שְׂפַת הַיְרִיעָה הַחֹבֶרֶת הַשֵּׁנִית

we'a'si'ta hha'mi'shim lu'la'ot al she'phat hai'ri'ah ha'e'hhat ha'qi'tso'nah ba'hho'va'ret wa'hha'mi'shim lu'la'ot al she'phat hai'ri'ah ha'hho've'ret ha'shey'nit

and~*you(ms)*~did~<u>DO</u> FIVE~s LOOP~s UPON LIP the~TENT-WALL the~UNIT the~OUTER in~the~COUPLING and~FIVE~s LOOP~s UPON LIP the~TENT-WALL the~COUPLING the~SECOND□	and you will (make) \fifty/ loops upon {the} lip {of} the (one) outer tent wall (with) the coupling, and \fifty/ loops upon {the} lip {of} the tent wall {of} the second coupling,□

26:11 וְעָשִׂיתָ קַרְסֵי נְחֹשֶׁת חֲמִשִּׁים וְהֵבֵאתָ אֶת הַקְּרָסִים בַּלֻּלָאֹת וְחִבַּרְתָּ אֶת הָאֹהֶל וְהָיָה אֶחָד

we'a'si'ta qar'sey ne'hho'shet hha'mi'shim we'hey'vey'ta et haq'ra'sim ba'lu'la'ot we'hhi'bar'ta et ha'o'hel we'hai'yah e'hhad

and~*you(ms)*~did~<u>DO</u> HOOK~s COPPER FIVE~s and~*you(ms)*~did~make~<u>COME</u> AT the~HOOK~s in~the~LOOP~s and~*you(ms)*~did~much~<u>COUPLE</u> AT the~TENT and~*he*~did~<u>EXIST</u> UNIT□	and you will (make) \fifty/ copper hooks, and you will [bring] the hooks in the loops, and you will couple the tent, and he will exist {as a} unit,□

26:12 וְסֶרַח הָעֹדֵף בִּירִיעֹת הָאֹהֶל חֲצִי הַיְרִיעָה הָעֹדֶפֶת תִּסְרַח עַל אֲחֹרֵי הַמִּשְׁכָּן

we'se'rahh ha'o'deyph bi'ri'ot ha'o'hel hha'tsi hai'ri'ah ha'o'de'phet tis'rahh al a'hho'rey

Revised Mechanical Translation Codes

(..) Alt Trans/App A   <..> Comp Phrase/App B   [..] Verb Form/App C   \../ Plural Form/App D
:..: Int Inf Abs |..| Past Perf Verb   {...} Added Word

~ 191 ~

ha'mish'kan

| and~OVERHANG the~EXCEED~ing/er(ms) in~ TENT-WALL~s the~TENT HALF the~TENT-WALL the~EXCEED~ing/er(fs) you(ms)~will~ OVERHANG UPON BACK~s the~DWELLING□ | and {the} overhang {of} the exceeding {part} in the tent walls {of} the tent, half {of} the tent wall, the exceeding {part}, you will overhang upon {the} backs {of} the dwelling,□ |

26:13 וְהָאַמָּה מִזֶּה וְהָאַמָּה מִזֶּה בָּעֹדֵף בְּאֹרֶךְ יְרִיעֹת הָאֹהֶל יִהְיֶה סָרוּחַ עַל צִדֵּי הַמִּשְׁכָּן מִזֶּה וּמִזֶּה לְכַסֹּתוֹ

we'ha'a'mah mi'zeh we'ha'a'mah mi'zeh ba'o'deyph be'o'rekh ye'ri'ot ha'o'hel yih'yeh sa'ru'ahh al tsi'dey ha'mish'kan mi'zeh u'mi'zeh le'kha'so'to

| and~the~FOREARM from~THIS and~the~ FOREARM from~THIS in~the~EXCEED~ ing/er(ms) in~LENGTH TENT-WALL~s the~ TENT he~will~EXIST OVERHANG~ed(ms) UPON SIDE~s the~DWELLING from~THIS and~from~THIS to~>~much~COVER-OVER~ him□ | and the forearm from this {side}, and the forearm from (that) {side}, in the exceeding {part} in {the} length {of the} tent walls {of} the tent, will (be) overhung upon {the} sides {of} the dwelling, from this {side} and from (that) {side} to cover him over,□ |

26:14 וְעָשִׂיתָ מִכְסֶה לָאֹהֶל עֹרֹת אֵילִם מְאָדָּמִים וּמִכְסֵה עֹרֹת תְּחָשִׁים מִלְמָעְלָה

we'a'si'ta mikh'seh la'o'hel o'rot ey'lim me'a'da'mim u'mikh'seyh o'rot te'hha'sim mil'ma'lah

| and~you(ms)~did~DO ROOF-COVERING to~ the~TENT SKIN~s BUCK~s be~much~BE-RED~ ing/er(mp) and~ROOF-COVERING SKIN~s TAHHASH~s from~to~UPWARD~unto□ | and you will (make) {a} roof covering (for) the tent, skins {of} bucks being red, and {a} roof covering {of} skins {of} tahhash* {on} <top>,□ |

26:15 וְעָשִׂיתָ אֶת הַקְּרָשִׁים לַמִּשְׁכָּן עֲצֵי שִׁטִּים עֹמְדִים

we'a'si'ta et haq'ra'shim la'mish'kan a'tsey shi'tim om'dim

| and~you(ms)~did~DO AT the~BOARD~s to~ the~DWELLING TREE~s ACACIA~s STAND~ ing/er(mp)□ | and you will (make) the boards (for) the dwelling {of} \wood/ {of} acacia standing {up},□ |

26:16 עֶשֶׂר אַמּוֹת אֹרֶךְ הַקָּרֶשׁ וְאַמָּה וַחֲצִי הָאַמָּה רֹחַב הַקֶּרֶשׁ הָאֶחָד

e'ser a'mot o'rekh ha'qa'resh we'a'mah wa'hha'tsi ha'a'mah ro'hhav ha'qe'resh ha'e'hhad

| TEN FOREARM~s LENGTH the~BOARD and~ FOREARM and~HALF the~FOREARM WIDTH the~BOARD the~UNIT□ | ten forearms {is the} length {of} the board, and {a} forearm and {a} half {a} forearm {is the} width {of} the (one) board,□ |

26:17 שְׁתֵּי יָדוֹת לַקֶּרֶשׁ הָאֶחָד מְשֻׁלָּבֹת אִשָּׁה אֶל אֲחֹתָהּ כֵּן תַּעֲשֶׂה לְכֹל קַרְשֵׁי הַמִּשְׁכָּן

---

* The Tahhash is an unknown species of animal.

Mechanical Translation Codes

| <u>WORD</u> – Verb | WORD – Noun | Word – Name | word – Pre/Suff | *word* – Conj. |

she'tey ya'dot la'qe'resh ha'e'hhad me'shu'la'vot i'shah el a'hho'tah keyn ta'a'seh le'khol qar'shey ha'mish'kan

TWO HAND~s to~the~BOARD the~UNIT *be~much*~<u>JOINED-TOGETHER</u>~*ing/er(fp)* WOMAN TO SISTER~her SO *you(ms)~will~*<u>DO</u> to~ALL BOARD~s the~DWELLING□	two hands* (for) the (one) board {for} being joined together, (each) to her sister, so you will (make) (for) all {the} boards {of} the dwelling,□

26:18 וְעָשִׂיתָ אֶת הַקְּרָשִׁים לַמִּשְׁכָּן עֶשְׂרִים קֶרֶשׁ לִפְאַת נֶגְבָּה תֵּימָנָה

we'a'si'ta et haq'ra'shim la'mish'kan es'rim qe'resh liph'at neg'bah tey'ma'nah

and~*you(ms)~did~*<u>DO</u> AT the~BOARD~s to~the~DWELLING TEN~s BOARD to~EDGE "Negev ^{PARCHED}"~unto SOUTH~unto□	and you will (make) the boards (for) the dwelling, \twenty/ boards (for) {the} edge unto {the} "Negev ^{Parched}", unto {the} south,□

26:19 וְאַרְבָּעִים אַדְנֵי כֶסֶף תַּעֲשֶׂה תַּחַת עֶשְׂרִים הַקֶּרֶשׁ שְׁנֵי אֲדָנִים תַּחַת הַקֶּרֶשׁ הָאֶחָד לִשְׁתֵּי יְדֹתָיו וּשְׁנֵי אֲדָנִים תַּחַת הַקֶּרֶשׁ הָאֶחָד לִשְׁתֵּי יְדֹתָיו

we'ar'ba'im ad'ney ke'seph ta'a'seh ta'hhat es'rim ha'qa'resh she'ney a'da'nim ta'hhat ha'qe'resh ha'e'hhad lish'tey ye'do'taw ush'ney a'da'nim ta'hhat ha'qe'resh ha'e'hhad lish'tey ye'do'taw

and~FOUR~s FOOTING~s SILVER *you(ms)~will~*<u>DO</u> UNDER TEN~s the~BOARD TWO FOOTING~s UNDER the~BOARD the~UNIT to~TWO HAND~s~him and~TWO FOOTING~s UNDER the~BOARD the~UNIT to~TWO HAND~s~him□	and you will (make) \forty/ footings {of} silver under \twenty/ {of} the board{s}, two footings under the (one) board (for) his two hands†, and two footings under the (other) board (for) his two hands,□

26:20 וּלְצֶלַע הַמִּשְׁכָּן הַשֵּׁנִית לִפְאַת צָפוֹן עֶשְׂרִים קָרֶשׁ

ul'tse'la ha'mish'kan ha'shey'nit liph'at tsa'phon es'rim qa'resh

and~to~RIB the~DWELLING the~SECOND to~EDGE NORTH TEN~s BOARD□	and (for) {the} second rib {of} the dwelling, to {the} north edge, {is} \twenty/ board{s},□

26:21 וְאַרְבָּעִים אַדְנֵיהֶם כָּסֶף שְׁנֵי אֲדָנִים תַּחַת הַקֶּרֶשׁ הָאֶחָד וּשְׁנֵי אֲדָנִים תַּחַת הַקֶּרֶשׁ הָאֶחָד

we'ar'ba'im ad'ney'hem ka'seph she'ney a'da'nim ta'hhat ha'qe'resh ha'e'hhad ush'ney a'da'nim ta'hhat ha'qe'resh ha'e'hhad

and~FOUR~s FOOTING~s~them(m) SILVER TWO FOOTING~s UNDER the~BOARD the~UNIT and~TWO FOOTING~s UNDER the~	and their \forty/ footings {of} silver, two footings under the (one) board, and two footings under the (other) board,□

---

* These "hands" are probably notched tenons which are cut into the board to join the boards together.

† These "hands" are probably notched tenons which are made to join the boards together.

Revised Mechanical Translation Codes

(..) Alt Trans/App A   <..> Comp Phrase/App B   [..] Verb Form/App C   \../ Plural Form/App D

:..: Int Inf Abs |..| Past Perf Verb   {...} Added Word

BOARD the~UNIT□

26:22

וּלְיַרְכְּתֵי הַמִּשְׁכָּן יָמָּה תַּעֲשֶׂה שִׁשָּׁה קְרָשִׁים

ul'yar'ke'tey ha'mish'kan ya'mah ta'a'seh shi'shah qe'ra'shim

and~to~FLANK~s2 the~DWELLING SEA~unto you(ms)~will~DO SIX BOARD~s□

and (for) {the} flanks* {of} the dwelling, unto the sea†, you will (make) six boards,□

26:23

וּשְׁנֵי קְרָשִׁים תַּעֲשֶׂה לִמְקֻצְעֹת הַמִּשְׁכָּן בַּיַּרְכָתָיִם

ush'ney qe'ra'shim ta'a'seh lim'quts'ot ha'mish'kan bai'yar'kha'ta'yim

and~TWO BOARD~s you(ms)~will~DO to~CORNER-POST~s the~DWELLING in~the~FLANK~s2□

and you will (make) two boards (for) {the} corner posts {of} the dwelling in the flanks,□

26:24

וְיִהְיוּ תֹאֲמִם מִלְמַטָּה וְיַחְדָּו יִהְיוּ תַמִּים עַל רֹאשׁוֹ אֶל הַטַּבַּעַת הָאֶחָת כֵּן יִהְיֶה לִשְׁנֵיהֶם לִשְׁנֵי הַמִּקְצֹעֹת יִהְיוּ

we'yih'yu to'a'mim mil'ma'tah we'yahh'daw yih'yu ta'mim al ro'sho el ha'ta'ba'at ha'e'hhat keyn yih'yeh lish'ney'hem lish'ney ha'miq'tso'ot yih'yu

and~they(m)~will~EXIST BE-DOUBLE~ing/er(mp) from~to~BENEATH and~TOGETHER they(m)~will~EXIST WHOLE UPON HEAD~him TO the~RING the~UNIT SO he~will~EXIST to~TWO~them(m) to~TWO the~BUTTRESS~s they(m)~will~EXIST□

and they will exist being double beneath, and together they will exist whole upon his head (for) the (one) ring, so he will exist (for) {the} two {of} them, (for) two {of} the buttresses they will exist,□

26:25

וְהָיוּ שְׁמֹנָה קְרָשִׁים וְאַדְנֵיהֶם כֶּסֶף שִׁשָּׁה עָשָׂר אֲדָנִים שְׁנֵי אֲדָנִים תַּחַת הַקֶּרֶשׁ הָאֶחָד וּשְׁנֵי אֲדָנִים תַּחַת הַקֶּרֶשׁ הָאֶחָד

we'hai'u she'mo'nah qe'ra'shim we'ad'ney'hem ke'seph shi'shah a'sar a'da'nim she'ney a'da'nim ta'hhat ha'qe'resh ha'e'hhad ush'ney a'da'nim ta'hhat ha'qe'resh ha'e'hhad

and~they~did~EXIST EIGHT BOARD~s and~FOOTING~s~them(m) SILVER SIX TEN FOOTING~s TWO FOOTING~s UNDER the~BOARD the~UNIT and~TWO FOOTING~s UNDER the~BOARD the~UNIT□

and eight boards will exist, and their footings {of} silver {are} <sixteen> footings, two footings under the (one) board and two footings under the (other) board,□

26:26

וְעָשִׂיתָ בְרִיחִם עֲצֵי שִׁטִּים חֲמִשָּׁה לְקַרְשֵׁי צֶלַע הַמִּשְׁכָּן הָאֶחָד

we'a'si'ta ve'ri'hhim a'tsey shi'tim hha'mi'shah le'qar'shey tse'la ha'mish'kan ha'e'hhad

and~you(ms)~did~DO WOOD-BAR~s TREE~s

and you will (make) wood bars {of} \wood/

---

* That is, "sides."
† Meaning "the west."

ACACIA~s FIVE to~BOARD~s RIB the~
DWELLING the~UNIT□

{of} acacia, five (for) {the} boards {of the}
(one) rib {of} the dwelling,□

26:27 נַחֲמִשָּׁה בְרִיחִם לְקַרְשֵׁי צֶלַע הַמִּשְׁכָּן הַשֵּׁנִית וַחֲמִשָּׁה בְרִיחִם לְקַרְשֵׁי
צֶלַע הַמִּשְׁכָּן לַיַּרְכָתַיִם יָמָּה

wa'hha'mi'shah ve'ri'hhim le'qar'shey tse'la ha'mish'kan ha'shey'nit wa'hha'mi'shah
ve'ri'hhim le'qar'shey tse'la ha'mish'kan lai'yar'kha'ta'yim ya'mah

and~FIVE WOOD-BAR~s to~BOARD~s RIB
the~DWELLING the~SECOND and~FIVE
WOOD-BAR~s to~BOARD~s RIB the~
DWELLING to~the~FLANK~s2 SEA~unto□

and five wood bars (for) {the} boards {of the}
second rib {of} the dwelling, and five wood
bars (for) {the} boards {of the} rib (for) the
flanks {of} the dwelling unto the sea*,□

26:28 וְהַבְּרִיחַ הַתִּיכֹן בְּתוֹךְ הַקְּרָשִׁים מַבְרִחַ מִן הַקָּצֶה אֶל הַקָּצֶה

we'ha'be'ri'ahh ha'ti'khon be'tokh haq'ra'shim mav'ri'ahh min ha'qa'tseh el ha'qa'tseh

and~the~WOOD-BAR the~MIDDLEMOST in~
MIDST the~BOARD~s make~<u>FLEE-AWAY</u>~
ing/er(ms) FROM the~EXTREMITY TO the~
EXTREMITY□

and the middlemost wood bar in {the} midst
{of} the boards {will} [reach] from the
extremity to the {other} end,□

26:29 וְאֵת הַקְּרָשִׁים תְּצַפֶּה זָהָב וְאֵת טַבְּעֹתֵיהֶם תַּעֲשֶׂה זָהָב בָּתִּים לַבְּרִיחִם
וְצִפִּיתָ אֶת הַבְּרִיחִם זָהָב

we'et haq'ra'shim te'tsa'peh za'hav we'et ta'be'o'tey'hem ta'a'seh za'hav ba'tim
la'be'ri'hhim we'tsi'pi'ta et ha'be'ri'hhim za'hav

and~AT the~BOARD~s you(ms)~will~much~
<u>OVERLAY</u> GOLD and~AT RING~s~them(m)
you(ms)~will~<u>DO</u> GOLD HOUSE~s to~the~
WOOD-BAR~s and~you(ms)~did~much~
<u>OVERLAY</u> AT the~WOOD-BAR~s GOLD□

and you will overlay the boards {with} gold,
and their rings you will (make) {with} gold,
houses‡ (for) the wood bars, and you will
overlay the wood bars {with} gold,□

26:30 וַהֲקֵמֹתָ אֶת הַמִּשְׁכָּן כְּמִשְׁפָּטוֹ אֲשֶׁר הָרְאֵיתָ בָּהָר

wa'ha'qey'mo'ta et ha'mish'kan ke'mish'pa'to a'sher har'ey'ta ba'har

and~you(ms)~did~make~<u>RISE</u> AT the~
DWELLING like~DECISION~him WHICH
you(ms)~did~be~make~<u>SEE</u> in~the~HILL□

and you will make the dwelling rise, like his
decision‡, which you were [shown] in the
hill,□

26:31 וְעָשִׂיתָ פָרֹכֶת תְּכֵלֶת וְאַרְגָּמָן וְתוֹלַעַת שָׁנִי וְשֵׁשׁ מָשְׁזָר מַעֲשֵׂה חֹשֵׁב
יַעֲשֶׂה אֹתָהּ כְּרֻבִים

---

* Meaning "the west."
† Or "housings."
‡ "Like his decision" means "according to the manner."

Revised Mechanical Translation Codes
(..) Alt Trans/App A   <..> Comp Phrase/App B   [..] Verb Form/App C   \../ Plural Form/App D
:..: Int Inf Abs |..| Past Perf Verb   {...} Added Word

we'a'si'ta pha'ro'khet te'khey'let we'ar'ga'man we'to'la'at sha'ni we'sheysh mash'zar
ma'a'seyh hho'sheyv ya'a'seh o'tah ke'ru'vim

and~*you(ms)~did~*<u>DO</u> TENT-CURTAIN BLUE and~PURPLE and~KERMES SCARLET and~ LINEN *be~*make~<u>TWIST-TOGETHER</u>~ *ing/er(ms)* WORK <u>THINK</u>~*ing/er(ms) he~will~* <u>DO</u> AT~her KERUV~s□	and you will (make) {a} tent curtain {of} blue and purple and kermes {of} scarlet and [twisted] linen, {a} work {of a} thinking*, he will (make) her {with} keruvs,□

26:32 וְנָתַתָּה אֹתָהּ עַל אַרְבָּעָה עַמּוּדֵי שִׁטִּים מְצֻפִּים זָהָב וָוֵיהֶם זָהָב עַל אַרְבָּעָה אַדְנֵי כָסֶף

we'na'ta'tah o'tah al ar'ba'ah a'mu'dey shi'tim me'tsu'pim za'hav wa'wey'hem za'hav al
ar'ba'ah ad'ney kha'seph

and~*you(ms)~did~*<u>GIVE</u>~^ AT~her UPON FOUR PILLAR~s ACACIA~s *be~much~*<u>OVERLAY</u>~*ing/er(ms)* GOLD PEG~s~them(m) GOLD UPON FOUR FOOTING~s SILVER□	and you will (place) her upon {the} four pillars {of} acacia, being overlaid {with} gold, their pegs {of} gold, upon {the} four footings {of} silver,□

26:33 וְנָתַתָּה אֶת הַפָּרֹכֶת תַּחַת הַקְּרָסִים וְהֵבֵאתָ שָׁמָּה מִבֵּית לַפָּרֹכֶת אֵת אֲרוֹן הָעֵדוּת וְהִבְדִּילָה הַפָּרֹכֶת לָכֶם בֵּין הַקֹּדֶשׁ וּבֵין קֹדֶשׁ הַקֳּדָשִׁים

we'na'ta'tah et ha'pa'ro'khet ta'hhat haq'ra'sim we'hey'vey'ta sham'mah mi'beyt
la'pa'ro'khet eyt a'ron ha'ey'dut we'hiv'di'lah ha'pa'ro'khet la'khem beyn ha'qo'desh
u'veyn qo'desh ha'qa'da'shim

and~*you(ms)~did~*<u>GIVE</u>~^ AT the~TENT-CURTAIN UNDER the~HOOK~s and~*you(ms)~ did~make~*<u>COME</u> THERE~unto from~HOUSE to~the~TENT-CURTAIN AT BOX the~ EVIDENCE and~ *she~did~make~*<u>SEPARATE</u> the~TENT-CURTAIN to~you(mp) BETWEEN the~SPECIAL and~BETWEEN SPECIAL the~ SPECIAL~s□	and you will (place) the tent curtain under the hooks, and you will [bring] unto there, (inside) the tent curtain, {the} box {of} the evidence, and the tent curtain will make {a} separat{ion} (for) you, between the special {place} and the special {place of} special {place}s,□

26:34 וְנָתַתָּ אֶת הַכַּפֹּרֶת עַל אֲרוֹן הָעֵדֻת בְּקֹדֶשׁ הַקֳּדָשִׁים

we'na'ta'ta et ha'ka'po'ret al a'ron ha'ey'dut be'qo'desh ha'qa'da'shim

and~*you(ms)~did~*<u>GIVE</u> AT the~LID UPON BOX the~EVIDENCE in~SPECIAL the~ SPECIAL~s□	and you will (place) the lid upon {the} box {of} the evidence in the special {place of} special {place}s,□

26:35 וְשַׂמְתָּ אֶת הַשֻּׁלְחָן מִחוּץ לַפָּרֹכֶת וְאֶת הַמְּנֹרָה נֹכַח הַשֻּׁלְחָן עַל צֶלַע הַמִּשְׁכָּן תֵּימָנָה וְהַשֻּׁלְחָן תִּתֵּן עַל צֶלַע צָפוֹן

we'sam'ta et ha'shul'hhan mi'hhuts la'pa'ro'khet we'et ham'no'rah no'khahh ha'shul'hhan

---

* This may be a work of an intricate design or made by "a thinker" in the sense of a designer.

al tse'la ha'mish'kan tey'ma'nah we'ha'shul'hhan ti'teyn al tse'la tsa'phon

and~you(ms)~did~<u>PLACE</u> AT the~TABLE from~OUTSIDE to~the~TENT-CURTAIN and~ AT the~LAMPSTAND IN-FRONT the~TABLE UPON RIB the~DWELLING SOUTH~unto and~ the~TABLE *you(ms)~will*~<u>GIVE</u> UPON RIB NORTH□	and you will place the table outside the tent curtain, and the lampstand in front {of} the table upon {the} rib {of} the dwelling unto {the} south, and the table you will (place) upon {the} rib {of the} north,□

26:36 וְעָשִׂיתָ מָסָךְ לְפֶתַח הָאֹהֶל תְּכֵלֶת וְאַרְגָּמָן וְתוֹלַעַת שָׁנִי וְשֵׁשׁ מָשְׁזָר מַעֲשֵׂה רֹקֵם

we'a'si'ta ma'sakh le'phe'tahh ha'o'hel te'khey'let we'ar'ga'man we'to'la'at sha'ni we'sheysh mash'zar ma'a'seyh ro'qeym

and~you(ms)~did~<u>DO</u> CANOPY to~OPENING the~TENT BLUE and~PURPLE and~KERMES SCARLET and~LINEN *be~make~*<u>TWIST-TOGETHER</u>*~ing/er(ms)* WORK <u>EMBROIDER</u>*~ing/er(ms)*□	and you will (make) {a} canopy (for) {an} opening {of} the tent {of} blue and purple and kermes {of} scarlet and [twisted] linen, {a} work {of} embroidering*,□

26:37 וְעָשִׂיתָ לַמָּסָךְ חֲמִשָּׁה עַמּוּדֵי שִׁטִּים וְצִפִּיתָ אֹתָם זָהָב וָוֵיהֶם זָהָב וְיָצַקְתָּ לָהֶם חֲמִשָּׁה אַדְנֵי נְחֹשֶׁת

we'a'si'ta la'ma'sakh hha'mi'shah a'mu'dey shi'tim we'tsi'pi'ta o'tam za'hav wa'wey'hem za'hav we'ya'tsaq'ta la'hem hha'mi'shah ad'ney ne'hho'shet

and~you(ms)~did~<u>DO</u> to~the~CANOPY FIVE PILLAR~s ACACIA~s and~you(ms)~did~ *much~*<u>OVERLAY</u> AT~them(m) GOLD PEG~s~ them(m) GOLD and~you(ms)~did~<u>POUR-DOWN</u> to~them(m) FIVE FOOTING~s COPPER□	and you will (make) (for) the canopy five pillars {of} acacia, and you will overlay them {with} gold, their pegs {of} gold, and you will pour down† (for) them five footings {of} copper,□

Chapter 27

27:1 וְעָשִׂיתָ אֶת הַמִּזְבֵּחַ עֲצֵי שִׁטִּים חָמֵשׁ אַמּוֹת אֹרֶךְ וְחָמֵשׁ אַמּוֹת רֹחַב רָבוּעַ יִהְיֶה הַמִּזְבֵּחַ וְשָׁלֹשׁ אַמּוֹת קֹמָתוֹ

we'a'si'ta et ha'miz'bey'ahh a'tsey shi'tim hha'meysh a'mot o'rekh we'hha'meysh a'mot ro'hhav ra'vu'a yih'yeh ha'miz'bey'ahh we'sha'losh a'mot qo'ma'to

and~you(ms)~did~<u>DO</u> AT the~ALTAR TREE~s ACACIA~s FIVE FOREARM~s LENGTH and~	and you will (make) the altar {of} \wood/ {of} acacia, five forearms {is the} length and five

---

* This word may also mean "an embroiderer."
† In this context, to "pour down" means to "cast" an object from a molten metal.

Revised Mechanical Translation Codes
(..) Alt Trans/App A   <..> Comp Phrase/App B   [..] Verb Form/App C   \../ Plural Form/App D
:..: Int Inf Abs |..| Past Perf Verb   {...} Added Word
~ 197 ~

FIVE FOREARM~s WIDTH <u>BE-SQUARE</u>~
ed(ms) he~will~<u>EXIST</u> the~ALTAR and~THREE
FOREARM~s HEIGHT~him□

forearms {is the} width, the altar will exist
squared, and three forearms {is} his height,□

27:2 וְעָשִׂיתָ קַרְנֹתָיו עַל אַרְבַּע פִּנֹּתָיו מִמֶּנּוּ תִּהְיֶיןָ קַרְנֹתָיו וְצִפִּיתָ אֹתוֹ נְחֹשֶׁת

we'a'si'ta qar'no'taw al ar'ba pi'no'taw mi'me'nu tih'yey'na qar'no'taw we'tsi'pi'ta o'to
ne'hho'shet

and~*you(ms)*~*did*~<u>DO</u> HORN~s~him UPON
FOUR CORNER~s~him FROM~him *they(f)*~
will~<u>EXIST</u> HORN~s~him and~*you(ms)*~*did*~
much~<u>OVERLAY</u> AT~him COPPER□

and you will (make) his* horns upon {the} four
{of} his corners, from him his horns will exist,
and you will overlay him {with} copper,□

27:3 וְעָשִׂיתָ סִּירֹתָיו לְדַשְּׁנוֹ וְיָעָיו וּמִזְרְקֹתָיו וּמִזְלְגֹתָיו וּמַחְתֹּתָיו לְכָל כֵּלָיו תַּעֲשֶׂה נְחֹשֶׁת

we'a'si'ta si'ro'taw le'dash'no we'ya'aw umiz're'qo'taw u'miz'le'go'taw u'mahh'to'taw
le'khol key'law ta'a'seh ne'hho'shet

and~*you(ms)*~*did*~<u>DO</u> POT~s~him to~
>~*much*~<u>MAKE-FAT</u>~him and~SHOVEL~s~
him and~SPRINKLING-BASIN~s~him and~
FORK~s~him and~FIRE-PAN~s~him to~ALL
ITEM~s~him *you(ms)*~*will*~<u>DO</u> COPPER□

and you will (make) his† pots (for) [removing
fat residue], and his shovels, and his sprinkling
basins, and his forks, and his fire pans, you will
(make) all his items {with} copper,□

27:4 וְעָשִׂיתָ לּוֹ מִכְבָּר מַעֲשֵׂה רֶשֶׁת נְחֹשֶׁת וְעָשִׂיתָ עַל הָרֶשֶׁת אַרְבַּע טַבְּעֹת נְחֹשֶׁת עַל אַרְבַּע קְצוֹתָיו

we'a'si'ta lo mikh'bar ma'a'seyh re'shet ne'hho'shet we'a'si'ta al ha're'shet ar'ba ta'be'ot
ne'hho'shet al ar'ba qe'tso'taw

and~*you(ms)*~*did*~<u>DO</u> to~him GRATE WORK
NETTING COPPER and~*you(ms)*~*did*~<u>DO</u>
UPON the~NETTING FOUR RING~s COPPER
UPON FOUR EXTREMITY~s~him□

and you will (make) (for) him‡ {a} grate work
{of} netting {with} copper, and you will (make)
upon the netting four rings {of} copper upon
his four extremities,□

27:5 וְנָתַתָּה אֹתָהּ תַּחַת כַּרְכֹּב הַמִּזְבֵּחַ מִלְּמָטָּה וְהָיְתָה הָרֶשֶׁת עַד חֲצִי הַמִּזְבֵּחַ

we'na'ta'tah o'tah ta'hhat kar'kov ha'miz'bey'ahh mil'ma'tah we'hai'tah ha're'shet ad
hha'tsi ha'miz'bey'ahh

---

* Referring to the "altar," a masculine word in Hebrew.
† Referring to the "altar," a masculine word in Hebrew.
‡ Referring to the "altar," a masculine word in Hebrew.

Mechanical Translation Codes

<u>WORD</u> – Verb	WORD – Noun	Word – Name	word – Pre/Suff	*word* – Conj.

and~you(ms)~did~<u>GIVE</u>~^ AT~her UNDER OUTER-RIM the~ALTAR from~to~<u>BENEATH</u> and~ she~did~<u>EXIST</u> the~NETTING UNTIL HALF the~ALTAR□

and you will (place) her* under {the} outer rim {of} the altar beneath, and the netting will exist <in the middle> {of} the altar,□

27:6 וְעָשִׂיתָ בַדִּים לַמִּזְבֵּחַ בַּדֵּי עֲצֵי שִׁטִּים וְצִפִּיתָ אֹתָם נְחֹשֶׁת

we'a'si'ta va'dim la'miz'bey'ahh ba'dey a'tsey shi'tim we'tsi'pi'ta o'tam ne'hho'shet

and~you(ms)~did~<u>DO</u> STICK~s to~the~ ALTAR STICK~s TREE~s ACACIA~s and~ you(ms)~did~much~<u>OVERLAY</u> AT~them(m) COPPER□

and you will (make) sticks (for) the altar, sticks {of} \wood/ {of} acacia, and you will overlay them {with} copper,□

27:7 וְהוּבָא אֶת בַּדָּיו בַּטַּבָּעֹת וְהָיוּ הַבַּדִּים עַל שְׁתֵּי צַלְעֹת הַמִּזְבֵּחַ בִּשְׂאֵת אֹתוֹ

we'hu'va et ba'daw ba'ta'ba'ot we'hai'u ha'ba'dim al she'tey tsal'ot ha'miz'bey'ahh bish'a'rey'kha o'to

and~he~did~be~make~<u>COME</u> AT STICK~s~ him in~the~RING~s and~they~did~<u>EXIST</u> the~STICK~s UPON ACACIA~s RIB~s the~ ALTAR in~>~<u>LIFT-UP</u> AT~him□

and his sticks will be [brought] in the rings, and the sticks will exist upon the acacia ribs {of} the altar in lift{ing} him† up,□

27:8 נְבוּב לֻחֹת תַּעֲשֶׂה אֹתוֹ כַּאֲשֶׁר הֶרְאָה אֹתְךָ בָּהָר כֵּן יַעֲשׂוּ

ne'vuv lu'hhot ta'a'seh o'to ka'a'sheyr her'ah ot'kha ba'har keyn ya'a'su

<u>HOLLOW-OUT</u>~ed(ms) SLAB~s you(ms)~will~ <u>DO</u> AT~him like~WHICH he~did~make~<u>SEE</u> AT~you(ms) in~the~HILL SO they(m)~will~ <u>DO</u>□

{with} hollowed out slabs you will (make) him, <just as> [shown] you in the hill, so they will do,□

27:9 וְעָשִׂיתָ אֵת חֲצַר הַמִּשְׁכָּן לִפְאַת נֶגֶב תֵּימָנָה קְלָעִים לֶחָצֵר שֵׁשׁ מָשְׁזָר מֵאָה בָאַמָּה אֹרֶךְ לַפֵּאָה הָאֶחָת

we'a'si'ta eyt hha'tsar ha'mish'kan liph'at ne'gev tey'ma'nah qe'la'im le'hha'tseyr sheysh mash'zar mey'ah va'a'mah o'rekh la'pey'ah ha'e'hhat

and~you(ms)~did~<u>DO</u> AT YARD the~ DWELLING to~EDGE "Negev ᴾᴬᴿᶜᴴᴱᴰ‚‚ SOUTH~ unto SLING~s to~the~YARD LINEN be~make~ <u>TWIST-TOGETHER</u>~ing/er(ms) HUNDRED in~ the~FOREARM LENGTH to~the~EDGE the~ UNIT□

and you will (make) {a} yard {of} the dwelling to {the} edge unto the "Negev ᴾᵃʳᶜʰᵉᵈ‚‚‡, slings (for) the yard {of} [twisted] linen, {a} hundred (by) the forearm {is the} length (for) the (one) edge,□

---

* Referring to the "netting," a feminine word in Hebrew.
† Referring to the "altar," a masculine word in Hebrew.
‡ That is the "south."

Revised Mechanical Translation Codes

(..) Alt Trans/App A   <..> Comp Phrase/App B   [..] Verb Form/App C   \..\ Plural Form/App D

:..: Int Inf Abs |..| Past Perf Verb   {...} Added Word

27:10 וְעַמֻּדָיו עֶשְׂרִים וְאַדְנֵיהֶם עֶשְׂרִים נְחֹשֶׁת וָוֵי הָעַמֻּדִים וַחֲשֻׁקֵיהֶם כָּסֶף

we'a'mu'daw es'rim we'ad'ney'hem es'rim ne'hho'shet wa'wey ha'a'mu'dim wa'hha'shu'qey'hem ka'seph

and~PILLAR~s~him TEN~s and~FOOTING~s~ them(m) TEN~s COPPER PEG~s the~PILLAR~s and~BINDER~s~them(m) SILVER□

and his \twenty/ pillars, and their \twenty/ footings {are of} copper, {the} pegs {of} the pillars and their binders {are of} silver,□

27:11 וְכֵן לִפְאַת צָפוֹן בָּאֹרֶךְ קְלָעִים מֵאָה אֹרֶךְ וְעַמֻּדָו עֶשְׂרִים וְאַדְנֵיהֶם עֶשְׂרִים נְחֹשֶׁת וָוֵי הָעַמֻּדִים וַחֲשֻׁקֵיהֶם כָּסֶף

we'kheyn liph'at tsa'phon ba'o'rekh qe'la'im mey'ah o'rekh we'a'mu'daw es'rim we'ad'ney'hem es'rim ne'hho'shet wa'wey ha'a'mu'dim wa'hha'shu'qey'hem ka'seph

and~SO to~EDGE NORTH in~the~LENGTH SLING~s HUNDRED LENGTH and~PILLAR~s~ him TEN~s and~FOOTING~s~them(m) TEN~s COPPER PEG~s the~PILLAR~s and~ BINDER~s~them(m) SILVER□

and so, (for) {the} edge {of the} north in the length, {the} slings {are a} hundred {in} length, and his \twenty/ pillars and their \twenty/ footings {of} copper, {the} pegs {of} the pillars and their binders {of} silver,□

27:12 וְרֹחַב הֶחָצֵר לִפְאַת יָם קְלָעִים חֲמִשִּׁים אַמָּה עַמֻּדֵיהֶם עֲשָׂרָה וְאַדְנֵיהֶם עֲשָׂרָה

we'ro'hhav he'hha'tseyr liph'at yam qe'la'im hha'mi'shim a'mah a'mu'dey'hem a'sa'rah we'ad'ney'hem a'sa'rah

and~WIDTH the~YARD to~EDGE SEA SLING~s FIVE~s FOREARM PILLAR~s~ them(m) TEN and~FOOTING~s~them(m) TEN□

and {the} width {of} the yard (for) the edge {of the} sea* {are the} slings {of} \fifty/ forearm{s}, their ten pillars and their ten footings,□

27:13 וְרֹחַב הֶחָצֵר לִפְאַת קֵדְמָה מִזְרָחָה חֲמִשִּׁים אַמָּה

we'ro'hhav he'hha'tseyr liph'at qeyd'mah miz'ra'hhah hha'mi'shim a'mah

and~WIDTH the~YARD to~EDGE EAST~unto SUNRISE~unto FIVE~s FOREARM□

and {the} width {of} the yard (for) unto {the} edge {of the} east, unto {the} sunrise, {is} \fifty/ forearm{s},□

27:14 וַחֲמֵשׁ עֶשְׂרֵה אַמָּה קְלָעִים לַכָּתֵף עַמֻּדֵיהֶם שְׁלֹשָׁה וְאַדְנֵיהֶם שְׁלֹשָׁה

wa'hha'meysh es'reyh a'mah qe'la'im la'ka'teyph a'mu'dey'hem she'lo'shah we'ad'ney'hem she'lo'shah

and~FIVE TEN FOREARM SLING~s to~the~ SHOULDER-PIECE PILLAR~s~them(m) THREE and~FOOTING~s~them(m) THREE□

and <fifteen> forearm{s are the} slings (for) the shoulder piece, their three pillars and their three footings,□

27:15 וְלַכָּתֵף הַשֵּׁנִית חֲמֵשׁ עֶשְׂרֵה קְלָעִים עַמֻּדֵיהֶם שְׁלֹשָׁה וְאַדְנֵיהֶם שְׁלֹשָׁה

---

* Meaning "the west."

Mechanical Translation Codes

<u>WORD</u> – Verb	WORD – Noun	Word – Name	word – Pre/Suff	*word* – Conj.

we'la'ka'teyph ha'shey'nit hha'meysh es'reyh qe'la'im a'mu'dey'hem she'lo'shah we'ad'ney'hem she'lo'shah

and~to~the~SHOULDER-PIECE the~SECOND FIVE TEN SLING~s PILLAR~s~them(m) THREE and~FOOTING~s~them(m) THREE□	and (for) the second shoulder piece {are} <fifteen> slings, their three pillars and their three footings,□

27:16 וּלְשַׁעַר הֶחָצֵר מָסָךְ עֶשְׂרִים אַמָּה תְּכֵלֶת וְאַרְגָּמָן וְתוֹלַעַת שָׁנִי וְשֵׁשׁ מָשְׁזָר מַעֲשֵׂה רֹקֵם עַמֻּדֵיהֶם אַרְבָּעָה וְאַדְנֵיהֶם אַרְבָּעָה

ul'sha'ar he'hha'tseyr ma'sakh es'rim a'mah te'khey'let we'ar'ga'man we'to'la'at sha'ni we'sheysh mash'zar ma'a'seyh ro'qeym a'mu'dey'hem ar'ba'ah we'ad'ney'hem ar'ba'ah

and~to~GATE the~YARD CANOPY TEN~s FOREARM BLUE and~PURPLE and~KERMES SCARLET and~LINEN be~make~TWIST-TOGETHER~ing/er(ms) WORK EMBROIDER~ing/er(ms) PILLAR~s~them(m) FOUR and~FOOTING~s~them(m) FOUR□	and (for) {the} gate {of} the yard {is a} canopy {of} \twenty/ forearm{s of} blue and purple and kermes {of} scarlet and [twisted] linen, {a} work {of} embroidering*, their four pillars and their four footings,□

27:17 כָּל עַמּוּדֵי הֶחָצֵר סָבִיב מְחֻשָּׁקִים כֶּסֶף וָוֵיהֶם כָּסֶף וְאַדְנֵיהֶם נְחֹשֶׁת

kol a'mu'dey he'hha'tseyr sa'viv me'hhu'sha'qim ke'seph wa'wey'hem ka'seph we'ad'ney'hem ne'hho'shet

ALL PILLAR~s the~YARD ALL-AROUND be~much~ATTACH~ing/er(mp) SILVER PEG~s~them(m) SILVER and~FOOTING~s~them(m) COPPER□	all {the} pillars {of} the yard all around {it}, being attached {with} silver, their pegs {of} silver and their footings {of} copper,□

27:18 אֹרֶךְ הֶחָצֵר מֵאָה בָאַמָּה וְרֹחַב חֲמִשִּׁים בַּחֲמִשִּׁים וְקֹמָה חָמֵשׁ אַמּוֹת שֵׁשׁ מָשְׁזָר וְאַדְנֵיהֶם נְחֹשֶׁת

o'rekh he'hha'tseyr mey'ah va'a'mah we'ro'hhav hha'mi'shim ba'hha'mi'shim we'qo'mah hha'meysh a'mot sheysh mash'zar we'ad'ney'hem ne'hho'shet

LENGTH the~YARD HUNDRED in~the~FOREARM and~WIDTH FIVE~s in~the~FIVE~s and~HEIGHT FIVE FOREARM~s LINEN be~make~TWIST-TOGETHER~ing/er(ms) and~FOOTING~s~them(m) COPPER□	{the} length {of} the yard {is a} hundred (by) the forearm, and {the} width {is} \fifty/ (by) the forearm{s}†, and {the} height {is} five forearms, {with} [twisted] linen and their footings {of} copper,□

27:19 לְכֹל כְּלֵי הַמִּשְׁכָּן בְּכֹל עֲבֹדָתוֹ וְכָל יְתֵדֹתָיו וְכָל יִתְדֹת הֶחָצֵר נְחֹשֶׁת

le'khol ke'ley ha'mish'kan be'khol a'vo'da'to we'khol ye'tey'do'taw we'khol yit'dot he'hha'tseyr ne'hho'shet

---

* This word may also mean "an embroiderer."

† The word בַּחֲמִשִּׁים (in fifty) is probably a scribal error and may originally have been written as בָאַמָּה (by the forearms).

Revised Mechanical Translation Codes

(..) Alt Trans/App A	<..> Comp Phrase/App B	[..] Verb Form/App C	\../ Plural Form/App D
:..: Int Inf Abs	|..| Past Perf Verb	{...} Added Word	

to~ALL ITEM~s the~DWELLING in~ALL SERVICE~him and~ALL TENT-PEG~s~him and~ALL TENT-PEG~s the~YARD COPPER□

to all {the} items {of} the dwelling, in all his service, and all his tent pegs, and all {the} tent pegs {of} the yard {are} copper,□

27:20

וְאַתָּה תְּצַוֶּה אֶת בְּנֵי יִשְׂרָאֵל וְיִקְחוּ אֵלֶיךָ שֶׁמֶן זַיִת זָךְ כָּתִית לַמָּאוֹר לְהַעֲלֹת נֵר תָּמִיד

we'a'tah te'tsa'weh et be'ney yis'ra'eyl we'yiq'hhu ey'ley'kha she'men za'yit zakh ka'tit la'ma'or le'ha'a'lot neyr ta'mid

and~YOU(ms) you(ms)~will~much~<u>DIRECT</u> AT SON~s "Yisra'el ^{he~will~TURN-ASIDE~+~MIGHTY-ONE}" and~they(m)~will~<u>TAKE</u> TO~you(ms) OIL OLIVE REFINED CRUSHED to~the~LUMINARY to~>~make~<u>GO-UP</u> LAMP CONTINUALLY□

and you, you will direct {the} sons {of} "Yisra'el ^{He turns El aside}", and they will take to you {the} refined {and} crushed oil {of the} olive (for) the luminary, to make {the} lamp go up* continually,□

27:21

בְּאֹהֶל מוֹעֵד מִחוּץ לַפָּרֹכֶת אֲשֶׁר עַל הָעֵדֻת יַעֲרֹךְ אֹתוֹ אַהֲרֹן וּבָנָיו מֵעֶרֶב עַד בֹּקֶר לִפְנֵי יְהֹוָה חֻקַּת עוֹלָם לְדֹרֹתָם מֵאֵת בְּנֵי יִשְׂרָאֵל

be'o'hel mo'eyd mi'hhuts la'pa'ro'khet a'sher al ha'ey'dut ya'a'rokh o'to a'ha'ron u'va'naw mey'e'rev ad bo'qer liph'ney YHWH hhu'qat o'lam le'do'ro'tam mey'eyt be'ney yis'ra'eyl

in~TENT APPOINTED from~OUTSIDE to~the~ TENT-CURTAIN WHICH UPON the~EVIDENCE he~will~<u>ARRANGE</u> AT~him "Aharon ^{LIGHT-BRINGER}" and~SON~s~him from~EVENING UNTIL MORNING to~FACE~s "Yhwh ^{he~will~BE}" RITUAL DISTANT to~GENERATION~s~ them(m) from~AT SON~s "Yisra'el ^{he~will~TURN-ASIDE~+~MIGHTY-ONE}"□

in {the} tent {of the} appointed {place}, outside the tent curtain, which is upon the evidence, "Aharon ^{Light bringer}", and his sons, will arrange him, from {the} evening until {the} morning <in front of> "Yhwh ^{He is}", {a} ritual {of a} distant {time} (for) their generations, from {the} sons {of} "Yisra'el ^{He turns El aside}",□

Chapter 28

28:1

וְאַתָּה הַקְרֵב אֵלֶיךָ אֶת אַהֲרֹן אָחִיךָ וְאֶת בָּנָיו אִתּוֹ מִתּוֹךְ בְּנֵי יִשְׂרָאֵל לְכַהֲנוֹ לִי אַהֲרֹן נָדָב וַאֲבִיהוּא אֶלְעָזָר וְאִיתָמָר בְּנֵי אַהֲרֹן

we'a'tah haq'reyv ey'ley'kha et a'ha'ron a'hhi'kha we'et ba'naw i'to mi'tokh be'ney yis'ra'eyl le'kha'ha'no li a'ha'ron na'dav wa'a'vi'hu el'a'zar we'i'ta'mar be'ney a'ha'ron

and~YOU(ms) !(ms)~make~<u>COME-NEAR</u> TO~ you(ms) AT "Aharon ^{LIGHT-BRINGER}" BROTHER~ you(ms) and~AT SON~s~him AT~him from~ MIDST SON~s "Yisra'el ^{he~will~TURN-ASIDE~+~MIGHTY-ONE}" to~>~much~<u>ADORN</u>~him to~me "Aharon ^{LIGHT-BRINGER}" "Nadav ^{he~did~OFFER-WILLINGLY}" and~"Aviyhu ^{FATHER~me~+~HE}" "Elazar

and you, [bring near] to you "Aharon ^{Light bringer}", your brother, and his sons (with) him, from {the} midst {of the} sons {of} "Yisra'el ^{He turns El aside}", to adorn him (for) me, "Nadav ^{He offered willingly}" and "Aviyhu ^{He is my father}", "Elazar ^{El helps}" and "Iytamar ^{Island of the date palm}", {the} sons {of} "Aharon ^{Light bringer}",□

---

* The word "go up" is referring to the rising flame of the lamp.

Mechanical Translation Codes

<u>WORD</u> – Verb	WORD – Noun	Word – Name	word – Pre/Suff	*word* – Conj.

MIGHTY-ONE~+~*he~did~*<u>HELP</u>„ and~"Iytamar ^{ISLAND~+~}

DATE-PALM„ SON~s "Aharon ^{LIGHT-BRINGER}„ ☐

28:2

וְעָשִׂיתָ בִגְדֵי קֹדֶשׁ לְאַהֲרֹן אָחִיךָ לְכָבוֹד וּלְתִפְאָרֶת

we'a'si'ta vig'dey qo'desh le'a'ha'ron a'hhi'kha le'kha'vod ul'tiph'a'ret

and~you(ms)~did~<u>DO</u> GARMENT~s SPECIAL to~"Aharon ^{LIGHT-BRINGER}„ BROTHER~you(ms) to~ARMAMENT and~to~DECORATION☐

and you will (make) garments {of} special{ness} (for) "Aharon ^{Light bringer}„, your brother, (for) armament and (for) decoration,☐

28:3

וְאַתָּה תְּדַבֵּר אֶל כָּל חַכְמֵי לֵב אֲשֶׁר מִלֵּאתִיו רוּחַ חָכְמָה וְעָשׂוּ אֶת בִּגְדֵי אַהֲרֹן לְקַדְּשׁוֹ לְכַהֲנוֹ לִי

we'a'tah te'da'beyr el kol hhakh'mey leyv a'sher mi'ley'tiw ru'ahh hhakh'mah we'a'su et big'dey a'ha'ron le'qad'sho le'kha'ha'no li

and~YOU(ms) *you(ms)~will~much~*<u>SPEAK</u> TO ALL SKILLED-ONE~s HEART WHICH *I~did~much~*<u>FILL</u>~him WIND SKILL and~*they~did~*<u>DO</u> AT GARMENT~s "Aharon ^{LIGHT-BRINGER}„ to~ >~*much~*<u>SET-APART</u>~him to~>~*much~* <u>ADORN</u>~him to~me☐

and you, you will speak to all {the} skilled ones {of} heart, (whom) I filled {with the} wind* {of} skill, and they will (make) {the} garments {of} "Aharon ^{Light bringer}„ to set him apart, to adorn him (for) me,☐

28:4

וְאֵלֶּה הַבְּגָדִים אֲשֶׁר יַעֲשׂוּ חֹשֶׁן וְאֵפוֹד וּמְעִיל וּכְתֹנֶת תַּשְׁבֵּץ מִצְנֶפֶת וְאַבְנֵט וְעָשׂוּ בִגְדֵי קֹדֶשׁ לְאַהֲרֹן אָחִיךָ וּלְבָנָיו לְכַהֲנוֹ לִי

we'ey'leh ha'be'ga'dim a'sher ya'a'su hho'shen we'ey'phod um'il ukh'to'net tash'beyts mits'ne'phet we'av'neyt we'a'su vig'dey qo'desh le'a'ha'ron a'hhi'kha ul'va'naw le'kha'ha'no li

and~THESE the~GARMENT~s WHICH *they(m)~will~*<u>DO</u> BREASTPLATE and~EPHOD and~CLOAK and~TUNIC WOVEN-MATERIAL TURBAN and~SASH and~*they~did~*<u>DO</u> GARMENT~s SPECIAL to~"Aharon ^{LIGHT-BRINGER}„ BROTHER~you(ms) and~to~SON~s~ him to~>~*much~*<u>ADORN</u>~him to~me☐

and these {are} the garments which they will (make), breastplate and ephod and cloak and tunic {of} woven material, turban and sash, and they will (make) garments {of} special{ness} (for) "Aharon ^{Light bringer}„, your brother, and (for) his sons, to adorn him (for) me,☐

28:5

וְהֵם יִקְחוּ אֶת הַזָּהָב וְאֶת הַתְּכֵלֶת וְאֶת הָאַרְגָּמָן וְאֶת תּוֹלַעַת הַשָּׁנִי וְאֶת הַשֵּׁשׁ

we'heym yiq'hhu et ha'za'hav we'et hat'khey'let we'et ha'ar'ga'man we'et to'la'at ha'sha'ni we'et ha'sheysh

and~THEY(m) *they(m)~will~*<u>TAKE</u> AT the~ GOLD and~AT the~BLUE and~AT the~ PURPLE and~AT KERMES the~SCARLET and~

and they, they will take the gold and the blue and the purple and {the} kermes {of} the scarlet and the linen,☐

---

* The wind, or breath, of an individual is his character.

Revised Mechanical Translation Codes

(..) Alt Trans/App A   <..> Comp Phrase/App B   [..] Verb Form/App C   \../ Plural Form/App D

:..: Int Inf Abs |..| Past Perf Verb   {...} Added Word

AT the~LINEN□

28:6

וְעָשׂוּ אֶת הָאֵפֹד זָהָב תְּכֵלֶת וְאַרְגָּמָן תּוֹלַעַת שָׁנִי וְשֵׁשׁ מָשְׁזָר מַעֲשֵׂה
חֹשֵׁב

we'a'su et ha'ey'phod za'hav te'khey'let we'ar'ga'man to'la'at sha'ni we'sheysh mash'zar
ma'a'seyh hho'sheyv

and~*they~did*~DO AT the~EPHOD GOLD BLUE and~PURPLE KERMES SCARLET and~ LINEN *be~make*~TWIST-TOGETHER~ *ing/er(ms)* WORK THINK~*ing/er(ms)*□	and they will (make) the ephod {with} gold, blue and purple, kermes {of} scarlet and [twisted] linen, {a} work {of a} thinking*,□

28:7

שְׁתֵּי כְתֵפֹת חֹבְרֹת יִהְיֶה לּוֹ אֶל שְׁנֵי קְצוֹתָיו וְחֻבָּר

she'tey khe'tey'phot hhov'rot yih'yeh lo el she'ney qe'tso'taw we'hhu'bar

TWO SHOULDER-PIECE~s COUPLE~*ing/er(fp)* *he~will*~EXIST *to~him* TO TWO EXTREMITY~s~*him* and~*he~did~be~much~* COUPLE□	he† will (have) two shoulder pieces coupl{ed together} (at) {the} two {of} his extremities, and he will be coupled,□

28:8

וְחֵשֶׁב אֲפֻדָּתוֹ אֲשֶׁר עָלָיו כְּמַעֲשֵׂהוּ מִמֶּנּוּ יִהְיֶה זָהָב תְּכֵלֶת וְאַרְגָּמָן
וְתוֹלַעַת שָׁנִי וְשֵׁשׁ מָשְׁזָר

we'hhey'shev a'phu'da'to a'sher a'law ke'ma'a'sey'hu mi'me'nu yih'yeh za'hav te'khey'let
we'ar'ga'man we'to'la'at sha'ni we'sheysh mash'zar

and~DECORATIVE-BAND EPHOD~*him* WHICH UPON~*him* like~WORK~*him* FROM~*him* *he~ will*~EXIST GOLD BLUE and~PURPLE and~ KERMES SCARLET and~LINEN *be~make*~ TWIST-TOGETHER~*ing/er(ms)*□	and {the} decorative band {of} his ephod, which {is} upon him, he will exist {just} like his work, gold, blue and purple and kermes {of} scarlet and [twisted] linen,□

28:9

וְלָקַחְתָּ אֶת שְׁתֵּי אַבְנֵי שֹׁהַם וּפִתַּחְתָּ עֲלֵיהֶם שְׁמוֹת בְּנֵי יִשְׂרָאֵל

we'la'qahh'ta et she'tey av'ney sho'ham u'phi'tahh'ta a'ley'hem she'mot be'ney yis'ra'eyl

and~*you(ms)~did*~TAKE AT TWO STONE~s ONYX and~*you(ms)~did~much~*OPEN UPON~*them(m)* TITLE~s SON~s "Yisra'el *he~ will*~TURN-ASIDE~+~MIGHTY-ONE*"□	and you will take {the} two stones {of the} onyx‡, and you will [engrave] upon them {the} titles {of the} sons {of} "Yisra'el ^{He turns El aside}",□

28:10

שִׁשָּׁה מִשְּׁמֹתָם עַל הָאֶבֶן הָאֶחָת וְאֶת שְׁמוֹת הַשִּׁשָּׁה הַנּוֹתָרִים עַל
הָאֶבֶן הַשֵּׁנִית כְּתוֹלְדֹתָם

shi'shah mish'mo'tam al ha'e'ven ha'e'hhat we'et she'mot ha'shi'shah ha'no'ta'rim al
ha'e'ven ha'shey'nit ke'tol'do'tam

---

* This may be a work of an intricate design or made by "a thinker" in the sense of a designer.
† Referring to the "Ephod," a masculine word in Hebrew.
‡ The "shoham" is unknown stone.

Mechanical Translation Codes

WORD – Verb	WORD – Noun	Word – Name	word – Pre/Suff	*word* – Conj.

SIX from~TITLE~s~them(m) UPON the~ STONE the~UNIT and~AT TITLE~s the~SIX the~be~<u>LEAVE-BEHIND</u>~ing/er(mp) UPON the~STONE the~SECOND like~BIRTHING~s~them(m)□

six from their titles upon the (one) stone and the six titles being left behind* upon the second stone, like† their birthings,□

28:11 מַעֲשֵׂה חָרַשׁ אֶבֶן פִּתּוּחֵי חֹתָם תְּפַתַּח אֶת שְׁתֵּי הָאֲבָנִים עַל שְׁמֹת בְּנֵי יִשְׂרָאֵל מֻסַבֹּת מִשְׁבְּצֹת זָהָב תַּעֲשֶׂה אֹתָם

ma'a'seyh hha'rash e'ven pi'tu'hhey hho'tam te'pha'tahh et she'tey ha'a'va'nim al she'mot be'ney yis'ra'eyl mu'sa'bot mish'be'tsot za'hav ta'a'seh o'tam

WORK ENGRAVER STONE CARVING~s SEAL *you(ms)~will~much~*<u>OPEN</u> AT TWO the~ STONE~s UPON TITLE~s SON~s "Yisra'el ^{he} <u>will~TURN-ASIDE</u>~+~MIGHTY-ONE*," be~*make~<u>GO-AROUND</u>~ing/er(fp) PLAIT~s GOLD *you(ms)~ will~*<u>DO</u> AT~them(m)□

{like the} work {of a} stone engraver, {like the} carvings {of a} seal, you will [engrave] the two stones (according to) {the} titles {of the} sons {of} "Yisra'el ^{He turns El aside}", you will (make) them [enclosed in] plaits {of} gold,□

28:12 וְשַׂמְתָּ אֶת שְׁתֵּי הָאֲבָנִים עַל כִּתְפֹת הָאֵפֹד אַבְנֵי זִכָּרֹן לִבְנֵי יִשְׂרָאֵל וְנָשָׂא אַהֲרֹן אֶת שְׁמוֹתָם לִפְנֵי יְהוָה עַל שְׁתֵּי כְתֵפָיו לְזִכָּרֹן

we'sam'ta et she'tey ha'a'va'nim al kit'phot ha'ey'phod av'ney zi'ka'ron liv'ney yis'ra'eyl we'na'sa a'ha'ron et she'mo'tam liph'ney YHWH al she'tey khe'tey'phaw le'zi'ka'ron

and~*you(ms)~did~*<u>PLACE</u> AT TWO the~ STONE~s UPON SHOULDER-PIECE~s the~ EPHOD STONE~s REMEMBRANCE to~SON~s "Yisra'el ^{he~will~TURN-ASIDE~+~MIGHTY-ONE}*," and~*he~ *did~*<u>LIFT-UP</u> "Aharon ^{LIGHT-BRINGER}*," AT TITLE~s~ them(m) to~FACE~s "Yhwh ^{he~will~<u>BE</u>}*," UPON TWO SHOULDER-PIECE~s~him to~ REMEMBRANCE□

and you will place the two stones upon {the} shoulder piece {of} the ephod, {to be} stones {of} remembrance (for) {the} sons {of} "Yisra'el ^{He turns El aside}", and "Aharon ^{Light bringer}" will lift up their titles <in front of> "Yhwh ^{He is}", upon his two shoulder pieces (for) {a} remembrance,□

28:13 וְעָשִׂיתָ מִשְׁבְּצֹת זָהָב

we'a'si'ta mish'be'tsot za'hav

and~*you(ms)~did~*<u>DO</u> PLAIT~s GOLD□

and you will (make) plaits {of} gold,□

28:14 וּשְׁתֵּי שַׁרְשְׁרֹת זָהָב טָהוֹר מִגְבָּלֹת תַּעֲשֶׂה אֹתָם מַעֲשֵׂה עֲבֹת וְנָתַתָּה אֶת שַׁרְשְׁרֹת הָעֲבֹתֹת עַל הַמִּשְׁבְּצֹת

ush'tey shar'she'rot za'hav ta'hor mig'ba'lot ta'a'seh o'tam ma'a'seyh a'vot we'na'ta'tah et shar'she'rot ha'a'vo'tot al ha'mish'be'tsot

and~TWO CHAIN~s GOLD PURE BOUNDARY~s *you(ms)~will~*<u>DO</u> AT~them(m)

and two chains {of} pure gold {are at the} boundaries, you will (make) them {a} work {of

---

* "six titles being left behind" means "the other six titles."
† Or "according to."

Revised Mechanical Translation Codes

(..) Alt Trans/App A	<..> Comp Phrase/App B	[..] Verb Form/App C	\..\ Plural Form/App D
:...: Int Inf Abs	|..| Past Perf Verb	{...} Added Word	

WORK THICK-CORD and~*you(ms)~did~* <u>GIVE</u>~^ AT CHAIN~s the~THICK-CORD~s UPON the~PLAIT~s☐	a} thick cord, and you will (place) {the} chains {of} thick cords upon the plaits,☐

28:15 וְעָשִׂיתָ חֹשֶׁן מִשְׁפָּט מַעֲשֵׂה חֹשֵׁב כְּמַעֲשֵׂה אֵפֹד תַּעֲשֶׂנּוּ זָהָב תְּכֵלֶת וְאַרְגָּמָן וְתוֹלַעַת שָׁנִי וְשֵׁשׁ מָשְׁזָר תַּעֲשֶׂה אֹתוֹ

we'a'si'ta hho'shen mish'pat ma'a'seyh hho'sheyv ke'ma'a'seyh ey'phod ta'a'se'nu za'hav te'khey'let we'ar'ga'man we'to'la'at sha'ni we'sheysh mash'zar ta'a'seh o'to

and~*you(ms)~did~*<u>DO</u> BREASTPLATE DECISION WORK <u>THINK</u>~*ing/er(ms)* like~ WORK EPHOD *you(ms)~will~*<u>DO</u>~him GOLD BLUE and~PURPLE and~KERMES SCARLET and~LINEN *be~make~*<u>TWIST-TOGETHER</u>~ *ing/er(ms) you(ms)~will~*<u>DO</u> AT~him☐	and you will (make) {a} breastplate {of} decision, {a} work {of} thinking*, like {the} work {of the} ephod you will (make) him, {with} gold, blue and purple and kermes {of} scarlet and [twisted] linen you will (make) him,☐

28:16 רָבוּעַ יִהְיֶה כָּפוּל זֶרֶת אָרְכּוֹ וְזֶרֶת רָחְבּוֹ

ra'vu'a yih'yeh ka'phul ze'ret ar'ko we'ze'ret rahh'bo

<u>BE-SQUARE</u>~*ed(ms) he~will~*<u>EXIST</u> <u>DOUBLE-OVER</u>~*ed(ms)* FINGER-SPAN LENGTH~him and~FINGER-SPAN WIDTH~him☐	he will exist squared, doubled over, {a} finger span {is} his length, and {a} finger span {is} his width,☐

28:17 וּמִלֵּאתָ בוֹ מִלֻּאַת אֶבֶן אַרְבָּעָה טוּרִים אָבֶן טוּר אֹדֶם פִּטְדָה וּבָרֶקֶת הַטּוּר הָאֶחָד

u'mi'ley'ta bo mi'lu'at e'ven ar'ba'ah tu'rim a'ven tur o'dem pit'dah u'va're'qet ha'tur ha'e'hhad

and~*you(ms)~did~much~*<u>FILL</u> in~him SETTING STONE FOUR ROW~s STONE ROW CARNELIAN OLIVINE and~EMERALD the~ ROW the~UNIT☐	and you will [set] in him setting{s of} stone†, four rows {of} stone, {a} row {of} carnelian, olivine and emerald {is} the (one) row,☐

28:18 וְהַטּוּר הַשֵּׁנִי נֹפֶךְ סַפִּיר וְיָהֲלֹם

we'ha'tur ha'shey'ni no'phekh sa'pir we'ya'ha'lom

and~the~ROW the~SECOND TURQUOISE LAPIS-LAZULI and~FLINT☐	and the second row {is} turquoise, lapis-lazuli and flint,☐

28:19 וְהַטּוּר הַשְּׁלִישִׁי לֶשֶׁם שְׁבוֹ וְאַחְלָמָה

---

* This may be a work of an intricate design or made by "a thinker" in the sense of a designer.

† The identification of these twelve stones is uncertain (see the dictionary entry for each stone for additional information).

Mechanical Translation Codes

<u>WORD</u> – Verb	WORD – Noun	Word – Name	word – Pre/Suff	*word* – Conj.

we'ha'tur hash'li'shi le'shem she'vo we'ahh'la'mah

and~the~ROW the~THIRD OPAL AGATE and~ AMETHYST☐

and the third row {is} opal, agate and amethyst,☐

28:20 וְהַטּוּר הָרְבִיעִי תַּרְשִׁישׁ וְשֹׁהַם וְיָשְׁפֵה מְשֻׁבָּצִים זָהָב יִהְיוּ בְּמִלּוּאֹתָם

we'ha'tur har'vi'i tar'shish we'sho'ham we'yash'pheyh me'shu'ba'tsim za'hav yih'yu be'mi'lu'o'tam

and~the~ROW the~FOURTH TOPAZ and~ ONYX and~JASPER be~much~WEAVE~ ing/er(mp) GOLD they(m)~will~EXIST in~ SETTING~s~them(m)☐

and the fourth row {is} topaz and onyx and jasper, being woven {with} gold they will exist in their settings,☐

28:21 וְהָאֲבָנִים תִּהְיֶיןָ עַל שְׁמֹת בְּנֵי יִשְׂרָאֵל שְׁתֵּים עֶשְׂרֵה עַל שְׁמֹתָם פִּתּוּחֵי חוֹתָם אִישׁ עַל שְׁמוֹ תִּהְיֶיןָ לִשְׁנֵי עָשָׂר שָׁבֶט

we'ha'a'va'nim tih'yey'na al she'mot be'ney yis'ra'eyl she'teym es'reyh al she'mo'tam pi'tu'hhey hho'tam ish al she'mo tih'yey'na lish'ney a'sar sha'vet

and~the~STONE~s they(f)~will~EXIST UPON TITLE~s SON~s "Yisra'el ^(he~will~TURN-ASIDE~+~MIGHTY-ONE)" TWO TEN UPON TITLE~s~them(m) CARVING~s SEAL MAN UPON TITLE~him they(f)~will~EXIST to~TWO TEN STAFF☐

and the stones will exist (according to) {the} titles {of the} sons {of} "Yisra'el ^(He turns El aside),, <twelve> (according to) their titles, carvings {of the} seal {of} (each) (according to) his title, they will exist (for) {the} <twelve> staff{s}*,☐

28:22 וְעָשִׂיתָ עַל הַחֹשֶׁן שַׁרְשֹׁת גַּבְלֻת מַעֲשֵׂה עֲבֹת זָהָב טָהוֹר

we'a'si'ta al ha'hho'shen shar'shot gav'lut ma'a'seyh a'vot za'hav ta'hor

and~you(ms)~did~DO UPON the~ BREASTPLATE CHAIN~s EDGING WORK THICK-CORD GOLD PURE☐

and you will (make) upon the breastplate chains, {the} edging {is a} work {of a} thick cord {of} pure gold,☐

28:23 וְעָשִׂיתָ עַל הַחֹשֶׁן שְׁתֵּי טַבְּעוֹת זָהָב וְנָתַתָּ אֶת שְׁתֵּי הַטַּבָּעוֹת עַל שְׁנֵי קְצוֹת הַחֹשֶׁן

we'a'si'ta al ha'hho'shen she'tey ta'be'ot za'hav we'na'ta'ta et she'tey ha'ta'ba'ot al she'ney qe'tsot ha'hho'shen

and~you(ms)~did~DO UPON the~ BREASTPLATE TWO RING~s GOLD and~ you(ms)~did~GIVE AT TWO the~RING~s UPON TWO EXTREMITY~s the~ BREASTPLATE☐

and you will (make) upon the breastplate two rings {of} gold, and you will (place) the two rings upon {the} two extremities {of} the breastplate,☐

28:24 וְנָתַתָּה אֶת שְׁתֵּי עֲבֹתֹת הַזָּהָב עַל שְׁתֵּי הַטַּבָּעוֹת אֶל קְצוֹת הַחֹשֶׁן

---

* Or "tribes."

Revised Mechanical Translation Codes

| (..) Alt Trans/App A | <..> Comp Phrase/App B | [..] Verb Form/App C | \../ Plural Form/App D |
| :..: Int Inf Abs | |..| Past Perf Verb | {...} Added Word | |

we'na'ta'tah et she'tey a'vo'tot ha'za'hav al she'tey ha'ta'ba'ot el qe'tsot ha'hho'shen

and~*you(ms)~did*~<u>GIVE</u>~^ AT TWO THICK-CORD~s the~GOLD UPON TWO the~RING~s TO EXTREMITY~s the~BREASTPLATE□

and you will (place) {the} two thick cords {of} gold upon {the} two rings (at) {the} extremities {of} the breastplate,□

28:25 וְאֵת שְׁתֵּי קְצוֹת שְׁתֵּי הָעֲבֹתֹת תִּתֵּן עַל שְׁתֵּי הַמִּשְׁבְּצוֹת וְנָתַתָּה עַל כִּתְפוֹת הָאֵפֹד אֶל מוּל פָּנָיו

we'eyt she'tey qe'tsot she'tey ha'a'vo'tot ti'teyn al she'tey ha'mish'be'tsot we'na'ta'tah al kit'phot ha'ey'phod el mul pa'naw

and~AT TWO EXTREMITY~s TWO the~THICK-CORD~s *you(ms)~will*~<u>GIVE</u> UPON TWO the~PLAIT~s and~*you(ms)~did*~<u>GIVE</u>~^ UPON SHOULDER-PIECE~s the~EPHOD TO FOREFRONT FACE~s~him□

and {the} two extremities {of} the two thick cords you will (place) upon the two plaits, and you will (place) upon {the} shoulder pieces {of} the ephod to {the} forefront {of} his face,□

28:26 וְעָשִׂיתָ שְׁתֵּי טַבְּעוֹת זָהָב וְשַׂמְתָּ אֹתָם עַל שְׁנֵי קְצוֹת הַחֹשֶׁן עַל שְׂפָתוֹ אֲשֶׁר אֶל עֵבֶר הָאֵפֹד בָּיְתָה

we'a'si'ta she'tey ta'be'ot za'hav we'sam'ta o'tam al she'ney qe'tsot ha'hho'shen al se'pha'to a'sher el ey'ver ha'ey'phod bai'tah

and~*you(ms)~did*~<u>DO</u> TWO RING~s GOLD and~*you(ms)~did*~<u>PLACE</u> AT~them(m) UPON TWO EXTREMITY~s the~BREASTPLATE UPON LIP~him WHICH TO OTHER-SIDE the~EPHOD HOUSE~unto□

and you will (make) two rings {of} gold, and you will place them upon {the} two extremities {of} the breastplate upon his lip, which {is} (on) {the} other side {of} the ephod, unto {the} (inside),□

28:27 וְעָשִׂיתָ שְׁתֵּי טַבְּעוֹת זָהָב וְנָתַתָּה אֹתָם עַל שְׁתֵּי כִתְפוֹת הָאֵפוֹד מִלְּמַטָּה מִמּוּל פָּנָיו לְעֻמַּת מַחְבַּרְתּוֹ מִמַּעַל לְחֵשֶׁב הָאֵפוֹד

we'a'si'ta she'tey ta'be'ot za'hav we'na'ta'tah o'tam al she'tey khit'phot ha'ey'phod mil'ma'tah mi'mul pa'naw le'u'mat mahh'bar'to mi'ma'al le'hhey'shev ha'ey'phod

and~*you(ms)~did*~<u>DO</u> TWO RING~s GOLD and~*you(ms)~did*~<u>GIVE</u>~^ AT~them(m) UPON TWO SHOULDER-PIECE~s the~EPHOD from~to~BENEATH from~FOREFRONT FACE~s~him to~ALONGSIDE JOINT~him from~UPWARD to~DECORATIVE-BAND the~EPHOD□

and you will (make) two rings {of} gold, and you will (place) them upon {the} two shoulder pieces {of} the ephod, beneath {the} forefront {of} his face, alongside his joint, <above> {the} decorative band {of} the ephod,□

28:28 וְיִרְכְּסוּ אֶת הַחֹשֶׁן מִטַּבְּעֹתָו אֶל טַבְּעֹת הָאֵפוֹד בִּפְתִיל תְּכֵלֶת לִהְיוֹת עַל חֵשֶׁב הָאֵפוֹד וְלֹא יִזַּח הַחֹשֶׁן מֵעַל הָאֵפוֹד

we'yir'ke'su et ha'hho'shen mi'ta'be'o'taw el ta'be'ot ha'ey'phod biph'til te'khey'let lih'yot al hhey'shev ha'ey'phod we'lo yi'zahh ha'hho'shen mey'al ha'ey'phod

and~*they(m)~will*~<u>TIE-ON</u> AT the~BREASTPLATE RING~s~him TO RING~s the~EPHOD in~CORD BLUE to~>~<u>EXIST</u> UPON

and they will tie on the breastplate {by} his rings to {the} rings {of} the ephod (with) {a} cord {of} blue, to exist upon {the} decorative

Mechanical Translation Codes

<u>WORD</u> – Verb	WORD – Noun	Word – Name	word – Pre/Suff	*word* – Conj.

DECORATIVE-BAND the~EPHOD and~NOT he~will~be~<u>LOOSEN</u> the~BREASTPLATE from~UPON the~EPHOD□

band {of} the ephod, and the breastplate will not be loosened from upon the ephod,□

28:29

וְנָשָׂא אַהֲרֹן אֶת שְׁמוֹת בְּנֵי יִשְׂרָאֵל בְּחֹשֶׁן הַמִּשְׁפָּט עַל לִבּוֹ בְּבֹאוֹ אֶל הַקֹּדֶשׁ לְזִכָּרֹן לִפְנֵי יְהוָה תָּמִיד

we'na'sa a'ha'ron et she'mot be'ney yis'ra'eyl be'hho'shen ha'mish'pat al li'bo be'vo'o el ha'qo'desh le'zi'ka'ron liph'ney YHWH ta'mid

and~he~did~<u>LIFT-UP</u> "Aharon ^{LIGHT-BRINGER}" AT TITLE~s SON~s "Yisra'el ^{he~will~TURN-ASIDE~+~MIGHTY-ONE}" in~BREASTPLATE the~DECISION UPON HEART~him in~>~<u>COME</u>~him TO the~SPECIAL to~REMEMBRANCE to~FACE~s "Yhwh ^{he~will~BE}" CONTINUALLY□

and "Aharon ^{Light bringer}" lifted up {the} titles {of the} sons {of} "Yisra'el ^{He turns El aside}" in {the} breastplate {of} the decision upon his heart, in his coming to the special {place} garments {of} special {place} (for) {a} remembrance <in front of> "Yhwh ^{He is}" continually,□

28:30

וְנָתַתָּ אֶל חֹשֶׁן הַמִּשְׁפָּט אֶת הָאוּרִים וְאֶת הַתֻּמִּים וְהָיוּ עַל לֵב אַהֲרֹן בְּבֹאוֹ לִפְנֵי יְהוָה וְנָשָׂא אַהֲרֹן אֶת מִשְׁפַּט בְּנֵי יִשְׂרָאֵל עַל לִבּוֹ לִפְנֵי יְהוָה תָּמִיד

we'na'ta'ta el hho'shen ha'mish'pat et ha'u'rim we'et ha'tu'mim we'hai'u al leyv a'ha'ron be'vo'o liph'ney YHWH we'na'sa a'ha'ron et mish'pat be'ney yis'ra'eyl al li'bo liph'ney YHWH ta'mid

and~you(ms)~did~<u>GIVE</u> TO BREASTPLATE the~DECISION AT the~"Uriym ^{LIGHT~s}" and~AT the~"Tumiym ^{FULL-STRENGTH~s}" and~they~did~<u>EXIST</u> UPON HEART "Aharon ^{LIGHT-BRINGER}" in~>~<u>COME</u>~him to~FACE~s "Yhwh ^{he~will~BE}" and~he~did~<u>LIFT-UP</u> "Aharon ^{LIGHT-BRINGER}" AT DECISION SON~s "Yisra'el ^{he~will~TURN-ASIDE~+~MIGHTY-ONE}" UPON HEART~him to~FACE~s "Yhwh ^{he~will~BE}" CONTINUALLY□

and you will (place) the "Uriym ^{Lights}" and the "Tumiym ^{Full strengths}" (on) {the} breastplate {of} the decision, and they will exist upon {the} heart {of} "Aharon ^{Light bringer}" in his coming <in front of> "Yhwh ^{He is}", and "Aharon ^{Light bringer}" will lift up {the} decision {of the} sons {of} "Yisra'el ^{He turns El aside}" upon his heart <in front of> "Yhwh ^{He is}" continually,□

28:31

וְעָשִׂיתָ אֶת מְעִיל הָאֵפוֹד כְּלִיל תְּכֵלֶת

we'a'si'ta et me'il ha'ey'phod ke'lil te'khey'let

and~you(ms)~did~<u>DO</u> AT CLOAK the~EPHOD ENTIRELY BLUE□

and you will (make) {the} cloak {of} the ephod entirely {of} blue,□

28:32

וְהָיָה פִי רֹאשׁוֹ בְּתוֹכוֹ שָׂפָה יִהְיֶה לְפִיו סָבִיב מַעֲשֵׂה אֹרֵג כְּפִי תַחְרָא יִהְיֶה לּוֹ לֹא יִקָּרֵעַ

we'hai'yah phi ro'sho be'to'kho sa'phah yih'yeh le'phiw sa'viv ma'a'seyh o'reyg ke'phi tahh'ra yih'yeh lo lo yi'qa'rey'a

---

Revised Mechanical Translation Codes

(..) Alt Trans/App A	<..> Comp Phrase/App B	[..] Verb Form/App C	\../ Plural Form/App D
:...: Int Inf Abs	|..| Past Perf Verb	{...} Added Word	

and~he~did~<u>EXIST</u> MOUTH HEAD~him in~
MIDST~him LIP *he~will*~<u>EXIST</u> to~MOUTH~
him ALL-AROUND WORK <u>BRAID</u>~ing/er(ms)
like~MOUTH COLLAR *he~will*~<u>EXIST</u> to~him
NOT *he~will*~be~<u>TEAR</u>□

and {a} mouth* {for} his head will exist in his
midst, {a} lip† will exist (for) his mouth all
around, {a} work {of} braiding‡, he will exist
(for) him like {the} mouth {of a} collar, he will
not be torn,□

28:33 וְעָשִׂיתָ עַל שׁוּלָיו רִמֹּנֵי תְּכֵלֶת וְאַרְגָּמָן וְתוֹלַעַת שָׁנִי עַל שׁוּלָיו סָבִיב
וּפַעֲמֹנֵי זָהָב בְּתוֹכָם סָבִיב

we'a'si'ta al shu'law ri'mo'ney te'khey'let we'ar'ga'man we'to'la'at sha'ni al shu'law sa'viv
u'pha'a'mo'ney za'hav be'to'kham sa'viv

and~*you(ms)*~did~<u>DO</u> UPON HEM~s~him
POMEGRANATE~s BLUE and~PURPLE and~
KERMES SCARLET UPON HEM~s~him ALL-
AROUND and~BELL~s GOLD in~MIDST~
them(m) ALL-AROUND□

and you will (make) upon his hems
pomegranates {of} blue and purple and
kermes {of} scarlet, upon his hems all around,
and bells {of} gold in their midst all around,□

28:34 פַּעֲמֹן זָהָב וְרִמּוֹן פַּעֲמֹן זָהָב וְרִמּוֹן עַל שׁוּלֵי הַמְּעִיל סָבִיב

pa'a'mon za'hav we'ri'mon pa'a'mon za'hav we'ri'mon al shu'ley ham'il sa'viv

BELL GOLD and~POMEGRANATE BELL GOLD
and~POMEGRANATE UPON HEM~s the~
CLOAK ALL-AROUND□

bell{s of} gold and pomegranate{s}, bell{s of}
gold and pomegranate{s}§ {are} upon {the}
hems {of} the cloak all around,□

28:35 וְהָיָה עַל אַהֲרֹן לְשָׁרֵת וְנִשְׁמַע קוֹלוֹ בְּבֹאוֹ אֶל הַקֹּדֶשׁ לִפְנֵי יְהוָה
וּבְצֵאתוֹ וְלֹא יָמוּת

we'hai'yah al a'ha'ron le'sha'reyt we'nish'ma qo'lo be'vo'o el ha'qo'desh liph'ney YHWH
uv'tsey'to we'lo ya'mut

and~he~did~<u>EXIST</u> UPON "Aharon <sup>LIGHT-
BRINGER</sup>" to~>~*much*~<u>MINISTER</u> and~he~did~
be~<u>HEAR</u> VOICE~him in~>~<u>COME</u>~him TO
the~SPECIAL to~FACE~s "Yhwh ^{*he~will*~<u>BE</u>}"
and~in~>~<u>GO-OUT</u>~him and~NOT *he~will*~
<u>DIE</u>□

and he will exist upon "Aharon ^{Light bringer}" to
minister, and his voice** will be heard in his
coming to the special {place}, <in front of>
"Yhwh ^{He is}", and in his go{ing} out and he will
not die,□

28:36 וְעָשִׂיתָ צִּיץ זָהָב טָהוֹר וּפִתַּחְתָּ עָלָיו פִּתּוּחֵי חֹתָם קֹדֶשׁ לַיהוָה

we'a'si'ta tsits za'hav ta'hor u'phi'tahh'ta a'law pi'tu'hhey hho'tam qo'desh la'YHWH

and~*you(ms)*~did~<u>DO</u> BLOSSOM GOLD PURE
and~*you(ms)*~did~*much*~<u>OPEN</u> UPON~him

and you will (make) {a} blossom {of} pure gold,
and you will [engrave] upon him carvings {of

---

* That is an "opening."

† That is an "edge" or a "border."

‡ May also be translated as a "braider."

§ The phrase "bells of gold and pomegranates" is written twice showing that they are to be
placed on the garment in series.

** Meaning the sound of the bells.

Mechanical Translation Codes

<u>WORD</u> – Verb   WORD – Noun   Word – Name   word – Pre/Suff   *word* – Conj.

CARVING~s SEAL SPECIAL to~"Yhwh ^{he~will~}_{BE}"□

a} seal, {a} special {thing} (for) "Yhwh ^{He is}",□

28:37

וְשַׂמְתָּ אֹתוֹ עַל פְּתִיל תְּכֵלֶת וְהָיָה עַל הַמִּצְנֶפֶת אֶל מוּל פְּנֵי הַמִּצְנֶפֶת יִהְיֶה

we'sam'ta o'to al pe'til te'khey'let we'hai'yah al ha'mits'na'phet el mul pe'ney ha'mits'ne'phet yih'yeh

and~you(ms)~did~<u>PLACE</u> AT~him UPON CORD BLUE and~he~did~<u>EXIST</u> UPON the~ TURBAN TO FOREFRONT FACE~s the~ TURBAN he~will~<u>EXIST</u>□

and you will place him upon {a} cord {of} blue, and he will exist upon the turban, to the forefront {of the} face {of} the turban he will exist,□

28:38

וְהָיָה עַל מֵצַח אַהֲרֹן וְנָשָׂא אַהֲרֹן אֶת עֲוֹן הַקֳּדָשִׁים אֲשֶׁר יַקְדִּישׁוּ בְּנֵי יִשְׂרָאֵל לְכָל מַתְּנֹת קָדְשֵׁיהֶם וְהָיָה עַל מִצְחוֹ תָּמִיד לְרָצוֹן לָהֶם לִפְנֵי יְהֹוָה

we'hai'yah al mey'tsahh a'ha'ron we'na'sa a'ha'ron et a'won ha'qa'da'shim a'sher yaq'di'shu be'ney yis'ra'eyl le'khol mat'not qad'shey'hem we'hai'yah al mits'hho ta'mid le'ra'tson la'hem liph'ney YHWH

and~he~did~<u>EXIST</u> UPON FOREHEAD "Aharon ^{LIGHT-BRINGER}" and~he~did~<u>LIFT-UP</u> "Aharon ^{LIGHT-BRINGER}" AT INIQUITY the~ SPECIAL~s WHICH they(m)~will~make~<u>SET-APART</u> SON~s "Yisra'el ^{he~will~<u>TURN-ASIDE</u>~+~MIGHTY-ONE}" to~ALL CONTRIBUTION SPECIAL~s~ them(m) and~he~did~<u>EXIST</u> UPON FOREHEAD~him CONTINUALLY to~ self-WILL to~them(m) to~FACE~s "Yhwh ^{he~will~<u>BE</u>}"□

and he will exist upon {the} forehead {of} "Aharon ^{Light bringer}", and "Aharon ^{Light bringer}" will lift up {the} iniquity {of} the special {thing}s, which {the} sons {of} "Yisra'el ^{He turns El aside}" set apart (for) all {the} contributions {of} their special {thing}s, and he will exist upon his forehead continually, (for) {the} self-will (for) them* <in front of> "Yhwh ^{He is}",□

28:39

וְשִׁבַּצְתָּ הַכְּתֹנֶת שֵׁשׁ וְעָשִׂיתָ מִצְנֶפֶת שֵׁשׁ וְאַבְנֵט תַּעֲשֶׂה מַעֲשֵׂה רֹקֵם

we'shi'bats'ta hak'to'net sheysh we'a'si'ta mits'ne'phet sheysh we'av'neyt ta'a'seh ma'a'seyh ro'qeym

and~you(ms)~did~much~<u>WEAVE</u> the~TUNIC LINEN and~you(ms)~did~<u>DO</u> TURBAN LINEN and~SASH you(ms)~will~DO WORK <u>EMBROIDER</u>~ing/er(ms)□

and you will weave the tunic {of} linen, and you will (make) {a} turban {of} linen, and you will (make) {a} sash, {a} work {of} embroidering†,□

28:40

וְלִבְנֵי אַהֲרֹן תַּעֲשֶׂה כֻתֳּנֹת וְעָשִׂיתָ לָהֶם אַבְנֵטִים וּמִגְבָּעוֹת תַּעֲשֶׂה לָהֶם לְכָבוֹד וּלְתִפְאָרֶת

we'liv'ney a'ha'ron ta'a'seh khu'ta'not we'a'si'ta la'hem av'ney'tim u'mig'ba'ot ta'a'seh

---

* The phrase "for the self-will for them" means "that they will be accepted."

† This word may also mean "an embroiderer."

Revised Mechanical Translation Codes

(..) Alt Trans/App A	<..> Comp Phrase/App B	[..] Verb Form/App C	\../ Plural Form/App D
:..: Int Inf Abs	|..| Past Perf Verb	{...} Added Word	

la'hem le'kha'vod ul'tiph'a'ret

and~to~SON~s "Aharon ^{LIGHT-BRINGER}„ you(ms)~will~<u>DO</u> TUNIC~s and~you(ms)~ did~<u>DO</u> to~them(m) SASH~s and~ HEADDRESS~s you(ms)~will~<u>DO</u> to~them(m) to~ARMAMENT and~to~DECORATION□

and (for) {the} sons {of} "Aharon ^{Light bringer}„ you will (make) tunics, and you will (make) (for) them sashes, and headdresses, you will (make) (for) them (for) armament and (for) decoration,□

28:41 וְהִלְבַּשְׁתָּ אֹתָם אֶת אַהֲרֹן אָחִיךָ וְאֶת בָּנָיו אִתּוֹ וּמָשַׁחְתָּ אֹתָם וּמִלֵּאתָ אֶת יָדָם וְקִדַּשְׁתָּ אֹתָם וְכִהֲנוּ לִי

we'hil'bash'ta o'tam et a'ha'ron a'hhi'kha we'et ba'naw i'to u'ma'shahh'ta o'tam u'mi'ley'ta et ya'dam we'qi'dash'ta o'tam we'khi'ha'nu li

and~you(ms)~did~make~<u>WEAR</u> AT~them(m) AT "Aharon ^{LIGHT-BRINGER}„ BROTHER~you(ms) and~AT SON~s~him AT~him and~you(ms)~ did~<u>SMEAR</u> AT~them(m) and~you(ms)~did~ much~<u>FILL</u> AT HAND~them(m) and~ you(ms)~did~much~<u>SET-APART</u> AT~them(m) and~they~did~much~<u>ADORN</u> to~me□

and you will [clothe] them, "Aharon ^{Light bringer}„ your brother and his sons (with) him, and you will smear them, and you will fill their hand*, and you will set them apart, and they will {be} adorned (for) me,□

28:42 וַעֲשֵׂה לָהֶם מִכְנְסֵי בָד לְכַסּוֹת בְּשַׂר עֶרְוָה מִמָּתְנַיִם וְעַד יְרֵכַיִם יִהְיוּ

wa'a'seyh la'hem mikh'ne'sey vad le'kha'sot be'sar er'wah mi'mat'na'yim we'ad ye'rey'kha'yim yih'yu

and~!(ms)~<u>DO</u> to~them(m) UNDERGARMENT~s STICK to~>~much~ <u>COVER-OVER</u> FLESH NAKEDNESS from~ WAIST~s and~UNTIL MIDSECTION~s they(m)~will~<u>EXIST</u>□

and (make) (for) them undergarments {of} (linen) to cover over {the} flesh {of} nakedness from {the} waists, and (unto) {the} midsection they will exist,□

28:43 וְהָיוּ עַל אַהֲרֹן וְעַל בָּנָיו בְּבֹאָם אֶל אֹהֶל מוֹעֵד אוֹ בְגִשְׁתָּם אֶל הַמִּזְבֵּחַ לְשָׁרֵת בַּקֹּדֶשׁ וְלֹא יִשְׂאוּ עָוֹן וָמֵתוּ חֻקַּת עוֹלָם לוֹ וּלְזַרְעוֹ אַחֲרָיו

we'hai'u al a'ha'ron we'al ba'naw be'vo'am el o'hel mo'eyd o ve'gish'tam el ha'miz'bey'ahh le'sha'reyt ba'qo'desh we'lo yish'u a'won wa'mey'tu hhu'qat o'lam lo ul'zar'o a'hha'raw

and~they~did~<u>EXIST</u> UPON "Aharon ^{LIGHT-BRINGER}„ and~UPON SON~s~him in~>~<u>COME</u>~ them(m) TO TENT APPOINTED OR in~ >~<u>DRAW-NEAR</u>~them(m) TO the~ALTAR to~ >~much~<u>MINISTER</u> in~the~SPECIAL and~ NOT they(m)~will~<u>LIFT-UP</u> INIQUITY and~ they~did~<u>DIE</u> RITUAL DISTANT to~him and~

and they will exist upon "Aharon ^{Light bringer}„ and upon his sons, in their coming to {the} tent {of the} appointed {place}, or in their draw{ing} near to the altar to minister in the special {place}, and they will not lift up iniquity (or) they will die, {it is a} ritual {of a} distant {time} (for) him and (for) his seed after him,□

---

* to "fill the hand" is an idiom of uncertain meaning, but the same phrase is used in Akkadian to mean the placing of a scepter (either literally or figuratively) in the hand of one being installed in a high office.

Mechanical Translation Codes

<u>WORD</u> – Verb	WORD – Noun	Word – Name	word – Pre/Suff	*word* – Conj.

to~SEED~him AFTER~him□

Chapter 29

29:1 וְזֶה הַדָּבָר אֲשֶׁר תַּעֲשֶׂה לָהֶם לְקַדֵּשׁ אֹתָם לְכַהֵן לִי לְקַח פַּר אֶחָד בֶּן
בָּקָר וְאֵילִם שְׁנַיִם תְּמִימִם

we'zeh ha'da'var a'sher ta'a'seh la'hem le'qa'deysh o'tam le'kha'heyn li le'qahh par e'hhad ben ba'qar we'ey'lim she'na'yim te'mi'mim

and~THIS the~WORD WHICH *you(ms)~will~*DO to~them(m) to~>~*much~*SET-APART AT~them(m) to~>~*much~*ADORN to~me *!(ms)~*TAKE BULL UNIT SON CATTLE and~BUCK~s TWO WHOLE~s□	and this {is} the (matter) which you will do (for) them to set them apart to {be} adorn{ed} (for) me, take (one) bull, {a} son {of the} cattle, and two whole bucks,□

29:2 וְלֶחֶם מַצּוֹת וְחַלֹּת מַצֹּת בְּלוּלֹת בַּשֶּׁמֶן וּרְקִיקֵי מַצּוֹת מְשֻׁחִים בַּשָּׁמֶן
סֹלֶת חִטִּים תַּעֲשֶׂה אֹתָם

we'le'hhem ma'tsot we'hha'lot ma'tsot be'lu'lot ba'she'men ur'qi'qey ma'tsot me'shu'hhim ba'sha'men so'let hhi'tim ta'a'seh o'tam

and~BREAD UNLEAVENED-BREAD~s and~PIERCED-BREAD~s UNLEAVENED-BREAD~s MIX~*ed(fp)* in~the~OIL and~THIN-BREAD~s UNLEAVENED-BREAD~s SMEAR~*ed(mp)* in~the~OIL FLOUR WHEAT~s *you(ms)~will~*DO AT~them(m)□	and unleavened bread and unleavened pierced bread mixed in the oil, and unleavened thin bread smeared in the oil, {from the} flour {of} wheat you will (make) them,□

29:3 וְנָתַתָּ אוֹתָם עַל סַל אֶחָד וְהִקְרַבְתָּ אֹתָם בַּסָּל וְאֵת הַפָּר וְאֵת שְׁנֵי
הָאֵילִם

we'na'ta'ta o'tam al sal e'hhad we'hiq'rav'ta o'tam ba'sal we'et ha'par we'eyt she'ney ha'ey'lim

and~*you(ms)~did~*GIVE AT~them(m) UPON BASKET UNIT and~*you(ms)~did~*make~COME-NEAR AT~them(m) in~the~BASKET and~AT the~BULL and~AT TWO the~BUCK~s□	and you will (place) them upon (one) basket, and you will make them come near (with) the basket and the bull and the two bucks,□

29:4 וְאֶת אַהֲרֹן וְאֶת בָּנָיו תַּקְרִיב אֶל פֶּתַח אֹהֶל מוֹעֵד וְרָחַצְתָּ אֹתָם בַּמָּיִם

we'et a'ha'ron we'et ba'naw taq'riv el pe'tahh o'hel mo'eyd we'ra'hhats'ta o'tam ba'ma'yim

and~AT "Aharon ^{LIGHT-BRINGER}" and~AT SON~s~him *you(ms)~will~*make~COME-NEAR TO OPENING TENT APPOINTED and~*you(ms)~*	and you will make "Aharon ^{Light bringer}" and his sons come near {the} opening {of the} tent {of the} appointed {place}, and you will bathe

did~<u>BATHE</u> AT~them(m) in~the~
WATER~s2□

them in the waters,□

29:5

וְלָקַחְתָּ אֶת הַבְּגָדִים וְהִלְבַּשְׁתָּ אֶת אַהֲרֹן אֶת הַכֻּתֹּנֶת וְאֵת מְעִיל
הָאֵפֹד וְאֶת הָאֵפֹד וְאֶת הַחֹשֶׁן וְאָפַדְתָּ לוֹ בְּחֵשֶׁב הָאֵפֹד

we'la'qahh'ta et ha'be'ga'dim we'hil'bash'ta et a'ha'ron et ha'ku'to'net we'eyt me'il
ha'ey'phod we'et ha'ey'phod we'et ha'hho'shen we'a'phad'ta lo be'hhey'shev ha'ey'phod

and~you(ms)~did~<u>TAKE</u> AT the~GARMENT~s
and~you(ms)~did~make~<u>WEAR</u> AT "Aharon
LIGHT-BRINGER" AT the~TUNIC and~AT CLOAK
the~EPHOD and~AT the~EPHOD and~AT
the~BREASTPLATE and~you(ms)~did~<u>GIRD</u>
to~him in~DECORATIVE-BAND the~EPHOD□

and you will take the garments, and you will
[clothe] "Aharon Light bringer" (with) the tunic
and (with) {the} cloak {of} the ephod and
(with) the ephod and (with) the breastplate,
and you will gird him (with) {the} decorative
band {of} the ephod,□

29:6

וְשַׂמְתָּ הַמִּצְנֶפֶת עַל רֹאשׁוֹ וְנָתַתָּ אֶת נֵזֶר הַקֹּדֶשׁ עַל הַמִּצְנָפֶת

we'sam'ta ha'mits'ne'phet al ro'sho we'na'ta'ta et ney'zer ha'qo'desh al ha'mits'na'phet

and~you(ms)~did~<u>PLACE</u> the~TURBAN
UPON HEAD~him and~you(ms)~did~<u>GIVE</u> AT
CROWN the~SPECIAL UPON the~TURBAN□

and you will place the turban upon his head,
and you will (place) the crown {of}
special{ness} upon the turban,□

29:7

וְלָקַחְתָּ אֶת שֶׁמֶן הַמִּשְׁחָה וְיָצַקְתָּ עַל רֹאשׁוֹ וּמָשַׁחְתָּ אֹתוֹ

we'la'qahh'ta et she'men ha'mish'hhah we'ya'tsaq'ta al ro'sho u'ma'shahh'ta o'to

and~you(ms)~did~<u>TAKE</u> AT OIL the~
OINTMENT and~you(ms)~did~<u>POUR-DOWN</u>
UPON HEAD~him and~you(ms)~did~<u>SMEAR</u>
AT~him□

and you will take the oil {of} ointment, and
you will pour {it} down upon his head, and you
will smear him,□

29:8

וְאֶת בָּנָיו תַּקְרִיב וְהִלְבַּשְׁתָּם כֻּתֳּנֹת

we'et ba'naw taq'riv we'hil'bash'tam ku'ta'not

and~AT SON~s~him you(ms)~will~make~
<u>COME-NEAR</u> and~you(ms)~did~make~
<u>WEAR</u>~them(m) TUNIC~s□

and you will make his sons come near, and
you will [clothe] them {with} tunics,□

29:9

וְחָגַרְתָּ אֹתָם אַבְנֵט אַהֲרֹן וּבָנָיו וְחָבַשְׁתָּ לָהֶם מִגְבָּעֹת וְהָיְתָה לָהֶם
כְּהֻנָּה לְחֻקַּת עוֹלָם וּמִלֵּאתָ יַד אַהֲרֹן וְיַד בָּנָיו

we'hha'gar'ta o'tam av'neyt a'ha'ron u'va'naw we'hha'vash'ta la'hem mig'ba'ot we'hai'tah
la'hem ke'hu'nah le'hhu'qat o'lam u'mi'ley'ta yad a'ha'ron we'yad ba'naw

and~you(ms)~did~<u>GIRD-UP</u> AT~them(m)
SASH "Aharon LIGHT-BRINGER" and~SON~s~him
and~you(ms)~did~<u>SADDLE</u> to~them(m)
HEADDRESS~s and~ she~did~<u>EXIST</u> to~

and you will gird up "Aharon Light bringer" and his
sons {with the} sash, and you will saddle them
{with the} headdresses, and {the}
administration will exist (for) them, {a} ritual

Mechanical Translation Codes

<u>WORD</u> – Verb   WORD – Noun   Word – Name   word – Pre/Suff   *word* – Conj.

~ 214 ~

them(m) ADMINISTRATION to~RITUAL DISTANT and~*you(ms)~did~much~*<u>FILL HAND</u> "Aharon ^{LIGHT-BRINGER}" and~HAND SON~s~him□

{of a} distant {time}, and you will fill {the} hand* {of} "Aharon ^{Light bringer}" and {the} hand {of} his sons,□

29:10 וְהִקְרַבְתָּ אֶת הַפָּר לִפְנֵי אֹהֶל מוֹעֵד וְסָמַךְ אַהֲרֹן וּבָנָיו אֶת יְדֵיהֶם עַל רֹאשׁ הַפָּר

we'hiq'rav'ta et ha'par liph'ney o'hel mo'eyd we'sa'makh a'ha'ron u'va'naw et ye'dey'hem al rosh ha'par

and~*you(ms)~did~make~*<u>COME-NEAR</u> AT the~BULL to~FACE~s TENT APPOINTED and~*he~did~*<u>SUPPORT</u> "Aharon ^{LIGHT-BRINGER}" and~SON~s~him AT HAND~s2~them(m) UPON HEAD the~BULL□

and you will make the bull come near <in front of> {the} tent {of the} appointed {place}, and "Aharon ^{Light bringer}", and his sons, will support their hands upon {the} head {of} the bull,□

29:11 וְשָׁחַטְתָּ אֶת הַפָּר לִפְנֵי יְהוָה פֶּתַח אֹהֶל מוֹעֵד

we'sha'hhat'ta et ha'par liph'ney YHWH pe'tahh o'hel mo'eyd

and~*you(ms)~did~*<u>SLAY</u> AT the~BULL to~FACE~s "Yhwh ^{he~will~BE}" OPENING TENT APPOINTED□

and you will slay the bull <in front of> "Yhwh ^{He is}" {at the} opening {of the} appointed {place},□

29:12 וְלָקַחְתָּ מִדַּם הַפָּר וְנָתַתָּה עַל קַרְנֹת הַמִּזְבֵּחַ בְּאֶצְבָּעֶךָ וְאֶת כָּל הַדָּם תִּשְׁפֹּךְ אֶל יְסוֹד הַמִּזְבֵּחַ

we'la'qahh'ta mi'dam ha'par we'na'ta'tah al qar'not ha'miz'bey'ahh be'ets'ba'e'kha we'et kol ha'dam tish'pokh el ye'sod ha'miz'bey'ahh

and~*you(ms)~did~*<u>TAKE</u> from~BLOOD the~BULL and~*you(ms)~did~*<u>GIVE</u>~^ UPON HORN~s the~ALTAR in~FINGER~you(ms) and~AT ALL the~BLOOD *you(ms)~will~*<u>POUR-OUT</u> TO FOUNDATION the~ALTAR□

and you will take from {the} blood {of} the bull and you will (place) {it} upon {the} horns {of} the altar (with) your finger, and you will pour out all the blood (at) {the} foundation {of} the altar,□

29:13 וְלָקַחְתָּ אֶת כָּל הַחֵלֶב הַמְכַסֶּה אֶת הַקֶּרֶב וְאֵת הַיֹּתֶרֶת עַל הַכָּבֵד וְאֵת שְׁתֵּי הַכְּלָיֹת וְאֶת הַחֵלֶב אֲשֶׁר עֲלֵיהֶן וְהִקְטַרְתָּ הַמִּזְבֵּחָה

we'la'qahh'ta et kol ha'hhey'lev ham'kha'sch et ha'qe'rev we'eyt hai'yo'te'ret al ha'ka'veyd we'eyt she'tey hak'la'yot we'et ha'hhey'lev a'sher a'ley'hen we'hiq'tar'ta ha'miz'bey'hhah

and~*you(ms)~did~*<u>TAKE</u> AT ALL the~FAT the~*much~*<u>COVER-OVER</u>~*ing/er(ms)* AT the~

and you will take all the covering fat, the within{s}† , and the lobe upon the heavy

---

* to "fill the hand" is an idiom of uncertain meaning, but the same phrase is used in Akkadian to mean the placing of a scepter (either literally or figuratively) in the hand of one being installed in a high office.

† The word "withins" mean the "insides."

WITHIN and~AT the~LOBE UPON the~HEAVY and~AT TWO the~KIDNEY~s and~AT the~ FAT WHICH UPON~them(f) and~*you(ms)*~ *did*~*make*~<u>BURN-INCENSE</u> the~ALTAR~ unto□

{one}*, and the two kidneys, and the fat which is upon them, and you will burn incense† unto the altar,□

29:14 וְאֶת בְּשַׂר הַפָּר וְאֶת עֹרוֹ וְאֶת פִּרְשׁוֹ תִּשְׂרֹף בָּאֵשׁ מִחוּץ לַמַּחֲנֶה חַטָּאת הוּא

we'et be'sar ha'par we'et o'ro we'et pir'sho tis'roph ba'eysh mi'hhuts la'ma'hha'neh hha'tat hu

and~AT FLESH the~BULL and~AT SKIN~him and~AT DUNG~him *you(ms)*~*will*~<u>CREMATE</u> in~the~FIRE from~OUTSIDE to~the~ CAMPSITE ERROR HE□

and you will cremate {the} flesh {of} the bull, and his skin, and his dung, in the fire outside the campsite, he {is an} error {offering},□

29:15 וְאֶת הָאַיִל הָאֶחָד תִּקָּח וְסָמְכוּ אַהֲרֹן וּבָנָיו אֶת יְדֵיהֶם עַל רֹאשׁ הָאָיִל

we'et ha'a'yil ha'e'hhad ti'qahh we'sam'khu a'ha'ron u'va'naw et ye'dey'hem al rosh ha'a'yil

and~AT the~BUCK the~UNIT *you(ms)*~*will*~<u>TAKE</u> and~*they*~*did*~<u>SUPPORT</u> "Aharon ^{LIGHT-BRINGER}" and~SON~s~him AT HAND~s2~ them(m) UPON HEAD the~BUCK□

and you will take the (one) buck, and "Aharon ^{Light bringer}" and his sons will support their hands upon {the} head {of} the buck,□

29:16 וְשָׁחַטְתָּ אֶת הָאַיִל וְלָקַחְתָּ אֶת דָּמוֹ וְזָרַקְתָּ עַל הַמִּזְבֵּחַ סָבִיב

we'sha'hhat'ta et ha'a'yil we'la'qahh'ta et da'mo we'za'raq'ta al ha'miz'bey'ahh sa'viv

and~*you(ms)*~*did*~<u>SLAY</u> AT the~BUCK and~ *you(ms)*~*did*~<u>TAKE</u> AT BLOOD~him and~ *you(ms)*~*did*~<u>SPRINKLE</u> UPON the~ALTAR ALL-AROUND□

and you will slay the buck, and you will take his blood and you will sprinkle {it} upon the altar all around,□

29:17 וְאֶת הָאַיִל תְּנַתֵּחַ לִנְתָחָיו וְרָחַצְתָּ קִרְבּוֹ וּכְרָעָיו וְנָתַתָּ עַל נְתָחָיו וְעַל רֹאשׁוֹ

we'et ha'a'yil te'na'tey'ahh lin'ta'hhaw we'ra'hhats'ta qir'bo ukh'ra'aw we'na'ta'ta al ne'ta'hhaw we'al ro'sho

and~AT the~BUCK *you(ms)*~*will*~*much*~ <u>DIVIDE-INTO-PIECES</u> to~PIECE~s~him and~

and you will divide the buck into pieces {according} to his pieces‡, and you will bathe

---

* "The heavy one" is the "liver," the heaviest organ of the body.
† The phrase "and you will burn incense" may also be interpreted as "and you will burn them as incense."
‡ "According to his pieces" means that the animal would be divided (cut) at each section (piece, joint).

Mechanical Translation Codes

<u>WORD</u> – Verb   WORD – Noun   Word – Name   word – Pre/Suff   *word* – Conj.

you(ms)~did~<u>BATHE</u> WITHIN~him and~
LEG~s~him and~you(ms)~did~<u>GIVE</u> UPON
PIECE~s~him and~UPON HEAD~him☐

his within{s}* and his legs, and you will (place)
{them} upon his pieces and upon his head,☐

29:18 וְהִקְטַרְתָּ אֶת כָּל הָאַיִל הַמִּזְבֵּחָה עֹלָה הוּא לַיהוָה רֵיחַ נִיחוֹחַ אִשֶּׁה
לַיהוָה הוּא

we'hiq'tar'ta et kol ha'a'yil ha'miz'bey'hhah o'lah hu la'YHWH rey'ahh ni'hho'ahh i'sheh
la'YHWH hu

and~you(ms)~did~make~<u>BURN-INCENSE</u> AT
ALL the~BUCK the~ALTAR~unto RISING HE
to~"Yhwh ^{he~will~<u>BE</u>}" AROMA SWEET FIRE-
OFFERING to~"Yhwh ^{he~will~<u>BE</u>}" HE☐

and you will burn {as} incense all {of} the buck
unto the altar, he {is a} rising {sacrifice} (for)
"Yhwh ^{He is}", {a} sweet aroma, he {is a} fire
offering (for) "Yhwh ^{He is}",☐

29:19 וְלָקַחְתָּ אֵת הָאַיִל הַשֵּׁנִי וְסָמַךְ אַהֲרֹן וּבָנָיו אֶת יְדֵיהֶם עַל רֹאשׁ הָאָיִל

we'la'qahh'ta eyt ha'a'yil ha'shey'ni we'sa'makh a'ha'ron u'va'naw et ye'dey'hem al rosh
ha'a'yil

and~you(ms)~did~<u>TAKE</u> AT the~BUCK the~
SECOND and~he~did~<u>SUPPORT</u> "Aharon
^{LIGHT-BRINGER}" and~SON~s~him AT HAND~s2~
them(m) UPON HEAD the~BUCK☐

and you will take the second buck, and
"Aharon ^{Light bringer}", and his sons, will support
their hands upon {the} head {of} the buck,☐

29:20 וְשָׁחַטְתָּ אֶת הָאַיִל וְלָקַחְתָּ מִדָּמוֹ וְנָתַתָּה עַל תְּנוּךְ אֹזֶן אַהֲרֹן וְעַל תְּנוּךְ
אֹזֶן בָּנָיו הַיְמָנִית וְעַל בֹּהֶן יָדָם הַיְמָנִית וְעַל בֹּהֶן רַגְלָם הַיְמָנִית
וְזָרַקְתָּ אֶת הַדָּם עַל הַמִּזְבֵּחַ סָבִיב

we'sha'hhat'ta et ha'a'yil we'la'qahh'ta mi'da'mo we'na'ta'tah al te'nukh o'zen a'ha'ron
we'al te'nukh o'zen ba'naw hai'ma'nit we'al bo'hen ya'dam hai'ma'nit we'al bo'hen
rag'lam hai'ma'nit we'za'raq'ta et ha'dam al ha'miz'bey'ahh sa'viv

and~you(ms)~did~<u>SLAY</u> AT the~BUCK and~
you(ms)~did~<u>TAKE</u> from~BLOOD~him and~
you(ms)~did~<u>GIVE</u>~^ UPON TIP EAR "Aharon
^{LIGHT-BRINGER}" and~UPON TIP EAR SON~s~him
the~RIGHT and~UPON THUMB HAND~
them(m) the~RIGHT and~UPON THUMB
FOOT~them(m) the~RIGHT and~you(ms)~
did~<u>SPRINKLE</u> AT the~BLOOD UPON the~
ALTAR ALL-AROUND☐

and you will slay the buck, and you will take
from his blood and you will (place) {it} upon
{the} tip {of the} ear {of} "Aharon ^{Light bringer}"
and upon {the} tip {of} the right ear {of} his
sons, and upon the right thumb {of} their
hands, and upon the right thumb {of} their
feet, and you will sprinkle the blood upon the
altar all around,☐

29:21 וְלָקַחְתָּ מִן הַדָּם אֲשֶׁר עַל הַמִּזְבֵּחַ וּמִשֶּׁמֶן הַמִּשְׁחָה וְהִזֵּיתָ עַל אַהֲרֹן
וְעַל בְּגָדָיו וְעַל בָּנָיו וְעַל בִּגְדֵי בָנָיו אִתּוֹ וְקָדַשׁ הוּא וּבְגָדָיו וּבָנָיו וּבִגְדֵי
בָנָיו אִתּוֹ

we'la'qahh'ta min ha'dam a'sher al ha'miz'bey'ahh u'mi'she'men ha'mish'hhah

---

* The word "withins" mean the "insides."

Revised Mechanical Translation Codes

(..) Alt Trans/App A	<..> Comp Phrase/App B	[..] Verb Form/App C	\../ Plural Form/App D
:..: Int Inf Abs	|..| Past Perf Verb	{...} Added Word	

we'hi'zey'ta al a'ha'ron we'al be'ga'daw we'al ba'naw we'al big'dey va'naw i'to we'qa'dash hu uv'ga'daw u'va'naw u'vig'dey va'naw i'to

and~*you(ms)*~*did*~<u>TAKE</u> FROM the~BLOOD WHICH UPON the~ALTAR and~from~OIL the~OINTMENT and~*you(ms)*~*did*~*make*~<u>SPATTER</u> UPON "Aharon ^{LIGHT-BRINGER}" and~ UPON GARMENT~s~him and~UPON SON~s~ him and~UPON GARMENT~s SON~s~him AT~him and~*he*~*did*~<u>SET-APART</u> HE and~ GARMENT~s~him and~SON~s~him and~ GARMENT~s SON~s~him AT~him□

and you will take from the blood which is upon the altar, and from {the} oil {of} the ointment, and you will spatter {it} upon "Aharon ^{Light bringer}" and upon his garments and upon his sons and upon {the} garments {of} his sons (with) him, and he* will set him apart, and his garments, and his sons, and {the} garments {of} his sons (with) him,□

29:22 וְלָקַחְתָּ מִן הָאַיִל הַחֵלֶב וְהָאַלְיָה וְאֶת הַחֵלֶב הַמְכַסֶּה אֶת הַקֶּרֶב וְאֵת יֹתֶרֶת הַכָּבֵד וְאֵת שְׁתֵּי הַכְּלָיֹת וְאֶת הַחֵלֶב אֲשֶׁר עֲלֵיהֶן וְאֵת שׁוֹק הַיָּמִין כִּי אֵיל מִלֻּאִים הוּא

we'la'qahh'ta min ha'a'yil ha'hhey'lev we'ha'al'yah we'et ha'hhey'lev ham'kha'seh et ha'qe'rev we'eyt yo'te'ret ha'ka'veyd we'eyt she'tey hak'la'yot we'et ha'hhey'lev a'sher a'ley'hen we'eyt shoq hai'ya'min ki eyl mi'lu'im hu

and~*you(ms)*~*did*~<u>TAKE</u> FROM the~BUCK the~FAT and~the~FAT-TAIL and~AT the~FAT the~*much*~<u>COVER-OVER</u>~*ing/er(ms)* AT the~ WITHIN and~AT LOBE the~HEAVY and~AT TWO the~KIDNEY~s and~AT the~FAT WHICH UPON~them(f) and~AT THIGH the~RIGHT-HAND GIVEN-THAT BUCK INSTALLATION~s HE□

and you will take from the buck the fat and the fat-tail and the covering fat and the within{s}† and {the} lobe {of} the heavy {one}‡ and the two kidneys and the fat which {is} upon them and the right thigh, given that {the} buck, he {is an} installation,□

29:23 וְכִכַּר לֶחֶם אַחַת וְחַלַּת לֶחֶם שֶׁמֶן אַחַת וְרָקִיק אֶחָד מִסַּל הַמַּצּוֹת אֲשֶׁר לִפְנֵי יְהוָה

we'khi'kar le'hhem a'hhat we'hha'lat le'hhem she'men a'hhat we'raqiq e'hhad mi'sal ha'ma'tsot a'sher liph'ney YHWH

and~ROUNDNESS BREAD UNIT and~ PIERCED-BREAD BREAD OIL UNIT and~THIN-BREAD UNIT from~BASKET the~ UNLEAVENED-BREAD~s WHICH to~FACE~s "Yhwh ^{he~will~<u>BE</u>}"□

and (one) round bread and (one) pierced bread {of} oil and (one) thin bread from {the} basket {of} the unleavened bread, which {is} <in front of> "Yhwh ^{He is}",□

29:24 וְשַׂמְתָּ הַכֹּל עַל כַּפֵּי אַהֲרֹן וְעַל כַּפֵּי בָנָיו וְהֵנַפְתָּ אֹתָם תְּנוּפָה לִפְנֵי יְהוָה

we'sam'ta ha'kol al ka'pey a'ha'ron we'al ka'pey va'naw we'hey'naph'ta o'tam te'nu'phah liph'ney YHWH

---

* Referring to the "blood," a masculine word in Hebrew.
† The word "within" means the "insides."
‡ "The heavy one" is the "liver," the heaviest organ of the body.

Mechanical Translation Codes

<u>WORD</u> – Verb	WORD – Noun	Word – Name	word – Pre/Suff	*word* – Conj.

and~you(ms)~did~<u>PLACE</u> the~ALL UPON PALM~s2 "Aharon ^{LIGHT-BRINGER}" and~UPON PALM~s2 SON~s~him and~you(ms)~did~make~<u>WAVE</u> AT~them(m) WAVING to~FACE~s "Yhwh ^{he~will~<u>BE</u>}"□

and you will place all {of it} upon {the} palms {of} "Aharon ^{Light bringer}" and upon {the} palms {of} his sons, and you will wave them {for a} wave {offer}ing <in front of> "Yhwh ^{He is}",□

29:25 וְלָקַחְתָּ אֹתָם מִיָּדָם וְהִקְטַרְתָּ הַמִּזְבֵּחָה עַל הָעֹלָה לְרֵיחַ נִיחֹחַ לִפְנֵי יְהוָה אִשֶּׁה הוּא לַיהוָה

we'la'qahh'ta o'tam mi'ya'dam we'hiq'tar'ta ha'miz'bey'hhah al ha'o'lah le'rey'ahh ni'hho'ahh liph'ney YHWH i'sheh hu la'YHWH

and~you(ms)~did~<u>TAKE</u> AT~them(m) from~HAND~them(m) and~you(ms)~did~make~<u>BURN-INCENSE</u> the~ALTAR~unto UPON the~RISING to~AROMA SWEET to~FACE~s "Yhwh ^{he~will~<u>BE</u>}" FIRE-OFFERING HE to~"Yhwh ^{he~will~<u>BE</u>}"□

and you will take them from their hand, and you will burn {them as} incense unto the altar, upon the rising {sacrifice} (for) {a} sweet aroma <in front of> "Yhwh ^{He is}", he {is a} fire offering (for) "Yhwh ^{He is}",□

29:26 וְלָקַחְתָּ אֶת הֶחָזֶה מֵאֵיל הַמִּלֻּאִים אֲשֶׁר לְאַהֲרֹן וְהֵנַפְתָּ אֹתוֹ תְּנוּפָה לִפְנֵי יְהוָה וְהָיָה לְךָ לְמָנָה

we'la'qahh'ta et he'hha'zeh mey'eyl ha'mi'lu'im a'sher le'a'ha'ron we'hey'naph'ta o'to te'nu'phah liph'ney YHWH we'hai'yah le'kha le'ma'nah

and~you(ms)~did~<u>TAKE</u> AT the~CHEST from~BUCK the~INSTALLATION~s WHICH to~"Aharon ^{LIGHT-BRINGER}" and~you(ms)~did~make~<u>WAVE</u> AT~him WAVING to~FACE~s "Yhwh ^{he~will~<u>BE</u>}" and~he~did~<u>EXIST</u> to~you(ms) to~SHARE□

and you will take the chest from {the} buck {of} the installation, which {is} (for) "Aharon ^{Light bringer}", and you will wave him {for a} wave {offer}ing <in front of> "Yhwh ^{He is}", and he will exist (for) you (for) {a} share,□

29:27 וְקִדַּשְׁתָּ אֵת חֲזֵה הַתְּנוּפָה וְאֵת שׁוֹק הַתְּרוּמָה אֲשֶׁר הוּנַף וַאֲשֶׁר הוּרָם מֵאֵיל הַמִּלֻּאִים מֵאֲשֶׁר לְאַהֲרֹן וּמֵאֲשֶׁר לְבָנָיו

we'qi'dash'ta eyt hha'zeyh hat'nu'phah we'eyt shoq hat'ru'mah a'sher hu'naph wa'a'sher hu'ram mey'eyl ha'mi'lu'im mey'a'sher le'a'ha'ron u'mey'a'sheyr le'va'naw

and~you(ms)~did~much~<u>SET-APART</u> AT CHEST the~WAVING and~AT THIGH the~OFFERING WHICH he~did~be~make~<u>WAVE</u> and~WHICH he~did~be~make~<u>RAISE</u> from~BUCK the~INSTALLATION~s from~WHICH to~"Aharon ^{LIGHT-BRINGER}" and~from~WHICH to~SON~s~him□

and you will set apart {the} chest {of} the wave {offer}ing and {the} thigh {of} the offering, which was waved and which was raised from {the} buck {of} the installation, (out of) which {is} (for) "Aharon ^{Light bringer}" and (out of) which {is} (for) his sons,□

29:28 וְהָיָה לְאַהֲרֹן וּלְבָנָיו לְחָק עוֹלָם מֵאֵת בְּנֵי יִשְׂרָאֵל כִּי תְרוּמָה הוּא וּתְרוּמָה יִהְיֶה מֵאֵת בְּנֵי יִשְׂרָאֵל מִזִּבְחֵי שַׁלְמֵיהֶם תְּרוּמָתָם לַיהוָה

we'hai'yah le'a'ha'ron ul'va'naw le'hhaq o'lam mey'eyt be'ney yis'ra'eyl ki te'ru'mah hu ut'ru'mah yih'yeh mey'eyt be'ney yis'ra'eyl mi'ziv'hhey shal'mey'hem te'ru'ma'tam

Revised Mechanical Translation Codes

(..) Alt Trans/App A	<..> Comp Phrase/App B	[..] Verb Form/App C	\../ Plural Form/App D
:..: Int Inf Abs	|..| Past Perf Verb	{...} Added Word	

la'YHWH

and~*he~did*~<u>EXIST</u> to~"Aharon ^{LIGHT-BRINGER}„ and~to~SON~s~him to~CUSTOM DISTANT from~AT SON~s "Yisra'el ^{he~will~<u>TURN-ASIDE</u>~+~MIGHTY-ONE}„ GIVEN-THAT OFFERING HE and~OFFERING *he~will*~<u>EXIST</u> from~AT SON~s "Yisra'el ^{he~will~<u>TURN-ASIDE</u>~+~MIGHTY-ONE}„ from~SACRIFICE~s COMPLETE~s~them(m) OFFERING~them(m) to~"Yhwh ^{he~will~<u>BE</u>}„□

and he will exist (for) "Aharon ^{Light bringer}„ and (for) his sons (for) {a} custom {of a} distant {time} from {the} sons {of} "Yisra'el ^{He turns El aside}„, given that he {is an} offering, and {the} offering will exist from {the} sons {of} "Yisra'el ^{He turns El aside}„, from their complete sacrifices, their offerings to "Yhwh ^{He is}„,□

29:29 וּבִגְדֵי הַקֹּדֶשׁ אֲשֶׁר לְאַהֲרֹן יִהְיוּ לְבָנָיו אַחֲרָיו לְמָשְׁחָה בָהֶם וּלְמַלֵּא בָם אֶת יָדָם

u'vig'dey ha'qo'desh a'sher le'a'ha'ron yih'yu le'va'naw a'hha'raw le'mash'hhah va'hem ul'ma'ley vam et ya'dam

and~GARMENT~s the~SPECIAL WHICH to~"Aharon ^{LIGHT-BRINGER}„ *they(m)~will*~<u>EXIST</u> to~SON~s~him AFTER~him to~>~<u>SMEAR</u> in~them(m) and~to~>~*much*~<u>FILL</u> in~them(m) AT HAND~them(m)□

and the garments {of} special{ness}, which {belong} to "Aharon ^{Light bringer}„, will exist (for) his sons after him, to {be} smear{ed} (with) them, and their hand to {be} fill{ed}* (with) them,□

29:30 שִׁבְעַת יָמִים יִלְבָּשָׁם הַכֹּהֵן תַּחְתָּיו מִבָּנָיו אֲשֶׁר יָבֹא אֶל אֹהֶל מוֹעֵד לְשָׁרֵת בַּקֹּדֶשׁ

shiv'at ya'mim yil'ba'sham ha'ko'heyn tahh'taw mi'ba'naw a'sher ya'vo el o'hel mo'eyd le'sha'reyt ba'qo'desh

SEVEN DAY~s *he~will*~<u>WEAR</u>~them(m) the~ADMINISTRATOR UNDER~him from~SON~s~him WHICH *he~will*~<u>COME</u> TO TENT APPOINTED to~>~*much*~<u>MINISTER</u> in~the~SPECIAL□

{for} seven days the administrator, from his sons, {that is} (in place of) him†, will wear them (when) he will come to {the} tent {of the} appointed {place}, to minister in the special {place},□

29:31 וְאֵת אֵיל הַמִּלֻּאִים תִּקָּח וּבִשַּׁלְתָּ אֶת בְּשָׂרוֹ בְּמָקֹם קָדֹשׁ

we'eyt eyl ha'mi'lu'im ti'qahh u'vi'shal'ta et be'sar'o be'ma'qom qa'dosh

and~AT BUCK the~INSTALLATION~s *you(ms)~will*~<u>TAKE</u> and~*you(ms)~did*~*much*~<u>BOIL</u> AT FLESH~him in~AREA UNIQUE□

and you will take {the} buck {of} the installation, and you will boil his flesh in the unique area,□

29:32 וְאָכַל אַהֲרֹן וּבָנָיו אֶת בְּשַׂר הָאַיִל וְאֶת הַלֶּחֶם אֲשֶׁר בַּסָּל פֶּתַח אֹהֶל מוֹעֵד

---

* to "fill the hand" is an idiom of uncertain meaning, but the same phrase is used in Akkadian to mean the placing of a scepter (either literally or figuratively) in the hand of one being installed in a high office.

† "That is in place of him" may be translated as "that takes his place."

Mechanical Translation Codes

<u>WORD</u> – Verb	WORD – Noun	Word – Name	word – Pre/Suff	*word* – Conj.

we'a'khal a'ha'ron u'va'naw et be'sar ha'a'yil we'et ha'le'hhem a'sher ba'sal pe'tahh o'hel mo'eyd

and~*he*~did~EAT "Aharon ^{LIGHT-BRINGER}" and~ SON~s~him AT FLESH the~BUCK and~AT the~BREAD WHICH in~the~BASKET OPENING TENT APPOINTED□

and "Aharon ^{Light bringer}", and his sons, will eat {the} flesh {of the} buck and the bread which {is} in the basket {at the} opening {of the} tent {of the} appointed {place},□

29:33 וְאָכְלוּ אֹתָם אֲשֶׁר כֻּפַּר בָּהֶם לְמַלֵּא אֶת יָדָם לְקַדֵּשׁ אֹתָם וְזָר לֹא יֹאכַל כִּי קֹדֶשׁ הֵם

we'akh'lu o'tam a'sher ku'par ba'hem le'ma'ley et ya'dam le'qa'deysh o'tam we'zar lo yo'khal ki qo'desh heym

and~*they*~did~EAT AT~them(m) WHICH *he*~ did~be~much~COVER in~them(m) to~ >~*much*~FILL AT HAND~them(m) to~ >~*much*~SET-APART AT~them(m) and~BE-STRANGE~*ing/er(ms)* NOT *he*~will~EAT GIVEN-THAT SPECIAL THEY(m)□

and they will eat them, which was {to} [make reconciliation] (with) them to fill their hand* to set them apart, and {a} stranger will not eat {it}, given that they {are a} special {thing},□

29:34 וְאִם יִוָּתֵר מִבְּשַׂר הַמִּלֻּאִים וּמִן הַלֶּחֶם עַד הַבֹּקֶר וְשָׂרַפְתָּ אֶת הַנּוֹתָר בָּאֵשׁ לֹא יֵאָכֵל כִּי קֹדֶשׁ הוּא

we'im yi'wa'teyr mi'be'sar ha'mi'lu'im u'min ha'le'hhem ad ha'bo'qer we'sa'raph'ta et ha'no'tar ba'eysh lo yey'a'kheyl ki qo'desh hu

and~IF *he*~will~be~LEAVE-BEHIND from~ FLESH the~INSTALLATION~s and~FROM the~ BREAD UNTIL the~MORNING and~*you(ms)*~ did~CREMATE AT the~be~LEAVE-BEHIND~ *ing/er(ms)* in~the~FIRE NOT *he*~will~be~EAT GIVEN-THAT SPECIAL HE□

and if (any){thing} is left behind from {the} flesh {of the} installation, and from the bread until the morning, (then) you will cremate {what is} being left behind in the fire, he will not be eaten given that he {is a} special {thing},□

29:35 וְעָשִׂיתָ לְאַהֲרֹן וּלְבָנָיו כָּכָה כְּכֹל אֲשֶׁר צִוִּיתִי אֹתָכָה שִׁבְעַת יָמִים תְּמַלֵּא יָדָם

we'a'si'ta le'a'ha'ron ul'va'naw ka'khah ke'khol a'sher tsi'wi'ti o'ta'khah shiv'at ya'mim te'ma'ley ya'dam

and~*you(ms)*~did~DO to~"Aharon ^{LIGHT-BRINGER}" and~to~SON~s~him like~IN-THIS-WAY like~ALL WHICH *I*~did~much~DIRECT AT~you(mp) SEVEN DAY~s *you(ms)*~will~

and you will do (for) "Aharon ^{Light bringer}" and (for) his sons <just like this>, {just} like all (that) I directed you, {for} seven days you will fill their hand*,□

---

* to "fill the hand" is an idiom of uncertain meaning, but the same phrase is used in Akkadian to mean the placing of a scepter (either literally or figuratively) in the hand of one being installed in a high office.

Revised Mechanical Translation Codes

(..) Alt Trans/App A   <..> Comp Phrase/App B   [..] Verb Form/App C   \../ Plural Form/App D
:...: Int Inf Abs |..| Past Perf Verb   {...} Added Word

much~<u>FILL</u> HAND~them(m)□   hand*,□

29:36   וּפַר חַטָּאת תַּעֲשֶׂה לַיּוֹם עַל הַכִּפֻּרִים וְחִטֵּאתָ עַל הַמִּזְבֵּחַ בְּכַפֶּרְךָ עָלָיו וּמָשַׁחְתָּ אֹתוֹ לְקַדְּשׁוֹ

u'phar hha'tat ta'a'seh la'yom al ha'ki'pu'rim we'hhi'tey'ta al ha'miz'bey'ahh be'kha'per'kha a'law u'ma'shahh'ta o'to le'qad'sho

and~BULL ERROR *you(ms)*~*will*~<u>DO</u> to~the~ DAY UPON the~ATONEMENT~s and~ *you(ms)*~*did*~*much*~<u>ERR</u> UPON the~ALTAR in~>~*much*~<u>COVER</u>~you(ms) UPON~him and~*you(ms)*~*did*~<u>SMEAR</u> AT~him to~ >~*much*~<u>SET-APART</u>~him□	and you will do {the} bull {of} error <daily> (concerning) the atonements, and you will [purge] upon the altar (with) your mak{ing} [reconciliation] upon him, and you will smear him (for) set{ting} him apart,□

29:37   שִׁבְעַת יָמִים תְּכַפֵּר עַל הַמִּזְבֵּחַ וְקִדַּשְׁתָּ אֹתוֹ וְהָיָה הַמִּזְבֵּחַ קֹדֶשׁ קָדָשִׁים כָּל הַנֹּגֵעַ בַּמִּזְבֵּחַ יִקְדָּשׁ

shiv'at ya'mim te'kha'peyr al ha'miz'bey'ahh we'qi'dash'ta o'to we'hai'yah ha'miz'bey'ahh qo'desh qa'da'shim kol ha'no'gey'a ba'miz'bey'ahh yiq'dash

SEVEN DAY~s *you(ms)*~*will*~*much*~<u>COVER</u> UPON the~ALTAR and~*you(ms)*~*did*~*much*~ <u>SET-APART</u> AT~him and~*he*~*did*~<u>EXIST</u> the~ ALTAR SPECIAL SPECIAL~s ALL the~<u>TOUCH</u>~ *ing/er(ms)* in~the~ALTAR *he*~*will*~<u>SET-APART</u>□	{for} seven days you will [make reconciliation] upon the altar, you will set him apart and the altar will exist {as a} special {thing of} special {thing}s, all the {ones} touching the altar will {be} set apart,□

29:38   וְזֶה אֲשֶׁר תַּעֲשֶׂה עַל הַמִּזְבֵּחַ כְּבָשִׂים בְּנֵי שָׁנָה שְׁנַיִם לַיּוֹם תָּמִיד

we'zeh a'sher ta'a'seh al ha'miz'bey'ahh ke'va'sim be'ney sha'nah she'na'yim la'yom ta'mid

and~THIS WHICH *you(ms)*~*will*~<u>DO</u> UPON the~ALTAR SHEEP~s SON~s YEAR TWO to~ the~DAY CONTINUALLY□	and this {is} (what) you will do upon the altar, two sheep, {a} son {of a} year✝, <daily>, continually,□

29:39   אֶת הַכֶּבֶשׂ הָאֶחָד תַּעֲשֶׂה בַבֹּקֶר וְאֵת הַכֶּבֶשׂ הַשֵּׁנִי תַּעֲשֶׂה בֵּין הָעַרְבָּיִם

et ha'ke'ves ha'e'hhad ta'a'seh va'bo'qer we'eyt ha'ke'ves ha'shey'ni ta'a'seh beyn ha'ar'ba'yim

AT the~SHEEP the~UNIT *you(ms)*~*will*~<u>DO</u> in~the~MORNING and~AT the~SHEEP the~ SECOND *you(ms)*~*will*~<u>DO</u> BETWEEN the~ EVENING~s□	you will do the (one) sheep in the morning, and you will do the second sheep between the evenings*,□

---

* to "fill the hand" is an idiom of uncertain meaning, but the same phrase is used in Akkadian to mean the placing of a scepter (either literally or figuratively) in the hand of one being installed in a high office.

✝ The phrase "son of a year" is an idiom meaning "a year old."

Mechanical Translation Codes

<u>WORD</u> – Verb	WORD – Noun	Word – Name	word – Pre/Suff	*word* – Conj.

29:40 וְעִשָּׂרֹן סֹלֶת בָּלוּל בְּשֶׁמֶן כָּתִית רֶבַע הַהִין וְנֵסֶךְ רְבִיעִת הַהִין יַיִן לַכֶּבֶשׂ הָאֶחָד

we'i'sa'ron so'let ba'lul be'she'men ka'tit re'va ha'hin we'ney'sekh re'vi'it ha'hin ya'yin la'ke'ves ha'e'hhad

and~ONE-TENTH FLOUR <u>MIX</u>~ed(*ms*) in~OIL CRUSHED QUARTER the~HIYN and~ POURING FOURTH the~HIYN WINE to~the~ SHEEP the~UNIT□	and one-tenth {part of} flour mixed in {a} quarter {of} the hiyn {of} crushed oil, and {a} pouring {of a} fourth {of} the hiyn {of} wine (for) the (one) sheep,□

29:41 וְאֵת הַכֶּבֶשׂ הַשֵּׁנִי תַּעֲשֶׂה בֵּין הָעַרְבָּיִם כְּמִנְחַת הַבֹּקֶר וּכְנִסְכָּהּ תַּעֲשֶׂה לָהּ לְרֵיחַ נִיחֹחַ אִשֶּׁה לַיהוָה

we'eyt ha'ke'ves ha'shey'ni ta'a'seh beyn ha'ar'ba'yim ke'min'hhat ha'bo'qer ukh'nis'kah ta'a'seh lah le'rey'ahh ni'hho'ahh i'sheh la'YHWH

and~AT the~SHEEP the~SECOND *you(ms)*~ will~<u>DO</u> BETWEEN the~EVENING~s like~ DONATION the~MORNING and~like~ POURING~her *you(ms)* will~<u>DO</u> to~her to~ AROMA SWEET FIRE-OFFERING to~"Yhwh *he~ will~<u>BE</u>*"□	and you will do the second sheep between the evenings**†** like {the} donation {of} the morning, and you will do her**‡** like her pouring, {it is} (for) {a} sweet aroma, {a} fire offering (for) "Yhwh ^He is^",□

29:42 עֹלַת תָּמִיד לְדֹרֹתֵיכֶם פֶּתַח אֹהֶל מוֹעֵד לִפְנֵי יְהוָה אֲשֶׁר אִוָּעֵד לָכֶם שָׁמָּה לְדַבֵּר אֵלֶיךָ שָׁם

o'lat ta'mid le'do'ro'tey'khem pe'tahh o'hel mo'eyd liph'ney YHWH a'sher i'wa'eyd la'khem sham'mah le'da'beyr ey'ley'kha sham

RISING CONTINUALLY to~GENERATION~s~ *you(mp)* OPENING TENT APPOINTED to~ FACE~s "Yhwh ^he~will~<u>BE</u>^" WHICH *I~will~be~* <u>APPOINT</u> to~you(mp) THERE~unto to~ >~*much*~<u>SPEAK</u> TO~*you(ms)* THERE□	{it is a} continual rising {sacrifice} (for) your generations {at the} opening {of the} tent {of the} appointed {place} <in front of> "Yhwh ^He is^", (where) I will be appointed to you there, to speak to you there,□

29:43 וְנֹעַדְתִּי שָׁמָּה לִבְנֵי יִשְׂרָאֵל וְנִקְדַּשׁ בִּכְבֹדִי

we'no'ad'ti sham'mah liv'ney yis'ra'eyl we'niq'dash bikh'vo'di

and~*I~did~be~*<u>APPOINT</u> THERE~unto to~ SON~s "Yisra'el ^he~will~<u>TURN-ASIDE</u>~+~MIGHTY-ONE^" and~*he~did~be~*<u>SET-APART</u> in~ARMAMENT~ me□	and I was appointed to {the} sons {of} "Yisra'el ^He turns El aside^" there, and he will be set apart (with) my armament,□

---

* The phrase "between the evenings" is of uncertain meaning but may be the time between sunset and dark.

† The phrase "between the evenings" is of uncertain meaning but may be the time between sunset and dark.

‡ Referring to the "donation," a feminine word in Hebrew.

Revised Mechanical Translation Codes

(..) Alt Trans/App A	<..> Comp Phrase/App B	[..] Verb Form/App C	\../ Plural Form/App D
:..: Int Inf Abs	|..| Past Perf Verb	{...} Added Word	

29:44 וְקִדַּשְׁתִּי אֶת אֹהֶל מוֹעֵד וְאֶת הַמִּזְבֵּחַ וְאֶת אַהֲרֹן וְאֶת בָּנָיו אֲקַדֵּשׁ לְכַהֵן לִי

we'qi'dash'ti et o'hel mo'eyd we'et ha'miz'bey'ahh we'et a'ha'ron we'et ba'naw a'qa'deysh le'kha'heyn li

and~I~did~much~<u>SET-APART</u> AT TENT APPOINTED and~AT the~ALTAR and~AT "Aharon ^{LIGHT-BRINGER}" and~AT SON~s~him I~will~much~<u>SET-APART</u> to~>~much~<u>ADORN</u> to~me□

and I will set apart {the} tent {of the} appointed {place} and the altar and "Aharon ^{Light bringer}" and his sons, I will set {them} apart to {be} adorn{ed} (for) me,□

29:45 וְשָׁכַנְתִּי בְּתוֹךְ בְּנֵי יִשְׂרָאֵל וְהָיִיתִי לָהֶם לֵאלֹהִים

we'sha'khan'ti be'tokh be'ney yis'ra'eyl we'hai'yi'ti la'hem ley'lo'him

and~I~did~<u>DWELL</u> in~MIDST SON~s "Yisra'el ^{he~will~TURN-ASIDE~+~MIGHTY-ONE}" and~I~did~<u>EXIST</u> to~them(m) to~"Elohiym ^{POWER~s}"□

and I will dwell in {the} midst {of the} sons {of} "Yisra'el ^{He turns El aside}", and I will exist (for) them (for) "Elohiym ^{Powers}",□

29:46 וְיָדְעוּ כִּי אֲנִי יְהוָה אֱלֹהֵיהֶם אֲשֶׁר הוֹצֵאתִי אֹתָם מֵאֶרֶץ מִצְרַיִם לְשָׁכְנִי בְתוֹכָם אֲנִי יְהוָה אֱלֹהֵיהֶם

we'yad'u ki a'ni YHWH e'lo'hey'hem a'sher ho'tsey'ti o'tam mey'e'rets mits'ra'yim le'shakh'ni ve'to'kham a'ni YHWH e'lo'hey'hem

and~they~did~<u>KNOW</u> GIVEN-THAT I "Yhwh ^{he~will~BE}" "Elohiym ^{POWER~s}"~them(m) WHICH I~did~make~<u>GO-OUT</u> AT~them(m) from~LAND "Mits'rayim ^{STRAIT~s2}" to~>~<u>DWELL</u>~me in~MIDST~them(m) I "Yhwh ^{he~will~BE}" "Elohiym ^{POWER~s}"~them(m)□

and they will know that I {am} "Yhwh ^{He is}" their "Elohiym ^{Powers}", (who) made them go out from {the} land {of} "Mits'rayim ^{Two straits}" (for) me {to} dwell in their midst, I {am} "Yhwh ^{He is}" their "Elohiym ^{Powers}",□

Chapter 30

30:1 וְעָשִׂיתָ מִזְבֵּחַ מִקְטַר קְטֹרֶת עֲצֵי שִׁטִּים תַּעֲשֶׂה אֹתוֹ

we'a'si'ta miz'bey'ahh miq'tar qe'to'ret a'tsey shi'tim ta'a'seh o'to

and~you(ms)~did~<u>DO</u> ALTAR PLACE-TO-BURN INCENSE TREE~s ACACIA~s you(ms)~will~<u>DO</u> AT~him□

and you will (make) {an} altar, {a} place to burn incense, you will (make) him {of} \wood/ {of} acacia,□

30:2 אַמָּה אָרְכּוֹ וְאַמָּה רָחְבּוֹ רָבוּעַ יִהְיֶה וְאַמָּתַיִם קֹמָתוֹ מִמֶּנּוּ קַרְנֹתָיו

a'mah ar'ko we'a'mah rahh'bo ra'vu'a yih'yeh we'a'ma'ta'yim qo'ma'to mi'me'nu qar'no'taw

FOREARM LENGTH~him and~FOREARM

{a} forearm {is} his length and {a} forearm {is}

Mechanical Translation Codes

<u>WORD</u> – Verb   WORD – Noun   Word – Name   word – Pre/Suff   *word* – Conj.

~ 224 ~

WIDTH~him <u>BE-SQUARE</u>~ed(ms) he~will~ <u>EXIST</u> and~FOREARM~s2 HEIGHT~him FROM~him HORN~s~him□

his width, he will exist squared, and two forearms {is} his height, from him {are} his horns,□

30:3 וְצִפִּיתָ אֹתוֹ זָהָב טָהוֹר אֶת גַּגּוֹ וְאֶת קִירֹתָיו סָבִיב וְאֶת קַרְנֹתָיו וְעָשִׂיתָ לּוֹ זֵר זָהָב סָבִיב

we'tsi'pi'ta o'to za'hav ta'hor et ga'go we'et qi'ro'taw sa'viv we'et qar'no'taw we'a'si'ta lo zeyr za'hav sa'viv

and~you(ms)~did~much~<u>OVERLAY</u> AT~him GOLD PURE AT ROOF~him and~AT WALL~s~ him ALL-AROUND and~AT HORN~s~him and~you(ms)~did~<u>DO</u> to~him MOLDING GOLD ALL-AROUND□

and you will overlay him {with} pure gold, his roof and his walls all around and his horns, and you will (make) (for) him {a} molding {of} gold all around,□

30:4 וּשְׁתֵּי טַבְּעֹת זָהָב תַּעֲשֶׂה לּוֹ מִתַּחַת לְזֵרוֹ עַל שְׁתֵּי צַלְעֹתָיו תַּעֲשֶׂה עַל שְׁנֵי צִדָּיו וְהָיָה לְבָתִּים לְבַדִּים לָשֵׂאת אֹתוֹ בָּהֵמָּה

ush'tey ta'be'ot za'hav ta'a'seh lo mi'ta'hhat le'zey'ro al she'tey tsal'o'taw ta'a'seh al she'ney tsi'daw we'hai'yah le'va'tim le'va'dim la'seyt o'to ba'hey'mah

and~TWO RING~s GOLD you(ms)~will~<u>DO</u> to~him from~UNDER to~MOLDING~him UPON TWO RIB~s~him you(ms)~will~<u>DO</u> UPON TWO SIDE~s~him and~he~did~<u>EXIST</u> to~HOUSE~s to~STICK~s to~>~<u>LIFT-UP</u> AT~ him in~THEY(m)□

and you will (make) two rings {of} gold (for) him under his molding upon his two ribs, you will (make) {them} upon his two sides, and he will exist (for) houses* (for) {the} sticks to lift him up in them,□

30:5 וְעָשִׂיתָ אֶת הַבַּדִּים עֲצֵי שִׁטִּים וְצִפִּיתָ אֹתָם זָהָב

we'a'si'ta et ha'ba'dim a'tsey shi'tim we'tsi'pi'ta o'tam za'hav

and~you(ms)~did~<u>DO</u> AT the~STICK~s TREE~s ACACIA~s and~you(ms)~did~much~ <u>OVERLAY</u> AT~them(m) GOLD□

and you will (make) the sticks {of} \wood/ {of} acacia, and you will overlay them {with} gold,□

30:6 וְנָתַתָּה אֹתוֹ לִפְנֵי הַפָּרֹכֶת אֲשֶׁר עַל אֲרֹן הָעֵדֻת לִפְנֵי הַכַּפֹּרֶת אֲשֶׁר עַל הָעֵדֻת אֲשֶׁר אִוָּעֵד לְךָ שָׁמָּה

we'na'ta'tah o'to liph'ney ha'pa'ro'khet a'sher al a'ron ha'ey'dut liph'ney ha'ka'po'ret a'sher al ha'ey'dut a'sher i'wa'eyd le'kha sham'mah

and~you(ms)~did~<u>GIVE</u>~^ AT~him to~ FACE~s the~TENT-CURTAIN WHICH UPON BOX the~EVIDENCE to~FACE~s the~LID WHICH UPON the~EVIDENCE WHICH I~will~ be~<u>APPOINT</u> to~you(ms) THERE~unto□

and you will (place) him <in front of> the tent curtain, which {is} upon {the} box {of} the evidence, <in front of> the lid, which {is} upon the evidence, (where) I will be appointed (for) you there,□

---

* Or "housings."

Revised Mechanical Translation Codes
(..) Alt Trans/App A   <..> Comp Phrase/App B   [..] Verb Form/App C   \../ Plural Form/App D
:...: Int Inf Abs |..| Past Perf Verb   {...} Added Word
~ 225 ~

30:7 וְהִקְטִיר עָלָיו אַהֲרֹן קְטֹרֶת סַמִּים בַּבֹּקֶר בַּבֹּקֶר בְּהֵיטִיבוֹ אֶת הַנֵּרֹת יַקְטִירֶנָּה

we'hiq'tir a'ha'ron qe'to'ret sa'mim ba'bo'qer ba'bo'qer be'hey'ti'vo et ha'ney'rot yaq'ti're'nah

and~he~did~make~BURN-INCENSE UPON~him "Aharon ^{LIGHT-BRINGER}" INCENSE AROMATIC-SPICE~s in~the~MORNING in~the~MORNING in~>~make~DO-WELL~him AT the~LAMP~s he~will~make~BURN-INCENSE~her□

and "Aharon ^{Light bringer}" will burn incense upon him, {an} incense {of} aromatic spices, morning (by) morning, in his mak{ing} the lamps do well* he will make her burn incense,□

30:8 וּבְהַעֲלֹת אַהֲרֹן אֶת הַנֵּרֹת בֵּין הָעַרְבַּיִם יַקְטִירֶנָּה קְטֹרֶת תָּמִיד לִפְנֵי יְהוָה לְדֹרֹתֵיכֶם

uv'ha'a'lot a'ha'ron et ha'ney'rot beyn ha'ar'ba'yim yaq'ti're'nah qe'to'ret ta'mid liph'ney YHWH le'do'ro'tey'khem

and~in~>~make~GO-UP "Aharon ^{LIGHT-BRINGER}" AT the~LAMP~s BETWEEN the~EVENING~s he~will~make~BURN-INCENSE~her INCENSE CONTINUALLY to~FACE~s "Yhwh ^{he~will~BE}" to~GENERATION~s~you(mp)□

and (with) "Aharon ^{Light bringer}" mak{ing} the lamp go up between the evenings†, he will make her burn incense, {a} continual incense <in front of> "Yhwh ^{He is}" (for) your generations,□

30:9 לֹא תַעֲלוּ עָלָיו קְטֹרֶת זָרָה וְעֹלָה וּמִנְחָה וְנֵסֶךְ לֹא תִסְּכוּ עָלָיו

lo ta'a'lu a'law qe'to'ret za'rah we'o'lah u'min'hhah we'ney'sekh lo tis'khu a'law

NOT you(mp)~will~make~GO-UP UPON~him INCENSE BE-STRANGE~ing/er(fs) and~RISING and~DONATION and~POURING NOT you(mp)~will~POUR UPON~him□

you will not make {an} incense {of a} stranger‡ go up upon him, and you will not pour upon him {a} rising {sacrifice} and {a} donation and {a} pouring,□

30:10 וְכִפֶּר אַהֲרֹן עַל קַרְנֹתָיו אַחַת בַּשָּׁנָה מִדַּם חַטַּאת הַכִּפֻּרִים אַחַת בַּשָּׁנָה יְכַפֵּר עָלָיו לְדֹרֹתֵיכֶם קֹדֶשׁ קָדָשִׁים הוּא לַיהוָה

we'khi'per a'ha'ron al qar'no'taw a'hhat ba'sha'nah mi'dam hha'tat ha'ki'pu'rim a'hhat ba'sha'nah ye'kha'peyr a'law le'do'ro'tey'khem qo'desh qa'da'shim hu la'YHWH

and~he~did~much~COVER "Aharon ^{LIGHT-BRINGER}" UPON HORN~s~him UNIT in~the~YEAR from~BLOOD ERROR the~ATONEMENT~s UNIT in~the~YEAR he~will~much~COVER UPON~him to~GENERATION~s~you(mp) SPECIAL SPECIAL~s

and "Aharon ^{Light bringer}" will [make reconciliation] upon his horns (one) {time} in the year from {the} blood {of} error {of} the atonement, (one) {time} in the year he will [make reconciliation] upon him (for) your generations, he {is a} special {thing of} special

---

* "Making the lamps do well" is probably referring to trimming the wicks so that they burn properly.

† The phrase "between the evenings" is of uncertain meaning but may be the time between sunset and dark.

‡ The phrase "incense of a stranger" could also be translated as "strange incense."

Mechanical Translation Codes

<u>WORD</u> – Verb	WORD – Noun	Word – Name	word – Pre/Suff	*word* – Conj.

HE to~"Yhwh ^{he~will~BE}"□

{thing}s (for) "Yhwh ^{He is}",□

30:11

וַיְדַבֵּר יְהֹוָה אֶל מֹשֶׁה לֵּאמֹר

wai'da'beyr YHWH el mo'sheh ley'mor

and~*he~will~much*~SPEAK "Yhwh ^{he~will~BE}" TO "Mosheh ^{PLUCKED-OUT}" to~>~SAY□

and "Yhwh ^{He is}" spoke to "Mosheh ^{Plucked out}" say{ing},□

30:12

כִּי תִשָּׂא אֶת רֹאשׁ בְּנֵי יִשְׂרָאֵל לִפְקֻדֵיהֶם וְנָתְנוּ אִישׁ כֹּפֶר נַפְשׁוֹ לַיהֹוָה בִּפְקֹד אֹתָם וְלֹא יִהְיֶה בָהֶם נֶגֶף בִּפְקֹד אֹתָם

ki ti'sa et rosh be'ney yis'ra'eyl liph'qu'dey'hem we'nat'nu ish ko'pher naph'sho la'YHWH biph'qod o'tam we'lo yih'yeh va'hem ne'geph biph'qod o'tam

GIVEN-THAT *you(ms)*~will~LIFT-UP AT HEAD SON~s "Yisra'el ^{he~will~TURN-ASIDE~+~MIGHTY-ONE}" to~REGISTER~*ed(mp)*~them(m) and~*they~ did*~GIVE MAN COVERING BEING~him to~ "Yhwh ^{he~will~BE}" in~>~REGISTER AT~them(m) and~NOT *he~will*~EXIST in~them(m) STRIKING in~>~REGISTER AT~them(m)□

given that you will lift up {the} head* {of the} sons {of} "Yisra'el ^{He turns El aside}" (for) them {to be} registered, and (each) will give {a} covering {of} his being to "Yhwh ^{He is}" (with) their register{ing}, and {a} striking† will not exist in them (with) their register{ing},□

30:13

זֶה יִתְּנוּ כָּל הָעֹבֵר עַל הַפְּקֻדִים מַחֲצִית הַשֶּׁקֶל בְּשֶׁקֶל הַקֹּדֶשׁ עֶשְׂרִים גֵּרָה הַשֶּׁקֶל מַחֲצִית הַשֶּׁקֶל תְּרוּמָה לַיהֹוָה

zeh yit'nu kol ha'o'veyr al hap'qu'dim ma'hha'tsit ha'she'qel be'she'qel ha'qo'desh es'rim gey'rah ha'she'qel ma'hha'tsit ha'she'qel te'ru'mah la'YHWH

THIS *they(m)*~will~GIVE ALL the~CROSS-OVER~*ing/er(ms)* UPON the~REGISTER~*ed(mp)* ONE-HALF the~SHEQEL in~SHEQEL the~SPECIAL TEN~s GERAH the~SHEQEL ONE-HALF the~SHEQEL OFFERING to~"Yhwh ^{he~will~BE}"□

this {is what} all the {ones} crossing over upon the registered will give, one-half {of} the sheqel, (with) the sheqel {of the} special {place}, \twenty/ gerah{s is} the sheqel, one-half {of} the sheqel {is the} offering (for) "Yhwh ^{He is}",□

30:14

כֹּל הָעֹבֵר עַל הַפְּקֻדִים מִבֶּן עֶשְׂרִים שָׁנָה וָמָעְלָה יִתֵּן תְּרוּמַת יְהֹוָה

kol ha'o'veyr al hap'qu'dim mi'ben es'rim sha'nah wa'ma'lah yi'teyn te'ru'mat YHWH

ALL the~CROSS-OVER~*ing/er(ms)* UPON the~REGISTER~*ed(mp)* from~SON TEN~s YEAR and~UPWARD~unto *he~will*~GIVE OFFERING "Yhwh ^{he~will~BE}"□

all the {ones} crossing over upon the registered, from {a} son {of} \twenty/ year{s}‡ and upward, will give {an} offering {of} "Yhwh ^{He is}",□

30:15

הֶעָשִׁיר לֹא יַרְבֶּה וְהַדַּל לֹא יַמְעִיט מִמַּחֲצִית הַשֶּׁקֶל לָתֵת אֶת תְּרוּמַת

---

* "Lift up the head" means to "count."
† That is a pestilence, plague or other disaster.
‡ "A son of twenty years" is an idiom meaning "twenty years old."

Revised Mechanical Translation Codes

(..) Alt Trans/App A   <..> Comp Phrase/App B   [..] Verb Form/App C   \../ Plural Form/App D
:..: Int Inf Abs |..| Past Perf Verb   {...} Added Word

יְהוָה לְכַפֵּר עַל נַפְשֹׁתֵיכֶם

he'a'sir lo yar'beh we'ha'dal lo yam'it mi'ma'hha'tsit ha'sha'qel la'teyt et te'ru'mat YHWH le'kha'peyr al naph'sho'tey'khem

the~RICH NOT *he~will~make~*<u>INCREASE</u> and~the~WEAK NOT *he~will~make~*<u>BE-LESS</u> from~ONE-HALF the~SHEQEL to~>~<u>GIVE</u> AT OFFERING "Yhwh *he~will~*<u>BE</u>" to~>~*much~*<u>COVER</u> UPON BEING~s~you(mp)□

the rich will not (give) {an} increase and the weak will not (give) less from {the} one-half {of} the sheqel, {it is} (for) giv{ing an} offering {of} "Yhwh ^(He is)" (for) mak{ing} [reconciliation] upon your beings,□

30:16 וְלָקַחְתָּ אֶת כֶּסֶף הַכִּפֻּרִים מֵאֵת בְּנֵי יִשְׂרָאֵל וְנָתַתָּ אֹתוֹ עַל עֲבֹדַת אֹהֶל מוֹעֵד וְהָיָה לִבְנֵי יִשְׂרָאֵל לְזִכָּרוֹן לִפְנֵי יְהוָה לְכַפֵּר עַל נַפְשֹׁתֵיכֶם

we'la'qahh'ta et ke'seph ha'ki'pu'rim mey'eyt be'ney yis'ra'eyl we'na'ta'ta o'to al a'vo'dat o'hel mo'eyd we'hai'yah liv'ney yis'ra'eyl le'zi'ka'ron liph'ney YHWH le'kha'peyr al naph'sho'tey'khem

and~*you(ms)~did~*<u>TAKE</u> AT SILVER the~ATONEMENT~s from~AT SON~s "Yisra'el *he~will~*<u>TURN-ASIDE</u>~+~MIGHTY-ONE" and~*you(ms)~did~*<u>GIVE</u> AT~him UPON SERVICE TENT APPOINTED and~*he~did~*<u>EXIST</u> to~SON~s "Yisra'el *he~will~*<u>TURN-ASIDE</u>~+~MIGHTY-ONE" to~REMEMBRANCE to~FACE~s "Yhwh *he~will~*<u>BE</u>" to~>~*much~*<u>COVER</u> UPON BEING~s~you(mp)□

and you will take {the} silver {of} the atonement from {the} sons {of} "Yisra'el ^(He turns El aside)", and you will give him* upon {the} service {of the} tent {of the} appointed {place}, and he will exist (for) {the} sons {of} "Yisra'el ^(He turns El aside)" (for) {a} remembrance <in front of> "Yhwh ^(He is)" (for) mak{ing} [reconciliation] upon your beings,□

30:17 וַיְדַבֵּר יְהוָה אֶל מֹשֶׁה לֵּאמֹר

wai'da'beyr YHWH el mo'sheh ley'mor

and~*he~will~much~*<u>SPEAK</u> "Yhwh *he~will~*<u>BE</u>" TO "Mosheh ^(PLUCKED-OUT)" to~>~<u>SAY</u>□

and "Yhwh ^(He is)" spoke to "Mosheh ^(Plucked out)" say{ing},□

30:18 וְעָשִׂיתָ כִּיּוֹר נְחֹשֶׁת וְכַנּוֹ נְחֹשֶׁת לְרָחְצָה וְנָתַתָּ אֹתוֹ בֵּין אֹהֶל מוֹעֵד וּבֵין הַמִּזְבֵּחַ וְנָתַתָּ שָׁמָּה מָיִם

we'a'si'ta ki'or ne'hho'shet we'kha'nu ne'hho'shet le'rahh'tsah we'na'ta'ta o'to beyn o'hel mo'eyd u'veyn ha'miz'bey'ahh we'na'ta'ta sham'mah ma'yim

and~*you(ms)~did~*<u>DO</u> CAULDRON COPPER and~BASE~him COPPER to~>~<u>BATHE</u> and~*you(ms)~did~*<u>GIVE</u> AT~him BETWEEN TENT APPOINTED and~BETWEEN the~ALTAR and~*you(ms)~did~*<u>GIVE</u> THERE~unto WATER~s2□

and you will (make) {a} cauldron {of} copper, and his base {of} copper, {it is} (for) bath{ing}, and you will (place) him between {the} tent {of the} appointed {place} and the altar, and you will (place) unto there {the} waters,□

30:19 וְרָחֲצוּ אַהֲרֹן וּבָנָיו מִמֶּנּוּ אֶת יְדֵיהֶם וְאֶת רַגְלֵיהֶם

we'ra'hha'tsu a'ha'ron u'va'naw mi'me'nu et ye'dey'hem we'et rag'ley'hem

---

* Referring to the "silver," a masculine word in Hebrew.

Mechanical Translation Codes

<u>WORD</u> – Verb	WORD – Noun	Word – Name	word – Pre/Suff	*word* – Conj.

and~*they*~*did*~BATHE "Aharon ^{LIGHT-BRINGER}" and~SON~s~him FROM~him AT HAND~s2~ them(m) and~AT FOOT~s2~them(m)□

and "Aharon ^{Light bringer}" and his sons will bathe from him, their hands and their feet,□

30:20

בְּבֹאָם אֶל אֹהֶל מוֹעֵד יִרְחֲצוּ מַיִם וְלֹא יָמֻתוּ אוֹ בְגִשְׁתָּם אֶל הַמִּזְבֵּחַ לְשָׁרֵת לְהַקְטִיר אִשֶּׁה לַיהוָה

be'vo'am el o'hel mo'eyd yir'hha'tsu ma'yim we'lo ya'mu'tu o ve'gish'tam el ha'miz'bey'ahh le'sha'reyt le'haq'tir i'sheh la'YHWH

in~>~COME~them(m) TO TENT APPOINTED *they(m)*~*will*~BATHE WATER~s2 and~NOT *they(m)*~*will*~DIE OR in~>~DRAW-NEAR~ them(m) TO the~ALTAR to~>~*much*~ MINISTER to~>~*make*~BURN-INCENSE FIRE-OFFERING to~"Yhwh ^{he~will~BE}"□

in their com{ing} to {the} tent {of the} appointed {place}, they will bathe {with} water and they will not die, or in their draw{ing} near to the altar to minister to burn incense, {it is a} fire offering (for) "Yhwh ^{He is}",□

30:21

וְרָחֲצוּ יְדֵיהֶם וְרַגְלֵיהֶם וְלֹא יָמֻתוּ וְהָיְתָה לָהֶם חָק עוֹלָם לוֹ וּלְזַרְעוֹ לְדֹרֹתָם

we'ra'hha'tsu ye'dey'hem we'rag'ley'hem we'lo ya'mu'tu we'hai'tah la'hem hhaq o'lam lo ul'zar'o le'do'ro'tam

and~*they*~*did*~BATHE HAND~s2~them(m) and~FOOT~s2~them(m) and~NOT *they(m)*~ *will*~DIE and~ she~*did*~EXIST to~them(m) CUSTOM DISTANT to~him and~to~SEED~him to~GENERATION~s~them(m)□

and they will bathe their hands and their feet and they will not die, and she* will exist (for) them {as a} custom {of a} distant {time}, (for) him and (for) his seed, (for) their generations,□

30:22

וַיְדַבֵּר יְהוָה אֶל מֹשֶׁה לֵּאמֹר

wai'da'beyr YHWH el mo'sheh ley'mor

and~*he*~*will*~*much*~SPEAK "Yhwh ^{he~will~BE}" TO "Mosheh ^{PLUCKED-OUT}" to~>~SAY□

and "Yhwh ^{He is}" spoke to "Mosheh ^{Plucked out}" say{ing},□

30:23

וְאַתָּה קַח לְךָ בְּשָׂמִים רֹאשׁ מָר דְּרוֹר חֲמֵשׁ מֵאוֹת וְקִנְּמָן בֶּשֶׂם מַחֲצִיתוֹ חֲמִשִּׁים וּמָאתָיִם וּקְנֵה בֹשֶׂם חֲמִשִּׁים וּמָאתָיִם

we'a'tah qahh le'kha be'sa'mim rosh mar de'ror hha'meysh mey'ot we'qin'man be'sem ma'haa'tsi'to hha'mi'shim u'mah'ta'yim uq'ney vo'sem hha'mi'shim u'mah'ta'yim

and~YOU(ms) !(ms)~TAKE to~you(ms) SWEET-SPICE~s HEAD MYRRH FREE-FLOWING FIVE HUNDRED~s and~CINNAMON SWEET-SPICE ONE-HALF~him FIVE~s and~ HUNDRED~s2 and~STALK SWEET-SPICE FIVE~s and~HUNDRED~s2□

and you, take (for) you {the} head† sweet spices, free flowing myrrh {will be} five hundred, and cinnamon {of} sweet spice {will be} one-half {of} him, {that is} \fifty/ and two hundred, and {a} stalk {of} sweet spice {will be} \fifty/ and two hundred,□

---

* Referring to the "custom," a feminine word in Hebrew.
† Meaning "chief" or "principle."

Revised Mechanical Translation Codes

(..) Alt Trans/App A	<..> Comp Phrase/App B	[..] Verb Form/App C	\../ Plural Form/App D
:...: Int Inf Abs	|..| Past Perf Verb	{...} Added Word	

30:24

וְקִדָּה חֲמֵשׁ מֵאוֹת בְּשֶׁקֶל הַקֹּדֶשׁ וְשֶׁמֶן זַיִת הִין

we'qi'dah hha'meysh mey'ot be'she'qel ha'qo'desh we'she'men za'yit hin

and~CASSIA FIVE HUNDRED~s in~SHEQEL the~SPECIAL and~OIL OLIVE HIYN□

and cassia {will be} five hundred, (by) the sheqel {of the} special {place}, and olive oil {will be a} hiyn,□

30:25

וְעָשִׂיתָ אֹתוֹ שֶׁמֶן מִשְׁחַת קֹדֶשׁ רֹקַח מִרְקַחַת מַעֲשֵׂה רֹקֵחַ שֶׁמֶן מִשְׁחַת קֹדֶשׁ יִהְיֶה

we'a'si'ta o'to she'men mish'hhat qo'desh ro'qahh mir'qa'hhat ma'a'seyh ro'qey'ahh she'men mish'hhat qo'desh yih'yeh

and~you(ms)~did~DO AT~him OIL OINTMENT SPECIAL SPICE-MIXTURE OINTMENT-MIXTURE WORK COMPOUND~ing/er(ms) OIL OINTMENT SPECIAL he~will~EXIST□

and you will (make) him {an} oil {of} ointment {of} special{ness}, {a} spice mixture, {an} ointment mixture, {a} work {of} compounding*, he will exist {as an} oil {of} ointment {of} special{ness},□

30:26

וּמָשַׁחְתָּ בוֹ אֶת אֹהֶל מוֹעֵד וְאֵת אֲרוֹן הָעֵדֻת

u'ma'shahh'ta bo et o'hel mo'eyd we'eyt a'ron ha'ey'dut

and~you(ms)~did~SMEAR in~him AT TENT APPOINTED and~AT BOX the~EVIDENCE□

and you will smear (with) him† {the} tent {of the} appointed {place}, and {the} box {of the} evidence,□

30:27

וְאֶת הַשֻּׁלְחָן וְאֶת כָּל כֵּלָיו וְאֶת הַמְּנֹרָה וְאֶת כֵּלֶיהָ וְאֵת מִזְבַּח הַקְּטֹרֶת

we'et ha'shul'hhan we'et kol key'law we'et ham'no'rah we'et key'ley'ah we'eyt miz'bahh haq'to'ret

and~AT the~TABLE and~AT ALL ITEM~s~him and~AT the~LAMPSTAND and~AT ITEM~s~her and~AT ALTAR the~INCENSE□

and the table and all his items, and the lampstand and her items, and {the} altar {of} the incense,□

30:28

וְאֶת מִזְבַּח הָעֹלָה וְאֶת כָּל כֵּלָיו וְאֶת הַכִּיֹּר וְאֶת כַּנּוֹ

we'et miz'bahh ha'o'lah we'et kol key'law we'et ha'ki'yor we'et ka'no

and~AT ALTAR the~RISING and~AT ALL ITEM~s~him and~AT the~CAULDRON and~AT BASE~him□

and the altar {of the} rising {sacrifice} and all his items, and {the} cauldron and his base,□

30:29

וְקִדַּשְׁתָּ אֹתָם וְהָיוּ קֹדֶשׁ קָדָשִׁים כָּל הַנֹּגֵעַ בָּהֶם יִקְדָּשׁ

---

* This may be a work of compounding, in the sense of a mixture, or made by a "compounder" in the sense of a mixer.
† The "him" is the oil in verse 24, a masculine word in Hebrew.

Mechanical Translation Codes

| <u>WORD</u> – Verb | WORD – Noun | Word – Name | word – Pre/Suff | *word* – Conj. |

we'qi'dash'ta o'tam we'hai'u qo'desh qa'da'shim kol ha'no'gey'a ba'hem yiq'dash

and~you(ms)~did~much~<u>SET-APART</u> AT~them(m) and~they~did~<u>EXIST</u> SPECIAL SPECIAL~s ALL the~<u>TOUCH</u>~ing/er(ms) in~them(m) he~will~<u>SET-APART</u>□

and you will set them apart, and they will exist {as a} special {thing of the} special {thing}s, all the {ones} touching them is set apart,□

30:30 וְאֶת־אַהֲרֹן וְאֶת־בָּנָיו תִּמְשָׁח וְקִדַּשְׁתָּ אֹתָם לְכַהֵן לִי

we'et a'ha'ron we'et ba'naw tim'shahh we'qi'dash'ta o'tam le'kha'heyn li

and~AT "Aharon ^{LIGHT-BRINGER}" and~AT SON~s~him you(ms)~will~<u>SMEAR</u> and~you(ms)~did~much~<u>SET-APART</u> AT~them(m) to~>~much~<u>ADORN</u> to~me□

and you will smear "Aharon ^{Light bringer}" and his sons, and you will set them apart to {be} adorn{ed} (for) me,□

30:31 וְאֶל־בְּנֵי יִשְׂרָאֵל תְּדַבֵּר לֵאמֹר שֶׁמֶן מִשְׁחַת־קֹדֶשׁ יִהְיֶה זֶה לִי לְדֹרֹתֵיכֶם

we'el be'ney yis'ra'eyl te'da'beyr ley'mor she'men mish'hhat qo'desh yih'yeh zeh li le'do'ro'tey'khem

and~TO SON~s "Yisra'el ^{he~will~TURN-ASIDE~+MIGHTY-ONE}" you(ms)~will~much~<u>SPEAK</u> to~>~<u>SAY</u> OIL OINTMENT SPECIAL he~will~<u>EXIST</u> THIS to~me to~GENERATION~s~you(mp)□

and to {the} sons {of} "Yisra'el ^{He turns El aside}" you will speak say{ing}, this oil {of} ointment {of} special{ness} will exist (for) me (for) your generations,□

30:32 עַל־בְּשַׂר אָדָם לֹא יִיסָךְ וּבְמַתְכֻּנְתּוֹ לֹא תַעֲשׂוּ כָּמֹהוּ קֹדֶשׁ הוּא קֹדֶשׁ יִהְיֶה לָכֶם

al be'sar a'dam lo yi'sakh uv'mat'kun'to lo ta'a'su ka'mo'hu qo'desh hu qo'desh yih'yeh la'khem

UPON FLESH HUMAN NOT he~will~<u>POUR-DOWN</u> and~in~SUM NOT you(mp)~will~<u>DO</u> like~THAT-ONE~him SPECIAL HE SPECIAL he~will~<u>EXIST</u> to~you(mp)□

upon {the} flesh {of the} human he is not poured, and (with) {the} sum* you will not (make) {it} like that one, he {is a} special {thing}, he will exist (for) you,□

30:33 אִישׁ אֲשֶׁר יִרְקַח כָּמֹהוּ וַאֲשֶׁר יִתֵּן מִמֶּנּוּ עַל־זָר וְנִכְרַת מֵעַמָּיו

ish a'sher yir'qahh ka'mo'hu wa'a'sher yi'teyn mi'me'nu al zar we'nikh'rat mey'a'maw

MAN WHICH he~will~<u>COMPOUND</u> like~THAT-ONE~him and~WHICH he~will~<u>GIVE</u> FROM~him UPON <u>BE-STRANGE</u>~ing/er(ms) and~he~did~be~<u>CUT</u> from PEOPLE~s~him□

{a} man (who) will compound like that one, and which will give from him upon {a} stranger, (then) he will be cut from his peoples,□

30:34 וַיֹּאמֶר יְהוָה אֶל־מֹשֶׁה קַח־לְךָ סַמִּים נָטָף וּשְׁחֵלֶת וְחֶלְבְּנָה סַמִּים וּלְבֹנָה זַכָּה בַּד בְּבַד יִהְיֶה

---

* Meaning the proportions mentioned in the previous verses.

Revised Mechanical Translation Codes

(..) Alt Trans/App A   <..> Comp Phrase/App B   [..] Verb Form/App C   \../ Plural Form/App D

:..: Int Inf Abs |..| Past Perf Verb   {...} Added Word

wai'yo'mer YHWH el mo'sheh qahh le'kha sa'mim na'taph ush'hhey'let we'hhel'be'nah sa'mim ul'vo'nah za'kah bad be'vad yih'yeh

| and~*he will*~<u>SAY</u> "Yhwh ^{*he will BE*}" TO "Mosheh ^{PLUCKED-OUT}" *I(ms)*~<u>TAKE</u> to~you(ms) AROMATIC-SPICE~s NATAPH and~ONYCHA and~GALBANUM AROMATIC-SPICE~s and~ FRANKINCENSE REFINED STICK in~STICK *he*~ *will*~<u>EXIST</u>□ | and "Yhwh ^{He is}" said to "Mosheh ^{Plucked out}", take (for) you aromatic spices, nataph and onycha and galbanum, aromatic spices and refined frankincense, he will exist (part) in (part)*,□ |

30:35 וְעָשִׂיתָ אֹתָהּ קְטֹרֶת רֹקַח מַעֲשֵׂה רוֹקֵחַ מְמֻלָּח טָהוֹר קֹדֶשׁ

we'a'si'ta o'tah qe'to'ret ro'qahh ma'a'seyh ro'qey'ahh me'mu'lahh ta'hor qo'desh

| and~*you(ms)*~*did*~<u>DO</u> AT~her INCENSE SPICE-MIXTURE WORK <u>COMPOUND</u>~ *ing/er(ms)* be~much~<u>SEASON</u>~*ing/er(ms)* PURE SPECIAL□ | and you will (make) her {an} incense, {a} spice mixture, {a} work {of} compounding†, {a} pure seasoning {of} special{ness},□ |

30:36 וְשָׁחַקְתָּ מִמֶּנָּה הָדֵק וְנָתַתָּה מִמֶּנָּה לִפְנֵי הָעֵדֻת בְּאֹהֶל מוֹעֵד אֲשֶׁר אִוָּעֵד לְךָ שָׁמָּה קֹדֶשׁ קָדָשִׁים תִּהְיֶה לָכֶם

we'sha'hhaq'ta mi'me'nah ha'zeyq we'na'ta'tah mi'me'nah liph'ney ha'ey'dut be'o'hel mo'eyd a'sher i'wa'eyd le'kha sham'mah qo'desh qa'da'shim tih'yeh la'khem

| and~*you(ms)*~*did*~<u>PULVERIZE</u> FROM~her >~*make*~<u>BEAT-IN-PIECES</u> and~*you(ms)*~*did*~ <u>GIVE</u>~^ FROM~her to~FACE~s the~EVIDENCE in~TENT APPOINTED WHICH *I*~*will*~be~ <u>APPOINT</u> to~you(ms) THERE~unto SPECIAL SPECIAL~s she~*will*~<u>EXIST</u> to~you(mp)□ | and you will pulverize (some of) her {into} pieces, and you will (place) (some of) her <in front of> the evidence in {the} tent {of the} appointed {place}, (where) I will be appointed (for) you there, she will exist (for) you {as a} special {thing of} special {thing}s,□ |

30:37 וְהַקְּטֹרֶת אֲשֶׁר תַּעֲשֶׂה בְּמַתְכֻּנְתָּהּ לֹא תַעֲשׂוּ לָכֶם קֹדֶשׁ תִּהְיֶה לְךָ לַיהוָה

we'haq'to'ret a'sher ta'a'seh be'mat'kun'tah lo ta'a'su la'khem qo'desh tih'yeh le'kha la'YHWH

| and~the~INCENSE WHICH *you(ms)*~*will*~<u>DO</u> in~SUM~her NOT *you(mp)*~*will*~<u>DO</u> to~ you(mp) SPECIAL she~*will*~<u>EXIST</u> to~you(ms) to~"Yhwh ^{*he will BE*}"□ | and the incense which you will (make) (with) her sum‡, you will not (make) (for) you, {it is a} special {thing}, she will exist (for) you (for) "Yhwh ^{He is}",□ |

30:38 אִישׁ אֲשֶׁר יַעֲשֶׂה כָמוֹהָ לְהָרִיחַ בָּהּ וְנִכְרַת מֵעַמָּיו

ish a'sher ya'a'seh kha'mo'ah le'ha'ri'ahh bah we'nikh'rat mey'a'maw

---

* "Part in part" means an equal portion of each.
† This may be a work of compounding, in the sense of a mixture, or made by a "compounder" in the sense of a mixer.
‡ Meaning the proportions mentioned in the previous verses.

Mechanical Translation Codes

| <u>WORD</u> – Verb | WORD – Noun | Word – Name | word – Pre/Suff | *word* – Conj. |

MAN WHICH *he~will~*<u>DO</u> like~THAT-ONE~ her to~>~*make~*<u>SMELL</u> in~her and~*he~did~* *be~*<u>CUT</u> from~PEOPLE~s~him◻

{a} man (who) will (make) {it} like that one, to smell (with)* her, (then) he will be cut from his peoples,◻

Chapter 31

31:1   וַיְדַבֵּר יְהוָה אֶל מֹשֶׁה לֵּאמֹר

wai'da'beyr YHWH el mo'sheh ley'mor

and~*he~will~*much~<u>SPEAK</u> "Yhwh *he~will~*<u>BE</u>" TO "Mosheh ^{PLUCKED-OUT}" to~>~<u>SAY</u>◻

and "Yhwh ^{He is}" spoke to "Mosheh ^{Plucked out}" say{ing},◻

31:2   רְאֵה קָרָאתִי בְשֵׁם בְּצַלְאֵל בֶּן אוּרִי בֶן חוּר לְמַטֵּה יְהוּדָה

re'eyh qa'ra'ti ve'sheym be'tsal'eyl ben u'ri ven hhur le'ma'teyh ye'hu'dah

!(ms)~<u>SEE</u> *I~did~*<u>CALL-OUT</u> in~TITLE "Betsaleyl ^{in~SHADOW~+~MIGHTY-ONE}" SON "Uriy ^{LIGHT~me}" SON "Hhur ^{CISTERN}" to~BRANCH "Yehudah ^{THANKSGIVING}"◻

see, I called out (by) title† "Betsaleyl ^{In the shadow of El}", son {of} "Uriy ^{My light}", son {of} "Hhur ^{Cistern}" {belonging} to {the} branch {of} "Yehudah ^{Thanksgiving}",◻

31:3   וָאֲמַלֵּא אֹתוֹ רוּחַ אֱלֹהִים בְּחָכְמָה וּבִתְבוּנָה וּבְדַעַת וּבְכָל מְלָאכָה

wa'a'ma'ley o'to ru'ahh e'lo'him be'hhakh'mah u'vit'vu'nah uv'da'at uv'khol me'la'khah

and~*I~will~*much~<u>FILL</u> AT~him WIND "Elohiym ^{POWER~s}" in~SKILL and~in~ INTELLIGENCE and~in~DISCERNMENT and~ in~ALL BUSINESS◻

and I filled him {with the} wind‡ {of} "Elohiym ^{Powers}", (with) skill and (with) intelligence and (with) discernment and (with) all {kinds of} business,◻

31:4   לַחְשֹׁב מַחֲשָׁבֹת לַעֲשׂוֹת בַּזָּהָב וּבַכֶּסֶף וּבַנְּחֹשֶׁת

lahh'shov ma'hha'sha'vot la'a'shot ba'za'hav u'va'ke'seph u'van'hho'shet

to~>~<u>THINK</u> INVENTION~s to~>~<u>DO</u> in~the~ GOLD and~in~the~SILVER and~in~the~ COPPER◻

to think {of} inventions, to (make) {things} (with) the gold and (with) the silver and (with) the copper,◻

31:5   וּבַחֲרֹשֶׁת אֶבֶן לְמַלֹּאת וּבַחֲרֹשֶׁת עֵץ לַעֲשׂוֹת בְּכָל מְלָאכָה

u'va'hha'ro'shet e'ven le'ma'lot u'va'hha'ro'shet eyts la'a'shot be'khol me'la'khah

---

* Probably meaning "the same as."

† The phrase "I called out by title Betsaleyl" can mean, "I called Betsaleyl by name," but can also be translated as "I met with the title (meaning character or person) of Betsaleyl," as the Hebrew verb קרא may mean to "call out" or to "meet."

‡ The wind, or breath, of an individual is his character.

Revised Mechanical Translation Codes

(..) Alt Trans/App A   <..> Comp Phrase/App B   [..] Verb Form/App C   \../ Plural Form/App D

:...: Int Inf Abs |..| Past Perf Verb   {...} Added Word

and~in~the~ENGRAVING STONE to~
>~*much*~FILL and~in~the~ENGRAVING TREE
to~>~*DO* in~ALL BUSINESS□

and (with) the engraving {of} stone (for)
fill{ing}, and (with) the engraving {of} tree{s}*
(for) (mak){ing things} (with) all {kinds of}
business,□

31:6   וַאֲנִי הִנֵּה נָתַתִּי אִתּוֹ אֵת אָהֳלִיאָב בֶּן אֲחִיסָמָךְ לְמַטֵּה דָן וּבְלֵב כָּל
חֲכַם לֵב נָתַתִּי חָכְמָה וְעָשׂוּ אֵת כָּל אֲשֶׁר צִוִּיתִךָ

wa'ani hin'neyh na'ta'ti i'to eyt a'ha'li'av ben a'hhi'sa'mak le'ma'teyh dan uv'leyv kol
hha'kham leyv na'ta'ti hhakh'mah we'a'su eyt kol a'sher tsi'wi'ti'kha

and~I LOOK *I~did~*GIVE AT~him AT "Ahaliyav
TENT~of~+~FATHER„ SON "Ahhiysamahh BROTHER~me~
+~he~did~SUPPORT„ to~BRANCH "Dan MODERATOR„
and~in~HEART ALL SKILLED-ONE HEART *I~
did~*GIVE SKILL and~*they~did~*DO AT ALL
WHICH *I~did~much~*DIRECT~you(ms)□

and look, I gave him "Ahaliyav Tent of father„, son
{of} "Ahhiysamahh My brother supports„, {belonging}
to {the} branch {of} "Dan Moderator„, and in {the}
heart {of} all {the} skilled one{s of} heart I gave
skill, and they will (make) all (that) I directed
you,□

31:7   אֵת אֹהֶל מוֹעֵד וְאֶת הָאָרֹן לָעֵדֻת וְאֶת הַכַּפֹּרֶת אֲשֶׁר עָלָיו וְאֵת כָּל כְּלֵי
הָאֹהֶל

eyt o'hel mo'eyd we'et ha'a'ron la'ey'dut we'et ha'ka'po'ret a'sher a'law we'eyt kol
ke'ley ha'o'hel

AT TENT APPOINTED and~AT the~BOX to~
the~EVIDENCE and~AT the~LID WHICH
UPON~him and~AT ALL ITEM~s the~TENT□

{the} tent {of the} appointed {place}, and the
box (for) the evidence, and the lid which {is}
upon him, and all {the} items {of} the tent,□

31:8   וְאֶת הַשֻּׁלְחָן וְאֶת כֵּלָיו וְאֶת הַמְּנֹרָה הַטְּהֹרָה וְאֶת כָּל כֵּלֶיהָ וְאֶת
מִזְבַּח הַקְּטֹרֶת

we'et ha'shul'hhan we'et key'law we'et ham'no'rah hat'ho'rah we'et kol key'ley'ah
we'eyt miz'bahh haq'to'ret

and~AT the~TABLE and~AT ITEM~s~him
and~AT the~LAMPSTAND the~PURE and~AT
ALL ITEM~s~her and~AT ALTAR the~
INCENSE□

and the table, and his items, and the pure
lampstand and all her items, and {the} altar
{of} the incense,□

31:9   וְאֶת מִזְבַּח הָעֹלָה וְאֶת כָּל כֵּלָיו וְאֶת הַכִּיּוֹר וְאֶת כַּנּוֹ

we'et miz'bahh ha'o'lah we'et kol key'law we'et ha'ki'yor we'et ka'no

and~AT ALTAR the~RISING and~AT ALL
ITEM~s~him and~AT the~CAULDRON and~
AT BASE~him□

and the altar {of the} rising {sacrifice} and all
his items, and the cauldron and his base,□

---

* When the Hebrew word עֵץ is written in the singular, as it is here, it always means tree or
trees. When it is written in the plural form, it always means "wood." If the original text read
עֵצִים, the plural form, then this would be translated as wood.

Mechanical Translation Codes

WORD – Verb	WORD – Noun	Word – Name	word – Pre/Suff	*word* – Conj.

31:10 וְאֵת בִּגְדֵי הַשְּׂרָד וְאֶת בִּגְדֵי הַקֹּדֶשׁ לְאַהֲרֹן הַכֹּהֵן וְאֶת בִּגְדֵי בָנָיו לְכַהֵן

we'eyt big'dey has'rad we'et big'dey ha'qo'desh le'a'ha'ron ha'ko'heyn we'et big'dey
va'naw le'kha'heyn

and~AT GARMENT~s the~BRAIDED-WORK and~AT GARMENT~s the~SPECIAL to~ "Aharon LIGHT-BRINGER" the~ADMINISTRATOR and~AT GARMENT~s SON~s~him to~ >~much~ADORN☐	and {the} garments {of} the braided work, and the garments {of} special{ness} (for) "Aharon Light bringer" the administrator, and {the} garments {of} his sons, {for them} to {be} adorn{ed},☐

31:11 וְאֵת שֶׁמֶן הַמִּשְׁחָה וְאֶת קְטֹרֶת הַסַּמִּים לַקֹּדֶשׁ כְּכֹל אֲשֶׁר צִוִּיתִךָ יַעֲשׂוּ

we'eyt she'men ha'mish'hhah we'et qe'to'ret ha'sa'mim la'qo'desh ke'khol a'sher
tsi'wi'ti'kha ya'a'su

and~AT OIL the~OINTMENT and~AT INCENSE the~AROMATIC-SPICE~s to~the~ SPECIAL like~ALL WHICH I~did~much~ DIRECT~you(ms) they(m)~will~DO☐	and the oil {of} ointment, and the incense {of} aromatic spices (for) the special {place}, {just} like all (that) I directed you, they will do,☐

31:12 וַיֹּאמֶר יְהוָה אֶל מֹשֶׁה לֵּאמֹר

wai'yo'mer YHWH el mo'sheh ley'mor

and~he~will~SAY "Yhwh he~will~BE" TO "Mosheh PLUCKED-OUT" to~>~SAY☐	and "Yhwh He is" said to "Mosheh Plucked out" say{ing},☐

31:13 וְאַתָּה דַּבֵּר אֶל בְּנֵי יִשְׂרָאֵל לֵאמֹר אַךְ אֶת שַׁבְּתֹתַי תִּשְׁמֹרוּ כִּי אוֹת הִוא בֵּינִי וּבֵינֵיכֶם לְדֹרֹתֵיכֶם לָדַעַת כִּי אֲנִי יְהוָה מְקַדִּשְׁכֶם

we'a'tah da'beyr el be'ney yis'ra'eyl ley'mor akh et sha'be'to'tai tish'moru ki ot hi bey'ni u'vey'ney'khem le'do'ro'tey'khem la'da'at ki a'ni YHWH me'qa'dish'khem

and~YOU(ms) !(ms)~much~SPEAK TO SON~s "Yisra'el he~will~TURN-ASIDE~+~MIGHTY-ONE" to~>~SAY SURELY AT CEASING~s~me you(mp)~will~ SAFEGUARD GIVEN-THAT SIGN she BETWEEN~me and~BETWEEN~you(mp) to~ GENERATION~s~you(mp) to~>~KNOW GIVEN-THAT I "Yhwh he~will~BE" much~SET- APART~ing/er(ms)~you(ms)☐	and you, speak to {the} sons {of} "Yisra'el He turns El aside" say{ing}, surely you will safeguard my ceasings given that she* {is a} sign between me and you (for) your generations, to know that I {am} "Yhwh He is" setting you apart,☐

31:14 וּשְׁמַרְתֶּם אֶת הַשַּׁבָּת כִּי קֹדֶשׁ הִוא לָכֶם מְחַלְלֶיהָ מוֹת יוּמָת כִּי כָּל הָעֹשֶׂה בָהּ מְלָאכָה וְנִכְרְתָה הַנֶּפֶשׁ הַהִוא מִקֶּרֶב עַמֶּיהָ

ush'mar'tem et ha'sha'bat ki qo'desh hi la'khem me'hhal'ley'ah mot yu'mat ki kol
ha'o'seh vah me'la'khah we'nikh're'tah ha'ne'phesh ha'hi mi'qe'rev a'mey'ah

---

* Referring to the "ceasing," a feminine word in Hebrew.

Revised Mechanical Translation Codes

(..) Alt Trans/App A	<..> Comp Phrase/App B	[..] Verb Form/App C	\../ Plural Form/App D
:..: Int Inf Abs	|..| Past Perf Verb	{...} Added Word	

and~*you(mp)*~*did*~SAFEGUARD AT the~ CEASING GIVEN-THAT SPECIAL she to~ you(mp) much~PIERCE~*ing/er(mp)*~her >~DIE *he*~*will*~*be*~*make*~DIE GIVEN-THAT ALL the~DO~*ing/er(ms)* in~her BUSINESS and~ she~*did*~*be*~CUT the~BEING the~ she from~WITHIN PEOPLE~s~her□

and you will safeguard the ceasing given that she* {is a} special {time} (for) you, {anyone} (mak)ing her [common] will :surely: be [killed] given that all the {ones} doing {a} business in her, (that) being will be cut from within her† peoples,□

31:15 שֵׁשֶׁת יָמִים יֵעָשֶׂה מְלָאכָה וּבַיּוֹם הַשְּׁבִיעִי שַׁבַּת שַׁבָּתוֹן קֹדֶשׁ לַיהוָה כָּל הָעֹשֶׂה מְלָאכָה בְּיוֹם הַשַּׁבָּת מוֹת יוּמָת

shey'shet ya'mim yey'a'seh me'la'khah u'va'yom hash'vi'i sha'bat sha'ba'ton qo'desh la'YHWH kol ha'o'seh me'la'khah be'yom ha'sha'bat mot yu'mat

SIX DAY~s *he*~*will*~*be*~DO BUSINESS and~in~ the~DAY the~SEVENTH CEASING REST-DAY SPECIAL to~"Yhwh *he*~*will*~BE" ALL the~DO~ *ing/er(ms)* BUSINESS in~DAY the~CEASING >~DIE *he*~*will*~*be*~*make*~DIE□

six days business‡ will be done, and in the seventh day {there will be a} ceasing, {a} rest day, {a} special {time} (for) "Yhwh He is", all the {ones} doing business in {the} day {of} the ceasing will :surely: be [killed],□

31:16 וְשָׁמְרוּ בְנֵי יִשְׂרָאֵל אֶת הַשַּׁבָּת לַעֲשׂוֹת אֶת הַשַּׁבָּת לְדֹרֹתָם בְּרִית עוֹלָם

we'sham'ru ve'ney yis'ra'eyl et ha'sha'bat la'a'shot et ha'sha'bat le'do'ro'tam be'rit o'lam

and~*they*~*did*~SAFEGUARD SON~s "Yisra'el *he*~*will*~TURN-ASIDE~+~MIGHTY-ONE" AT the~CEASING to~>~DO AT the~CEASING to~ GENERATION~s~them(m) COVENANT DISTANT□

and {the} sons {of} "Yisra'el He turns El aside" will safeguard the ceasing, to do the ceasing to their generations, {it is a} covenant {of a} distant {time},□

31:17 בֵּינִי וּבֵין בְּנֵי יִשְׂרָאֵל אוֹת הִוא לְעֹלָם כִּי שֵׁשֶׁת יָמִים עָשָׂה יְהוָה אֶת הַשָּׁמַיִם וְאֶת הָאָרֶץ וּבַיּוֹם הַשְּׁבִיעִי שָׁבַת וַיִּנָּפַשׁ

bey'ni u'veyn be'ney yis'ra'eyl ot hi le'o'lam ki shey'shet ya'mim a'sah YHWH et ha'sha'ma'yim we'et ha'a'rets u'va'yom hash'vi'i sha'vat wai'yi'na'phash

BETWEEN~me and~BETWEEN SON~s "Yisra'el *he*~*will*~TURN-ASIDE~+~MIGHTY-ONE" SIGN she to~DISTANT GIVEN-THAT SIX DAY~s *he*~*did*~ DO "Yhwh *he*~*will*~BE" AT the~SKY~s2 and~AT the~LAND and~in~the~DAY the~SEVENTH *he*~*did*~CEASE and~*he*~*will*~BREATHE-DEEPLY□

between me and {the} sons {of} "Yisra'el He turns El aside", she§ {is a} sign (for) {a} distant {time} given that {in} six days "Yhwh He is" (made) the skies and the land, and in the seventh day he ceased and he breathed deeply**,□

---

* Referring to the "ceasing," a feminine word in Hebrew.
† Referring to the "being," a feminine word in Hebrew.
‡ It appears the word יֵעָשֶׂה is written defectively. The verb יַעֲשֶׂה identifies the subject of the verb as a masculine singular (he). However, the word "business," the subject of the verb, is a feminine singular word.
§ Referring to the "ceasing," a feminine word in Hebrew.
** "Breathed deeply" means to take a break, to refresh oneself.

Mechanical Translation Codes

WORD – Verb	WORD – Noun	Word – Name	word – Pre/Suff	*word* – Conj.

31:18 וַיִּתֵּן אֶל מֹשֶׁה כְּכַלֹּתוֹ לְדַבֵּר אִתּוֹ בְּהַר סִינַי שְׁנֵי לֻחֹת הָעֵדֻת לֻחֹת אֶבֶן כְּתֻבִים בְּאֶצְבַּע אֱלֹהִים

wai'yi'teyn el mo'sheh ke'kha'lo'to le'da'beyr i'to be'har si'nai she'ney lu'hhot ha'ey'dut lu'hhot e'ven ke'tu'vim be'ets'ba e'lo'him

and~*he~will*~<u>GIVE</u> TO "Mosheh ^{PLUCKED-OUT}" like~>~*much*~<u>FINISH</u>~him to>~*much*~ <u>SPEAK</u> AT~him in~HILL "Sinai ^{SHARP-THORN~s~me}" TWO SLAB~s the~EVIDENCE SLAB~s STONE <u>WRITE</u>~*ed(mp)* in~FINGER "Elohiym ^{POWER~s}"□

and he gave to "Mosheh ^{Plucked out}", (as) he finished speak{ing} (with) him in {the} hill {of} "Sinai ^{My sharp thorns}", {the} two slabs {of} the evidence, {the} slabs {of} stone written (with) {the} finger {of} "Elohiym ^{Powers}",□

Chapter 32

32:1 וַיַּרְא הָעָם כִּי בֹשֵׁשׁ מֹשֶׁה לָרֶדֶת מִן הָהָר וַיִּקָּהֵל הָעָם עַל אַהֲרֹן וַיֹּאמְרוּ אֵלָיו קוּם עֲשֵׂה לָנוּ אֱלֹהִים אֲשֶׁר יֵלְכוּ לְפָנֵינוּ כִּי זֶה מֹשֶׁה הָאִישׁ אֲשֶׁר הֶעֱלָנוּ מֵאֶרֶץ מִצְרַיִם לֹא יָדַעְנוּ מֶה הָיָה לוֹ

wai'yar ha'am ki vo'sheysh mo'sheh la're'det min ha'har wai'yi'qa'heyl ha'am al a'ha'ron wai'yom'ru ey'law qum a'seyh la'nu e'lo'him a'sher yeyl'khu le'pha'ney'nu ki zeh mo'sheh ha'ish a'sher he'e'la'nu mey'e'rets mits'ra'yim lo ya'dey'nu meh hai'yah lo

and~*he~will*~<u>SEE</u> the~PEOPLE GIVEN-THAT *he~did~much*~<u>BE-ASHAMED</u> "Mosheh ^{PLUCKED-OUT}" to>~*much*~<u>GO-DOWN</u> FROM the~HILL and~*he~will*~*be*~<u>ROUND-UP</u> the~PEOPLE UPON "Aharon ^{LIGHT-BRINGER}" and~*they(m)*~ *will*~<u>SAY</u> TO~him *!(ms)*~<u>RISE</u> *!(ms)*~<u>DO</u> to~us "Elohiym ^{POWER~s}" WHICH *they(m)~will*~<u>WALK</u> to~FACE~s~us GIVEN-THAT THIS "Mosheh ^{PLUCKED-OUT}" the~MAN WHICH *he~did~make*~ <u>GO-UP</u>~us from~LAND "Mits'rayim ^{STRAIT~s2}" NOT *we~did*~<u>KNOW</u> WHAT *he~did*~<u>EXIST</u> to~ him□

and the people saw that "Mosheh ^{Plucked out}" [refrained] to go down from the hill, and the people were rounded up upon "Aharon ^{Light bringer}" and they said to him, rise, (make) (for) us "Elohiym ^{Powers}" * Which will walk <in front of> us, given that this "Mosheh ^{Plucked out}", the man which made us go up from {the} land {of} "Mits'rayim ^{Two straits}", we do not know what (came to pass) to him,□

32:2 וַיֹּאמֶר אֲלֵהֶם אַהֲרֹן פָּרְקוּ נִזְמֵי הַזָּהָב אֲשֶׁר בְּאָזְנֵי נְשֵׁיכֶם בְּנֵיכֶם וּבְנֹתֵיכֶם וְהָבִיאוּ אֵלָי

---

* When the word "Elohiym," a plural word, is used as the subject of a verb, the verb normally identifies the subject as a masculine singular. Therefore, the word "Elohiym" is being used in a singular sense. However, in this verse, the verb "walk" identifies the subject of the verb, "Elohiym," as a masculine plural noun. This may simply be an alternate grammatical verb and noun construct, or the word Elohiym is meant to be understood as a plural in this verse. (Compare with Exodus 32:4, 32:5 and 32:8.)

Revised Mechanical Translation Codes

(..) Alt Trans/App A   <..> Comp Phrase/App B   [..] Verb Form/App C   \\../ Plural Form/App D
:..: Int Inf Abs |..| Past Perf Verb   {...} Added Word

wai'yo'mer a'ley'hem a'ha'ron par'qu niz'mey ha'za'hav a'sher be'az'ney ne'shey'khem be'ney'khem uv'no'tey'khem we'ha'vi'u ey'lai

and~*he~will*~<u>SAY</u> TO~them(m) "Aharon ^{LIGHT-BRINGER}" !(mp)~much~<u>TEAR-OFF</u> ORNAMENTAL-RING~s the~GOLD WHICH in~ EAR~s2 WOMAN~s~you(mp) SON~s~ you(mp) and~DAUGHTER~s~you(mp) and~ !(mp)~*make*~<u>COME</u> TO~me□

and "Aharon ^{Light bringer}" said to them, tear off {the} ornamental rings {of} gold which {are} in {the} ears {of} your women, your sons and your daughters and [bring] {them} to me,□

32:3 וַיִּתְפָּרְקוּ כָּל הָעָם אֶת נִזְמֵי הַזָּהָב אֲשֶׁר בְּאָזְנֵיהֶם וַיָּבִיאוּ אֶל אַהֲרֹן

wai'yit'par'qu kol ha'am et niz'mey ha'za'hav a'sher be'az'ney'hem wai'ya'vi'u el a'ha'ron

and~*they(m)~will~* self~<u>TEAR-OFF</u> ALL the~ PEOPLE AT ORNAMENTAL-RING~s the~GOLD WHICH in~EAR~s2~them(m) and~*they(m)~ will*~*make*~<u>COME</u> TO "Aharon ^{LIGHT-BRINGER}"□

and the people tore off {the} ornamental rings {of} gold which {were} in their ears and they [brought] {them} to "Aharon ^{Light bringer}",□

32:4 וַיִּקַּח מִיָּדָם וַיָּצַר אֹתוֹ בַּחֶרֶט וַיַּעֲשֵׂהוּ עֵגֶל מַסֵּכָה וַיֹּאמְרוּ אֵלֶּה אֱלֹהֶיךָ יִשְׂרָאֵל אֲשֶׁר הֶעֱלוּךָ מֵאֶרֶץ מִצְרָיִם

wai'yi'qahh mi'ya'dam wai'ya'tsar o'to ba'hhe'ret wai'ya'a'sey'hu ey'gel ma'sey'khah wai'yom'ru ey'leh e'lo'hey'kha yis'ra'eyl a'sher he'e'lu'kha mey'e'rets mits'ra'yim

and~*he~will*~<u>TAKE</u> from~HAND~them(m) and~*he~will*~<u>SMACK</u> AT~him in~the~ ENGRAVING-TOOL and~*he~will*~<u>DO</u>~him BULLOCK CAST-IMAGE and~*they(m)~will*~ <u>SAY</u> THESE "Elohiym ^{POWER~s}~you(ms) "Yisra'el ^{*he~will*~<u>TURN-ASIDE</u>~+~MIGHTY-ONE}" WHICH *they~did~make*~<u>GO-UP</u>~you(ms) from~ LAND "Mits'rayim ^{STRAIT~s2}"□

and he took {them} from their hand, and he smacked him (with) the engraving tool, and he (made) him {into a} cast image {of a} bullock, and they said, "Yisra'el ^{He turns El aside}", these {are} your "Elohiym ^{Powers}"* which made you go up from {the} land {of} "Mits'rayim ^{Two straits}",□

32:5 וַיַּרְא אַהֲרֹן וַיִּבֶן מִזְבֵּחַ לְפָנָיו וַיִּקְרָא אַהֲרֹן וַיֹּאמַר חַג לַיהוָה מָחָר

wai'yar a'ha'ron wai'yi'ven miz'bey'ahh le'pha'naw wai'yiq'ra a'ha'ron wai'yo'mar hhag la'YHWH ma'hhar

and~*he~will*~<u>SEE</u> "Aharon ^{LIGHT-BRINGER}" and~ *he~will*~<u>BUILD</u> ALTAR to~FACE~s~him and~ *he~will*~<u>CALL-OUT</u> "Aharon ^{LIGHT-BRINGER}" and~ *he~will*~<u>SAY</u> FEAST to~"Yhwh ^{*he~will*~<u>BE</u>}" TOMORROW□

and "Aharon ^{Light bringer}" saw {it} and he built {an} altar <in front of> him†, and "Aharon ^{Light bringer}" called out and he said, tomorrow {is a} feast to "Yhwh ^{He is}",□

---

* The word "Elohiym" is being used as a masculine plural noun in this verse, as it is modified with the masculine plural pronoun "these." However, the image representing the "Elohiym" is a single bullock. (Compare with Exodus 32:1, 32:5 and 32:8.)

† In this verse the "Elohiym" is being identified with a masculine singular pronoun. (Compare with Exodus 32:1, 32:4 and 32:8.)

Mechanical Translation Codes

<u>WORD</u> – Verb	WORD – Noun	Word – Name	word – Pre/Suff	*word* – Conj.

32:6

וַיַּשְׁכִּימוּ מִמָּחֳרָת וַיַּעֲלוּ עֹלֹת וַיַּגִּשׁוּ שְׁלָמִים וַיֵּשֶׁב הָעָם לֶאֱכֹל וְשָׁתוֹ
וַיָּקֻמוּ לְצַחֵק

wai'yash'ki'mu mi'ma'hha'rat wai'ya'a'lu o'lot wai'ya'gi'shu she'la'mim wai'yey'shev ha'am
le'e'khol we'sha'to wai'ya'qu'mu le'tsa'hheyq

and~they(m)~will~make~DEPART-EARLY
from~MORROW and~they(m)~will~make~
GO-UP RISING and~they(m)~will~make~
DRAW-NEAR COMPLETE~s and~he~will~
SETTLE the~PEOPLE to~>~EAT and~>~GULP
and~they(m)~will~RISE to~>~much~
LAUGH□

and they departed early <the next day>, and
they made {a} rising {sacrifice} go up, and they
made complete {sacrifice}s draw near, and the
people settled to eat and gulp, and they rose
to [mock],□

32:7

וַיְדַבֵּר יְהוָה אֶל מֹשֶׁה לֶךְ רֵד כִּי שִׁחֵת עַמְּךָ אֲשֶׁר הֶעֱלֵיתָ מֵאֶרֶץ
מִצְרָיִם

wai'da'beyr YHWH el mo'sheh lekh reyd ki shi'hheyt am'kha a'sher he'e'ley'ta mey'e'rets
mits'ra'yim

and~he~will~much~SPEAK "Yhwh ^{he~will~BE}"
TO "Mosheh ^{PLUCKED-OUT}" !(ms)~WALK !(ms)~
GO-DOWN GIVEN-THAT he~did~much~
DAMAGE PEOPLE~you(ms) WHICH you(ms)~
did~make~GO-UP from~LAND "Mits'rayim
^{STRAIT~s2}"□

and "Yhwh ^{He is}" spoke to "Mosheh ^{Plucked out}",
walk, go down, given that your people, which
you made go up from {the} land {of}
"Mits'rayim ^{Two straits}", {are} damaged,□

32:8

סָרוּ מַהֵר מִן הַדֶּרֶךְ אֲשֶׁר צִוִּיתִם עָשׂוּ לָהֶם עֵגֶל מַסֵּכָה וַיִּשְׁתַּחֲווּ לוֹ
וַיִּזְבְּחוּ לוֹ וַיֹּאמְרוּ אֵלֶּה אֱלֹהֶיךָ יִשְׂרָאֵל אֲשֶׁר הֶעֱלוּךָ מֵאֶרֶץ מִצְרָיִם

sa'ru ma'heyr min ha'de'rekh a'sher tsi'wi'tim a'su la'hem ey'gel ma'sey'khah
wai'yish'ta'hhaw lo wai'yiz'be'hhu lo wai'yom'ru ey'leh e'lo'hey'kha yis'ra'eyl a'sher
he'e'lu'kha mey'e'rets mits'ra'yim

they~did~TURN-ASIDE QUICKLY FROM the~
ROAD WHICH I~did~much~DIRECT~them(m)
they~did~DO to~them(m) BULLOCK CAST-
IMAGE and~they(m)~will~self~BEND-DOWN
to~him and~they(m)~will~SACRIFICE to~him
and~they(m)~will~SAY THESE "Elohiym
^{POWER~s}~you(ms) "Yisra'el ^{he~will~TURN-ASIDE+~}
^{MIGHTY-ONE}" WHICH they~did~make~GO-UP~
you(ms) from~LAND "Mits'rayim ^{STRAIT~s2}"□

they quickly turned aside from the road which
I directed them, they (made) (for) them{selves
a} cast image {of a} bullock, and they bent
{them}selves down to him* and they
sacrificed to him, and they said, "Yisra'el ^{He turns}
^{El aside}", these† {are} your "Elohiym ^{Powers}",
which made you go up from {the} land {of}
"Mits'rayim ^{Two straits}",□

---

* The pronoun "him," identifies the word "Elohiym" as a masculine singular noun. In addition,
the image representing the "Elohiym" is a single bullock. (Compare with Exodus 32:1, 32:4 and
32:5 and the following Footnote.)
† The word "Elohiym" is identified as a masculine plural noun, as it is modified with the
masculine plural pronoun "these." (Compare with the previous Footnote and Exodus 32:1, 32:4
and 32:5.)

Revised Mechanical Translation Codes

| (..) Alt Trans/App A | <...> Comp Phrase/App B | [..] Verb Form/App C | \../ Plural Form/App D |
| :...: Int Inf Abs | |..| Past Perf Verb | {...} Added Word | |

32:9 וַיֹּאמֶר יְהֹוָה אֶל מֹשֶׁה רָאִיתִי אֶת הָעָם הַזֶּה וְהִנֵּה עַם קְשֵׁה עֹרֶף הוּא

wai'yo'mer YHWH el mo'sheh ra'i'ti et ha'am ha'zeh we'hin'neyh am qe'sheyh o'reph hu

and~he~will~<u>SAY</u> "Yhwh ^{he~will~<u>BE</u>}" TO "Mosheh ^{PLUCKED-OUT}" I~did~<u>SEE</u> AT the~PEOPLE the~THIS and~LOOK PEOPLE HARD NECK HE□

and "Yhwh ^{He is}" said to "Mosheh ^{Plucked out}", I saw this people and look, he* {is a} hard neck{ed} people,□

32:10 וְעַתָּה הַנִּיחָה לִּי וְיִחַר אַפִּי בָהֶם וַאֲכַלֵּם וְאֶעֱשֶׂה אוֹתְךָ לְגוֹי גָּדוֹל

we'a'tah ha'ni'hhah li we'yi'hhar a'pi va'hem wa'a'kha'leym we'e'e'seh ot'kha le'goi ga'dol

and~NOW !(fs)~make~<u>REST</u> to~me and~he~will~<u>FLARE-UP</u> NOSE~me in~them(m) and~I~will~much~<u>FINISH</u>~them(m) and~I~will~<u>DO</u> AT~you(ms) to~NATION GREAT□

and now [leave] me, and my nose will flare up† in them, and I will finish‡ them, and I will (make) you {in}to {a} great nation,□

32:11 וַיְחַל מֹשֶׁה אֶת פְּנֵי יְהֹוָה אֱלֹהָיו וַיֹּאמֶר לָמָה יְהֹוָה יֶחֱרֶה אַפְּךָ בְּעַמֶּךָ אֲשֶׁר הוֹצֵאתָ מֵאֶרֶץ מִצְרַיִם בְּכֹחַ גָּדוֹל וּבְיָד חֲזָקָה

wai'hhal mo'sheh et pe'ney YHWH e'lo'haw wai'yo'mer la'mah YHWH ye'hhe'reh ap'kha be'a'me'kha a'sher ho'tsey'ta mey'e'rets mits'ra'yim be'kho'ahh ga'dol uv'yad hha'za'qah

and~he~will~much~<u>TWIST</u> "Mosheh ^{PLUCKED-OUT}" AT FACE~s "Yhwh ^{he~will~<u>BE</u>}" "Elohiym ^{POWER~s}~him and~he~will~<u>SAY</u> to~WHAT "Yhwh ^{he~will~<u>BE</u>}" he~will~<u>FLARE-UP</u> NOSE~you(ms) in~PEOPLE~you(ms) WHICH you(ms)~did~make~<u>GO-OUT</u> from~LAND "Mits'rayim ^{STRAIT~s2}" in~STRENGTH GREAT and~in~HAND FORCEFUL□

and "Mosheh ^{Plucked out}" twisted§ {the} face {of} "Yhwh ^{He is}" his "Elohiym ^{Powers}", and he said, "Yhwh ^{He is}", <why> is your nose flared up** (with) your people, which you made go out from {the} land {of} "Mits'rayim ^{Two straits}", (with) great strength and (with) {a} forceful hand?□

32:12 לָמָה יֹאמְרוּ מִצְרַיִם לֵאמֹר בְּרָעָה הוֹצִיאָם לַהֲרֹג אֹתָם בֶּהָרִים וּלְכַלֹּתָם מֵעַל פְּנֵי הָאֲדָמָה שׁוּב מֵחֲרוֹן אַפֶּךָ וְהִנָּחֵם עַל הָרָעָה לְעַמֶּךָ

la'mah yom'ru mits'ra'yim ley'mor be'ra'ah ho'tsi'am la'ha'rog o'tam be'ha'rim ul'kha'lo'tam mey'al pe'ney ha'a'da'mah shuv mey'hha'ron a'pe'kha we'hi'na'hheym al ha'ra'ah le'a'me'kha

to~WHAT they(m)~will~<u>SAY</u> "Mits'rayim ^{STRAIT~s2}" to~>~<u>SAY</u> in~DYSFUNCTIONAL he~did~make~<u>GO-OUT</u>~them(m) to~>~<u>KILL</u> AT~

<why> will "Mits'rayim ^{Two straits}" say say{ing}, in dysfunction he made them go out to kill them in {the} hills and to finish them from

---

* Referring to the "people," a masculine singular word in Hebrew.
† The "flaring of the nose" is an idiom for a fierce anger.
‡ The context implies that the word "finish" means to "destroy."
§ The root of the Hebrew word ויחל may be חול (to twist), חלל (to pierce) or חלה (to be sick).

** The "flaring of the nose" is an idiom for a fierce anger.

Mechanical Translation Codes

<u>WORD</u> – Verb	WORD – Noun	Word – Name	word – Pre/Suff	*word* – Conj.

them(m) in~HILL~s and~to~>~*much*~<u>FINISH</u>~ them(m) from~UPON FACE~s the~GROUND *!(ms)*~<u>TURN-BACK</u> from~BURNING-WRATH NOSE~you(ms) and~*!(ms)*~be~<u>COMFORT</u> UPON the~<u>DYSFUNCTIONAL</u> to~PEOPLE~you(ms)□

upon {the} face {of} the ground*? turn back from {the} burning wrath {of} your nose, and [repent] (concerning) the dysfunction (for) your people,□

32:13 זְכֹר לְאַבְרָהָם לְיִצְחָק וּלְיִשְׂרָאֵל עֲבָדֶיךָ אֲשֶׁר נִשְׁבַּעְתָּ לָהֶם בָּךְ וַתְּדַבֵּר אֲלֵהֶם אַרְבֶּה אֶת זַרְעֲכֶם כְּכוֹכְבֵי הַשָּׁמָיִם וְכָל הָאָרֶץ הַזֹּאת אֲשֶׁר אָמַרְתִּי אֶתֵּן לְזַרְעֲכֶם וְנָחֲלוּ לְעֹלָם

ze'khor le'av'raham le'yits'hhaq ul'yis'ra'eyl a'va'dey'kha a'sher nish'ba'ta la'hem bakh wat'da'beyr a'ley'hem ar'beh et zar'a'khem ke'khokh'vey ha'sha'ma'yim we'khol ha'a'rets ha'zot a'sher a'mar'ti e'teyn le'zar'a'khem we'na'hha'lu le'o'lam

!(ms)~<u>REMEMBER</u> to~"Avraham ^{FATHER~+~LIFTED}" to~"Yits'hhaq ^{he~will~LAUGH}" and~to~ "Yisra'el ^{he~will~TURN-ASIDE~+~MIGHTY-ONE}" SERVANT~s~you(ms) WHICH you(ms)~did~be~<u>SWEAR</u> to~them(m) in~you(ms) and~ you(ms)~will~*much*~<u>SPEAK</u> TO~them(m) *I*~will~make~<u>INCREASE</u> AT SEED~you(mp) like~ STAR~s the~SKY~s2 and~ALL the~LAND the~ THIS WHICH *I*~did~<u>SAY</u> *I*~will~<u>GIVE</u> to~SEED~you(mp) and~*they*~did~<u>INHERIT</u> to~ DISTANT□

remember "Avraham ^{Father lifted}", "Yits'hhaq ^{He laughs}" and "Yisra'el ^{He turns El aside}" your servants, which you swore to them (by) your{self}, and you spoke to them, I will make your seed increase like {the} stars {of} the skies, and all this land, which I said I will give to your seed and they will inherit {it} to {a} distant {time},□

32:14 וַיִּנָּחֶם יְהוָה עַל הָרָעָה אֲשֶׁר דִּבֶּר לַעֲשׂוֹת לְעַמּוֹ

wai'yi'na'hhem YHWH al ha'ra'ah a'sher di'ber la'a'shot le'a'mo

and~*he*~will~be~<u>COMFORT</u> "Yhwh ^{he~will~BE}" UPON the~<u>DYSFUNCTIONAL</u> WHICH *he*~did~ *much*~<u>SPEAK</u> to~>~<u>DO</u> to~PEOPLE~him□

and "Yhwh ^{He is}" [repented] upon the dysfunction, which he spoke to do to his people,□

32:15 וַיִּפֶן וַיֵּרֶד מֹשֶׁה מִן הָהָר וּשְׁנֵי לֻחֹת הָעֵדֻת בְּיָדוֹ לֻחֹת כְּתֻבִים מִשְּׁנֵי עֶבְרֵיהֶם מִזֶּה וּמִזֶּה הֵם כְּתֻבִים

wai'yi'phen wai'yey'red mo'sheh min ha'har ush'ney lu'hhot ha'ey'dut be'ya'do lu'hhot ke'tu'vim mish'ney ev'rey'hem mi'zeh u'mi'zeh heym ke'tu'vim

and~*he*~will~<u>TURN</u> and~*he*~will~<u>GO-DOWN</u> "Mosheh ^{PLUCKED-OUT}" FROM the~HILL and~ TWO SLAB~s the~<u>EVIDENCE</u> in~HAND~him SLAB~s <u>WRITE</u>~*ed(mp)* from~TWO OTHER-SIDE~them(m) from~THIS and~from~THIS THEY(m) <u>WRITE</u>~*ed(mp)*□

and "Mosheh ^{Plucked out}" turned, and he went down from the hill, and {the} two slabs {of} the evidence {were} in his hand, {the} slabs written (on) their two sides, (on) this {side} and (on) (that) {side} they {were} written,□

---

* The phrase "to finish them from upon the face of the ground" means "to remove them from the land."

Revised Mechanical Translation Codes

(..) Alt Trans/App A   <..> Comp Phrase/App B   [..] Verb Form/App C   \../ Plural Form/App D
:..: Int Inf Abs |..| Past Perf Verb   {...} Added Word

~ 241 ~

32:16 וְהַלֻּחֹת מַעֲשֵׂה אֱלֹהִים הֵמָּה וְהַמִּכְתָּב מִכְתַּב אֱלֹהִים הוּא חָרוּת עַל הַלֻּחֹת

we'ha'lu'hhot ma'a'seyh e'lo'him hey'mah we'ha'mikh'tav mikh'tav e'lo'him hu hha'rut al ha'lu'hhot

and~the~SLAB~s WORK "Elohiym ᴾᴼᵂᴱᴿ~s" THEY(m) and~the~THING-WRITTEN THING-WRITTEN "Elohiym ᴾᴼᵂᴱᴿ~s" HE <u>ENGRAVE</u>~ed(ms) UPON the~SLAB~s□

and the slabs, they {are the} work {of} "Elohiym ᴾᵒʷᵉʳˢ", and the thing written {was a} thing written {of} "Elohiym ᴾᵒʷᵉʳˢ", he engraved upon the slabs,□

32:17 וַיִּשְׁמַע יְהוֹשֻׁעַ אֶת קוֹל הָעָם בְּרֵעֹה וַיֹּאמֶר אֶל מֹשֶׁה קוֹל מִלְחָמָה בַּמַּחֲנֶה

wai'yish'ma ye'ho'shu'a et qol ha'am be'rey'oh wai'yo'mer el mo'sheh qol mil'hha'mah ba'ma'hha'neh

and~he~will~<u>HEAR</u> "Yehoshu'a ᴱˣᴵˢᵀᴵᴺᴳ~+~ʰᵉ~ʷⁱˡˡ~<u>ᴿᴱˢᶜᵁᴱ</u>" AT VOICE the~PEOPLE in~LOUD-NOISE and~he~will~<u>SAY</u> TO "Mosheh ᴾᴸᵁᶜᴷᴱᴰ-ᴼᵁᵀ" VOICE BATTLE in~the~CAMPSITE□

and "Yehoshu'a ʸᵃʰ ʷⁱˡˡ ʳᵉˢᶜᵘᵉ" heard {the} voice {of} the people (with) {a} loud noise, and he said to "Mosheh ᴾˡᵘᶜᵏᵉᵈ ᵒᵘᵗ", {it is the} voice {of} battle in the campsite,□

32:18 וַיֹּאמֶר אֵין קוֹל עֲנוֹת גְּבוּרָה וְאֵין קוֹל עֲנוֹת חֲלוּשָׁה קוֹל עֲנוֹת אָנֹכִי שֹׁמֵעַ

wai'yo'mer eyn qol a'not ge'vu'rah we'eyn qol a'not hha'lu'shah qol a'not a'no'khi sho'mey'a

and~he~will~<u>SAY</u> WITHOUT VOICE >~<u>ANSWER</u> BRAVERY and~WITHOUT VOICE >~<u>ANSWER</u> DEFEAT VOICE >~<u>ANSWER</u> I <u>HEAR</u>~ing/er(ms)□

and he said, {it is} not {a} voice {in} answer {of} bravery, {it is} not {a} voice {in} answer {of} defeat, {it is a} voice {in} answer {of wine}* {that} I {am} hearing,□

32:19 וַיְהִי כַּאֲשֶׁר קָרַב אֶל הַמַּחֲנֶה וַיַּרְא אֶת הָעֵגֶל וּמְחֹלֹת וַיִּחַר אַף מֹשֶׁה וַיַּשְׁלֵךְ מִיָּדָו אֶת הַלֻּחֹת וַיְשַׁבֵּר אֹתָם תַּחַת הָהָר

wai'hi ka'a'sheyr qa'rav el ha'ma'hha'neh wai'yar et ha'ey'gel um'hho'lot wai'yi'hhar aph mo'sheh wai'yash'leykh mi'ya'daw et ha'lu'hhot wai'sha'beyr o'tam ta'hhat ha'har

and~he~will~<u>EXIST</u> like~WHICH he~did~<u>COME-NEAR</u> TO the~CAMPSITE and~he~will~<u>SEE</u> AT the~BULLOCK and~DANCE~s and~he~will~<u>FLARE-UP</u> NOSE "Mosheh ᴾᴸᵁᶜᴷᴱᴰ-ᴼᵁᵀ" and~he~will~make~<u>THROW-OUT</u> from~HAND~him AT the~SLAB~s and~he~will~<u>CRACK</u> AT~them(m) UNDER the~HILL□

and (it) (came to pass) <just as> he came near to the campsite, and he saw the bullock and {the} dances, and {the} nose {of} "Mosheh ᴾˡᵘᶜᵏᵉᵈ ᵒᵘᵗ" flared up†, and he threw out the slabs from his hand, and he cracked them under‡ the hill,□

---

* The text appears to be missing a word, possibly "rejoicing, but the Septuagint has "wine."
† The "flaring of the nose" is an idiom for a fierce anger.
‡ "Under the hill" meaning "at the bottom of the hill."

Mechanical Translation Codes

| <u>WORD</u> – Verb | WORD – Noun | Word – Name | word – Pre/Suff | *word* – Conj. |

32:20 וַיִּקַּח אֶת הָעֵגֶל אֲשֶׁר עָשׂוּ וַיִּשְׂרֹף בָּאֵשׁ וַיִּטְחַן עַד אֲשֶׁר דָּק וַיִּזֶר עַל פְּנֵי הַמַּיִם וַיַּשְׁקְ אֶת בְּנֵי יִשְׂרָאֵל

wai'yi'qahh et ha'ey'gel a'sher a'su wai'yish'roph ba'eysh wai'yit'hhan ad a'sher daq wai'yi'zer al pe'ney ha'ma'yim wai'ya'sheq et be'ney yis'ra'eyl

and~he~will~<u>TAKE</u> AT the~BULLOCK WHICH *they~did~*<u>DO</u> and~he~will~<u>CREMATE</u> in~ the~FIRE and~*he~will~*<u>GRIND</u> UNTIL WHICH *he~did~*<u>BEAT-IN-PIECES</u> and~*he~will~* <u>DISPERSE</u> UPON FACE~s the~WATER~s2 and~*he~will~make~*<u>DRINK</u> AT SON~s "Yisra'el *he~will~*<u>TURN-ASIDE</u>~+~MIGHTY-ONE" □

and he took the bullock which they (made) and he cremated {it} in the fire, and he ground {it} until he was beat in pieces, and he dispersed {it} upon {the} face {of} the waters, and he made {the} sons {of} "Yisra'el He turns El aside" drink {it},□

32:21 וַיֹּאמֶר מֹשֶׁה אֶל אַהֲרֹן מֶה עָשָׂה לְךָ הָעָם הַזֶּה כִּי הֵבֵאתָ עָלָיו חֲטָאָה גְדֹלָה

wai'yo'mer mo'sheh el a'ha'ron meh a'sah le'kha ha'am ha'zeh ki hey'vey'ta a'law hha'ta'ah ge'do'lah

and~he~will~<u>SAY</u> "Mosheh PLUCKED-OUT" TO "Aharon LIGHT-BRINGER" WHAT *he~did~*<u>DO</u> to~ you(ms) the~PEOPLE the~THIS GIVEN-THAT *you(ms)~did~make~*<u>COME</u> UPON~him ERROR GREAT□

and "Mosheh Plucked out" said to "Aharon Light bringer", what did this people do to you? given that you brought upon him* {a} great error,□

32:22 וַיֹּאמֶר אַהֲרֹן אַל יִחַר אַף אֲדֹנִי אַתָּה יָדַעְתָּ אֶת הָעָם כִּי בְרָע הוּא

wai'yo'mer a'ha'ron al yi'hhar aph a'do'ni a'tah ya'da'ta et ha'am ki ve'ra hu

and~he~will~<u>SAY</u> "Aharon LIGHT-BRINGER" DO-NOT *he~will~*<u>FLARE-UP</u> NOSE LORD~me YOU(ms) *you(ms)~did~*<u>KNOW</u> AT the~ PEOPLE GIVEN-THAT in~DYSFUNCTIONAL HE□

and "Aharon Light bringer" said, do not {let the} nose {of} my lord flare up†, you, you know the people given that he‡ {is} in dysfunction,□

32:23 וַיֹּאמְרוּ לִי עֲשֵׂה לָנוּ אֱלֹהִים אֲשֶׁר יֵלְכוּ לְפָנֵינוּ כִּי זֶה מֹשֶׁה הָאִישׁ אֲשֶׁר הֶעֱלָנוּ מֵאֶרֶץ מִצְרַיִם לֹא יָדַעְנוּ מֶה הָיָה לוֹ

wai'yom'ru li a'seyh la'nu e'lo'him a'sher yeyl'khu le'pha'ney'nu ki zeh mo'sheh ha'ish a'sher he'e'la'nu mey'e'rets mits'ra'yim lo ya'dey'nu mch hai'yah lo

and~*they(m)~will~*<u>SAY</u> to~me !(ms)~<u>DO</u> to~ us "Elohiym POWER~s" WHICH *they(m)~will~* <u>WALK</u> to~FACE~s~us GIVEN-THAT THIS "Mosheh PLUCKED-OUT" the~MAN WHICH *he~*

and they said to me, (make) (for) us "Elohiym Powers"§ which will walk <in front of> us, given that this "Mosheh Plucked out", the man which made us go up from {the} land {of}

---

* Referring to the "people," a masculine singular word in Hebrew.
† The "flaring of the nose" is an idiom for a fierce anger.
‡ Referring to the "people," a masculine singular word in Hebrew.
§ See Exodus 32:1

Revised Mechanical Translation Codes

(..) Alt Trans/App A	<..> Comp Phrase/App B	[..] Verb Form/App C	\../ Plural Form/App D
:..: Int Inf Abs	|..| Past Perf Verb	{...} Added Word	

did~make~<u>GO-UP</u>~us from~LAND
"Mits'rayim ^{STRAIT~s2}" NOT we~did~<u>KNOW</u>
WHAT he~did~<u>EXIST</u> to~him□

"Mits'rayim ^{Two straits}", we do not know what
(came to pass) to him,□

32:24 נֹאמַר לָהֶם לְמִי זָהָב הִתְפָּרָקוּ וַיִּתְּנוּ לִי וָאַשְׁלִכֵהוּ בָאֵשׁ וַיֵּצֵא הָעֵגֶל הַזֶּה

wa'o'mar la'hem le'khol za'hav hit'pa'ra'qu wai'yit'nu li wa'ash'li'khey'hu va'eysh
wai'yey'tsey ha'ey'gel ha'zeh

and~I~will~<u>SAY</u> to~them(m) to~WHO GOLD
!(mp)~ self~<u>TEAR-OFF</u> and~they(m)~will~
<u>GIVE</u> to~me and~I~will~make~<u>SEND</u>~him in~
the~FIRE and~he~will~<u>GO-OUT</u> the~
BULLOCK the~THIS□

and I said to them, who{ever has} gold, tear
{it} off {of your}self, and they gave {it} to me,
and I sent him in the fire, and this bullock
went out,□

32:25 וַיַּרְא מֹשֶׁה אֶת הָעָם כִּי פָרֻעַ הוּא כִּי פְרָעֹה אַהֲרֹן לְשִׁמְצָה בְּקָמֵיהֶם

wai'yar mo'sheh et ha'am ki pha'ru'a hu ki phe'ra'oh a'ha'ron le'shim'tsah
be'qa'mey'hem

and~he~will~<u>SEE</u> "Mosheh ^{PLUCKED-OUT}" AT
the~PEOPLE GIVEN-THAT <u>LOOSE</u>~ed(ms) HE
GIVEN-THAT he~did~<u>LOOSE</u>~him "Aharon
^{LIGHT-BRINGER}" to~<u>WHISPER</u> in~<u>RISE</u>~
ing/er(mp)~them(m)□

and "Mosheh ^{Plucked out}" saw the people, given
that he* {is} loosened†, given that "Aharon
^{Light bringer}" loosened him to whisper in their
risers‡,□

32:26 וַיַּעֲמֹד מֹשֶׁה בְּשַׁעַר הַמַּחֲנֶה וַיֹּאמֶר מִי לַיהוָה אֵלַי וַיֵּאָסְפוּ אֵלָיו כָּל בְּנֵי לֵוִי

wai'ya'a'mod mo'sheh be'sha'ar ha'ma'hha'neh wai'yo'mer mi la'YHWH ey'lai
wai'yey'as'phu ey'law kol be'ney ley'wi

and~he~will~<u>STAND</u> "Mosheh ^{PLUCKED-OUT}" in~
GATE the~CAMPSITE and~he~will~<u>SAY</u> WHO
to~"Yhwh ^{he~will~<u>BE</u>}" TO~me and~they(m)~
will~<u>GATHER</u> TO~him ALL SON~s "Lewi
^{JOINING~me}"□

and "Mosheh ^{Plucked out}" stood in {the} gate {of}
the campsite, and he said, who {is} (for)
"Yhwh ^{He is}"? {come} to me, and all {the} sons
{of} "Lewi ^{My joining}" gathered to him,□

32:27 וַיֹּאמֶר לָהֶם כֹּה אָמַר יְהוָה אֱלֹהֵי יִשְׂרָאֵל שִׂימוּ אִישׁ חַרְבּוֹ עַל יְרֵכוֹ עִבְרוּ וָשׁוּבוּ מִשַּׁעַר לָשַׁעַר בַּמַּחֲנֶה וְהִרְגוּ אִישׁ אֶת אָחִיו וְאִישׁ אֶת רֵעֵהוּ וְאִישׁ אֶת קְרֹבוֹ

wai'yo'mer la'hem koh a'mar YHWH e'lo'hey yis'ra'eyl si'mu ish hhar'bo al ye'rey'kho
iv'ru wa'shu'vu mi'sha'ar la'sha'ar ba'ma'hha'neh we'hir'gu ish et a'hhiw we'ish et
rey'ey'hu we'ish et qe'ro'vo

and~he~will~<u>SAY</u> to~them(m) IN-THIS-WAY

and he said to them, in this way "Yhwh ^{He is}"

---

* Referring to the "people," a masculine singular word in Hebrew.
† Probably referring to the peoples loosening of their clothes and, or, inhibitions.
‡ The meaning of the phrase "to whisper in their risers" is uncertain.

Mechanical Translation Codes

<u>WORD</u> – Verb	WORD – Noun	Word – Name	word – Pre/Suff	*word* – Conj.

he~did~SAY "Yhwh ^{he~will~BE} "Elohiym
POWER~s" "Yisra'el ^{he~will~TURN-ASIDE~+~MIGHTY-ONE},"
!(mp)~PLACE MAN SWORD~him UPON
MIDSECTION~him !(mp)~CROSS-OVER and~
!(mp)~TURN-BACK from~GATE to~GATE in~
the~CAMPSITE and~!(mp)~KILL MAN AT
BROTHER~him and~MAN AT COMPANION~
him and~MAN AT NEAR~him□

{the} "Elohiym ^{Powers}" {of} "Yisra'el ^{He turns El aside},"
said, (each) {will} place his sword upon his
midsection*, cross over and turn back from
{one} gate to {the other} gate in the campsite,
and kill (each) his brother, and (each) his
companion, and (each) his near {one},□

32:28 וַיַּעֲשׂוּ בְנֵי לֵוִי כִּדְבַר מֹשֶׁה וַיִּפֹּל מִן הָעָם בַּיּוֹם הַהוּא כִּשְׁלֹשֶׁת אַלְפֵי אִישׁ

wai'ya'a'su ve'ney ley'wi kid'var mo'sheh wai'yi'pol min ha'am ba'yom ha'hu kish'lo'shet
al'phey ish

and~they(m)~will~DO SON~s "Lewi ^{JOINING~me}" like~WORD "Mosheh ^{PLUCKED-OUT}" and~he~
will~FALL FROM the~PEOPLE in~the~DAY
the~HE like~THREE THOUSAND~s MAN□

and {the} sons {of} "Lewi ^{My joining}" did {just} like
{the} word {of} "Mosheh ^{Plucked out}", and (about)
three thousand men fell from the people in
(that) day,□

32:29 וַיֹּאמֶר מֹשֶׁה מִלְאוּ יֶדְכֶם הַיּוֹם לַיהוָה כִּי אִישׁ בִּבְנוֹ וּבְאָחִיו וְלָתֵת עֲלֵיכֶם הַיּוֹם בְּרָכָה

wai'yo'mer mo'sheh mil'u yed'khem hai'yom la'YHWH ki ish biv'no uv'a'hhiw we'la'teyt
a'ley'khem hai'yom be'ra'kha

and~he~will~SAY "Mosheh ^{PLUCKED-OUT}"
!(mp)~FILL HAND~you(mp) the~DAY to~
"Yhwh ^{he~will~BE}" GIVEN-THAT MAN in~SON~
him and~in~BROTHER~him and~to~>~GIVE
UPON~you(mp) the~DAY PRESENT□

and "Mosheh ^{Plucked out}" said, fill your hand†
<today> (for) "Yhwh ^{He is}",□

32:30 וַיְהִי מִמָּחֳרָת וַיֹּאמֶר מֹשֶׁה אֶל הָעָם אַתֶּם חֲטָאתֶם חֲטָאָה גְדֹלָה וְעַתָּה אֶעֱלֶה אֶל יְהוָה אוּלַי אֲכַפְּרָה בְּעַד חַטַּאתְכֶם

wai'hi mi'ma'hha'rat wai'yo'mer mo'sheh el ha'am a'tem hha'ta'tem hha'ta'ah ge'do'lah
we'a'tah e'e'leh el YHWH u'lai a'khap'rah be'ad hha'ta'te'khem

and~he~will~EXIST from~MORROW and~he~
will~SAY "Mosheh ^{PLUCKED-OUT}" TO the~
PEOPLE YOU(mp) you(mp)~did~ERR ERROR
GREAT and~NOW I~will~GO-UP TO "Yhwh
^{he~will~BE}" POSSIBLY I~will~much~COVER~^
ROUND-ABOUT ERROR~you(mp)□

and (it) (came to pass) <the next day>, and
"Mosheh ^{Plucked out}" said to the people, you,
you erred {a} great error, and now I will go up
to "Yhwh ^{He is}", possibly I will cover {it}
(concerning) your error,□

---

* "Place his sword upon his midsection" means to "strap a sword onto the waist."
† to "fill the hand" is an idiom of uncertain meaning, but the same phrase is used in Akkadian
to mean the placing of a scepter (either literally or figuratively) in the hand of one being
installed in a high office.

Revised Mechanical Translation Codes

(..) Alt Trans/App A	<..> Comp Phrase/App B	[..] Verb Form/App C	\../ Plural Form/App D
:..: Int Inf Abs	|..| Past Perf Verb	{...} Added Word	

32:31 וַיָּשָׁב מֹשֶׁה אֶל יְהוָה וַיֹּאמַר אָנָּא חָטָא הָעָם הַזֶּה חֲטָאָה גְדֹלָה וַיַּעֲשׂוּ לָהֶם אֱלֹהֵי זָהָב

wai'ya'shav mo'sheh el YHWH wai'yo'mar a'nah hha'ta ha'am ha'zeh hha'ta'ah ge'do'lah wai'ya'a'su la'hem e'lo'hey za'hav

and~he~will~TURN-BACK "Mosheh PLUCKED-OUT" TO "Yhwh he~will~BE" and~he~will~SAY PLEASE he~did~ERR the~PEOPLE the~THIS ERROR GREAT and~they(m)~will~DO to~ them(m) "Elohiym POWER~s" GOLD□

and "Mosheh Plucked out" turned back to "Yhwh He is" and he said, please, this people erred {a} great error, and they (made) (for) them{selves} "Elohiym Powers" {of} gold,□

32:32 וְעַתָּה אִם תִּשָּׂא חַטָּאתָם וְאִם אַיִן מְחֵנִי נָא מִסִּפְרְךָ אֲשֶׁר כָּתָבְתָּ

we'a'tah im ti'sa hha'ta'tam we'im a'yin me'hhey'ni na mi'siph're'kha a'sher ka'tav'ta

and~NOW IF you(ms)~will~LIFT-UP ERROR~ them(m) and~IF WITHOUT !(ms)~WIPE-AWAY~me PLEASE from~SCROLL~you(ms) WHICH you(ms)~did~WRITE□

and now, if you will lift up their error, (but) if (not), please wipe me away from your scroll which you wrote,□

32:33 וַיֹּאמֶר יְהוָה אֶל מֹשֶׁה מִי אֲשֶׁר חָטָא לִי אֶמְחֶנּוּ מִסִּפְרִי

wai'yo'mer YHWH el mo'sheh mi a'sher hha'ta li em'hhe'nu mi'siph'ri

and~he~will~SAY "Yhwh he~will~BE" TO "Mosheh PLUCKED-OUT" WHO WHICH he~did~ ERR to~me I~will~WIPE-AWAY~him from~ SCROLL~me□

and "Yhwh He is" said to "Mosheh Plucked out", who {is it} (that) erred to me? I will wipe him away from my scroll,□

32:34 וְעַתָּה לֵךְ נְחֵה אֶת הָעָם אֶל אֲשֶׁר דִּבַּרְתִּי לָךְ הִנֵּה מַלְאָכִי יֵלֵךְ לְפָנֶיךָ וּבְיוֹם פָּקְדִי וּפָקַדְתִּי עֲלֵהֶם חַטָּאתָם

we'a'tah leykh ne'hheyh et ha'am el a'sher di'bar'ti lakh hin'neyh mal'a'khi yey'leykh le'pha'ney'kha uv'yom paq'di u'pha'qad'ti a'ley'hem hha'ta'tam

and~NOW !(ms)~WALK !(ms)~GUIDE AT the~PEOPLE TO WHICH I~did~much~SPEAK to~you(fs) LOOK MESSENGER~me he~will~ WALK to~FACE~s~you(ms) and~in~DAY >~REGISTER~me and~I~did~REGISTER UPON~them(m) ERROR~them(m)□

and now, walk, guide the people to (where) I spoke to you, look, my messenger will walk <in front of> you, and in {the} day {of} my register{ing}, (then) I will register upon them their error,□

32:35 וַיִּגֹּף יְהוָה אֶת הָעָם עַל אֲשֶׁר עָשׂוּ אֶת הָעֵגֶל אֲשֶׁר עָשָׂה אַהֲרֹן

wai'yi'goph YHWH et ha'am al a'sher a'su et ha'ey'gel a'sher a'sah a'ha'ron

and~he~will~SMITE "Yhwh he~will~BE" AT the~ PEOPLE UPON WHICH they~did~DO AT the~ BULLOCK WHICH he~did~DO "Aharon LIGHT-BRINGER"□

and "Yhwh He is" smote the people (according to) (who) (made) the bullock, which "Aharon Light bringer" (made),□

Mechanical Translation Codes

UNDERLINE_WORD – Verb   WORD – Noun   Word – Name   word – Pre/Suff   *word* – Conj.

~ 246 ~

Chapter 33

33:1

וַיְדַבֵּר יְהוָה אֶל מֹשֶׁה לֵךְ עֲלֵה מִזֶּה אַתָּה וְהָעָם אֲשֶׁר הֶעֱלִיתָ מֵאֶרֶץ
מִצְרָיִם אֶל הָאָרֶץ אֲשֶׁר נִשְׁבַּעְתִּי לְאַבְרָהָם לְיִצְחָק וּלְיַעֲקֹב לֵאמֹר
לְזַרְעֲךָ אֶתְּנֶנָּה

wai'da'beyr YHWH el mo'sheh leykh a'leyh mi'zeh a'tah we'ha'am a'sher he'e'li'ta
mey'e'rets mits'ra'yim el ha'a'rets a'sher nish'ba'ti le'av'ra'ham le'yits'hhaq ul'ya'a'qov
ley'mor le'zar'a'kha et'ne'nah

and~he~will~much~<u>SPEAK</u> "Yhwh ^{he~will~<u>BE</u>}"
TO "Mosheh ^{PLUCKED-OUT}" !(ms)~<u>WALK</u> !(ms)~
<u>GO-UP</u> from~THIS YOU(ms) and~the~
PEOPLE WHICH *you(ms)~did~make*~<u>GO-UP</u>
from~LAND "Mits'rayim ^{STRAIT~s2}" TO the~
LAND WHICH *I~did~be*~<u>SWEAR</u> to~"Avraham
^{FATHER~+~LIFTED}" to~"Yits'hhaq ^{he~will~<u>LAUGH</u>}" and~
to~"Ya'aqov ^{he~will~<u>RESTRAIN</u>}" to~>~<u>SAY</u> to~
SEED~you(ms) *I~will*~<u>GIVE</u>~her□

and "Yhwh ^{He is}" spoke to "Mosheh ^{Plucked out}",
walk, go up from this {place}, you and the
people which you made go up from {the} land
{of} "Mits'rayim ^{Two straits}", which I swore to
"Avraham ^{Father lifted}" to "Yits'hhaq ^{He laughs}" and
to "Ya'aqov ^{He restrains}" say{ing}, I will give her*
to your seed,□

33:2

וְשָׁלַחְתִּי לְפָנֶיךָ מַלְאָךְ וְגֵרַשְׁתִּי אֶת הַכְּנַעֲנִי הָאֱמֹרִי וְהַחִתִּי וְהַפְּרִזִּי
הַחִוִּי וְהַיְבוּסִי

we'sha'lahh'ti le'pha'ney'kha mal'akh we'gey'rash'ti et ha'ke'na'a'ni ha'e'mo'ri we'ha'hhi'ti
we'ha'pe'ri'zi ha'hhi'wi we'hai'vu'si

and~*I~did*~<u>SEND</u> to~FACE~s~you(ms)
MESSENGER and~*I~did*~much~<u>CAST-OUT</u> AT
the~"Kena'an ^{LOWERED}"~of the~"Emor ^{SAYER}"~
of and~the~"Hhet ^{TREMBLING-IN-FEAR}"~of and~
the~"Perez ^{PEASANT}"~of the~"Hhiw ^{TOWN}"~of
and~the~"Yevus ^{he~will~<u>TRAMPLE-DOWN</u>}"~of□

and I will send {a} messenger <in front of>
you, and I will cast out the {one} of "Kena'an
^{Lowered}", the {one} of "Emor ^{Sayer}" and the {one}
of "Hhet ^{Trembling in fear}" and the {one} of "Perez
^{Peasant}", the {one} of "Hhiw ^{Town}" and the {one}
of "Yevus ^{He will trample down}",□

33:3

אֶל אֶרֶץ זָבַת חָלָב וּדְבָשׁ כִּי לֹא אֶעֱלֶה בְּקִרְבְּךָ כִּי עַם קְשֵׁה עֹרֶף אַתָּה
פֶּן אֲכֶלְךָ בַּדָּרֶךְ

el e'rets za'vat hha'lav ud'vash ki lo e'e'leh be'qir'be'kha ki am qe'sheyh o'reph a'tah
pen a'khel'kha ba'da'rekh

TO LAND <u>ISSUE</u>~*ing/er(fs)* FAT and~HONEY
GIVEN-THAT NOT *I~will*~<u>GO-UP</u> in~WITHIN~
you(ms) GIVEN-THAT PEOPLE HARD NECK
YOU(ms) OTHERWISE *I~will*~much~<u>FINISH</u>~

to {a} land issuing fat† and honey‡, given that
I will not go up <among> you, given that you
{are a} hard neck{ed} people, otherwise, I will

---

* Referring to the "land," a feminine word in Hebrew.
† Or "milk."
‡ The Hebrew word בש means a "sticky mass" and can also mean "dates" from the palm tree.

Revised Mechanical Translation Codes

(..) Alt Trans/App A   <..> Comp Phrase/App B   [..] Verb Form/App C   \\../ Plural Form/App D
:..: Int Inf Abs |..| Past Perf Verb   {...} Added Word

~ 247 ~

you(ms) in~the~ROAD□   finish* you in the road,□

33:4 וַיִּשְׁמַע הָעָם אֶת הַדָּבָר הָרָע הַזֶּה וַיִּתְאַבָּלוּ וְלֹא שָׁתוּ אִישׁ עֶדְיוֹ עָלָיו

wai'yish'ma ha'am et ha'da'var ha'ra ha'zeh wai'yit'a'ba'lu we'lo sha'tu ish ed'yo a'law

and~*he~will*~<u>HEAR</u> the~PEOPLE AT the~ WORD the~DYSFUNCTIONAL the~THIS and~ *they(m)~will~* self~<u>MOURN</u> and~NOT *they~ did~*<u>SET-DOWN</u> MAN TRAPPINGS~him UPON~him□

and the people heard this dysfunctional word, and they mourned, and (each) did not set down† his trappings upon him,□

33:5 וַיֹּאמֶר יְהוָה אֶל מֹשֶׁה אֱמֹר אֶל בְּנֵי יִשְׂרָאֵל אַתֶּם עַם קְשֵׁה עֹרֶף רֶגַע אֶחָד אֶעֱלֶה בְקִרְבְּךָ וְכִלִּיתִיךָ וְעַתָּה הוֹרֵד עֶדְיְךָ מֵעָלֶיךָ וְאֵדְעָה מָה אֶעֱשֶׂה לָּךְ

wai'yo'mer YHWH el mo'sheh e'mor el be'ney yis'ra'eyl a'tem am qe'sheyh o'reph re'ga e'hhad e'e'leh ve'qir'be'kha we'khi'li'to'kha we'a'tah ho'reyd ed'ye'kha mey'a'ley'kha we'eyd'ah mah e'e'seh lakh

and~*he~will*~<u>SAY</u> "Yhwh *he~will~*<u>BE</u>" TO "Mosheh ^{PLUCKED-OUT}" *!(ms)~*<u>SAY</u> TO SON~s "Yisra'el *he~will~*<u>TURN-ASIDE</u>~+~<u>MIGHTY-ONE</u>" YOU(mp) PEOPLE HARD NECK MOMENT UNIT *I~will~* <u>GO-UP</u> in~WITHIN~you(ms) and~*I~will~* much~<u>FINISH</u>~you(ms) and~NOW *!(ms)~* make~<u>GO-DOWN</u> TRAPPINGS~you(ms) from~UPON~you(ms) and~*I~will~*<u>KNOW</u>~^ WHAT *I~will~*<u>DO</u> to~you(fs)□

and "Yhwh ^{He is}" said to "Mosheh ^{Plucked out}", say to {the} sons {of} "Yisra'el ^{He turns El aside}", you {are a} hard neck{ed} people, I will go up <among> you (one) moment, and I will finish‡ you, and now, make your trappings go down§ from upon you, and I will know what I will do to you,□

33:6 וַיִּתְנַצְּלוּ בְנֵי יִשְׂרָאֵל אֶת עֶדְיָם מֵהַר חוֹרֵב

wai'yit'nats'lu ve'ney yis'ra'eyl et ed'yam me'har hho'reyv

and~*they(m)~will~* self~<u>DELIVER</u> SON~s "Yisra'el *he~will~*<u>TURN-ASIDE</u>~+~<u>MIGHTY-ONE</u>" AT TRAPPINGS~them(m) from~HILL "Hhorev ^{PARCHING-HEAT}"□

and {the} sons {of} "Yisra'el ^{He turns El aside}" delivered** their trappings (by) {the} hill {of} "Hhorev ^{Parching heat}",□

33:7 וּמֹשֶׁה יִקַּח אֶת הָאֹהֶל וְנָטָה לוֹ מִחוּץ לַמַּחֲנֶה הַרְחֵק מִן הַמַּחֲנֶה וְקָרָא לוֹ אֹהֶל מוֹעֵד וְהָיָה כָּל מְבַקֵּשׁ יְהוָה יֵצֵא אֶל אֹהֶל מוֹעֵד אֲשֶׁר מִחוּץ לַמַּחֲנֶה

u'mo'sheh yi'qahh et ha'o'hel we'na'tah lo mi'hhuts la'ma'hha'neh har'hheyq min ha'ma'hha'neh we'qa'ra lo o'hel mo'eyd we'hai'yah kol me'va'qeysh YHWH yey'tsey el

---

* The context implies that the word "finish" means to "destroy."
† "Set down" in this context means to "put on."
‡ The context implies that the word "finish" means to "destroy."
§ "make your trappings go down" in this context means to "take off your trappings."
** The context implies that the word "delivered" means "removed."

Mechanical Translation Codes

<u>WORD</u> – Verb	WORD – Noun	Word – Name	word – Pre/Suff	*word* – Conj.

o'hel mo'eyd a'sher mi'hhuts la'ma'hha'neh

and~"Mosheh ^{PLUCKED-OUT}" he~will~<u>TAKE</u> AT the~TENT and~he~did~<u>EXTEND</u> to~him from~<u>OUTSIDE</u> to~the~CAMPSITE >~make~ <u>BE-FAR</u> FROM the~CAMPSITE and~he~did~ <u>CALL-OUT</u> to~him TENT APPOINTED and~he~ did~<u>EXIST</u> ALL much~<u>SEARCH-OUT</u>~ ing/er(ms) "Yhwh ^{he~will~}<u>BE</u>" he~will~<u>GO-OUT</u> TO TENT APPOINTED WHICH from~<u>OUTSIDE</u> to~the~CAMPSITE□	and "Mosheh ^{Plucked out}" will take the tent and he will extend* him outside {of} the campsite, far from the campsite, and he will call out to him {at the} tent {of the} appointed {place}†, and (it) will (come to pass), {the ones} searching out "Yhwh ^{He is}" will go out to {the} tent {of the} appointed {place}, which {is} outside {of} the campsite,□

33:8 וְהָיָה כְּצֵאת מֹשֶׁה אֶל הָאֹהֶל יָקוּמוּ כָּל הָעָם וְנִצְּבוּ אִישׁ פֶּתַח אָהֳלוֹ וְהִבִּיטוּ אַחֲרֵי מֹשֶׁה עַד בֹּאוֹ הָאֹהֱלָה

we'hai'yah ke'tseyt mo'sheh el ha'o'hel ya'qu'mu kol ha'am we'nits'bu ish pe'tahh a'ha'lo we'hi'bi'tu a'hha'rey mo'sheh ad bo'o ha'o'he'lah

and~he~did~<u>EXIST</u> like~>~<u>GO-OUT</u> "Mosheh ^{PLUCKED-OUT}" TO the~TENT they(m)~will~<u>RISE</u> ALL the~PEOPLE and~they~did~be~<u>STAND-UP</u> MAN OPENING TENT~him and~they~did~ make~<u>STARE</u> AFTER "Mosheh ^{PLUCKED-OUT}" UNTIL >~<u>COME</u>~him the~TENT~unto□	and (it) will (come to pass), {when} "Mosheh ^{Plucked out}" {is} (about) {to} go out to the tent, all the people will rise, and they will stand up, (each) {at the} opening {of} his tent, and they will stare after "Mosheh ^{Plucked out}", until his com{ing} unto the tent,□

33:9 וְהָיָה כְּבֹא מֹשֶׁה הָאֹהֱלָה יֵרֵד עַמּוּד הֶעָנָן וְעָמַד פֶּתַח הָאֹהֶל וְדִבֶּר עִם מֹשֶׁה

we'hai'yah ke'vo mo'sheh ha'o'he'lah yey'reyd a'mud he'a'nan we'a'mad pe'tahh ha'o'hel we'di'ber im mo'sheh

and~he~did~<u>EXIST</u> like~>~<u>COME</u> "Mosheh ^{PLUCKED-OUT}" the~TENT~unto he~will~<u>GO-DOWN</u> PILLAR the~CLOUD and~he~did~ <u>STAND</u> OPENING the~TENT and~he~did~ much~<u>SPEAK</u> WITH "Mosheh ^{PLUCKED-OUT}"□	and (it) will (come to pass), {when} "Mosheh ^{Plucked out}" {is} (about) {to} come unto the tent, {the} pillar {of} the cloud will go down, and he‡ will stand {at the} opening {of} the tent, and he will speak with "Mosheh ^{Plucked out}",□

33:10 וְרָאָה כָל הָעָם אֶת עַמּוּד הֶעָנָן עֹמֵד פֶּתַח הָאֹהֶל וְקָם כָּל הָעָם וְהִשְׁתַּחֲווּ אִישׁ פֶּתַח אָהֳלוֹ

we'ra'ah khol ha'am et a'mud he'a'nan o'meyd pe'tahh ha'o'hel we'qam kol ha'am we'hish'ta'hha'wu ish pe'tahh a'ha'lo

and~he~did~<u>SEE</u> ALL the~PEOPLE AT PILLAR the~CLOUD <u>STAND</u>~ing/er(ms) OPENING	and all the people saw {the} pillar {of} the cloud standing {at the} opening {of} the tent,

---

* That is, stretch out, to set up.

† The phrase "and he will call out to him at the tent of the appointed place" could also be translated as "and he called him the tent of the appointed place."

‡ Referring to the "pillar," a masculine word in Hebrew.

Revised Mechanical Translation Codes

(..) Alt Trans/App A	<..> Comp Phrase/App B	[..] Verb Form/App C	\../ Plural Form/App D
:...: Int Inf Abs	|..| Past Perf Verb	{...} Added Word	

the~TENT and~*he~did*~<u>RISE</u> ALL the~PEOPLE and~*they~did*~ self~<u>BEND-DOWN</u> MAN OPENING TENT~him□

and all the people rose, and they bent {them}selves down, (each) {at the} opening {of} his tent,□

33:11

וַיְדַבֵּר יְהוָה אֶל מֹשֶׁה פָּנִים אֶל פָּנִים כַּאֲשֶׁר יְדַבֵּר אִישׁ אֶל רֵעֵהוּ וְשָׁב אֶל הַמַּחֲנֶה וּמְשָׁרְתוֹ יְהוֹשֻׁעַ בִּן נוּן נַעַר לֹא יָמִישׁ מִתּוֹךְ הָאֹהֶל

we'di'ber YHWH el mo'sheh pa'nim el pa'nim ka'a'sheyr ye'da'beyr ish el rey'ey'hu we'shav el ha'ma'hha'neh um'shar'to ye'ho'shu'a bin nun na'ar lo ya'mish mi'tokh ha'o'hel

and~*he~did~much*~<u>SPEAK</u> "Yhwh ^{he~will~BE}" TO "Mosheh ^{PLUCKED-OUT}" FACE~s TO FACE~s like~WHICH *he~will~much*~<u>SPEAK</u> MAN TO COMPANION~him and~*he~did*~<u>TURN-BACK</u> TO the~CAMPSITE and~*much*~<u>MINISTER</u>~*ing/er(ms)*~him "Yehoshu'a ^{EXISTING~+~he~will~RESCUE}" SON "Nun ^{CONTINUE}" YOUNG-MAN NOT *he~will~make*~<u>MOVE-AWAY</u> from~MIDST the~TENT□

and "Yhwh ^{He is}" spoke to "Mosheh ^{Plucked out}" face to face, <just as> {a} man will speak to his companion, and he turned back to the campsite, and his minister, "Yehoshu'a ^{Yah will rescue}", {the} son {of} "Nun ^{Continue}", {a} young man, will not move away from {the} midst {of} the tent,□

33:12

וַיֹּאמֶר מֹשֶׁה אֶל יְהוָה רְאֵה אַתָּה אֹמֵר אֵלַי הַעַל אֶת הָעָם הַזֶּה וְאַתָּה לֹא הוֹדַעְתַּנִי אֵת אֲשֶׁר תִּשְׁלַח עִמִּי וְאַתָּה אָמַרְתָּ יְדַעְתִּיךָ בְשֵׁם וְגַם מָצָאתָ חֵן בְּעֵינָי

wai'yo'mer mo'sheh el YHWH re'eyh a'tah o'meyr ey'lai ha'al et ha'am ha'zeh we'a'tah lo ho'da'ta'ni eyt a'sher tish'lahh i'mi we'a'tah a'mar'ta ye'da'ti'kha ve'sheym we'gam ma'tsa'ta hheyn be'ey'nai

and~*he~will*~<u>SAY</u> "Mosheh ^{PLUCKED-OUT}" TO "Yhwh ^{he~will~BE}" !*(ms)*~<u>SEE</u> YOU(ms) <u>SAY</u>~*ing/er(ms)* TO~me !*(ms)~make*~<u>GO-UP</u> AT the~PEOPLE the~THIS and~YOU(ms) NOT *you(ms)~did~make*~<u>KNOW</u>~me AT WHICH *you(ms)~will*~<u>SEND</u> WITH~me and~YOU(ms) *you(ms)~did*~<u>SAY</u> *I~did*~<u>KNOW</u>~*you(ms)* in~TITLE and~ALSO *you(ms)~did*~<u>FIND</u> BEAUTY in~EYE~s2~me□

and "Mosheh ^{Plucked out}" said to "Yhwh ^{He is}", see, you {are} saying to me, make this people go up, and you, you did not make me know (who) you will send with me, and you, you said, I know you (by) title*, and also you found beauty† in my eyes,□

33:13

וְעַתָּה אִם נָא מָצָאתִי חֵן בְּעֵינֶיךָ הוֹדִעֵנִי נָא אֶת דְּרָכֶךָ וְאֵדָעֲךָ לְמַעַן אֶמְצָא חֵן בְּעֵינֶיךָ וּרְאֵה כִּי עַמְּךָ הַגּוֹי הַזֶּה

we'a'tah im na ma'tsa'ti hheyn be'ey'ney'kha ho'di'ey'ni na et de'ra'khe'kha we'ey'da'a'kha le'ma'an em'tsa hheyn be'ey'ney'kha ur'eyh ki am'kha ha'goi ha'zeh

---

* "I know you by title" is an idiom meaning "I know your character," or "I know all about you."

† "Find beauty" means to "be accepted."

Mechanical Translation Codes

<u>WORD</u> – Verb	WORD – Noun	Word – Name	word – Pre/Suff	*word* – Conj.

and~NOW IF PLEASE *I~did~*<u>FIND</u> BEAUTY in~ EYE~s2~you(ms) *!(ms)~make~*<u>KNOW</u>~me PLEASE AT ROAD~you(ms) and~*I~will~* <u>KNOW</u>~you(ms) to~THAT *I~will~*<u>FIND</u> BEAUTY in~EYE~s2~you(ms) and~*!(ms)~*<u>SEE</u> GIVEN-THAT PEOPLE~you(ms) the~NATION the~THIS□

and now, please, if I find beauty* in your eyes, please, make me know your road†, and I will know you, (so) that I will find beauty‡ in your eyes and see that your people {are} this nation,□

33:14

וַיֹּאמַר פָּנַי יֵלֵכוּ וַהֲנִחֹתִי לָךְ

wai'yo'mar pa'nai yey'ley'khu wa'ha'ni'hho'ti lakh

and~*he~will~*<u>SAY</u> FACE~s~me *they(m)~will~* <u>WALK</u> and~*I~did~make~*<u>REST</u> to~you(fs)□

and he said, my face will walk§, and I will make {a} rest (for) you**,□

33:15

וַיֹּאמֶר אֵלָיו אִם אֵין פָּנֶיךָ הֹלְכִים אַל תַּעֲלֵנוּ מִזֶּה

wai'yo'mer ey'law im eyn pa'ney'kha hol'khim al ta'a'ley'nu mi'zeh

and~*he~will~*<u>SAY</u> TO~him IF WITHOUT FACE~s~you(ms) <u>WALK</u>~*ing/er(mp)* DO-NOT *you(ms)~will~make~*<u>GO-UP</u>~us from~THIS□

and he said to him, if your face {is} (not) walking, do not make us go up from this {place},□

33:16

וּבַמֶּה יִוָּדַע אֵפוֹא כִּי מָצָאתִי חֵן בְּעֵינֶיךָ אֲנִי וְעַמֶּךָ הֲלוֹא בְּלֶכְתְּךָ עִמָּנוּ וְנִפְלִינוּ אֲנִי וְעַמְּךָ מִכָּל הָעָם אֲשֶׁר עַל פְּנֵי הָאֲדָמָה

u'va'meh yi'wa'da ey'pho ki ma'tsa'ti hheyn be'ey'ney'kha a'ni we'a'me'kha ha'lo be'lekh'te'kha i'ma'nu we'niph'li'nu a'ni we'am'kha mi'kol ha'am a'sher al pe'ney ha'a'da'mah

and~in~WHAT *he~will~be~*<u>KNOW</u> THEN GIVEN-THAT *I~did~*<u>FIND</u> BEAUTY in~EYE~s2~ you(ms) I and~PEOPLE~you(ms) ?~NOT in~ >~<u>WALK</u>~you(ms) WITH~us and~*we~did~* *be~*<u>BE-DISTINCT</u> I and~PEOPLE~you(ms) from~ALL the~PEOPLE WHICH UPON FACE~s the~GROUND□

and how will (it) be known then that I, and your people, found beauty†† in your eyes? {is it} not (with) your walk{ing} with us? (then) I and your people will be distinct (out of) all the people which {are} upon {the} face {of} the ground,□

33:17

וַיֹּאמֶר יְהוָה אֶל מֹשֶׁה גַּם אֶת הַדָּבָר הַזֶּה אֲשֶׁר דִּבַּרְתָּ אֶעֱשֶׂה כִּי מָצָאתָ חֵן בְּעֵינַי וָאֵדָעֲךָ בְּשֵׁם

wai'yo'mer YHWH el mo'sheh gam et ha'da'var ha'zeh a'sher di'bar'ta e'e'seh ki ma'tsa'ta hheyn be'ey'nai wa'e'da'a'kha be'shem

---

* "Find beauty" means to "be accepted."
† "Know your road" is an idiom meaning "teach me your ways."
‡ "Find beauty" means to "be accepted."
§ "My face will walk" means "my presence will go."
** "Make a rest for you" may be translated as "give you rest."
†† "Find beauty" means to "be accepted."

Revised Mechanical Translation Codes
(..) Alt Trans/App A   <..> Comp Phrase/App B   [..] Verb Form/App C   \../ Plural Form/App D
:..: Int Inf Abs |..| Past Perf Verb   {...} Added Word

ma'tsa'ta hheyn be'ey'nai wa'ey'da'a'kha be'sheym

and~he~will~SAY "Yhwh ^{he~will~BE}" TO "Mosheh ^{PLUCKED-OUT}" ALSO AT the~WORD the~THIS WHICH *you(ms)~did~much~*SPEAK *l~will~*DO GIVEN-THAT *you(ms)~did~*FIND BEAUTY in~EYE~s2~me and~*l~will~*KNOW~ you(ms) in~TITLE☐

and "Yhwh ^{He is}" said to "Mosheh ^{Plucked out}", also this word which you spoke, I will do, given that you found beauty* in my eyes, and I know you (by) title†,☐

33:18

וַיֹּאמַר הַרְאֵנִי נָא אֶת כְּבֹדֶךָ

wai'yo'mar har'ey'ni na et ke'vo'de'kha

and~he~will~SAY !(ms)~make~SEE~me PLEASE AT ARMAMENT~you(ms)☐

and he said, please make me see your armament,☐

33:19   וַיֹּאמֶר אֲנִי אַעֲבִיר כָּל טוּבִי עַל פָּנֶיךָ וְקָרָאתִי בְשֵׁם יְהוָה לְפָנֶיךָ וְחַנֹּתִי אֶת אֲשֶׁר אָחֹן וְרִחַמְתִּי אֶת אֲשֶׁר אֲרַחֵם

wai'yo'mer a'ni a'a'vir kol tu'vi al pa'ney'kha we'qa'ra'ti ve'sheym YHWH le'pha'ney'kha we'hha'no'ti et a'sher a'hhon we'ri'hham'ti et a'sher a'ra'hhey m

and~he~will~SAY I *l~will~*make~CROSS-OVER ALL FUNCTIONAL~me UPON FACE~s~ you(ms) and~*l~did~*CALL-OUT in~TITLE "Yhwh ^{he~will~BE}" to~FACE~s~you(ms) and~*l~did~*SHOW-BEAUTY AT WHICH *l~will~*SHOW-BEAUTY and~*l~did~much~*HAVE-COMPASSION AT WHICH *l~will~much~*HAVE-COMPASSION☐

and he said, I will make all my function cross over upon your face, and I will call out "Yhwh ^{He is}" (by) title‡ <in front of> you, and I will show beauty§ (to) (who) I will show beauty**, and I will have compassion (to) (who) I will have compassion,☐

33:20   וַיֹּאמֶר לֹא תוּכַל לִרְאֹת אֶת פָּנָי כִּי לֹא יִרְאַנִי הָאָדָם וָחָי

wai'yo'mer lo tu'khal lir'ot et pa'nai ki lo yir'a'ni ha'a'dam wa'hhai

and~he~will~SAY NOT *you(ms)~will~*BE-ABLE to~>~SEE AT FACE~s~me GIVEN-THAT NOT he~will~SEE~me the~HUMAN and~he~will~ LIVE☐

and he said, you will not be able to see my face, given that the human will not see me and live,☐

33:21   וַיֹּאמֶר יְהוָה הִנֵּה מָקוֹם אִתִּי וְנִצַּבְתָּ עַל הַצּוּר

---

* "Find beauty" means to "be accepted."
† "I know you by title" is an idiom meaning "I know your character," or "I know all about you."

‡ The phrase "I will call out Yhwh by title" can mean, "I will call Yhwh by name," but can also be translated as "and I will meet with the title (meaning character or person) of Yhwh," as the Hebrew verb קרא may mean to "call out" or to "meet."
§ To "show beauty" means to "show acceptance."
** To "show beauty" means to "show acceptance."

Mechanical Translation Codes

| <u>WORD</u> – Verb | WORD – Noun | Word – Name | word – Pre/Suff | *word* – Conj. |

wai'yo'mer YHWH hin'neyh ma'qom i'ti we'ni'tsav'ta al ha'tsur

and~*he~will*~SAY "Yhwh *he~will~*<u>BE</u>" LOOK AREA AT~me and~*you(ms)~did~be~*<u>STAND-UP</u> UPON the~BOULDER□

and "Yhwh *He is*" said, look, {an} area {is} (by) me, and you will be stand{ing} up upon the boulder,□

33:22 וְהָיָה בַּעֲבֹר כְּבֹדִי וְשַׂמְתִּיךָ בְּנִקְרַת הַצוּר וְשַׂכֹּתִי כַפִּי עָלֶיךָ עַד עָבְרִי

we'hai'yah ba'a'vor ke'vo'di we'sam'ti'kha be'niq'rat ha'tsur we'sa'ko'ti kha'pi a'ley'kha ad av'ri

and~*he~did~*<u>EXIST</u> in~>~<u>CROSS-OVER</u> ARMAMENT~me and~*l~did~*<u>PLACE</u>~you(ms) in~<u>FISSURE</u> the~BOULDER and~*l~did~* <u>FENCE-AROUND</u> PALM~me UPON~you(ms) UNTIL >~<u>CROSS-OVER</u>~me□

and (it) will (come to pass) (with) {the} cross{ing} over {of} my armament, and I will place you in {the} fissure {of} the boulder, and I will fence my palm* around you until I cross over,□

33:23 וַהֲסִרֹתִי אֶת כַּפִּי וְרָאִיתָ אֶת אֲחֹרָי וּפָנַי לֹא יֵרָאוּ

wa'ha'si'ro'ti et ka'pi we'ra'i'ta et a'hho'rai u'phanaw lo yey'ra'u

and~*l~did~make~*<u>TURN-ASIDE</u> AT PALM~me and~*you(ms)~did~*<u>SEE</u> AT BACK~s~me and~ FACE~s~me NOT *they(m)~will~be~*<u>SEE</u>□

and I will make my palm† turn aside and you will see my backs‡, (but) my face will not [appear],□

Chapter 34

34:1 וַיֹּאמֶר יְהֹוָה אֶל מֹשֶׁה פְּסָל לְךָ שְׁנֵי לֻחֹת אֲבָנִים כָּרִאשֹׁנִים וְכָתַבְתִּי עַל הַלֻּחֹת אֶת הַדְּבָרִים אֲשֶׁר הָיוּ עַל הַלֻּחֹת הָרִאשֹׁנִים אֲשֶׁר שִׁבַּרְתָּ

wai'yo'mer YHWH el mo'sheh pe'sal le'kha she'ney lu'hhot a'va'nim ka'ri'sho'nim we'kha'tav'ti al ha'lu'hhot et had'va'rim a'sher hai'u al ha'lu'hhot ha'ri'sho'nim a'sher shi'bar'ta

and~*he~will*~SAY "Yhwh *he~will~*<u>BE</u>" TO "Mosheh ^{PLUCKED-OUT}" !(ms)~<u>SCULPT</u> to~ you(ms) TWO SLAB~s STONE~s like~FIRST~s and~*l~did~*<u>WRITE</u> UPON the~SLAB~s AT the~ WORD~s WHICH *they~did~*<u>EXIST</u> UPON the~ SLAB~s like~FIRST~s WHICH *you(ms)~did~* <u>CRACK</u>□

and "Yhwh *He is*" said to "Mosheh ^{Plucked out}", sculpt (for) your{self} two slabs {of} stone like {the} first {one}s, and I will write upon the slabs the words, which existed upon the slabs, like {the} first {one}s, which you cracked,□

---

* This may be the palm of a hand, a palm tree or anything that is palm-shaped.

† This may be the palm of a hand, a palm tree or anything that is palm-shaped.

‡ The phrase "my backs" may also be translated as "behind me."

Revised Mechanical Translation Codes

(..) Alt Trans/App A	<..> Comp Phrase/App B	[..] Verb Form/App C	\../ Plural Form/App D
:..: Int Inf Abs	|..| Past Perf Verb	{...} Added Word	

34:2 וְהְיֵה נָכוֹן לַבֹּקֶר וְעָלִיתָ בַבֹּקֶר אֶל הַר סִינַי וְנִצַּבְתָּ לִי שָׁם עַל רֹאשׁ הָהָר

weh'yey na'khon la'bo'qer we'a'li'ta va'bo'qer el har si'nai we'ni'tsav'ta li sham al rosh ha'har

and~!(ms)~<u>EXIST</u> be~<u>PREPARE</u>~ing/er(ms) to~the~MORNING and~you(ms)~did~<u>GO-UP</u> in~the~MORNING TO HILL "Sinai ^{SHARP-THORN~s~me}" and~you(ms)~did~be~<u>STAND-UP</u> to~me THERE UPON HEAD the~HILL□

and <be ready> (for) the morning, and you will go up in the morning to {the} hill {of} "Sinai ^{My sharp thorns}", and you will stand up to me there upon {the} head {of} the hill,□

34:3 וְאִישׁ לֹא יַעֲלֶה עִמָּךְ וְגַם אִישׁ אַל יֵרָא בְּכָל הָהָר גַּם הַצֹּאן וְהַבָּקָר אַל יִרְעוּ אֶל מוּל הָהָר הַהוּא

we'ish lo ya'a'leh i'makh we'gam ish al yey'ra be'khol ha'har gam ha'tson we'ha'ba'qar al yir'u el mul ha'har ha'hu

and~MAN NOT he~will~<u>GO-UP</u> WITH~you(fs) and~ALSO MAN DO-NOT he~will~be~<u>SEE</u> in~ALL the~HILL ALSO the~FLOCKS and~the~CATTLE DO-NOT they(m)~will~<u>FEED</u> TO FOREFRONT the~HILL the~HE□

and (no) man will go up with you, and also, do not {let a} man [appear] in all the hill, also do not {let} the flocks and the cattle feed (on) {the} forefront {of} (that) hill,□

34:4 וַיִּפְסֹל שְׁנֵי לֻחֹת אֲבָנִים כָּרִאשֹׁנִים וַיַּשְׁכֵּם מֹשֶׁה בַבֹּקֶר וַיַּעַל אֶל הַר סִינַי כַּאֲשֶׁר צִוָּה יְהוָה אֹתוֹ וַיִּקַּח בְּיָדוֹ שְׁנֵי לֻחֹת אֲבָנִים

wai'yiph'sol she'ney lu'hhot a'va'nim ka'ri'sho'nim wai'yash'keym mo'sheh va'bo'qer wai'ya'al el har si'nai ka'a'sheyr tsi'wah YHWH o'to wai'yi'qahh be'ya'do she'ney lu'hhot a'va'nim

and~he~will~<u>SCULPT</u> TWO SLAB~s STONE~s like~FIRST~s and~he~will~make~<u>DEPART-EARLY</u> "Mosheh ^{PLUCKED-OUT}" in~the~MORNING and~he~will~<u>GO-UP</u> TO HILL "Sinai ^{SHARP-THORN~s~me}" like~WHICH he~did~much~<u>DIRECT</u> "Yhwh ^{he~will~BE}" AT~him and~he~will~<u>TAKE</u> in~HAND~him TWO SLAB~s STONE~s□

and he sculpted two slabs {of} stone like {the} first {one}s, and "Mosheh ^{Plucked out}" departed early in the morning, and he went up to {the} hill {of} "Sinai ^{My sharp thorns}", <just as> "Yhwh ^{He is}" directed him, and he took in his hand {the} two slabs {of} stone,□

34:5 וַיֵּרֶד יְהוָה בֶּעָנָן וַיִּתְיַצֵּב עִמּוֹ שָׁם וַיִּקְרָא בְשֵׁם יְהוָה

wai'yey'red YHWH be'a'nan wai'yit'ya'tseyv i'mo sham wai'yiq'ra ve'sheym YHWH

Mechanical Translation Codes

<u>WORD</u> – Verb	WORD – Noun	Word – Name	word – Pre/Suff	*word* – Conj.

and~he~will~GO-DOWN "Yhwh ^{he~will~BE}" in~ CLOUD and~he~will~ self~STATION WITH~ him THERE and~he~will~CALL-OUT in~TITLE "Yhwh ^{he~will~BE}"□

and "Yhwh ^{He is}" went down in {the} cloud, and he stationed {him}self with him there, and he called out "Yhwh ^{He is}" (by) title*,□

34:6 וַיַּעֲבֹר יְהוָה עַל פָּנָיו וַיִּקְרָא יְהוָה יְהוָה אֵל רַחוּם וְחַנּוּן אֶרֶךְ אַפַּיִם וְרַב חֶסֶד וֶאֱמֶת

wai'ya'a'vor YHWH al pa'naw wai'yiq'ra YHWH YHWH eyl ra'hhum we'hha'nun e'rek a'pa'yim we'rav hhe'sed we'e'met

and~he~will~CROSS-OVER "Yhwh ^{he~will~BE}" UPON FACE~s~him and~he~will~CALL-OUT "Yhwh ^{he~will~BE}" "Yhwh ^{he~will~BE}" MIGHTY-ONE COMPASSIONATE and~GRACIOUS SLOW NOSE~s2 and~ABUNDANT KINDNESS and~TRUTH□

and "Yhwh ^{He is}" crossed over upon his face, and he called out, "Yhwh ^{He is}", "Yhwh ^{He is}", {the} mighty one†, compassionate and gracious, slow {of} \nostrils/‡, and abundant {in} kindness and truth,□

34:7 נֹצֵר חֶסֶד לָאֲלָפִים נֹשֵׂא עָוֹן וָפֶשַׁע וְחַטָּאָה וְנַקֵּה לֹא יְנַקֶּה פֹּקֵד עֲוֹן אָבֹת עַל בָּנִים וְעַל בְּנֵי בָנִים עַל שִׁלֵּשִׁים וְעַל רִבֵּעִים

no'tseyr hhe'sed la'a'la'phim no'sey a'won wa'phe'sha we'hha'ta'ah we'na'qeyh lo ye'na'qeh po'qeyd a'won a'vot al ba'nim we'al be'ney va'nim al shi'ley'shim we'al ri'bey'im

PRESERVE~ing/er(ms) KINDNESS to~the~ THOUSAND~s LIFT-UP~ing/er(ms) INIQUITY and~TRANSGRESSION and~ERROR and~ >~much~ACQUIT NOT he~will~much~ ACQUIT REGISTER~ing/er(ms) INIQUITY FATHER~s UPON SON~s and~UPON SON~s SON~s UPON THIRD-GENERATION~s and~ UPON FOURTH-GENERATION~s□

preserving kindness to the thousands, lifting up§ iniquity and transgression and error, (but) he will not :completely: acquit**, registering {the} iniquity {of the} fathers upon {the} sons and upon {the} sons {of the} sons, upon {the} third generations and upon {the} fourth generation,□

34:8 וַיְמַהֵר מֹשֶׁה וַיִּקֹּד אַרְצָה וַיִּשְׁתָּחוּ

wai'ma'heyr mo'sheh wai'yi'qod ar'tsah wai'yish'ta'hhu

and~he~will~much~HURRY "Mosheh ^{PLUCKED-}

and "Mosheh ^{Plucked out}" hurried and he bowed

---

* The phrase "he called out Yhwh by title" can mean, "he called Yhwh by name," but can also be translated as "and he met with the title (meaning character or person) of Yhwh," as the Hebrew verb קרא may mean to "call out" or to "meet."

† The phrase וַיִּקְרָא יְהוָה יְהוָה may also be translated as "and Yhwh called out, Yhwh is a mighty one" or "and Yhwh called out Yhwh the mighty one."

‡ "Slow of nostrils" is an idiom meaning "patient."

§ "lifting up" means "forgiving."

** Another possible translation for "but he will not completely acquit" is "but he will not acquit the guilty," where the word "guilty" comes from the Septuagint and assumes this word is missing from the Hebrew text.

Revised Mechanical Translation Codes

(..) Alt Trans/App A	<..> Comp Phrase/App B	[..] Verb Form/App C	\../ Plural Form/App D
:...: Int Inf Abs	|..| Past Perf Verb	{...} Added Word	

OUT„ and~he~will~BOW-THE-HEAD LAND~ unto and~he~will~ self~BEND-DOWN▢

the head unto {the} land and he bent {him}self down,▢

34:9 וַיֹּאמֶר אִם נָא מָצָאתִי חֵן בְּעֵינֶיךָ אֲדֹנָי יֵלֶךְ נָא אֲדֹנָי בְּקִרְבֵּנוּ כִּי עַם קְשֵׁה עֹרֶף הוּא וְסָלַחְתָּ לַעֲוֺנֵנוּ וּלְחַטָּאתֵנוּ וּנְחַלְתָּנוּ

wai'yo'mer im na ma'tsa'ti hheyn be'ey'ney'kha a'do'nai yey'lekh na a'do'nai be'qir'bey'nu ki am qe'sheyh o'reph hu we'sa'lahh'ta la'a'o'ney'nu ul'hha'ta'tey'nu un'hhal'ta'nu

and~he~will~SAY IF PLEASE I~did~FIND BEAUTY in~EYE~s2~you(ms) "Adonai ^{LORD~s~me}" he~will~WALK PLEASE "Adonai ^{LORD~s~me}" in~WITHIN~us GIVEN-THAT PEOPLE HARD NECK HE and~you(ms)~will~FORGIVE to~ INIQUITY~us and~to~ERROR~us and~ you(ms)~did~INHERIT~us▢

and he said, please, if I found beauty* in your eyes "Adonai ^{My lords}", please, "Adonai ^{My lords}" will walk <among> us, given that he† {is a} hard neck{ed} people, and you will forgive our iniquity and our error, and you will inherit us,▢

34:10 וַיֹּאמֶר הִנֵּה אָנֹכִי כֹּרֵת בְּרִית נֶגֶד כָּל עַמְּךָ אֶעֱשֶׂה נִפְלָאֹת אֲשֶׁר לֹא נִבְרְאוּ בְכָל הָאָרֶץ וּבְכָל הַגּוֹיִם וְרָאָה כָל הָעָם אֲשֶׁר אַתָּה בְקִרְבּוֹ אֶת מַעֲשֵׂה יְהוָה כִּי נוֹרָא הוּא אֲשֶׁר אֲנִי עֹשֶׂה עִמָּךְ

wai'yo'mer hin'neyh a'no'khi ko'reyt be'rit ne'ged kol am'kha e'e'seh niph'la'ot a'sher lo niv're'u be'khol ha'a'rets uv'khol ha'go'yim we'ra'ah khol ha'am a'sher a'tah ve'qir'bo et ma'a'seyh YHWH ki no'ra hu a'sher a'ni o'seh i'makh

and~he~will~SAY LOOK I CUT~ing/er(ms) COVENANT OPPOSITE ALL PEOPLE~you(ms) I~will~DO be~PERFORM~ing/er(fp) WHICH NOT they~did~be~FATTEN in~ALL the~LAND and~in~ALL the~NATION~s and~he~did~SEE ALL the~PEOPLE WHICH YOU(ms) in~ WITHIN~him AT WORK "Yhwh ^{he~will~BE}" GIVEN-THAT be~FEAR~ing/er(ms) HE WHICH I DO~ing/er(ms) WITH~you(fs)▢

and he said, look, I {am} cutting {a} covenant (before) all your people, I will do [performances], which {has} not been fattened‡ in all the land and in all the nations, and all the people, which you {are} <among>, will see {the} work {of} "Yhwh ^{He is}", given that (what) I {am} doing with you, {is to} be fear{ed},▢

34:11 שְׁמָר לְךָ אֵת אֲשֶׁר אָנֹכִי מְצַוְּךָ הַיּוֹם הִנְנִי גֹרֵשׁ מִפָּנֶיךָ אֶת הָאֱמֹרִי וְהַכְּנַעֲנִי וְהַחִתִּי וְהַפְּרִזִּי וְהַחִוִּי וְהַיְבוּסִי

she'mar le'kha eyt a'sher a'no'khi me'tsa'we'kha hai'yom hin'ni go'reysh mi'pa'ney'kha et ha'e'mo'ri we'hak'na'a'ni we'ha'hhi'ti we'ha'pe'ri'zi we'ha'hhi'wi we'hai'vu'si

!(ms)~SAFEGUARD to~you(ms) AT WHICH I much~DIRECT~ing/er(ms)~you(ms) the~DAY LOOK~me CAST-OUT~ing/er(ms) from~

safeguard (for) you (what) I {am} directing you <today>, look {at} me casting out from your face§ the {one} of "Emor ^{Sayer}" and the {one} of

---

* "Find beauty" means to "be accepted."
† Referring to the "people," a masculine word in Hebrew.
‡ "Has not been fattened "means that it has not been done before."
§ "From your face" is an idiom meaning "from your presence."

Mechanical Translation Codes

<u>WORD</u> – Verb	WORD – Noun	Word – Name	word – Pre/Suff	*word* – Conj.

FACE~s~you(ms) AT the~"Emor ^{SAYER}"~of and~the~"Kena'an ^{LOWERED}"~of and~the~ "Hhet ^{TREMBLING-IN-FEAR}"~of and~the~"Perez ^{PEASANT}"~of and~the~"Hhiw ^{TOWN}"~of and~ the~"Yevus ^{he~will~TRAMPLE-DOWN}"~of□

"Emor ^{Sayer}" and the {one} of "Kena'an ^{Lowered}" and the {one} of "Hhet ^{Trembling in fear}" and the {one} of "Perez ^{Peasant}" and the {one} of "Hhiw ^{Town}" and the {one} of "Yevus ^{He will trample down}",□

34:12 הִשָּׁמֶר לְךָ פֶּן תִּכְרֹת בְּרִית לְיוֹשֵׁב הָאָרֶץ אֲשֶׁר אַתָּה בָּא עָלֶיהָ פֶּן יִהְיֶה לְמוֹקֵשׁ בְּקִרְבֶּךָ

hi'sha'mer le'kha pen tikh'rot be'rit le'yo'sheyv ha'a'rets a'sher a'tah ba a'ley'ah pen yih'yeh le'mo'qeysh be'qir'be'kha

!(ms)~be~<u>SAFEGUARD</u> to~you(ms) OTHERWISE you(ms)~will~<u>CUT</u> COVENANT to~<u>SETTLE</u>~ing/er(ms) the~LAND WHICH YOU(ms) <u>COME</u>~ing/er(ms) UPON~her OTHERWISE he~will~<u>EXIST</u> to~SNARE in~ WITHIN~you(ms)□

be safeguard{ed} to your{self}, otherwise you will cut {a} covenant (for) {a} settler {of} the land which you {are} coming upon, otherwise he will exist (for) {a} snare <among> you,□

34:13 כִּי אֶת מִזְבְּחֹתָם תִּתֹּצוּן וְאֶת מַצֵּבֹתָם תְּשַׁבֵּרוּן וְאֶת אֲשֵׁרָיו תִּכְרֹתוּן

ki et miz'be'hho'tam ti'to'tsun we'et ma'tsey'vo'tam te'sha'bey'run we'et a'shey'raw tikh'ro'tun

GIVEN-THAT AT ALTAR~s~them(m) you(mp)~ will~<u>BREAK-DOWN</u>~must and~AT MONUMENT~s~them(m) you(mp)~will~ much~<u>CRACK</u>~must and~AT GROVE~s~him you(mp)~will~<u>CUT</u>~must□

given that their altars you must break down, and their monuments you must [shatter], and his groves you must cut,□

34:14 כִּי לֹא תִשְׁתַּחֲוֶה לְאֵל אַחֵר כִּי יְהוָה קַנָּא שְׁמוֹ אֵל קַנָּא הוּא

ki lo tish'ta'hha'weh le'eyl a'hheyr ki YHWH qa'na she'mo eyl qa'na hu

GIVEN-THAT NOT you(ms)~will~ self~<u>BEND-DOWN</u> to~MIGHTY-ONE OTHER GIVEN-THAT "Yhwh ^{he~will~BE}" ZEALOUS TITLE~him MIGHTY-ONE ZEALOUS HE□

given that you will not bend {your}self down to {an}other mighty one, given that "Yhwh ^{He is}" {is} zealous, his title {is the} mighty one, he {is} zealous,□

34:15 פֶּן תִּכְרֹת בְּרִית לְיוֹשֵׁב הָאָרֶץ וְזָנוּ אַחֲרֵי אֱלֹהֵיהֶם וְזָבְחוּ לֵאלֹהֵיהֶם וְקָרָא לְךָ וְאָכַלְתָּ מִזִּבְחוֹ

pen tikh'rot be'rit le'yo'sheyv ha'a'rets we'za'nu a'hha'rey e'lo'hey'hem we'zav'hhu ley'lo'hey'hem we'qa'ra le'kha we'a'khal'ta mi'ziv'hho

OTHERWISE you(ms)~will~<u>CUT</u> COVENANT to~<u>SETTLE</u>~ing/er(ms) the~LAND and~they~ did~<u>BE-A-WHORE</u> AFTER "Elohiym ^{POWER~s}"~ them(m) and~they~did~<u>SACRIFICE</u> to~ "Elohiym ^{POWER~s}"~them(m) and~he~did~ <u>CALL-OUT</u> to~you(ms) and~you(ms)~did~

otherwise you will cut {a} covenant (for) {a} settler {of} the land, and they will be a whore after their "Elohiym ^{Powers}", and they will sacrifice to their "Elohiym ^{Powers}", and he will call out to you and you will eat {of} his altar,□

Revised Mechanical Translation Codes

(..) Alt Trans/App A	<..> Comp Phrase/App B	[..] Verb Form/App C	\../ Plural Form/App D
:...: Int Inf Abs	|..| Past Perf Verb	{...} Added Word	

EAT ALTAR~him□

34:16   וְלָקַחְתָּ מִבְּנֹתָיו לְבָנֶיךָ וְזָנוּ בְנֹתָיו אַחֲרֵי אֱלֹהֵיהֶן וְהִזְנוּ אֶת בָּנֶיךָ אַחֲרֵי אֱלֹהֵיהֶן

we'la'qahh'ta mi'be'no'taw le'va'ney'kha we'za'nu ve'no'taw a'hha'rey e'lo'hey'hen
we'hiz'nu et ba'ney'kha a'hha'rey e'lo'hey'hen

and~*you(ms)~did*~TAKE from~
DAUGHTER~s*him to~SON~s*you(ms) and~
they~did~BE-A-WHORE DAUGHTER~s*him
AFTER "Elohiym ᴾᴼᵂᴱᴿ~ˢ*~them(f) and~*they~
did~make*~BE-A-WHORE AT SON~s*you(ms)
AFTER "Elohiym ᴾᴼᵂᴱᴿ~ˢ*~them(f)□

and you will take from his daughters (for) your
sons, and his daughters will be a whore after
their "Elohiym ᴾᵒʷᵉʳˢ", and they will make your
sons be a whore after their "Elohiym ᴾᵒʷᵉʳˢ",□

34:17   אֱלֹהֵי מַסֵּכָה לֹא תַעֲשֶׂה לָּךְ

e'lo'hey ma'sey'khah lo ta'a'seh lakh

"Elohiym ᴾᴼᵂᴱᴿ~ˢ" CAST-IMAGE NOT *you(ms)~*
will*~DO to~you(fs)□

you will not (make) (for) you {an} "Elohiym
ᴾᵒʷᵉʳˢ" {of a} cast image,□

34:18   אֶת חַג הַמַּצוֹת תִּשְׁמֹר שִׁבְעַת יָמִים תֹּאכַל מַצּוֹת אֲשֶׁר צִוִּיתִךָ לְמוֹעֵד חֹדֶשׁ הָאָבִיב כִּי בְּחֹדֶשׁ הָאָבִיב יָצָאתָ מִמִּצְרָיִם

et hhag ha'ma'tsot tish'mor shiv'at ya'mim to'khal ma'tsot a'sher tsi'wi'ti'kha le'mo'eyd
hho'desh ha'a'viv ki be'hho'desh ha'a'viv ya'tsa'ta mi'mits'ra'yim

AT FEAST the~UNLEAVENED-BREAD~s
you(ms)~will~SAFEGUARD SEVEN DAY~s
you(ms)~will~EAT UNLEAVENED-BREAD~s
WHICH *I~did~much*~DIRECT~you(ms) to~
APPOINTED NEW-MOON the~GREEN-GRAIN
GIVEN-THAT in~NEW-MOON the~GREEN-
GRAIN *you(ms)~did*~GO-OUT from~
"Mits'rayim ˢᵀᴿᴬᴵᵀ~ˢ²"□

you will safeguard {the} feast {of the}
unleavened bread, seven days you will eat
{the} unleavened bread which I directed you
(for) {an} appointed {time in the} (month) {of}
the green grain, given that in {the} (month)
{of} the green grain you went out from
"Mits'rayim ᵀʷᵒ ˢᵗʳᵃⁱᵗˢ",□

34:19   כָּל פֶּטֶר רֶחֶם לִי וְכָל מִקְנְךָ תִּזָּכָר פֶּטֶר שׁוֹר וָשֶׂה

kol pe'ter re'hhem li we'khol miq'ne'kha ti'za'khar pe'ter shor wa'seh

ALL BURSTING BOWELS to~me and~ALL
LIVESTOCK~you(ms) *you(ms)~will*~be~
REMEMBER BURSTING OX and~RAM□

all {the} bursting {of the} bowels* {is} (for) me,
all your livestock, the males† bursting {of the}
ox and ram,□

34:20   וּפֶטֶר חֲמוֹר תִּפְדֶּה בְשֶׂה וְאִם לֹא תִפְדֶּה וַעֲרַפְתּוֹ כֹּל בְּכוֹר בָּנֶיךָ תִּפְדֶּה וְלֹא יֵרָאוּ פָנַי רֵיקָם

---

* The "bursting of the bowels" is the childbirths.
† The Hebrew word תִּזָּכָר means "you will be remembered," but the context implies that this
word may have originally been written as הַזָּכָר meaning "the male."

Mechanical Translation Codes

<u>WORD</u> – Verb	WORD – Noun	Word – Name	word – Pre/Suff	*word* – Conj.

u'phe'ter hha'mor tiph'deh ve'sheh we'im lo tiph'deh wa'a'raph'to kol be'khor
ba'ney'kha tiph'deh we'lo yey'ra'u pha'nai rey'qam

and~BURSTING DONKEY *you(ms)~will~* <u>RANSOM</u> in~RAM and~IF NOT *you(ms)~will~* <u>RANSOM</u> and~*you(ms)~did~*<u>BEHEAD</u>~him ALL FIRSTBORN SON~s~*you(ms)* *you(ms)~* *will~*<u>RANSOM</u> and~NOT *they(m)~will~be~* <u>SEE</u> FACE~s~me EMPTINESS□	and {the} bursting{s of the} donkey you will ransom (with) {a} ram, and if you will not ransom {it} (then) you will behead* him, all {the} firstborn {of} your sons you will ransom and they will not [appear] (in front of)† me empty,□

34:21 שֵׁשֶׁת יָמִים תַּעֲבֹד וּבַיּוֹם הַשְּׁבִיעִי תִּשְׁבֹּת בֶּחָרִישׁ וּבַקָּצִיר תִּשְׁבֹּת

shey'shet ya'mim ta'a'vod u'va'yom hash'vi'i tish'bot be'hha'rish u'va'qa'tsir tish'bot

SIX DAY~s *you(ms)~will~*<u>SERVE</u> and~in~the~ DAY the~SEVENTH *you(ms)~will~*<u>CEASE</u> in~ PLOWING and~in~HARVEST *you(ms)~will~* <u>CEASE</u>□	six days you will serve and in the seventh day you will cease (with) {the} plowing, and (with) {the} harvesting you will cease,□

34:22 וְחַג שָׁבֻעֹת תַּעֲשֶׂה לְךָ בִּכּוּרֵי קְצִיר חִטִּים וְחַג הָאָסִיף תְּקוּפַת הַשָּׁנָה

we'hhag sha'vu'ot ta'a'seh le'kha bi'ku'rey qe'tsir hhi'tim we'hhag ha'a'siph te'qu'phat ha'sha'nah

and~FEAST WEEK~s *you(ms)~will~*<u>DO</u> to~ *you(ms)* FIRSTFRUIT~s HARVEST WHEAT~s and~FEAST the~GATHERING CIRCUIT the~ YEAR□	and you will do {the} feast {of} weeks (for) you, firstfruits {of the} harvest {of the} wheat, and {a} feast {of the} gathering {at the} circuit‡ {of} the year,□

34:23 שָׁלֹשׁ פְּעָמִים בַּשָּׁנָה יֵרָאֶה כָּל זְכוּרְךָ אֶת פְּנֵי הָאָדֹן יְהוָה אֱלֹהֵי יִשְׂרָאֵל

sha'losh pe'a'mim ba'sha'nah yey'ra'eh kol zekhur'kha et pe'ney ha'a'don YHWH e'lo'hey yis'ra'eyl

THREE FOOTSTEP~s in~the~YEAR *he~will~* *be~*<u>SEE</u> ALL MEN~*you(ms)* AT FACE~s the~ LORD "Yhwh *he~will~*<u>BE</u>" "Elohiym *POWER~s*" "Yisra'el *he~will~*<u>TURN-ASIDE</u>~+~MIGHTY-ONE*"* □	three footsteps§ in the year all your men will [appear] at {the} face {of} the lord "Yhwh *He is*" {the} "Elohiym *Powers*" {of} "Yisra'el *He turns El aside*",□

34:24 כִּי אוֹרִישׁ גּוֹיִם מִפָּנֶיךָ וְהִרְחַבְתִּי אֶת גְּבֻלֶךָ וְלֹא יַחְמֹד אִישׁ אֶת אַרְצְךָ בַּעֲלֹתְךָ לֵרָאוֹת אֶת פְּנֵי יְהוָה אֱלֹהֶיךָ שָׁלֹשׁ פְּעָמִים בַּשָּׁנָה

---

* This Hebrew verb can mean to "behead" or "break the neck."

† The word פְּנֵי appears to be missing the prefix ל (to). As it is written, the sentence could be translated as "and my face will not appear empty."

‡ Or "end."

§ Or "times."

ki o'rish go'yim mi'pa'ney'kha we'hir'hhav'ti et ge'vu'le'kha we'lo yahh'mod ish et ar'tse'kha ba'a'lot'kha ley'ra'ot et pe'ney YHWH e'lo'hey'kha sha'losh pe'a'mim ba'sha'nah

GIVEN-THAT *I~will~make~*POSSESS NATION~s from~FACE~s~you(ms) and~*I~ did~make~*WIDEN AT BORDER~you(ms) and~NOT *he~will~*CRAVE MAN AT LAND~ you(ms) in~>~GO-UP~you(ms) to~>~*be~*SEE AT FACE~s "Yhwh *he~will~BE*" "Elohiym POWER~s*"~ you(ms) THREE FOOTSTEP~s in~the~YEAR□

given that I will [dispossess] {the} nations from your face, and I will widen your border{s}, and {a} man will not crave your land (with) you go{ing} up to [appear] at {the} face "Yhwh He is" your "Elohiym Powers" three footsteps* in the year,□

34:25

לֹא תִשְׁחַט עַל חָמֵץ דַּם זִבְחִי וְלֹא יָלִין לַבֹּקֶר זֶבַח חַג הַפָּסַח

lo tish'hhat al hha'meyts dam ziv'hhi we'lo ya'lin la'bo'qer ze'vahh hhag ha'pa'sahh

NOT *you(ms)~will~*SLAY UPON LEAVENED-BREAD BLOOD SACRIFICE~me and~NOT *he~ will~*STAY-THE-NIGHT to~the~MORNING SACRIFICE FEAST the~"Pesahh HOPPING"□

you will not slay {the} blood {of} my sacrifice upon {the} leavened bread, and {the} sacrifice {of the} feast {of} the "Pesahh hopping" will not stay the night to the morning,□

34:26

רֵאשִׁית בִּכּוּרֵי אַדְמָתְךָ תָּבִיא בֵּית יְהוָה אֱלֹהֶיךָ לֹא תְבַשֵּׁל גְּדִי בַּחֲלֵב אִמּוֹ

rey'shit bi'ku'rey ad'mat'kha ta'vi beyt YHWH e'lo'hey'kha lo te'va'sheyl ge'di ba'hha'leyv i'mo

SUMMIT FIRSTFRUIT~s GROUND~you(ms) *you(ms)~will~make~*COME HOUSE "Yhwh *he~ will~BE*" "Elohiym POWER~s*"~you(ms) NOT *you(ms)~will~much~*BOIL MALE-KID in~the~ FAT MOTHER~him□

you will [bring] {the} summit† {of the} firstfruits {of} your ground {to the} house {of} "Yhwh He is" your "Elohiym Powers", you will not boil {a} male kid in the fat‡ {of} his mother,□

34:27

וַיֹּאמֶר יְהוָה אֶל מֹשֶׁה כְּתָב לְךָ אֶת הַדְּבָרִים הָאֵלֶּה כִּי עַל פִּי הַדְּבָרִים הָאֵלֶּה כָּרַתִּי אִתְּךָ בְּרִית וְאֶת יִשְׂרָאֵל

wai'yo'mer YHWH el mo'sheh ke'tav le'kha et had'va'rim ha'ey'leh ki al pi had'va'rim ha'ey'leh ka'ra'ti it'kha be'rit we'et yis'ra'eyl

and~*he~will~*SAY "Yhwh *he~will~BE*" TO "Mosheh PLUCKED-OUT*" *!(ms)~*WRITE to~ you(ms) AT the~WORD~s the~THESE GIVEN-THAT UPON MOUTH the~WORD~s the~ THESE *I~did~*WRITE AT~you(ms) COVENANT

and "Yhwh He is" said to "Mosheh Plucked out", write (for) your{self} these words, given that (according to) {the} mouth {of} these words, I wrote you and "Yisra'el He turns El aside" {a} covenant,□

---

* Or "times."

† "The summit of the firstfruits" may mean the "first" or the "best" of the firstfruits.

‡ Or "milk."

Mechanical Translation Codes

WORD – Verb	WORD – Noun	Word – Name	word – Pre/Suff	word – Conj.

and~AT "Yisra'el" ^{he~will~}TURN-ASIDE~+~MIGHTY-ONE„□

34:28

וַיְהִי שָׁם עִם יְהוָה אַרְבָּעִים יוֹם וְאַרְבָּעִים לַיְלָה לֶחֶם לֹא אָכַל וּמַיִם
לֹא שָׁתָה וַיִּכְתֹּב עַל הַלֻּחֹת אֵת דִּבְרֵי הַבְּרִית עֲשֶׂרֶת הַדְּבָרִים

wai'hi sham im YHWH ar'ba'im yom we'ar'ba'im lai'lah le'hhem lo a'khal u'ma'yim lo
sha'tah wai'yikh'tov al ha'lu'hhot eyt div'rey ha'be'rit a'se'ret had'va'rim

and~he~will~EXIST THERE WITH "Yhwh ^{he~will~BE}„ FOUR~s DAY and~FOUR~s NIGHT BREAD NOT he~did~EAT and~WATER~s2 NOT he~did~GULP and~he~will~WRITE UPON the~SLAB~s AT WORD~s the~COVENANT TEN the~WORD~s□

and he existed there with "Yhwh ^{He is}„ \forty/ day{s} and \forty/ night{s}, he did not eat bread and he did not gulp water, and he wrote upon the slabs {the} words {of} the covenant, ten {of} the words*,□

34:29

וַיְהִי בְּרֶדֶת מֹשֶׁה מֵהַר סִינַי וּשְׁנֵי לֻחֹת הָעֵדֻת בְּיַד מֹשֶׁה בְּרִדְתּוֹ מִן
הָהָר וּמֹשֶׁה לֹא יָדַע כִּי קָרַן עוֹר פָּנָיו בְּדַבְּרוֹ אִתּוֹ

wai'hi be're'det mo'sheh me'har si'nai ush'ney lu'hhot ha'ey'dut be'yad mo'sheh
be'rid'to min ha'har u'mo'sheh lo ya'da ki qa'ran or pa'naw be'da'be'ro i'to

and~he~will~EXIST in~>~GO-DOWN "Mosheh ^{PLUCKED-OUT}„ from~HILL "Sinai ^{SHARP-THORN~s~me}„ and~TWO SLAB~s the~EVIDENCE in~HAND "Mosheh ^{PLUCKED-OUT}„ in~>~GO-DOWN~him FROM the~HILL and~"Mosheh ^{PLUCKED-OUT}„ NOT he~did~KNOW GIVEN-THAT he~did~HAVE-HORNS SKIN FACE~s~him in~>~much~SPEAK~him AT~him□

and (it) (came to pass) (with) "Mosheh ^{Plucked out}„ go{ing} down from {the} hill {of} "Sinai ^{My sharp thorns}„, and {the} two slabs {of} the evidence {were} in {the} hand {of} "Mosheh ^{Plucked out}„, (with) his go{ing} down from the hill, and "Mosheh ^{Plucked out}„ |had| not known that {the} skin {of} his face had horns† (with) his speak{ing} (with) him,□

34:30

וַיַּרְא אַהֲרֹן וְכָל בְּנֵי יִשְׂרָאֵל אֶת מֹשֶׁה וְהִנֵּה קָרַן עוֹר פָּנָיו וַיִּירְאוּ
מִגֶּשֶׁת אֵלָיו

wai'yar a'ha'ron we'khol be'ney yis'ra'eyl et mo'sheh we'hin'neyh qa'ran or pa'naw
wai'yir'u mi'ge'shet ey'law

and~he~will~SEE "Aharon ^{LIGHT-BRINGER}„ and~ALL SON~s "Yisra'el ^{he~will~TURN-ASIDE~+~MIGHTY-ONE}„ AT "Mosheh ^{PLUCKED-OUT}„ and~LOOK he~did~HAVE-HORNS SKIN FACE~s~him and~they(m)~will~FEAR from~>~DRAW-NEAR

and "Aharon ^{Light bringer}„, and all {the} sons {of} "Yisra'el ^{He turns El aside}„, saw "Mosheh ^{Plucked out}„, and look, {the} skin {of} his face had horns‡, and they feared (to) draw near to him,□

---

* This Hebrew word can also be translated as "matters."

† The Hebrew phrase קָרַן עוֹר פָּנָיו literally means "the skin of his face had horns," but many interpret this figuratively to mean that "rays of light" came from his face. An amazing sight in either case.

‡ The Hebrew phrase קָרַן עוֹר פָּנָיו literally means "the skin of his face had horns," but many interpret this figuratively to mean that "rays of light" came from his face. An amazing sight in either case.

Revised Mechanical Translation Codes

(..) Alt Trans/App A   <..> Comp Phrase/App B   [..] Verb Form/App C   \../ Plural Form/App D
:...: Int Inf Abs |..| Past Perf Verb   {...} Added Word

TO~him□

34:31 וַיִּקְרָא אֲלֵהֶם מֹשֶׁה וַיָּשֻׁבוּ אֵלָיו אַהֲרֹן וְכָל הַנְּשִׂאִים בָּעֵדָה וַיְדַבֵּר מֹשֶׁה אֲלֵהֶם

wai'yiq'ra a'ley'hem mo'sheh wai'ya'shu'vu ey'law a'ha'ron we'khol han'so'im ba'ey'dah wai'da'beyr mo'sheh a'ley'hem

and~he~will~<u>CALL-OUT</u> TO~them(m) "Mosheh ^{PLUCKED-OUT}" and~they(m)~will~ <u>TURN-BACK</u> TO~him "Aharon ^{LIGHT-BRINGER}" and~ALL the~CAPTAIN~s in~the~COMPANY and~he~will~much~<u>SPEAK</u> "Mosheh ^{PLUCKED-OUT}" TO~them(m)□

and "Mosheh ^{Plucked out}" called out to them, and "Aharon ^{Light bringer}" and all the captains in the company turned back to him, and "Mosheh ^{Plucked out}" spoke to them,□

34:32 וְאַחֲרֵי כֵן נִגְּשׁוּ כָּל בְּנֵי יִשְׂרָאֵל וַיְצַוֵּם אֵת כָּל אֲשֶׁר דִּבֶּר יְהֹוָה אִתּוֹ בְּהַר סִינָי

we'a'hha'rey kheyn nig'shu kol be'ney yis'ra'eyl wai'tsa'weym eyt kol a'sher di'ber YHWH i'to be'har si'nai

and~AFTER SO they~did~be~<u>DRAW-NEAR</u> ALL SON~s "Yisra'el ^{he~will~TURN-ASIDE~+~MIGHTY-ONE}" and~he~will~much~<u>DIRECT</u>~them(m) AT ALL WHICH he~did~much~<u>SPEAK</u> "Yhwh ^{he~will~BE}" AT~him in~HILL "Sinai ^{SHARP-THORN~s~me}"□

and <afterward> all {the} sons {of} "Yisra'el ^{He turns El aside}" were drawn near, and he directed them (with) all which "Yhwh ^{He is}" spoke (with) him in {the} hill {of} "Sinai ^{My sharp thorns}",□

34:33 וַיְכַל מֹשֶׁה מִדַּבֵּר אִתָּם וַיִּתֵּן עַל פָּנָיו מַסְוֶה

wai'khal mo'sheh mi'da'beyr i'tam wai'yi'teyn al pa'naw mas'weh

and~he~will~much~<u>FINISH</u> "Mosheh ^{PLUCKED-OUT}" >~much~<u>SPEAK</u> AT~them(m) and~he~ will~<u>GIVE</u> UPON FACE~s~him HOOD□

and "Mosheh ^{Plucked out}" finished speak{ing} (with) them, and he (placed) {a} hood upon his face,□

34:34 וּבְבֹא מֹשֶׁה לִפְנֵי יְהֹוָה לְדַבֵּר אִתּוֹ יָסִיר אֶת הַמַּסְוֶה עַד צֵאתוֹ וְיָצָא וְדִבֶּר אֶל בְּנֵי יִשְׂרָאֵל אֵת אֲשֶׁר יְצֻוֶּה

uv'vo mo'sheh liph'ney YHWH le'da'beyr i'to ya'sir et ha'mas'weh ad tsey'to we'ya'tsa we'di'ber el be'ney yis'ra'eyl eyt a'sher ye'tsu'weh

and~in~>~<u>COME</u> "Mosheh ^{PLUCKED-OUT}" to~ FACE~s "Yhwh ^{he~will~BE}" to~>~much~<u>SPEAK</u> AT~him he~will~make~<u>TURN-ASIDE</u> AT the~ HOOD UNTIL >~<u>GO-OUT</u>~him and~he~will~ <u>GO-OUT</u> and~he~did~much~<u>SPEAK</u> TO SON~s "Yisra'el ^{he~will~TURN-ASIDE~+~MIGHTY-ONE}" AT WHICH he~will~be~much~<u>DIRECT</u>□

and (with) "Mosheh ^{Plucked out}" com{ing} to {the} face {of} "Yhwh ^{He is}" to speak (with) him, he turned aside the hood until his go{ing} out, and he went out and he spoke to {the} sons {of} "Yisra'el ^{He turns El aside}" (with) (what) he directed,□

34:35 וְרָאוּ בְנֵי יִשְׂרָאֵל אֶת פְּנֵי מֹשֶׁה כִּי קָרַן עוֹר פְּנֵי מֹשֶׁה וְהֵשִׁיב מֹשֶׁה אֶת

Mechanical Translation Codes

<u>WORD</u> – Verb   WORD – Noun   Word – Name   word – Pre/Suff   *word* – Conj.

~ 262 ~

הַמַּסְוֶה עַל פָּנָיו עַד בֹּאוֹ לְדַבֵּר אִתּוֹ

we'ra'u ve'ney yis'ra'eyl et pe'ney mo'sheh ki qa'ran or pe'ney mo'sheh we'hey'shiv mo'sheh et ha'mas'weh al pa'naw ad bo'o le'da'beyr i'to

and~they~did~SEE SON~s "Yisra'el ^{he~will~TURN-ASIDE~+~MIGHTY-ONE}" AT FACE~s "Mosheh ^{PLUCKED-OUT}" GIVEN-THAT he~did~HAVE-HORNS SKIN FACE~s "Mosheh ^{PLUCKED-OUT}" and~he~did~make~TURN-BACK "Mosheh ^{PLUCKED-OUT}" AT the~HOOD UPON FACE~s~him UNTIL >~COME~him to~>~much~SPEAK AT~him□

and {the} sons {of} "Yisra'el ^{He turns El aside}" saw {the} face {of} "Mosheh ^{Plucked out}", given that {the} skin {of the} face {of} "Mosheh ^{Plucked out}" had horns*, and "Mosheh ^{Plucked out}" turned back the hood upon his face until his com{ing} to speak (with) him,□

Chapter 35

35:1

וַיַּקְהֵל מֹשֶׁה אֶת כָּל עֲדַת בְּנֵי יִשְׂרָאֵל וַיֹּאמֶר אֲלֵהֶם אֵלֶּה הַדְּבָרִים אֲשֶׁר צִוָּה יְהוָה לַעֲשֹׂת אֹתָם

wai'yaq'heyl mo'sheh et kol a'dat be'ney yis'ra'eyl wai'yo'mer a'ley'hem ey'leh had'va'rim a'sher tsi'wah YHWH la'a'shot o'tam

and~he~will~ROUND-UP "Mosheh ^{PLUCKED-OUT}" AT ALL COMPANY SON~s "Yisra'el ^{he~will~TURN-ASIDE~+~MIGHTY-ONE}" and~he~will~SAY TO~them(m) THESE the~WORD~s WHICH he~did~much~DIRECT "Yhwh ^{he~will~BE}" to~>~DO AT~them(m)□

and "Mosheh ^{Plucked out}" rounded up all {the} company {of the} sons {of} "Yisra'el ^{He turns El aside}", and he said to them, these {are} the words which "Yhwh ^{He is}" directed them to do†,□

35:2

שֵׁשֶׁת יָמִים תֵּעָשֶׂה מְלָאכָה וּבַיּוֹם הַשְּׁבִיעִי יִהְיֶה לָכֶם קֹדֶשׁ שַׁבַּת שַׁבָּתוֹן לַיהוָה כָּל הָעֹשֶׂה בוֹ מְלָאכָה יוּמָת

shey'shet ya'mim tey'a'seh me'la'khah u'va'yom hash'vi'i yih'yeh la'khem qo'desh sha'bat sha'ba'ton la'YHWH kol ha'o'seh bo me'la'khah yu'mat

SIX DAY~s she~will~be~DO BUSINESS and~in~the~DAY the~SEVENTH he~will~EXIST to~you(mp) SPECIAL CEASING REST-DAY to~"Yhwh ^{he~will~BE}" ALL the~DO~ing/er(ms) in~him BUSINESS he~will~be~make~DIE□

six days business will be done, and in the seventh day {a} special {time} will exist (for) you, {it is a} ceasing, {a} rest day (for) "Yhwh ^{He is}", (any){one} doing business in him‡ will be [killed],□

---

* The Hebrew phrase קָרַן עוֹר פְּנֵי מֹשֶׁה literally means "the skin of the face of Mosheh had horns," but many interpret this figuratively to mean that "rays of light" came from his face. An amazing sight in either case.

† Context implies that the pronoun "them" is in error and should be "you."

‡ Referring to the "day," a masculine word in Hebrew.

Revised Mechanical Translation Codes

| (..) Alt Trans/App A | <..> Comp Phrase/App B | [..] Verb Form/App C | \../ Plural Form/App D |
| :..: Int Inf Abs | \|..\| Past Perf Verb | {...} Added Word | |

35:3 לֹא תְבַעֲרוּ אֵשׁ בְּכֹל מֹשְׁבֹתֵיכֶם בְּיוֹם הַשַּׁבָּת

lo te'va'a'ru eysh be'khol mosh'vo'tey'khem be'yom ha'sha'bat

NOT you(mp)~will~much~<u>BURN</u> FIRE in~ALL SETTLING~s~you(mp) in~DAY the~<u>CEASING</u>□

you will not [ignite] {a} fire in (any) {of} your settlings in {the} day {of} the ceasing,□

35:4 וַיֹּאמֶר מֹשֶׁה אֶל כָּל עֲדַת בְּנֵי יִשְׂרָאֵל לֵאמֹר זֶה הַדָּבָר אֲשֶׁר צִוָּה יְהוָה לֵאמֹר

wai'yo'mer mo'sheh el kol a'dat be'ney yis'ra'eyl ley'mor zeh ha'da'var a'sher tsi'wah YHWH ley'mor

and~he~will~<u>SAY</u> "Mosheh ^{PLUCKED-OUT}" TO ALL COMPANY SON~s "Yisra'el ^{he~will~TURN-ASIDE~+~MIGHTY-ONE}" to~>~<u>SAY</u> THIS the~WORD WHICH he~did~much~<u>DIRECT</u> "Yhwh ^{he~will~BE}" to~>~<u>SAY</u>□

and "Mosheh ^{Plucked out}" said to all {the} company {of the} sons {of} "Yisra'el ^{He turns El aside}" say{ing}, this {is} the word which "Yhwh ^{He is}" directed say{ing},□

35:5 קְחוּ מֵאִתְּכֶם תְּרוּמָה לַיהוָה כֹּל נְדִיב לִבּוֹ יְבִיאֶהָ אֵת תְּרוּמַת יְהוָה זָהָב וָכֶסֶף וּנְחֹשֶׁת

qe'hhu mey'it'khem te'ru'mah la'YHWH kol ne'div li'bo ye'vi'e'ah eyt te'ru'mat YHWH za'hav wa'ke'seph un'hho'shet

!(mp)~<u>TAKE</u> from~AT~you(mp) OFFERING to~"Yhwh ^{he~will~BE}" ALL WILLING HEART~him he~will~make~<u>COME</u>~her AT OFFERING "Yhwh ^{he~will~BE}" GOLD and~SILVER and~COPPER□

take from you {an} offering (for) "Yhwh ^{He is}", all willing {of} his heart will [bring] {the} offering {of} "Yhwh ^{He is}", gold, and silver, and copper,□

35:6 וּתְכֵלֶת וְאַרְגָּמָן וְתוֹלַעַת שָׁנִי וְשֵׁשׁ וְעִזִּים

ut'khey'let we'ar'ga'man we'to'la'at sha'ni we'sheysh we'i'zim

and~BLUE and~PURPLE and~KERMES SCARLET and~LINEN and~SHE-GOAT~s□

and blue, and purple, and kermes {of} scarlet, and linen, and she-goats*,□

35:7 וְעֹרֹת אֵילִם מְאָדָּמִים וְעֹרֹת תְּחָשִׁים וַעֲצֵי שִׁטִּים

we'o'rot ´ey'lim me'a'da'mim we'o'rot te'hha'sim wa'a'tsey shi'tim

and~SKIN~s BUCK~s be~much~<u>BE-RED</u>~ing/er(mp) and~SKIN~s TAHHASH~s and~TREE~s ACACIA~s□

and skins {of} bucks being red, and skins {of} tahhashs†, and acacia \wood/,□

35:8 וְשֶׁמֶן לַמָּאוֹר וּבְשָׂמִים לְשֶׁמֶן הַמִּשְׁחָה וְלִקְטֹרֶת הַסַּמִּים

---

* Specifically, the hair of the she-goats.

† The Tahhash is an unknown species of animal.

Mechanical Translation Codes

<u>WORD</u> – Verb	WORD – Noun	Word – Name	word – Pre/Suff	*word* – Conj.

we'she'men la'ma'or uv'sha'mim le'she'men ha'mish'hhah we'liq'to'ret ha'sa'mim

and~OIL to~the~LUMINARY and~in~SWEET-SPICE~s to~OIL the~OINTMENT and~to~INCENSE the~AROMATIC-SPICE~s□

and oil (for) the luminary, and (with) sweet spices (for) the oil {of} ointment and (for) {the} incense {of} aromatic spices,□

35:9

וְאַבְנֵי שֹׁהַם וְאַבְנֵי מִלֻּאִים לָאֵפוֹד וְלַחֹשֶׁן

we'av'ney sho'ham we'av'ney mi'lu'im la'ey'phod we'lahh'shen

and~STONE~s ONYX and~STONE~s INSTALLATION~s to~the~EPHOD and~to~the~BREASTPLATE□

and stones {of the} onyx*, and stones {of the} installations (for) the ephod and (for) the breastplate,□

35:10

וְכָל חֲכַם לֵב בָּכֶם יָבֹאוּ וְיַעֲשׂוּ אֵת כָּל אֲשֶׁר צִוָּה יְהוָה

we'khol hha'kham leyv ba'khem ya'vo'u we'ya'a'su eyt kol a'sher tsi'wah YHWH

and~ALL SKILLED-ONE HEART in~you(mp) *they(m)~will~*COME and~*they(m)~will~*DO AT ALL WHICH *he~did~much~*DIRECT "Yhwh *he~will~*BE"□

and all {the} skilled one{s of} heart (with) you will come, and they will (make) all which "Yhwh ^He is^ directed,□

35:11

אֵת הַמִּשְׁכָּן אֶת אָהֳלוֹ וְאֶת מִכְסֵהוּ אֶת קְרָסָיו וְאֶת קְרָשָׁיו אֶת בְּרִיחָו אֶת עַמֻּדָיו וְאֶת אֲדָנָיו

et ha'mish'kan et a'ha'lo we'et mikh'sey'hu et qe'ra'saw we'et qe'ra'shaw et be'ri'hhaw et a'mu'daw we'et a'da'naw

AT the~DWELLING AT TENT~him and~AT ROOF-COVERING~him AT HOOK~s~him and~AT BOARD~s~him AT WOOD-BAR~s~him AT PILLAR~s~him and~AT FOOTING~s~him□

the dwelling, his tent, his roof covering, his hooks and his boards, his wood bars, his pillars and his footings,□

35:12

אֶת הָאָרֹן וְאֶת בַּדָּיו אֶת הַכַּפֹּרֶת וְאֵת פָּרֹכֶת הַמָּסָךְ

et ha'a'ron we'et ba'daw et ha'ka'po'ret we'eyt pa'ro'khet ha'ma'sakh

AT the~BOX and~AT STICK~s~him AT the~LID and~AT TENT-CURTAIN the~CANOPY□

the box and his sticks, the lid, and {the} tent curtain {of} the canopy,□

35:13

אֶת הַשֻּׁלְחָן וְאֶת בַּדָּיו וְאֶת כָּל כֵּלָיו וְאֵת לֶחֶם הַפָּנִים

et ha'shul'hhan we'et ba'daw we'et kol key'law we'eyt le'hhem ha'pa'nim

AT the~TABLE and~AT STICK~s~him and~AT ALL ITEM~s~him and~AT BREAD the~FACE~s□

the table and his sticks and all his items, and {the} bread {of} the face,□

---

* The "shoham" is unknown stone.

Revised Mechanical Translation Codes

(..) Alt Trans/App A	<..> Comp Phrase/App B	[..] Verb Form/App C	\../ Plural Form/App D
:..: Int Inf Abs	|..| Past Perf Verb	{...} Added Word	

35:14

וְאֶת מְנֹרַת הַמָּאוֹר וְאֶת כֵּלֶיהָ וְאֶת נֵרֹתֶיהָ וְאֵת שֶׁמֶן הַמָּאוֹר

we'et me'no'rat ha'ma'or we'et key'ley'ah we'et ney'ro'te'yah we'eyt she'men ha'ma'or

and~AT LAMPSTAND the~LUMINARY and~ AT ITEM~s~her and~AT LAMP~s~her and~AT OIL the~LUMINARY☐	and {the} lampstand {of} the luminary and all her items and her lamps, and {the} oil {of} the luminary,☐

35:15

וְאֶת מִזְבַּח הַקְּטֹרֶת וְאֶת בַּדָּיו וְאֵת שֶׁמֶן הַמִּשְׁחָה וְאֵת קְטֹרֶת הַסַּמִּים וְאֶת מָסַךְ הַפֶּתַח לְפֶתַח הַמִּשְׁכָּן

we'et miz'bahh haq'to'ret we'et ba'daw we'eyt she'men ha'mish'hhah we'eyt qe'to'ret ha'sa'mim we'et ma'sakh ha'pe'tahh le'phe'tahh ha'mish'kan

and~AT ALTAR the~INCENSE and~AT STICK~s~him and~AT OIL the~OINTMENT and~AT INCENSE the~AROMATIC-SPICE~s and~AT CANOPY the~OPENING to~OPENING the~DWELLING☐	and {the} altar {of} the incense and his sticks, and the oil {of} ointment, and the incense {of} aromatic spices, and {the} canopy {of} the opening (for) {the} opening {of} the dwelling,☐

35:16

אֵת מִזְבַּח הָעֹלָה וְאֶת מִכְבַּר הַנְּחֹשֶׁת אֲשֶׁר לוֹ אֶת בַּדָּיו וְאֶת כָּל כֵּלָיו אֶת הַכִּיֹּר וְאֶת כַּנּוֹ

eyt miz'bahh ha'o'lah we'et mikh'bar han'hho'shet a'sher lo et ba'daw we'et kol key'law et ha'ki'yor we'et ka'no

AT ALTAR the~RISING and~AT GRATE the~ COPPER WHICH to~him AT STICK~s~him and~AT ALL ITEM~s~him AT the~CAULDRON and~AT BASE~him☐	the altar {of the} rising {sacrifice}, and the copper grate which {is} (for) him, his sticks and all his items, the cauldron and his base,☐

35:17

אֵת קַלְעֵי הֶחָצֵר אֶת עַמֻּדָיו וְאֶת אֲדָנֶיהָ וְאֵת מָסַךְ שַׁעַר הֶחָצֵר

eyt qal'ey he'hha'tseyr et a'mu'daw we'et a'da'ney'ah we'eyt ma'sakh sha'ar he'hha'tseyr

AT SLING~s the~YARD AT PILLAR~s~him and~AT FOOTING~s~her and~AT CANOPY GATE the~YARD☐	{the} slings {of} the yard, his pillars and her footings, and the canopy {of the} gate {of the} yard,☐

35:18

אֶת יִתְדֹת הַמִּשְׁכָּן וְאֶת יִתְדֹת הֶחָצֵר וְאֶת מֵיתְרֵיהֶם

et yit'dot ha'mish'kan we'et yit'dot he'hha'tseyr we'et meyt'rey'hem

AT TENT-PEG~s the~DWELLING and~AT TENT-PEG~s the~YARD and~AT STRING~s~ them(m)☐	{the} tent pegs {of} the dwelling, and {the} tent pegs {of} the yard, and their strings,☐

35:19

אֶת בִּגְדֵי הַשְּׂרָד לְשָׁרֵת בַּקֹּדֶשׁ אֶת בִּגְדֵי הַקֹּדֶשׁ לְאַהֲרֹן הַכֹּהֵן וְאֶת בִּגְדֵי בָנָיו לְכַהֵן

et big'dey has'rad le'sha'reyt ba'qo'desh et big'dey ha'qo'desh le'a'ha'ron ha'ko'heyn we'et big'dey va'naw le'kha'heyn

AT GARMENT~s the~BRAIDED-WORK to~ >~*much*~MINISTER in~the~SPECIAL AT GARMENT~s the~SPECIAL to~"Aharon LIGHT-BRINGER" the~ADMINISTRATOR and~AT GARMENT~s SON~s~him to~>~*much*~ADORN□

{the} garments {of} the braided work to minister in the special {place}, the garments {of} special{ness} (for) "Aharon Light bringer" the administrator, and {the} garments {of} his sons to {be} adorn{ed},□

35:20 וַיֵּצְאוּ כָּל עֲדַת בְּנֵי יִשְׂרָאֵל מִלִּפְנֵי מֹשֶׁה

wai'yeyts'u kol a'dat be'ney yis'ra'eyl mi'liph'ney mo'sheh

and~they(m)~*will*~GO-OUT ALL COMPANY SON~s "Yisra'el *he~will*~TURN-ASIDE~+~MIGHTY-ONE" from~to~FACE~s "Mosheh PLUCKED-OUT"□

and all {the} company {of the} sons {of} "Yisra'el He turns El aside" will go out from <in front of> "Mosheh Plucked out",□

35:21 וַיָּבֹאוּ כָּל אִישׁ אֲשֶׁר נְשָׂאוֹ לִבּוֹ וְכֹל אֲשֶׁר נָדְבָה רוּחוֹ אֹתוֹ הֵבִיאוּ אֶת תְּרוּמַת יְהֹוָה לִמְלֶאכֶת אֹהֶל מוֹעֵד וּלְכָל עֲבֹדָתוֹ וּלְבִגְדֵי הַקֹּדֶשׁ

wai'ya'vo'u kol ish a'sher ne'sa'o li'bo we'khol a'sher nad'vah ru'hho o'to hey'vi'u et te'ru'mat YHWH lim'le'khet o'hel mo'eyd ul'khol a'vo'da'to ul'vig'dey ha'qo'desh

and~they(m)~*will*~COME ALL MAN WHICH *he~did*~LIFT-UP~him HEART~him and~ALL WHICH *she~did*~OFFER-WILLINGLY WIND~him AT~him *they~did~make*~COME AT OFFERING "Yhwh *he~will*~BE" to~BUSINESS TENT APPOINTED and~to~ALL SERVICE~him and~to~GARMENT~s the~SPECIAL□

and they will come, (every) man which lifted up his heart and all (whose) wind* willingly offered him, they [brought] {the} offering {of} "Yhwh He is" (for) {the} business {of the} tent {of the} appointed {place}, and (for) all his service, and (for) the garments {of} special{ness},□

35:22 וַיָּבֹאוּ הָאֲנָשִׁים עַל הַנָּשִׁים כֹּל נְדִיב לֵב הֵבִיאוּ חָח וָנֶזֶם וְטַבַּעַת וְכוּמָז כָּל כְּלִי זָהָב וְכָל אִישׁ אֲשֶׁר הֵנִיף תְּנוּפַת זָהָב לַיהֹוָה

wai'ya'vo'u ha'a'na'shim al ha'na'shim kol ne'div leyv hey'vi'u hhahh wa'ne'zem we'ta'ba'at we'khu'maz kol ke'li za'hav we'khol ish a'sher hey'niph te'nu'phat za'hav la'YHWH

and~they(m)~*will*~COME the~MAN~s UPON the~WOMAN~s ALL WILLING HEART *they~did~make*~COME NOSE-RING and~ORNAMENTAL-RING and~RING and~ARM-BAND ALL ITEM~s GOLD and~ALL MAN WHICH *he~did*~WAVE WAVING GOLD to~ "Yhwh *he~will*~BE"□

and they will come, the men (also) the women, all willing {of} heart |had| [brought] nose ring{s} and ornamental ring{s} and ring{s} and arm band{s}, all items {of} gold, and (every) man which waved {a} wave {offer}ing {of} gold to "Yhwh He is",□

35:23 וְכָל אִישׁ אֲשֶׁר נִמְצָא אִתּוֹ תְּכֵלֶת וְאַרְגָּמָן וְתוֹלַעַת שָׁנִי וְשֵׁשׁ וְעִזִּים וְעֹרֹת אֵילִם מְאָדָּמִים וְעֹרֹת תְּחָשִׁים הֵבִיאוּ

we'khol ish a'sher nim'tsa i'to te'khey'let we'ar'ga'man we'to'la'at sha'ni we'sheysh

---

* The wind, or breath, of an individual is his character.

Revised Mechanical Translation Codes

(..) Alt Trans/App A   <..> Comp Phrase/App B   [..] Verb Form/App C   \..\/ Plural Form/App D

:..: Int Inf Abs |..| Past Perf Verb   {...} Added Word

we'i'zim we'o'rot ey'lim me'a'da'mim we'o'rot te'hha'sim hey'vi'u

and~ALL MAN WHICH *he~did~be~*FIND AT~ him BLUE and~PURPLE and~KERMES SCARLET and~LINEN and~SHE-GOAT~s and~ SKIN~s BUCK~s *be~much~*BE-RED~ *ing/er(mp)* and~SKIN~s TAHHASH~s *they~ did~*make~COME□	and (every) man which was found (with) blue, and purple, and kermes {of} scarlet, and linen, and she-goats*, and skins {of} bucks being red, and skins {of} tahhashs†, they [brought] {it},□

35:24 כָּל מֵרִים תְּרוּמַת כֶּסֶף וּנְחֹשֶׁת הֵבִיאוּ אֵת תְּרוּמַת יְהוָה וְכֹל אֲשֶׁר נִמְצָא אִתּוֹ עֲצֵי שִׁטִּים לְכָל מְלֶאכֶת הָעֲבֹדָה הֵבִיאוּ

kol mey'rim te'ru'mat ke'seph un'hho'shet hey'vi'u eyt te'ru'mat YHWH we'khol a'sher nim'tsa i'to a'tsey shi'tim le'khol me'le'khet ha'a'vo'dah hey'vi'u

ALL *make~*RAISE~*ing/er(ms)* OFFERING SILVER and~COPPER *they~did~*make~COME AT OFFERING "Yhwh *he~will~*BE" and~ALL WHICH *he~did~be~*FIND AT~him TREE~s ACACIA~s to~ALL BUSINESS the~SERVICE *they~did~*make~COME□	(any) {one} raising {an} offering {of} silver and copper [brought] {the} offering {of} "Yhwh He is", and (any) {one} which was found (with) acacia \wood/ (for) all {the} business {of} the service, they [brought] {it},□

35:25 וְכָל אִשָּׁה חַכְמַת לֵב בְּיָדֶיהָ טָווּ וַיָּבִיאוּ מַטְוֶה אֶת הַתְּכֵלֶת וְאֶת הָאַרְגָּמָן אֶת תּוֹלַעַת הַשָּׁנִי וְאֶת הַשֵּׁשׁ

we'khol i'shah hhakh'mat leyv be'ya'dey'ah ta'wu wai'ya'vi'u mat'weh et hat'khey'let we'et ha'ar'ga'man et to'la'at ha'sha'ni we'et ha'sheysh

and~ALL WOMAN SKILLED-ONE HEART in~ HAND~s*her *they~did~*SPIN and~*they(m)~ will~*make~COME YARN AT the~BLUE and~ AT the~PURPLE AT KERMES the~SCARLET and~AT the~LINEN□	and (every) woman skilled {of} heart spun (with) her hands, and they [brought] yarn, the blue, and the purple, kermes {of} scarlet, and the linen,□

35:26 וְכָל הַנָּשִׁים אֲשֶׁר נָשָׂא לִבָּן אֹתָנָה בְּחָכְמָה טָווּ אֶת הָעִזִּים

we'khol ha'na'shim a'sher na'sa li'ban o'ta'nah be'hhakh'mah ta'wu et ha'i'zim

and~ALL the~WOMAN~s WHICH *he~did~* LIFT-UP HEART~them(f) AT~them(f) in~SKILL *they~did~*SPIN AT the~SHE-GOAT~s□	and all the women (whose) heart lifted them up in skill, they spun the she-goats‡,□

35:27 וְהַנְּשִׂאָם הֵבִיאוּ אֵת אַבְנֵי הַשֹּׁהַם וְאֵת אַבְנֵי הַמִּלֻּאִים לָאֵפוֹד וְלַחֹשֶׁן

we'han'si'im hey'vi'u eyt av'ney ha'sho'ham we'eyt av'ney ha'mi'lu'im la'ey'phod we'lahh'shen

and~the~CAPTAIN~s *they~did~*make~COME	and the captains [brought] {the} stones {of}

---

* Specifically, the hair of the she-goats.
† The Tahhash is an unknown species of animal.
‡ Specifically, the hair of the she-goats.

Mechanical Translation Codes

<u>WORD</u> – Verb	WORD – Noun	Word – Name	word – Pre/Suff	*word* – Conj.

AT STONE~s the~ONYX and~AT STONE~s the~INSTALLATION~s to~the~EPHOD and~ to~the~BREASTPLATE□

the onyx* and {the} stones {of} the installations (for) the ephod and (for) the breastplate,□

35:28 וְאֶת הַבֹּשֶׂם וְאֶת הַשֶּׁמֶן לְמָאוֹר וּלְשֶׁמֶן הַמִּשְׁחָה וְלִקְטֹרֶת הַסַּמִּים

we'et ha'bo'sem we'et ha'sha'men le'ma'or ul'she'men ha'mish'hhah we'liq'to'ret ha'sa'mim

and~AT the~SWEET-SPICE and~AT the~OIL to~the~LUMINARY and~to~OIL the~ OINTMENT and~to~INCENSE the~ AROMATIC-SPICE~s□

and the sweet spice, and the oil (for) the luminary and (for) the oil {of} ointment and (for) the incense {of} aromatic spices,□

35:29 כָּל אִישׁ וְאִשָּׁה אֲשֶׁר נָדַב לִבָּם אֹתָם לְהָבִיא לְכָל הַמְּלָאכָה אֲשֶׁר צִוָּה יְהוָה לַעֲשׂוֹת בְּיַד מֹשֶׁה הֵבִיאוּ בְנֵי יִשְׂרָאֵל נְדָבָה לַיהוָה

kol ish we'i'shah a'sher na'dav li'bam o'tam le'ha'vi le'khol ham'la'khah a'sher tsi'wah YHWH la'a'shot be'yad mo'sheh hey'vi'u ve'ney yis'ra'eyl ne'da'vah la'YHWH

ALL MAN and~WOMAN WHICH _he~did~_ <u>OFFER-WILLINGLY</u> HEART~them(m) AT~ them(m) to~>~_make~_<u>COME</u> to~ALL the~ BUSINESS WHICH _he~did~much~_<u>DIRECT</u> "Yhwh _he~will~_<u>BE</u>" to~>~<u>DO</u> in~HAND "Mosheh PLUCKED-OUT" _they~did~make~_<u>COME</u> SON~s "Yisra'el _he~will~_<u>TURN-ASIDE</u>~+~MIGHTY-ONE" FREEWILL-OFFERING to~"Yhwh _he~will~_<u>BE</u>"□

(every) man and woman (whose) heart willingly offered them to [bring] {things} (for) all the business which "Yhwh He is" directed to do (by) {the} hand {of} "Mosheh Plucked out", {the} sons {of} "Yisra'el He turns El aside" [brought] {a} freewill offering (for) "Yhwh He is",□

35:30 וַיֹּאמֶר מֹשֶׁה אֶל בְּנֵי יִשְׂרָאֵל רְאוּ קָרָא יְהוָה בְּשֵׁם בְּצַלְאֵל בֶּן אוּרִי בֶן חוּר לְמַטֵּה יְהוּדָה

wai'yo'mer mo'sheh el be'ney yis'ra'eyl re'u qa'ra YHWH be'sheym be'tsal'eyl ben u'ri ven hhur le'ma'teyh ye'hu'dah

and~_he~will~_<u>SAY</u> "Mosheh PLUCKED-OUT" TO SON~s "Yisra'el _he~will~_<u>TURN-ASIDE</u>~+~MIGHTY-ONE" !(mp)~<u>SEE</u> _he~did~_<u>CALL-OUT</u> "Yhwh _he~will~_<u>BE</u>" in~TITLE "Betsaleyl in~SHADOW~+~MIGHTY-ONE" SON "Uriy LIGHT~me" SON "Hhur CISTERN" to~BRANCH "Yehudah THANKSGIVING"□

and "Mosheh Plucked out" said to {the} sons {of} "Yisra'el He turns El aside", see, "Yhwh He is" called out (by) title "Betsaleyl In the shadow of El"†, son {of} "Uriy My light", son {of} "Hhur Cistern", {belonging} to {the} branch {of} "Yehudah Thanksgiving",□

35:31 וַיְמַלֵּא אֹתוֹ רוּחַ אֱלֹהִים בְּחָכְמָה בִּתְבוּנָה וּבְדַעַת וּבְכָל מְלָאכָה

wai'ma'ley o'to ru'ahh e'lo'him be'hhakh'mah bit'vu'nah uv'da'at uv'khol me'la'khah

---

* The "shoham" is unknown stone.

† The phrase "Yhwh called out by title Betsaleyl " can mean, "I called Betsaleyl by name," but can also be translated as "I met with the title (meaning character or person) of Betsaleyl," as the Hebrew verb קרא may mean to "call out" or to "meet."

Revised Mechanical Translation Codes

(..) Alt Trans/App A	<..> Comp Phrase/App B	[..] Verb Form/App C	\../ Plural Form/App D
:..: Int Inf Abs	|..| Past Perf Verb	{...} Added Word	

and~*he~will~much*~<u>FILL</u> AT~him WIND
"Elohiym ^{POWER~s}" in~SKILL in~INTELLIGENCE
and~in~DISCERNMENT and~in~ALL
BUSINESS□

and he filled him {with the} wind* {of}
"Elohiym ^{Powers}", (with) skill, (with) intelligence,
and (with) discernment, and (with) all
business,□

35:32 וְלַחְשֹׁב מַחֲשָׁבֹת לַעֲשֹׂת בַּזָּהָב וּבַכֶּסֶף וּבַנְּחֹשֶׁת

we'lahh'shov ma'hha'sha'vot la'a'shot ba'za'hav u'va'ke'seph u'van'hho'shet

and~to~>~<u>THINK</u> INVENTION~s to~>~<u>DO</u> in~
the~GOLD and~in~the~SILVER and~in~the~
COPPER□

and to think inventions to make {things} (with)
the gold and (with) the silver and (with) the
copper,□

35:33 וּבַחֲרֹשֶׁת אֶבֶן לְמַלֹּאת וּבַחֲרֹשֶׁת עֵץ לַעֲשֹׂות בְּכָל מְלֶאכֶת מַחֲשָׁבֶת

u'va'hha'ro'shet e'ven le'ma'lot u'va'hha'ro'shet eyts la'a'shot be'khol me'le'khet ma'hha'sha'vet

and~in~the~ENGRAVING STONE to~
>~*much*~<u>FILL</u> and~in~the~ENGRAVING TREE
to~>~<u>DO</u> in~ALL BUSINESS INVENTION□

and (with) the engraving {of} stone to fill
{things}, and (with) the engraving {of} tree{s}†
to (make) {things} (with) all {the} business {of}
invention,□

35:34 וּלְהוֹרֹת נָתַן בְּלִבּוֹ הוּא וְאָהֳלִיאָב בֶּן אֲחִיסָמָךְ לְמַטֵּה דָן

ul'ho'rot na'tan be'li'bo hu we'a'ha'li'av ben a'hhi'sa'mak le'ma'teyh dan

and~to~>~*make*~<u>THROW</u> *he~did*~<u>GIVE</u> in~
HEART~him HE and~"Ahaliyav ^{TENT~of~+~FATHER}"
SON "Ahhiysamahh ^{BROTHER~me~+~he~did~SUPPORT}"
to~BRANCH "Dan ^{MODERATOR}"□

and he (placed) in his heart to [teach], he and
"Ahaliyav ^{Tent of father}", son {of} "Ahhiysamahh <sup>My
brother supports</sup>", belonging to {the} branch {of}
"Dan ^{Moderator}",□

35:35 מִלֵּא אֹתָם חָכְמַת לֵב לַעֲשֹׂות כָּל מְלֶאכֶת חָרָשׁ וְחֹשֵׁב וְרֹקֵם בַּתְּכֵלֶת
וּבָאַרְגָּמָן בְּתוֹלַעַת הַשָּׁנִי וּבַשֵּׁשׁ וְאֹרֵג עֹשֵׂי כָּל מְלָאכָה וְחֹשְׁבֵי מַחֲשָׁבֹת

mi'ley o'tam hhakh'mat leyv la'a'shot kol me'le'khet hha'rash we'hho'sheyv we'ro'qeym
bat'khey'let u'va'ar'ga'man be'to'la'at ha'sha'ni u'va'sheysh we'o'reyg o'sey kol me'la'khah
we'hhosh'vey ma'hha'sha'vot

he~did~much~<u>FILL</u> AT~them(m) SKILL HEART
to~>~<u>DO</u> ALL BUSINESS ENGRAVER and~
<u>THINK</u>~*ing/er(ms)* and~<u>EMBROIDER</u>~

he filled them {with the} skill {of} heart to do
all {the} business {of the} engraver and
thinking‡, and embroidering* (with) blue, and

---

* The wind, or breath, of an individual is his character.
† When the Hebrew word עֵץ is written in the singular, as it is here, it always means tree or
trees. When it is written in the plural form, it always means "wood." If the original text read
עֵצִים, the plural form, then this would be translated as wood.
‡ This may be a work of an intricate design or made by "a thinker" in the sense of a designer.

Mechanical Translation Codes

<u>WORD</u> – Verb	WORD – Noun	Word – Name	word – Pre/Suff	*word* – Conj.

ing/er(ms) in~the~BLUE and~in~the~PURPLE in~KERMES the~SCARLET and~in~the~LINEN and~BRAID~ing/er(ms) DO~ing/er(mp) ALL BUSINESS THINK~ing/er(mp) INVENTION~s□

embroidering* (with) blue, and (with) purple, (with) kermes {of} the scarlet, and (with) the linen, and {the} braider, {for} doing all {the} business {of} thinking† {of} inventions,□

Chapter 36

36:1 וְעָשָׂה בְצַלְאֵל וְאָהֳלִיאָב וְכֹל אִישׁ חֲכַם לֵב אֲשֶׁר נָתַן יְהֹוָה חָכְמָה וּתְבוּנָה בָּהֵמָּה לָדַעַת לַעֲשֹׂת אֵת כָּל מְלֶאכֶת עֲבֹדַת הַקֹּדֶשׁ לְכֹל אֲשֶׁר צִוָּה יְהֹוָה

we'a'sah ve'tsal'eyl we'a'ha'li'av we'khol ish hha'kham leyv a'sher na'tan YHWH hhakh'mah ut'vu'nah ba'hey'mah la'da'at la'a'shot et kol me'le'khet a'vo'dat ha'qo'desh le'khol a'sher tsi'wah YHWH

and~he~did~DO "Betsaleyl in~SHADOW~+~MIGHTY-ONE" and~"Ahaliyav TENT~of~+~FATHER" and~ALL MAN SKILLED-ONE HEART WHICH he~did~GIVE "Yhwh he~will~BE" SKILL and~INTELLIGENCE in~THEY(m) to~>~KNOW to~>~DO AT ALL BUSINESS SERVICE the~SPECIAL to~ALL WHICH he~did~much~DIRECT "Yhwh he~will~BE"□

and "Betsaleyl In the shadow of El", and "Ahaliyav Tent of father", and all {the} men skilled {of} heart, which "Yhwh He is" gave skill and intelligence in them, to know {how} to (make) all {the} business {of} the service {of the} special {place}, to (make) {things} (for) all which "Yhwh He is" directed,□

36:2 וַיִּקְרָא מֹשֶׁה אֶל בְּצַלְאֵל וְאֶל אָהֳלִיאָב וְאֶל כָּל אִישׁ חֲכַם לֵב אֲשֶׁר נָתַן יְהֹוָה חָכְמָה בְּלִבּוֹ כֹּל אֲשֶׁר נְשָׂאוֹ לִבּוֹ לְקָרְבָה אֶל הַמְּלָאכָה לַעֲשֹׂת אֹתָהּ

wai'yiq'ra mo'sheh el be'tsal'eyl we'el a'ha'li'av we'el kol ish hha'kham leyv a'sher na'tan YHWH hhakh'mah be'li'bo kol a'sher ne'sa'o li'bo le'qar'vah el ham'la'khah la'a'shot o'tah

and~he~will~CALL-OUT "Mosheh PLUCKED-OUT" TO "Betsaleyl in~SHADOW~+~MIGHTY-ONE" and~TO "Ahaliyav TENT~of~+~FATHER" and~TO ALL MAN SKILLED-ONE HEART WHICH he~did~GIVE "Yhwh he~will~BE" SKILL in~HEART~him ALL WHICH he~did~LIFT-UP~him HEART~him to~>~COME-NEAR TO the~BUSINESS to~>~DO AT~her□

and "Mosheh Plucked out" called out to "Betsaleyl In the shadow of El", and "Ahaliyav Tent of father", and all {the} men skilled {of} heart, which "Yhwh He is" gave skill in his heart, all (whose) heart lifted him up, to come near to the business to do her‡,□

---

* This word may also mean "an embroiderer."
† This may be a work of an intricate design or made by "a thinker" in the sense of a designer.
‡ Referring to the "business," a feminine word in Hebrew.

Revised Mechanical Translation Codes

(..) Alt Trans/App A	<..> Comp Phrase/App B	[..] Verb Form/App C	\../ Plural Form/App D
:..: Int Inf Abs	|..| Past Perf Verb	{...} Added Word	

36:3 וַיִּקְחוּ מִלִּפְנֵי מֹשֶׁה אֵת כָּל הַתְּרוּמָה אֲשֶׁר הֵבִיאוּ בְּנֵי יִשְׂרָאֵל לִמְלֶאכֶת
עֲבֹדַת הַקֹּדֶשׁ לַעֲשֹׂת אֹתָהּ וְהֵם הֵבִיאוּ אֵלָיו עוֹד נְדָבָה בַּבֹּקֶר בַּבֹּקֶר

wai'yiq'hhu mi'liph'ney mo'sheh eyt kol hat'ru'mah a'sher hey'vi'u be'ney yis'ra'eyl
lim'le'khet a'vo'dat ha'qo'desh la'a'shot o'tah we'heym hey'vi'u ey'law od ne'da'vah
ba'bo'qer ba'bo'qer

and~they(m)~will~TAKE from~to~FACE~s
"Mosheh PLUCKED-OUT" AT ALL the~OFFERING
WHICH they~did~make~COME SON~s
"Yisra'el he~will~TURN-ASIDE~+~MIGHTY-ONE" to~
BUSINESS SERVICE the~SPECIAL to~>~DO
AT~her and~THEY(m) they~did~make~COME
TO~him YET-AGAIN FREEWILL-OFFERING in~
the~MORNING in~the~MORNING□

and they took from <in front of> "Mosheh
Plucked out" all the offering{s} which {the} sons {of}
"Yisra'el He turns El aside" [brought] (for) {the}
business {of the} service {of the} special {place},
to do her*, and they, they [brought] to him
(more) freewill offering{s}, morning (by)
morning,□

36:4 וַיָּבֹאוּ כָּל הַחֲכָמִים הָעֹשִׂים אֵת כָּל מְלֶאכֶת הַקֹּדֶשׁ אִישׁ אִישׁ
מִמְּלַאכְתּוֹ אֲשֶׁר הֵמָּה עֹשִׂים

wai'ya'vo'u kol ha'hha'kha'mim ha'o'sim eyt kol me'le'khet ha'qo'desh ish ish mim'lakh'to
a'sher hey'mah o'sim

and~they(m)~will~COME ALL the~SKILLED-
ONE~s the~DO~ing/er(mp) AT ALL BUSINESS
the~SPECIAL MAN MAN from~BUSINESS~
him WHICH THEY(m) DO~ing/er(mp)□

and all the skilled ones, the {one}s doing all the
business {of the} special {place}, came, (each)
man from his business which they {were}
doing,□

36:5 וַיֹּאמְרוּ אֶל מֹשֶׁה לֵאמֹר מַרְבִּים הָעָם לְהָבִיא מִדֵּי הָעֲבֹדָה לַמְּלָאכָה
אֲשֶׁר צִוָּה יְהוָה לַעֲשֹׂת אֹתָהּ

wai'yom'ru el mo'sheh ley'mor mar'bim ha'am le'ha'vi mi'dey ha'a'vo'dah lam'la'khah
a'sher tsi'wah YHWH la'a'shot o'tah

and~they(m)~will~SAY TO "Mosheh PLUCKED-
OUT" to~>~SAY make~INCREASE-IN-
NUMBER~ing/er(mp) the~PEOPLE to~
>~make~COME from~SUFFICIENT the~
SERVICE to~the~BUSINESS WHICH he~did~
much~DIRECT "Yhwh he~will~BE" to~>~DO AT~
her□

and they said to "Mosheh Plucked out" say{ing},
the people {are} making {an} increase in
number to [bring] (more than) {is} sufficient
{for} the service (for) the business, which
"Yhwh He is" directed to do her†,□

36:6 וַיְצַו מֹשֶׁה וַיַּעֲבִירוּ קוֹל בַּמַּחֲנֶה לֵאמֹר אִישׁ וְאִשָּׁה אַל יַעֲשׂוּ עוֹד
מְלָאכָה לִתְרוּמַת הַקֹּדֶשׁ וַיִּכָּלֵא הָעָם מֵהָבִיא

wai'tsaw mo'sheh wai'ya'a'vi'ru qol ba'ma'hha'neh ley'mor ish we'i'shah al ya'a'su od
me'la'khah lit'ru'mat ha'qo'desh wai'yi'ka'ley ha'am mey'ha'vi

and~he~will~much~DIRECT "Mosheh PLUCKED-
OUT" and~they(m)~will~make~CROSS-OVER

and "Mosheh Plucked out" directed, and they
made {the} voice cross over in the campsite

---

* Referring to the "business," a feminine word in Hebrew.
† Referring to the "business," a feminine word in Hebrew.

Mechanical Translation Codes

WORD – Verb	WORD – Noun	Word – Name	word – Pre/Suff	word – Conj.

VOICE in~the~CAMPSITE to~>~SAY MAN and~WOMAN DO-NOT they(m)~will~DO YET-AGAIN BUSINESS to~OFFERING the~SPECIAL and~he~will~be~RESTRICT the~PEOPLE from~>~make~COME□

saying, do not {let a} man (or) woman do (more) business (for) the offering {of the} special {place}, and the people were restricted from [bring]{ing},□

36:7 וְהַמְּלָאכָה הָיְתָה דַיָּם לְכָל הַמְּלָאכָה לַעֲשׂוֹת אֹתָהּ וְהוֹתֵר

we'ham'la'khah hai'tah da'yam le'khol ham'la'khah la'a'shot o'tah we'ho'teyr

and~the~BUSINESS she~did~EXIST SUFFICIENT~them(m) to~ALL the~BUSINESS to~>~DO AT~her and~>~make~LEAVE-BEHIND□

and the business (was) sufficient (for) all the business to do her*, and {some was} left behind,□

36:8 וַיַּעֲשׂוּ כָל חֲכַם לֵב בְּעֹשֵׂי הַמְּלָאכָה אֶת הַמִּשְׁכָּן עֶשֶׂר יְרִיעֹת שֵׁשׁ מָשְׁזָר וּתְכֵלֶת וְאַרְגָּמָן וְתוֹלַעַת שָׁנִי כְּרֻבִים מַעֲשֵׂה חֹשֵׁב עָשָׂה אֹתָם

wai'ya'a'su khol hha'kham leyv be'o'shey ham'la'khah et ha'mish'kan e'ser ye'ri'ot sheysh mash'zar ut'khey'let we'ar'ga'man we'to'la'at sha'ni ke'ru'vim ma'a'seyh hho'sheyv a'sah o'tam

and~they(m)~will~DO ALL SKILLED-ONE HEART in~DO ing/er(mp) the~BUSINESS AT the~DWELLING TEN TENT-WALL~s LINEN be~make~TWIST-TOGETHER~ing/er(ms) and~BLUE and~PURPLE and~KERMES SCARLET KERUV~s WORK THINK~ing/er(ms) he~did~DO AT~them(m)□

and all {the} skilled one{s of} heart (with) doing the business (with) the dwelling (made) ten tent walls {of} [twisted] linen {with} blue, and purple, and kermes {of} scarlet, keruvs, {with} keruvs {of a} work {of} thinking†, he (made) them,□

36:9 אֹרֶךְ הַיְרִיעָה הָאַחַת שְׁמֹנֶה וְעֶשְׂרִים בָּאַמָּה וְרֹחַב אַרְבַּע בָּאַמָּה הַיְרִיעָה הָאֶחָת מִדָּה אַחַת לְכָל הַיְרִיעֹת

o'rekh hai'ri'ah ha'a'hhat she'mo'neh we'es'rim ba'a'mah we'ro'hhav ar'ba ba'a'mah hai'ri'ah ha'e'hhat mi'dah a'hhat le'khol hai'ri'ot

LENGTH the~TENT-WALL the~UNIT EIGHT and~TEN~s in~the~FOREARM and~WIDTH FOUR in~the~FOREARM the~TENT-WALL the~UNIT MEASUREMENT UNIT to~ALL the~TENT-WALL~s□

{the} length {of} the (one) tent wall {is} eight and \twenty/ (by) the forearm, and {the} width {is} four (by) the forearm, the (one) tent wall measurement {is} (one) (for) all the tent walls,□

36:10 וַיְחַבֵּר אֶת חֲמֵשׁ הַיְרִיעֹת אַחַת אֶל אֶחָת וְחָמֵשׁ יְרִיעֹת חִבַּר אַחַת אֶל אֶחָת

wai'hha'beyr et hha'meysh hai'ri'ot a'hhat el e'hhat we'hha'meysh ye'ri'ot hhi'bar a'hhat

---

* Referring to the "business," a feminine word in Hebrew.
† This may be a work of an intricate design or made by "a thinker" in the sense of a designer.

Revised Mechanical Translation Codes
(..) Alt Trans/App A   <..> Comp Phrase/App B   [..] Verb Form/App C   \../ Plural Form/App D
:..: Int Inf Abs |..| Past Perf Verb   {...} Added Word
~ 273 ~

el e'hhat

and~*he~will~much*~<u>COUPLE</u> AT FIVE the~ TENT-WALL~s UNIT TO UNIT and~FIVE TENT-WALL~s *he~did~much*~<u>COUPLE</u> UNIT TO UNIT□	and he will couple five {of} the tent walls unit to unit, and five tent walls he will couple unit to unit,□

36:11　וַיַּעַשׂ לֻלְאֹת תְּכֵלֶת עַל שְׂפַת הַיְרִיעָה הָאֶחָת מִקָּצָה בַּמַּחְבָּרֶת כֵּן עָשָׂה בִּשְׂפַת הַיְרִיעָה הַקִּיצוֹנָה בַּמַּחְבֶּרֶת הַשֵּׁנִית

wai'ya'as lul'ot te'khey'let al she'phat hai'ri'ah ha'e'hhat mi'qa'tsah ba'mahh'ba'ret keyn a'sah bis'phat hai'ri'ah ha'qi'tso'nah ba'mahh'be'ret ha'shey'nit

and~*he~will*~<u>DO</u> LOOP~s BLUE UPON LIP the~TENT-WALL the~UNIT from~EXTREMITY in~the~JOINT SO *he~did*~<u>DO</u> in~LIP the~ TENT-WALL the~OUTER in~the~JOINT the~ SECOND□	and he (made) loops {of} blue upon {the} lip {of} the (one) tent wall from {the} extremity in the joint, so he did (with) {the} lip {of} the outer tent wall in the second joint,□

36:12　חֲמִשִּׁים לֻלָאֹת עָשָׂה בַּיְרִיעָה הָאֶחָת וַחֲמִשִּׁים לֻלָאֹת עָשָׂה בִּקְצֵה הַיְרִיעָה אֲשֶׁר בַּמַּחְבֶּרֶת הַשֵּׁנִית מַקְבִּילֹת הַלֻּלָאֹת אַחַת אֶל אֶחָת

hha'mi'shim lu'la'ot a'sah bai'ri'ah ha'e'hhat wa'hha'mi'shim lu'la'ot a'sah biq'tseyh hai'ri'ah a'sher ba'mahh'be'ret ha'shey'nit maq'bi'lot ha'lu'la'ot a'hhat el e'hhat

FIVE~s LOOP~s *he~did*~<u>DO</u> in~the~TENT-WALL the~UNIT and~FIVE~s LOOP~s *he~did*~<u>DO</u> in~EXTREMITY the~TENT-WALL WHICH in~the~JOINT the~SECOND *make*~<u>RECEIVE</u>~ *ing/er*(fp) the~LOOP~s UNIT TO UNIT□	he (made) five loops in the (one) tent wall, and he (made) five loops in {the} extremity {of} the tent wall which {is} in the second joint receiving the loops unit to unit,□

36:13　וַיַּעַשׂ חֲמִשִּׁים קַרְסֵי זָהָב וַיְחַבֵּר אֶת הַיְרִיעֹת אַחַת אֶל אַחַת בַּקְּרָסִים וַיְהִי הַמִּשְׁכָּן אֶחָד

wai'ya'as hha'mi'shim qar'sey za'hav wai'hha'beyr et hai'ri'ot a'hhat el a'hhat baq'ra'sim wai'hi ha'mish'kan e'hhad

and~*he~will*~<u>DO</u> FIVE~s HOOK~s GOLD and~ *he~will~much*~<u>COUPLE</u> AT the~TENT-WALL~s UNIT TO UNIT in~the~HOOK~s and~ *he~will*~<u>EXIST</u> the~DWELLING UNIT□	and he (made) five hooks {of} gold, and he coupled the tent walls unit to unit in the hooks, and he existed {as} (one) dwelling,□

36:14　וַיַּעַשׂ יְרִיעֹת עִזִּים לְאֹהֶל עַל הַמִּשְׁכָּן עַשְׁתֵּי עֶשְׂרֵה יְרִיעֹת עָשָׂה אֹתָם

wai'ya'as ye'ri'ot i'zim le'o'hel al ha'mish'kan ash'tey es'reyh ye'ri'ot a'sah o'tam

and~*he~will*~<u>DO</u> TENT-WALL~s SHE-GOAT~s to~TENT UPON the~DWELLING ONE TEN TENT-WALL~s *he~did*~<u>DO</u> AT~them(m)□	and he (made) {the} tent walls {of} she-goats* (for) {a} tent upon the dwelling, he (made) <eleven> tent walls,□

---

* Specifically, the hair of the she-goats.

Mechanical Translation Codes

<u>WORD</u> – Verb	WORD – Noun	Word – Name	word – Pre/Suff	*word* – Conj.

36:15 אֹ֣רֶךְ הַיְרִיעָ֣ה הָֽאַחַ֗ת שְׁלֹשִׁים֙ בָּֽאַמָּ֔ה וְאַרְבַּ֣ע אַמּ֗וֹת רֹ֚חַב הַיְרִיעָ֣ה הָֽאֶחָ֔ת מִדָּ֥ה אַחַ֖ת לְעַשְׁתֵּ֥י עֶשְׂרֵ֖ה יְרִיעֹֽת

o'rekh hai'ri'ah ha'a'hhat she'lo'shim ba'a'mah we'ar'ba a'mot ro'hhav hai'ri'ah ha'e'hhat mi'dah a'hhat le'ash'tey es'reyh ye'ri'ot

LENGTH the~TENT-WALL the~UNIT THREE~s in~the~FOREARM and~FOUR FOREARM~s WIDTH the~TENT-WALL the~UNIT MEASUREMENT UNIT to~ONE TEN TENT-WALL~s□	{the} length {of} the (one) tent wall {is} \thirty/ (by) the forearm, and four forearms {is the} width, the (one) tent wall measurement {is} (one) (for) {the} <eleven> tent walls,□

36:16 וַיְחַבֵּ֛ר אֶת־חֲמֵ֥שׁ הַיְרִיעֹ֖ת לְבָ֑ד וְאֶת־שֵׁ֥שׁ הַיְרִיעֹ֖ת לְבָֽד

wai'hha'beyr et hha'meysh hai'ri'ot le'vad we'et sheysh hai'ri'ot le'vad

and~he~will~much~COUPLE AT FIVE the~TENT-WALL~s to~STICK and~AT SIX the~TENT-WALL~s to~STICK□	and he coupled five {of} the tent walls <alone> and six {of} the tent walls <alone>,□

36:17 וַיַּ֜עַשׂ לֻֽלָאֹ֣ת חֲמִשִּׁ֗ים עַ֚ל שְׂפַ֣ת הַיְרִיעָ֔ה הַקִּיצֹנָ֖ה בַּמַּחְבָּ֑רֶת וַחֲמִשִּׁ֣ים לֻֽלָאֹ֗ת עָשָׂה֙ עַל־שְׂפַ֣ת הַיְרִיעָ֔ה הַחֹבֶ֖רֶת הַשֵּׁנִֽית

wai'ya'as lu'la'ot hha'mi'shim al she'phat hai'ri'ah ha'qi'tso'nah ba'mahh'ba'ret wa'hha'mi'shim lu'la'ot a'sah al she'phat hai'ri'ah ha'hho've'ret ha'shey'nit

and~he~will~DO LOOP~s FIVE~s UPON LIP the~TENT-WALL the~OUTER in~the~JOINT and~FIVE~s LOOP~s he~did~DO UPON LIP the~TENT-WALL the~COUPLING the~SECOND□	and he (made) \fifty/ loops upon {the} lip {of} the outer tent wall in the joint, and \fifty/ loops he (made) upon {the} lip {of} the tent wall {of} the second coupling,□

36:18 וַיַּ֛עַשׂ קַרְסֵ֥י נְחֹ֖שֶׁת חֲמִשִּׁ֑ים לְחַבֵּ֥ר אֶת־הָאֹ֖הֶל לִֽהְיֹ֥ת אֶחָֽד

wai'ya'as qar'sey ne'hho'shet hha'mi'shim le'hha'beyr et ha'o'hel lih'yot e'hhad

and~he~will~DO HOOK~s COPPER FIVE~s to~>~much~COUPLE AT the~TENT to~>~EXIST UNIT□	and he (made) \fifty/ copper hooks (for) coupl{ing} the tent to exist {as a} unit,□

36:19 וַיַּ֤עַשׂ מִכְסֶה֙ לָאֹ֔הֶל עֹרֹ֥ת אֵילִ֖ם מְאָדָּמִ֑ים וּמִכְסֵ֛ה עֹרֹ֥ת תְּחָשִׁ֖ים מִלְמָֽעְלָה

wai'ya'as mikh'seh la'o'hel o'rot ey'lim me'a'da'mim u'mikh'seyh o'rot te'hha'sim mil'ma'lah

and~he~will~DO ROOF-COVERING to~the~TENT SKIN~s BUCK~s be~much~BE-RED~	and he made {a} roof covering (for) the tent {from} skins {of} bucks being red, and {a} roof

---

Revised Mechanical Translation Codes

(..) Alt Trans/App A   <..> Comp Phrase/App B   [..] Verb Form/App C   \../ Plural Form/App D

:..: Int Inf Abs |..| Past Perf Verb   {...} Added Word

ing/er(mp) and~ROOF-COVERING SKIN~s TAHHASH~s from~to~UPWARD~unto□

covering {from} skins {of} tahhashs* {on} <top>,□

36:20

וַיַּעַשׂ אֶת הַקְּרָשִׁים לַמִּשְׁכָּן עֲצֵי שִׁטִּים עֹמְדִים

wai'ya'as et haq'ra'shim la'mish'kan a'tsey shi'tim om'dim

and~*he~will*~<u>DO</u> AT the~BOARD~s to~the~ DWELLING TREE~s ACACIA~s <u>STAND</u>~ ing/er(mp)□

and he (made) the boards (for) the dwelling {of} acacia \wood/, standing**†**,□

36:21

עֶשֶׂר אַמֹּת אֹרֶךְ הַקָּרֶשׁ וְאַמָּה וַחֲצִי הָאַמָּה רֹחַב הַקֶּרֶשׁ הָאֶחָד

e'ser a'mot o'rekh ha'qa'resh we'a'mah wa'hha'tsi ha'a'mah ro'hhav ha'qe'resh ha'e'hhad

TEN FOREARM~s LENGTH the~BOARD and~ FOREARM and~HALF the~FOREARM WIDTH the~BOARD the~UNIT□

ten forearms {is the} length {of} the board, and {a} forearm and {a} half {of} the forearm {is the} width {of} the (one) board,□

36:22

שְׁתֵּי יָדֹת לַקֶּרֶשׁ הָאֶחָד מְשֻׁלָּבֹת אַחַת אֶל אֶחָת כֵּן עָשָׂה לְכֹל קַרְשֵׁי הַמִּשְׁכָּן

she'tey ya'dot la'qe'resh ha'e'hhad me'shu'la'vot a'hhat el e'hhat keyn a'sah le'khol qar'shey ha'mish'kan

TWO HAND~s to~the~BOARD the~UNIT *be~ much*~<u>JOINED-TOGETHER</u>~*ing/er(fp)* UNIT TO UNIT SO *he~did*~<u>DO</u> to~ALL BOARD~s the~DWELLING□

two hands**‡** (for) the (one) board {for} being joined together unit to unit, so he (made) (for) all {the} boards {of} the dwelling,□

36:23

וַיַּעַשׂ אֶת הַקְּרָשִׁים לַמִּשְׁכָּן עֶשְׂרִים קְרָשִׁים לִפְאַת נֶגֶב תֵּימָנָה

wai'ya'as et haq'ra'shim la'mish'kan es'rim qe'ra'shim liph'at ne'gev tey'ma'nah

and~*he~will*~<u>DO</u> AT the~BOARD~s to~the~ DWELLING TEN~s BOARD~s to~EDGE "Negev PARCHED" SOUTH~unto□

and he (made) the boards (for) the dwelling, \twenty/ boards to {the} edge unto the "Negev Parched"**§**,□

36:24

וְאַרְבָּעִים אַדְנֵי כֶסֶף עָשָׂה תַּחַת עֶשְׂרִים הַקְּרָשִׁים שְׁנֵי אֲדָנִים תַּחַת הַקֶּרֶשׁ הָאֶחָד לִשְׁתֵּי יְדֹתָיו וּשְׁנֵי אֲדָנִים תַּחַת הַקֶּרֶשׁ הָאֶחָד לִשְׁתֵּי יְדֹתָיו

we'ar'ba'im ad'ney ke'seph a'sah ta'hhat es'rim haq'ra'shim she'ney a'da'nim ta'hhat ha'qe'resh ha'e'hhad lish'tey ye'do'taw ush'ney a'da'nim ta'hhat ha'qe'resh ha'e'hhad

---

* The Tahhash is an unknown species of animal.
† The contextual meaning of this word is uncertain. It may mean "standing acacia wood" or "acacia wood standing up."
‡ These "hands" are probably notched tenons which are cut into the board to join the boards together.
§ That is the "south."

Mechanical Translation Codes

<u>WORD</u> – Verb	WORD – Noun	Word – Name	word – Pre/Suff	*word* – Conj.

lish'tey ye'do'taw

and~FOUR~s FOOTING~s SILVER *he~did~*<u>DO</u> UNDER TEN~s the~BOARD~s TWO FOOTING~s UNDER the~BOARD the~UNIT to~TWO HAND~s~him and~TWO FOOTING~s UNDER the~BOARD the~UNIT to~TWO HAND~s~him□	and \forty/ footings {of} silver he (made) under the \twenty/ boards, two footings under the (one) board (for) his two hands* and two footings under the (other) board (for) his two hands,□

36:25   וּלְצֶלַע הַמִּשְׁכָּן הַשֵּׁנִית לִפְאַת צָפוֹן עָשָׂה עֶשְׂרִים קְרָשִׁים

ul'tse'la ha'mish'kan ha'shey'nit liph'at tsa'phon a'sah es'rim qe'ra'shim

and~to~RIB the~DWELLING the~SECOND to~ EDGE NORTH *he~did~*<u>DO</u> TEN~s BOARD~s□	and (for) {the} second rib {of} the dwelling, (at) {the} north edge, he (made) \twenty/ boards,□

36:26   וְאַרְבָּעִים אַדְנֵיהֶם כָּסֶף שְׁנֵי אֲדָנִים תַּחַת הַקֶּרֶשׁ הָאֶחָד וּשְׁנֵי אֲדָנִים תַּחַת הַקֶּרֶשׁ הָאֶחָד

we'ar'ba'im ad'ney'hem ka'seph she'ney a'da'nim ta'hhat ha'qe'resh ha'e'hhad ush'ney a'da'nim ta'hhat ha'qe'resh ha'e'hhad

and~FOUR~s FOOTING~s~them(m) SILVER TWO FOOTING~s UNDER the~BOARD the~ UNIT and~TWO FOOTING~s UNDER the~ BOARD the~UNIT□	and their \forty/ footings {of} silver, two footings under the (one) board and two footings under the (other) board,□

36:27   וּלְיַרְכְּתֵי הַמִּשְׁכָּן יָמָּה עָשָׂה שִׁשָּׁה קְרָשִׁים

ul'yar'ke'tey ha'mish'kan ya'mah a'sah shi'shah qe'ra'shim

and~to~FLANK~s2 the~DWELLING SEA~unto *he~did~*<u>DO</u> SIX BOARD~s□	and (for) {the} two flanks {of} the dwelling unto the sea† he (made) six boards,□

36:28   וּשְׁנֵי קְרָשִׁים עָשָׂה לִמְקֻצְעֹת הַמִּשְׁכָּן בַּיַּרְכָתָיִם

ush'ney qe'ra'shim a'sah lim'quts'ot ha'mish'kan bai'yar'kha'ta'yim

and~TWO BOARD~s *he~did~*<u>DO</u> to~CORNER- POST~s the~DWELLING in~the~FLANK~s2□	and two boards he (made) (for) {the} corner posts {of} the dwelling in the two flanks,□

36:29   וְהָיוּ תוֹאֲמָם מִלְמַטָּה וְיַחְדָּו יִהְיוּ תַמִּים אֶל רֹאשׁוֹ אֶל הַטַּבַּעַת הָאֶחָת כֵּן עָשָׂה לִשְׁנֵיהֶם לִשְׁנֵי הַמִּקְצֹעֹת

we'hai'u to'a'mim mil'ma'tah we'yahh'daw yih'yu ta'mim el ro'sho el ha'ta'ba'at ha'e'hhat keyn a'sah lish'ney'hem lish'ney ha'miq'tso'ot

and~*they~did~*<u>EXIST</u> BE-DOUBLE~*ing/er*(mp)	and they existed being double beneath, and

---

* These "hands" are probably notched tenons which are cut into the board to join the boards together.

† Meaning "the west."

from~to~BENEATH and~TOGETHER~him
they(m)~will~<u>EXIST</u> WHOLE TO HEAD~him
TO the~RING the~UNIT SO he~did~<u>DO</u> to~
TWO~them(m) to~TWO the~BUTTRESS~s□

together they existed whole to his head (for)
the (one) ring, so he did exist (for) {the} two
{of} them, (for) two {of} the buttresses,□

36:30 וְהָיוּ שְׁמֹנָה קְרָשִׁים וְאַדְנֵיהֶם כֶּסֶף שִׁשָּׁה עָשָׂר אֲדָנִים שְׁנֵי אֲדָנִים תַּחַת הַקֶּרֶשׁ הָאֶחָד

we'hai'u she'mo'nah qe'ra'shim we'ad'ney'hem ke'seph shi'shah a'sar a'da'nim she'ney
a'da'nim she'ney a'da'nim ta'hhat ha'qe'resh ha'e'hhad

and~they~did~<u>EXIST</u> EIGHT BOARD~s and~
FOOTING~s~them(m) SILVER SIX TEN
FOOTING~s TWO FOOTING~s TWO
FOOTING~s UNDER the~BOARD the~UNIT□

and eight boards and their footings {of} silver
existed, <sixteen> footings, two footings {under
the one board, and}* two footings under the
(other) board,□

36:31 וַיַּעַשׂ בְּרִיחֵי עֲצֵי שִׁטִּים חֲמִשָּׁה לְקַרְשֵׁי צֶלַע הַמִּשְׁכָּן הָאֶחָת

wai'ya'as be'ri'hhey a'tsey shi'tim hha'mi'shah le'qar'shey tse'la ha'mish'kan ha'e'hhat

and~he~will~<u>DO</u> WOOD-BAR~s TREE~s
ACACIA~s FIVE to~BOARD~s RIB the~
DWELLING the~UNIT□

and he (made) wood bars {of} acacia \wood/,
five (for) {the} boards {of} the (one) rib {of} the
dwelling,□

36:32 וַחֲמִשָּׁה בְרִיחִם לְקַרְשֵׁי צֶלַע הַמִּשְׁכָּן הַשֵּׁנִית וַחֲמִשָּׁה בְרִיחִם לְקַרְשֵׁי הַמִּשְׁכָּן לַיַּרְכָתַיִם יָמָּה

wa'hha'mi'shah ve'ri'hhim le'qar'shey tse'la ha'mish'kan ha'shey'nit wa'hha'mi'shah
ve'ri'hhim le'qar'shey ha'mish'kan lai'yar'kha'ta'yim ya'mah

and~FIVE WOOD-BAR~s to~BOARD~s RIB
the~DWELLING the~SECOND and~FIVE
WOOD-BAR~s to~BOARD~s the~DWELLING
to~the~FLANK~s2 SEA~unto□

and five wood bars (for) {the} boards {of} the
second rib {of} the dwelling, and five wood bars
(for) {the} boards {of} the two flanks {of} the
dwelling unto {the} sea†,□

36:33 וַיַּעַשׂ אֶת הַבְּרִיחַ הַתִּיכֹן לִבְרֹחַ בְּתוֹךְ הַקְּרָשִׁים מִן הַקָּצֶה אֶל הַקָּצֶה

wai'ya'as et ha'be'ri'ahh ha'ti'khon liv'ro'ahh be'tokh haq'ra'shim min ha'qa'tseh el
ha'qa'tseh

and~he~will~<u>DO</u> AT the~WOOD-BAR the~
MIDDLEMOST to~>~<u>FLEE-AWAY</u> in~MIDST
the~BOARD~s FROM the~EXTREMITY TO
the~EXTREMITY□

and he (made) the middlemost wood bar to
flee away‡ in {the} midst {of} the boards from
the extremity to the {other} extremity,□

36:34 וְאֶת הַקְּרָשִׁים צִפָּה זָהָב וְאֶת טַבְּעֹתָם עָשָׂה זָהָב בָּתִּים לַבְּרִיחִם וַיְצַף אֶת הַבְּרִיחִם זָהָב

---

* The Hebrew text appears to be missing this phrase (compare with Exodus 36:26).
† Meaning "the west."
‡ "Flee away" probably means "pass through."

Mechanical Translation Codes

<u>WORD</u> – Verb	WORD – Noun	Word – Name	word – Pre/Suff	*word* – Conj.

we'et haq'ra'shim tsi'pah za'hav we'et ta'be'o'tam a'sah za'hav ba'tim la'be'ri'hhim wai'tsaph et ha'be'ri'hhim za'hav

and~AT the~BOARD~s *he~did~much~* <u>OVERLAY</u> GOLD and~AT RING~s~them(m) *he~did~* <u>DO</u> GOLD HOUSE~s to~the~WOOD-BAR~s and~*he~will~much~* <u>OVERLAY</u> AT the~ WOOD-BAR~s GOLD□	and he overlaid the boards {with} gold, and he (made) their rings {with} gold, houses* (for) the wood bars, and he overlaid the wood bars {with} gold,□

36:35 וַיַּעַשׂ אֶת הַפָּרֹכֶת תְּכֵלֶת וְאַרְגָּמָן וְתוֹלַעַת שָׁנִי וְשֵׁשׁ מָשְׁזָר מַעֲשֵׂה חֹשֵׁב עָשָׂה אֹתָהּ כְּרֻבִים

wai'ya'as et ha'pa'ro'khet te'khey'let we'ar'ga'man we'to'la'at sha'ni we'sheysh mash'zar ma'a'seyh hho'sheyv a'sah o'tah ke'ru'vim

and~*he~will~* <u>DO</u> AT the~TENT-CURTAIN BLUE and~PURPLE and~KERMES SCARLET and~LINEN *be~make~* <u>TWIST-TOGETHER</u>~ *ing/er(ms)* WORK <u>THINK</u>~*ing/er(ms)* *he~did~* <u>DO</u> AT~her KERUV~s□	and he (made) the tent curtain {with} blue, and purple, and kermes {of} scarlet, and [twisted] linen, {with} keruvs {of a} work {of} thinking†, he (made) her‡,□

36:36 וַיַּעַשׂ לָהּ אַרְבָּעָה עַמּוּדֵי שִׁטִּים וַיְצַפֵּם זָהָב וָוֵיהֶם זָהָב וַיִּצֹק לָהֶם אַרְבָּעָה אַדְנֵי כָסֶף

wai'ya'as lah ar'ba'ah a'mu'dey shi'tim wai'tsa'peym za'hav wa'wey'hem za'hav wai'yi'tsoq la'hem ar'ba'ah ad'ney kha'seph

and~*he~will~* <u>DO</u> to~her FOUR PILLAR~s ACACIA~s and~*he~will~much~* <u>OVERLAY</u>~ them(m) GOLD PEG~s~them(m) GOLD and~ *he~will~* <u>POUR-DOWN</u> to~them(m) FOUR FOOTING~s SILVER□	and he (made) (for) her four pillars {of} acacia, and he overlaid them {with} gold, their pegs {with} gold, and he poured down§ (for) them four footings {of} silver,□

36:37 וַיַּעַשׂ מָסָךְ לְפֶתַח הָאֹהֶל תְּכֵלֶת וְאַרְגָּמָן וְתוֹלַעַת שָׁנִי וְשֵׁשׁ מָשְׁזָר מַעֲשֵׂה רֹקֵם

wai'ya'as ma'sakh le'phe'tahh ha'o'hel te'khey'let we'ar'ga'man we'to'la'at sha'ni we'sheysh mash'zar ma'a'seyh ro'qeym

and~*he~will~* <u>DO</u> CANOPY to~OPENING the~ TENT BLUE and~PURPLE and~KERMES SCARLET and~LINEN *be~make~* <u>TWIST-TOGETHER</u>~*ing/er(ms)* WORK <u>EMBROIDER</u>~ *ing/er(ms)*□	and he (made) {a} canopy (for) {the} opening {of} the tent {of} blue, and purple, and kermes {of} scarlet, and [twisted] linen, {a} work {of} embroidering**,□

---

* Or "housings."

† This may be a work of an intricate design or made by "a thinker" in the sense of a designer.

‡ Referring to the "tent curtain," a feminine word in Hebrew.

§ In this context, to "pour down" means to "cast" an object from a molten metal.

** This word may also mean "an embroiderer."

Revised Mechanical Translation Codes

(..) Alt Trans/App A   <..> Comp Phrase/App B   [..] Verb Form/App C   \../ Plural Form/App D

:...: Int Inf Abs |..| Past Perf Verb   {...} Added Word

36:38 וְאֶת עַמּוּדָיו חֲמִשָּׁה וְאֶת וָוֵיהֶם וְצִפָּה רָאשֵׁיהֶם וַחֲשֻׁקֵיהֶם זָהָב וְאַדְנֵיהֶם חֲמִשָּׁה נְחֹשֶׁת

we'et a'mu'daw hha'mi'shah we'et wa'wey'hem we'tsi'pah ra'shey'hem wa'hha'shu'qey'hem za'hav we'ad'ney'hem hha'mi'shah ne'hho'shet

and~AT PILLAR~s~him FIVE and~AT PEG~s~ them(m) and~*he~did~much~*<u>OVERLAY</u> HEAD~s~them(m) and~BINDER~s~them(m) GOLD and~FOOTING~s~them(m) FIVE COPPER□

and his five pillars and their pegs, and he overlaid their heads and their binders {with} gold, and their five footings {with} copper,□

Chapter 37

37:1 וַיַּעַשׂ בְּצַלְאֵל אֶת הָאָרֹן עֲצֵי שִׁטִּים אַמָּתַיִם וָחֵצִי אָרְכּוֹ וְאַמָּה וָחֵצִי רָחְבּוֹ וְאַמָּה וָחֵצִי קֹמָתוֹ

wai'ya'as be'tsal'eyl et ha'a'ron a'tsey shi'tim a'ma'ta'yim wa'hhey'tsi ar'ko we'a'mah wa'hhey'tsi rahh'bo we'a'mah wa'hhey'tsi qo'ma'to

and~*he~will~*DO "Betsaleyl ^{in~SHADOW~+~MIGHTY-ONE}" AT the~BOX TREE~s ACACIA~s FOREARM~s2 and~HALF LENGTH~him and~ FOREARM and~HALF WIDTH~him and~ FOREARM and~HALF HEIGHT~him□

and "Betsaleyl ^{In the shadow of El}" (made) the box {of} acacia \wood/, two forearms and {a} half {is} his length, and {a} forearm and {a} half {is} his width, and {a} forearm and {a} half {is} his height,□

37:2 וַיְצַפֵּהוּ זָהָב טָהוֹר מִבַּיִת וּמִחוּץ וַיַּעַשׂ לוֹ זֵר זָהָב סָבִיב

wai'tsa'pey'hu za'hav ta'hor mi'ba'yit u'mi'hhuts wai'ya'as lo zeyr za'hav sa'viv

and~*he~will~much~*<u>OVERLAY</u>~him GOLD PURE from~HOUSE and~from~OUTSIDE and~*he~will~*DO to~him MOLDING GOLD ALL-AROUND□

and he overlaid him {with} pure gold, from {the} (inside) and from {the} outside, and he (made) (for) him {a} molding {of} gold all around,□

37:3 וַיִּצֹק לוֹ אַרְבַּע טַבְּעֹת זָהָב עַל אַרְבַּע פַּעֲמֹתָיו וּשְׁתֵּי טַבָּעֹת עַל צַלְעוֹ הָאֶחָת וּשְׁתֵּי טַבָּעֹת עַל צַלְעוֹ הַשֵּׁנִית

wai'yi'tsoq lo ar'ba ta'be'ot za'hav al ar'ba pa'a'mo'taw ush'tey ta'ba'ot al tsal'o ha'e'hhat ush'tey ta'ba'ot al tsal'o ha'shey'nit

and~*he~will~*<u>POUR-DOWN</u> to~him FOUR RING~s GOLD UPON FOUR FOOTSTEP~s~him and~TWO RING~s UPON RIB~him the~UNIT and~TWO RING~s UPON RIB~him the~ SECOND□

and he poured down* (for) him four rings {of} gold upon his four footsteps† and two rings upon his (one) rib, and two rings upon his second rib,□

---

* In this context, to "pour down" means to "cast" an object from a molten metal.
† Or "feet."

Mechanical Translation Codes

<u>WORD</u> – Verb   WORD – Noun   Word – Name   word – Pre/Suff   *word* – Conj.

~ 280 ~

37:4 וַיַּעַשׂ בַּדֵּי עֲצֵי שִׁטִּים וַיְצַף אֹתָם זָהָב

wai'ya'as ba'dey a'tsey shi'tim wai'tsaph o'tam za'hav

and~*he*~*will*~<u>DO</u> STICK~s TREE~s ACACIA~s and~*he*~*will*~much~<u>OVERLAY</u> AT~them(m) GOLD□	and he (made) sticks {of} acacia \wood/, and he overlaid them {with} gold,□

37:5 וַיָּבֵא אֶת הַבַּדִּים בַּטַּבָּעֹת עַל צַלְעֹת הָאָרֹן לָשֵׂאת אֶת הָאָרֹן

wai'ya'vey et ha'ba'dim ba'ta'ba'ot al tsal'ot ha'a'ron la'seyt et ha'a'ron

and~*he*~*will*~make~<u>COME</u> AT the~STICK~s in~the~RING~s UPON RIB~s the~BOX to~ >~<u>LIFT-UP</u> AT the~BOX□	and he [brought] the sticks in the rings upon {the} ribs {of} the box to lift up the box,□

37:6 וַיַּעַשׂ כַּפֹּרֶת זָהָב טָהוֹר אַמָּתַיִם וָחֵצִי אָרְכָּהּ וְאַמָּה וָחֵצִי רָחְבָּהּ

wai'ya'as ka'po'ret za'hav ta'hor a'ma'ta'yim wa'hhey'tsi ar'kah we'a'mah wa'hhey'tsi rahh'bah

and~*he*~*will*~<u>DO</u> LID GOLD PURE FOREARM~s2 and~HALF LENGTH~her and~ FOREARM and~HALF WIDTH~her□	and he (made) {a} lid {of} pure gold, two forearms and {a} half {is} her length, and {a} forearm and {a} half {is} her width,□

37:7 וַיַּעַשׂ שְׁנֵי כְרֻבִים זָהָב מִקְשָׁה עָשָׂה אֹתָם מִשְּׁנֵי קְצוֹת הַכַּפֹּרֶת

wai'ya'as she'ney khe'ru'vim za'hav miq'shah a'sah o'tam mish'ney qe'tsot ha'ka'po'ret

and~*he*~*will*~<u>DO</u> TWO KERUV~s GOLD BEATEN-WORK *he*~*did*~<u>DO</u> AT~them(m) from~TWO EXTREMITY~s the~LID□	and he (made) two keruvs {of} gold, {a} beaten work, he (made) them from {the} two extremities {of} the lid,□

37:8 כְּרוּב אֶחָד מִקָּצָה מִזֶּה וּכְרוּב אֶחָד מִקָּצָה מִזֶּה מִן הַכַּפֹּרֶת עָשָׂה אֶת הַכְּרֻבִים מִשְּׁנֵי קְצוֹותוֹ

ke'ruv e'hhad mi'qa'tsah mi'zeh ukh'ruv e'hhad mi'qa'tsah mi'zeh min ha'ka'po'ret a'sah et hak'ru'vim mish'ney qits'wo'to

KERUV UNIT from~EXTREMITY from~THIS and~KERUV UNIT from~EXTREMITY from~ THIS FROM the~LID *he*~*did*~<u>DO</u> AT the~ KERUV~s from~TWO EXTREMITY~s~him□	(one) keruv from this extremity, and {the} (other) keruv from (that) extremity, from the lid he (made) the keruvs, from {the} two end{s of} his extremities*,□

37:9 וַיִּהְיוּ הַכְּרֻבִים פֹּרְשֵׂי כְנָפַיִם לְמַעְלָה סֹכְכִים בְּכַנְפֵיהֶם עַל הַכַּפֹּרֶת וּפְנֵיהֶם אִישׁ אֶל אָחִיו אֶל הַכַּפֹּרֶת הָיוּ פְּנֵי הַכְּרֻבִים

wai'yih'yu hak'ru'vim por'sey khe'na'pha'yim le'ma'lah sokh'khim be'khan'phey'hem al ha'ka'po'ret uph'ney'hem ish el a'hhiw el ha'ka'po'ret hai'u pe'ney hak'ru'vim

and~*they*(m)~*will*~<u>EXIST</u> the~KERUV~s	and the keruvs (were) spreading out {the}

---

* The Hebrew word קְצוֹותוֹ is written defectively and should be written as קְצוֹתָיו.

Revised Mechanical Translation Codes

(..) Alt Trans/App A   <..> Comp Phrase/App B   [..] Verb Form/App C   \../ Plural Form/App D

:..: Int Inf Abs |..| Past Perf Verb   {...} Added Word

SPREAD-OUT~*ing/er*(mp) WING~s2 to~ UPWARD~*unto* FENCE-AROUND~*ing/er*(mp) in~WING~s~them(m) UPON the~LID and~ FACE~s~them(m) MAN TO BROTHER~him TO the~LID *they~did~*EXIST FACE~s the~ KERUV~s□

wings <above>, fencing around (with) their wings upon the lid, and their faces (each) to his brother, {the} faces {of} the keruvs will exist to{ward} the lid,□

37:10 וַיַּעַשׂ אֶת הַשֻּׁלְחָן עֲצֵי שִׁטִּים אַמָּתַיִם אָרְכּוֹ וְאַמָּה רָחְבּוֹ וְאַמָּה וָחֵצִי קֹמָתוֹ

wai'ya'as et ha'shul'hhan a'tsey shi'tim a'ma'ta'yim ar'ko we'a'mah rahh'bo we'a'mah wa'hhey'tsi qo'ma'to

and~*he~will~*DO AT the~TABLE TREE~s ACACIA~s FOREARM~s2 LENGTH~him and~ FOREARM WIDTH~him and~FOREARM and~ HALF HEIGHT~him□

and he (made) the table {of} acacia \wood/, two forearms {is} his length, and {a} forearm {is} his width, and {a} forearm and {a} half {is} his height,□

37:11 וַיְצַף אֹתוֹ זָהָב טָהוֹר וַיַּעַשׂ לוֹ זֵר זָהָב סָבִיב

wai'tsaph o'to za'hav ta'hor wai'ya'as lo zeyr za'hav sa'viv

and~*he~will~much~*OVERLAY AT~him GOLD PURE and~*he~will~*DO to~him MOLDING GOLD ALL-AROUND□

and he overlaid him {with} pure gold, and he (made) (for) him {a} molding {of} gold all around,□

37:12 וַיַּעַשׂ לוֹ מִסְגֶּרֶת טֹפַח סָבִיב וַיַּעַשׂ זֵר זָהָב לְמִסְגַּרְתּוֹ סָבִיב

wai'ya'as lo mis'ge'ret to'phahh sa'viv wai'ya'as zeyr za'hav le'mis'gar'to sa'viv

and~*he~will~*DO to~him RIM HAND-SPAN ALL-AROUND and~*he~will~*DO MOLDING GOLD to~RIM~him ALL-AROUND□

and he (made) (for) him {a} rim {a} hand span all around, and he made {a} molding {of} gold (for) him all around,□

37:13 וַיִּצֹק לוֹ אַרְבַּע טַבְּעֹת זָהָב וַיִּתֵּן אֶת הַטַּבָּעֹת עַל אַרְבַּע הַפֵּאֹת אֲשֶׁר לְאַרְבַּע רַגְלָיו

wai'yi'tsoq lo ar'ba ta'be'ot za'hav wai'yi'teyn et ha'ta'ba'ot al ar'ba ha'pey'ot a'sher le'ar'ba rag'law

and~*he~will~*POUR-DOWN to~him FOUR RING~s GOLD and~*he~will~*GIVE AT the~ RING~s UPON FOUR the~EDGE~s WHICH to~ FOUR FOOT~s2~him□

and he poured down* (for) him four rings {of} gold, and he (placed) the rings upon the four edges which {is} (for) his four feet,□

37:14 לְעֻמַּת הַמִּסְגֶּרֶת הָיוּ הַטַּבָּעֹת בָּתִּים לַבַּדִּים לָשֵׂאת אֶת הַשֻּׁלְחָן

le'u'mat ha'mis'ge'ret hai'u ha'ta'ba'ot ba'tim la'ba'dim la'seyt et ha'shul'hhan

to~ALONGSIDE the~RIM *they~did~*EXIST

the rings existed alongside the rim, houses*

---

* In this context, to "pour down" means to "cast" an object from a molten metal.

Mechanical Translation Codes

the~RING~s HOUSE~s to~the~STICK~s to~
>~LIFT-UP AT the~TABLE□

(for) the sticks to lift up the table,□

37:15 וַיַּעַשׂ אֶת הַבַּדִּים עֲצֵי שִׁטִּים וַיְצַף אֹתָם זָהָב לָשֵׂאת אֶת הַשֻּׁלְחָן

wai'ya'as et ha'ba'dim a'tsey shi'tim wai'tsaph o'tam za'hav la'seyt et ha'shul'hhan

and~he~will~DO AT the~STICK~s TREE~s
ACACIA~s and~he~will~much~OVERLAY AT~
them(m) GOLD to~>~LIFT-UP AT the~
TABLE□

and he (made) the sticks {of} acacia \wood/,
and he overlaid them {with} gold to lift up the
table,□

37:16 וַיַּעַשׂ אֶת הַכֵּלִים אֲשֶׁר עַל הַשֻּׁלְחָן אֶת קְעָרֹתָיו וְאֶת כַּפֹּתָיו וְאֶת
מְנַקִּיֹּתָיו וְאֶת הַקְּשָׂוֹת אֲשֶׁר יֻסַּךְ בָּהֵן זָהָב טָהוֹר

wai'ya'as et ha'key'lim a'sher al ha'shul'hhan et qe'a'ro'taw we'et ka'po'taw we'eyt
me'na'qi'yo'taw we'et haq'sa'ot a'sher yu'sakh ba'heyn za'hav ta'hor

and~he~will~DO AT the~ITEM~s WHICH
UPON the~TABLE AT PLATTER~s~him and~
AT PALM~s~him and~AT SACRIFICIAL-
BOWL~s~him and~AT the~JUG~s WHICH he~
will~be~make~POUR in~them(f) GOLD
PURE□

and he (made) the items which {are} upon the
table, his platters, and his palms**†** and his
sacrificial bowls and his jugs, which will be
{for} pour{ing} (with) them, {and he made
them with}**‡** pure gold,□

37:17 וַיַּעַשׂ אֶת הַמְּנֹרָה זָהָב טָהוֹר מִקְשָׁה עָשָׂה אֶת הַמְּנֹרָה יְרֵכָהּ וְקָנָהּ
גְּבִיעֶיהָ כַּפְתֹּרֶיהָ וּפְרָחֶיהָ מִמֶּנָּה הָיוּ

wai'ya'as et ham'no'rah za'hav ta'hor miq'shah a'sah et ham'no'rah ye'rey'khah
we'qa'nah ge'vi'ey'ah kaph'to'rey'ah uph'ra'hhey'ah mi'me'nah hai'u

and~he~will~DO AT the~LAMPSTAND GOLD
PURE BEATEN-WORK he~did~DO AT the~
LAMPSTAND MIDSECTION~her and~STALK~
her BOWL~s~her KNOB~s~her and~BUD~s~
her FROM~her they~did~EXIST□

and he (made) the lampstand {with} pure
gold, {a} beaten work, and he (made) the
lampstand, her midsection, and her stalk, her
bowls, her knobs and her buds existed (out of)
her**§**,□

37:18 וְשִׁשָּׁה קָנִים יֹצְאִים מִצִּדֶּיהָ שְׁלֹשָׁה קְנֵי מְנֹרָה מִצִּדָּהּ הָאֶחָד וּשְׁלֹשָׁה
קְנֵי מְנֹרָה מִצִּדָּהּ הַשֵּׁנִי

we'shi'shah qa'nim yots'lm mi'tsi'dey'ah she'lo'shah qe'ney me'no'rah mi'tsi'dah
ha'e'hhad ush'lo'shah qe'ney me'no'rah mi'tsi'dah ha'shey'ni

and~SIX STALK~s GO-OUT~ing/er(mp) from~
SIDE~s~her THREE STALK~s LAMPSTAND
from~SIDE~her the~UNIT and~THREE

and six stalks {are} going out from her sides,
three stalks {of the} lampstand (out of) her
(one) side, and three stalks {of} the lampstand

---

* Or "housings."
† That is, "spoons."
‡ The end of this verse appears to be missing "he made them" (compare with Exodus 25:29).
§ "out of her" means that each of these parts is beaten (molded) out of the one piece.

Revised Mechanical Translation Codes

(..) Alt Trans/App A   <..> Comp Phrase/App B   [..] Verb Form/App C   \../ Plural Form/App D
:..: Int Inf Abs |..| Past Perf Verb   {...} Added Word

STALK~s LAMPSTAND from~SIDE~her the~
SECOND□

(out of) her second side,□

37:19 שְׁלֹשָׁה גְבִעִים מְשֻׁקָּדִים בַּקָּנֶה הָאֶחָד כַּפְתֹּר וָפֶרַח וּשְׁלֹשָׁה גְבִעִים מְשֻׁקָּדִים בְּקָנֶה אֶחָד כַּפְתֹּר וָפָרַח כֵּן לְשֵׁשֶׁת הַקָּנִים הַיֹּצְאִים מִן הַמְּנֹרָה

she'lo'shah ge'vi'im me'shu'qa'dim ba'qa'neh ha'e'hhad kaph'tor wa'phe'rahh ush'lo'shah ge'vi'im me'shu'qa'dim be'qa'neh e'hhad kaph'tor wa'pha'rahh keyn le'shey'shet ha'qa'nim hai'yots'im min ham'no'rah

THREE BOWL~s *be~much*~BE-ALMOND-
SHAPED~*ing/er*(*mp*) in~the~STALK the~UNIT
KNOB and~BUD and~THREE BOWL~s *be~
much*~BE-ALMOND-SHAPED~*ing/er*(*mp*) in~
STALK UNIT KNOB and~BUD SO to~SIX the~
STALK~s the~GO-OUT~*ing/er*(*mp*) FROM
the~LAMPSTAND□

three bowls, being almond shaped in the stalk
{of} the (one) {with a} knob and {a} bud, and
three bowls, being almond shaped in the stalk
{of} the (other) {with a} knob and {a} bud, so
{it is} (for) the six stalks going out from the
lampstand,□

37:20 וּבַמְּנֹרָה אַרְבָּעָה גְבִעִים מְשֻׁקָּדִים כַּפְתֹּרֶיהָ וּפְרָחֶיהָ

u'vam'no'rah ar'ba'ah ge'vi'im me'shu'qa'dim kaph'to'rey'ah uph'ra'hhey'ah

and~in~the~LAMPSTAND FOUR BOWL~s *be~
much*~BE-ALMOND-SHAPED~*ing/er*(*mp*)
KNOB~s~her and~BUD~s~her□

and in the lampstand {are} four bowls being
almond shaped {with} her knobs and her
buds,□

37:21 וְכַפְתֹּר תַּחַת שְׁנֵי הַקָּנִים מִמֶּנָּה וְכַפְתֹּר תַּחַת שְׁנֵי הַקָּנִים מִמֶּנָּה וְכַפְתֹּר תַּחַת שְׁנֵי הַקָּנִים מִמֶּנָּה לְשֵׁשֶׁת הַקָּנִים הַיֹּצְאִים מִמֶּנָּה

we'khaph'tor ta'hhat she'ney ha'qa'nim mi'me'nah we'khaph'tor ta'hhat she'ney ha'qa'nim mi'me'nah we'khaph'tor ta'hhat she'ney ha'qa'nim mi'me'nah le'shey'shet ha'qa'nim hai'yots'im mi'me'nah

and~KNOB UNDER TWO the~STALK~s
FROM~her and~KNOB UNDER TWO the~
STALK~s FROM~her and~KNOB UNDER TWO
the~STALK~s FROM~her to~SIX the~STALK~s
the~GO-OUT~*ing/er*(*mp*) FROM~her□

and {a} knob under two {of} the stalks (out of)
her, and {a} knob under two {of} the stalks
(out of) her, and {a} knob under two {of} the
stalks (out of) her, (for) the six stalks going out
from her,□

37:22 כַּפְתֹּרֵיהֶם וּקְנֹתָם מִמֶּנָּה הָיוּ כֻּלָּהּ מִקְשָׁה אַחַת זָהָב טָהוֹר

kaph'to'rey'hem uq'no'tam mi'me'nah hai'u ku'lah miq'shah a'hhat za'hav ta'hor

KNOB~s~them(*m*) and~STALK~s~them(*m*)
FROM~her *they~did*~EXIST ALL~her BEATEN-
WORK UNIT GOLD PURE□

their knobs and their stalks (out of) her, all {of}
her will exist {as} (one) beaten work {of} pure
gold,□

37:23 וַיַּעַשׂ אֶת נֵרֹתֶיהָ שִׁבְעָה וּמַלְקָחֶיהָ וּמַחְתֹּתֶיהָ זָהָב טָהוֹר

wai'ya'as et ney'ro'te'yah shiv'ah u'mal'qa'hhey'ah u'mahh'to'tey'ah za'hav ta'hor

Mechanical Translation Codes

<u>WORD</u> – Verb	WORD – Noun	Word – Name	word – Pre/Suff	*word* – Conj.

and~he~will~<u>DO</u> AT LAMP~s~her SEVEN
and~TONG~s~her and~FIRE-PAN~s~her
GOLD PURE☐

and he (made) her seven lamps, and her
tongs, and her fire pans, {with} pure gold,☐

37:24

כִּכַּר זָהָב טָהוֹר עָשָׂה אֹתָהּ וְאֵת כָּל כֵּלֶיהָ

ki'kar za'hav ta'hor a'sah o'tah we'eyt kol key'ley'ah

KIKAR GOLD PURE he~did~<u>DO</u> AT~her and~
AT ALL ITEM~s~her☐

{a} kikar {of} pure gold he (made) her and all
her items,☐

37:25

וַיַּעַשׂ אֶת מִזְבַּח הַקְּטֹרֶת עֲצֵי שִׁטִּים אַמָּה אָרְכּוֹ וְאַמָּה רָחְבּוֹ רָבוּעַ
וְאַמָּתַיִם קֹמָתוֹ מִמֶּנּוּ הָיוּ קַרְנֹתָיו

wai'ya'as et miz'bahh haq'to'ret a'tsey shi'tim a'mah ar'ko we'a'mah rahh'bo ra'vu'a
we'a'ma'ta'yim qo'ma'to mi'me'nu hai'u qar'no'taw

and~he~will~<u>DO</u> AT ALTAR the~INCENSE
TREE~s ACACIA~s FOREARM LENGTH~him
and~FOREARM WIDTH~him <u>BE-SQUARE</u>~
ed(ms) and~FOREARM~s2 HEIGHT~him
FROM~him they~did~<u>EXIST</u> HORN~s~him☐

and he (made) the altar {of} incense {of}
acacia \wood/, {a} forearm {is} his length, and
{a} forearm {is} his width, {it is} squared, and
two forearms {is} his height, (out of) him
existed his horns,☐

37:26

וַיְצַף אֹתוֹ זָהָב טָהוֹר אֶת גַּגּוֹ וְאֶת קִירֹתָיו סָבִיב וְאֶת קַרְנֹתָיו וַיַּעַשׂ
לוֹ זֵר זָהָב סָבִיב

wai'tsaph o'to za'hav ta'hor et ga'go we'et qi'ro'taw sa'viv we'et qar'no'taw wai'ya'as lo
zeyr za'hav sa'viv

and~he~will~much~<u>OVERLAY</u> AT~him GOLD
PURE AT ROOF~him and~AT WALL~s~him
ALL-AROUND and~AT HORN~s~him and~he~
will~<u>DO</u> to~him MOLDING GOLD ALL-
AROUND☐

and he overlaid him {with} pure gold, his roof,
and his walls all around, and his horns, and he
(made) (for) him {a} molding {of} gold all
around,☐

37:27

וּשְׁתֵּי טַבְּעֹת זָהָב עָשָׂה לוֹ מִתַּחַת לְזֵרוֹ עַל שְׁתֵּי צַלְעֹתָיו עַל שְׁנֵי צִדָּיו
לְבָתִּים לְבַדִּים לָשֵׂאת אֹתוֹ בָּהֶם

ush'tey ta'be'ot za'hav a'sah lo mi'ta'hhat le'zey'ro al she'tey tsal'o'taw al she'ney
tsi'daw le'va'tim le'va'dim la'seyt o'to ba'hem

and~TWO RING~s GOLD he~did~<u>DO</u> to~him
from~UNDER to~MOLDING~him UPON TWO
RIB~s~him UPON TWO SIDE~s~him to~
HOUSE~s to~STICK~s to~<u>LIFT UP</u> AT~him
in~them(m)☐

and he (made) two rings {of} gold (for) him
under his molding upon his two ribs, upon his
two sides, (for) houses* (for) {the} sticks to lift
him up (with) them,☐

37:28

וַיַּעַשׂ אֶת הַבַּדִּים עֲצֵי שִׁטִּים וַיְצַף אֹתָם זָהָב

---

* Or "housings."

Revised Mechanical Translation Codes

(..) Alt Trans/App A   <..> Comp Phrase/App B   [..] Verb Form/App C   \../ Plural Form/App D
:...: Int Inf Abs |..| Past Perf Verb   {...} Added Word

wai'ya'as et ha'ba'dim a'tsey shi'tim wai'tsaph o'tam za'hav

and~*he~will*~<u>DO</u> AT the~STICK~s TREE~s ACACIA~s and~*he~will*~much~<u>OVERLAY</u> AT~ them(m) GOLD□	and he (made) the sticks {of} acacia \wood/, and he overlaid them {with} gold,□

37:29 וַיַּעַשׂ אֶת שֶׁמֶן הַמִּשְׁחָה קֹדֶשׁ וְאֶת קְטֹרֶת הַסַּמִּים טָהוֹר מַעֲשֵׂה רֹקֵחַ

wai'ya'as et she'men ha'mish'hhah qo'desh we'et qe'to'ret ha'sa'mim ta'hor ma'a'seyh ro'qey'ahh

and~*he~will*~<u>DO</u> AT OIL the~OINTMENT SPECIAL and~AT INCENSE the~AROMATIC-SPICE~s PURE WORK <u>COMPOUND</u>~ *ing/er(ms)*□	and he (made) the oil {of} ointment {of} special{ness}, and {the} pure incense {of} the aromatic spices, {the} work {of} compounding*,□

Chapter 38

38:1 וַיַּעַשׂ אֶת מִזְבַּח הָעֹלָה עֲצֵי שִׁטִּים חָמֵשׁ אַמּוֹת אָרְכּוֹ וְחָמֵשׁ אַמּוֹת רָחְבּוֹ רָבוּעַ וְשָׁלֹשׁ אַמּוֹת קֹמָתוֹ

wai'ya'as et miz'bahh ha'o'lah a'tsey shi'tim hha'meysh a'mot ar'ko we'hha'meysh a'mot rahh'bo ra'vu'a we'sha'losh a'mot qo'ma'to

and~*he~will*~<u>DO</u> AT ALTAR the~RISING TREE~s ACACIA~s FIVE FOREARM~s LENGTH~ him and~FIVE FOREARM~s WIDTH~him <u>BE-SQUARE</u>~*ed(ms)* and~THREE FOREARM~s HEIGHT~him□	and he (made) the altar {of the} rising {sacrifice of} acacia \wood/, five forearms {is} his length, and five forearms {is} his width, {it is} square, and three forearms {is} his height,□

38:2 וַיַּעַשׂ קַרְנֹתָיו עַל אַרְבַּע פִּנֹּתָיו מִמֶּנּוּ הָיוּ קַרְנֹתָיו וַיְצַף אֹתוֹ נְחֹשֶׁת

wai'ya'as qar'no'taw al ar'ba pi'no'taw mi'me'nu hai'u qar'no'taw wai'tsaph o'to ne'hho'shet

and~*he~will*~<u>DO</u> HORN~s~him UPON FOUR CORNER~s~him FROM~him *they~did*~<u>EXIST</u> HORN~s~him and~*he~will*~much~<u>OVERLAY</u> AT~him COPPER□	and he (made) his horns upon his four corners, (out of) him his horns will exist, and he overlaid him {with} copper,□

38:3 וַיַּעַשׂ אֶת כָּל כְּלֵי הַמִּזְבֵּחַ אֶת הַסִּירֹת וְאֶת הַיָּעִים וְאֶת הַמִּזְרָקֹת אֶת הַמִּזְלָגֹת וְאֶת הַמַּחְתֹּת כָּל כֵּלָיו עָשָׂה נְחֹשֶׁת

wai'ya'as et kol ke'ley ha'miz'bey'ahh et ha'si'rot we'et hai'ya'im we'et ha'miz'ra'qot et ha'miz'la'got we'et ha'mahh'tot kol key'law a'sah ne'hho'shet

and~*he~will*~<u>DO</u> AT ALL ITEM~s the~ALTAR	and he (made) all {the} items {of} the altar, the

---

* This may be a work of compounding, in the sense of a mixture, or made by a "compounder" in the sense of a mixer.

Mechanical Translation Codes

<u>WORD</u> – Verb	WORD – Noun	Word – Name	word – Pre/Suff	*word* – Conj.

AT the~POT~s and~AT the~SHOVEL~s and~
AT the~SPRINKLING-BASIN~s AT the~FORK~s
and~AT the~FIRE-PAN~s ALL ITEM~s~him
he~did~<u>DO</u> COPPER□

pots, and the shovels, and the sprinkling
basins, the forks, and the fire pans, he (made)
all his items {with} copper,□

38:4 וַיַּעַשׂ לַמִּזְבֵּחַ מִכְבָּר מַעֲשֵׂה רֶשֶׁת נְחֹשֶׁת תַּחַת כַּרְכֻּבּוֹ מִלְמַטָּה עַד חֶצְיוֹ

wai'ya'as la'miz'bey'ahh mikh'bar ma'a'seyh re'shet ne'hho'shet ta'hhat kar'ku'bo
mil'ma'tah ad hhets'yo

and~he~will~<u>DO</u> to~the~ALTAR GRATE
WORK NETTING COPPER UNDER OUTER-
RIM~him from~to~BENEATH UNTIL HALF~
him□

and he (made) (for) the altar {a} grate work
{of} netting {with} copper under his outer rim,
from beneath (unto) his half,□

38:5 וַיִּצֹק אַרְבַּע טַבָּעֹת בְּאַרְבַּע הַקְּצָוֹת לְמִכְבַּר הַנְּחֹשֶׁת בָּתִּים לַבַּדִּים

wai'yi'tsoq ar'ba ta'ba'ot be'ar'ba haq'tsa'ot le'mikh'bar han'hho'shet ba'tim la'ba'dim

and~he~will~<u>POUR-DOWN</u> FOUR RING~s in~
FOUR the~EXTREMITY~s to~GRATE the~
COPPER HOUSE~s to~the~STICK~s□

and he poured down* four rings in four
extremities (for) the copper grate, houses†
(for) the sticks,□

38:6 וַיַּעַשׂ אֶת הַבַּדִּים עֲצֵי שִׁטִּים וַיְצַף אֹתָם נְחֹשֶׁת

wai'ya'as et ha'ba'dim a'tsey shi'tim wai'tsaph o'tam ne'hho'shet

and~he~will~<u>DO</u> AT the~STICK~s TREE~s
ACACIA~s and~he~will~much~<u>OVERLAY</u> AT~
them(m) COPPER□

and he (made) the sticks {of} acacia \wood/,
and he overlaid them {with} copper,□

38:7 וַיָּבֵא אֶת הַבַּדִּים בַּטַּבָּעֹת עַל צַלְעֹת הַמִּזְבֵּחַ לָשֵׂאת אֹתוֹ בָּהֶם נְבוּב לֻחֹת עָשָׂה אֹתוֹ

wai'ya'vey et ha'ba'dim ba'ta'ba'ot al tsal'ot ha'miz'bey'ahh la'seyt o'to ba'hem ne'vuv
lu'hhot a'sah o'to

and~he~will~make~<u>COME</u> AT the~STICK~s
in~the~RING~s UPON RIB~s the~ALTAR to~
>~<u>LIFT-UP</u> AT~him in~them(m) <u>HOLLOW-
OUT</u>~ed(ms) SLAB~s he~did~<u>DO</u> AT~him□

and he [brought] the sticks in the rings upon
{the} ribs {of} the altar to lift him up (with)
them, he (made) him {with} hollowed out
slabs,□

38:8 וַיַּעַשׂ אֵת הַכִּיּוֹר נְחֹשֶׁת וְאֵת כַּנּוֹ נְחֹשֶׁת בְּמַרְאֹת הַצֹּבְאֹת אֲשֶׁר צָבְאוּ פֶּתַח אֹהֶל מוֹעֵד

wai'ya'as eyt ha'ki'yor ne'hho'shet we'eyt ka'no ne'hho'shet be'mar'ot ha'tsov'ot a'sher
tsav'u pe'tahh o'hel mo'eyd

---

* In this context, to "pour down" means to "cast" an object from a molten metal.
† Or "housings."

Revised Mechanical Translation Codes

(..) Alt Trans/App A	<..> Comp Phrase/App B	[..] Verb Form/App C	\../ Plural Form/App D
:..: Int Inf Abs	|..| Past Perf Verb	{...} Added Word	

and~*he~will~*<u>DO</u> AT the~CAULDRON COPPER
and~AT BASE~him COPPER in~REFLECTION~s
the~<u>MUSTER</u>~*ing/er(fp)* WHICH *they~did~*
<u>MUSTER</u> OPENING TENT APPOINTED□

and he (made) the cauldron {with} copper,
and his base {with} copper, (with) reflections
{of} the musterers (who) muster {at the}
opening {of the} tent {of the} appointed
{place},□

38:9 וַיַּעַשׂ אֶת הֶחָצֵר לִפְאַת נֶגֶב תֵּימָנָה קַלְעֵי הֶחָצֵר שֵׁשׁ מָשְׁזָר מֵאָה בָּאַמָּה

wai'ya'as et he'hha'tseyr liph'at ne'gev tey'ma'nah qal'ey he'hha'tseyr sheysh mash'zar mey'ah ba'a'mah

and~*he~will~*<u>DO</u> AT the~YARD to~EDGE
"Negev ^{PARCHED}" SOUTH~unto SLING~s the~
YARD LINEN *be~make~*<u>TWIST-TOGETHER</u>~
ing/er(ms) HUNDRED in~the~FOREARM□

and he (made) the yard to {the} "Negev
Parched", unto {the} south, slings {of} the yard
{are of} [twisted] linen, {a} hundred (by) the
forearm,□

38:10 עַמּוּדֵיהֶם עֶשְׂרִים וְאַדְנֵיהֶם עֶשְׂרִים נְחֹשֶׁת וָוֵי הָעַמּוּדִים וַחֲשֻׁקֵיהֶם כָּסֶף

a'mu'dey'hem es'rim we'ad'ney'hem es'rim ne'hho'shet wa'wey ha'amu'dim wa'hha'shu'qey'hem ka'seph

PILLAR~s~them(m) TEN~s and~FOOTING~s~
them(m) TEN~s COPPER PEG~s the~PILLAR~s
and~BINDER~s~them(m) SILVER□

their \twenty/ pillars and their \twenty/
footings {of} copper, {the} pegs {of} the pillars
and their binders {of} silver,□

38:11 וְלִפְאַת צָפוֹן מֵאָה בָאַמָּה עַמּוּדֵיהֶם עֶשְׂרִים וְאַדְנֵיהֶם עֶשְׂרִים נְחֹשֶׁת וָוֵי הָעַמּוּדִים וַחֲשֻׁקֵיהֶם כָּסֶף

we'liph'at tsa'phon mey'ah va'a'mah a'mu'dey'hem es'rim we'ad'ney'hem es'rim ne'hho'shet wa'wey ha'amu'dim wa'hha'shu'qey'hem ka'seph

and~to~EDGE NORTH HUNDRED in~the~
FOREARM PILLAR~s~them(m) TEN~s and~
FOOTING~s~them(m) TEN~s COPPER PEG~s
the~PILLAR~s and~BINDER~s~them(m)
SILVER□

and to {the} north edge, {a} hundred (by) the
forearm, their \twenty/ pillars and their
\twenty/ footings {of} copper, {the} pegs {of}
the pillars and their binders {of} silver,□

38:12 וְלִפְאַת יָם קְלָעִים חֲמִשִּׁים בָּאַמָּה עַמּוּדֵיהֶם עֲשָׂרָה וְאַדְנֵיהֶם עֲשָׂרָה וָוֵי הָעַמֻּדִים וַחֲשׁוּקֵיהֶם כָּסֶף

we'liph'at yam qe'la'im hha'mi'shim ba'a'mah a'mu'dey'hem a'sa'rah we'ad'ney'hem a'sa'rah wa'wey ha'a'mu'dim wa'hha'shu'qey'hem ka'seph

and~to~EDGE SEA SLING~s FIVE~s in~the~
FOREARM PILLAR~s~them(m) TEN and~
FOOTING~s~them(m) TEN PEG~s the~
PILLAR~s and~BINDER~s~them(m) SILVER□

and to {the} edge {of the} sea*, \fifty/ slings
(by) the forearm, their ten pillars and their ten
footings, {the} pegs {of} the pillars and their
silver binders,□

---

* Meaning "the west."

38:13

וְלִפְאַת קֵדְמָה מִזְרָחָה חֲמִשִּׁים אַמָּה

we'liph'at qeyd'mah miz'ra'hhah hha'mi'shim a'mah

and~to~EDGE EAST~unto SUNRISE~unto FIVE~s FOREARM☐

and to {the} edge unto {the} east, unto {the} sunrise, {it is} \fifty/ forearm{s},☐

38:14

קְלָעִים חֲמֵשׁ עֶשְׂרֵה אַמָּה אֶל הַכָּתֵף עַמּוּדֵיהֶם שְׁלֹשָׁה וְאַדְנֵיהֶם שְׁלֹשָׁה

qe'la'im hha'meysh es'reyh a'mah el ha'ka'teyph a'mu'dey'hem she'lo'shah we'ad'ney'hem she'lo'shah

SLING~s FIVE TEN FOREARM TO the~ SHOULDER-PIECE PILLAR~s~them(m) THREE and~FOOTING~s~them(m) THREE☐

{the} slings {are} <fifteen> forearm{s} (for) the shoulder piece, their three pillars and their three footings,☐

38:15

וְלַכָּתֵף הַשֵּׁנִית מִזֶּה וּמִזֶּה לְשַׁעַר הֶחָצֵר קְלָעִים חֲמֵשׁ עֶשְׂרֵה אַמָּה עַמֻּדֵיהֶם שְׁלֹשָׁה וְאַדְנֵיהֶם שְׁלֹשָׁה

we'la'ka'teyph ha'shey'nit mi'zeh u'mi'zeh le'sha'ar he'hha'tseyr qe'la'im hha'meysh es'reyh a'mah a'mu'dey'hem she'lo'shah we'ad'ney'hem she'lo'shah

and~to~the~SHOULDER-PIECE the~SECOND from~THIS and~from~THIS to~GATE the~ YARD SLING~s FIVE TEN FOREARM PILLAR~s~ them(m) THREE and~FOOTING~s~them(m) THREE☐

and (for) the second shoulder piece, from this {one} and from (that) {one}, (for) {the} gate {of} the yard {are} slings, <fifteen> forearm{s}, their three pillars and their three footings,☐

38:16

כָּל קַלְעֵי הֶחָצֵר סָבִיב שֵׁשׁ מָשְׁזָר

kol qal'ey he'hha'tseyr sa'viv sheysh mash'zar

ALL SLING~s the~YARD ALL-AROUND LINEN *be~make~*__TWIST-TOGETHER__*~ing/er(ms)*☐

all {the} slings {of} the yard all around {are of} [twisted] linen,☐

38:17

וְהָאֲדָנִים לָעַמֻּדִים נְחֹשֶׁת וָוֵי הָעַמּוּדִים וַחֲשׁוּקֵיהֶם כֶּסֶף וְצִפּוּי רָאשֵׁיהֶם כָּסֶף וְהֵם מְחֻשָּׁקִים כֶּסֶף כֹּל עַמֻּדֵי הֶחָצֵר

we'ha'a'da'nim la'a''mu'dim ne'hho'shet wa'wey ha'amu'dim wa'hha'shu'qey'hem ke'seph we'tsi'pui ra'shey'hem ka'seph we'heym me'hhu'sha'qim ke'seph kol a'mu'dey he'hha'tseyr

and~the~FOOTING~s to~the~PILLAR~s COPPER PEG~s the~PILLAR~s and~ BINDER~s~them(m) SILVER and~METAL-PLATING HEAD~s~them(m) SILVER and~ THEY(m) *be~much~*__ATTACH__*~ing/er(mp)* SILVER ALL PILLAR~s the~YARD☐

and the footings (for) the pillars {of} copper, {the} pegs {of} the pillars and their binders {of} silver, and {the} metal plating {of} their heads {of} silver, and all {the} pillars {of} the yard {are} being attached {with} silver,☐

38:18

וּמָסַךְ שַׁעַר הֶחָצֵר מַעֲשֵׂה רֹקֵם תְּכֵלֶת וְאַרְגָּמָן וְתוֹלַעַת שָׁנִי וְשֵׁשׁ מָשְׁזָר וְעֶשְׂרִים אַמָּה אֹרֶךְ וְקוֹמָה בְרֹחַב חָמֵשׁ אַמּוֹת לְעֻמַּת קַלְעֵי

Revised Mechanical Translation Codes

(..) Alt Trans/App A   <..> Comp Phrase/App B   [..] Verb Form/App C   \../ Plural Form/App D

:..: Int Inf Abs |..| Past Perf Verb   {...} Added Word

הֶחָצֵר

u'ma'sakh sha'ar he'hha'tseyr ma'a'seyh ro'qeym te'khey'let we'ar'ga'man we'to'la'at
sha'ni we'sheysh mash'zar we'es'rim a'mah o'rekh we'qol ve'ro'hhav hha'meysh a'mot
le'u'mat qal'ey he'hha'tseyr

and~CANOPY GATE the~YARD WORK
EMBROIDER~ing/er(ms) BLUE and~PURPLE
and~KERMES SCARLET and~LINEN be~make~
TWIST-TOGETHER~ing/er(ms) and~TEN~s
FOREARM LENGTH and~HEIGHT in~WIDTH
FIVE FOREARM~s to~ALONGSIDE SLING~s
the~YARD□

and the canopy {of the} gate {of the} yard {is
a} work {of} embroidering* {with} blue, and
purple, and kermes {of} scarlet, and [twisted]
linen, and \twenty/ forearm{s is the} length,
and {the} height (with) {the} width {is} five
forearms alongside {the} slings {of} the yard,□

38:19 וְעַמֻּדֵיהֶם אַרְבָּעָה וְאַדְנֵיהֶם אַרְבָּעָה נְחֹשֶׁת וָוֵיהֶם כֶּסֶף וְצִפּוּי
רָאשֵׁיהֶם וַחֲשֻׁקֵיהֶם כָּסֶף

we'a'mu'dey'hem ar'ba'ah we'ad'ney'hem ar'ba'ah ne'hho'shet wa'wey'hem ke'seph
we'tsi'pui ra'shey'hem wa'hha'shu'qey'hem ka'seph

and~PILLAR~s~them(m) FOUR and~
FOOTING~s~them(m) FOUR COPPER PEG~s~
them(m) SILVER and~METAL-PLATING
HEAD~s~them(m) and~BINDER~s~them(m)
SILVER□

and their four pillars and their four footings
{of} copper, their pegs {of} silver, and the
metal plating {of} their heads and their
binders {of} silver,□

38:20 וְכָל הַיְתֵדֹת לַמִּשְׁכָּן וְלֶחָצֵר סָבִיב נְחֹשֶׁת

we'khol hai'tey'dot la'mish'kan we'le'hha'tser sa'viv ne'hho'shet

and~ALL the~TENT-PEG~s to~the~
DWELLING and~to~YARD ALL-AROUND
COPPER□

and all the tent pegs (for) the dwelling and
(for) {the} yard all around {of} copper,□

38:21 אֵלֶּה פְקוּדֵי הַמִּשְׁכָּן מִשְׁכַּן הָעֵדֻת אֲשֶׁר פֻּקַּד עַל פִּי מֹשֶׁה עֲבֹדַת הַלְוִיִּם
בְּיַד אִיתָמָר בֶּן אַהֲרֹן הַכֹּהֵן

ey'leh phe'qudey ha'mish'kan mish'kan ha'ey'dut a'sher pu'qad al pi mo'sheh a'vo'dat
hal'wi'yim be'yad i'ta'mar ben a'ha'ron ha'ko'heyn

THESE REGISTER~ed(mp) the~DWELLING
DWELLING the~EVIDENCE WHICH he~did~
be~much~REGISTER UPON MOUTH "Mosheh
PLUCKED-OUT" SERVICE the~"Lewi JOINING~me"~s
in~HAND "Iytamar ISLAND~+~DATE-PALM" SON
"Aharon LIGHT-BRINGER" the~ADMINISTRATOR□

these {are} registered {of} the dwelling, {the}
dwelling {of} the evidence which he registered
(according to) {the} mouth {of} "Mosheh Plucked
out", {the} service {of} the {one}s {of} "Lewi My
joining", (by) {the} hand {of} "Iytamar Island of the
date palm", {the} son {of} "Aharon Light bringer", the
administrator,□

38:22 וּבְצַלְאֵל בֶּן אוּרִי בֶן חוּר לְמַטֵּה יְהוּדָה עָשָׂה אֵת כָּל אֲשֶׁר צִוָּה יְהוָה

---

* This word may also mean "an embroiderer."

Mechanical Translation Codes

| <u>WORD</u> – Verb | WORD – Noun | Word – Name | word – Pre/Suff | *word* – Conj. |

אֶת מֹשֶׁה

uv'tsal'eyl ben u'ri ven hhur le'ma'teyh ye'hu'dah a'sah eyt kol a'sher tsi'wah YHWH et mo'sheh

and~"Betsaleyl ^{in~SHADOW~+~MIGHTY-ONE}" SON "Uriy ^{LIGHT~me}" SON "Hhur ^{CISTERN}" to~BRANCH "Yehudah ^{THANKSGIVING}" he~did~<u>DO</u> AT ALL WHICH he~did~much~<u>DIRECT</u> "Yhwh ^{he~will~<u>BE</u>}" AT "Mosheh ^{PLUCKED-OUT}"□	and "Betsaleyl ^{In the shadow of El}", {the} son {of} "Uriy ^{My light}", {the} son {of} "Hhur ^{Cistern}", {belonging} to {the} branch {of} "Yehudah ^{Thanksgiving}", |had| (made) all which "Yhwh ^{He is}" directed "Mosheh ^{Plucked out}",□

38:23 וְאִתּוֹ אָהֳלִיאָב בֶּן אֲחִיסָמָךְ לְמַטֵּה דָן חָרָשׁ וְחֹשֵׁב וְרֹקֵם בַּתְּכֵלֶת וּבָאַרְגָּמָן וּבְתוֹלַעַת הַשָּׁנִי וּבַשֵּׁשׁ

we'i'to a'ha'li'av ben a'hhi'sa'mak le'ma'teyh dan hha'rash we'hho'sheyv we'ro'qeym bat'khey'let u'va'ar'ga'man uv'to'la'at ha'sha'ni u'va'sheysh

and~AT~him "Ahaliyav ^{TENT~of~+~FATHER}" SON "Ahhiysamahh ^{BROTHER~me~+~he~did~<u>SUPPORT</u>}" to~BRANCH "Dan ^{MODERATOR}" ENGRAVER and~<u>THINK</u>~ing/er(ms) and~EMBROIDER~ing/er(ms) in~the~BLUE and~in~the~PURPLE and~in~the~KERMES the~SCARLET and~in~the~LINEN□	and (with) him {is} "Ahaliyav ^{Tent of father}", {the} son {of} "Ahhiysamahh ^{My brother supports}", {belonging} to {the} branch {of} "Dan ^{Moderator}", {an} engraver, and {a} thinker, and {an} embroiderer (with) the blue, and (with) the purple, and (with) the kermes {of} the scarlet, and (with) the linen,□

38:24 כָּל הַזָּהָב הֶעָשׂוּי לַמְּלָאכָה בְּכֹל מְלֶאכֶת הַקֹּדֶשׁ וַיְהִי זְהַב הַתְּנוּפָה תֵּשַׁע וְעֶשְׂרִים כִּכָּר וּשְׁבַע מֵאוֹת וּשְׁלֹשִׁים שֶׁקֶל בְּשֶׁקֶל הַקֹּדֶשׁ

kol ha'za'hav he'a'su'i lam'la'khah be'khol me'le'khet ha'qo'desh wai'hi ze'hav hat'nu'phah tey'sa we'es'rim ki'kar ush'va mey'ot ush'lo'shim she'qel be'she'qel ha'qo'desh

ALL the~GOLD the~<u>DO</u>~ed(ms) to~the~BUSINESS in~ALL BUSINESS the~SPECIAL and~he~will~<u>EXIST</u> GOLD the~WAVING NINE and~TEN~s KIKAR and~SEVEN HUNDRED~s and~THREE~s SHEQEL in~SHEQEL the~SPECIAL□	all the gold (used) (for) the business in all the business {of the} special {place}, {the} gold {of} the wave {offer}ing (was) nine and \twenty/ kikar{s}, and seven hundred and \thirty/ sheqel{s} (by) the sheqel {of the} special {place},□

38:25 וְכֶסֶף פְּקוּדֵי הָעֵדָה מְאַת כִּכָּר וְאֶלֶף וּשְׁבַע מֵאוֹת וַחֲמִשָּׁה וְשִׁבְעִים שֶׁקֶל בְּשֶׁקֶל הַקֹּדֶשׁ

we'khe'seph pe'qu'dey ha'ey'dah me'at ki'kar we'eleph ush'va mey'ot wa'hha'mi'shah we'shiv'im she'qel be'she'qel ha'qo'desh

and~SILVER <u>REGISTER</u>~ed(mp) the~COMPANY HUNDRED KIKAR and~THOUSAND and~SEVEN HUNDRED~s and~FIVE and~SEVEN~s SHEQEL in~SHEQEL the~SPECIAL□	and {the} silver registered {of} the company, {a} hundred kikar, and {a} thousand and seven hundred and five and \seventy/ sheqel{s} (by) the sheqel {of the} special {place},□

38:26 בֶּקַע לַגֻּלְגֹּלֶת מַחֲצִית הַשֶּׁקֶל בְּשֶׁקֶל הַקֹּדֶשׁ לְכֹל הָעֹבֵר עַל הַפְּקֻדִים

Revised Mechanical Translation Codes

(..) Alt Trans/App A   <..> Comp Phrase/App B   [..] Verb Form/App C   \../ Plural Form/App D
:..: Int Inf Abs |..| Past Perf Verb   {...} Added Word

מִבֶּן עֶשְׂרִים שָׁנָה וָמַעְלָה לְשֵׁשׁ מֵאוֹת אֶלֶף וּשְׁלֹשֶׁת אֲלָפִים וַחֲמֵשׁ מֵאוֹת וַחֲמִשִּׁים

be'qa la'gul'go'let ma'hha'tsit ha'she'qel be'she'qel ha'qo'desh le'khol ha'o'veyr al hap'qu'dim mi'ben es'rim sha'nah wa'ma'lah le'sheysh mey'ot e'leph ush'lo'shet a'la'phim wa'hha'meysh mey'ot wa'hha'mi'shim

BEQA to~the~SKULL ONE-HALF the~SHEQEL in~SHEQEL the~SPECIAL to~ALL the~<u>CROSS-OVER</u>~ing/er(ms) UPON the~<u>REGISTER</u>~ed(mp) from~SON TEN~s YEAR and~UPWARD~unto to~SIX HUNDRED~s THOUSAND and~THREE THOUSAND~s and~FIVE HUNDRED~s and~FIVE~s□	{a} beqa (for) the skull*, one-half {of} the sheqel (by) the sheqel {of the} special {place} (for) all the {one}s crossing over upon the registered, from {a} son {of} \twenty/ year{s}† and upward, to {the} six hundred thousand and three thousand and five hundred and \fifty/,□

38:27 וַיְהִי מְאַת כִּכַּר הַכֶּסֶף לָצֶקֶת אֵת אַדְנֵי הַקֹּדֶשׁ וְאֵת אַדְנֵי הַפָּרֹכֶת מְאַת אֲדָנִים לִמְאַת הַכִּכָּר כִּכָּר לָאָדֶן

wai'hi me'at ki'kar ha'ke'seph la'tse'qet eyt ad'ney ha'qo'desh we'eyt ad'ney ha'pa'ro'khet me'at a'da'nim lim'at ha'ki'kar ki'kar la'a'den

and~he~will~<u>EXIST</u> HUNDRED KIKAR the~SILVER to~>~<u>POUR-DOWN</u> AT FOOTING~s the~SPECIAL and~AT FOOTING~s the~TENT-CURTAIN HUNDRED FOOTING~s to~HUNDRED the~KIKAR KIKAR to~the~FOOTING□	and {a} hundred kikar{s of} silver existed (for) pour{ing} down‡ the footings {of the} special {place}, and {the} footings {of} the tent curtain, {a} hundred footings (for) the hundred kikar{s}, {a} kikar (for) {a} footing,□

38:28 וְאֶת הָאֶלֶף וּשְׁבַע הַמֵּאוֹת וַחֲמִשָּׁה וְשִׁבְעִים עָשָׂה וָוִים לָעַמּוּדִים וְצִפָּה רָאשֵׁיהֶם וְחִשַּׁק אֹתָם

we'et ha'e'leph ush'va ha'mey'ot wa'hha'mi'shah we'shiv'im a'sah wa'wim la'a'mu'dim we'tsi'pah ra'shey'hem we'hhi'shaq o'tam

and~AT the~THOUSAND and~SEVEN the~HUNDRED~s and~FIVE and~SEVEN~s he~did~<u>DO</u> PEG~s to~the~PILLAR~s and~he~did~much~<u>OVERLAY</u> HEAD~s~them(m) and~he~did~much~<u>ATTACH</u> AT~them(m)□	and (with) the thousand and seven hundred and five and \seventy/ {sheqels}§ he (made) {the} pegs (for) the pillars, and he overlaid their heads and he attached them,□

38:29 וּנְחֹשֶׁת הַתְּנוּפָה שִׁבְעִים כִּכָּר וְאַלְפַּיִם וְאַרְבַּע מֵאוֹת שָׁקֶל

un'hho'shet hat'nu'phah shiv'im ki'kar we'al'pa'yim we'ar'ba mey'ot sha'qel

and~COPPER the~WAVING SEVEN~s KIKAR and~THOUSAND~s2 and~FOUR HUNDRED~s SHEQEL□	and {the} copper {of} the wave {offer}ing {was} \seventy/ kikar{s} and two thousand and four hundred sheqel{s},□

---

* Meaning "individual."

† "A son of twenty years" is an idiom meaning "twenty years old."

‡ In this context, to "pour down" means to "cast" an object from a molten metal.

§ The text appears to be missing this word.

Mechanical Translation Codes

<u>WORD</u> – Verb	WORD – Noun	Word – Name	word – Pre/Suff	*word* – Conj.

38:30 וַיַּעַשׂ בָּהּ אֶת אַדְנֵי פֶּתַח אֹהֶל מוֹעֵד וְאֵת מִזְבַּח הַנְּחֹשֶׁת וְאֶת מִכְבַּר הַנְּחֹשֶׁת אֲשֶׁר לוֹ וְאֵת כָּל כְּלֵי הַמִּזְבֵּחַ

wai'ya'as bah et ad'ney pe'tahh o'hel mo'eyd we'eyt miz'bahh han'hho'shet we'et mikh'bar han'hho'shet a'sher lo we'eyt kol ke'ley ha'miz'bey'ahh

and~*he~will~*<u>DO</u> in~her AT FOOTING~s OPENING TENT APPOINTED and~AT ALTAR the~COPPER and~AT GRATE the~COPPER WHICH to~him and~AT ALL ITEM~s the~ ALTAR□

and he (made) in her {the} footings {of the} opening {of the} tent {of the} appointed {place}, and {the} copper altar, and the copper grate which {belongs} to him and all {the} items {of} the altar,□

38:31 וְאֵת אַדְנֵי הֶחָצֵר סָבִיב וְאֶת אַדְנֵי שַׁעַר הֶחָצֵר וְאֵת כָּל יִתְדֹת הַמִּשְׁכָּן וְאֶת כָּל יִתְדֹת הֶחָצֵר סָבִיב

we'et ad'ney he'hha'tseyr sa'viv we'et ad'ney sha'ar he'hha'tseyr we'eyt kol yit'dot ha'mish'kan we'et kol yit'dot he'hha'tseyr sa'viv

and~AT FOOTING~s the~YARD ALL-AROUND and~AT FOOTING~s GATE the~YARD and~AT ALL TENT-PEG~s the~DWELLING and~AT ALL TENT-PEG~s the~YARD ALL-AROUND□

and {the} footings {of the} yard all around, and {the} footings {of the} gate {of} the yard, and all {the} tent pegs {of} the dwelling, and all {the} tent pegs {of} the yard all around,□

Chapter 39

39:1 וּמִן הַתְּכֵלֶת וְהָאַרְגָּמָן וְתוֹלַעַת הַשָּׁנִי עָשׂוּ בִגְדֵי שְׂרָד לְשָׁרֵת בַּקֹּדֶשׁ וַיַּעֲשׂוּ אֶת בִּגְדֵי הַקֹּדֶשׁ אֲשֶׁר לְאַהֲרֹן כַּאֲשֶׁר צִוָּה יְהֹוָה אֶת מֹשֶׁה

u'min hat'khey'let we'ha'ar'ga'man we'to'la'at ha'sha'ni a'su vig'dey se'rad le'sha'reyt ba'qo'desh wai'ya'a'su et big'dey ha'qo'desh a'sher le'a'ha'ron ka'a'sheyr tsi'wah YHWH et mo'sheh

and~FROM the~BLUE and~the~PURPLE and~ KERMES the~SCARLET *they~did~*<u>DO</u> GARMENT~s BRAIDED-WORK to~>~*much~* <u>MINISTER</u> in~the~SPECIAL and~*they(m)~* *will~*<u>DO</u> AↃ GARMENT~s the~SPECIAL WHICH to~"Aharon ^{LIGHT-BRINGER}" like~WHICH *he~did~* *much~*<u>DIRECT</u> "Yhwh ^{*he~will~*<u>BE</u>}" AT "Mosheh ^{PLUCKED-OUT}"□

and from the blue, and the purple, and {the} kermes {of} the scarlet they (made) {the} garments {of} braided work, to minister in the special {place}, and they (made) the garments {of} special{ness} which {are} (for) "Aharon ^{Light bringer}", <just as> "Yhwh ^{He is}" directed "Mosheh ^{Plucked out}",□

39:2 וַיַּעַשׂ אֶת הָאֵפֹד זָהָב תְּכֵלֶת וְאַרְגָּמָן וְתוֹלַעַת שָׁנִי וְשֵׁשׁ מָשְׁזָר

wai'ya'as et ha'ey'phod za'hav te'khey'let we'ar'ga'man we'to'la'at sha'ni we'sheysh mash'zar

and~*he~will~*<u>DO</u> AT the~EPHOD GOLD BLUE and~PURPLE and~KERMES SCARLET and~

and he (made) the ephod {of} gold, blue, and purple, and kermes {of} scarlet, and [twisted]

Revised Mechanical Translation Codes

(..) Alt Trans/App A	<..> Comp Phrase/App B	[..] Verb Form/App C	\../ Plural Form/App D
:..: Int Inf Abs	|..| Past Perf Verb	{...} Added Word	

LINEN *be~make~*<u>TWIST-TOGETHER</u>~   linen,□
ing/er(ms)□

39:3   וַיְרַקְּעוּ אֶת פַּחֵי הַזָּהָב וְקִצֵּץ פְּתִילִם לַעֲשׂוֹת בְּתוֹךְ הַתְּכֵלֶת וּבְתוֹךְ
הָאַרְגָּמָן וּבְתוֹךְ תּוֹלַעַת הַשָּׁנִי וּבְתוֹךְ הַשֵּׁשׁ מַעֲשֵׂה חֹשֵׁב

wai'raq'u et pa'hhey ha'za'hav we'qi'tseyts pe'ti'lim la'a'shot be'tokh hat'khey'let uv'tokh
ha'ar'ga'man uv'tokh to'la'at ha'sha'ni uv'tokh ha'sheysh ma'a'seyh hho'sheyv

and~they(m)~will~<u>HAMMER</u> AT WIRE~s *the~* GOLD *and~he~did~*<u>SEVER</u> CORD~s *to~>~*<u>DO</u> *in~*MIDST *the~*BLUE *and~in~*MIDST *the~* PURPLE *and~in~*MIDST KERMES *the~* SCARLET *and~in~*MIDST *the~*LINEN WORK <u>THINK</u>~*ing/er(ms)*□	and they hammered {the} wires {of} gold, and he severed {the} cords to (use) in {the} midst {of} the blue, and in {the} midst {of} the purple, and in {the} midst {of the} kermes {of} the scarlet, and in {the} midst {of} the linen, {a} work {of} thinking*,□

39:4   כְּתֵפֹת עָשׂוּ לוֹ חֹבְרֹת עַל שְׁנֵי קִצְווֹתוֹ חֻבָּר

ke'tey'phot a'su lo hhov'rot al she'ney qits'wo'to hhu'bar

SHOULDER-PIECE~s *they~did~*<u>DO</u> *to~*him <u>COUPLE</u>~*ing/er(fp)* UPON TWO EXTREMITY~s~him <u>COUPLE</u>~*ed(ms)*□	they (made) {the} shoulder pieces (for) him, {a} coupling, upon his two extremities† {it is} coupled,□

39:5   וְחֵשֶׁב אֲפֻדָּתוֹ אֲשֶׁר עָלָיו מִמֶּנּוּ הוּא כְּמַעֲשֵׂהוּ זָהָב תְּכֵלֶת וְאַרְגָּמָן
וְתוֹלַעַת שָׁנִי וְשֵׁשׁ מָשְׁזָר כַּאֲשֶׁר צִוָּה יְהוָה אֶת מֹשֶׁה

we'hhey'shev a'phu'da'to a'sher a'law mi'me'nu hu ke'ma'a'sey'hu za'hav te'khey'let
we'ar'ga'man we'to'la'at sha'ni we'sheysh mash'zar ka'a'sheyr tsi'wah YHWH et mo'sheh

*and~*DECORATIVE-BAND EPHOD~him WHICH UPON~him FROM~him HE *like~*WORK~him GOLD BLUE *and~*PURPLE *and~*KERMES SCARLET *and~*LINEN *be~make~*<u>TWIST-TOGETHER</u>~*ing/er(ms)* *like~*WHICH *he~did~* *much~*<u>DIRECT</u> "Yhwh ^{*he~will~*<u>BE</u>}" AT "Mosheh ^{PLUCKED-OUT}"□	and {the} decorative band {of} his ephod, which {is} upon him, he {is just} like his work, {of} gold, blue, and purple, and kermes {of} scarlet, and [twisted] linen, <just as> "Yhwh ^{He is}" directed "Mosheh ^{Plucked out}",□

39:6   וַיַּעֲשׂוּ אֶת אַבְנֵי הַשֹּׁהַם מֻסַבֹּת מִשְׁבְּצֹת זָהָב מְפֻתָּחֹת פִּתּוּחֵי חוֹתָם
עַל שְׁמוֹת בְּנֵי יִשְׂרָאֵל

wai'ya'a'su et av'ney ha'sho'ham mu'sa'bot mish'be'tsot za'hav me'phu'ta'hhot pi'tu'hhey
hho'tam al she'mot be'ney yis'ra'eyl

and~they(m)~will~<u>DO</u> AT STONE~s *the~* ONYX *be~make~*<u>GO-AROUND</u>~*ing/er(fp)* PLAIT~s GOLD *be~much~*<u>OPEN</u>~*ing/er(fp)* CARVING~s SEAL UPON TITLE~s SON~s	and they (made) {the} stones {of} the onyx‡, [enclosed in] plaits {of} gold, being [engraved] {as} carvings {of a} seal (according to) {the} titles {of the} sons {of} "Yisra'el ^{He turns El aside}",□

---

* This may be a work of an intricate design or made by "a thinker" in the sense of a designer.
† The Hebrew word קְצוֹתוֹ is written defectively and should be written as קְצוֹתָיו.
‡ The "shoham" is unknown stone.

Mechanical Translation Codes

<u>WORD</u> – Verb	WORD – Noun	Word – Name	word – Pre/Suff	*word* – Conj.

"Yisra'el ^{he~will~TURN-ASIDE~+~MIGHTY-ONE}"□

39:7 וַיָּשֶׂם אֹתָם עַל כִּתְפֹת הָאֵפֹד אַבְנֵי זִכָּרוֹן לִבְנֵי יִשְׂרָאֵל כַּאֲשֶׁר צִוָּה יְהֹוָה אֶת מֹשֶׁה

wai'ya'sem o'tam al kit'phot ha'ey'phod av'ney zi'ka'ron liv'ney yis'ra'eyl ka'a'sheyr tsi'wah YHWH et mo'sheh

and~he~will~<u>PLACE</u> AT~them(m) UPON SHOULDER-PIECE~s the~EPHOD STONE~s REMEMBRANCE to~SON~s "Yisra'el ^{he~will~<u>TURN-ASIDE</u>~+~MIGHTY-ONE}" like~WHICH he~did~ much~<u>DIRECT</u> "Yhwh ^{he~will~<u>BE</u>}" AT "Mosheh ^{PLUCKED-OUT}"□	and he placed them upon {the} shoulder pieces {of} the ephod, stones {of} remembrance (for) {the} sons {of} "Yisra'el ^{He turns El aside}", <just as> "Yhwh ^{He is}" directed "Mosheh ^{Plucked out}",□

39:8 וַיַּעַשׂ אֶת הַחֹשֶׁן מַעֲשֵׂה חֹשֵׁב כְּמַעֲשֵׂה אֵפֹד זָהָב תְּכֵלֶת וְאַרְגָּמָן וְתוֹלַעַת שָׁנִי וְשֵׁשׁ מָשְׁזָר

wai'ya'as et ha'hho'shen ma'a'seyh hho'sheyv ke'ma'a'seyh ey'phod za'hav te'khey'let we'ar'ga'man we'to'la'at sha'ni we'sheysh mash'zar

and~he~will~<u>DO</u> AT the~BREASTPLATE WORK <u>THINK</u>~ing/er(ms) like~WORK EPHOD GOLD BLUE and~PURPLE and~KERMES SCARLET and~LINEN be~make~<u>TWIST-TOGETHER</u>~ing/er(ms)□	and he (made) the breastplate, {a} work {of} thinking*, like {the} work {of the} ephod {of} gold, blue, and purple, and kermes {of} scarlet, and [twisted] linen,□

39:9 רָבוּעַ הָיָה כָּפוּל עָשׂוּ אֶת הַחֹשֶׁן זֶרֶת אָרְכּוֹ וְזֶרֶת רָחְבּוֹ כָּפוּל

ra'vu'a hai'yah ka'phul a'su et ha'hho'shen ze'ret ar'ko we'ze'ret rahh'bo ka'phul

<u>BE-SQUARE</u>~ed(ms) he~did~<u>EXIST</u> <u>DOUBLE-OVER</u>~ed(ms) they~did~<u>DO</u> AT the~ BREASTPLATE FINGER-SPAN LENGTH~him and~FINGER-SPAN WIDTH~him <u>DOUBLE-OVER</u>~ed(ms)□	he existed squared, doubled over they (made) the breastplate, {a} finger span {is} his length, and {a} finger span {is} his width, doubled over,□

39:10 וַיְמַלְאוּ בוֹ אַרְבָּעָה טוּרֵי אָבֶן טוּר אֹדֶם פִּטְדָה וּבָרֶקֶת הַטּוּר הָאֶחָד

wai'mal'u bo ar'ba'ah tu'rey a'ven tur o'dem pit'dah u'va're'qet ha'tur ha'e'hhad

and~they(m)~will~much~<u>FILL</u> in~him FOUR ROW~s STONE ROW CARNELIAN OLIVINE and~EMERALD the~ROW the~UNIT□	and they [set] in him four rows {of} stone†, {a} row {of} carnelian, olivine and emerald {is} the (one) row,□

---

* This may be a work of an intricate design or made by "a thinker" in the sense of a designer.

† The identification of these twelve stones is uncertain (see the dictionary entry for each stone for additional information).

Revised Mechanical Translation Codes

(..) Alt Trans/App A   <..> Comp Phrase/App B   [..] Verb Form/App C   \../ Plural Form/App D
:..: Int Inf Abs |..| Past Perf Verb   {...} Added Word

39:11

וְהַטּוּר הַשֵּׁנִי נֹפֶךְ סַפִּיר וְיָהֲלֹם

we'ha'tur ha'shey'ni no'phekh sa'pir we'ya'ha'lom

and~the~ROW the~SECOND TURQUOISE LAPIS-LAZULI and~FLINT□

and the second row {is} turquoise, lapiz-lazuli and flint,□

39:12

וְהַטּוּר הַשְּׁלִישִׁי לֶשֶׁם שְׁבוֹ וְאַחְלָמָה

we'ha'tur hash'li'shi le'shem she'vo we'ahh'la'mah

and~the~ROW the~THIRD OPAL AGATE and~ AMETHYST□

and the third row {is} opal, agate and amethyst,□

39:13

וְהַטּוּר הָרְבִיעִי תַּרְשִׁישׁ שֹׁהַם וְיָשְׁפֵה מוּסַבֹּת מִשְׁבְּצֹת זָהָב בְּמִלֻּאֹתָם

we'ha'tur har'vi'i tar'shish sho'ham we'yash'pheyh mu'sa'bot mish'be'tsot za'hav be'mi'lu'o'tam

and~the~ROW the~FOURTH TOPAZ ONYX and~JASPER be~make~GO-AROUND~ ing/er(fp) PLAIT~s GOLD in~SETTING~s~ them(m)□

and the fourth row {is} topaz and onyx and jasper, being woven {with} gold they will exist in their settings,.□

39:14

וְהָאֲבָנִים עַל שְׁמֹת בְּנֵי יִשְׂרָאֵל הֵנָּה שְׁתֵּים עֶשְׂרֵה עַל שְׁמֹתָם פִּתּוּחֵי חֹתָם אִישׁ עַל שְׁמוֹ לִשְׁנֵים עָשָׂר שָׁבֶט

we'ha'a'va'nim al she'mot be'ney yis'ra'eyl heyn'nah she'teym es'reyh al she'mo'tam pi'tu'hhey hho'tam ish al she'mo lish'neym a'sar sha'vet

and~the~STONE~s UPON TITLE~s SON~s "Yisra'el ^(he~will~<u>TURN-ASIDE</u>~+~MIGHTY-ONE)″ THEY(f) TWO TEN UPON TITLE~s~them(m) CARVING~s SEAL MAN UPON TITLE~him to~ TWO TEN STAFF□

and the stones {were} (according to) {the} titles {of the} sons {of} "Yisra'el ^(He turns El aside)″, <twelve> (according to) their titles, carvings {of the} seal {of} (each) (according to) his title, they will exist (for) {the} <twelve> staff{s}*,□

39:15

וַיַּעֲשׂוּ עַל הַחֹשֶׁן שַׁרְשְׁרֹת גַּבְלֻת מַעֲשֵׂה עֲבֹת זָהָב טָהוֹר

wai'ya'a'su al ha'hho'shen shar'she'rot gav'lut ma'a'seyh a'vot za'hav ta'hor

and~they(m)~will~<u>DO</u> UPON the~ BREASTPLATE CHAIN~s EDGING WORK THICK-CORD GOLD PURE□

and they (made) upon the breastplate chains, {the} edging {is a} work {of a} thick cord {of} pure gold,□

39:16

וַיַּעֲשׂוּ שְׁתֵּי מִשְׁבְּצֹת זָהָב וּשְׁתֵּי טַבְּעֹת זָהָב וַיִּתְּנוּ אֶת שְׁתֵּי הַטַּבָּעֹת עַל שְׁנֵי קְצוֹת הַחֹשֶׁן

wai'ya'a'su she'tey mish'be'tsot za'hav ush'tey ta'be'ot za'hav wai'yit'nu et she'tey ha'ta'ba'ot al she'ney qe'tsot ha'hho'shen

---

* Or "tribes."

Mechanical Translation Codes

<u>WORD</u> – Verb	WORD – Noun	Word – Name	word – Pre/Suff	*word* – Conj.

and~*they(m)~will*~<u>DO</u> TWO PLAIT~s GOLD and~TWO RING~s GOLD and~*they(m)~will*~<u>GIVE</u> AT TWO the~RING~s UPON TWO EXTREMITY~s the~BREASTPLATE☐

and they (made) two plaits {of} gold, and two rings {of} gold, and they (placed) the two rings upon {the} two extremities {of} the breastplate,☐

39:17 וַיִּתְּנוּ שְׁתֵּי הָעֲבֹתֹת הַזָּהָב עַל שְׁתֵּי הַטַּבָּעֹת עַל קְצוֹת הַחֹשֶׁן

wai'yit'nu she'tey ha'a'vo'tot ha'za'hav al she'tey ha'ta'ba'ot al qe'tsot ha'hho'shen

and~*they(m)~will*~<u>GIVE</u> TWO the~THICK-CORD~s the~GOLD UPON TWO the~RING~s UPON EXTREMITY~s the~BREASTPLATE☐

and they (placed) {the} two thick cords {of} gold upon {the} two rings, upon {the} extremities {of} the breastplate,☐

39:18 וְאֵת שְׁתֵּי קְצוֹת שְׁתֵּי הָעֲבֹתֹת נָתְנוּ עַל שְׁתֵּי הַמִּשְׁבְּצֹת וַיִּתְּנֻם עַל כִּתְפֹת הָאֵפֹד אֶל מוּל פָּנָיו

we'eyt she'tey qe'tsot she'tey ha'a'vo'tot nat'nu al she'tey ha'mish'be'tsot wai'yit'num al kit'phot ha'ey'phod el mul pa'naw

and~AT TWO EXTREMITY~s TWO the~THICK-CORD~s *they~did*~<u>GIVE</u> UPON TWO the~PLAIT~s and~*they(m)~will*~<u>GIVE</u>~them(m) UPON SHOULDER-PIECE~s the~EPHOD TO FOREFRONT FACE~s~him☐

and {the} two extremities {of} the two thick cords, they (placed) upon the two plaits, and they (placed) upon {the} shoulder pieces {of} the ephod, to {the} forefront {of} his face,☐

39:19 וַיַּעֲשׂוּ שְׁתֵּי טַבְּעֹת זָהָב וַיָּשִׂימוּ עַל שְׁנֵי קְצוֹת הַחֹשֶׁן עַל שְׂפָתוֹ אֲשֶׁר אֶל עֵבֶר הָאֵפֹד בָּיְתָה

wai'ya'a'su she'tey ta'be'ot za'hav wai'ya'si'mu al she'ney qe'tsot ha'hho'shen al se'pha'to a'sher el ey'ver ha'ey'phod bai'tah

and~*they(m)~will*~<u>DO</u> TWO RING~s GOLD and~*they(m)~will*~<u>PLACE</u> UPON TWO EXTREMITY~s the~BREASTPLATE UPON LIP~him WHICH TO OTHER-SIDE the~EPHOD HOUSE~unto☐

and they (made) two rings {of} gold, and they placed {them} upon {the} two extremities {of} the breastplate upon his lip, which {is} (on) {the} other side {of} the ephod, unto {the} (inside),☐

39:20 וַיַּעֲשׂוּ שְׁתֵּי טַבְּעֹת זָהָב וַיִּתְּנֻם עַל שְׁתֵּי כִתְפֹת הָאֵפֹד מִלְמַטָּה מִמּוּל פָּנָיו לְעֻמַּת מַחְבַּרְתּוֹ מִמַּעַל לְחֵשֶׁב הָאֵפֹד

wai'ya'a'su she'tey ta'be'ot za'hav wai'yit'num al she'tey khit'phot ha'ey'phod mil'ma'tah mi'mul pa'naw le'u'mat mahh'bar'to mi'ma'al le'hhey'shev ha'ey'phod

and~*they(m)~will*~<u>DO</u> TWO RING~s GOLD and~*they(m)~will*~<u>GIVE</u>~them(m) UPON TWO SHOULDER-PIECE~s the~EPHOD from~to~BENEATH from~FOREFRONT FACE~s~him to~ALONGSIDE JOINT~him from~UPWARD to~DECORATIVE-BAND the~EPHOD☐

and they (made) two rings {of} gold, and they (placed) them upon {the} two shoulder pieces {of} the ephod, beneath {the} forefront {of} his face, alongside his joint, <above> {the} decorative band {of} the ephod,☐

39:21 וַיִּרְכְּסוּ אֶת הַחֹשֶׁן מִטַּבְּעֹתָיו אֶל טַבְּעֹת הָאֵפֹד בִּפְתִיל תְּכֵלֶת לִהְיֹת

Revised Mechanical Translation Codes

(..) Alt Trans/App A   <..> Comp Phrase/App B   [..] Verb Form/App C   \../ Plural Form/App D
:..: Int Inf Abs |..| Past Perf Verb   {...} Added Word

עַל חֵשֶׁב הָאֵפֹד וְלֹא יִזַּח הַחֹשֶׁן מֵעַל הָאֵפֹד כַּאֲשֶׁר צִוָּה יְהוָה אֶת מֹשֶׁה

wai'yir'ke'su et ha'hho'shen mi'ta'be'o'taw el ta'be'ot ha'ey'phod biph'til te'khey'let lih'yot al hhey'shev ha'ey'phod we'lo yi'zahh ha'hho'shen mey'al ha'ey'phod ka'a'sheyr tsi'wah YHWH et mo'sheh

and~*they(m)~will*~<u>TIE-ON</u> AT the~ BREASTPLATE RING~s~him TO RING~s the~ EPHOD in~CORD BLUE to~>~<u>EXIST</u> UPON DECORATIVE-BAND the~EPHOD and~NOT *he~will~be*~<u>LOOSEN</u> the~BREASTPLATE from~UPON the~EPHOD like~WHICH *he~ did~much~*<u>DIRECT</u> "Yhwh ^{*he~will~*<u>BE</u>}" AT "Mosheh ^{PLUCKED-OUT}"□	and they tied on the breastplate {by} his rings to {the} rings {of} the ephod (with) {a} cord {of} blue, to exist upon {the} decorative band {of} the ephod, and the breastplate will not be loosened from upon the ephod, <just as> "Yhwh ^{He is}" directed "Mosheh ^{Plucked out}",□

39:22

וַיַּעַשׂ אֶת מְעִיל הָאֵפֹד מַעֲשֵׂה אֹרֵג כְּלִיל תְּכֵלֶת

wai'ya'as et me'il ha'ey'phod ma'a'seyh o'reyg ke'lil te'khey'let

and~*he~will*~<u>DO</u> AT CLOAK the~EPHOD WORK <u>BRAID</u>~*ing/er(ms)* ENTIRELY BLUE□	and he (made) {the} cloak {of} the ephod, {a} work {of} braiding*, entirely {with} blue,□

39:23

וּפִי הַמְּעִיל בְּתוֹכוֹ כְּפִי תַחְרָא שָׂפָה לְפִיו סָבִיב לֹא יִקָּרֵעַ

u'phi ham'il be'to'kho ke'phi tahh'ra sa'phah le'phiw sa'viv lo yi'qa'rey'a

and~MOUTH the~CLOAK in~MIDST~him like~MOUTH COLLAR LIP to~MOUTH~him ALL-AROUND NOT *he~will~be*~<u>TEAR</u>□	and {the} mouth† {of} the cloak in his midst, like {the} mouth {of the} collar, {a} lip‡ (for) his mouth all around, he will not be torn,□

39:24

וַיַּעֲשׂוּ עַל שׁוּלֵי הַמְּעִיל רִמּוֹנֵי תְּכֵלֶת וְאַרְגָּמָן וְתוֹלַעַת שָׁנִי מָשְׁזָר

wai'ya'a'su al shu'ley ham'il ri'mo'ney te'khey'let we'ar'ga'man we'to'la'at sha'ni mash'zar

and~*they(m)~will*~<u>DO</u> UPON HEM~s the~ CLOAK POMEGRANATE~s BLUE and~PURPLE and~KERMES SCARLET *be~make~*<u>TWIST-TOGETHER</u>~*ing/er(ms)*□	and they (made) upon {the} hems {of} the cloak pomegranates {of} blue, and purple, and kermes {of} scarlet, {and} [twisted] {linen}§,□

39:25

וַיַּעֲשׂוּ פַעֲמֹנֵי זָהָב טָהוֹר וַיִּתְּנוּ אֶת הַפַּעֲמֹנִים בְּתוֹךְ הָרִמֹּנִים עַל שׁוּלֵי הַמְּעִיל סָבִיב בְּתוֹךְ הָרִמֹּנִים

wai'ya'a'su pha'a'mo'ney za'hav ta'hor wai'yit'nu et ha'pa'a'mo'nim be'tokh ha'ri'mo'nim al shu'ley ham'il sa'viv be'tokh ha'ri'mo'nim

and~*they(m)~will*~<u>DO</u> BELL~s GOLD PURE and~*they(m)~will*~<u>GIVE</u> AT the~BELL~s in~	and they (made) bell{s of} pure gold and they (placed) the bells in {the} midst {of} the

---

* May also be translated as a "braider."

† Or "opening."

‡ Or "edge."

§ This word appears to be missing from the text.

Mechanical Translation Codes

<u>WORD</u> – Verb	WORD – Noun	Word – Name	word – Pre/Suff	*word* – Conj.

MIDST the~POMEGRANATE~s UPON HEM~s the~CLOAK ALL-AROUND in~MIDST the~POMEGRANATE~s□

pomegranate{s} upon {the} hems {of} the cloak all around in {the} midst {of} the pomegranate{s},□

39:26

פַּעֲמֹן וְרִמֹּן פַּעֲמֹן וְרִמֹּן עַל שׁוּלֵי הַמְּעִיל סָבִיב לְשָׁרֵת כַּאֲשֶׁר צִוָּה יְהוָה אֶת מֹשֶׁה

pa'a'mon we'ri'mon pa'a'mon we'ri'mon al shu'ley ham'il sa'viv le'sha'reyt ka'a'sheyr tsi'wah YHWH et mo'sheh

BELL and~POMEGRANATE BELL and~POMEGRANATE UPON HEM~s the~CLOAK ALL-AROUND to~>~much~MINISTER like~WHICH he~did~much~DIRECT "Yhwh ^he~will~BE^" AT "Mosheh ^PLUCKED-OUT^"□

bell and pomegranate, bell and pomegranate* {are} upon {the} hems {of} the cloak all around to minister, <just as> "Yhwh ^He is^" directed "Mosheh ^Plucked out^",□

39:27

וַיַּעֲשׂוּ אֶת הַכָּתְנֹת שֵׁשׁ מַעֲשֵׂה אֹרֵג לְאַהֲרֹן וּלְבָנָיו

wai'ya'a'su et ha'kat'not sheysh ma'a'seyh o'reyg le'a'ha'ron ul'va'naw

and~they(m)~will~DO AT the~TUNIC~s LINEN WORK BRAID~ing/er(ms) to~"Aharon ^LIGHT-BRINGER^" and~to~SON~s~him□

and they (made) the tunics {of} linen, {a} work {of} braiding† (for) "Aharon ^Light bringer^" and (for) his sons,□

39:28

וְאֵת הַמִּצְנֶפֶת שֵׁשׁ וְאֶת פַּאֲרֵי הַמִּגְבָּעֹת שֵׁשׁ וְאֶת מִכְנְסֵי הַבָּד שֵׁשׁ מָשְׁזָר

we'eyt ha'mits'ne'phet sheysh we'et pa'a'rey ha'mig'ba'ot sheysh we'et mikh'ne'sey ha'bad sheysh mash'zar

and~AT the~TURBAN LINEN and~AT BONNET~s the~HEADDRESS LINEN and~AT UNDERGARMENT~s the~STICK LINEN be~make~TWIST-TOGETHER~ing/er(ms)□

and the turban {of} linen and {the} bonnets {of} the headdress {of} linen, and {the} undergarments {of} (linen), [twisted] linen,□

39:29

וְאֶת הָאַבְנֵט שֵׁשׁ מָשְׁזָר וּתְכֵלֶת וְאַרְגָּמָן וְתוֹלַעַת שָׁנִי מַעֲשֵׂה רֹקֵם כַּאֲשֶׁר צִוָּה יְהוָה אֶת מֹשֶׁה

we'et ha'av'neyt sheysh mash'zar ut'khey'let we'ar'ga'man we'to'la'at sha'ni ma'a'seyh ro'qeym ka'a'sheyr tsi'wah YHWH et mo'sheh

and~AT the~SASH LINEN be~make~TWIST-TOGETHER~ing/er(ms) and~BLUE and~PURPLE and~KERMES SCARLET WORK EMBROIDER~ing/er(ms) like~WHICH he~did~much~DIRECT "Yhwh ^he~will~BE^" AT "Mosheh

and the sash {of} [twisted] linen, and blue, and purple, and kermes {of} scarlet, {a} work {of} embroidering‡, <just as> "Yhwh ^He is^" directed "Mosheh ^Plucked out^",□

---

* The phrase "bells and pomegranate" is written twice showing that they are to be placed on the garment in series.
† May also be translated as a "braider."
‡ This word may also mean "an embroiderer."

Revised Mechanical Translation Codes

(..) Alt Trans/App A   <..> Comp Phrase/App B   [..] Verb Form/App C   \../ Plural Form/App D
:..: Int Inf Abs |..| Past Perf Verb   {...} Added Word

PLUCKED-OUT„□

39:30 וַיַּעֲשׂוּ אֶת צִיץ נֵזֶר הַקֹּדֶשׁ זָהָב טָהוֹר וַיִּכְתְּבוּ עָלָיו מִכְתַּב פִּתּוּחֵי חוֹתָם קֹדֶשׁ לַיהוָה

wai'ya'a'su et tsits ney'zer ha'qo'desh za'hav ta'hor wai'yikh'te'vu a'law mikh'tav pi'tu'hhey hho'tam qo'desh la'YHWH

and~*they(m)~will*~<u>DO</u> AT BLOSSOM CROWN the~SPECIAL GOLD PURE and~*they(m)~will*~<u>WRITE</u> UPON~him THING-WRITTEN CARVING~s SEAL SPECIAL to~"Yhwh *he~will~*<u>BE</u>„□

and they (made) the blossom {of the} crown {of} special{ness of} pure gold, and they wrote upon him {a} thing written, carvings {of a} seal, {a} special {thing} (for) "Yhwh *He is*„,□

39:31 וַיִּתְּנוּ עָלָיו פְּתִיל תְּכֵלֶת לָתֵת עַל הַמִּצְנֶפֶת מִלְמָעְלָה כַּאֲשֶׁר צִוָּה יְהוָה אֶת מֹשֶׁה

wai'yit'nu a'law pe'til te'khey'let la'teyt al ha'mits'ne'phet mil'ma'lah ka'a'sheyr tsi'wah YHWH et mo'sheh

and~*they(m)~will*~<u>GIVE</u> UPON~him CORD BLUE to~>~<u>GIVE</u> UPON the~TURBAN from~ to~UPWARD~unto like~WHICH *he~did~ much*~<u>DIRECT</u> "Yhwh *he~will~*<u>BE</u>„ AT "Mosheh PLUCKED-OUT„□

and they (placed) upon him {a} cord {of} blue, to (place) upon {the} <top> {of} the turban from <above>, <just as> "Yhwh *He is*„ directed "Mosheh *Plucked out*„,□

39:32 וַתֵּכֶל כָּל עֲבֹדַת מִשְׁכַּן אֹהֶל מוֹעֵד וַיַּעֲשׂוּ בְּנֵי יִשְׂרָאֵל כְּכֹל אֲשֶׁר צִוָּה יְהוָה אֶת מֹשֶׁה כֵּן עָשׂוּ

wa'tey'khel kol a'vo'dat mish'kan o'hel mo'eyd wai'ya'a'su be'ney yis'ra'eyl ke'khol a'sher tsi'wah YHWH et mo'sheh keyn a'su

and~ *she~will*~<u>FINISH</u> ALL SERVICE DWELLING TENT APPOINTED and~*they(m)~ will*~<u>DO</u> SON~s "Yisra'el *he~will~*<u>TURN-ASIDE</u>~+~ MIGHTY-ONE„ like~ALL WHICH *he~did~much*~ <u>DIRECT</u> "Yhwh *he~will~*<u>BE</u>„ AT "Mosheh PLUCKED-OUT„ SO *they~did~*<u>DO</u>□

and all {the} service {of the} dwelling {of the} tent {of the} appointed {place was} finished, and {the} sons {of} "Yisra'el *He turns El aside*„ (made) {it just} like (what) "Yhwh *He is*„ directed "Mosheh *Plucked out*„, so they (made),□

39:33 וַיָּבִיאוּ אֶת הַמִּשְׁכָּן אֶל מֹשֶׁה אֶת הָאֹהֶל וְאֶת כָּל כֵּלָיו קְרָסָיו קְרָשָׁיו בְּרִיחָו וְעַמֻּדָיו וַאֲדָנָיו

wai'ya'vi'u et ha'mish'kan el mo'sheh et ha'o'hel we'et kol key'law qe'ra'saw qe'ra'shaw be'ri'hhaw we'a'mu'daw we'a'da'naw

and~*they(m)~will*~make~<u>COME</u> AT the~ DWELLING TO "Mosheh PLUCKED-OUT„ AT the~ TENT and~AT ALL ITEM~s~him HOOK~s~him BOARD~s~him WOOD-BAR~s~him and~ PILLAR~s~him and~FOOTING~s~him□

and they [brought] the dwelling to "Mosheh *Plucked out*„, the tent and all his items, his hooks, his boards, his wood bars, and his pillars, and his footings,□

Mechanical Translation Codes

<u>WORD</u> – Verb	WORD – Noun	Word – Name	word – Pre/Suff	*word* – Conj.

39:34

וְאֶת מִכְסֵה עוֹרֹת הָאֵילִם הַמְאָדָּמִים וְאֶת מִכְסֵה עֹרֹת הַתְּחָשִׁים וְאֵת פָּרֹכֶת הַמָּסָךְ

we'et mikh'seyh o'rot ha'ey'lim ham'a'da'mim we'et mikh'seyh o'rot hat'hha'shim we'eyt pa'ro'khet ha'ma'sakh

and~AT ROOF-COVERING SKIN~s the~ BUCK~s the~*be~much~*<u>BE-RED</u>~ing/er(mp) and~AT ROOF-COVERING SKIN~s the~ TAHHASH~s and~AT TENT-CURTAIN the~ CANOPY□

and {the} roof covering {of} skins {of} the bucks being red, and the roof covering {of} skins {of} the tahhash*, and {the} tent curtain {of} the canopy,□

39:35

אֶת אֲרוֹן הָעֵדֻת וְאֶת בַּדָּיו וְאֵת הַכַּפֹּרֶת

et a'ron ha'ey'dut we'et ba'daw we'eyt ha'ka'po'ret

AT BOX the~EVIDENCE and~AT STICK~s~him and~AT the~LID□

{the} box {of} the evidence and his sticks and the lid,□

39:36

אֶת הַשֻּׁלְחָן אֶת כָּל כֵּלָיו וְאֵת לֶחֶם הַפָּנִים

et ha'shul'hhan et kol key'law we'eyt le'hhem ha'pa'nim

AT the~TABLE AT ALL ITEM~s~him and~AT BREAD the~FACE~s□

the table (with) all his items, and {the} bread {of} the face,□

39:37

אֶת הַמְּנֹרָה הַטְּהֹרָה אֶת נֵרֹתֶיהָ נֵרֹת הַמַּעֲרָכָה וְאֶת כָּל כֵּלֶיהָ וְאֵת שֶׁמֶן הַמָּאוֹר

et ham'no'rah hat'ho'rah et ney'ro'te'yah ney'rot ha'ma'a'ra'kha we'et kol key'ley'ah we'eyt she'men ha'ma'or

AT the~LAMPSTAND the~PURE AT LAMP~s~ her LAMP~s the~RANK and~AT ALL ITEM~s~ her and~AT OIL the~LUMINARY□

the pure lampstand, (with) her lamps, the lamp {of} rank†, and all her items, and {the} oil {of} the luminary,□

39:38

וְאֵת מִזְבַּח הַזָּהָב וְאֵת שֶׁמֶן הַמִּשְׁחָה וְאֵת קְטֹרֶת הַסַּמִּים וְאֵת מָסַךְ פֶּתַח הָאֹהֶל

we'eyt miz'bahh ha'za'hav we'eyt she'men ha'mish'hhah we'eyt qe'to'ret ha'sa'mim we'eyt ma'sakh pe'tahh ha'o'hel

and~AT ALTAR the~GOLD and~AT OIL the~ OINTMENT and~AT INCENSE the~ AROMATIC-SPICE~s and~AT CANOPY OPENING the~TENT□

and {the} altar {of} gold, and {the} oil {of} ointment, and the incense {of} aromatic spices, and {the} canopy {of the} opening {of} the tent,□

39:39

אֶת מִזְבַּח הַנְּחֹשֶׁת וְאֶת מִכְבַּר הַנְּחֹשֶׁת אֲשֶׁר לוֹ אֶת בַּדָּיו וְאֶת כָּל כֵּלָיו אֶת הַכִּיֹּר וְאֶת כַּנּוֹ

---

* The Tahhash is an unknown species of animal.

† "The lamp of rank" means "the row of lamps."

Revised Mechanical Translation Codes

(..) Alt Trans/App A   <..> Comp Phrase/App B   [..] Verb Form/App C   \../ Plural Form/App D

:..: Int Inf Abs |..| Past Perf Verb   {...} Added Word

eyt miz'bahh han'hho'shet we'et mikh'bar han'hho'shet a'sher lo et ba'daw we'et kol key'law et ha'ki'yor we'et ka'no

AT ALTAR the~COPPER and~AT GRATE the~COPPER WHICH to~him AT STICK~s~him and~AT ALL ITEM~s~him AT the~CAULDRON and~AT BASE~him□	the altar {of} copper, and the grate {of} copper which {is} (for) him, his sticks, and all his items, the cauldron and his base,□

39:40 אֶת קַלְעֵי הֶחָצֵר אֶת עַמֻּדֶיהָ וְאֶת אֲדָנֶיהָ וְאֶת הַמָּסָךְ לְשַׁעַר הֶחָצֵר אֶת מֵיתָרָיו וִיתֵדֹתֶיהָ וְאֶת כָּל כְּלֵי עֲבֹדַת הַמִּשְׁכָּן לְאֹהֶל מוֹעֵד

eyt qal'ey he'hha'tseyr et a'mudey'ah we'et a'da'ney'ah we'et ha'ma'sakh le'sha'ar he'hha'tseyr et mey'ta'raw wi'tey'do'tey'ah we'eyt kol ke'ley a'vo'dat ha'mish'kan le'o'hel mo'eyd

AT SLING~s the~YARD AT PILLAR~s~her and~AT FOOTING~s~her and~AT the~CANOPY to~GATE the~YARD AT STRING~s~him and~TENT-PEG~s~her and~AT ALL ITEM~s SERVICE the~DWELLING to~TENT APPOINTED□	{the} slings {of} the yard, her pillars and her footings, and the canopy (for) {the} gate {of} the yard, his strings, and her tent pegs, and all {the} items {of the} service {of the} dwelling, (for) {the} tent {of the} appointed {place},□

39:41 אֶת בִּגְדֵי הַשְּׂרָד לְשָׁרֵת בַּקֹּדֶשׁ אֶת בִּגְדֵי הַקֹּדֶשׁ לְאַהֲרֹן הַכֹּהֵן וְאֶת בִּגְדֵי בָנָיו לְכַהֵן

et big'dey has'rad le'sha'reyt ba'qo'desh et big'dey ha'qo'desh le'a'ha'ron ha'ko'heyn we'et big'dey va'naw le'kha'heyn

AT GARMENT~s the~BRAIDED-WORK to~>~much~<u>MINISTER</u> in~the~SPECIAL AT GARMENT~s the~SPECIAL to~"Aharon ^{LIGHT-BRINGER}" the~ADMINISTRATOR and~AT GARMENT~s SON~s~him to~>~much~<u>ADORN</u>□	the garments {of} braided work to minister in the special {place}, the garments {of} special{ness} (for) "Aharon ^{Light bringer}" the administrator, and {the} garments {of} his sons to adorn {them},□

39:42 כְּכֹל אֲשֶׁר צִוָּה יְהֹוָה אֶת מֹשֶׁה כֵּן עָשׂוּ בְּנֵי יִשְׂרָאֵל אֵת כָּל הָעֲבֹדָה

ke'khol a'sher tsi'wah YHWH et mo'sheh keyn a'su be'ney yis'ra'eyl eyt kol ha'a'vo'dah

like~ALL WHICH *he~did~much~*<u>DIRECT</u> "Yhwh *^{he~will~}<u>BE</u>*" AT "Mosheh ^{PLUCKED-OUT}" SO *they~did~*<u>DO</u> SON~s "Yisra'el *^{he~will~}<u>TURN-ASIDE</u>~+~MIGHTY-ONE*" AT ALL the~SERVICE□	{just} like all (that) "Yhwh ^{He is}" directed "Mosheh ^{Plucked out}", so {the} sons {of} "Yisra'el ^{He turns El aside}" (made) all the service,□

39:43 וַיַּרְא מֹשֶׁה אֶת כָּל הַמְּלָאכָה וְהִנֵּה עָשׂוּ אֹתָהּ כַּאֲשֶׁר צִוָּה יְהֹוָה כֵּן עָשׂוּ וַיְבָרֶךְ אֹתָם מֹשֶׁה

wai'yar mo'sheh et kol ham'la'khah we'hin'neyh a'su o'tah ka'a'sheyr tsi'wah YHWH keyn a'su wai'va'rekh o'tam mo'sheh

and~he~will~<u>SEE</u> "Mosheh ^{PLUCKED-OUT}" AT ALL the~<u>BUSINESS</u> and~<u>LOOK</u> they~did~<u>DO</u> AT~ her like~<u>WHICH</u> he~did~much~<u>DIRECT</u> "Yhwh ^{he~will~<u>BE</u>}" SO they~did~<u>DO</u> and~he~ will~much~<u>KNEEL</u> AT~them(m) "Mosheh ^{PLUCKED-OUT}"□

and "Mosheh ^{Plucked out}" saw all the business, and look, they (made) her* <just as> "Yhwh ^{He is}" directed, so they (made) {it}, and "Mosheh ^{Plucked out}" [respected] them,□

Chapter 40

40:1

וַיְדַבֵּר יְהֹוָה אֶל מֹשֶׁה לֵּאמֹר

wai'da'beyr YHWH el mo'sheh ley'mor

and~he~will~much~<u>SPEAK</u> "Yhwh ^{he~will~<u>BE</u>}" TO "Mosheh ^{PLUCKED-OUT}" to~>~<u>SAY</u>□

and "Yhwh ^{He is}" spoke to "Mosheh ^{Plucked out}" say{ing},□

40:2

בְּיוֹם הַחֹדֶשׁ הָרִאשׁוֹן בְּאֶחָד לַחֹדֶשׁ תָּקִים אֶת מִשְׁכַּן אֹהֶל מוֹעֵד

be'yom ha'hho'desh ha'ri'shon be'e'hhad la'hho'desh ta'qim et mish'kan o'hel mo'eyd

in~DAY the~NEW-MOON the~FIRST in~UNIT to~the~NEW-MOON you(ms)~will~make~ <u>RISE</u> AT DWELLING TENT APPOINTED□

in the first new moon†, (on) the (first) {day of} the new moon, you will make {the} dwelling {of the} tent {of the} appointed {place} rise,□

40:3

וְשַׂמְתָּ שָׁם אֵת אֲרוֹן הָעֵדוּת וְסַכֹּתָ עַל הָאָרֹן אֶת הַפָּרֹכֶת

we'sam'ta sham eyt a'ron ha'ey'dut we'sa'ko'ta al ha'a'ron et ha'pa'ro'khet

and~you(ms)~did~<u>PLACE</u> THERE AT BOX the~ EVIDENCE and~you(ms)~did~<u>FENCE-AROUND</u> UPON the~BOX AT the~TENT-CURTAIN□

and you will place {the} box {of} the evidence there, and you will fence around the box (with) the tent curtain,□

40:4

וְהֵבֵאתָ אֶת הַשֻּׁלְחָן וְעָרַכְתָּ אֶת עֶרְכּוֹ וְהֵבֵאתָ אֶת הַמְּנֹרָה וְהַעֲלֵיתָ אֶת נֵרֹתֶיהָ

we'hey'vey'ta et ha'shul'hhan we'a'rakh'ta et er'ko we'hey'vey'ta et ham'no'rah weha'a'ley'ta et ney'ro'te'yah

and~you(ms)~did~make~<u>COME</u> AT the~ TABLE and~you(ms)~did~<u>ARRANGE</u> AT ARRANGEMENT~him and~you(ms)~did~

and you will [bring] the table, and you will arrange his arrangement, and you will [bring] the lampstand, and you will [bring up] her

---

* Referring to the "business," a feminine word in Hebrew.

† The phrase בְּאֶחָד לַחֹדֶשׁ always means "the first day of the new moon" (compare with Exodus 40:17). Therefore, it appears that the phrase בְּיוֹם הַחֹדֶשׁ הָרִאשׁוֹן is written defectively and should be written as בְּחֹדֶשׁ הָרִאשׁוֹן (in the first new moon).

Revised Mechanical Translation Codes

(..) Alt Trans/App A	<..> Comp Phrase/App B	[..] Verb Form/App C	\../ Plural Form/App D
:..: Int Inf Abs	|..| Past Perf Verb	{...} Added Word	

make~<u>COME</u> AT the~LAMPSTAND and~
you(ms)~*did*~*make*~<u>GO-UP</u> AT LAMP~s~
her□

lamps,□

40:5

וְנָתַתָּה אֶת מִזְבַּח הַזָּהָב לִקְטֹרֶת לִפְנֵי אֲרוֹן הָעֵדֻת וְשַׂמְתָּ אֶת מָסַךְ הַפֶּתַח לַמִּשְׁכָּן

we'na'ta'tah et miz'bahh ha'za'hav liq'to'ret liph'ney a'ron ha'ey'dut we'sam'ta et ma'sakh ha'pe'tahh la'mish'kan

and~*you(ms)*~*did*~<u>GIVE</u>~^ AT ALTAR the~GOLD to~INCENSE to~FACE~s BOX the~EVIDENCE and~*you(ms)*~*did*~<u>PLACE</u> AT CANOPY the~OPENING to~the~DWELLING□

and you will (place) the altar {of} gold (for) {the} incense (for) {the} face {of the} box {of} the evidence, and you will place {the} canopy {of} the opening (for) the dwelling,□

40:6

וְנָתַתָּה אֵת מִזְבַּח הָעֹלָה לִפְנֵי פֶּתַח מִשְׁכַּן אֹהֶל מוֹעֵד

we'na'ta'tah eyt miz'bahh ha'o'lah liph'ney pe'tahh mish'kan o'hel mo'eyd

and~*you(ms)*~*did*~<u>GIVE</u>~^ AT ALTAR the~RISING to~FACE~s OPENING DWELLING TENT APPOINTED□

and you will (place) the altar {of the} rising {sacrifice} to {the} face {of the} opening {of the} dwelling {of the} tent {of the} appointed {place},□

40:7

וְנָתַתָּ אֶת הַכִּיֹּר בֵּין אֹהֶל מוֹעֵד וּבֵין הַמִּזְבֵּחַ וְנָתַתָּ שָׁם מָיִם

we'na'ta'ta et ha'ki'yor beyn o'hel mo'eyd u'veyn ha'miz'bey'ahh we'na'ta'ta sham ma'yim

and~*you(ms)*~*did*~<u>GIVE</u> AT the~CAULDRON BETWEEN TENT APPOINTED and~BETWEEN the~ALTAR and~*you(ms)*~*did*~<u>GIVE</u> THERE WATER~s2□

and you will (place) the cauldron between {the} tent {of the} appointed {place} and the altar, and you will (place) water {in} there,□

40:8

וְשַׂמְתָּ אֶת הֶחָצֵר סָבִיב וְנָתַתָּ אֶת מָסַךְ שַׁעַר הֶחָצֵר

we'sam'ta et he'hha'tseyr sa'viv we'na'ta'ta et ma'sakh sha'ar he'hha'tseyr

and~*you(ms)*~*did*~<u>PLACE</u> AT the~YARD ALL-AROUND and~*you(ms)*~*did*~<u>GIVE</u> AT CANOPY GATE the~YARD□

and you will place the yard all around, and you will (place) the canopy {of the} gate {of the} yard,□

40:9

וְלָקַחְתָּ אֶת שֶׁמֶן הַמִּשְׁחָה וּמָשַׁחְתָּ אֶת הַמִּשְׁכָּן וְאֶת כָּל אֲשֶׁר בּוֹ וְקִדַּשְׁתָּ אֹתוֹ וְאֶת כָּל כֵּלָיו וְהָיָה קֹדֶשׁ

we'la'qahh'ta et she'men ha'mish'hhah u'ma'shahh'ta et ha'mish'kan we'et kol a'sher bo we'qi'dash'ta o'to we'et kol key'law we'hai'yah qo'desh

and~*you(ms)*~*did*~<u>TAKE</u> AT OIL the~OINTMENT and~*you(ms)*~*did*~<u>SMEAR</u> AT the~DWELLING and~AT ALL WHICH in~him and~*you(ms)*~*did*~*much*~<u>SET-APART</u> AT~him and~AT ALL ITEM~s~him and~*he*~*did*~<u>EXIST</u>

and you will take the oil {of} ointment, and you will smear the dwelling and all which {is} in him, and you will set him, and all his items, apart, and he will exist {as a} special {thing},□

Mechanical Translation Codes

<u>WORD</u> – Verb	WORD – Noun	Word – Name	word – Pre/Suff	*word* – Conj.

SPECIAL□

40:10

וּמָשַׁחְתָּ אֶת מִזְבַּח הָעֹלָה וְאֶת כָּל כֵּלָיו וְקִדַּשְׁתָּ אֶת הַמִּזְבֵּחַ וְהָיָה הַמִּזְבֵּחַ קֹדֶשׁ קָדָשִׁים

u'ma'shahh'ta et miz'bahh ha'o'lah we'et kol key'law we'qi'dash'ta et ha'miz'bey'ahh we'hai'yah ha'miz'bey'ahh qo'desh qa'da'shim

and~*you(ms)~did~*SMEAR AT ALTAR the~ RISING and~AT ALL ITEM~s~him and~ *you(ms)~did~much~*SET-APART AT the~ ALTAR and~*he~did~*EXIST the~ALTAR SPECIAL SPECIAL~s□

and you will smear the altar {of the} rising {sacrifice} and all his items, and you will set the altar apart, and the altar, {a} special {thing of} special {thing}s, will exist,□

40:11

וּמָשַׁחְתָּ אֶת הַכִּיֹּר וְאֶת כַּנּוֹ וְקִדַּשְׁתָּ אֹתוֹ

u'ma'shahh'ta et ha'ki'yor we'et ka'no we'qi'dash'ta o'to

and~*you(ms)~did~*SMEAR AT the~ CAULDRON and~AT BASE~him and~ *you(ms)~did~much~*SET-APART AT~him□

and you will smear the cauldron and his base, and you will set him apart,□

40:12

וְהִקְרַבְתָּ אֶת אַהֲרֹן וְאֶת בָּנָיו אֶל פֶּתַח אֹהֶל מוֹעֵד וְרָחַצְתָּ אֹתָם בַּמָּיִם

we'hiq'rav'ta et a'ha'ron we'et ba'naw el pe'tahh o'hel mo'eyd we'ra'hhats'ta o'tam ba'ma'yim

and~*you(ms)~did~make~*COME-NEAR AT "Aharon ^LIGHT-BRINGER^" and~AT SON~s~him TO OPENING TENT APPOINTED and~*you(ms)~ did~*BATHE AT~them(m) in~the~ WATER~s2□

and you will [bring near] "Aharon ^Light bringer^" and his sons to {the} opening {of the} tent {of the} appointed {place}, and you will bathe them in the water,□

40:13

וְהִלְבַּשְׁתָּ אֶת אַהֲרֹן אֵת בִּגְדֵי הַקֹּדֶשׁ וּמָשַׁחְתָּ אֹתוֹ וְקִדַּשְׁתָּ אֹתוֹ וְכִהֵן לִי

we'hil'bash'ta et a'ha'ron eyt big'dey ha'qo'desh u'ma'shahh'ta o'to we'qi'dash'ta o'to we'khi'heyn li

and~*you(ms)~did~make~*WEAR ΛT "Aharon ^LIGHT-BRINGER^" AT GARMENT~s the~SPECIAL and~*you(ms)~did~*SMEAR AT~him and~ *you(ms)~did~much~*SET-APART AT~him and~*he~did~much~*ADORN to~me□

and you will [clothe] "Aharon ^Light bringer^" (with) the garments {of} special{ness}, and you will smear him, and you will set him apart, and he will {be} adorned (for) me,□

40:14

וְאֶת בָּנָיו תַּקְרִיב וְהִלְבַּשְׁתָּ אֹתָם כֻּתֳּנֹת

we'et ba'naw taq'riv we'hil'bash'ta o'tam ku'ta'not

and~AT SON~s~him *you(ms)~will~make~* COME-NEAR and~*you(ms)~did~make~*WEAR

and you will [bring near] his sons, and you will [clothe] them {with} tunics,□

Revised Mechanical Translation Codes

(..) Alt Trans/App A   <..> Comp Phrase/App B   [..] Verb Form/App C   \../ Plural Form/App D
:..: Int Inf Abs |..| Past Perf Verb   {...} Added Word

AT~them(m) TUNIC~s□

40:15 וּמָשַׁחְתָּ אֹתָם כַּאֲשֶׁר מָשַׁחְתָּ אֶת אֲבִיהֶם וְכִהֲנוּ לִי וְהָיְתָה לִהְיֹת לָהֶם מָשְׁחָתָם לִכְהֻנַּת עוֹלָם לְדֹרֹתָם

u'ma'shahh'ta o'tam ka'a'sheyr ma'shahh'ta et a'vi'hem we'khi'ha'nu li we'hai'tah lih'yot la'hem mash'hha'tam likh'hu'nat o'lam le'do'ro'tam

and~you(ms)~did~<u>SMEAR</u> AT~them(m) like~ WHICH you(ms)~did~<u>SMEAR</u> AT FATHER~ them(m) and~they~did~much~<u>ADORN</u> to~ me and~ she~did~<u>EXIST</u> to~>~<u>EXIST</u> to~ them(m) >~<u>SMEAR</u>~them(m) to~ ADMINISTRATION DISTANT to~ GENERATION~s~them(m)□	and you will smear them <just as> you smeared their father, and they will {be} adorned (for) me, and their smear{ing} will :surely: exist (for) them, (for) {an} administration {of a} distant {time}, (for) their generations,□

40:16 וַיַּעַשׂ מֹשֶׁה כְּכֹל אֲשֶׁר צִוָּה יְהוָה אֹתוֹ כֵּן עָשָׂה

wai'ya'as mo'sheh ke'khol a'sher tsi'wah YHWH o'to keyn a'sah

and~he~will~<u>DO</u> "Mosheh ^{PLUCKED-OUT}" like~ ALL WHICH he~did~much~<u>DIRECT</u> "Yhwh ^{he~ will~BE}" AT~him SO he~did~<u>DO</u>□	and "Mosheh ^{Plucked out}" did {just} like all (that) "Yhwh ^{He is}" directed him, so he did,□

40:17 וַיְהִי בַּחֹדֶשׁ הָרִאשׁוֹן בַּשָּׁנָה הַשֵּׁנִית בְּאֶחָד לַחֹדֶשׁ הוּקַם הַמִּשְׁכָּן

wai'hi ba'hho'desh ha'ri'shon ba'sha'nah ha'shey'nit be'e'hhad la'hho'desh hu'qam ha'mish'kan

and~he~will~<u>EXIST</u> in~the~NEW-MOON the~ FIRST in~the~YEAR the~SECOND in~UNIT to~ the~NEW-MOON he~did~be~make~<u>RISE</u> the~DWELLING□	and (it) (came to pass), in the first new moon, in the second year, (on) {the} (first) {day of} the new moon, the dwelling was made {to} rise,□

40:18 וַיָּקֶם מֹשֶׁה אֶת הַמִּשְׁכָּן וַיִּתֵּן אֶת אֲדָנָיו וַיָּשֶׂם אֶת קְרָשָׁיו וַיִּתֵּן אֶת בְּרִיחָיו וַיָּקֶם אֶת עַמּוּדָיו

wai' ya'qem mo'sheh et ha'mish'kan wai'yi'teyn et a'da'naw wai'ya'sem et qe'ra'shaw wai'yi'teyn et be'ri'hhaw wai' ya'qem et a'mu'daw

and~he~will~make~<u>RISE</u> "Mosheh ^{PLUCKED-OUT}" AT the~DWELLING and~he~will~<u>GIVE</u> AT FOOTING~s~him and~he~will~<u>PLACE</u> AT BOARD~s~him and~he~will~<u>GIVE</u> AT WOOD-BAR~s~him and~he~will~make~<u>RISE</u> AT PILLAR~s~him□	and "Mosheh ^{Plucked out}" made the dwelling rise, and he (placed) his footings, and he (placed) his boards, and he (placed) his wood bars, and he made his pillars rise,□

40:19 וַיִּפְרֹשׂ אֶת הָאֹהֶל עַל הַמִּשְׁכָּן וַיָּשֶׂם אֶת מִכְסֵה הָאֹהֶל עָלָיו מִלְמָעְלָה כַּאֲשֶׁר צִוָּה יְהוָה אֶת מֹשֶׁה

wai'yiph'ros et ha'o'hel al ha'mish'kan wai'ya'sem et mikh'seyh ha'o'hel a'law mil'ma'lah ka'a'sheyr tsi'wah YHWH et mo'sheh

and~*he~will*~<u>SPREAD-OUT</u> AT the~TENT UPON the~DWELLING and~*he~will*~<u>PLACE</u> AT ROOF-COVERING the~TENT UPON~him from~to~UPWARD~unto like~WHICH *he~did~much*~<u>DIRECT</u> "Yhwh ^{he~will~<u>BE</u>}" AT "Mosheh ^{PLUCKED-OUT}"□	and he spread out the tent upon the dwelling, and he placed {the} roof covering {of} the tent upon {the} <top> {of} him, <just as> "Yhwh ^{He is}" directed "Mosheh ^{Plucked out}",□

40:20   וַיִּקַּח וַיִּתֵּן אֶת הָעֵדֻת אֶל הָאָרֹן וַיָּשֶׂם אֶת הַבַּדִּים עַל הָאָרֹן וַיִּתֵּן אֶת הַכַּפֹּרֶת עַל הָאָרֹן מִלְמָעְלָה

wai'yi'qahh wai'yi'teyn et ha'ey'dut el ha'a'ron wai'ya'sem et ha'ba'dim al ha'a'ron wai'yi'teyn et ha'ka'po'ret al ha'a'ron mil'ma'lah

and~*he~will*~<u>TAKE</u> and~*he~will*~<u>GIVE</u> AT the~EVIDENCE TO the~BOX and~*he~will*~<u>PLACE</u> AT the~STICK*s UPON the~BOX and~*he~will*~<u>GIVE</u> AT the~LID UPON the~BOX from~to~UPWARD~unto□	and he took, and he (placed) the evidence to* the box, and he placed the sticks upon the box, and he (placed) the lid upon {the} <top> {of} the box,□

40:21   וַיָּבֵא אֶת הָאָרֹן אֶל הַמִּשְׁכָּן וַיָּשֶׂם אֵת פָּרֹכֶת הַמָּסָךְ וַיָּסֶךְ עַל אֲרוֹן הָעֵדוּת כַּאֲשֶׁר צִוָּה יְהֹוָה אֶת מֹשֶׁה

wai'ya'vey et ha'a'ron el ha'mish'kan wai'ya'sem eyt pa'ro'khet ha'ma'sakh wai'ya'sekh al a'ron ha'ey'dut ka'a'sheyr tsi'wah YHWH et mo'sheh

and~*he~will~make*~<u>COME</u> AT the~BOX TO the~DWELLING and~*he~will*~<u>PLACE</u> AT TENT-CURTAIN the~CANOPY and~*he~will*~<u>FENCE-AROUND</u> UPON BOX the~EVIDENCE like~WHICH *he~did~much*~<u>DIRECT</u> "Yhwh ^{he~will~<u>BE</u>}" AT "Mosheh ^{PLUCKED-OUT}"□	and he [brought] the box to the dwelling, and he (placed) {the} tent curtain {of} the canopy, and he fenced around upon {the} box {of} the evidence, <just as> "Yhwh ^{He is}" directed "Mosheh ^{Plucked out}",□

40:22   וַיִּתֵּן אֶת הַשֻּׁלְחָן בְּאֹהֶל מוֹעֵד עַל יֶרֶךְ הַמִּשְׁכָּן צָפֹנָה מִחוּץ לַפָּרֹכֶת

wai'yi'teyn et ha'shul'hhan be'o'hel mo'eyd al ye'rekh ha'mish'kan tsa'pho'nah mi'hhuts la'pa'ro'khet

and~*he~will*~<u>GIVE</u> AT the~TABLE in~TENT APPOINTED UPON MIDSECTION the~DWELLING NORTH~unto from~OUTSIDE to~the~TENT-CURTAIN□	and he (placed) the table in {the} tent {of the} appointed {place}, upon the midsection {of} the dwelling, unto the north, outside the tent curtain,□

40:23   וַיַּעֲרֹךְ עָלָיו עֵרֶךְ לֶחֶם לִפְנֵי יְהֹוָה כַּאֲשֶׁר צִוָּה יְהֹוָה אֶת מֹשֶׁה

wai'ya'a'rokh a'law ey'rekh le'hhem liph'ney YHWH ka'a'sheyr tsi'wah YHWH et mo'sheh

and~*he~will*~<u>ARRANGE</u> UPON~him	and he arranged upon him {the} bread (for)

---

* Probably meaning "inside."

Revised Mechanical Translation Codes

(..) Alt Trans/App A   <..> Comp Phrase/App B   [..] Verb Form/App C   \../ Plural Form/App D
:..: Int Inf Abs |..| Past Perf Verb   {...} Added Word

ARRANGEMENT BREAD to~FACE~s "Yhwh ^{he~} ^{will~}<u>BE</u>" like~WHICH he~did~much~<u>DIRECT</u> "Yhwh ^{he~will~}<u>BE</u>" AT "Mosheh ^{PLUCKED-OUT}",□

{the} face {of} "Yhwh ^{He is}", <just as> "Yhwh ^{He is}" directed "Mosheh ^{Plucked out}",□

40:24 וַיָּשֶׂם אֶת הַמְּנֹרָה בְּאֹהֶל מוֹעֵד נֹכַח הַשֻּׁלְחָן עַל יֶרֶךְ הַמִּשְׁכָּן נֶגְבָּה

wai'ya'sem et ham'no'rah be'o'hel mo'eyd no'khahh ha'shul'hhan al ye'rekh ha'mish'kan neg'bah

and~he~will~<u>PLACE</u> AT the~LAMPSTAND in~ TENT APPOINTED IN-FRONT the~TABLE UPON MIDSECTION the~DWELLING "Negev ^{PARCHED}"~unto□

and he placed the lampstand in {the} tent {of the} appointed {place}, in front {of} the table, upon the midsection {of} the dwelling, unto {the} "Negev ^{Parched}"*,□

40:25 וַיַּעַל הַנֵּרֹת לִפְנֵי יְהוָה כַּאֲשֶׁר צִוָּה יְהוָה אֶת מֹשֶׁה

wai'ya'al ha'ney'rot liph'ney YHWH ka'a'sheyr tsi'wah YHWH et mo'sheh

and~he~will~make~<u>GO-UP</u> the~LAMP~s to~ FACE~s "Yhwh ^{he~will~}<u>BE</u>" like~WHICH he~did~ much~<u>DIRECT</u> "Yhwh ^{he~will~}<u>BE</u>" AT "Mosheh ^{PLUCKED-OUT}",□

and he made the lamps go up† to {the} face {of} "Yhwh ^{He is}", <just as> "Yhwh ^{He is}" directed "Mosheh ^{Plucked out}",□

40:26 וַיָּשֶׂם אֶת מִזְבַּח הַזָּהָב בְּאֹהֶל מוֹעֵד לִפְנֵי הַפָּרֹכֶת

wai'ya'sem et miz'bahh ha'za'hav be'o'hel mo'eyd liph'ney ha'pa'ro'khet

and~he~will~<u>PLACE</u> AT ALTAR the~GOLD in~ TENT APPOINTED to~FACE~s the~TENT-CURTAIN□

and he placed the altar {of} gold in {the} tent {of the} appointed {place}, to {the} face {of} the tent curtain,□

40:27 וַיַּקְטֵר עָלָיו קְטֹרֶת סַמִּים כַּאֲשֶׁר צִוָּה יְהוָה אֶת מֹשֶׁה

wai'yaq'teyr a'law qe'to'ret sa'mim ka'a'sheyr tsi'wah YHWH et mo'sheh

and~he~will~make~<u>BURN-INCENSE</u> UPON~ him INCENSE AROMATIC-SPICE~s like~ WHICH he~did~much~<u>DIRECT</u> "Yhwh ^{he~will~} <u>BE</u>" AT "Mosheh ^{PLUCKED-OUT}",□

and he burned incense upon him, {an} incense {of} aromatic spices, <just as> "Yhwh ^{He is}" directed "Mosheh ^{Plucked out}",□

40:28 וַיָּשֶׂם אֶת מָסַךְ הַפֶּתַח לַמִּשְׁכָּן

wai'ya'sem et ma'sakh ha'pe'tahh la'mish'kan

and~he~will~<u>PLACE</u> AT CANOPY the~OPENING to~ the~DWELLING□

and he placed {the} canopy {of} the opening to the dwelling,□

40:29 וְאֵת מִזְבַּח הָעֹלָה שָׂם פֶּתַח מִשְׁכַּן אֹהֶל מוֹעֵד וַיַּעַל עָלָיו אֶת הָעֹלָה וְאֶת הַמִּנְחָה כַּאֲשֶׁר צִוָּה יְהוָה אֶת מֹשֶׁה

---

* That is the "south."

† "Made her lamps go up" means to light the wicks.

Mechanical Translation Codes

<u>WORD</u> – Verb	WORD – Noun	Word – Name	word – Pre/Suff	*word* – Conj.

we'eyt miz'bahh ha'o'lah sham pe'tahh mish'kan o'hel mo'eyd wai'ya'al a'law et ha'o'lah we'et ha'min'hhah ka'a'sheyr tsi'wah YHWH et mo'sheh

and~AT ALTAR the~RISING *he~did* PLACE OPENING DWELLING TENT APPOINTED and~*he~will~make~* GO-UP UPON~him AT the~RISING and~AT the~ DONATION like~WHICH *he~did~much* DIRECT "Yhwh *he~will~BE*" AT "Mosheh PLUCKED-OUT"□

and the altar {of the} rising {sacrifice} he placed {at the} opening {of the} dwelling {of the} appointed {place}, and he made the rising {sacrifice} and the donation go up upon him, <just as> "Yhwh He is" directed "Mosheh Plucked out",□

40:30 וַיָּשֶׂם אֶת הַכִּיֹּר בֵּין אֹהֶל מוֹעֵד וּבֵין הַמִּזְבֵּחַ וַיִּתֵּן שָׁמָּה מַיִם לְרָחְצָה

wai'ya'sem et ha'ki'yor beyn o'hel mo'eyd u'veyn ha'miz'bey'ahh wai'yi'teyn sham'mah ma'yim le'rahh'tsah

and~*he~will~* PLACE AT the~CAULDRON BETWEEN TENT APPOINTED and~BETWEEN the~ALTAR and~ *he~will~* GIVE THERE~unto WATER~s2 to~>~BATHE□

and he placed the cauldron between {the} tent {of the} appointed {place} and the altar, and he (placed) {the} water to bathe unto there,□

40:31 וְרָחֲצוּ מִמֶּנּוּ מֹשֶׁה וְאַהֲרֹן וּבָנָיו אֶת יְדֵיהֶם וְאֶת רַגְלֵיהֶם

we'ra'hha'tsu mi'me'nu mo'sheh we'a'ha'ron u'va'naw et ye'dey'hem we'et rag'ley'hem

and~*they~did~* BATHE FROM~him "Mosheh PLUCKED-OUT" and~"Aharon LIGHT-BRINGER" and~SON~s2~him AT HAND~s2~them(m) and~AT FOOT~s2~them(m)□

and they will bathe from him*, "Mosheh Plucked out" and "Aharon Light bringer" and his sons, their hands and their feet,□

40:32 בְּבֹאָם אֶל אֹהֶל מוֹעֵד וּבְקָרְבָתָם אֶל הַמִּזְבֵּחַ יִרְחָצוּ כַּאֲשֶׁר צִוָּה יְהוָה אֶת מֹשֶׁה

be'vo'am el o'hel mo'eyd uv'qar'va'tam el ha'miz'bey'ahh yir'hha'tsu ka'a'sheyr tsi'wah YHWH et mo'sheh

in~>~COME~them(m) TO TENT APPOINTED and~in~ >~COME-NEAR~them(m) TO the~ALTAR *they(m)~ will~* BATHE like~WHICH *he~did~much* DIRECT "Yhwh *he~will~BE*" AT "Mosheh PLUCKED-OUT"□

in their com{ing} to {the} tent {of the} appointed {place}, and in their coming near to the altar, they will bathe, <just as> "Yhwh He is" directed "Mosheh Plucked out",□

40:33 וַיָּקֶם אֶת הֶחָצֵר סָבִיב לַמִּשְׁכָּן וְלַמִּזְבֵּחַ וַיִּתֵּן אֶת מָסַךְ שַׁעַר הֶחָצֵר וַיְכַל מֹשֶׁה אֶת הַמְּלָאכָה

wai' ya'qem et he'hha'tseyr sa'viv la'mish'kan we'la'miz'bey'ahh wai'yi'teyn et ma'sakh sha'ar he'hha'tseyr wai'khal mo'sheh et ham'la'khah

and~*he~will~make~* RISE AT the~YARD ALL AROUND to~the~DWELLING and~to~the~ALTAR and~*he~will~* GIVE AT CANOPY GATE the~YARD and~*he~will~ much* FINISH "Mosheh PLUCKED-OUT" AT the~ BUSINESS□

and he made the yard all around rise to the dwelling, and to the altar he (placed) the canopy {of the} gate {of the} yard, and "Mosheh Plucked out" finished the business,□

40:34 וַיְכַס הֶעָנָן אֶת אֹהֶל מוֹעֵד וּכְבוֹד יְהוָה מָלֵא אֶת הַמִּשְׁכָּן

wai'khas he'a'nan et o'hel mo'eyd ukh'vod YHWH ma'ley et ha'mish'kan

---

* Referring to the "cauldron," a masculine word in Hebrew.

Revised Mechanical Translation Codes

(..) Alt Trans/App A   <..> Comp Phrase/App B   [..] Verb Form/App C   \../ Plural Form/App D

:..: Int Inf Abs |..| Past Perf Verb   {...} Added Word

and~*he~will~much*~<u>COVER-OVER</u> the~CLOUD AT TENT APPOINTED and~ARMAMENT "Yhwh ^{he~will~BE}" *he~did*~<u>FILL</u> AT the~DWELLING□

and the cloud covered over {the} tent {of the} appointed {place}, and {the} armament {of} "Yhwh ^{He is}" filled the dwelling,□

40:35 וְלֹא יָכֹל מֹשֶׁה לָבוֹא אֶל אֹהֶל מוֹעֵד כִּי שָׁכַן עָלָיו הֶעָנָן וּכְבוֹד יְהוָה מָלֵא אֶת הַמִּשְׁכָּן

we'lo ya'khol mo'sheh la'vo el o'hel mo'eyd ki sha'khan a'law he'a'nan ukh'vod YHWH ma'ley et ha'mish'kan

and~NOT *he~did*~<u>BE-ABLE</u> "Mosheh ^{PLUCKED-OUT}" *to~*>~<u>COME</u> TO TENT APPOINTED GIVEN-THAT *he~did*~<u>DWELL</u> UPON~him the~CLOUD and~ARMAMENT "Yhwh ^{he~will~BE}" *he~did*~<u>FILL</u> AT the~DWELLING□

and "Mosheh ^{Plucked out}" was not able to come to {the} tent {of the} appointed {place}, given that the cloud dwelled upon him, and {the} armament {of} "Yhwh ^{He is}" |had| filled the dwelling,□

40:36 וּבְהֵעָלוֹת הֶעָנָן מֵעַל הַמִּשְׁכָּן יִסְעוּ בְּנֵי יִשְׂרָאֵל בְּכֹל מַסְעֵיהֶם

uv'hey'a'lot he'a'nan mey'al ha'mish'kan yis'u be'ney yis'ra'eyl be'khol mas'ey'hem

and~*in~*>~*be*~<u>GO-UP</u> the~CLOUD from~UPON the~DWELLING *they(m)~will*~<u>JOURNEY</u> SON~s "Yisra'el ^{he will~TURN-ASIDE~+~MIGHTY-ONE}" *in~*ALL BREAKING-CAMP~s~them(m)□

and in {the} go{ing} up {of} the cloud from upon the dwelling, {the} sons {of} "Yisra'el ^{He turns El aside}" will journey in all their breaking camps*,□

40:37 וְאִם לֹא יֵעָלֶה הֶעָנָן וְלֹא יִסְעוּ עַד יוֹם הֵעָלֹתוֹ

we'im lo yey'a'leh he'a'nan we'lo yis'u ad yom hey'a'lo'to

and~IF NOT *he~will*~*be*~<u>GO-UP</u> the~CLOUD and~NOT *they(m)~will*~<u>JOURNEY</u> UNTIL DAY >~*be*~<u>GO-UP</u>~him□

and if the cloud will not go up, (then) they will not journey until {the} day {of} his go{ing} up,□

40:38 כִּי עֲנַן יְהוָה עַל הַמִּשְׁכָּן יוֹמָם וְאֵשׁ תִּהְיֶה לַיְלָה בּוֹ לְעֵינֵי כָל בֵּית יִשְׂרָאֵל בְּכָל מַסְעֵיהֶם

ki a'nan YHWH al ha'mish'kan yo'mam we'eysh tih'yeh lai'lah bo le'ey'ney khol beyt yis'ra'eyl be'khol mas'ey'hem

GIVEN-THAT CLOUD "Yhwh ^{he~will~BE}" UPON the~DWELLING DAYTIME and~FIRE *she~will*~<u>EXIST</u> NIGHT *in~*him *to~*EYE~s2 ALL HOUSE "Yisra'el ^{he will~TURN-ASIDE~+~MIGHTY-ONE}" *in~*ALL BREAKING-CAMP~s~them(m)□

given that {the} cloud {of} "Yhwh ^{He is}" is upon the dwelling {in the} daytime, and fire will exist in him {in the} night to {the} eyes {of} all {the} house {of} "Yisra'el ^{He turns El aside}" in all their breaking camps†,□

---

* "In all their breaking camps" mean "whenever they break camp."
† "In all their breaking camps" mean "whenever they break camp."

Mechanical Translation Codes

<u>WORD</u> – Verb	WORD – Noun	Word – Name	word – Pre/Suff	*word* – Conj.

Dictionary

Nouns and Verbs

ABIDE: Anc Heb: 𐤀𐤅𐤄 Mod Heb: נוה / nu-ah; **Definition:** To dwell restfully and peacefully. [AHLB: 1305-J (V) / Strong's: 5115] **Concordance:** 15:2

ABODE: Anc Heb: 𐤀𐤅𐤄 Mod Heb: נוה / na-weh (mas); **Definition:** The dwelling place of man (home), god (mountain) or animal (pasture or stable). [AHLB: 1305-J (N) / Strong's: 5116] **Concordance:** 15:13

ABUNDANCE: Anc Heb: 𐤓𐤅𐤁 Mod Heb: רוב / rov (mas); **Definition:** An ample quantity of number (many) or plentiful supply of strength (great). [AHLB: 1439-J (N) / Strong's: 7230] **Concordance:** 15:7

ABUNDANT: Anc Heb: 𐤓𐤁 Mod Heb: רב / rav (mas); **Definition:** Great plenty or supply of numbers (many) or strength (great). One who is abundant in authority such as a master or teacher. Also, an archer as one abundant with arrows. [AHLB: 1439-A (N) / Strong's: 7227, 7228, 7229] **Concordance:** 1:9 2:23 5:5 9:28 12:38 19:21 23:2{2} 34:6

ACACIA: Anc Heb: 𐤔𐤈𐤄 Mod Heb: שטה / shit-tah (fem); **Definition:** A thorny tree commonly found in the Near East. In its plural form can mean wood or boards from the tree. [AHLB: 1469-A (N¹) / Strong's: 7848] **Concordance:** 25:5 25:10 25:13 25:23 25:28 26:15 26:26 26:32 26:37 27:1 27:6 27:7 30:1 30:5 35:7 35:24 36:20 36:31 36:36 37:1 37:4 37:10 37:15 37:25 37:28 38:1 38:6

ACQUIRED: Anc Heb: 𐤌𐤒𐤍𐤄 Mod Heb: מקנה / miq-nah (fem); **Definition:** What is accumulated in the sense of gathering to build a nest. What is obtained as one's own. Often used in the context of purchasing. [AHLB: 1428-H (h¹) / Strong's: 4736] **Concordance:** 12:44 17:3

ACQUIT: Anc Heb: 𐤍𐤒𐤄 Mod Heb: נקה / na-qah; **Definition:** To declare one innocent of a crime or oath. [AHLB: 1318-H (V) / Strong's: 5343, 5352] **Concordance:** 20:7 21:19 34:7{2}

ACT-TREACHEROUSLY: Anc Heb: 𐤁𐤂𐤃 Mod Heb: בגד / ba-gad; **Definition:** To perform an action covertly or with the intent to deceive. [AHLB: 2004 (V) / Strong's: 898] **Concordance:** 21:8

ADD: Anc Heb: 𐤉𐤎𐤐 Mod Heb: יסף / ya-saph; **Definition:** To augment something by increasing it in amount or supply. The hiphil (causative) form means "again." [AHLB: 1339-L (V) / Strong's: 3254, 3255] **Concordance:** 1:10 5:7 8:25 9:28 9:34 10:28 10:29 11:6 14:13

ADMINISTRATION: Anc Heb: 𐤊𐤄𐤅𐤍𐤄 Mod Heb: כהונה / ke-hu-nah (fem); **Definition:** The collective members from the tribe of Levi who administrate over the tent of meeting or the temple. [AHLB: 1244-G (d¹) / Strong's: 3550] **Concordance:** 29:9 40:15

ADMINISTRATOR: Anc Heb: 𐤊𐤄𐤅𐤍 Mod Heb: כוהן / ko-heyn (mas); **Definition:** One who manages the affairs and activities of an organization. The administrators (often translated as "priest") of Israel are Levites who manage the Tent of Meeting, and later the Temple, as well as teach the people the teachings and directions of YHWH, and perform other duties, such as the inspection of people and structures for disease. [AHLB: 1244-G (g) / Strong's: 3548, 3549] **Concordance:** 2:16 3:1 18:1 19:6 19:22 19:24 29:30 31:10 35:19 38:21 39:41

ADORATION: Anc Heb: 𐤕𐤄𐤋𐤄 Mod Heb: תהילה / te-hi-lah (fem); **Definition:** To praise or to be boastful. [AHLB: 1104-A (ie¹) / Strong's: 8416] **Concordance:** 15:11

ADORN: Anc Heb: שׁראל Mod Heb: כהן / ka-han; **Definition:** To put on special ornaments or garments for a special office or event. (see Isaiah 61:10). [AHLB: 1244-G (V) / Strong's: 3547] **Concordance:** 28:1 28:3 28:4 28:41 29:1 29:44 30:30 31:10 35:19 39:41 40:13 40:15

AFFLICT: Anc Heb: ‎%‎ Mod Heb: ענה / a-nah; **Definition:** To oppress severely so as to cause persistent suffering or anguish in the sense of making dark. [AHLB: 1359-H (V) / Strong's: 6031, 6033] **Concordance:** 1:11 1:12 10:3 20:16 22:21 22:22{2}

AFFLICTION: Anc Heb: ‎ר‎ Mod Heb: עני / a-ni (mas); **Definition:** The cause of persistent suffering, pain or distress. [AHLB: 1359-A (f) / Strong's: 6040, 6041] **Concordance:** 3:7 3:17 4:31 22:24

AFTER: Anc Heb: ‎ר‎ Mod Heb: אחרי / a-hhar-i (mas); Alt Sp: אחר **Definition:** A time to come beyond another event. [AHLB: 1181-C (N) / Strong's: 310, 311] **Concordance:** 3:1 3:20 5:1 7:25 10:14 11:1 11:5 11:8 14:4 14:8 14:9 14:10 14:17 14:19{2} 14:23 14:28 15:20 18:2 23:2{2} 23:13 28:43 29:29 33:8 34:15 34:16{2} 34:32

AGATE: Anc Heb: ‎שׁבו‎ Mod Heb: שבו / she-vo (fem); **Definition:** Probably the Agate, a variety of quartz that may be gray, light blue, orange, red or black in color. The Septuagint uses achates meaning Agate. [AHLB: 1462-A (q) / Strong's: 7618] **Concordance:** 28:19 39:12

AGONY: Anc Heb: ‎חיל‎ Mod Heb: חיל / hhil (mas); חילה / hhi-lah (fem); **Definition:** A state of being in emotional or physical turmoil or pain. [AHLB: 1173-M (N) / Strong's: 2427] **Concordance:** 15:14

ALL: Anc Heb: ‎כול‎ Mod Heb: כול / kol (mas); **Definition:** The whole of a group. [AHLB: 1242-J (N) / Strong's: 3605, 3606] **Concordance:** 1:5 1:6{2} 1:14{2} 1:22{3} 3:20 4:19 4:21 4:28{2} 4:29 4:30 5:12 6:29 7:2 7:19{2} 7:20 7:21 7:24 7:27 7:29 8:12 8:13{2} 8:20 9:4 9:6 9:9{2} 9:11 9:14{2} 9:16 9:19{2} 9:22{2} 9:24 9:25{4} 10:5 10:6{2} 10:12{2} 10:13{2} 10:14{2} 10:15{5} 10:19 10:22 10:23 11:5{2} 11:6 11:7 11:8{2} 11:10 12:3 12:6 12:12{2} 12:15 12:16{2} 12:19 12:20{2} 12:21 12:29{2} 12:30{2} 12:33 12:41 12:42 12:43 12:44 12:47 12:48{2} 12:50 13:2{2} 13:7 13:12{2} 13:13{2} 13:15{3} 14:4 14:7{2} 14:9 14:17 14:20 14:21 14:23 14:28 15:15 15:20 15:26{2} 16:1 16:2 16:3 16:6 16:9 16:10 16:22 16:23 17:1 18:1 18:8{2} 18:9 18:11 18:12 18:14{2} 18:21 18:22{3} 18:23 18:24 18:25 18:26{2} 19:5{2} 19:7 19:8{2} 19:11 19:12 19:16 19:18{2} 20:1 20:4 20:9 20:10 20:11 20:17 20:18 20:24 21:30 22:8{2} 22:9 22:18 22:21 23:13 23:17 23:22 23:27{2} 24:3{4} 24:4 24:7 24:8 25:2 25:9{2} 25:22 25:36 25:39 26:2 26:17 27:3 27:17 27:19{4} 28:3 28:38 29:12 29:13 29:18 29:24 29:35 29:37 30:13 30:14 30:27 30:28 30:29 31:3 31:5 31:6{2} 31:7 31:8 31:9 31:11 31:14 31:15 32:3 32:13 32:26 33:7 33:8 33:10{2} 33:16 33:19 34:3 34:10{4} 34:19{2} 34:20 34:23 34:30 34:31 34:32{2} 35:1 35:2 35:3 35:4 35:5 35:10{2} 35:13 35:16 35:20 35:21{3} 35:22{3} 35:23 35:24{3} 35:25 35:26 35:29{2} 35:31 35:33 35:35{2} 36:1{3} 36:2{2} 36:3 36:4{2} 36:7 36:8 36:9 36:22 37:22 37:24 38:3{2} 38:16 38:17 38:20 38:22 38:24{2} 38:26 38:30 38:31{2} 39:32{2} 39:33 39:36 39:37 39:39 39:40 39:42{2} 39:43 40:9{2} 40:10 40:16 40:36 40:38{2}

ALL-AROUND: Anc Heb: ‎סביב‎ Mod Heb: סביב / sa-viv (mas); סביבה / se-vi-vah (fem); **Definition:** On all sides; enclose so as to surround; in rotation or succession. A circling or bordering about the edge. [AHLB: 1324-B (b) / Strong's: 5439] **Concordance:** 7:24 16:13 19:12 25:11 25:24 25:25{2} 27:17 28:32 28:33{2} 28:34 29:16 29:20 30:3{2} 37:2 37:11 37:12{2} 37:26{2} 38:16 38:20 38:31{2} 39:23 39:25 39:26 40:8 40:33

ALLIED: Anc Heb: ‎קהת‎ Mod Heb: קהת / qe-hat (mas); **Definition:** To be a part of. [AHLB: 1439-G (V) / Strong's: n/a]

ALONGSIDE: Anc Heb: ‎עומת‎ Mod Heb: עומת / u-mat (fem); **Definition:** To stand with, or next to, someone or something. [AHLB: 1358-J (N^2) / Strong's: 5980] **Concordance:** 25:27 28:27 37:14 38:18 39:20

ALSO: Anc Heb: ᴍᴌ Mod Heb: גם / gam (mas); **Definition:** In addition to. The idea of a gathering of objects or ideas. [AHLB: 1059-A (N) / Strong's: 1571] **Concordance:** 1:10 2:19 3:9 4:9 4:10{3} 4:14 5:2 5:14{2} 6:4 6:5 7:11{2} 7:23 8:17 8:28 10:24 10:25 10:26 11:3 12:31{2} 12:32{3} 12:38 12:39 18:18{2} 18:23 19:9 19:22 21:29 21:35 33:12 33:17 34:3{2}

ALTAR: Anc Heb: ᴍᴎᴢᴙᴍ Mod Heb: מזבח / miz-bey-ahh (mas); **Definition:** The place of sacrifice. [AHLB: 2117 (h) / Strong's: 4196] **Concordance:** 17:15 20:24 20:25 20:26 21:14 24:4 24:6 27:1{2} 27:5{2} 27:6 27:7 28:43 29:12{2} 29:13 29:16 29:18 29:20 29:21 29:25 29:36 29:37{3} 29:38 29:44 30:1 30:18 30:20 30:27 30:28 31:8 31:9 32:5 34:13 34:15 35:15 35:16 37:25 38:1 38:3 38:4 38:7 38:30{2} 39:38 39:39 40:5 40:6 40:7 40:10{3} 40:26 40:29 40:30 40:32 40:33

AMETHYST: Anc Heb: ᴪᴍᴌᴍᴍ₯ Mod Heb: אחלמה / ahh-la-mah (fem); **Definition:** Probably the Amethyst, a violet form of quartz. The Septuagint uses Amethystos. [AHLB: 2164 (n^1) / Strong's: 306] **Concordance:** 28:19 39:12

ANSWER: Anc Heb: ᴪᴌᴓ Mod Heb: ענה / a-nah; **Definition:** Something written or spoken in reply to a question. [AHLB: 1520-H (V) / Strong's: 6030, 6032] **Concordance:** 4:1 15:21 19:8 19:19 23:2 24:3 32:18{3}

APPAREL: Anc Heb: ᴪᴜᴍᴎᴙ Mod Heb: שימלה / sim-lah (fem); **Definition:** Something that clothes or adorns. As forming to the image of the body. [AHLB: 2489 (e^1) / Strong's: 8071] **Concordance:** 3:22 12:34 12:35 19:10 19:14 22:26

APPEARANCE: Anc Heb: ᴪᴙᴍᴍ Mod Heb: מראה / mar-e (mas); **Definition:** What is seen or is in sight. [AHLB: 1438-H (a) / Strong's: 4758] **Concordance:** 3:3 24:17

APPOINT: Anc Heb: ᴙᴓᴜ Mod Heb: יעד / ya-ad; **Definition:** To arrange, fix or set in place, to determine a set place or time to meet. [AHLB: 1349-L (V) / Strong's: 3259] **Concordance:** 21:8 21:9 25:22 29:42 29:43 30:6 30:36

APPOINTED: Anc Heb: ᴙᴓᴝᴍ Mod Heb: מועד / mo-eyd (mas); **Definition:** Persons, places or things that are fixed or officially set. [AHLB: 1349-L (a) / Strong's: 4150, 4151] **Concordance:** 9:5 13:10 23:15 27:21 28:43 29:4 29:10 29:11 29:30 29:32 29:42 29:44 30:16 30:18 30:20 30:26 30:36 31:7 33:7{2} 34:18 35:21 38:8 38:30 39:32 39:40 40:2 40:6 40:7 40:12 40:22 40:24 40:26 40:29 40:30 40:32 40:34 40:35

APPOINTED-TIME: Anc Heb: ᴜᴓ Mod Heb: עת / eyt (fem); **Definition:** A fixed or officially set event, occasion or date. [AHLB: 1367-A (N) / Strong's: 6256] **Concordance:** 9:18 18:22 18:26

APPORTION: Anc Heb: ᴓᴜᴎ Mod Heb: חלק / hha-laq; **Definition:** To divide and mete out according to a plan among the appropriate recipients. [AHLB: 2167 (V) / Strong's: 2505] **Concordance:** 15:9

APPROACH: Anc Heb: ᴪᴝᴓ Mod Heb: אנה / a-nah; **Definition:** To come near or nearer to. [AHLB: 1014-H (V) / Strong's: 579] **Concordance:** 21:13

ARCH: Anc Heb: ᴌᴌ Mod Heb: גב / gav (com); Alt Sp: גו **Definition:** A curved object. The bowing of the back as when digging. Also any high arched or convex thing such as the eyebrow or the rim of a wheel. [AHLB: 1048-A (N) / Strong's: 1354, 1355, 1458, 1460, 1610] **Concordance:** 21:3{2} 21:4

AREA: Anc Heb: ᴍᴝᴓᴍ Mod Heb: מקום / ma-qom (mas); **Definition:** An indefinite region or expanse; a particular part of a surface or body. [AHLB: 1427-J (a) / Strong's: 4725] **Concordance:** 3:5 3:8 16:29 17:7 18:23 20:24 21:13 23:20 29:31 33:21

ARM: Anc Heb: ᴪᴙᴓᴢ Mod Heb: זרוע / ze-ro-a (fem); **Definition:** The human upper limb as representing power. [AHLB: 2139 (c) / Strong's: 2220] **Concordance:** 6:6 15:16

ARMAMENT: Anc Heb: ᴙᴝᴜᴎᴎ Mod Heb: כבוד / ka-vod (mas); **Definition:** The arms and equipment of a soldier or military unit. From a root meaning "heavy" and often paralleled with other weapons. [AHLB: 2246 (c) / Strong's: 3519] **Concordance:** 16:7 16:10 24:16 24:17 28:2 28:40 29:43 33:18 33:22 40:34 40:35

ARM-BAND: Anc Heb: Mod Heb: כומז / ku-maz (mas); **Definition:** An insignia or emblem showing loyalty or ownership. [AHLB: 2263 (o) / Strong's: 3558] **Concordance:** 35:22

ARM-FOR-BATTLE: Anc Heb: Mod Heb: חמש / hha-mash; **Definition:** To grab weapons in preparation for battle. [AHLB: 2176 (d) / Strong's: 2571] **Concordance:** 13:18

ARMY: Anc Heb: Mod Heb: צבא / tse-va (fem); **Definition:** A large organized group mustered together and armed for war or service. [AHLB: 1393-E (N) / Strong's: 6635] **Concordance:** 6:26 7:4 12:17 12:41 12:51

AROMA: Anc Heb: Mod Heb: ריח / ri-ahh (fem); **Definition:** A distinctive pervasive and usually pleasant or savory smell or odor. [AHLB: 1445-M (N) / Strong's: 7381, 7382] **Concordance:** 5:21 29:18 29:25 29:41

AROMATIC-SPICE: Anc Heb: Mod Heb: סם / sam (mas); **Definition:** A spice that is pleasing to the nose. [AHLB: 1473-A (N) / Strong's: 5561] **Concordance:** 25:6 30:7 30:34{2} 31:11 35:8 35:15 35:28 37:29 39:38 40:27

ARRANGE: Anc Heb: Mod Heb: ערך / a-rakh; **Definition:** To set something in order or into a correct or suitable configuration, sequence or adjustment. [AHLB: 2576 (V) / Strong's: 6186] **Concordance:** 27:21 40:4 40:23

ARRANGEMENT: Anc Heb: Mod Heb: ערך / ey-rekh (mas); **Definition:** Set in a row or in order according to rank or age. In parallel. Arranged items in juxtaposition. [AHLB: 2576 (N) / Strong's: 6187] **Concordance:** 40:4 40:23

ASSEMBLY: Anc Heb: Mod Heb: קהל / qa-hal (mas); **Definition:** A large group, as a gathering of the flock of sheep to the shepherd. [AHLB: 1426-G (N) / Strong's: 6951] **Concordance:** 12:6 16:3

ASSOCIATION: Anc Heb: Mod Heb: חברון / hhev-ron (mas); **Definition:** A relationship between two persons, places or objects that connects them together. [AHLB: n/a / Strong's: n/a] **Concordance:** *Used in names only.*

AT: Anc Heb: Mod Heb: את / et (mas); **Definition:** A function word to indicate presence or occurrence, a goal of an implied or indicated action, etc. Commonly used as a grammatical tool to identify the direct object of a verb. [AHLB: 1022-A (N) / Strong's: 853, 854, 3487] **Concordance:** 1:1 1:7 1:8 1:11{2} 1:12 1:13 1:14{2} 1:16{2} 1:17{2} 1:18 1:21 2:1 2:2 2:3 2:5{2} 2:6 2:7 2:8 2:9{2} 2:12 2:14 2:15{2} 2:16 2:17 2:19 2:20 2:21{2} 2:22 2:24{5} 2:25 3:1{2} 3:3 3:7{3} 3:9{2} 3:10 3:11 3:12{2} 3:16{3} 3:17 3:19 3:20{3} 3:21 3:22 4:15{3} 4:17{2} 4:19 4:20{3} 4:21{2} 4:23{2} 4:25 4:28{2} 4:29 4:30 4:31{2} 5:1 5:2{3} 5:4 5:5 5:6{2} 5:8 5:19 5:20{3} 5:21 5:23 6:4{4} 6:5{3} 6:6{3} 6:7{2} 6:8{4} 6:11 6:13 6:20{3} 6:23{5} 6:25 6:26 6:27 6:29 7:2{2} 7:3{3} 7:4{3} 7:5{2} 7:6 7:9 7:10 7:12 7:16 7:20 7:25 7:26 7:27 8:1{2} 8:2{2} 8:3 8:4 8:10 8:11 8:12{2} 8:13{2} 8:14 8:17{3} 8:18 8:22 8:24 8:25 8:28{2} 9:1 9:6 9:7 9:10{2} 9:12 9:13 9:14 9:15{3} 9:16 9:19{2} 9:20{3} 9:21{2} 9:22 9:23 9:25{3} 9:28 9:29{2} 9:33 9:35 10:1{2} 10:2{2} 10:4 10:5{4} 10:7{2} 10:8{3} 10:10{2} 10:11{4} 10:12{2} 10:13{2} 10:15{3} 10:17 10:19 10:20{2} 10:22 10:23 10:24 10:26{2} 10:27 11:1{2} 11:2{2} 11:3 11:10{3} 12:6 12:7 12:8 12:11{2} 12:13 12:14 12:17{3} 12:23{2} 12:24 12:25 12:27{2} 12:28 12:31 12:32 12:34 12:36{2} 12:38 12:39 12:44 12:47 12:48 12:50{2} 12:51 13:3{2} 13:5 13:7 13:10 13:17 13:18 13:19{5} 14:4 14:5 14:6{2} 14:8 14:9 14:10 14:12{2} 14:13{2} 14:16{2} 14:17 14:20 14:21{3} 14:24 14:25 14:26 14:27{2} 14:28{2} 14:30{2} 14:31{2} 15:1 15:19 15:20 15:22 16:3{2} 16:5 16:6 16:7{2} 16:8 16:9 16:12 16:13 16:21 16:23{3} 16:24 16:31 16:32{3} 16:33 16:35{2} 17:2 17:3{3} 17:5{2} 17:7 17:13{2} 17:14 18:1{2} 18:2 18:3 18:8{2} 18:10{2} 18:13 18:14 18:16{2} 18:19 18:20{5} 18:22{2} 18:23 18:25 18:26{2} 18:27 19:4{2} 19:5 19:7 19:8 19:9 19:12 19:14

19:17 19:23 20:1 20:7{3} 20:8 20:11{5} 20:12{2} 20:18{4} 20:20 20:23 20:24{5} 20:25 21:5{3} 21:6 21:7 21:18 21:20{2} 21:26{2} 21:28{3} 21:35{4} 22:4 22:5 22:22 22:23 22:24{2} 22:30 23:9 23:10{2} 23:15 23:16 23:22{2} 23:25{3} 23:26 23:27{3} 23:28{4} 23:30 23:31{2} 23:33{2} 24:3{2} 24:4 24:5 24:8 24:10 24:11 24:12 24:15 25:2{2} 25:3 25:9{3} 25:11 25:13 25:14{2} 25:16 25:18 25:19 25:21{2} 25:22{3} 25:24 25:26 25:27 25:28{3} 25:29 25:37{2} 25:39{2} 26:1{2} 26:6 26:7 26:9{3} 26:11{2} 26:15 26:18 26:29{3} 26:30 26:31 26:32 26:33{2} 26:34 26:35{2} 26:37 27:1 27:2 27:5 27:6 27:7{2} 27:8{2} 27:9 27:20 27:21{2} 28:1{3} 28:3 28:5{5} 28:6 28:9 28:10 28:11{2} 28:12{2} 28:14{2} 28:15 28:23 28:24 28:25 28:26 28:27 28:28 28:29 28:30{3} 28:31 28:37 28:38 28:41{7} 29:1 29:2 29:3{4} 29:4{3} 29:5{6} 29:6 29:7{2} 29:8 29:9 29:10{2} 29:11 29:12 29:13{5} 29:14{3} 29:15{2} 29:16{2} 29:17 29:18 29:19{2} 29:20{2} 29:21{2} 29:22{6} 29:24 29:25 29:26{2} 29:27{2} 29:28{2} 29:29 29:31{2} 29:32{2} 29:33{3} 29:34 29:35 29:36 29:37 29:39{2} 29:41 29:44{4} 29:46 30:1 30:3{4} 30:4 30:5{2} 30:6 30:7 30:8 30:12{3} 30:15 30:16{3} 30:18 30:19{2} 30:25 30:26{2} 30:27{5} 30:28{4} 30:29 30:30{3} 30:35 31:3 31:6{3} 31:7{4} 31:8{5} 31:9{4} 31:10{3} 31:11{2} 31:13 31:14 31:16{2} 31:17{2} 31:18 32:3 32:4 32:9 32:10 32:11 32:12 32:13 32:17 32:19{3} 32:20{2} 32:22 32:25 32:27{3} 32:34 32:35{2} 33:2 33:4 33:6 33:7 33:10 33:12{2} 33:13 33:17 33:18 33:19{2} 33:20 33:21 33:23{2} 34:1 34:4 34:10 34:11{2} 34:13{3} 34:16 34:18 34:23 34:24{3} 34:27{3} 34:28 34:29 34:30 34:32{2} 34:33 34:34{3} 34:35{3} 35:1{2} 35:5{2} 35:10 35:11{8} 35:12{4} 35:13{4} 35:14{4} 35:15{5} 35:16{6} 35:17{4} 35:18{3} 35:19{3} 35:21{2} 35:23 35:24{2} 35:25{4} 35:26{2} 35:27{2} 35:28{2} 35:29 35:31 35:35 36:1 36:2 36:3{2} 36:4 36:5 36:7 36:8{2} 36:10 36:13 36:14 36:16{2} 36:18 36:20 36:23 36:33 36:34{3} 36:35{2} 36:38{2} 37:1 37:4 37:5{2} 37:7 37:8 37:10 37:11 37:13 37:14 37:15{3} 37:16{5} 37:17{2} 37:23 37:24{2} 37:25 37:26{4} 37:27 37:28{2} 37:29{2} 38:1 38:2 38:3{6} 38:6{2} 38:7{3} 38:8{2} 38:9 38:22{2} 38:23 38:27{2} 38:28{2} 38:30{4} 38:31{4} 39:1{2} 39:2 39:3 39:5 39:6 39:7{2} 39:8 39:9 39:16 39:18 39:21{2} 39:22 39:25 39:26 39:27 39:28{3} 39:29{2} 39:30 39:31 39:32 39:33{3} 39:34{3} 39:35{3} 39:36{3} 39:37{4} 39:38{4} 39:39{6} 39:40{6} 39:41{3} 39:42{2} 39:43{3} 40:2 40:3{2} 40:4{4} 40:5{2} 40:6 40:7 40:8{2} 40:9{5} 40:10{3} 40:11{3} 40:12{3} 40:13{4} 40:14{2} 40:15{2} 40:16 40:18{5} 40:19{3} 40:20{3} 40:21{3} 40:22 40:23 40:24 40:25 40:26 40:27 40:28 40:29{4} 40:30 40:31{2} 40:32 40:33{3} 40:34{2} 40:35

ATONEMENT: Anc Heb: ℘צ﹥ﬦﬡ Mod Heb: כיפור / ki-pur (mas); **Definition:** An act of paying the price to release the debt or person. A covering over of transgression. [AHLB: 2283 (ed) / Strong's: 3725] **Concordance:** 29:36 30:10 30:16

ATTACH: Anc Heb: ﹍ﬗ﬘ﬧ Mod Heb: חשק / hha-shaq; **Definition:** To bring one's self into an association with another. To have an attachment to another. [AHLB: 2219 (V) / Strong's: 2836] **Concordance:** 27:17 38:17 38:28

ATTACK: Anc Heb: ﬗ﬘℘ Mod Heb: איב / a-yav; **Definition:** To be antagonistic or unfriendly to another. An action taken by an enemy. [AHLB: 1002-M (V) / Strong's: 340, 341] **Concordance:** 15:6 15:9 23:4 23:22{2} 23:27

AT-THAT-TIME: Anc Heb: ﬤℐ Mod Heb: אז / az (mas); **Definition:** A specified moment or time. [AHLB: 1007-A (N) / Strong's: 227] **Concordance:** 4:10 4:26 5:23 9:24 12:44 12:48 15:1 15:15

AT-THIS-POINT: Anc Heb: ﬡﬗℐﬡ Mod Heb: הלום / ha-lom (mas); **Definition:** To indicate a specific moment or place in time. [AHLB: 1104-K (p) / Strong's: 1988] **Concordance:** 3:5

AUNT: Anc Heb: ﬡℐﬤﬡ Mod Heb: דודה / do-dah (fem); **Definition:** The sister of one's father or mother. One who is loved. [AHLB: 1073-J (N[1]) / Strong's: 1733] **Concordance:** 6:20

AVENGE: Anc Heb: ﬗℐﬧ Mod Heb: נקם / na-qam; **Definition:** To take vengeance for or on behalf of another; to gain satisfaction for a wrong by punishing the wrongdoer; to pursue and kill one who has murdered. [AHLB: 2433 (V) / Strong's: 5358] **Concordance:** 21:20{2} 21:21

AWE: Anc Heb: ⵟⵎⵎⵐ Mod Heb: פַחַד / pa-hhad (mas) **Definition:** As shaking when in the presence of an awesome sight. [AHLB: 2598 (N) / Strong's: 6343, 6344] **Concordance:** 15:16

AWL: Anc Heb: ⵐⵎⵎⵐ Mod Heb: מַרְצֵעַ / mar-tsey-a (mas); **Definition:** A sharp pointed tool for piercing holes in leather or the skin. [AHLB: 2791 (N) / Strong's: 4836] **Concordance:** 21:6

BACK: Anc Heb: ⵐⵎⵐ Mod Heb: אָחוֹר / a-hhor (mas); **Definition:** The part of the body that is behind. To be in the rear of or behind something. [AHLB: 1181-C (c) / Strong's: 268] **Concordance:** 26:12 33:23

BAKE: Anc Heb: ⵐⵐ Mod Heb: אָפָה / a-phah; **Definition:** To cook using dry heat, especially in an oven. [AHLB: 1017-H (V) / Strong's: 644] **Concordance:** 12:39 16:23{2}

BALDING: Anc Heb: ⵎⵎⵐ Mod Heb: קֹרֵחַ / qo-rahh (mas); **Definition:** The top of the head void of any hair. [AHLB: n/a / Strong's: n/a] **Concordance:** *Used in names only.*

BARLEY: Anc Heb: ⵐⵎⵐ Mod Heb: שְׂעוֹרָה / se-o-rah (fem); **Definition:** A crop used as food, and for determining the month of Aviv. [AHLB: 2494 (c¹) / Strong's: 8184] **Concordance:** 9:31{2}

BASE: Anc Heb: ⵐⵐ Mod Heb: כֵּן / keyn (mas); **Definition:** The bottom or foundation which provides support. A person's home or family as being a base. A species of gnat. [AHLB: 1244-A (N) / Strong's: 3653] **Concordance:** 30:18 30:28 31:9 35:16 38:8 39:39 40:11

BASKET: Anc Heb: ⵐⵐ Mod Heb: סַל / sal (mas); **Definition:** A receptacle made of interwoven materials such as reeds. [AHLB: 1334-A (N) / Strong's: 5536] **Concordance:** 29:3{2} 29:23 29:32

BATHE: Anc Heb: ⵐⵎⵐ Mod Heb: רָחַץ / ra-hhats; **Definition:** To cleanse by being immersed in, or washing with, water. [AHLB: 2764 (V) / Strong's: 7364, 7365] **Concordance:** 2:5 29:4 29:17 30:18 30:19 30:20 30:21 40:12 40:30 40:31 40:32

BATTLE: Anc Heb: ⵐⵎⵎⵐ Mod Heb: מִלְחָמָה / mil-hha-mah (fem); **Definition:** A struggle between two armies. [AHLB: 2305 (h¹) / Strong's: 4421] **Concordance:** 1:10 13:17 15:3 17:16 32:17

BE: Anc Heb: ⵐⵐⵐ Mod Heb: הָוָה / ha-wah; **Definition:** To exist or have breath. That which exists has breath. In Hebrew thought the breath is the character of someone or something. Just as a man has character, so do objects. [AHLB: 1097-J (V) / Strong's: 1933, 1934]

BE-ABLE: Anc Heb: ⵐⵎⵐ Mod Heb: יָכֹל / ya-khal; **Definition:** To successfully prevail, overcome or endure. [AHLB: 1242-L (V) / Strong's: 3201, 3202] **Concordance:** 2:3 7:21 7:24 8:14 9:11 10:5 12:39 15:23 18:18 18:23 19:23 33:20 40:35

BE-ABUNDANT: Anc Heb: ⵎⵐⵐ Mod Heb: עָצַם / a-tsam; **Definition:** To be strong in might or numbers. From the abundant number of bones in the body. [AHLB: 2569 (V) / Strong's: 6105] **Concordance:** 1:7 1:20

BE-ALMOND-SHAPED: Anc Heb: ⵐⵎⵐ Mod Heb: שָׁקַד / sha-qad; **Definition:** An object that is in the form of an almond. [AHLB: 2872 (V) / Strong's: 8246] **Concordance:** 25:33{2} 25:34 37:19{2} 37:20

BE-AMAZED: Anc Heb: ⵐⵎⵐ Mod Heb: חָדָה / hha-dah; **Definition:** To be overwhelmed with surprise or sudden wonder; astonished greatly. [AHLB: 1165-H (V) / Strong's: 2302] **Concordance:** 18:9

BE-AN-IN-LAW: Anc Heb: ⵐⵎⵐ Mod Heb: חָתַן / hha-tan; **Definition:** To have a relationship with another through marriage. [AHLB: 2224 (V) / Strong's: 2859] **Concordance:** 3:1 4:18 18:1 18:2 18:5 18:6 18:7 18:8 18:12{2} 18:14 18:15 18:17 18:24 18:27

BEARD: Anc Heb: ⌐⌐⌐ Mod Heb: זקן / za-qeyn (mas); **Definition:** The hair that grows on a man's face. A long beard as a sign of old age and wisdom. An elder as a bearded one. [AHLB: 2132 (N) / Strong's: 2205, 2206] **Concordance:** 3:16 3:18 4:29 10:9 12:21 17:5 17:6 18:12 19:7 24:1 24:9 24:14

BE-ASHAMED: Anc Heb: ⌐⌐⌐ Mod Heb: בוש / bush; **Definition:** Feeling shame, guilt or disgrace; to be dried up with shame. [AHLB: 1044-J (V) / Strong's: 954] **Concordance:** 32:1

BEAST: Anc Heb: ⌐⌐⌐ Mod Heb: בהמה / be-hey-mah (fem); **Definition:** An animal as distinguished from man or a plant. A tall or large creature. [AHLB: 1036-G (N^1) / Strong's: 929, 930] **Concordance:** 8:13 8:14 9:9 9:10 9:19 9:22 9:25 11:5 11:7 12:12 12:29 13:2 13:12 13:15 19:13 20:10 22:9 22:18

BEATEN-WORK: Anc Heb: ⌐⌐⌐ Mod Heb: מקשה / miq-shah (fem); **Definition:** To be shaped into a specific form by an outside force such as a hammer. [AHLB: 1435-H (h^1) / Strong's: 4749] **Concordance:** 25:18 25:31 25:36 37:7 37:17 37:22

BEAT-IN-PIECES: Anc Heb: ⌐⌐⌐ Mod Heb: דקק / da-qaq; **Definition:** To crush or beat something into thin or small pieces. [AHLB: 1080-B (V) / Strong's: 1854, 1855] **Concordance:** 30:36 32:20

BEAUTY: Anc Heb: ⌐⌐⌐ Mod Heb: חן / hheyn (mas); **Definition:** The qualities in a person or thing that give pleasure to the senses. Someone or something that is desired, approved, favored or in agreement by another. [AHLB: 1175-A (N) / Strong's: 2580] **Concordance:** 3:21 11:3 12:36 33:12 33:13{2} 33:16 33:17 34:9

BE-A-WHORE: Anc Heb: ⌐⌐⌐ Mod Heb: זנה / za-nah **Definition:** A woman who practices promiscuous sexual behavior, especially for hire. [AHLB: 1152-H (V) / Strong's: 2181] **Concordance:** 34:15 34:16{2}

BE-BITTER: Anc Heb: ⌐⌐⌐ Mod Heb: מרר / ma-rar; **Definition:** Having a harsh, disagreeably acrid taste. One of the four basic taste sensations. [AHLB: 1296-B (V) / Strong's: 4843] **Concordance:** 1:14 23:21

BE-BOLD: Anc Heb: ⌐⌐⌐ Mod Heb: עוז / uz; **Definition:** To be fearless and daring; courageous. [AHLB: 1352-J (V) / Strong's: 5756] **Concordance:** 9:19

BE-CHILDLESS: Anc Heb: ⌐⌐⌐ Mod Heb: שכל / sha-khal; **Definition:** To be without children through miscarriage, barrenness or loss of children. [AHLB: 2836 (V) / Strong's: 7921] **Concordance:** 23:26

BE-CORRECT: Anc Heb: ⌐⌐⌐ Mod Heb: צדק / tsa-daq; **Definition:** To walk on the right path without losing the way. [AHLB: 2658 (V) / Strong's: 6663] **Concordance:** 23:7

BED: Anc Heb: ⌐⌐⌐ Mod Heb: מטה / mit-tah (fem); **Definition:** A place for sleeping. Spread out sheet for sleeping. [AHLB: 1308-A (h^1) / Strong's: 4296] **Concordance:** 7:28

BE-DISTINCT: Anc Heb: ⌐⌐⌐ Mod Heb: פלה / pa-lah; **Definition:** To be clearly distinguished. To have a marked difference. To be prominent; separated out completely. [AHLB: 1380-H (V) / Strong's: 6395] **Concordance:** 8:18 9:4 11:7 33:16

BE-DOUBLE: Anc Heb: ⌐⌐⌐ Mod Heb: תאם / ta-am; **Definition:** To have two identical pieces placed together. Also to bear twins as doubles. [AHLB: 1496-D (V) / Strong's: 8382] **Concordance:** 26:24 36:29

BE-DYSFUNCTIONAL: Anc Heb: ⌐⌐⌐ Mod Heb: רעע / ra-a; **Definition:** Impaired or abnormal filling of purpose; to act wrongly by injuring or doing an evil action. [AHLB: 1460-B (V) / Strong's: 4827, 7489] **Concordance:** 5:22 5:23

BE-EMINENT: Anc Heb: ⌐⌐⌐ Mod Heb: אדר / a-dar; **Definition:** To be large in size or stature. [AHLB: 1089-C (V) / Strong's: 142] **Concordance:** 15:6 15:11

BE-FACE-TO-FACE: Anc Heb: ⌐⌐ᒪ Mod Heb: נגד / na-gad; **Definition:** To face another. The hiphil (causative) form means "tell" in the sense of speaking face to face. [AHLB: 2372 (V) / Strong's: 5046, 5047] **Concordance:** 4:28 13:8 14:5 16:22 19:3 19:9

BE-FAR: Anc Heb: ⌐ Mod Heb: רחק / ra-hhaq; **Definition:** To be distant, a long way off. [AHLB: 2765 (V) / Strong's: 7368] **Concordance:** 8:24{2} 23:7 33:7

BEFORE: Anc Heb: ⌐ Mod Heb: טרם / te-rem (mas); **Definition:** What precedes another event. [AHLB: 2244 (N) / Strong's: 2962] **Concordance:** 1:19 9:30 10:7 12:34

BE-HARD: Anc Heb: ⌐ Mod Heb: קשה / qa-shah; **Definition:** To be difficult; not easily penetrated; not easily yielding to pressure. [AHLB: 1435-H (V) / Strong's: 7185] **Concordance:** 7:3 13:15

BEHEAD: Anc Heb: ⌐ Mod Heb: ערף / a-raph; **Definition:** To sever the neck from the body. Also, to break the neck. [AHLB: 2580 (V) / Strong's: 6202] **Concordance:** 13:13 34:20

BE-HEAVY: Anc Heb: ⌐ Mod Heb: כבד / ka-vad; **Definition:** To be great in weight, wealth or importance. The piel (intensive) form means "honor." [AHLB: 2246 (V) / Strong's: 3513] **Concordance:** 5:9 8:11 8:28 9:7 9:34 10:1 14:4 14:17 14:18 20:12

BEING: Anc Heb: ⌐ Mod Heb: נפש / ne-phesh (fem); **Definition:** The whole of a person, god or creature including the body, mind, emotion, character and inner parts. [AHLB: 2424 (N) / Strong's: 5315] **Concordance:** 1:5{2} 4:19 12:4 12:15 12:16 12:19 15:9 16:16 21:23{2} 21:30 23:9 30:12 30:15 30:16 31:14

BE-LESS: Anc Heb: ⌐ Mod Heb: מעט / ma-at; **Definition:** To be fewer or diminished in size or amount. [AHLB: 2347 (V) / Strong's: 4591] **Concordance:** 12:4 16:17 16:18 30:15

BELITTLE: Anc Heb: ⌐ Mod Heb: קלל / qa-lal; **Definition:** To regard or portray as less impressive or important; to be light in weight; to curse or despise in the sense of making light. [AHLB: 1426-B (V) / Strong's: 7043] **Concordance:** 18:22 21:17 22:27

BELL: Anc Heb: ⌐ Mod Heb: פעמן / pa-a-mon (mas); **Definition:** An instrument used to call to attention or to a warning. From its rhythmic ringing. [AHLB: 2623 (m) / Strong's: 6472] **Concordance:** 28:33 28:34{2} 39:25{2} 39:26{2}

BELONGING: Anc Heb: ⌐ Mod Heb: פוט / put (mas); **Definition:** To acquire ownership or authority over, something or someone owned by another. [AHLB: n/a / Strong's: n/a] **Concordance:** Used in names only.

BEND-DOWN: Anc Heb: ⌐ Mod Heb: שחה / sha-hhah; **Definition:** To pay homage to another one by bowing low or getting on the knees with the face to the ground. [AHLB: 1468-H (V) / Strong's: 7812] **Concordance:** 4:31 11:8 12:27 18:7 20:5 23:24 24:1 32:8 33:10 34:8 34:14

BENEATH: Anc Heb: ⌐ Mod Heb: מטה / mat-tah (mas); **Definition:** Below; in a lower place, position or state. As under a stretched out sheet. [AHLB: 1308-H (a) / Strong's: 4295] **Concordance:** 26:24 27:5 28:27 36:29 38:4 39:20

BE-OVERSHADOWED: Anc Heb: ⌐ Mod Heb: צלל / tsa-lal; **Definition:** To be sunk down into a dark depth. [AHLB: 1403-B (V) / Strong's: 6749, 6751] **Concordance:** 15:10

BEQA: Anc Heb: ⌐ Mod Heb: בקע / be-qa (mas); **Definition:** A dry weight measure equal to one-half shekel weight. [AHLB: 2034 (N) / Strong's: 1235] **Concordance:** 38:26

BE-RED: Anc Heb: ⌐ Mod Heb: אדם / a-dam; **Definition:** To be ruddy. To have a dark reddish color. [AHLB: 1082-C (V) / Strong's: 119] **Concordance:** 25:5 26:14 35:7 35:23 36:19 39:34

BE-SATISFIED: Anc Heb: ⟨anc⟩ Mod Heb: שבע / sa-va; **Definition:** To be filled full or to overflowing; to have a complete amount. [AHLB: 2461 (V) / Strong's: 7646] **Concordance:** 16:8 16:12

BE-SILENT: Anc Heb: ⟨anc⟩ Mod Heb: דמם / da-mam (mas); **Definition:** To come to a standstill in speech or deed. To be quiet; refrain from speech or action. [AHLB: 1082-B (N) / Strong's: 1826] **Concordance:** 15:16

BE-SKILLED: Anc Heb: ⟨anc⟩ Mod Heb: חכם / hha-kham; **Definition:** To be able to decide or discern between good and bad, right and wrong; to act correctly in thought and action. [AHLB: 2159 (V) / Strong's: 2449] **Concordance:** 1:10

BE-SOUR: Anc Heb: ⟨anc⟩ Mod Heb: חמץ / hha-mats; **Definition:** To be fermented by adding leaven to bread. Also, sour in taste, thought or action. [AHLB: 2173 (V) / Strong's: 2556] **Concordance:** 12:19 12:20 12:34 12:39

BE-SQUARE: Anc Heb: ⟨anc⟩ Mod Heb: רבע / ra-va; **Definition:** Any four sided object. Also, to go down on the hands and knees, to be on all fours. [AHLB: 2744 (V) / Strong's: 7250, 7251] **Concordance:** 27:1 28:16 30:2 37:25 38:1 39:9

BEST: Anc Heb: ⟨anc⟩ Mod Heb: מיטב / may-tav (mas); **Definition:** Excelling all others; most, largest; most productive or good, utility or satisfaction. [AHLB: 1186-L (k) / Strong's: 4315] **Concordance:** 22:4{2}

BE-STRANGE: Anc Heb: ⟨anc⟩ Mod Heb: זור / zur; **Definition:** To be separated out from others; to be scattered abroad. [AHLB: 1158-J (V) / Strong's: 2114] **Concordance:** 29:33 30:9 30:33

BETROTH: Anc Heb: ⟨anc⟩ Mod Heb: ארש / a-ras; **Definition:** A promise or contract of impending marriage. To request a woman for marriage. [AHLB: 1458-C (V) / Strong's: 781] **Concordance:** 22:15

BETWEEN: Anc Heb: ⟨anc⟩ Mod Heb: בין / beyn (mas); **Definition:** In the time, space or interval that separates. [AHLB: 1037-M (N) / Strong's: 996, 997, 1143] **Concordance:** 8:19{2} 9:4{2} 11:7{2} 12:6 13:9 13:16 14:2{2} 14:20{2} 16:1{2} 16:12 18:16{2} 22:10 25:22 26:33{2} 29:39 29:41 30:8 30:18{2} 31:13{2} 31:17{2} 40:7{2} 40:30{2}

BE-WARM: Anc Heb: ⟨anc⟩ Mod Heb: חמם / hha-mam; **Definition:** To glow; project extreme heat. To be heated, either internally or externally, such as from the sun or a fire. [AHLB: 1174-B (V) / Strong's: 2552] **Concordance:** 16:21

BINDER: Anc Heb: ⟨anc⟩ Mod Heb: חשוק / hha-shuq (mas); **Definition:** Attached around something. [AHLB: 2219 (d) / Strong's: 2838] **Concordance:** 27:10 27:11 36:38 38:10 38:11 38:12 38:17 38:19

BIRD: Anc Heb: ⟨anc⟩ Mod Heb: ציפור / tsi-por (fem); **Definition:** A creature distinguished by a body covering of feathers and wings as forelimbs. [AHLB: 2685 (c) / Strong's: 6833]

BIRTH: Anc Heb: ⟨anc⟩ Mod Heb: שגר / she-ger (fem); **Definition:** What is brought forth from the womb. [AHLB: 2816 (N) / Strong's: 7698] **Concordance:** 13:12

BIRTHED: Anc Heb: ⟨anc⟩ Mod Heb: ילוד / yi-lud (mas); **Definition:** What is given birth to; a baby human or animal that is brought from the womb into the open world. [AHLB: 1257-L (c) / Strong's: 3209] **Concordance:** 1:22

BIRTHING: Anc Heb: ⟨anc⟩ Mod Heb: תולדה / tol-dah (fem); **Definition:** The act or process of bringing forth offspring from the womb. Total of the children born within an era. [AHLB: 1257-L (i^3) / Strong's: 8435] **Concordance:** 6:16 6:19 28:10

BITTER: Anc Heb: ⟨anc⟩ Mod Heb: מר / mar (mas); **Definition:** A difficult taste or experience. [AHLB: 1296-A (N) / Strong's: 4751, 4752] **Concordance:** 15:23

BITTER-HERBS: Anc Heb: ᕙᕙᘉᗩᕙᗪᗺᗺ Mod Heb: ממרור / mam-ror (mas); **Definition:** Edible plants, that when eaten brings tears to the eyes. [AHLB: 1296-B (ac) / Strong's: 4472] **Concordance:** 12:8

BITTERNESS: Anc Heb: ᕙᗪᗺᗺ Mod Heb: מרר / ma-rar (mas); **Definition:** Having a harsh, disagreeably acrid taste. [AHLB: n/a / Strong's: n/a] **Concordance:** *Used in names only.*

BLAZING: Anc Heb: ⊗ᕙᑡᐸ Mod Heb: להט / la-hat (mas); **Definition:** To burn, flash or shine brightly. Also used for the magic of magicians. [AHLB: 1262-G (N) / Strong's: 3858] **Concordance:** 7:11

BLIND: Anc Heb: ᕙᕙᐸ Mod Heb: עור / i-weyr (mas); **Definition:** A darkness of the eye. [AHLB: 1526-J (N) / Strong's: 5787] **Concordance:** 4:11

BLIND: Anc Heb: ᕙᕙᐸ Mod Heb: עור / a-war; **Definition:** To become dark of site through blindness or the putting out of the eyes. [AHLB: 1526-J (V) / Strong's: 5786] **Concordance:** 23:8

BLISTER: Anc Heb: ᑡ⊙ᕙ⊙⊙ᑡ/ Mod Heb: אבעבועה / a-va-bu-ah (fem); **Definition:** A swelling irritation that festers on the skin. An inflammatory pustule as an eruption. [AHLB: 1039-C (Id^1) / Strong's: 76] **Concordance:** 9:9 9:10

BLOOD: Anc Heb: ᗺᐸᑣ Mod Heb: דם / dam (mas); **Definition:** The red fluid that circulates through body. [AHLB: 1082-A (N) / Strong's: 1818] **Concordance:** 4:9 4:25 4:26 7:17 7:19{2} 7:20 7:21 12:7 12:13{2} 12:22{2} 12:23 22:1 22:2 23:18 24:6{2} 24:8{2} 29:12{2} 29:16 29:20{2} 29:21 30:10 34:25

BLOSSOM: Anc Heb: ᘉᕙ⊙ᗺ Mod Heb: ציץ / tsits (mas); **Definition:** To sprout a flower on a tree or plant that will produce edible fruit. [AHLB: 1409-M (N) / Strong's: 6731] **Concordance:** 28:36 39:30

BLOW: Anc Heb: ⊙ᒐᒐᕙ Mod Heb: נשף / na-shaph; **Definition:** To expel air from the mouth. [AHLB: 2444 (V) / Strong's: 5398] **Concordance:** 15:10

BLUE: Anc Heb: ᕙ/ᒐᒐᕙ Mod Heb: תכלת / te-khey-let (fem); **Definition:** A color that is created with the use of a dye. [AHLB: 1242-A (i^2) / Strong's: 8504] **Concordance:** 25:4 26:1 26:4 26:31 26:36 27:16 28:5 28:6 28:8 28:15 28:28 28:31 28:33 28:37 35:6 35:23 35:25 35:35 36:8 36:11 36:35 36:37 38:18 38:23 39:1 39:2 39:3 39:5 39:8 39:21 39:22 39:24 39:29 39:31

BOARD: Anc Heb: ᒐᒐᗺᕙ Mod Heb: קרש / qe-resh (mas); **Definition:** A plank of wood often used to wall off an area or restrict access. [AHLB: 2736 (N) / Strong's: 7175] **Concordance:** 26:15 26:16{2} 26:17{2} 26:18{2} 26:19{3} 26:20 26:21{2} 26:22 26:23 26:25{3} 26:26 26:27{2} 26:28 26:29 35:11 36:20 36:21{2} 36:22{2} 36:23{2} 36:24{3} 36:25 36:26{2} 36:27 36:28 36:30{2} 36:31 36:32{2} 36:33 36:34 39:33 40:18

BOIL: Anc Heb: ᕙᒐᒐᗺ Mod Heb: בשל / ba-shal; **Definition:** To generate bubbles of vapor when heated; to cook a meat in water. The hiphil (causative) form means "ripen." [AHLB: 2043 (V) / Strong's: 1310] **Concordance:** 12:9 16:23{2} 23:19 29:31 34:26

BOILED: Anc Heb: ᕙᒐᒐᗺ Mod Heb: בשל / ba-sheyl (mas); **Definition:** Meat or other edible that is cooked in water over a fire. [AHLB: 2043 (N) / Strong's: 1311] **Concordance:** 12:9

BOILS: Anc Heb: ᑡᒐᒐᗺᕙ Mod Heb: שחין / she-hhin (mas); **Definition:** A festering under the skin. Pits in the skin from disease. [AHLB: 1468-A (s) / Strong's: 7822] **Concordance:** 9:9 9:10 9:11{2}

BOLDNESS: Anc Heb: ᘉᕙᐸ Mod Heb: עז / oz (mas); **Definition:** Knowing one's position or authority and standing in it. Strengthened and protected from danger. [AHLB: 1352-J (N) / Strong's: 5797] **Concordance:** 15:2 15:13

BONDWOMAN: Anc Heb: ✡ᕬᕩ Mod Heb: אמה / a-mah (fem); **Definition:** A female slave. One who is bound to another. [AHLB: 1013-A (N¹) / Strong's: 519] **Concordance:** 2:5 20:10 20:17 21:7 21:20 21:26 21:27 21:32 23:12

BONE: Anc Heb: ᕬᕬᕩᕬᕩ Mod Heb: עצם / e-tsem (mas); **Definition:** The hard tissue of which the skeleton is chiefly composed. As a numerous amount. [AHLB: 2569 (N) / Strong's: 6106] **Concordance:** 12:17 12:41 12:46 12:51 13:19{2} 24:10

BONNET: Anc Heb: ᕩᕩᕬᕩ Mod Heb: פאר / pe-eyr (mas); **Definition:** A piece of cloth that is wound around the head as a decoration. [AHLB: 1388-D (N) / Strong's: 6287] **Concordance:** 39:28

BOOTH: Anc Heb: ✡ᕬᕩᕬᕩ Mod Heb: סוכה / su-kah (fem); **Definition:** A temporary shelter; a small enclosure; dwelling place. [AHLB: 1333-J (N¹) / Strong's: 5521]

BORDER: Anc Heb: ᕩᕬᕩᕬᕩ Mod Heb: גבול / ge-vul (mas); **Definition:** The outer edge of a region. Also the area within the borders. [AHLB: 2049 (d) / Strong's: 1366] **Concordance:** 7:27 10:4 10:14 10:19 13:7 23:31 34:24

BORE-THROUGH: Anc Heb: ᕬᕩᕬᕩ Mod Heb: רצע / ra-tsa; **Definition:** To pierce with a sharp object. [AHLB: 2791 (V) / Strong's: 7527] **Concordance:** 21:6

BOSOM: Anc Heb: ᕩᕬᕩᕬᕩ Mod Heb: חיק / hheyq (mas); Alt Sp: חק, חוק **Definition:** The human chest, especially the front side. [AHLB: 1163-M (N) / Strong's: 2436] **Concordance:** 4:6{2} 4:7{3}

BOTTOM: Anc Heb: ᕩᕬᕩᕬᕩ Mod Heb: רפיד / re-phid (mas); **Definition:** The lowest or deepest part of anything. [AHLB: 2785 (b¹) / Strong's: n/a]

BOULDER: Anc Heb: ᕬᕩᕬᕩ Mod Heb: צור / tsur (mas); **Definition:** A large rock used as a weapon or a rock cliff used as a place of defense. Also flint, a very hard rock that when fractured forms a razor sharp edge and used for knives, spears or arrowheads. [AHLB: 1411-J (N) / Strong's: 6697] **Concordance:** 17:6{2} 33:21 33:22

BOUND: Anc Heb: ᕩᕬᕩ Mod Heb: גבל / na-val; **Definition:** To be defined by a border. [AHLB: 2049 (V) / Strong's: 1379] **Concordance:** 19:12 19:23

BOUNDARY: Anc Heb: ✡ᕩᕬᕩᕬᕩ Mod Heb: מגבלה / mig-be-let (fem); **Definition:** Marks the outer edge, the end, of a definite area or region. Idiomatically used for an entire region. [AHLB: 2049 (h¹) / Strong's: 4020] **Concordance:** 28:14

BOWELS: Anc Heb: ᕬᕬᕩ Mod Heb: רחם / re-hhem (mas); **Definition:** The large intestines as encompassed about by the torso. Compassion as coming from the bowels. [AHLB: 2762 (N) / Strong's: 7356, 7358, 7359] **Concordance:** 13:2 13:12 13:15 34:19

BOWL: Anc Heb: ᕬᕩᕬᕩ Mod Heb: גביע / ga-vi-a (mas); **Definition:** A concave vessel especially for holding liquids. As with high sides. [AHLB: 2051 (b) / Strong's: 1375] **Concordance:** 25:31 25:33{2} 25:34 37:17 37:19{2} 37:20

BOW-THE-HEAD: Anc Heb: ᕩᕬᕩᕬᕩ Mod Heb: קדד / qa-dad; **Definition:** To lower the head as a sign of respect. [AHLB: 1418-B (V) / Strong's: 6915] **Concordance:** 4:31 12:27 34:8

BOX: Anc Heb: ᕩᕬᕩᕩ Mod Heb: ארון / a-ron (mas); **Definition:** A rigid rectangular receptacle often with a cover. Any box-shaped object. [AHLB: 1020-H (j) / Strong's: 727] **Concordance:** 25:10 25:14{2} 25:15 25:16 25:21{2} 25:22 26:33 26:34 30:6 30:26 31:7 35:12 37:1 37:5{2} 39:35 40:3{2} 40:5 40:20{3} 40:21{2}

BOY: Anc Heb: ᕩᕬᕩᕬ Mod Heb: ילד / ye-led (mas); **Definition:** A male child from birth to puberty. [AHLB: 1257-L (N) / Strong's: 3206] **Concordance:** 1:17 1:18 2:3 2:6{2} 2:7 2:8 2:9{2} 2:10 21:4 21:22

BRAID: Anc Heb: ᘯ⌐⍝ Mod Heb: ארג / a-rag; **Definition:** To twist, entwine or weave several pieces together in parallel to become one. [AHLB: 1440-C (V) / Strong's: 707] **Concordance:** 28:32 35:35 39:22 39:27

BRAIDED-WORK: Anc Heb: ⌐ᘯ≼ Mod Heb: שרד / se-red (mas); **Definition:** Finely made articles of clothing made by weaving together fibers. [AHLB: 2506 (N) / Strong's: 8278, 8279] **Concordance:** 31:10 35:19 39:1 39:41

BRAMBLE: Anc Heb: ⍝Y⊶ Mod Heb: קוץ / qots (mas); **Definition:** A rough, prickly vine or shrub. Thorn. [AHLB: 1432-J (N) / Strong's: 6975] **Concordance:** 22:5

BRANCH: Anc Heb: ⍦⊗⋀ Mod Heb: מטה / ma-teh (mas); **Definition:** A branch used as a staff. Also, a tribe as a branch of the family. [AHLB: 1285-H (N) / Strong's: 4294] **Concordance:** 4:2 4:4 4:17 4:20 7:9 7:10 7:12{3} 7:15 7:17 7:19 7:20 8:1 8:12 8:13 9:23 10:13 14:16 17:5 17:9 21:20 31:2 31:6 35:30 35:34 38:22 38:23

BRAVERY: Anc Heb: ⍦ᘯY⊔⌐ Mod Heb: גבורה / ge-vo-rah (fem); **Definition:** An act of defending one's property, convictions or beliefs. Control through physical strength. [AHLB: 2052 (d[1]) / Strong's: 1369, 1370] **Concordance:** 32:18

BREAD: Anc Heb: ⋀⍟⍝⌐ Mod Heb: לחם / le-hhem (mas); **Definition:** Baked and leavened food primarily made of flour or meal. [AHLB: 2305 (N) / Strong's: 3899, 3900, 3901] **Concordance:** 2:20 16:3 16:4 16:8 16:12 16:15 16:22 16:29 16:32 18:12 23:25 25:30 29:2 29:23{2} 29:32 29:34 34:28 35:13 39:36 40:23

BREAD-CAKE: Anc Heb: ⍦⍝Y⍟ Mod Heb: עוגה / u-gah (fem); **Definition:** Cakes baked on hot stones. [AHLB: 1348-A (N[1]) / Strong's: 5692] **Concordance:** 12:39

BREAK-DOWN: Anc Heb: ⍝⌐⍦ Mod Heb: נתץ / na-tats; **Definition:** To demolish an elevated object; to tear down. [AHLB: 2454 (V) / Strong's: 5422] **Concordance:** 34:13

BREAKING-CAMP: Anc Heb: ⍟≼⍝⋀ Mod Heb: מסע / mas-sah (mas); **Definition:** The packing up of camp for the purpose of beginning a journey. [AHLB: 2413 (a) / Strong's: 4550, 4551] **Concordance:** 17:1 40:36 40:38

BREAK-OUT: Anc Heb: ⍝ᘯ⊂ Mod Heb: פרץ / pa-rats; **Definition:** To be spread out wide or widespread. [AHLB: 2642 (V) / Strong's: 6555] **Concordance:** 1:12 19:22 19:24

BREAST: Anc Heb: ⌐⍳⍝ Mod Heb: שד / shad (mas); **Definition:** Milk-producing glandular organs situated on the front part of the chest in the female; the fore part of the body between the neck and the abdomen. Also a goat-idol from the teats of the goat. [AHLB: 1464-A (N) / Strong's: 7699, 7700]

BREASTPLATE: Anc Heb: ⍳⍲Y⍟⍟ Mod Heb: חושן / hho-shen (mas); **Definition:** An ornamental plate worn by the High Priest that held stones representing the twelve tribes of Israel and the Urim and Thummim. [AHLB: 1182-J (m) / Strong's: 2833] **Concordance:** 25:7 28:4 28:15 28:22 28:23{2} 28:24 28:26 28:28{2} 28:29 28:30 29:5 35:9 35:27 39:8 39:9 39:15 39:16 39:17 39:19 39:21{2}

BREATHE-DEEPLY: Anc Heb: ⍲⊶⍦ Mod Heb: נפש / na-phash; **Definition:** To relax and breath in deeply to refresh oneself. To take a breather. [AHLB: 2424 (V) / Strong's: 5314] **Concordance:** 23:12 31:17

BRIBE: Anc Heb: ⌐⍟⍳⍲ Mod Heb: שחד / sha-hhad (mas); **Definition:** To buy a favor or service that would be otherwise out of reach. [AHLB: 2822 (N) / Strong's: 7810] **Concordance:** 23:8{2}

BRICK: Anc Heb: ⍦⍳⍟⌐ Mod Heb: לבנה / le-vey-nah (fem); **Definition:** A building material typically rectangular and of moist clay hardened by heat. [AHLB: 2303 (N[1]) / Strong's: 3840, 3843] **Concordance:** 1:14 5:7 5:8 5:16 5:18 5:19 24:10

BRIDE-PRICE: Anc Heb: ⲟⲙⲩ̄ⲙ Mod Heb: מוהר / mo-har (mas); **Definition:** A payment given by or in behalf of a prospective husband to the bride's family. [AHLB: 1296-G (g) / Strong's: 4119] **Concordance:** 22:16

BRIGHTNESS: Anc Heb: ⲫⲁⲟⲩⲩ Mod Heb: שיפרה / shiph-rah (fem); **Definition:** Harmonized and in balance. Cheerful. [AHLB: 2869 (e^1) / Strong's: 8235]

BRING-FORTH: Anc Heb: ⲧⲟⲩⲥ Mod Heb: ילד / ya-lad; **Definition:** To issue out; to bring forth children, either by the woman who bears them or the man who fathers them. The piel (intensive) form means "act-as-midwife." [AHLB: 1257-L (V) / Strong's: 3205] **Concordance:** 1:15 1:16 1:17 1:18 1:19{3} 1:20 1:21 2:2 2:22 6:20 6:23 6:25 21:4

BROTHER: Anc Heb: ⲙⲟⲩ Mod Heb: אח / ahh (mas); **Definition:** A male who has the same parents as another or shares one parent with another. One who stands between the enemy and the family, a protector. [AHLB: 1008-A (N) / Strong's: 251, 252, 1889] **Concordance:** 1:6 2:11{2} 4:14 4:18 7:1 7:2 10:23 16:15 25:20 28:1 28:2 28:4 28:41 32:27 32:29 37:9

BRUISE: Anc Heb: ⲟⲙⲟ Mod Heb: פצע / pe-tsah (mas); **Definition:** An injury involving rupture of small blood vessels and discoloration without a skin break. The dark coloring of the skin caused by being hit or smashed. [AHLB: 2628 (N) / Strong's: 6482] **Concordance:** 21:25{2}

BUCK: Anc Heb: ⲥⲟⲩⲟⲩ Mod Heb: איל / a-yil (mas); **Definition:** The large males of a flock of sheep or heard of deer. By extension, anything of strength including a chief, pillar (as the strong support of a building), or oak tree (one of the strongest of the woods). [AHLB: 1012-M (N) / Strong's: 352, 353, 354] **Concordance:** 15:15 25:5 26:14 29:1 29:3 29:15{2} 29:16 29:17 29:18 29:19{2} 29:20 29:22{2} 29:26 29:27 29:31 29:32 35:7 35:23 36:19 39:34

BUD: Anc Heb: ⲙⲟ̄ⲟ Mod Heb: פרח / pe-rahh (mas); **Definition:** The beginning of a flower that bursts from the plant. [AHLB: 2636 (N) / Strong's: 6525] **Concordance:** 25:31 25:33{2} 25:34 37:17 37:19{2} 37:20

BUDDING: Anc Heb: ⲥⲩⲟⲟⲟⲩⲃ Mod Heb: גיבעול / giv-ol (mas); **Definition:** To sprout flowers or blooms. To come into a fullness. [AHLB: 3006 / Strong's: 1392] **Concordance:** 9:31

BUILD: Anc Heb: ⲫⲁⲥ Mod Heb: בנה / ba-nah; **Definition:** To construct a building, home or family. [AHLB: 1037-H (V) / Strong's: 1124, 1129] **Concordance:** 1:11 17:15 20:25 24:4 32:5

BUILD-UP: Anc Heb: ⲥⲥⲟ Mod Heb: סלל / sa-lal; **Definition:** To raise the elevation of the bank of a river or a highway. To raise one up higher than others. [AHLB: 1334-B (V) / Strong's: 5549] **Concordance:** 9:17

BULL: Anc Heb: ⲟⲟ Mod Heb: פר / par (mas); **Definition:** A large male un-castrated bovine. [AHLB: 1388-A (N) / Strong's: 6499] **Concordance:** 24:5 29:1 29:3 29:10{2} 29:11 29:12 29:14 29:36

BULLOCK: Anc Heb: ⲥⲟⲟⲃ Mod Heb: עגל / ey-gel (mas); **Definition:** A young bull. Also, insinuating strength. [AHLB: 2524 (N) / Strong's: 5695] **Concordance:** 32:4 32:8 32:19 32:20 32:24 32:35

BULRUSH: Anc Heb: ⲥⲁⲙⲩⲃ Mod Heb: גומא / go-me (mas); **Definition:** A reed that grows in, or on the edge of, a pond or river. [AHLB: 1059-E (N) / Strong's: 1573] **Concordance:** 2:3

BUNCH: Anc Heb: ⲫⲟ̄ⲩⲃⲩ Mod Heb: אגודה / a-gu-dah (fem); **Definition:** A group of men or things bound together. [AHLB: 1050-J (n^1) / Strong's: 92] **Concordance:** 12:22

BURDEN: Anc Heb: ⲫⲥⲟⲟ Mod Heb: סבלה / se-va-lah (fem); **Definition:** The heavy load carried in bondage. [AHLB: 2460 (N^1) / Strong's: 5450] **Concordance:** 1:11 2:11 5:4 5:5 6:6 6:7

BURN: Anc Heb: ⲟⲟⲟ Mod Heb: בער / ba-ar; **Definition:** To undergo rapid combustion or consume fuel in such a way as to give off heat, gases, and, usually, light; be on fire. [AHLB: 2028 (V) / Strong's: 1197] **Concordance:** 3:2 3:3 22:4{2} 22:5 35:3

BURN-INCENSE: Anc Heb: ⊗⊕ Mod Heb: קטר / qa-tar; **Definition:** To light a sacrifice or aromatic plant on fire creating smoke, often aromatic. [AHLB: 2705 (V) / Strong's: 6999, 7000] **Concordance:** 29:13 29:18 29:25 30:7{2} 30:8 30:20 40:27

BURNING: Anc Heb: ⊕⊗ Mod Heb: בערה / be-ey-rah (fem); **Definition:** Something that is aflame with fire. [AHLB: 2028 (N¹) / Strong's: 1200] **Concordance:** 22:5

BURNING-WRATH: Anc Heb: ⊗ Mod Heb: חרון / hha-ron (mas); **Definition:** A fierce anger. [AHLB: 1181-A (j) / Strong's: 2740] **Concordance:** 15:7 32:12

BURSTING: Anc Heb: ⊗⊕ Mod Heb: פטר / pe-ter (mas); **Definition:** A sudden and forceful release or issuing out. [AHLB: 2604 (N) / Strong's: 6363] **Concordance:** 13:2 13:12{2} 13:13 13:15 34:19{2} 34:20

BURST-OUT: Anc Heb: ⊗ Mod Heb: פרה / pa-rahh; **Definition:** To be larger, fuller, or more crowded; to break out or break forth as a blooming flower or the wings of a bird. [AHLB: 2636 (V) / Strong's: 6524] **Concordance:** 9:9 9:10

BUSINESS: Anc Heb: ⊗ Mod Heb: מלאכה / me-la-khah (fem); **Definition:** The principal occupation of one's life. A service. [AHLB: 1264-D (k¹) / Strong's: 4399] **Concordance:** 12:16 20:9 20:10 22:7 22:10 31:3 31:5 31:14 31:15{2} 35:2{2} 35:21 35:24 35:29 35:31 35:33 35:35{2} 36:1 36:2 36:3 36:4{2} 36:5 36:6 36:7{2} 36:8 38:24{2} 39:43 40:33

BUT: Anc Heb: ⊗ Mod Heb: אולם / u-lam (com); **Definition:** On the contrary. An outcome desired in the sense of joining. [AHLB: 1254-J (p) / Strong's: 199] **Concordance:** 9:16

BUTCHER: Anc Heb: ⊗ Mod Heb: טבח / ta-vahh; **Definition:** One who slaughters animals or dresses their flesh. [AHLB: 2227 (V) / Strong's: 2873] **Concordance:** 21:37

BUTTRESS: Anc Heb: ⊗ Mod Heb: מקצוע / miq-tso-a (mas); **Definition:** A support or prop. Wall or abutment built to support another wall on the outside, when very high or loaded with a heavy structure. [AHLB: 2725 (hc) / Strong's: 4740] **Concordance:** 26:24 36:29

BY: Anc Heb: ⊗ Mod Heb: עימד / i-mad (mas); **Definition:** In proximity to. The sense of standing with another. [AHLB: 2550 (e) / Strong's: 5978] **Concordance:** 17:2

CALL-OUT: Anc Heb: ⊗ Mod Heb: קרא / qa-ra; **Definition:** To raise one's voice or speak to someone loudly and with urgency; to give, a name; to meet in the sense of being called to a meeting; to have an encounter by chance; to read in the sense of calling out words. [AHLB: 1434-E (V) / Strong's: 7121, 7123] **Concordance:** 1:18 2:7 2:8 2:10 2:20 2:22 3:4 7:11 8:4 8:21 9:27 10:16 10:24 12:21 12:31 15:23 16:31 17:7 17:15 19:3 19:7 19:20 24:7 24:16 31:2 32:5 33:7 33:19 34:5 34:6 34:15 34:31 35:30 36:2

CAMEL: Anc Heb: ⊗ Mod Heb: גמל / ga-mal (com); **Definition:** Either of two ruminant mammals used as draft animals in the desert. The produce of the fields were tied in large bundles and transported on camels. [AHLB: 2070 (N) / Strong's: 1581] **Concordance:** 9:3

CAMP: Anc Heb: ⊗ Mod Heb: חנה / hha-nah; **Definition:** To erect temporary shelters (as tents) together; to stop for the night and pitch the tents. [AHLB: 1175-H (V) / Strong's: 2583] **Concordance:** 13:20 14:2{2} 14:9 15:27 17:1 18:5 19:2{2}

CAMPSITE: Anc Heb: ⊗ Mod Heb: מחנה / me-hha-neh (mas); **Definition:** A place suitable for or used as the location of a camp. The inhabitants of a camp. [AHLB: 1175-H (a) / Strong's: 4264] **Concordance:** 14:19 14:20{2} 14:24{2} 16:13{2} 19:16 19:17 29:14 32:17 32:19 32:26 32:27 33:7{3} 33:11 36:6

CANOPY: Anc Heb: ⊗ Mod Heb: מסך / ma-sak (mas); **Definition:** The covering of a temporary shelter. [AHLB: 1333-A (a) / Strong's: 4539] **Concordance:** 26:36 26:37 27:16 35:12 35:15 35:17 36:37 38:18 39:34 39:38 39:40 40:5 40:8 40:21 40:28 40:33

CAPTAIN: Anc Heb: ⊗ Mod Heb: נשיא / na-si (mas); **Definition:** A military leader; the commander of a unit or a body of troops. The leader of a family, tribe or people as one who carries the burdens of the people. [AHLB: 1314-E (b) / Strong's: 5387] **Concordance:** 16:22 22:27 34:31 35:27

CAPTIVE: Anc Heb: ᛌᛒᛑ Mod Heb: שבי / she-vi (fem); **Definition:** A person who is enslaved or dominated. [AHLB: 1462-H (f) / Strong's: 7628] **Concordance:** 12:29

CAPTURE: Anc Heb: ᛌᛒᛑ Mod Heb: שבה / sha-vah; **Definition:** The act of catching, winning, or gaining control by force, stratagem, or guile; to take one away from his homeland as an involuntary prisoner. [AHLB: 1462-H (V) / Strong's: 7617] **Concordance:** 22:9

CARNELIAN: Anc Heb: ᛉᛏᛮᚥ Mod Heb: אודם / o-dem (fem); **Definition:** Probably the Carnelian, a reddish brown gemstone. The Hebrew word is from a root meaning red or reddish. Another possible translation is Jasper. [AHLB: 1082-C (g) / Strong's: 124] **Concordance:** 28:17 39:10

CARVING: Anc Heb: ᛑᛏᛮᚥ Mod Heb: פיתוח / pi-tu-ahh (mas); **Definition:** A cutting into a solid material, such as wood or stone, to engrave a design or writing. [AHLB: 2649 (ed) / Strong's: 6603] **Concordance:** 28:11 28:21 28:36 39:6 39:14 39:30

CASSIA: Anc Heb: ᚥᛑᛮᛂ Mod Heb: קידה / qi-dah (fem); **Definition:** The tree, wood or spice which is used in anointing oils and perfumes. [AHLB: 1418-M (N^1) / Strong's: 6916] **Concordance:** 30:24

CAST-DOWN: Anc Heb: ᛋᛂᚥ Mod Heb: הרס / ha-ras; **Definition:** To ruin or break into pieces by throwing or pulling down. [AHLB: 1452-F (V) / Strong's: 2040] **Concordance:** 15:7 19:21 19:24 23:24{2}

CAST-IMAGE: Anc Heb: ᚥᛂᛮᛒᛮ Mod Heb: מסכה / ma-sey-khah (fem); **Definition:** A molten metal that is poured in a cast to form images. [AHLB: 2412 (a^1) / Strong's: 4541] **Concordance:** 32:4 32:8 34:17

CAST-OFF: Anc Heb: ᛋᛑᛮ Mod Heb: נשל / na-shal; **Definition:** To remove with force and intention. [AHLB: 2442 (V) / Strong's: 5394] **Concordance:** 3:5

CAST-OUT: Anc Heb: ᛋᚥᛂ Mod Heb: גרש / ga-rash; **Definition:** To drive out, expel, thrust away. [AHLB: 2089 (V) / Strong's: 1644] **Concordance:** 2:17 6:1 10:11 11:1{2} 12:39 23:28 23:29 23:30 23:31 33:2 34:11

CATTLE: Anc Heb: ᛂᛒᛑ Mod Heb: בקר / ba-qar (mas); Alt Sp: בעיר **Definition:** Domesticated bovine animals. Strong beasts used to break the soil with plows. [AHLB: 2035 (N) / Strong's: 1165, 1241] **Concordance:** 9:3 10:9 10:24 12:32 12:38 20:24 21:37 22:4 29:1 34:3

CAULDRON: Anc Heb: ᛂᛏᛮᚥ Mod Heb: כיור / ki-or (mas); **Definition:** A large kettle or boiler, of copper or other metal. A smelting pot. [AHLB: 1250-J (e) / Strong's: 3595] **Concordance:** 30:18 30:28 31:9 35:16 38:8 39:39 40:7 40:11 40:30

CEASE: Anc Heb: ᛂᛒᛑ Mod Heb: שבת / sha-vat; **Definition:** To come to an end; to die out; to stop an activity for the purpose of rest or celebration. [AHLB: 2812 (V) / Strong's: 7673] **Concordance:** 5:5 12:15 16:30 23:12 31:17 34:21{2}

CEASING: Anc Heb: ᛂᛒᛑ Mod Heb: שבת / sha-bat (fem); **Definition:** A stopping of work or activity; An activity curtailed before completion. The seventh day of the week (often translated as Sabbath) when all business ceases for rest and celebration. [AHLB: 2812 (N) / Strong's: 7674, 7676] **Concordance:** 16:23 16:25 16:26 16:29 20:8 20:10 20:11 21:19 31:13 31:14 31:15{2} 31:16{2} 35:2 35:3

CENTER: Anc Heb: ᛑᚥᛮᚥᛮ Mod Heb: חצות / hha-tsot (fem); **Definition:** The middle of something. [AHLB: 1179-A (N^3) / Strong's: 2676] **Concordance:** 11:4

CHAIN: Anc Heb: ᚥᛂᛮᛂᛮ Mod Heb: שרשרה / shar-she-rah (fem); Alt Sp: שרשה **Definition:** A strand of linked metal loops. [AHLB: 1480-D (l^1) / Strong's: 8331, 8333] **Concordance:** 28:14{2} 28:22 39:15

CHAMBER: Anc Heb: 𐤒𐤃𐤓 Mod Heb: חדר / hhe-der (mas); **Definition:** A bedroom; a natural or artificial enclosed space or cavity. Place surrounded by walls. An inner place as hidden or secret. [AHLB: 2150 (N) / Strong's: 2315] **Concordance:** 7:28

CHARGE: Anc Heb: 𐤕𐤔𐤌𐤓𐤕 Mod Heb: משמרת / mish-me-ret (fem); **Definition:** A person or thing committed to the care of another. What is given to be watched over and protected. [AHLB: 2853 (h²) / Strong's: 4931] **Concordance:** 12:6 16:23 16:32 16:33 16:34

CHARIOT: Anc Heb: 𐤌𐤓𐤊𐤁𐤄 Mod Heb: מרכבה / mer-ka-vah (fem); **Definition:** A light, two-wheeled battle vehicle for one or two persons, usually drawn by two horses and driven from a standing position. [AHLB: 2769 (k¹) / Strong's: 4818] **Concordance:** 14:25 15:4

CHEST: Anc Heb: 𐤇𐤆𐤄 Mod Heb: חזה / hha-zeh (mas); **Definition:** The breast containing heart. What is prominently visible. The breast of an animal used for a sacrifice. [AHLB: 1168-H (N) / Strong's: 2373] **Concordance:** 29:26 29:27

CHIEF: Anc Heb: 𐤀𐤋𐤅𐤐 Mod Heb: אלוף / a-luph (mas); **Definition:** Accorded highest rank or office; of greatest importance, significance, or influence. One who is yoked to another to lead and teach. [AHLB: 2001 (d) / Strong's: 441] **Concordance:** 15:15

CHILD-OF-THE-SUN: Anc Heb: 𐤓𐤏𐤌𐤎𐤎 Mod Heb: רעמסס / ra-me-seys (mas); **Definition:** A word of Egyptian origins. [AHLB: **4018** / Strong's: n/a] **OF-**THE-SUN:

CHILDREN: Anc Heb: 𐤈𐤐 Mod Heb: טף / taph (mas); **Definition:** The offspring of the parent or descendents of a patron. More than one child. [AHLB: 1201-A (N) / Strong's: 2945] **Concordance:** 10:10 10:24 12:37

CHOOSE: Anc Heb: 𐤁𐤇𐤓 Mod Heb: בחר / ba-hhar; **Definition:** To select freely and after consideration. [AHLB: 2012 (V) / Strong's: 977] **Concordance:** 14:7 17:9 18:25

CHOSEN: Anc Heb: 𐤌𐤁𐤇𐤓 Mod Heb: מבחר / miv-hhar (mas); **Definition:** One who is the object of choice or of divine favor. [AHLB: 2012 (h) / Strong's: 4005] **Concordance:** 15:4

CINNAMON: Anc Heb: 𐤒𐤍𐤌𐤅𐤍 Mod Heb: קנמון / qi-na-mon (mas); **Definition:** A spice from the bark of a small evergreen tree. The essential oil is of great price. [AHLB: 2716 (j) / Strong's: 7076] **Concordance:** 30:23

CIRCUIT: Anc Heb: 𐤕𐤒𐤅𐤐𐤄 Mod Heb: תקופה / te-qu-phah (fem); **Definition:** A going around in a circle. To return to a starting point in the sense of going full circle. [AHLB: 1431-J (i¹) / Strong's: 8622] **Concordance:** 34:22

CIRCUMCISE: Anc Heb: 𐤌𐤅𐤋 Mod Heb: מול / mul; **Definition:** To cut off the foreskin of a male. [AHLB: 1288-J (V) / Strong's: 4135] **Concordance:** 12:44 12:48

CIRCUMCISION: Anc Heb: 𐤌𐤅𐤋𐤄 Mod Heb: מולה / mu-lah (fem); **Definition:** The removal of the front part of the male sexual organ. [AHLB: 1288-J (N¹) / Strong's: 4139] **Concordance:** 4:26

CISTERN: Anc Heb: 𐤊𐤅𐤓 Mod Heb: כור / kor (mas); Alt Sp: בור **Definition:** An artificial reservoir for storing water. A hole or well as dug out. [AHLB: 1250-J (N) / Strong's: 953, 2352, 2356, 3564] **Concordance:** 12:29 21:33{2} 21:34

CITY: Anc Heb: 𐤏𐤉𐤓 Mod Heb: עיר / ir (mas); **Definition:** An inhabited place of greater size, population, or importance than a town or village. Usually protected by a wall. [AHLB: 1526-M (N) / Strong's: 5892] **Concordance:** 1:11 9:29 9:33

CITY-OF-JUSTICE: Anc Heb: 𐤐𐤉𐤕𐤌 Mod Heb: פיתום / pi-tom (mas); **Definition:** A word of Egyptian origins. [AHLB: **4015** / Strong's: n/a] **OF-**JUSTICE:

CLEANLINESS: Anc Heb: 𐤈𐤄𐤓 Mod Heb: טוהר / to-har (mas); **Definition:** The act of being free from dirt or immorality. Free from foreign elements. [AHLB: 1204-G (g) / Strong's: 2892] **Concordance:** 24:10

CLEAVE: Anc Heb: ⊷•ᴟ Mod Heb: בקע / ba-qa; **Definition:** To divide by or as if by a cutting blow; to separate into distinct parts; to break, cut or divide something in half. [AHLB: 2034 (V) / Strong's: 1234] **Concordance:** 14:16 14:21

CLOAK: Anc Heb: ⊿⊶ᴑᴟᴟ Mod Heb: מעיל / me-il (mas); **Definition:** A loose outer garment worn over other clothes both by men and women. [AHLB: 1357-M (k) / Strong's: 4598] **Concordance:** 28:4 28:31 28:34 29:5 39:22 39:23 39:24 39:25 39:26

CLOUD: Anc Heb: ⵏⵏ⼃ Mod Heb: ענן / a-nan (mas); **Definition:** A visible mass of particles of water or ice in the form of fog, mist, or haze suspended usually at a considerable height in the air. [AHLB: 1359-B (N) / Strong's: 6050, 6051] **Concordance:** 13:21 13:22 14:19 14:20 14:24 16:10 19:9 19:16 24:15 24:16{2} 24:18 33:9 33:10 34:5 40:34 40:35 40:36 40:37 40:38

COLLAR: Anc Heb: ⼂ᴑ⼄ᴟᵀ Mod Heb: תחרא / tahh-ra (mas); **Definition:** The hole in the middle of a rectangular garment for the head to pass through. An area reinforced around the neck opening. [AHLB: 1181-E (i) / Strong's: 8473] **Concordance:** 28:32 39:23

COLLECT: Anc Heb: ᴜᴜᴜ•ᴑ Mod Heb: קשש / qa-shash; **Definition:** To gather up straw, stubble or sticks. [AHLB: 1435-B (V) / Strong's: 7197] **Concordance:** 5:7 5:12

COLLECTION: Anc Heb: ⼂Ყ•ᴑᴟᴟ Mod Heb: מקוה / miq-weh (mas); **Definition:** An accumulation of objects or material. A collection of water (a pool, pond or sea) or horses (herd). [AHLB: 1419-J (h) / Strong's: 4723] **Concordance:** 7:19

COME: Anc Heb: ⼂Ყᴟᴟ Mod Heb: בוא / bo; **Definition:** To move toward something; approach; enter. This can be understood as to come or to go. The hiphil (causative) form means "bring." [AHLB: 1024-J (V) / Strong's: 935] **Concordance:** 1:1{2} 1:19 2:10 2:16 2:17 2:18{2} 3:1 3:9 3:13 3:18 4:6{2} 5:1 5:15 5:23 6:8 6:11 7:10 7:23 7:26 7:28 8:20 9:1 10:1 10:3 10:4 10:26 11:1 12:23 12:25 13:5 13:11 14:16 14:17 14:20 14:22 14:23 14:28 15:17 15:19 15:23 15:27 16:1 16:5 16:22 16:35{2} 17:8 17:12 18:5 18:6 18:7 18:12 18:15 18:16 18:19 18:22 18:23 18:26 19:1 19:2 19:4 19:7 19:9 20:20 20:24 21:3 22:8 22:12 22:14 22:25 23:19 23:20 23:23 23:27 24:3 24:18 25:14 26:11 26:33 27:7 28:29 28:30 28:35 28:43 29:30 30:20 32:2 32:3 32:21 33:8 33:9 34:12 34:26 34:34 34:35 35:5 35:10 35:21{2} 35:22{2} 35:23 35:24{2} 35:25 35:27 35:29{2} 36:3{2} 36:4 36:5 36:6 37:5 38:7 39:33 40:4{2} 40:21 40:32 40:35

COME-NEAR: Anc Heb: ᴟᴑ•ᴑ Mod Heb: קרב / qa-rav; **Definition:** To come close by or near to. [AHLB: 2729 (V) / Strong's: 7126, 7127] **Concordance:** 3:5 12:48 14:10 14:20 16:9 22:7 28:1 29:3 29:4 29:8 29:10 32:19 36:2 40:12 40:14 40:32

COME-UP: Anc Heb: ᴟᴑ•ᴚ Mod Heb: זרח / za-rahh; **Definition:** To rise up, as the sun does at the horizon. [AHLB: 2135 (V) / Strong's: 2224] **Concordance:** 22:2

COMFORT: Anc Heb: ᴧᴟᴑᴟᴧ Mod Heb: נחם / na-hham; **Definition:** Consolation in time of trouble or worry; to give solace in time of difficulty or sorrow. The niphal (passive) form means "repent." [AHLB: 2392 (V) / Strong's: 5162] **Concordance:** 13:17 32:12 32:14

COMMIT-ADULTERY: Anc Heb: ⊸⟩Ⴟᴧ Mod Heb: נאף / na-aph; **Definition:** To perform voluntary violation of the marriage bed. [AHLB: 2365 (V) / Strong's: 5003] **Concordance:** 20:14

COMPANION: Anc Heb: ⊛ᴟ Mod Heb: רע / ra (mas); **Alt Sp:** ריע **Definition:** One that accompanies another. As a close companion. [AHLB: 1453-A (N) / Strong's: 7453] **Concordance:** 2:13 11:2 18:7 18:16 20:16 20:17{3} 21:14 21:18 21:35 22:6 22:7 22:8 22:9 22:10 22:13 22:25 32:27 33:11

COMPANY: Anc Heb: ᵠᵀ⊛ Mod Heb: עדה / ey-dah (fem); **Definition:** A group of persons or things for carrying on a project or undertaking; a group with a common testimony. May also mean a witness or testimony. [AHLB: 1349-A (N[1]) / Strong's: 5712, 5713] **Concordance:** 12:3 12:6 12:19 12:47 16:1 16:2 16:9 16:10 16:22 17:1 34:31 35:1 35:4 35:20 38:25

COMPASSIONATE: Anc Heb: ᗰᏓᗰᏂᎧ Mod Heb: רחום / ra-hhum (mas); **Definition:** Being sympathetic, and understanding. A protecting from harm. [AHLB: 2762 (d) / Strong's: 7349] **Concordance:** 34:6

COMPEL: Anc Heb: ᗰᎧᎩᎩᎩ Mod Heb: אוץ / uts; **Definition:** To drive or urge forcefully or irresistibly. A pressing into an action or narrow place. [AHLB: 1018-J (V) / Strong's: 213] **Concordance:** 5:13

COMPLETE: Anc Heb: ᗰᎧᎩᎩᎩ Mod Heb: שלם / she-lem (mas); **Definition:** Having all necessary parts, elements or steps. A state of being whole or full. Left unaltered and whole in its original functional state without removing or adding to it. To finish. A sacrifice or offering given to bring about peace. [AHLB: 2845 (N) / Strong's: 8001, 8002, 8003] **Concordance:** 20:24 24:5 29:28 32:6

COMPLETENESS: Anc Heb: ᗰᎧᎩᎩᎩ Mod Heb: שלום / sha-lom (mas); **Definition:** Something that has been finished or made whole. A state of being complete. [AHLB: 2845 (c) / Strong's: 7965] **Concordance:** 4:18 18:7 18:23

COMPLETION: Anc Heb: ᎩᎩᎩᎩ Mod Heb: כלה / ka-lah (fem); **Definition:** The act or process of completing. This can be in a positive sense or negative, such as in a failure. [AHLB: 1242-A (N^1) / Strong's: 3617] **Concordance:** 11:1

COMPOUND: Anc Heb: ᏂᎧᎩᎩ Mod Heb: רקח / ra-qahh; **Definition:** The combining of two or more ingredients to achieve the desired substance. [AHLB: 2795 (V) / Strong's: 7543] **Concordance:** 30:25 30:33 30:35 37:29

CONCEAL: Anc Heb: ᎩᎧᎩᎩ Mod Heb: צפן / tsa-phan; **Definition:** To hide to prevent discovery. [AHLB: 2683 (V) / Strong's: 6845] **Concordance:** 2:2 2:3

CONCEIVE: Anc Heb: ᎩᎧᎩ Mod Heb: הרה / a-rah; **Definition:** To become pregnant with young. [AHLB: 1112-H (V) / Strong's: 2029] **Concordance:** 2:2

CONCERNING: Anc Heb: ᎩᎩᎧᎩᎩ Mod Heb: אודות / o-dot (fem); **Definition:** Regarding. Marked interest or regard usually arising through a personal tie or relationship. A turning over and bringing together of a thought. [AHLB: 1004-J (N^3) / Strong's: 182] **Concordance:** 18:8

CONCLUSION: Anc Heb: ᎧᎩᎧ Mod Heb: קץ / qeyts (mas); **Definition:** To come to an end. The end of a time period or place or the end of something. The border of a country as its edges. [AHLB: 1432-A (N) / Strong's: 7093] **Concordance:** 12:41

CONFUSE: Anc Heb: ᗰᗰᎧᎩ Mod Heb: המם / ha-mam; **Definition:** To cause trouble and confusion through a great noise such as with trumpets. [AHLB: 1105-B (V) / Strong's: 2000] **Concordance:** 14:24 23:27

CONSENT: Anc Heb: ᎩᎧᎩᎩ Mod Heb: אבה / a-vah; **Definition:** To give approval; to be in concord in opinion or sentiment; agreement as to action or opinion; to be willing to go somewhere or do something. [AHLB: 1028-C (V) / Strong's: 14] **Concordance:** 10:27

CONSISTENCY: Anc Heb: ᎩᎩᎧᎩ Mod Heb: איתן / ey-tan (mas); **Definition:** Agreement or harmony of parts or features; showing steady conformity to character, profession, belief, or custom. [AHLB: 1497-C (e) / Strong's: 386] **Concordance:** 14:27

CONTENTION: Anc Heb: ᎩᎧᎩᎩᗰ Mod Heb: מריבה / me-ri-vah (fem); **Definition:** An act or instance of striving or struggling against great difficulty or opposition. [AHLB: 1439-M (k^1) / Strong's: 4808]

CONTINUALLY: Anc Heb: ᎩᎩᎩᗰᎩ Mod Heb: תמיד / ta-mid (mas); **Definition:** Happening without interruption or cessation; continuous in time. [AHLB: 1280-M (b) / Strong's: 8548] **Concordance:** 25:30 27:20 28:29 28:30 28:38 29:38 29:42 30:8

CONTINUE: Anc Heb: ᎩᎩᎩ Mod Heb: נון / nun (mas); **Definition:** Maintain the action, to forge ahead with intention. [AHLB: n/a / Strong's: n/a] **Concordance:** *Used in names only.*

CONTRIBUTION: Anc Heb: 𐤌𐤕𐤍𐤄 Mod Heb: מתנה / mat-nah (fem); **Definition:** What is given or supplied in common with others. [AHLB: 2451 (a^1) / Strong's: 4978, 4979] **Concordance:** 28:38

COPPER: Anc Heb: 𐤍𐤇𐤔𐤕 Mod Heb: נחושת / ne-hho-shet (fem); **Definition:** A malleable, ductile, metallic element having a characteristic reddish-brown color. A precious metal. [AHLB: 2395 (c^2) / Strong's: 5178] **Concordance:** 25:3 26:11 26:37 27:2 27:3 27:4{2} 27:6 27:10 27:11 27:17 27:18 27:19 30:18{2} 31:4 35:5 35:16 35:24 35:32 36:18 36:38 38:2 38:3 38:4 38:5 38:6 38:8{2} 38:10 38:11 38:17 38:19 38:20 38:29 38:30{2} 39:39{2}

CORD: Anc Heb: 𐤐𐤕𐤋 Mod Heb: פתיל / pa-til (mas); **Definition:** A long slender flexible material made of several strands woven or twisted together. Made of twisted fibers. [AHLB: 2650 (b) / Strong's: 6616] **Concordance:** 28:28 28:37 39:3 39:21 39:31

CORIANDER: Anc Heb: 𐤂𐤃 Mod Heb: גד / gad (mas); **Definition:** A class of plants with seeds which are in the form of the size of a peppercorn. They are used medicinally and as a spice. Likened to the manna in its form and color. [AHLB: 1050-A (N) / Strong's: 1407] **Concordance:** 16:31

CORNER: Anc Heb: 𐤐𐤍𐤄 Mod Heb: פינה / pin-nah (fem); **Definition:** The point where two lines meet. [AHLB: 1382-M (N^1) / Strong's: 6438] **Concordance:** 27:2 38:2

CORNER-POST: Anc Heb: 𐤌𐤒𐤑𐤏𐤄 Mod Heb: מקוצעה / me-quts-ah (fem); **Definition:** The strongest point from where the rest of the structure is built from. As scraped out with a plane. [AHLB: 2725 (ko^1) / Strong's: 4742] **Concordance:** 26:23 36:28

CORRECT: Anc Heb: 𐤑𐤃𐤒 Mod Heb: צדיק / tsa-diq (mas); **Definition:** To make or set right. Conforming to fact, standard or truth. [AHLB: 2658 (b) / Strong's: 6662] **Concordance:** 9:27 23:7 23:8

COUNT: Anc Heb: 𐤎𐤐𐤓 Mod Heb: ספר / sa-phar; **Definition:** To find the total number of units involved by naming the numbers in order up to and including. The piel (intensive) form means "recount." [AHLB: 2500 (V) / Strong's: 5608] **Concordance:** 9:16 10:2 18:8 24:3

COUPLE: Anc Heb: 𐤇𐤁𐤓 Mod Heb: חבר / hha-var; **Definition:** To bind by joining or coupling together. [AHLB: 2143 (V) / Strong's: 2266] **Concordance:** 26:3{2} 26:6 26:9 26:11 28:7{2} 36:10{2} 36:13 36:16 36:18 39:4{2}

COUPLING: Anc Heb: 𐤇𐤁𐤓𐤕 Mod Heb: חוברת / hho-be-ret (fem); **Definition:** To bring together as a unit. [AHLB: 2143 (g^2) / Strong's: 2279] **Concordance:** 26:4 26:10{2} 36:17

COVENANT: Anc Heb: 𐤁𐤓𐤉𐤕 Mod Heb: ברית / be-rit (fem); **Definition:** A solemn and binding agreement between two or more parties especially for the performance of some action. Often instituted through a sacrifice. [AHLB: 1043-H (N^4) / Strong's: 1285] **Concordance:** 2:24 6:4 6:5 19:5 23:32 24:7 24:8 31:16 34:10 34:12 34:15 34:27 34:28

COVER: Anc Heb: 𐤊𐤐𐤓 Mod Heb: כפר / ka-phar; **Definition:** To afford protection or security; to hide from sight or knowledge; to cover over as with a lid. [AHLB: 2283 (V) / Strong's: 3722] **Concordance:** 29:33 29:36 29:37 30:10{2} 30:15 30:16 32:30

COVERING: Anc Heb: 𐤊𐤐𐤓 Mod Heb: כופר / ko-pher (mas); **Definition:** Something that covers or conceals. A covering such as pitch or a monetary covering such as a bribe or ransom. A "village" as a covering. [AHLB: 2283 (g) / Strong's: 3723, 3724] **Concordance:** 21:30 30:12

COVER-OVER: Anc Heb: 𐤊𐤎𐤄 Mod Heb: כסה / ka-sah; Alt Sp: כשה **Definition:** To prevent disclosure or recognition of; to place out of sight; to completely cover over or hide. [AHLB: 1245-H (V) / Strong's: 3680, 3780] **Concordance:** 8:2 10:5 10:15 14:28 15:5 15:10 16:13 21:33 24:15 24:16 26:13 28:42 29:13 29:22 40:34

CRACK: Anc Heb: ᔕᔕᗑ Mod Heb: שבר / sha-var; **Definition:** To break open, apart or into pieces. The piel (intensive) form means "shatter." [AHLB: 2811 (V) / Strong's: 7665, 8406] **Concordance:** 9:25 12:46 22:9 22:13 23:24{2} 32:19 34:1 34:13

CRAVE: Anc Heb: ᖰᗑ Mod Heb: חמד / hha-mad; **Definition:** To have a strong or inward desire for something. [AHLB: 2169 (V) / Strong's: 2530] **Concordance:** 20:17{2} 34:24

CREMATE: Anc Heb: ᗑᔕ Mod Heb: שרף / sa-raph; Alt Sp: שרף **Definition:** To reduce a dead body, or other object, to ashes by burning. [AHLB: 2512 (V) / Strong's: 5635, 8313] **Concordance:** 12:10 29:14 29:34 32:20

CROSS-OVER: Anc Heb: ᖰᗑᗑ Mod Heb: עבר / a-var; **Definition:** To pass from one side to the other; to go across a river or through a land; to transgress in the sense of crossing over. [AHLB: 2520 (V) / Strong's: 5674, 5675] **Concordance:** 12:12 12:23 13:12 15:16{2} 17:5 30:13 30:14 32:27 33:19 33:22{2} 34:6 36:6 38:26

CROWN: Anc Heb: ᖰᗑᗑ Mod Heb: נזר / ne-zer (mas); **Definition:** An object showing Kingship or authority. Also, a sign upon the head as a sign of dedication. [AHLB: 2390 (N) / Strong's: 5145] **Concordance:** 29:6 39:30

CRUSHED: Anc Heb: ᗑᗑ Mod Heb: כתית / ka-tit (mas); **Definition:** The pressing of the olive to extract the oil. [AHLB: 1252-B (b) / Strong's: 3795] **Concordance:** 27:20 29:40

CRY: Anc Heb: ᖰᗑ Mod Heb: צעקה / tse-a-qah (fem); **Definition:** To utter loudly; to shout; to shed tears, often noisily. A loud crying or calling out. [AHLB: 2679 (N^1) / Strong's: 6818] **Concordance:** 3:7 3:9 11:6 12:30 22:22

CRY-OUT: Anc Heb: ᖰᗑ Mod Heb: צעק / tsa-aq; **Definition:** To cry or call out loudly. [AHLB: 2679 (V) / Strong's: 6817] **Concordance:** 5:8 5:15 8:8 14:10 14:15 15:25 17:4 22:22{2} 22:26

CUPPED-HAND: Anc Heb: ᖰᗑ Mod Heb: חופן / hho-phen (mas); **Definition:** The cup shape of the palm. [AHLB: 2190 (g) / Strong's: 2651] **Concordance:** 9:8

CURDLE: Anc Heb: ᖰᗑ Mod Heb: קפא / qa-pha; **Definition:** To change into curd; coagulate; congeal. To spoil; turn sour. [AHLB: 1431-E (V) / Strong's: 7087] **Concordance:** 15:8

CUSTOM: Anc Heb: ᖰᗑ Mod Heb: חוק / hhuq (mas); **Definition:** A usage or practice common to many or to a particular place or class or habitual with an individual. [AHLB: 1180-J (N) / Strong's: 2706] **Concordance:** 5:14 12:24 15:25 15:26 18:16 18:20 29:28 30:21

CUT: Anc Heb: ᗑᔕ Mod Heb: כרת / ka-rat; **Definition:** To penetrate with a sharp edged instrument. [AHLB: 2291 (V) / Strong's: 3772] **Concordance:** 4:25 8:5 12:15 12:19 23:32 24:8 30:33 30:38 31:14 34:10 34:12 34:13 34:15

CUT-SHARPLY: Anc Heb: ᖰᗑ Mod Heb: חרץ / hha-rats; **Definition:** To divide or slice with a sharp instrument. To make a decision in the sense of dividing between two choices. [AHLB: 2209 (V) / Strong's: 2782] **Concordance:** 11:7

DAMAGE: Anc Heb: ᖰᗑᗑ Mod Heb: שחת / sha-hhat; **Definition:** To bring to ruin by destruction; to destroy through disfigurement or corruption. [AHLB: 2830 (V) / Strong's: 7843, 7844] **Concordance:** 8:20 12:23 21:26 32:7

DANCE: Anc Heb: ᖰᗑᗑ Mod Heb: מחולה / me-hho-lah (fem); **Definition:** Twisting, skipping, or leaping with joy. To rejoice in expression of thanksgiving for religious worship or festivity. [AHLB: 1173-J (k^1) / Strong's: 4246] **Concordance:** 15:20 32:19

DARKEN: Anc Heb: ᖰᗑᗑ Mod Heb: חשך / hha-shak; **Definition:** To be deprived of light. To be dark as night. [AHLB: 2215 (V) / Strong's: 2821] **Concordance:** 10:15

DARKNESS: Anc Heb: ᖰᗑᗑ Mod Heb: חושך / hho-shekh (mas); **Definition:** The state of being dark. As the darkness of a moonless night. [AHLB: 2215 (g) / Strong's: 2822] **Concordance:** 10:21{2} 10:22 14:20

DASH-TO-PIECES: Anc Heb: ᛢᛞᛜᛗ Mod Heb: רעץ / ra-ats; **Definition:** To shatter into pieces by force. [AHLB: 2783 (V) / Strong's: 7492] **Concordance:** 15:6

DATE-PALM: Anc Heb: ᛢᛗᛏ Mod Heb: תמר / ta-mar (mas); **Definition:** The tree that produces the date. An erect tree as a pillar. [AHLB: 2896 (N) / Strong's: 8558] **Concordance:** 15:27

DAUGHTER: Anc Heb: ᛏᛚᛠ Mod Heb: בת / bat (fem); **Definition:** A female having the relation of a child to parent. A village that resides outside of the city walls; as "the daughter of the city." [AHLB: 1037-A (N²) / Strong's: 1323] **Concordance:** 1:16 1:22 2:1 2:5 2:7 2:8 2:9 2:10 2:16 2:20 2:21 3:22 6:23 6:25 10:9 20:10 21:4 21:7 21:9 21:31 32:2 34:16{2}

DAY: Anc Heb: ᛗᛟᛝᛃ Mod Heb: יום / yom (mas); **Definition:** The time of light between one night and the next one. Usually in the context of daylight hours but may also refer to the entire day or even a season. [AHLB: 1220-J (N) / Strong's: 3117, 3118] **Concordance:** 2:11 2:13 2:18 2:23 3:18 5:3 5:6 5:13{2} 5:14 5:19{2} 6:28 7:25 8:18 8:23 9:18 10:6{2} 10:13 10:22 10:23 10:28 12:6 12:14 12:15{4} 12:16{2} 12:17{2} 12:18{2} 12:19 12:41 12:51 13:3 13:4 13:6{2} 13:7 13:8 13:10{2} 14:13{2} 14:30 15:22 16:1 16:4{2} 16:5{3} 16:22 16:25{3} 16:26{2} 16:27 16:29{3} 16:30 19:1 19:10 19:11{2} 19:15 19:16 20:8 20:9 20:10 20:11{3} 20:12 21:21{2} 22:29{2} 23:12{2} 23:15 23:26 24:16{2} 24:18 29:30 29:35 29:36 29:37 29:38 31:15{3} 31:17{2} 32:28 32:29{2} 32:34 34:11 34:18 34:21{2} 34:28 35:2{2} 35:3 40:2 40:37

DAYTIME: Anc Heb: ᛗᛗᛟᛝᛃ Mod Heb: יומם / yo-mam (mas); **Definition:** The time of the day when the sun is shining. [AHLB: 1220-J (p) / Strong's: 3119] **Concordance:** 13:21{2} 13:22 40:38

DEAL-DECEITFULLY: Anc Heb: ᛞᛏᛌ Mod Heb: התל / ha-tal; **Definition:** To give as one's portion by a false impression. [AHLB: 1495-F (V) / Strong's: 2048] **Concordance:** 8:25

DEATH: Anc Heb: ᛏᛁᛗ Mod Heb: מות / mot (mas); **Definition:** A permanent cessation of all vital functions; the end of life. [AHLB: 1298-J (N) / Strong's: 4192, 4193, 4194] **Concordance:** 10:17

DECEIVE: Anc Heb: ᛒᛚᛌᛁ Mod Heb: נשא / na-sha; **Alt Sp:** נשה **Definition:** To cause to accept as true or valid what is false or invalid. Can also mean usury in the sense of a deception. In the participle form can mean creditor in the sense of imposition. [AHLB: 1320-E (V) / Strong's: 5377, 5378, 5383] **Concordance:** 22:24

DECIDE: Anc Heb: ᛟᛜᛚ Mod Heb: שפט / sha-phat; **Definition:** To make a determination in a dispute or wrong doing. [AHLB: 2864 (V) / Strong's: 8199, 8200] **Concordance:** 2:14 5:21 18:13 18:16 18:22{2} 18:26{2}

DECISION: Anc Heb: ᛟᛜᛚᛗ Mod Heb: משפט / mish-pat (mas); **Definition:** A pronounced opinion. [AHLB: 2864 (h) / Strong's: 4941] **Concordance:** 15:25 21:1 21:9 21:31 23:6 24:3 26:30 28:15 28:29 28:30{2}

DECORATE: Anc Heb: ᛢᛒᛟᛜ Mod Heb: פאר / pa-ar; **Definition:** To apply ornamentation to show distinguishment or distinction. To stand out; being seen in a good light. To boast, in the sense of decorating the self with words. [AHLB: 1388-D (V) / Strong's: 6286] **Concordance:** 8:5

DECORATION: Anc Heb: ᛢᛒᛟᛜᛏ Mod Heb: תפארה / tiph-a-rah (fem); **Alt Sp:** תפארת **Definition:** Ornamentation that shows position, distinguishment or distinction. [AHLB: 1388-D (i¹) / Strong's: 8597] **Concordance:** 28:2 28:40

DECORATIVE-BAND: Anc Heb: ᛞᛚᛒᛂ Mod Heb: חשב / hhy-shev (mas); **Definition:** An adornment with designs used to decorate or tie an article of clothing. [AHLB: 2213 (N) / Strong's: 2805] **Concordance:** 28:8 28:27 28:28 29:5 39:5 39:20 39:21

DEEP-SEA: Anc Heb: ᛗᛟᛂᛏ Mod Heb: תהום / te-hom (fem); **Definition:** Extending far from some surface or area; in difficulty or distress. Deep and tumultuous water. A subterranean body of water. [AHLB: 1105-J (i) / Strong's: 8415] **Concordance:** 15:5

DEFEAT: Anc Heb: 𐤇𐤋𐤅𐤔𐤄 Mod Heb: חלושה / hha-lu-shah (fem); **Definition:** Overcome or weakened by an outside force. [AHLB: 2168 (d^1) / Strong's: 2476] **Concordance:** 32:18

DELAY: Anc Heb: 𐤀𐤇𐤓 Mod Heb: אחר / a-hhar; **Definition:** To stop, detain or hinder for a time. [AHLB: 1181-C (V) / Strong's: 309] **Concordance:** 22:28

DELIVER: Anc Heb: 𐤍𐤑𐤋 Mod Heb: נצל / na-tsal; **Definition:** To set free; to take and hand over to or leave for another. [AHLB: 2428 (V) / Strong's: 5337, 5338] **Concordance:** 2:19 3:8 3:22 5:23{2} 6:6 12:27 12:36 18:4 18:8 18:9 18:10{2} 33:6

DEPART: Anc Heb: 𐤓𐤔𐤏 Mod Heb: רשע / ra-sha; **Definition:** To go astray from the correct path and become lost; to act against a law or teaching as one who has gone astray. The hiphil (causative) form means "convict." [AHLB: 2799 (V) / Strong's: 7561] **Concordance:** 22:8

DEPART-EARLY: Anc Heb: 𐤔𐤊𐤌 Mod Heb: שכם / sha-kham; **Definition:** Literally, to put a load on the shoulder to go away or leave early. [AHLB: 2837 (V) / Strong's: 7925] **Concordance:** 8:16 9:13 24:4 32:6 34:4

DEPTH: Anc Heb: 𐤌𐤑𐤅𐤋𐤄 Mod Heb: מצולה / me-tso-lah (fem); **Definition:** The bottom of a deep body of water. [AHLB: 1403-J (k^1) / Strong's: 4688] **Concordance:** 15:5 15:8

DESOLATE: Anc Heb: 𐤔𐤌𐤌𐤄 Mod Heb: שממה / she-ma-mah (fem); **Definition:** Vacant or void of required sources for life. [AHLB: 1473-B (N^1) / Strong's: 8077] **Concordance:** 23:29

DESTRUCTION: Anc Heb: 𐤌𐤔𐤇𐤕 Mod Heb: משחית / mash-hhit (mas); **Definition:** To completely destroy with force. To tear or bring down. [AHLB: 2830 (ab) / Strong's: 4889] **Concordance:** 12:13

DEVOTED: Anc Heb: 𐤇𐤍𐤊 Mod Heb: חנוך / hha-nokh (mas); **Definition:** Immersed in activity for a specific task. [AHLB: n/a / Strong's: n/a] **Concordance:** *Used in names only.*

DEW: Anc Heb: 𐤈𐤋 Mod Heb: טל / tal (mas); **Definition:** Moisture condensed on the surfaces of cool bodies or objects, especially at night. [AHLB: 1196-A (N) / Strong's: 2919, 2920] **Concordance:** 16:13 16:14

DIE: Anc Heb: 𐤌𐤅𐤕 Mod Heb: מות / mut; **Definition:** To pass from physical life; to pass out of existence; to come to an end through death. The hiphil (causative) form means "kill." [AHLB: 1298-J (V) / Strong's: 4191] **Concordance:** 1:6 1:16 2:23 4:19 4:24 7:18 7:21 8:9 9:4 9:6{2} 9:7 9:19 10:28 11:5 12:30 12:33 14:11 14:12 14:30 16:3{2} 17:3 19:12{2} 20:19 21:12{3} 21:14 21:15{2} 21:16{2} 21:17{2} 21:18 21:20 21:28 21:29{2} 21:34 21:35{2} 21:36 22:1 22:9 22:13 22:18{2} 28:35 28:43 30:20 30:21 31:14{2} 31:15{2} 35:2

DIG: Anc Heb: 𐤊𐤓𐤄 Mod Heb: כרה / ka-rah; **Definition:** To break or loosen earth with an instrument or tool. To bargain in the sense of digging. [AHLB: 1250-H (V) / Strong's: 3735, 3738, 3739] **Concordance:** 21:33

DIG-OUT: Anc Heb: 𐤇𐤐𐤓 Mod Heb: חפר / hha-phar; **Definition:** To dig something out of the ground. To dig into something as if searching. To confuse in the sense of being dug out. [AHLB: 2192 (V) / Strong's: 2658, 2659] **Concordance:** 7:24

DIMINISH: Anc Heb: 𐤇𐤎𐤓 Mod Heb: חסר / hha-sar; **Definition:** To make less or cause to appear less; to lessen the authority, dignity, or reputation of. Be lacking or to decrease. [AHLB: 2187 (V) / Strong's: 2637] **Concordance:** 16:18

DIP: Anc Heb: 𐤈𐤁𐤋 Mod Heb: טבל / ta-val; **Definition:** To plunge or immerse momentarily or partially, as under the surface of a liquid, to moisten, cool, or coat. [AHLB: 2228 (V) / Strong's: 2881] **Concordance:** 12:22

DIRECT: Anc Heb: 𐤑𐤅𐤄 Mod Heb: צוה / tsa-wah; **Definition:** To cause to turn, move, or point undeviatingly or to follow a straight course; give instructions or orders for a path to be taken. [AHLB: 1397-H (V) / Strong's: 6680] **Concordance:** 1:22 4:28 5:6 6:13 7:2 7:6 7:10 7:20 12:28 12:50 16:16 16:24 16:32 16:34 18:23 19:7 23:15 25:22 27:20 29:35 31:6 31:11 32:8 34:4

34:11 34:18 34:32 34:34 35:1 35:4 35:10 35:29 36:1 36:5 36:6 38:22 39:1 39:5 39:7 39:21 39:26 39:29 39:31 39:32 39:42 39:43 40:16 40:19 40:21 40:23 40:25 40:27 40:29 40:32

DIRECTIVE: Anc Heb: 𐤑𐤅𐤌 Mod Heb: מצוה / mits-wah (fem); **Definition:** Serving or intended to guide, govern, or influence; serving to point direction. [AHLB: 1397-H (h¹) / Strong's: 4687] **Concordance:** 15:26 16:28 20:6 24:12

DISCERNMENT: Anc Heb: 𐤕𐤏𐤃 Mod Heb: דעת / da-at (fem); **Definition:** The quality of being able to grasp and comprehend what is obscure. An intimacy with a person, idea or concept. [AHLB: 1085-A (N²) / Strong's: 1847] **Concordance:** 31:3 35:31

DISGUSTING: Anc Heb: 𐤕𐤏𐤁𐤄 Mod Heb: תועבה / to-ey-vah (fem); **Definition:** Something highly distasteful that arouses marked aversion in one. [AHLB: 2897 (g¹) / Strong's: 8441] **Concordance:** 8:22{2}

DISPERSE: Anc Heb: 𐤆𐤓𐤄 Mod Heb: זרה / za-rah; **Definition:** To separate or remove to a distance apart from each other; to diffuse or cause to break into different parts. [AHLB: 1158-H (V) / Strong's: 2219] **Concordance:** 32:20

DISPUTE: Anc Heb: 𐤓𐤉𐤁 Mod Heb: ריב / riv (mas); **Definition:** Bitter, sometimes violent conflict or dissension. [AHLB: 1439-M (N) / Strong's: 7379] **Concordance:** 17:7 23:2 23:3 23:6

DISPUTE: Anc Heb: 𐤓𐤉𐤁 Mod Heb: ריב / riv; Alt Sp: רוב **Definition:** To engage in argument; to dispute or chide another in harassment or trial. [AHLB: 1439-M (V) / Strong's: 7378] **Concordance:** 17:2{2} 21:18

DISSOLVE: Anc Heb: 𐤌𐤅𐤂 Mod Heb: מוג / mug; **Definition:** To loose the bonds of something. To make something disappear. [AHLB: 1279-J (V) / Strong's: 4127] **Concordance:** 15:15

DISTANCE: Anc Heb: 𐤓𐤇𐤅𐤒 Mod Heb: רחוק / ra-hhoq (mas); **Definition:** Separation in space or time. A distant place or time. [AHLB: 2765 (c) / Strong's: 7350] **Concordance:** 2:4 20:18 20:21 24:1

DISTANT: Anc Heb: 𐤏𐤅𐤋𐤌 Mod Heb: עולם / o-lam (mas); **Definition:** A far off place or time. The past or future, as a time hidden from the present. [AHLB: 2544 (g) / Strong's: 5769] **Concordance:** 3:15 12:14 12:17 12:24 14:13 15:18 19:9 21:6 27:21 28:43 29:9 29:28 30:21 31:16 31:17 32:13 40:15

DIVIDE: Anc Heb: 𐤇𐤑𐤄 Mod Heb: חצה / hha-tsah; **Definition:** To separate into two or more parts, areas or groups. To divide in half. [AHLB: 1179-H (V) / Strong's: 2673] **Concordance:** 21:35{2}

DIVIDE-INTO-PIECES: Anc Heb: 𐤍𐤕𐤇 Mod Heb: נתח / na-tahh; **Definition:** To sever or part into sections To distribute or to bestow in parts or shares. [AHLB: 2449 (V) / Strong's: 5408] **Concordance:** 29:17

DO: Anc Heb: 𐤏𐤔𐤄 Mod Heb: עשה / a-sah; **Definition:** To bring to pass; to bring about; to act or make. [AHLB: 1360-H (V) / Strong's: 6213] **Concordance:** 1:17 1:18 1:21 2:4 3:16 3:20 4:15 4:17 4:21 4:30 5:8 5:9{2} 5:15 5:16 6:1 7:6{2} 7:10 7:11 7:20 7:22 8:3 8:9 8:13 8:14 8:20 8:22 8:27 9:5 9:6 10:25 11:10 12:12 12:16{2} 12:28{2} 12:35 12:39 12:47 12:48{2} 12:50{2} 13:8 14:4 14:5 14:11 14:13 14:31 15:11 15:26 16:17 17:4 17:6 17:10 18:1 18:8 18:9 18:14{2} 18:17 18:18 18:20 18:23 18:24 19:4 19:8 20:4 20:6 20:9 20:10 20:11 20:23{2} 20:24 20:25 21:9 21:11 21:31 22:29 23:11 23:12 23:22 23:24 24:3 24:7 25:8 25:9 25:10 25:11 25:13 25:17 25:18{2} 25:19{2} 25:23 25:24 25:25{2} 25:26 25:28 25:29{2} 25:31{2} 25:37 25:39 25:40 26:1{2} 26:4{2} 26:5{2} 26:6 26:7{2} 26:10 26:11 26:14 26:15 26:17 26:18 26:19 26:22 26:23 26:26 26:29 26:31{2} 26:36 26:37 27:1 27:2 27:3{2} 27:4{2} 27:6 27:8{2} 27:9 28:2 28:3 28:4{2} 28:6 28:11 28:13 28:14 28:15{3} 28:22 28:23 28:26 27:27 28:31 28:33 28:36 28:39{2} 28:40{3} 28:42 29:1 29:2 29:35 29:36 29:38 29:39{2} 29:41{2} 30:1{2} 30:3 30:4{2} 30:5 30:18 30:25 30:32 30:35 30:37{2} 30:38 31:4 31:5 31:6 31:11 31:14 31:15{2} 31:16 31:17 32:1 32:4

~ 333 ~

32:8 32:10 32:14 32:20 32:21 32:23 32:28 32:31 32:35{2} 33:5 33:17 34:10{2} 34:17 34:22 35:1 35:2{2} 35:10 35:29 35:32 35:33 35:35{2} 36:1{2} 36:2 36:3 36:4{2} 36:5 36:6 36:7 36:8{3} 36:11{2} 36:12{2} 36:13 36:14{2} 36:17{2} 36:18 36:19 36:20 36:22 36:23 36:24 36:25 36:27 36:28 36:29 36:31 36:33 36:34 36:35{2} 36:36 36:37 37:1 37:2 37:4 37:6 37:7{2} 37:8 37:10 37:11 37:12{2} 37:15 37:16 37:17{2} 37:23 37:24 37:25 37:26 37:27 37:28 37:29 38:1 38:2 38:3{2} 38:4 38:6 38:7 38:8 38:9 38:22 38:24 38:28 38:30 39:1{2} 39:2 39:3 39:4 39:6 39:8 39:9 39:15 39:16 39:19 39:20 39:22 39:24 39:25 39:27 39:30 39:32{2} 39:42 39:43{2} 40:16{2}

DOG: Anc Heb: ⑃⌇Ⴑ Mod Heb: כלב / ke-lev (mas); **Definition:** An unclean four-footed animal. Also meaning contempt or reproach. [AHLB: 2259 (N) / Strong's: 3611] **Concordance:** 11:7 22:30

DOMINATE: Anc Heb: ⌇⊗Ⴑ Mod Heb: שטר / sha-tar; **Definition:** To govern or prevail over as a magistrate; to be in ultimate control; to establish order. [AHLB: 2833 (V) / Strong's: 7860] **Concordance:** 5:6 5:10 5:14 5:15 5:19

DONATION: Anc Heb: ⽏╫⅃⌇Ⴑ Mod Heb: מנחה / min-hhah (fem); **Definition:** The act of making a gift or a free contribution. What is brought to another as a gift. [AHLB: 1307-A (h[1]) / Strong's: 4503, 4504] **Concordance:** 29:41 30:9 40:29

DONKEY: Anc Heb: ⍬ⵁ⌇╫╫ Mod Heb: חמור / hha-mor (mas); **Definition:** A male ass. [AHLB: 2175 (c) / Strong's: 2543, 2565] **Concordance:** 4:20 9:3 13:13 20:17 21:33 22:3 22:8 22:9 23:4 23:5 23:12 34:20

DO-NOT: Anc Heb: ⅃⌇ Mod Heb: אל / al (mas); **Definition:** The negative of an alternative choice. To be without; to not be. [AHLB: 1254-A (N) / Strong's: 408, 409, 3809] **Concordance:** 3:5 5:9 8:25 10:28 12:9 14:13 16:19 16:29 19:15 19:24 20:19 20:20 23:1 23:7 23:21 32:22 33:15 34:3{2} 36:6

DOOR: Anc Heb: †⌇╫ Mod Heb: דלת / de-let (fem); **Definition:** A means of access; usually a swinging or sliding barrier by which an entry is closed and opened. [AHLB: 1081-A (N[2]) / Strong's: 1817] **Concordance:** 21:6

DOORPOST: Anc Heb: ⽏╫⍬╫╫ Mod Heb: מזוזה / me-zu-zah (fem); **Definition:** The supporting frame or single post around a door or gate. [AHLB: 1145-J (k[1]) / Strong's: 4201] **Concordance:** 12:7 12:22 12:23 21:6

DOUBLE: Anc Heb: ⽏⌇Ⴑ╫ Mod Heb: משנה / mish-neh (mas); **Definition:** To make twice as great or as many. As a second or a multiple of two. [AHLB: 1474-H (h) / Strong's: 4932] **Concordance:** 16:5 16:22

DOUBLE-OVER: Anc Heb: ⌇⌇Ⴑ Mod Heb: כפל / ka-phal; **Definition:** To bend at the waist or middle. [AHLB: 2280 (V) / Strong's: 3717] **Concordance:** 26:9 28:16 39:9{2}

DOUGH: Anc Heb: ⌇⊙⌇╫ Mod Heb: בצק / ba-tseyq (mas); **Definition:** A mass of flour and water that rises when yeast is added and is then baked into bread or cakes. [AHLB: 2032 (N) / Strong's: 1217] **Concordance:** 12:34 12:39

DO-WELL: Anc Heb: ⊗⌇ Mod Heb: יטב / ya-tav; **Definition:** To do something necessary; to be good, in the sense of being "functional." [AHLB: 1186-L (V) / Strong's: 3190, 3191] **Concordance:** 1:20 30:7

DRAW: Anc Heb: ⌇⌇Ⴑ╫ Mod Heb: משך / ma-shakh; **Definition:** To pull up or out of a receptacle or place; to draw or pull something out; to prolong in the sense of drawing out time; to draw out a sound from a horn. [AHLB: 2358 (V) / Strong's: 4900] **Concordance:** 12:21 19:13

DRAWING-NEAR: Anc Heb: ⌇Ⴑ⍬⌇ Mod Heb: גושן / go-shen (mas); **Definition:** To come or be brought close. [AHLB: n/a / Strong's: n/a] **Concordance:** *Used in names only.*

DRAW-NEAR: Anc Heb: ᘇᒪᐣ Mod Heb: נגש / na-gash; **Definition:** To bring close to another. [AHLB: 2379 (V) / Strong's: 5066] **Concordance:** 19:15 19:22 20:21 21:6{2} 24:2{2} 24:14 28:43 30:20 32:6 34:30 34:32

DRAW-OUT: Anc Heb: ᐟYᑎ Mod Heb: רוק / ruq; **Definition:** To empty. To arm oneself by unsheathing a sword in the sense of emptying the scabbard. Acting in vain; empty-handed. [AHLB: 1456-J (V) / Strong's: 7324] **Concordance:** 15:9

DRAW-UP: Anc Heb: ᒥᐟᑐ Mod Heb: דלה / da-lah; **Definition:** To bale up. To lift the bucket out of the well for drawing water. [AHLB: 1081-H (V) / Strong's: 1802] **Concordance:** 2:16 2:19{2}

DRINK: Anc Heb: ᕀᐧᒡ Mod Heb: שקה / sha-qah; **Definition:** To swallow liquid, whether of man or of the land. [AHLB: 1479-H (V) / Strong's: 8248] **Concordance:** 2:16 2:17 2:19 32:20

DRIVE: Anc Heb: ᒪᕀᐣ Mod Heb: נהג / na-hag; **Definition:** To set or keep in motion; to press or force into an activity, course, or direction. [AHLB: 1302-G (V) / Strong's: 5090] **Concordance:** 3:1 10:13 14:25

DROP-DOWN: Anc Heb: ᕀᑐᐣ Mod Heb: נתך / na-tak; **Definition:** To pour down, pour out to the ground or into a vessel. To pour out anger to another. [AHLB: 2450 (V) / Strong's: 5413] **Concordance:** 9:33

DRY-GROUND: Anc Heb: ᕀᒡᒥᐠ Mod Heb: יבשה / ya-ba-shah (fem); **Definition:** Land that has become dried, parched or void of water. [AHLB: 1044-L (N^1) / Strong's: 3004] **Concordance:** 4:9 14:16 14:22 14:29 15:19

DRY-LAND: Anc Heb: ᑐᒡᒥᐠ Mod Heb: יבשת / ya-be-shet (fem); **Definition:** An area void of water. [AHLB: 1044-L (N^2) / Strong's: 3006, 3007] **Concordance:** 4:9

DUNG: Anc Heb: ᒡᑎᐩ Mod Heb: פרש / pe-resh (mas); **Definition:** The excrement of animals or humans. Manure or refuse. [AHLB: 2644 (N) / Strong's: 6569] **Concordance:** 29:14

DUST: Anc Heb: ᐟᒬᐤ Mod Heb: אבק / a-vaq (mas); **Definition:** Fine particles of earth or other material that are easily disturbed to create a cloud. [AHLB: 1042-C (N) / Strong's: 80] **Concordance:** 9:9

DWELL: Anc Heb: ᐣᒡᒡ Mod Heb: שכן / sha-khan; **Definition:** To remain for a time; to live as a resident; to stay or sit in one location for an indeterminate duration. [AHLB: 2838 (V) / Strong's: 7931, 7932] **Concordance:** 24:16 25:8 29:45 29:46 40:35

DWELLER: Anc Heb: ᐣᒡᒡ Mod Heb: שכן / she-khen (mas); **Definition:** The resident of a region. Also a habitation, the place of residence. [AHLB: 2838 (N) / Strong's: 7933, 7934] **Concordance:** 3:22 12:4

DWELLING: Anc Heb: ᐣᒡᒡᒧ Mod Heb: משכן / mish-kan (mas); **Definition:** A place of habitation or residence. [AHLB: 2838 (h) / Strong's: 4907, 4908] **Concordance:** 25:9 26:1 26:6 26:7 26:12 26:13 26:15 26:17 26:18 26:20 26:22 26:23 26:26 26:27{2} 26:30 26:35 27:9 27:19 35:11 35:15 35:18 36:8 36:13 36:14 36:20 36:22 36:23 36:25 36:27 36:28 36:31 36:32{2} 38:20 38:21{2} 38:31 39:32 39:33 39:40 40:2 40:5 40:6 40:9 40:17 40:18 40:19 40:21 40:22 40:24 40:28 40:29 40:33 40:34 40:35 40:36 40:38

DYSFUNCTIONAL: Anc Heb: ᐠᑎ Mod Heb: רע / ra (com); **Definition:** Impaired or abnormal action other than that for which a person or thing is intended. Something that does not function within its intended purpose. [AHLB: 1460-A (N) / Strong's: 7451, 7455] **Concordance:** 5:19 10:10 21:8 23:2 32:12{2} 32:14 32:22 33:4

EAR: Anc Heb: ᐣᙾᐤᐧ Mod Heb: אוזן / o-zen (fem); **Definition:** The organ of hearing; so named from its broad shape. [AHLB: 1152-C (g) / Strong's: 241] **Concordance:** 10:2 11:2 17:14 21:6 24:7 29:20{2} 32:2 32:3

EAST: Anc Heb: ᴀᴍ⊤⚬ Mod Heb: קדם / qe-dem (mas); **Definition:** The general direction of sunrise. As in front when facing the rising sun. Also, the ancient past. [AHLB: 2698 (N) / Strong's: 6924] **Concordance:** 27:13 38:13

EAST-WIND: Anc Heb: ᴀᴍ⅃⊤⚬ Mod Heb: קדים / qa-dim (mas); **Definition:** The wind that comes from the east. Toward the east as the origin of the east wind. [AHLB: 2698 (b) / Strong's: 6921] **Concordance:** 10:13{2} 14:21

EAT: Anc Heb: ᴊᗩ Mod Heb: אכל / a-khal; **Definition:** To consume food; to destroy. A devouring of a fire. [AHLB: 1242-C (V) / Strong's: 398, 399] **Concordance:** 2:20 3:2 10:5{2} 10:12 10:15 12:4 12:7 12:8{2} 12:9 12:11{2} 12:15{2} 12:16 12:18 12:19 12:20{2} 12:43 12:44 12:45 12:46 12:48 13:3 13:6 13:7 15:7 16:3 16:8 16:12 16:16 16:18 16:21 16:25 16:32 16:35{2} 18:12 21:28 22:5 22:30 23:11{2} 23:15 24:11 24:17 29:32 29:33{2} 29:34 32:6 34:15 34:18 34:28

EDGE: Anc Heb: ⵯᗽⵗ Mod Heb: פאה / pey-ah (fem); **Definition:** The border or boundary of an object or a region. The thin cutting edge of a blade. [AHLB: 1369-A (N^1) / Strong's: 6285] **Concordance:** 25:26 26:18 26:20 27:9{2} 27:11 27:12 27:13 36:23 36:25 37:13 38:9 38:11 38:12 38:13

EDGING: Anc Heb: ⵗ Mod Heb: גבלות / gav-lut (fem); **Definition:** Furnished with a border or trim. Added to a garment for ornamentation. [AHLB: 2049 (N^3) / Strong's: 1383] **Concordance:** 28:22 39:15

EIGHT: Anc Heb: ⵗ Mod Heb: שמונה / she-mo-nah (mas); שמונה / she-mo-neh (fem); **Definition:** The ordinal number eight. May represent fullness from its connection to root meaning fat or rich. [AHLB: 2850 (c) / Strong's: 8083, 8084] **Concordance:** 7:7{2} 26:2 26:25 36:9 36:30

EIGHTH: Anc Heb: ⵗ Mod Heb: שמיני / she-mi-ni (mas); **Definition:** A cardinal number. [AHLB: 2850 (bf) / Strong's: 8066] **Concordance:** 22:29

EMBROIDER: Anc Heb: ᴀᴍ⚬ Mod Heb: רקם / ra-qam; **Definition:** To decorate with ornamental and colorful needlework. [AHLB: 2796 (V) / Strong's: 7551] **Concordance:** 26:36 27:16 28:39 35:35 36:37 38:18 38:23 39:29

EMERALD: Anc Heb: ⵗ Mod Heb: ברקת / ba-re-qet (fem); **Definition:** Possibly the Emerald, a green variety of Beryl. The Hebrew word is from a root meaning to flash or shimmer, while the Septuagint uses Smaragdos meaning a green stone. Other possible translations are Beryl or Quartz. [AHLB: 2041 (N^2) / Strong's: 1304] **Concordance:** 28:17 39:10

EMINENT: Anc Heb: ⵗ Mod Heb: אדיר / a-dir (mas); **Definition:** What exerts power and status. Someone or something that is wide in authority or majesty. [AHLB: 1089-C (b) / Strong's: 117] **Concordance:** 15:10

EMPTINESS: Anc Heb: ᴀᴍ⚬⅃ᴿ Mod Heb: ריקם / rey-qam (mas); **Definition:** Lack of contents which should be present. Void of contents or purpose. [AHLB: 1456-M (p) / Strong's: 7387] **Concordance:** 3:21 23:15 34:20

ENCOUNTER: Anc Heb: ⵗ Mod Heb: פגש / pa-gash; **Definition:** To meet or come in contact with another person. A meeting between two hostile factions; to engage in conflict with. [AHLB: 2594 (V) / Strong's: 6298] **Concordance:** 4:24 4:27

ENGRAVE: Anc Heb: †ᴿ Mod Heb: חרת / hha-rat; **Definition:** To mark, scratch, or scrape. To chisel or cut figures, letters, or devices on stone or metal. [AHLB: 2212 (V) / Strong's: 2801] **Concordance:** 32:16

ENGRAVER: Anc Heb: ⵗ Mod Heb: חרש / hhe-resh (mas); **Definition:** A sculptor or carver who engraves wood, stone or metal. [AHLB: 2211 (N) / Strong's: 2791, 2796] **Concordance:** 28:11 35:35 38:23

ENGRAVING: Anc Heb: Mod Heb: חרושת / hha-ro-shet (fem); **Definition:** A scratching or carving in stone, metal or wood. [AHLB: 2211 (c^2) / Strong's: 2799] **Concordance:** 31:5{2} 35:33{2}

ENGRAVING-TOOL: Anc Heb: Mod Heb: חרט / hhe-ret (mas); **Definition:** A tool making markings or inscriptions by carving on stone, metal or wood. A stylus for inscribing a clay tablet. [AHLB: 2203 (N) / Strong's: 2747] **Concordance:** 32:4

ENQUIRE: Anc Heb: Mod Heb: שאל / sha-al; **Definition:** To ask about; to search into; to seek to understand what is not known. The hiphil (causative) form means "grant." [AHLB: 1472-D (V) / Strong's: 7592, 7593] **Concordance:** 3:22 11:2 12:35 12:36 13:14 18:7 22:13

ENTANGLED: Anc Heb: Mod Heb: בוך / buk; **Definition:** Twisted together or interwoven in a confused manner. Involved. [AHLB: 1034-J (V) / Strong's: 943] **Concordance:** 14:3

ENTIRELY: Anc Heb: Mod Heb: כליל / ka-lil (mas); **Definition:** A state of being complete. All of it. No missing parts; complete by including everything. [AHLB: 1242-B (b) / Strong's: 3632] **Concordance:** 28:31 39:22

EPHOD: Anc Heb: Mod Heb: אפוד / e-phod (mas); אפודה / e-phu-dah (fem); **Definition:** An apron-like vestment having two shoulder straps and ornamental attachments for securing the breastplate, worn with a waistband by the high priest. [AHLB: 1372-C (c) / Strong's: 642, 646] **Concordance:** 25:7 28:4 28:6 28:8 28:12 28:15 28:25 28:26 28:27{2} 28:28{3} 28:31 29:5{3} 35:9 35:27 39:2 39:5 39:7 39:8 39:18 39:19 39:20{2} 39:21{3} 39:22

EPIDEMIC: Anc Heb: Mod Heb: דבר / de-ver (mas); **Definition:** A wide spread disease effecting man or animal. A pestilence. [AHLB: 2093 (N) / Strong's: 1698] **Concordance:** 5:3 9:3 9:15

ERR: Anc Heb: Mod Heb: חטא / hha-ta; **Definition:** To miss the target, whether a literal target or a goal that is aimed for. The piel (intensive) form means "reconcile." [AHLB: 1170-E (V) / Strong's: 2398] **Concordance:** 9:27 9:34 10:16 20:20 23:33 29:36 32:30 32:31 32:33

ERROR: Anc Heb: Mod Heb: חטאה / hha-ta-a (fem); Alt Sp: חטאת **Definition:** An act or condition of ignorant or imprudent deviation from a code of behavior. A missing of the target in the sense of making a mistake. The sacrifice, which by transference, becomes the sin. [AHLB: 1170-E (N^1) / Strong's: 2401, 2402, 2403] **Concordance:** 5:16 10:17 29:14 29:36 30:10 32:21 32:30{2} 32:31 32:32 32:34 34:7 34:9

ESCAPE: Anc Heb: Mod Heb: פליטה / pe-ley-tah (fem) **Definition:** To get away, especially from confinement. [AHLB: 2609 (b1) / Strong's: 6413] **Concordance:** 10:5

ESTIMATE: Anc Heb: Mod Heb: כסס / ka-sas; **Definition:** To make an approximate count or reckoning. [AHLB: 1245-B (V) / Strong's: 3699] **Concordance:** 12:4

EVENING: Anc Heb: Mod Heb: ערב / e-rev (mas); **Definition:** The latter part and close of the day and the early part of the night. Dark of the evening or dark-skinned people. Also the willow from its dark color. [AHLB: 2907 (N) / Strong's: 6153, 6155] **Concordance:** 12:6 12:18{2} 16:6 16:8 16:12 16:13 18:13 18:14 27:21 29:39 29:41 30:8

EVICTED: Anc Heb: Mod Heb: גרשון / ger-shon (mas); **Definition:** To be removed or thrown from with force. To dispossess, exile, dismiss. [AHLB: n/a / Strong's: n/a] **Concordance:** *Used in names only.*

EVIDENCE: Anc Heb: Mod Heb: עדות / ey-dut (fem); **Definition:** That which proves or disproves something; something that makes plain or clear; an indication or sign. [AHLB: 1349-A (N^3) / Strong's: 5715] **Concordance:** 16:34 25:16 25:21 25:22 26:33 26:34 27:21 30:6{2} 30:26 30:36 31:7 31:18 32:15 34:29 38:21 39:35 40:3 40:5 40:20 40:21

EXCEED: Anc Heb: Mod Heb: עדף / a-raph; **Definition:** Running over, filled beyond capacity. [AHLB: 2529 (V) / Strong's: 5736] **Concordance:** 16:18 16:23 26:12{2} 26:13

EXCEPT: Anc Heb: ⲙⲧⲗⲃ Mod Heb: בילתי / bil-ti (mas); **Definition:** With the exclusion of from the whole. The whole with the exception of one or more. [AHLB: 2021 (ef) / Strong's: 1115] **Concordance:** 8:18 8:25 9:17 20:20 22:19

EXCUSE-ME: Anc Heb: ⲃⲓ Mod Heb: בי / bi (mas); **Definition:** To exact neither punishment nor redress for one's self and interrupting. Used as an introduction for an entreaty or request. [AHLB: 1033-A (N) / Strong's: 994] **Concordance:** 4:10 4:13

EXIST: Anc Heb: ⲃⲏⲏ Mod Heb: היה / ha-yah; **Definition:** To have real being whether material or spiritual; to have breath. [AHLB: 1097-M (V) / Strong's: 1961] **Concordance:** 1:5{2} 1:10 1:21 2:10 2:11 2:22 2:23 3:1 3:12 3:14{2} 3:21 4:3 4:4 4:8 4:9{3} 4:12 4:15 4:16{3} 4:24 5:13 6:7 6:28 7:1 7:9 7:10 7:12 7:19{2} 7:21 8:11 8:12 8:13{2} 8:14 8:18 8:19 9:3 9:9{2} 9:10 9:11 9:18 9:22 9:24{3} 9:26 9:28 9:29 10:6 10:7 10:10 10:13 10:14{2} 10:21 10:22 10:23 11:6{2} 12:4 12:5 12:6 12:13{2} 12:14 12:16 12:25 12:26 12:29 12:30 12:41{2} 12:48 12:49 12:51 13:5 13:9{2} 13:11 13:12 13:14 13:15 13:16 13:17 14:20 14:24 15:2 16:5{2} 16:10 16:13{2} 16:22 16:24 16:26 16:27 17:11 17:12 18:3 18:13 18:16 18:19{2} 18:22 19:5 19:6 19:11 19:15 19:16{3} 19:19 20:3 20:20 21:4 21:22 21:23 21:34 21:36 22:10 22:20 22:23 22:24 22:26 22:29 22:30 23:1 23:2 23:9 23:26 23:29 23:33 24:12 24:18 25:15 25:20{2} 25:27 25:31 25:36 26:3 26:6 26:11 26:13 26:24{4} 26:25 27:1 27:2 27:5 27:7 28:7 28:8 28:16 28:20 28:21{2} 28:28 28:30 28:32{3} 28:35 28:37{2} 28:38{2} 28:42 28:43 29:9 29:26 29:28{2} 29:29 29:37 29:45 30:2 30:4 30:12 30:16 30:21 30:25 30:29 30:31 30:32 30:34 30:36 30:37 32:1 32:19 32:23 32:30 33:7 33:8 33:9 33:22 34:1 34:2 34:12 34:28 34:29 35:2 36:7 36:13 36:18 36:29{2} 36:30 37:9{2} 37:14 37:17 37:22 37:25 38:2 38:24 38:27 39:9 39:21 40:9 40:10 40:15{2} 40:17 40:38

EXISTING: Anc Heb: ⲏ Mod Heb: יה / yah (mas); **Definition:** Set in place. To be fixed with permanence or continuance. To continue in being. [AHLB: n/a / Strong's: n/a] **Concordance:** *Used in names only.*

EXTEND: Anc Heb: ⲏⲟⲧ Mod Heb: נטה / na-tah; **Definition:** To set up camp by stretching out the cover of the tent; to extend or stretch in length. [AHLB: 1308-H (V) / Strong's: 5186] **Concordance:** 6:6 7:5 7:19 8:1 8:2 8:12 8:13 9:22 9:23 10:12 10:13 10:21 10:22 14:16 14:21 14:26 14:27 15:12 23:2{2} 23:6 33:7

EXTREMITY: Anc Heb: ⲏⲟⲙⲟ Mod Heb: קצה / qa-tseh (mas); קצה / qa-tsah (fem); **Definition:** The most distant end of something; the corner or edge. [AHLB: 1432-H (N) / Strong's: 7097, 7098] **Concordance:** 13:20 16:35 19:12 25:18 25:19{3} 26:4 26:5 26:28{2} 27:4 28:7 28:23 28:24 28:25 28:26 36:11 36:12 36:33{2} 37:7 37:8{3} 38:5 39:4 39:16 39:17 39:18 39:19

EYE: Anc Heb: ⲟⲗⲙⲟ Mod Heb: עין / a-yin (fem); **Definition:** The organ of sight or vision that tears when a person weeps. A spring that weeps water out of the ground. [AHLB: 1359-M (N) / Strong's: 5869, 5870] **Concordance:** 3:21 4:30 5:21{2} 7:20{2} 8:22 9:8 10:5 10:15 11:3{3} 12:36 13:9 13:16 14:10 15:26 15:27 17:6 19:11 21:8 21:24{2} 21:26{3} 24:17 33:12 33:13{2} 33:16 33:17 34:9 40:38

EYPHAH: Anc Heb: ⲟⲗⲙⲏ Mod Heb: איפה / ey-phah (fem); **Definition:** A dry standard of measure equal to 3 se'ahs or 10 omers. The same as the liquid measure bath which is about 9 imperial gallons or 40 liters. [AHLB: 1017-M (N[1]) / Strong's: 374] **Concordance:** 16:36

FACE: Anc Heb: ⲏⲙⲟ Mod Heb: פנה / pa-neh (mas); **Definition:** The front part of the human head; outward appearance. One present, in the sense of being in the face of another. Always written in the plural form. [AHLB: 1382-H (N) / Strong's: 3942, 6440] **Concordance:** 1:12 2:15 3:6 3:7 4:3 4:21 6:12 6:30 7:9 7:10{2} 8:16 8:20 9:10 9:11{2} 9:13 9:30 10:3 10:10 10:11 10:14 10:28{2} 10:29 11:10 13:21 13:22 14:2{2} 14:9 14:19{2} 14:25 16:9 16:14 16:33 16:34 17:5 17:6 18:12 19:7 19:18 20:3 20:20 21:1 23:15 23:17 23:20 23:21 23:23 23:27 23:28{2} 23:29 23:30 23:31 25:20{2} 25:30{2} 25:37 26:9 27:21 28:12 28:25 28:27 28:29 28:30{2} 28:35 28:37

28:38 29:10 29:11 29:23 29:24 29:25 29:26 29:42 30:6{2} 30:8 30:16 30:36 32:1 32:5 32:11 32:12 32:20 32:23 32:34 33:2 33:11{2} 33:14 33:15 33:16 33:19{2} 33:20 33:23 34:6 34:11 34:20 34:23 34:24{2} 34:29 34:30 34:33 34:34 34:35{3} 35:13 35:20 36:3 37:9{2} 39:18 39:20 39:36 40:5 40:6 40:23 40:25 40:26

FADE: Anc Heb: ᒉᗱᔓ Mod Heb: נבל / na-val; **Definition:** To degrade a person, action or object. To droop or pass away. To wither away as a leaf. To wear out of strength. To act unproductively. [AHLB: 2369 (V) / Strong's: 5034] **Concordance:** 18:18{2}

FALL: Anc Heb: ᒉᐁᔓ Mod Heb: נפל / na-phal; **Definition:** To leave an erect position suddenly and involuntarily; to descend freely by the force of gravity. [AHLB: 2421 (V) / Strong's: 5307, 5308] **Concordance:** 15:16 19:21 21:18 21:27 21:33 32:28

FALSE: Anc Heb: ᐤᦲᐃ Mod Heb: שקר / she-qer (mas); **Definition:** A deliberate lie. An expression of a non-truth. [AHLB: 2879 (N) / Strong's: 8267] **Concordance:** 5:9 20:16 23:7

FALSENESS: Anc Heb: ᒉᎩᐃ Mod Heb: שוא / sha-weh (com); **Definition:** Words or actions that are not true or are empty. A Deception. Lacking value and content. [AHLB: 1461-J (N) / Strong's: 7723] **Concordance:** 20:7{2} 23:1

FAMILY: Anc Heb: ᏜᐁᦲᎲ Mod Heb: משפחה / mish-pa-hhah (fem); **Definition:** A group of persons of common ancestry. A group of people joined together by certain convictions or common affiliation. [AHLB: 2863 (h^1) / Strong's: 4940] **Concordance:** 6:14 6:15 6:17 6:19 6:24 6:25 12:21

FAT: Anc Heb: ᎲᒉᏜ Mod Heb: חלב / hhe-lev (mas); **Definition:** Animal tissue consisting of cells distended with greasy or oily matter; adipose tissue. The fat of an animal as the choicest part. Also milk; A white fatty liquid secreted by cows, sheep and goats, and used for food or as a source of butter, cheeses, yogurt, etc. [AHLB: 2160 (N) / Strong's: 2459, 2461] **Concordance:** 3:8 3:17 13:5 23:18 23:19 29:13{2} 29:22{3} 33:3 34:26

FATHER: Anc Heb: Ꮂᒉ Mod Heb: אב / av (mas); **Definition:** A man who has begotten a child. The provider and support to the household. The ancestor of a family line. The patron of a profession or art. [AHLB: 1002-A (N) / Strong's: 1, 2] **Concordance:** 2:16 2:18 3:6 3:13 3:15 3:16 4:5 6:14 6:25 10:6{3} 12:3 13:5 13:11 15:2 18:4 20:5 20:12 21:15 21:17 22:16 34:7 40:15

FAT-TAIL: Anc Heb: ᏜᒉᎲᒉ Mod Heb: אליה / al-yah (fem); **Definition:** The fat part of a sheep's rump considered an Eastern delicacy. [AHLB: 1012-A (b^1) / Strong's: 451] **Concordance:** 29:22

FATTEN: Anc Heb: ᒉᐤᎲ Mod Heb: ברא / ba-ra; **Definition:** To make more substantial, fleshy or plump; to fill up. The filling of the earth in Genesis 1 with the sun, moon, plants and animals. The filling of man with breath and the image of God. [AHLB: 1043-E (V) / Strong's: 1254] **Concordance:** 34:10

FEAR: Anc Heb: ᒉᐤᏠ Mod Heb: ירא / ya-ra; **Definition:** To be afraid of; to have a strong emotion caused by anticipation or awareness of danger; to dread what is terrible or revere what is respected. [AHLB: 1227-E (V) / Strong's: 3372] **Concordance:** 1:17 1:21 2:14 3:6 9:20 9:30 14:10 14:13 14:31 15:11 20:20 34:10 34:30

FEARFUL: Anc Heb: ᒉᐤᏠ Mod Heb: ירא / ya-rey (mas); **Definition:** Full of fear or dread. [AHLB: 1227-E (N) / Strong's: 3373] **Concordance:** 18:21

FEARFULNESS: Anc Heb: ᏜᒉᐤᏠ Mod Heb: יראה / yi-rah (fem); **Definition:** Inclined to be afraid. [AHLB: 1227-E (N^1) / Strong's: 3374] **Concordance:** 20:20

FEAST: Anc Heb: ᎲᏠᎲ Mod Heb: חג / hhag (mas); **Definition:** A commemoration of a special event with dancing, rejoicing, and sharing of food. A ceremony of joy and thanksgiving. A festival with a magnificent meal which is shared with a number of guests. [AHLB: 1164-A (N) / Strong's: 2282] **Concordance:** 10:9 12:14 13:6 23:15 23:16{2} 23:18 32:5 34:18 34:22{2} 34:25

FEED: Anc Heb: ⟨glyphs⟩ Mod Heb: רעה / ra-ah; **Definition:** To give food to; to provide feed or pasture to the flock. Commonly used in the participle form meaning a feeder or shepherd. [AHLB: 1453-H (V) / Strong's: 7462] **Concordance:** 2:17 2:19 3:1 34:3

FENCE-AROUND: Anc Heb: ⟨glyphs⟩ Mod Heb: שכך / sa-khak; **Definition:** To surround with a wall of protection or covering. To encompass completely. [AHLB: 1333-B (V) / Strong's: 5526] **Concordance:** 25:20 33:22 37:9 40:3 40:21

FIELD: Anc Heb: ⟨glyphs⟩ Mod Heb: שדה / sa-deh (mas); **Definition:** An open land area free of trees and buildings. A level plot of ground. [AHLB: 1326-H (N) / Strong's: 7704] **Concordance:** 1:14 8:9 9:3 9:19{2} 9:21 9:22 9:25{3} 10:5 10:15 16:25 22:4{3} 22:5 22:30 23:11 23:16{2} 23:29

FIGHT: Anc Heb: ⟨glyphs⟩ Mod Heb: לחם / la-hham; **Definition:** To make war; to battle as to destruction; to attempt to defeat, subdue, or destroy an enemy by blows or weapons. A struggle for victory. [AHLB: 2305 (V) / Strong's: 3898] **Concordance:** 1:10 14:14 14:25 17:8 17:9 17:10

FILL: Anc Heb: ⟨glyphs⟩ Mod Heb: מלא / ma-la; **Definition:** To occupy to the full capacity. The piel (intensive) form means "fulfill." [AHLB: 1288-E (V) / Strong's: 4390, 4391] **Concordance:** 1:7 2:16 7:25 8:17 10:6 15:9 23:26 28:3 28:17 28:41 29:9 29:29 29:33 29:35 31:3 31:5 32:29 35:31 35:33 35:35 39:10 40:34 40:35

FILLING: Anc Heb: ⟨glyphs⟩ Mod Heb: מלוא / me-lo (mas); Alt Sp: מלו **Definition:** An act or instance of filling; something used to fill a cavity, container, or depression. [AHLB: 1288-E (c) / Strong's: 4393] **Concordance:** 9:8 16:32 16:33

FIND: Anc Heb: ⟨glyphs⟩ Mod Heb: מצא / ma-tsa; **Definition:** To come upon, often accidentally; to meet with; to discover and secure through searching. [AHLB: 1294-E (V) / Strong's: 4291, 4672] **Concordance:** 5:11 9:19 12:19 15:22 16:25 16:27 18:8 21:16 22:1 22:3{2} 22:5 22:6 22:7 33:12 33:13{2} 33:16 33:17 34:9 35:23 35:24

FINE: Anc Heb: ⟨glyphs⟩ Mod Heb: ענש / a-nash; **Definition:** A financial penalty made for an offense or damages. [AHLB: 2560 (V) / Strong's: 6064] **Concordance:** 21:22{2}

FINGER: Anc Heb: ⟨glyphs⟩ Mod Heb: אצבע / ets-ba (fem); **Definition:** The extension of the hand. Can be used to point. [AHLB: 2655 (n) / Strong's: 676, 677] **Concordance:** 8:15 29:12 31:18

FINGER-SPAN: Anc Heb: ⟨glyphs⟩ Mod Heb: זרת / ze-ret (fem); **Definition:** The span of the fingers, often used as a measurement. [AHLB: 1158-A (N^2) / Strong's: 2239] **Concordance:** 28:16{2} 39:9{2}

FINISH: Anc Heb: ⟨glyphs⟩ Mod Heb: כלה / ka-lah; **Definition:** To bring to an end; terminate; to complete an action, event. [AHLB: 1242-H (V) / Strong's: 3615] **Concordance:** 5:13 5:14 31:18 32:10 32:12 33:3 33:5 34:33 39:32 40:33

FIRE: Anc Heb: ⟨glyphs⟩ Mod Heb: אש / eysh (fem); **Definition:** The phenomenon of combustion manifested by heat, light and flame. [AHLB: 1021-A (N) / Strong's: 784, 785] **Concordance:** 3:2{2} 9:23 9:24 12:8 12:9 12:10 13:21 13:22 14:24 19:18 22:5 24:17 29:14 29:34 32:20 32:24 35:3 40:38

FIRE-OFFERING: Anc Heb: ⟨glyphs⟩ Mod Heb: אישה / i-sheh (mas); **Definition:** A sacrifice that is placed in a fire as an offering. [AHLB: 1021-H (e) / Strong's: 801] **Concordance:** 29:18 29:25 29:41 30:20

FIRE-PAN: Anc Heb: ⟨glyphs⟩ Mod Heb: מחתה / mahh-tah (fem); **Definition:** A tray for carrying hot coals. [AHLB: 1183-A (a^1) / Strong's: 4289] **Concordance:** 25:38 27:3 37:23 38:3

FIRMNESS: Anc Heb: ⟨glyphs⟩ Mod Heb: אמונה / e-mu-nah (fem); **Definition:** Securely fixed in place. [AHLB: 1290-C (d^1) / Strong's: 530] **Concordance:** 17:12

FIRST: Anc Heb: ᐃᏔᏕᏮ Mod Heb: ריאשון / ri-shon (mas); **Definition:** The head of a time or position. [AHLB: 1458-D (ej) / Strong's: 7223] **Concordance:** 4:8 12:2 12:15{2} 12:16 12:18 34:1{2} 34:4 40:2 40:17

FIRSTBORN: Anc Heb: ᐃᎺᏔᏕᏮ Mod Heb: בכור / be-khor (mas); **Definition:** The firstborn offspring, usually a son, of a man or animal. The prominent one. [AHLB: 2016 (c) / Strong's: 1060] **Concordance:** 4:22 4:23 6:14 11:5{4} 12:12 12:29{4} 13:2 13:13 13:15{4} 22:28 34:20

FIRSTFRUIT: Anc Heb: ᐃᎺᏔᏕᏮ Mod Heb: ביכור / bi-khor (mas); **Definition:** The first gathered fruits of a harvest; the first results of an undertaking. [AHLB: 2016 (ed) / Strong's: 1061] **Concordance:** 23:16 23:19 34:22 34:26

FISH: Anc Heb: ᏔᏔ Mod Heb: דג / dag (mas); דגה / da-gah (fem); Alt Sp: דאג **Definition:** An aquatic animal. Only fish with scales and fins are considered fit for food (clean). [AHLB: 1072-A (N) / Strong's: 1709, 1710] **Concordance:** 7:18 7:21

FISSURE: Anc Heb: ᏔᏤᏕᏮ Mod Heb: נקרה / nik-rah (fem); **Definition:** A division, causing to become two pieces instead of one. A cleft or narrow chasm. [AHLB: 2436 (N^1) / Strong's: 5366] **Concordance:** 33:22

FIST: Anc Heb: ᏔᏤᏕᏮᏮ Mod Heb: אגרוף / eg-roph (mas); **Definition:** Clenched fingers into the palm of the hand. [AHLB: 2088 (nc) / Strong's: 106] **Concordance:** 21:18

FIVE: Anc Heb: ᏔᏤᏕᏮᏮᏮ Mod Heb: חמשה / hha-mi-shah (mas); חמש / hha-meysh (fem); **Definition:** An ordinal number, from the number of fingers on a hand. [AHLB: 2176 (N) / Strong's: 2568, 2572] **Concordance:** 16:1 18:21 18:25 21:37 26:3{2} 26:5{2} 26:6 26:9 26:10{2} 26:11 26:26 26:27{2} 26:37{2} 27:1{2} 27:12 27:13 27:14 27:15 27:18{3} 30:23{3} 30:24 36:10{2} 36:12{2} 36:13 36:16 36:17{2} 36:18 36:31 36:32{2} 36:38{2} 38:1{2} 38:12 38:13 38:14 38:15 38:18 38:25 38:26{2} 38:28

FLAKE-OFF: Anc Heb: ᏔᏤᏕᏮ Mod Heb: חספס / hhas-phas; **Definition:** To scale off particles from an object. [AHLB: **3017** / Strong's: 2636] **Concordance:** 16:14

FLAMING: Anc Heb: ᏔᏤᏕᏮ Mod Heb: חרי / hha-ri (mas); **Definition:** A visible fire, usually used in the sense of a fierce anger. [AHLB: 1181-A (f) / Strong's: 2750] **Concordance:** 11:8

FLANK: Anc Heb: ᏔᏤᏕᏮ Mod Heb: ירכה / yar-khah (fem); **Definition:** The hollow of the loins between the legs. [AHLB: 1448-L (N^1) / Strong's: 3410, 3411] **Concordance:** 26:22 26:23 26:27 36:27 36:28 36:32

FLARE-UP: Anc Heb: ᏔᏤᏕᏮ Mod Heb: חרה / hha-rah; **Definition:** To become suddenly excited or angry; to break out suddenly. Burn with a fierce anger. [AHLB: 1181-H (V) / Strong's: 2734] **Concordance:** 4:14 22:23 32:10 32:11 32:19 32:22

FLASH: Anc Heb: ᏔᏤᏕᏮ Mod Heb: ברק / ba-raq (mas); **Definition:** The bright light shining off the edge of a sword. The bright light of lightning. [AHLB: 2041 (N) / Strong's: 1300] **Concordance:** 19:16

FLAVOR: Anc Heb: ᏔᏤᏕᏮ Mod Heb: טעם / ta-am (mas); **Definition:** The taste of a food or the perception of a person's behavior. [AHLB: 2236 (N) / Strong's: 2940, 2941, 2942] **Concordance:** 16:31

FLAX: Anc Heb: ᏔᏤᏕᏮ Mod Heb: פשתה / pish-teh (fem); **Definition:** A plant in which its fibers are used in manufacturing articles of clothing. Also used to make wicks, cords, and bands. Linseed, linseed oil, and oilcake are useful products of the same plant. [AHLB: 2648 (N^1) / Strong's: 6593, 6594] **Concordance:** 9:31{2}

FLEE: Anc Heb: ᏔᏤᏕᏮ Mod Heb: נוס / nus; **Definition:** To run away, often from danger or evil; to hurry toward a place of safety; to flee to any safe place such as a city or mountain. [AHLB: 1314-J (V) / Strong's: 5127] **Concordance:** 4:3 9:20 14:25 14:27 21:13

FLEE-AWAY: Anc Heb: ⲙⲫⲗⲁ Mod Heb: ברח / ba-rahh; **Definition:** To run away from. [AHLB: 2038 (V) / Strong's: 1272] **Concordance:** 2:15 14:5 26:28 36:33

FLESH: Anc Heb: ⲫⲗⲁ Mod Heb: בשר / ba-sar (fem); **Definition:** The soft parts of a human or animal, composed primarily of skeletal muscle. Skin and muscle or the whole of the person. Meat as food. [AHLB: 2025 (N) / Strong's: 1154, 1320, 1321] **Concordance:** 4:7 12:8 12:46 16:3 16:8 16:12 21:28 22:30 28:42 29:14 29:31 29:32 29:34 30:32

FLINT: Anc Heb: ⲙⲩⳡⳃⲗ Mod Heb: יהלום / ya-ha-lom (mas); **Definition:** Possibly the flint, a form of quartz of a brown, gray or black color. Other possible translations are onyx and diamond. [AHLB: 1104-L (qp) / Strong's: 3095] **Concordance:** 28:18 39:11

FLOCKS: Anc Heb: ⳡⲩⲟⲙ Mod Heb: צון / tson (fem); Alt Sp: צאן **Definition:** Groups of birds or animals assembled or herded together. [AHLB: 1405-J (N) / Strong's: 6629] **Concordance:** 2:16 2:17 2:19 3:1{2} 9:3 10:9 10:24 12:21 12:32 12:38 20:24 21:37 22:29 34:3

FLOUR: Anc Heb: ✝ⳃⲩⳃ Mod Heb: סולת / so-let (fem); **Definition:** Finely ground meal of grain used for making bread. [AHLB: 1334-J (N^2) / Strong's: 5560] **Concordance:** 29:2 29:40

FLOW: Anc Heb: ⳃⲍⳡ Mod Heb: נזל / na-zal; **Definition:** To stream or gush a liquid substance. To run like water. [AHLB: 2387 (V) / Strong's: 5140] **Concordance:** 15:8

FOOD: Anc Heb: ✿ⳃ�ⳃⲩ Mod Heb: אכלה / akh-lah (fem); **Definition:** Something that nourishes, sustains, or supplies. For giving sustenance and making one whole. [AHLB: 1242-C (N^1) / Strong's: 402] **Concordance:** 16:15

FOOT: Anc Heb: ⳃⲗⲁ Mod Heb: רגל / re-gel (fem); **Definition:** The terminal part of the leg upon which the human, animal or object stands. [AHLB: 2749 (N) / Strong's: 7271, 7272] **Concordance:** 3:5 4:25 11:8 12:11 21:24{2} 23:14 24:10 25:26 29:20 30:19 30:21 37:13 40:31

FOOTING: Anc Heb: ⳡⲗⲩ Mod Heb: אדן / e-den (mas); **Definition:** Ground or basis for a firm foundation. That which sustains a stable position. [AHLB: 1083-C (N) / Strong's: 134] **Concordance:** 26:19{3} 26:21{3} 26:25{4} 26:32 26:37 27:10 27:11 27:12 27:14 27:15 27:16 27:17 27:18 35:11 35:17 36:24{3} 36:26{3} 36:30{4} 36:36 36:38 38:10 38:11 38:12 38:14 38:15 38:17 38:19 38:27{4} 38:30 38:31{2} 39:33 39:40 40:18

FOOTSTEP: Anc Heb: ⲙⲟⲟ Mod Heb: פעם / pa-am (fem); **Definition:** A stroke of time as a rhythmic beating of time, one moment after the other. A moment in time. A foot or leg in the sense of stepping. [AHLB: 2623 (N) / Strong's: 6471] **Concordance:** 8:28 9:14 9:27 10:17 23:17 25:12 34:23 34:24 37:3

FORCE: Anc Heb: ⳃⲀⳃⳛ Mod Heb: חיל / hha-yil (mas); **Definition:** The pressure exerted to make a piercing. [AHLB: 1173-M (N) / Strong's: 2428, 2429] **Concordance:** 14:4 14:9 14:17 14:28 15:4 18:21 18:25

FORCEFUL: Anc Heb: ⲟⲁⳛ Mod Heb: חזק / hha-zaq (com); **Definition:** A strong grip on something to refrain or support. Driven with force. Acting with power. [AHLB: 2152 (N) / Strong's: 2389, 2390, 2391] **Concordance:** 3:19 6:1{2} 10:19 13:9 19:16 19:19 32:11

FOREARM: Anc Heb: ✿ⲙⲙⳃⳡ Mod Heb: אמה / am-mah (fem); **Definition:** A linear standard of measure equal to the length of the forearm. [AHLB: 1013-A (N^1) / Strong's: 520] **Concordance:** 25:10{3} 25:17{2} 25:23{3} 26:2{2} 26:8{2} 26:13{2} 26:16{3} 27:1{3} 27:9 27:12 27:13 27:14 27:16 27:18{2} 30:2{3} 36:9{2} 36:15{2} 36:21{3} 37:1{3} 37:6{2} 37:10{3} 37:25{3} 38:1{3} 38:9 38:11 38:12 38:13 38:14 38:15 38:18{2}

FOREFRONT: Anc Heb: ⳃⲩⲙ Mod Heb: מול / mul (mas); **Definition:** In front of or at the head of, in space or time. [AHLB: 1288-J (N) / Strong's: 4136] **Concordance:** 18:19 26:9 28:25 28:27 28:37 34:3 39:18 39:20

FOREHEAD: Anc Heb: ⲙⲟⲙⲙ Mod Heb: מצח / mey-tsahh (mas); **Definition:** The part of the face which extends from the hair on the top of the head to the eyes. Impudence, confidence, or assurance. The seat of boldness of speech and actions. [AHLB: 2350 (N) / Strong's: 4696] Concordance: 28:38{2}

FOREIGN: Anc Heb: ⲗⲥⲁⲗ Mod Heb: נכרי / na-khri (mas); נכריה / na-khri-yah (fem); **Definition:** Situated outside one's own country. Alien in character. A strange person, place or thing as being unrecognized. [AHLB: 2406 (f) / Strong's: 5237] **Concordance:** 2:22 18:3 21:8

FOREIGNER: Anc Heb: ⲗⲥⲁ Mod Heb: נכר / ney-khar (mas); **Definition:** A person belonging to or owing allegiance to a foreign country. [AHLB: 2406 (N) / Strong's: 5235, 5236] Concordance: 12:43

FORESKIN: Anc Heb: ⲣⲟ⳥ Mod Heb: ערלה / ar-lah (fem); **Definition:** A fold of skin that covers the end of the penis. [AHLB: 2577 (N¹) / Strong's: 6190] **Concordance:** 4:25

FORGIVE: Anc Heb: ⲙⳬⲁ Mod Heb: סלח / sa-lahh; **Definition:** To pardon; to overlook an offense and treat the offender as not guilty. [AHLB: 2482 (V) / Strong's: 5545] **Concordance:** 34:9

FORK: Anc Heb: ⲓⳬⲙⲙ Mod Heb: מזלג / maz-leyg (mas); **Definition:** An implement, or tool with multiple prongs or tines. [AHLB: 2122 (a) / Strong's: 4207] **Concordance:** 27:3 38:3

FORTUNE: Anc Heb: ⳬⳬ Mod Heb: גד / gad (mas); **Definition:** A store of material possessions. [AHLB: 1050-A (N) / Strong's: 1409]

FOUND: Anc Heb: ⳬⲁⳬ Mod Heb: יסד / ya-sad; **Definition:** To lay a foundation of a house, place or plan. [AHLB: 1326-L (V) / Strong's: 3245] **Concordance:** 9:18

FOUNDATION: Anc Heb: ⳬⳬⲁ Mod Heb: יסוד / ye-sod (fem); **Definition:** A supporting and level base of a building or structure which lies on or in the ground. [AHLB: 1326-L (c) / Strong's: 3247] **Concordance:** 29:12

FOUR: Anc Heb: ⲟⲙⳬⲁⳬ Mod Heb: ארבעה / ar-ba-ah (mas); ארבע / ar-ba (fem); **Definition:** An ordinal number. [AHLB: 2744 (n) / Strong's: 702, 703, 705] **Concordance:** 12:6 12:18 12:40 12:41 16:35 21:37 24:18{2} 25:12{2} 25:26{3} 25:34 26:2 26:8 26:19 26:21 26:32{2} 27:2 27:4{2} 27:16{2} 28:17 34:28{2} 36:9 36:15 36:24 36:26 36:36{2} 37:3{2} 37:13{3} 37:20 38:2 38:5{2} 38:19{2} 38:29 39:10

FOURTH: Anc Heb: ⳬⲟⳬⲁ Mod Heb: רביעי / re-vi-i (mas); **Definition:** A cardinal number. [AHLB: 2744 (bf) / Strong's: 7243, 7244] **Concordance:** 28:20 29:40 39:13

FOURTH-GENERATION: Anc Heb: ⲟⳬⲁ Mod Heb: ריבע / ri-va (mas); **Definition:** A great-great grandchild, as a descendant of the fourth generation. [AHLB: 2744 (e) / Strong's: 7256] Concordance: 20:5 34:7

FRANKINCENSE: Anc Heb: ⳬⳬⲩⳬⲟ Mod Heb: לבונה / le-vo-nah (fem); **Definition:** A resin or gum that is a residue from the bark of a particular ash or fir tree. Used as incense, perfume, or with an offering. [AHLB: 2303 (c¹) / Strong's: 3828] Concordance: 30:34

FREE: Anc Heb: ⳬⳬⲟⳬⲙ Mod Heb: חפשי / hhaph-shi (mas); **Definition:** Released from bondage or burden of obligation. Emancipation. [AHLB: 2193 (f) / Strong's: 2670] **Concordance:** 21:2 21:5 21:26 21:27

FREE-FLOWING: Anc Heb: ⳬⲟⳬⳬ Mod Heb: דרור / de-ror (fem); **Definition:** To flow without hindrances. [AHLB: 1089-B (c) / Strong's: 1865] **Concordance:** 30:23

FREELY: Anc Heb: ⲙⳬⳬⲙ Mod Heb: חנם / hhi-nam (mas); **Definition:** Having no restrictions. A work or action that is performed without wages or without cause. [AHLB: 1175-A (p) / Strong's: 2600] **Concordance:** 21:2 21:11

FREEWILL-OFFERING: Anc Heb: ⳬⳬⲟⳬ Mod Heb: נדבה / ne-da-vah (fem); **Definition:** A voluntary or spontaneous gift as an offering out of respect or devotion. [AHLB: 2380 (N¹) / Strong's: 5071] Concordance: 35:29 36:3

FRIEND: Anc Heb: ᛏᛦᛪᛉ Mod Heb: רעות / re-ut (fem); **Definition:** A female companion as one who is close. [AHLB: 1453-A (N³) / Strong's: 7468] **Concordance:** 11:2

FROG: Anc Heb: ᛆᛏᛪᛉᛏ Mod Heb: צפרדע / tse-phar-dey-a (mas); **Definition:** A four-legged amphibious animal. [AHLB: n/a / Strong's: 6854] **Concordance:** 7:27 7:28 7:29 8:1 8:2 8:3 8:4 8:5 8:7 8:8 8:9

FROM: Anc Heb: ᛣᛏᛒᛙ Mod Heb: מין / min (mas); Alt Sp: מני **Definition:** A function word indicating a starting point or origin. [AHLB: 1290-A (h) / Strong's: 4480, 4481] **Concordance:** 1:9 1:10 2:7 2:10 2:23{2} 3:8 4:9 4:26 5:8 7:18 7:21 8:4 8:5 8:7 8:9{3} 9:15 9:18 10:5{2} 10:26 12:5{2} 12:7 12:9 12:10{2} 12:22 12:33 12:46{2} 14:12 16:4 16:16 16:19 16:20 16:27 16:32 17:6 18:13 18:14 18:18 19:3 19:14 19:17 19:21 20:22 23:16 25:15 25:19 25:31 25:33 25:35{4} 25:36 26:28 27:2 28:8 29:21 29:22 29:34 30:2 30:19 30:33 30:36{2} 32:1 32:8 32:15 32:28 33:7 34:29 36:33 37:8 37:17 37:19 37:21{4} 37:22 37:25 38:2 39:1 39:5 40:31

FULL-STRENGTH: Anc Heb: ᛉᛦᛏ Mod Heb: תום / tom (mas); **Definition:** Someone or something that is whole or complete. Full in power or force. One who is mature. [AHLB: 1496-J (N) / Strong's: 8537] **STRENGTH:**

FUNCTIONAL: Anc Heb: ᛙᛦᛟ Mod Heb: טוב / tov (com); **Definition:** Fulfilling the action for which a person or thing is specially fitted or used, or for which a thing exists. Something that functions within its intended purpose. Also goods as Items, produce or other essentials needed for survival. [AHLB: 1186-J (N) / Strong's: 2896, 2898] **Concordance:** 2:2 3:8 14:12 18:9 18:17 33:19

FURNACE: Anc Heb: ᛣᛒᛲᛟ Mod Heb: כיבשן / kiv-shan (mas); **Definition:** An enclosed structure in which heat is produced. [AHLB: 2251 (em) / Strong's: 3536] **Concordance:** 9:8 9:10 19:18

GALBANUM: Anc Heb: ᛴᛣᛲᛘ Mod Heb: חלבנה / hhel-be-nah (fem); **Definition:** An odoriferous resin used in incense. A choice ingredient used in the Temple incense or oil. [AHLB: 2160 (m¹) / Strong's: 2464] **Concordance:** 30:34

GARMENT: Anc Heb: ᛏᛓᛘ Mod Heb: בגד / be-ged (mas); **Definition:** An article of clothing for covering. [AHLB: 2004 (N) / Strong's: 899] **Concordance:** 28:2 28:3 28:4{2} 29:5 29:21{4} 29:29 31:10{3} 35:19{3} 35:21 39:1{2} 39:41{3} 40:13

GATE: Anc Heb: ᛉᛪᛒ Mod Heb: שער / sha-ar (mas); **Definition:** The opening in a wall or fence through which livestock or people pass. Can be the gatekeeper. Also sha'ar, a unit of measurement. [AHLB: 2862 (N) / Strong's: 8179, 8651, 8652] **Concordance:** 20:10 27:16 32:26 32:27{2} 35:17 38:15 38:18 38:31 39:40 40:8 40:33

<u>GATHER</u>: Anc Heb: ᛆᛟᛘᛞ Mod Heb: אסף / a-saph; **Definition:** To bring together; to accumulate and place in readiness. [AHLB: 1339-C (V) / Strong's: 622] **Concordance:** 3:16 4:29 9:19 23:10 23:16 32:26

GATHERED-UP: Anc Heb: ᛆᛟ Mod Heb: לק / laq (mas); **Definition:** To bring together. Acquire. [AHLB: n/a / Strong's: n/a] **Concordance:** *Used in names only.*

GATHERING: Anc Heb: ᛆᛙᛘᛞ Mod Heb: אסיף / a-siph (mas); **Definition:** That which has been brought together. [. [AHLB: 1339-C (b) / Strong's: 614] **Concordance:** 23:16 34:22

GENERATION: Anc Heb: ᛉᛦᛏ Mod Heb: דור / dor (mas); **Definition:** A body of living beings constituting a single step in the line of descent from an ancestor. [AHLB: 1089-J (N) / Strong's: 1755, 1859] **Concordance:** 1:6 3:15{2} 12:14 12:17 12:24 12:42 16:32 16:33 17:16{2} 27:21 29:42 30:8 30:10 30:21 30:31 31:13 31:16 40:15

GERAH: Anc Heb: ᛴᛪᛒ Mod Heb: גרה / ge-rah (fem); **Definition:** A dry weight measure equal to a 20th part of a shekel. [AHLB: 1066-A (N¹) / Strong's: 1626] **Concordance:** 30:13

GIRD: Anc Heb: ᵴᵒ⟩⟨ Mod Heb: אפד / a-phad; **Definition:** To pull in closely to the body. To wrap around. To tie on the ephod. [AHLB: 1372-C (V) / Strong's: 640] **Concordance:** 29:5

GIRD-UP: Anc Heb: ᴺ⊓ Mod Heb: חגר / hha-gar; **Definition:** To bind the loose portions of clothing into a belt or sash to prepare to go to war; to be bound with arms for war. [AHLB: 2147 (V) / Strong's: 2296] **Concordance:** 12:11 29:9

GIVE: Anc Heb: ᵞᵗ⟨ Mod Heb: נתן / na-tan; **Definition:** To make a present; to present a gift; to grant, allow or bestow by formal action. [AHLB: 2451 (V) / Strong's: 5414] **Concordance:** 2:9 2:21 3:19 3:21 5:7 5:10 5:16 5:18{2} 5:21 6:4 6:8{2} 7:1 7:4 7:9 9:23 10:25 11:3 12:7 12:23 12:25 12:36 13:5 13:11 16:3 16:8 16:15 16:29{2} 16:33 17:2 18:25 20:12 21:4 21:19 21:22 21:23 21:30 21:32 22:6 22:9 22:16 22:28 22:29 23:27 23:31 24:12 25:12 25:16{2} 25:21{3} 25:26 25:30 26:32 26:33 26:34 26:35 27:5 28:14 28:23 28:24 28:25{2} 28:27 28:30 29:3 29:6 29:12 29:17 29:20 30:6 30:12 30:13 30:14 30:15 30:16 30:18{2} 30:33 30:36 31:6{2} 31:18 32:13 32:24 32:29 33:1 34:33 35:34 36:1 36:2 37:13 39:16 39:17 39:18{2} 39:20 39:25 39:31{2} 40:5 40:6 40:7{2} 40:8 40:18{2} 40:20{2} 40:22 40:30 40:33

GIVE-ADVICE: Anc Heb: ᵒ⟨ᵒᵘ Mod Heb: יעץ / ya-ats; **Definition:** To assist another by providing wise counsel. [AHLB: 1363-L (V) / Strong's: 3272, 3289] **Concordance:** 18:19

GIVE-AN-EAR: Anc Heb: ᵞᵃ⟨ Mod Heb: אזן / a-zan; **Definition:** To pay attention to a voice or sound; to hear with thoughtful attention and obedience. [AHLB: 1152-C (V) / Strong's: 238, 239] **Concordance:** 15:26

GIVEN-THAT: Anc Heb: ⟩ᵘ Mod Heb: כי / ki (mas); **Definition:** Prone or disposed to according to what preceded. A reference to the previous or following context. [AHLB: 1240-A (N) / Strong's: 3588] **Concordance:** 1:10 1:19{2} 1:21 2:2 2:10 2:12 2:22 3:4 3:5 3:6 3:7 3:11{2} 3:12{2} 3:19 3:21 4:1 4:5 4:10 4:14 4:19 4:25 4:31{2} 5:8 5:11 6:1 6:7 7:5 7:9 7:17 7:24 8:6 8:11 8:17 8:18 8:22 9:2 9:11 9:14{2} 9:15 9:29 9:30 9:31 9:32 9:34 10:1 10:2 10:4 10:7 10:9 10:10 10:11 10:26 10:28 12:9 12:15 12:17 12:19 12:25 12:26 12:30 12:33 12:39{2} 12:48 13:3 13:5 13:9 13:11 13:14 13:15 13:16 13:17{2} 13:19 14:4 14:5{2} 14:12 14:13 14:18 14:25 15:1 15:19 15:21 15:23 15:26 16:3 16:6 16:7 16:8 16:9 16:12 16:15 16:25 16:29 17:14 17:16 18:1 18:3 18:4 18:11{2} 18:15 18:16 18:18 19:5 19:11 19:13 19:23 20:5 20:7 20:11 20:20 20:22 20:25 21:2 21:7 21:14 21:18 21:20 21:21 21:22 21:26 21:28 21:33{2} 21:35 21:36 21:37 22:4 22:5 22:6 22:8 22:9 22:13 22:15 22:20 22:22 22:26{3} 23:4 23:5 23:7 23:8 23:9 23:15 23:21{2} 23:22 23:23 23:24 23:31 23:33{2} 29:22 29:28 29:33 29:34 29:46 30:12 31:13{2} 31:14{2} 31:17 32:1{2} 32:7 32:21 32:22 32:23 32:25{2} 32:29 33:3{2} 33:13 33:16 33:17 33:20 34:9 34:10 34:13 34:14{2} 34:18 34:24 34:27 34:29 34:35 40:35 40:38

GLIMMERING: Anc Heb: ᵞᵃᵒⱽ Mod Heb: להבה / leh-ha-vah (fem); Alt Sp: להבהת, לבה / **Definition:** The flash of light from a fire or metal. [AHLB: 1255-G (N[1]) / Strong's: 3827, 3852] **Concordance:** 3:2

GNAT: Anc Heb: ᵞᵘ Mod Heb: כן / keyn (mas); **Definition:** A small flying insect. [AHLB: 1244-A (N) / Strong's: 3654] **Concordance:** 8:12 8:13{2} 8:14{2}

GO-AROUND: Anc Heb: ⊔ᵘᵃ Mod Heb: סבב / sa-vav; **Definition:** To circle completely around something. [AHLB: 1324-B (V) / Strong's: 5437] **Concordance:** 13:18 28:11 39:6 39:13

GOBLET: Anc Heb: ᵞᵇⱽ Mod Heb: אגן / a-nan (mas); **Definition:** A cup for containing liquids. [AHLB: 1060-C (N) / Strong's: 101] **Concordance:** 24:6

GO-DOWN: Anc Heb: ⊓ᵃᵘ Mod Heb: ירד / ya-rad; **Definition:** To go or come lower from a higher place. The hiphil (causative) form means "bring down." [AHLB: 1441-L (V) / Strong's: 3381] **Concordance:** 2:5 3:8 9:19 11:8 15:5 19:11 19:14 19:18 19:20 19:21 19:24 19:25 32:1 32:7 32:15 33:5 33:9 34:5 34:29{2}

GOLD: Anc Heb: ⱳ⚐⚏ Mod Heb: זהב / za-hav (mas); **Definition:** A malleable yellow metallic element that is used especially in coins, jewelry, and dentures. A precious metal. [AHLB: 1140-G (N) / Strong's: 1722, 2091] **Concordance:** 3:22 11:2 12:35 20:23 25:3 25:11{2} 25:12 25:13 25:17 25:18 25:24{2} 25:25 25:26 25:28 25:29 25:31 25:36 25:38 25:39 26:6 26:29{3} 26:32{2} 26:37{2} 28:5 28:6 28:8 28:11 28:13 28:14 28:15 28:20 28:22 28:23 28:24 28:26 28:27 28:33 28:34{2} 28:36 30:3{2} 30:4 30:5 31:4 32:2 32:3 32:24 32:31 35:5 35:22{2} 35:32 36:13 36:34{3} 36:36{2} 36:38 37:2{2} 37:3 37:4 37:6 37:7 37:11{2} 37:12 37:13 37:15 37:16 37:17 37:22 37:23 37:24 37:26{2} 37:27 37:28 38:24{2} 39:2 39:3 39:5 39:6 39:8 39:13 39:15 39:16{2} 39:17 39:19 39:20 39:25 39:30 39:38 40:5 40:26

GO-OUT: Anc Heb: ⅄⌂↶↝ Mod Heb: יצא / ya-tsa; **Definition:** To go, come or issue forth. [AHLB: 1392-L (V) / Strong's: 3318, 3319] **Concordance:** 1:5 2:11 2:13 3:10 3:11 3:12 4:6 4:7 4:14 5:10 5:20 6:6 6:7 6:13 6:26 6:27 7:4 7:5 7:15 8:8 8:14 8:16 8:25 8:26 9:29 9:33 10:6 10:18 11:4 11:8{3} 12:17 12:22 12:31 12:39 12:41 12:42 12:46 12:51 13:3{2} 13:4 13:8 13:9 13:14 13:16 14:8 14:11 15:20 15:22 16:1 16:3 16:4 16:6 16:27 16:29 16:32 17:6 17:9 18:1 18:7 19:1 19:17 20:2 21:2 21:3{2} 21:4 21:5 21:7{2} 21:11 21:22 22:5 23:15 23:16 25:32 25:33 25:35 28:35 29:46 32:11 32:12 32:24 33:7 33:8 34:18 34:34{2} 35:20 37:18 37:19 37:21

GORE: Anc Heb: ⌂⅃⅃⅄ Mod Heb: נגח / na-gahh; **Definition:** To stab with the horns. [AHLB: 2373 (V) / Strong's: 5055] **Concordance:** 21:28 21:31{2} 21:32

GORER: Anc Heb: ⌂⅃⅃⅄ Mod Heb: נגח / na-gahh (mas); **Definition:** An ox that is known to gore with the horns. [AHLB: 2373 (N) / Strong's: 5056] **Concordance:** 21:29 21:36

GO-UP: Anc Heb: ⚐⅃⌐ Mod Heb: עלה / a-lah; **Definition:** To go, come or bring higher. The hiphil (causative) form means "bring up." [AHLB: 1357-H (V) / Strong's: 5924, 5927] **Concordance:** 1:10 2:23 3:8 3:17 7:28 7:29 8:1 8:2 8:3 10:12 10:14 12:38 13:18 13:19 16:13 16:14 17:3 17:10 19:3 19:12 19:13 19:18 19:20 19:23 19:24{2} 20:26 24:1 24:2 24:5 24:9 24:12 24:13 24:15 24:18 25:37 27:20 30:8 30:9 32:1 32:4 32:6 32:7 32:8 32:23 32:30 33:1{2} 33:3 33:5 33:12 33:15 34:2 34:3 34:4 34:24 40:4 40:25 40:29 40:36 40:37{2}

GRACIOUS: Anc Heb: ⅄↶⚏ Mod Heb: חנון / hha-nun (mas); **Definition:** Pleasantly kind, benevolent, and courteous. [AHLB: 1175-B (d) / Strong's: 2587] **Concordance:** 22:26 34:6

GRAIN-STALK: Anc Heb: ⚐↷↝ Mod Heb: קמה / qa-mah (fem); **Definition:** The tall stem of cereal crops. [AHLB: 1427-A (N^1) / Strong's: 7054] **Concordance:** 22:5

GRASP: Anc Heb: ↝⍁⌐↷ Mod Heb: חוזק / hho-zeq (mas); **Definition:** A firm hold or grip. [AHLB: 2152 (g) / Strong's: 2392] **Concordance:** 13:3 13:14 13:16

GRATE: Anc Heb: ⍜⚒⚏↷ Mod Heb: מכבר / mikh-bar (mas); **Definition:** An agricultural device, like a sieve, used to separate the grain form the stem. [AHLB: 2250 (h) / Strong's: 4345] **Concordance:** 27:4 35:16 38:4 38:5 38:30 39:39

GRAVE: Anc Heb: ⍜⌐↷ Mod Heb: קבר / qe-ver (mas); **Definition:** An excavation for the burial of a body. [AHLB: 2696 (N) / Strong's: 6913] **Concordance:** 14:11

GREAT: Anc Heb: ⅃⋎⌐⅃ Mod Heb: גדול / ga-dol (mas); **Definition:** Something with increased size, power or authority. [AHLB: 2054 (c) / Strong's: 1419] **Concordance:** 3:3 6:6 7:4 11:3 11:6 12:30 14:31 15:16 18:11 18:22 32:10 32:11 32:21 32:30 32:31

GREAT-HOUSE: Anc Heb: ⚐⌂⍜⌐⍜ Mod Heb: פרעה / par-o (mas); **Definition:** A word of Egyptian origins. [AHLB: **4016** / Strong's: n/a] **HOUSE:**

GREEN: Anc Heb: ↝⌐⅄ Mod Heb: ירק / ye-req (mas); **Definition:** A color somewhat less yellow than that of fresh growing grass and of that part of the spectrum between blue and yellow. The color of grasses and herbs as thin. [AHLB: 1456-L (N) / Strong's: 3418, 3419] **Concordance:** 10:15

GREEN-GRAIN: Anc Heb: ⲟⲩⲗⲩⲟ Mod Heb: אביב / a-viv (mas); **Definition:** Fresh young stalks of standing grain. Also the name of a month in the Hebrew calendar. [AHLB: 1002-B (b) / Strong's: 24] **Concordance:** 9:31 13:4 23:15 34:18{2}

GRIND: Anc Heb: ⲗⲟⲟ⊗ Mod Heb: טחן / ta-hhan; **Definition:** To reduce to fine particles through abrasion. [AHLB: 2231 (V) / Strong's: 2912] **Concordance:** 32:20

GROANING: Anc Heb: ⲯⲟⲗⲩⲏ Mod Heb: נאקה / ne-a-qah (fem); **Definition:** To voice a deep, inarticulate sound, as of pain, grief, or displeasure. [AHLB: 1318-D (N[1]) / Strong's: 5009] **Concordance:** 2:24 6:5

GROPE: Anc Heb: ⲩⲩⲩⲩⲙ Mod Heb: משש / ma-shash; **Definition:** To feel about blindly or uncertainly in search of something. A groping around in the darkness to find something. [AHLB: 1297-B (V) / Strong's: 4184, 4959] **Concordance:** 10:21

GROUND: Anc Heb: ⲯⲙⲟⲧⲗⲩ Mod Heb: אדמה / a-da-mah (fem); **Definition:** The surface of the earth. From its reddish color. [AHLB: 1082-C (N[1]) / Strong's: 127] **Concordance:** 3:5 8:17 10:6 20:12 20:24 23:19 32:12 33:16 34:26

GROVE: Anc Heb: ⲯⲟⲩⲩⲗⲩ Mod Heb: אשרה / a-shey-rah (fem); **Definition:** An area of planted trees. Trees planted in a straight line. [AHLB: 1480-C (N) / Strong's: 842] **Concordance:** 34:13

GUIDE: Anc Heb: ⲯⲟⲟⲏ Mod Heb: נחה / na-hhah; **Definition:** One who leads or directs another in his way. [AHLB: 1307-H (V) / Strong's: 5148] **Concordance:** 13:17 13:21 15:13 32:34

GULP: Anc Heb: ⲯⳁⲩⲩ Mod Heb: שתה / sha-tah; **Definition:** To drink plentifully; to swallow hurriedly or greedily or in one swallow. [AHLB: 1482-H (V) / Strong's: 8354, 8355] **Concordance:** 7:18 7:21 7:24{2} 15:23 15:24 17:1 17:2 17:6 24:11 32:6 34:28

HABITATION: Anc Heb: ⲯⳁⲨⲟ Mod Heb: עונה / o-nah (fem); **Definition:** A place of residences. An abode. [AHLB: 1359-J (N[1]) / Strong's: 5772] **Concordance:** 21:10

HAILSTONES: Anc Heb: ⲧⲟⲟⲟ Mod Heb: ברד / ba-rad (mas); **Definition:** A precipitation in the form of irregular pellets or balls of ice. [AHLB: 2037 (N) / Strong's: 1259] **Concordance:** 9:18 9:19 9:22 9:23{2} 9:24{2} 9:25{2} 9:26 9:28 9:29 9:33 9:34 10:5 10:12 10:15

HALF: Anc Heb: ⲩⲟⲙⲟ Mod Heb: חצי / hha-tsi (mas); **Definition:** An equal part of something divided into two pieces. [AHLB: 1179-A (f) / Strong's: 2677] **Concordance:** 12:29 24:6{2} 25:10{3} 25:17{2} 25:23 26:12 26:16 27:5 36:21 37:1{3} 37:6{2} 37:10 38:4

HAMMER: Anc Heb: ⲟⲟⲟⲟ Mod Heb: רקע / ra-qa; **Definition:** To beat a malleable metal with a hammer to make thin sheets. [AHLB: 2797 (V) / Strong's: 7554] **Concordance:** 39:3

HAND: Anc Heb: ⲟⲩⲩ Mod Heb: יד / yad (fem); Alt Sp: יך **Definition:** The terminal, functional part of the forelimb. Hand with the ability to work, throw and give thanks. [AHLB: 1211-A (N) / Strong's: 3027, 3028, 3197] **Concordance:** 2:5 2:19 3:8 3:19 3:20 4:2 4:4{2} 4:6{3} 4:7{2} 4:13 4:17 4:20 4:21 5:21 6:1{2} 6:8 7:4 7:5 7:15 7:17 7:19 8:1 8:2 8:13 9:3 9:15 9:22 9:35 10:12 10:21 10:22 10:25 12:11 13:3 13:9{2} 13:14 13:16{2} 14:8 14:16 14:21 14:26 14:27 14:30 14:31 15:9 15:17 15:20 16:3 17:5 17:9 17:11{2} 17:12{3} 17:16 18:9 18:10{3} 19:13 21:13 21:16 21:20 21:24{2} 22:3 22:7 22:10 23:1 23:31 24:11 26:17 26:19{2} 28:41 29:9{2} 29:10 29:15 29:19 29:20 29:25 29:29 29:33 29:35 30:19 30:21 32:4 32:11 32:15 32:19 32:29 34:4 34:29 35:25 35:29 36:22 36:24{2} 38:21 40:31

HAND-SPAN: Anc Heb: ⲟⲟ⊗ Mod Heb: טפח / te-phahh (mas); **Definition:** A linear standard of measure that is equal to the span of the fingers of the hand. [AHLB: 2238 (N) / Strong's: 2947] **Concordance:** 25:25 37:12

HAPPY: Anc Heb: ⲟⲩⲩⲗⲩ Mod Heb: אשר / a-sheyr (mas); **Definition:** A feeling of joy or satisfaction. [AHLB: 1480-C (N) / Strong's: 835]

HARD: Anc Heb: 𐤒𐤔𐤄 Mod Heb: קשה / qa-sheh (fem); **Definition:** Not easily penetrated; resistant to stress; firm; lacking in responsiveness. [AHLB: 1435-H (N) / Strong's: 7186] **Concordance:** 1:14 6:9 18:26 32:9 33:3 33:5 34:9

HARM: Anc Heb: 𐤀𐤎𐤍 Mod Heb: אסון / a-son (mas); **Definition:** Physical or mental damage; injury. The pain from the thorn. [AHLB: 1336-C (c) / Strong's: 611] **Concordance:** 21:22 21:23

HARVEST: Anc Heb: 𐤒𐤑𐤓 Mod Heb: קציר / qa-tsir (mas); **Definition:** The season for gathering agricultural crops. Time when the plants are severed from their roots to be used for seed or food. [AHLB: 2727 (b) / Strong's: 7105] **Concordance:** 23:16 34:21 34:22

HASTE: Anc Heb: 𐤇𐤐𐤆𐤍 Mod Heb: חיפזון / hhi-pha-zon (mas); **Definition:** A hurried action. [AHLB: 2188 (ej) / Strong's: 2649] **Concordance:** 12:11

HATE: Anc Heb: 𐤔𐤍𐤀 Mod Heb: שנא / sa-na; **Definition:** Intense hostility and aversion, usually deriving from fear, anger, or sense of injury; extreme dislike or antipathy. [AHLB: 1336-E (V) / Strong's: 8130, 8131] **Concordance:** 1:10 18:21 20:5 23:5

HAVE-COMPASSION: Anc Heb: 𐤓𐤇𐤌 Mod Heb: רחם / ra-hham; **Definition:** To have a feeling of deep sympathy and sorrow for another who is stricken by misfortune, accompanied by a strong desire to alleviate the suffering. [AHLB: 2762 (V) / Strong's: 7355] **Concordance:** 33:19{2}

HAVE-HORNS: Anc Heb: 𐤒𐤓𐤍 Mod Heb: קרן / qa-ran; **Definition:** One of a pair of bony processes that arise from the head of many animals, sometimes used as a wind instrument. The horn-shaped protrusions of the altar or a musical instrument. [AHLB: 2732 (V) / Strong's: 7160] **Concordance:** 34:29 34:30 34:35

HE: Anc Heb: 𐤄𐤅𐤀 Mod Heb: הוא / hu (mas); **Definition:** The male who is neither speaker nor hearer. [AHLB: 1093-J (N) / Strong's: 1931, 1932] **Concordance:** 1:6 1:10 1:16 2:2 3:5 4:14{2} 4:16{2} 5:6 6:26 6:27 8:18 9:34 10:13 12:2 12:4 12:11 12:16 12:27 12:30 12:42{2} 13:2 13:8 13:17 14:30 16:15{3} 16:23 16:29 16:31 16:36 18:5 18:14 21:3 21:4 21:21 21:29 21:36 22:8 22:14 29:14 29:18{2} 29:21 29:22 29:25 29:28 29:34 30:10 30:32 32:9 32:16 32:22 32:25 32:28 34:3 34:9 34:10 34:14 35:34 39:5

HEAD: Anc Heb: 𐤓𐤀𐤔 Mod Heb: ראש / rosh (mas); Alt Sp: ריש **Definition:** The top of the body. A person in authority or role of leader. The top, beginning or first of something. [AHLB: 1458-D (N) / Strong's: 7217, 7218, 7389] **Concordance:** 6:14 6:25 12:2 12:9 17:9 17:10 18:25 19:20{2} 24:17 26:24 28:32 29:6 29:7 29:10 29:15 29:17 29:19 30:12 30:23 34:2 36:29 36:38 38:17 38:19 38:28

HEADDRESS: Anc Heb: 𐤌𐤂𐤁𐤏𐤕 Mod Heb: מגבעת / mig-ba-at (fem); **Definition:** A bowl shaped covering for the head. A covering for protection. [AHLB: 2051 (hb²) / Strong's: 4021] **Concordance:** 28:40 29:9 39:28

HEAL: Anc Heb: 𐤓𐤐𐤀 Mod Heb: רפא / ra-pha; Alt Sp: רפה **Definition:** To restore to health or wholeness. [AHLB: 1454-E (V) / Strong's: 7495] **Concordance:** 15:26 21:19{2}

HEAP: Anc Heb: 𐤍𐤃 Mod Heb: נד / neyd (mas); **Definition:** A large pile dirt or rubbish. [AHLB: 1303-A (N) / Strong's: 5067] **Concordance:** 15:8

HEAR: Anc Heb: 𐤔𐤌𐤏 Mod Heb: שמע / sha-ma; **Definition:** To perceive or apprehend by the ear; to listen to with attention. [AHLB: 2851 (V) / Strong's: 8085, 8086] **Concordance:** 2:15 2:24 3:7 3:18 4:1 4:8 4:9 4:31 5:2 6:5 6:9 6:12{2} 6:30 7:4 7:13 7:16 7:22 8:11 8:15 9:12 11:9 15:14 15:26{2} 16:7 16:8 16:9 16:12 16:20 18:1 18:19 18:24 19:5{2} 19:9 20:19 22:22{2} 22:26 23:13 23:21 23:22{2} 24:7 28:35 32:17 32:18 33:4

HEARER: Anc Heb: 𐤔𐤌𐤏𐤅𐤍 Mod Heb: שימעון / shi-mon (mas); **Definition:** One who listens. The one who acts upon what he has heard. [AHLB: n/a / Strong's: n/a] **Concordance:** *Used in names only.*

HEART: Anc Heb: Mod Heb: לב / leyv (mas); **Definition:** Literally, the vital organ which pumps blood, but, also seen as the seat of thought; the mind. [AHLB: 1255-A (N) / Strong's: 1079, 3820, 3821] **Concordance:** 4:14 4:21 7:3 7:13 7:14 7:22 7:23 8:11 8:15 8:28 9:7 9:12 9:14 9:21 9:34 9:35 10:1{2} 10:20 10:27 11:10 14:4 14:8 14:17 15:8 25:2 28:3 28:29 28:30{2} 31:6{2} 35:5 35:10 35:21 35:22 35:25 35:26 35:29 35:34 35:35 36:1 36:2{3} 36:8

HEAVINESS: Anc Heb: Mod Heb: כבדות / ke-vey-dut (fem); **Definition:** A physical or spiritual weight. A sadness or burden. [AHLB: 2246 (N^3) / Strong's: 3517] **Concordance:** 14:25

HEAVY: Anc Heb: Mod Heb: כבד / ka-ved (fem); **Definition:** Having great weight. Something that is weighty. May also be grief or sadness in the sense of heaviness. Also, the liver as the heaviest of the organs. [AHLB: 2246 (N) / Strong's: 3515, 3516] **Concordance:** 4:10{2} 7:14 8:20 9:3 9:18 9:24 10:14 12:38 17:12 18:18 19:16 29:13 29:22

HEIGHT: Anc Heb: Mod Heb: קומה / qo-mah (fem); **Definition:** The highest part or most advanced point; the condition of being tall or high. In the sense of being raised up. [AHLB: 1427-J (N^1) / Strong's: 6967] **Concordance:** 25:10 25:23 27:1 27:18 30:2 37:1 37:10 37:25 38:1 38:18

HELP: Anc Heb: Mod Heb: עזר / e-zer (mas); **Definition:** One that helps. Who comes to assist with a trouble or burden. [AHLB: 2535 (N) / Strong's: 5828] **Concordance:** 18:4

HELP: Anc Heb: Mod Heb: עזר / a-zar; **Definition:** To give assistance or support to. [AHLB: 2535 (V) / Strong's: 5826]

HEM: Anc Heb: Mod Heb: שול / shul (mas); **Definition:** The outer edge of a garment. [AHLB: 1472-J (N) / Strong's: 7757] **Concordance:** 28:33{2} 28:34 39:24 39:25 39:26

HERB: Anc Heb: Mod Heb: עשב / ey-sev (fem); **Definition:** The grasses and plants of the field used for their medicinal, savory, or aromatic qualities. [AHLB: 2561 (N) / Strong's: 6211, 6212] **Concordance:** 9:22 9:25 10:12 10:15{2}

HEWN-STONE: Anc Heb: Mod Heb: גזית / ga-zit (fem); **Definition:** Stones that are sheered or chipped to form flat sides or an object. [AHLB: 1053-A (N^4) / Strong's: 1496] **Concordance:** 20:25

HIDE: Anc Heb: Mod Heb: סתר / sa-tar; Alt Sp: שתר **Definition:** To put out of sight; to conceal from view; to keep secret. Hide or conceal. [AHLB: 2516 (V) / Strong's: 5641, 5642, 8368] **Concordance:** 3:6

HILL: Anc Heb: Mod Heb: הר / har (mas); **Definition:** A rounded natural elevation of land lower than a mountain. [AHLB: 1112-A (N) / Strong's: 2022] **Concordance:** 3:1 3:12 4:27 15:17 18:5 19:2 19:3 19:11 19:12{2} 19:13 19:14 19:16 19:17 19:18{2} 19:20{3} 19:23{2} 20:18 24:4 24:12 24:13 24:15{2} 24:16 24:17 24:18{2} 25:40 26:30 27:8 31:18 32:1 32:12 32:15 32:19 33:6 34:2{2} 34:3{2} 34:4 34:29{2} 34:32

HIRE: Anc Heb: Mod Heb: שכר / sha-khar; **Definition:** Payment for labor or personal services; to engage the personal service of another. [AHLB: 2479 (V) / Strong's: 7936]

HIRELING: Anc Heb: Mod Heb: שכיר / se-khir (mas); **Definition:** One who is hired for service and receives compensation. [AHLB: 2479 (b) / Strong's: 7916] **Concordance:** 12:45 22:14

HIT: Anc Heb: Mod Heb: נכה / na-khah; **Definition:** To deliver a blow by action; to strike with the hand; to clap, kill or harm. [AHLB: 1310-H (V) / Strong's: 5221] **Concordance:** 2:11 2:12 2:13 3:20 5:14 5:16 7:17 7:20 7:25 8:12 8:13 9:15 9:25{2} 9:31 9:32 12:12 12:13 12:29 17:5 17:6 21:12 21:15 21:18 21:19 21:20 21:26 22:1

HIYN: Anc Heb: Mod Heb: הין / hin (mas); **Definition:** A liquid measure equal to about 5 quarts (6 liters). [AHLB: 1106-M (N) / Strong's: 1969] **Concordance:** 29:40{2} 30:24

HOARFROST: Anc Heb: 𐤔𐤟‑𐤀 Mod Heb: כפור / ke-phor (mas); **Definition:** A covering of small ice crystals, formed from frozen water vapor. [AHLB: 2283 (c) / Strong's: 3713] **Concordance:** 16:14

HOLD-A-FEAST: Anc Heb: ⌂⌂ Mod Heb: חגג / hha-gag; **Definition:** The act of performing a celebration. [AHLB: 1164-B (V) / Strong's: 2287] **Concordance:** 5:1 12:14{2} 23:14

HOLLOW-OUT: Anc Heb: 𐤍𐤁 Mod Heb: נבב / na-vav; **Definition:** To form by making something hollow. [AHLB: 1301-B (V) / Strong's: 5014] **Concordance:** 27:8 38:7

HONEY: Anc Heb: 𐤃𐤁𐤔 Mod Heb: דבש / de-vash (mas); **Definition:** A sweet material elaborated out of the nectar of flowers in the honey sac of various bees. Also, dates as a thick, sticky and sweet food. [AHLB: 2094 (N) / Strong's: 1706] **Concordance:** 3:8 3:17 13:5 16:31 33:3

HOOD: Anc Heb: 𐤌𐤎𐤅𐤄 Mod Heb: מסוה / mas-weh (mas); **Definition:** A covering of the entire head and face. [AHLB: 1327-J (a) / Strong's: 4533] **Concordance:** 34:33 34:34 34:35

HOOK: Anc Heb: 𐤒𐤓𐤎 Mod Heb: קרס / qe-res (mas); **Definition:** A straight piece of wood or metal that is bent at one end. [AHLB: 2733 (N) / Strong's: 7165] **Concordance:** 26:6{2} 26:11{2} 26:33 35:11 36:13{2} 36:18 39:33

HOP: Anc Heb: 𐤐𐤎𐤇 Mod Heb: פסח / pa-sahh; **Definition:** To jump from one position to another. Also, to be lame, as one who hops on one leg. [AHLB: 2618 (V) / Strong's: 6452] **Concordance:** 12:13 12:23 12:27

HOPPING: Anc Heb: 𐤐𐤎𐤇 Mod Heb: פסח / pe-sahh (mas); **Definition:** The feast celebrating the "hopping" (usually called "Passover" but more literally means "hop over"). [AHLB: n/a / Strong's: n/a] **Concordance:** Used in names only.

HORDE: Anc Heb: 𐤏𐤓𐤁 Mod Heb: ערוב / a-rov (mas); **Definition:** A large swarm of flies in the sense of a mixture. Also used for a large group of people. [AHLB: 2573 (c) / Strong's: 6157] **Concordance:** 8:17{2} 8:18 8:20{2} 8:25 8:27

HORN: Anc Heb: 𐤒𐤓𐤍 Mod Heb: קרן / qe-ren (fem); **Definition:** One of a pair of bony processes that arise from the head of many animals and used as a wind instrument. The horns of an animal or a musical instrument in the shape of a horn. [AHLB: 2732 (N) / Strong's: 7161, 7162] **Concordance:** 27:2{2} 29:12 30:2 30:3 30:10 37:25 37:26 38:2{2}

HORNET: Anc Heb: 𐤑𐤓𐤏𐤄 Mod Heb: צירעה / tsir-ah (fem); **Definition:** A flying insect with a stinger that is capable of causing serious injury or death to one that is stung. [AHLB: 2691 (e[1]) / Strong's: 6880] **Concordance:** 23:28

HORSE: Anc Heb: 𐤎𐤅𐤎 Mod Heb: סוס / sus (mas); **Definition:** A domesticated animal used as a beast of burden, a draft animal or for riding. [AHLB: 1337-J (N) / Strong's: 5483] **Concordance:** 9:3 14:9 14:23 15:1 15:19 15:21

HORSEMAN: Anc Heb: 𐤐𐤓𐤔 Mod Heb: פרש / pa-rash (mas); **Definition:** One that rides a horse. [AHLB: 2644 (N) / Strong's: 6571] **Concordance:** 14:9 14:17 14:18 14:23 14:26 14:28 15:19

HOUSE: Anc Heb: 𐤁𐤉𐤕 Mod Heb: בית / beyt (mas); **Definition:** The structure or the family, as a household that resides within the house. A housing. Within. [AHLB: 1045-M (N) / Strong's: 1004, 1005] **Concordance:** 1:1 1:21 2:1 3:22 6:14 7:23 7:28{2} 8:5 8:7 8:9 8:17{2} 8:20{2} 9:19 9:20 10:6{3} 12:3{2} 12:4{2} 12:7 12:13 12:15 12:19 12:22 12:23 12:27{2} 12:29 12:30 12:46{2} 13:3 13:14 16:31 19:3 20:2 20:17 22:6 22:7 23:19 25:11 25:27 26:29 26:33 28:26 30:4 34:26 36:34 37:2 37:14 37:27 38:5 39:19 40:38

HOW: Anc Heb: 𐤀𐤉𐤊 Mod Heb: איך / eykh (mas); Alt Sp: איכה **Definition:** In what way or manner; by what means. [AHLB: 1010-A (N) / Strong's: 349] **Concordance:** 6:12 6:30

HOW-LONG: Anc Heb: 𐤌𐤕𐤉 Mod Heb: מתי / ma-tai (mas); **Definition:** An unknown duration of time. [AHLB: 1298-A (f) / Strong's: 4970] **Concordance:** 8:5 10:3 10:7

HUMAN: Anc Heb: ᵐᵃᵈᵃᵐ Mod Heb: אדם / a-dam (mas); **Definition:** Of, relating to, or characteristic of man. The first man. All of mankind as the descendants of the first man. [AHLB: 1082-C (N) / Strong's: 120] **Concordance:** 4:11 8:13 8:14 9:9 9:10 9:19 9:22 9:25 12:12 13:2 13:13 13:15 30:32 33:20

HUNDRED: Anc Heb: ᵐᵉʸᵃ Mod Heb: מאה / mey-ah (fem); Alt Sp: מאיה **Definition:** A specific number but also a large amount without any reference to a specific number. [AHLB: 1277-A (N^1) / Strong's: 3967, 3969] **Concordance:** 6:16 6:18 6:20 12:37 12:40 12:41 14:7 18:21 18:25 27:9 27:11 27:18 30:23{3} 30:24 38:9 38:11 38:24 38:25{2} 38:26{2} 38:27{3} 38:28 38:29

HUNGER: Anc Heb: ᵃⁿᵃ Mod Heb: רעב / ra-eyv (mas); **Definition:** A craving or urgent need for food. [AHLB: 2777 (N) / Strong's: 7457, 7458] **Concordance:** 16:3

HURRY: Anc Heb: ᵐᵃʰᵃʳ Mod Heb: מהר / ma-har; **Definition:** To carry or cause to go with haste. [AHLB: 1296-G (V) / Strong's: 4116, 4117] **Concordance:** 2:18 10:16 12:33 22:15{2} 34:8

HYSSOP: Anc Heb: ᵉʸᶻᵒᵛ Mod Heb: אזוב / ey-zov (mas); **Definition:** An aromatic herb whose twigs were used in ceremonial sprinkling. [AHLB: 1140-C (c) / Strong's: 231] **Concordance:** 12:22

I: Anc Heb: ᵃⁿⁱ Mod Heb: אני / a-ni (com); Alt Sp: אנוכי **Definition:** A person aware of possessing a personal identity in self-reference. [AHLB: n/a / Strong's: 576, 589, 595] **Concordance:** 2:9 3:6 3:11 3:12 3:13 3:19 4:10{2} 4:11 4:12 4:15 4:21 4:23 6:2 6:5 6:6 6:7 6:8 6:12 6:29{2} 6:30 7:3 7:5 7:17{2} 7:27 8:18 8:24 8:25 9:14 9:27 10:1 10:2 11:4 12:12 13:15 14:4 14:17 14:18 15:26 16:12 17:9 18:6 19:9 20:2 20:5 22:26 23:20 25:9 29:46{2} 31:6 31:13 32:18 33:16{2} 33:19 34:10{2} 34:11

IF: Anc Heb: ᵃⁱᵐ Mod Heb: אים / im (mas); **Definition:** Allowing that; on condition that. A desire to bind two ideas together. [AHLB: 1013-M (N) / Strong's: 518] **Concordance:** 1:16{2} 4:8 4:9 7:27 8:17 9:2 10:4 12:4 12:9 13:13 15:26 16:4 17:7 18:23 19:5 19:13{2} 20:25 21:3{2} 21:4 21:5 21:8 21:9 21:10 21:11 21:19 21:21 21:23 21:27 21:29 21:30 21:32 22:1 22:2{2} 22:3 22:6 22:7{2} 22:10 22:11 22:12 22:14{2} 22:16 22:22{2} 22:24 22:25 23:22 29:34 32:32{2} 33:13 33:15 34:9 34:20 40:37

IMMIGRANT: Anc Heb: ᵖᵉˡᵉˢʰᵉᵗ Mod Heb: פלשת / pe-le-shet (fem); **Definition:** Someone from outside of the homeland. Someone who migrated from another land or country. [AHLB: n/a / Strong's: n/a] **Concordance:** *Used in names only.*

INCENSE: Anc Heb: ᵠᵉᵗᵒʳᵉᵗ Mod Heb: קטורת / qe-to-ret (fem); **Definition:** Usually made of several spices and or fruits, etc. To emit a fragrance. Used at the altar as a sweet savor. [AHLB: 2705 (c^2) / Strong's: 7004] **Concordance:** 25:6 30:1 30:7 30:8 30:9 30:27 30:35 30:37 31:8 31:11 35:8 35:15{2} 35:28 37:25 37:29 39:38 40:5 40:27

INCREASE: Anc Heb: ᵃʳᵃᵛᵃ Mod Heb: רבה / ra-vah; **Definition:** To become progressively greater; to multiply by the production of young; to be abundant of number, strength or authority. [AHLB: 1439-H (V) / Strong's: 7235, 7236] **Concordance:** 1:7 1:10 1:12 1:20 7:3 11:9 16:17 16:18 30:15 32:13

INCREASE-IN-NUMBER: Anc Heb: ᵃʳᵃᵛᵃᵛ Mod Heb: רבב / ra-vav; **Definition:** To become progressively greater; to multiply by the production of young. Multiply. Also, meaning "to shoot" from the abundant arrows of the archer. [AHLB: 1439-B (V) / Strong's: 7231, 7232] **Concordance:** 23:29 36:5

INFECT: Anc Heb: ᵗˢᵃʳᵃ Mod Heb: צרע / tsa-ra; **Definition:** To taint or contaminate with something that affects quality, character, or condition unfavorably. To be infected with leprosy, mildew or mold. [AHLB: 2691 (V) / Strong's: 6879] **Concordance:** 4:6

IN-FRONT: Anc Heb: ⁿᵒᵏʰᵃʰ Mod Heb: נוכח / no-khahh (mas); **Definition:** Before or opposite to something. [AHLB: 2403 (g) / Strong's: 5227] **Concordance:** 14:2 26:35 40:24

INHERIT: Anc Heb: 𐤍𐤄𐤋 Mod Heb: נחל / na-hhal; **Definition:** A passing down of properties, wealth or blessings to the offspring. [AHLB: 2391 (V) / Strong's: 5157] **Concordance:** 23:30 32:13 34:9

INHERITANCE: Anc Heb: 𐤍𐤄𐤋𐤐 Mod Heb: נחלה / na-hha-lah (fem); **Definition:** The acquisition of a possession from past generations. [AHLB: 2391 (N[1]) / Strong's: 5159] **Concordance:** 15:17

INIQUITY: Anc Heb: 𐤏𐤅𐤍 Mod Heb: עוון / a-won (mas); **Definition:** Gross injustice; wickedness. The result of twisted actions. [AHLB: 1512-A (m) / Strong's: 5771] **Concordance:** 20:5 28:38 28:43 34:7{2} 34:9

IN-LAW: Anc Heb: 𐤇𐤕𐤍 Mod Heb: חתן / hha-tan (mas); **Definition:** One related by marriage. [AHLB: 2224 (N) / Strong's: 2860] **Concordance:** 4:25 4:26

INNOCENT: Anc Heb: 𐤍𐤒𐤉 Mod Heb: נקי / na-qi (mas); Alt Sp: נקיא **Definition:** Free from guilt or sin. A state of innocence as an infant. [AHLB: 1318-A (f) / Strong's: 5355] **Concordance:** 21:28 23:7

INSTALLATION: Anc Heb: 𐤌𐤋𐤀 Mod Heb: מלוא / mi-lu (mas); **Definition:** Placed in its proper and permanent position. [AHLB: 1288-E (ed) / Strong's: 4394] **Concordance:** 25:7 29:22 29:26 29:27 29:31 29:34 35:9 35:27

INTELLIGENCE: Anc Heb: 𐤕𐤁𐤍 Mod Heb: תבון / ta-vun (mas); תבונה / te-vu-nah (fem); **Definition:** The ability to learn, reason, plan and build. [AHLB: 1037-J (i) / Strong's: 8394] **Concordance:** 31:3 35:31 36:1

INTENTION: Anc Heb: 𐤏𐤁𐤅𐤓 Mod Heb: עבור / a-vur (mas); **Definition:** As a crossing over from one idea to another. [AHLB: 2520 (d) / Strong's: 5668] **Concordance:** 9:14 9:16{2} 13:8 19:9 20:20{2}

INTERCEDE: Anc Heb: 𐤏𐤕𐤓 Mod Heb: עתר / a-tar; **Definition:** To intervene between parties to reconcile differences. Supplicate on the behalf of another. [AHLB: 2910 (V) / Strong's: 6279] **Concordance:** 8:4 8:5 8:24 8:25 8:26 9:28 10:17 10:18

IN-THIS-WAY: Anc Heb: 𐤊𐤅𐤄 Mod Heb: כוה / ko (mas); Alt Sp: ככוה **Definition:** To do something in a certain manner; a reference to the previous or following context. [AHLB: 1235-A (N) / Strong's: 3541, 3542, 3602] **Concordance:** 2:12{2} 3:14 3:15 4:22 5:1 5:10 5:15 7:16 7:17 7:26 8:16 9:1 9:13 10:3 11:4 12:11 19:3 20:22 29:35 32:27

INVENTION: Anc Heb: 𐤌𐤇𐤔𐤁𐤐 Mod Heb: מחשבה / ma-hha-sha-vah (fem); **Definition:** A product of the imagination. Designing or planning of inventions or plans. [AHLB: 2213 (a[1]) / Strong's: 4284] **Concordance:** 31:4 35:32 35:33 35:35

ISLAND: Anc Heb: 𐤀𐤉 Mod Heb: אי / iy (mas); **Definition:** A tract of land surrounded by water. [AHLB: 1014-A (f) / Strong's: 336, 339]

ISSUE: Anc Heb: 𐤆𐤅𐤁 Mod Heb: זוב / zuv; **Definition:** To flow out; to go, pass, or flow out; emerge. [AHLB: 1140-J (V) / Strong's: 2100] **Concordance:** 3:8 3:17 13:5 33:3

ITEM: Anc Heb: 𐤊𐤋𐤉 Mod Heb: כלי / ke-li (mas); **Definition:** A utensil or implement usually for carrying or storing various materials. [AHLB: 1242-A (f) / Strong's: 3627] **Concordance:** 3:22{2} 11:2{2} 12:35{2} 22:6 25:9 25:39 27:3 27:19 30:27{2} 30:28 31:7 31:8{2} 31:9 35:13 35:14 35:16 35:22 37:16 37:24 38:3{2} 38:30 39:33 39:36 39:37 39:39 39:40 40:9 40:10

JASPER: Anc Heb: 𐤉𐤔𐤐𐤄 Mod Heb: ישפה / yash-phey (fem); **Definition:** Probably the Jasper which may be red, yellow or brown in color. The Septuagint uses Iaspis meaning Jasper. Other possible translations are Ruby, Hyacinth and Emerald. [AHLB: 1477-L (N[1]) / Strong's: 3471] **Concordance:** 28:20 39:13

JEWEL: Anc Heb: 𐤎𐤂𐤋𐤄 Mod Heb: סגולה / se-gu-lah (fem); **Definition:** A precious stone. Something of value. [AHLB: 2465 (d[1]) / Strong's: 5459] **Concordance:** 19:5

JOIN: Anc Heb: ⲫⲧⳑ Mod Heb: לוה / la-wah; **Definition:** To bind together. [AHLB: 1259-J (V) / Strong's: 3867] **Concordance:** 22:24

JOINED-TOGETHER: Anc Heb: ⳗⳑⳡ Mod Heb: שלב / sha-lav; **Definition:** Two becoming one purposely. [AHLB: 2840 (V) / Strong's: 7947] **Concordance:** 26:17 36:22

JOINING: Anc Heb: ⲧⳑ Mod Heb: לו / law (mas); **Definition:** The attachment of objects through binding together. [AHLB: n/a / Strong's: n/a] **Concordance:** Used in names only.

JOINT: Anc Heb: †ⲷⲙⲙⲙ Mod Heb: מחברת / mahh-be-ret (fem); **Definition:** The point at which two opposing objects meet. [AHLB: 2143 (a²) / Strong's: 4225] **Concordance:** 26:4 26:5 28:27 36:11{2} 36:12 36:17 39:20

JOURNEY: Anc Heb: ⲟⳍⳡ Mod Heb: נסע / na-sa; **Definition:** To travel or pass from one place to another; to break camp and begin a journey. [AHLB: 2413 (V) / Strong's: 5265] **Concordance:** 12:37 13:20 14:10 14:15 14:19{2} 15:22 16:1 17:1 19:2 40:36 40:37

JUDGE: Anc Heb: ⳑⳡⳑⲷ Mod Heb: פליל / pa-lil (mas); **Definition:** One who presides over a dispute. [AHLB: 1380-B (b) / Strong's: 6414] **Concordance:** 21:22

JUDGMENT: Anc Heb: ⊗⳽ⳡ Mod Heb: שפט / she-phet (mas); **Definition:** Reward for action, good or bad. An aspect of determining the outcome. [AHLB: 2864 (N) / Strong's: 8201] **Concordance:** 6:6 7:4 12:12

JUG: Anc Heb: ⲫⳍⳡ Mod Heb: קשה / qa-sah (fem); **Definition:** A vessel used for storage of water, grain, etc. [AHLB: 1245-A (N¹) / Strong's: 7184] **Concordance:** 25:29 37:16

JUICE: Anc Heb: ⲟⲙⳡⳡ Mod Heb: דמע / de-ma (mas); **Definition:** The liquid that seeps out of the fruit. [AHLB: 2106 (N) / Strong's: 1831] **Concordance:** 22:28

KEEP-SECRET: Anc Heb: ⳡⲙⳡ Mod Heb: כחד / ka-hhad; **Definition:** To refrain from disclosing information. [AHLB: 2255 (V) / Strong's: 3582] **Concordance:** 9:15 23:23

KEEP-SILENT: Anc Heb: ⳡⲷⲙ Mod Heb: חרש / hha-rash; **Definition:** To stand still and be silent. [AHLB: 2211 (V) / Strong's: 2790] **Concordance:** 14:14

KERMES: Anc Heb: ⲟⳑⳇ† Mod Heb: תולע / to-la (mas); **Definition:** The 'coccus ilicis,' a worm used for medicinal purposes as well as for making a crimson dye. [AHLB: 1269-L (i) / Strong's: 8438] **Concordance:** 16:20 25:4 26:1 26:31 26:36 27:16 28:5 28:6 28:8 28:15 28:33 35:6 35:23 35:25 35:35 36:8 36:35 36:37 38:18 38:23 39:1 39:2 39:3 39:5 39:8 39:24 39:29

KERUV: Anc Heb: ⳡⲫⲷⳡ Mod Heb: כרוב / ke-ruv (mas); **Definition:** A supernatural creature, identified in other Semitic cultures as a winged lion, a Griffin. [AHLB: n/a / Strong's: 3742] **Concordance:** 25:18 25:19{3} 25:20{2} 25:22 26:1 26:31 36:8 36:35 37:7 37:8{3} 37:9{2}

KIDNEY: Anc Heb: ⲫⳑⳡⳡ Mod Heb: כליה / kil-yah (fem); **Definition:** An organ of the body. The seat of emotion in Hebraic thought. [AHLB: 1242-A (f¹) / Strong's: 3629] **Concordance:** 29:13 29:22

KIKAR: Anc Heb: ⲫⳡⳡⳡ Mod Heb: כיכר / ki-kar (fem); **Definition:** A dry standard of measure. Usually rendered as "talent" in most translations, however the word talent is a transliteration of the Greek word talanton (a Greek coin) used in the Greek Septuagint for the Hebrew word "kikar." [AHLB: 2258 (e) / Strong's: 3603] **Concordance:** 25:39 37:24 38:24 38:25 38:27{3} 38:29

KILL: Anc Heb: ⳑⲫⲫ Mod Heb: הרג / ha-rag; **Definition:** To deprive of life; to slaughter. [AHLB: 1440-F (V) / Strong's: 2026] **Concordance:** 2:14{2} 2:15 4:23 5:21 13:15 21:14 22:23 23:7 32:12 32:27

KINDNESS: Anc Heb: ⲧⲫⲙ Mod Heb: חסד / hhe-sed (mas); **Definition:** Of a sympathetic nature; quality or state of being sympathetic. In the sense of bowing the neck to another as a sign of kindness. [AHLB: 2181 (N) / Strong's: 2617] **Concordance:** 15:13 20:6 34:6 34:7

KING: Anc Heb: ꟿ Mod Heb: מֶלֶךְ / me-lekh (mas); **Definition:** The male ruler of a nation or city state. [AHLB: 2340 (N) / Strong's: 4428, 4430, 4431] **Concordance:** 1:8 1:15 1:17 1:18 2:23 3:18 3:19 5:4 6:11 6:13 6:27 6:29 14:5 14:8

KINGDOM: Anc Heb: ꟿ Mod Heb: מַמְלָכָה / mam-la-khah (fem); **Definition:** The area under the control of a king. [AHLB: 2340 (a¹) / Strong's: 4467] **Concordance:** 19:6

KISS: Anc Heb: ꟿ Mod Heb: נשק / na-shaq; **Definition:** To touch together as when kissing with the lips or in battle with weapons. [AHLB: 2445 (V) / Strong's: 5401] **Concordance:** 4:27 18:7

KNEADING-BOWL: Anc Heb: ꟿ Mod Heb: מִשְׁאֶרֶת / mish-eret (fem); **Definition:** The vessel used for mixing bread dough. [AHLB: 1342-D (h²) / Strong's: 4863] **Concordance:** 7:28 12:34

KNEEL: Anc Heb: ꟿ Mod Heb: ברך / ba-rakh; **Definition:** To bend the knee, to kneel in homage or to drink water. The piel (intensive) form means "respect," in the sense of kneeling before another. [AHLB: 2039 (V) / Strong's: 1288, 1289] **Concordance:** 12:32 18:10 20:11 20:24 23:25 39:43

KNOB: Anc Heb: ꟿ Mod Heb: כפתור / kaph-tor (mas); **Definition:** An ornamental round lump or protuberance on the surface or at the end of something. [AHLB: **3025** / Strong's: 3730] **Concordance:** 25:31 25:33{2} 25:34 25:35{3} 25:36 37:17 37:19{2} 37:20 37:21{3} 37:22

KNOLL: Anc Heb: ꟿ Mod Heb: גיבעה / giv-ah (fem); **Definition:** A small round hill. [AHLB: 2051 (N¹) / Strong's: 1389] **Concordance:** 17:9 17:10

KNOW: Anc Heb: ꟿ Mod Heb: ידע / ya-da; **Definition:** To have an intimate and personal understanding; to have an intimate relationship with another person. [AHLB: 1085-L (V) / Strong's: 3045, 3046] **Concordance:** 1:8 2:4 2:14 2:25 3:7 3:19 4:14 5:2 6:3 6:7 7:5 7:17 8:6 8:18 9:14 9:29 9:30 10:2 10:7 10:26 11:7 14:4 14:18 16:6 16:12 16:15 18:11 18:16 18:20 21:36 23:9 29:46 31:13 32:1 32:22 32:23 33:5 33:12{2} 33:13{2} 33:16 33:17 34:29 36:1

LAMP: Anc Heb: ꟿ Mod Heb: נר / ner (mas); **Definition:** A container for an inflammable liquid, as oil, which is burned at a wick as a means of illumination. [AHLB: 1319-A (N) / Strong's: 5216] **Concordance:** 25:37{2} 27:20 30:7 30:8 35:14 37:23 39:37{2} 40:4 40:25

LAMPSTAND: Anc Heb: ꟿ Mod Heb: מנורה / me-no-rah (fem); **Definition:** A platform, sometimes elevated, for holding a lamp. [AHLB: 1319-J (k¹) / Strong's: 4501] **Concordance:** 25:31{2} 25:32{2} 25:33 25:34 25:35 26:35 30:27 31:8 35:14 37:17{2} 37:18{2} 37:20 39:37 40:4 40:24

LAND: Anc Heb: ꟿ Mod Heb: אֶרֶץ / e-rets (fem); **Definition:** The solid part of the earth's surface. The whole of the earth or a region. [AHLB: 1455-C (N) / Strong's: 772, 776, 778] **Concordance:** 1:7 1:10 2:15 2:22 3:8{3} 3:17{2} 4:3{2} 4:20 5:5 5:12 6:1 6:4{2} 6:8 6:11 6:13 6:26 6:28 7:2 7:3 7:4 7:19 7:21 8:1 8:2 8:3 8:10 8:12{2} 8:13{3} 8:18{2} 8:20{2} 8:21 9:5 9:9{2} 9:14 9:15 9:16 9:22{2} 9:23{2} 9:24 9:25 9:26 9:29 9:33 10:5{2} 10:12{3} 10:13{2} 10:14 10:15{4} 10:21 10:22 11:3 11:5 11:6 11:9 11:10 12:1 12:12{2} 12:13 12:17 12:19 12:25 12:29 12:33 12:41 12:42 12:48 12:51 13:5{2} 13:11 13:15 13:17 13:18 14:3 15:12 16:1 16:3 16:6 16:14 16:32 16:35{2} 18:3 18:27 19:1 19:5 20:2 20:4{2} 20:11 22:20 23:9 23:10 23:26 23:29 23:30 23:31 23:33 29:46 31:17 32:1 32:4 32:7 32:8 32:11 32:13 32:23 33:1{2} 33:3 34:8 34:10 34:12 34:15 34:24

LAPIS LAZULI: Anc Heb: ꟿ Mod Heb: סַפִּיר / sa-phir (mas); **Definition:** Probably the Lapis Lazuli which is similar to the color of the Sapphire. While the Hebrew word is saphiyr, the origin of the word Sapphire, the Sapphire was unknown until the Roman period. [AHLB: 2500 (b) / Strong's: 5601] **Concordance:** 24:10 28:18 39:11

LAST: Anc Heb: ᐯᐯᒲᐯ Mod Heb: אחרון / a-hha-ron (mas); **Definition:** In, to or toward the back. To be in back of, at the rear or following after something. [AHLB: 1181-C (j) / Strong's: 314] **Concordance:** 4:8

LATE: Anc Heb: ᐯᐟᐟᐯ Mod Heb: אפיל / a-phil (mas); **Definition:** The latter part of the day, in the sense of night as being dark. The latter part of a season. At or near the end. [AHLB: 1380-C (b) / Strong's: 648] **Concordance:** 9:32

LAUGH: Anc Heb: ᐯᒲᐯ Mod Heb: צחק / tsa-hhaq; **Definition:** To show mirth, joy, or scorn with a smile and chuckle or explosive sound. [AHLB: 2660 (V) / Strong's: 6711] **Concordance:** 32:6

LAY-DOWN: Anc Heb: ᐯᒲᐯ Mod Heb: שכב / sha-khav; **Definition:** To give up; to lie down for copulation, rest or sleep. [AHLB: 2834 (V) / Strong's: 7901] **Concordance:** 22:15 22:18 22:26

LAYING-PLACE: Anc Heb: ᐯᒲᐯ Mod Heb: משכב / mish-kav (mas); **Definition:** The location one lays for rest or sleep. [AHLB: 2834 (h) / Strong's: 4903, 4904] **Concordance:** 7:28 21:18

LAY-IN-WAIT: Anc Heb: ᐯᒲᐯ Mod Heb: צדה / tsa-dah; **Definition:** To hide in ambush. [AHLB: 1395-H (V) / Strong's: 6658] **Concordance:** 21:13

LEAD: Anc Heb: ᐯᒲᐯ Mod Heb: עופרת / o-phe-ret (fem); **Definition:** A very heavy metal that is commonly melted and poured into casts to make statues or other objects. [AHLB: 2565 (g²) / Strong's: 5777] **Concordance:** 15:10

LEAD: Anc Heb: ᐯᒲᐯ Mod Heb: נהל / na-hal; **Definition:** To guide on a way, especially by going in advance. The flock directed to the pasture at the end of the journey. [AHLB: 1311-G (V) / Strong's: 5095] **Concordance:** 15:13

LEADER: Anc Heb: ᐯᒲᐯ Mod Heb: אציל / a-tsil (fem); **Definition:** One who is in charge or in command of others. [AHLB: 1403-C (b) / Strong's: 678] **Concordance:** 24:11

LEAVE: Anc Heb: ᐯᒲᐯ Mod Heb: עזב / a-zav; **Definition:** To go away from; to neglect. [AHLB: 2532 (V) / Strong's: 5800] **Concordance:** 2:20 9:21 23:5{3}

LEAVE-BEHIND: Anc Heb: ᐯᒲᐯ Mod Heb: יתר / ya-tar; **Definition:** To set aside; to retain or hold over to a future time or place; to leave a remainder. [AHLB: 1480-L (V) / Strong's: 3498] **Concordance:** 10:15{2} 12:10{2} 16:19 16:20 28:10 29:34{2} 36:7

LEAVE-IN-PLACE: Anc Heb: ᐯᒲᐯ Mod Heb: יצג / ya-tsag; **Definition:** To put something in a place. [AHLB: 1394-L (V) / Strong's: 3322] **Concordance:** 10:24

LEAVEN: Anc Heb: ᐯᒲᐯ Mod Heb: שאור / se-or (mas); **Definition:** The element that causes bread to rise, such as salt or yeast. [AHLB: 1342-D (c) / Strong's: 7603] **Concordance:** 12:15 12:19 13:7

LEAVENED-BREAD: Anc Heb: ᐯᒲᐯ Mod Heb: חמץ / hha-mets (mas); **Definition:** Dough that has had leaven added to make a sour bread. [AHLB: 2173 (N) / Strong's: 2557] **Concordance:** 12:15 13:3 13:7 23:18 34:25

LEFT-HAND: Anc Heb: ᐯᒲᐯ Mod Heb: שמואל / se-mol (mas); **Definition:** The left hand, side or direction. [AHLB: 3036 / Strong's: 8040] **Concordance:** 14:22 14:29

LEG: Anc Heb: ᐯᒲᐯ Mod Heb: כרע / ka-ra (fem); **Definition:** The appendage from the ankle to the hip and bends at the knee. [AHLB: 2290 (N) / Strong's: 3767] **Concordance:** 12:9 29:17

LENGTH: Anc Heb: ᐯᒲᐯ Mod Heb: אורך / o-rekh (mas); **Definition:** A measured distance or dimension. [AHLB: 1448-C (g) / Strong's: 753] **Concordance:** 25:10 25:17 25:23 26:2 26:8 26:13 26:16 27:1 27:9 27:11{2} 27:18 28:16 30:2 36:9 36:15 36:21 37:1 37:6 37:10 37:25 38:1 38:18 39:9

LET-ALONE: Anc Heb: ᐯᒲᐯ Mod Heb: נטש / na-tash; **Definition:** To be left behind by those who leave. [AHLB: 2401 (V) / Strong's: 5203] **Concordance:** 23:11

LID: Anc Heb: ⲧⲁⲩ≂ш Mod Heb: כפורת / ka-po-ret (fem); **Definition:** The cover of a box or other container. [AHLB: 2283 (c²) / Strong's: 3727] **Concordance:** 25:17 25:18 25:19 25:20{2} 25:21 25:22 26:34 30:6 31:7 35:12 37:6 37:7 37:8 37:9{2} 39:35 40:20

LIEUTENANT: Anc Heb: ⲩⲩ▵∪ш Mod Heb: שליש / sha-lish (mas); Alt Sp: שלוש **Definition:** A leader who is responsible for a group of thirty. [AHLB: 2847 (b) / Strong's: 7991] **Concordance:** 14:7 15:4

LIFTED: Anc Heb: ⲙ🙰ⲁ Mod Heb: רהם / ra-ham (mas); **Definition:** Raised up in position or in exaltation. [AHLB: n/a / Strong's: n/a] **Concordance:** *Used in names only.*

LIFT-UP: Anc Heb: ⳑ🙰ⲁ Mod Heb: נסא / na-sa; Alt Sp: נשא **Definition:** To lift up a burden or load and carry it; to lift up camp and begin a journey; to forgive in the sense of removing the offense. [AHLB: 1314-E (V) / Strong's: 4984, 5375, 5376] **Concordance:** 6:8 10:13 10:17 10:19 12:34 14:10 18:22 19:4 20:7{2} 23:1 23:21 25:14 25:27 25:28 27:7 28:12 28:29 28:30 28:38 28:43 30:4 30:12 32:32 34:7 35:21 35:26 36:2 37:5 37:14 37:15 37:27 38:7

LIGHT: Anc Heb: ⲁⳛⳑ Mod Heb: אור / or (com); **Definition:** The illumination from the sun, moon, stars, fire, candle or other source. [AHLB: 1020-J (N) / Strong's: 216, 217] **Concordance:** 10:23

LIGHT: Anc Heb: ⲁⳛⳑ Mod Heb: אור / or; **Definition:** To shine with an intense light; be or give off light; to be bright. [AHLB: 1020-J (V) / Strong's: 215] **Concordance:** 13:21 14:20 25:37

LIGHT-BRINGER: Anc Heb: ⳑ🙰ⲁⳑ Mod Heb: אהרון / a-ha-ron (mas); **Definition:** One who carries light into the darkness. [AHLB: n/a / Strong's: n/a] **Concordance:** *Used in names only.*

LINEN: Anc Heb: шшш Mod Heb: שש / sheysh (mas); Alt Sp: ששי **Definition:** Fabric made of flax and noted for its strength, coolness and luster. A white cloth. Also, marble from its whiteness. [AHLB: 1481-A (N) / Strong's: 7893, 8336] **Concordance:** 25:4 26:1 26:31 26:36 27:9 27:16 27:18 28:5 28:6 28:8 28:15 28:39{2} 35:6 35:23 35:25 35:35 36:8 36:35 36:37 38:9 38:16 38:18 38:23 39:2 39:3 39:5 39:8 39:27 39:28{3} 39:29

LINGER: Anc Heb: 🙰🙰ⲙ Mod Heb: מהה / ma-hah (mas); **Definition:** To be slow in parting or in quitting something. [AHLB: 1281-B (N) / Strong's: 4102] **Concordance:** 12:39

LINTEL: Anc Heb: ⊂ⳛ◎шшⲙ Mod Heb: משקוף / mash-qoph (mas); **Definition:** A horizontal architectural member supporting the weight above an opening, as a window or a door. [AHLB: 2877 (ac) / Strong's: 4947] **Concordance:** 12:7 12:22 12:23

LIP: Anc Heb: 🙰◎≂≼ Mod Heb: שפה / sa-phah (fem); **Definition:** The rim or edge of the mouth or other opening. Language, as spoken from the lips. [AHLB: 1339-A (N¹) / Strong's: 8193] **Concordance:** 2:3 6:12 6:30 7:15 14:30 26:4{2} 26:10{2} 28:26 28:32 36:11{2} 36:17{2} 39:19 39:23

LIVE: Anc Heb: 🙰ⳛ▥ Mod Heb: חיה / hhay-yah; **Definition:** To be alive and continue alive. Have life within. The revival of life gained from food or other necessity. The piel (intensive) form means "keep alive." [AHLB: 1171-H (V) / Strong's: 2418, 2421, 2425] **Concordance:** 1:16 1:17 1:18 1:22 19:13 22:17 33:20

LIVELY: Anc Heb: 🙰ⳛ▥ Mod Heb: חיה / hhay-eh (mas); **Definition:** Having the vigor of life. [AHLB: 1171-H (N) / Strong's: 2422] **Concordance:** 1:19

LIVESTOCK: Anc Heb: 🙰◎ⲙ Mod Heb: מקנה / miq-neh (mas); **Definition:** Animals kept or raised for use or pleasure. What is purchased or possessed. [AHLB: 1428-H (h) / Strong's: 4735] **Concordance:** 9:3 9:4{2} 9:6{2} 9:7 9:19 9:20 9:21 10:26 12:38 34:19

LIVING: Anc Heb: ⳛⳛ▥ Mod Heb: חי / hhai (mas); חיה / hhai-yah (fem); **Definition:** The quality that distinguishes a vital and functional being from a dead body. Literally the stomach. Also, used idiomatically of living creatures, especially in conjunction with land, ground or field.

[AHLB: 1171-A (N) / Strong's: 2416, 2417] **Concordance:** 1:14 4:18 6:16 6:18 6:20 21:35 22:3 23:11 23:29

LOAD: Anc Heb: 𐤉𐤔𐤌 Mod Heb: משא / ma-sa (mas); **Definition:** Something that is lifted up and carried. The lifting up of the voice in song. [AHLB: 1314-E (a) / Strong's: 4853] **Concordance:** 23:5

LOATHE: Anc Heb: ꞯ𐤓𐤒 Mod Heb: קוץ / quts; **Definition:** To dislike greatly and often with disgust. To be sickened as if pierced by a thorn. [AHLB: 1432-J (V) / Strong's: 6973] **Concordance:** 1:12

LOBE: Anc Heb: 𐤕𐤓𐤕𐤉 Mod Heb: יותרת / yo-te-ret (fem); **Definition:** The extended point of the liver. [AHLB: 1503-L (g²) / Strong's: 3508] **Concordance:** 29:13 29:22

LOCUST: Anc Heb: 𐤄𐤁𐤓𐤀 Mod Heb: ארבה / ar-beh (mas); **Definition:** A six legged insect having short antennae and commonly migrating in swarms that strip the vegetation from large areas. [AHLB: 1439-H (n) / Strong's: 697] **Concordance:** 10:4 10:12 10:13 10:14{2} 10:19{2}

LOOK: Anc Heb: 𐤄𐤍𐤄 Mod Heb: הינה / hi-ney (mas); **Definition:** To ascertain by the use of one's eyes. [AHLB: 1106-H (e) / Strong's: 2009] **Concordance:** 1:9 2:6 2:13 3:2 3:4 3:9 3:13 4:6 4:7 4:14 4:23 5:16 7:15 7:16 7:17 7:27 8:16 8:17 8:25 9:3 9:7 9:18 10:4 14:10 14:17 16:4 16:10 16:14 17:6 19:9 23:20 24:8 24:14 31:6 32:9 32:34 33:21 34:10 34:11 34:30 39:43

LOOK-DOWN: Anc Heb: 𐤐𐤒𐤔 Mod Heb: שקף / sha-qaph; **Definition:** To look out and down as through a window. [AHLB: 2877 (V) / Strong's: 8259] **Concordance:** 14:24

LOOP: Anc Heb: 𐤄𐤀𐤋𐤋 Mod Heb: לולאה / lu-lah (fem); **Definition:** A circular object that is open in the middle. [AHLB: 1265-E (o¹) / Strong's: 3924] **Concordance:** 26:4 26:5{3} 26:10{2} 26:11 36:11 36:12{3} 36:17{2}

LOOSE: Anc Heb: 𐤏𐤓𐤐 Mod Heb: פרע / pa-ra; **Definition:** To uncover, remove or let go. Such as to make naked by removing clothing. To uncover the head. [AHLB: 2641 (V) / Strong's: 6544] **Concordance:** 5:4 32:25{2}

LOOSEN: Anc Heb: 𐤇𐤇𐤆 Mod Heb: זחח / za-hhahh; **Definition:** To make less tight; slacken or relax. To untie or remove. [AHLB: 1146-B (V) / Strong's: 2118] **Concordance:** 28:28 39:21

LORD: Anc Heb: 𐤍𐤃𐤀 Mod Heb: אדון / a-don (mas); **Definition:** The ruler as the foundation to the community. [AHLB: 1083-C (c) / Strong's: 113] **Concordance:** 21:4{2} 21:5 21:6{2} 21:8 21:32 23:17 32:22 34:23

LOST: Anc Heb: 𐤏𐤔𐤓 Mod Heb: רשע / re-sha (mas); **Definition:** Departed from the correct path or way. [AHLB: 2799 (N) / Strong's: 7562, 7563] **Concordance:** 2:13 9:27 23:1 23:7

LOST-THING: Anc Heb: 𐤄𐤃𐤁𐤀 Mod Heb: אבדה / a-vey-dah (fem); **Definition:** An object that is missing or misplaced. [AHLB: 1027-C (N¹) / Strong's: 9] **Concordance:** 22:8

LOUD-NOISE: Anc Heb: 𐤏𐤓 Mod Heb: רוע / rey-a (mas); **Definition:** A loud, confused, constant noise or sound [AHLB: 1460-A (N) / Strong's: 7452] **Concordance:** 32:17

LOVE: Anc Heb: 𐤁𐤄𐤀 Mod Heb: אהב / a-hav; **Definition:** To provide and protect that which is given as a privilege. An intimacy of action and emotion. Strong affection for another arising from personal ties. [AHLB: 1094-C (V) / Strong's: 157] **Concordance:** 20:6 21:5

LOWERED: Anc Heb: 𐤍𐤏𐤍𐤊 Mod Heb: כנען / ke-na-an (mas); **Definition:** Brought down. [AHLB: n/a / Strong's: n/a] **Concordance:** Used in names only.

LOWER-PART: Anc Heb: 𐤉𐤕𐤇𐤕 Mod Heb: תחתי / tahh-ti (mas); **Definition:** The part beneath. A low place. [AHLB: 2892 (f) / Strong's: 8482] **Concordance:** 19:17

LUMINARY: Anc Heb: 𐤓𐤀𐤌 Mod Heb: מאור / ma-or (mas); **Definition:** That which gives off light. [AHLB: 1020-J (a) / Strong's: 3974] **Concordance:** 25:6 27:20 35:8 35:14{2} 35:28 39:37

LYING-DOWN: Anc Heb: 𐤔𐤊𐤁𐤄 Mod Heb: שכבה / she-kha-vah (fem); **Definition:** A laying with another in copulation. Something spread out. [AHLB: 2834 (N¹) / Strong's: 7902] **Concordance:** 16:13 16:14

MAGGOT: Anc Heb: 𐤓𐤌𐤄 Mod Heb: רימה / ri-mah (fem); **Definition:** The larvae of flies. [AHLB: 1450-M (N¹) / Strong's: 7415] **Concordance:** 16:24

MAGICIAN: Anc Heb: 𐤇𐤓𐤈𐤌 Mod Heb: חרטום / hhar-tom (mas); **Definition:** One who performs tricks of illusion and sleight of hand. Writes magical circles and lines. [AHLB: 2203 (qp) / Strong's: 2748, 2749] **Concordance:** 7:11 7:22 8:3 8:14 8:15 9:11{2}

MAGNIFY: Anc Heb: 𐤂𐤃𐤋 Mod Heb: גדל / ga-dal; **Definition:** To increase in size or one's position of honor. [AHLB: 2054 (V) / Strong's: 1431] **Concordance:** 2:10 2:11

MAID: Anc Heb: 𐤔𐤐𐤇𐤄 Mod Heb: שפחה / shiph-hhah (fem); **Definition:** An unmarried young woman. [AHLB: 2863 (e¹) / Strong's: 8198] **Concordance:** 11:5

MAJESTY: Anc Heb: 𐤂𐤀𐤅𐤍 Mod Heb: גאון / ga-on (mas); **Definition:** Elevated to a higher position. Supreme greatness or authority. [AHLB: 1047-A (j) / Strong's: 1347] **Concordance:** 15:7

MAKE: Anc Heb: 𐤐𐤏𐤋 Mod Heb: פעל / pa-al; **Definition:** To perform a task of physical labor. [AHLB: 2622 (V) / Strong's: 6466] **Concordance:** 15:17

MAKE-BRICKS: Anc Heb: 𐤋𐤁𐤍 Mod Heb: לבן / la-van; **Definition:** To shape moist clay or earth into blocks for construction purposes. Can also mean to be "white." [AHLB: 2303 (V) / Strong's: 3835] **Concordance:** 5:7 5:14

MAKE-FAT: Anc Heb: 𐤃𐤔𐤍 Mod Heb: דשן / da-shan; **Definition:** To make or become large with fat tissue. [AHLB: 2115 (V) / Strong's: 1878] **Concordance:** 27:3

MAKE-RESTITUTION: Anc Heb: 𐤔𐤋𐤌 Mod Heb: שלם / sha-lam; **Definition:** To restore or make right through action, payment or restoration to a rightful owner. [AHLB: 2845 (V) / Strong's: 7999, 8000] **Concordance:** 21:34 21:36{2} 21:37 22:2{2} 22:3 22:4 22:5{2} 22:6 22:8 22:10 22:11 22:12 22:13{2} 22:14

MALE: Anc Heb: 𐤆𐤊𐤓 Mod Heb: זכר / za-khar (mas); **Definition:** Being the gender who begets offspring. One who acts and speaks for the family. [AHLB: 2121 (N) / Strong's: 1798, 2145] **Concordance:** 12:5 12:48 13:12 13:15

MALE-KID: Anc Heb: 𐤂𐤃𐤉 Mod Heb: גדי / ge-di (mas); **Definition:** A young goat. [AHLB: 1510-A (f) / Strong's: 1423] **Concordance:** 23:19 34:26

MAN: Anc Heb: 𐤀𐤉𐤔 Mod Heb: איש / ish (mas); **Definition:** An adult male human. As mortal. Also, used to mean "each" in the sense of an individual. [AHLB: 2003 (b) / Strong's: 376, 377] **Concordance:** 1:1 2:1 2:11{2} 2:12 2:13 2:14 2:19 2:20 2:21 4:10 4:19 5:9 7:12 10:7 10:23{2} 11:2 11:3 11:7 12:3 12:4 12:22 12:44 15:3 16:15 16:16{2} 16:18 16:19 16:20 16:21 16:29{2} 17:9 18:7 18:16 18:21{2} 18:25 19:13 21:7 21:12 21:14 21:16 21:18{2} 21:20 21:22 21:26 21:28 21:29 21:33{2} 21:35 21:37 22:4 22:6{2} 22:9 22:13 22:15 22:30 25:2 25:20 28:21 30:12 30:33 30:38 32:1 32:23 32:27{4} 32:28 32:29 33:4 33:8 33:10 33:11 34:3{2} 34:24 35:21 35:22{2} 35:23 35:29 36:1 36:2 36:4{2} 36:6 37:9 39:14

MANY: Anc Heb: 𐤌𐤀𐤃 Mod Heb: מאוד / me-od (mas); **Definition:** A large but indefinite number. An abundance of things (many, much, great), actions (complete, wholly, strong, quick) or character (very). [AHLB: 1004-J (k) / Strong's: 3966] **Concordance:** 1:7{2} 1:20 9:3 9:18 9:24 10:14 10:19 11:3 12:38 14:10 19:16 19:18 19:19

MARKER: Anc Heb: 𐤈𐤅𐤈𐤐𐤄 Mod Heb: טוטפה / to-ta-phah (fem); **Definition:** A mark or emblem used to identify a purpose. [AHLB: 2233 (g¹) / Strong's: 2903] **Concordance:** 13:16

MASTER: Anc Heb: ᴊᴏᴍ Mod Heb: בעל / ba-al (mas); **Definition:** Having chief authority; a workman qualified to teach apprentices. [AHLB: 2027 (N) / Strong's: 1167, 1169] **Concordance:** 21:3 21:22 21:28 21:29{2} 21:34{2} 21:36 22:7 22:10 22:11 22:13 22:14 24:14

MEASURE: Anc Heb: ᴛᴛᴍ Mod Heb: מדד / ma-dad; **Definition:** To determine the length of something by comparing it to a standard of measure. [AHLB: 1280-B (V) / Strong's: 4058] **Concordance:** 16:18

MEASURED-AMOUNT: Anc Heb: ᴌᴡᴛ Mod Heb: תוכן / to-khen (mas); **Definition:** A calculated measurement of weight. [AHLB: 2893 (g) / Strong's: 8506] **Concordance:** 5:18

MEASUREMENT: Anc Heb: ᴘᴛᴍ Mod Heb: מדה / mi-dah (fem); **Definition:** A size or distance that is determined by comparing to a standard of measure. [AHLB: 1280-A (N^1) / Strong's: 4060, 4061] **Concordance:** 26:2 26:8 36:9 36:15

MEET: Anc Heb: ᴘᴀᴏ Mod Heb: קרה / qa-rah; Alt Sp: קרא **Definition:** To come into the presence of; to go to meet another; to have a chance encounter. [AHLB: 1434-H (V) / Strong's: 7122, 7125, 7136] **Concordance:** 1:10 3:18 4:14 4:27 5:3 5:20 7:15 14:27 18:7 19:17

MEETING: Anc Heb: ᴘᴀᴏᴍ Mod Heb: מקרה / miq-rah (mas); **Definition:** A planned or accidental coming together. An encounter. [AHLB: 1434-H (h) / Strong's: 4744, 4745] **Concordance:** 12:16{2}

MELT-AWAY: Anc Heb: ᴀᴀᴍ Mod Heb: מסס / ma-sas; **Definition:** To become liquefied by warmth or heat. Also, the dissolving of the heart through fear or discouragement. [AHLB: 1291-B (V) / Strong's: 4549] **Concordance:** 16:21

MEMORIAL: Anc Heb: ᴀᴡᴌᴢ Mod Heb: זכר / zey-kher (mas); **Definition:** A remembering based on a past event often through an annual festival. [AHLB: 2121 (N) / Strong's: 2143] **Concordance:** 3:15 17:14

MEN: Anc Heb: ᴀᴡᴌᴢ Mod Heb: זכור / za-khur (mas); **Definition:** Male persons. [AHLB: 2121 (d) / Strong's: 2138] **Concordance:** 23:17 34:23

MESSENGER: Anc Heb: ᴡᴌᴊᴍ Mod Heb: מלאך / mal-akh (mas); **Definition:** One who bears a message or runs an errand. Walks for another. [AHLB: 1264-D (a) / Strong's: 4397, 4398] **Concordance:** 3:2 14:19 23:20 23:23 32:34 33:2

METAL-PLATING: Anc Heb: ᴊᴙᴏᴢ Mod Heb: צפוי / tsi-phu-i (mas); **Definition:** Thin layers of metals used to cover materials to give the look of metal. A hammered out sheet of gold used to overlay something. [AHLB: 1155-A (rf) / Strong's: 6826] **Concordance:** 38:17 38:19

MIDDLEMOST: Anc Heb: ᴌᴡᴊᴛ Mod Heb: תיכון / ti-khon (mas); **Definition:** The absolute center. [AHLB: 1494-M (j) / Strong's: 8484] **Concordance:** 26:28 36:33

MIDSECTION: Anc Heb: ᴡᴀᴊ Mod Heb: ירך / ya-rey-akh (fem); **Definition:** The lower abdomen and back. [AHLB: 1448-L (N) / Strong's: 3409] **Concordance:** 1:5 25:31 28:42 32:27 37:17 40:22 40:24

MIDST: Anc Heb: ᴡᴛ Mod Heb: תוך / ta-wek (mas); **Definition:** The center or middle of the whole. [AHLB: 1494-J (N) / Strong's: 8432] **Concordance:** 2:5 3:2 3:4 7:5 9:24 11:4 12:31 12:49 14:16 14:22 14:23 14:27 14:29 15:19 24:16 24:18 25:8 26:28 28:1 28:32 28:33 29:45 29:46 33:11 36:33 39:3{4} 39:23 39:25{2}

MIGHTY-ONE: Anc Heb: ᴊᴌ Mod Heb: אל / el (mas); **Definition:** One who holds authority over others, such as a judge, chief or god. In the sense of being yoked to one another. [AHLB: 1012-A (N) / Strong's: 410] **Concordance:** 6:3 15:2 15:11 20:5 34:6 34:14{2}

MILLSTONE: Anc Heb: ᴘᴀᴀ Mod Heb: רחה / re-hheh (mas); **Definition:** A large circular stone that is revolved on top of another stone to grind grain into flour. [AHLB: 1445-H (N) / Strong's: 7347] **Concordance:** 11:5

MIND: Anc Heb: ⲙⲏⲛ Mod Heb: לבב / ley-vav (mas); **Definition:** Literally, the vital organ which pumps blood, but, also seen as the seat of thought; the mind. [AHLB: 1255-B (N) / Strong's: 3824, 3825] **Concordance:** 14:5

MINISTER: Anc Heb: ⲧⲏⲛ Mod Heb: שרת / sha-rat; **Definition:** To give aid or service; to be in service to another. [AHLB: 2884 (V) / Strong's: 8334] **Concordance:** 24:13 28:35 28:43 29:30 30:20 33:11 35:19 39:1 39:26 39:41

MISERY: Anc Heb: ⲙⲏⲛ Mod Heb: מכאוב / makh-ov (mas); **Definition:** An agony of the heart. [AHLB: 1232-D (ac) / Strong's: 4341] **Concordance:** 3:7

MIX: Anc Heb: ⲗⲗⲙ Mod Heb: בלל / ba-lal; **Definition:** To combine in one mass; to mingle together. [AHLB: 1035-B (V) / Strong's: 1101] **Concordance:** 29:2 29:40

MIXTURE: Anc Heb: ⲙⲏⲛ Mod Heb: ערב / ey-rev (mas); **Definition:** Two or more elements to create one new element. Also the woof in weaving from its mixing of colors. [AHLB: 2573 (N) / Strong's: 6154] **Concordance:** 12:38

MODERATOR: Anc Heb: ⲛⲧ Mod Heb: דן / dan (mas); **Definition:** A judge. One who presides over a dispute. [AHLB: n/a / Strong's: n/a] **Concordance:** *Used in names only.*

MOLDING: Anc Heb: ⲛⲙ Mod Heb: זר / zeyr (mas); **Definition:** Material used to encompass an area or to enhance or beautify. Spread or scattered over a large area. [AHLB: 1158-A (N) / Strong's: 2213] **Concordance:** 25:11 25:24 25:25 30:3 30:4 37:2 37:11 37:12 37:26 37:27

MOMENT: Anc Heb: ⲙⲛⲗ Mod Heb: רגע / re-ga (mas); **Definition:** A single point in time. A wink of the eye. [AHLB: 2752 (N) / Strong's: 7281, 7282] **Concordance:** 33:5

MONUMENT: Anc Heb: ⲙⲛⲧⲗⲙ Mod Heb: מצבה / ma-tsey-vah (fem); **Definition:** A lasting evidence, reminder, or example of someone or something. As standing tall and firm. [AHLB: 2426 (a¹) / Strong's: 4676] **Concordance:** 23:24 24:4 34:13

MOON: Anc Heb: ⲙⲛⲗ Mod Heb: ירח / ye-rey-ahh (mas); **Definition:** The second brightest object in the sky which reflects the sun's light. Also, a month by counting its cycles. [AHLB: 1445-L (N) / Strong's: 3391, 3393, 3394] **Concordance:** 2:2

MORNING: Anc Heb: ⲛⲧⲙ Mod Heb: בוקר / bo-qer (mas); **Definition:** The time from sunrise to noon. Breaking of daylight. [AHLB: 2035 (g) / Strong's: 1242] **Concordance:** 7:15 8:16 9:13 10:13 12:10{2} 12:22 14:24 14:27 16:7 16:8 16:12 16:13 16:19 16:20 16:21{2} 16:23 16:24 18:13 18:14 19:16 23:18 24:4 27:21 29:34 29:39 29:41 30:7{2} 34:2{2} 34:4 34:25 36:3{2}

MORROW: Anc Heb: ⲧⲙⲛⲗⲙ Mod Heb: מחרת / ma-hha-ret (fem); **Definition:** The next day. At a time following. [AHLB: 1181-A (a²) / Strong's: 4283] **Concordance:** 9:6 18:13 32:6 32:30

MORTAR: Anc Heb: ⲙⲛⲧⲙ Mod Heb: חומר / hho-mer (mas); **Definition:** A thick and slimy soil used to join bricks or for making bricks. [AHLB: 2175 (g) / Strong's: 2563] **Concordance:** 1:14

MOTHER: Anc Heb: ⲙⲗ Mod Heb: אם / eym (fem); **Definition:** A female parent. Maternal tenderness or affection. One who fulfills the role of a mother. [AHLB: 1013-A (N) / Strong's: 517] **Concordance:** 2:8 20:12 21:15 21:17 22:29 23:19 34:26

MOURN: Anc Heb: ⲗⲙⲗ Mod Heb: אבל / a-val; **Definition:** To feel or express grief or sorrow. [AHLB: 1035-C (V) / Strong's: 56] **Concordance:** 33:4

MOUTH: Anc Heb: ⲍⲙ Mod Heb: פה / peh (mas); **Definition:** The opening through which food enters the body. Any opening. [AHLB: 1373-A (N) / Strong's: 6310] **Concordance:** 4:10 4:11 4:12 4:15{3} 4:16 12:4 13:9 16:16 16:18 16:21 17:1 17:13 23:13 28:32{3} 34:27 38:21 39:23{3}

MOVE-AWAY: Anc Heb: ⲙⲛⲗⲙ Mod Heb: מוש / mush; **Definition:** To pass from one place or position to another. [AHLB: 1297-J (V) / Strong's: 4185] **Concordance:** 13:22 33:11

MOVING: Anc Heb: ⲙⲛⲗⲙ Mod Heb: מוש / mush (mas); **Definition:** What has passed from one place to another. [AHLB: n/a / Strong's: n/a] **Concordance:** *Used in names only.*

MURDER: Anc Heb: Mod Heb: רצח / ra-tshahh; **Definition:** A killing committed with malice aforethought, characterized by deliberation or premeditation. [AHLB: 2790 (V) / Strong's: 7523] **Concordance:** 20:13

MURMUR: Anc Heb: Mod Heb: לון / lun; **Definition:** To make a low or indistinct sound, esp. Continuously. To complain in a low tone, usually in private. [AHLB: 1451-J (V) / Strong's: 3885] **Concordance:** 15:24 16:2 16:7 16:8 17:3

MURMURING: Anc Heb: Mod Heb: תלונה / te-lu-nah (fem); **Definition:** A continuously low or indistinct sound. A complaining in low tones, usually in private. [AHLB: 1451-J (i^1) / Strong's: 8519] **Concordance:** 16:7 16:8{2} 16:9 16:12

MUSIC: Anc Heb: Mod Heb: זימרת / zim-rat (fem); **Definition:** An art of sound in time that expresses ideas and emotions in significant forms through the elements of rhythm, melody, harmony, and color. [AHLB: 2124 (e^2) / Strong's: 2176] **Concordance:** 15:2

MUSTER: Anc Heb: Mod Heb: צבא / tsa-va; **Definition:** To gather together a group for service, work or war. [AHLB: 1393-E (V) / Strong's: 6633] **Concordance:** 38:8{2}

MUTE: Anc Heb: Mod Heb: אילם / i-leym (mas); **Definition:** Inability to speak. A bound up tongue. [AHLB: 1266-C (e) / Strong's: 483] **Concordance:** 4:11

MYRRH: Anc Heb: Mod Heb: מור / mor (mas); **Definition:** A sweet smelling spice. Used as an exchange due to its monetary value. [AHLB: 1296-J (N) / Strong's: 4753] **Concordance:** 30:23

NAKEDNESS: Anc Heb: Mod Heb: ערוה / er-wah (fem); **Definition:** The state of being without clothing. Idiomatic for sexual relations. [AHLB: 1365-K (N^1) / Strong's: 6172, 6173] **Concordance:** 20:26 28:42

NATAPH: Anc Heb: Mod Heb: נטף / na-taph (mas); **Definition:** An unknown precious stone. [AHLB: 2399 (N) / Strong's: 5198] **Concordance:** 30:34

NATION: Anc Heb: Mod Heb: גוי / goy (mas); **Definition:** A community of people of one or more nationalities and having a more or less defined territory and government. The people as the back, or body of the nation. [AHLB: 1052-A (f) / Strong's: 1471] **Concordance:** 9:24 19:6 32:10 33:13 34:10 34:24

NATIVE: Anc Heb: Mod Heb: אזרח / ez-rahh (mas); **Definition:** Born and raised in the Land. [AHLB: 2135 (n) / Strong's: 249] **Concordance:** 12:19 12:48 12:49

NEAR: Anc Heb: Mod Heb: קרוב / qa-rov (mas); **Definition:** Close to; at or within a short distance from. Also, a kin, as a near relative. [AHLB: 2729 (c) / Strong's: 7138] **Concordance:** 12:4 13:17 32:27

NECK: Anc Heb: Mod Heb: עורף / o-reph (mas); **Definition:** The part of a person that connects the head with the body. [AHLB: 2580 (N) / Strong's: 6203] **Concordance:** 23:27 32:9 33:3 33:5 34:9

NEEDY: Anc Heb: Mod Heb: אביון / ev-yon (mas); **Definition:** In a condition of need or want. [AHLB: 1033-C (j) / Strong's: 34] **Concordance:** 23:6 23:11

NESHER: Anc Heb: Mod Heb: נשר / ne-sher (mas); **Definition:** An unknown bird, but probably a hawk or eagle. [AHLB: 2446 (N) / Strong's: 5403, 5404] **Concordance:** 19:4

NETTING: Anc Heb: Mod Heb: רשת / re-shet (fem); **Definition:** A sheet of meshed fabric, cord or metal. [AHLB: 1458-A (N^2) / Strong's: 7568] **Concordance:** 27:4{2} 27:5 38:4

NEW: Anc Heb: Mod Heb: חדש / hha-dash (mas); **Definition:** Something that is new, renewed, restored or repaired. [AHLB: 2151 (N) / Strong's: 2319, 2323] **Concordance:** 1:8

NEW-MOON: Anc Heb: Mod Heb: חודש / hho-desh (mas); **Definition:** The moon phase when the thin crescent first appears and is perceived as the renewal of the moon. The first day of the month. Also, a month as the interval between crescents. [AHLB: 2151 (g) / Strong's: 2320] **Concordance:** 12:2{3} 12:3 12:6 12:18{2} 13:4 13:5 16:1 19:1 23:15 34:18{2} 40:2{2} 40:17{2}

NIGHT: Anc Heb: ل٭ل / Mod Heb: ליל / la-yil (mas); Alt Sp: לילה; **Definition:** The time from dusk to dawn. The hours associated with darkness and sleep. [AHLB: 1265-M (N) / Strong's: 3915] **Concordance:** 10:13 11:4 12:8 12:12 12:29 12:30 12:31 12:42{2} 13:21{2} 13:22 14:20{2} 14:21 24:18 34:28 40:38

NIGHT-WATCH: Anc Heb: ٭لسمر٭ Mod Heb: אשמורה / ash-mu-rah (fem); **Definition:** An increment of time during the night when guards watch the area. [AHLB: 2853 (nd[1]) / Strong's: 821] **Concordance:** 14:24

NINE: Anc Heb: ٭شت Mod Heb: תשע / ti-sha (mas); תשע / tey-sha (fem); **Definition:** An ordinal number. The total number of hours in an ancient day or night. [AHLB: 1476-A (i) / Strong's: 8672, 8673] **Concordance:** 38:24

NOBLE: Anc Heb: ٭٭ Mod Heb: סר / sar (mas); Alt Sp: שר **Definition:** Possessing outstanding qualities or properties. Of high birth or exalted rank. One who has authority. May also mean "heavy" from the weight of responsibility on one in authority. [AHLB: 1342-A (N) / Strong's: 5620, 8269] **Concordance:** 1:11 2:14 18:21{4} 18:25{4}

NORTH: Anc Heb: ٭٭ Mod Heb: צפון / tsa-phon (fem); **Definition:** From the North Star which is watched for direction. [AHLB: 1408-A (j) / Strong's: 6828] **Concordance:** 26:20 26:35 27:11 36:25 38:11 40:22

NOSE: Anc Heb: ٭٭ Mod Heb: אף / aph (mas); **Definition:** The organ bearing the nostrils on the anterior of the face. The nostrils when used in the plural form. Also meaning anger from the flaring of the nostrils when angry. [AHLB: 1017-A (N) / Strong's: 639] **Concordance:** 4:14 11:8 15:8 22:23 32:10 32:11 32:12 32:19 32:22 34:6

NOSE-RING: Anc Heb: ٭٭ Mod Heb: חח / hhahh (mas); Alt Sp: חחי **Definition:** A round piece of jewelry, usually of a metal, that is pierced through the nose or lip. [AHLB: 1169-A (N) / Strong's: 2397] **Concordance:** 35:22

NOT: Anc Heb: ٭لو٭ Mod Heb: לא / lo (mas); Alt Sp: לוה **Definition:** A function word to stand for the negative. As being without. [AHLB: 1254-J (N) / Strong's: 3808] **Concordance:** 1:8 1:17 1:19 2:3 3:3 3:19{2} 3:21 4:1{3} 4:8{2} 4:9{2} 4:10 4:11 4:14 4:21 5:2{2} 5:7 5:8 5:14 5:18 5:19 5:23 6:3 6:9 6:12 7:4 7:13 7:16 7:21 7:22 7:23 7:24 8:11 8:14 8:15 8:22{2} 8:24 8:27 8:28 9:4 9:6 9:7{2} 9:11 9:12 9:18 9:19 9:21 9:24 9:26 9:28 9:29 9:32 9:33 9:35 10:5 10:6 10:11 10:14{2} 10:15 10:19 10:20 10:23{2} 10:26{2} 10:27 10:29 11:6{2} 11:7 11:9 11:10 12:10 12:13 12:16 12:19 12:20 12:22 12:23 12:39{3} 12:43 12:45 12:46{2} 12:48 13:3 13:7{2} 13:13 13:17 13:22 14:12 14:13 14:20 14:28 15:22 15:23 15:26 16:4 16:8 16:15 16:18{2} 16:20 16:24{2} 16:25 16:26 16:27 18:17 18:18 19:13{2} 19:23 20:3 20:4 20:5{2} 20:7{2} 20:10 20:13 20:14 20:15 20:16 20:17{2} 20:23{2} 20:25 20:26{2} 21:5 21:7 21:8{2} 21:10 21:11 21:13 21:18 21:21 21:22 21:28 21:29 21:33 21:36 22:7{2} 22:10{2} 22:12 22:14 22:15 22:17 22:20{2} 22:21 22:24{2} 22:27{2} 22:28 22:30 23:1 23:2{2} 23:3 23:6 23:7 23:8 23:9 23:13{2} 23:15 23:18{2} 23:19 23:21 23:24{3} 23:26 23:29 23:32 23:33 24:2{2} 24:11 25:15 28:28 28:32 28:35 28:43 29:33 29:34 30:9{2} 30:12 30:15{2} 30:20 30:21 30:32{2} 30:37 32:1 32:23 33:3 33:4 33:11 33:12 33:16 33:20{2} 33:23 34:3 34:7 34:10 34:14 34:17 34:20{2} 34:24 34:25{2} 34:26 34:28{2} 34:29 35:3 39:21 39:23 40:35 40:37{2}

NOW: Anc Heb: ٭ت٭ Mod Heb: עתה / a-tah (mas); **Definition:** At the present time or moment. [AHLB: 1367-H (N) / Strong's: 6258] **Concordance:** 3:9 3:10 3:18 4:12 5:5 5:18 6:1 9:15 9:18 9:19 10:17 18:11 18:19 19:5 32:10 32:30 32:32 32:34 33:5 33:13

NUMBER: Anc Heb: ⲁ◦ᏋᎷ Mod Heb: מספר / mis-phar (mas); **Definition:** A sum of units. Counting as a recording. [AHLB: 2500 (h) / Strong's: 4557] **Concordance:** 16:16 23:26

NUMEROUS: Anc Heb: ᎷᎩᎧⲛ◦ Mod Heb: עצום / a-tsum (mas); **Definition:** Involving more than one. [AHLB: 2569 (d) / Strong's: 6099] **Concordance:** 1:9

OFFERED-WILLINGLY: Anc Heb: �29Ꭸˋ Mod Heb: נדב / na-dav (mas); **Definition:** Given of one's free will without recompense. [AHLB: n/a / Strong's: n/a] **Concordance:** *Used in names only.*

OFFERING: Anc Heb: ⲯᎷᎩᎧᵻ Mod Heb: תרומה / te-ru-mah (fem); **Definition:** A donation presented to another. [AHLB: 1450-J (i¹) / Strong's: 8641] **Concordance:** 25:2{2} 25:3 29:27 29:28{3} 30:13 30:14 30:15 35:5{2} 35:21 35:24{2} 36:3 36:6

OFFER-WILLINGLY: Anc Heb: �29Ꭸˋ Mod Heb: נדב / na-dav; **Definition:** To give from a willing heart. [AHLB: 2380 (V) / Strong's: 5068, 5069] **Concordance:** 25:2 35:21 35:29

OIL: Anc Heb: ˋᎷᎢᏔ Mod Heb: שמן / she-men (mas); **Definition:** A semi-liquid, often oily and thick. Usually olive oil and used as a medicinal ointment. Also, meaning fat or rich. [AHLB: 2850 (N) / Strong's: 8081, 8082] **Concordance:** 25:6{2} 27:20 29:2{2} 29:7 29:21 29:23 29:40 30:24 30:25{2} 30:31 31:11 35:8{2} 35:14 35:15 35:28{2} 37:29 39:37 39:38 40:9

OINTMENT: Anc Heb: ⲯᎢᎢᏔᎷᎷ Mod Heb: משחה / mash-hhah (fem); **Definition:** An oil or other liquid that is smeared on an animal or person for healing or dedication. [AHLB: 2357 (N¹) / Strong's: 4888] **Concordance:** 25:6 29:7 29:21 30:25{2} 30:31 31:11 35:8 35:15 35:28 37:29 39:38 40:9

OINTMENT-MIXTURE: Anc Heb: ᵻᎢᎧˍᎧᎩᎷᎷ Mod Heb: מרקחת / mir-qa-hhat (fem); **Definition:** A mixture of spices for an ointment or perfume. [AHLB: 2795 (h²) / Strong's: 4842] **Concordance:** 30:25

OLIVE: Anc Heb: ᵻᏈ△ᵴ Mod Heb: זית / za-yit (mas); **Definition:** The fruit or the tree. The fruit of the olive is used for food and as a source of oil. [AHLB: 1160-M (N) / Strong's: 2132] **Concordance:** 23:11 27:20 30:24

OLIVINE: Anc Heb: ⲯᎢ⊗ᏈˍᎧ Mod Heb: פיטדה / pit-dah (fem); **Definition:** Probably the Olivine, a green gemstone. The Septuagint uses the word topazios, but the Topaz was unknown at the time of the Exodus. Another possible meaning of this word is Chrysolite. [AHLB: 2603 (e¹) / Strong's: 6357] **Concordance:** 28:17 39:10

OMER: Anc Heb: ⲁᎷᎩᎧ Mod Heb: עומר / o-mer (mas); **Definition:** A dry measure equal to one tenth of an ephah (about two liters). [AHLB: 2554 (g) / Strong's: 6016] **Concordance:** 16:16 16:18 16:22 16:32 16:33 16:36

ONE: Anc Heb: ᏈᎢᏔᎧ Mod Heb: עשתי / ash-tey (com); **Definition:** Existing, acting, or considered as a single unit, entity, or individual. [AHLB: 2586 (f) / Strong's: 6249] **Concordance:** 26:7 26:8 36:14 36:15

ONE-HALF: Anc Heb: ᵻᏈˍᎧᎷᎷᎷ Mod Heb: מחצית / ma-hha-tsit (fem); **Definition:** A portion that is equal to the remainder. [AHLB: 1179-A (a⁴) / Strong's: 4276] **Concordance:** 30:13{2} 30:15 30:23 38:26

ONE-TENTH: Anc Heb: ˋᎩᎨᎧ Mod Heb: עשרון / i-sa-ron (mas); **Definition:** An equal part of something divided into ten parts. [AHLB: 2563 (j) / Strong's: 6241] **Concordance:** 29:40

ON-FOOT: Anc Heb: ᏈᏈᏞᎨ Mod Heb: רגלי / rag-li (mas); **Definition:** A soldier, messenger or traveler who moves on foot. [AHLB: 2749 (f) / Strong's: 7273] **Concordance:** 12:37

ONLY: Anc Heb: ◦Ꭸ Mod Heb: רק / raq (mas); **Definition:** A single instance or thing and nothing more or different. [AHLB: 1456-A (N) / Strong's: 7535] **Concordance:** 8:5 8:7 8:24 8:25 9:26 10:17 10:24 21:19

ONYCHA: Anc Heb: †√ᛑᛚᛜ Mod Heb: שחלת / she-hhey-let (fem); **Definition:** An unknown precious stone. [AHLB: 2824 (N²) / Strong's: 7827] **Concordance:** 30:34

ONYX: Anc Heb: ᛜᛟᛉᛚ Mod Heb: שוהם / sho-ham (mas); **Definition:** Probably the Onyx, a form of quartz that may be of any color. The Septuagint uses beryllios (Beryl). Another possible translation is the Malachite. [AHLB: 1473-G (g) / Strong's: 7718] **Concordance:** 25:7 28:9 28:20 35:9 35:27 39:6 39:13

OPAL: Anc Heb: ᛜᛜᛚᛚ Mod Heb: לשם / le-shem (mas); **Definition:** Possibly the Opal, which may be found in a wide variety of colors. Other possible translates are Amber, Jacinth, Agate or Amethyst. [AHLB: 2324 (N) / Strong's: 3958] **Concordance:** 28:19 39:12

OPEN: Anc Heb: ᛜᛏ Mod Heb: פתח / pa-tahh; **Definition:** To open up as opening a gate or door; to have no confining barrier. The piel (intensive) form means "engrave." [AHLB: 2649 (V) / Strong's: 6605, 6606] **Concordance:** 2:6 21:33 28:9 28:11 28:36 39:6

OPENING: Anc Heb: ᛜᛏ Mod Heb: פתח / pe-tahh (mas); **Definition:** Something that is open, as an entrance or opening of a tent, house or city. [AHLB: 2649 (N) / Strong's: 6607, 6608] **Concordance:** 12:22 12:23 26:36 29:4 29:11 29:32 29:42 33:8 33:9 33:10{2} 35:15{2} 36:37 38:8 38:30 39:38 40:5 40:6 40:12 40:28 40:29

OPPOSITE: Anc Heb: ᛏᛚ Mod Heb: נגד / ne-ged (mas); **Definition:** Something in front of; on the other side; in the presence of. [AHLB: 2372 (N) / Strong's: 5048, 5049] **Concordance:** 10:10 19:2 34:10

OR: Anc Heb: Υ Mod Heb: או / o (mas); **Definition:** An alternative or optional desire. [AHLB: 1006-A (N) / Strong's: 176] **Concordance:** 4:11{4} 5:3 19:13 21:4 21:6 21:18 21:20 21:21 21:26 21:27 21:28 21:29 21:31{2} 21:32 21:33{2} 21:36 21:37{2} 22:4 22:5{2} 22:6 22:9{4} 22:13 23:4 28:43 30:20

ORNAMENTAL-RING: Anc Heb: ᛜᛉᛚ Mod Heb: נזם / ne-zem (mas); **Definition:** A circular band worn as an ornament. [AHLB: 2388 (N) / Strong's: 5141] **Concordance:** 32:2 32:3 35:22

ORPHAN: Anc Heb: ᛜΥᛏ Mod Heb: יתום / ya-tom (mas); **Definition:** Having no mother or father. [AHLB: 1496-L (c) / Strong's: 3490] **Concordance:** 22:21 22:23

OTHER: Anc Heb: ᛜᛉ Mod Heb: אחר / a-hhar (mas); **Definition:** One that remains of two or more. A time, person or thing that follows after. [AHLB: 1181-C (N) / Strong's: 312, 317] **Concordance:** 20:3 21:10 22:4 34:14

OTHER-SIDE: Anc Heb: ᛜᛜ Mod Heb: עבר / ey-ver (mas); **Definition:** As being across from this side. [AHLB: 2520 (N) / Strong's: 5676] **Concordance:** 25:37 28:26 32:15 39:19

OTHERWISE: Anc Heb: ᛚ Mod Heb: פן / peyn (mas); **Definition:** In a different manner or way. [AHLB: 1382-A (N) / Strong's: 6435] **Concordance:** 1:10 5:3 13:17 19:21 19:22 19:24 20:19 23:29 23:33 33:3 34:12{2} 34:15

OUTCRY: Anc Heb: ᛜᛟᛜ Mod Heb: שועה / shaw-ah (fem); **Definition:** An expression of need, or help or injustice. A loud wail from distress. [AHLB: 1476-J (N¹) / Strong's: 7775] **Concordance:** 2:23

OUTER: Anc Heb: ᛚᛟᛜ Mod Heb: קיצון / qi-tson (mas); **Definition:** The furthest from the center. The end. [AHLB: 1432-A (ej) / Strong's: 7020] **Concordance:** 26:4 26:10 36:11 36:17

OUTER-GARMENT: Anc Heb: ᛟᛜᛚ Mod Heb: שלמה / sal-mah (fem); **Definition:** Garments worn over top of other garments. [AHLB: 2483 (N) / Strong's: 8008] **Concordance:** 22:8 22:25

OUTER-RIM: Anc Heb: ᛜᛟᛜᛜ Mod Heb: כרכוב / kar-kov (mas); **Definition:** The out edge of something. [AHLB: **3027** / Strong's: 3749] **Concordance:** 27:5 38:4

OUTSIDE: Anc Heb: ᕟᕐᒣ Mod Heb: חוץ / hhuts (mas); **Definition:** A place or region beyond an enclosure or barrier. [AHLB: 1179-J (N) / Strong's: 2351] **Concordance:** 12:46 21:19 25:11 26:35 27:21 29:14 33:7{2} 37:2 40:22

OVEN: Anc Heb: ᕟᕟ Mod Heb: תנור / ta-nur (mas); **Definition:** A chamber used for baking, heating or drying. As a lamp for cooking. [AHLB: 1319-J (i) / Strong's: 8574] **Concordance:** 7:28

OVERCOME: Anc Heb: ᕟᕟ Mod Heb: גבר / ga-var; **Definition:** To get the better of. Be successful in strength or authority. [AHLB: 2052 (V) / Strong's: 1396] **Concordance:** 17:11{2}

OVERHANG: Anc Heb: ᕟᕟ Mod Heb: סרח / se-rahh (mas); **Definition:** What is left over. A remnant. Residue or overhanging. [AHLB: 2507 (N) / Strong's: 5629] **Concordance:** 26:12

OVERHANG: Anc Heb: ᕟᕟ Mod Heb: סרח / sa-rah; **Definition:** To proceed beyond any given or supposed limit or measure. To extend beyond proper bounds. To be superfluous. [AHLB: 2507 (V) / Strong's: 5628] **Concordance:** 26:12 26:13

OVERLAY: Anc Heb: ᕟᕟ Mod Heb: צפה / tsa-phah; **Definition:** To cover with a different material, usually with gold. [AHLB: 1408-H (V) / Strong's: 6823] **Concordance:** 25:11{2} 25:13 25:24 25:28 26:29{2} 26:32 26:37 27:2 27:6 30:3 30:5 36:34{2} 36:36 36:38 37:2 37:4 37:11 37:15 37:26 37:28 38:2 38:6 38:28

OVERTAKE: Anc Heb: ᕟᕟ Mod Heb: נסג / na-sag; **Definition:** To catch up with; to remove in the sense of taking over. [AHLB: 2410 (V) / Strong's: 5253, 5381] **Concordance:** 14:9 15:9

OVERTURN: Anc Heb: ᕟᕟ Mod Heb: הפך / hha-phak; **Definition:** To turn something over or upside down, as if pouring out its contents. [AHLB: 1379-F (V) / Strong's: 2015] **Concordance:** 7:15 7:17 7:20 10:19 14:5

OX: Anc Heb: ᕟᕟ Mod Heb: שור / shor (mas); **Definition:** A domestic bovine animal used for pulling heavy loads. [AHLB: 1480-J (N) / Strong's: 7794, 8450] **Concordance:** 20:17 21:28{3} 21:29{2} 21:32{2} 21:33 21:35{3} 21:36{3} 21:37{2} 22:3 22:8 22:9 22:29 23:4 23:12 34:19

PALM: Anc Heb: ᕟᕟ Mod Heb: כף / kaph (fem); **Definition:** A tropical tree with fan-shaped leaves. Part of the hand or foot between the base of the digits and the wrist or ankle. A palm-shaped object. [AHLB: 1247-A (N) / Strong's: 3709, 3710] **Concordance:** 4:4 9:29 9:33 25:29 29:24{2} 33:22 33:23 37:16

PARCHED: Anc Heb: ᕟᕟ Mod Heb: נגב / ne-gev (mas); **Definition:** A dry and arid region, a desert. [AHLB: 2371 (N) / Strong's: n/a]

PARCHING-HEAT: Anc Heb: ᕟᕟ Mod Heb: חורב / hho-rev (mas); **Definition:** To shrivel or toast with intense heat. [AHLB: 2199 (g) / Strong's: 2721] **HEAT:**

PASTE: Anc Heb: ᕟᕟ Mod Heb: חמר / hha-mar; **Definition:** To smear a paste such as mortar on bricks or tar on a boat. [AHLB: 2175 (V) / Strong's: 2560] **Concordance:** 2:3

PATTERN: Anc Heb: ᕟᕟ Mod Heb: תבנית / tav-nit (fem); **Definition:** A model or instructions detailing a construction. [AHLB: 1037-H (if²) / Strong's: 8403] **Concordance:** 25:9{2} 25:40

PEASANT: Anc Heb: ᕟᕟ Mod Heb: פרז / pa-raz (mas); **Definition:** One of lower rank, or value, usually dwelling in a town without walls. [AHLB: 2635 (N) / Strong's: 6518]

PEDESTAL: Anc Heb: ᕟᕟ Mod Heb: מכונה / me-kho-nah (fem); **Definition:** A base that is firm and functions as a supports. [AHLB: 1244-A (kc¹) / Strong's: 4350] **Concordance:** 15:17

PEG: Anc Heb: ᕟᕟ Mod Heb: וו / waw (mas); **Definition:** A peg, nail or hook as used for attaching one thing to another. [AHLB: 1121-A (N) / Strong's: 2053] **Concordance:** 26:32 26:37 27:10 27:11 27:17 36:36 36:38 38:10 38:11 38:12 38:17 38:19 38:28

PEOPLE: Anc Heb: ᕟᕟ Mod Heb: עם / am (mas); **Definition:** A large group of men or women. [AHLB: 1358-A (N) / Strong's: 5971, 5972] **Concordance:** 1:9{2} 1:20 1:22 3:7 3:10 3:12 3:21

4:16 4:21 4:30 4:31 5:1 5:4 5:5 5:6 5:7 5:10{2} 5:12 5:16 5:22 5:23{2} 6:7 7:4 7:14 7:16 7:26
7:28 7:29 8:4{2} 8:5 8:7 8:16 8:17{2} 8:18 8:19{2} 8:25{2} 8:27 8:28 9:1 9:7 9:13 9:14 9:15
9:17 9:27 10:3 10:4 11:2 11:3{2} 11:8 12:27 12:31 12:33 12:34 12:36 13:3 13:17{2} 13:18
13:22 14:5{2} 14:6 14:13 14:31 15:13 15:14 15:16{2} 15:24 16:4 16:27 16:30 17:1 17:2 17:3{2}
17:4 17:5 17:6 17:13 18:1 18:10 18:13{2} 18:14{3} 18:15 18:18 18:19 18:21 18:22 18:23 18:25
18:26 19:5 19:7 19:8{2} 19:9{2} 19:10 19:11 19:12 19:14{2} 19:15 19:16 19:17 19:21 19:23
19:24 19:25 20:18{2} 20:20 20:21 21:8 22:24 22:27 23:11 23:27 24:2 24:3{2} 24:7 24:8 30:33
30:38 31:14 32:1{2} 32:3 32:6 32:7 32:9{2} 32:11 32:12 32:14 32:17 32:21 32:22 32:25 32:28
32:30 32:31 32:34 32:35 33:1 33:3 33:4 33:5 33:8 33:10{2} 33:12 33:13 33:16{3} 34:9 34:10{2}
36:5 36:6

PERCEIVE: Anc Heb: ✦⊐ᄆ Mod Heb: חזה / hha-zah; **Definition:** To be able to understand on a higher level; to see something that is not physically present. [AHLB: 1168-H (V) / Strong's: 1957, 2370, 2372] **Concordance:** 18:21 24:11

PERFORATE: Anc Heb: ᄊᆰᄆ Mod Heb: חרם / hha-ram; **Definition:** To fill with holes. To make holes. [AHLB: 2206 (V) / Strong's: 2763] **Concordance:** 22:19

PERFORM: Anc Heb: ᆨᏙᆮ Mod Heb: פלא / pa-la; **Definition:** To do a wondrous action that shows ones might. [AHLB: 1380-E (V) / Strong's: 6381] **Concordance:** 3:20 34:10

PERFORMANCE: Anc Heb: ᆨᏙᆮ Mod Heb: פלא / pe-le (mas); **Definition:** A wondrous action. [AHLB: 1380-E (N) / Strong's: 6382] **Concordance:** 15:11

PERFORMING: Anc Heb: ᆨᏙᆮ Mod Heb: פלוא / pa-lu (mas); **Definition:** The act of doing, displaying, or creating. [AHLB: n/a / Strong's: n/a] **Concordance:** Used in names only.

PERISH: Anc Heb: ᄆᏙᆰ Mod Heb: אבד / a-vad; **Definition:** To be separated from the whole, life or functionality. [AHLB: 1027-C (V) / Strong's: 6, 7] **Concordance:** 10:7

PESTILENCE: Anc Heb: ✦ᆰᆱᄊ Mod Heb: מגפה / ma-gey-phah (fem); **Definition:** A plague or other disaster that smites people or beasts. [AHLB: 2377 (k¹) / Strong's: 4046] **Concordance:** 9:14

PICK-UP: Anc Heb: ⊗ᆮᏙ Mod Heb: לקט / la-qat; **Definition:** To take hold of and lift up; to gather together. [AHLB: 2320 (V) / Strong's: 3950] **Concordance:** 16:4 16:5 16:16 16:17 16:18 16:21 16:22 16:26 16:27

PIECE: Anc Heb: ᄆ Mod Heb: נתח / ney-tahh (mas); **Definition:** A part of the original. What has been cut from the whole. [AHLB: 2449 (N) / Strong's: 5409] **Concordance:** 29:17{2}

PIERCE: Anc Heb: ᏙᏙᄆ Mod Heb: חלל / hha-lal **Definition:** To run into or through as with a pointed weapon or tool; pierce a hole through; to begin in the sense of pressing in. [AHLB: 1173-B (V) / Strong's: 2490] **Concordance:** 20:25 31:14

PIERCED-BREAD: Anc Heb: ✦Ꮩᄆ Mod Heb: חלה / hha-lah (fem); **Definition:** Bread that has many holes, as perforated. [AHLB: 1173-A (N¹) / Strong's: 2471] **Concordance:** 29:2 29:23

PILE: Anc Heb: ᄊᆰ Mod Heb: ערם / a-ram; **Definition:** To mound up in a heap. [AHLB: 2578 (V) / Strong's: 6192] **Concordance:** 15:8

PILE-UP: Anc Heb: ᆰᄊ Mod Heb: צבר / tsa-var; **Definition:** To heap something up in a mound. [AHLB: 2656 (V) / Strong's: 6651] **Concordance:** 8:10

PILGRIMAGE: Anc Heb: ᆰᆱᄊ Mod Heb: מגור / ma-gur (mas); **Definition:** A journey of a pilgrim; the course of life on earth. One who travels in a strange land. The pilgrimage or the dwelling place of a stranger. [AHLB: 1066-J (d) / Strong's: 4033] **Concordance:** 6:4

PILLAR: Anc Heb: ᄆᏙᆰ Mod Heb: עמוד / a-mud (mas); **Definition:** A standing upright post or column. [AHLB: 2550 (d) / Strong's: 5982] **Concordance:** 13:21{2} 13:22{2} 14:19 14:24 26:32 26:37 27:10{2} 27:11{2} 27:12 27:14 27:15 27:16 27:17 33:9 33:10 35:11 35:17 36:36 36:38 38:10{2} 38:11{2} 38:12{2} 38:14 38:15 38:17{3} 38:19 38:28 39:33 39:40 40:18

PITCH: Anc Heb: Mod Heb: זפת / ze-phet (fem); **Definition:** A sticky substance used to seal wood from water leakage. [AHLB: 1155-A (N^2) / Strong's: 2203] **Concordance:** 2:3

PLACE: Anc Heb: Mod Heb: סים / sim; Alt Sp: סום **Definition:** To put or set in a particular place, position, situation, or relation. [AHLB: 1335-J (V) / Strong's: 3455, 7760, 7761] **Concordance:** 1:11 2:3{2} 2:14 3:22 4:11{2} 4:15 4:21 5:8 5:14 8:8 8:19 9:5 9:21 10:2 14:21 15:25 15:26{2} 17:12 17:14 18:21 19:7 21:1 21:13 22:24 24:6 26:35 28:12 28:26 28:37 29:6 29:24 32:27 33:22 39:7 39:19 40:3 40:5 40:8 40:18 40:19 40:20 40:21 40:24 40:26 40:28 40:29 40:30

PLACE-OF-LODGING: Anc Heb: Mod Heb: מלון / ma-lon (mas); **Definition:** An establishment for lodging and entertaining travelers. A place for spending the night. [AHLB: 1267-J (a) / Strong's: 4411] **Concordance:** 4:24

PLACE-TO-BURN: Anc Heb: Mod Heb: מקטר / miq-tar (mas); **Definition:** A specific location used for burning incense. [AHLB: 2705 (h) / Strong's: 4729] **Concordance:** 30:1

PLAGUE: Anc Heb: Mod Heb: נגע / ne-ga (mas); **Definition:** An epidemic disease causing high mortality. An epidemic or other sore or illness as a touch from God. [AHLB: 2376 (N) / Strong's: 5061] **Concordance:** 11:1

PLAIT: Anc Heb: Mod Heb: משבצה / mish-be-tsah (fem); **Definition:** A woven or checkered work. [AHLB: 2809 (h^1) / Strong's: 4865] **Concordance:** 28:11 28:13 28:14 28:25 39:6 39:13 39:16 39:18

PLANT: Anc Heb: Mod Heb: נטע / na-ta; **Definition:** To put or set into the ground for growth; to establish plants in the sense of setting into place in the soil. [AHLB: 2398 (V) / Strong's: 5193] **Concordance:** 15:17

PLATTER: Anc Heb: Mod Heb: קערה / qe-a-rah (fem); **Definition:** A large plate, serving dish. [AHLB: 2719 (N^1) / Strong's: 7086] **Concordance:** 25:29 37:16

PLEASE: Anc Heb: Mod Heb: נא / na (mas); Alt Sp: אנא **Definition:** A pleading or request for something. To make another happy or gratified. [AHLB: 1300-A (N) / Strong's: 577, 4994] **Concordance:** 3:3 3:18 4:6 4:13 4:18 5:3 10:11 10:17 11:2 32:31 32:32 33:13{2} 33:18 34:9{2}

PLOWING: Anc Heb: Mod Heb: חריש / hha-rish (mas); **Definition:** Breaking up the ground in order to plant a crop. The time of plowing. [AHLB: 2211 (b) / Strong's: 2758] **Concordance:** 34:21

PLOWSHARE: Anc Heb: Mod Heb: את / yet (mas); **Definition:** The cutting point of a plow. [AHLB: 1022-A (N) / Strong's: 855]

PLUCKED-OUT: Anc Heb: Mod Heb: מושה / mo-sheh (mas); **Definition:** What is drawn or pulled out. [AHLB: n/a / Strong's: n/a] **Concordance:** *Used in names only.*

PLUCK-OUT: Anc Heb: Mod Heb: משה / ma-shah; **Definition:** To draw or pull out. [AHLB: 1297-H (V) / Strong's: 4871] **Concordance:** 2:10

POMEGRANATE: Anc Heb: Mod Heb: רמון / ri-mon (mas); **Definition:** A sweet deep red fruit prolific with seeds. A symbol of compassion and love. [AHLB: 1450-A (j) / Strong's: 7416] **Concordance:** 28:33 28:34{2} 39:24 39:25{2} 39:26{2}

POOL: Anc Heb: Mod Heb: אגם / a-gam (mas); **Definition:** A collection of water, either natural or manmade. Once (Jeremiah 51:32) used for the reeds which line the pond. [AHLB: 1059-C (N) / Strong's: 98, 99] **Concordance:** 7:19 8:1

POSSESS: Anc Heb: Mod Heb: ירש / ya-rash; **Definition:** To come into possession of or receive especially as a right or divine portion; to receive from an ancestor at his death; to take possession, either by seizing or through inheritance. [AHLB: 1458-L (V) / Strong's: 3423] **Concordance:** 15:9 34:24

POSSESSION: Anc Heb: 𐤌𐤓𐤔𐤄 Mod Heb: מורשה / mo-ra-shah (fem); **Definition:** Something that is personally owned. [AHLB: 1458-L (a¹) / Strong's: 4181] **Concordance:** 6:8

POSSIBLY: Anc Heb: 𐤀𐤅𐤋𐤉 Mod Heb: אולי / u-lai (com); **Definition:** Being within the limits of ability, capacity, or realization. A possible outcome. To desire what you are without in the sense of joining. [AHLB: 1254-J (f) / Strong's: 194] **Concordance:** 32:30

POT: Anc Heb: 𐤎𐤉𐤓 Mod Heb: סיר / sir (mas); **Definition:** A vessel used for cooking or storing. [AHLB: 1342-M (N) / Strong's: 5518] **Concordance:** 16:3 27:3 38:3

POUR: Anc Heb: 𐤍𐤎𐤊 Mod Heb: נסך / na-sakh; **Definition:** To cause to flow in a stream; to give full expression to. [AHLB: 2412 (V) / Strong's: 5258, 5259, 5260] **Concordance:** 25:29 30:9 37:16

POUR-DOWN: Anc Heb: 𐤉𐤑𐤒 Mod Heb: יצק / ya-tsaq; Alt Sp: יסק **Definition:** To send a liquid from a container into another container or onto a person or object; to pour molten metal into a cast. [AHLB: 1410-L (V) / Strong's: 3251, 3332] **Concordance:** 25:12 26:37 29:7 30:32 36:36 37:3 37:13 38:5 38:27

POURING: Anc Heb: 𐤍𐤎𐤊 Mod Heb: נסך / ne-sak (mas); **Definition:** A liquid poured out as an offering or the pouring of a molten metal to form images. [AHLB: 2412 (N) / Strong's: 5261, 5262] **Concordance:** 29:40 29:41 30:9

POUR-OUT: Anc Heb: 𐤔𐤐𐤊 Mod Heb: שפך / sha-phakh; **Definition:** To let flow a liquid, often the blood of an animal in sacrifice or a man. [AHLB: 2865 (V) / Strong's: 8210] **Concordance:** 4:9 29:12

POWDER: Anc Heb: 𐤏𐤐𐤓 Mod Heb: עפר / a-phar (mas); **Definition:** Matter in a fine particulate state. An abundant amount of powdery substance as dust or ash. [AHLB: 2565 (N) / Strong's: 6083] **Concordance:** 8:12 8:13{2}

POWER: Anc Heb: 𐤀𐤋𐤅𐤄 Mod Heb: אלוה / e-lo-ah (mas); **Definition:** Possession of control, authority, or influence over others; physical might. The power or might of one who rules or teaches. One who yokes with another. Often applies to rulers or a god. The plural form is used for the name Elohiym, meaning "powers." [AHLB: 1012-H (c) / Strong's: 430, 433]

PRECIPITATE: Anc Heb: 𐤌𐤈𐤓 Mod Heb: מטר / ma-tar; **Definition:** To rain or snow. [AHLB: 2336 (V) / Strong's: 4305] **Concordance:** 9:18 9:23 16:4

PRECIPITATION: Anc Heb: 𐤌𐤈𐤓 Mod Heb: מטר / ma-tar (mas); **Definition:** A rain, snow or exceptionally heavy dew. [AHLB: 2336 (N) / Strong's: 4306] **Concordance:** 9:33 9:34

PREGNANT: Anc Heb: 𐤄𐤓𐤄 Mod Heb: הרה / ha-reh (fem); Alt Sp: הרי **Definition:** Containing unborn young within the body. [AHLB: 1112-H (N¹) / Strong's: 2030] **Concordance:** 21:22

PREPARE: Anc Heb: 𐤊𐤅𐤍 Mod Heb: כון / kun; **Definition:** To put in proper condition or readiness. The piel (intensive) form means "establish." [AHLB: 1244-J (V) / Strong's: 3559] **Concordance:** 8:22 15:17 16:5 19:11 19:15 23:20 34:2

PRESENT: Anc Heb: 𐤁𐤓𐤊𐤄 Mod Heb: ברכה / be-ra-khah (fem); **Definition:** A gift given to another in respect as if on bended knee. Also, a pool of water as a place where one kneels down to drink from. [AHLB: 2039 (N¹) / Strong's: 1293, 1295] **Concordance:** 32:29

PRESERVE: Anc Heb: 𐤍𐤑𐤓 Mod Heb: נצר / na-tsar; **Definition:** To watch over or guard for protection. [AHLB: 2429 (V) / Strong's: 5341] **Concordance:** 34:7

PRESS-IN: Anc Heb: 𐤑𐤓𐤓 Mod Heb: צרר / tsa-rar; **Definition:** To confine or restrict in a tight place. [AHLB: 1411-B (V) / Strong's: 6887] **Concordance:** 12:34 23:22

PRESS-OUT-OIL: Anc Heb: 𐤑𐤄𐤓 Mod Heb: צהר / tsa-har; **Definition:** Extracting the fluids from the olive. [AHLB: 1411-G (V) / Strong's: 6671] **OUT-OIL:**

PRISONER: Anc Heb: ⲁⲭⲉⲗ⳧ Mod Heb: אסיר / a-sir (mas); **Definition:** One who is bound or confined. [AHLB: 1342-C (b) / Strong's: 615, 616]

PRODUCE: Anc Heb: ⲣⲁⲟ Mod Heb: פרי / pe-ri (mas); **Definition:** Agricultural products, especially fresh fruits and vegetables. The harvested product of a crop. [AHLB: 1388-H (f) / Strong's: 6529] **Concordance:** 10:15

PRODUCTION: Anc Heb: ⳧ⳡⲩⲧ Mod Heb: תבואה / te-vu-ah (fem); **Definition:** Total output of a commodity or an industry. An increase of produce, usually of fruit. [AHLB: 1024-J (i^1) / Strong's: 8393] **Concordance:** 23:10

PROFIT: Anc Heb: ⲟⲙⲩ Mod Heb: בצע / be-tsa (mas); **Definition:** A valuable return; to derive benefit. The taking of money or something of value through force in the sense of cutting. [AHLB: 2031 (N) / Strong's: 1215] **Concordance:** 18:21

<u>**PROLONG:**</u> Anc Heb: ⲱⲁⲗ⳧ Mod Heb: ארך / a-rak; **Definition:** To lengthen or delay. [AHLB: 1448-C (V) / Strong's: 748, 749] **Concordance:** 20:12

PROPHET: Anc Heb: ⳧ⲗⲧⳡ Mod Heb: נביא / na-vi (mas); **Definition:** One who utters the words or instructions of Elohiym that are received through a vision or dream. [AHLB: 1301-E (b) / Strong's: 5029, 5030] **Concordance:** 7:1

PROPHETESS: Anc Heb: ⳧ⳡⲗⲧⳡ Mod Heb: נביאה / na-vi-ah (fem); **Definition:** One gifted with more than ordinary spiritual and moral insight. Who brings forth the inner fruit. [AHLB: 1301-E (b^1) / Strong's: 5031] **Concordance:** 15:20

PROTECTION: Anc Heb: ⲟⲧⳡⲭ Mod Heb: סיתר / si-tar (mas); **Definition:** Shielded from harm or destruction, in the sense of being hidden. [AHLB: n/a / Strong's: n/a] **Concordance:** *Used in names only.*

<u>**PROVIDE:**</u> Anc Heb: ⲟⳡⲗ Mod Heb: יהב / ya-hav; **Definition:** To give what is due; to grant or allow permission. [AHLB: 1094-L (V) / Strong's: 3051, 3052] **Concordance:** 1:10

PROVISIONS: Anc Heb: ⳧ⲧⲗⲙ⳦ Mod Heb: צידה / tsi-dah (fem); **Definition:** A stock of needed materials. The produce of the hunt. Also, used for "food" in general. [AHLB: 1395-M (N^1) / Strong's: 6720] **Concordance:** 12:39

<u>**PULVERIZE:**</u> Anc Heb: ⲱⲙⲟ Mod Heb: שחק / sha-hhaq; **Definition:** To continually beat something to make it small or turn to powder. [AHLB: 2828 (V) / Strong's: 7833] **Concordance:** 30:36

<u>**PURCHASE:**</u> Anc Heb: ⳧ⲗⲟ Mod Heb: קנה / qa-nah; **Definition:** To acquire ownership or occupation through an exchange. [AHLB: 1428-H (V) / Strong's: 7066, 7069] **Concordance:** 15:16 21:2

PURE: Anc Heb: ⲟⲩ⳦ⲟ Mod Heb: טהור / ta-hor (mas); **Definition:** Unmixed with any other matter. A man, animal or object that is free of impurities or is not mixed. [AHLB: 1204-G (c) / Strong's: 2889, 2890] **Concordance:** 25:11 25:17 25:24 25:29 25:31 25:36 25:38 25:39 28:14 28:22 28:36 30:3 30:35 31:8 37:2 37:6 37:11 37:16 37:17 37:22 37:23 37:24 37:26 37:29 39:15 39:25 39:30 39:37

PURPLE: Anc Heb: ⳡⲙⲅⲗⲭ Mod Heb: ארגמן / ar-ga-man (mas); **Definition:** A reddish-blue color used to dye yarn and used in weaving. [AHLB: 1440-C (pm) / Strong's: 713] **Concordance:** 25:4 26:1 26:31 26:36 27:16 28:5 28:6 28:8 28:15 28:33 35:6 35:23 35:25 35:35 36:8 36:35 36:37 38:18 38:23 39:1 39:2 39:3 39:5 39:8 39:24 39:29

<u>**PURSUE:**</u> Anc Heb: ⲟⲧⲙ⳦ Mod Heb: רדף / ra-daph; **Definition:** To follow in order to overtake, capture, kill, or defeat; to pursue in chase or persecution. [AHLB: 2755 (V) / Strong's: 7291] **Concordance:** 14:4 14:8 14:9 14:23 15:9

<u>**PUSH:**</u> Anc Heb: ⲅⲙⳡ Mod Heb: נגש / na-gas; **Definition:** To drive oxen or men. [AHLB: 2375 (V) / Strong's: 5065] **Concordance:** 3:7 5:6 5:10 5:13 5:14

QUAIL: Anc Heb: Yּ√≼ Mod Heb: שלו / se-law (fem); Alt Sp: שליו **Definition:** A small bird used as a food. [AHLB: 1334-K (N) / Strong's: 7958] **Concordance:** 16:13

QUARREL: Anc Heb: ּ√┴╥ᴀᴀ Mod Heb: מדין / mid-yan (mas); **Definition:** A rather loud verbal disagreement. [AHLB: 1083-A (hb) / Strong's: 4079]

QUARTER: Anc Heb: ⌐ᴥᴀ Mod Heb: רבע / re-va (mas); **Definition:** One portion from the whole that has been divided into four equal parts. One side of a four sided square. A fourth. [AHLB: 2744 (N) / Strong's: 7252, 7253] **Concordance:** 29:40

QUICKLY: Anc Heb: ᴔ≼ᴀᴀ Mod Heb: מהר / ma-heyr (mas); **Definition:** To act on a matter as soon as possible. [AHLB: 1296-G (N) / Strong's: 4118] **Concordance:** 32:8

QUIETNESS: Anc Heb: †ᴆᴧ Mod Heb: נחת / na-hhat (fem); **Definition:** Without noise, without making a sound. [AHLB: 1307-A (N^2) / Strong's: 5183]

RAIMENT: Anc Heb: †Y≼ᴥ Mod Heb: כסות / ke-sut (fem); **Definition:** Clothing; garments. [AHLB: 1245-A (N^3) / Strong's: 3682] **Concordance:** 21:10 22:26

RAISE: Anc Heb: ᴀᴀYᴀ Mod Heb: רום / rum; **Definition:** To lift something up. [AHLB: 1450-J (V) / Strong's: 7311, 7313] **Concordance:** 7:20 14:8 14:16 15:2 16:20 17:11 29:27 35:24

RAISED: Anc Heb: ᴀᴀᴀ Mod Heb: רם / ram (mas); **Definition:** Lifted up in position or in exaltation. [AHLB: n/a / Strong's: n/a] **Concordance:** *Used in names only.*

RAM: Anc Heb: ⯑≼ Mod Heb: שה / seh (mas); Alt Sp: זה **Definition:** A member of a flock of sheep or goats. [AHLB: 1327-A (N) / Strong's: 2089, 7716] **Concordance:** 12:3{2} 12:4{2} 12:5 13:13 21:37{2} 22:3 22:8 22:9 34:19 34:20

RAM-HORN: Anc Heb: ⌐⌐Yᴧᴧ Mod Heb: שופר / sho-phar (mas); **Definition:** The horn of ram made into a trumpet that emits a bright and beautiful sound. [AHLB: 2869 (g) / Strong's: 7782] **Concordance:** 19:16 19:19 20:18

RAMPART: Anc Heb: ⯑ᴀᴀYᴛᴛ Mod Heb: חומה / hho-mah (fem); **Definition:** A fortified enclosure. [AHLB: 1174-J (N^1) / Strong's: 2346] **Concordance:** 14:22 14:29

RANK: Anc Heb: ⯑ᴧ≼⌐⌐ᴀᴀ Mod Heb: מערכה / ma-a-ra-khah (fem); **Definition:** A row, line, or series of things or persons. [AHLB: 2576 (a^1) / Strong's: 4634] **Concordance:** 39:37

RANSOM: Anc Heb: †Yᴛᴛ⌐ Mod Heb: פדות / pe-dut (fem); **Definition:** The act of requiring, or paying, a price for something that was stolen or wrongfully taken. [AHLB: 1372-A (N^3) / Strong's: 6304] **Concordance:** 8:19

RANSOM: Anc Heb: ⯑ᴛᴛ⌐ Mod Heb: פדה / pa-dah; **Definition:** To Pay the price stipulated, to retrieve what has been stolen or wrongfully taken. [AHLB: 1372-H (V) / Strong's: 6299] **Concordance:** 13:13{3} 13:15 21:8 34:20{3}

RANSOM-PRICE: Anc Heb: ּ√Yᴛᴛ⌐ Mod Heb: פדיון / pid-yon (mas); Alt Sp: פדיום **Definition:** A stipulated amount given to retrieve what has been stolen or wrongfully taken. [AHLB: 1372-A (fj) / Strong's: 6306] **Concordance:** 21:30

RAW: Anc Heb: ᴥᴧ Mod Heb: נא / na (mas); **Definition:** Uncooked meat. Meat that is not fit for consumption. [AHLB: 1300-A (N) / Strong's: 4995] **Concordance:** 12:9

REACH: Anc Heb: ⌐ᴧ⌐ Mod Heb: פנע / pa-ga; **Definition:** To touch or grasp; to get up to or as far as; to come together in meeting by chance; to give or place in the sense of a meeting. [AHLB: 2592 (V) / Strong's: 6293] **Concordance:** 5:3 5:20 23:4

RECEIVE: Anc Heb: √ᴛᴗᴏ Mod Heb: קבל / qa-val; **Definition:** To take or accept what has been given. [AHLB: 2693 (V) / Strong's: 6901, 6902] **Concordance:** 26:5 36:12

RED: Anc Heb: ᴀᴀYᴛ√ Mod Heb: אדום / a-dom (mas); **Definition:** Of the color red. Ruddy; florid. [AHLB: 1082-C (c) / Strong's: 122]

REDDISH-GRAY: Anc Heb: ⲁⲙⲟⲩⲁ Mod Heb: צוהר / tso-hhar (mas); **Definition:** A dark grayish ruddy color. [AHLB: n/a / Strong's: n/a] **Concordance:** *Used in names only.*

REDEEM: Anc Heb: ⳑⲟⳑ Mod Heb: גאל / ga-al; **Definition:** To buy back. Restore one to his original position or avenge his death. In the participle form this verb means "avenger," as it is the role of the nearest relative to buy back one in slavery or avenge his murder. [AHLB: 1058-D (V) / Strong's: 1350] **Concordance:** 6:6 15:13

REEDS: Anc Heb: ⲟⲩⲁ Mod Heb: סוף / suph (mas); **Definition:** The plants that grow at the edge, or lip, of a river or pond. This word can also mean the edge or conclusion of something. [AHLB: 1339-J (N) / Strong's: 5488, 5490, 5491] **Concordance:** 2:3 2:5 10:19 13:18 15:4 15:22 23:31

REFINED: Anc Heb: ⳑⲁ Mod Heb: זך / zak (mas); **Definition:** An oil or other substance that is free of impurities. Also, a person without impurities. [AHLB: 1149-A (N) / Strong's: 2134] **Concordance:** 27:20 30:34

REFLECTION: Anc Heb: ⳑⲟⲁⲙ Mod Heb: מראה / mar-ah (fem); **Definition:** The return of light or sound waves from a surface; production of an image as by a mirror. [AHLB: 1438-A (a^1) / Strong's: 4759] **Concordance:** 38:8

REFUSE: Anc Heb: ⳑⲟⲙ Mod Heb: מאן / ma-an; **Definition:** To express one's self as being unwilling to accept. [AHLB: 1290-D (V) / Strong's: 3985] **Concordance:** 4:23 7:14 10:3 16:28 22:16{2}

REFUSING: Anc Heb: ⳑⲟⲙ Mod Heb: מאן / ma-eyn (mas); **Definition:** Rejection of a proposal, denial. [AHLB: 1290-D (N) / Strong's: 3986, 3987] **Concordance:** 7:27 9:2 10:4

REGISTER: Anc Heb: ⲧⲟ⳽ Mod Heb: פקד / pa-qad; **Definition:** To indicate or show acknowledgement of someone or something; to document or count another. [AHLB: 2630 (V) / Strong's: 6485] **Concordance:** 3:16{2} 4:31 13:19{2} 20:5 30:12{3} 30:13 30:14 32:34{2} 34:7 38:21{2} 38:25 38:26

REGULATE: Anc Heb: ⳑⲩⲙⲙ Mod Heb: משל / ma-shal; **Definition:** To govern or correct according to rule; to bring order, method, or uniformity to; to compare one thing to another in the sense of a rule of measurement, often as a proverb or parable. [AHLB: 2359 (V) / Strong's: 4910, 4911] **Concordance:** 21:8

REIGN: Anc Heb: ⳑⲩⲙ Mod Heb: מלך / ma-lakh; **Definition:** To rule over a kingdom as king or queen. [AHLB: 2340 (V) / Strong's: 4427] **Concordance:** 15:18

REJOICE: Anc Heb: ⳑⲙⲙⲁ Mod Heb: שמח / sa-mahh; **Definition:** To be happy, glad. [AHLB: 2487 (V) / Strong's: 8055] **Concordance:** 4:14

RELEASE: Anc Heb: ⲟⲙⲩⲩ Mod Heb: שמט / sha-mat; **Definition:** To let go by dropping or shaking loose. [AHLB: 2849 (V) / Strong's: 8058] **Concordance:** 23:11

RELIEF: Anc Heb: ⳑⲟⲩⲙⳑ Mod Heb: ישועה / ye-shu-ah (fem); **Definition:** A deliverance or freedom from a trouble, burden or danger. [AHLB: 1476-L (d^1) / Strong's: 3444] **Concordance:** 14:13 15:2

REMAIN: Anc Heb: ⳑⳑⲩⲙ Mod Heb: שאר / sha-ar; **Definition:** To continue unchanged; to stay behind. [AHLB: 1480-D (V) / Strong's: 7604] **Concordance:** 8:5 8:7 8:27 10:5 10:12 10:19 10:26 14:28

REMAINDER: Anc Heb: ⳑⲧⲩ Mod Heb: יתר / ye-ter (mas); **Definition:** A remaining group, part or trace. [AHLB: 1480-L (N) / Strong's: 3499] **Concordance:** 10:5 23:11

REMAINS: Anc Heb: ⳑⳑⲩⲙ Mod Heb: שאר / she-ar (mas); **Definition:** What is left behind, a residue. A relative as a remnant. Flesh as what remains after death. [AHLB: 1480-D (N) / Strong's: 7605, 7606, 7607] **Concordance:** 21:10

REMEMBER: Anc Heb: ⵉⵡⵛⴵ Mod Heb: זכר / za-khar; **Definition:** To bring to mind or think of again; to act or speak on behalf of another. Remember in thought as a memorial or mention through speech. The hiphil (causative) form means "mention." [AHLB: 2121 (V) / Strong's: 2142] **Concordance:** 2:24 6:5 13:3 20:8 20:24 23:13 32:13 34:19

REMEMBRANCE: Anc Heb: ⵉⵢⴰⵡⵛⴵ Mod Heb: זיכרון / zikh-ron (mas); **Definition:** A recalling of a past event. Also, an action based on a past event. [AHLB: 2121 (ej) / Strong's: 1799, 2146] **Concordance:** 12:14 13:9 17:14 28:12{2} 28:29 30:16 39:7

REMOVE-THE-COVER: Anc Heb: ⵣⴵⵍ Mod Heb: גלה / ga-lah; **Definition:** To reveal something by exposing it. Usually to be exposed from the removal of clothing. [AHLB: 1357-H (V) / Strong's: 1540, 1541] **Concordance:** 20:26

REPORT: Anc Heb: ⵐⵡⴰⵍ Mod Heb: שמע / shey-ma (mas); **Definition:** An account or statement of an event or happening. What is heard. [AHLB: 2851 (N) / Strong's: 8088] **Concordance:** 23:1

REPRODUCE: Anc Heb: ⵣⴰⵐ Mod Heb: פרה / pa-rah; **Definition:** To produce new individuals of the same kind; to be abundant in fruit. [AHLB: 1388-H (V) / Strong's: 6509] **Concordance:** 1:7 23:30

RESCUE: Anc Heb: ⵐⵡⴵ Mod Heb: ישע / ya-sha; **Definition:** To free or deliver from a trouble, burden or danger. [AHLB: 1476-L (V) / Strong's: 3467] **Concordance:** 2:17 14:30

RESEMBLANCE: Anc Heb: ⵣⵉⵢⵡⵜ Mod Heb: תמונה / te-mu-nah (fem); **Definition:** To be of like kind. Having attributes that are similar in shape, size or value. [AHLB: 1290-J (i¹) / Strong's: 8544] **Concordance:** 20:4

RESIDENT: Anc Heb: ⵉⵢⵣⵢⴵ Mod Heb: זבולון / ze-vu-lan (mas); **Definition:** One who abides or dwells in a place or area. [AHLB: n/a / Strong's: n/a] **Concordance:** *Used in names only.*

RESPITE: Anc Heb: ⵣⴰⵢⵐ Mod Heb: רוחה / re-wa-hhah (fem); **Definition:** A relief from labor, punishment or trouble. [AHLB: 1445-J (N¹) / Strong's: 7309] **Concordance:** 8:11

REST: Anc Heb: ⵐⵢⵉ Mod Heb: נוח / nu-ahh; **Definition:** Freedom from activity or labor. To rest from trouble or labor. [AHLB: 1307-J (V) / Strong's: 5117] **Concordance:** 10:14 16:23 16:24 16:33 16:34 17:11 20:11 23:12 32:10 33:14

REST-DAY: Anc Heb: ⵉⵢⵜⵡⵐ Mod Heb: שבתון / sha-ba-ton (mas); **Definition:** A day when work and normal activities are halted. [AHLB: 2812 (j) / Strong's: 7677] **Concordance:** 16:23 31:15 35:2

RESTRAIN: Anc Heb: ⵐⵙⵍ Mod Heb: עקב / a-qav; **Definition:** To prevent from doing. Hold back, in the sense of grabbing the heel. [AHLB: 2571 (V) / Strong's: 6117]

RESTRICT: Anc Heb: ⵣⵣⵐ Mod Heb: כלא / ka-la; **Definition:** To confine within bounds. Hold back or prevent someone or something. [AHLB: 1242-E (V) / Strong's: 3607] **Concordance:** 36:6

RIB: Anc Heb: ⵣⵣⴰ Mod Heb: צל / tsey-la (fem); Alt Sp: צלע **Definition:** Any of the paired bony or cartilaginous bones that stiffen the walls of the thorax and protect the organs beneath. A ridge of a hill from its similar shape to a rib. Also, the side. [AHLB: 2664 (N) / Strong's: 5967, 6763] **Concordance:** 25:12{2} 25:14 26:20 26:26 26:27{2} 26:35{2} 27:7 30:4 36:25 36:31 36:32 37:3{2} 37:5 37:27 38:7

RICH: Anc Heb: ⵐⵡⵉⵐ Mod Heb: עשיר / a-shir (mas); **Definition:** Having wealth or great possessions; abundantly supplied with resources, means, or funds. [AHLB: 2585 (b) / Strong's: 6223] **Concordance:** 30:15

RIDE: Anc Heb: ⵐⵡⵐⵣ Mod Heb: רכב / ra-khav; **Definition:** To sit and travel in any conveyance; to sit astride an animal, wagon or chariot. [AHLB: 2769 (V) / Strong's: 7392] **Concordance:** 4:20 15:1 15:21

RIGHT: Anc Heb: ﹌ Mod Heb: ימני / ye-ma-ni (mas); **Definition:** A direction as in to the right. [AHLB: 1290-L (f) / Strong's: 3233] **Concordance:** 29:20{3}

RIGHT-HAND: Anc Heb: ﹌ Mod Heb: ימין / ya-min (fem); **Definition:** The hand on the right side of a person. Also, a direction as in to the right. [AHLB: 1290-L (b) / Strong's: 3225] **Concordance:** 14:22 14:29 15:6{2} 15:12 29:22

RIM: Anc Heb: ﹌ Mod Heb: מסגרת / mis-ge-ret (fem); **Definition:** The edge of a region, hole, etc. , in the sense of enclosing. [AHLB: 2467 (h^2) / Strong's: 4526] **Concordance:** 25:25{2} 25:27 37:12{2} 37:14

RING: Anc Heb: ﹌ Mod Heb: טבעת / ta-ba-at (fem); **Definition:** A circular band of metal or other durable material. Also the signet ring containing the mark of the owner that is sunk into a lump of clay as a seal. [AHLB: 2229 (N^2) / Strong's: 2885] **Concordance:** 25:12{3} 25:14 25:15 25:26{2} 25:27 26:24 26:29 27:4 27:7 28:23{2} 28:24 28:26 28:27 28:28{2} 30:4 35:22 36:29 36:34 37:3{3} 37:5 37:13{2} 37:14 37:27 38:5 38:7 39:16{2} 39:17 39:19 39:20 39:21{2}

RIPE-FRUIT: Anc Heb: ﹌ Mod Heb: מלאה / me-ley-ah (fem); **Definition:** Fruit that has come to full maturity and fit for eating. [AHLB: 1288-E (N^1) / Strong's: 4395] **Concordance:** 22:28

RISE: Anc Heb: ﹌ Mod Heb: קום / qum; **Definition:** To assume an upright position; to raise or rise up; to continue or establish. [AHLB: 1427-J (V) / Strong's: 6965, 6966] **Concordance:** 1:8 2:17 6:4 10:23 12:30 12:31 15:7 21:19 24:13 26:30 32:1 32:6 32:25 33:8 33:10 40:2 40:17 40:18{2} 40:33

RISE-UP: Anc Heb: ﹌ Mod Heb: גאה / ga-ah; **Definition:** To lift or grow up high. [AHLB: 1051-D (V) / Strong's: 1342] **Concordance:** 15:1{2} 15:21{2}

RISING: Anc Heb: ﹌ Mod Heb: עולה / o-lah (fem); Alt Sp: גולה **Definition:** A rising of smoke from a burnt offering. Captivity in the sense of placing a yoke on the captives. [AHLB: 1357-J (N^1) / Strong's: 1473, 5930] **Concordance:** 10:25 18:12 20:24 24:5 29:18 29:25 29:42 30:9 30:28 31:9 32:6 35:16 38:1 40:6 40:10 40:29{2}

RITUAL: Anc Heb: ﹌ Mod Heb: חוקה / hhu-qah (fem); **Definition:** A repeating of the same actions. A custom. [AHLB: 1180-J (N^1) / Strong's: 2708] **Concordance:** 12:14 12:17 12:43 13:10 27:21 28:43 29:9

RIVER: Anc Heb: ﹌ Mod Heb: נהר / na-har (mas); **Definition:** A natural stream of water of considerable volume. The life-giving water that washes over the soil. [AHLB: 1319-G (N) / Strong's: 5103, 5104] **Concordance:** 7:19 8:1 23:31

ROAD: Anc Heb: ﹌ Mod Heb: דרך / de-rek (mas); **Definition:** A route or path for traveled or walked. The path or manner of life. [AHLB: 2112 (N) / Strong's: 1870] **Concordance:** 3:18 4:24 5:3 8:23 13:17 13:18 13:21 18:8 18:20 23:20 32:8 33:3 33:13

ROAST: Anc Heb: ﹌ Mod Heb: צלי / tsa-li (mas); **Definition:** A meat that is cooked over a fire. [AHLB: 1403-H (f) / Strong's: 6748] **Concordance:** 12:8 12:9

ROCK-WALL: Anc Heb: ﹌ Mod Heb: שור / shur (mas); **Definition:** A wall made of rocks or stones for protection. [AHLB: 1480-J (N) / Strong's: 7790, 7791, 7792] **WALL:**

ROD: Anc Heb: ﹌ Mod Heb: מקל / ma-qeyl (mas); מקלה / maq-lah (fem); **Definition:** A long and slender bar of wood. A staff for walking. [AHLB: 1426-A (a) / Strong's: 4731] **Concordance:** 12:11

ROOF: Anc Heb: ﹌ Mod Heb: גג / gag (mas); **Definition:** The covering of a dwelling place. [AHLB: 1049-A (N) / Strong's: 1406] **Concordance:** 30:3 37:26

ROOF-COVERING: Anc Heb: ﹌ Mod Heb: מכסה / mikh-seh (mas); **Definition:** Material used for a top or covering of a building. What covers something. [AHLB: 1245-H (h) / Strong's: 4372] **Concordance:** 26:14{2} 35:11 36:19{2} 39:34{2} 40:19

ROUND-ABOUT: Anc Heb: ⲧⲟⲱⲟⲩ Mod Heb: בעד / ba-ad (mas); **Definition:** A circuitous way or route. [AHLB: 1349-A (N) / Strong's: 1157] **Concordance:** 8:24 32:30

ROUNDNESS: Anc Heb: ꙉꙍꙑꙑꙍ Mod Heb: כיכר / ki-kar (fem); **Definition:** Cylindrical; something as a circle, globe or ring that is round. A round thing or place. A round loaf of bread. The plain, as a round piece of land. [AHLB: 2258 (e) / Strong's: 3603] **Concordance:** 29:23

ROUND-UP: Anc Heb: ⳺⳩⳾ Mod Heb: קהל / qa-hal; **Definition:** To gather together a flock, herd or group of people. [AHLB: 1426-G (V) / Strong's: 6950, 7035] **Concordance:** 32:1 35:1

ROW: Anc Heb: ꙍ⳧⊗ Mod Heb: טור / tur (mas); **Definition:** Set or placed in a line. A mountain range as a row. [AHLB: 1204-J (N) / Strong's: 2905, 2906] **Concordance:** 28:17{3} 28:18 28:19 28:20 39:10{3} 39:11 39:12 39:13

SACRIFICE: Anc Heb: ꙏꙍⲟⲱꙎ Mod Heb: זבה / ze-vahh (mas); **Definition:** An animal killed for an offering. [AHLB: 2117 (N) / Strong's: 1685, 2077] **Concordance:** 10:25 12:27 18:12 23:18 24:5 29:28 34:25{2}

SACRIFICE: Anc Heb: ꙏꙍⲟⲱꙎ Mod Heb: זבה / za-vahh; **Definition:** An act of offering to deity something precious; to kill an animal for an offering. [AHLB: 2117 (V) / Strong's: 1684, 2076] **Concordance:** 3:18 5:3 5:8 5:17 8:4 8:21 8:22{2} 8:23 8:24 8:25 13:15 20:24 22:19 23:18 24:5 32:8 34:15

SACRIFICIAL-BOWL: Anc Heb: ꓕⲗ⳹Ꙏꙏꙏ Mod Heb: מנקית / me-na-qit (fem); **Definition:** A vessel used to hold the required sacrifice. From the shape of a bowl that holds liquids like a breast that holds milk. [AHLB: 1318-A (k⁴) / Strong's: 4518] **Concordance:** 25:29 37:16

SADDLE: Anc Heb: ꙡꙡꙎꙏ Mod Heb: חבש / hha-bash; **Definition:** A shaped mounted support on which an object can travel; to bind up with a saddle. [AHLB: 2144 (V) / Strong's: 2280] **Concordance:** 29:9

SAFEGUARD: Anc Heb: ꙏꙍⲙꙑꙡ Mod Heb: שמר / sha-mar; **Definition:** The act or the duty of protecting or defending; to watch over or guard in the sense of preserving or protecting. [AHLB: 2853 (V) / Strong's: 8104] **Concordance:** 10:28 12:17{2} 12:24 12:25 13:10 15:26 16:28 19:5 19:12 20:6 21:29 21:36 22:6 22:9 23:13 23:15 23:20 23:21 31:13 31:14 31:16 34:11 34:12 34:18

SAFEGUARDING: Anc Heb: ꙏꙭ⳩ꙍꙗ⳹ꙡ Mod Heb: שימור / shi-mur (mas); **Definition:** To keep safe. To protect. [AHLB: 2853 (d) / Strong's: 8107] **Concordance:** 12:42{2}

SANCTUARY: Anc Heb: ꙡꙡⲧ⳺ꙍꙏꙡ Mod Heb: מקדש / miq-dash (mas); **Definition:** A place set apart for a special purpose. [AHLB: 2700 (h) / Strong's: 4720] **Concordance:** 15:17 25:8

SAND: Anc Heb: ꙩꙍꙡꙡ Mod Heb: חול / hhul (mas); **Definition:** Loose granular material from the disintegration of rocks and consisting of particles not as fine as silt and used in mortar. Sand is used as an abrasive ingredient for drilling by placing it in the hole being drilled. [AHLB: 1173-J (N) / Strong's: 2344] **Concordance:** 2:12

SANDAL: Anc Heb: ꙩꙍⲟ⳹ Mod Heb: נעל / na-al (fem); **Definition:** A shoe consisting of a sole strapped to the foot. [AHLB: 2415 (N) / Strong's: 5275] **Concordance:** 3:5 12:11

SASH: Anc Heb: ⊗ꙡꙍⲟꙑꙙ Mod Heb: אבנט / av-neyt (mas); **Definition:** A waistband worn around the waist. [AHLB: 2022 (n) / Strong's: 73] **Concordance:** 28:4 28:39 28:40 29:9 39:29

SATISFACTION: Anc Heb: ⲟꙏꙍꙡꙔ Mod Heb: שבע / so-va (mas) **Definition:** The state of being content. [AHLB: 2461 (g) / Strong's: 7648] **Concordance:** 16:3

SAY: Anc Heb: ꙩꙍꙏꙙ Mod Heb: אמר / a-mar; **Definition:** To speak chains of words that form sentences. [AHLB: 1288-C (V) / Strong's: 559, 560] **Concordance:** 1:9 1:15 1:16 1:18 1:19 1:22 2:6 2:7 2:8 2:9 2:10 2:13 2:14{3} 2:18 2:19 2:20 2:22 3:3 3:4{2} 3:5 3:6 3:7 3:11 3:12 3:13{4} 3:14{3} 3:15{2} 3:16{2} 3:17 3:18 4:1{2} 4:2{2} 4:3 4:4 4:6 4:7 4:10 4:11 4:13 4:14 4:18{2} 4:19 4:21 4:22{2} 4:23 4:25 4:26 4:27 5:1{2} 5:2 5:3 5:4 5:5 5:6 5:8 5:10{3} 5:13 5:14 5:15 5:16

5:17{2} 5:19 5:21 5:22 6:1 6:2 6:6 6:10 6:12 6:26 6:29 6:30 7:1 7:8{2} 7:9{2} 7:14 7:16{2} 7:17 7:19{2} 7:26{3} 8:1{2} 8:4 8:5 8:6{2} 8:12{2} 8:15 8:16{3} 8:21 8:22 8:23 8:24 8:25 9:1{2} 9:5 9:8 9:13{3} 9:22 9:27 9:29 10:1 10:3{2} 10:7 10:8 10:9 10:10 10:12 10:16 10:21 10:24 10:25 10:28 10:29 11:1 11:4{2} 11:8 11:9 12:1{2} 12:3 12:21 12:26 12:27 12:31 12:33 12:43 13:1 13:3 13:8 13:14{2} 13:17 13:19 14:1 14:3 14:5 14:11 14:12 14:13 14:15 14:25 14:26 15:1{2} 15:9 15:24 15:26 16:3 16:4 16:6 16:8 16:9{2} 16:11 16:12 16:15{2} 16:19 16:23 16:25 16:28 16:32 16:33 17:2{2} 17:3 17:4 17:5 17:7 17:9 17:10 17:14 17:16 18:3 18:6 18:10 18:14 18:15 18:17 18:24 19:3{2} 19:8 19:9 19:10 19:12 19:15 19:21 19:23{2} 19:24 19:25 20:1 20:19 20:20 20:22{2} 21:5{2} 22:8 23:13 24:1 24:3 24:7 24:8 24:12 24:14 25:1 30:11 30:17 30:22 30:31 30:34 31:1 31:12{2} 31:13 32:1 32:2 32:4 32:5 32:8 32:9 32:11 32:12{2} 32:13 32:17 32:18 32:21 32:22 32:23 32:24 32:26 32:27{2} 32:29 32:30 32:31 32:33 33:1 33:5{2} 33:12{3} 33:14 33:15 33:17 33:18 33:19 33:20 33:21 34:1 34:9 34:10 34:27 35:1 35:4{3} 35:30 36:5{2} 36:6 40:1

SAYER: Anc Heb: Mod Heb: אמור / e-mor (mas); **Definition:** One who speaks words. Possibly a prophet or psalmist. [AHLB: n/a / Strong's: n/a] **Concordance:** *Used in names only.*

SCARLET: Anc Heb: Mod Heb: שני / sha-ni (mas); **Definition:** Any of various bright reds. [AHLB: 1474-A (f) / Strong's: 8144] **Concordance:** 25:4 26:1 26:31 26:36 27:16 28:5 28:6 28:8 28:15 28:33 35:6 35:23 35:25 35:35 36:8 36:35 36:37 38:18 38:23 39:1 39:2 39:3 39:5 39:8 39:24 39:29

<u>**SCATTER-ABROAD**</u>**:** Anc Heb: Mod Heb: פוץ / puts; **Definition:** To sow, cast or fling widely. [AHLB: 1386-J (V) / Strong's: 6327] **Concordance:** 5:12

SCRAWNY: Anc Heb: Mod Heb: דק / daq (mas); **Definition:** Wasted away physically. [AHLB: 1088-A (N) / Strong's: 1851] **Concordance:** 16:14{2}

SCROLL: Anc Heb: Mod Heb: ספר / se-pher (mas); **Definition:** A document or record written on sheets of papyrus, leather or parchment and rolled up for storage. [AHLB: 2500 (N) / Strong's: 5609, 5612, 5613] **Concordance:** 17:14 24:7 32:32 32:33

<u>**SCULPT**</u>**:** Anc Heb: Mod Heb: פסל / pa-sal **Definition:** To carve or chisel out a figure from wood or stone. [AHLB: 2619 (V) / Strong's: 6458] **Concordance:** 34:1 34:4

SCULPTURE: Anc Heb: Mod Heb: פסל / pe-sel (mas); **Definition:** A figurine that is formed and shaped from stone, wood or clay. [AHLB: 2619 (N) / Strong's: 6459] **Concordance:** 20:4

SEA: Anc Heb: Mod Heb: ים / yam (mas); **Definition:** A large body of water. Also, the direction of the great sea (the Mediterranean), the west. [AHLB: 1220-A (N) / Strong's: 3220, 3221] **Concordance:** 10:19{2} 13:18 14:2{2} 14:9 14:16{2} 14:21{3} 14:22 14:23 14:26 14:27{3} 14:28 14:29 14:30 15:1 15:4{2} 15:8 15:10 15:19{3} 15:21 15:22 20:11 23:31{2} 26:22 26:27 27:12 36:27 36:32 38:12

SEAL: Anc Heb: Mod Heb: חותם / hho-tam (mas); **Definition:** A seal used officially to give personal authority to a document. A signature ring or cylinder with the owner's seal that is pressed into clay to show ownership. [AHLB: 2223 (g) / Strong's: 2368] **Concordance:** 28:11 28:21 28:36 39:6 39:14 39:30

SEARCHING: Anc Heb: Mod Heb: מחתרת / mahh-te-ret (fem); **Definition:** A digging up to uncover something hidden. [AHLB: 2226 (a^2) / Strong's: 4290] **Concordance:** 22:1

<u>**SEARCH-OUT**</u>**:** Anc Heb: Mod Heb: בקש / ba-qash; **Definition:** To intently look for someone or something until the object of the search is found. [AHLB: 2036 (V) / Strong's: 1245] **Concordance:** 2:15 4:19 4:24 10:11 33:7

<u>**SEASON**</u>**:** Anc Heb: Mod Heb: מלח / ma-lahh; **Definition:** To season with salt to enhance the flavor. [AHLB: 2338 (V) / Strong's: 4414, 4415] **Concordance:** 30:35

SEAT: Anc Heb: שׁוﬔﬗ﬘ Mod Heb: כִּסֵא / ki-sey (mas); Alt Sp: כִּסֵה **Definition:** A special chair of one in eminence. Usually a throne or seat of authority. [AHLB: 1245-E (e) / Strong's: 3678, 3764] **Concordance:** 11:5 12:29

SECOND: Anc Heb: ﬓﬗ﬘ Mod Heb: שֵׁנִי / shey-ni (com); **Definition:** A cardinal number. [AHLB: 1474-H (f) / Strong's: 8145] **Concordance:** 1:15 2:13 16:1 25:12 25:32 26:4 26:5 26:10 26:20 26:27 27:15 28:10 28:18 29:19 29:39 29:41 36:11 36:12 36:17 36:25 36:32 37:3 37:18 38:15 39:11 40:17

SECRET: Anc Heb: ⊗ﬔ Mod Heb: לָט / lat (mas); **Definition:** That which is unknown or hidden. [AHLB: 1262-A (N) / Strong's: 3909] **Concordance:** 7:22 8:3 8:14

SECURE: Anc Heb: ﬗ﬘ﬔﬗ Mod Heb: אָמַן / a-man; **Definition:** Solidly fixed in place; to stand firm in the sense of a support. Not subject to change or revision. The hiphil (causative) form means "support." [AHLB: 1290-C (V) / Strong's: 539, 540] **Concordance:** 4:1 4:5 4:8{2} 4:9 4:31 14:31 19:9

SEE: Anc Heb: ﬥﬔﬗ Mod Heb: רָאָה / ra-ah; **Definition:** To take notice; to perceive something or someone; to see visions. The niphal (passive) form means "appear" and the hiphil (causative) form means "show." [AHLB: 1438-H (V) / Strong's: 7200, 7202, 7207, 7212] **Concordance:** 1:16 2:2 2:5 2:6 2:11{2} 2:12 2:25 3:2{2} 3:3 3:4{2} 3:7{2} 3:9 3:16 4:1 4:5 4:14 4:18 4:21 4:31 5:19 5:21 6:1 6:3 7:1 8:11 9:16 9:34 10:5 10:6 10:10 10:23 10:28{2} 10:29 12:13 12:23 13:7{2} 13:17 14:13{3} 14:30 14:31 16:7 16:10 16:15 16:29 16:32 18:14 19:4 19:21 20:18{2} 20:22 22:9 23:5 23:15 23:17 24:10 25:9 25:40{2} 26:30 27:8 31:2 32:1 32:5 32:9 32:19 32:25 33:10 33:12 33:13 33:18 33:20{2} 33:23{2} 34:3 34:10 34:20 34:23 34:24 34:30 34:35 35:30 39:43

SEED: Anc Heb: ⊙ﬗﬕ Mod Heb: זֶרַע / ze-ra (mas); **Definition:** The grains or ripened ovules of plants used for sowing. Scattered in the field to produce a crop. The singular word can be used for one or more. Also, the descendants of an individual, either male or female. [AHLB: 2137 (N) / Strong's: 2233, 2234] **Concordance:** 16:31 28:43 30:21 32:13{2} 33:1

SEEING: Anc Heb: ﬗﬔﬗﬕ Mod Heb: פִּקֵּחַ / pi-qey-ahh (mas); **Definition:** One who is able to see with the eyes. [AHLB: 2631 (N) / Strong's: 6493] **Concordance:** 4:11 23:8

SEEK: Anc Heb: ﬥﬗ﬘ﬕ Mod Heb: דָּרַשׁ / da-rash; **Definition:** To look for or search for something or for answers. The niphal (passive) form means "require." [AHLB: 2114 (V) / Strong's: 1875] **Concordance:** 18:15

SEIZE: Anc Heb: ﬗﬔﬕﬗ Mod Heb: חָזַק / hha-zaq; **Definition:** To possess or take by force; grab hold tightly; to refrain or support by grabbing hold. [AHLB: 2152 (V) / Strong's: 2388] **Concordance:** 4:4 4:21 7:13 7:22 8:15 9:2 9:12 9:35 10:20 10:27 11:10 12:33 14:4 14:8 14:17

SELF-WILL: Anc Heb: ﬥﬔﬗﬕ Mod Heb: רָצוֹן / ra-tson (mas); **Definition:** Used to express determination, insistence, persistence, or willfulness. One's desire. [AHLB: 1455-H (j) / Strong's: 7522] **Concordance:** 28:38

SELL: Anc Heb: ﬗ﬘ﬔﬗ Mod Heb: מָכַר / ma-khar; **Definition:** To give up property to another for money or another valuable compensation. [AHLB: 2337 (V) / Strong's: 4376] **Concordance:** 21:7 21:8 21:16 21:35 21:37 22:2

SEND: Anc Heb: ﬗﬔﬗ﬘ﬕ Mod Heb: שָׁלַח / sha-lahh; **Definition:** To cause to go; to direct, order, or request to go. [AHLB: 2842 (V) / Strong's: 7971, 7972] **Concordance:** 2:5 3:10 3:12 3:13 3:14 3:15 3:20{2} 4:4{2} 4:13{2} 4:21 4:23{2} 4:28 5:1 5:2{2} 5:22 6:1 6:11 7:2 7:14 7:16{2} 7:26 7:27 8:4 8:16 8:17{2} 8:24 8:25 8:28 9:1 9:2 9:7{2} 9:13 9:14 9:15 9:17 9:19 9:27 9:28 9:35 10:3 10:4 10:7 10:10 10:20 10:27 11:1{2} 11:10 12:33 13:15 13:17 14:5 15:7 18:27 21:26 21:27 22:4 22:7 22:10 23:20 23:27 23:28 24:5 24:11 32:24 33:2 33:12

SEND-OFF: Anc Heb: ﬗﬔﬗ﬘ﬕ Mod Heb: שִׁלּוּחַ / shi-lu-ahh (mas); **Definition:** To send away a person or gift. [AHLB: 2842 (ed) / Strong's: 7964] **Concordance:** 18:2

SEPARATE: Anc Heb: ᴊᴛᴍ Mod Heb: בדל / ba-dal; **Definition:** To set or keep apart. [AHLB: 2005 (V) / Strong's: 914] **Concordance:** 26:33

SERPENT: Anc Heb: ᴧᴍ Mod Heb: נחש / na-hhash (mas); **Definition:** A poisonous snake that hisses, creeps and bites. [AHLB: 2395 (N) / Strong's: 5175] **Concordance:** 4:3 7:15

SERVANT: Anc Heb: ᴛᴍᴄ Mod Heb: עבד / e-ved (mas); **Definition:** One who provides a service to another, as a slave, bondservant or hired hand. [AHLB: 2518 (N) / Strong's: 5649, 5650, 5652] **Concordance:** 4:10 5:15 5:16{2} 5:21 7:10 7:20 7:28 7:29 8:5 8:7 8:17 8:20 8:25 8:27 9:14 9:20{2} 9:21 9:30 9:34 10:1 10:6 10:7 11:3 11:8 12:30 12:44 13:3 13:14 14:5 14:31 20:2 20:10 20:17 21:2 21:5 21:7 21:20 21:26 21:27 21:32 32:13

SERVE: Anc Heb: ᴛᴍᴄ Mod Heb: עבר / a-var; **Definition:** To provide a service to another, as a servant or slave or to work at a profession. [AHLB: 2518 (V) / Strong's: 5647, 5648] **Concordance:** 1:13 1:14 3:12 4:23 5:18 6:5 7:16 7:26 8:16 9:1 9:13 10:3 10:7 10:8 10:11 10:24 10:26{2} 12:31 13:5 14:5 14:12{2} 20:5 20:9 21:2 21:6 23:24 23:25 23:33 34:21

SERVICE: Anc Heb: ᴦᴛᴍᴄ Mod Heb: עבודה / a-vo-dah (fem); **Definition:** Labor provided by a servant or slave. [AHLB: 2518 (c¹) / Strong's: 5656] **Concordance:** 1:14{3} 2:23{2} 5:9 5:11 6:6 6:9 12:25 12:26 13:5 27:19 30:16 35:21 35:24 36:1 36:3 36:5 38:21 39:32 39:40 39:42

SET-APART: Anc Heb: ᴧᴛᴦ Mod Heb: קדש / qa-dash; **Definition:** To move or place someone or something separate from the whole for a special purpose. [AHLB: 2700 (V) / Strong's: 6942] **Concordance:** 13:2 19:10 19:14 19:22 19:23 20:8 20:11 28:3 28:38 28:41 29:1 29:21 29:27 29:33 29:36 29:37{2} 29:43 29:44{2} 30:29{2} 30:30 31:13 40:9 40:10 40:11 40:13

SET-DOWN: Anc Heb: ᴛᴦᴦ Mod Heb: שית / shit; **Definition:** To cause to sit down; to lay down. [AHLB: 1482-M (V) / Strong's: 7896] **Concordance:** 7:23 10:1 21:22 21:30{2} 23:1 23:31 33:4

SETTING: Anc Heb: ᴦᴦᴦᴍ Mod Heb: מלואה / mi-lu-ah (fem); **Definition:** A recess for filling with a stone or other ornament. [AHLB: 1288-E (ed¹) / Strong's: 4396] **Concordance:** 28:17 28:20 39:13

SETTLE: Anc Heb: ᴦᴦᴍ Mod Heb: ישב / ya-shav; **Definition:** To stay in a dwelling place for the night or for long periods of time; to sit down. [AHLB: 1462-L (V) / Strong's: 3427, 3488] **Concordance:** 2:15{2} 2:21 11:5 12:29 12:40 15:14 15:15 15:17 16:3 16:29 16:35 17:12 18:13 18:14 23:31 23:33 24:14 32:6 34:12 34:15

SETTLING: Anc Heb: ᴦᴦᴦᴍ Mod Heb: מושב / mo-shav (mas); **Definition:** The place of sitting, resting or dwelling, usually temporarily. [AHLB: 1462-L (a) / Strong's: 4186] **Concordance:** 10:23 12:20 12:40 35:3

SEVEN: Anc Heb: ᴄᴦᴍᴍ Mod Heb: שבעה / shiv-ah (mas); שבע / she-va (fem); **Definition:** An ordinal number. [AHLB: 2808 (N) / Strong's: 7651, 7657, 7655] **Concordance:** 1:5 2:16 6:16 6:20 7:25 12:15 12:19 13:6 13:7 15:27 22:29 23:15 24:1 24:9 25:37 29:30 29:35 29:37 34:18 37:23 38:24 38:25{2} 38:28{2} 38:29

SEVENTH: Anc Heb: ᴧᴄᴦᴍᴍ Mod Heb: שביעי / she-vi-i (mas); **Definition:** A cardinal number. [AHLB: 2808 (bf) / Strong's: 7637] **Concordance:** 12:15 12:16 13:6 16:26 16:27 16:29 16:30 20:10 20:11 21:2 23:11 23:12 24:16 31:15 31:17 34:21 35:2

SEVER: Anc Heb: ᴄᴧᴦ Mod Heb: קצץ / qa-tsats **Definition:** To make an end of something by cutting it off. [AHLB: 1432-B (V) / Strong's: 7082, 7112, 7113] **Concordance:** 39:3

SHADOW: Anc Heb: ᴊᴧᴦ Mod Heb: צל / tseyl (mas); **Definition:** The dark figure cast on a surface by a body intercepting the rays from a light source. [AHLB: 1403-A (N) / Strong's: 6738]

SHAKE: Anc Heb: ᴄᴧᴦ Mod Heb: רגז / ra-gaz; **Definition:** To tremble in fear or anger. [AHLB: 2748 (V) / Strong's: 7264, 7265] **Concordance:** 15:14

SHAKE-OFF: Anc Heb: ᔐᔑ Mod Heb: נער / na-ar; **Definition:** To violently shake back and forth to throw something off. To overthrow. [AHLB: 2458 (V) / Strong's: 5286, 5287] **Concordance:** 14:27

SHAKING-IN-FEAR: Anc Heb: ᔐᔑᔗ Mod Heb: רעד / ra-ad (mas); רעדה / re-a-dah (fem); **Definition:** Being physically effected by shivering or shaking from a dreadful event. [AHLB: 2778 (N) / Strong's: 7461] **Concordance:** 15:15

SHARE: Anc Heb: ᔐᔑᔗ Mod Heb: מן / mahn (mas); מנה / ma-nah (fem); **Definition:** A portion that is provided to a group or person to meet their needs. [AHLB: 1290-A (N¹) / Strong's: 4490] **Concordance:** 29:26

SHARP-STONE: Anc Heb: ᔐᔑᔗ Mod Heb: צור / tsor (mas); **Definition:** A piece of stone from obsidian, flint or chert that forms a narrow and sharp edge when flaked off. [AHLB: 1411-J (N) / Strong's: 6864] **Concordance:** 4:25

SHARP-THORN: Anc Heb: ᔐᔑ Mod Heb: צן / tseyn (mas); **Definition:** A pointed, piercing object. [AHLB: 1336-A (N) / Strong's: 6791] **THORN:**

SHE: Anc Heb: ᔐᔑᔗ Mod Heb: היא / hi (fem); Alt Sp: הוא **Definition:** The female who is neither the speaker nor the one addressed. [AHLB: 1093-J (N) / Strong's: 1931, 1932] **Concordance:** 1:16 3:8 8:15 12:15 12:19 22:26{2} 31:13 31:14{2} 31:17

SHEEP: Anc Heb: ᔐᔑᔗ Mod Heb: כשב / ke-sev (mas); Alt Sp: כבש **Definition:** A mammal related to the goat domesticated for its flesh and wool. [AHLB: 2273 (N) / Strong's: 3532, 3775] **Concordance:** 12:5 29:38 29:39{2} 29:40 29:41

SHE-GOAT: Anc Heb: ᔐᔑ Mod Heb: עז / eyz (fem); **Definition:** A female goat. [AHLB: 1513-A (N) / Strong's: 5795, 5796] **Concordance:** 12:5 25:4 26:7 35:6 35:23 35:26 36:14

SHEQEL: Anc Heb: ᔐᔑᔗ Mod Heb: שקל / she-qel (mas); **Definition:** A chief Hebrew weight standard of measurement. [AHLB: 2874 (N) / Strong's: 8255, 8625] **Concordance:** 21:32 30:13{4} 30:15 30:24 38:24{2} 38:25{2} 38:26{2} 38:29

SHORTNESS: Anc Heb: ᔐᔑᔗ Mod Heb: קוצר / qo-tser (mas); **Definition:** Short in patience. [AHLB: 2727 (g) / Strong's: 7115] **Concordance:** 6:9

SHOULDER: Anc Heb: ᔐᔑᔗ Mod Heb: שכם / she-khem (mas); **Definition:** Capacity for bearing a task or blame. The shoulders as the place where loads are placed. [AHLB: 2837 (N) / Strong's: 7926] **Concordance:** 12:34

SHOULDER-PIECE: Anc Heb: ᔐᔑᔗ Mod Heb: כתף / ka-teyph (fem); **Definition:** The part of an object that acts like a shoulder. [AHLB: 2299 (N) / Strong's: 3802] **Concordance:** 27:14 27:15 28:7 28:12{2} 28:25 28:27 38:14 38:15 39:4 39:7 39:18 39:20

SHOUTING: Anc Heb: ᔐᔑᔗ Mod Heb: אוהד / o-had (mas); **Definition:** Raising of the voice to show authority, anger or gladness. [AHLB: n/a / Strong's: n/a] **Concordance:** *Used in names only.*

SHOVEL: Anc Heb: ᔐᔑ Mod Heb: יע / ya (mas); **Definition:** A flat tray attached to a handle for scooping up hot coals. [AHLB: 1223-A (N) / Strong's: 3257] **Concordance:** 27:3 38:3

SHOW-BEAUTY: Anc Heb: ᔐᔑᔗ Mod Heb: חנן / hha-nan; **Definition:** To give or show beauty, grace or mercy to another. The hitpael (reflexive) form means "beseech." [AHLB: 1175-B (V) / Strong's: 2589, 2603, 2604] **Concordance:** 33:19{2}

SHOW-PITY: Anc Heb: ᔐᔑᔗ Mod Heb: חמל / hha-mal; **Definition:** To have compassion; to sympathize. [AHLB: 2171 (V) / Strong's: 2550] **Concordance:** 2:6

SHUT: Anc Heb: ᔐᔑᔗ Mod Heb: סגר / sa-gar; Alt Sp: סכר **Definition:** To close or block an opening. [AHLB: 2467 (V) / Strong's: 5462, 5463, 5534] **Concordance:** 14:3

SICKNESS: Anc Heb: 𐤔𐤂𐤌𐤌 Mod Heb: מחלה / ma-hha-leh (mas); מחלה / ma-hha-lah (fem); **Definition:** A physical or emotional illness. Weakened. [AHLB: 1173-H (a) / Strong's: 4245] **Concordance:** 15:26 23:25

SIDE: Anc Heb: 𐤄𐤂𐤌 Mod Heb: צד / tsad (mas); **Definition:** An area next to something. [AHLB: 1395-A (N) / Strong's: 6654, 6655] **Concordance:** 25:32{3} 26:13 30:4 37:18{3} 37:27

SIGH: Anc Heb: 𐤄𐤋𐤏 Mod Heb: אנח / a-nah; **Definition:** Exhaling of breath as in relief. To breath out as a desire for rest. [AHLB: 1307-C (V) / Strong's: 584] **Concordance:** 2:23

SIGN: Anc Heb: 𐤕𐤅𐤋 Mod Heb: אות / ot (fem); **Definition:** The motion, gesture, or mark representing an agreement between two parties. A wondrous or miraculous sign. [AHLB: 1022-J (N) / Strong's: 226, 852] **Concordance:** 3:12 4:8{2} 4:9 4:17 4:28 4:30 7:3 8:19 10:1 10:2 12:13 13:9 13:16 31:13 31:17

SILENT: Anc Heb: 𐤔𐤓𐤌 Mod Heb: חרש / hhey-reysh (mas); **Definition:** A state of speechlessness or extreme quiet. [AHLB: 2211 (N) / Strong's: 2795] **Concordance:** 4:11

SILVER: Anc Heb: 𐤎𐤔𐤊 Mod Heb: כסף / ke-seph (mas); **Definition:** A soft metal capable of a high degree of polish used for coinage, implements and ornaments. A desired and precious metal. [AHLB: 2277 (N) / Strong's: 3701, 3702] **Concordance:** 3:22 11:2 12:35 12:44 20:23 21:11 21:21 21:32 21:34 21:35 22:6 22:16 22:24 25:3 26:19 26:21 26:25 26:32 27:10 27:11 27:17{2} 30:16 31:4 35:5 35:24 35:32 36:24 36:26 36:30 36:36 38:10 38:11 38:12 38:17{3} 38:19{2} 38:25 38:27

SIMMER: Anc Heb: 𐤃𐤅𐤆 Mod Heb: זוד / zud; Alt Sp: זיד **Definition:** To cook a soup over a fire. To be heated with pride or anger. [AHLB: 1142-J (V) / Strong's: 2102, 2103] **Concordance:** 18:11 21:14

SING: Anc Heb: 𐤓𐤅𐤔 Mod Heb: שיר / shir; Alt Sp: שור **Definition:** To express one's voice in a melody or to music. [AHLB: 1480-M (V) / Strong's: 7891] **Concordance:** 15:1{2} 15:21

SINGEING: Anc Heb: 𐤔𐤅𐤉𐤋 Mod Heb: כויה / ke-wi-yah (fem); **Definition:** A burning of the skin or hair. [AHLB: 1235-J (f¹) / Strong's: 3555] **Concordance:** 21:25{2}

SINK: Anc Heb: 𐤏𐤁𐤈 Mod Heb: טבע / ta-va; **Definition:** To fall, drop, or descend down to a lower level. [AHLB: 2229 (V) / Strong's: 2883] **Concordance:** 15:4

SINK-DOWN: Anc Heb: 𐤄𐤐𐤓 Mod Heb: רפה / ra-phah; **Definition:** To drop down; to be slack or idle due to weakness, illness or laziness. The niphal (passive) form means "lazy." [AHLB: 1454-H (V) / Strong's: 7503] **Concordance:** 4:26 5:8 5:17{2}

SISTER: Anc Heb: 𐤕𐤅𐤇𐤋 Mod Heb: אחות / a-hhot (fem); **Definition:** A female person having the same parents or parent as another person. [AHLB: 1008-A (N³) / Strong's: 269] **Concordance:** 2:4 2:7 6:23 15:20 26:3{2} 26:5 26:6 26:17

SIX: Anc Heb: 𐤔𐤔𐤄 Mod Heb: ששה / shi-shah (mas); שש / sheysh (fem); **Definition:** An ordinal number. [AHLB: 1481-A (N) / Strong's: 8337, 8346, 8353, 8361] **Concordance:** 12:37 14:7 16:26 20:9 20:11 21:2 23:10 23:12 24:16 25:32 25:33 25:35 26:9 26:22 26:25 28:10{2} 31:15 31:17 34:21 35:2 36:16 36:27 36:30 37:18 37:19 37:21 38:26

SIXTH: Anc Heb: 𐤉𐤔𐤔 Mod Heb: שישי / shi-shi (com); **Definition:** A cardinal number. [AHLB: 1481-A (ef) / Strong's: 8345] **Concordance:** 16:5 16:22 16:29 26:9

SKILL: Anc Heb: 𐤄𐤌𐤊𐤇 Mod Heb: חכמה / hhakh-mah (fem); **Definition:** The ability to decide or discern between good and bad, right and wrong. [AHLB: 2159 (N¹) / Strong's: 2451, 2452] **Concordance:** 28:3 31:3 31:6 35:26 35:31 35:35 36:1 36:2

SKILLED-ONE: Anc Heb: 𐤌𐤊𐤇 Mod Heb: חכם / hha-kham (mas); **Definition:** A person characterized by a deep understanding of a craft. [AHLB: 2159 (N) / Strong's: 2450] **Concordance:** 7:11 28:3 31:6 35:10 35:25 36:1 36:2 36:4 36:8

SKIN: Anc Heb: 𐤏𐤅𐤓 Mod Heb: עור / or (mas); **Definition:** The integument covering men or animals, as well as leather made from animal skins. The husk of a seed. [AHLB: 1365-J (N) / Strong's: 5784, 5785] **Concordance:** 22:26 25:5{2} 26:14{2} 29:14 34:29 34:30 34:35 35:7{2} 35:23{2} 36:19{2} 39:34{2}

SKULL: Anc Heb: 𐤕𐤂𐤋𐤂𐤋 Mod Heb: גולגולת / gul-go-let (fem); **Definition:** The bones of the head. The roundness of the head or skull. Also a census by the counting of heads. [AHLB: 1058-A (I²) / Strong's: 1538] **Concordance:** 16:16 38:26

SKY: Anc Heb: 𐤔𐤌𐤉𐤌 Mod Heb: שמה / sha-mah (mas); **Definition:** The upper atmosphere that constitutes an apparent great vault or arch over the earth. Place of the winds. [AHLB: 1473-A (N) / Strong's: 8064, 8065] **Concordance:** 9:8 9:10 9:22 9:23 10:21 10:22 16:4 17:14 20:4 20:11 20:22 24:10 31:17 32:13

SLAB: Anc Heb: 𐤋𐤅𐤇 Mod Heb: לוח / lu-ahh (mas); **Definition:** A wood or stone tablet or plank. Often used for writing. [AHLB: 1261-J (N) / Strong's: 3871] **Concordance:** 24:12 27:8 31:18{2} 32:15{2} 32:16{2} 32:19 34:1{3} 34:4{2} 34:28 34:29 38:7

SLAY: Anc Heb: 𐤔𐤇𐤈 Mod Heb: שחט / sha-hhat; **Definition:** To strike, beat or kill. [AHLB: 2823 (V) / Strong's: 7819, 7820] **Concordance:** 12:6 12:21 29:11 29:16 29:20 34:25

SLING: Anc Heb: 𐤒𐤋𐤏 Mod Heb: קלע / qe-la (mas); **Definition:** A weapon made of a pouch that is attached to two long cords and used for throwing stones. Also something that hangs like a sling. [AHLB: 2709 (N) / Strong's: 7050, 7051] **Concordance:** 27:9 27:11 27:12 27:14 27:15 35:17 38:9 38:12 38:14 38:15 38:16 38:18 39:40

SLOW: Anc Heb: 𐤀𐤓𐤊 Mod Heb: ארך / a-reykh (mas); **Definition:** Capable of calmly awaiting an outcome or result. [AHLB: 1448-C (N) / Strong's: 750] **Concordance:** 34:6

SMACK: Anc Heb: 𐤑𐤅𐤓 Mod Heb: צור / tsur; Alt Sp: זור **Definition:** To strike or push as an attack. [AHLB: 1411-J (V) / Strong's: 2115, 6696] **Concordance:** 23:22 32:4

SMALL: Anc Heb: 𐤒𐤈𐤍 Mod Heb: קטן / qa-tan (mas); **Definition:** Someone or something that is not very large in size, importance, age or significance. [AHLB: 2703 (N) / Strong's: 6996] **Concordance:** 18:22 18:26

SMALL-AMOUNT: Anc Heb: 𐤌𐤏𐤈 Mod Heb: מעט / me-at (mas); **Definition:** Something that is few or small in size or amount. [AHLB: 2347 (N) / Strong's: 4592] **Concordance:** 17:4 23:30{2}

SMEAR: Anc Heb: 𐤌𐤔𐤇 Mod Heb: משה / ma-shahh; **Definition:** To overspread with oil for medical treatment or as a sign of authority. [AHLB: 2357 (V) / Strong's: 4886] **Concordance:** 28:41 29:2 29:7 29:29 29:36 30:26 30:30 40:9 40:10 40:11 40:13 40:15{3}

SMELL: Anc Heb: 𐤓𐤅𐤇 Mod Heb: רוח / ra-wahh; **Definition:** The odor or scent of a thing. As carried on the wind. To be "refreshed", as when taking in a deep breath. [AHLB: 1445-J (V) / Strong's: 7304, 7306] **Concordance:** 30:38

SMITE: Anc Heb: 𐤍𐤂𐤐 Mod Heb: נגף / na-gaph; **Definition:** To deliver a hit with the intent to harm; to bring a plague in the sense of a striking. [AHLB: 2377 (V) / Strong's: 5062] **Concordance:** 7:27 12:22 12:23{2} 12:27 21:22 21:35 32:35

SMOKE: Anc Heb: 𐤏𐤔𐤍 Mod Heb: עשן / a-sheyn (mas); **Definition:** The gaseous products of combustion. [AHLB: 2583 (N) / Strong's: 6226, 6227] **Concordance:** 19:18{2} 20:18

SMOKE: Anc Heb: 𐤏𐤔𐤍 Mod Heb: עשן / a-shan; **Definition:** To emit a gaseous cloud when burning. [AHLB: 2583 (V) / Strong's: 6225] **Concordance:** 19:18

SNAP: Anc Heb: 𐤒𐤑𐤐 Mod Heb: קצף / qa-tsaph; **Definition:** To make a sudden closing; to break suddenly with a sharp sound; to splinter a piece of wood; to lash out in anger as a splintering. [AHLB: 2726 (V) / Strong's: 7107, 7108] **Concordance:** 16:20

SNARE: Anc Heb: ⊔⊸•Ɏ⋏⋏ Mod Heb: מוקש / mo-qeysh (mas); **Definition:** A trap laid with bait to capture an animal or person. An entrapment. [AHLB: 1435-L (a) / Strong's: 4170] **Concordance:** 10:7 23:33 34:12

SNORTING: Anc Heb: ⍟Ɏ⊐⍑ Mod Heb: נחור / na-hhor (mas); **Definition:** A forcing of the breath violently through the nostrils with a loud, harsh sound. [AHLB: n/a / Strong's: n/a] **Concordance:** Used in names only.

SNOW: Anc Heb: ⊑Ʋ⊔⊔ Mod Heb: שלג / she-leg (mas); **Definition:** A precipitation of water in the form of ice crystals. [AHLB: 2841 (N) / Strong's: 7950, 8517] **Concordance:** 4:6

SO: Anc Heb: ꞁ�111 Mod Heb: כן / keyn (mas); **Definition:** In a manner or way indicated or suggested. What comes before or after another event. [AHLB: 1244-A (N) / Strong's: 3651, 3652] **Concordance:** 1:12{2} 3:20 5:8 5:17 6:6 6:9 7:6 7:10 7:11 7:20 7:22 8:3 8:13 8:14 8:20 8:22 10:10 10:11 10:14{2} 10:29 11:1 11:8 12:28 12:50 13:15 14:4 15:23 16:17 16:29 17:6 20:11 22:29 23:11 25:9 25:33 26:4 26:17 26:24 27:8 27:11 34:32 36:11 36:22 36:29 37:19 39:32 39:42 39:43 40:16

SOJOURN: Anc Heb: ⍟Ɏ⌂ Mod Heb: גור / gur; **Definition:** To stay as a temporary resident. Travel in a strange land. Also, the extended meaning of "to be afraid" of a stranger. [AHLB: 1066-J (V) / Strong's: 1481] **Concordance:** 3:22 6:4 12:48 12:49

SOJOURNER: Anc Heb: ⊔⊔⋏Ɏ† Mod Heb: תושב / to-shav (mas); **Definition:** One who stays temporarily. Travels from place to place. [AHLB: 1462-L (i) / Strong's: 8453] **Concordance:** 12:45

SON: Anc Heb: ꞁ⊔ Mod Heb: בן / ben (mas); **Definition:** A male offspring. This can be the son of the father or a later male descendant. One who continues the family line. [AHLB: 1037-A (N) / Strong's: 1121, 1123, 1247, 1248] **Concordance:** 1:1 1:7 1:9 1:12 1:13 1:16 1:22 2:2 2:10 2:22 2:23 2:25 3:9 3:10 3:11 3:13 3:14 3:15 3:22 4:20 4:22 4:23{2} 4:25 4:29 4:31 5:14 5:15 5:19 6:5 6:6 6:9 6:11 6:12 6:13{2} 6:14 6:15{2} 6:16 6:17 6:18 6:19 6:21 6:22 6:24 6:25 6:26 6:27 7:2 7:4 7:5 7:7{2} 9:4 9:6 9:26 9:35 10:2{3} 10:9 10:20 10:23 11:7 11:10 12:5 12:26 12:27 12:28 12:31 12:35 12:37 12:40 12:42 12:43 12:50 12:51 13:2 13:8 13:13 13:14 13:15 13:18 13:19 14:2 14:3 14:8{2} 14:10{2} 14:15 14:16 14:22 14:29 15:1 15:19 16:1 16:2 16:3 16:6 16:9 16:10 16:12 16:15 16:17 16:35 17:1 17:3 17:7 18:3 18:5 18:6 19:1 19:3 19:6 20:5 20:10 20:22 21:4 21:5 21:9 21:31 22:23 22:28 23:12 24:5 24:11 24:17 25:2 25:22 27:20 27:21{2} 28:1{3} 28:4 28:9 28:11 28:12 28:21 28:29 28:30 28:38 28:40 28:41 28:43 29:1 29:4 29:8 29:9{2} 29:10 29:15 29:19 29:20 29:21{4} 29:24 29:27 29:28{3} 29:29 29:30 29:32 29:35 29:38 29:43 29:44 29:45 30:12 30:14 30:16{2} 30:19 30:30 30:31 31:2{2} 31:6 31:10 31:13 31:16 31:17 32:2 32:20 32:26 32:28 32:29 33:5 33:6 33:11 34:7{3} 34:16{2} 34:20 34:30 34:32 34:34 34:35 35:1 35:4 35:19 35:20 35:29 35:30{3} 35:34 36:3 38:21 38:22{2} 38:23 38:26 39:6 39:7 39:14 39:27 39:32 39:41 39:42 40:12 40:14 40:31 40:36

SONG: Anc Heb: ⍟>⊔⊔ Mod Heb: שיר / shir (mas) שירה / shi-rah (fem) **Definition:** The act or art of singing. [AHLB: 1480-M (N) / Strong's: 7892] **Concordance:** 15:1

SOOT: Anc Heb: ⊏⋗⊸◦ Mod Heb: פיח / pi-ahh (mas); **Definition:** Residue left after burning. [AHLB: 1376-M (N) / Strong's: 6368] **Concordance:** 9:8 9:10

SORCERY: Anc Heb: ⊶⊔⊔� Mod Heb: כשף / ka-shaph; **Definition:** To perform supernatural magic. [AHLB: 2293 (V) / Strong's: 3784] **Concordance:** 7:11 22:17

SOUTH: Anc Heb: ꞁ⋏⊸⋗† Mod Heb: תימן / tey-man (fem); **Definition:** To the right of one when facing the east, the rising sun. [AHLB: 1290-L (i) / Strong's: 8486] **Concordance:** 26:18 26:35 27:9 36:23 38:9

SOW: Anc Heb: ⊙⍑⋢ Mod Heb: זרע / za-ra; **Definition:** To spread seeds on the ground; to plant a crop. [AHLB: 2137 (V) / Strong's: 2232] **Concordance:** 23:10 23:16

SPATTER: Anc Heb: 𐤍𐤆𐤄 Mod Heb: נזה / na-zah; **Definition:** To ceremonially sprinkle water or oil on something that is being dedicated. [AHLB: 1306-H (V) / Strong's: 5137] **Concordance:** 29:21

SPEAK: Anc Heb: 𐤃𐤁𐤓 Mod Heb: דבר / da-var; **Definition:** A careful arrangement of words or commands said orally. [AHLB: 2093 (V) / Strong's: 1696] **Concordance:** 1:17 4:10 4:12 4:14{2} 4:15 4:16 4:30{2} 5:23 6:2 6:9 6:10 6:11 6:12 6:13 6:27 6:28 6:29{3} 7:2{2} 7:7 7:9 7:13 7:22 8:11 8:15 9:1 9:12 9:35 10:29 11:2 12:3 12:25 12:31 12:32 13:1 14:1 14:2 14:12 14:15 16:10 16:11 16:12 16:23 19:6 19:8 19:9 19:19 20:1 20:19{2} 20:22 23:22 24:3 24:7 25:1 25:2 25:22 28:3 29:42 30:11 30:17 30:22 30:31 31:1 31:13 31:18 32:7 32:13 32:14 32:34 33:1 33:9 33:11{2} 33:17 34:29 34:31 34:32 34:33 34:34{2} 34:35 40:1

SPECIAL: Anc Heb: 𐤒𐤃𐤔 Mod Heb: קודש / qo-desh (mas); **Definition:** A person, item, time or place that has the quality of being unique; Separated from the rest for a special purpose. [AHLB: 2700 (g) / Strong's: 6944] **Concordance:** 3:5 12:16{2} 15:11 15:13 16:23 22:30 26:33{3} 26:34{2} 28:2 28:4 28:29 28:35 28:36 28:38{2} 28:43 29:6 29:29 29:30 29:33 29:34 29:37{2} 30:10{2} 30:13 30:24 30:25{2} 30:29{2} 30:31 30:32{2} 30:35 30:36{2} 30:37 31:10 31:11 31:14 31:15 35:2 35:19{2} 35:21 36:1 36:3 36:4 36:6 37:29 38:24{2} 38:25 38:26 38:27 39:1{2} 39:30{2} 39:41{2} 40:9 40:10{2} 40:13

SPELT: Anc Heb: 𐤊𐤎𐤌𐤕 Mod Heb: כוסמת / ku-se-met (fem); **Definition:** A wheat like grain with what looks like trimmed hair. [AHLB: 2276 (o^2) / Strong's: 3698] **Concordance:** 9:32

SPICE-MIXTURE: Anc Heb: 𐤓𐤒𐤇 Mod Heb: רוקח / ro-qahh (mas); **Definition:** A mixture of spices for an ointment or perfume. [AHLB: 2795 (g) / Strong's: 7545] **Concordance:** 30:25 30:35

SPIN: Anc Heb: 𐤈𐤅𐤄 Mod Heb: טוה / ta-wah; **Definition:** To revolve in a circle without moving forward. [AHLB: 1189-J (V) / Strong's: 2901] **Concordance:** 35:25 35:26

SPIT-UPON: Anc Heb: 𐤉𐤓𐤒 Mod Heb: ארר / a-rar; **Definition:** To eject saliva, usually on another in spite or disrespect. [AHLB: 1457-C (V) / Strong's: 779] **Concordance:** 22:27

SPLENDID: Anc Heb: 𐤐𐤅𐤏 Mod Heb: פועה / pu-ah (fem); **Definition:** Someone or something that is exceptional. A wonder. [AHLB: n/a / Strong's: n/a] **Concordance:** *Used in names only.*

SPLIT-HOOF: Anc Heb: 𐤐𐤓𐤎 Mod Heb: פרסה / par-sah (fem); **Definition:** The hard covering of a clean animals foot that is divided into two parts. [AHLB: 2640 (N^1) / Strong's: 6541] **Concordance:** 10:26

SPOIL: Anc Heb: 𐤔𐤋𐤋 Mod Heb: שלל / sha-lal (mas); **Definition:** Plunder taken from an enemy in war or robbery. To impair the quality or effect of. [AHLB: 1472-B (N) / Strong's: 7998] **Concordance:** 15:9

SPREAD-OUT: Anc Heb: 𐤐𐤓𐤔 Mod Heb: פרש / pa-rash; **Definition:** To expand beyond a starting point; to be easily and plainly understood in the sense of being spread out to see. [AHLB: 2644 (V) / Strong's: 6566, 6567, 6568] **Concordance:** 9:29 9:33 25:20 37:9 40:19

SPREAD-WIDE: Anc Heb: 𐤐𐤕𐤄 Mod Heb: פתה / pa-tah; **Definition:** To lay out in a large area. The piel (intensive) form means "persuade." [AHLB: 1390-H (V) / Strong's: 6601] **Concordance:** 22:15

SPRING-UP: Anc Heb: 𐤑𐤌𐤇 Mod Heb: צמח / tsa-mahh; **Definition:** To grow up as a plant. [AHLB: 2666 (V) / Strong's: 6779] **Concordance:** 10:5

SPRINKLE: Anc Heb: 𐤆𐤓𐤒 Mod Heb: זרק / za-raq; **Definition:** To drip a liquid, usually water or blood. [AHLB: 2138 (V) / Strong's: 2236] **Concordance:** 9:8 9:10 24:6 24:8 29:16 29:20

SPRINKLING-BASIN: Anc Heb: 𐤌𐤆𐤓𐤒 Mod Heb: מזרק / miz-raq (mas); **Definition:** A container of liquid that is used to drip the liquid. [AHLB: 2138 (h) / Strong's: 4219] **Concordance:** 27:3 38:3

SPROUT-UP: Anc Heb: ᒐᐸ Mod Heb: נפג / ne-pheg (mas); **Definition:** A word of unknown meaning. [AHLB: n/a / Strong's: n/a] **Concordance:** *Used in names only.*

SQUEEZE: Anc Heb: ᐧᒧᒪᐣ Mod Heb: לחץ / la-hhats; **Definition:** To exert pressure either physically or emotionally. [AHLB: 2307 (V) / Strong's: 3905] **Concordance:** 3:9 22:20 23:9

SQUEEZING: Anc Heb: ᐧᒧᒪᐣ Mod Heb: לחץ / la-hhats (mas); **Definition:** Pressure being exerted, either physically or emotionally. [AHLB: 2307 (N) / Strong's: 3906] **Concordance:** 3:9

STACK: Anc Heb: ᒣᐧᐁᒐᐸ Mod Heb: גדיש / ga-dish (mas); **Definition:** A pile of grain or dirt. [AHLB: 2058 (b) / Strong's: 1430] **Concordance:** 22:5

STAFF: Anc Heb: ⊗ᒧᒪ Mod Heb: שבט / she-vet (mas); **Definition:** A walking stick made from the branch of a tree. Also, a tribe as a branch of the family. [AHLB: 2805 (N) / Strong's: 7625, 7626] **Concordance:** 24:4 28:21 39:14

STAGGER: Anc Heb: ᐊᒥᐸ Mod Heb: נוע / nu-a; **Definition:** To reel from side to side; to wag or shake back and forth or up and down; to wander as staggering about. [AHLB: 1322-J (V) / Strong's: 5128] **Concordance:** 20:18

STALK: Anc Heb: ᒍᐧᒣᒧ Mod Heb: קנה / qa-neh (mas); **Definition:** The main stem and support of a plant. [AHLB: 1428-H (N) / Strong's: 7070] **Concordance:** 25:31 25:32{3} 25:33{3} 25:35{4} 25:36 30:23 37:17 37:18{3} 37:19{3} 37:21{4} 37:22

STAND: Anc Heb: ᐟᒧᒪᐁ Mod Heb: עמד / a-mad; **Definition:** To rise, raise or set in a place. [AHLB: 2550 (V) / Strong's: 5975, 5976] **Concordance:** 3:5 8:18 9:10 9:11 9:16 9:28 14:19 17:6 18:13 18:23 20:18 20:21 21:21 26:15 32:26 33:9 33:10 36:20

STANDARD: Anc Heb: ᐯᐸ Mod Heb: נס / neys (mas); **Definition:** A flag that hangs from a pole with the insignia of a tribe or army. Also, a sail. [AHLB: 1314-A (N) / Strong's: 5251]

STAND-UP: Anc Heb: ᒧᐁᐸ Mod Heb: נצב / na-tsav; **Definition:** To be vertical in position; to stand tall and erect; to set in place. [AHLB: 2426 (V) / Strong's: 5324] **Concordance:** 5:20 7:15 8:16 9:13 15:8 17:9 18:14 19:17 33:8 33:21 34:2

STAR: Anc Heb: ᒧᒧᒧᒣ Mod Heb: כוכב / ko-khav (mas) **Definition:** A natural luminous body visible in the night sky. [AHLB: 1232-B (g) / Strong's: 3556] **Concordance:** 32:13

STARE: Anc Heb: ⊗ᒧᐸ Mod Heb: נבט / na-vat; **Definition:** To carefully look; to make a close inspection. [AHLB: 2367 (V) / Strong's: 5027] **Concordance:** 3:6 33:8

STATION: Anc Heb: ᒧᒧᐁ Mod Heb: יצב / ya-tsav; **Definition:** To stand firm and in place. [AHLB: 1393-L (V) / Strong's: 3320, 3321] **Concordance:** 2:4 14:13 34:5

STAVE: Anc Heb: ᒍᐧᒧᒧᒧ Mod Heb: משענה / mish-ey-nah (fem); **Definition:** A staff made from a sapling or branch. A support for walking. [AHLB: 2861 (h^1) / Strong's: 4938] **Concordance:** 21:19

STAY-THE-NIGHT: Anc Heb: ᐧᐸᒪ Mod Heb: לון / lun; Alt Sp: לין **Definition:** To remain or stay through the night. [AHLB: 1267-J (V) / Strong's: 3885] **Concordance:** 23:18 34:25

STEAL: Anc Heb: ᒧᐸᒐ Mod Heb: גנב / ga-nav; **Definition:** To wrongfully take the property of another; rob. [AHLB: 2073 (V) / Strong's: 1589] **Concordance:** 20:15 21:16 21:37 22:6 22:11{2}

STEP: Anc Heb: ᒍᐧᒧᒧᒧ Mod Heb: מעלה / ma-a-lah (fem); **Definition:** A straight or stepped incline for ascending and descending. [AHLB: 1357-A (a^1) / Strong's: 4609] **Concordance:** 20:26

STERILE: Anc Heb: ᒍᐧᐁᒧ Mod Heb: עקר / a-qar (mas); **Definition:** Failing to produce or incapable of producing offspring, fruit or spores. Being without children in the sense of being plucked of fruit. [AHLB: 2905 (N) / Strong's: 6135] **Concordance:** 23:26

STICK: Anc Heb: ᴍᴍ Mod Heb: בד / bad (mas); **Definition:** A branch or staff as separated from the tree. Linen cloth, from its stiff and divided fibers. Often used in the idiom "to his/her own stick" meaning alone or self. [AHLB: 1027-A (N) / Strong's: 905, 906] **Concordance:** 12:16 12:37 18:14 18:18 22:19 22:26 24:2 25:13 25:14 25:15 25:27 25:28 26:9{2} 27:6{2} 27:7{2} 28:42 30:4 30:5 30:34{2} 35:12 35:13 35:15 35:16 36:16{2} 37:4 37:5 37:14 37:15 37:27 37:28 38:5 38:6 38:7 39:28 39:35 39:39 40:20

STINK: Anc Heb: ᴍᴍ Mod Heb: באש / ba-ash; **Definition:** To emit a bad odor or be loathsome. [AHLB: 1044-D (V) / Strong's: 887, 888] **Concordance:** 5:21 7:18 7:21 8:10 16:20 16:24

STIR: Anc Heb: ᴍᴍ Mod Heb: בהל / ba-hal; **Definition:** To disturb the quiet of; agitate. [AHLB: 1035-G (V) / Strong's: 926, 927] **Concordance:** 15:15

STONE: Anc Heb: ᴍᴍ Mod Heb: אבן / e-ven (fem); **Definition:** A piece of rock, often in the context of building material. [AHLB: 1037-C (N) / Strong's: 68, 69] **Concordance:** 7:19 15:5 15:16 17:12 20:25 21:18 24:12 25:7{2} 28:9 28:10{2} 28:11{2} 28:12{2} 28:17{2} 28:21 31:5 31:18 34:1 34:4{2} 35:9{2} 35:27{2} 35:33 39:6 39:7 39:10 39:14

STONE: Anc Heb: ᴍᴍ Mod Heb: סקל / sa-qal; **Definition:** To gather stones for stoning. The act of throwing rocks with the intention of killing. To remove stones from a road or field. [AHLB: 2502 (V) / Strong's: 5619] **Concordance:** 8:22 17:4 19:13{2} 21:28{2} 21:29 21:32

STONE-STOOL: Anc Heb: ᴍᴍ Mod Heb: אובן / o-ven (mas); **Definition:** A platform made of stone and used by a potter or a midwife. [AHLB: 1037-C (N) / Strong's: 70] **Concordance:** 1:16

STOOL: Anc Heb: ᴍᴍ Mod Heb: כס / keys (mas); **Definition:** A seat or throne. [AHLB: 1245-A (N) / Strong's: 3676] **Concordance:** 17:16

STOREHOUSE: Anc Heb: ᴍᴍ Mod Heb: מסכנה / mis-ke-nah (fem); **Definition:** Places for storing foods or other items for future benefit. [AHLB: 2478 (h^1) / Strong's: 4543] **Concordance:** 1:11

STRAIGHT: Anc Heb: ᴍᴍ Mod Heb: ישר / ya-shar (mas); **Definition:** Without a bend, angle, or curve. A straight line, path or thought. The cord of the bow as stretched taught. [AHLB: 1480-L (N) / Strong's: 3477] **Concordance:** 15:26

STRAIT: Anc Heb: ᴍᴍ Mod Heb: מצר / mey-tsar (mas); **Definition:** A narrow tight place or situation. [AHLB: 1411-A (k) / Strong's: 4712]

STRANGER: Anc Heb: ᴍᴍ Mod Heb: גר / ger (mas); Alt Sp: גיר **Definition:** A foreigner; a person or thing unknown or with whom one is unacquainted. [AHLB: 1066-A (N) / Strong's: 1616] **Concordance:** 2:22 12:19 12:48 12:49 18:3 20:10 22:20{2} 23:9{3} 23:12

STRAW: Anc Heb: ᴍᴍ Mod Heb: תבן / te-ven (mas); **Definition:** Stalks of grain after threshing; dry, stalky plant residue. When more permanent structures were built, they were constructed of stones and bricks made of clay and straw; replacing the tent panels as the main component of construction for dwellings. [AHLB: 1037-A (i) / Strong's: 8401] **Concordance:** 5:7{2} 5:10 5:11 5:12 5:13 5:16 5:18

STREAM: Anc Heb: ᴍᴍ Mod Heb: יאור / ye-or (mas); **Definition:** A body of running water; any body of flowing water. [AHLB: 1227-D (N) / Strong's: 2975] **Concordance:** 1:22 2:3 2:5{2} 4:9{2} 7:15 7:17 7:18{3} 7:19 7:20{2} 7:21{3} 7:24{2} 7:25 7:28 8:1 8:5 8:7 17:5

STRENGTH: Anc Heb: ᴍᴍ Mod Heb: כוח / ko-ahh (mas); **Definition:** The quality or state of being strong. [AHLB: 1238-J (N) / Strong's: 3581] **Concordance:** 9:16 15:6 32:11

STRETCH-OUT: Anc Heb: ᴍᴍ Mod Heb: רבץ / ra-vats; **Definition:** To lie or stretch out as to rest; to crouch down to hide for an ambush. [AHLB: 2745 (V) / Strong's: 7257] **Concordance:** 23:5

STRIKING: Anc Heb: ⟞ᒐ Mod Heb: נגף / ne-geph (mas); **Definition:** The act of being hit. A plague as hitting the people. [AHLB: 2377 (N) / Strong's: 5063] **Concordance:** 12:13 30:12

STRING: Anc Heb: ᔕᒐᔕ Mod Heb: מישר / mey-shar (mas); **Definition:** A cord or rope, as straight. Also a straight line, path or thought. [AHLB: 1480-L (k) / Strong's: 4339, 4340] **Concordance:** 35:18 39:40

STRIPED-BRUISE: Anc Heb: ⧆⟋ᒐᔕ Mod Heb: חבורה / hha-bu-rah (fem); **Definition:** Marks made by ropes binding the wrist or lashes with a rope. [AHLB: 2143 (d¹) / Strong's: 2250] **Concordance:** 21:25{2}

STRONG: Anc Heb: ⟋ᒐ Mod Heb: עז / az (mas); **Definition:** Having or marked by great physical strength. [AHLB: 1352-A (N) / Strong's: 5794] **Concordance:** 14:21

STRUGGLE: Anc Heb: ⧆ᔕᒐ Mod Heb: נצה / na-tsah; **Definition:** The act of trying to achieve the goal, but with hindrances. [AHLB: 1317-H (V) / Strong's: 5327] **Concordance:** 2:13 21:22

STUBBLE: Anc Heb: ᒐᔕ Mod Heb: קש / qash (mas); **Definition:** What is left after the stalk has been removed. [AHLB: 1435-A (N) / Strong's: 7179] **Concordance:** 5:12 15:7

SUBMERGE: Anc Heb: ᔕᒐ⊗ Mod Heb: טמן / ta-man; **Definition:** To hide by burying or to cover. [AHLB: 2234 (V) / Strong's: 2934] **Concordance:** 2:12

SUBTLETY: Anc Heb: ⧆ᒐᔕ Mod Heb: ערמה / ar-mah (fem); **Definition:** Performance that calls no attention to its self. To act in craftiness or prudence. [AHLB: 2908 (N¹) / Strong's: 6193, 6195] **Concordance:** 21:14

SUCKLE: Anc Heb: ᒐᔕ Mod Heb: ינק / ya-naq; **Definition:** To give milk to from the breast or udder. The hiphil (ver b) (causative) form means "nurse." [AHLB: 1318-L (V) / Strong's: 3243] **Concordance:** 2:7{2} 2:9{2}

SUFFICIENT: Anc Heb: ᒐᔕ Mod Heb: די / dai (mas); **Definition:** An amount that is not lacking. What is enough. [AHLB: 1079-A (N) / Strong's: 1767] **Concordance:** 36:5 36:7

SUM: Anc Heb: ᒐᔕᔕᒐ Mod Heb: מתכונת / mat-ko-net (fem); **Definition:** The total amount. An amount weighed out. [AHLB: 2893 (ac²) / Strong's: 4971] **Concordance:** 5:8 30:32 30:37

SUMMIT: Anc Heb: ᒐᔕᔕ Mod Heb: ראשית / rey-shit (fem); **Definition:** The head, top or beginning of a place, such as a river or mountain, or a time, such as an event. The point at which something starts; origin, source. [AHLB: 1458-D (N⁴) / Strong's: 7225] **Concordance:** 23:19 34:26

SUN: Anc Heb: ᔕᒐᔕ Mod Heb: שמש / she-mesh (fem); **Definition:** The luminous body around which the earth revolves and from which it receives heat and light. [AHLB: 2854 (N) / Strong's: 8121, 8122] **Concordance:** 16:21 17:12 22:2 22:25

SUNRISE: Anc Heb: ᒐᔕᔕ Mod Heb: מזרה / miz-rah (mas); **Definition:** When the first light of the sun comes over the horizon. An eastward direction as the place of the rising sun. [AHLB: 2135 (h) / Strong's: 4217] **Concordance:** 27:13 38:13

SUPPORT: Anc Heb: ᔕᒐ Mod Heb: סמך / sa-makh; **Definition:** To uphold or defend; to hold up or serve as a foundation or prop for. [AHLB: 2488 (V) / Strong's: 5564] **Concordance:** 29:10 29:15 29:19

SUPPRESS: Anc Heb: ⧆ᒐ Mod Heb: ינה / ya-nah; **Definition:** To cause to be brought low by force, hindered. [AHLB: 1304-L (V) / Strong's: 3238] **Concordance:** 22:20

SURELY: Anc Heb: ᒐᔕ Mod Heb: אכן / a-kheyn (mas); Alt Sp: אך **Definition:** In a sure manner. To be firm in something. [AHLB: 1244-C (N) / Strong's: 389, 403] **Concordance:** 2:14 10:17 12:15 12:16 21:21 31:13

SURROUNDED-BY-A-WALL: Anc Heb: ⳤⲩⲟⲱⲱⲭ Mod Heb: חצרון / hhets-ron (mas); **Definition:** To be surrounded, encompassed, by a wall of stone or thorns for protection. [AHLB: n/a / Strong's: n/a] **Concordance:** *Used in names only.*

SWALLOW: Anc Heb: ⲟⲩⳑⲙ Mod Heb: בלע / ba-la; **Definition:** To pass through the mouth and move into the esophagus to the stomach. [AHLB: 2020 (V) / Strong's: 1104] **Concordance:** 7:12 15:12

SWARM: Anc Heb: ⲁⲟⲣⲱⲱ Mod Heb: שרץ / sha-rats; **Definition:** To move, as a large mass of creatures. [AHLB: 2881 (V) / Strong's: 8317] **Concordance:** 1:7 7:28

SWEAR: Anc Heb: ⲟⳤⲱ Mod Heb: שבע / sha-va; **Definition:** To completely submit to a promise or oath with words and spoken seven times. [AHLB: 2808 (V) / Strong's: 7650] **Concordance:** 13:5 13:11 13:19{2} 32:13 33:1

SWEARING: Anc Heb: ⳨ⲟⲩⳑⲱⲱ Mod Heb: שבועה / she-vu-ah (fem); **Definition:** The act of taking an oath. [AHLB: 2808 (d¹) / Strong's: 7621] **Concordance:** 22:10

SWEET: Anc Heb: ⲱⲩⲱⲱⳤ Mod Heb: ניחוח / ni-hho-ahh (mas); **Definition:** Pleasing to the taste. Not sour, bitter or salty. Something that smells pleasing. [AHLB: 1310-B (bc) / Strong's: 5207, 5208] **Concordance:** 29:18 29:25 29:41

SWEET-SPICE: Anc Heb: ⲁ⳨ⲩⲱ Mod Heb: בוסם / bo-sem (mas); **Definition:** An aromatic spice that is pleasing to the nose. [AHLB: 2024 (g) / Strong's: 1314] **Concordance:** 25:6 30:23{3} 35:8 35:28

SWELL: Anc Heb: ⳤⲧ⳨ Mod Heb: הדר / ha-dar; **Definition:** Someone or something that is wide in size or majesty. To honor. To puff up. [AHLB: 1089-F (V) / Strong's: 1921, 1922] **Concordance:** 23:3

SWORD: Anc Heb: ⲱⳤⲃⳑ Mod Heb: חרב / hhe-rev (fem); **Definition:** A weapon with a long blade for cutting or thrusting. [AHLB: 2199 (N) / Strong's: 2719] **Concordance:** 5:3 5:21 15:9 17:13 18:4 20:25 22:23 32:27

TABLE: Anc Heb: ⳑⲱⳑⲩⲱ Mod Heb: שולחן / shul-hhan (mas); **Definition:** A flat surface, usually made of wood and with four legs, for laying out the meal to be eaten. [AHLB: 2842 (om) / Strong's: 7979] **Concordance:** 25:23 25:27 25:28 25:30 26:35{3} 30:27 31:8 35:13 37:10 37:14 37:15 37:16 39:36 40:4 40:22 40:24

TAHHASH: Anc Heb: ⲱⲱⲱⳁ Mod Heb: תחש / ta-hhash (mas); **Definition:** An unknown species of animal. [AHLB: 2891 (N) / Strong's: 8476] **Concordance:** 25:5 26:14 35:7 35:23 36:19 39:34

TAIL: Anc Heb: ⳤⳑⲍ Mod Heb: זנב / na-nav (mas); **Definition:** The hindmost flexible appendage of an animal. [AHLB: 2125 (N) / Strong's: 2180] **Concordance:** 4:4

TAKE: Anc Heb: ⲱⲟⳑ Mod Heb: לקח / la-qahh; **Definition:** To receive what is given; to gain possession by seizing. [AHLB: 2319 (V) / Strong's: 3947] **Concordance:** 2:1 2:3 2:5 2:9 4:9{2} 4:17 4:20{2} 4:25 5:11 6:7 6:20 6:23 6:25 7:9 7:15 7:19 9:8 9:10 9:24 10:26 12:3 12:4 12:5 12:7 12:21 12:22 12:32 13:19 14:6 14:7 14:11 15:20 16:16 16:33 17:5{2} 17:12 18:2 18:12 21:10 21:14 22:10 23:8 24:6 24:7 24:8 25:2{2} 25:3 27:20 28:5 28:9 29:1 29:5 29:7 29:12 29:13 29:15 29:16 29:19 29:20 29:21 29:22 29:25 29:26 29:31 30:16 30:23 30:34 32:4 32:20 33:7 34:4 34:16 35:5 36:3 40:9 40:20

TAKE-AS-A-PLEDGE: Anc Heb: ⳑⲩ⳨ Mod Heb: חבל / hha-val; **Definition:** To receive an object in exchange for a promise. [AHLB: 2141 (V) / Strong's: 2254, 2255] **Concordance:** 22:25{2}

TAKE-AWAY: Anc Heb: ⲟⲁⳑ Mod Heb: גרע / ga-ra; **Definition:** To scrape off or clip. To impair or degrade. [AHLB: 2087 (V) / Strong's: 1639] **Concordance:** 5:8 5:11 5:19 21:10

TAKE-HOLD: Anc Heb: ⲍⲱⲍⳑ Mod Heb: אחז / a-hhaz; **Definition:** To have possession or ownership of; to keep in restraint; to have or maintain in one's grasp; to grab something and keep hold of it. [AHLB: 1168-C (V) / Strong's: 270] **Concordance:** 4:4 15:14 15:15

TAKE-UPON: Anc Heb: ⳑⳑⲗⳤ Mod Heb: יאל / ya-al; **Definition:** The placing of a yoke on the shoulders to perform work or undertake a task. [AHLB: 1012-L (V) / Strong's: 2974] **Concordance:** 2:21

TAMBOURINE: Anc Heb: ⳤⲩ† Mod Heb: תוף / toph (mas); **Definition:** A shallow, one-headed drum with loose disks at the sides played by shaking, striking with the hand, or rubbing with the thumb. [AHLB: 1500-J (N) / Strong's: 8596] **Concordance:** 15:20{2}

TANIYN: Anc Heb: ⳑ† Mod Heb: תנין / ta-nin (mas); Alt Sp: תן **Definition:** A large unknown serpent like creature. [AHLB: 1497-A (N) / Strong's: 8565, 8577] **Concordance:** 7:9 7:10 7:12

TAR: Anc Heb: ⳤⲙⲙ⳧ Mod Heb: חמר / hhey-mar (mas); **Definition:** A dark and thick liquid that floats to the surface of water and is used as a waterproof covering for boats. [AHLB: 2175 (N) / Strong's: 2561, 2562, 2564] **Concordance:** 2:3 8:10{2}

TASK-WORK: Anc Heb: ⲙⳤⲙ Mod Heb: מס / mas (mas); **Definition:** A forced labor or service. [AHLB: 1291-A (N) / Strong's: 4522, 4523] **Concordance:** 1:11

TASTE-SWEET: Anc Heb: ⳤⲙ†⳨ Mod Heb: מתק / ma-taq; **Definition:** To have a pleasant taste to the mouth. [AHLB: 2364 (V) / Strong's: 4985, 4988] **Concordance:** 15:25

TEACHING: Anc Heb: ⲧⳡⲙ† Mod Heb: תורה / to-rah (fem); **Definition:** Acquired knowledge or skills that mark the direction one is to take in life. A straight direction. Knowledge passed from one person to another. [AHLB: 1227-H (i^1) / Strong's: 8451] **Concordance:** 12:49 13:9 16:4 16:28 18:16 18:20 24:12

TEAR: Anc Heb: ⳤⳡⳤ Mod Heb: קרע / qa-ra; **Definition:** To rip into pieces. [AHLB: 2734 (V) / Strong's: 7167] **Concordance:** 28:32 39:23

TEAR-INTO-PIECES: Anc Heb: ⳤⳡ⊗ Mod Heb: טרף / ta-raph; **Definition:** To tear into pieces as a predator does to its prey; to rip a cloth into pieces. [AHLB: 2245 (V) / Strong's: 2963] **Concordance:** 22:12{2}

TEAR-OFF: Anc Heb: ⳨ⳡⳤ Mod Heb: פרק / pa-raq; **Definition:** To remove reluctantly. [AHLB: 2643 (V) / Strong's: 6561, 6562] **Concordance:** 32:2 32:3 32:24

TEN: Anc Heb: ⳤ⳧⳨ Mod Heb: עשרה / a-sa-rah (mas); עשר / e-ser (fem); **Definition:** Ten in number. [AHLB: 2563 (N) / Strong's: 6235, 6236, 6240, 6242, 6243] **Concordance:** 12:6 12:18{2} 15:27 16:1 18:21 18:25 24:4{2} 26:1 26:2 26:7 26:8 26:16 26:18 26:19 26:20 26:25 27:10{2} 27:11{2} 27:12{2} 27:14 27:15 27:16 28:21{2} 30:13 30:14 34:28 36:8 36:9 36:14 36:15 36:21 36:23 36:24 36:25 36:30 38:10{2} 38:11{2} 38:12{2} 38:14 38:15 38:18 38:24 38:26 39:14{2}

TENT: Anc Heb: ⳑ⳪ⲩⳑ Mod Heb: אוהל / o-hel (mas); **Definition:** The black, goat hair dwelling of the nomad. [AHLB: 1104-C (g) / Strong's: 168] **Concordance:** 16:16 18:7 26:7 26:9 26:11 26:12 26:13 26:14 26:36 27:21 28:43 29:4 29:10 29:11 29:30 29:32 29:42 29:44 30:16 30:18 30:20 30:26 30:36 31:7{2} 33:7{3} 33:8{3} 33:9{2} 33:10{2} 33:11 35:11 35:21 36:14 36:18 36:19 36:37 38:8 38:30 39:32 39:33 39:38 39:40 40:2 40:6 40:7 40:12 40:19{2} 40:22 40:24 40:26 40:29 40:30 40:32 40:34 40:35

TENT-CURTAIN: Anc Heb: †ⲱⳡⳤ⳨ Mod Heb: פרוכת / pa-ro-khet (fem); **Definition:** A wall of fabric or hung from the roof to make a dividing of a room. [AHLB: 2638 (c^2) / Strong's: 6532] **Concordance:** 26:31 26:33{3} 26:35 27:21 30:6 35:12 36:35 38:27 39:34 40:3 40:21 40:22 40:26

TENTH: Anc Heb: ⳡⳤ⳪⳨ Mod Heb: עשירי / a-si-ri (mas); **Definition:** A cardinal number. [AHLB: 2563 (bf) / Strong's: 6224] **Concordance:** 16:36

TENTH-ONE: Anc Heb: ⲣⳡ⳨ Mod Heb: עשור / a-sor (mas); **Definition:** That which occupies the tenth position in a sequence. [AHLB: 2563 (c) / Strong's: 6218] **Concordance:** 12:3

TENT-PEG: Anc Heb: ⼟✝⼧⼚ Mod Heb: יתד / ya-teyd (fem); **Definition:** An instrument used to secure the corners and sides of the tent to the ground. [AHLB: 1487-L (N) / Strong's: 3489] **Concordance:** 27:19{2} 35:18{2} 38:20 38:31{2} 39:40

TENT-WALL: Anc Heb: ✡⌖⼬⼝⼚ Mod Heb: יריעה / ye-ri-a (fem); **Definition:** The goat hair curtain that forms the walls of the tent. [AHLB: 1440-L (N) / Strong's: 3407] **Concordance:** 26:1 26:2{3} 26:3{2} 26:4{2} 26:5{2} 26:6 26:7{2} 26:8{3} 26:9{3} 26:10{2} 26:12{2} 26:13 36:8 36:9{3} 36:10{2} 36:11{2} 36:12{2} 36:13 36:14{2} 36:15{3} 36:16{2} 36:17{2}

TERMINATE: Anc Heb: ⼮⼍⼳ Mod Heb: חדל / hha-dal; **Definition:** To stop or refrain from continuing an action. [AHLB: 2148 (V) / Strong's: 2308] **Concordance:** 9:29 9:33 9:34 14:12 23:5

TERROR: Anc Heb: ✡⌳⼦⼳ Mod Heb: אימה / ey-mah (fem); **Definition:** A state of intense fear. [AHLB: 1220-C (N[1]) / Strong's: 367] **Concordance:** 15:16 23:27

TEST: Anc Heb: ✡⚒⼈ Mod Heb: נסה / na-sah; **Definition:** A critical examination, observation, or evaluation; trial. [AHLB: 1314-H (V) / Strong's: 5254] **Concordance:** 15:25 16:4 17:2 17:7 20:20

THANKSGIVING: Anc Heb: ✡⼮Y✡⼚ Mod Heb: יהודה / ye-hu-dah (mas); **Definition:** An expression of thanks through shouting. [AHLB: n/a / Strong's: n/a] **Concordance:** *Used in names only.*

THAT: Anc Heb: ⼂⌖⼤ Mod Heb: מען / ma-an (mas); **Definition:** The person, thing, or idea indicated, mentioned, or understood from the situation. A close watching. [AHLB: 1359-A (a) / Strong's: 4616] **Concordance:** 1:11 4:5 8:6 8:18 9:16 9:29 10:1 10:2 11:7 11:9 13:9 16:4 16:32 20:12 23:12 33:13

THAT-ONE: Anc Heb: Y⼤ Mod Heb: מו / mo (mas); **Definition:** Being the person, thing, or idea specified, mentioned, or understood. [AHLB: 1282-A (N) / Strong's: 1119, 3644, 3926] **Concordance:** 9:14 9:18 9:24 10:14 11:6{2} 15:5 15:8 15:11{2} 30:32 30:33 30:38

THEFT: Anc Heb: ✡⼡⌳⼪ Mod Heb: גנבה / ge-ney-vah (fem); **Definition:** The unlawful taking of another's property. [AHLB: 2073 (N[1]) / Strong's: 1591] **Concordance:** 22:2 22:3

THEN: Anc Heb: Y⼂⼾ Mod Heb: אפו / ey-pho (mas); **Definition:** An inquiry of a time or place. [AHLB: 1374-C (N) / Strong's: 645] **Concordance:** 33:16

THERE: Anc Heb: ⼾⼴⼝ Mod Heb: שם / sham (mas); **Definition:** Used to identify another place. [AHLB: 1473-A (N) / Strong's: 8033, 8536] **Concordance:** 8:18 9:26 10:26 12:13 12:30 15:25{2} 15:27{2} 16:33 17:3 17:6 18:5 19:2 20:21 21:13 21:33 24:12 25:22 26:33 29:42{2} 29:43 30:6 30:18 30:36 34:2 34:5 34:28 40:3 40:7 40:30

THERE-IS: Anc Heb: ⼴⼴⼚ Mod Heb: יש / yeysh (mas); **Alt Sp:** אש **Definition:** Something that exists. [AHLB: 1228-A (N) / Strong's: 786, 3426] **Concordance:** 17:7

THESE: Anc Heb: ⼮✤ Mod Heb: אלה / ey-lah (mas); **Alt Sp:** אל **Definition:** The persons, things, or ideas present or near in place, time, or thought or just mentioned. A grammatical tool used to identify something specific in the sense of looking toward a sight. [AHLB: 1104-A (N) / Strong's: 411, 412, 428, 429, 459, 479] **Concordance:** 1:1 4:9 6:14{2} 6:15 6:16 6:19 6:24 6:25 10:1 11:8 11:10 19:6 19:7 20:1 21:1 21:11 24:8 25:39 28:4 32:4 32:8 34:27{2} 35:1 38:21

THEY(f): Anc Heb: ⼞⼾✤ Mod Heb: הנה / hey-nah (fem); **Definition:** The plural of "she." [AHLB: 1093-J (N) / Strong's: 2007, 3860] **Concordance:** 1:19 9:32 39:14

THEY(m): Anc Heb: ⼤⼾✤ Mod Heb: חמה / hey-mah (mas); **Definition:** The plural of "he." [AHLB: 1093-J (N) / Strong's: 1992, 1994] **Concordance:** 2:11 2:23 5:7 5:8{3} 6:27 7:11 8:17 14:3 15:23 18:22 18:26 19:13 24:2 28:5 29:33 30:4 32:15 32:16 36:1 36:3 36:4 38:17

THICK: Anc Heb: ⊔ﬞ Mod Heb: עב / av (com); **Definition:** Heavily compacted material, such as a cloud, forest or thicket, and is filled with darkness. [AHLB: 1508-A (N) / Strong's: 5645] **Concordance:** 19:9

THICK-CORD: Anc Heb: ﬢﬞ Mod Heb: עבות / a-vot (fem); **Definition:** A rope or other woven object that is tightly wrapped. [AHLB: 1508-A (N^3) / Strong's: 5687, 5688] **Concordance:** 28:14{2} 28:22 28:24 28:25 39:15 39:17 39:18

THICK-DARKNESS: Anc Heb: ⌐ﬞ Mod Heb: ערפל / a-ra-phel (mas); **Definition:** A heavy darkness that can be felt. [AHLB: **3067** / Strong's: 6205] **Concordance:** 20:21

THICK-GLOOMINESS: Anc Heb: ⌐ﬞ Mod Heb: אפלה / a-phey-lah (fem); **Definition:** A heavy darkness that brings about sadness or depression. [AHLB: 1380-C (N^1) / Strong's: 653] **Concordance:** 10:22

THIEF: Anc Heb: ⊔ﬞ Mod Heb: גנב / ga-nav (mas); **Definition:** One who steals the property of another. [AHLB: 2073 (N) / Strong's: 1590] **Concordance:** 22:1 22:6 22:7

THIGH: Anc Heb: ﬣﬞ Mod Heb: שוק / shuq (fem); **Definition:** The upper part of the leg of a man or animal. Also a street. [AHLB: 1479-J (N) / Strong's: 7784, 7785] **Concordance:** 29:22 29:27

THIN-BREAD: Anc Heb: ﬤﬞ Mod Heb: רקיק / ra-qiq (mas); **Definition:** Dough that has been spread thin before baked. [AHLB: 1456-B (b) / Strong's: 7550] **Concordance:** 29:2 29:23

THING-WRITTEN: Anc Heb: ⊔ﬞ Mod Heb: מכתב / mikh-tav (mas); **Definition:** A composition that has been recorded by the written words. [AHLB: 2295 (h) / Strong's: 4385] **Concordance:** 32:16{2} 39:30

THINK: Anc Heb: ⊔ﬞ Mod Heb: חשב / hha-shav; **Definition:** To plan or design a course of action, item or invention. [AHLB: 2213 (V) / Strong's: 2803, 2804] **Concordance:** 26:1 26:31 28:6 28:15 31:4 35:32 35:35{2} 36:8 36:35 38:23 39:3 39:8

THIRD: Anc Heb: ﬥﬞ Mod Heb: שלישי / she-li-shi (mas); **Definition:** The third within the order. [AHLB: 2847 (bf) / Strong's: 7992, 8523] **Concordance:** 19:1 19:11{2} 19:16 28:19 39:12

THIRD-GENERATION: Anc Heb: ﬥﬞ Mod Heb: שילש / shi-leysh (mas); **Definition:** The third increment within the sequence. [AHLB: 2847 (e) / Strong's: 8029] **Concordance:** 20:5 34:7

THIRST: Anc Heb: ﬦﬞ Mod Heb: צמא / tsa-mey (mas); **Definition:** The lack of sufficient water. [AHLB: 1404-E (N) / Strong's: 6771, 6772] **Concordance:** 17:3

THIRST: Anc Heb: ﬦﬞ Mod Heb: צמא / tsa-ma; **Definition:** To lack sufficient water. [AHLB: 1404-E (V) / Strong's: 6770] **Concordance:** 17:3

THIS: Anc Heb: ﬧﬞ Mod Heb: זה / zeh (mas); זאת / zot (fem); **Definition:** A person, thing, or idea present or near in place, time, or thought or just mentioned. As prominent or pointed out. [AHLB: 1143-A (N) / Strong's: 1454, 1668, 1768, 1791, 1797, 1836, 2063, 2088, 2090, 2097] **Concordance:** 1:18 2:6 2:9 2:15 2:20 3:3 3:12{2} 3:15{2} 3:21 4:2 4:17 5:22{2} 5:23 7:17 7:23 8:19 8:28 9:5 9:6 9:14 9:16 10:6 10:7 10:17 11:1{2} 12:2 12:3 12:6 12:8 12:12 12:14 12:17{2} 12:24 12:25 12:26 12:41 12:42 12:43 12:51 13:3{2} 13:5{2} 13:8 13:10 13:14 13:19 14:5 14:11 14:12 14:20{2} 15:1 15:2 16:3{2} 16:16 16:32 17:3 17:4 17:12{2} 17:14 18:14 18:18 18:23{2} 19:1 21:31 22:8 24:14 25:3 25:19{2} 26:13{4} 29:1 29:38 30:13 30:31 32:1 32:9 32:13 32:15{2} 32:21 32:23 32:24 32:31 33:1 33:4 33:12 33:13 33:15 33:17 35:4 37:8{2} 38:15{2}

THORN-BUSH: Anc Heb: ﬨﬞ Mod Heb: סנה / se-neh (mas); **Definition:** A plant, bush or tree, that grows thorns. [AHLB: 1336-H (N) / Strong's: 5572] **Concordance:** 3:2{3} 3:3 3:4

THOUGH: Anc Heb: ﬩ﬞ Mod Heb: הן / heyn (mas); **Definition:** However; nevertheless. In spite of the fact of. A possible or desired location. To bring attention to an event. [AHLB: 1106-A (N) / Strong's: 581, 2004, 2005, 2006, 3861] **Concordance:** 4:1 5:5 6:12 6:30 8:22

THOUSAND: Anc Heb: ⲟⳑⲩ Mod Heb: אֶלֶף / e-leph (mas); **Definition:** Ten times one hundred in amount or number. [AHLB: 2001 (N) / Strong's: 505, 506] **Concordance:** 12:37 18:21 18:25 20:6 32:28 34:7 38:25 38:26{2} 38:28 38:29

THREE: Anc Heb: ⲗⳑⲩⲗⲗ Mod Heb: שְׁלוֹשָׁה / she-lo-shah (mas); שָׁלוֹשׁ / she-losh (fem); **Definition:** A total of three in number or amount. [AHLB: 2847 (c) / Strong's: 7969, 7970] **Concordance:** 2:2 3:18 5:3 6:16 6:18{2} 6:20 7:7 8:23 10:22 10:23 12:40 12:41 15:22 19:15 21:11 21:32 23:14 23:17 25:32{2} 25:33{2} 26:8 27:1 27:14{2} 27:15{2} 32:28 34:23 34:24 36:15 37:18{2} 37:19{2} 38:1 38:14{2} 38:15{2} 38:24 38:26

THREE-DAYS-AGO: Anc Heb: ⲙⳑⲩⲗⲗⲟ-ⲗⲗ Mod Heb: שִׁלְשׁוֹם / shil-shom (mas); **Definition:** Literally the day before yesterday, but used as an idiom for the past. [AHLB: 2847 (eqp) / Strong's: 8032] **Concordance:** 4:10 5:7 5:8 5:14 21:29 21:36

THROW: Anc Heb: ⲯⲟⲗ Mod Heb: ירה / ya-rah; Alt Sp: ירא **Definition:** To propel through the air by a forward motion; to drizzle as a throwing down of water; to teach in the sense of throwing or pointing a finger in a straight line as the direction one is to walk. The hiphil (causative) form means "teach." [AHLB: 1227-H (V) / Strong's: 3384] **Concordance:** 4:12 4:15 15:4 15:25 19:13{2} 24:12 35:34

THROW-DOWN: Anc Heb: ⲯⲟⲗⲟ Mod Heb: רמה / ra-mah; **Definition:** To lead astray; to deliver to an enemy by treachery; to reveal unintentionally. [AHLB: 1450-H (V) / Strong's: 7411, 7412] **Concordance:** 15:1 15:21

THROW-OUT: Anc Heb: ⲩⲗⲗⲗ Mod Heb: שׁלך / sha-lakh; **Definition:** To remove from a place, usually in a sudden or unexpected manner; to cast out, down or away. [AHLB: 2844 (V) / Strong's: 7993] **Concordance:** 1:22 4:3{2} 7:9 7:10 7:12 15:25 22:30 32:19

THRUST: Anc Heb: ⲟⲟ-ⲧ Mod Heb: תקע / ta-qa; **Definition:** To push or drive with force a pole into the ground, such as when setting up the tent; to blow the trumpet in the sense of throwing out the sound. [AHLB: 2902 (V) / Strong's: 8628] **Concordance:** 10:19

THUMB: Anc Heb: ⲗⲯⲩⲟ Mod Heb: בֹּהֶן / bo-hen (fem); **Definition:** The opposable digit of the hand. Also the big toe of the foot. Perceived as the builder because of its unique abilities. [AHLB: 1037-G (N) / Strong's: 931] **Concordance:** 29:20{2}

TIE-ON: Anc Heb: Ⳡⲩⲟ Mod Heb: רכס / ra-khas; **Definition:** To attach or bind one object to another by tying them together. [AHLB: 2771 (V) / Strong's: 7405] **Concordance:** 28:28 39:21

TIE-UP: Anc Heb: ⲟⲯⳑ Mod Heb: אסר / a-sar **Definition:** To wrap or fasten with a cord. [AHLB: 1342-C (V) / Strong's: 631] **Concordance:** 14:6

TIP: Anc Heb: ⲩⲯⲧ Mod Heb: תְּנוּךְ / te-nuk (mas); **Definition:** The pointed end of an object. [AHLB: 1310-J (i) / Strong's: 8571] **Concordance:** 29:20{2}

TITLE: Anc Heb: ⲙⲗⲗ Mod Heb: שֵׁם / sheym (mas); **Definition:** A word given to an individual or place denoting its character. The character of an individual or place. [AHLB: 1473-A (N) / Strong's: 8034, 8036] **Concordance:** 1:1 1:15{2} 2:10 2:22 3:13 3:15 5:23 6:3 6:16 9:16 15:3 15:23 16:31 17:7 17:15 18:3 18:4 20:7{2} 20:24 23:13 23:21 28:9 28:10{2} 28:11 28:12 28:21{3} 28:29 31:2 33:12 33:17 33:19 34:5 34:14 35:30 39:6 39:14{3}

TO: Anc Heb: ⳑⲟ Mod Heb: אֵל / el (mas); **Definition:** Used as a function word to indicate movement or an action or condition suggestive of progress toward a place, person, or thing reached. [AHLB: 1104-A (N) / Strong's: 413] **Concordance:** 1:9 1:17 1:19{2} 2:7 2:11 2:18 2:20 2:23 3:1 3:2 3:4 3:6 3:8{3} 3:9 3:10 3:11{2} 3:13{4} 3:14{2} 3:15{3} 3:16{2} 3:17{2} 3:18{2} 4:1 4:2 4:4 4:5 4:7{2} 4:10{2} 4:11 4:15 4:16 4:18{2} 4:19 4:21 4:22 4:23 4:27 4:30 5:1 5:4 5:10 5:15 5:21 5:22 5:23 6:1 6:2{2} 6:3{3} 6:8 6:9{2} 6:10 6:11 6:12 6:13{4} 6:27 6:28 6:29{3} 6:30 7:1 7:2 7:4 7:7 7:8{2} 7:9{2} 7:10 7:13 7:14 7:15 7:16{2} 7:19{2} 7:22 7:23 7:26{3} 8:1{2} 8:4 8:8 8:11 8:12{2} 8:15{2} 8:16{2} 8:21 8:23 8:25 8:26 9:1{3} 9:8{2} 9:12{2} 9:13{2} 9:14 9:20

9:21 9:22 9:27 9:28 9:29{2} 9:33 10:1{2} 10:3{2} 10:7 10:8{2} 10:10 10:12 10:18 10:21 10:24 11:1 11:8 11:9{2} 12:1{2} 12:3 12:4 12:21 12:22{2} 12:23 12:25 12:26 12:43 13:1 13:3 13:5 13:11 13:14 14:1 14:2 14:5 14:10 14:11 14:12 14:13 14:15{3} 14:20 14:23 14:24 14:26 15:13 15:22 15:25{2} 16:1 16:3{2} 16:4 16:6 16:9{2} 16:10{2} 16:11 16:12 16:15{2} 16:19 16:20 16:23 16:28 16:33 16:34 16:35{2} 17:4 17:5 17:9 17:14 18:5{2} 18:6{2} 18:15 18:16 18:17 18:19 18:22 18:26 18:27 19:3{2} 19:4 19:6 19:8 19:9{3} 19:10{2} 19:14 19:15{2} 19:20{2} 19:21{2} 19:22 19:23{2} 19:24{2} 19:25{2} 20:19 20:20 20:21 20:22{2} 20:24 21:6{3} 22:6 22:7 22:9 22:22 22:26 23:13 23:17 23:20 23:23 23:27 24:1{2} 24:2 24:11 24:12{2} 24:13 24:14{3} 24:15 24:16 24:18 25:1 25:2 25:16{2} 25:20{2} 25:21{2} 25:22 26:3{2} 26:5 26:6 26:9 26:17 26:24 26:28 27:20 28:1 28:3 28:7 28:24 28:25 28:26 28:28 28:29 28:30 28:35 28:37 28:43{2} 29:4 29:12 29:30 29:42 30:11 30:17 30:20{2} 30:22 30:31 30:34 31:1 31:12 31:13 31:18 32:1 32:2{2} 32:3 32:7 32:9 32:13 32:17 32:19 32:21 32:26{2} 32:30{2} 32:31 32:33 32:34 33:1{2} 33:3 33:5{2} 33:7 33:8 33:11{4} 33:12{2} 33:15 33:17 34:1 34:2 34:3 34:4 34:27 34:30 34:31{3} 34:34 35:1 35:4 35:30 36:2{4} 36:3 36:5 36:10{2} 36:12 36:13 36:22 36:29{2} 36:33 37:9{2} 38:14 39:18 39:19 39:21 39:33 40:1 40:12 40:20 40:21 40:32{2} 40:35

TOGETHER: Anc Heb: ⌂⌂ᴗ⌐ Mod Heb: יחד / ya-hhad (mas); Alt Sp: יחדו **Definition:** In or into one place, mass, collection, or group. [AHLB: 1165-L (N) / Strong's: 3162] **Concordance:** 19:8 26:24 36:29

TOMORROW: Anc Heb: ☌⌐ᴗᴥ⌐ Mod Heb: מחר / ma-hhar (fem); **Definition:** The next day. At a time following. [AHLB: 1181-A (a) / Strong's: 4279] **Concordance:** 8:6 8:19 8:25 9:5 9:18 10:4 13:14 16:23 17:9 19:10 32:5

TONG: Anc Heb: ⌐⌐ᴗ⌐ᴥ⌐ Mod Heb: מלקח / mel-qahh (mas); **Definition:** An instrument used for grasping, having two arms working together. A tool for taking coals out of the fire. [AHLB: 2319 (a) / Strong's: 4457] **Concordance:** 25:38 37:23

TONGUE: Anc Heb: ⌐⌐ᴗᴗᴗ Mod Heb: לשון / la-shon (mas); **Definition:** A fleshy moveable process on the floor of the mouth used in speaking and eating. Also, language as a tongue. [AHLB: 2325 (c) / Strong's: 3956] **Concordance:** 4:10 11:7

TOOTH: Anc Heb: ᴗᴗ⌐ Mod Heb: שׁן / sheyn (com); **Definition:** Hard bony appendages on the jaws used for chewing food and forming of sounds when talking. [AHLB: 1474-A (N) / Strong's: 8127, 8128] **Concordance:** 21:24{2} 21:27{3}

TOPAZ: Anc Heb: ⌐⌐ᴗᴗᴗ✝ Mod Heb: תרשיש / tar-shish (mas); **Definition:** Possibly the Topaz, which may be yellow, gray, white, pink, green or blue in color. Other possible translations are Beryl, Lapis Lazuli, Amber, Jasper, Serpentine, Olivine, or Flint. [AHLB: 1458-B (ib) / Strong's: 8658] **Concordance:** 28:20 39:13

TORCH: Anc Heb: ⌐⌐ᴥ⌐ᴗ⌐ Mod Heb: לפיד / la-pid (mas); **Definition:** A burning stick of resinous wood. Also, lightning as a torch in the night sky. [AHLB: 2317 (b) / Strong's: 3940] **Concordance:** 20:18

TORN: Anc Heb: ✲⌐ᴥ⊗ Mod Heb: טרפה / te-rey-phah (fem); **Definition:** Pulled apart. Flesh that is torn. [AHLB: 2245 (N[1]) / Strong's: 2966] **Concordance:** 22:12 22:30

TOUCH: Anc Heb: ᴥ⌐⌐ᴗ Mod Heb: נגע / na-ga; **Definition:** To lay hands upon; to touch or strike; to be touched by a plague. [AHLB: 2376 (V) / Strong's: 5060] **Concordance:** 4:25 19:12{2} 19:13 29:37 30:29

TOWER: Anc Heb: ᴗ⌐⌐ᴗᴥ⌐ᴥᴥ Mod Heb: מגדל / mig-dal (mas); **Definition:** A structure higher than its diameter and high relative to its surroundings. Place of great size. [AHLB: 2054 (h) / Strong's: 4026]

TOWN: Anc Heb: ✲⌐⌐ᴥᴥᴥ Mod Heb: חוה / hha-wah (fem); **Definition:** A small village. [AHLB: 1167-A (N[1]) / Strong's: 2333]

TRAMPLE-DOWN: Anc Heb: ⊀ΥΩ Mod Heb: בוס / bus; **Definition:** To purposely destroy by stomping upon to break or smash. [AHLB: 1038-J (V) / Strong's: 947] **DOWN:**

TRANSGRESSION: Anc Heb: ⊙ɰ⊙ Mod Heb: פשע / pe-sha (mas); **Definition:** The exceeding of due bounds or limits. [AHLB: 2647 (N) / Strong's: 6588] **Concordance:** 22:8 23:21 34:7

TRAPPINGS: Anc Heb: ⊁ᵪ⊙ Mod Heb: עדי / a-di (mas); **Definition:** Articles of dress or adornment that often witness to a person's position or rank. [AHLB: 1349-A (f) / Strong's: 5716] **Concordance:** 33:4 33:5 33:6

TREE: Anc Heb: ⌒⊙ Mod Heb: עץ / eyts (mas); **Definition:** A woody perennial plant with a supporting stem or trunk and multiple branches. Meaning "wood" when written in the plural form. [AHLB: 1363-A (N) / Strong's: 636, 6086, 6097] **Concordance:** 7:19 9:25 10:5 10:15{2} 15:25 25:5 25:10 25:13 25:23 25:28 26:15 26:26 27:1 27:6 30:1 30:5 31:5 35:7 35:24 35:33 36:20 36:31 37:1 37:4 37:10 37:15 37:25 37:28 38:1 38:6

TREMBLE: Anc Heb: ⌐ᴀɱ Mod Heb: חרד / hha-rad; **Definition:** To shake involuntarily; shiver. [AHLB: 2201 (V) / Strong's: 2729] **Concordance:** 19:16 19:18

TREMBLING-IN-FEAR: Anc Heb: †ᴀ Mod Heb: חת / hhet (mas); **Definition:** A physical reaction, such as shivering, in fear or dread. [AHLB: 1183-A (N) / Strong's: 2844] **IN-FEAR:**

TRIAL: Anc Heb: ⊀⌐ɰ Mod Heb: מסה / ma-sah (fem); **Definition:** The act of trying, testing, or putting to the proof. [AHLB: 1314-A (a¹) / Strong's: 4531]

TROUBLE: Anc Heb: ⊀⌐Ⴑ† Mod Heb: תלאה / te-la-ah (fem); **Definition:** A difficulty that brings about weariness. [AHLB: 1258-D (i¹) / Strong's: 8513] **Concordance:** 18:8

TROUGH: Anc Heb: ⊗ⴑᴀ Mod Heb: רהט / ra-hat (mas); **Definition:** A long, shallow often V-shaped receptacle for the drinking water or food of domestic animals. [AHLB: 1446-G (N) / Strong's: 7298] **Concordance:** 2:16

TRUMPET: Anc Heb: Ⴑᴑᴦ Mod Heb: יובל / yo-vel (mas); **Definition:** An instrument of flowing air to make a sound. Also, the horn of a ram as used as a trumpet. [AHLB: 1035-L (g) / Strong's: 3104] **Concordance:** 19:13

TRUTH: Anc Heb: †Ɱᴑ Mod Heb: אמת / e-met (fem); **Definition:** The state of being the case. Fact. What is firm. Accurately so. [AHLB: 1290-C (N²) / Strong's: 571] **Concordance:** 18:21 34:6

TUB: Anc Heb: ⌒⊀ Mod Heb: סף / saph (mas); **Definition:** A container with a lip. The lip of the door. [AHLB: 1339-A (N) / Strong's: 5592] **Concordance:** 12:22{2}

TUNIC: Anc Heb: †ᵪᵼɰ Mod Heb: כתנת / ke-to-net (fem); **Definition:** A simple slip-on garment with or without sleeves. [AHLB: 2298 (c²) / Strong's: 3801] **Concordance:** 28:4 28:39 28:40 29:5 29:8 39:27 40:14

TURBAN: Anc Heb: †⊙ᴀɰ Mod Heb: מצנפת / mits-ne-phet (fem); **Definition:** A cloth that is wrapped around the head. [AHLB: 2673 (h²) / Strong's: 4701] **Concordance:** 28:4 28:37{2} 28:39 29:6{2} 39:28 39:31

TURN: Anc Heb: ⊁ᵪ⊙ Mod Heb: פנה / pa-nah; **Definition:** To rotate or revolve; to face another direction; to turn the face; to turn directions; to turn something back or away. [AHLB: 1382-H (V) / Strong's: 6437] **Concordance:** 2:12 7:23 10:6 14:27 16:10 32:15

TURN-ASIDE: Anc Heb: ᴀᵪ⊀ Mod Heb: סור / sur; Alt Sp: שור **Definition:** To change the location, position, station, or residence; to remove. The hiphil (causative) form means "remove." [AHLB: 1342-J (V) / Strong's: 5493, 7787] **Concordance:** 3:3 3:4 8:4 8:7 8:25 8:27 10:17 14:25 23:25 25:15 32:8 33:23 34:34

TURN-BACK: Anc Heb: ɰᵪɰ Mod Heb: שוב / shuv; **Definition:** To return to a previous place or state. [AHLB: 1462-J (V) / Strong's: 7725, 8421] **Concordance:** 4:7{3} 4:18{2} 4:19 4:20 4:21

5:22 10:8 13:17 14:2 14:26 14:27 14:28 15:19 19:8 21:34 22:25 23:4{2} 24:14 32:12 32:27 32:31 33:11 34:31 34:35

TURQUOISE: Anc Heb: ש❤Yꟸ Mod Heb: נוֹפֶךְ / no-phek (mas); **Definition:** Possibly the Turquoise, a blue to green stone that was commonly mined in the Near East. The Septuagint has Anthrax meaning coal. Other possible translations are Carbuncle, Garnet, Emerald and Malachite. [AHLB: 2420 (g) / Strong's: 5306] **Concordance:** 28:18 39:11

TWIST: Anc Heb: ꟸYꟸ Mod Heb: חוּל / hhul; Alt Sp: חִיל **Definition:** A winding or wrapping together; entwined in pain or joy. [AHLB: 1173-J (V) / Strong's: 2342] **Concordance:** 32:11

TWIST-BACKWARDS: Anc Heb: ꟸꟸ❤ Mod Heb: סָלַף / sa-laph; **Definition:** A path that winds back on itself. To twist words or actions away from their proper context. [AHLB: 2485 (V) / Strong's: 5557] **Concordance:** 23:8

TWIST-TOGETHER: Anc Heb: ꟸꟸ❤ Mod Heb: שָׁזַר / sha-zar; **Definition:** To wrap separate pieces together forming one unit. [AHLB: 2821 (V) / Strong's: 7806] **Concordance:** 26:1 26:31 26:36 27:9 27:16 27:18 28:6 28:8 28:15 36:8 36:35 36:37 38:9 38:16 38:18 39:2 39:5 39:8 39:24 39:28 39:29

TWO: Anc Heb: ꟸꟸ❤ Mod Heb: שְׁנַיִם / she-na-yim (mas); שְׁתַּיִם / she-ta-yim (fem); **Definition:** An ordinal number. [AHLB: 1474-H (N) / Strong's: 8147, 8578, 8648] **Concordance:** 2:13 4:9 12:7 12:22 12:23 15:27 16:22 18:3 18:6 22:3 22:6 22:8{2} 22:10 24:4{2} 25:12{2} 25:18{2} 25:19 25:22 25:35{3} 26:17 26:19{4} 26:21{2} 26:23 26:24{2} 26:25{2} 28:7{2} 28:9 28:11 28:12{2} 28:14 28:21{2} 28:23{3} 28:24{2} 28:25{3} 28:26{2} 28:27{2} 29:1 29:3 29:13 29:22 29:38 30:4{3} 31:18 32:15{2} 34:1 34:4{2} 34:29 36:22 36:24{4} 36:26{2} 36:28 36:29{2} 36:30{2} 37:3{2} 37:7{2} 37:8 37:21{3} 37:27{3} 39:4 39:14{2} 39:16{4} 39:17{2} 39:18{3} 39:19{2} 39:20{2}

UNAWARE: Anc Heb: ꟸꟸ❤ Mod Heb: בְּלִי / be-li (mas); **Definition:** Without design, attention, preparation, or premeditation. [AHLB: 1035-A (f) / Strong's: 1097] **Concordance:** 14:11

UNCIRCUMCISED: Anc Heb: ꟸꟸ❤ Mod Heb: עָרֵל / a-reyl (mas); **Definition:** A male with a foreskin. [AHLB: 2577 (N) / Strong's: 6189] **Concordance:** 6:12 6:30 12:48

UNDER: Anc Heb: ꟸꟸꟸ Mod Heb: תַּחַת / ta-hhat (mas); **Definition:** Beneath. Below or underneath. Also, to be underneath in the sense of being in place of something else. [AHLB: 2892 (N) / Strong's: 8478, 8479] **Concordance:** 6:6 6:7 10:23 16:29 17:12 17:14 18:10 20:4{2} 21:20 21:23 21:24{4} 21:25{3} 21:26 21:27 21:36 21:37{2} 23:5 24:4 24:10 25:35{3} 26:19{3} 26:21{2} 26:25{2} 26:33 27:5 29:30 30:4 32:19 36:24{3} 36:26{2} 36:30 37:21{3} 37:27 38:4

UNDERGARMENT: Anc Heb: ꟸꟸꟸ❤ Mod Heb: מִכְנָס / mikh-nas (mas); **Definition:** Garment worn under another garment that is bundled up. [AHLB: 2267 (h) / Strong's: 4370] **Concordance:** 28:42 39:28

UNIQUE: Anc Heb: ꟸꟸꟸ❤ Mod Heb: קָדוֹשׁ / qa-dosh (mas); **Definition:** Someone or something that has, or has been given the quality of specialness, and has been separated from the rest for a special purpose. [AHLB: 2700 (c) / Strong's: 6918] **Concordance:** 19:6 29:31

UNIT: Anc Heb: ꟸꟸꟸ❤ Mod Heb: אֶחָד / e-hhad (mas); אַחַת / e-hhat (fem); **Definition:** A unit within the whole, a unified group. A single quantity. [AHLB: 1165-C (N) / Strong's: 259] **Concordance:** 1:15 8:27 9:6 9:7 10:19 11:1 12:18 12:46 12:49 14:28 16:22 16:33 17:12{2} 18:3 18:4 23:29 24:3 25:12 25:19{2} 25:32 25:33{2} 25:36 26:2{3} 26:4 26:5 26:6 26:8{3} 26:10 26:11 26:16 26:17 26:19{2} 26:21{2} 26:24 26:25{2} 26:26 27:9 28:10 28:17 29:1 29:3 29:15 29:23{3} 29:39 29:40 30:10{2} 33:5 36:9{3} 36:10{4} 36:11 36:12{3} 36:13{3} 36:15{3} 36:18 36:21 36:22{3} 36:24{2} 36:26{2} 36:29 36:30 36:31 37:3 37:8{2} 37:18 37:19{2} 37:22 39:10 40:2 40:17

UNLEAVENED-BREAD: Anc Heb: 𐤀𐤅𐤔𐤌 Mod Heb: מצה / mats-tsah (fem); **Definition:** A hard and flat bread or cake made without yeast. [AHLB: 1294-B (N^1) / Strong's: 4682] **Concordance:** 12:8 12:15 12:17 12:18 12:20 12:39 13:6 13:7 23:15{2} 29:2{3} 29:23 34:18{2}

UNTIL: Anc Heb: 𐤃𐤏 Mod Heb: עד / ad (mas); **Definition:** The conclusion of a determinate period of time. Also, again; a repetition of time, either definite or indefinite; another time; once more. [AHLB: 1349-A (N) / Strong's: 5703, 5704, 5705] **Concordance:** 7:16 9:7 9:18 9:25 10:3 10:6 10:7 10:26 11:5 11:7 12:6 12:10{2} 12:12 12:15 12:18 12:22 12:24 12:29 13:15 14:13 14:28 15:16{2} 15:18 16:19 16:20 16:23 16:24 16:28 16:35{2} 17:12 18:13 18:14 22:3{2} 22:8 22:25 23:18 23:30 23:31{2} 24:14 27:5 27:21 28:42 29:34 32:20 33:8 33:22 34:34 34:35 38:4 40:37

UPHOLD: Anc Heb: 𐤊𐤌𐤕 Mod Heb: תמך / ta-makh; **Definition:** To give support or to steady. [AHLB: 2895 (V) / Strong's: 8551] **Concordance:** 17:12

UPON: Anc Heb: 𐤏𐤋 Mod Heb: על / al (mas); **Definition:** To be on or over in the sense of the yoke that is placed on the neck of the ox. [AHLB: 1357-A (N) / Strong's: 5921, 5922] **Concordance:** 1:8 1:10 1:11 1:16 2:3 2:5{2} 2:6 2:14 2:15 3:5{2} 3:12 3:18 3:22{2} 4:20 5:3 5:8{2} 5:9 5:14 5:17 5:21 6:26 7:5 7:15 7:17 7:19{5} 7:28 8:1{4} 8:2 8:3 8:5 8:8 8:17 8:18 9:9{3} 9:19 9:22{4} 9:23{2} 10:6 10:12{2} 10:13 10:14 10:17 10:21{2} 10:22 10:28 11:1{2} 11:5 12:4 12:7{3} 12:8 12:9{2} 12:13{2} 12:23{3} 12:27 12:29 12:33 12:34 12:51 13:9 13:15 13:16 14:2 14:3 14:7 14:9{2} 14:16 14:21 14:26{4} 14:27 14:30 15:16 15:19 15:23 15:24 15:26 15:27 16:2{2} 16:3 16:5 16:7{2} 16:8{3} 16:14{2} 16:20 16:29 17:1 17:3 17:6 17:7{2} 17:9 17:12 17:16 18:8 18:9 18:11 18:13 18:14 18:21 18:22 18:23 18:25 19:4 19:11 19:16 19:18 19:20 20:3 20:5{3} 20:11 20:12 20:20 20:24 20:25 20:26{2} 21:14 21:19 21:22 21:30{2} 22:2 22:8{6} 22:24 23:2 23:13 23:18 23:29 24:6 24:8{2} 24:16 25:11 25:12{3} 25:14 25:19 25:20 25:21 25:22{2} 25:26 25:30 25:37 26:4 26:7 26:10{2} 26:12 26:13 26:24 26:32{2} 26:34 26:35{2} 27:2 27:4{2} 27:7 27:21 28:8 28:9 28:10{2} 28:11 28:12{2} 28:14 28:21{3} 28:22 28:23{2} 28:24 28:25{2} 28:26{2} 28:27 28:28{2} 28:29 28:30{2} 28:33{2} 28:34 28:35 28:36 28:37{2} 28:38{2} 28:43{2} 29:3 29:6{2} 29:7 29:10 29:12 29:13{2} 29:15 29:16 29:17{2} 29:19 29:20{5} 29:21{5} 29:22 29:24{2} 29:25 29:36{3} 29:37 29:38 30:4{2} 30:6{2} 30:7 30:9{2} 30:10{2} 30:13 30:14 30:15 30:16{2} 30:32 30:33 31:7 32:1 32:12{2} 32:14 32:16 32:20 32:21 32:27 32:29 32:34 32:35 33:4 33:5 33:16 33:19 33:21 33:22 34:1{2} 34:2 34:6 34:7{4} 34:12 34:25 34:27 34:28 34:33 34:35 35:22 36:11 36:14 36:17{2} 37:3{3} 37:5 37:9 37:13 37:16 37:27{2} 38:2 38:7 38:21 38:26 39:4 39:5 39:6 39:7 39:14{3} 39:15 39:16 39:17{2} 39:18{2} 39:19{2} 39:20 39:21{2} 39:24 39:25 39:26 39:30 39:31{2} 40:3 40:19{2} 40:20{2} 40:21 40:22 40:23 40:24 40:27 40:29 40:35 40:36 40:38

UPWARD: Anc Heb: 𐤌𐤏𐤋 Mod Heb: מעל / ma-al (mas); **Definition:** In a direction from lower to higher. [AHLB: 1357-A (a) / Strong's: 4605] **Concordance:** 20:4 25:20 25:21 26:14 28:27 30:14 36:19 37:9 38:26 39:20 39:31 40:19 40:20

USURY: Anc Heb: 𐤍𐤔𐤊 Mod Heb: נשך / ne-shek (mas); **Definition:** The lending or practice of lending money at an exorbitant interest. [AHLB: 2441 (N) / Strong's: 5392] **Concordance:** 22:24

VALUE: Anc Heb: 𐤌𐤊𐤎𐤄 Mod Heb: מכסה / mikh-sah (fem); **Definition:** The number assigned according to its amount, importance or need. [AHLB: 1245-A (h^1) / Strong's: 4373] **Concordance:** 12:4

VEHICLE: Anc Heb: 𐤓𐤊𐤁 Mod Heb: רכב / re-khev (mas); **Definition:** A wheeled transport such as a wagon or chariot used for transportation. Also, the top millstone as a wheel that rides on top of the lower millstone. [AHLB: 2769 (N) / Strong's: 7393, 7395] **Concordance:** 14:6 14:7{2} 14:9 14:17 14:18 14:23 14:26 14:28 15:19

VESSEL: Anc Heb: 𐤕𐤁𐤄 Mod Heb: תבה / tey-vah (fem); **Definition:** A floating container for holding items. Used for the basket that carried Mosheh down the Nile river and the boat made by Noah. [AHLB: 1028-A (i) / Strong's: 8392] **Concordance:** 2:3 2:5

VINEYARD: Anc Heb: 𐤊𐤓𐤌 Mod Heb: כרם / ke-rem (mas); **Definition:** A planting of grapevines. [AHLB: 2288 (N) / Strong's: 3754] **Concordance:** 22:4{2} 23:11

VIOLENCE: Anc Heb: 𐤇𐤌𐤎 Mod Heb: חמס / hha-mas (mas); **Definition:** Exertion of physical force so as to injure or abuse. A violent shaking. [AHLB: 2172 (N) / Strong's: 2555] **Concordance:** 23:1

VIRGIN: Anc Heb: 𐤁𐤕𐤅𐤋𐤄 Mod Heb: בתולה / be-tu-lah (fem); **Definition:** An unmarried young woman who is absolutely chaste. [AHLB: 2045 (d^1) / Strong's: 1330] **Concordance:** 22:15 22:16

VOICE: Anc Heb: 𐤒𐤅𐤋 Mod Heb: קול / qol (mas); **Definition:** The faculty of utterance. Sound of a person, musical instrument, the wind, thunder, etc. [AHLB: 1426-J (N) / Strong's: 6963] **Concordance:** 3:18 4:1 4:8{2} 4:9 5:2 9:23 9:28 9:29 9:33 9:34 15:26 18:19 18:24 19:5 19:16{2} 19:19{2} 20:18{2} 23:21 23:22 24:3 28:35 32:17{2} 32:18{3} 36:6

WAFER: Anc Heb: 𐤑𐤐𐤇𐤕 Mod Heb: צפיחת / tsa-pi-hhit (fem); **Definition:** Small thinly baked bread. [AHLB: 2682 (b^4) / Strong's: 6838] **Concordance:** 16:31

WAGE: Anc Heb: 𐤔𐤊𐤓 Mod Heb: שכר / se-kher (mas); **Definition:** The reward or price paid for one's labor. [AHLB: 2479 (N) / Strong's: 7938, 7939] **Concordance:** 2:9 22:14

WAIST: Anc Heb: 𐤌𐤕𐤍 Mod Heb: מתן / ma-ten (mas); **Definition:** The slender part of the body above the hips. [AHLB: 2363 (N) / Strong's: 4975] **Concordance:** 12:11 28:42

WALK: Anc Heb: 𐤄𐤋𐤊 Mod Heb: הלך / ha-lakh; **Definition:** To move along on foot; walk a journey; to go. Also, customs as a lifestyle that is walked or lived. [AHLB: 1264-F (V) / Strong's: 1946, 1980, 1981, 3212] **Concordance:** 2:1 2:5 2:7 2:8{2} 2:9 3:10 3:11 3:16 3:18 3:19 3:21{2} 4:12 4:18{3} 4:19 4:21 4:27{2} 4:29 5:3 5:4 5:7 5:8 5:11 5:17 5:18 7:15 8:21 8:23 8:24 9:23 10:8{2} 10:9{2} 10:11 10:24{2} 10:26 10:28 12:28 12:31 12:32 13:21{2} 14:19{2} 14:21 14:29 15:19 15:22 16:4 17:5 18:20 18:27 19:10 19:19 19:24 21:19 23:23 32:1 32:7 32:23 32:34{2} 33:1 33:14 33:15 33:16 34:9

WALL: Anc Heb: 𐤒𐤉𐤓 Mod Heb: קיר / qir (mas); **Definition:** A permanent upright construction having a length much greater than the thickness and presenting a continuous surface, may be constructed of a curtain, earth, rocks or hewed stones. Used for shelter, protection, or privacy, or to subdivide interior space. [AHLB: 1434-M (N) / Strong's: 2426, 7023] **Concordance:** 30:3 37:26

WANDER: Anc Heb: 𐤕𐤏𐤄 Mod Heb: תעה / ta-ah; **Definition:** To go astray due to deception or influence. [AHLB: 1499-H (V) / Strong's: 8582] **Concordance:** 23:4

WARN: Anc Heb: 𐤆𐤄𐤓 Mod Heb: זהר / za-har; **Definition:** To urge or advise to be careful. To caution. [AHLB: 1158-G (V) / Strong's: 2094, 2095] **Concordance:** 18:20

WARRIOR: Anc Heb: 𐤂𐤁𐤓 Mod Heb: גבר / ge-ver (mas); **Definition:** One of great strength in battle, such as a warrior. One who is strong in authority, such as a master. [AHLB: 2052 (N) / Strong's: 1397, 1399, 1400] **Concordance:** 10:11 12:37

WASH: Anc Heb: 𐤊𐤁𐤎 Mod Heb: כבס / ka-vas; **Definition:** To immerse articles of clothing into a cleaning solution and agitate them, usually by treading upon them, to clean them; to clean the body. [AHLB: 2249 (V) / Strong's: 3526] **Concordance:** 19:10 19:14

WASTELAND: Anc Heb: 𐤇𐤓𐤁𐤄 Mod Heb: חרבה / hhar-bah (fem); **Definition:** Barren or uncultivated land. Also a dry land. [AHLB: 2199 (N^1) / Strong's: 2723, 2724] **Concordance:** 14:21

WATER: Anc Heb: ℱ𝗆 Mod Heb: מה / mah (mas); **Definition:** The Liquid of streams, ponds and seas or stored in cisterns or jars. The necessary liquid that is drank. [AHLB: 1281-A (N) / Strong's: 4325] **Concordance:** 2:10 4:9{2} 7:15 7:17 7:18 7:19{2} 7:20{2} 7:21 7:24{2} 8:2 8:16 12:9 14:21 14:22 14:26 14:28 14:29 15:8 15:10 15:19 15:22 15:23 15:25{2} 15:27{2} 17:1 17:2 17:3 17:6 20:4 23:25 29:4 30:18 30:20 32:20 34:28 40:7 40:12 40:30

WAVE: Anc Heb: ⌐Y\ Mod Heb: נוף / nuph; **Definition:** To move an object, such as hammer or a sacrifice, back and forth. [AHLB: 1316-J (V) / Strong's: 5130] **Concordance:** 20:25 29:24 29:26 29:27 35:22

WAVING: Anc Heb: ℱ⌐Y\† Mod Heb: תנופה / te-nu-phah (fem); **Definition:** The action of moving an object, such as hammer or a sacrifice, back and forth. [AHLB: 1316-J (i[1]) / Strong's: 8573] **Concordance:** 29:24 29:26 29:27 35:22 38:24 38:29

WE: Anc Heb: Y\⍺ Mod Heb: אנו / a-nu (com); Alt Sp: נחנו, אנחנו **Definition:** I and the rest of a group. [AHLB: n/a / Strong's: 580, 586, 587, 5168] **Concordance:** 10:26 16:7 16:8

WEAK: Anc Heb: ⍂⎺ Mod Heb: דל / dal (mas); **Definition:** One who dangles the head in poverty or hunger. [AHLB: 1081-A (N) / Strong's: 1800] **Concordance:** 23:3 30:15

WEAKEN: Anc Heb: ⊔⍂⊞ Mod Heb: חלש / hha-lash; **Definition:** To reduce in strength. [AHLB: 2168 (V) / Strong's: 2522] **Concordance:** 17:13

WEAR: Anc Heb: ⊔⊔⍂ Mod Heb: לבש / la-vash; **Definition:** To cover with cloth or clothing; to provide with clothing; put on clothing. The hiphil (causative) form means "clothe." [AHLB: 2304 (V) / Strong's: 3847, 3848] **Concordance:** 28:41 29:5 29:8 29:30 40:13 40:14

WEARY: Anc Heb: ℱ⍂⍀ Mod Heb: לאה / la-ah; **Definition:** Exhausted in strength, endurance, vigor or freshness. [AHLB: 1258-D (V) / Strong's: 3811] **Concordance:** 7:18

WEAVE: Anc Heb: ⍺⊔⊔ Mod Heb: שבץ / sha-vats; **Definition:** To interlace (threads, yarns, strips, fibrous material, etc.) so as to form a fabric or material. [AHLB: 2809 (V) / Strong's: 7660] **Concordance:** 28:20 28:39

WEEK: Anc Heb: ⌐Y⊞⊔⊔ Mod Heb: שבוע / sha-vu-a (mas); **Definition:** A period of time consisting of seven days or seven years. [AHLB: 2808 (d) / Strong's: 7620] **Concordance:** 34:22

WEEP: Anc Heb: ℱ⊔⊔⍀ Mod Heb: בכה / ba-khah; **Definition:** To express deep sorrow, especially by shedding tears. [AHLB: 1034-H (V) / Strong's: 1058] **Concordance:** 2:6

WEIGH: Anc Heb: ⍂⊸⊔⊔ Mod Heb: שקל / sha-qal; **Definition:** To ascertain the heaviness of by a balance or scale. Weigh out, usually of silver for payment. [AHLB: 2874 (V) / Strong's: 8254] **Concordance:** 22:16

WELL: Anc Heb: ℱ⍂⊔⊔ Mod Heb: באר / be-eyr (fem); **Definition:** A dug-out hole, usually a well or cistern. [AHLB: 1250-D (N) / Strong's: 875] **Concordance:** 2:15

WHAT: Anc Heb: ℱ𝗆 Mod Heb: מה / mah (mas); **Definition:** Interrogative expressing inquiry about the identity, nature, or value of an object. Something that is unknown; can also be why, when or how. [AHLB: 1281-A (N) / Strong's: 3964, 4100, 4101, 4479] **Concordance:** 2:4 2:13 2:20 3:13{2} 4:2 5:4 5:15 5:22{2} 10:26 12:26 13:14 14:5 14:11 14:15 15:24 16:7 16:8 16:15 17:2{2} 17:3 17:4 18:14 22:26 32:1 32:11 32:12 32:21 32:23 33:5 33:16

WHEAT: Anc Heb: ℱ⊗⍀⊞ Mod Heb: חיטה / hhi-tah (fem); **Definition:** A cereal grain that yields a fine white flour, the chief ingredient of bread. [AHLB: 2177 (e[1]) / Strong's: 2406, 2591] **Concordance:** 9:32 29:2 34:22

WHEEL: Anc Heb: ⍀⌐Y⍂ Mod Heb: אופן / o-phen (mas); **Definition:** A circular frame or disk arranged to revolve on an axis, as on a wagon or chariot. [AHLB: 1382-C (g) / Strong's: 212] **Concordance:** 14:25

WHERE: Anc Heb: ⟨ᵧ⟩ Mod Heb: אי / ey (mas); Alt Sp: איה, איפוה **Definition:** At, in, or to what place. [AHLB: 1010-A (N) / Strong's: 335, 346, 351, 375] **Concordance:** 2:20

WHEREIN: Anc Heb: ⟨ᵧ⟩ Mod Heb: זו / zu (com); **Definition:** A person, thing, or idea present or near in place, time, or thought or just mentioned. [AHLB: 1143-A (N) / Strong's: 2098] **Concordance:** 15:13 15:16

WHEREVER: Anc Heb: ⟨ᵧ⟩ Mod Heb: אן / an (mas); Alt Sp: אנה **Definition:** Anywhere at all. A search for a person, place or time. [AHLB: 1014-A (N) / Strong's: 575] **Concordance:** 16:28

WHICH: Anc Heb: ⟨ᵧ⟩ Mod Heb: אשר / a-sheyr (mas); **Definition:** Or who, what or that. This word links the action of the sentence to the one doing the action. [AHLB: 1480-C (N) / Strong's: 834] **Concordance:** 1:8 1:12 1:14 1:15 1:17 2:14 3:5 3:7 3:9 3:14 3:20 4:9 4:12 4:15 4:17 4:18 4:21 4:28{2} 4:30 5:2 5:8 5:11 5:13 5:14 5:21 6:1 6:4 6:5 6:8 6:26 6:29 7:2 7:6 7:10 7:13 7:15 7:17{2} 7:18 7:20{3} 7:21 7:22 8:8 8:11 8:15 8:17 8:18 8:23 9:3 9:12 9:18 9:19{2} 9:21 9:24 9:25 9:26 9:35 10:2{2} 10:6 10:10 10:12 10:15 11:5 11:6 11:7 11:8 12:7 12:13 12:16 12:22{2} 12:25{2} 12:27 12:28 12:29 12:30 12:32 12:39 12:40 12:50 13:3 13:5 13:11 13:12 14:12 14:13{2} 14:31 15:26 16:1 16:5{2} 16:8 16:15 16:16{2} 16:23{3} 16:24 16:32{2} 16:34 17:5 17:10 17:11{2} 18:1 18:3 18:5 18:8{2} 18:9{2} 18:10{2} 18:11 18:14{2} 18:17 18:18 18:20 18:24 19:4 19:6 19:7 19:8 19:16 19:18 20:2 20:4{3} 20:7 20:10 20:11 20:12 20:17 20:21 20:24 20:26 21:1 21:8 21:13{2} 21:22 21:30 22:8{2} 22:15 23:13 23:15 23:16 23:20 23:22 23:27 23:30 24:3 24:7 24:8 24:12 24:14 25:2 25:3 25:9 25:16 25:21 25:22{2} 25:26 25:29 25:40 26:5 26:30 27:8 27:21 28:3 28:4 28:8 28:26 28:38 29:1 29:13 29:21 29:22 29:23 29:26 29:27{4} 29:29 29:30 29:32 29:33 29:35 29:38 29:42 29:46 30:6{3} 30:33{2} 30:36 30:37 30:38 31:6 31:7 31:11 32:1{2} 32:2 32:3 32:4 32:7 32:8{2} 32:11 32:13{2} 32:14 32:19 32:20{2} 32:23{2} 32:32 32:33 32:34 32:35{2} 33:1{2} 33:7 33:11 33:12 33:16 33:17 33:19{2} 34:1{2} 34:4 34:10{3} 34:11 34:12 34:18 34:32 34:34 35:1 35:4 35:10 35:16 35:21{2} 35:22 35:23 35:24 35:26 35:29{2} 36:1{2} 36:2{2} 36:3 36:4 36:5 36:12 37:13 37:16{2} 38:8 38:21 38:22 38:30 39:1{2} 39:5{2} 39:7 39:19 39:21 39:26 39:29 39:31 39:32 39:39 39:42 39:43 40:9 40:15 40:16 40:19 40:21 40:23 40:25 40:27 40:29 40:32

WHIP: Anc Heb: ⟨ᵧ⟩ Mod Heb: פרך / pe-rek (mas); **Definition:** To strike, in punishment or anger with a rope or cord. [AHLB: 2638 (N) / Strong's: 6531] **Concordance:** 1:13 1:14

WHISPER: Anc Heb: ⟨ᵧ⟩ Mod Heb: שימצה / shim-tsah (fem); **Definition:** To talk in a low quiet voice. [AHLB: 2852 (e^1) / Strong's: 8103] **Concordance:** 32:25

WHITE: Anc Heb: ⟨ᵧ⟩ Mod Heb: לבן / la-van (com); **Definition:** Free from color. [AHLB: 2303 (N) / Strong's: 3836] **Concordance:** 16:31

WHO: Anc Heb: ⟨ᵧ⟩ Mod Heb: מי / mi (mas); **Definition:** What or which person or persons. Someone that is unknown. [AHLB: 1286-A (N) / Strong's: 4310] **Concordance:** 2:14 3:11 4:11{2} 5:2 10:8{2} 15:11{2} 16:3 24:14 32:24 32:26 32:33

WHOLE: Anc Heb: ⟨ᵧ⟩ Mod Heb: תמים / ta-mim (mas); **Definition:** Free of wound or injury; free of defect or impairment; having all its proper parts or components. [AHLB: 1496-B (b) / Strong's: 8549] **Concordance:** 12:5 26:24 29:1 36:29

WHY: Anc Heb: ⟨ᵧ⟩ Mod Heb: מדוע / ma-du-a (mas); **Definition:** For what cause, purpose or reason for which. [AHLB: 1085-J (a) / Strong's: 4069] **Concordance:** 1:18 2:18 3:3 5:14 18:14

WIDE: Anc Heb: ⟨ᵧ⟩ Mod Heb: רחב / ra-hhav (com); **Definition:** Having great extent or breadth. [AHLB: 2759 (N) / Strong's: 7338, 7342] **Concordance:** 3:8

WIDEN: Anc Heb: ⟨ᵧ⟩ Mod Heb: רחב / ra-hhav; **Definition:** To increase the size of an area wide; large; roomy. [AHLB: 2759 (V) / Strong's: 7337] **Concordance:** 34:24

WIDOW: Anc Heb: ✼ℓﬔﬔⵎℓⴹ Mod Heb: אלמנה / al-ma-nah (fem); **Definition:** A woman who has lost her husband by death. As bound in grief. [AHLB: 1266-C (m¹) / Strong's: 490] Concordance: 22:21 22:23

WIDTH: Anc Heb: ⵡⴹⵎⵈⵐ Mod Heb: רוחב / ro-hhav (mas); **Definition:** Largeness of extent or scope. From the width of a road. [AHLB: 2759 (g) / Strong's: 7341] **Concordance:** 25:10 25:17 25:23 26:2 26:8 26:16 27:1 27:12 27:13 27:18 28:16 30:2 36:9 36:15 36:21 37:1 37:6 37:10 37:25 38:1 38:18 39:9

WILDERNESS: Anc Heb: ⵇⵡⴹⵎⵎ Mod Heb: מדבר / mid-bar (mas); **Definition:** A tract or region uncultivated and uninhabited by human beings. Place of order, a sanctuary. [AHLB: 2093 (h) / Strong's: 4057] **Concordance:** 3:1 3:18 4:27 5:1 5:3 7:16 8:23 8:24 13:18 13:20 14:3 14:11 14:12 15:22{2} 16:1 16:2 16:3 16:10 16:14 16:32 17:1 18:5 19:1 19:2{2} 23:31

WILLING: Anc Heb: ⵡⴹⵐⵕ Mod Heb: נדיב / na-div (mas); **Definition:** To give honor or offering out of one's own free will. [AHLB: 2380 (b) / Strong's: 5081] **Concordance:** 35:5 35:22

WIND: Anc Heb: ⵎⵈⵐ Mod Heb: רוח / ru-ahh (fem); **Definition:** A natural movement of air; breath. The breath of man, animal or God. The character. A space in between. [AHLB: 1445-J (N) / Strong's: 7305, 7307] **Concordance:** 6:9 10:13{2} 10:19 14:21 15:8 15:10 28:3 31:3 35:21 35:31

WINE: Anc Heb: ⵝⵡⴹⵕ Mod Heb: יין / ya-yin (mas); **Definition:** Fermented juice of fresh grapes. From the mire in the wine. [AHLB: 1221-M (N) / Strong's: 3196] **Concordance:** 29:40

WING: Anc Heb: ⵘⵝⵡ Mod Heb: כנף / ka-naph (fem); **Definition:** An appendage that allows an animal, bird or insect to fly. Also, the wings of a garment. [AHLB: 2269 (N) / Strong's: 3671] **Concordance:** 19:4 25:20{2} 37:9{2}

WIPE-AWAY: Anc Heb: ✼ⵎⵎ Mod Heb: מחה / ma-hhah; **Definition:** To remove by drying or sweeping away through rubbing; to polish in the sense of a vigorous rubbing; erase. [AHLB: 1284-H (V) / Strong's: 4229] **Concordance:** 17:14{2} 32:32 32:33

WIRE: Anc Heb: ⵎⵙ Mod Heb: פח / pahh (mas); **Definition:** A slender, string-like piece or filament of relatively rigid or flexible metal often used for snares. [AHLB: 1376-A (N) / Strong's: 6341] **Concordance:** 39:3

WITH: Anc Heb: ⵎⵕⵙ Mod Heb: עים / im (mas); **Definition:** Through the idea of being together in a group. [AHLB: 1358-M (N) / Strong's: 5868, 5973, 5974] **Concordance:** 3:12 4:12 4:15{2} 8:8 8:25 8:26 9:33 10:6 10:10 10:18 10:24 10:26 11:8 13:19 14:6 17:2 17:8 18:6 18:12 18:18 18:19 19:9 19:24 20:19{2} 20:22 21:3 21:14 22:11 22:13{2} 22:14 22:15 22:18 22:24 22:29 23:1 23:5 24:2 24:8 24:14 33:9 33:12 33:16 34:3 34:5 34:10 34:28

WITHIN: Anc Heb: ⵡⵙⵎ Mod Heb: קרב / qe-rev (mas); **Definition:** In the sense of being close or in the interior of. An approaching. [AHLB: 2729 (N) / Strong's: 7130, 7131] **Concordance:** 3:20 8:18 10:1 12:9 17:7 23:21 23:25 29:13 29:17 29:22 31:14 33:3 33:5 34:9 34:10 34:12

WITHOUT: Anc Heb: ⵝⵡⴹⵐ Mod Heb: אין / a-yin (mas); **Definition:** A lacking of something or the inability to do or have something. The search for a place of unknown origin. [AHLB: 1014-M (N) / Strong's: 369, 370, 371] **Concordance:** 2:12 3:2 5:10 5:11 5:16 8:6 8:17 9:14 12:30{2} 14:11 17:1 17:7 21:11 22:1 22:2 22:9 22:13 32:18{2} 32:32 33:15

WITNESS: Anc Heb: ⵎⵙ Mod Heb: עד / eyd (fem); **Definition:** Attestation of a fact or event. An object, person or group that affords evidence. [AHLB: 1349-A (N) / Strong's: 5707] **Concordance:** 20:16 22:12 23:1

WOMAN: Anc Heb: ✼ⵎⵐⵐⵐⴹ Mod Heb: אישה / i-shah (fem); **Definition:** An adult female person. As mortal. [AHLB: 2003 (b¹) / Strong's: 802] **Concordance:** 1:19 2:2 2:7 2:9 3:22 4:20 6:20 6:23 6:25 11:2 15:20 18:2 18:5 18:6 19:15 20:17 21:3{2} 21:4{2} 21:5 21:22{2} 21:28 21:29 22:15 22:23 26:3{2} 26:5 26:6 26:17 32:2 35:22 35:25 35:26 35:29 36:6

WONDER: Anc Heb: †⊂Υ⅄ Mod Heb: מופת / mo-phet (mas); **Definition:** An amazing sight or event that causes one to be dismayed. Something out of the ordinary. [AHLB: 1390-L (a) / Strong's: 4159] **Concordance:** 4:21 7:3 7:9 11:9 11:10

WOOD-BAR: Anc Heb: ⅄⅄ Mod Heb: בריח / be-ri-ahh (mas); **Definition:** Round wooden dowels. [AHLB: 2038 (b) / Strong's: 1280, 1281] **Concordance:** 26:26 26:27{2} 26:28 26:29{2} 35:11 36:31 36:32{2} 36:33 36:34{2} 39:33 40:18

WORD: Anc Heb: ⅄ Mod Heb: דבר / da-var (mas); **Definition:** An arrangement of words, ideas or concepts to form sentences. An action in the sense of acting out an arrangement. A plague as an act. [AHLB: 2093 (N) / Strong's: 1697] **Concordance:** 1:18 2:14 2:15 4:10 4:15 4:28 4:30 5:9 5:11 5:13 5:19 8:6 8:8 8:9 8:27 9:4 9:5 9:6 9:20 9:21 12:24 12:35 14:12 16:4 16:16 16:32 18:11 18:14 18:16 18:17 18:18 18:19 18:22{2} 18:23 18:26{2} 19:6 19:7 19:8 19:9 20:1 22:8{2} 23:7 23:8 24:3{2} 24:4 24:8 24:14 29:1 32:28 33:4 33:17 34:1 34:27{2} 34:28{2} 35:1 35:4

WORK: Anc Heb: ⅄ Mod Heb: מעשה / ma-a-seh (mas); **Definition:** Activity where one exerts strength or faculties to do or perform something. An action. [AHLB: 1360-H (a) / Strong's: 4639] **Concordance:** 5:4 5:13 18:20 23:12 23:16{2} 23:24 24:10 26:1 26:31 26:36 27:4 27:16 28:6 28:8 28:11 28:14 28:15{2} 28:22 28:32 28:39 30:25 30:35 32:16 34:10 36:8 36:35 36:37 37:29 38:4 38:18 39:3 39:5 39:8{2} 39:15 39:22 39:27 39:29

WORK-OVER: Anc Heb: ⅃⅃⊙ Mod Heb: עלל / a-lal; **Definition:** To carefully and thoroughly perform a task such as gleaning a field. Also, to mock or abuse in the sense of walking over another. [AHLB: 1357-B (V) / Strong's: 5953, 5954] **Concordance:** 10:2

WOVEN-BASKET: Anc Heb: †⅄⊗⅄⊗ Mod Heb: צינצנת / tsin-tse-net (fem); **Definition:** A container made from multiple pieces of material entwined together into one unit. [AHLB: 1198-A (el^2) / Strong's: 6803] **Concordance:** 16:33

WOVEN-MATERIAL: Anc Heb: ⊙⅄⅄† Mod Heb: תשבץ / tash-beyts (mas); **Definition:** Material made from weaving threads of fibers together to become a solid piece. [AHLB: 2809 (i) / Strong's: 8665] **Concordance:** 28:4

WRAP-AROUND: Anc Heb: ⅄Υ⊙ Mod Heb: עוד / ud; **Definition:** To enclose; to repeat or do again what has been said or done. The hiphil (causative) form means "warn." [AHLB: 1349-J (V) / Strong's: 5749] **Concordance:** 19:21 19:23 21:29

WRESTLING: Anc Heb: ⅃Υ†⊂⅄ Mod Heb: נפתול / naph-tul (mas); **Definition:** To contend by grappling with to throw one's opponent off balance. [AHLB: 3034 / Strong's: 5319]

WRITE: Anc Heb: ⅄†⅄ Mod Heb: כתב / ka-tav; **Definition:** To describe one's thoughts or instruction in a form that is readable. [AHLB: 2295 (V) / Strong's: 3789, 3790] **Concordance:** 17:14 24:4 24:12 31:18 32:15{2} 32:32 34:1 34:27{2} 34:28 39:30

YARD: Anc Heb: ⅄Υ⅄ Mod Heb: חצר / hha-tser (mas); **Definition:** The grounds of a building or group of buildings. Villages outside of the larger cities, as "the yard of the city." A courtyard as outside the house. [AHLB: 2197 (N) / Strong's: 2691] **Concordance:** 8:9 27:9{2} 27:12 27:13 27:16 27:17 27:18 27:19 35:17{2} 35:18 38:9{2} 38:15 38:16 38:17 38:18{2} 38:20 38:31{3} 39:40{2} 40:8{2} 40:33{2}

YARN: Anc Heb: ⅄Υ⊗⅄ Mod Heb: מטוה / mat-weh (mas); **Definition:** Fibers that are spun together to form one strand. [AHLB: 1189-J (a) / Strong's: 4299] **Concordance:** 35:25

YEAR: Anc Heb: ⅄⅃⅄ Mod Heb: שנה / sha-neyh (fem); **Definition:** The period of around 365 solar days. [AHLB: 1474-A (N^1) / Strong's: 8140, 8141] **Concordance:** 6:16{2} 6:18{2} 6:20{2} 7:7{2} 12:2 12:5 12:40{2} 12:41{2} 16:35 21:2 23:10 23:14 23:16 23:17 23:29 29:38 30:10{2} 30:14 34:22 34:23 34:24 38:26 40:17

YELL-OUT: Anc Heb: ⊸⊚⌇ Mod Heb: זעק / za-aq; **Definition:** To call out in a louder than normal voice; to declare; to cry out for help. [AHLB: 2131 (V) / Strong's: 2199, 2200] **Concordance:** 2:23

YESTERDAY: Anc Heb: ᴠᴠ⋀⋀† Mod Heb: תמול / te-mul (mas); **Definition:** On the day last past. Idiomatic for a time past. [AHLB: 1288-J (i) / Strong's: 8543] **Concordance:** 4:10 5:7 5:8 5:14{2} 21:29 21:36

YET-AGAIN: Anc Heb: ⌐ᴥ⊚ Mod Heb: עוד / od (mas); **Definition:** A repeating of something. [AHLB: 1349-J (N) / Strong's: 5750, 5751] **Concordance:** 2:3 3:15 4:6 4:18 9:2 9:17 9:29 10:29 11:1 14:13 17:4 36:3 36:6

YOU(mp): Anc Heb: ⋀⋀†ᴑ Mod Heb: אתם / a-tem (mas); **Definition:** Pronoun, second person, masculine plural. [AHLB: n/a Strong's: 859] **Concordance:** 5:11 5:17{2} 10:11 12:13 12:22 12:31 13:4 14:14 16:8 19:4 19:6 20:22 23:9 32:30 33:5

YOU(ms): Anc Heb: ⊠†ᴑ Mod Heb: אתה / a-tah (mas); **Definition:** Pronoun, second person, masculine singular. [AHLB: n/a Strong's: 607, 608] **Concordance:** 2:14 3:5 3:18 4:16 4:25 7:2 7:27 9:2 9:30 10:4 10:25 11:8 14:16 18:14{2} 18:17 18:18 18:19{2} 18:21 19:23 19:24 20:10 20:19 24:1 25:40 27:20 28:1 28:3 30:23 31:13 32:22 33:1 33:3 33:12{3} 34:10 34:12

YOUNG-MAIDEN: Anc Heb: ⊠⋀ᴠ⊚ Mod Heb: עלמה / al-mah (fem); **Definition:** A young female of marriageable age or newly married as at the prime age for work. [AHLB: 1357-A (p[1]) / Strong's: 5959] **Concordance:** 2:8

YOUNG-MAN: Anc Heb: ⋒⊚⟍ Mod Heb: נער / na-ar (mas); **Definition:** A male that has moved from youth to young adulthood. [AHLB: 2418 (N) / Strong's: 5288, 5289] **Concordance:** 2:6 10:9 24:5 33:11

YOUNG-WOMAN: Anc Heb: ⊠⋒⊚⟍ Mod Heb: נערה / na-a-rah (fem); **Definition:** A female that has moved from youth to young adulthood. [AHLB: 2418 (N[1]) / Strong's: 5291] **Concordance:** 2:5

ZEALOUS: Anc Heb: ᴠ⟍⊸ Mod Heb: קנא / qa-nah (mas); **Definition:** Someone who is insistent on reaching the desired outcome. Single minded. One who is protective over someone or something. [AHLB: 1428-E (N) / Strong's: 7067] **Concordance:** 20:5 34:14{2}

Prefixes and Suffixes

?~: Anc Heb: 𐤄 Mod Heb: ה / ah **Definition:** The interrogative hey converting the sentence into a question.

and~: Anc Heb: Y Mod Heb: ו / we **Definition:** The conjunction meaning and. Often used as the vav consecutive meaning that when prefixed to a verb it will usually reverse the tense of the verb.

from~: Anc Heb: 𐤌 Mod Heb: מ / me **Definition:** A preposition meaning from.

in~: Anc Heb: 𐤁 Mod Heb: ב / be **Definition:** A preposition meaning in or with.

like~: Anc Heb: 𐤊 Mod Heb: כ / ke **Definition:** A preposition meaning like.

the~: Anc Heb: 𐤄 Mod Heb: ה / ha **Definition:** The definite article meaning "the".

to~: Anc Heb: 𐤋 Mod Heb: ל / le **Definition:** A preposition meaning to or for.

which~: Anc Heb: 𐤔 Mod Heb: ש / she **Definition:** A preposition meaning which or who.

~^: Anc Heb: 𐤄 Mod Heb: ה / h **Definition:** Paragogic Hey; added to the ordinary forms of words, to express additional emphasis, or some change in the sense.

~her: Anc Heb: 𐤄 Mod Heb: ה / ah **Definition:** Third person feminine singular pronoun (her) also used as a possessive pronoun (of him or his).

~him: Anc Heb: Y Mod Heb: ו / o **Definition:** Third person masculine singular pronoun (him) also used as a possessive pronoun (of him or his).

~me: Anc Heb: 𐤉 Mod Heb: י / i **Definition:** First person common singular pronoun (me), also used as a possessive pronoun (of me or my).

~must: Anc Heb: 𐤍 Mod Heb: ן / n **Definition:** Paragogic Nun; emphasises the intensity of action of the verb.

~of: Anc Heb: 𐤉 Mod Heb: י / i **Definition:** Identifies the noun as possessive.

~s: Anc Heb: 𐤌𐤉𐤕Y Mod Heb: ים (mas) ות (fem) / im (mas) ot (fem) **Definition:** Identifies the noun as a quantitative or qualitative plural.

~s2: Anc Heb: 𐤌𐤉 Mod Heb: ים / yim **Definition:** Identifies the noun as a dual plural.

~them(f): Anc Heb: 𐤍𐤄 Mod Heb: הן / hen **Definition:** Third person feminine plural pronoun (them) also used as a possessive pronoun (of them or their).

~them(m): Anc Heb: 𐤌𐤄 Mod Heb: הם / hem **Definition:** Third person masculine plural pronoun (them) also used as a possessive pronoun (of them or their).

~unto: Anc Heb: 𐤄 Mod Heb: ה / ah **Definition:** Directional Hey; implies movement toward the location identified in the word this suffix is attached to.

~us: Anc Heb: Y𐤍 Mod Heb: נו / nu **Definition:** First person common plural pronoun (we), also used as a possessive pronoun (of us or our).

~you(fp): Anc Heb: 𐤍𐤊 Mod Heb: כן / khen **Definition:** Second person feminine plural pronoun (you), also used as a possessive pronoun (of you or your).

~you(fs): Anc Heb: 𐤊 Mod Heb: ך / ek **Definition:** Second person feminine singular pronoun (you), also used as a possessive pronoun (of you or your).

~you(mp): Anc Heb: 𐤌𐤊 Mod Heb: כם / khem **Definition:** Second person masculine plural pronoun (you), also used as a possessive pronoun (of you or your).

~you(ms): Anc Heb: 𐤔𐤊 Mod Heb: ך / kha **Definition:** Second person masculine singular pronoun (you), also used as a possessive pronoun (of you or your).

Verb Conjugations

~+~: Identifies a compound name (used in the translation of names only).

!(fp)~: Identifies the verb as a feminine plural imperative.

!(fs)~: Identifies the verb as a feminine singular imperative.

!(mp)~: Identifies the verb as a masculine plural imperative.

!(ms)~: Identifies the verb as a masculine singular imperative.

>~: Identifies the verb form as infinitive.

be~: Identifies the voice of the verb as passive.

did~: Identifies the tense of the verb as perfect.

he~: Identifies the subject of the verb as third person masculine singular.

I~: Identifies the subject of the verb as first person common singular.

make~: Identifies the the mood of the verb as causative.

much~: Identifies the the mood of the verb as intensive.

self~: Identifies the voice of the verb as reflexive.

she~: Identifies the subject of the verb as third person feminine singular.

they(f)~: Identifies the subject of the verb as third person feminine plural.

they(m)~: Identifies the subject of the verb as third person masculine plural.

they~: Identifies the subject of the verb as third person common plural.

we~: Identifies the subject of the verb as first person common plural.

will~: Identifies the tense of the verb as imperfect.

you(fp)~: Identifies the subject of the verb as second person feminine plural.

you(fs)~: Identifies the subject of the verb as second person feminine singular.

you(mp)~: Identifies the subject of the verb as second person masculine plural.

you(ms)~: Identifies the subject of the verb as second person masculine singular.

~ed(fp): Feminine plural verb passive participle denoting an action.

~ed(fs): Feminine singular verb passive participle denoting an action.

~ed(mp): Masculine plural verb passive participle denoting an action.

~ed(ms): Masculine singular verb passive participle denoting an action.

~ing/er(fp): Feminine plural verb participle denoting an action or one of action.

~ing/er(fs): Feminine singular verb participle denoting an action or one of action.

~ing/er(mp): Masculine plural verb participle denoting an action or one of action.

~ing/er(ms): Masculine singular verb participle denoting an action or one of action.

Names

Adonai: Anc Heb: ـلٮٮﻰ Mod Heb: אדוני / a-do-ni (mas); **Meaning:** My lords [Strong's: 136] Concordance: 4:10 4:13 5:22 15:17 34:9{2}

Ahaliyav: Anc Heb: ﻡﻝﻯﻝﭗﻝ Mod Heb: אהליאב / a-ha-li-av (mas); **Meaning:** Tent of father [Strong's: 171] Concordance: 31:6 35:34 36:1 36:2 38:23

Aharon: Anc Heb: ﻝﻯﭖﻝ Mod Heb: אהרון / a-ha-ron (mas); **Meaning:** Light bringer; Uncertain meaning but related to the word for light. [Strong's: 175] **Concordance:** 4:14 4:27 4:28 4:29 4:30 5:1 5:4 5:20 6:13 6:20 6:23 6:25 6:26 6:27 7:1 7:2 7:6 7:7 7:8 7:9 7:10{2} 7:12 7:19 7:20 8:1 8:2 8:4 8:8 8:12 8:13 8:21 9:8 9:27 10:3 10:8 10:16 11:10 12:1 12:28 12:31 12:43 12:50 15:20 16:2 16:6 16:9 16:10 16:33 16:34 17:10 17:12 18:12 19:24 24:1 24:9 24:14 27:21 28:1{3} 28:2 28:3 28:4 28:12 28:29 28:30{2} 28:35 28:38{2} 28:40 28:41 28:43 29:4 29:5 29:9{2} 29:10 29:15 29:19 29:20 29:21 29:24 29:26 29:27 29:28 29:29 29:32 29:35 29:44 30:7 30:8 30:10 30:19 30:30 31:10 32:1 32:2 32:3 32:5{2} 32:21 32:22 32:25 32:35 34:30 34:31 35:19 38:21 39:1 39:27 39:41 40:12 40:13 40:31

Ahhiysamahh: Anc Heb: ﺵﻡﺱﻯﺡﻝ Mod Heb: אחיסמך / a-hhi-sa-mak (mas); **Meaning:** My brother supports; May also mean "My brother of support." [Strong's: 294] **Concordance:** 31:6 35:34 38:23

Amaleq: Anc Heb: ـﻝﻡﻉ Mod Heb: עמלק / a-me-leq (mas); **Meaning:** People gathered up [Strong's: 6002, 6003] **Concordance:** 17:8 17:9 17:10 17:11 17:13 17:14 17:16

Amiynadav: Anc Heb: ﺏﺩﻝﻯﻡﻉ Mod Heb: עמינדב / a-mi-na-dav (mas); **Meaning:** My people offered willingly [Strong's: 5992] **Concordance:** 6:23

Amram: Anc Heb: ﻡﺭﻡﻉ Mod Heb: עמרם / am-ram (mas); **Meaning:** People raised [Strong's: 6019] **Concordance:** 6:18 6:20{2}

Asher: Anc Heb: ﺭﺵﻝ Mod Heb: אשר / a-sher (mas); **Meaning:** Happy [Strong's: 836] Concordance: 1:4

Asiyr: Anc Heb: ﺭﻯﺱﻝ Mod Heb: אסיר / a-sir (mas); **Meaning:** Prisoner [Strong's: 617] Concordance: 6:24

Aviyasaph: Anc Heb: ﻭﭖﺱﻯﺏﻝ Mod Heb: אביאסף / avi-a-saph (mas); **Meaning:** My father gathers [Strong's: 23] **Concordance:** 6:24

Aviyhu: Anc Heb: ﻝﻭﻯﻩﻝ Mod Heb: אביהוא / avi-hu (mas); **Meaning:** He is my father [Strong's: 30] **Concordance:** 6:23 24:1 24:9 28:1

Avraham: Anc Heb: ﻡﻩﺭﺏﻝ Mod Heb: אברהם / av-ra-ham (mas); **Meaning:** Father lifted [Strong's: 85] **Concordance:** 2:24 3:6 3:15 3:16 4:5 6:3 6:8 32:13 33:1

Ba'al-Tsephon: Anc Heb: ﻝﻭﻉﺹﻝﻉﺏ Mod Heb: בעל·צפון / ba-al tse-hon (mas); **Meaning:** Master of the north [Strong's: 1189] **Concordance:** 14:2 14:9

Betsaleyl: Anc Heb: ﻝﻯﻝﺹﺏ Mod Heb: בצלאל / be-tsa-leyl (mas); **Meaning:** In the shadow of El [Strong's: 1212] **Concordance:** 31:2 35:30 36:1 36:2 37:1 38:22

Binyamin: Anc Heb: ﻥﻯﻡﻯﻥﺏ Mod Heb: בנימין / bin-ya-min (mas); **Meaning:** Son of the right hand [Strong's: 1144] **Concordance:** 1:3

Dan: Anc Heb: ﻥﺩ Mod Heb: דן / dan (mas); **Meaning:** Moderator [Strong's: 1835] Concordance: 1:4 31:6 35:34 38:23

Edom: Anc Heb: ﻡﻭﺩﻝ Mod Heb: אדום / e-dom (mas); **Meaning:** Red [Strong's: 123] Concordance: 15:15

Ehyeh: Anc Heb: 𐤀𐤄𐤉𐤄 Mod Heb: אהיה / eh-yeh (mas); **Meaning:** I exist; Used only once (Exodus 3:14) where it is used as a proper name. [Strong's: n/a] **Concordance:** 3:14

Elazar: Anc Heb: 𐤀𐤋𐤏𐤆𐤓 Mod Heb: אלעזר / el-a-zar (mas); **Meaning:** El helps [Strong's: 499] **Concordance:** 6:23 6:25 28:1

Eli'ezer: Anc Heb: 𐤀𐤋𐤉𐤏𐤆𐤓 Mod Heb: אליעזר / e-li-e-zer (mas); **Meaning:** My El helps; Can also mean "Mighty one of help." [Strong's: 461] **Concordance:** 18:4

Eliysheva: Anc Heb: 𐤀𐤋𐤉𐤔𐤁𐤏 Mod Heb: אלישבע / e-li-she-va (fem); **Meaning:** My El swears [Strong's: 472] **Concordance:** 6:23

Eliytsaphan: Anc Heb: 𐤀𐤋𐤉𐤑𐤐𐤍 Mod Heb: אליצפן / e-li-tsa-phan (mas); **Meaning:** My El conceals [Strong's: 469] **Concordance:** 6:22

Elohiym: Anc Heb: 𐤀𐤋𐤄𐤉𐤌 Mod Heb: אלוהים / e-lo-him (mas); **Meaning:** Powers [Strong's: 430] **Concordance:** 1:17 1:20 1:21 2:23 2:24{2} 2:25{2} 3:1 3:4 3:6{5} 3:11 3:12 3:13{2} 3:14 3:15{5} 3:16{2} 3:18{2} 4:5{4} 4:16 4:20 4:27 5:1 5:3{2} 5:8 6:2 6:7{2} 7:1 7:16 8:6 8:15 8:21 8:22 8:23 8:24 9:1 9:13 9:28 9:30 10:3 10:7 10:8 10:16 10:17 10:25 10:26 12:12 13:17{2} 13:18 13:19 14:19 15:2 15:26 16:12 17:9 18:1 18:4 18:5 18:11 18:12{2} 18:15 18:16 18:19{3} 18:21 18:23 19:3 19:17 19:19 20:1 20:2 20:3 20:5 20:7 20:10 20:12 20:19 20:20 20:21 20:23{2} 21:6 21:13 22:7 22:8{2} 22:19 22:27 23:13 23:19 23:24 23:25 23:32 23:33 24:10 24:11 24:13 29:45 29:46{2} 31:3 31:18 32:1 32:4 32:8 32:11 32:16{2} 32:23 32:27 32:31 34:15{2} 34:16{2} 34:17 34:23 34:24 34:26 35:31

Elqanah: Anc Heb: 𐤀𐤋𐤒𐤍𐤄 Mod Heb: אלקנה / el-qa-nah (mas); **Meaning:** El purchased [Strong's: 511] **Concordance:** 6:24

Emor: Anc Heb: 𐤀𐤌𐤓 Mod Heb: אמור / e-mor (mas); **Meaning:** Sayer [Strong's: 567] **Concordance:** 3:8 3:17 13:5 23:23 33:2 34:11

Ever: Anc Heb: 𐤏𐤁𐤓 Mod Heb: עבר / e-ver (mas); **Meaning:** Other side [Strong's: 5677, 5680, 5681, 5682] **Concordance:** 1:15 1:16 1:19 2:6 2:7 2:11 2:13 3:18 5:3 7:16 9:1 9:13 10:3 21:2

Eyliym: Anc Heb: 𐤀𐤉𐤋𐤉𐤌 Mod Heb: אילים / ey-lim (mas); **Meaning:** Bucks [Strong's: 362] **Concordance:** 15:27 16:1{2}

Eytam: Anc Heb: 𐤀𐤉𐤕𐤌 Mod Heb: אתם / ey-tam (mas); **Meaning:** Their plowshare. [Strong's: 864] **Concordance:** 13:20

Gad: Anc Heb: 𐤂𐤃 Mod Heb: גד / gad (mas); **Meaning:** Fortune [Strong's: 1410] **Concordance:** 1:4

Gershom: Anc Heb: 𐤂𐤓𐤔𐤌 Mod Heb: גרשום / ger-shom (mas); **Meaning:** Evicted [Strong's: 1647] **Concordance:** 2:22 18:3

Gershon: Anc Heb: 𐤂𐤓𐤔𐤍 Mod Heb: גרשון / ger-shon (mas); **Meaning:** Evicted [Strong's: 1648] **Concordance:** 6:16 6:17

Goshen: Anc Heb: 𐤂𐤔𐤍 Mod Heb: גושן / go-shen (mas); **Meaning:** Drawing near [Strong's: 1657] **Concordance:** 8:18 9:26

Hhanokh: Anc Heb: 𐤇𐤍𐤊 Mod Heb: חנוך / hha-nokh (mas); **Meaning:** Devoted [Strong's: 2585] **Concordance:** 6:14

Hhet: Anc Heb: 𐤇𐤕 Mod Heb: חת / hhet (mas); **Meaning:** Trembling in fear [Strong's: 2845, 2850] **Concordance:** 3:8 3:17 13:5 23:23 23:28 33:2 34:11

Hhetsron: Anc Heb: 𐤇𐤑𐤓𐤍 Mod Heb: חצרון / hhets-ron (mas); **Meaning:** Surrounded by a wall [Strong's: 2696] **Concordance:** 6:14

Hhevron: Anc Heb: 𐤇𐤁𐤓𐤍 Mod Heb: חברון / hhev-ron (mas); **Meaning:** Association [Strong's: 2275, 2276] **Concordance:** 6:18

Hhiw: Anc Heb: 𐤉𐤅𐤇 Mod Heb: חיו / hhiw (mas); **Meaning:** Town [Strong's: 2340] Concordance: 3:8 3:17 13:5 23:23 23:28 33:2 34:11

Hhorev: Anc Heb: 𐤁𐤓𐤇 Mod Heb: חורב / hho-rev (mas); **Meaning:** Parching heat [Strong's: 2722] Concordance: 3:1 17:6 33:6

Hhur: Anc Heb: 𐤓𐤅𐤇 Mod Heb: חור / hhur (mas); **Meaning:** Cistern [Strong's: 2354] Concordance: 17:10 17:12 24:14 31:2 35:30 38:22

Iytamar: Anc Heb: 𐤓𐤌𐤕𐤉𐤀 Mod Heb: איתמר / it-mar (mas); **Meaning:** Island of the date palm [Strong's: 385] Concordance: 6:23 28:1 38:21

Karmi: Anc Heb: 𐤉𐤌𐤓𐤊 Mod Heb: כרמי / kar-mi (mas); **Meaning:** My vineyard [Strong's: 3756] Concordance: 6:14

Kena'an: Anc Heb: 𐤍𐤏𐤍𐤊 Mod Heb: כנען / ke-na-an (mas); **Meaning:** Lowered [Strong's: 3667, 3669] Concordance: 3:8 3:17 6:4 6:15 13:5 13:11 15:15 16:35 23:23 23:28 33:2 34:11

Lewi: Anc Heb: 𐤉𐤅𐤋 Mod Heb: לוי / le-wi (mas); **Meaning:** My joining [Strong's: 3878, 3879, 3881] Concordance: 1:2 2:1{2} 4:14 6:16{2} 6:19 6:25 32:26 32:28 38:21

Liyvniy: Anc Heb: 𐤉𐤍𐤁𐤋 Mod Heb: ליבני / liv-ni (mas); **Meaning:** My white [Strong's: 3845] Concordance: 6:17

Mahh'liy: Anc Heb: 𐤉𐤋𐤇𐤌 Mod Heb: מחלי / mahh-li (mas); **Meaning:** My Sickness [Strong's: 4249] Concordance: 6:19

Mahn: Anc Heb: 𐤍𐤌 Mod Heb: מן / man (mas); **Meaning:** Share; The bread-like substance provided to the Israelites while in the wilderness. The actual meaning of this word is uncertain but can mean "stringed instrument," "from," or "portion." [Strong's: 4478] Concordance: 16:15 16:31 16:33 16:35{2}

Marah: Anc Heb: 𐤄𐤓𐤌 Mod Heb: מרה / ma-rah (fem); **Meaning:** Bitter [Strong's: 4785] Concordance: 15:23{3}

Masah: Anc Heb: 𐤄𐤎𐤌 Mod Heb: מסה / ma-sah (fem); **Meaning:** Trial [Strong's: 4532] Concordance: 17:7

Merari: Anc Heb: 𐤉𐤓𐤓𐤌 Mod Heb: מררי / me-ra-ri (mas); **Meaning:** My bitterness [Strong's: 4847] Concordance: 6:16 6:19

Meriyvah: Anc Heb: 𐤄𐤁𐤉𐤓𐤌 Mod Heb: מריבה / me-ri-vah (fem); **Meaning:** Contention [Strong's: 4809] Concordance: 17:7

Mid'yan: Anc Heb: 𐤍𐤉𐤃𐤌 Mod Heb: מידין / mid-yan (mas); **Meaning:** Quarrel [Strong's: 4080] Concordance: 2:15 2:16 3:1 4:19 18:1

Migdol: Anc Heb: 𐤋𐤅𐤃𐤂𐤌 Mod Heb: מגדול / mig-dol (mas); **Meaning:** Tower [Strong's: 4024] Concordance: 14:2

Mir'yam: Anc Heb: 𐤌𐤉𐤓𐤌 Mod Heb: מירים / mir-yam (fem); **Meaning:** Bitter sea; Can also mean "rebellion." [Strong's: 4813] Concordance: 15:20 15:21

Mits'rayim: Anc Heb: 𐤌𐤉𐤓𐤑𐤌 Mod Heb: מצרים / mits-ra-yim (fem); **Meaning:** Two straits [Strong's: 4713, 4714] Concordance: 1:1 1:5 1:8 1:13 1:15 1:17 1:18 1:19 2:11 2:12 2:14 2:19 2:23 3:7 3:8 3:9 3:10 3:11 3:12 3:16 3:17 3:18 3:19 3:20 3:21 3:22 4:18 4:19 4:20 4:21 5:4 5:12 6:5 6:6 6:7 6:11 6:13{2} 6:26 6:27{2} 6:28 6:29 7:3 7:4{2} 7:5{2} 7:11 7:18 7:19{2} 7:21{2} 7:22 7:24 8:1 8:2{2} 8:3 8:12 8:13 8:17 8:20 8:22{2} 9:4 9:6 9:9{2} 9:11 9:18 9:22{2} 9:23 9:24 9:25 10:2 10:6 10:7 10:12{2} 10:13 10:14{2} 10:15 10:19 10:21 10:22 11:1 11:3{2} 11:4 11:5 11:6 11:7 11:9 12:1 12:12{3} 12:13 12:17 12:23 12:27{2} 12:29 12:30{2} 12:33 12:35 12:36{2} 12:39{2} 12:40 12:41 12:42 12:51 13:3 13:8 13:9 13:14 13:15 13:16 13:17 13:18 14:4 14:5 14:7 14:8 14:9 14:10 14:11{2} 14:12{3} 14:13 14:17 14:18 14:20 14:23 14:24{2} 14:25{2}

14:26 14:27{2} 14:30{2} 14:31 15:26 16:1 16:3 16:6 16:32 17:3 18:1 18:8 18:9 18:10{2} 19:1 19:4 20:2 22:20 23:9 23:15 29:46 32:1 32:4 32:7 32:8 32:11 32:12 32:23 33:1 34:18

Miysha'eyl: Anc Heb: ꝟ𐤋ꟷꟷ𐤌 Mod Heb: מישאל / mi-sha-eyl (mas); **Meaning:** Who enquired [Strong's: 4332] **Concordance:** 6:22

Mo'av: Anc Heb: 𐤟𐤋ꟻ𐤌 Mod Heb: מואב / mo-av (mas); **Meaning:** That one is father [Strong's: 4124] **Concordance:** 15:15

Mosheh: Anc Heb: 𐤔ꟷ𐤟𐤌 Mod Heb: מושה / mo-sheh (mas); **Meaning:** Plucked out [Strong's: 4872] **Concordance:** 2:10 2:11 2:14 2:15{2} 2:17 2:21{2} 3:1 3:3 3:4{2} 3:6 3:11 3:13 3:14 3:15 4:1 4:3 4:4 4:10 4:14 4:18{2} 4:19 4:20{2} 4:21 4:27 4:28 4:29 4:30 5:1 5:4 5:20 5:22 6:1 6:2 6:9{2} 6:10 6:12 6:13 6:20 6:26 6:27 6:28 6:29 6:30 7:1 7:6 7:7 7:8 7:10 7:14 7:19 7:20 7:26 8:1 8:4 8:5 8:8{2} 8:9 8:12 8:16 8:21 8:22 8:25 8:26 8:27 9:1 9:8{2} 9:10 9:11 9:12 9:13 9:22 9:23 9:27 9:29 9:33 9:35 10:1 10:3 10:8 10:9 10:12 10:13 10:16 10:21 10:22 10:24 10:25 10:29 11:1 11:3 11:4 11:9 11:10 12:1 12:21 12:28 12:31 12:35 12:43 12:50 13:1 13:3 13:19 14:1 14:11 14:13 14:15 14:21 14:26 14:27 14:31 15:1 15:22 15:24 16:2 16:4 16:6 16:8 16:9 16:11 16:15 16:19 16:20{2} 16:22 16:24 16:25 16:28 16:32 16:33 16:34 17:2{2} 17:3 17:4 17:5 17:6 17:9 17:10{2} 17:11 17:12 17:14 17:15 18:1{2} 18:2{2} 18:5{2} 18:6 18:7 18:8 18:12{2} 18:13{2} 18:14 18:15 18:17 18:24 18:25 18:26 18:27 19:3 19:7 19:8 19:9{2} 19:10 19:14 19:17 19:19 19:20{2} 19:21 19:23 19:25 20:19 20:20 20:21 20:22 24:1 24:2 24:3 24:4 24:6 24:8 24:9 24:12 24:13{2} 24:15 24:16 24:18{2} 25:1 30:11 30:17 30:22 30:34 31:1 31:12 31:18 32:1{2} 32:7 32:9 32:11 32:15 32:17 32:19 32:23 32:25 32:26 32:28 32:29 32:30 32:31 32:33 33:1 33:5 33:7 33:8{2} 33:9{2} 33:11 33:12 33:17 34:1 34:4 34:8 34:27 34:29{3} 34:30 34:31{2} 34:33 34:34 34:35{3} 35:1 35:4 35:20 35:29 35:30 36:2 36:3 36:5 36:6 38:21 38:22 39:1 39:5 39:7 39:21 39:26 39:29 39:31 39:32 39:33 39:42 39:43{2} 40:1 40:16 40:18 40:19 40:21 40:23 40:25 40:27 40:29 40:31 40:32 40:33 40:35

Mushiy: Anc Heb: ꟷꟷ𐤟𐤌 Mod Heb: מושי / mu-shi (mas); **Meaning:** My moving [Strong's: 4187] **Concordance:** 6:19

Nadav: Anc Heb: 𐤁𐤃ꟻ Mod Heb: נדב / na-dav (mas); **Meaning:** He offered willingly [Strong's: 5070] **Concordance:** 6:23 24:1 24:9 28:1

Nahhshon: Anc Heb: ꟻ𐤟ꟷ𐤄ꟻ Mod Heb: נחשון / nahh-shon (mas); **Meaning:** Diviner [Strong's: 5177] **Concordance:** 6:23

Naphtali: Anc Heb: ꟷꟷ𐤕ꟻ Mod Heb: נפתלי / naph-ta-li (mas); **Meaning:** My wrestling [Strong's: 5321] **Concordance:** 1:4

Negev: Anc Heb: 𐤁ꟷꟻ Mod Heb: נגב / ne-gev (mas); **Meaning:** Parched; A desert region in the southern part of the land of Israel. [Strong's: 5045] **Concordance:** 26:18 27:9 36:23 38:9 40:24

Nepheg: Anc Heb: ꟷꟻꟻ Mod Heb: נפג / ne-pheg (mas); **Meaning:** Sprout up [Strong's: 5298] **Concordance:** 6:21

Nun: Anc Heb: ꟻ𐤟ꟻ Mod Heb: נון / nun (mas); **Meaning:** Continue [Strong's: 5126] **Concordance:** 33:11

Ohad: Anc Heb: 𐤃𐤄ꟻ𐤏 Mod Heb: אוהד / o-had (mas); **Meaning:** Shouting [Strong's: 161] **Concordance:** 6:15

Palu: Anc Heb: ꟻ𐤟ꟻ𐤏 Mod Heb: פלוא / pa-lu (mas); **Meaning:** Performing [Strong's: 6396] **Concordance:** 6:14

Paroh: Anc Heb: 𐤄𐤏𐤓ꟻ𐤏 Mod Heb: פרעה / par-oh (mas); **Meaning:** Great house [Strong's: 6547] **Concordance:** 1:11 1:19 1:22 2:5 2:7 2:8 2:9 2:10 2:15{2} 3:10 3:11 4:21 4:22 5:1 5:2 5:5 5:6 5:10 5:14 5:15 5:20 5:21 5:23 6:1 6:11 6:12 6:13 6:27 6:29 6:30 7:1 7:2 7:3 7:4 7:7 7:9{2} 7:10{2} 7:11 7:13 7:14 7:15 7:20 7:22 7:23 7:26 8:4 8:5 8:8{2} 8:11 8:15{2} 8:16 8:20

8:21 8:24 8:25{2} 8:26 8:27 8:28 9:1 9:7{2} 9:8 9:10 9:12 9:13 9:20 9:27 9:33 9:34 9:35 10:1 10:3 10:6 10:7 10:8 10:11 10:16 10:18 10:20 10:24 10:27 10:28 11:1 11:3 11:5 11:8 11:9 11:10{2} 12:29 12:30 13:15 13:17 14:3 14:4{2} 14:5 14:8 14:9 14:10 14:17 14:18 14:23 14:28 15:4 15:19 18:4 18:8 18:10

Peleshet: Anc Heb: ⊬ா−/⊂ Mod Heb: פלשת / pe-le-shet (fem); **Meaning:** Immigrant [Strong's: 6429, 6430] **Concordance:** 13:17 15:14 23:31

Perez: Anc Heb: ௬ௐ⊂ Mod Heb: פרץ / pe-rez (mas); **Meaning:** Peasant; Meaning one who dwells in a village. [Strong's: 6522] **Concordance:** 3:8 3:17 23:23 33:2 34:11

Pesahh: Anc Heb: □◄⊂ Mod Heb: פסח / pe-sahh (mas); **Meaning:** Hopping; The day of deliverance from Egypt. Also the feast remembering this day and the lamb that is sacrificed for this feast. [Strong's: 6453] **Concordance:** 12:11 12:21 12:27 12:43 12:48 34:25

Pitom: Anc Heb: ⋏Y⊢⊿⊂ Mod Heb: פיתום / pi-tom (mas); **Meaning:** City of justice [Strong's: 6619] **Concordance:** 1:11

Piy-Hahhiyrot: Anc Heb: ⊦Yௐ⊿□❊⊿⊸⊂ Mod Heb: פי·החירות / pi ha-hhi-rot (mas); **Meaning:** Mouth of the cisterns [Strong's: 6367] **Concordance:** 14:2 14:9

Piynhhas: Anc Heb: ◄□⊿⊸⊂ Mod Heb: פינחס / pin-hhas (mas); **Meaning:** Mouth of the serpent [Strong's: 6372] **Concordance:** 6:25

Pu'ah: Anc Heb: ❊⊙Y⊂ Mod Heb: פועה / pu-ah (fem); **Meaning:** Splendid [Strong's: 6326] **Concordance:** 1:15

Puthiy'eyl: Anc Heb: ⊿/⅄⊿⊗Y⊂ Mod Heb: פוטיאל / pu-ti-eyl (mas); **Meaning:** Belonging of El [Strong's: 6317] **Concordance:** 6:25

Qehat: Anc Heb: ⊦❊•⊷ Mod Heb: קהת / qe-hat (mas); **Meaning:** Allied [Strong's: 6955] **Concordance:** 6:16 6:18{2}

Qorahh: Anc Heb: □௬Y•⊷ Mod Heb: קורח / qo-rahh (mas); **Meaning:** Balding [Strong's: 7141] **Concordance:** 6:21 6:24{2}

Ra'meses: Anc Heb: ◄◄⋏⊙௬ Mod Heb: רעמסס / ra-me-seys (mas); **Meaning:** Child of the sun [Strong's: 7486] **Concordance:** 1:11 12:37

Rephiydiym: Anc Heb: ⋏⊿⊢⊿⊸௬ Mod Heb: רפידים / re-phi-dim (mas); **Meaning:** Bottom [Strong's: 7508] **Concordance:** 17:1 17:8 19:2

Re'u'el: Anc Heb: ⊿/⅄Y⊙௬ Mod Heb: רעואל / re-u-eyl (mas); **Meaning:** Companion of El [Strong's: 7467] **Concordance:** 2:18

Re'uven: Anc Heb: ৲⍽⅄⊿௬ Mod Heb: ראובן / re-u-veyn (mas); **Meaning:** See a son [Strong's: 7205] **Concordance:** 1:2 6:14{2}

Shaddai: Anc Heb: ⊿⊢ாш Mod Heb: שדי / shad-dai (mas); **Meaning:** My breasts [Strong's: 7706] **Concordance:** 6:3

Sha'ul: Anc Heb: ⊿/⅄/ш Mod Heb: שאול / sha-ul (mas); **Meaning:** Enquired [Strong's: 7586] **Concordance:** 6:15

Shimon: Anc Heb: ৲Y⊙⋏⊿ш Mod Heb: שימעון / shi-mon (mas); **Meaning:** Hearer [Strong's: 8095] **Concordance:** 1:2 6:15{2}

Shiphrah: Anc Heb: ❊௬⊂⊿ш Mod Heb: שיפרה / shiph-rah (fem); **Meaning:** Brightness [Strong's: 8236] **Concordance:** 1:15

Shiymiy: Anc Heb: ⊿⊙⋏⊿ш Mod Heb: שימעי / shi-mi (mas); **Meaning:** My report [Strong's: 8096] **Concordance:** 6:17

Shur: Anc Heb: ௬Yш Mod Heb: שור / shur (mas); **Meaning:** Rock wall [Strong's: 7793] **Concordance:** 15:22

Sin: Anc Heb: ⟨symbol⟩ Mod Heb: סין / sin (mas); **Meaning:** Sharpt thorn [Strong's: 5513] Concordance: 16:1 17:1

Sinai: Anc Heb: ⟨symbol⟩ Mod Heb: סיני / si-nai (mas); **Meaning:** My sharp thorns [Strong's: 5514] Concordance: 16:1 19:1 19:2 19:11 19:18 19:20 19:23 24:16 31:18 34:2 34:4 34:29 34:32

Sitriy: Anc Heb: ⟨symbol⟩ Mod Heb: סיתרי / sit-ri (mas); **Meaning:** My protection [Strong's: 5644] Concordance: 6:22

Sukhot: Anc Heb: ⟨symbol⟩ Mod Heb: סוכות / su-khot (mas); **Meaning:** Booths [Strong's: 5523] Concordance: 12:37 13:20

Tsiporah: Anc Heb: ⟨symbol⟩ Mod Heb: ציפורה / tsi-po-rah (fem); **Meaning:** Bird [Strong's: 6855] Concordance: 2:21 4:25 18:2

Tsohhar: Anc Heb: ⟨symbol⟩ Mod Heb: צוחר / tso-hhar (mas); **Meaning:** Reddish gray [Strong's: 6714] Concordance: 6:15

Tumiym: Anc Heb: ⟨symbol⟩ Mod Heb: תומים / tu-mim (mas); **Meaning:** Full strengths [Strong's: 8550] Concordance: 28:30

Uriy: Anc Heb: ⟨symbol⟩ Mod Heb: אורי / u-ri (mas); **Meaning:** My light [Strong's: 221] Concordance: 31:2 35:30 38:22

Uriym: Anc Heb: ⟨symbol⟩ Mod Heb: אורים / u-rim (mas); **Meaning:** Lights [Strong's: 224] Concordance: 28:30

Uziy'eyl: Anc Heb: ⟨symbol⟩ Mod Heb: עוזיאל / u-zi-eyl (mas); **Meaning:** My boldness is El [Strong's: 5816] Concordance: 6:18 6:22

Ya'aqov: Anc Heb: ⟨symbol⟩ Mod Heb: יעקוב / ya-a-qov (mas); **Meaning:** He restrains [Strong's: 3290] Concordance: 1:1 1:5 2:24 3:6 3:15 3:16 4:5 6:3 6:8 19:3 33:1

Yah: Anc Heb: ⟨symbol⟩ Mod Heb: יה / yah (mas); **Meaning:** Existing; The actual pronunciation of this name is not certain but probably "Yah." [Strong's: 3050] Concordance: 15:2 17:16

Yakhin: Anc Heb: ⟨symbol⟩ Mod Heb: יכין / ya-khin (mas); **Meaning:** He will prepare [Strong's: 3199] Concordance: 6:15

Yamin: Anc Heb: ⟨symbol⟩ Mod Heb: ימין / ya-min (mas); **Meaning:** Right hand [Strong's: 3226] Concordance: 6:15

Yehoshu'a: Anc Heb: ⟨symbol⟩ Mod Heb: יהושע / ye-ho-shu-a (mas); **Meaning:** Yah will rescue [Strong's: 3091] Concordance: 17:9 17:10 17:13 17:14 24:13 32:17 33:11

Yehudah: Anc Heb: ⟨symbol⟩ Mod Heb: יהודה / ye-hu-dah (mas); **Meaning:** Thanksgiving [Strong's: 3063] Concordance: 1:2 31:2 35:30 38:22

Yemu'el: Anc Heb: ⟨symbol⟩ Mod Heb: ימואל / ye-mu-eyl (mas); **Meaning:** Day of El [Strong's: 3223] Concordance: 6:15

Yeter: Anc Heb: ⟨symbol⟩ Mod Heb: יתר / ye-ter (mas); **Meaning:** Remainder; Only used once (Exodus 4:18) and may be a misspelling or alternative for the name Yitro. [Strong's: n/a] Concordance: 4:18

Yevus: Anc Heb: ⟨symbol⟩ Mod Heb: יבוס / ye-vus (mas); **Meaning:** He will trample down [Strong's: 2982, 2983] Concordance: 3:8 3:17 13:5 23:23 33:2 34:11

Yhwh: Anc Heb: ⟨symbol⟩ Mod Heb: יהוה / Yhwh (mas); **Meaning:** He is; The actual pronunciation of this name is not certain. [Strong's: 3068] **Concordance:** 3:2 3:4 3:7 3:15 3:16 3:18{2} 4:1 4:2 4:4 4:5 4:6 4:10 4:11{2} 4:14 4:19 4:21 4:22 4:24 4:27 4:28 4:30 4:31 5:1 5:2{2} 5:3 5:17 5:21 5:22 6:1 6:2 6:3 6:6 6:7 6:8 6:10 6:12 6:13 6:26 6:28 6:29{2} 6:30 7:1 7:5 7:6 7:8 7:10 7:13 7:14 7:16 7:17{2} 7:19 7:20 7:22 7:25 7:26{2} 8:1 8:4{2} 8:6 8:8 8:9 8:11 8:12 8:15 8:16{2} 8:18 8:20 8:22 8:23 8:24 8:25{2} 8:26 8:27 9:1{2} 9:3 9:4 9:5{2} 9:6 9:8 9:12{2} 9:13{2} 9:20 9:21 9:22 9:23{2} 9:27 9:28 9:29{2} 9:30 9:33 9:35 10:1 10:2 10:3 10:7 10:8 10:9 10:10

10:11 10:12 10:13 10:16 10:17 10:18 10:19 10:20 10:21 10:24 10:25 10:26{2} 10:27 11:1 11:3
11:4 11:7 11:9 11:10 12:1 12:11 12:12 12:14 12:23{2} 12:25 12:27 12:28 12:29 12:31 12:36
12:41 12:42{2} 12:43 12:48 12:50 12:51 13:1 13:3 13:5 13:6 13:8 13:9{2} 13:11 13:12{2} 13:14
13:15{2} 13:16 13:21 14:1 14:4 14:8 14:10 14:13 14:14 14:15 14:18 14:21 14:24 14:25 14:26
14:27 14:30 14:31{3} 15:1{2} 15:3{2} 15:6{2} 15:11 15:16 15:17 15:18 15:19 15:21 15:25{2}
15:26{2} 16:3 16:4 16:6 16:7{2} 16:8{3} 16:9 16:10 16:11 16:12 16:15 16:16 16:23{2} 16:25
16:28 16:29 16:32 16:33 16:34 17:1 17:2 17:4 17:5 17:7{2} 17:14 17:16 18:1 18:8{2} 18:9
18:10 18:11 19:3 19:7 19:8{2} 19:9{2} 19:10 19:11 19:18 19:20{2} 19:21{2} 19:22{2} 19:23
19:24{2} 20:2 20:5 20:7{2} 20:10 20:11{2} 20:12 20:22 22:10 22:19 23:17 23:19 23:25 24:1
24:2 24:3{2} 24:4 24:5 24:7 24:8 24:12 24:16 24:17 25:1 27:21 28:12 28:29 28:30{2} 28:35
28:36 28:38 29:11 29:18{2} 29:23 29:24 29:25{2} 29:26 29:28 29:41 29:42 29:46{2} 30:8 30:10
30:11 30:12 30:13 30:14 30:15 30:16 30:17 30:20 30:22 30:34 30:37 31:1 31:12 31:13 31:15
31:17 32:5 32:7 32:9 32:11{2} 32:14 32:26 32:27 32:29 32:30 32:31 32:33 32:35 33:1 33:5
33:7 33:11 33:12 33:17 33:19 33:21 34:1 34:4 34:5{2} 34:6{3} 34:10 34:14 34:23 34:24 34:26
34:27 34:28 34:32 34:34 35:1 35:2 35:4 35:5{2} 35:10 35:21 35:22 35:24 35:29{2} 35:30
36:1{2} 36:2 36:5 38:22 39:1 39:5 39:7 39:21 39:26 39:29 39:30 39:31 39:32 39:42 39:43 40:1
40:16 40:19 40:21 40:23{2} 40:25{2} 40:27 40:29 40:32 40:34 40:35 40:38

Yhwh-Nisiy: Anc Heb: ◄·Ƴ♐Ɏ↲ Mod Heb: יהוה·ניסי / Yhwh ni-si (mas); **Meaning:** Yhwh is
my standard [Strong's: 3071] **Concordance:** 17:15

Yisra'el: Anc Heb: ⳑ⅄ⲙ≮↲ Mod Heb: יסראל / yis-ra-eyl (mas); He turns El aside [Strong's: 3478,
3479] **Concordance:** 1:1 1:7 1:9 1:12 1:13 2:23 2:25 3:9 3:10 3:11 3:13 3:14 3:15 3:16 3:18
4:22 4:29 4:31 5:1 5:2{2} 5:14 5:15 5:19 6:5 6:6 6:9 6:11 6:12 6:13{2} 6:14 6:26 6:27 7:2 7:4
7:5 9:4{2} 9:6 9:7 9:26 9:35 10:20 10:23 11:7{2} 11:10 12:3 12:6 12:15 12:19 12:21 12:27
12:28 12:31 12:35 12:37 12:40 12:42 12:47 12:50 12:51 13:2 13:18 13:19 14:2 14:3 14:5
14:8{2} 14:10{2} 14:15 14:16 14:19 14:20 14:22 14:25 14:29 14:30{2} 14:31 15:1 15:19 15:22
16:1 16:2 16:3 16:6 16:9 16:10 16:12 16:15 16:17 16:31 16:35 17:1 17:5 17:6 17:7 17:8 17:11
18:1{2} 18:8 18:9 18:12 18:25 19:1 19:2 19:3 19:6 20:22 24:1 24:4 24:5 24:9 24:10 24:11
24:17 25:2 25:22 27:20 27:21 28:1 28:9 28:11 28:12 28:21 28:29 28:30 28:38 29:28{2} 29:43
29:45 30:12 30:16{2} 30:31 31:13 31:16 31:17 32:4 32:8 32:13 32:20 32:27 33:5 33:6 34:23
34:27 34:30 34:32 34:34 34:35 35:1 35:4 35:20 35:29 35:30 36:3 39:6 39:7 39:14 39:32 39:42
40:36 40:38

Yis'sas'khar: Anc Heb: ⲙ⊞⩊≮≮↲ Mod Heb: יששכר / yeysh-sa-khar (mas); **Meaning:** There is a
wage [Strong's: 3485] **Concordance:** 1:3

Yitro: Anc Heb: Ƴ⩊+↲ Mod Heb: יתרו / yit-ro (mas); **Meaning:** His remainder [Strong's: 3503]
Concordance: 3:1 4:18 18:1 18:2 18:5 18:6 18:9 18:10 18:12

Yits'har: Anc Heb: ⩊⅌⌁↲ Mod Heb: יצהר / yits-har (mas); **Meaning:** He presses out oil
[Strong's: 3324] **Concordance:** 6:18 6:21

Yits'hhaq: Anc Heb: •⌆⅌↲ Mod Heb: יצחק / yits-hhaq (mas); **Meaning:** He laughs [Strong's:
3327] **Concordance:** 2:24 3:6 3:15 3:16 4:5 6:3 6:8 32:13 33:1

Yokheved: Anc Heb: ⊕Ⴑ⩊⅃Ɏ↲ Mod Heb: יוכבד / yo-khe-ved (fem); **Meaning:** Yah is heavy
[Strong's: 3115] **Concordance:** 6:20

Yoseph: Anc Heb: ⌂≮Ƴ↲ Mod Heb: יוסף / yo-seph (mas); **Meaning:** Adding [Strong's: 3130]
Concordance: 1:5 1:6 1:8 13:19

Zevulun: Anc Heb: ⅂Ƴ⩌⊞⌃ Mod Heb: זבולון / ze-vu-lun (mas); **Meaning:** Resident [Strong's:
2074] **Concordance:** 1:3

Zikh'riy: Anc Heb: ↲⩊⊞⌃⌃ Mod Heb: זיכרי / zikh-ri (mas); **Meaning:** My memorial [Strong's:
2147] **Concordance:** 6:21

Appendix A – Alternate translations

(about) - like~

(according to) - UPON

(act) - self~

(allow) - GIVE

(also) - UPON

(among) - in~

(and) - ALSO

(any) - ALL

(any) - he~

(as) - like~

(as) - and~

(as) - to~

(at) - from~

(at) - TO

(be) - EXIST

(because) - UPON

(because) - GIVEN-THAT

(because) - WHICH

(before) - OPPOSITE

(behind) - AFTER

(beyond) - UNTIL

(both) - ALSO

(but) - and~

(but) - GIVEN-THAT

(by) - UPON

(by) - in~

(by) - to~

(by) - from~

(by) - UNTIL

(by) - UNDER

(by) - AT

(came to pass) - EXIST

(causes) - make~

(come to pass) - EXIST

(come) - PROVIDE

(concerning) - UPON

(concerning) - ROUND-ABOUT

(continue) - YET-AGAIN

(each) - WOMAN

(each) - MAN

(even) - UNTIL

(even) - YET-AGAIN

(ever) - YET-AGAIN

(every) - ALL

(first) - UNIT

(for) - to~

(for) - TO

(for) - UNTIL

(give) - make~

(great) - MANY

(greatly) - MANY

(have) - EXIST

(here) - LOOK

(however) - SURELY

(if) - GIVEN-THAT

(in place of) - UNDER

(in place) - FOREFRONT

(in) - THERE

(inside) - HOUSE

(it) - he~

(linen) - STICK

(look) - SEE

(made) - GIVE

(make) - GIVE

(make) - DO

(matter) - WORD

(middle) - HALF

(month) - NEW-MOON

(more than) - from~

(more) - YET-AGAIN

(more) - MANY

(no) - WITHOUT

(not yet) - BEFORE

(not) - WITHOUT

(not) - EXCEPT

(nothing) - WITHOUT

(on) - in~

(on) - from~

(on) - TO

(one) - MAN

(one) - UNIT

(only) - SURELY

(or) - and~

(or) - IF

(other) - UNIT

(out of) - from~

(over) - UPON

(over) - in~

(part) - STICK

(place) - GIVE

(placed) - GIVE

(rather than) - from~

(saw) - LOOK

(since) - THOUGH

(so) - to~

(some of) - from~

(still) - YET-AGAIN

(take) - make~

(that way) - IN-THIS-WAY

(that) - GIVEN-THAT

(that) - WHICH

(that) - SHE

(that) - THIS

(that) - HE

(then) - and~

(thing) - WORD

(this) - HE

(those) - THEY(m)

(thus) - SO

(times) - FOOT~s2

(to) - in~

(to) - AT

(unto) - UNTIL

(use) - DO

(used) - DO

(very) - MANY

(was) - EXIST

(were) - EXIST

(when) - GIVEN-THAT

(when) - WHICH

(where) - WHICH

(which is when) - WHICH

(who) - WHICH

(whom) - WHICH

(why) - WHAT

(with) - UPON

(with) - in~

(with) - to~

(with) - AT

(with) - BY

Appendix B – Compound Phrases

<above> - from~to~UPWARD

<above> - to~UPWARD~unto

<afterward> - AFTER SO

<alone> - to~STICK

<among> - ALL to~

<among> - in~WITHIN

<aside> - to~STICK

<at all times> - in~ALL APPOINTED-
    TIME

<away from> - from~WITH

<be ready> - EXIST
    be~PREPARE~ing/er(ms)

<because of this> - to~SO

<before> - like~from~

<before> - to~FROM

<behind> - from~AFTER

<below> - from~UNDER

<but> - and~THOUGH

<by not> - to~EXCEPT

<daily> - DAY DAY

<daily> - to~the~DAY

<eleven> - ONE TEN

<even though> - GIVEN-THAT WHICH

<everyone> - to~ALL BEING

<fifteen> - FIVE TEN

<fourteen> - FOUR TEN

<here> - in~THIS

<himself> - ARCH~him

<how long> - UNTIL WHEREVER

<how> - in~WHAT

<in a moment> - YET-AGAIN SMALL-
    AMOUNT

<in front of> - to~FACE~s

<in the middle> - UNTIL HALF

<instead> - GIVEN-THAT IF

<just as> - like~WHICH

<just like this> - like~IN-THIS-WAY

<lack of> - UNAWARE WITHOUT

<little by little> - SMALL-AMOUNT
    SMALL-AMOUNT

<on account of> - UPON
    CONCERNING~s

<only> - to~STICK

<or not> - IF WITHOUT

<previously> - YESTERDAY THREE-
    DAYS-AGO

<self> - to~STICK

<since> - ALSO from~

<single one> - UNTIL UNIT

<sixteen> - SIX TEN

<still> - UNTIL IN-THIS-WAY

<than what is needed> - from~>~EXIST

<that alone> - to~STICK

<that> - to~WHICH

<the next day> - from~MORROW

<there is enough> - and~ABUNDANT
    from~>~EXIST

<therefore> - UPON SO

<this time> - the~FOOTSTEP

<this> - THAT-ONE~him

<today> - the~DAY

<top> - from~to~UPWARD~unto

<twelve> - TWO TEN

<what is the reason> - to~WHAT THIS

<why> - to~WHAT

<without> - and~NOT in~

Appendix C – Verb Forms

[abused] - self~WORK-OVER

[again] - make~ADD

[agree] - make~TAKE-UPON

[appear] - be~SEE

[appeared] - be~SEE

[be brought near] - be~COME-NEAR

[bring near] - make~COME-NEAR

[bring out] - make~GO-OUT

[bring up] - make~GO-UP

[bring] - make~COME

[brought up] - make~GO-UP

[brought] - make~COME

[clothe] - make~WEAR

[common] - much~PIERCE

[convict] - make~DEPART

[delivers] - much~APPROACH

[destroy] - make~PERFORATE

[dispossess] - make~POSSESS

[enclosed in] - be~make~GO-
    AROUND~ing/er(fp)

[engrave] - much~OPEN

[engraved] - much~OPEN

[follow] - EXIST AFTER

[fulfill] - much~FILL

[go well] - make~DO-WELL

[grant] - make~ENQUIRE

[hide] - make~KEEP-SECRET

[honor] - much~BE-HEAVY

[ignite] - much~BURN

[keep alive] - much~LIVE

[kept alive] - much~LIVE

[kill] - make~DIE

[killed] - make~DIE

[kills] - make~DIE

[lazy] - be~SINK-DOWN

[leave] - make~REST

[leaven] - make~BE-SOUR~ing/er(fs)

[left] - make~REST

[left] - make~REMAIN

[loan] - make~JOIN

[make reconciliation] - much~COVER

[midwife] - much~BRING-
    FORTH~ing/er(fs)

[midwives] - much~BRING-
    FORTH~ing/er(fp)

[miscarry] - much~BE-
    CHILDLESS~ing/er(fs)

[mock] - much~LAUGH

[nurse] - make~SUCKLE~ing/er(fs)

[nurse] - make~SUCKLE

[nursed] - make~SUCKLE

[performances] -
    be~PERFORM~ing/er(fp)

[persuade] - much~SPREAD-WIDE

[point] - make~THROW

[prepare] - be~PREPARE

[provoke] - make~BE-BITTER

[purge] - much~ERR

[reach] - make~FLEE-AWAY~ing/er(ms)

[recount] - much~COUNT

[recounted] - much~COUNT

[refrained] - much~BE-ASHAMED

[remove] - make~TURN-ASIDE

[removing fat residue] -
    >~much~MAKE-FAT

[repent] - be~COMFORT

[repented] - be~COMFORT

[respect] - much~KNEEL

[respected] - KNEEL~ed(ms)

[return] - make~TURN-BACK

[returned] - make~TURN-BACK

[seek refuge] - make~BE-BOLD

[set] - much~FILL

[shatter] - much~CRACK

[shattered] - much~CRACK

[show] - make~SEE

[showed] - make~SEE

[shown] - make~SEE

[support] - make~SECURE

[supported] - make~BE-FIRM

[take] - make~WALK

[teach] - make~THROW

[tell] - make~BE-FACE-TO-FACE

[told] - make~BE-FACE-TO-FACE

[tremble] - SHAKE~must

[trembled] - SHAKE~must

[turn away from] - make~EXTEND

[twisted] - be~make~TWIST-
TOGETHER~ing/er(ms)

[uncover] - be~REMOVE-THE-COVER

[wage war] - be~FIGHT

[waged war] - be~FIGHT

[warn] - make~WRAP-AROUND

[warned] - make~WRAP-AROUND

Appendix D – Plural Forms

\bloodshed/ - BLOOD~s
\eighty/ - EIGHT~s
\fifty/ - FIVE~s
\forty/ - FOUR~s
\life/ - LIVING~s
\nostrils/ - NOSE~s2
\seventy/ - SEVEN~s
\thirty/ - THREE~s
\thunder/ - VOICE~s
\twenty/ - TEN~s
\underneath/ - UNDER~s
\wood/ - TREE~s

Appendix E – Pronunciation Guide

a	like the "a" in father	n	like the "n" in no
ai	like the "ai" in aisle	o	like the "o" in cold
b	like the "b" in boy	p	like the "p" in pie
d	like the "d" in dog	ph	like the "ph" in phone
e	like the "e" in egg	q	like the "k" in kite
ey	like the "ey" in grey	r	like the "r" in road
g	like the "g" in go	s	like the "s" in sit
h	like the "h" in hello	sh	like the "sh" in shine
hh	like the "ch" in the name Bach	t	like the "t" in tie
i	like the "i" in machine	u	like the "u" in tune
k	like the "k" in kite	v	like the "v" in vine
kh	like the "ch" in the name Bach	w	like the "w" in wood*
l	like the "l" in lake	y	like the "y" in yellow
m	like the "m" in me	z	like the "z" in zebra

---

* In the Modern Hebrew language the sixth letter of the Hebrew alphabet, the letter "vav," is pronounced as a "v." However, linguistic, textual and historical evidence suggests that this letter was originally pronounced as a "w."

Appendix F – Changes from Genesis to Exodus

Genesis to Exodus

The words following "Gen" are the translation of words used in the Mechanical Translation in *A Mechanical Translation of the Book of Genesis* that have been revised since its publication. The new translation, which is used in the Mechanical Translation of this book, follows "Ex."

Gen: Account-of **-->** **Ex:** Sake-of
Gen: Around **-->** **Ex:** All-around
Gen: Ashamed **-->** **Ex:** Be-ashamed
Gen: Assembled-flock **-->** **Ex:** Assembly
Gen: Barley **-->** **Ex:** Grain-seeds
Gen: Behind **-->** **Ex:** Last
Gen: Be-firm **-->** **Ex:** Secure
Gen: Be-insubstantial **-->** **Ex:** Belittle
Gen: Betray **-->** **Ex:** Throw-down
Gen: Blossom **-->** **Ex:** Grape-blossom
Gen: Branch **-->** **Ex:** Twig
Gen: Bronze **-->** **Ex:** Copper
Gen: Burst **-->** **Ex:** Crack
Gen: Chan **-->** **Ex:** Necklace
Gen: Clothe **-->** **Ex:** Wear
Gen: Compassionate **-->** **Ex:** Pitiful
Gen: Conceal **-->** **Ex:** Cover-over
Gen: Counsel **-->** **Ex:** Confidence
Gen: Distant **-->** **Ex:** Further
Gen: Emaciated **-->** **Ex:** Scrawny
Gen: Feast **-->** **Ex:** Banquet
Gen: Fixed **-->** **Ex:** Prepare
Gen: Foolish **-->** **Ex:** Confident
Gen: Glow **-->** **Ex:** Light
Gen: Guard **-->** **Ex:** Safeguard
Gen: Hold **-->** **Ex:** Take-hold
Gen: Hollow **-->** **Ex:** Depression
Gen: Honor **-->** **Ex:** Armament
Gen: Hostile **-->** **Ex:** Attack

Gen: Inherit **-->** **Ex:** Possess
Gen: Instrument **-->** **Ex:** Item
Gen: Judge **-->** **Ex:** Decide
Gen: Judgment **-->** **Ex:** Decision
Gen: Kingdom-place **-->** **Ex:** Kingdom
Gen: Later **-->** **Ex:** Tomorrow
Gen: Lie **-->** **Ex:** Deal-falsely
Gen: Life **-->** **Ex:** Living
Gen: Listen **-->** **Ex:** Give-an-ear
Gen: Loin-covering **-->** **Ex:** Loin-wrap
Gen: Magnificence **-->** **Ex:** Great
Gen: Multiple **-->** **Ex:** Numerous
Gen: Myrrh **-->** **Ex:** Ladanum
Gen: Nothing **-->** **Ex:** Anything
Gen: Occupation **-->** **Ex:** Business
Gen: On-account-of **-->** **Ex:** Intention
Gen: Outcry **-->** **Ex:** Yell
Gen: Possession **-->** **Ex:** Material
Gen: Prepare **-->** **Ex:** Be-ready
Gen: Priest **-->** **Ex:** Administrator
Gen: Quarrel **-->** **Ex:** Strive
Gen: Ram **-->** **Ex:** Ram
Gen: Relate **-->** **Ex:** Be-an-in-law
Gen: Rescue **-->** **Ex:** Relief
Gen: Resting-place **-->** **Ex:** Oasis
Gen: Revolution **-->** **Ex:** Transgression
Gen: Rider **-->** **Ex:** Vehicle
Gen: Ring **-->** **Ex:** Ornamental-ring
Gen: Seethe **-->** **Ex:** Simmer

Gen: Set --> **Ex:** Leave-in-place

Gen: Sheaf --> **Ex:** Bound-sheaf

Gen: Signet --> **Ex:** Seal

Gen: Stand-erect --> **Ex:** Stand-up

Gen: Stave --> **Ex:** Branch

Gen: Stretch --> **Ex:** Extend

Gen: Strife --> **Ex:** Dispute

Gen: Stroke-of-time --> **Ex:** Footstep

Gen: Strong-one --> **Ex:** Buck

Gen: Tear-away --> **Ex:** Tear-off

Gen: Thing-of-sacrifice --> **Ex:** Sacrifice

Gen: Tomorrow --> **Ex:** Morrow

Gen: Tread-upon --> **Ex:** Wash

Gen: Trouble --> **Ex:** Persecution

Gen: Visit --> **Ex:** Register

Gen: Wash --> **Ex:** Bathe

Gen: Will --> **Ex:** Self-will

Gen: Wise --> **Ex:** Skilled-one

Gen: Wrestle --> **Ex:** Wrestling

Exodus to Genesis

Ex: Administrator --> **Gen:** Priest

Ex: All-around --> **Gen:** Around

Ex: Anything --> **Gen:** Nothing

Ex: Armament --> **Gen:** Honor

Ex: Assembly --> **Gen:** Assembled-flock

Ex: Attack --> **Gen:** Hostile

Ex: Banquet --> **Gen:** Feast

Ex: Bathe --> **Gen:** Wash

Ex: Be-an-in-law --> **Gen:** Relate

Ex: Be-ashamed --> **Gen:** Ashamed

Ex: Belittle --> **Gen:** Be-insubstantial

Ex: Be-ready --> **Gen:** Prepare

Ex: Bound-sheaf --> **Gen:** Sheaf

Ex: Branch --> **Gen:** Stave

Ex: Buck --> **Gen:** Strong-one

Ex: Business --> **Gen:** Occupation

Ex: Confidence --> **Gen:** Counsel

Ex: Confident --> **Gen:** Foolish

Ex: Copper --> **Gen:** Bronze

Ex: Cover-over --> **Gen:** Conceal

Ex: Crack --> **Gen:** Burst

Ex: Deal-falsely --> **Gen:** Lie

Ex: Decide --> **Gen:** Judge

Ex: Decision --> **Gen:** Judgment

Ex: Depression --> **Gen:** Hollow

Ex: Dispute --> **Gen:** Strife

Ex: Extend --> **Gen:** Stretch

Ex: Footstep --> **Gen:** Stroke-of-time

Ex: Further --> **Gen:** Distant

Ex: Give-an-ear --> **Gen:** Listen

Ex: Grain-seeds --> **Gen:** Barley

Ex: Grape-blossom --> **Gen:** Blossom

Ex: Great --> **Gen:** Magnificence

Ex: Intention --> **Gen:** On-account-of

Ex: Item --> **Gen:** Instrument

Ex: Kingdom --> **Gen:** Kingdom-place

Ex: Ladanum --> **Gen:** Myrrh

Ex: Last --> **Gen:** Behind

Ex: Leave-in-place --> **Gen:** Set

Ex: Light --> **Gen:** Glow

Ex: Living --> **Gen:** Life

Ex: Loin-wrap --> **Gen:** Loin-covering

Ex: Material --> **Gen:** Possession

Ex: Morrow --> **Gen:** Tomorrow

Ex: Necklace --> **Gen:** Chan

Ex: Numerous --> **Gen:** Multiple

Ex: Oasis --> **Gen:** Resting-place

Ex: Ornamental-ring --> **Gen:** Ring

Ex: Persecution **--> Gen:** Trouble

Ex: Pitiful **--> Gen:** Compassionate

Ex: Possess **--> Gen:** Inherit

Ex: Prepare **--> Gen:** Fixed

Ex: Ram **--> Gen:** Ram

Ex: Register **--> Gen:** Visit

Ex: Relief **--> Gen:** Rescue

Ex: Sacrifice **--> Gen:** Thing-of-sacrifice

Ex: Safeguard **--> Gen:** Guard

Ex: Sake-of **--> Gen:** Account-of

Ex: Scrawny **--> Gen:** Emaciated

Ex: Seal **--> Gen:** Signet

Ex: Self-will **--> Gen:** Will

Ex: Simmer **--> Gen:** Seethe

Ex: Skilled-one **--> Gen:** Wise

Ex: Stand-up **--> Gen:** Stand-erect

Ex: Strive **--> Gen:** Quarrel

Ex: Take-hold **--> Gen:** Hold

Ex: Tear-off **--> Gen:** Tear-away

Ex: Throw-down **--> Gen:** Betray

Ex: Tomorrow **--> Gen:** Later

Ex: Transgression **--> Gen:** Revolution

Ex: Twig **--> Gen:** Branch

Ex: Vehicle **--> Gen:** Rider

Ex: Wash **--> Gen:** Tread-upon

Ex: Wear **--> Gen:** Clothe

Ex: Wrestling **--> Gen:** Wrestle

Ex: Yell **--> Gen:** Outcry

Bibliography

Hebrew Language, Culture and Thought

Benner, Jeff A.; Ancient Hebrew Lexicon of the Bible (College Station, TX: Vitural Bookworm, 2005)

Boman, Thorleif; Hebrew Thought Compared with Greek (N.Y., W.W. Norton and Company, 1960)

Chase, Mary Ellen; Life and Language in the Old Testament (N.Y., W. W. Norton and Company Inc. 1955)

Clark, Matityahu; Etymological Dictionary of Biblical Hebrew (Jerusalem, New York: Feldheim Publishing, 1999)

Cole, Donald Powell; Nomads of the Nomads, (Arlington Heights, Ill., Harlan Davidson, Inc., 1975)

Davidson, Benjamin; The Analytical Hebrew and Chaldee Lexicon, (London, Samuel Bagster)

Gesenius' Hebrew Grammar, (London, Oxford Press, 2nd English Ed. 1910)

Halley, Henry H.; Halley's Bible Handbook (Grand Rapids, Mi: Zondervan, 24th)

Harper, William R.; Elements of Hebrew, (N.Y., Charles Scribner's Sons, 1895)

Heaton, E. W.; Everyday life in Old Testament times, (New York, Charles Scribners, 1956)

Holman Bible Dictionary, (Nashville, Holman, 1991)

Horowitz, Edward; How the Hebrew Language Grew (KTAV, 1960)

Lion Encyclopedia of the Bible, The, (Tring England, Lion, new rev. ed.1986)

Miller, Madeleine S., and Miller, J. Lane; Encyclopedia of Bible Life (New York: Harper & Brothers, 1944)

New Westminster Dictionary of the Bible, The, (Philadelphia, Westminster, 1976)

NIV Compact Dictionary of the Bible, (Grand Rapids, Zondervan, 1989)

Packer, J.I., Tenney, Merril C., White Jr., William; Nelson's Illustrated Encyclopedia of Bible Facts (Nashville: Thomas Nelson, 1995) Madelene S. Miller and J. Lane Miller, Harper's Bible Dictionary, (New York, Harper, 1973)

Smith, William; Smith's Bible Dictionary (Grand Rapids, Mi.: Zondervan, 1948)

Strong, James; New Strong's Concise Dictionary of the Words in the Hebrew Bible, (Nashville, Nelson, 1995)

Unger, Merrill F.; Unger's Bible Dictionary, (Chicago, Moody, 1977)

Vine, W. E., Unger, Merrill F., White, William; Vine's Expository Dictionary of Biblical Words, (Nashville, Nelson, 1985)

Wright, Fred H.; Manners and Customs of Bible Lands (Chicago: Moody, 1983)

Bibles

Biblia Hebraica Leningradensia

Biblia Hebraica Stutgartensia

Greek Septuagint Translation of the Old Testament

The American Standard Version of the Bible

The King James Version of the Bible

The Stone Edition Tanach (Brooklyn, Mesorah Publications Ltd., 1996)

Young's Literal Translation of the Bible

www.ingramcontent.com/pod-product-compliance
Lightning Source LLC
Chambersburg PA
CBHW050402110426
42812CB00006BA/1771